A Short History
of the Movies

Gerald Mast, DECEASED
Formerly of the University of Chicago

A Short History of the Movies

FIFTH EDITION

REVISED BY
Bruce F. Kawin
University of Colorado at Boulder

Macmillan Publishing Company
New York

Maxwell Macmillan Canada
Toronto

Editor: D. Anthony English
Production Supervisor: Marcia Craig
Production Manager: Valerie A. Sawyer
Cover Designer: Sheree Goodman

This book was set in Baskerville by Progressive Typographers, Inc., and printed and bound by
R. R. Donnelley, Crawfordsville. The cover was printed by Phoenix Color Corp.

Macmillan Publishing Company
866 Third Avenue, New York, New York 10022

Macmillan Publishing Company is part of the
Maxwell Communication Group of Companies.

Maxwell Macmillan Canada, Inc.
1200 Eglinton Avenue East, Suite 200
Don Mills, Ontario M3C 3N1

LIBRARY OF CONGRESS CATALOGING-IN-PUBLICATION DATA

Mast, Gerald
    A short history of the movies / Gerald Mast. — 5th ed. / revised
  by Bruce F. Kawin.
        p.   cm.
    Includes bibliographical references and index.
    ISBN 0-02-377070-8 (paper)   0-02-580510-x (cloth)
    1. Motion pictures—History.   I. Kawin, Bruce F.
  II. Title.
  PN1993.5.A1M39   1992
  791.43′09—dc20   90-28627
                                                     CIP

Printing: 3 4 5 6 7   Year: 2 3 4 5 6 7 8

Foreword

When Gerald Mast died in 1988 at the age of 48, the fourth edition of *A Short History of the Movies* was the nation's most highly respected and widely used textbook for college courses in film history. He had not begun work on this fifth edition, nor left any instructions concerning it. At the request of Gerald's agent, Rick Balkin, and his family and publisher, I have revised this classic text and updated it to the beginning of the 1990s.

Gerald and I met in 1982 at an international film conference in Hawaii, which ended with a literal hurricane. For the previous eight or nine years, I had been one of the many professors who had used his book in class and had suggested revisions by mail; once we became friends, that process accelerated and became mutual. His pre-publication reading of my own textbook, *How Movies Work,* was the toughest and the most generous it received; that same year, he was generous enough to thank Tag Gallagher and me at length for our help on the fourth edition of the *Short History.* For Gerald Mast had a generous mind, one that ranged widely and precisely over the whole of the humanities. His knowledge of film was both awesome and playful, and I can't think of anyone with whom it was more *fun* to talk about movies—and what, for Gerald, always went with them: music and dance, literature and philosophy, human beings. He was deeply interested in art and in people, and his many books showed us what it meant to interweave and integrate those concerns into a vision of human potential.

Bruce F. Kawin

Preface

From its first edition, Gerald Mast's *A Short History of the Movies* helped to focus the field of film studies; it has its own role in film history. Comprehensively conceived, evocatively illustrated, and eminently readable, drawing useful generalizations and analyzing key works in depth, it became the foundation for the modern film history course. And as the field developed, so did the book.

With each new edition, the *Short History* grew longer and more comprehensive. This new edition breaks with tradition in one respect: It is not significantly longer than its predecessor. Playing the role of a respectful but aggressive editor, I have had to take one word out for nearly every word put in, mostly by tightening the prose and doing some very careful trimming.

No vital material has been taken out; in fact, a great deal has been added. Many of the discussions, such as those of *The Birth of a Nation, Greed,* and *The Last Laugh,* have been invisibly revised to make their essential points more clear, to enrich the analysis, and to fix the occasional problem. More attention is paid to women filmmakers (for example, Lois Weber and Dorothy Arzner are included for the first time) and to such pioneers as black filmmaker Oscar Micheaux.

In response to developments in the field, the perspective offered by new or newly discovered works, and my own sense of what simply had to be covered in this book, I have expanded the discussions of such key directors as John Cassavetes, Abel Gance, D. W. Griffith, John Huston, Chris Marker, G. W. Pabst, Michael Powell, Martin Scorsese, Agnès Varda, and Orson Welles, while making room for such relative newcomers as John Carpenter, David Cronenberg, Terry Gilliam, Jim Jarmusch, Spike Lee, Ridley Scott, Luis Valdez, and Zhang Yimou.

In addition to the most significant recent films, movies new to this edition range from *Tokyo Story* to *Detour,* and from *The Night of the Hunter* to *Night of the Living Dead.* The final chapter now includes more information about how today's movies are produced (the film business) and consumed (often the video business), about sequels and stereo, about colorization and restoration, and about American studios in the era of the corporate takeover. Although much of the new writing naturally comes at the end, the book has been revised and updated throughout.

I have taken the liberty of correcting known errors, whether typographical or factual, especially in regard to names, titles, and dates. To take a few representative examples: I've changed the date of *Strike* from 1924 to 1925, the name DeSica to De Sica, David Lynch's citizenship from British to American, and the title *Trees and Flowers* to *Flowers and Trees*. *It's a Wonderful Life* now reads *It's A Wonderful Life*, which is how it appears in the movie. The hundreds of such changes—and more elemental ones, such as the revised explanation of the phi phenomenon—required painstaking research, and for a good cause: to make what is still the shortest in-depth survey of film history as accurate as possible.

In response to those who critiqued the fourth edition at the publisher's request, I have modified some of the more opinionated passages, cleaned up the occasional sexist usage, and expanded the range of inquiry without sacrificing Gerald's emphasis on *auteurs*—the artists whose breakthroughs and masterpieces made history. Nonfiction, animated, and avant-garde films receive relatively more attention this time, and technical matters are presented with greater precision. Over 75 stills have been added, and not just from recent movies; previously used stills have been double-checked for frontality and sequence. All the illustrations have been numbered for easy reference, and most of the captions have been rewritten for clarity. This is also the first edition to contain a glossary. For all these changes, right or wrong, I take full responsibility.

But this is still Gerald Mast's book—in structure, in spirit, in its concentration on the directors of narrative films, and in most of its analyses, arguments, and wording. The fifth edition is arranged exactly like the fourth, and every movie is taken up in the order Gerald carefully determined, with additional titles inserted chronologically.

As each edition has, future editions of the *Short History* will continue to improve in accuracy and scope and to respond to new ideas and developments, whether theoretical or technical, political or artistic.

In his prefaces Gerald always warmly thanked those who contributed to this book through its many editions. There are those who helped him in preparing the manuscripts: Joe Adamson, Richard Meran Barsam, Madeline Cook, Jeanne Eichenseer, Antonín J. Liehm, Steven Jack, Richard Dyer MacCann, John Matthew, Ned McLeroy, Leonard Quart, William Reiter, Burnell Y. Sitterly, and Tom Wittenberg. There are those who helped him see films or collect stills: Mary Corliss (of the Museum of Modern Art/Film Stills Archive), Walter J. Dauler (of Audio-Brandon Films), Darrell Flugg, Bill Franz, Murray Glass (of Em Gee Films), Steven Harvey, Peter Meyer (formerly of Janus Films and now of Corinth Films), the late Adam Reilly, Emily Sieger, and Charles Silver (of the Museum of Modern Art). The fourth edition owed much to the efforts of editor Paul O'Connell and readers Tag Gallagher and myself. For reviewing the fourth edition, or the fifth prior to publication, both the publisher and I are grateful to Professor Kay Beck, Georgia State University; Mike Bloebaun, Pasadena City College; Professor Robert Carringer, University of Illinois, Urbana; Professor Harold Castleton, Concordia College, Minnesota; Professor Judith Cornes, Odessa College, Texas; Professor Alan B. Eaker, University of South Florida; Professor Daniel Greenberg, Oakland Community College; Professor Robert Hoskins, James Madison University/Harrisonburg, Virginia; Dr. Paul Kending, University of Wisconsin-Superior; Dr. Steven Rauscher, University of New Haven, Connecticut; Professor Larry Rochelle, Johnson County Community College/Kansas; and Professor William Wolf, William Wolf Features, Inc./New York.

As usual, the photographs that accompany the text are either frame enlargements (also called blowups), which may be blurry, but capture a literal shot of a film, or production stills, taken on the set with a still camera and often posed, so that they rarely duplicate a literal view of a film, but always look better in a book. For their help in obtaining the new stills, I am deeply grateful to Mary Corliss and Terry Geesken of the Museum of Modern Art/Film Stills Archive; to the restorer of *Lawrence of Arabia*, Robert A. Harris of Biograph Entertainment; to Helen LaVarre of Columbia Pictures; and to Martin Scorsese. For their help in granting or facilitating permission to use the new stills (for specifics and formal copyright notices, see "Acknowledgments" at the end of the volume), I wish to express special thanks to Herbert Nusbaum and Joan Pierce of MGM/UA Communications Co. and Julia Judge of Scorsese Productions.

Finally, let me thank those who helped me get through what turned out to be an immense job: Bruce Bassoff, Stan Brakhage, Ray Carney, David Cook, Steve Englund, Suranjan Ganguly, David James, Marian Keane, Marsha Kinder, Frank and Celeste McConnell, Bill McLeod, Charles Middleton, Howie Movshovitz, Jim Palmer, Donald Richie, and William Van Wert, and, at Macmillan, editors Tony English and Diane Kraut, who worked hard on this book, as well as Valerie Sawyer and Marcia Craig, who saw it through production.

B. F. K.

Contents

Introductory Assumptions

The first audience watched a motion picture flicker on a screen in 1895, less than one hundred years ago. In that short time the movies have developed from a simple recording device—the first films merely captured a scenic or not-so-scenic view—to a complex art and business. The first movie audiences were delighted to see that it was possible to record a moving scene on film; today we debate the desirability, rather than the possibility, of capturing an image. The important question for the first film audiences was, "Is the image discernible?" rather than, "Is the image meaningful?" From the simple beginning of turning a camera on to record a scene, filmmakers have learned that their art depends on the way their cameras shape the scene they are recording. Analogous to the novel, the completed narrative film is not just a story, but a story told in a certain way, and it is impossible to separate what is told from how it is told. Just as novelists discovered that narrative technique can be either subtly invisible —as in Flaubert or Hemingway—or intrusively self-conscious—as in Joyce or Faulkner —so too the filmmaker can construct a lucid, apparently artless story or a complex, almost chaotic maze for traveling to the story. The wonder is that while the evolution of narrative

fiction can be traced back to Homer, the movies have evolved such complex techniques in less than a century.

No one takes the movies more for granted than the present generation of moviegoers who grew up with the polished sound, color, wide-screen films of the past thirty-five years. Although the current "film generation" may prefer seeing movies to reading novels, or making movies to writing poetry, and has pushed the movies into university curricula, it is surprisingly ignorant of the evolution of movie art—especially surprising since each student filmmaker lives through the historical evolution of film in learning the craft. The student begins by trying to record technically correct pictures on film, perfecting the ability to obtain clearly focused, properly exposed images. The student then realizes the power of different pictorial compositions, the strategies of long shots and close-ups, the effects of different lenses and filters, and the power of editing in creating a film's meaning and tone. The student's first film is often a black-and-white silent film with musical accompaniment— precisely the kind of film that evolved during the first thirty-five years of film history. Only after gaining some confidence with this kind of film does the new filmmaker experiment with color and synchronized sound.

The history of the movies is, first of all, the history of a new art. Though it has affinities with fiction, drama, dance, painting, photography, and music, like each of these kindred arts it has a "poetics" of its own. When the early films turned from scenic views to fictional stories, directors assumed that the "poetics" of the film were similar to those of the stage. Stage acting, stage movement, stage stories, stage players, and stage perspectives dominated early story films. The camera was assumed to be a passive spectator in a theatre audience, and just as the spectator has only one seat, the camera had only one position from which to shoot a scene.

Time and experimentation revealed that the camera was anchored by analogy alone—and that the analogy was false. The scene—the locale—is the basic unit of the stage because space in the theatre is so concrete. The audience sits here, the characters play there, the scenery is fixed in space behind the action. But space in the film is completely elastic; only the screen is fixed, not the action on it. Directors discovered that the unit of a film is the shot, not the scene, that shots can be joined together in any number of combinations to produce whole scenes, and that scenes can be varied and juxtaposed and paralleled in any number of ways. Unity of place, a rather basic and practical principle of the stage, does not apply to the movie. More applicable is what the earliest film theorist, Hugo Münsterberg, called a "unity of action," an appropriate succession of images that produces the desired narrative continuity, the intended meaning, and the appropriate emotional tension of the film as a whole. By the end of the silent era this principle had been not only discovered, but demonstrated.

The discovery of sound raised doubts about the discoveries of the preceding thirty years. Once again the analogy with the stage was suspected; once again stage actors, stage writers, stage directors, and stage techniques flooded the movies. And once again, the analogy was found to be false. Just as the stage is anchored visually in space, so too is it anchored by sound. Sounds come from the speaker's mouth; you see both speaker and mouth. But movies were

free to show any kind of picture while the words came from the speaker's mouth. Synchronization of picture and sound also allowed for the disjunction of picture and sound. Further, the freedom of the movies from spatial confinement allowed a greater freedom in the kinds of sounds they could use: natural sound effects, musical underscoring, distortion effects, private thoughts, and so forth. Whereas the history of the silent film could be summarized as the discovery of the different means of producing an evocative *succession* of visual images, the history of the sound film is the discovery of the different means of producing an evocative *integration* of visual images and sound.

Just as the history of the novel is, to some extent, a catalogue of important novels, the history of film as an art centers on important films. In film history, a discussion of the significant films is especially relevant, for the individual films are not only milestones on a historical path, but also significant artistic discoveries that almost immediately influenced other filmmakers. Although Shakespeare drew from Seneca and Brecht from Shakespeare, even more immediate was the influence of Griffith on Ford or Bergman on Woody Allen. Without years of stage tradition to draw on, film artists have drawn on the exciting discoveries of their contemporaries. The internationalism of film distribution has always guaranteed the rapid dispersal of any significant discovery.

In order to keep track of this dispersal of discoveries, it is necessary to know when a particular film was released—that is, when it was first shown to a public audience—for that is usually the earliest that it could have influenced audiences and other filmmakers. This is much like learning the publication date of a novel rather than its completion date or the number of years it took to complete. (One could date James Joyce's *Ulysses* 1914–1921, the years he wrote it, or 1921, the year he finished it; but it was first published in February, 1922 and is regularly dated 1922.) In this book, the date that follows a film's title is, in almost all cases, the year the film was *released in its country of origin*. If a film was released long after it was completed, both the completion and release dates are given. If it has become customary to refer to a particular film by the year in which most of it was shot (*Caligari*, 1919; *Breathless*, 1959), but it came out the following year, both dates are given. And both dates are given if the release date is so early in the year as to be misleading; a film released on January 8, 1929, like Dziga Vertov's *The Man with a Movie Camera*, ought to be considered a 1928 work as well as a 1929 release. If it matters when a foreign film opened in the United States and affected American audiences, the U.S. release date is also provided; Fellini's *La dolce vita* won an Oscar in 1961, but came out in Italy in 1960. In any case, most films open the year they are completed and do perfectly well with one date.

The majority of film historians subscribe to a basic, if far from absolute, assumption: The very best films have generally resulted from the clear vision and unifying intelligence of a single, controlling mind with primary responsibility for the whole film. Just as there is only one conductor per orchestra or one architect per structure, there can be only one dominant creator of a movie. The *"auteur* theory," as defined by François Truffaut in France and Andrew Sarris in America, identifies the director (whose personal artistic signature is evident in the work) as a film's "author" or dominant creator. Whether the *auteur* improvises the whole film as it goes along—as Chaplin did—or works according to a preconceived and scripted plan, a single mind shapes and controls the work of film art. The difficulty with movies, however, is that their very massiveness, expense, and complexity work against their having such an *auteur*. The director is frequently no more than a mechanic, bolting together a machine (often infernal) designed by someone else.

But if the best movies are usually dominated by an *auteur*, it is also true that any movie represents an immensely collaborative venture. There are examples of very good movies with two co-directors (Gene Kelly and Stanley Donen, Michael Powell and Emeric Pressburger, Ján Kadár and Elmar Klos). Many of the best directors work in frequent partnership with the same scriptwriter (Frank Capra with Robert Riskin, John Ford with Dudley Nichols, Howard Hawks with Jules Furthman, William Faulkner, or Ben Hecht), or the same cameraman (Ingmar Bergman with Sven Nykvist, William Wyler with Gregg Toland, Sergei Eisenstein with Eduard Tisse, D. W. Griffith with Billy Bitzer), or assistant director (Truffaut with Suzanne Schiffman), or composer (Alfred Hitchcock with Bernard Herrmann, Federico Fellini with Nino Rota). Even Charles Chaplin, perhaps the most singular creator of a large body of films, worked with a single cameraman, Rollie H. Totheroh, for over three decades. To study a dozen or so films by a single screenwriter, or composer, or cameraman would surely reveal as consistent and distinguishable a personality as a dozen or so films by a single director. To speak of a film's *auteur* is both to describe a creative fact and to manipulate a useful metaphor.

Those who view the film as an inferior artistic medium most frequently argue that the conditions of making a commercial film nullify its chances for artistic success. To see the history of films as several dozen "Great Movies" is to simplify the history. All movies, great or small, have been made in the context of the entire film industry. Any film history that intends to reveal the genesis of today's film world must, in addition to discussing the film as art, discuss three related problems that have always influenced the artistic product—and continue to influence it today: the film as business, the film as cultural product and commodity, and the film as machinery.

Movies today are a billion-dollar business. The choice of directors, stars, and scripts is in the hands of businesspeople, not in the heads of artists. The company that invests $30 million in a picture ought to be able to insure the safety of its investment. Commercial values outweigh artistic ones. The name Hollywood, for some synonymous with glamor, is for others synonymous with selling out. For decades Hollywood's commercial crassness has served American novelists—from F. Scott Fitzgerald and Nathanael West to Gore Vidal—as a metaphor for the vulgar emptiness of the American Dream. If the gifted young director today seems to face a distasteful dilemma—sell out or get out—directors have faced the same problem for over seventy-five years.

The awesome financial pressures of Hollywood are partly responsible for the growing number of independent and underground films and videos—just as Broadway production demands are responsible for the Off-Broadway and Off-Off-Broadway theatres. Young filmmakers and video artists often prefer to work alone, their sole expense equipment and film (or tape). These filmmakers are, in a sense, regressing to the earliest period of film history. But every artistic innovation since then has ironically necessitated spending more money. If lighting was a step forward in film toning, it also required spending money on lighting equipment and on people who knew how to control it. If acting was to be improved, proven actors had to be retained. And as actors supplied greater proofs, they demanded higher salaries. Longer films required more film, more actors, more story material, and more publicity to insure a financial return on the greater investment. It took only twenty-five years for the movies to progress from cheap novelty to big business.

Why do movies cost so much to make? Put the question this way: How much would you expect to pay if you employed an army of the most specialized artisans at their trade for a period of, say, three to six months? Making a commercial feature film is an immense feat of social engineering; to justify the cost of that feat, the resulting movie must generate some kind of return, some social profit—financial (in the capitalist West), cultural (in the Communist and Third World countries), or both. Even in the West the movies provide an informal forum for cultural discussion, and even in the East the movies must observe the constraints of budgets and schedules. Despite the greater (and more highly publicized) cost of making movies, the theories of fiscal and cultural responsibility apply no less to the publication of a newspaper, a novel, or a scholarly journal than to films. All of them are produced for some kind of profit.

Making a film is such a massive and complex task it is a wonder that an artistically whole movie can be made at all. The huge sums of money required to finance a movie merely reflect the hugeness of the task of taking a movie from story idea to final print. Shooting is painfully slow. It takes time to perfect each setup: Lights must be carefully focused and toned, the shot's composition must be attractive and ap-

propriate, the set must be dressed, background actors (extras) must be coordinated with the action of the principals, actors must have mastered their interpretations of lines so that a single shot fits into the dramatic fabric of the whole film, make-up must be correct, costumes coordinated, and so forth. Because it takes so much time to set up a shot, producers economize by shooting all scenes together that require the same location, set, or setup, regardless of their position in the film's continuity. But even with such economies, to get three minutes of screen time "in the can" is a hard, well-organized day's work. Sometimes, on location with mammoth spectacle pictures, a whole day can be devoted to a fifteen-second piece of the finished film—the sun, the caravans, the camels, the soldiers, and the gypsy maidens must be caught just as they reach their proper places. A movie's production budget is calculated on the number of days it will take to shoot, the average expense for a color film being in excess of $250,000 per day. Even the ten-minute student film can cost over $1,000 for film stock and laboratory expenses alone—exclusive of the original cost of the equipment.

Because movies cost so much to make, the companies that spend that money are understandably concerned about getting it back. The only way to retrieve expenses is with sales—selling tickets, leasing television rights to networks or cable franchises, selling videocassettes and laserdiscs outright.

The film artist not only is at the mercy of expensive machines and services but also is dependent on the consent of the entertained. The history of the movies as a business is inextricably linked with the history of the movies as a mass entertainment medium. To get the public to spend its money at the box office, the producer must give the public what it wants or make the public want what it gets. History indicates that the public has gotten some of both. The crassest movie maxim is the famous,"The box office is never wrong." The validity of the maxim depends on the kinds of questions you ask the box office to answer.

Just as film art has changed radically in the course of its history, so too film audiences have changed. The first movie patrons in America were also patrons of vaudeville houses and variety shows. When those audiences tired of the same kinds of film programs, the movies found a home with lower- and working-class patrons. Small theatres sprang up in the poor sections and commercial districts of cities; admission was a nickel or dime. The rich and educated saw movies only as an afternoon or evening of slumming. As film art and craft improved, larger and more expensive movie theatres opened in the respectable entertainment centers of the cities. Films tried to appeal to a wide range of tastes and interests, much as television does today. In this period there was little consciousness of movies as an art; they were mass entertainment. And as with today's network television, the educated, the literati, and the serious shunned them. H. L. Mencken sardonically lauded the movies as the appropriate artistic attainment of the American "boob-oisie." Similes linking movies with tastelessness and movie patrons with morons continually popped up in fiction and articles of the 1920s and 1930s.

This discussion of the evolving audiences for movies indicates the close connection between the movies as cultural artifacts and conditions in American culture as a whole. Particular cultural conditions influence, if not dictate, the particular qualities and quantities of films in any given era. For a specific movie to become a major hit at a specific time indicates, at least partially, the cultural fact that a sufficient number of people wanted, needed, demanded, or responded to just that film then. To compare *Mr. Smith Goes to Washington* of 1939, with *The Best Years of Our Lives* of 1946, with *Rebel Without a Cause* of 1955, with *The Graduate* of 1967, with *Saturday Night Fever* of 1977, and with *Flashdance* of 1983 is to write a history of American culture over the past five decades. Any history of the movies must both take account of and account for these cultural shifts and conditions.

But if movies convey an overt and explicit cultural content — a war-torn society attempting to heal its wounds in *The Best Years of Our Lives* or a working-class woman attempting to express and distinguish herself in *Flashdance* — they can also convey covert and "invisible" ideological messages. It was precisely this fear of covert ideological contamination that led to the inquiries of the House Un-American Activities Committee in the years following World War II. More recently, many contemporary film theorists, following the lead of French Marxist historians and critics like Louis Althusser and Roland Barthes, have attempted to expose the unspoken, assumed cultural values of films — values that seem so obviously true for that culture that they are accepted as inevitable, normal, and natural rather than as constructs of the culture itself. For example, happiness in an American film is so equated with a synthesis of material comfort (home, job, car, stereo) and spiritual contentment (almost inevitably a monogamous romantic relationship) that any alternative ideas of happiness (or even a critique of the idea of happiness itself) are automatically unthinkable. Television (even its new cable stations) is so completely structured around commercials that the very idea of buying becomes natural; it doesn't matter exactly what it is the viewer buys, just so the viewer understands that life itself consists of buying something or other, and that nearly anything can be a commodity.

This ideological analysis has been especially useful to feminist critics and theorists who seek the underlying sources of sexist thinking in our cultural history. Women in American films seem banished to the kitchen or the pedestal; either they stir the soup on the stove or they gaze down on us as goddesses of love and beauty, mythic Circes and Venuses like Greta Garbo, Marlene Dietrich, and Marilyn Monroe. Following the psychoanalytic theories of Jacques Lacan, many feminist film theorists explicate the way that women in most American movies have traditionally served as voyeuristic objects presented by male directors for the pleasurable gaze of male spectators. Although one need not accept the radical analyses and proposals of such contemporary theory, there is no question that such discussions of movies have made contemporary Americans more conscious and self-conscious about the cultural and moral values we previously took for granted.

Another radical approach to film theory suggests that our very way of looking at the

Fig. 1-1

Fig. 1-2

The movies as mirror of American social history. Fig. 1-1: social institutions responsive to human needs and challenges (Jean Arthur in the U.S. Senate of **Mr. Smith Goes to Washington,** *1939). Fig. 1-2: Three returning servicemen view the land they fought to save (from left, Dana Andrews, Fredric March, and Harold Russell in* **The Best Years of Our Lives,** *1946).*

world, of seeing nature, reality, and all the persons and things within it, is itself a cultural construct. The principles of Renaissance perspective—of a deep receding space presented for the eye of the single, privileged viewer—have been ground into the lenses of cameras. Others have argued that bourgeois culture privileges a single sense—sight—over all others. The apparently innocent act of "seeing the world"—whether through our eyes or through a lens—is not at all innocent since both the seeing and the seen are cultural constructs. Hence, a final influence on the movies, important to any discussion of their history, is the dependence of film art on machines.

Appropriately enough, our technological century has produced an art that depends on technology. The first filmmakers were not artists but tinkerers. The same spirit that produced a light bulb and a telephone produced a movie camera and projector. The initial goal in making a movie was not to create beauty but to display a scientific curiosity. The invention of the first cameras and projectors set a trend that was to repeat itself with the introduction of every new movie invention: The invention was first exploited as a novelty in itself and only later integrated as one tool in making the whole film. The first movie camera merely exploited its ability to capture images of moving things. The first synchronized sound films exploited the audience's excitement at hearing the words that the actor's lips were mouthing. Most of the first color films were merely colorful, many of the first wide-screen films merely wide.

No other art is so tied to machines. Some of the most striking artistic effects are the products of expanding film technology. For example, the awesome compositions in depth and shadow of Orson Welles's *Citizen Kane* (1941) are partially the result of the studios' conversion to brighter arc lamps, the introduction of specially coated lenses, and the development of high-speed, fine-grain film stocks, all of which made it possible for *Kane*'s cinematographer, Gregg Toland, to "stop down" the lens (in other words, since there was now more light on the set and the film was more sensitive, he could narrow the lens's aperture) and achieve much greater depth of field. Research has converted the camera from an erratic, hand-cranked film grinder to a smooth, precise clockwork. Research has silenced the camera's noise without using clumsy, bulky devices to baffle the clatter. Research has developed faster and faster black-and-white stocks, enabling greater flexibility in lighting, composition, and shooting conditions. Research has developed color film stocks that are not only brilliant in recording color but also can provide different effects for different artistic purposes. Research has improved sound recording and sound reproduction, developed huge cranes and dollies, perfected a wide assortment of laboratory processes and effects, and invented special lenses and special projectors and special filters. Film equipment is so sophisticated that no film artist can master all of it; yet despite the difficulties of money and machine, movies have become the dominant art of the century.

This short history will follow the road the movies have traveled to get here. To keep a history even this "short" has required several decisions. First, this history aims at revealing significant trends and turns along the road rather than detailing exhaustive lists of titles, directors, and dates. For further reading and detail, the reader is strongly advised to consult the Appendix.

Second, because the history of the American film is most relevant to American readers, this short history allots more space to a discussion of American movie practices. But although American films are the dominant force in the film world, to write a history of the art that neglects the influences of non-American films is impossible. The reader must bear in mind, however, that the non-American films that have had the most impact on the film art and audiences of America represent a tiny fraction of total foreign production. The "art films" of Renoir, Truffaut, Antonioni, Bertolucci, Kurosawa, and Mizoguchi represent something like 2 or 3 percent of feature film production in France, Italy, or Japan. The run-of-the-mill overseas production is far less remarkable—in both visual style and technical expertise—than the typical American production. While only the most extraordinary foreign films are screened in America, audiences overseas see and enjoy even the average American product.

Third, this history concentrates on the fiction film almost exclusively. The aesthetic principles of the nonfiction (documentary) film are different enough from those of the fiction (or narrative or story) film that the documentary or factual film, like the animated film or the avant-garde film, deserves a separate study of its own.

Finally, the reader must realize precisely what this book of history (and any book of history) really is—not a collection of all the facts that must be accepted and ingested as absolute truth but a selection of facts that have been fitted into an interpretive pattern. A history is inevitably a telling, a narrative, a story; after all, five-sevenths of the word *history* is *story*. This story is perpetually revised and rethought: New data are selected, old data rejected or reinterpreted, new ways of viewing those data

adopted. Like plays, novels, and movies, histories are stories told to a particular audience at a particular time, embodying the values, hopes, ideals, and commitments of those times.

The reader of this history is urged, therefore, not simply to swallow the assertions of this text but to probe and reflect upon the taste and texture of the morsels she or he has been asked to chew. Histories of movies, no less than the movies themselves, construct a view of the world and of human experience. We all inhabit a present in which the goal is not simply to accept the world as constructed but to *deconstruct* that pattern—as the French philosopher, Jacques Derrida, and his followers argue—the better to understand exactly what that construction is, how it works, what it assumes, which contradictions it comprises, and what it implies as a consequence.

2

Birth

Some film historians trace the origin of movies to cave paintings, to Balinese shadow puppets, or to Plato's mythic Cave of the Shadows in Book VII of *The Republic*. Many theorists find a particular aptness in Plato's mass of spectators, entranced by the flickering shadows of objects on the cave wall that are merely projections of the light behind them, diverted from the real objects they would see if they could only ascend from the shadow-show to examine them in the light itself. The nonmetaphoric history of the movies, however, begins with the steps leading to the invention of the movie camera and projector.

The nineteenth-century mechanical mind created machines for travel, machines for work, machines for the home, and, in the process, machines for entertainment. In the second third of the nineteenth century, three kinds of mechanical experimentation began that, by the end of the century, had combined to create the motion picture: research in the phenomenon of persistence of vision, developments in still photography, and increasing public interest in mechanized entertainments.

Persistence of Vision

Movies are an optical illusion. We believe we are watching completely continuous, fluid motion on the screen. In fact, we watch short, discontinuous bits of the motion, which the eye sees as continuous because of the way the eye sees and the way the brain interprets that information.

When darkness follows a bright image, the light receptors in the eye (whose action diminishes rapidly but does not instantly shut off) retain the image for a fraction of a second, so that the retina briefly continues to send the last visual information it received to the brain. If it did not, we would be conscious of the hundreds of times a day that the eyelids blink. The mind has no consciousness of blinking because, although the lids cover the eyeball for a fraction of a second, the preblink image is retained. The same principle accounts for the way that a flashlight rotated in a circle in the darkness appears to produce a circle of light. The retina blurs the individual points of light into a circular figure. This optical phenomenon is known as *persistence of vision*.

9

If the eye saw sixteen individual but related images of a moving object in rapid succession, the brain would connect the pieces to make a single, fluid sequence out of them. Persistence of vision accounts for why we do not notice the "blinks" between frames, but each frame is still seen, correctly, as an unmoving image. A second process, first explained in 1916 by psychologist and film theorist Hugo Münsterberg and later called the *phi phenomenon*, mentally fills in the gaps (the motions that took place between exposures, when the shutter was closed) so that we hallucinate, or believe that we see, a continuous action rather than a series of frozen motion-fragments. For the brain, the instantaneous leap from one position to another is a paradox—like the quantum leap, whereby an electron may be now at one distance from the atom's nucleus and then at another, without having crossed the space between those positions—that can be resolved only by presuming that movement *had* to have taken place between the successive frames, then creating and "seeing" it.

Persistence of vision and the phi phenomenon make movie action seem as fluid and uninterrupted as live action. The movie camera exposes one frame at a time; each frame is a single, fixed, still photograph. The stroboscopic succession of frames produces the appearance of movement. To record each image, the camera stops the film while the shutter is open—in most cases, for about one-fiftieth of a second. Then the film is advanced to the next frame while the shutter is closed and no light can enter the camera. At sound speed (the standard projection rate since the late 1920s), the shutter exposes twenty-four of these images each second. Simple mathematics indicates that one second of film thus exposed contains only 24/50ths of a second of exposed action and 26/50ths of a second of darkness (of blinking) between the frames. Whereas, in viewing, a second of film appears to be an uninterrupted line, ————, it is really a discontinuous one, - - - - - - - -. The eye and the mind fill in the blank spaces. Ironically, just over half the time we spend watching a film, the screen is literally blank, devoid of any shadowy images at all.

Persistence of vision, known by the ancients, was investigated and demonstrated by Euro-

pean thinkers and tinkerers between 1820 and 1835. One of the early discussions of the phenomenon was by Peter Mark Rôget, author of the famous thesaurus. An English scientist, Sir John Herschel, bet a friend that he could show the head and tail of a shilling at the same time. And then Sir John spun the coin. The eye blurred the spinning sides of the coin into a single image. In 1825, Dr. John Ayrton Paris had developed a little toy based on this same spinning-coin principle. On one side of a circular board was a parrot, on the other an empty cage. By holding the board by two attached straps and then spinning it, the viewer saw the parrot inside the cage. Again, two images had melted into one. Paris called his little toy the Thaumatrope (from the Greek "wonder turning").

Four years later, in 1829, Joseph Antoine Ferdinand Plateau published his investigations on persistence of vision, and three years after that (1832) he marketed his own toy to demonstrate his theoretical research. Painted on a flat, circular piece of board were individual designs in slightly varying positions. When the board was grasped by a handle, held up in front of a mirror, and then spun, the individual designs became a continuous, animated sequence. In order to see the designs moving (rather than as a blur), the viewer looked into the mirror through little slits cut into the circular board of the toy. Plateau called his toy the Phenakistoscope (from the Greek "deceptive viewer"). Plateau's research was important, for in the course of it he discovered that sixteen images per second were an optimal number for producing continuous movement (below twelve frames per second, the intermittent darkness is perceived as blatant "flickering," and the stills appear still). The early filmmakers would also discover the utility of sixteen frames per second. In addition, Plateau's machine required moments of darkness, of nonimage, in order to make the images appear to move. The eye needed momentary resting time to soak in the images. A successful projector would not be invented until an analogy to Plateau's slits was discovered.

A German inventor, Simon Ritter von Stampfer, developed the same machine as Plateau's Phenakistoscope in the same year; he called it the Stroboscope (light and dark in rapid alternation, from the Greek "alternating viewer"). Based on the same principle as the Phenakistoscope and Stroboscope, many refined versions of this toy appeared throughout the nineteenth century. In 1834, William George Horner created a stroboscopic machine that used a circular drum rather than a flat circular board. Exchangeable paper strips would fit inside the circular drum. When the viewer looked through the slits in the drum, which allowed instants of darkness, the pictures on the spinning paper strips appeared in delightfully sequential motion. Horner first called his toy the Daedelum, then the Zoötrope (or Zoetrope, from the Greek "life turning").

Also in 1834, Baron Franz von Uchatius began combining stroboscopic toys with the magic lantern—a candle-powered slide projector. Uchatius lined up a series of projectors side by side and focused them on the same screen. In each lantern was a glass slide with a slightly different phase of movement. By running with a torch from lantern to lantern, Uchatius threw an apparent sequence of movement on the screen. The result was the progenitor of the animated cartoon. Uchatius's experiments with lanterns continued, and by 1853 he had developed a Projecting Phenakistoscope, combining a phenakistoscopic disc with a single magic lantern. When the operator spun the disc, the lantern threw the sequential animated movement on the screen.

By the end of the nineteenth century, hundreds of variations on these toys abounded, each with its own name, either simple or ornate: Praxinoscope, Choreutoscope, Wheel of Life. All of these stroboscopic toys shared, in addition to their common use of persistence of vision, several traits that were to continue as trends in later movie history. Most striking was the inventors' passion for fancy Greek and Latin names to dignify their dabblings: Thaumatrope, Phenakistoscope, Viviscope, Zoetrope. (There was also a Getthemoneygraph.) This passion for nominal embroidery would later dominate the first era of motion pictures—Kinetoscope, Bioscope, Vitascope, Cinématographe—and beyond it—Technicolor, CinemaScope, television, stereophony, video. Also striking is the simultaneity

Fig. 2-1
Early persistence of vision toys: the Thaumatrope, a Zoötrope wheel with paper strip, and (left rear) a primitive version of what would become a Mutoscope.

of discoveries by different men in different countries, primarily in France, England, Germany, and the United States. Such simultaneous experimenting produced a confusion that would continue throughout the century, so that even today these four countries each claim to have invented the motion picture. The claim of each chauvinistic historian can be supported with solid evidence. The validity of each claim is contingent upon whether one defines the motion picture as invented when it was conceived, when it was patented, when it was photographed on film, or when it was projected in public.

All the stroboscopic experiments and toys used drawn figures. Before the movies could progress from stroboscopic toy to motion pictures of the natural world, the means to record the natural world had to be discovered.

Photography

Before there could be motion pictures, there had to be pictures. A moving picture was born from the union of the stroboscopic toys and the still photograph. The principle of photography dates back at least to the Renaissance and Leonardo da Vinci's drawing of a *camera obscura*. This device—literally translated as dark room or chamber—was a completely dark enclosure that admitted light only through a small hole. The *camera obscura* projected an inverted reproduction of the scene facing it on the wall opposite. After a lens was introduced to brighten and sharpen the image, all the *camera obscura* needed to become a camera was a photographic plate to replace the wall. Nineteenth-century scientists set out in pursuit of this plate that could fix the inverted image permanently.

As early as 1816, Joseph Nicéphore Niépce, a Frenchman, used metal plates to capture rather fuzzy and temporary images, which he called Heliographs. In the 1830s, the English inventor William Henry Fox Talbot began his research in paper printing—the principle of the photographic negative, and with it, the reproducible photograph. But it was another Frenchman, Louis Jacques Mandé Daguerre, the late Niépce's partner, who in 1839 determined the future of photography by making clear, sharp, permanent images on silvered copperplate. (The very first Daguerreotype, a picture of the artist's studio, was taken in 1837, but the invention was announced and verified in 1839.) The exposure time required for an image was fifteen minutes, so the first sitters for Daguerreotypes had to pose motionless for fifteen minutes, their heads propped up to keep from wiggling. Before photography could become more practical, exposure time would have to be cut. There obviously could be no motion pictures, which require multiple exposures per second, until the photographic material was sensitive enough to permit such shutter speeds. (Indeed, the first still cameras used the lens cap as a shutter.) After Daguerre's and Talbot's perfecting of the basic principles, photographic stocks became faster (more photosensitive), permitting a three-minute exposure by 1841. Before thirty years had passed, the shutter had been invented, and faster photographic plates allowed for exposures of fractions of a second.

The first attempts at motion photography were posed stills that simulated continuous action. The stills were then projected with a Projecting Phenakistoscope to give the appearance of movement. But a real motion picture required a continuous live action to be first analyzed into its component units and then resynthesized, rather than a simple synthesis of static, posed bits of action. The first man to break a continuous action into discrete photographic units was an Englishman transplanted to California, Eadweard Muybridge. Muybridge, whose career was as bizarre as the spelling of his first name, was a vagabond photographer and inventor who had been entangled in a divorce and murder scandal. In 1872, he was hired by the governor of California, Leland Stanford, to help win a $25,000 bet. Stanford, an avid horse breeder and racer, bet a friend that at some point in the racehorse's stride all four hooves left the ground. In 1877, after faster exposures became possible, Muybridge set up twenty-four cameras in a row along the racing track. He attached a string to each camera shutter and stretched the string across the track. He chalked numerals and lines on a board behind the track to measure the horse's progress. Stanford's horse then galloped down the track, tripping the wires, and Mr. Stanford won $25,000 that had cost him only $40,000 to win.

For the next twenty years, Muybridge perfected his multiple-camera technique. He increased his battery of cameras from twelve (in the earliest experiments) to forty-eight. He used faster, more sensitive plates. He added white horizontal and vertical lines on a black background to increase the impression of motion. He shot motion sequences of horses and elephants and tigers, of nude women and wrestling men and dancing couples. He mounted his photographs on a Phenakistoscope wheel and combined the wheel with the magic lantern for public projections of his work in 1879. He called his invention—a variation on Uchatius's Projecting Phenakistoscope—the Zoöpraxiscope (from the Greek "life-constructing viewer"). Muybridge traveled to Europe, where he gave special showings of the Zoöpraxiscope to admiring scientists and

Fig. 2-2
Muybridge's leaping horse.

photographers. However, Muybridge's later refinements never surpassed the importance of his first set of motion photographs. Continuous motion had been divided into distinct frames, but it had not yet been photographed by a single camera.

One of Muybridge's hosts in Paris was another scientist, Etienne-Jules Marey, who was experimenting with motion photography. In 1882, Marey was the first to shoot multiple pictures with a single camera. "Shoot" applies quite literally to Marey's experiment, for his camera looked like a shotgun. The photographic gun used a long barrel for its lens and a circular chamber containing a single glass photographic plate. The circular plate rotated

twelve times in the chamber during a single second of shooting, leaving all twelve exposures arranged in a ring around the glass plate. Whereas Muybridge had gone from one camera to another, each loaded with a glass plate that had been coated with a light-sensitive emulsion, Marey moved one plate through one camera. Like Muybridge, Marey photographed men and animals: runners, jumpers, fencers, trotting horses, falling cats, flying gulls. But Marey's Chronophotographs (from the Greek "writing time with light") produced a much more fluid analysis of motion, the finished print resembling a surreal multiple exposure. In 1888, Marey replaced the glass plate with paper roll film, allowing more and faster exposures.

Photography had reached the threshold of motion pictures.

To produce a movie that was more than a one- or two-second snippet of activity, a material had to be developed that could accommodate not twelve or forty or one hundred images, as Marey's eventually did, but thousands. In 1884, George Eastman began his experiments with celluloid and with paper roll film, the latter for use in his Kodak still camera. By 1888, photography, which had been the sole property of professionals, had become any person's hobby (Kodak's slogan was "You push the button, we do the rest"). Eastman's 1889 celluloid film became the natural material for further experiments in motion photography. This American discovery of celluloid film shifts the history of the movies back across the Atlantic from France.

Thomas Edison

Appropriately enough, the American father of the movies is the ultimate representative of the ingenious, pragmatic American inventor – businessperson — Thomas Alva Edison. The supreme tinkerer threw his support behind the new craze of motion photography. But Edison gave the motion picture little more than support. Although he assigned employees and laboratory space to the photographic project, he himself gave motion pictures little thought, an oversight that was later to cost him both prestige and money. Edison's real interest in motion pictures was to provide visual accompaniment for the phonograph he had invented earlier — in effect, a kind of MTV. His original idea was to etch tiny photographs on a wax cylinder in much the same way that sound was recorded on his phonograph cylinders. The same cylinder would contain both sound and picture and could be reproduced by a single machine. The idea was theoretically attractive, but the practical problem of reducing pictures to pinpoints was unsolvable.

In 1887, George Eastman replicated the celluloid roll film that had been invented and patented by the Reverend Hannibal Goodwin. Its cellulose nitrate base was perfected by an Eastman chemist named Henry M. Reichen-

bach, and Eastman began to produce and market strips and rolls of celluloid film in 1889. The film was transparent, thin, strong, and of the same width and quality from one batch to another, thanks to George Eastman's great skill at designing efficient, effective means of manufacturing and merchandising. In 1892, the Eastman Dry Plate and Film Company (founded 1881) took the name by which it is still known, the Eastman Kodak Company.

Edison's director of the motion picture project, William Kennedy Laurie Dickson — who invented the camera and viewer for which Edison took credit and who, sometime between 1889 and 1891, made the first American movie (he may well have made *the* first movies) — persuaded the "Wizard" to abandon cylinders for celluloid. At first, Dickson bought sheets of celluloid film from inventor John Carbutt and cut them into strips. He sent his first order to Eastman in late 1889.

Success did not come quickly. Edison traveled to Europe in 1889, leaving Dickson in charge of perfecting the motion picture apparatus. On Edison's return in October, Dickson claims to have greeted his boss with a film projected on a screen and roughly synchronized with sound. Dickson called the machine the Kineto-phonograph (from the Greek "motion – sound recorder"). Unfortunately, no evidence other than Dickson's claim exists for this amazingly early synchronization of picture and sound. If Dickson had developed such equipment by 1889, Edison would surely have filed for a patent — but he did not file any movie-related patents until 1891.

The earliest pieces of existing film can be traced to no earlier than 1890 (unless one calls Le Prince's 1888 paper-roll fragments films), and the earliest whole film on record at the Library of Congress is *Fred Ott's Sneeze* (also called *Record of a Sneeze*), which a contemporary magazine article describes as having been shot in 1891 but whose copyright date is 1894. According to legend, one of Edison's mechanics, Fred Ott, was a comical fellow who could sneeze on cue. Dickson selected Fred as the subject for one of his celluloid strips, probably in late 1893. The strips Dickson shot before *Fred Ott's Sneeze* no longer survive. The Dick-

Fig. 2-3
The business of invention: George Eastman (left) and Thomas Edison, posing in 1927.

son film Edison showed when he demonstrated the Kinetoscope for the first time—in May, 1891, to the National Federation of Women's Clubs—showed a man who bowed, smiled, waved his hands to demonstrate natural motion, and gracefully took off his hat.

Once Fred's sneeze was "in the can," the problem confronting Edison was how to share that sneeze with the public. Edison, who worried about the poor quality of projected images, decided on direct viewing. Rather than seeing an image projected for large groups, the individual customer would put an eye to the hole of a machine and view the single filmstrip inside it. Edison's decision was based on his integrity as an inventor as well as on his greed as a businessman. He saw the greater clarity of reproduction in the little peephole machine,

and he was sure he would make more money from the novelty if it were displayed to one person at a time rather than to a hall full of people. Edison so underestimated the potential of moving pictures that he refused to spend $150 to extend his American patent rights to England and Europe. His shortsightedness would cost him more than $150.

In 1891 Edison applied for patents on his camera, the Kinetograph (from the Greek "motion writer"), and his peephole viewer, the Kinetoscope (from the Greek "motion viewer"); previously he had been calling both machines the Kinetograph, to complement his Phonograph. The patents were not granted until two years later, just in time for display at the Columbian Exposition, the Chicago World's Fair of 1893. By 1894, Edison was marketing

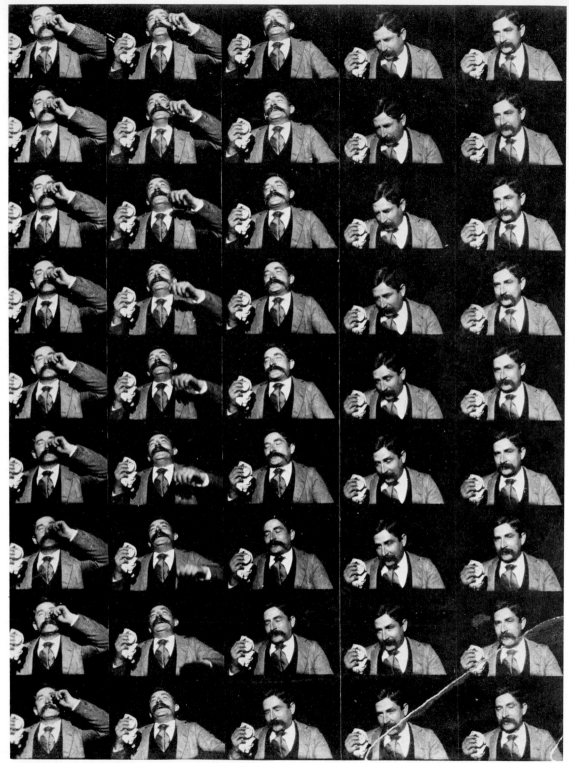

Fig. 2-4
Fred Ott's Sneeze, *the earliest whole film on record.*

A Kinetoscope Parlor: phonographs on the left (complete with handkerchiefs for wiping the earpieces), Kinetoscopes on the right.

Fig. 2-5

his own machines through a firm fronted by Norman Raff and Frank Gammon; Kinetoscope Parlors, turn-of-the-century ancestors of today's video arcades, showing Fred's sneeze and other items, began to spring up all over the United States. Rows of battery-run, nickel-in-the-slot Kinetoscope machines beckoned the customer to peek at the new marvel of mechanically recorded life.

The requirements and design of the Kinetoscope strongly influenced the hundreds of films Dickson shot for it. Wound around spools inside the Kinetoscope, the film's ending led continuously into its beginning, exactly as the Phenakistoscope wheels or Zoetrope strips had done. The space inside the Kinetoscope box limited the length of a filmstrip to fifty feet, and since Edison's cameras and viewers ran at forty or more frames per second (forty six according to his patent, but Edison refused to be bound by that number in legal testimony), the Kinetoscope contained less than a half-minute of action. The films for these machines were not edited; whatever Dickson shot became the finished film. The most popular filmstrips were

bits of dancing, juggling, or clowning, of natural wonders from all over the world, and even of staged historical events.

Despite the crudeness of the first Edison films—and despite his blunder about projection—Edison left his mark on the future of film. Most important was the decision to use perforations (sprocket holes) on the sides of the film to control its motion past the shutter. The Edison–Dickson perforations quickly became the standard throughout the world and were known as the American Perforation. Edison and Dickson also fathered the movie studio. In order to produce films for the Kinetoscope Parlors, in 1893 Dickson built a small room especially for motion pictures adjacent to the Edison laboratories. Because the outside of the studio was protected with black tar paper (to exclude unwanted light), the room quickly became known as the Black Maria, at that time slang for paddy wagon. Dickson mounted his camera on a trolley inside the Black Maria so that it could move closer or further away, depending on the subject of the film. The camera, however, never changed position during the

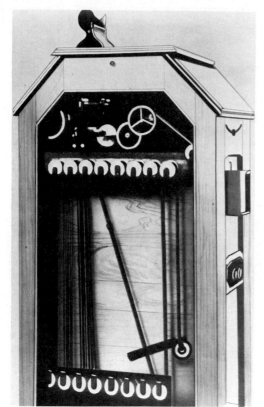

Fig. 2-6
The Kinetoscope mechanism.

machine. For these steps the history of film travels back across the Atlantic.

Projection

The problem of projecting motion pictures was surprisingly difficult to solve. After the principles of motion photography had been discovered and a camera developed to demonstrate the principles, one would have thought that projecting the images would come easily. In fact, early projection attempts produced blurry images, ripped film, and a great deal of noise. Edison's decision to shelve projection was as much a realization of difficulties as a business blunder. On the other hand, it was clear to other inventors that a projected motion picture was the next evolutionary step. For hundreds of years audiences had delighted in mechani-

shooting. To light the action, the Black Maria's roof opened to catch the sunlight. The whole studio—actually a shooting stage—could be rotated to catch the sun, so that the scene would always be sufficiently lit.

The disadvantages of the Black Maria are obvious. The room was really a small sunlit theatre with the camera as single spectator. There was even a specified stage area where the juggler, dancer, comic, or animal performed. Mobility was further curtailed by the bulky heaviness of Dickson's camera because of Edison's insistence on using electricity rather than a hand crank to run it, so that the machine remained perpetually indoors and inert.

To free the camera from its cage and the filmstrip from its peephole box were the next essential steps in the evolution of the movie

Fig. 2-7
The first movie studio: Edison's Black Maria (1893). The first studio with glass walls and roof was built by Méliès in 1897.

cally projected shows. Even before photography, audiences had sat in darkened rooms and watched puppets' shadows or projected images on a screen.

The invention of the magic lantern is attributed to Father Athanasius Kircher who, in 1646, made drawings of a box that could reproduce images by means of a light passing through a lens. That box was the ancestor of today's slide projector. In the eighteenth century, showmen trooped across Europe giving magic lantern shows, projecting drawings and, much later, photographs for paying customers. From the beginning, the magic lanternists sought to make their static images move. They developed lantern slides with moving parts and moving patterns. They used multiple lanterns to give the impression of depth and sequence. The most famous of these multiple-lantern shows was the Phantasmagoria, in which ghosts and spirits were made to move, appear, and disappear with the aid of moving lanterns and mirrors. The stroboscopic toys of the nineteenth century further enlarged the lanternist's bag of motion tricks.

The last in the string of pre-movie projection entertainments was the movie's closest ancestor—the photo play. In the late nineteenth century, Alexander Black, an American author and lecturer, combined the magic lantern slide, photography, and narration to produce a complete play with live narrator, live actors, and pictorial slides. Unlike the stroboscopic lantern shows, the goal of these entertainments was not the visual novelty of reproduced motion but the realization of the same stories and dramas that drew audiences to the live theatre. One of Black's photo plays lasted a full two hours and contained as many as four slides a minute, based on the same kind of melodramatic plot and suffering characters that the early movies (which were often called "photoplays") would themselves use.

By the late nineteenth century, several other audience entertainments combined visual images, the play of light, and the telling of a story. The Panorama presented a huge painted mural, which evolved from day to dusk to night to dawn to day again, while the action moved across the variously illuminated surfaces of the picture. The movies have paid homage to their Panorama ancestors—examples include the lighting changes on a scenic backdrop in Chaplin's *Monsieur Verdoux* and Hitchcock's *Rope*. The Diorama was an even more complicated version of the same kind of show, capable of presenting two different pictures (and, therefore, capable of scene changes) by rotating the seated audience itself from a view of one large mural to the other.

Even the late nineteenth-century theatre was devoted to spectacular visual and mechanical effects. The conversion from oil lighting to the more controllable gas and, finally, to totally malleable electricity, coupled with the invention of elaborately mechanized scene-changing devices, led to such spectacular visual effects on stage as chases, last-minute rescues, dazzling transformations of one scene into another, and even the rapid shifts of visual setting that the movies would later codify as the cross-cut.

Such predecessors clearly indicated the potential popularity of projected movie shows. The problem was to develop a machine that could project the filmstrips. Two specific difficulties had deterred Edison: The projector needed a light source powerful enough to make the projected image clear and distinct, and the film needed to run smoothly and regularly past that light source without ripping, rattling, or burning. One of the first successful projections was made by a Virginia family of adventurer-inventors, the Lathams. Major Woodville Latham, former officer in the Confederate Army and former chemistry instructor, together with his two dashing sons, Gray and Otway, invented a camera and projecting machine in 1895 (called either the Panoptikon or the Eidoloscope) that produced better results than Edison's. The Lathams doubled the width of Edison's film to approximately 70mm. The bigger film produced a clearer, brighter, sharper picture. Although the Lathams gave a few showings in southern cities and in New York, their stay in the temptingly big city converted the younger Lathams from scientists to playboys. The Lathams and their invention ended in the obscurity of financial disaster.

A successful projector had to do more than just enlarge the film. It had to feed and take up film on reels rather than run the film as a necessarily short, continuous loop, and it required a totally new principle of moving the film past the gate. The new principle, discovered and developed in Europe rather than America, used an intermittent movement of the film rather than a continuous one. Each frame stopped momentarily in front of the lamp and was then succeeded by the next frame, which stopped, and then the next, which stopped, and so forth. Thanks to Dickson's perforations, the Kinetograph had used intermittent movement to stop the film during exposure, but the Kinetoscope had moved the film continuously (behind a rotating, slotted shutter that allowed a glimpse of each frame as the film rolled by). Intermittent movement in the projector allowed a clear, sharp image, for the stationary frame used the available light more economically.

The intermittent motion was, in principle, precisely the same as the slits in the Phenakistoscope; rather than a continuous succession of whirring images, each image was separated from the others into an individual piece of the whole. Although the intermittent movement of the film frames past the projection gate solved the problem of insufficient illumination, it could not cure the disease of ripping film without a tiny adjustment to take the tension off the jerkily speeding film. That adjustment was to create a small loop of excess film just before the gate, easing the tension from the feeding reel. Because the initial loop was used — and patented — by the Lathams for their camera (but, ironically, not their projector), it became known around the world as the *Latham Loop*, which all movie cameras and projectors still use today, in most cases both before and after the gate. The loop also provided a key legal loophole that allowed Edison — once he bought the rights — to drag his competitors into court for almost a decade, attempting to get back the money he had lost from his initial patenting mistakes.

The single problem caused by intermittent projection was the possibility of burning the highly flammable nitrate film that remained momentarily stationary in the gate. To solve this problem, the intermittent motion projector required some kind of cooling system to protect the film. Today, despite all the changes and improvements in movie equipment, our projectors are the same in principle as those invented in the final years of the nineteenth century.

As early as November, 1888, a Frenchman working in England, Louis Aimé Augustin Le Prince (Dickson's only competition for the title of Inventor of the Movies), patented machines that both shot and projected motion pictures (two of which, taken in October, 1888, survive), using intermittent motion in both processes. He also shot several filmstrips with a machine that used perforated film and a much slower film speed than Edison's (twenty frames per second). Le Prince's influence on the history of film is minor, however, for in 1890 he — and his equipment and films — mysteriously disappeared from a train between Dijon and Paris; he was never found. In 1893, an Englishman, William Friese-Greene, patented a combination camera–projector. Because the same machine that shot the films also projected them, and because cameras had always used intermittent motion, intermittent motion for projection was guaranteed. Unfortunately, there is no evidence that this early machine ever successfully photographed or projected any films. The two most significant projectors were developed by men who began, ironically, by buying Edison Kinetographs and analyzing them. Edison's oversight in neglecting European rights allowed an Englishman, R. W. Paul, and, more importantly, two French brothers, appropriately named Lumière (French for "light"), to invent a functional projector and build a more functional camera.

Auguste Marie Louis Nicolas Lumière, the elder, and Louis Jean Lumière, the younger and more important of the two inventor brothers, started dabbling with Edison's Kinetoscope and Kinetograph in 1894. Their father, an avid photographer, had founded a factory in Lyon for manufacturing photographic plates and, later, celluloid film. Interested by the new motion photography, these scientist–industrialist–mechanic brothers developed their own machine within a year. Unlike Edison's bulky indoor camera, the Lumière camera was portable; it could be carried any-

The Lumières' first film:
Workers Leaving the Lumière Factory.

Fig. 2-8

where. The operator turned a hand crank rather than pushed an electric button. It used 35mm film. In addition, the same machine that shot the pictures also printed and projected them. While the machine admitted light through its lens during filming, it projected light through its lens during projection. Intermittent motion was guaranteed for movie photography, printing, and projection.

Early in 1895 the Lumière brothers shot their first film, *Workers Leaving the Lumière Factory.* Beginning in March of the same year, the Lumières projected this film and several others to private, specially invited audiences of scientists and friends throughout Europe. The first movie theatre opened to the paying public on December 28, 1895 in the basement room of the Grand Café in Paris. This date marks the generally accepted birthday of the movies. The Lumières showed several films, among them *Workers Leaving the Lumière Factory*, a Lumière baby's meal (*Le Repas de bébé*, the first home movie), a comical incident about a gardener's getting his face doused through a boy's prank (*L'Arroseur arrosé*, the first narrative film, happily a comedy), and a train rushing into a railway station (*L'Arrivée d'un train en gare*). The last film provoked the most reaction, as the au-

dience shrieked and ducked when it saw the train hurtling toward them. In Jean-Luc Godard's *Les Carabiniers*—Godard packs his films with historical tidbits—a farm boy watches his first movie, which is also a train arriving at a station, using the same camera angle and diagonal composition as the Lumières' film. The boy ducks, just as the first movie audiences did in the café theatre. Audiences would have to learn how to watch movies.

The Lumière discovery of 1895 established the brothers as the most influential and important men in motion pictures in the world, eclipsing the power and prestige of Edison's Kinetograph and Kinetoscope. Within five years, the light of the Lumières would also fade. The brothers were more interested in the scientific curiosity of their discovery than the art or business of it, although eventually their film catalogue included over one thousand filmstrips for purchase. The Lumières sent the first camera crews all over the globe, recording the most interesting scenes and cities of the earth for the delight and instruction of a public who would never be able to travel to such places on their own. Theirs were the first films to be shown in India, Japan, and other countries, inspiring film industries and filmgoing around the world.

From Russia and Sweden to Guatemala and Senegal, the Lumières were the Johnny Appleseeds of cinema; in this respect (among others) their importance far exceeds that of Edison. Despite their brief hegemony, the Lumière brothers established patterns and practices that have remained standard throughout the history of film. The Lumières set the film width at 35mm, still the standard width of film today. They also established the film speed of sixteen frames per second, a functional silent speed until the invention of sound required a faster one for better sound reproduction. The slower film speed allowed their projector to run more quietly and dependably. Edison, maintaining the visual superiority of the forty-plus frames per second of his Kinetoscope, scoffed that the Lumière speed would destroy the sensation of continuous movement; only a year later Edison himself adopted the Lumière speed for his projector. And a final Lumière contribution was the fancy name they coined for their invention—the Cinématographe (from the Greek "motion recorder" or "kinetic writer"); it is one of the few Greco-Latin names to survive the first era of invention. In many countries today, the movies are the cinema, and shooting is cinematography.

Almost simultaneously with the Lumières, experimenters in England, Germany, and America were making progress on their own machines. In England, Robert William Paul and Birt Acres each borrowed Edison's unpatented machines as a basis for their own significant discoveries. In Berlin, Max and Emil Skladanowsky entertained audiences with their Bioskop (or Bioscope), a camera and projector they had developed independently of any other invention. In America, a young inventor named Thomas Armat independently discovered the Lumière principle that all film movement should be intermittent. It was Armat who discovered the efficacy of the small loop to relax the film's tension, and Armat who added the Latham Loop to his projector. Early in 1896, Thomas Armat and Thomas Edison came to a business agreement. Edison would sell Armat's projector as his own invention, enhancing the prestige and sales potential of the machine. Armat would silently receive a percentage of the sales. The Edison company announced its

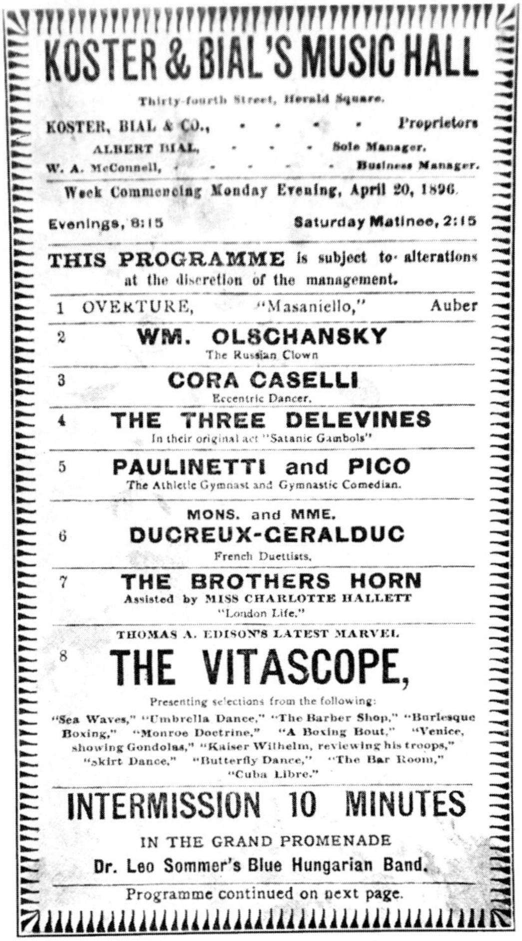
KOSTER & BIAL'S MUSIC HALL

Thirty-fourth Street, Herald Square.

KOSTER, BIAL & CO., ... Proprietors
ALBERT BIAL, ... Sole Manager.
W. A. McConnell, ... Business Manager.

Week Commencing Monday Evening, April 20, 1896.

Evenings, 8:15 Saturday Matinee, 2:15

THIS PROGRAMME is subject to alterations at the discretion of the management.

1 OVERTURE, "Masaniello," Auber

2 WM. OLSCHANSKY
The Russian Clown

3 CORA CASELLI
Eccentric Dancer.

4 THE THREE DELEVINES
In their original act "Satanic Gambols"

5 PAULINETTI and PICO
The Athletic Gymnast and Gymnastic Comedian.

6 MONS. and MME. DUCREUX-GERALDUC
French Duettists.

7 THE BROTHERS HORN
Assisted by MISS CHARLOTTE HALLETT
"London Life."

8 THOMAS A. EDISON'S LATEST MARVEL
THE VITASCOPE,
Presenting selections from the following:
"Sea Waves," "Umbrella Dance," "The Barber Shop," "Burlesque Boxing," "Monroe Doctrine," "A Boxing Bout," "Venice, showing Gondolas," "Kaiser Wilhelm, reviewing his troops," "Skirt Dance," "Butterfly Dance," "The Bar Room," "Cuba Libre."

INTERMISSION 10 MINUTES
IN THE GRAND PROMENADE
Dr. Leo Sommer's Blue Hungarian Band.

Programme continued on next page.

Fig. 2-9
The program for the Vitascope's debut at Koster & Bial's Music Hall in 1896.

latest invention, the Vitascope ("life viewer"), a projecting version of the "Wizard's" Kinetoscope.

The first public showing of a projected motion picture in the United States is difficult to fix. The Lathams projected a boxing film to a paying audience in May, 1895. Thomas Armat demonstrated his projector in Richmond, Virginia, before selling it to Edison. Several other American inventors—Jean-Aimé le Roy, Eugene Lauste, Herman Casler, C. Francis Jenkins—also demonstrated projection machines to limited audiences as early as 1891. The first Edison projection for a paying audience was on

April 23, 1896, at Koster & Bial's Music Hall on 34th Street and Broadway in New York City —the present site of Macy's. The "amazing Vitascope" was only one act in a vaudeville bill; movies became a typical part of vaudeville shows in the United States until they started filling their own theatres shortly after the turn of the century.

For the first Vitascope program, Edison converted several of his Kinetoscope strips for the projector; he also pirated a few of the R. W. Paul films from England. One good piracy deserved another. As with the first Lumière showings, the most exciting films were those with action that came straight out at the audience. During the showing of a filmstrip of *The Beach at Dover*, patrons in the front rows ran screaming from their seats, afraid they were about to be drenched. Those cynics who were unimpressed were sure that the film had been shot in New Jersey.

The First Films

The first film audiences were amazed to see that living, moving action could be projected on an inert screen by a machine. Frank Norris's novel *McTeague* (which became the basis of Erich von Stroheim's *Greed*) affectionately records an immigrant family's first experience of the Vitascope in a vaudeville theatre, certain that the images were produced by some kind of conventional magic trick. It was an illusion all right, but not a conventional one—an illusion that allowed them to see the world as it had never been seen before.

It is easy to forget the way the world looked to our ancestors of a century ago—a world without automobiles, airplanes, television, radio, and movies. How could an American view life in London? How could a Frenchman ever view the Pacific Ocean? How could one person in a single lifetime ever expect to view the tropics, the frigid north, the many cities of the world, and its various mountains, plains, seas, and deserts? Except for the few who could afford the time and cost of laborious travel, it was impossible to experience the sights of all these places. True, there were paintings—but they were idealized impressions. And there

were photographs—even three-dimensional photographed images in relief for stereopticon viewers. But none of these images moved (and, in a very real sense, life can be equated with movement—that is one meaning of "animate").

The movies were very much a part of the process that has produced what today seems a global culture—our ability to view and to travel to any place on earth in less time than it would take a person to travel twenty miles two centuries ago. Newspapers (which rose to cultural prominence in the mid-eighteenth century), the train (a development of the early nineteenth century), the photograph (in the mid-nineteenth century), automobile, airplane, telephone, radio, television—these are the media of transportation and communication that have metaphorically shrunk the world and have practically erased the distances between its inhabitants. At the center of this communication-transportation process—temporally and spiritually—are the movies.

The first films understandably exploited their visual wonder. The films that Louis Lumière shot for the Cinématographe and that Dickson's successors at Edison shot for the Vitascope were similar. A movie lasted between fifteen and ninety seconds. The camera was stationed in a single spot, turned on to record the action, and then turned off when the action had finished. These films were really "home movies"—unedited scenery, family activity, or posed action—that depended for their effect on the same source as today's home movies—the wonder of seeing something familiar and transitory reproduced in an unfamiliar and permanent way. Nowhere is the home-movie-like quality of the first films more obvious than in the Lumières' *Le Repas de bébé* (*Feeding Baby*, or *Baby's Breakfast*), which has been duplicated uncounted times by later generations of parents with their own 8mm or video equipment.

A major difference between the first Edison films and the first Lumière films is that the Lumières' have more of this home-movie quality of merely turning the camera on to record the events that happened to occur around it. The Edison films, despite their initial lack of editing and plot, were gropings toward a fictional, theatrical film, many of them shot in-

Fig. 2-10

A "home movie": the Lumières'
Feeding Baby; *Mr. and Mrs. Auguste*
Lumière with their daughter.

Fig. 2-11

The freedom of the outdoors and the
excitement of motion: the Lumières'
Boat Leaving the Port.

doors. The Lumière films, with a nose for the news, roamed around outdoors: They were freer, less stilted, better composed, more active.

The categories of the Lumières' catalogue indicate their conception of what the filmstrip would provide its audience. The catalogue breaks its films into different kinds of "views" —mere visual actualities—General Views, Comic Views, Military Views, Views of Diverse Countries. The most interesting views are those containing the most interesting patterns of movement: a boat struggling out to sea against the waves, the charge of a line of cavalry horses, the demolition of a wall.

One of the most celebrated Lumière films is the comic jest *L'Arroseur arrosé* (*The Sprinkler Sprinkled*, or *Watering the Gardener*). This incident—staged, but shot outdoors—contains the seeds of what was to blossom into one of the most important contributions of the silent film: physical comedy. While a man waters a garden, a boy sneaks behind him and steps on the hose. The flow of water stops, the gardener looks into the nozzle to see what's wrong, and the boy steps off the hose. Water gushes into the gar-

*John Rice and May Irwin enact
their kiss.*

Fig. 2-12

dener's face; the boy laughs. The gardener catches the boy, drags him back into camera range (since the camera refuses to pan to follow the action), spanks him, and resumes his watering.

This little film contains many elements of a comic art that would soon mature: The gag is completely physical; despite the improbability of the result, the causes are clear and credible; the butt of the joke is the victim of circumstances of which he is unaware; despite the victim's ignorance and innocence, the audience participates in the joke with the boy, laughing when the gardener gets drenched; the comic punishment (the spanking) is a blow to the ego more than to the body; the comic participants have obvious one-dimensional traits and roles so that complexity of character cannot interfere with the force of the jest; and the original situation is restored after the comic disruption. Above all, the comic incident is fictitious, even though Auguste and particularly Louis Lumière are correctly considered the fathers of the nonfiction film (the *actualité*, or direct, unbiased look at reality—as well as its successor, the documentary, which is organized to express a conviction or make a point about the factual material it presents).

For all their appearance of recording unstaged, spontaneous, real events, the Lumière films subtly incorporate the conventions of two artistic traditions that would powerfully influence the movies to follow. First, the Lumière films are very carefully composed, with symmetrical balancing of the left and right edges of the frame and interplay between the foreground and the deep space perspectives of the reargroound (especially for those actions that move directly toward the camera). As still photographers, the Lumières had borrowed these compositional patterns from Western representational painting—as most early photographers did.

Second, the Lumière films organize their filmed events as little stories according to the most basic narrative pattern of beginning, middle, and end. The Lumière films, as brief as they are, do not usually begin with the event or action in progress. Instead, the camera establishes the scene before that action starts; then the event occurs from start to finish; and only after the movement has terminated does the camera quit the scene. The very first Lumière film, *Workers Leaving the Lumière Factory*, establishes this pattern. As the film begins, the large double doors of the factory are closed. They swing open for the camera, almost like the curtain rising in the theatre, and the workers pour out. Some move off frame to the right and some to the left (for compositional balance and to avoid hitting the camera), some manipulate "props" (a bicycle), and some are accompanied by a companion (a dog). In one of the very earliest examples, the movies showed their affinity for machines and animals as well as people. Only after the workers have all left the factory do the double doors begin to swing shut, concluding the film with the suggestion of the event's ending and the curtain's falling. However innocent and lifelike such a film might seem, it is not at all unstaged, unplanned, or unstructured.

The early Edison films lack the outdoor freshness and freedom of those produced by the Lumières; Edison's fail to understand and exploit the wonder and beauty of watching the world at work and at play, at rest and in motion. Typical is the staged heaviness of the first special-effects film, *The Execution of Mary, Queen of Scots* (1895), directed for Edison's peephole viewer by Alfred Clark, who got Dickson's job when Dickson left Edison. In less than a half-minute of film, besheeted guards lead Mary to the block, push her on it, and whack off her head.

Despite its primitive quality, two elements of this originally terrifying film are worth special attention. First, the camera clearly thinks of itself as a spectator in the theatre. It watches from a fixed angle, a good seat. The characters move left and right in a single plane, rather than using the full depth that films were later to discover. Further, the film has a strong sense of entrance and exit, two more stage devices the mature film would discard. This stage mentality would continue to influence the movies for over fifteen years. Second, the film shows one clear realization of the potential of the film medium. After Mary (a male actor) sets her head on the block, the camera stops to allow a dummy to be substituted for Mary and be decapitated. The ability to stop the action and start it again without any apparent break (which makes *Mary* the first two-shot-long Edison film, though it is made to look like a single shot; a few frames were snipped from the end of the

actor shot and the start of the dummy shot, and a splice was made) is one of the advantages that the camera enjoys over the stage. Within a very few years, a French magician, Georges Méliès, would make much of this camera advantage.

A second interesting Edison film, and certainly the most famous of the early ones, is *The Irwin–Rice Kiss*. Shot originally for the Kinetoscope in 1896, this kiss, when projected on the large screen, excited the first wave of moralistic reaction to movie romance, which has remained a constant in film history. John C. Rice and May Irwin were the romantic leads in *The Widow Jones*, a current Broadway stage success; the Edison Company got them to perform their climactic kiss in the Black Maria. When moralists and reformers saw their large, projected mouths meet in lascivious embrace, they showered the newspapers with letters and the politicians with petitions. Upon seeing *The Kiss* today, the viewer would probably find more obscenity in the dumpy unattractiveness of the two bussers than in their "torrid" smooch.

Although Lumière specialized in actualities and Edison in theatrical and staged scenes, the success of each company in its particular genre led to imitations by the other. Edison's *Washday Troubles* (1898) is a clear descendant of Lumière's gardener film, substituting a washtub of soapy water for Lumière's hose. After seeing Edison's success with historical scenes, Lumière began staging those such as *Marat* and *Robespierre* in 1897. In addition to borrowing successful formulas — a practice that would continue throughout movie history and into television programming — the two companies literally stole each other's films, made up duplicate prints (dupes) or reshot them without significant changes, and sold them as their own. In addition to competing with and stealing from each other, Edison and Lumière faced competition and thievery from rivals who were springing up in England, America, and France. The next ten years of film history would be a decade of commercial lawlessness as well as aesthetic discovery.

3

Film Narrative,
Commercial Expansion

The two film rulers of 1895, Lumière and Edison, would encounter crafty and powerful competitors within a year. In France, the Lumière superiority was attacked by an artist on one side and by industrialists on the other. Georges Méliès, owner – prestidigitator of the Théâtre Robert-Houdin, saw the movies as a means of inflating his bag of magical tricks. He immediately recognized the cinematic possibilities for fantasy and illusion. In 1896 he asked the Lumières to sell him a camera and projector. When the Lumières, who insisted on licensing their own franchises to shoot and show their own kinds of actualities, refused to sell a Cinématographe, he bought one of R. W. Paul's Theatrographs in London. Méliès shot his first film of illusory tricks, *A Game of Cards,* in the spring of 1896. By 1902, Méliès was supplying the world with films and the Lumières had almost ceased production.

Two other Frenchmen, Charles Pathé and Léon Gaumont, also began building huge film empires in 1896, several colonies of which still exist today. Charles Pathé and his three brothers formed Pathé Frères, which began by copying the familiar Lumière formulas of "views" and "actualities." But the Pathé goal was not entertainment but conquest: to control all branches of the French film industry. Within a very few years Pathé embraced everything to do with motion pictures; it manufactured cameras and projectors, manufactured raw film stock (after acquiring George Eastman's European patent rights), produced the filmstrips, and owned a chain of theatres for showing them. The American film industry would grope hesitatingly toward this monolithic vertical integration that the Pathés quickly realized. Léon Gaumont's perceptions were similar; he founded a film empire whose activities ranged from manufacturing machine parts to collecting receipts at the theatre door.

The English film between 1896 and 1906 was perhaps the most innovative in the world. R. W. Paul, who had been displaying the products of his Theatrograph (which he later renamed the Animatograph) for almost a year, began attracting other inventor – photographers to experiment with moving pictures. This group became known as the "school of Brighton." G. A. Smith, James Williamson, and Cecil Hepworth made significant and rapid

27

progress with the principles of editing and composition, realizing that the effect of a filmed story was a function of the way the individual shots were composed and stitched together. Until the emergence of D. W. Griffith some ten years later, the films of these British directors were the most visually imaginative on the screen, precisely because they had discovered the importance of editing for both building a story and driving its rhythms.

An American, Charles Urban, joined the native Englishmen to enrich the British film further in this period. Urban, who had tried unsuccessfully to peddle his Edison-imitation camera (called the Bioscope) in America, journeyed to London to try his luck there. Fearing the stigma of Americanism, Urban christened his London concern the Warwick Trading Company. Despite the name, the Urban company pioneered in its production of scientific films using microcinematography and in its development of the first successful color process, which Urban called Kinemacolor (1908, based largely on the discoveries of G. A. Smith). These British pioneers discovered the elements of film construction that Griffith would later fuse into more powerful movie chemistry: the close-up, the cross-cut, the traveling shot, and the pan shot. It is not clear whether the Brighton school or Méliès first discovered superimposition.

In the United States, artistic and industrial progress was much slower than in England or France. The era of tinkering, piracy, and imitation lasted until after the turn of the twentieth century. By 1897, however, the two companies that would share the power with Edison — Biograph and Vitagraph — had begun making and showing films. The American Mutoscope and Biograph Company (American Biograph for short) manufactured both a peepshow machine and a projecting machine that outperformed Edison's. The primary inventive intelligence behind "Biograph" ("life recorder"), as the company was to be called, was Edison's own film pioneer, W. K. L. Dickson. Dickson had left Edison in 1895 because of tensions and dissatisfaction to go to work for the Lathams; when he found the social life of the Lathams too "fast" (according to his own legal testimony), he went on to become the

"D" of the K.M.C.D. Syndicate later in 1895. The early film companies often took their names from the initials of their owners; Dickson's initial joined Eugene Koopman's, Henry Marvin's, and Herman Casler's.

The K.M.C.D.'s first project was the Mutoscope, their peephole machine, whose effectiveness put the Kinetoscope out of business. Like the Kinetoscope, the Mutoscope offered a series of moving photographs to the eyes of a single viewer. Unlike the Kinetoscope's celluloid frames, however, the Mutoscope pictures were large photographs mounted on individual cards. When the viewer flipped the series of cards with a hand crank, they were held still for an instant by a hook, allowing a good steady view of each frame and producing the same appearance of movement as a motion picture. The large picture cards made the Mutoscope pictures clearer, more detailed, and more lifelike than the Kinetoscope's. The hand crank added to the viewer's pleasure by allowing the motion to go slower, go faster, or stop. The ultimate testimony to the Mutoscope is that of all the archaic and outdated machines of the invention era, it survives most prominently today — in penny arcades and amusement parks — delighting children with some of the same photographs that their great-grandparents flicked through over ninety years ago. The machine has also survived in "adult" book stores, engaging patrons with a type of photographic entertainment that could not have been envisioned by the Messrs. K.M.C.D.

The K.M.C.D. motion picture machine also bested its Edison opponent. Like the Latham projector, the Biograph used much larger film than Edison's or the Lumières' (a single frame would fill a 4 × 5 inch Mutoscope card). Dickson adopted this large-format film not merely to improve photographic clarity but also to circumvent Edison's patents on all methods of transporting the smaller gauges of film. Dickson, in effect, invented the motion picture twice. The similarity of the oversized film implies that Dickson may have developed the Latham machine as well as the Biograph. The Biograph camera's huge pictures could either be mounted on Mutoscope cards or, when combined with its intermittent-motion projector, throw the sharpest, clearest images that

Fig. 3-1
The Mutoscope.

As he had done at Edison's West Orange laboratories, Dickson built a special studio for shooting staged scenes. The first Biograph studio was outdoors, on the roof of the Biograph Company's offices near Broadway and 14th Street in New York City. As in the Black Maria, the stage of Dickson's roof theatre rotated to keep the sun at the best lighting angle. From this nuts-and-bolts beginning the company evolved that was to give its name to moving pictures in some parts of the world (in Danish the cinema is still called the *biograf*; both Chicago and London still have theatres called the Biograph) and that was to launch the careers of D. W. Griffith, Mack Sennett, Mary Pickford, the Gish sisters, and many others.

Edison's second major competitor was the Vitagraph Company, which had a less spectacular career than Biograph but a longer one. Vitagraph's founder and director of production was J. Stuart Blackton, another Americanized Englishman, who began as a reporter and cartoonist for the *New York World*. Blackton first became interested in moving pictures when he visited Edison at the Black Maria; he even performed his sketching act for Edison's Kinetograph. Edison soon leased Blackton a Vitascope franchise. Blackton repaid Edison's kindnesses by copying Edison's machine and making pictures on his own. Realizing the appeal of the Edison company, Blackton and his partners, William "Pop" Rock and Albert E. Smith, chose a name for their company that was as close to Edison's as the law would allow. Vitagraph's first film, *Burglar on the Roof* (1897), was appropriately filmed on the rooftop of their office building in Chelsea. For several years Manhattan rooftops doubled as film studios. Another interesting early Vitagraph film was *Tearing Down the Spanish Flag* (1898), an attempt to capitalize on the Spanish-American War. Although the film claimed to have been shot in the heat of battle, Blackton actually staged it in the heat of Manhattan on his friendly rooftop.

Others all over the country were catching the movie craze, assembling machines, and capturing images. In Chicago, three men began tinkering independently: George Kleine, George K. Spoor, and "Colonel" Selig. Kleine would one day become the "K" of the Kalem

had yet been seen on a screen. (Later Biograph movies were shot on standard 35mm stock. Films shot for the Mutoscope were called "mutoscopes"; those shot for projection were called "biographs.") Dickson's films were also more interesting and active than Edison's: the Empire State Express (yet another thrilling train shot), President McKinley receiving a letter at home, the actor Joseph Jefferson performing scenes from his famous *Rip Van Winkle*.

(K.L.M.) Company that produced the first *Ben-Hur* in 1907. Spoor would one day become the "S" of Essanay (S&A) who, with his partner, G. M. ("Broncho Billy") Anderson, would shoot the first series of westerns. William Selig, who liked to be called "Colonel," modeled the Selig Standard Camera and the Polyscope projector on the Lumière Cinématographe; in 1907 he sent a crew to Los Angeles to shoot parts of *The Count of Monte Cristo,* the first filming done in Hollywood. In Philadelphia, Sigmund Lubin began several tricky activities, including "duping" (illegally duplicating) films made by others to eliminate the problem of paying for them and re-enacting events like a heavyweight title bout or the Oberammergau Passion Play on his Philadelphia rooftop. He even precisely re-enacted film hits like *The Great Train Robbery.* Movie projectionists trooped across the country with their filmstrips much as the magic lanternists had trooped across Europe with their slides a century earlier. One of these projectionists toured the Caribbean, drawing audiences and applause with the unauthorized adopted name of Thomas Edison, Jr.; his real name was Edwin S. Porter.

Narrative

Despite the frenzy of movie activity in the United States, the films did not change much until 1902 or 1903. New films imitated the successes of earlier ones; like television and film producers today, the earliest film producers copied successful formulas. The new films were longer, of course, freed from the fifty-foot limit of the Kinetoscope box. But the same rushing trains, ocean and mountain views, one-joke pranks, and historical vignettes dominated the screen. Audiences began to yawn at these same predictable film subjects. The motion picture, formerly the highlight of a vaudeville bill, became the "chaser," the part of the program that was so dull that it chased the old audience out so that the new one could file in. By 1900 the movies were suffering the first of a series of business crises.

The rope that pulled the movies from the abyss was the development of a new kind of screen entertainment. The rope-abyss image is

an apt one, for the new kind of movie, the story film, was to use this and similar heart-stopping devices to weave its spell. The movies were born into the age of theatrical producer David Belasco; they have never quite outgrown that heritage. The Belasco theatre era traded on extreme emotional effects—violent tears, violent suspense, violent laughter. The two dominant theatre genres were melodrama and farce; they were to become the two dominant film genres as well. The most respected playwrights were Scribe and Sardou, Jones and Pinero, Dion Boucicault, Bronson Howard, Augustin Daly, and Belasco himself. In these plays, good and evil were as clearly distinct as black type on a white page. Though evil triumphed over good for the first two hours of the play, good miraculously won out in the last fifteen minutes. Melodrama was a world of pathos, not of tragedy, of fears and tears, not of ideas. No action was irreversible; no matter what mistake the good-hearted character made, it would eventually be erased by his or her essential goodness. The era's farce was just as extroverted; a series of comic mistakes would arise, entangle, and explode until the denouement put all the pieces of the puzzle together. There was no reason a film could not tell the same kinds of stories.

The problem was to translate these dramatic stories into film terms. There had been early attempts at screen narrative (Blackton's *Burglar on the Roof,* for example). But these early narrative films merely pieced together the same kinds of static, unedited scenes that were shot for the first Kinetoscope—expanding the fifty-foot strip to a whole reel. A good example of one of these films is *Pullman Honeymoon* (1898). This Edison product (shot in the large multi-set studio that replaced the Black Maria) records a series of events that might take place in one of George Pullman's sleeping cars between porters and passengers, lovers, comics, bandits, and the police. The film is strikingly inert. The movie set is a stage set: The berths line the frame at left and right; the center aisle of the Pullman car serves as the stage-center playing area. Although the film lasts almost ten minutes, the camera never shifts its viewing angle nor its distance from any of the action. As in the earlier Edison strips, the camera is the single spectator at a staged play. The only noticeable participation of the camera in the action is that it stops after each incident and then starts again. But the slight jumps between the scenes indicate that the filmmaker tried (and failed) to make these gaps invisible, to keep the camera from participating in the event, refusing to exploit the cinema's ability to manipulate time. Further, because the film uses only one setup, the effect is ploddingly static; the passive camera never picks out any details; no action, character, or object is made to be more important than anything else.

The Frenchman, Georges Méliès, was a much better film storyteller, precisely because he exploited the very difference between time in nature and in the cinema that *Pullman Honeymoon* tried to cover up. The Méliès films owe their superiority to the wild imagination and subtle debunking humor of their master. Méliès was by trade a magician; just as earlier magicians had adopted the magic lantern, Méliès adopted moving pictures. He saw that the camera's ability to stop and start again (stop-motion photography, an effect achieved in the camera rather than through cutting) brought the magician's two greatest arts to perfection — disappearance and conversion. Anything could be converted into anything else; anything could vanish.

One of Méliès's greatest and most enjoyable films, *The Conjuror* (1899), is nothing but one fast minute of disappearances and transformations. The magician (played by Méliès himself) vanishes, his lady assistant vanishes, she turns into snow, he turns into her, and she turns into him. Pure cinema — as pure in its own way as its opposite, the realism of Lumière. That same year, Méliès made *The Dreyfus Affair,* the first movie since *The Execution of Mary, Queen of Scots* to consist of more than one shot (*Dreyfus* has ten scenes, each one — like *every* Méliès scene — a single shot, usually incorporating stop-motion effects, taken by an unmoving camera), the twenty-scene *Cinderella,* and ten or twenty others. Between 1896 (when he founded the Star Film Company) and 1913, he made about five hundred amazing movies, of which fewer than one hundred forty survive. He was cer-

tainly the first Frenchman, and probably the first filmmaker, to use superimposition (multiple exposure), hand-painting (a dab of red on the photographed dress, orange on the fire, blue on the curtain, every single frame), the dissolve, and time-lapse photography. Even allowing for the earlier *The Execution of Mary, Queen of Scots* and *Watering the Gardener* (whose possibilities neither Clark nor Lumière pursued further), the position of Méliès as the father of the special effects film — and every cinematic use of the fantastic — is beyond challenge, and the narrative film itself belongs on the list of his credits.

Griffith said "I owe everything to him."

In *The Magic Lantern* (1903), Méliès compared the art of the magician to that of the filmmaker. (Ingmar Bergman would draw much the same metaphorical parallel decades later in *The Magician,* 1958, and *Fanny and Alexander,* 1982.) *The Magic Lantern* contains its own little history of Western visual representation and dramatic art. First, the lantern projects a static landscape (a recreation of the painter's art); then it projects a pair of lovers in fancy wigs and costumes (a recreation of the aristocratic theatre); finally, the lantern projects the magician himself and his clownlike servant (an image of the common people, of movies themselves). These reflexive films-within-the film demonstrate at a very early date the filmmaker's conscious equation of cinema, comedy, and magic. The magic box, like a new kind of circus-clown car, is impossibly full of figures, for it can capture, store, and present any image in a world of images.

Méliès was the first filmmaker to light films from the side as well as from above, thanks to the glass walls and roof of the studio he built at Montreuil (just outside Paris) in 1897. Like Dickson's Black Maria, the Montreuil studio relied on sunlight — artificial lighting truly adequate for cinematography was not introduced until 1904 — but its glass walls allowed a richer, more fully modeled lighting plan and washed out the top-lit shadows characteristic of earlier studio work. In 1899 Méliès was the first to diffuse, or soften, light by filtering it through cotton sheets or rippled glass; not until 1902 did any other studio (Pathé) begin to use dif-

fused lighting, and it took Edison and Biograph
another two years to catch up.

Méliès's most famous work is the thirty-
scene *A Trip to the Moon* (1902), which successfully combines his fantasy and his humor into
a naïvely charming film full of trick effects.
Méliès parodies the intellectual doings of aca-
demics in the opening scene as a crazy professor
(Méliès again) earnestly demonstrates his points
and makes his ideological opponents disappear.
Méliès's parody of the intelligentsia continues
in his later *The Doctor's Secret* (1910) and *The
Conquest of the Pole* (1912). Delightfully whimsical in *A Trip to the Moon* are the rocket ship's
landing with a splat in the eye of the man in the
moon, the lines of chorus girls who wave goodbye to the moonship and lend their faces to the
seven stars of the Pleiades, and the jumpy gymnastics of the moon creatures who go up in
puffs of smoke when the scientists whack them
with their umbrellas. In *A Trip to the Moon*,
stars and planets twirl about the heads of the
sleeping scientists, and the explorers gesticulate
with delight when they see the earth rise.

There was a previous tendency for film his-

torians, most interested in establishing editing
as the essential cinematic operation, to dispar-
age the work of Méliès. True enough, for all his
visual playfulness, he was still very much a stage
creator, shaping effects for a passive camera,
delighting in the play of plaster, pulleys, and
paint. The earth's rising was contrived by pulling up the earth and pulling down the rear part
of the moon's crust; the ship's landing on the
moon was contrived by moving the moon closer
to the camera, not by moving the camera closer
to the moon. Méliès clearly saw the film as parallel to a stageplay, and he referred to his technique as making "artificially arranged scenes."
The structure of *A Trip to the Moon* reveals his
thinking: Though the film shifts locations
(*Pullman Honeymoon* did not), each scene is
presented in a single, unedited shot. Even so,
The Conjuror reminds us that the camera could
be turned off and on many times during a single Méliès "shot."

Méliès also composes the scenes as on a
stage; he is conscious of limited depth, of entrances and exits. This staging is weakest in
those scenes in which the performers merely
line up in a row across the screen. The staginess
of Méliès's technique is especially clear in his
Oriental fantasy film, *The Palace of the Arabian
Nights* (1905), in which we can see the trap
doors opening, the wires pulling, and the cardboard scenery sliding.

Méliès took great pride in his scenic decor
and effects, which he painted and plastered and
conceived himself. In that respect alone he
must be recognized as the father of art direction. Theatricality aside, however, Méliès's
camera tricks relied completely on his realization of the essential difference between natural
time, which is perfectly continuous, and cinematic time, which seems continuous in projection, even if it was not so in filming.

Film theorists of a later generation —
particularly Siegfried Kracauer and André
Bazin — observed that Méliès and his contemporary, Louis Lumière, established the two
potential directions of the cinema in the very
infancy of the art: Lumière's realism (the rendering of the world as it is) and Méliès's fantasy
(the recreation of the world — or creation of
any world — through the filmmaker's imagination). Interestingly, these theorists find

Méliès's A Trip to the Moon: *A chorus line bids farewell to the space ship.*

Fig. 3-3

Lumière's realism the more legitimate path. But such a judgment overlooks the fact that, in contrast to the often impersonal filmstrips of Lumière, the Méliès films reveal a wit behind the camera's lens still capable of producing laughter and delight in an audience that has seen nine decades of later films. The Méliès films abound in surreal surprises and audacious sight-gags-in-time (unlike the later custard pie, which is a sight-gag-in-space), clearly demonstrating that a motion picture could result from the human acts of creation and imagination, do far more than record physical reality, and even lie.

After 1899, Méliès's peak year as a creative artist and as a businessman was 1902. His trademark, the star, was seen all over the world. That star steadily declined in the first decade of the century, if only because his painstakingly personal artisanship could not compete with the factory methods of Gaumont and Pathé. By 1914 he had lost his audience, made his last film, turned his studio into a theatre where he went back to performing magic tricks, and disappeared from the screen like one of the moon creatures in his most famous film. Fourteen years later a journalist discovered him selling toys and candy at a kiosk in the Gare Montparnasse. His fame and films (some of which Méliès himself had destroyed out of bitterness; most of the rest had been requisitioned by the military during World War I and melted down for boot heels — call it disappearance and conversion) were revived. After receiving the Legion of Honor as well as a small pension from his admirers, he died in 1938.

Méliès had an immense influence on other directors in France and all over the world. Porter's *Dream of a Rarebit Fiend* (1906) is as indebted to Méliès as it is to the hallucinatory comic strip (*Dreams of the Rarebit Fiend*) by Winsor McCay, who himself went on to make animated films (including *Gertie the Dinosaur*, 1909 and 1914). The second most imaginative French filmmaker of the decade, Emile Cohl, also delighted in the irrational surprises of a world of tricks. Cohl applied the tricks that Méliès played with the natural world to animated drawings. The surreal illogic of the Cohl cartoons is much closer in spirit to the wild transformations of objects in the early Disney cartoons or in the trippy *Yellow Submarine* (1968) than to the more realistic later Disney cartoon. Like his American contemporary,

Fig. 3-4
Cohl's **The Joyous Microbes**: *the disease of drunkenness.*

McCay, Cohl delighted in converting one kind of drawn figure into another: a stick that becomes a man that becomes a window, an angry woman whose head rolls off and turns into a parrot, a pool cue that becomes a straw. In *The Joyous Microbes* (1909), tiny microbic dots flow together to depict the diseases they supposedly cause. In another witty Cohl film, *The Neo-Impressionist Painter* (1910), a painter tries to sell his very arty abstract canvases to a buyer (the film is still topical today). As he describes each painting, the events and qualities he discusses come alive in line drawings on the canvas.

Méliès's success also influenced the films of Ferdinand Zecca. Zecca, who was director of production at Pathé in the first decade of the century, made films in all the popular genres: social commentaries, farces, and melodramas. But Zecca also made trick films like *Whence Does He Come?* (1904) in which a man leaps out of the sea and begins putting on clothes that also leap out at him. Méliès's influence is also clear in many of Zecca's chase films. The chase was almost obligatory in the first decade of the century; the excitement of people running after other people compensated for the stasis of the camera. Zecca was one of the masters of the chase, but he added new excitement when he combined the chase with trick shots. In *Slippery Jim* (1905), the police chase a criminal who successfully eludes them because he has the ability to disappear, to appear in two or three places at once, to fly in the air on a bicycle, to unscrew his feet and remove the fetters, and to wriggle out of any container or bind. Méliès's success accounts for the trick films of G. A. Smith and Charles Urban in England, for special effects films in Denmark and Germany, and, in fact, for everything from Edwin S. Porter's *Dream of a Rarebit Fiend* to Victor Sjøstrøm's *The Phantom Chariot* (1920, released 1921) and George Lucas's *Star Wars* (1977).

One of the most influential French filmmakers in the first decade of the twentieth century was more famous for his performing than for his directing of the films in which he starred. Max Linder was the first internationally famous star of motion pictures and the first film clown. *A Skater's Debut* in 1906, in which a clumsy man meets a pair of ice skates for the first time, was also the debut of a comic character, Max, who was to become the leading figure of hundreds of comic one- and two-reel films over the next decade. By 1910 Linder's yearly salary had jumped to over one million francs, and his face had become one of the most familiar in Europe. Linder, like Chaplin, Keaton, Lloyd, and Langdon who followed him, was a tiny man, and he used his smallness deliberately to contrast with the bigger opponents and obstacles he frequently faced. Linder's dancing moustache and dandyish mannerisms with hat and cane also set a pattern that Chaplin would follow (and expand). Linder specialized in drunken routines (also a Chaplin specialty) as in *Max and the Quinquina* (1911), in which a woozy Max makes a series of comic mistakes with both people and houses. He also specialized in debunking the intellectual, pretentious, and arty (like Méliès before him and Sennett after) as in *Max Plays at Drama* (c. 1912), which parodies classical tragedy and romantic melodrama, primarily by means of delightful anachronisms.

Because of his European popularity and American anonymity, the Essanay company brought Max to America in 1917 after Chaplin had left them. Both Max and Essanay soon failed. Although the films he made in America were slick and funny (especially the features, *Seven Years Bad Luck,* 1921, and *The Three Must-Get-Theres,* 1922), they never recaptured the popularity of his earlier, cruder, but livelier films in Europe.

In the French films of Linder and Zecca— as in the films of Méliès—one shot equalled one scene; the finished film was a series of scenes, not of shots. Each scene progressed chronologically, following the central character about. There were no leaps in time or space, no ellipses in the sequence of events. The camera was invariably distant enough from the playing to include the full bodies of all the players.

Then came Edwin S. Porter. After Porter returned from the Caribbean, he paid a visit to his "father," Mr. Edison, Sr., and asked for a job. Edison hired him as a cameraman; within a few years Porter became director of production for Edison's film company.

As a projectionist, Porter had often shown *A Trip to the Moon;* from it he learned that a film's action could continue from one scene to the next—that a picture could tell, as he put it, "a story in continuity form"; he was sure that would "draw the customers back to the theatres." His work, which directly prepared the way for Griffith's, showed that actions could be made to appear continuous from one *shot* to the next, that it was unnecessary to show scenes from beginning to end, and that a movie could cover events taking place simultaneously in different locations.

Porter's two most important films were released in 1903. *The Life of an American Fireman* (shot late in 1902) begins with the fireman-hero falling asleep, the subject of his reveries appearing in a superimposed white space near his head (a vignette, or "dream balloon"). This was the first time any film had attempted to present a character's thoughts, converting part of the movie screen into a "mindscreen"; later, Griffith revealed the logic of simply *cutting* to the character's mental visions (a full-frame mindscreen).

As the fireman dreams of a mother and child, then wakes—worried about those who may be in danger from fire at the moment— there is a cut to a close-up (in today's terms, a "close shot," but in any case the first that Porter had ever integrated into a narrative) of a fire alarm box and a hand setting off the alarm. The scene changes again to the fire station as the men tumble out of their beds (in response to the alarm, implying causal continuity from shot to shot), slide down the pole (in one shot, and reach the ground floor in the next), and rush out on their horse-drawn fire engines. The scenes of the fire brigade charging out of the station and down the street were bits of stock footage that Porter cut into the narrative (another first).

Up to this point, Porter's editing shows far more fluidity than Méliès's or Zecca's; he cuts freely—if a bit slowly—from place to place and from full shot to close shot, allowing the logic of the story rather than the scene-by-scene progress of the focal characters to determine the editing plan. In the film's final scene—the fireman rescuing a mother and baby from the burning house—Porter may have taken an even more imaginative step. There are two surviving versions of the film, referred to as "the copyright version" and "the cross-cut version"; each does the rescue scene differently.

In both versions the rescue scene is shown from two vantage points or setups—from inside the house (the woman and child awaiting rescue) and from outside it (the firemen setting up a ladder and saving them). In the copyright version, the audience sees the entire rescue and the putting out of the fire first from inside the house, then repeated in its entirety from outside the house.

The paper prints submitted for copyright were notoriously unconcerned about film continuity. Before 1912, films were not protected by copyright law, but still photographs were, since they could be printed on paper. Film companies solved this legal problem by sending individual still photographs of every frame of the movie on a roll of paper (called a "paper print"; see Figure 2-4 for an example). When doing so, they frequently omitted continuity devices (for example, printed titles) and even

Fig. 3-5

Fig. 3-6
Porter's **The Life of an American Fireman:** *the interior and exterior views of the rescue process.*

ignored the continuity of the film's narrative (copyrighting the film in the order in which the scenes were shot, rather than assembled, since their order was irrelevant to protecting the individual photographs). Because all the action outside the house was shot in one continuous take, it naturally appears in the paper print as one shot, as does the scene inside the house. This version violates chronology and common

sense by making the firemen go through the rescue twice.

The cross-cut version, which survived on film (but not in a 1903 print), is more comprehensible and daring. It cuts back and forth between the interior and the exterior of the house —that is, intercuts the two takes into a thirteen-shot sequence—turning the two place-bound setups into the coherent narration of a single temporal process. The fireman climbs up the ladder (outside), steps into the room and saves the woman (inside), climbs down the ladder with her and then up again when the woman tells him about the baby (outside), gets the baby (inside), and so on. Porter seems to have realized that the basis of film construction was not the scene but the sequence of shots that could be built into a scene.

The question is, did he edit the film that way? Which of these copies represents the film as it was originally released? The answer (established by film historian Charles Musser) turns out to be that the copyright version corresponds to the release version. The cross-cut version was re-edited (not by Porter) in the Griffith era. The fact that to cut back and forth between the interior and exterior views would have been logical does not mean that Porter thought of it in 1902. Nevertheless, *The Life of an American Fireman* remains a crucial link in the evolution of film narrative—for the way it integrated the alarm close-up into the firehouse actions, for the first attempt to film a dream, and for other reasons already mentioned. One not yet mentioned is that no matter how it was edited, the final rescue sequence reveals Porter's perception of what the Soviets later called "creative geography." The outdoor shots were clearly shot outside a real house and the indoor shots just as obviously inside a studio. Porter seems to have intuited that the cinema's narrative logic creates a unity of place where none exists in nature. As later theorists have demonstrated, we make sense of a narrative, a story, not merely on the basis of the action as presented but on the interplay between those events and our mental ability to connect them into a meaningful chronological sequence. Porter's constructing the rescue process from two distinct views demanded that we mentally connect them into a single logical process—and the interior and exterior shots into views of a single building.

Porter's later film of 1903, *The Great Train Robbery,* makes even greater use of this interplay between filmed event and mental connection, and probably owes its terrific success— the single most popular film in America prior to 1912—to it. The first series of shots in the film shows the same kind of step-by-step, one-shot-one-scene editing of the Méliès films. The outlaws enter the telegraph office and tie up the operator, board the train as it stops for water, rob the mail car and shoot the railroad man, seize the locomotive, unhook it from the rest of the train, rob all the passengers and shoot one who tries to escape, run to the locomotive and chug off, get off the locomotive and run to their horses in the woods. Up to this point in the film any director might have made it, except for the flow and careful detail of the narrative sequences and the beauty and vitality of the outdoor shots. The very last scene of the sequence reveals a new editing idea. It is clearly an elliptical jump in time (from when the outlaws started their escape in the train to when they stopped the train and got off to find and mount their horses), and it contains a pan shot that follows the outlaws through the woods.

But the next shot identifies the director's cinematic imagination more clearly. He *cuts back* to the opening scene, the telegraph office, and shows the discovery of the assaulted operator. Although the cut may be a backward leap in time and certainly deserts the spatial focus of the film (the outlaws and their getaway, which we understand to be an action that continues, unshown, while we watch the operator be revived), it makes perfect sense in the story's continuity. It answers the question the audience naturally asks: How will the outlaws be caught? Porter's next shot reveals yet another ellipsis. Rather than sticking with the new focal characters (the operator and, presumably, his daughter), it jumps to a barn dance, into which the operator and the girl eventually enter to tell their tale. And then another ellipsis. The posse is tailing the outlaws in the woods. Again, the audience makes the connecting links that the director has purposely omitted. Porter was

demonstrating a familiar artistic maxim in film form: The most effective way to shape a work is to omit the inessential. Although Porter may have discovered the power of ellipsis accidentally (according to legend, he was running out of film and needed to economize), the finished film demonstrates that power nonetheless.

In the film's final shoot-out, three of the four bandits meet overacted, hands-in-the-air, pirouette-and-fall deaths. The fourth had already fallen off his horse in the chase scene. Ironically, this one gunman who did not know how to ride (he even had trouble mounting up in an earlier scene) later became the world's first cowboy star: "Broncho Billy" Anderson (né Max Aronson), who also played the passenger who pirouetted to his death in the foreground. Apart from these stagey deaths, the film's cinematic showmanship is evident in the final shot—a close-up of a bandit firing at the audience—which was intentionally unrelated to the whole film and could, according to the Edison catalogue, be shown before or after the rest of the movie. Like 3-D of later years, the shot thrilled customers with a direct assault. For the next five years, it became almost obligatory to end a film with a close-up of its major figure (*The Boy Detective* and *Her First Adventure,* two Biograph films of 1908, are good examples) all because of the success of the device in *The Great Train Robbery.*

For all the understandable later attention to the editing of this landmark film, one other source of its power cannot be overlooked. Like the earliest Lumière films, *The Great Train Robbery* is a film of documentation, much as *The Life of an American Fireman* is a film about a job. It is almost a little textbook called "How to Rob a Train"—first you tie up the telegraph operator so he can't send a warning, then you climb aboard the train when it stops for water, then you unhook the locomotive from the passenger cars so the passengers can't escape, and so forth. Many of the earliest moral fears about the movies arose from their ability to teach audiences how to perform daring crimes in precise and clear detail. Interestingly enough, not until the serials of Louis Feuillade in France, a decade after Porter's *Train Robbery,* did films do as good a job at documenting the precise

Fig. 3-7

Fig. 3-8
The Great Train Robbery. *Fig. 3-7: composition that hides the robbers on the far left of the frame; Fig. 3-8: the murder of a fleeing passenger, composed in depth along a diagonal.*

methods of the forces of law at catching criminals. In *The Great Train Robbery*, for example, there is considerable fuzziness about exactly how the posse discovered where the train robbers were. Porter, like Lumière, came to films

from photography, and Porter's most important film reveals the photographer's commitment to documentation.

Porter's other films do not show the same freshness in cutting or composition as *The Great Train Robbery*. His version of *Uncle Tom's Cabin*, also 1903, is completely bound by the stage and staging. His *Dream of a Rarebit Fiend* (1906), despite its comedy and visual inventiveness, its relatively fluid use of long and close shots, its nearly film-long dream, and a highly original use of superimposition and the moving camera to show how it feels to be drunk, otherwise simply reverts to the Méliès formula. Perhaps the freedom of being outdoors influenced Porter's editing and shooting plan in *The Great Train Robbery*.

One of the striking characteristics of American films before 1910 (including Griffith's) is that their outdoor shots look vital and fresh while the indoor shots look static, flat, and dead. Once outdoors, the accidental attractions of nature compensated for the filmmaker's lack of craft and consciousness. Many of Porter's studio films, like those of his contemporaries, revert to the principles of the films shot in the Black Maria. One reason, of course, is that the early films invested so little money and visual care in production. Nature didn't require an investment. Another reason is that the slowness of early film stock (with an ASA the equivalent of something like 8) and lenses could only render the world in depth outdoors, where there was plenty of available light.

While Porter was developing the tools of continuity and ellipsis in America, the "school of Brighton" was making similar and even more rapid progress in England. Cecil Hepworth's *Rescued by Rover* (1905) is one of the most energetically edited pre-Griffith films, a decided advance over Porter in narrative construction and rhythm. In the first expositional shot, a nurse wheeling a baby carriage insults a gypsy woman, who vows revenge. In the second shot, a carefully blocked sequence with a camera pan —a general strategy that would later be described as *plan-séquence*, the complicated blocking of a lengthy shot—the gypsy steals the baby as the nurse chats with a beau. Then Hepworth makes a huge elliptical jump. Rather

The Great Train Robbery: *the freedom of the outdoors and the visual assertion of the frame's depth.*

Fig. 3-9

than sticking with nurse, watching her discover the loss and run home to tell baby's parents, the film's third shot begins with nurse bursting into the family living room to tell her news. As she recites her tale, Rover, the family collie, listens intently; he jumps out the window in search of the stolen baby.

Then begins the most remarkable sequence in the film: a series of individual shots documenting Rover's finding baby, returning to tell his master, and leading master back to baby. The sequence unfolds in the following shots: (1) Rover jumps out of window; (2) runs down the street toward camera; (3) turns corner; (4) swims across stream toward camera (with a delightful moment as Rover shakes himself off after emerging from the water); (5) searches a row of shanty doors; (6) cut to inside shanty where gypsy sits guzzling booze; gypsy exits, Rover enters, nuzzles baby; (7) Rover runs out door of shanty, same setup as 5; (8) swims across stream away from camera, same setup as 4; (9) runs around corner, away from camera, same setup as 3; (10) runs down street away from camera, same setup as 2; (11) jumps into house window, same setup as 1; (12) cut to inside house, Rover "tells" master; (13) Rover and master run down street, same setup as 2 and 10; (14) Rover and master cross stream, same setup as 4 and 8; (15) Rover leads master to door of shanty, same setup as 5 and 7;

(16) master finds baby, takes her out of shanty; gypsy returns to find baby gone; she is comforted by baby's clothes and her bottle of booze. In the film's final scene baby, master, mistress, and Rover are happily united in their living room; Hepworth has elliptically omitted the process of returning home, knowing that the sequence was not necessary to the emotional tension of the film.

Hepworth's careful editing of *Rescued by Rover* produced two effects that had not been achieved before, which communicated themselves to the audience by completely cinematic means. His careful use of the same setups to mark Rover's progress both toward and away from baby firmly implanted in the audience's mind exactly where Rover was in relation to the object of the rescue (the gypsy hovel) and the agent of the rescue (the master's house). Without any titles or explanations, the audience had a complete understanding of the rescue process. Second, this documentation produced not only awareness but suspense. Because the audience knew where Rover's path was leading, it could participate in the excitement of Rover's finally reaching the end of it. Hepworth increased this excitement with the dynamic fluidity of cuts from one setup to the next. Although the locations were undoubtedly far apart, the impression produced by Hepworth's cutting was that Rover ran continuously from one

Fig. 3-10
Rescued by Rover: *The precise establishment of locations, the repetition of setups, and the consistent direction of movement within the frame produce both awareness of the process and emotional participation in the event.*

location to the next. Hepworth cut consistently as Rover was in motion across the frame (Eisenstein and Pabst would later develop the power of cutting on movement), impelling the viewer's eye into the next shot and producing both fluid continuity and visual energy.

Perhaps the ultimate testimony to the quality of the primitive British films can be seen in the satirical comedy *A Suffragette in Spite of Himself.* Produced by the new British branch of the Edison Company in 1912, this little film is the story of a male chauvinist who inadvertently carries a profeminist sign on his back all around London, the sign having been stuck there by some pranksterish boys. (The film is a clear extension of the Lumière prank film, effectively complicated by detailed characterization and social satire.) The film's acting is so subtle, its satire so relevant, its plot construction and editing so fluid, its composition so interesting (one shot even uses extreme depth of field with both foreground action inside a room and rearground action outside a window that might be said to anticipate Renoir), its visual texture so consistent between indoor and outdoor shots, that it was far superior to any of the contemporary offerings of the parent Edison Company.

Despite the slower pace of visual and narrative discovery in the American films of the period, the years from 1903 to 1908—in effect between Porter's *Train Robbery* and Griffith's directorial debut—laid the foundation on which Griffith built. Porter cleverly combined live-action comedy and animation in *The Whole Dam Family and the Dam Dog* (1905); he used metaphoric lighting, a firelight's glow, for the final old-age scene of *The Seven Ages* (1905), predating Griffith's famous use of the same visual metaphor in *The Drunkard's Reformation* four years later; and Porter also made some of the earliest American film dramas of social commentary, such as *The Kleptomaniac* (1905), which contrasts the one kind of law that applies to a poor and needy thief and the other kind that applies to a rich, disturbed one. Griffith would make much of such "contrasts" in *Intolerance.*

Even before Griffith, the Biograph company had been producing the most interesting American films on the market. There were frantic seriocomic chases, clearly modeled on Zecca's, like *Personal* (1904), *The Lost Child* (1904), and *Tom, Tom, the Piper's Son* (1905). Within a half decade, two directors at this same studio would refine these chases into their purer but opposite types—D. W. Griffith's last-minute rescues and Mack Sennett's physical farces. Biograph also made films of ingenious thefts, like *The Great Jewel Mystery* (1905), in which the thief hides in a coffin on a train, and *The Silver Wedding* (1906), which concludes with a chase through the city sewers. The bizarre narrative twists and imaginative characterizations of the thieves in these films foreshadow the same sort of narrative imagination in the serials of the French filmmaker Louis Feuillade a decade later, and the 1920s gangster silents of Fritz Lang.

Also in this period at Biograph, G. W. ("Billy") Bitzer, the man who was to shoot all of Griffith's most inventive and important films, had begun to master the art of cinematography, most notably in *Tom, Tom, the Piper's Son.* In *A Kentucky Feud* (1905), Bitzer's photography creates the appropriate visual setting for a tale of the Hatfields and McCoys; in *The Black Hand* (1906), a tale of organized crime, Bitzer juxtaposes scenes shot on sets with actual location shooting on Seventh Avenue in New York City. Biograph's *The Paymaster* (1906) may well use available light more creatively and beautifully than any other American film before 1908; especially effective are Bitzer's capturing the reflections of light on the river and his shots inside an old mill, lit entirely by oblique streams of light pouring through its window.

For all the power of this film photographically, there is something incomprehensible about its continuity—particularly without the explanatory intertitles that were not copyrighted with the photographs (but were of course included in the original release prints). The pictures by themselves fail to accomplish the storytelling task.

It is especially difficult to determine who exactly is doing what to whom and why— not merely that the characters' motivations are fuzzy, but that it is almost impossible to decipher who the characters are, since the camera works so far away from the people and their faces. As the French semiologist Christian Metz has argued, narrative films cannot begin to develop connotative power until they establish denotative clarity. Later films would begin to develop character only when they began to individuate characters with closer photographic views.

Of course, one question frequently debated among later film theorists is precisely why these early films gravitated toward narrative, toward storytelling, in the first place. Why didn't films remain depictions of real events and places in the world or depictions of abstract visual qualities of light, shape, and form? Some theorists suggest that films only began to tell stories as an act of commercial exploitation, because uneducated audiences were willing to consume these primitive fictional shows. The union of film and narrative might have been an example of the capitalist ethic at work: selling the public all that it will buy and bear. Others point out film's roots in documentation—that it was a small step to move from documenting real events, like the arrival of a train, to fictional ones, like the robbing of a train.

Still others suggest there was something inevitable about film's movement into storytelling, a clear outgrowth of nineteenth-century fiction and drama, which themselves sought the paradoxical union of two opposites—the telling of absolutely fictional and unreal stories within a visual, social, and psychological environment that seemed absolutely real and true to human experience. Movies seemed an ideal medium for combining the fictional tale with the real or realistic setting.

Whatever the theoretical, material, or spiritual reasons, between 1895 and 1908 movies changed from static, one-shot "views" to increasingly fluid sequences of visually effective shots that produced a continuous—if not necessarily complex or evocative—narrative. The next evolution of narrative would require a master with a firmer and bolder sense, not so much of the individual cinematic elements but of the means to synthesize them into clearer, more credible, and more powerful narrative wholes. It would require a man not only with a strong visual sense, inherited from observing the accomplishments of Western painting, but also with a strong feeling for the plays and novels of the previous century. D. W. Griffith would display those senses before the end of 1909.

Business Wars

While moviemakers gradually discovered the elements of film construction, American movie exhibitors gradually converted commercial chaos into order. In the last five years of the nineteenth century, the American picture business enjoyed the protection of neither law nor professional ethics. Cameramen and exhibitors blatantly ignored machine patents, pirating and duplicating any instrument that could make them money. Even more vulnerable were the filmstrips themselves, which were not yet protected *as films* by copyright laws. The French and English films were the most vulnerable; although many Méliès films were shown in the United States, his Star Film Company made no money from the prints that had been smuggled out of France and duped in America. Piracy had become so pervasive that film companies pasted their identifying logo on the sets themselves. The Edison trademark can be clearly seen on a burning wall of *The Life of an American Fireman,* and the American Biograph monogram, the letters AB in a circle ⒶⒷ, has even been pasted on the street organ of *Her First Adventure* and is easy to spot throughout *The Lonely Villa.* A cold war that on occasion became a hot one entangled all producers and exhibitors of motion pictures.

In 1899, for example, Biograph set up a huge battery of hot lights on Coney Island to record the Jeffries–Sharkey fight. The film would be the first to use electricity instead of sunlight. While the Biograph camera was grinding away in the front row, the Vitagraph camera was grinding away twenty rows back. When the Biograph boys discovered the Vitagraph camera, they sent a crew of Pinkerton detectives to seize the machine and film. The fight fans surrounding the Vitagraph camera, unaware of the causes of the attack, manfully protected their neighbor, producing more action outside the ring than in it. Eventually Vitagraph's Albert E. Smith recorded the whole fight, smuggled the film out of the arena, and developed it that night in the Vitagraph lab.

The next morning Smith discovered that the pirated film had itself been pirated out of the lab by some late-night delegates of the Edison company. Ironically, although Biograph went to the trouble and expense of lighting the fight, Vitagraph and Edison (both eventually released prints of it) were the only ones to make any money on it.

In December of 1897, Thomas Edison served his first legal writ, announcing his intention to eliminate all competitors in motion pictures. Edison, in the next ten years, would bring suit against any company that used a loop of film in either a projection machine or camera, claiming he owned the rights to all loops because of the Armat patent on the Latham Loop, the generic name for all loops in all film machines. Edison's private detectives roamed the country searching for shooting companies, serving any they discovered with legal writs or extralegal wreckage. Edison steadily coerced the smaller companies into accepting his terms, eventually bringing suit against the big ones like Biograph.

Then Thomas Armat, dissatisfied with Edison's taking full credit for the Vitascope, took to the courts. Edison had double-crossed Armat commercially by manufacturing his own projecting machine, the Projecting Kinetoscope, just two years after marketing Armat's. Armat, like Edison, brought suit against everyone who used his loop projector; he also sued Edison. Biograph, meanwhile, was preparing its own legal dossiers. With some careful bargaining it bought both the Armat patents and the Latham patents, thereby arming itself with plenty of paper ammunition to use against Edison. For ten years the motion picture companies busied themselves with suits and countersuits. Some five hundred legal actions were taken, over two hundred of them making their way into court. The reams of court testimony from this era proved to be valuable for the film historian, if for no one else.

While the company lawyers were busy at each other's legal throats, the movie companies continued making and selling an ever-increasing number of films. Originally, when movies were part of vaudeville bills or amusement arcades, the film company sold the finished picture directly to the exhibitor at between five and twenty-five cents per foot, depending on the expenses of the film, its potential popularity, whether it was hand-colored, and so forth. The exhibitor then owned the film and could show it until the print wore out, then buy a new one.

But a new exhibiting development, just after the turn of the century, produced a new distributing practice. In 1902, an enterprising Los Angeles showman opened a small theatre in a store specifically for the purpose of showing motion pictures. Thomas L. Tally's Electric Theatre was the first permanent movie theatre in the United States. More and more of these store theatres sprang up until, in June of 1905, a Pittsburgh store theatre opened that was a bit plushier, accompanied its showings with a piano, and charged its customers a nickel. It was the first nickelodeon, or "nickel theatre." Within three or four years there were over five thousand nickelodeons in the United States. So popular were they that in 1908 it was estimated that they drew 80 million admissions every week (at a time when the entire population of the United States was about 100 million).

The permanent movie theatre forced a fundamental change in the relationship of the movie exhibitor and movie producer. The nickelodeon required a large number of films each week; about six films of one or one-half reel each [at sixteen frames per second (16 fps), a full reel—one thousand feet of 35mm film—lasted about sixteen minutes] made up a single hour-long program, and to keep the customers coming, programs had to change several times a week, if not daily. The theatre owner had no use for owning a film outright; after several showings, the regular patrons would not want to see it again. Between the film producer and the film exhibitor stepped a middleman who either bought the film or leased it from the producer and then rented it to the many exhibitors. The exhibitor paid less money for a larger supply of films; the producer was certain of selling films. The three-part structure of the American film industry—the producer who makes the film, the distributor who arranges for its most effective circulation, and the exhibitor who shows it in the theatre—worked out well for all parties. That structure, with some wrinkles, survives today.

Fig. 3-11

The beckoning lure of an
early nickelodeon.

Edison tried to use this three-level structure to control the chaotic American film world. It was particularly important to work out a treaty between the two top competitors, Edison and Biograph, along with the key people and companies allied with each of them. Pressure, threats, bankruptcy, and collusion led to a combining of the nine leading film companies of 1908 — Edison, Biograph, Vitagraph, Essanay, Lubin, Selig, Kalem, Méliès, and Pathé (the latter two had both begun producing in America) — along with inventor Thomas Armat and distributor George Kleine (the im-porter of Gaumont and Urban productions). The combine, called the Motion Picture Patents Company, was incorporated on September 9, 1908 and activated on December 18, 1908; Méliès was added to the group on July 20, 1909. The members of the combine agreed to share the legal rights to their various machine and film patents, to buttress each other's business procedures, and to keep all other parties and machine parts out of the film business permanently. The Motion Picture Patents Company could make its rules stick because it also agreed not to sell or lease to any distributor who bought a film from any other company. The exchange (distributor) that wanted to handle Patent Company films—the best pictures then on the market—could not handle any other company's films. Further, the Patent Company made an exclusive contract (on January 1, 1909) with George Eastman's factory; Eastman would sell perforated raw film stock to the Patent Company and only to the Patent Company. The Patent Company was such a big account that Eastman could not afford to sell to interlopers. After ten years of piracy and bickering, the "War of the Patents" was over. American film production was the exclusive property of nine companies: They leased their films only to those distributors who would accept their terms and pay their fees; and these "licensed" film exchanges, soon to become amalgamated as the powerful General Film Company, rented only to exhibitors who paid a weekly licensing fee ($2.00) and agreed to show Patent Company pictures exclusively. From first shot to final showing, law and order had theoretically come to motion pictures.

Having temporarily ended the warfare within the industry, the Motion Picture Patents Company sought to silence the increasing moral clamor outside it. The staggering success and popularity of the nickelodeons, the huge numbers of Americans who had caught the "nickel madness," troubled the moral principles of both amateur advocates and professional politicians. As early as 1907, states and cities began to establish either censorship boards to assure the cleanliness of film content, licensing boards to assure the cleanliness and safety of motion picture theatres, or both. These boards became commercially troublesome for an increasingly national industry. What if a film were acceptable in New York but not in Chicago? What if a film were acceptable in Pennsylvania but not in Philadelphia? To silence its critics, as well as to ensure the commercial health of its product, the infant motion picture industry took the first step of the kind it would take throughout its history when faced with a moral attack that endangered its financial welfare—it established its own censorship board to control film content. The National Board of Censorship, founded in 1908 (in 1915 it changed its name to the more tolerant-sounding National Board of Review), did not put an end to troublesome state and local censorship actions, but it greatly reduced their inconsistencies by establishing standards and principles that most of them could (and did) accept.

Less fortunate for the Motion Picture Patents Company and its General Film Company was the rebellion of some distributors and exhibitors within the industry itself against this monopolistic control. It eliminated bargaining, it eliminated profits from duping, it raised prices. Within months after the peace had been signed in 1908, two distributors, William Swanson of Chicago and Carl Laemmle of New York, decided to "go independent." The two pacesetters urged other film exchanges to follow their example. The Patent War had ended; the Trust War had begun.

The independent distributor faced one problem: obtaining films to distribute that were not made by a Patent Company studio. One of the obvious solutions was for a distributor to turn producer. Carl Laemmle, film exchange-man, became Carl Laemmle, film producer, and gave birth to the organization that would eventually become Universal Pictures. William Fox, distributor and theatre owner, became William Fox, producer, and the organization that would eventually become Twentieth Century-Fox was born. Fox also retaliated against the Patent Company by suing them and their General Film Company as an illegal trust. The lawyers were back in the movie business—to stay.

For all of Teddy Roosevelt's historical reputation as a "trust buster," it was the new Wilson administration that joined Fox's suit against the Film Trust in 1913. Governmental agencies had learned at this early date that they could attract maximum publicity in the press and interest in the public by attacking a popular and glamorous industry like the movies— exactly as the House Un-American Activities Committee realized decades later. By 1913 Americans had really come to care about the movies.

Until 1915 movie companies fought in the courts and fought in the streets. Jeremiah J. Kennedy, a major executive of the Patent Company, sent gangs of gentlemen to visit unlicensed studios, shooting holes in cameras and leaving bits of wreckage about for calling cards. Despite the strong-arm tactics of the Trust, the Independents prospered. Adam Kessel and Charles Bauman, two former bookies, formed the New York Motion Picture Company, which eventually founded the film careers of Thomas Ince, Mack Sennett, and Charles Chaplin. Edwin S. Porter left Edison to go independent, making films for his own Rex Company; it would one day be swallowed by Paramount. Most successful of all the Independents was Laemmle's Independent Motion Picture Company (known as IMP).

The Trust's solid barriers sprung other leaks. Unable to buy film stock from Eastman, the Independents bought stock from English and French factories. In addition, legitimate licensed film companies and film exchanges ran unlicensed, independent companies and exchanges on the side. When the smoke of this second film war had cleared, by late 1915, not only had the Motion Picture Patents Company been busted in court as an illegal trust (it disbanded in 1917, when the case was finally settled), but also the individual companies that formed the Trust were dying or dead. The independent companies, for reasons that we will see, propelled the movies into their next era. Three of the independent companies (Fox, Universal, and Paramount) survive today. The last of the original Trust companies, Vitagraph, was swallowed by Warner Bros. in 1925.

The Film d'Art

An important film influence was to make itself felt toward the end of the new century's first decade. In 1907, a French film company announced the intention of creating a serious, artistic cinema, of bringing together on film the most important playwrights, directors, actors, composers, and painters of the period. The company, which rather pretentiously called itself the Société Film d'Art, produced its first film in 1908 — *The Assassination of the Duke of Guise*. Featuring actors from the Comédie Française and incidental music by Saint-Saëns, the film was hailed as introducing the nobility and seriousness of the stage to the film. Ironically, the Film d'Art ran the movies headlong

back into the theatre: theatrical staging, unedited scenes, theatrical acting, theatrical set painting. It was the first in a series of attempts to produce "canned theatre," the most recent of which was the American Film Theater of the mid-1970s with its filmed productions of plays like *The Iceman Cometh* and *A Delicate Balance.*

The first of these Films d'Art to be seen in the United States was *Queen Elizabeth* (1912), featuring Sarah Bernhardt and members of the Comédie Française, directed by Louis Mercanton. This bombastic film version of Elizabeth's love for Essex, whom she must eventually send to the block, reveals all the plodding staginess of the Film d'Art technique. Characters enter and exit from right and left; groups of soldiers, ladies in waiting, or courtiers stand immobile in the background, just as they are supposed to do on the stage; the actors, Bernhardt included, indulge in a grotesque series of facial grimaces, finger gesticulations, arm swingings, fist clenchings, breast thumpings (once even raising dust from the costume), and quadruple takes. And yet these were among the most skillful stage actors in the world!

One clear lesson of the Film d'Art was that stage acting and film acting were incompatible. The stage, which puts small performers in a large hall, requires larger, more demonstrative movements. The artificiality of this demonstrativeness does not show in a theatre for two reasons: First, the live performance sustains the gestures with the "vibrations," the vitality of the living performer's presence, which assimilates gesture as only one part of a whole performance; second, the performer's voice adds another living note that makes facial expression and gesticulation also merely parts of a whole. In the Film d'Art of *Queen Elizabeth,* gesture and grimace were not parts but the wholes themselves.

The way to improve film acting was not just to make the actors underplay but to let cinematic technique help the actors act. A camera can move in so close to an actor's face that the blinking of an eye or the flicker of a smile can become a significant and sufficient gesture. Or the field of view can cut from the actor to the subject of the actor's thoughts or attention,

Sarah Bernhardt in Queen
Elizabeth: stage composition
and stage acting, with no help
from the camera.

Fig. 3-12

thereby revealing the emotion without requiring a grotesque, overstated thump on the chest. Film acting before Griffith—and before his greatest star, Lillian Gish—not only in the Film d'Art but in Méliès and Porter and Hepworth as well, had been so bad precisely because the camera had not yet learned to help the actors.

In *Queen Elizabeth*, for example, there is a scene in which Elizabeth bids adieu to Essex (he's off for Ireland) and then, after all the court has left, she sinks down on her throne in abject sorrow. The entire scene—adieu, exit, sorrow—is filmed in one setup. The single, frozen take is ridiculous, unresponsive to the developing action, and even unrelated to the theatrical composition of the scene.

Although the Film d'Art had nothing to do with film art, it had a lot to do with the direction that film art would take. *Queen Elizabeth*, despite its leaden technique, was a huge success. That success launched the career of its American distributor, Adolph Zukor, who decided to form an American Film d'Art called Famous Players in Famous Plays, which would eventually become Paramount Pictures. Its success also proved that quality pictures and, more important, *long* pictures could make money. It was to the advantage of the Motion Picture Patents Company to maintain the theory that audiences would not sit through a single picture of over fifteen minutes, for the whole film business they had solidified was built on programs of one-reel pictures. The General Film Company could not distribute any film longer than two reels, since it served the nickelodeons exclusively. *Queen Elizabeth*, a three-reeler, squashed the Trust myths. And D. W. Griffith's three-hour epics were only two years away.

4

Griffith

David Wark Griffith never intended to make movies. The accidental path that eventually led him to films stretched from his rural Kentucky home to selling books, picking hops in California, reporting for a Louisville newspaper, and finally writing and acting for the legitimate stage. The young Griffith had decided he was a playwright. One of his plays, *The Fool and the Girl,* even played two tepid weeks in Washington and Baltimore. Like the movies themselves, Griffith's dramatic apprenticeship was rooted in the world of Belasco. It would be Griffith who would most successfully translate the Belasco effects for the screen—melodrama, suspense, pathos, purity. Although today there is a certain pejorativeness in the term that press agents concocted to describe Griffith—"the Belasco of the screen"—there is an ironic aptness in the label that was not then apparent. Griffith began with the same dramatic structures, the same sentimental characters, and the same moral assumptions of the Belasco stage, and he never deserted them, even when his audiences did.

Griffith's playwriting ultimately brought him to the movies. Like all stage actors, Griffith regarded the moving pictures as an artistic slum. But he had written an adaptation of

Tosca, which he failed to peddle as a stageplay. He then decided to try to sell it to the pictures. In 1907, over thirty and out of work, he took his manuscript up to the new Edison studios in the Bronx. The film companies had deserted city rooftops for more spacious and secretive quarters in the Bronx and Brooklyn. Edwin S. Porter, by then head of production at Edison, thought Griffith's *Tosca,* with its many scenes and lengthy plot, too heady for the movies (this was five years before the Film d'Art's *Queen Elizabeth*). Instead of buying Griffith's script, Porter offered him an acting job at five dollars a day. Griffith, recently married to Linda Arvidson, needed the money and took the job. But he insisted on playing under the assumed name of Lawrence Griffith, thinking he would save his real name for the day when one of his plays opened on Broadway. Things would work out differently.

Apprenticeship

In Griffith's first role for Porter he played a lumberjack (a very thin lumberjack!) and father in *The Eagle's Nest* (also known as *Rescued from an Eagle's Nest*), produced by Porter and directed by J. Searle Dawley. When his wife

48

*D. W. Griffith: a portrait of the
artist as a film director.*

Fig. 4-1

informed him that baby had been swooped
away by a huge bird, Griffith scaled the bird's
mountain lair (shot partly inside a studio and
partly outdoors on location, like *The Life of an
American Fireman),* fought the puppet eagle to
the death, and brought baby back home. This
melodramatic film was not without significance
for Griffith's later career. First, Edwin S.
Porter provided Griffith's introduction to film
technique. Porter was the American director
before Griffith who best understood the power
and logic of editing in building a story. Second,
the melodramatic plot was to find its reincarnations in Griffith's movies throughout his career,

from the early short films to the long epics and
later features. Whether Griffith acquired the
taste for the last-minute rescue from the
Belasco stage or the Porter screen, by the time
he started to direct his own films that taste had
become his own.

After a short career with Edison, Griffith
took a job at Biograph, performing the same
kinds of acting chores for the head of production there, Wallace C. ("Old Man")
McCutcheon. By 1908, the devouring nickelodeon's demand for films was so great that Biograph needed to step up production to several
reels per week and therefore needed another

director. Griffith, whose imagination had been spotted by Biograph cameraman Arthur Marvin (brother of co-owner Henry Marvin), was offered the job. Griffith wasn't sure he wanted it. He was content with the daily five-dollar wage; failure as a director might cost him the steady income from acting. Biograph promised him that he could go back to acting if he failed as a director. The sincerity of the promise was never tested. Griffith directed his first film, *The Adventures of Dollie,* in June, 1908.

The Adventures of Dollie displays Griffith's thorough knowledge of the successful formulas of the past. Dollie's one-reel adventures are terribly familiar. An insulted gypsy takes vengeance on a family by kidnapping baby Dollie and hiding her in a water cask. As the gypsies ride away, the cask falls off the wagon and into a stream, where it moves steadily toward the vicious rapids. Dollie eventually escapes a watery death when her cries attract the attention of a nearby boy who is fishing; the picture ends with the inevitable happy family reunion. Griffith uses two motifs that had become standard in filmed melodrama: the spurned gypsy's revenge and the perilous danger to an innocent child. Its clear ancestors are films like *Rescued by Rover, The Eagle's Nest, The Lost Child* — in which a mother thinks her baby has been spirited away by a gypsy and runs off in pursuit —

and *Her First Adventure* (1908), Biograph's own version of the *Rover* film, made just three months before Griffith's *Dollie.* The dangerous rapids would recur in later Griffith films, most notably in *Way Down East*, made twelve years later, in which Lillian Gish floats ominously toward the falls on an ice cake.

Although Griffith's film sticks to extremely conventional narrative material, he handles those conventions with a narrative fluidity and symmetry uncommon in films of the period. Griffith establishes the agent of Dollie's rescue, the boy fisherman, in the first shot. He walks along the river bank and away from the camera at the same time that Dollie and her family walk toward the camera. This narrative linking in the film's opening shot makes the action's resolution more probable and logical. The final sequence with the floating cask also flows more continuously and rhythmically (using the consistent direction of motion across the frame and cutting on movement) than is usual for films of 1908. And the film's most interestingly planned shot is a deep-focus long shot that shows a farmer cutting grain as the gypsy runs through the field with Dollie in his grasp. Because the farmer is occupied with his task and submerged in the tall stalks, he cannot and does not see the mischief that passes so near him. The shot gives the convincing feeling that these

Fig. 4-2

The opening shot of **The Adventures of Dollie.**

episodes of movie fiction have been plucked out of the random and continuous flow of life itself.

It was this paradox of film narrative—that films look so spontaneously real and natural and yet are so fictional and patterned—that Griffith would develop and master in the five years that followed. His general method would be to push each of these paradoxical qualities to its extreme—to make filmed life look as natural and random as real life and yet to make filmed stories as carefully structured and patterned as any well-constructed fictions.

Griffith, shouldering the production demand of directing several one-reel pictures every week, had been given an ideal laboratory for experimentation and development. Between 1908 and 1913, clearly Griffith's apprenticeship period, he directed over four hundred and fifty films for Biograph, giving him the opportunity to test a new idea immediately, see whether and how it worked, and then return to the technique the next week and develop it further. Griffith did not innovate abstractly; he could test each method day by day in front of and with the camera, rejecting what failed, refining what worked. Griffith's discoveries were empirical, not theoretical. Those discoveries embraced every component of visual, black-and-white cinematic technique.

Griffith realized that the content of the shot should determine the camera's relationship to it, whereas the accepted shot in the film world of 1908 was what would be called the full shot or far shot today. This shot necessarily included the full figures of all the characters in the scene, plus enough of the scenery to show the audience exactly where the characters were and how carefully the set had been painted. This standard shot enjoyed the official blessing of the Motion Picture Patents Company, whose reasoning seemed sensible: Why should the public pay the full price to see half an actor? Griffith revealed the effectiveness of showing half of an actor, a corner of a set, or even smaller portions.

In his apprentice years, Griffith developed a full series of different shooting perspectives. Beginning with the standard full shot, he moved the camera closer to the players to produce the medium shot—including, say, two

actors from the knees up (a shot later christened the "American shot"). And then the camera moved still closer to produce the close shot, including only the head and shoulders of a single actor; the close-up, revealing only a hand or face; and the extreme close-up, showing perhaps just an eye. Griffith also saw that he could move the camera in the other direction, further away from the actors. He produced the long shot—a much more distant view of one or more players—which emphasized more of the scenic environment than the far shot. And then he moved the camera still further from the players, producing the extreme long shot that would emphasize huge vistas and panoramas rather than the human figures.

Griffith was not, of course, the first to use these shots. Many of the Lumière "views" were of vast panoramas. *Fred Ott's Sneeze* and the opening-or-closing shot of *The Great Train Robbery* both used medium to close shots. G. A. Smith's *A Big Swallow* (1900) uses an extreme close-up of a man's mouth (he was supposedly swallowing the camera), and Porter's *The Life of an American Fireman* used a close-up insert of a fire-alarm box. But these earlier films used the nonstandard shot for some special photographic or narrative effect (as even the term *insert* implies). Griffith made all of these shots standard and combined them into sequential wholes, proving that the very idea of standardness was a cinematic lie. One could cut freely between long and medium, close and medium, close and long to produce a whole scene. Griffith broke the theatrical scene into the cinematic unit of shots.

In a sense, his method really was another kind of analogy with the stage, but a much more subtle one than earlier film directors had perceived. Although a scene on the stage is anchored in immovable space, it really is a series of shifting "beats," of emotional pivots and pirouettes, of thrusts and parries, of comings together and splittings apart. Despite the stasis of the setting and the audience's viewing angle, the theatrical scene is not static; it is constantly shifting, changing, and evolving. Griffith translated these stage "beats" into film terms. When the mood shifted, when the emotions changed, the camera shifted. It caught that intimate moment when a single member of a group made up his or her mind to take a significant emotional leap; it caught the smallness of a solitary soldier in the midst of a huge army on a vast battlefield. Griffith discovered that the narrative content of the scene, not the location of the scene, determined the correct placement of the camera and the correct moment to cut from one perspective to another. This discovery is frequently called the "grammar and rhetoric" of film because Griffith discovered that—as with words—there was a way of combining film shots to produce clarity, power, and meaning.

Griffith discovered, at the same time, the power of two moving-camera shots: the pan shot and the traveling shot. Again, both of these shots had been used before. There were pans in the "school of Brighton" films and in *The Great Train Robbery*. There were traveling shots in early Lumière views (a trip through Venice by gondola in 1897) and in an American film show called Hales Tours in which the audience sat in a theatre designed as a railroad car and watched films of moving scenery actually shot from a moving railroad car. But Griffith realized that these special shots were just two more potential units in creating the whole. The panoramic shot, or pan, with its horizontal sweeps from left to right or right to left, not only is functional for following the moving action but also transfers its feeling of sweeping movement to the viewer. The eye is sensitive to such shifts in the field of vision, and it telegraphs this sensitivity to the brain, which translates it into a physical sensation. The traveling shot (sometimes called a track shot or tracking shot because the camera's platform often rolled along, railroad style, on tracks) produces an even more magnified sensation of physical movement: the perfect tool for communicating the internal excitement of people riding rushing trains and galloping horses and racing wagons. Griffith integrated these two moving shots into his cinematic rhetoric, using their special emotional qualities when his narrative needed those effects. Griffith's restraint in using the traveling shot—reserved for brief and occasional movements in the midst of a climactic chase or "race for life"—shows how thoroughly he understood its kinetic power.

Griffith also realized that, just as the camera was not the servant of space, neither was the final editing of a film the servant of space or time. Most of the early films had followed a focal character slavishly from place to place, unable to leap to other places and other people regardless of the needs of the narrative. Griffith discovered that two places vastly separate in space or time could be brought together in the audience's mind. This back-and-forth editing technique, called the cross-cut (or parallel cut, switchback, or several other synonyms), which produced closeness out of distance, became a standard Griffith tool, fulfilling several primary functions. The cut could be a leap in space (from the victims of an attack to their potential rescuers) to increase the audience's suspense or awareness, a leap in time (to contrast a happy moment with a sad one, or modern with ancient behavior), or a leap controlled by a character's mind (from the face of a sad girl to a shot of her husband lying dead on the battlefield) to reveal the character's motivations or perceptions. Such cross-cuts were attempts to interrelate and explore contrasts and parallels as well as to mirror internal human sensation in a concrete, externalized, visual form—either the fear and frenzy of a rescue from a violent attack or a reflective reverie in a quiet moment of joy or melancholy. A fourth kind of Griffith cross-cut served a more symbolic and intellectual purpose. In *A Corner in Wheat* (1909), Griffith cross-cut between a lavish and lively banquet for the rich and a frozen portrait of the poor, waiting in line for a meager loaf of bread. The cross-cut clearly and effectively underlined the injustice of these simultaneous social conditions. When the Biograph management wondered whether audiences would be able to understand these shifts, Griffith's answer revealed both his insight and his influences: "Doesn't Dickens write that way?"

Griffith had learned, by trial and experience, what the earliest film theorist, Hugo Münsterberg, had discovered by watching movies at almost the same time: Films were capable of mirroring not only physical activities but mental processes. Films could recreate the activities of the mind: the focusing of attention on one object or another (by means of a close-up), the recalling of memories or projecting of

Fig. 4-3

Fig. 4-4
A Corner in Wheat: *Griffith's cross-cut from the banquet table of the rich to the bread line of the poor.*

those events. Griffith's "discovery" was far more than a mere technique or assortment of devices; it was the way to make film narrative, storytelling with moving images, *consistently coherent.*

While Griffith's narratives learned to leap from space to space, they also began to deepen the texture of life within each of those spaces. Not content with the two-dimensional settings that dominated the interior scenes of most American films of the era (so flat that many painted their furniture and props onto the backdrop), Griffith insisted on making his interior scenes appear as three-dimensional as his outdoor ones. He thrust desks and tables into the shooting area, perpendicular to the walls of the set and to the frame line, rather than lining them up parallel to the walls, as they would be on the stage. He pushed pieces of furniture out at oblique angles to the set, the camera, and each other, and he shoved chairs, tables, and vases close to the camera itself, further increasing the sense of depth in the cramped quarters where the early Biograph films were shot. By 1909 Griffith's sense of the difference between theatrical and cinematic space was so clear that he could shoot a film, *The Drunkard's Reformation,* that used the device of a play-within-a-film and depended on our perceiving the contrast between shallow and deep space. By mid-1909 he was also taking his cast and crew out of New York City to shoot on location, first in upstate New York and later (1910) in California.

Griffith's innovations went beyond the camera and the editing table. Almost simultaneous with Griffith's debut in films came the debut of the electric light in the studios. Artificial lighting gradually replaced the sun's harsh and inconstant performances. When film companies left Manhattan rooftops for the Bronx and Brooklyn, they also left behind the sun and muslin sheets that diffused its glare. But the first film directors merely used the new arc lights as though they were the sun — to produce bright, even, untuned light with no regard to the tonal and narrative requirements of the scene. Does the scene take place indoors or out? During night or day? Should it feel harsh or gentle, cool or warm? Griffith — and G. W. ("Billy") Bitzer, the cameraman who shot

imaginings (by means of a flashback, flash forward, or mindscreen), the division of interest (by means of the cross-cut). Griffith had come to realize, much more firmly and consistently than Porter before him, the importance of the interplay between events presented on the screen and the spectator's mental synthesis of

Griffith's greatest works and taught him the ropes much as cinematographer Gregg Toland later taught director Orson Welles — realized the importance of such questions and the ways lighting could be effective in answering them. But neither the flat, even sunlight nor all the arcs on full blast could duplicate the texture and atmosphere of indoor life, let alone create a mood or explore a character. And so — though they were not the first to do this (Porter did it in *The Seven Ages,* 1905, and Griffith had seen a similar effect while acting in Biograph's 1908 *The Music Master*) — Griffith and Bitzer lit *The Dunkard's Reformation* with a dim, flickering, low-angle light that convincingly imitated a fire's glow, giving the scene the look of real life and creating a hearth that was tonally and metaphorically related to the film's plot: the drunkard's returning from the theatre to the warmth and comfort of home and family.

Pippa Passes (also 1909, but six months and sixty-eight movies later) had much subtler and more ambitious lighting effects — including indicating the passage of time, from sunrise to night, with artificial light alone, and using light to characterize Pippa's personality as well as her room; *Pippa* was also Griffith's first attempt to tell four stories in one movie (in this case, Pippa's plus three that she passes by and affects). *Pippa Passes,* the first movie to be reviewed individually by the *New York Times,* was based on a poem by Robert Browning. Griffith often adapted classic stories, novels, plays, and even poems (a particularly difficult challenge, requiring perfect manipulation of texture, rhythm, and tone) for the screen because he was sure that both he and the cinema could deal with great, complex material and important questions. Griffith's complete mastery of tonal lighting would culminate in 1919 with *Broken Blossoms,* which is dependent on lighting effects not only for its atmosphere and tone but also for the metaphoric contrast that underlies the film's moral system.

Griffith was as innovative with people as with machines. First, he demanded underacting: no more huge gestures and demonstrative poses. Of course, because he had developed the expressive power of his camera and editing, he had the tools to allow a player to underact and still be understood. Second, he showed a much greater attention to selecting actors to play the roles, realizing that in a photographic medium, which depicts only visible surfaces, the actor's physical type was as crucial as acting style in the conveying of internal emotional and intellectual states.

Third, he developed a lexicon of gesture and movement, stylized enough to be clear and evocative, yet subtle enough to seem real and unaffected. As early as *A Corner in Wheat* (1909), there is a basic stylistic difference in the movement and gesture of the poor and rich folks. While the poor farm people and customers at the bakery move slowly and glidingly, with open, fluid hand gestures, the rich Wheat King and his cronies move briskly, with sharp, pointed, grasping hand gestures. This contrast between their styles of movement culminates in the awesome *tableau vivant* (resembling what today would be called a freeze-frame), when the movement of the poor becomes so slow that it stops altogether.

Fourth, Griffith shocked his employers with what they considered an obvious waste of time — rehearsals. The actors rehearsed the scenes before Griffith shot them. In an era when directors could scream their instructions during the shooting, Griffith's method seemed extravagant and unnecessary. It was crucial. Finally, Griffith realized the applicability of one of the key artistic principles of the stage: A whole production requires an ensemble, not a collection of individual players. Griffith began building the Biograph stock company as a cohesive group of talented, attuned performers. His success is reflected in the number of important screen actors that Griffith's stock company produced, either for his own films or for the films of others. Mary Pickford, Lionel Barrymore, Lillian and Dorothy Gish, Mae Marsh, Blanche Sweet, Harry Carey, Henry B. Walthall, Robert Harron, and Donald Crisp all had worked for Griffith by 1913.

A close look at three Griffith one-reelers reveals his growing mastery of the film form. In *The Lonely Villa* (1909), Griffith's skill in cutting adds excitement to a melodramatic trifle about a wife and children who are attacked by two intruders in her home. Early in the film, the fluid and rhythmic cutting adds pace to a rather clumsy exposition that establishes the husband's

Fig. 4-5

Fig. 4-6

The Lonely Villa: Griffith's cross-cutting — the husband gallops to the rescue . . . of the family under attack at home.

leaving home while the two assailants hide outside in the bushes. The opening sequence is full of match cuts — shots from different angles and distances that have been assembled to give the impression of fluid, continuous movement — as the husband walks through the house and out the front door. These match cuts also establish — as systematically as the repeated locations in *Rescued by Rover* — the various domains of the house: the hallways and rooms that will play significant roles in the film's climactic sequence as the family retreats further and further from the intruders (the steady retreat into the protective depths of the home would become a consistent Griffith motif).

That climactic sequence reveals the power of Griffith's cross-cut. As the intruders begin their assault, Griffith cuts to the husband, many miles distant and ignorant of the danger to his family. The wife retreats to the telephone to inform her husband; Griffith cuts to the husband receiving the call, firmly linking the two distant locations in the narrative flow despite the separation in time and space. Griffith then cuts back and forth between the besieged wife trying to hold out against the attackers and the husband furiously driving home to the rescue. Griffith tightens the screws by cutting each shot shorter and shorter, increasing the excitement

and suspense. When the husband arrives home — just in time — the audience feels as much relief as the besieged wife; we, like her, relax after the driving finish.

The Lonedale Operator (1911) drives to its climax both more forcefully and more personally. The whole film shows a surer and more fluid technique than *The Lonely Villa*. The exposition, establishing the relationship of the girl (Blanche Sweet) and her beau, and that he is a railroad engineer and she a telegraph operator, is much clearer and more detailed than the exposition in the earlier film. The acting is much quieter, much more natural; the scene in which he proposes to her is humanly credible and warmly touching. Griffith captures the girl's spirit and her joy as she unexpectedly leaps on one of the railroad tracks and walks, tightrope-style, on the track while she talks to her beau. As soon as she and the beau separate, he to his engine and she to her telegraph office, Griffith builds toward the climax with a series of fluid match cuts showing her entering the office — door by door, as in *Villa* — and setting to work.

Once the attack begins on her and her office, Griffith begins his relentless and rhythmic cross-cutting, which alternates among three clearly established locales: the attackers on the outside trying to get further and further into the office, the operator inside the office trying to protect herself from the assault, and the speeding train (traveling shot) on its way to answer the distress signal that the operator intelligently wired to the next station. Griffith cuts with increasing rapidity from outside to inside to train, outside, inside, train, until the beau arrives just in time to find his sweetheart holding the culprits at bay with a "pistol" that is revealed in close-up to be a wrench (a definitive use of the close-up to show something important that cannot be seen or fully appreciated from a distance). The woman has brains as well as energy. She also has a sense of humor; she cheerfully acknowledges the comic, mock-gallant bow that the two vanquished but admiring tramps extend to her at the film's conclusion. Griffith was beginning to make his women not merely frail victims but forceful, clever, and able human beings who could take care of themselves when they had to.

Both of these films are pure stories of suspense with similar devices, although the later one has more human detail, greater realistic texture, and stronger narrative construction. *The New York Hat* (1912) dispenses with the melodramatic, suspenseful rescue altogether. With a screenplay by teenager Anita Loos (her first, for which she received $15 and an offer to write more), featuring Mary Pickford and Lionel Barrymore, *The New York Hat* is the story of the birth of love. Young Mary longs to escape her drab life and clothing, to attract a gentleman's eye. The young reverend of the parish (Barrymore) buys her a stylish hat from New York that she fancies. The town biddies start gossiping, linking Mary and the reverend in sin. The father tears up the hat with a cruelty that anticipates *Broken Blossoms.* Finally the reverend silences their talk with a letter from Mary's dying mother asking him to look after the girl. He takes advantage of this opportunity to declare his romantic intentions; she accepts his proposal of marriage.

To establish Mary's longing for a hat, Griffith breaks down an expositional scene between Mary and her father into two different setups, alternating between a medium two-shot (a shot with two equally important figures) that includes both Mary and her father and a close-up of Mary alone making wistful faces in a mirror. The two alternating setups in the scene establish the crucial emotional premise of the exposition: the gulf between Mary's little-girl relationship with her moralistic father and Mary's womanly longing to be pretty. And Griffith makes the mirror a key leitmotif of the film, for when Mary finally gets her hat, she returns to the mirror (and the camera to precisely the same setup) to see how charming she looks. Griffith similarly breaks the hat-buying scene into several significant setups: from Mary's point of view (desiring the hat), from the reverend's point of view (seeing she wants the hat), and then a close two-shot when he makes the purchase, bringing their two heads together, instantly suggesting the direction of their affections.

The film is full of other sensitive human touches. Mary's faces in the mirror are coy and charming; the snide, interfering town gossips are perfect comic caricatures. Griffith would draw fuller portraits of such nosy, close-minded, holier-than-thou women in *Intolerance* and *Way Down East.* Most personal of all in the film is the disdainful flick of the head that the all-male church elders give, in unison, to the self-righteous gossips. Griffith is also thumbing his own nose at these morally nearsighted ladies of reform and "uplift." One must remember that in 1912 feminism was associated not only with female suffrage but also with a moral cause that appalled Griffith (who cared intensely about freedom of expression)—temperance. The Women's Christian Temperance Union was the most powerful feminist organization in America, and its social pressure would lead to the Volstead Act and Prohibition by the end of the decade.

With a film like *The New York Hat,* Griffith had gone as far and as deeply as he could with the fifteen-minute picture. Those five years of one-reel films show Griffith laying the foundation not only for his technical achievements but also for the themes and motifs that would dominate his later films. He had made films about periods of American history (such as *1776, or The Hessian Renegades,* 1909), films about the contemporary social problems of poverty and vice (such as *What Shall We Do With Our Old?,* 1910, released 1911, and *The Musketeers of Pig*

Fig. 4-7
The New York Hat: *The gentlemen thumb their noses at the gossipy matrons (the second from the right is Mae Marsh).*

performed, the Bible his mother and father had taught him.

Although no member of the audience yet knew Griffith's name (no Patent Company director or actor received screen credit until after 1912), they all knew that Biograph pictures were the best on the market. So did Griffith. By 1913, he wanted to break loose from the one-reel limit on his thoughts. (He had earlier made two-reel films, but the General Film Company insisted on releasing them in two parts, one reel at a time. By popular demand, however, Griffith's 1911 two-reeler, *Enoch Arden,* based on the poem by Tennyson, had been shown as a single film shortly after it had been released as two; his first two-reeler, *His Trust* and *His Trust Fulfilled,* shot in 1910 and released separately in 1911, had no such luck.) Now that Griffith had discovered how to say things with cinema, he found he had things he wanted to say.

Griffith's longer films use the earlier innovations to assimilate and communicate more complex material. And that material was, as he saw it, simply the Truth. He wanted the images on the screen to illuminate his personal vision of good and evil. Griffith was not the cinema's first technician; he was its first moralist, poet, *auteur,* and master storyteller. A cliché in the criticism of Griffith is that his moral system is essentially that of the Victorian patriarchal

Alley, 1912), films that were stylistically careful adaptations of literary classics (Shakespeare, Poe, Tennyson, Browning, Longfellow) and contemporary novels (Frank Norris, Helen Hunt Jackson). Griffith had also begun making moral-religious allegories—Satan as the source of all human error and misery (*The Devil,* 1908); the inevitable choice between the life of sensual pleasure and the life of home and family (*The Two Paths,* 1910, released 1911); the incompatibility of goodness and the realities of human existence (*The Way of the World,* 1910). Griffith particularly excelled at the close and affectionate study of American rural life—either the gently comic, tender study of rural customs and courtship, as in *A Country Cupid* (1911), or the compassionate view of the difficulty of rural living and survival, as in *A Corner in Wheat.* The latter film also provided a very early conscious reference to a specific painting—Jean-François Millet's "The Sowers." Griffith was obviously bringing his entire nineteenth-century background into the movies—the paintings he had seen, the novels he had read, the plays he had

Fig. 4-8
A Corner in Wheat: *an image of the natural unity of man, beast, and field, based on Millet's painting "The Sowers." The rest of the movie is based on Frank Norris's story "A Deal in Wheat."*

Fig. 4-9

Fig. 4-10

Griffith's framing in The Musketeers of Pig Alley. Fig. 4-9: the tension of the oversized close-up (Elmer Booth and Harry Carey); Fig. 4-10: the social implication of money that arrives anonymously (to Elmer Booth) at the side of the frame.

sentimentalist. The positive values are social order, peace, intellectual freedom, loyalty, the home and family, womanhood/motherhood, and marital fidelity. The negative values are, correspondingly, social change, war, censorship, treachery, the high life, sexual license, and the broken home. But these specific values are really consequences of Griffith's central vision rather than the vision itself.

The two poles of Griffith's moral world are gentleness and violence. From gentleness come all the virtues of Woman, Peace, and the Home. The figures of gentleness are almost always female. Griffith's young women are luminous, soft, sweet, honest, springy, childlike, at times symbols of a delicate ideal rather than living, breathing creatures — but they can also be independent, brave, tough, and resourceful (like the Mountain Girl in *Intolerance*). Some of his women are monsters, too, and many are victims. For if Griffith saw gentleness as the ideal, he also saw cruelty, lust, and violence as the reality. The figures of oppression and violence are almost always male, though his men can also be dedicated, honorable, valiant, and even gentle. In *Broken Blossoms,* for example, the hero is a loving, intelligent, kind, religious, artistically sensitive pacifist and the villain is a stupid, violent lout who beats his gentle, long-suffering daughter to death; it is a pacifist tale of the destruction of love and tenderness — of broken blossoms.

Griffith's difficulty was integrating his vision into his melodramatic, plotty films. All too often Griffith fell back on two artificial devices that seemed superimposed on the films rather than an integral part of them. One of them was literally superimposed. He often thrust allegorical meanings on the films by superimposing angels and visions up in the heavens to comment on the earthly action. His allegory also extended to giving characters allegorical names — the Dear One, the Friendless One, Evil Eye. A second Griffith device was to soup up the film's meaning with purple, rhetorical titles that told the audience what moral conclusions it should draw from the actions it was about to witness. The titles constantly tell us that war's slaughter is *bitter* and *useless* (italics Griffith's), that women turn to social reform when they can no longer turn a man's fancy, that "the loom

of fate weaves death." Griffith's titles (also called intertitles or title cards) were far more florid and didactic than the titles in other films of the era. Some of them even had footnotes. Griffith's last-minute rescues were so exciting partly because they required no titles at all.

Several four-reel films that Griffith shot between the one-reelers of 1912 and the epic films of 1914 – 16 show both his artistry in transition and his difficulties in wedding moral significance to film action. *Judith of Bethulia* (filmed 1913, released 1914) was the last film Griffith made for Biograph. Just before *Judith,* he made one of his best two-reel Biographs, *The Battle at Elderbush Gulch* (released 1914), a western shot in California that had *no* difficulty in unifying action and moral significance. *Judith,* however, is a curious mixture of cinematic strengths and weaknesses. Because Griffith felt self-conscious about his biblical style and subject, his actors were much more stilted and much less carefully observed than in *The New York Hat.* Griffith's rendering of the evil of the invader, Holofernes, is formulaic and hollow. The "orgies" in his tent, metaphoric for the man's evil mind, are represented as a series of clumsy and unevocative semihula dances by the "Maids of the Fishes." Those Fish Maidens revealed a flaw in Griffith's vision that was to persist throughout his film career. Although Griffith knew what purity and goodness were, he either never really knew or could not honestly depict what sin and degeneracy were all about. The abstractness of the lives of sin and degeneracy that people lead in his films (a different matter from the cruelty, violence, and horror he dramatized so well) derive from the moralistic abstractions of Victorian melodrama, as in his little allegorical homily, *The Two Paths,* which signifies sin by dancing while holding a cocktail.

Balancing the film's artificiality and the thinness of the characters is Griffith's skill at cutting and construction. His opening expositional sequence effectively establishes the peacefulness and fertility of life in Bethulia, the importance of the well to its survival, and the thickness of the town walls for its defense. Here is Griffith's civilized ideal of peace and gentleness. Then Griffith introduces the conqueror Holofernes and his army, the forces of violent destruction. The branches in the foreground part, revealing the awesome hordes ready to descend on peaceful Bethulia.

Griffith magnifies the horrifying intensity of the battle scenes with his skillful cross-cutting from inside the walls to outside and back again. These battle scenes clearly show Griffith warming up for the huge sequences in *The Birth of a Nation*, although in *Judith* the battles feel pinched and confined by being anchored to the walls of the city, a problem he would solve in *Intolerance*. Much freer is Griffith's cutting at the end of the film when the attacking hordes, without their leader, retreat in chaos. Griffith cuts from one shot in which the horses and men run furiously from screen right to screen left to the next in which men and horses stream down a hill at the top of screen left into a valley that is at the bottom of screen right. This collision of contrary movements would not only dominate the battles in *The Birth of a Nation* but would also contribute to Eisenstein's theory of the shock value of colliding images.

Also noteworthy in the film are the crosscuts between the Bethulians starving inside the walls and Judith inside Holofernes's tent preparing to ease their starvation (clearly a variation of the last-minute rescue), and the cuts between Judith's hesitation before killing Holofernes, with whom she has fallen in love, and her vision of her own starving people (the vision that ultimately moves her to commit the murder). Despite Griffith's continuing technical skill and despite the film's vastness, it remains a rather tepid and artificial production.

Judith of Bethulia was Griffith's longest film yet, but it was by no means the first feature film. The term "feature," first used to describe any multiple-reel film, soon came to mean any film that was at least one hour long; at silent speed that meant at least four reels. The first feature film was made in Australia in 1906: *The Story of the Kelly Gang*, a four-reel movie about outlaw Ned Kelly, who wore a suit of armor, was directed by Charles Tait. The first feature made by Carl Laemmle's Universal Film Company (later Universal) was the six-reel *Traffic in Souls* (1913), directed—without Laemmle's approval—by George Loane Tucker; a powerful film about the prostitution racket, with the

tough, uncompromising look of urban rather than studio reality, it caused audiences literally to fight for seats. Since the nickelodeons refused to show features, being geared entirely toward the exhibition of one- and two-reelers, features were shown in legitimate theatres at higher prices (a quarter for *Traffic in Souls*, a dollar for *Quo vadis?*). Griffith was unaware of *The Story of the Kelly Gang* and the Australian features that followed it, but he certainly saw *Traffic in Souls* as well as two extraordinary spectacles imported from Italy: Enrico Guazzoni's *Quo vadis?* (1912, U.S. release 1913, eight reels) and Giovanni Pastrone's masterful *Cabiria* (1914, twelve reels).

By late 1913, Griffith's innovativeness and the growing lengths and costs of his films had irked Biograph into kicking him upstairs, making him director of studio production and relieving him of the opportunity to direct films personally. But Griffith wanted to make feature films—and the irony was, so did Biograph, which had noted the commercial success of *Queen Elizabeth;* they just didn't want to make long Griffith films. Thoroughly angry, Griffith left Biograph for an independent company, Mutual/Reliance-Majestic (the production company was Reliance-Majestic; Mutual was the distributor), signing a contract with producer Harry Aitken that gave him the freedom to make one picture of his own each year in addition to several program pictures of the company's choosing. (During that first year with Mutual, 1914, Griffith shot four features, each about five reels long: *The Battle of the Sexes; The Escape; Home, Sweet Home;* and *The Avenging Conscience*.) It was a new beginning for Griffith; it was the end for Biograph, which folded in 1915. When Griffith left for Mutual and California, he took Bitzer with him as well as nearly the entire Griffith stock company of actors. He also took out a full-page ad in the *New York Dramatic Mirror* in which he identified himself as the director of "all great Biograph successes," of which he listed 151 (out of the 455 movies he made at Biograph from 1908 to 1913, counting the two-reelers, whether released separately or together, as one film each). Griffith plainly asserted the right of the director to be called a film's creator, and his personal right to be credited with "revolutionizing Motion Picture drama and founding the modern technique of the art."

One of Griffith's program pictures for Mutual, *Home, Sweet Home*, showed where Griffith had been and indicated where he was to go. Like the later *Intolerance*, *Home, Sweet Home* uses four strands of action. Unlike the later film, Griffith does not weave the strands together but keeps them separate, using only the leitmotif of the song, "Home, Sweet Home," to unite the four stories, just as the wandering Pippa's song unites the incidents of *Pippa Passes*. In the framing story of *Home, Sweet Home*, the composer of the famous song, John Howard Payne, deserts home, mother, and sweetheart for the big city. There he falls to wenching, drinking, degeneracy, and poverty, summoning up just enough of his old home spirit to write his famous song. Payne later dies of unspecified causes in a foreign land, and his hometown sweetheart dies at the same time, presumably from ESP.

The second story in the film is the most delightful. An Eastern slicker falls in love with the earthy, out-west hashslinger, Apple Pie Mary, played energetically by Mae Marsh. Griffith adds a human, comic touch when Mary first sees the slicker; she immediately starts pulling the curlers out of her hair, revealing her attraction to him. When he later returns to her, she goes through the curler business again. In this section, the Easterner is about to reject Apple Pie Mary (two different worlds) when he hears a fiddler playing "Home, Sweet Home." He rushes back to her—a delightful reunion scene with her crawling under the bed to hide from him—and they marry to live happily ever after. Interestingly, this section, the comic, earthy, rural sequence of the film, is the most entertaining part of it; Griffith repeatedly demonstrates that his best film subjects are those he intimately knew and loved.

The third section of *Home, Sweet Home* is a melodramatic Cain-and-Abel story in which brother murders brother. Their mother, about to commit suicide after the dual slaughter, hears another fiddler playing "Home, Sweet Home." She gives up her thoughts of suicide and continues living, now resigned to life. The fourth section of the film is a domestic tale of potential marital infidelity. A young wife flirts with a lascivious admirer; as she is about to run off with him to a sinful amour, she hears a fiddler playing "Home, Sweet Home." (Those fiddlers are everywhere.) She rejects the lover and returns to her husband, and in the next shot we see the happy couple, aged and gray, surrounded by a bushel of kids.

The implication of all three stories is clearly that Mr. Payne's song, despite his faulty life, did great good. The film's epilogue picks up this moral nail and drives it home. We return to Payne in some unclear locale; he is either slaving away in Hell or fighting in a foreign war in which he met his death. Payne's hometown sweetheart (played by Lillian Gish) appears to him as a white diaphanous angel, superimposed in the heavens. Her image multiplies until there are many images of her fluttering and floating and beckoning from up there; Payne's image flutters up to join hers. The point Griffith makes is obviously that the results of the man's work cancel out the depravity of the man's life; furthermore, that Payne had the potential for good in him (he could write such a song), but the potential was corrupted by decadent, big-city life. There is obviously much that is soft-headed in the film. Griffith announces with his opening title that the film is allegorical and not biographical; but the slender, melodramatic stories and the artificial unifying device (that fiddle) cannot support the film's ponderous theme.

Another transitional film, *The Avenging Conscience*, Griffith's adaptation of Poe's "Annabel Lee" and "The Tell-Tale Heart," is much more intriguing and successful. In his study of the early motion pictures, the American poet Vachel Lindsay used this Griffith film as a demonstration of the psychological power and intensity of the cinema. Less historically grandiose than *Judith of Bethulia*, less allegorically grandiose than *Home, Sweet Home*, *The Avenging Conscience* concentrates exclusively and intensely on the internal derangement and paranoid suspicions of the man (Henry B. Walthall) who believes he has murdered his guardian. Although Griffith awakens Walthall from his nightmare at the end of the film (Poe's actual murder becomes a Griffith dream), the nightmarish mood the film sustains for as long as the dream lasts is a chillingly impressive accomplishment. Despite his aspiration to cinematic Ideas, Griffith would remain a master of cinematic Emotion.

The Birth of a Nation and *Intolerance*

For his own independent project for 1914, Griffith chose a novel by Thomas Dixon, *The Clansman.* The book appealed to Griffith for several reasons. It was a vast story, covering the final years in the graceful life of the old South before the Civil War; the turbulent, violent years of war; and the painful, political years of Reconstruction, during which the Ku Klux Klan arose to defend the rights of the whites. Griffith also used material from the stage version of *The Clansman* and from another Dixon novel, *The Leopard's Spots,* all of which were extremely racist. Griffith, a Southerner whose father served in the Confederate Army, was attracted by Dixon's slant. Dixon, also a Southerner, saw the Reconstruction era as a period of chaos in which the "civilized" white South, presented as the gallant underdog, struggled but survived. It was this film, with dangerous social and political implications, that Griffith set out to make. Shooting began on the Fourth of July, 1914.

No one on the set knew exactly what Griffith's film was all about. Griffith used no shooting script, creating all details of the vast cinema pageant out of his head as he went along. The players only knew that the project was vast: It took six weeks to rehearse and nine weeks to shoot, an incredible amount of time in an era when most films were cranked out in a week. It required thousands of men and animals and countless huge and detailed indoor sets. Its cost, $110,000, was the most ever invested in a motion picture. At the film's official premiere in Clune's Auditorium in Los Angeles on February 8, 1915, audiences finally saw how huge Griffith's plan and project were. The thirteen-reel film was still called *The Clansman* at that opening. When the author of the novel finally saw the film, however, Dixon

told Griffith, in his enthusiasm, that the original title was too tame. Griffith should call his film *The Birth of a Nation.* His point was that the nation was truly born only when the whites of the North and South united "in defense of their Aryan birthright."

The retitled version opened in New York on March 3, 1915, still thirteen reels long. But in response to social protests, Griffith deleted about nine minutes from the film (footage that has never been recovered), leaving it just over twelve reels long.

The Birth of a Nation is as much a document of American social history as of film history. Though President Wilson, a former historian at Princeton, described the film as "like history written with lightning," its action openly praises the Ku Klux Klan. Wilson may well have offered the simile simply to help his old school chum, Dixon. The film, which contributed significantly to the resurgence of the modern Klan in this century, is a very difficult morsel for today's liberal or social activist to swallow. It was just as difficult for the liberals of 1915. The NAACP; the president of Harvard, Jane Addams; and liberal politicians all damned the work for its bigoted, racist portrayal of the Negro. The film was suppressed in some cities for fear of race riots; politicians spoke for or against it according to their dependence on the black vote. At a revival of the film some ten years after its original opening, mobs poured into Chicago to see it as well as to attend a Ku Klux Klan convention. With all of the controversy over the film, it might be wise to look at Griffith's handling of the black man and woman a bit more closely before moving on to the cinematic qualities of the film.

First, a close examination of the film reveals that two of the three villains—Lynch (the false reformer) and Sarah (Stoneman's mistress)—are not pure Negroes but mulattoes. Both possess qualities that Griffith had already damned in whites—hypocrisy, selfishness, social reforming, and sexual license. That they were mulattoes indicates that Griffith's main target was not the blacks but miscegenation—an objective of the third villain, a black soldier named Gus, when he forces his attentions on a southern white girl. (His marriage proposal—a rape in the novel—causes Flora, "the little pet

Fig. 4-11

The Birth of a Nation: *Griffith's "historical facsimile" of Ford's Theatre.*

sister," to throw herself off a cliff to her death; in the novel, and perhaps in the censored footage, Gus is castrated by the KKK when they kill him.) The miscegenation theme flows through the movie like a poisonous river—in the scenes of the lecherous black legislature, in signs at the black-dominated polling place, in Lynch's attraction to Elsie (Lillian Gish) and Gus's to Flora (Mae Marsh). The mixing of bloods is the source of evil. Griffith's stance against miscegenation stems from an assumption about blacks and whites that is perhaps more central to the film's offensiveness. For Griffith, whites are whites and blacks blacks; the white race is naturally superior; each race has "its own place." If Griffith's view seems outrageous—well, it is. Not every masterpiece is "politically correct," and part of dealing with *The Birth of a Nation* lies in examining, rather than explaining away, how offensive it is. Although Griffith recognized that slavery was the root of America's racial problems, his solution (proposed in part of the censored footage, an ending originally meant to balance the all-white harmony of the

surviving conclusion) was to send the blacks back to Africa.

There are good blacks and bad blacks in Griffith's film. The good ones are the "faithful souls" who work in the fields, "know their place," and stay with their white family after the war. *Gone With the Wind,* twenty-four years newer fashioned than *The Birth of a Nation* and still adored by the public, makes the same distinction between good and bad "darkies." Perhaps Griffith's most offensive scene is the one in which the empty state legislature suddenly (with the aid of a dissolve) springs to life, full of black lawmakers with bare feet on desks, swilling booze, and eating—what else?—fried chicken while they eye the white women in the gallery. But Griffith's treatment of these blacks is not an isolated expression of racial prejudice; it is a part of his lifelong distrust of the "evils" of social change and disruption. And on a purely technical level, this legislature scene is a visual marvel!

The brilliance of *The Birth of a Nation* is that it is both strikingly complex and tightly whole.

Fig. 4-12

Fig. 4-13
From war's fury to "War's Peace."

It is a film of brilliant parts carefully tied together by the driving line of the film's narrative. Its hugeness of conception, its acting, its sets, its cinematic devices had not been equalled by any film before it and would not be surpassed by many that followed it. Yet surprisingly, for such an obviously big picture, it is also a highly personal and intimate one. Its small moments are as impressive as its big ones. Though Griffith summarizes an entire historical era in the evolution of the nation in general and the South in particular, his summary adopts a human focus: two families, one from the North (the Stonemans), one from the South (the Camerons), who, despite the years of death and suffering, survive the Civil War and Reconstruction. The eventual marriage between the two white families becomes a symbol or emblem for Griffith's view of the united nation. Love, courage, sincerity, and natural affection triumph over social movements and selfish reformers. The close observation of people and their most intimate feelings, the techniques of which Griffith had been developing for five years, propels the film, not its huge battle scenes, its huge dances and political meetings, or its detailed "historical facsimiles" of Ford's Theater and the Appomattox courthouse. The big scenes serve as the violent social realities with which the gentle, loving people must contend.

Even in the mammoth battle sequences Griffith never deserts his human focus. His rhythmic and energetic editing constantly alternates between distant, extreme long shots of the battles and close concentration on the individual men who are fighting. Griffith takes the time for such touches as his cut from the living, fighting soldiers to a shot of the motionless dead ones who have found "war's peace," his cuts from the valiant human effort on the Union side to shots of a similar effort on the Confederate, including Ben Cameron's heroic charge of the Union lines, ramming the Southern flag down the barrel of a Union cannon. Griffith increases the power, the violence, the energy of these battle sequences with his sensitivity to cutting on contrary movement across the frame, to cutting in rhythm with the action, and to cutting to different distances and angles that mirror the points of view of the different

Ben Cameron (Henry B. Walthall) rams the Confederate flag down the throat of the Union cannon.

Fig. 4-14

participants. But in the midst of such violence, Griffith takes time for quiet, tender moments: the moment when the two boys, one Cameron and one Stoneman, die in each other's arms; the moment in which a weeping mother on a hilltop views the destructiveness of the invading army in the valley.

This shot, one of the most celebrated in the film, shows Griffith's control of the masking- or irising-effect, another of the innovations he developed in his apprentice years. The iris-shot masks a certain percentage of the frame, concentrating the viewer's attention completely on a circle or rectangle or some other shape of light within the blackened screen rectangle; for an example, see Figure 4-12. The iris, analogous to the theatre spotlight or today's zoom lens, either shrinks the audience's focus from the whole field to a single point or expands our focus from the single point to the whole field. In *The Birth of a Nation*'s famous iris shot,

Griffith begins tightly on the weeping mother's face and then irises out to reveal the awesome army below her, the cause of her sorrow. This use of the mask shot to reveal cause and effect is only one of many in the picture.

Griffith often uses animals as symbols or to define his characters and their emotional states. In the early sequence depicting the gentle, peaceful life of the old South (analogous to the opening sequence of *Judith of Bethulia*), Griffith shows Doctor Cameron gently stroking two puppies. Significantly, one of the puppies is black and the other white; it is also significant that a kitten soon begins to play with the pups and starts a fight. The dogs become visual metaphors for Griffith's idealized prewar South, a happy mixture of different races and social classes, able to work out their own problems; the cat is the intrusive outsider who hurts the white pup. Later in the film Griffith cross-cuts between the two lovers, Elsie and Ben,

Fig. 4-15
*The street as emotional barometer: the total emptiness
and loneliness of the "Little Colonel's" return from
the war.*

gently playing with a dove while the savage
Lynch mistreats a dog. The attitudes of the
characters toward animals ultimately reveal
their attitudes toward people.

Another of Griffith's artistic devices is his
use of the main street in the town of Piedmont
as a barometer of the film's emotional and social tensions. At the film's opening the street is
full of people and carriages: active, sociable,
friendly. As the Confederate soldiers first
march off to war, the street becomes a carnival:
fireworks, cheering townspeople, rhythmic columns of men on horses. When "the little Colonel" (Ben Cameron) returns home after the
war, the street is desolate, ruined, dusty, dead.
And finally, when the town is overrun with
carpetbaggers and reconstructionists, drunken
gangs of black men rove the street; the street
has become a very unfriendly, ungentle place.
By capturing human emotion in concrete visual
images Griffith successfully renders human
feeling rather than a parody of feeling, as in
Queen Elizabeth.

The Birth of a Nation is part mammoth spectacle and part touching human drama. It is also

part melodrama and part allegorical vision.
Griffith never deserts the constructional principles of his early melodramatic one-reelers as
the means to keep his story moving. The suspense and excitement of Griffith's cross-cutting
create the dramatic tension of many of the sequences: the attack of a band of black renegades (significantly their captain is white) on the
defenseless town and the Cameron home (and
women); the assassination of Lincoln in Ford's
Theatre; the rapacious Gus chasing the littlest
Cameron girl through the woods until she falls
to her death. The most thrilling sequence of all
is, appropriately, the final one in which Griffith
gives us not one but two last-minute rescues.
Not only does Griffith cross-cut from the victims to the potential agents of their rescue, he
cuts between two sets of victims and their common saviors—the Ku Klux Klan—furiously
galloping forth to eradicate the forces of rapine
and death. Not only is this rescue sequence
Griffith's most complex up to this point, it is
also his most sensitive to the kinetic excitement
of editing rhythms and the moving camera.

But after the dust from the galloping climax
has settled, Griffith celebrates the peaceful
union of Elsie Stoneman and Ben Cameron
with a superimposed allegorical pageant in the
heavens. Elsie and Ben see Christ replacing the
military general (Alexander the Great?); Christ
cuts the Gordian knot and all humanity rejoices
as the City of God replaces the Kingdoms of
the Earth. There are several remarkable things
about this closing vision: its audacity, its irrelevance, and the passion and sincerity of Griffith's
commitment to it. But exactly how is this City
of God to become a reality? Certainly not by the
efforts of the Ku Klux Klan alone. It is the evil
in the human soul that must be exorcised. And
once again Griffith reveals his nearsightedness
in probing what he considers evil.

The evil in the film is instigated by three
people. They are evil (1) because they are evil,
or (2) because they have mixed blood. They
succeed in doing evil because they entice the
naturally good, but easily tempted, Congress-
man Stoneman to the abolitionist cause. His
temptation stems from his vanity despite his
physical deformity (Griffith brilliantly uses a
club foot, parallel to the classic deformity of
Shakespeare's Richard III, and an ill-fitting wig

to define these traits), and from the "fatal weakness" of being sexually attracted to his mulatto housekeeper. According to the film's action, the chaos of the Civil War was the direct result of the nation's Stonemans who became entangled in an evil of which they were totally ignorant or that they unwisely thought they could control. Even granting Griffith this preposterous premise, how is one to be sure the future contains no Stonemans? And how can one abolish slavery without abolition? *The Birth of a Nation*'s final vision is an innocent and mystical wish rather than the intellectual consequence of what preceded it. The film remains solid as human drama and cinematic excitement, flimsy as abstract social theory.

Right after *The Birth of a Nation*, Griffith made *The Mother and the Law* (1915, released 1919), a tightly constructed melodrama starring Mae Marsh (the Dear One), Bobby Harron (the Boy), and Miriam Cooper (the Friendless One); it indicted reformers and big business while telling a powerful story of love, loss, and endurance. Aitken and Griffith, who had set up their own company (Epoch) to finance and distribute *The Birth of a Nation,* had by now left Mutual for the Triangle Film Corporation, whose big three were Griffith, Thomas Ince, and Mack Sennett. But the controversy over *The Birth* led to Griffith's pulling *The Mother and the Law* from Triangle's release schedule; instead he and Aitken set up another separate company (Wark) to produce *Intolerance* (1916).

Griffith's treatment of blacks provoked public condemnation, even riots. The criticism stung Griffith deeply, since he felt he had gone to some trouble to present good and bad blacks *and* whites, as he had watered down or cut out the novel's most inflammatory, racist passages. (What he kept of Dixon's prose included "the opal gates of death"; what he left out sounded like this, and his reasons for deleting it are obvious: "For a thick-lipped, flat-nosed, spindle-shanked negro, exuding his nauseating animal odour, to shout in derision over the hearths and homes of white men and women is an atrocity too monstrous for belief." The KKK had permanently disbanded in 1869, and Dixon nostalgically dedicated his 1905 "historical romance," *The Clansman,* to the memory of his "Scotch-Irish" uncle, a "Grand Titan Of The

Fig. 4-16
Ben (Walthall) and Elsie (Lillian Gish) see the City of God replacing the strife of the world.

Invisible Empire"; unfortunately, *The Birth of a Nation* used the medium so powerfully that Griffith's film unexpectedly but indisputably inspired the birth of the twentieth-century Klan in late 1915.) Griffith began defending himself against the charges of bigotry and hatred; he angrily protested the film's suppression in several cities and wrote *The Rise and Fall of Free Speech in America,* a pamphlet that championed the "Freedom of the Screen." *Intolerance* was to be his cinematic defense, his pamphlet in film form against intellectual censorship. Fortunately for Griffith, *The Birth of a Nation* became the first authentic blockbuster in film history, earning untold millions of dollars; he would need his entire share of that money for *Intolerance,* its cost nearly half a million dollars ($493,800), its release length fourteen reels (his longest film, between 13,500 and 13,700 feet [of 35mm film, which has 16 frames per foot], not all of which survives), its conception so vast that it was to *The Birth of a Nation* as *The Birth of a Nation* was to *Judith of Bethulia.*

Intolerance was not one story, but four. In Belshazzar's Babylon (sixth century B.C.), the evil high priest conspires against the wise and just ruler, betraying the city to the Persian conqueror, Cyrus; by the end of this story, every

Fig. 4-17
Intolerance: *the immensity of the walls of Babylon.*

"good" character is dead. In Judea, the close-minded Pharisees intrigue against Jesus; ultimately, the gentle savior is sent to the cross. In Reformation France (sixteenth century A.D.), ambitious courtiers persuade the Catholic king to slaughter all the Protestant Huguenots on St. Bartholomew's Day, a massacre that includes the rape and murder of a young Protestant and the killing of her fiancé. In twentieth-century America (the "Modern Story," which used to be *The Mother and the Law*), strikers are gunned down, a Boy is falsely convicted of murder, and his wife loses her baby thanks to the meddling of a group of reformers; the facts eventually surface to save the Boy from the gallows.

Instead of telling one story after the other, as in *Home, Sweet Home,* Griffith tells these stories all at once, interweaving them—and 2,500 years of history—into an intellectual and emotional argument, a demonstration that love, diversity, and the little guy have always had to struggle against the overwhelming forces of hypocrisy, intolerance, and oppression. Because the colliding, streaming, *juxtaposed fragments* of these stories implied an *idea* that went beyond the "moral" of each individual story, making the whole greater than and different from the sum of its parts, *Intolerance* is recognized as the cinema's first great Modernist experiment in what Sergei Eisenstein would later call intellectual (or dialectical) montage. Indeed, Griffith's editing influenced the Soviets as much as his psychological lighting and control of *mise-en-scène* influenced the Germans; if *The Birth of a Nation* set the course for the American cinema, *Intolerance* did so for the Soviet cinema and *Broken Blossoms* for the German. The next American film to be organized this complexly would be *Citizen Kane* (1941); the next to be structured as a dialectical montage would be *The Godfather Part II* (1974).

The four stories are tied together by their consistent theme: the machinations of the selfish, the frustrated, and the inferior; the divisiveness of religious and political beliefs; the constant triumph of injustice over justice; the pervasiveness of violence and viciousness through the centuries. Also tying the stories together is Griffith's brilliant control of editing, which keeps all the parallels in the stories quite clear, and which creates an even more spectacular climax than that of *The Birth of a Nation*. In *Intolerance,* there are four frenzied climaxes; the excitement in each of the narrative lines reinforces the others, all of them driving furiously to their breathtaking conclusions. Griffith's last-minute rescues cross-cut through the centuries.

And finally, tying the four stories together, much as Pippa did, is a symbolic mother-woman, rocking a cradle, bathed in a shaft of light, representing the eternal evolution of humanity through time and fate (the three Fates sit behind her), fulfilling the purpose of the creator. This woman, inspired by Whitman's lines, "Endlessly rocks the cradle, Uniter of Here and Hereafter," is a figure of peace, of light, of fertility (flowers bloom in her cradle at the end of the film), of ultimate goodness that will eventually triumph. She is played by Lillian Gish, who assisted Griffith in the editing of *Intolerance.*

The film's bigness is obvious: the high walls of Babylon, the hugeness of the palace (and the immense tracking shot that Griffith uses to span it), the battle sequences, the care with each of the film's periods and styles. The costumes, the lighting, the acting styles, the decor, and even the intertitles are so distinct in each of the four epochs that viewers know exactly whether they are in the squalid, drab poverty of a contemporary slum, the elegant tastefulness of the French court, or the garishness of ancient Babylon. But as with *The Birth of a Nation,* *Intolerance* is a big film that works because of its little, intimate moments. The film revolves around the faces of women—from the bubbling, jaunty, comically vital face of the Mountain Girl in the Babylonian Story to the luminous, tear-stained, soulful faces of Brown Eyes in the French Story and the little Dear One in the Modern Story. *Intolerance* makes it perfectly clear that social chaos takes its toll on the women, who are the helpless sufferers of its violence. Significantly, Griffith's mother-symbol of historical continuity is also necessarily a woman. Along with the close-ups of faces, the film is equally attentive to close-ups of hands, particularly in the Modern Story: the Dear One's wrenched hands as the callous court pronounces judgment on her husband; her hand

Fig. 4-18

Fig. 4-19

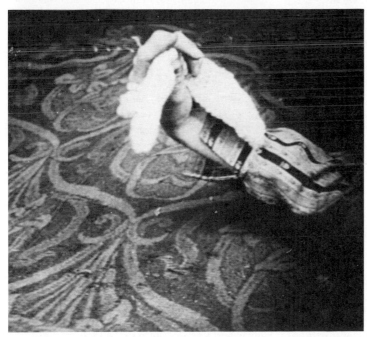

Fig. 4-20

Intolerance: *the faces of women.*
Fig. 4-18: The Mountain Girl
(Constance Talmadge). Fig. 4-19:
The little Dear One (Mae Marsh).
Fig. 4-20: The poignant detail —
losing consciousness, the Dear
One grasps the bootie of her stolen
baby.

grasping her imprisoned husband's cap, a tender memory of his warm presence; her hand clutching one of her baby's booties after the social uplifters have carried the infant away.

The film is also rich in the same kind of metaphoric detail found in *The Birth of a Nation*. The Dear One shows her humanity and tenderness as she lovingly throws grain to her chickens; when she moves to the oppressive city she keeps a single flower in her flat, a metaphor for all that is beautiful and natural and alive. (Flowers become the same kind of symbol of love and beauty in *Broken Blossoms*.) Yet another touching detail is the little cart pulled by two white doves in the Babylon sequence — a metaphor for the tender, fragile love between Belshazzar and his queen and for the peaceful ways of their court. After the two and the Mountain Girl have been slain, Griffith hauntingly irises out to a shot of the tiny cart and doves, a touching evocation of a beauty that was but is no longer.

Griffith's technique is as effective at conveying hatred as it is at evoking tenderness. A deeply felt film, *Intolerance* makes it clear what Griffith detests: those who meddle and destroy, those who take advantage of the poor, schemers, hypocrites, and monsters of lust and power. One of Griffith's devices of caricature is the cross-cut — particularly effective in the sequence in which he captures the cold inhumanity of the factory owner. Griffith cuts from the shots of the workers being mowed down by military or hired gunfire (violent, quick cutting, frenetic) to a shot of the owner of the factory sitting alone in his vast office (a long shot, perfectly still, that emphasizes the size of the office and the moral smallness of the big businessman). The contrast clearly defines the man's unsympathetic inhumanity to his slaughtered workers. Nine years later Eisenstein would build a whole film, *Strike,* out of such cross-cuts.

Although Griffith's dislikes are clear, the intellectual cement uniting the four stories (and the rocking cradle) is a bit muddy. The film could as easily have been called "Injustice" or "Intrigue" as *Intolerance*. Griffith was interested in the word "intolerance" because he felt himself the victim of it. But in none of the four stories does intolerance seem so much the cause of evil as blind human selfishness, nastiness, and

ambition (exactly as in *The Birth of a Nation*). And when the film ends with its almost obligatory optimistic vision — more superimposed angels in the heavens; the fields of the prison dissolve into fields of flowers; flowers bloom in the cradle — we once again witness an interpolated wish rather than a consequence of the film's action. Though there may be hope in the Boy's last-minute reprieve, it hardly seems enough to balance a whole film of poverty, destruction, suffering, and injustice.

The audience of 1916 found the film confusing and unpleasant. Unlike *The Birth of a Nation*, *Intolerance* aroused no social protest; worse, it aroused little audience interest of any kind. Perhaps the film was unpopular because it asked too much from its audience. Or perhaps the film was a victim of historical accident, its obviously pacifistic statement being totally antipathetic to a nation preparing itself emotionally to send its soldiers "Over There." Thomas Ince's pacifist bombast, *Civilization*, had made money only six months earlier. Whatever the reason, *Intolerance* was a financial disaster, costing Griffith all his profits from *The Birth of a Nation*. The failure of *Intolerance* began Griffith's financial dependence on other producers and businessmen, from which he would never recover.

1917–1931

The cliché of Griffith criticism is that with *Intolerance* the director reached a peak from which the only direction was down. The final years of Griffith's career are often dismissed as years of repetition, a retreat into sentimentality, and a lack of attention to audience tastes. There is some truth in the cliché. In the final period of his career, Griffith was less of an innovator; the cinematic advances of his youth had solidified into a stable, controlled mastery of the film form beyond which he rarely went. Some of his major pictures seem more striking in their parts than in their wholes today: *Hearts of the World* (1918), *America* (1924). After the financial fiasco of *Intolerance*, Griffith also had to look to his wallet, a concern that led to uninspired and uncommitted program pictures to fulfill contracts: *The Idol Dancer* (1920), *One Exciting Night* (1922, dull), *Sally of the Sawdust*

(1925, with W. C. Fields), *That Royle Girl* (1926, also with Fields), and perhaps a dozen more.

In 1917 Griffith went to Europe with Billy Bitzer, Robert Harron, Lillian and Dorothy Gish, and other members of his brilliant ensemble—who had, under his guidance, refined the arts of cinematography and film acting to an extent unparalleled in film history, just as Griffith had gone beyond all previous editing techniques in establishing absolutely that the shot, not the scene, was the basis of film construction, and had learned how to break down and reconstruct actions, placing the emphasis wherever he wished (on a hand, a twitch, a prop, a mood), so that *Queen Elizabeth* hardly seems to have been made on the same planet as *Intolerance,* let alone a mere four years before. Their object in Europe was to film the First World War (1914–1918) for Artcraft, a production company headed by Adolph Zukor, whose films were released by Famous Players-Lasky, soon to be reorganized as Paramount. Designed as a propaganda film for the British war effort and to show Americans what the suffering and valor of the war were all about, the twelve-reel *Hearts of the World* deserted the labyrinth of *Intolerance* for the relatively linear narrative style Griffith was to use till the end of his career. This decidedly unpacifist film, one of whose aims was to urge America to join the war, aroused and manipulated emotion in the manner of *The Birth of a Nation*—but without causing riots (by the time the film came out, America was in the war anyway). There is no significant change in the propagandistic narrative formula when the KKK, charging to the rescue, becomes the cavalry or anyone or anything the movie has made the audience like.

Some of the Artcraft films Griffith made between 1917 and 1919 were among his finest work. Aside from *Hearts of the World,* they were six or seven reels long. The best of them used a relatively small narrative canvas; their simple stories were told with rich emotion and plain humor, unpretentious lyricism and sudden suspense, all perfectly controlled. *A Romance of Happy Valley* (1918, released 1919), *True Heart Susie* (1919), and *The Greatest Question* (1919, made not for Artcraft but for his next employer, First National)—all of them set in something like rural Kentucky, shot by Bitzer,

and starring Lillian Gish and Bobby Harron (who died in 1920)—let Griffith work with material he knew and loved. These are melodramas, often contrived, but the people in them feel real and so do their problems (ambition, fidelity, death, the search for simplicity and happiness, the war against evil and deceit, the need to see into people's hearts). The sincerity of Griffith's engagement with these films—their settings, characters, and moral questions—is apparent and rewarding. Between *True Heart Susie* and *The Greatest Question* he made his lyrical masterpiece, *Broken Blossoms,* and his only full-length western, *Scarlet Days* (starring Richard Barthelmess). He bought *Broken Blossoms* back from Zukor and released it through United Artists, an independent distribution company that he, Charles Chaplin, Mary Pickford, and Douglas Fairbanks founded in 1919. For *Broken Blossoms,* which cost $3 to see (*The Birth* had cost $2 in its big-city runs; normal films cost well under a dollar) and which made a mint, Griffith designed a system of lights, concealed above and below the screen, that would wash across the image and add their colors to those that were already on the tinted and toned print—a music of light that perfectly complemented and was coordinated with the music that he co-wrote for the film. (*The Birth* and *Intolerance* had also been tinted—blue for night scenes, sepia for interiors, and so on—and accompanied by an orchestra playing music co-written by Griffith, but no film before or since had those lights; the machine was reconstructed in 1980, and Lillian Gish toured the country with it, showing *Broken Blossoms* in its original form to a new generation.)

In 1920, at the studio he had set up in Mamaroneck, New York, he made two awful films (*The Idol Dancer* and *The Love Flower*) and the classic melodrama *Way Down East.* He followed that with *Dream Street* (1921, a lyrical allegory with haunting, intriguing moments), *Orphans of the Storm* (1921, a twelve-reel melodrama set in the French Revolution, his last film with either of the Gish sisters), *The White Rose* (1923, a deeply moving film starring Mae Marsh), the clunker *America,* the superb *Isn't Life Wonderful?* (1924, starring Carol Dempster; significantly, the last film for which he wrote the script), five more clunkers, and his last silent, *Lady of the Pavements* (1929), a great-looking love story starring Lupe Velez and photographed by Karl Struss, *assisted* by Bitzer.

Part of the story here is that Griffith and Bitzer found it difficult to work together after 1920; at times Bitzer worked alongside other cinematographers (notably Hendrik Sartov, who began by doing soft-focus shots for *Broken Blossoms* and co-shooting *Way Down East*), but there were many films (*Isn't Life Wonderful?* among them) that Bitzer did not shoot at all. Griffith also lost some of his top players in the early 1920s—most crucially Lillian Gish, who later became a producer at MGM (five films including *The Wind,* 1928) and continued her acting career for the rest of the history of the cinema. Griffith's new leading lady, Carol Dempster, was watchable in *Dream Street,* very good in *Isn't Life Wonderful?*, but otherwise simply a terrible actress with bad posture, no subtlety, and a kind of hungry vanity. Unlike Gish, she could not "carry" a picture, let alone deliver a compelling close-up—but Griffith kept using her, as she was doubtless using him. Griffith's artistic and personal judgment began to falter, which is why Bitzer grew impatient with him. Along with this, it should be remembered that Griffith lost his principal writer (himself) after 1924; the films declined markedly when he worked from others' scripts.

As an example of bad artistic judgment and financial troubles, the following should suffice: Griffith cut into the negative of *Intolerance* in 1919, without making a copy first, in order to assemble two features, *The Mother and the Law* and *The Fall of Babylon* (with a ridiculous ending in which the unkilled Mountain Girl falls in love with the weak, treacherous man she avoided throughout the film, and they leave the ruins of Babylon together). Aside from how bad *The Fall of Babylon* was, and how reasonable a business decision it was to release *The Mother and the Law* on its own, the point is that the negative of *Intolerance* was all but destroyed. Two reels' worth of footage was lost, most of it forever. He made this idiotic, desperate decision the same year he released four masterpieces (*A Romance of Happy Valley, True Heart Susie, Broken Blossoms,* and *The Greatest Question*) and helped found United Artists.

Despite Griffith's troubles, at least two of the late films rank in power and interest just behind the two great epics. In fact, *Broken Blossoms* and *Way Down East* are more entertaining and easier for today's audiences to sit through than either *The Birth* or *Intolerance* (let alone *Judith of Bethulia*).

Broken Blossoms is Griffith's most polished, most finished gem, a tight triangle story of one woman between two men. Out of this triangle come the film's values, rather than from Griffith's subtitles and allegorical visions. If the film is less weighty than the epics, it is also less pretentious. To shift terms, one could call *The Birth of a Nation* an epic, *Intolerance* a film essay or tract, and *Broken Blossoms* a lyric—an emotional poem made to be sung. Like so many Griffith films, *Broken Blossoms* is an adaptation of a work of fiction—Thomas Burke's "The Chink and the Child," from his collection *Limehouse Nights.* As with *The Clansman,* Griffith took another man's work and made it his own, as the film's metaphoric title so clearly shows (the cleaned-up subtitle, however, was "The Yellow Man and the Girl").

The film is Griffith's gentlest, his most explicit and poetic hymn to gentleness. The typical Griffith film shows violence destroying gentleness; the focus of the films is usually on the violent disrupters: war, social upheaval, union protests, political chicanery, sexual debauches. In *Broken Blossoms,* the aura of ideal gentleness dominates the action, punctuated by the violent jabs of the real world. The gentle man in the film comes from the Orient to bring the message of the gentle Buddha to the vicious, violent men of the West. Once he arrives in London's dockside slum, Limehouse, Cheng Huan (Richard Barthelmess) runs into the "sordid realities of life"—gambling, whoring, opium smoking—that constitute life in the West. He virtually gives up.

Then in the film's second section, Griffith switches to the female figure of gentleness, Lucy (Lillian Gish). Raised by the prize fighter, Battling Burrows (Donald Crisp), Lucy is an unloved child who spends her time wandering around the Limehouse district, trying to scrape up enough tin foil to buy herself a flower. Flowers are the primary visual metaphor for gentleness in the film, as the title indicates. Lucy's gentleness, however, like Cheng Huan's, runs into sordid realities. Her reality is her father, Burrows, a brute who uses Lucy as both slavish servant and defenseless punching bag. One of the most poignant touches in the film is Burrows's insistence that Lucy smile for him, regardless of her real feelings. Since she is unable to summon a genuine smile, she uses two fingers to force one.

The next section of the film necessarily brings the two gentle figures together. Cheng Huan is attracted by Lucy's gentle purity, which he instantly perceives. They first meet, appropriately, over the purchase of a flower. She later collapses in his shop after a terrific beating by her father. Cheng Huan enthrones her in his room as a Princess of Flowers, and the two celebrate a brief but beautiful union of gentle love. Lucy even smiles without the aid of her fingers for the first time, and Cheng Huan's one weak moment of animal lust (brilliantly communicated by a painfully tight close-up) is soon conquered by his realization of the ideal perfection of his guest and their relationship.

But the realities break in upon the ideal. Burrows finds her at Cheng Huan's, trashes the place, drags her back to their slum room, and begins his inevitable attack. She retreats to a closet; he smashes it open with an axe, and Griffith creates one of the most accurate renditions of human frenzy in screen history as Lucy frantically starts rushing in a circle inside the closet—trapped, flustered, terrified. The death of all three characters is imminent. Lucy dies from this final beating, Cheng Huan shoots Burrows and then stabs himself. Blossoms, despite their loveliness, cannot survive for long in the soil of mortality.

Griffith suffuses the film with the atmosphere of dreams and haze. Richard Barthelmess and Lillian Gish have perfectly harmonious faces of inner calm and peace. Their acting is so restrained and so perfectly matched that the two feel like a single being. Griffith also succeeds in giving the abusive father both energy and credibility. Griffith makes the prize fighter walk, stand, sway, stagger like an animal in the ring. After Cheng Huan shoots Burrows, Griffith adds one of those observant touches that brilliantly makes the moment come to life. Burrows, reeling under the shot, instinctively puts up his dukes and begins dizzily jabbing at his opponent; after a few weak and faltering feints, Burrows collapses. This realistic yet symbolic, emblematic detail at the moment of death—for once Griffith gives his villain as much naturalistic attention as his heroes—parallels Lucy's final living gesture in which she uses two fingers to poke her face into a last smile.

Griffith's lighting also sustains the film's mood; *Broken Blossoms* remains one of the most beautifully lit films in screen history, supported by the beautiful color tinting and toning of its original 35mm prints. The lighting of scenes in Cheng Huan's shop and room is an atmospheric blend of beams of light and pools of shadow. Lillian Gish, as the Princess, becomes luminous, surrounded by the gray and black regions of her flowery kingdom. Griffith uses low-key lighting exclusively for these scenes. The lighting is not only atmospheric, it is also a precise visual translation of the film's metaphoric contrast between gentleness and violence. While Lucy is enthroned in Cheng Huan's room, Battling Burrows fights his title match. Griffith cross-cuts between the place of love—the room—and the place of hate—the ring. The boxing ring is harshly lit with bright, even white light; the room is suffused with shafts and shadows. Although *Broken Blossoms* asks a lot less of its audience than the earlier epics, it keeps its promises.

Way Down East, although more uneven than *Broken Blossoms*, contains sections that are as fine as anything Griffith ever did. The most famous sequence in the film is the climax, the last minute rescue of Anna Moore (Lillian Gish), floating steadily toward the deadly falls. Anna Moore's unfortunate sexual error—to have "married" a rogue in a bogus ceremony and then borne him a child who died, in all of which she was honorable and innocent—has been discovered by her adopted down-east (Maine) family; she rushes out of their house into a blinding blizzard, the savagery of the wind and snow becoming visual metaphors for the chaos and misery in her own heart and the heartlessness of her oppressors. Then Griffith's cross-cutting, his most enduring tool, drives the film's climax by alternating among three separate but related locations: Anna Moore alone in the storm, prostrate on a moving ice floe; her down-east boyfriend (Richard Barthelmess)

Fig. 4-21
Broken Blossoms: *Cheng Huan (Richard Barthelmess) and Lucy (Lillian Gish) in their luminous Kingdom of Peace.*

searching for her—the agent of her rescue; and the ominous falls, toward which the ice is moving—the danger from which she must be saved. The falls that Griffith used for this sequence were none other than Niagara Falls; Griffith merely spliced in bits of stock footage. Here was the ultimate proof of the logic of cross-cutting: Although the actress was really nowhere near any falls (especially Niagara), the audience felt her nearness because of the cuts and narrative links that bound the three locations. Soviet filmmakers would soon seize on this editing principle, naming it "creative geography."

The uneven, weaker parts of *Way Down East* are the plotty remnants of the original stage melodrama, whose rights Griffith purchased for $175,000 (far more than the entire budget of *The Birth of a Nation* and a sure indication of the film industry's rising costs). Everything in *Way*

Down East related to the evil doings of the rich folks reveals the artificial, heavy, and abstract hand of Griffith trying to depict a life-style for which he had neither sympathy nor understanding. After all, rich people have more things to do with their money than hold fancy-dress balls, act snobbish toward the pure of heart but poor of purse, and seduce innocent virgins with fake marriage vows. But the film has two compensating virtues. First, there is the face of Lillian Gish: radiant, luminous, determined, charming, alive. If the problems that the plot gives her seem contrived, the touching reactions of her eyes and mouth make sense of them. Griffith knew the power of the Gish face; he rivets our gaze on it with close-up after close-up, most of them key-lit to give her hair that shiny, diaphanous glow. The real action of the film takes place not in society but on the Gish face.

Fig. 4-22

Fig. 4-23

Griffith on location. Fig. 4-22: directing a race for life in Intolerance; *the driver, Tod Browning, later directed* Dracula *and* Freaks. *Fig. 4-23: with Billy Bitzer (left) in the snow of* Way Down East.

The second virtue of the film is Griffith's tender, careful, comic observation of down-east life. He loves the warmth of these rural people, their pettiness, laziness, and short-sightedness as well as their sincerity, simplicity, and compassion. In down-east life Griffith saw a mirror for the gentle and fertile life of the South (which he had depicted in the opening section of *The Birth of a Nation*) before the violence of military and political wars ripped that life asunder, demonstrating again that no director could more convincingly and carefully render the things he knew and loved, or could more stiltedly render the things he gathered from Victorian conventions and literary clichés.

There are several theories that attempt to explain Griffith's creative decay in the final years of his career. Perhaps he ran out of ideas, both technically and intellectually. The solidifying of his cinematic technique may have contributed to the congealing of his ability to make exciting, moving, powerful films. Or he might not have found the right challenge. There might never have been an *Intolerance* to equal or surpass *The Birth of a Nation* if the controversy over the first epic hadn't fired Griffith's anger and imagination. He may well have been unable to do his best work in regimented studios. Indeed, *Isn't Life Wonderful?* is so fine partly because it was shot outside any studio, on location in Germany during its disastrous postwar hyperinflation (where a bushel of banknotes *might* buy a loaf of bread; the exchange rate in 1923 rose to 4.2 trillion marks per dollar); shot on the streets, with many non-professionals in the cast, *Isn't Life Wonderful?* is the first precursor of neorealism. It was also his last independent production until *The Struggle*.

Another popular theory is that Griffith's ideas had become outmoded in the twenties. The flapper morality of the Jazz Age rejected the sentimentality of Griffith's Victorianism. Belasco's melodrama had been supplanted by urbane, domestic comedy-dramas of sexual

Fig. 4-24

Fig. 4-25

Waiting in line for food during a period of disastrous inflation. Fig. 4-24: Isn't Life Wonderful? (1924), shot on location in Germany by Griffith, anticipated many of the techniques and values of the neorealists; here Carol Dempster (fourth from the left, in wide-brimmed hat) checks to see how much the price of pork has gone up since she first got on line. Fig. 4-25: The Joyless Street (1925), set in Vienna during the same economic disaster, shot on a set by G. W. Pabst. Note the striking differences between street and studio realism.

innuendo and visual wit. The high life of dancing while holding a cocktail, which Griffith depicted so blackly and so clumsily, was exactly what audiences vicariously wanted to experience. Griffith no longer gave the public what it wanted.

The truth probably lies somewhere among the various theories. Griffith certainly seemed to be running out of creative gas. As his pictures became more and more formulaic, he was more and more dependent on public acceptance of his formulas—but his formulas, as formulas, were ten to twenty years out of date. The Griffith mastery when he was working at the top of his powers could make Victorian formulas exciting; *Broken Blossoms* and *Way Down East,* both heavily Victorian and sentimental and both released in the early years of the Jazz Age, were huge box-office successes—as big as Griffith ever had. When the mastery flagged, however, audiences saw the bare bones of sentimentality and took themselves to other pictures.

The final years of Griffith's career were scarred by his disastrous fling with the sound picture. In *Abraham Lincoln* (1930), a film that won high praise at the time, he returned to American history—but the result was stylistically inept and narratively inert. *The Struggle*

(1931) was a fervent, sentimental, sociological study of alcoholism and one man's struggle to overcome it. The screenplay was by John Emerson and Anita Loos, who had gotten her start with *The New York Hat;* the sound recording was of high quality. The budget was low, so the film was shot on the streets of New York and looks it; *The Struggle* has a tough flavor of suffering and authenticity. It also, in typical Griffith fashion, blames alcoholism on Prohibition, which converted a beer- and wine-drinking nation to whiskey. Audiences laughed it off the screen in a week.

The Hollywood brass was convinced that Griffith—without whom none of them would have had a job—was old-fashioned, that his day was done. He spent his final seventeen years barred from an art that he had practically fashioned by himself. He received an honorary Oscar in 1935, but the only job he got was as a consultant on purely visual acting for Hal Roach's *One Million B.C.* (1940), parts of which he appears to have directed; since the cave people in that film grunt and gesture rather than speak, Roach needed someone to teach the movies how *not* to talk. Public praise for his achievements could not ease the bitterness of his rejection by the business. He died broke and alone in Hollywood in 1948.

5

The Comics: Mack Sennett and the Chaplin Shorts

In 1907, the year that Griffith took his ride on the "El" up to the Edison studios in the Bronx, Mack Sennett took the same ride for the same purpose. Like Griffith, Sennett then wandered from Edison to Biograph to take up a longer residence there. Like Griffith, Sennett later moved from his apprenticeship at Biograph to maturity as an independent producer and director. Sennett even worked for Griffith at Biograph, as director, actor, and writer (he wrote the script for Griffith's *The Lonely Villa*). In his years with Griffith, Sennett absorbed many lessons on cutting, shooting, and construction. Sennett would later repay his teacher both by adopting his fluid cutting methods and by parodying Griffith's plots and last-minute rescues. Unlike Griffith, however, Sennett always wanted to make comic films. For years he tried to get Biograph to let him make a comedy about cops. He finally got his chance with his own independent company, Keystone, in 1912.

Krazy Keystones

The marriage that Sennett effected between visual, physical, burlesque comedy and the si-

lent film was one of those happy, inevitable unions. The purely visual film medium was perfectly suited to the purely visual comic gags that Sennett concocted. The popularity of the Lumières' first comedy, *L'Arroseur arrosé*, foreshadowed the future of the physical gag. Although there were comic films before Sennett — particularly the comic surprises of the trick films and the energy of the chase films — no one before him so forcefully revealed the comic effects of motion, of human bodies and machines and inanimate objects hurtling across the screen and colliding. It may not be coincidence that one of the most famous essays on comedy — Henri Bergson's *Le Rire* (1900) — was contemporary with the early films. Sennett — and later Chaplin, Keaton, Lloyd, Laurel and Hardy, et cetera — would unknowingly apply the Bergson theories. No theoretical aesthetic ever had the advantage of such concrete and convincing data. The Bergsonian principle that Sennett best demonstrated was that the source of the comic was the conversion of a human being into a machine. We laugh at the mechanical, inelastic motions of a man who fails to alter his responses to suit some change in the environment: the man who slips on a banana peel but continues walking as if no peel were under him until he inevitably falls. Further, we cannot laugh if we have any real fears for the man's safety; we must view him externally as a kind of imperishable machine rather than as a man who can suffer pain and broken bones and bruises.

This conversion of people into moving objects is at the center of Sennett's comic technique. The characters zip across the screen like mechanical toys, crashing and colliding into bricks, pies, walls, furniture, and one another. Sennett furthers the impression of human machines by undercranking the camera. He saw that by recording the action at only eight to twelve frames per second and then projecting it at sixteen or twenty, the action became so speeded up that the effect became even more artificial, more frantic, and, hence, more comical. In one Sennett film, *A Clever Dummy* (1917), Ben Turpin actually plays a robot. There is rarely a sense of the Sennett characters as people; reflection and feeling are human activities they never experience, and their individuation is strictly by physical type—fat, thin, short, tall, dark, fair, male, female. The use of people as objects rather than as feeling, thinking beings makes them perfectly suited to run into trouble with the other objects and machines in their universe. Whatever terrific collisions they suffer, we know that the injury will be no more serious than a dent in an automobile fender. Although many Sennett characters brandish guns, the audience knows that a bullet is no more lethal than a kick in the pants or a pie in the face. Their automobiles smash into each other at fifty miles an hour, their boats sink, their roller-coaster cars fly off the tracks, they fall down wells, they fall off roofs. Disasters resulting in death in the real world produce only a few dazed moments in the Sennett world (or, for that matter, in the world of the animated cartoon, where a character can be massacred in one shot and fine in the next). No damage is permanent. If we thought these characters were feeling real pain, we couldn't laugh at them.

Like Griffith, Sennett depended heavily on improvisation. A rough plot outline was the basis for staff meetings each week when Sennett, the cast, and the crew would get together to see what zany bits they could inject into the story line. Sennett liked to have an imaginative outside observer, whom he called his "wild card" or "joker," sit in on the staff meetings to toss out the wildest, most farfetched and irrelevant gags he could think up. After a series of gags had been hammered together in the meeting, there was further improvisation in the course of the shooting. Sennett adhered to only one principle of construction: A gag had to begin, develop, and finish itself off within a hundred seconds. Because Sennett cared so little about whole plots—the individual gag was the beginning and end of his cinematic technique—the films are loosely structured, held together only by the pace of the movement within them. The stories seldom go anywhere; they end when the series of gags has been played out. One of the most common Sennett endings is for the clashing characters to end up dazed and exhausted or doused in a pool of water, the ocean, or a well, as in *Tillie's Punctured Romance*, *The Surf Girl*, and *The Masquerader*. When the characters are all wet, the action simply stops.

Sennett films usually conform to one of three structural patterns. In one of the most common, Sennett takes some conventional, almost melodramatic plot—the kind that Griffith often used—and then peppers it with gags wherever he can. The plot merely serves as a kind of string to tie the gags together, or a clothesline on which to hang them. The second kind of Sennett structure is even less plotty and could best be described as "riffing"—taking some place or situation and then running through all the gags that might occur there. The third Sennett structure is more whole than the first two. Sennett had a great taste for parodying both the styles and the themes of other famous directors and pictures. In the parody pictures, Sennett not only used individual gags but shaped the whole film in accordance with the model he was burlesquing.

Sennett's first feature-length film, *Tillie's Punctured Romance* (1914, six reels), is a good example of the formulaic plot that merely strings gags together. The completely conventional story concerns a farm girl who falls prey to the false advances of a city slicker; he wants her only for her money. She leaves the farm for the evil city, inherits money from an uncle who is presumed dead, gets mixed up with rich city folk, has troubles with her fiancé who has another girlfriend, and finally discovers his duplicity.

Tillie, the farm girl, is played by the enormous Marie Dressler (in her first film role); her city-slicker boyfriend is the small and skinny Chaplin (before he adopted the tramp character exclusively). Sennett plays with the disproportion in their sizes, showing Tillie besting her beau in all sorts of contests in which Charlie winds up with a brick or a stone or a boot hitting him in the head or seat of the pants. The "other woman" in the film is played by Mabel Normand, a coy and subtle comedienne who indulges in her own comic shenanigans as a fake waitress at Tillie's grand ball. Sennett includes a hilarious dance number with the tiny Charlie and the immense Tillie, he adds a hilarious drunken "elephant" sequence when Tillie overindulges in a café, he draws on the incompetent Keystone cops for the final chase, and he throws all the main characters off the Santa Monica pier and into the Pacific Ocean to end the film. The plot becomes irrelevant; the best things in the film are the gratuitous gags, the surprises that Sennett throws in. That which is gratuitous ultimately becomes that which is essential.

Mabel's Dramatic Career (1913) has the same kind of structure. Mabel (Normand), a country gal, and Mack (Sennett), her country swain, are in love. (Sennett acted in his films, too, usually portraying the oafish, sluggish country boy.) Mack's mother objects to the match. The story is further complicated by another woman who arrives from the city and steals Mack's heart away from Mabel. Mack gets his ring back from Mabel, and Mabel slinks sadly off toward the big city. Some unspecified time later, Mack journeys to the city and sees a nickelodeon displaying Mabel's picture. (Many of the early film comedies were about the film business itself.) Mack goes into the theatre to see the show; he sees Mabel attacked by the villain (Ford Sterling) in a typical film melodrama. Mack, who does not realize he is watching a fiction, fails to keep his aesthetic distance. He pulls out his sixshooter and starts firing at the screen, scaring

the shocked customers out of the theatre. Mack also runs out and catches a glimpse of the screen villain at home; naturally, off-screen Ford is a kindly father and husband. But Mack starts shooting again. Someone douses him with a pail of water, and the film just stops once the menace has been soaked.

The Sennett "riffing" films are even more fun; the director does not pay even lip service to story values. These films are structured as a pure series of gags, held together only by pace and by the general locale or situation (the same could be said of an avalanche). Several of the films Chaplin made for Sennett use the riffing structure. In *The Masquerader* (1914), Sennett and Chaplin pull as many gags as they can on the premise that a disruptive actor on a movie set can wreak havoc in a studio. Chaplin plays the actor; the director boots him out; Charlie sneaks back in as a seductive woman; chaos follows until Charlie winds up soaked in a well and the riffing stops. *The Rounders* (1914) riffs on the troubles that two drunks (Chaplin and Roscoe "Fatty" Arbuckle, two obviously contrasting physical types) can get into, and on the reactions of their two shrewish wives. *Getting Acquainted* (1914) riffs on the theme of flirtation and mashing in the park.

The Surf Girl (1916) is one of the zaniest of the riffing pictures. The two-reeler takes the beach as its starting point and then runs off every gag it can imagine in a beach setting. Sennett uses the ocean, a swimming pool, a roller coaster, a ferris wheel, a beach-front saloon, dressing rooms for changing into bathing suits, showers, beach cabañas, an amusement park, an aviary, motorboats, whatever. The strong man with the hammer not only rings the gong but sends a fellow surfer flying up the gauge and off into the sea. The swimming pool is a crowded casserole of frantic aquatics— Sennett's undercranked camera makes the pool activities a kind of water ballet turned St. Vitus' dance. An immensely fat man rolls down a slide and into the pool. Everyone in the pool (Sennett uses reverse motion of the camera brilliantly) is vomited out of the water by the impact of the fat man's splash. The two lifeguards, courting a young lady, discover that an ostrich has swallowed her locket. They chase and ride the awkward bird until it disgorges the chain. Another lifeguard, swinging on the rings over the pool, loses his pants; the lady who has been pushing him flies off with the pants into the pool.

This wild mêlée of gags and movement ends with a great anticlimactic joke. The cops hustle all the soaked, brawling surfers into the paddy wagon. As the wagon pulls into the station, the top part strikes the roof of the entrance and separates from the chassis. (Those incompetent cops can't even build the right-sized garage.) The surfer-felons slowly walk away from the cops, using the top part of the paddy wagon as a shell and cover for their retreat. As the dozen or so legs walk off, looking like a huge beetle, the film comes to a halt. Despite its title, there is no surf girl in the picture.

The Sennett parody films are less zany but more whole. Parodying the latest movie hit was a staple of the comic shorts, just as parodying the film hits of the past became a staple of comedy in the 1970s and of comedies, melodramas, and adventure and horror films in the 1980s. Chaplin parodied *Carmen* in 1915, the same year that two serious versions of the story were released; there were parodies of stage and filmed melodrama: for example, Vitagraph's delightful *Goodness Gracious;* both Sennett and Hal Roach parodied hits like *The Iron Horse (The Iron Nag)* and *The Covered Wagon (The Uncovered Wagon, Two Wagons Both Covered).* Some of Sennett's best parodies were of Griffith, not only of his melodramatic stories but also of his famous last-minute rescues. An early parody of Griffith, *Barney Oldfield's Race for a Life* (1913), features a villain (played by Ford Sterling) who ties the young damsel (Mabel Normand) to the railroad tracks and then steals a train for the express purpose of running over her. Her boyfriend, played by Sennett, is flying to the rescue in an automobile. The cops, also alerted to the danger, furiously pump to the rescue on a handcar. Sennett, in the best Griffith tradition, cuts among four locales: Mabel on the tracks, anxious; Ford in the train, gleefully looking forward to squashing Mabel; Mack and Barney in the auto; the cops on the handcar. Sennett pokes fun at Griffith by drawing out this rescue to an impossible length; the train, which we know is not very far from Mabel's bound body, takes forever to get to it,

Fig. 5-1

Fig. 5-2

The Surf Girl. *Fig. 5-1: fun in the pool; Fig. 5-2: the police wagon as beetle.*

just long enough for Mack and the cops to get there in time.

Teddy at the Throttle (1917) parodies not only Griffith's cross-cuts but also his plots. The story is a triangle. The young man (Bobby Vernon)

Barney Oldfield's Race for a Life: *Ford Sterling has Mabel Normand tied to the tracks in an exaggerated parody of melodramatic gesture and acting.*

Fig. 5-3

drops his true girlfriend for the rich society gal; the young man is being manipulated by the villain (Wallace Beery), who thinks he will make money from the society match. The society gal (large) drags the young man (small) out into an unbelievably intense storm — with winds that blow the clothes off the guests at a fancy ball

Fig. 5-4
Barney Oldfield's Race for a Life: *Mack Sennett and Mabel Normand.*

when the door opens, with oceans of rain driving down, with pools of mud several feet deep. She is insistent on getting married pronto. The true girl (Gloria Swanson), who has discovered the deception, pursues them. When Gloria is tied to the railroad tracks by the villain, her dog, Teddy, carries a scribbled message (which she miraculously managed to write while tied up) explaining her terrible plight to her boyfriend. Then comes the Griffith cutting: from Gloria tied to the tracks, to the train chugging toward her, to the agent of her rescue (the dog), who finds the boyfriend and leads him back to Gloria. Gloria is, of course, saved just in time, and Teddy continues his canine heroism by treeing the nasty villain.

The Sennett films set a comic standard for zaniness, non sequitur, and physical activity that has served as a model ever since — for, among others, René Clair, Richard Lester, Mel Brooks, Chuck Jones, and the Monty Python troupe. Not as technical a cinematic innovator as Griffith, Sennett still realized that the tricks the camera could play with motion were highly suited to physical comedy. In a sense, Sennett's method took Méliès's stop-action principle one step further by combining rapid physical activity with the camera's tricks.

By as early as 1915 Sennett had become exclusively a producer who no longer directed films personally. In 1916 he scrapped his independently funky Keystone Company to begin producing comedies for the giants like First National, Paramount, and Pathé. His films became more expensive and polished, losing much of the improvisational, slap-dash and slap-happy quality of the Keystones that starred Chaplin, Normand, Sterling, Arbuckle, Chester Conklin, and Mack Swain. But Sennett's parody still created hilarious 1920s films that starred the cross-eyed antihero, Ben Turpin, the antithesis of movie glamor and romance. Sennett's devotion to frantic movement, irrational surprises, and impossible nonsense created films that starred Billy Bevan, supported by incredibly agile machines like leaping tin lizzies and flipping airplanes, or by menacingly awesome beasts like wild lions and even a viciously snapping oyster. Although Sennett produced sound shorts, his importance died with the silent film, which was his natural medium. The particular qualities of the Sennett style become most obvious when compared with the completely different method and emphasis of his most distinguished disciple.

Charlie

In 1913, the English stage comedian Charles Chaplin was touring American vaudeville stages with a music-hall act, Fred Karno's English Pantomime Troupe (also called Fred Karno's Speechless Comedians and Fred Karno's London Comedians, a troupe that included Stan Laurel). Either Harry Aitken, who was Griffith's and Sennett's partner, or Adam Kessel, the bookmaker-turned-owner of the Keystone Company, or Mabel Normand and Sennett saw Chaplin's performance as a comic drunk in Karno's *A Night in an English Music Hall.* Keystone offered Chaplin a job, believing Chaplin's gymnastic talents were perfectly suited to Sennett's athletic menagerie. Chaplin wasn't sure he wanted to work in that zoo; he shared the prejudice of many stage performers against working in films, suspecting, with his typical hard-headedness, the impermanence of a novelty that seemed more monkey business than show business. After Chaplin drove Kessel's offer up from $75 to $150 a week, including a one-year guarantee, he decided the risk was worth it. He appeared on the Sennett lot in

December of 1913. His first Sennett film was *Making A Living* (1914, directed poorly by Henry Lehrman); Chaplin hated it.

Sennett immediately tried to use Chaplin as one more cog in his factory of human puppets. Sennett capitalized on Chaplin's gymnastic abilities: his ability to fall and stagger and roll and bounce off both people and the floor. Chaplin's smallness was the perfect foil for the fatness of Arbuckle or the hugeness of Dressler. In *The Knockout* (1914, like all Chaplin's Keystone films), Chaplin makes a brief appearance as referee in a boxing match, ducking, sliding, squirming, and falling between the punching pugilists and the ropes. This was Chaplin as pure physical comic. Sennett used the same gymnastic potential in *The Rounders* and *Tango Tangles,* in which Chaplin recreates his drunk act from Karno's troupe.

But tension soon developed between Chaplin and Sennett. Sennett's rapid, pure-motion principle bothered Chaplin, who wanted to add character and individuality to his gymnastics. As early as his second and third Keystone films, *Mabel's Strange Predicament* and *Kid Auto Races at Venice* (the latter shot after *Mabel* but released before it), Chaplin began to evolve the tramp character, borrowing the idea of using a cane and hat from the earlier French film comic, Max Linder, borrowing an old pair of Ford Sterling's shoes (much too big for Charlie's feet) and an old pair of Fatty Arbuckle's oversized pants. He also used a small derby that belonged to Arbuckle's father-in-law, Charles Avery's small jacket, and Mack Swain's false moustache (which he shortened considerably) — all found in the Keystone dressing room. Such individuation was both unwanted and unneeded in Sennett's mechanical world. Sennett neither took the time nor placed the camera close enough to make such characterization count. After only one year with Sennett, the little clown with the bowler hat, baggy pants, reedy cane, and floppy shoes had become one of the most familiar figures and faces in the entire United States. He had also, in April of 1914, become a director. Chaplin directed 19 of the 35 films he acted in at Keystone; in most cases he wrote what he directed. From 1915 on, he wrote and directed and usually edited every one of his films. For the record, the first

Keystone he wrote and directed was *Twenty Minutes of Love;* the second was *Caught in the Rain.* In between those films, Mabel Normand directed *Caught in a Cabaret* (all 1914).

A brief recounting of contractual facts and figures will summarize his meteoric rise to fame, fortune, power, and artistic maturity over the five years between 1913 and 1918. From $150 a week as a Sennett pawn in 1914, Chaplin signed a one-year contract with the Essanay (S & A) Company of Chicago for ten times the amount of his Keystone contract: $1,250 per week, plus a $10,000 bonus upon signing—a total of $75,000 for 1915. He turned down Sennett's comparatively chintzy 500 percent raise to $750 a week (Sennett typically lost his stars when he refused to pay them their market value). In 1916, Chaplin signed a contract for yet another ten times the amount of the previous year's agreement—$10,000 per week plus a $150,000 bonus, a total of $670,000 for the year—with the Mutual Corporation (it took him 18 months to fulfill this contract for 12 films). In late 1917 he signed a contract with First National for an even million dollars (at almost the same time that Mary Pickford signed her first million-dollar contract, the first time such fabulous sums entered Hollywood legend). Each of these contractual arrangements brought Chaplin more money and more creative independence—to write, direct, produce, and even own the rights to his films (as he did, beginning in 1918).

Such awesome numbers indicate not only the general expansion of the movie industry (in 1914, Mack Sennett could make an entire one-reel comedy for $1,000 or less) but also the personal accomplishment of a man who became history's first truly international superstar and the first maker of movies (and comic movies at that) acknowledged as a genius and primary influence by an entire generation of twentieth-century artists and intellectuals.

Temperamentally, Chaplin never could see comedy as Sennett saw it. For Sennett, the comic world was a realm of silly surfaces; for Chaplin, the comic world provided the means to examine the serious world of human needs and societal structures. For Sennett, comedy was an end; for Chaplin, it was a means. Chaplin revealed another dimension of Bergson's

Fig. 5-5

Fig. 5-6

Chaplin's appearance in his first Keystone releases. Fig. 5-5: as an English type with an animatedly dancing cane in Making A Living; *Fig. 5-6: in his tramp costume for* Kid Auto Races at Venice.

theory of comedy in *Le Rire*—a moral force to correct the mechanical and inelastic constrictions of social norms.

Chaplin's own experience played a tremendous role in shaping his outlook. With his father and mother separated and his mother battling ill health and insanity, Chaplin spent almost two years of his Dickensian childhood in a workhouse for the poor. The boy in the workhouse quickly perceived the power of wealth and social status. The young Chaplin was an outsider, beyond the embrace of social and material comforts. The screen character he created, Charlie (the French call him Charlot), is also an outsider. He is a tramp, a criminal, an immigrant, a worker—someone excluded from the beautiful life. And yet Charlie yearns desperately for that life. He longs for money, for love, for legitimacy, for social station, for etiquette, for superiority, for recognition. Ironically, Charlie as outsider serves to show both the gleaming attractiveness of the beautiful life for those who don't have it and the false emptiness of the beautiful life for those who do. Chaplin was mature enough as an artist to show the ambivalence of power and wealth, its attractiveness and its emptiness, an ambivalence that Chaplin the man felt when he became rich and powerful.

The Chaplin comic aesthetic was radically different from Sennett's. The cliché is that Chaplin slowed down Sennett's dizzy pace. He did slow it down, but he did so to put something else in. The structures of the films reveal a key shift. If Sennett's films are merely strings of gags, Chaplin's films are structured as three or four beads on a string. Like Sennett's, Chaplin's film structures break into clear and distinct pieces. But where Sennett's pieces are 30 to 90 seconds long, Chaplin's are 5 to 10 minutes long. He exhausts a comic situation or location completely rather than flipping from gag to gag. His classic Essanay film *The Tramp* (1915), in which Chaplin first demonstrates a complete consciousness of his clown persona, breaks into four clear sections: Charlie the tramp protecting the pretty girl from other, meaner tramps; Charlie as farmhand on the girl's farm; Charlie foiling the other tramps' plot to rob the farm; and Charlie losing the girl when her wealthy boyfriend arrives. A later film he made for Mutual—*The Adventurer* (1917), whose plot resembles much of *City Lights*—also breaks into four clear sections: Charlie's escape from the police; Charlie's rescue of the drowning rich man; Charlie's attempt to join the *haut monde*

at the rich man's swank party; and Charlie's second escape from the police when the rich man betrays him, coupled with his expulsion from the house by the pretty rich girl.

The shift in film structure from the gag to the scene demands that each of the sequences be more detailed, richer, fuller; each focuses attention on either the social situation or the conflict of characters and their values within it, rather than on the gags alone. The gags actually define the characters. When Charlie twirls his cane at a fancy party (in *The Count,* 1916) and then accidentally stabs the turkey, which he inadvertently swings above his head, he defines his sociable attempts to be suave and his frustrating lack of success at it. Charlie's sly and jaunty crap shooting and card shuffling when surrounded by big, mean opponents (*The Immigrant,* 1917) show he has guts as well as style. Despite the size of his opponents and the social obstacles, Charlie insists on enjoying the last laugh or the last kick in the pants. His attempts to enjoy the last boot are not only ingenious and funny, they also define his pluck. Though Charlie is comically incompetent at mastering the social graces of the *haut monde,* he consistently makes up for his lack of etiquette with his wiry toughness and his pragmatic cleverness. Chaplin's gags alone define Charlie's ironic synthesis of naïve innocence and pragmatic pluck.

Another dimension of the mature Chaplin tramp is that, despite the toughness, opportunism, and dishonesty that help him survive, he has a kind and generous heart. He demonstrates this trait repeatedly by using a Griffith-like woman who evokes Charlie's milder qualities: blonde, ethereal, and kind, instantly perceiving the redeeming characteristics in the unworldly tramp. From 1915 to 1922 Chaplin used the same actress, Edna Purviance, to portray her.

For Chaplin, the woman was not just a sentimental character—although she certainly was that; she was also a metaphor for natural human beauty uncorrupted by social definitions and unburied by material possessions. In film after film Charlie shows his affinity with the naturally good and beautiful spirit by allying with her against those who can do him more material good. In *The Tramp* and *Police* (1916), he

Fig. 5-7
Easy Street: *the runt and the giant (Charlie and Eric Campbell).*

refuses to ally with fellow robbers and protects Edna instead. In *The Tramp* and *The Immigrant,* he retrieves Edna's stolen money and, without letting her know it, slips it back into her pocket. And yet Chaplin's sense of character and reality is such that after stuffing a whole wad of bills in Edna's pocket, he thinks better of it and takes a few back for himself.

Chaplin's characters also comment on the assumed values of the society that produces such people. The villain in the Mutual Chaplin films is invariably Eric Campbell, a huge brute of a man whose superblack, upturned eyebrows look as though they alone contained enough poison to kill a man Charlie's size. Like Sennett, Chaplin uses physical types for comic effect. Unlike Sennett, the physical type also implies moral, social, and psychological values. Eric Campbell, the heavy, is invariably a member of the film's social in-group; he naturally hates Charlie because Charlie is not a member of that group. Eric is the physical giant in *Easy Street* (1917), a very uneasy street that values physical

toughness alone; Charlie is the contrasting runt. Eric is the waiter in *The Immigrant* who enjoys pommeling those patrons who are only ten cents short of paying the bill; Charlie is the diner without any money. Eric is the lecherous rich man in *The Rink* (1916); Charlie is the poor waiter (but terrific skater!). If the social "ins" are as brutal, as coarse, as empty, as vicious as Eric, then there is some human value in being "out," like Charlie.

Consistent with his social view, Chaplin's cops are very different from Sennett's incompetent and cockeyed loons. Though not precisely what would be called, in the argot of a later generation, "pigs," Chaplin's cops were not very far from it. In *Police,* the cops spend their time leisurely motoring to answer an emergency call for help; they drink tea and fluff their uniforms and show no concern at all for Edna's distress. Ultimately it is Charlie, one of the two robbers, who protects Edna against his own partner. The cops in *The Adventurer* are not as satirical, but they do shoot rifles at the escaping Charlie, and their bullets, unlike those in Sennett comedies, look as though they might hurt somebody. In the First National three-reel film, *A Dog's Life* (1918), the only crimes that the neighborhood cop finds interesting are those committed by a hungry Charlie, desperately seeking something to eat.

The short Chaplin films—like the later features—contain ironic and pointed social commentary in the action as well as in the characters. The comedies treat several controversial themes that we might think the exclusive property of our own generation: drug addiction, poverty, hunger, crime on the streets, homosexuality, religious hypocrisy. In *Police,* Charlie learns that those who want him to go straight only intend to eliminate him as a competitor. He discovers that the preacher who urges him to reform has stolen a man's watch that Charlie considered stealing but didn't because of the preacher's sermon. In *The Immigrant,* Charlie juxtaposes the Statue of Liberty with a cattle boat full of immigrants. As soon as a title announces, "The land of liberty," government officials rope all the immigrants together and start checking their identification tags. Men in uniform are inevitably damned in the Chaplin shorts, whether the uniform is a policeman's, a fireman's, a government official's, or a banker's.

Aside from *The Immigrant, Easy Street* may be the most socially conscious of the early short films. In the opening sequence, Charlie gets uplifted in the Hope Mission, singing hymns and feasting on Edna's pure face. He is so uplifted that he gives back the collection box he has stolen. The inspired Charlie goes off into the world only to discover that it is a vicious place, full of hunger, poverty, thieves, drug addicts, bullies, and rapists; Easy Street is not so easy, a jungle world of animals striving to survive. Charlie as a cop in the slums (now an outcast *because of* the uniform) subdues all the foes of goodness, ironically inspired to perform his heroic deeds by a shot of dope. In the final sequence, the den of thieves has been miraculously transformed into the New Hope Mission; all the thugs, including the ominous Eric Campbell, have dressed in their Sunday suits and Sunday smiles, all of them marching meekly and politely into the mission for their own uplifting.

This contrived, Pollyannaish ending is Chaplin's deliberate way of reducing social optimism to absurdity. The social evils admit of no easy solutions; in fact, they seem to admit of no solutions at all. As Brecht's *Threepenny Opera* put it ten years later with its similarly contrived happy ending, "Victoria's messenger does not come riding often." Chaplin's endings frequently imply this social dimension of false happiness and solution, as in *The Vagabond* and *A Dog's Life*. In *The Bank* (1915) and *Shoulder Arms* (1918), Charlie wakes up only to discover that the happy ending literally was a dream. The other typical Chaplin ending (*The Tramp, The Adventurer*), less socially pointed but more poignant than the faked happy ones, shows Charlie losing in the end, shuffling off down the road again after failing to satisfy his longings.

Though the social and moral implications of the Chaplin shorts are striking, Chaplin never deserts the objective tool of comedy for making his points. One of the most brilliant examples is the beginning of *The Bank.* Charlie strides into the bank, goes directly to the safe, twirls the dials of the huge safe, checking his cuff to

Fig. 5-8

Fig. 5-9

Easy Street: *Charlie gets uplifted in the mission (Fig. 5-8), feasting on the face of Edna Purviance (Fig. 5-9).*

make sure that he remembers the combination, finally opens the door of the safe, steps in, and brings out his mop and pail. Not only does Charlie demonstrate the difference between capital and labor, but he does it in a stunning surprise of our expectations. At the beginning of *The Immigrant,* people are lying about the boat, obviously seasick. The camera cuts to Charlie, leaning over the side of the pitching ship. We expect he is sick like all his fellow passengers. Then he turns around, proudly displaying the fish he has just caught. In *The Tramp,* he enters walking down a dusty road; a car rushes by, spraying him with dust—another contrast of rich and poor. Charlie takes out a brush, whisks himself off, buffs his fingernails, and continues on his way. The spunky tramp is a fastidious gentleman—in himself, a perfect comic contrast. As an integrator of contrasts, of the good-bad, sneaky-brave, poor-rich, lucky and out of luck in all of us, Chaplin's tramp crossed worlds and, through laughter and pathos, brought people and worlds together.

An essential element of Chaplin's comic technique—and that of every other silent comedian—was the ingenious use of objects, something at which Chaplin was a master. Unlike Sennett, Chaplin did not use objects simply as comic weapons (the pie in the face); the object could be either weapon or tool, could define the character using it, could be used in a surprising and unfamiliar way, could foul Charlie up or help him out. If Chaplin's favorite structure was to exhaust a situation of some length before moving on to the next, one way to exhaust a situation was to exhaust all the objects in it. And in exhausting an object, Chaplin frequently transformed it into a completely different thing—not by stopping the camera, as Méliès had, but simply by manipulating the object in a witty and unexpected way. Chaplin, like Méliès, was a kind of magician, but his was a magic without camera tricks.

Chaplin's most famous short film with objects is *One A.M.* (1916). With the exception of a cab driver in the first sequence, Charlie is the only character in the film—except for a roomful of objects. In this film Charlie returns to one of his favorite incarnations, the drunk; the play with objects begins in the first section when the

drunken Charlie, returning from a night on the town, gets tangled with the taxi door and then with the taxi meter. Charlie can't find the key to his front door so he climbs in the window, stepping in a goldfish bowl as he does so. Inside the house he finds the key in his vest pocket. Back out the window he goes (foot in the goldfish bowl again) so that he can enter properly through the door.

In the film's second section—Charlie in the living room—Chaplin uses every piece of inanimate matter with which the set has been decorated. He feels he is being attacked by the tiger rug on the floor. He tries to walk on a circular table toward a bottle of booze and seltzer; the table spins giddily and Charlie walks a treadmill, unable to reach the booze as he spins faster and faster. He tries to walk up the stairs only to discover himself at the bottom again. Second and third tries to ascend end with him rolled up in the rug covering the stairs. He finally succeeds in getting upstairs by climbing a coatrack.

Then, in the third section—Charlie and the bed—the game with objects culminates in a five-minute duel between the drunken tramp and a Murphy bed, which seems to operate according to its own laws. The bed flips down, flips up, reverses itself, loses its frame, bounces, rises, falls as it pleases. Charlie finally beds down in the bathtub. With the bed, Chaplin has succeeded in bringing an inanimate object to life. Though he excludes living people to play against in *One A.M.,* Chaplin has not excluded living opponents, who draw their breath of life from the power of cinema to record an event over and over again, until the choreographed interaction and movement are perfect. (Chaplin's films were expensive to make because he called for so many retakes.) Chaplin refuses to cut during the final duel with the bed; except for one cut-away, the whole episode is a single long take. The lack of cutting rivets our attention on the two combatants. All consciousness of the cinematic medium disappears.

The Pawnshop (1916) is another short masterwork of comic objects. Charlie and a rival worker sling baking dough at each other in the kitchen. When the boss walks in, Charlie nonchalantly starts kneading the dough and then

One A.M.: *Charlie and the tiger rug.*

Fig. 5-10

suavely runs it through the wringer of the washing machine. He later tries to dry the dishes by running cups and saucers through the wringer. When he tries to eat one of Edna's doughnuts, it seems a bit heavy to him. He transforms the doughnut into a dumbbell by doing weight-lifting exercises with it and then blithely caps his routine by tossing it in the air to catch on his plate. The dumbbell-doughnut smashes the plate to bits and crashes through to the floor.

Among *The Pawnshop*'s other objects are an immense ladder that Charlie uses as a seesaw, a birdcage that he uses as a hatrack, a piece of string that he transforms into a tightrope, and a fishbowl that he mistakes for a chamber pot. But the film's culminating transformation of an object is Charlie's dismembering a clock that a needy customer (Albert Austin) has brought in to pawn. Probing the value of the clock, Charlie's deft part-by-part dissection combines the methods of the jeweler (do its parts seem

real or fake?), the surgeon (is it sound? are its reflexes good?), and the shopper for meat (do the contents smell fresh?) or cloth (how many yards of material does it contain?). After the innards of the clock lie in front of him, Charlie winds its shell, and its parts begin to dance (in typical Chaplin style, he does not use Méliès's stop-action tricks but a magnet to propel the pieces without camera trickery). Then Charlie adopts the method of the gardener, spraying the jittering "bugs" with oil to exterminate them. Finally, he scrapes the clock's mauled contents into the customer's hat and hands the rubble back to him with a shake of the head: Sorry; it won't do.

Charlie's careful dissection and examination of the clock reveal the most remarkable trait of his physical comedy. Despite its confinement to photographing mere physical surfaces (an inevitable consequence of photography itself), Chaplin's comedy was extremely internalized, suggesting the thought and feeling beneath

Fig. 5-11

Fig. 5-12
The Pawnshop: *the clock as patient (Fig. 5-11) and as jewel (Fig. 5-12). Charlie and Albert Austin.*

those visible surfaces. His comedy was also the most sensation-centered of any physical comedian, implying the operations of all the senses (quite an accomplishment in an art apparently confined to the single sense of sight). Charlie perpetually reveals how things smell (either pleasant, the way he sniffs the aroma of a hot dog in the opening scene of *A Dog's Life,* or unpleasant, the way he checks the bottoms of his shoes when he steps into the tiny room packed with children in *Easy Street*); how they taste (the soapy mop and sudsy coffee in *The Bank*); how they sound (the contrast between his violin music and the brass band in the opening sequence of *The Vagabond*); and how they feel to the touch (in *City Lights,* just the touch of the tramp's hand leads the formerly blind flower seller to recognize her benefactor). As the film theorist Rudolph Arnheim pointed out in 1933, Chaplin's inability to manipulate any sensory data other than visual images stimulated his imaginative depiction of all the missing senses.

As opposed to D. W. Griffith's sharp contrast of idealized goodness and idealized evil, Chaplin examined the inherent contradictions within the definitions of good and evil in bourgeois industrial society. The comic tramp was himself a walking contradiction, a figure who loathed (and feared) the falsity of the established order and who yearned toward the purity of the ideal, but also envied the comforts and rewards of the established society and realized that he had better administer a kick unto others before they kicked unto him. This tension between naïveté and instinctive, tough pragmatism in the Charlie tramp produces the moral ambivalence of the mature Chaplin films: the contrast between societal definitions of paternity and more human ones in *The Kid* (1921, his first feature), the ambivalent contrasts between rich and poor in *City Lights* (1931), and the choice between civilization and nature in *Modern Times* (1936). In his first four years, Chaplin created and developed the character whom he would use to explore the cultural landscape of civilization itself.

Most unlike discussions of Griffith, discussion of Chaplin's contribution to the cinema focuses on what he does *on* film rather than *with* film. Whereas Griffith combined the devices of cinema into a coherent narrative medium, Chaplin advanced the art by making all consciousness of the cinematic medium disappear so completely that we concentrate on the photographic subject rather than the process. This does not mean (as many have claimed) that Chaplin was "uncinematic," that he was ignorant of the means of manipulating the cinematic language. Quite the opposite. One indeed manipulates a language skillfully when all consciousness of manipulation disappears and the language serves solely to communicate the subject matter with complete lucidity. Chaplin's insistence on unobtrusive, middle-distance composition and restrained, seamless editing sustains the spell of his performance by producing his hypnotic magic without sleight-of-hand.

Chaplin's early films demonstrated not only the magic of a human performance on film, but also the appeal of the performer on the minds of his public. Millions of new fans in America rushed to the novelty shops that sold mechanical dolls and plaster statuettes in the tramp's image, much as later generations of kiddies have bought Mouseketeer and *Star Wars* paraphernalia. Chaplin was the very first national and international craze generated by the motion picture industry. (The craze that came next would be Chaplin's only serious rival — Mickey Mouse.) There were popular songs, like "Oh Those Charlie Chaplin Feet," some of which even crossed the Atlantic to the trenches of France, like "The Moon Shines Bright on Charlie Chaplin." Chaplin's face, figure, and icons (bowler, cane, shoes, moustache) became more familiar to more people all over the globe than any previous face and figure in history. Chaplin hobnobbed with the most famous figures of his generation — Albert Einstein, Winston Churchill, H. G. Wells, Mahatma Gandhi. George Bernard Shaw proclaimed him the only authentic genius the cinema ever produced. The talented young writers, artists, and composers of his generation all grew up as his ardent fans — James Joyce, Samuel Beckett, Bertolt Brecht, Hart Crane, Fernand Léger, Pablo Picasso, Erik Satie.

If there was a single quality that most struck this generation of admirers, it was Chaplin's tremendous range, his paradoxical combina-

tions of diametrically opposed human sentiments and reactions. Charlie was a terrific cynic (especially when some preacher came toward him with a sob story), but he could also be touched by their stories (as he is in *Police*, *Easy Street*, and *The Pawnshop*). He could be tough as nails when he booted an opponent in the butt or bashed an assailant in the face, but he could gaze with rhapsodic rapture on the face of tender female beauty. He could be crude and earthily vulgar (with repeated references to the sounds and smells of the human body's least polite organic functions) and he could be a romantic poet (his favorite symbol, as it was for Griffith, was the fragile but lovely flower). He was a total outsider to bourgeois middle-class propriety and its institutions, both above it in his gentlemanly disdain and below it in his destitute station. (One can only imagine his horror at the IBM advertising campaign that exploits his image but rejects his view of the world.) But Charlie understood the comforts and bases of those institutions as well as their constrictions. They simply weren't for the likes of him, who belonged everywhere and nowhere at all on earth.

By 1918, the time of his million-dollar contract with First National, a firm that only distributed and exhibited films, Chaplin had become a totally independent producer and the owner of his own film studio, staffed with associates like his brother (and business manager) Sydney, Rollie Totheroh (his cameraman), Henry Bergman and Chuck Reisner (his assistants), Edna Purviance (his leading lady), and Albert Austin (his deadpan character man). Many of them would never work for anyone else and would remain under contract to Chaplin even when he wasn't shooting a picture.

With First National, the later phases of his career began — with silent and sound feature films. Like D. W. Griffith, Chaplin made longer and more famous films after his apprenticeship period; and like Griffith, Chaplin's complex later works reveal the increasing self-consciousness and control of the mature artist. Although these later and longer works were invaluable and unique contributions to film art, Chaplin never exerted a greater cultural influence, both in America and abroad, than in those first four years between 1914 and 1918.

6

Movie Czars and Movie Stars

Griffith, Sennett, and Chaplin were three of the most important figures of the moving picture's second major period, 1908–1919. The first, 1894–1907, was dominated by Edison (and Dickson and Porter), Lumière, and Méliès. The year 1908, the year Griffith started making pictures, marks one boundary; the start of the 1920s marks the other, beginning a third period that would end with the coming of sound. The 1920s would see Keaton, Gance, Murnau, Dreyer, Eisenstein, and von Stroheim—and, of course, new work by Griffith, Chaplin, and Sennett.

After trailing the art and industries of England and France in the first years of commercial filmmaking, the American film asserted its dominance in the years just preceding World War I and, with the help of that war (and the films of Griffith, Sennett, and Chaplin; the star system; and the beginnings of the studio system), established a commercial supremacy that has never been challenged. The secret of the American rise was both art and industry. The increasing demand of American audiences to see moving pictures, the increasing admissions at the nickelodeons, led, in turn, to greater demands on production and more opportunities to experiment and to invent methods that were

better than the competition's. The art of a Griffith was partially the result of the audience's demand that the Biograph studio turn out two, three, or more reels a week. The necessity of just making films allowed Griffith's imagination to discover ways of making them better. His discoveries, in turn, produced greater popularity and esteem for the movies, and hence further demands for more films and for better films. The success of a Chaplin worked in the same circular way.

World War I came at an opportune time for the American film industry. In 1914, just as the American film imagination had begun to swell, the war came along to kill off the European film industry. The chemicals that produced raw film stock were also the essential ingredients of gunpowder. The European governments, given the choice of guns or movies, made the "obvious" decision. American films, suddenly without any competitors, ruled the screens of America and Europe during the war and just after it. When the film industries of France, Germany, Russia, and Scandinavia finally recovered, their roles in world film production were as fertile, imaginative innovators rather than as equal competitors with the big-dollar doings of Hollywood. By 1918, the

American film had become, as it has remained, the dominant cinema force in the world.

Wealth began pouring into the American film business with the appearance of the nickelodeons in 1905, converting that business into a powerful industry and pushing it to untangle the legal and commercial chaos of its infancy. In 1910, the war against the Trust was raging as the impish Independents valiantly kept fighting and producing pictures. Ten years later all but one of the original Trust companies had folded, and the leaders of the opposition had themselves become more tyrannical and powerful than their earlier Establishment adversaries. Carl Laemmle, William Fox, Adolph Zukor, Jesse Lasky, Marcus Loew, Samuel Goldfish, Lewis J. Selznick, and Louis B. Mayer were all lucky enough to be in the right place at the right time. They were fortunate to be running a studio or buying up theatres at the moment when everyone in America started going to the movies and when everyone abroad went to American movies because there were few others. These men, who became the first movie moguls, had outlasted their Trust competitors —the Motion Picture Patents Company— simply because they rode the crest of the new wave of film merchandising rather than trying to dam it.

The business of the Trust's distributor was to market one-hour programs of short films for the little nickelodeons; the new feature films, lasting up to two hours, were for more genuine and comfortable theatres devoted to and equipped for a full evening's entertainment. To produce fifty-two feature films a year (the equivalent of one film program per week) required a huge permanent staff of actors, writers, directors, and technicians; a major investment in equipment; a complex administrative office for scheduling the shooting and selling the films; and large, comfortable theatres. Zukor, Goldfish, Laemmle, Fox, and some others made the investment; many of the Trust companies could not or did not, certain that the new feature craze was a passing fancy. The fancy never passed; the Trust companies did.

Although the Trust officially lost the public battle in the courts in 1917, it had already lost the war to such opponents as *Queen Elizabeth,* *Traffic in Souls, Cabiria, The Squaw Man, Tillie's Punctured Romance,* and *The Birth of a Nation.* The public wanted to see feature films.

Stars Over Hollywood

The years between 1910 and 1920 determined the direction the American film industry would take. By 1915 the film program consisted of a single feature film supplemented by a short or two, the same practice that survives today (with or without the short). A second current practice was born at the same time—the star system. In the healthy days of the Trust, no Biograph actor ever received screen credit. Performers were known either by the names of the characters they played—"Little Mary"—or by the studio—the Biograph Girl. There even seems to have been some doubt in the minds of the earliest patrons about whether they were watching a dramatization or real life. The confusion in the mind of the country boy about fiction or reality in *Mabel's Dramatic Career* may have been quite common a few years earlier.

Biograph opposed giving screen credit for the same short-sighted commercial reasons that it opposed the feature film: Star actors would cost more than anonymous faces on a screen. The reasoning was quite correct. But the Independents reasoned that although a star would cost more, a film with a star would earn more. As with the feature film, the Independents had the stronger argument: To make more it was necessary to spend more. The Independents launched their career by stealing the Biograph Girl in 1910 and featuring her in IMP pictures under her real name—Florence Lawrence. They did the same with "Little Mary" Pickford, King Baggott, Arthur Johnson, and many other formerly anonymous Biograph players. The power of the star system, begun by the Independents, was such that in 1917—only a few years after its inception—two stars, Chaplin and Pickford, were vying with producers and with each other to become the highest paid performers in the business, both of them signing contracts for over $1,000,000. And every major producer in the industry was trying to sign them and pay them that million.

The movie star, no longer an anonymous character in a film but a human being in his or her own right, instantly seized the imagination of the American public. In 1912, just after audiences started learning their favorites' names, America's first motion picture fan magazine, *Photoplay,* appeared. It and subsequent fan magazines featured pictures, stories, and interviews that made the figure on the screen an even more intimate and personal being for each member of the audience. Producing companies needed publicity departments to sell the stars as well as the pictures to the public. In the middle of the second decade of the century, the exotic and erotic activities of the stars first became items of household gossip. One of the earliest and most impressive of the grand publicity jobs was Fox's packaging of the "lusty, seductive siren," Theda Bara, who made her debut in *A Fool There Was* (1915). Born in Cincinnati as Theodosia Goodman, she was transformed by Fox publicists into an Arabian beauty clad in black who survived less on oxygen and victuals than by wrecking homes and devouring men. She was a mystic semisorceress; her name, they pointed out, bore an anagrammatical relationship to death (Theda) and Arab (Bara); the blood of the Ptolemies flowed in her veins; and her astrological signs matched Cleopatra's. The character she played—a sexual vampire—was abbreviated to vamp, adding a new noun and verb to the English language. More significant than all the drivel of the Bara legend was the fact that the public loved the drivel and swallowed it, obviously because it wanted to. Movie publicists had discovered the ease of selling something the public wanted to buy. And Bara, along with a movie star of a very different type, the cowboy dandy, Tom Mix, established Fox as a major production power—their attractive presences mythified by the studio's publicity mills.

Later film theorists have speculated about the appeal, value, and utility of movie stars, both in American film and American culture. For some critics, movie stars are a commodity of industrial production, another means for the film industry to package and market its products to the public. For others, movie stars are symptomatic of certain ills in American culture—they are beautiful but shallow, powerful visual presences with little actual ability. Movie actors have frequently been compared unfavorably with stage actors, since film stars often seem to play one role—an on-screen persona very close to their off-screen style—over and over again. Still other critics see this unity and consistency of star personality as the most interesting and powerful accomplishment of movie stars: Movie stars do not so much play characters (as stage actors do); they *are* the characters. The movie star capitalizes on an essential paradox of movies—that they are fictional truths. A movie star is also a fictional truth, a fictional character in a fictional narrative, and yet a real human being with a powerful and familiar persona. As commodity, actor, and persona, the movie star had become a powerful component of American cultural experience by 1915.

The greatest stars of the silent films created their own images and types; the lesser stars merely filled the patterns that the great stars had already sketched. There were imitations of Mary Pickford's spunky, good-hearted, pranksterish little girl with the golden curls. There were sultry sirens in the Theda Bara image, many of them imported from Europe. There were gentle, soulful juveniles—Richard Barthelmess, Charles Ray. There were exotic Latin leading men—Rudolph Valentino, Ramon Novarro. Perhaps even Douglas Fairbanks's conversion from zippy American go-getter to swarthy swashbuckler in the twenties was the result of the influence of this new sexual type. There were lecherous, jaded roués, often from decadent foreign shores—Erich von Stroheim, Owen Moore, Adolphe Menjou. There were stars from the opera, the stage, and even the swimming pool—Geraldine Farrar, Mary Garden, Alla Nazimova, Annette Kellerman. There was the basically pure woman who was inevitably tainted by experience (Lillian Gish); there was the stubborn, sophisticated, and often tragic lady (Gloria Swanson); there was the strong, competent, virile male (Thomas Meighan); there was the serious, tough cowboy with the sad eyes (William S. Hart); there was the fat man (John Bunny, Fatty Arbuckle), and the little man

Fig. 6-1

Fig. 6-2

Fig. 6-3

Early archetypes. Fig. 6-1: the vamp, Theda Bara; Fig. 6-2: the rough good–bad man of the frontier, William S. Hart; Fig. 6-3: the cowboy dandy, Tom Mix.

(Chaplin, Harold Lloyd, Buster Keaton), and the everyman (Lou Chaney). The star and not the play became the thing that caught the consciousness of the public. Hollywood also used the star to catch the public's wallet.

The third major development of the American film's second decade was the move west. As early as 1907, production companies—perhaps evading the law or the Patents Company wrecking crews—discovered the felicities of southern California. According to the colorful (if not completely reliable) film historian, Terry Ramsaye, during the Trust War, the independent companies took advantage of California's distance from the Trust headquarters in New York and its closeness to the Mexican border, where the company could quickly flee with its negatives and machines. But gradually the genuine virtues of California struck the filmmakers. The vast, open plains, the dependability of the sun, the nearby mountains and deserts and ocean, all attracted the eyes of men whose art depended on the power of the visual. D. W. Griffith brought his company west in the winters of 1910, 1911, and 1912. *The Birth of a Nation* and *Intolerance* were both shot in California.

By 1915 most of the film companies had permanently settled down to business in the Los Angeles suburbs—known colloquially and generically as Hollywood but in fact including such diverse areas of the Los Angeles basin as Culver City, Burbank, and North Hollywood. Real estate speculators, who suddenly discovered that miles of apparently useless land were of great use to the movie men, sold it to them by the tens of thousands of acres, at absurdly reasonable prices. Vast studios, like Thomas Ince's Inceville (which became MGM) and Carl Laemmle's Universal City, with rows of shooting studios, office buildings, storage buildings, back lots (for the outdoor sets), and even vast ranches completely stocked with cattle and horses and other beasts of the field, sprang up near Los Angeles. The founding of the movie capital was the result of three coincidental accidents: weather, topography, and real estate values. Enjoying the harvests of chance, the accidental emperors of the new film world now ruled vast, tangible empires.

The Emperors and Their Rule

The most significant accident in the history of the American film is that this first generation of influential movie producers, those gentlemen who made the concrete decisions about the artistic and moral values worthy of inclusion in films, were themselves deficient in formal education and aesthetic judgment. The first Hollywood producers were not just businessmen; they were, according to their biographers, a very specific breed of businessmen. Most of them were either Jewish immigrants from Germany or Russia or Poland, or the sons of Jewish immigrants. Most of them came to the movies by accident. They sold herring or furs or gloves or second-hand clothes. They jumped from these businesses into running amusement parks and penny arcades just when Edison's Kinetoscope and Biograph's Mutoscope were bringing new life to the novelty business.

There were two reasons Jewish immigrants could thrive in this business, and they were the same reasons that Jews thrived in another contemporary entertainment business—the writing, publishing, and selling of popular music on New York's 28th Street, known colloquially as Tin Pan Alley. First, these were new businesses that had not evolved their structures of corporate control that always tend to keep newcomers out. Second, they were the kinds of risky, "illegitimate" businesses that respectable businessmen and social prejudice always allowed the Jews to run—like the lending of money in Medieval and Renaissance Europe.

When movies left the peep-show box for the screen, these arcade owners converted their stores into nickelodeons. They built more and more of these theatres, which became more and more plush. Soon they began producing films for their theatres, what with the pressures of the Trust and its licensing fees. Such was the series of small steps by which a Goldfish or Zukor or Mayer climbed out of the ghetto and into a multi-million-dollar throne of power over national artistic tastes. It is the same route that later generations of disadvantaged Americans have travelled; for many, the quickest and most glamorous road to the American Dream of fame and fortune is show business (sports, rock music, television, and movies).

It is doubtful that a first generation of producer-aesthete intellectuals would have made better movies (look at the likes of *Queen Elizabeth*); but this first generation of movie men and movie values left a legacy of sacrificing taste for dollars—or equating them—that Hollywood films have never completely shed. And they never really can. The costs of making and distributing a movie demand that it appeal to a great many people. The curse and the glory of a popular art is that it is intended for large audiences over the entire social spectrum. Movie executives, then as now, make guesses (often based more on hope than information) about popular appeal.

By 1915—even as early as 1908—there were three types of movie executives, and the differences among them reveal the structure of the American film industry as a whole. Out in Hollywood, the most famous of the movie moguls were those who controlled the actual production of films; they were the film producers and studio heads whose private lives and personal salaries made the headlines. Back in New York, on the East Coast, were the parent companies, whose executives supervised not the making of films but budgeting the entire operation of the studio, marketing its products, reinvesting its revenues, and managing its assets as profitably as possible. Then, scattered throughout the country were the owners of theatres and theatre chains who needed films from the studios and returned to them the revenues that the film companies needed to make more films. The three-tiered structure of the American film industry—production, distribution (or management), and exhibition—evolved in the middle years of the century's second decade.

The most powerful film company of the silent era was Paramount Pictures. Paramount was the child of Adolph Zukor, the final stage in the evolution of his Famous Players in Famous Plays. Zukor, who began by distributing *Queen Elizabeth*, jumped aboard the feature-film wagon at the very beginning—one of the chief reasons for his success. Zukor's Famous Players company initiated three kinds of pictures: Class A (with stage stars and stage properties, the arty films), Class B (with established screen players), and Class C (cheap, quick features). Zukor discovered that the Class B films, the ones with Mary Pickford, were far more popular than the high-toned Class A. Zukor dropped the stagy films and made Class Bs exclusively. He soon absorbed Jesse Lasky's Feature Play Company (creating Famous Players-Lasky in 1916), Lewis J. Selznick's Picture Company, Edwin S. Porter's Rex Pictures, Pallas Pictures, and Morosco Pictures; he also absorbed a distributing exchange called Paramount Pictures, which eventually gave its name to the final amalgamation. Zukor bested his competition by buying it out. The huge company then had the power and the money to hire the most popular stars and demand the highest fees from exhibitors who wanted the films of its stars.

Zukor had been working in a steady, octopal manner, snatching up theatres as well as studios and exchanges. One of Zukor's commercial innovations was the system of block booking. The theatre owner had to agree to buy all of Zukor's products to get any of them. If he wanted Mary Pickford or William S. Hart, he had to buy all fifty-two weekly programs from Paramount. But even block booking, tyrannical as it was, was less efficient than owning the theatres. The studio owner not only had to produce films but had to guarantee that each of them would be shown. What better guarantee than to own the theatres to show them?

Another powerful combine emerged in the mid-twenties: Metro-Goldwyn-Mayer. The monolith was assembled by theatre owner Marcus Loew, who wanted to control the profit from the pictures that he showed in his vast national chain of theatres. In 1924, Loew bought the struggling Metro Picture Company and the struggling Goldwyn Picture Company. Loew then put Louis B. Mayer, another theatre owner recently turned producer, in charge of production at MGM. Mayer brought with him a young assistant, Irving Thalberg, to supervise the shooting of the pictures. (In other words, Mayer was the executive in charge of the production—as opposed to the distribution—arm of the studio, and Thalberg was in charge of the actual activity of film production, planning, approving, and supervising the making of

Fig. 6-4

Fig. 6-5

A SHORT HISTORY OF THE MOVIES

Fig. 6-6

A gallery of stars. Fig. 6-4: "Little Mary" Pickford in
The Love Light *(note how the huge sets and furniture*
make her seem truly little); Fig. 6-5: the demure
Lillian Gish with the slickly brilliantined Rod La
Rocque; Fig. 6-6: a cool Gloria Swanson.

all MGM films.) With these individual parts,
Loew assembled the most solid film factory in
America. Anchored by his chain of classy and
genteel theatres, Loew's MGM studio began to
manufacture the kind of classy and genteel
films that would perfectly mesh the ambiance
of the environment to the tone of the entertainment within it. MGM took over the
Goldwyn lot to shoot its films (Goldwyn had
earlier taken it over from Ince); that studio then
distributed its films to all of the Loew theatres.
Loew, like Zukor, had succeeded in creating
the kind of vertically integrated empire that
Gaumont and Pathé had established twenty
years earlier; he controlled all three branches
of the theatrical film business: production, distribution, and exhibition.

Understandably, the theatre owner did not
enjoy the strong-arm pressures of block booking or the unavailability of those popular films
that had been made by the studios for their own
theatres. In 1917, a group of theatre owners
joined together specifically as an antidote to
Zukor's commercial poison, calling themselves
the First National Exhibitors Circuit. First National, managed by W. W. Hodkinson (himself
elbowed out of Paramount by Zukor) and J. D.
Williams, intended to diminish the power of the
film production companies in filmmaking, just
as the film production companies were trying to
diminish the independent exhibitor's. First National contracted with individual stars (Chaplin,
for example, and Harry Langdon) to make pictures for their theatres. The star gained independence and financial backing; the theatre
owner gained the lucrative products of popular,
established stars. The idea was so felicitous that
First National was among the three great
powers of the 1920s film world.

Yet another new wrinkle was the emergence
of the artist as producer. If film producers
could turn theatre owners and if theatre owners
could turn producers, then artists could also
turn producers and work for themselves. In
1919, D. W. Griffith, Charles Chaplin, Mary
Pickford, and Douglas Fairbanks joined together to form the United Artists Corporation.
Each would produce his or her own films (Griffith's first UA film was *Broken Blossoms;* Chaplin's was *A Woman of Paris,* 1923), which would
then be distributed by the common company,
United Artists. United Artists owned neither
studio nor theatre; it was exclusively a distributing organization for pictures made elsewhere.
However flimsy such an organization seemed
compared to the giants like Paramount and
First National, the company survived, eventually merging with MGM (in 1981). The idea
for United Artists was years ahead of its time,
foreshadowing the commercial practices of the
1960s and 1970s. Today, the major studios
themselves are primarily distributors for pictures that have been made by independent
producers.

The Hollywood film studios of the 1920s
had traveled a long way from Edison's Black
Maria — and even from the glass-walled studio
of Méliès; now they made their own light. Vast
expanses of land and a complex maze of buildings had replaced the single little tar-paper
shack that pirouetted with the sun. The Hollywood studio had become an entertainment factory. The contemporary of one of the most
famous innovations in American industry,

Fig. 6-7
The four United Artists after the signing (from a contemporary newsreel): from left, Fairbanks, Griffith, Pickford, and Chaplin.

Henry Ford's assembly line for the manufacture of automobiles, the movie studio manufactured entertainment on an assembly line. Like Ford's plant, the Hollywood studio broke the manufacture of its product into a series of operations, and each cell of the whole organism fulfilled its particular function. There was a specific section for writers in the studio —those who conceived the original story ideas, those who wrote the final scenarios, and even those who created the film's intertitles, a separate and highly developed art of its own. There was a specific section for costuming, one for the construction of sets, and another for the care and maintenance of the increasingly complicated equipment, still another for the shooting of the films, and one for publicizing, marketing, and financing the finished product. The arts of the costumer, the cinematographer, the art director, the electrician, and the writer had become as significant as the contributions of the director and actor.

As the film studio evolved, so did the movie theatre. Almost simultaneous with the birth of the feature film came the huge, plush theatre to glorify the longer films and show them in comfort. The same feature phenomenon that enriched the studios enriched the theatres. The

earlier nickelodeons were small and often dirty; the new feature-length movies left these little stores for huge theatres on Broadway. The first of the new palaces was the Strand, constructed on Broadway in 1914, followed immediately by the Vitagraph (now the multiplex Criterion). The new theatres could accommodate over two thousand patrons, who trod on carpeted floors and relaxed in plush, padded chairs. The manager of the Strand Theatre, Samuel L. Rothafel (né Rothapfel), soon went on to buy, build, and conceive huge movie palaces of his own. Roxy (his nickname) opened or salvaged a string of mammoth New York houses: the Rialto, Rivoli, Capitol, Roxy, and the Radio City Music Hall, his finale and *chef d'oeuvre*. Roxy brought the same tone of quasi-gentility to the movie theatre that his colleagues, like Zukor and Mayer, brought to the films themselves. Roxy supplemented the film showing with symphony orchestras, corps de ballets, live variety acts, and, at Radio City, the last survivor of the Roxy era, the legendary Rockettes. Whereas vaudeville had supported the movies in their first years in America, the movies had now begun to support vaudeville.

Roxy decorated the insides of his theatres with the same kinds of flouncing that he used for the film showings. The ushers wore colorful silken uniforms that matched the carpets and walls, consistent with the theatre's architectural motif. The theatre walls offered ornate carvings in stone, brass, and wood; gargoyles stared from the balconies; plaster copies of Greek statues (attired in fig leaves) gazed down from trellised cupolas, bathed in a red or green floodlight. The Roxy of the West Coast, Sid Grauman, paid as much attention to the outsides of his theatres as Roxy paid to the inside. His Chinese Theatre welcomed the patron with a complex system of pagoda roofs and Oriental carvings—and the cement footprints of the stars; his Egyptian Theatre offered patrons a waterfall and a wishing well as they walked in the door. In the 1950s, *The King and I* opened at the Chinese and *The Ten Commandments* at the Egyptian. The Roxies of the midwest, Balaban and Katz, gave the same grand treatment to the many theatres in their chain, pulling out all the stops for their glorious flagship, The Chicago. Even the smaller neighborhood theatre imitated the attractions of the movie palaces—electric stars twinkled in their stucco heavens as plaster copies of Greek gods and goddesses stared down from an Olympus decorated as a Spanish hacienda.

The pretentiousness, the tacky splendor of these movie houses today (those that have survived urban renewal and gentrification) seems metaphoric of most of the films they showed on their screens. It is tempting to see the movies' move from the nickelodeon to the movie palace as its move out of the working class and into middle-class respectability. While moviegoing, from its beginnings, had been far more a middle-class pastime in Europe, where much higher ticket prices kept poorer citizens away, American movies mingled with the urban working classes from the start. The social fact, however, is probably not so much that American movies deserted the working classes but that prospering American workers themselves had begun their upward mobility toward more middle-class comforts and attitudes. The movies simply accompanied them.

Morality

The movies have waged a perpetual cold war with the forces of religion and righteousness. In 1896, the moralists denounced the improprieties of *The Irwin-Rice Kiss*. *Fatima* (1897), which depicted the bumps and grinds of a noted cooch dancer of the day, so offended some members of certain communities that exhibitors superimposed broad white stripes across the screen to cover the areas where Fatima displayed her most lascivious wares. Without question, the censored version of the film is far more offensive and obscene than the original since the two heavily streaked regions of the frame inform the viewer quite precisely which areas of the body should be considered nasty.

Throughout the nickelodeon era the movies had been criticized as cultivators of iniquity; the theatres had been attacked as unsavory or unsafe. The protests of the moralistic few did not deter the entertainment-minded many from going to the nickelodeons. The parallels between the twentieth-century moralistic controversy over the movies (still continuing today) and the sixteenth-century moralistic contro-

Fig. 6-8

Fig. 6-9

Early film censorship: the 1897 hoochy-coochy dancer Fatima, without and with her censorship stripes.

versy over the Elizabethan theatre (also criticized as a breeder of licentiousness and laziness) are striking. The movie cold war suddenly became a hot one in the early 1920s.

First, the content of films, reflecting the new materialism and moral relativism of the decade, became spicier and more suggestive. The sentimental films of the Griffith era had not disappeared; Griffith's own films, Mary Pickford's, and pictures like Henry King's *Tol'able David* perpetuated the tradition of innocence, purity, courage, and honor. But alongside these Victorian films were others suggesting that lust was indeed a human emotion, that married couples indulged in extramarital flirtations (at the least), and that the urbane and wealthy and lustful were not inevitably evil and unhappy. The new materialistic audience (who spent as much as two dollars to get into the plush movie palace) enjoyed films that idolized the material as well as the spiritual. The sermonizers intensified their letter-writing and speech-making campaigns with concerted public action. Clergymen and laymen united to form panels and committees that would not exactly censor films, but would advise parishioners and the public about which films to see and which to avoid. Behind the censorship drives of some of these organizations lay a thinly veiled anti-Semitism (a parallel with the subtly anti-Semitic campaigns against the Hollywood "Reds" some thirty years later). The moral deficiencies of the movies were yet another strategem of the Jewish infidels, once again poisoning the wells of a Christian nation. Against such attacks, the moral statements and strictures of the industry's own National Board of Review (its name changed from the National Board of Censorship in 1915 and its power undermined by the busting of the Trust that created it) were inadequate and powerless.

The moral ambiguities of the offerings on the screen were soon accompanied by the scandalous doings of the motion picture people off the screen. In the early twenties, several national scandals rocked the film industry far more severely than had the letters and speeches of the zealots. Hollywood did not just sell pictures to the public; it sold the stars who sold the pictures. Scandal in the life of a star was more serious than any extramarital wink on the screen. In 1920, Mary Pickford, "America's Sweetheart," quietly went to Nevada with her husband, Owen Moore, to get a divorce. Three weeks later "Little Mary" married her male counterpart in innocence and purity, Douglas Fairbanks. The public was not shocked by the divorce alone, since Hollywood divorces had already become old news. But this divorce, followed by the abrupt marriage of these two sup-

posedly healthy, happy, all-American people, was something special. The Pickford–Fairbanks marriage was further complicated by the possibility that the divorce proceeding had been improperly executed ("Little Mary" eventually avoided the stain of bigamy). Though Doug and Mary had done nothing illegal, their illicit premarital romance seemed to contradict their screen purity. The tremendous public interest in this petty domestic affair clearly revealed the new social importance of the film industry and its vulnerability to attack by newspaper headlines.

In 1921, two consecutive Fatty Arbuckle scandals fed the headlines. In July of that year newspapers reported a mysterious Arbuckle party in Massachusetts that had taken place in 1917. The mysterious detail was that the district attorney of a Massachusetts county had received a $100,000 gift just after the party. The public wondered what the district attorney had discovered that was worth such a sum to keep quiet. Then in September 1921, Arbuckle threw a second party, this one in San Francisco's St. Francis Hotel. The next morning one of Arbuckle's guests, Virginia Rappe, was found dead in her hotel room. A week later Arbuckle gave himself up to the police, was eventually tried for involuntary manslaughter, and, after three trials (the first two ending with hung juries), was finally found not guilty. His innocence in the eyes of the law did not affect his standing in the eyes of the moralists.

The Hollywood producers, acceding to the cries of the preachers, barred the evil Fatty from pictures. The great comedian worked in very few films, usually in small roles (for example, James Cruze's bitter 1923 satire, *Hollywood*), although he continued to direct comic shorts under the assumed (and sarcastic) name of Will B. Good! The moguls threw Arbuckle to the moralists, hoping to still the hissing tongues; the money men back East preferred a safe surrender to a possibly unsettling and certainly unprofitable confrontation. Some thirty years later the film industry made an identical choice when it refused to defend "the Hollywood Ten" against the red-baiters and then instituted its blacklist.

In 1922, "handsome" Wallace Reid died suddenly and mysteriously, generating a posthumous scandal when the newspapers discovered he had used drugs. Early in the same year, a minor director, William Desmond Taylor, was found dead in his apartment, another scandal with a vague mixture of sex, murder, and drugs. The Taylor murder hurt the careers of Mabel Normand, the pretty comedienne, and Mary Miles Minter, a little-girl imitation of Mary Pickford, who were both friends of the director. The press, satisfying the hunger of its readers, turned these friendships into something salacious. There was no defense against vague rumor and veiled innuendo. Two more careers were thrown to the yapping dogs to keep them quiet.

Such notoriety brought the film business to the attention of the United States Congress and to the edge of federal censorship—the last thing any producer wanted. The industry decided once again to clean its own house, to serve as its own censorship body. Recalling the success of the baseball owners at finding a moralistic commissioner, the esteemed Judge Landis, to cleanse the "Black Sox" scandals, the film producers sought their own respected commissioner. In 1922, they found Will H. Hays, President Harding's campaign manager, postmaster general of the United States, Presbyterian elder, and Republican. Hays became president of the Motion Picture Producers and Distributors of America (MPPDA), an organization supported and financed by all the major

Moguls and Morals—from left: Irving Thalberg, Louis B. Mayer, Will Hays, and Harry Rapf on the MGM lot.

Fig. 6-10

film companies in America. It became known colloquially as the Hays Office, and he headed it for over twenty years. In 1945, the MPPDA became the MPAA (Motion Picture Association of America), and Hays was succeeded by Eric Johnston, who headed the MPAA until 1966, when Jack Valenti became president. Rather than taking concrete censorship actions, the Hays Office sought to counter bad publicity with good, to keep the press from magnifying its tales of Hollywood debauches, to regularize business procedures, and to encourage producers to submit their films voluntarily for prerelease examination. The loose, informal advising of the Hays Office in the twenties was another in a series of successful Hollywood attempts to keep films out of the hands of government censors, a strategy that would be duplicated by the enforcement of the much less loose and informal Hollywood Production Code of the 1930s and the MPAA Rating System that was set up in 1968 and is still in force.

Films and Filmmakers, 1910–1928

The ever-increasing problem of the American film director was how to make an individualized, special film in a factory system geared toward standardization and mass production. The Griffith era of anarchy and improvisation was rapidly passing, even as Griffith himself went to work for Zukor. For a director to assemble his own company and begin production without a shooting script and production schedule became unthinkable. Rather than being the artistic creator of his own films, the director was more and more expected to be the mechanic who hammered together the machine that others, the producer and writer, had earlier designed. Griffith himself noted with dismay the widening gap between producer and director, between the business of making a film and the art of making a film. Each film, rather than being an important work in itself, became only one unit of the studio's yearly output. Though the films had gotten longer and the film business more complex, studio owners considered only the total yearly product, exactly as they did in the Patents Company days

of the one-reeler. This industrialization of the film business is most relevant to the career of Thomas Ince, Griffith's contemporary and one of the most interesting American producers and directors of noncomic films before 1919.

Ince's films are almost the paradigmatic opposites of Griffith's. Whereas Griffith's technique aimed at developing the characters, their emotions, and the metaphoric implications of the action, Ince concentrated ruthlessly on the narrative flow. Ince was as avid a film editor as Griffith, but whereas Griffith cut to develop rhythm, emotion, and ideas, Ince cut to keep the story moving. Griffith's interest was primarily in why the characters did something and what that implied symbolically; Ince's focused almost exclusively on what they did. Ince's pretentiously symbolic *Civilization* (1916) is an obvious exception. However, more typical of Ince is a film like *The Coward* (1915), a Civil War story that avoids all the symbolic freight of *The Birth of a Nation* (1915) to concentrate exclusively on one young man's earning his "red badge of courage." The titles of the films (the specificity of Ince's, abstractness of Griffith's) are indicative.

The openness and movement that Griffith used for battle scenes and chases were the bases of Ince's films: the stagecoach sweeping down a mountain trail flanked by mountains and plains and sagebrush, the Indians pursuing, the posse galloping across the prairies, the Indians' circle of death as they revolve about the isolated victims, the dust and smoke and powder of the gun battle (a brilliant translation of sound into visual imagery), the dust of the horses' hooves, the silhouettes of the tribe of Apaches on the mesa awaiting the moment to join the attack. One of the most common (and beautiful) Ince images is smoke—the swirling, enveloping movement of gunpowder or dust, shot through refractive beams of light. The producer Ince's most able director of these early westerns was Francis Ford, whose crisp, deep-focus shots established the photographic conventions of the western. Ince's productions also popularized one of the western's most enduring character types, the good–bad man—embodied by William S. Hart. A little too tough, stubborn and ornery, sometimes even on the wrong side of the law, he could always be depended on to do the right thing in a crunch.

Contemporary with the nostalgic painting and sculpture of Frederick Remington and the pulp stories of Zane Grey, these Ince and Ford films depict a western frontier that was already disappearing under the tracks and ties of civilization (just as movies themselves had invaded the West and were the most likely place for the old cowhands to find employment). Ince, Ford, and Hart would later pass on these legacies — the power of movement within vast western vistas and the dignity of the good–bad men who inhabit these spaces — to their successors: Ford's younger brother, John, as well as Howard Hawks, Sam Peckinpah, and many others.

As a supervisor of production, in effect a producer, Ince could keep his finger on several different film projects at the same time. Although it was a split that Griffith found distasteful, many of the current generation of directors (Steven Spielberg, for example) have, like Ince and Sennett, alternated between directing and producing. Unlike Griffith, Ince insisted on a detailed shooting script, which he eventually approved and stamped "Shoot as is." The Ince director then went about the business of constructing from the producer's blueprint. Ince supplemented the shooting script with a detailed production breakdown and schedule, making sure that all people and animals and equipment went to the right place at the right time for the fewest number of hours. If Griffith was the cinema's first real director, Ince was its first important producer, instituting the system that divided the artistic responsibility for a film between two people — or camps. Ince showed the future studio heads how to run a studio.

Ironically, Ince's career waned in the studio era itself. He was the hardest hit by the failure of the Triangle Film Corporation, which depended on his films and his Culver City studio. In 1915, the president of the Mutual Film Corporation, Harry Aitken, was ousted by his partner, John R. Freuler, in a power struggle. Aitken, who personally owned the Mutual contracts of Griffith, Sennett, and Ince, took the three with him to build the Triangle Film Cor-

poration, with the three important directors as the tips of the triangle. But Griffith produced several weak program pictures, and Sennett's and Ince's drawing powers were feebler than they had been. The triangle collapsed in 1919. Ince, the movie man of system and efficiency, died mysteriously (on William Randolph Hearst's yacht) in 1924, just when the era of system and efficiency had officially arrived with the Mayer–Thalberg rule at MGM, which stood on Ince's old lot.

The films of Douglas Fairbanks also reveal the changing values of Hollywood. Fairbanks broke into films with Griffith at Triangle; the young actor was so athletic, so bouncy, so perpetually in motion, that Griffith gave up on him and suggested he go see Mr. Sennett. Triangle eventually let Fairbanks go his own way, pairing him with writer Anita Loos, her director–husband, John Emerson, and cameraman Victor Fleming. Between 1915 and 1920, the group produced a series of breezy, parodic, energetic comedies that combined the star's athleticism, energy, and sincerity with the writer's and director's wit and style. The early Fairbanks films — like the utterly outrageous *The Mystery of the Leaping Fish* (1916) — are refreshing surprises. They are parodies that make fun of a personality trait (American snobbishness, the fascination with royalty, the hunger for publicity, the ambition to achieve the impossible) or a genre of films (the western, the mystery, the melodrama). Doug is the center of the parody, the magnified version of whatever the film is satirizing. But Doug, because of his naïveté and enthusiasm, because of his obvious love of life and people, always succeeds in engaging our sympathies at the same time that we may be laughing at him. Loos and Emerson took advantage of the way that Doug overdid everything; they made a virtue of overdoing. And Doug's athleticism, his physical exhilaration, his constant movement, become a delight to watch. Doug's acting technique seemed to center around such questions as: why enter a room through a door when you can jump in through the window? why walk up a flight of stairs when you can swing upstairs on a lighting fixture, or vault through a hole in the downstairs ceiling?

One of the key contrasts in his early films is between the dull, routine, banal life Doug must live in conventional society and the imaginative, free, vigorous life he wants to live. Fairbanks was the foe of the dull and regimented; the row upon row of similar desks in the button factory of *Reaching for the Moon* (1917) was an image of everything he hated. The physical emphasis of Doug's talent also led the star to value the source of the physical, the body. Doug supplemented his on-screen cleanliness with magazine articles lauding the healthy life and disparaging the unhealthy lures of drink, tobacco, and gluttony.

The later Fairbanks films of the twenties— *The Mark of Zorro* (1920, where he leads a real, not imaginary, double life), *Robin Hood* (1922), *The Thief of Bagdad* (1924), and *The Black Pirate* (1926, shot in two-strip Technicolor)—make quite a contrast with these earlier, breezy ones. Doug is still a great athlete; he still has his smile and energy. But he is no longer a contemporary American trying to strike a blend between his own imaginative impulses and the conventions of society. Doug has been transported to faraway, romantic lands of long ago. He is free to perform exotic deeds, and although he is usually some kind of thief, he is not, paradoxically, dishonest. In addition to sparking his daring exploits, the faroff themes and places allow Doug to become an explicit sex symbol, gliding through most of the films without his shirt, with limbs clearly defined by a pair of tights or slightly exposed by the scanty cloth that teasingly covers his middle.

No two directors more clearly show the problems of the filmmaker in the 1920s than Erich von Stroheim and Cecil B. DeMille. As were Griffith and Ince a few years earlier, the two are almost paradigms for the whole industry. Von Stroheim (he added the "von" himself and may be referred to as Stroheim or as von Stroheim; the same is true of Josef von Sternberg, except that his "von" was added by a producer) gave the public what he wanted, DeMille gave it what he thought it wanted. Von Stroheim was a ruthless realist committed to his art and his vision; DeMille was willing to throw in any faddish or striking hokum. Von Stroheim's greatest tools were close observation and detail, DeMille's were size and splash. De-

Mille was a big producer; von Stroheim's tragedy was that he had to depend on producers. Von Stroheim's films, despite their adult themes, were controlled by the director's taste and intelligence; DeMille's films had everything but taste and intelligence.

Both DeMille and von Stroheim served several apprentice years before emerging as major directors. DeMille shot his first film, *The Squaw Man* (1914), for Jesse Lasky's Feature Play Company in 1913; it was the first feature-length western shot in Hollywood. The Lasky company was formed by Lasky, DeMille, and Samuel Goldfish in 1913; in 1916 it merged with Zukor's company, Famous Players (founded 1912), to become Famous Players-Lasky. (In 1922, Goldfish left to form a new company with Edgar Selwyn; "Gold" + "wyn" became Goldwyn, and Goldfish soon named himself after the studio. With Goldfish gone, Zukor consolidated Famous Players-Lasky and several other companies into Paramount, for which DeMille directed most of his films.) DeMille began keeping track of national trends and tastes. Von Stroheim began as a studio adviser on European military details and an assistant to (and player for) Griffith, then began playing vicious "Huns" (dubbed "the man you love to hate"), and finally, in 1919, persuaded Carl Laemmle to let him write, direct, and perform in his own films.

The two films that most clearly reveal the differences in the two men are DeMille's *Male and Female* and von Stroheim's *Blind Husbands*. Both were released in 1919; both capitalized on the new audience interest in sexual amours and the doings of the rich. Both suggested the importance of sex in human relationships. There the similarities stop. *Male and Female* is a lavish, pretentious, and inconsistent examination of the class question, which seems to suggest both that masters may marry their servants and that masters may not marry their servants. Although some of the film's confusion stems from the J. M. Barrie play DeMille was adapting, *The Admirable Crichton* (to be adapted again by Lina Wertmüller in 1975 as *Swept Away . . .*), the most dazzling stupidities are DeMille's "additions." For example, the film begins with a sequence that does not exist in the original play, a series of shots of oceans and

Fig. 6-11
The Americano gone exotic—Douglas Fairbanks in **The Thief of Bagdad.**

the Grand Canyon, followed by a biblical quote, "God created man in his own image." Both the quotation and this whole Creation sequence are irrelevant to anything that follows in the film. The stentorian seriousness of the DeMille beginning—the implication that the film one was about to see was Very Significant Art and might even come directly from God—was a consistent DeMille trait that continued into the sound era. Much of DeMille's work

uses the Bible to dignify its distinctly lay interests.

DeMille then plunges into the affairs of a contemporary British household, spending most of his time showing the elegance of Gloria Swanson taking a bath (scented with rose water), the water temperature being checked carefully by her maid, Gloria striding carefully and sliding gently into the sunken tub. One of DeMille's titles asks why shouldn't the bathroom express as much elegance as anything else in life, and his even asking such a question is at the heart of what is empty about the film (although DeMille's materialistic Jazz-Age audiences must surely have been delighted to see the answer). Meanwhile, DeMille contrasts the high-falutin' ways of Lady Mary (Gloria), who rejects a piece of toast because it is too soft, with the simple ways of Tweeny, her maid. Simple Tweeny is in love with the butler, Crichton (Thomas Meighan). But, alas, he is not simple; he loves Lady Mary; he reads aloud poetry that Tweeny cannot understand but Lady Mary can.

Then the whole family takes a yachting trip and runs aground. A title tells us that they have sailed into "uncharted seas," but we recognize Catalina. Now that the group must survive on a desert isle, DeMille can add yet another locale and style of decor to the film. Having already filmed the Creation and a chic English drawing-room comedy, he can go about filming a kind of Swiss Family Robinson. On the island, it turns out that he who is lower class in one society is upper class in another. Crichton, the butler, becomes the king of the group and they become his servants, simply because he is competent and fit to survive, while they are all numbskulls trying to play at being posh in the wilderness. The only unaltered element is that Crichton still loves Mary (now no longer a Lady), and she discovers that she loves him. One night, fearing for her safety, Crichton follows her to the haunt of the lions where he slays a beast that is about to attack her. The male and female vow their love. And now DeMille throws in the kitchen sink.

There is an instantaneous and unmotivated cut to some Oriental dream kingdom, presumably Babylon (the scene does not exist, of course, in Barrie's play). The motivation for the shift is the line of poetry that Crichton and Mary have read in the film (Barrie uses the line just once, but DeMille repeats it several times so you don't miss it), "If I were a king of Babylon. . . ." DeMille is not one to leave his ifs iffy. In this Babylon sequence, Crichton is indeed king, and Mary, a title informs us, is a Christian slave. The fact that Babylon had evaporated hundreds of years before Christ

does not offend DeMille's sense of history. Despite the irrelevance of the shift, DeMille can trade in the cave man, leopard skin costumes of the island sequence for the lavish, gaudy silks and satins of Hollywood's version of Babylon.

The film is clearly one of the bastard progeny of *Intolerance* in its combination of different epochs in a single film. But in *Male and Female*, the diversity is pointless and pretentious, and the moralizing is hypocritical. Such moral spinelessness became a staple of DeMille's career. His racy films (like *Why Change Your Wife?*, 1920, and *Forbidden Fruit*, 1922) flirt with naughtiness and sell conventionality; his religious films flirt with righteousness and sell lewdness. In both versions of *The Ten Commandments* (1923 and 1956), DeMille was more interested in the splashy sinful doings around the golden calf than in the righteous thunder and lightning on the mountain.

Von Stroheim's *Blind Husbands* is a far less complicated story than *Male and Female*. A doctor and his wife travel to the Alps; he pays her insufficient sexual attention. A German military officer (played by von Stroheim) sees the young wife and desires her; she cannot stop herself from desiring him, for she has no other outlet for her desires. The husband's blindness finally clears up; on a climactic hiking trip, the two males confront each other on the pinnacle, and the lecherous rival perishes, more a victim of the mountains and of fate than of the husband. The power of the film lies in von Stroheim's reduction of the quantity of incidents (quantity was DeMille's credo) in order to develop the quality, the feeling, the texture of the incidents he includes. Von Stroheim was such a master of *mise-en-scène* (see definition below) that his films remain powerful even if they were recut (actually, massacred) by lesser talents after having been taken out of von Stroheim's hands; we can still see what's *in the shot* and respond to that. Details develop the film's emotional dynamics: the calm husband's pipe; the wife's provocative ankles and shoes; the German's handling of his monocle and his careful primping with brush, comb, and vaporizer of cologne to make himself sexually attractive; the soulful tune that Margaret (the wife) plays on the piano, joined by von Steuben (the German) on the violin, which shows both her loneliness and her desire (we need no sound to hear the kind of tune the two are playing).

Von Stroheim's attention to detail inevitably allows him the luxury and subtlety of understatement. Several of the seduction scenes between von Steuben and Margaret take place in rooms, or hallways, or fields where a cross can distantly but clearly be seen in the background; von Stroheim never cuts to a close-up of the cross. The one way to turn subtle symbolism into overstated twaddle would have been to force us to read the crosses symbolically. Von Stroheim, a mature artist, knows the power of allusion and understatement.

The director's technique owes its greatest debt to his first master, Griffith. Like Griffith, his two principal tools are editing (montage) and the creation of atmosphere (*mise-en-scène:* what is provided and arranged within a shot; what is made to be the scene, or put into it as a photographable element). Von Stroheim's care with sets, lighting, costumes, and decor is so meticulous in creating his seamy world that you can almost smell it. In *Blind Husbands,* the details of the inn courtyard, of the dining room with its posters and crockery, of the individual bedrooms (so important to the film's plot), of the fog and mist on the pinnacle, all contribute to the tone of the film and the power of each scene.

Von Stroheim's care extended to his editing of the films, further developing Griffith's devices of the cross-cut (to show parallel events in different places at the same time) and the subjective cut (to show the mental projection of a character: what is in his or her mind's eye at a particular moment). In *Blind Husbands,* von Stroheim's cross-cutting develops both tension and irony. For example, he shows the doctor delivering a baby at the same time that von Steuben courts his wife, obviously trying to perform the act that produces babies. The most striking subjective cut in *Blind Husbands* comes just after the husband has discovered the Prussian's designs on his wife. Von Stroheim suddenly cuts to a menacing, spot-lit head of the German looming out of the darkness until it fills the frame; it leers grotesquely and points an accusing finger at the doctor.

The grotesque, the ugly, and the psychologically disturbed are dominant motifs in his work. André Bazin described von Stroheim's "one simple rule for direction": "Take a close look at the world, keep on doing so, and in the end it will lay bare for you all its cruelty and ugliness." Von Stroheim's films are populated with physical cripples and mental defectives (whose like the screen would not see until Tod Browning's *Freaks* and Luis Buñuel's *Land Without Bread*—both 1932 and both banned), but even beneath the surfaces of his more elegant characters—their polished manners, white gloves, and spray perfume—there is animal rapacity, viciousness, obsessive desire, and the brutal will to power. In von Stroheim's Naturalistic worldview, heredity, instinct, psychopathology, environment, and economics determine behavior, which he observes with the sharp eye of a realist—but a realist to whom all the resources of Expressionism are available. That may sound paradoxical, but it is exact.

In *Foolish Wives* (1921, which Universal hyped as "the first million dollar picture" and cut from just over 21 to just over 14 reels before releasing it in 1922; now only 7½ reels survive), a fake Russian Count (von Stroheim) attempts to rape a helpless, mentally retarded young woman. At the end of the film, her father kills the "Count" and dumps his body into the sewer so it can be swept out to sea with the other garbage.

Foolish Wives made von Stroheim world famous. When Jean Renoir saw it, he decided to make movies instead of ceramics. Like *Blind Husbands* and *The Devil's Pass Key* (1920, now lost), and even his later *The Merry Widow* (1925), *Foolish Wives* was extremely popular with audiences who appreciated its careful examination of bedroom tensions. The haughty independence of its director was less popular with the heads of studios and their flunkies. Erich von Stroheim was a completist, a perfectionist, an idealist who took film and its possibilities absolutely seriously; he was forced to work with executives (much like those who run Hollywood today) who maintained that they had an instinct for show business and knew better than anyone else what made a good picture—or had experience with budgets and could recognize an

Fig. 6-12

Fig. 6-13
Foolish Wives: *Erich von Stroheim (as the bogus Russian Count) defines his murderousness on the pistol range (Fig. 6-12); then he sets his sexual sights on a mentally retarded young woman (Fig. 6-13).*

advisable investment. Most of them regarded von Stroheim as an egomaniac whose projects always needed to be brought under control. Irving Thalberg, who was to become MGM's most creative production executive before his early death, hated von Stroheim as much as his

work. When Thalberg was Carl Laemmle's assistant at Universal, he removed von Stroheim from *Merry-Go-Round* (1922) in the middle of shooting, firing him for his "inefficient" (that is, perfectionistic and uncompromising) production methods, his wasteful expenditures on "invisible" details (which were actually quite visible in the convincing realism and texture of the film), and his insubordination (von Stroheim said they often "crossed swords"). At MGM, Thalberg would get the chance to fire von Stroheim again—and beyond that, to destroy his greatest work, in one of film history's true horror stories, the re-editing of *Greed* (1924).

Von Stroheim had long wanted to film a complete novel, and the one he chose—by Frank Norris, a writer he knew Griffith admired, for his story "A Deal in Wheat" had been the basis of *A Corner in Wheat*—was *McTeague, A Story of San Francisco* (1899). In 1922 he interested Samuel Goldwyn in backing the project and was hired by the Goldwyn Company, whose slogan was "the author and the play are the thing."

McTeague attracted von Stroheim for many reasons. It was uncompromisingly realistic, psychologically intriguing, and structured like a greased slide to Hell. Norris's view of the human dog matched that of von Stroheim, who consistently depicted human behavior in animal terms. Like von Stroheim, Norris was a realist (to be specific, a Naturalist in the tradition of Emile Zola) with a taste for the pathological. Many of von Stroheim's films and Norris's novels are about people who fall victim to traps they have set for themselves without knowing it, people whose very lives are traps. Further, the novel's family of German immigrants roughly paralleled von Stroheim's own heritage (he was born in Vienna, the son of a Jewish hatter from Prussia), and the novel's familiar San Francisco and Oakland settings appealed to a man who had lived there before going to Hollywood. He did not, as it is often said, set out to film *McTeague* page by page; his script includes most of the novel but changes and adds a great deal, and where the novel was entirely realistic, the film was that and more. Shot entirely on location—that is, without a single studio set—in an era of studio shooting, it was also an experiment in Expressionism; it observed behavior from the outside, as tightly and scrupulously as the job has ever been done, but it also dipped into the mind and displayed its contents.

With cast and crew (the cinematographers were Ben F. Reynolds and William H. Daniels), von Stroheim went to San Francisco to shoot on the very streets named in the novel, and even to Death Valley (in the summer!) to obtain absolutely authentic details. One of the stars, Jean Hersholt, had to be hospitalized after the grueling takes in Death Valley. The film took seven months to shoot and cost $470,000; then von Stroheim edited it for months.

The original version of *McTeague*—previewed to two journalists, who wrote about what they saw, and one director—ran forty-two reels, a mere nine hours at 20 frames per second (in the teens and 1920s, silent speed varied from 16 to 24 fps, depending on the year and the camera operator; 16, 18, and 20 fps were common speeds). That first audience felt they had seen the greatest movie ever made or likely to be made. Von Stroheim himself shortened the film to twenty-four reels (just over five hours, considered the "director's version"), to be shown in two parts, with a dinner break after the wedding sequence. His friend at Metro, Rex Ingram (who had been the third member of that first audience), cut the film to eighteen reels and forbade von Stroheim to let anyone take another foot out of it. By this time the Maria/Zerkow and Baker/Grannis stories, to be discussed below, had been trimmed drastically but not deleted, and the film was still in two parts.

Meanwhile, as mentioned earlier, the Goldwyn Company—without Goldwyn, who had been forced out by his partners but who soon founded Samuel Goldwyn Productions entirely on his own—merged in 1924 with Metro Pictures (which was owned by Marcus Loew of Loew's Inc., the man who arranged the merger) and with Louis B. Mayer Productions, forming Metro-Goldwyn-Mayer. Mayer hired Thalberg away from Universal and put him directly in charge of production. All this made *McTeague* an MGM property and put von Stroheim at Thalberg's mercy, which was not a good place to be. Fully backed up by Mayer, Thalberg

turned the film over to the MGM story and editing departments; under the loose supervision of June Mathis, a hack cutter and title-writer named Joseph W. Farnham—who had not read the book or the script—completed the hatchet job. What was left of a long, tight masterpiece was a mess; von Stroheim said the cutter had nothing on his mind but a hat. *McTeague* was retitled *Greed* and made to open with a bad poem about gold. The nearly three-hour prologue was cut to less than five minutes. Mathis and/or Farnham wrote idiotic intertitles to patch up some of the glaring holes that had been created in the story's continuity and in the characters' motivations. In addition, many scenes were shuffled out of order, and three Expressionist shots—out of all those sequences, many of which had presented the dreams and hallucinations of a crazy junkman, obsessed with discovering a 100-plate service of solid gold, but some of which had used grotesque shadows and figures to convey the violence and madness of the waking world—were randomly cut into the realistic footage as "symbolic" commentary on the greed of the characters. *Greed* was released at ten reels ($2\frac{1}{4}$ hours with no intermission—in some cases, after all this cutting, on a double bill!), no copies of the earlier versions were made, and except for the ten reels used in *Greed*, the negative was destroyed along with all the outtakes so that the silver might be retrieved from the celluloid.

The *Greed* that exists (the release version) must therefore be judged on the strength of its parts rather than as a whole. For one who hasn't read Norris's novel, the film's narrative (certainly its details) is almost incomprehensible. The concrete process of the dissolution of the relationship between the dentist, John McTeague (Mac), and his wife, Trina Sieppe, makes no sense in the film, for in the novel Norris carefully charts it by moving the couple to shabbier and shabbier living quarters—a practice followed in von Stroheim's script (which was faithful to the novel but not afraid to add a feature-length prologue, a funeral at a wedding, or a second pet bird). Each degradation in their physical surroundings implies or contributes to their bodily, emotional, moral, and psychological degradation. But in *Greed*, although we may notice that the walls of the

Fig. 6-14
On location: Gibson Gowland (left) and ZaSu Pitts in
Greed.

McTeague household change as the film pro-
gresses, we never know exactly when, why, and
where the couple has moved, or how the delicate Trina became so rough and sloppy. Although in one shot we may notice that Trina's
bandaged hand is lacking several fingers, we
never learn from the film that she lost them
because they became infected as a result of her
husband's biting them. The dissolution from
happy marriage to vicious, insane combat—
which is, both psychologically and economically, the meticulously observed subject of at
least half of the novel (and of the screenplay)—
barely exists in the film.

Another reason this sense of gradual,
inevitable dissolution is lost is that the ten-reel
version had to do without two other "love"
relationships in the novel that undoubtedly
seemed superfluous to a hack writer and cutter
but that are really essential. The relationship
between Trina (ZaSu Pitts, in one of the silent
screen's greatest performances) and Mac
(Gibson Gowland) is bounded, on the one hand,
by old Grannis and Miss Baker, a couple of
timid old folks who carry on a pure, genteel,
unphysical love affair, and, on the other, by
Zerkow (the junkman) and Maria Macapa, two
slovenly human beasts whose "love" is based

on Zerkow's almost sexual pleasure in listening
to the equally insane Maria's story of her hoard
of gold. Maria remains in the released film only
long enough to sell Trina the fateful lottery
ticket; Zerkow is deleted entirely. All that remains of their "love story" are a few shots of
skeletal, photographically distorted arms playing with distorted treasures; taken out of the
Maria–Zerkow context and applied to Trina,
these shots seem irrelevant and pretentious. In
the novel, we understand the original love of
Mac and Trina, together with their originally
rational view of money, as a median between
the sexual timidity and parsimony of the old
folks and the crazed passion of the gold lovers.
Trina begins as Miss Baker's close friend,
somewhat repulsed by Maria's crudeness, and
gradually drifts into becoming Maria's confi-
dante. Mac and Trina even move into the
squalid hovel where Zerkow and Maria lived
(and which became vacant when Zerkow cut
Maria's throat). Without the two poles of these
other couples, *Greed* has no barometer to measure the direction and degree of decay in the
central couple; it is a triptych missing its outer
panels.

Despite the incoherence of *Greed* as a whole,
many of the sequences are visual and dramatic
marvels, and the *mise-en-scène* survives within
the surviving shots. The wedding ceremony is
a mixture of the comic and the somber: a delightful parody of wedding customs that is
overshadowed by the sight of a funeral cortege
through an open window (a great use of deep
focus and a clear premonition of the direction
the marriage will take). The scene in which
Trina realizes that she is alone—with no one
to protect her except the stranger who is her
animal-sensual husband—is a touching examination of her feelings. The mad scene that climaxes her perverse confusion of money and
sex, where she lies naked in bed with her gold,
is both daring and terrifying as well as cinematically unprecedented. Von Stroheim's use of
animal symbolism, particularly his likening the
envious Marcus Schouler (Jean Hersholt) to
the sneaky cat that constantly prowls about the
cage of McTeague's more complexly symbolic
birds, is quite effective. And most awesome visually are the endless wastes of Death Valley—
a seeming infinity of caked sand and dust under

a pitiless, dead sky—the ultimate stopping place on a journey in which a dead metal seems the only goal worth pursuing.

That same vision dominates even the fluffy trifle that Thalberg assigned von Strohcim after *Greed*. *The Merry Widow* (1925) was a safe property, a Viennese operetta that Thalberg was sure von Stroheim could not destroy. Von Stroheim apparently did not destroy it; the film was one of his greatest commercial successes. But von Stroheim, in adapting this operetta fairy tale, devotes a disproportionate amount of attention to the widow's first husband (before she became a widow) rather than her resulting merry widowhood. The husband is a deformed cripple (von Stroheim accentuates the deformity) with a very obvious sexual fetish; he is attracted to healthy feet—a theme that von Stroheim develops with pointed cutting. Worse, he is so excited on his wedding night that he collapses and dies on top of his bride, worn out from dragging his gnarled body up to the bed of love. Von Stroheim's handling of this unsavory relationship is not exactly operetta fare. Another brilliant stroke is his depiction of the mental attitudes of the widow's three suitors. All three come to watch her perform at the theatre; all three stare at her through opera glasses. Then von Strohcim cuts to the object of their stares: the cripple watches her feet; the lecherous suitor watches her groin; the young hero watches her face. Such naturalistic touches turned Franz Lehár's operetta into a salacious parody of an operetta.

Because his production methods seemed extravagant, because he seemed mean and tyrannical, unwholesome and unpleasant, Erich von Stroheim was very easy to fire, even if his films made money. *The Merry Widow* was his last film for MGM and MGM's first big hit. He went to work for Zukor and had as little success with him as with Thalberg. After two very interesting projects of 1926–1929, *The Wedding March* (which starred von Stroheim, ZaSu Pitts, and Fay Wray; began as a production for Pat Powers's independent company, Celebrity Pictures; became a Paramount picture when Zukor bought Powers out; and was drastically cut before its 1928 release—although we now have the benefit of von Stroheim's 1957 recut of the first half of what was to have been a two-part

Fig. 6-15
The wedding scene of **Greed**, *with the funeral procession outside on the street below.*

film) and *Queen Kelly* (produced by Gloria Swanson, who fired him too), Erich von Stroheim directed only one other film, *Walking Down Broadway* (1932, released 1933 as *Hello Sister!* after much tampering and reshooting by others). For the next twenty-five years von Stroheim continued acting in films—one of the many ways his career anticipates that of Orson Welles—most memorably as von Rauffenstein in *Grand Illusion* (directed by Renoir, whose entire career and aesthetic he had decisively influenced) and as Max, the chauffeur and former movie director, in Billy Wilder's *Sunset Boulevard* (1950). The irony of this late film was not only that von Stroheim played a character whose career echoed his own (the filmclips Norma Desmond screens in the movie are from his own *Queen Kelly*), but also that he played the devoted servant of Gloria Swanson, who was with him at the stormy end of his Hollywood road.

Another interesting and important descendant of Griffith's methods was Henry King's *Tol'able David*. The Soviet director V. I. Pudovkin found King's use of cutting to build a scene as instructive and effective as Griffith's. *Tol'able David* (1921) is a very powerful film in which King, the student of Griffith and the employee of Ince, combines the best of both masters. King's world in *Tol'able David* is similar to Griffith's Kentucky: rural, homey, gently comic, touching, pastoral. Into the peaceful world come the violent figures from outside, three fugitives from justice, who are as vicious, as nasty, as psychotically mean as Battling Burrows—or, for that matter, as the degenerate families in Sam Peckinpah's *Straw Dogs* (1971) and Wes Craven's *The Hills Have Eyes* (1977). Like Griffith, King defines the characters by their responses to animals (Pudovkin called it the use of the "plastic material"): David lovingly plays with his dog, Rocket; the invaders consider stoning a sleeping cat and eventually kill Rocket out of pure meanness.

King shows how to bring a story alive with significant and memorable detail by manipulating the visual, "plastic material." Richard Barthelmess, Griffith's own figure of gentleness and sincerity, plays David; his face and presence contribute greatly to the charm, warmth, and sympathy of the story. King's cutting consistently drives the emotions of the tale; the horror of the injury to David's brother, Alan, and its impact on Rose, his wife, come alive as King repeatedly cuts from the crippled, helpless Alan in bed to a shot of Rose, sitting in a rocking chair, holding their new infant, rocking relentlessly back and forth, back and forth. King's cutting transforms the emotionally neutral act of rocking into a moment of pain, of determination, of savagery, of misery, as the shots of the invalid in bed create the emotional climate for the wife's silent rocking. This rocking is far more successful than that of the cradle in *Intolerance* because the human focus and the specific causes and effects of the act of rocking are so much more concrete.

Also effective in the film are its details of brutality, which clash, intentionally, with the sweeter strains of the picture. Unlike Griffith and more like Ince, King actually depicted malicious violence on the screen: the death of David's dog, Hatburn's digging his finger into the gunshot wound in David's shoulder, the excruciating, exhausting pain of David's final fight with the Hatburn Goliaths. Even in Griffith's *Broken Blossoms*, the beatings of Lucy were more implied than graphically depicted. Also Ince-like is the irreversibility of the disaster that has befallen the characters. Unlike the damage done in *Way Down East*, the pieces of David's life can never be patched together again. His dog and father are dead, and his brother is an incurable invalid; there can be no miraculous resuscitations. His home is gone; his innocence will never return.

Oscar Micheaux, born in Metropolis, Illinois in 1884, was one of the earliest black filmmakers. He published his first book, the autobiographical *The Conquest*, in 1913 at his own expense. Four years later, he and black actor Noble Johnson formed the Lincoln Motion Picture Company, but Johnson's agent (or existing contracts) kept them from making any films; that was Micheaux's last brush with Hollywood, and what he did was brush it off. He became a one-man studio, based primarily in Manhattan but active in the Midwest and elsewhere. Between 1918 and 1948 Micheaux single-handedly wrote, produced, directed, edited, and distributed more than thirty features for the Micheaux Film Corporation.

His first picture, *The Homesteader* (1918), was based on his first novel. Six years later he made *Birthright*, an answer to *The Birth of a Nation*. Resenting the way Hollywood portrayed blacks (whether they were cast as servants, in comic roles, or picking cotton—as they usually were—he found the actors "ugly"), Micheaux filled his films with beautiful women, decent and handsome men, and children who were as attractive and perceptive as Hollywood's white kids. Though his films did very good business around the country, and great business in Latin America, Micheaux was particularly aware that his films were needed in the South, where black audiences had no other opportunity to see blacks who (like many rich blacks in the big cities of the North) lived in penthouses, had servants, and went out to the best nightclubs; only in Micheaux's films could they see black actors playing leading roles and, as Micheaux actress Bee Freeman put it, "really dressed up, really living, and talking like people talk." Each of his films proudly featured "An All Colored Cast"; he had a company of well-known actors recruited from Harlem and from Broadway.

He also included a showgirl scene in almost every film (regardless of plot relevance, deliberately for the black men in the southern audience), using cabaret dancers or acts from the Cotton Club—shooting late at night, after the clubs had closed and the dancers had been picked up in a bus and taken to wherever they might be shooting. And "wherever" describes it, for Micheaux would shoot in churches, cabarets, lobbies, railroad stations—anything he could get, including farmhouses when he was shooting on the road.

Though he did not drive (and so hired a chauffeur), Micheaux was on the road much of the time, raising money for his pictures, lining up bookings, and sometimes shooting on location. "A genius able to talk anyone out of their shirts," as actor Lorenzo Tucker (his "Valentino") described him, Micheaux might simply drive into a town, raise local money for shooting part or all of a movie, shoot there with locals for actors, show the film there, and add it to the collection of films he drove or shipped around the country. Often in the South, late on Saturday night in a regular movie house, a Micheaux film might be shown after the regular feature—because Micheaux would be in town with it.

But the majority of his films were made in big cities, on tight, precise budgets and with smart showmanship. Among his more important talkies were *The Exile* (1931, about a black man from Chicago who goes to South Dakota and falls in love with a white woman—who fortunately turns out to be partly black; a subplot involves a black woman who owns a club in Chicago and has an Ethiopian suitor), *Ten Minutes to Live* (1932), *God's Step Children* (1938, about a light-skinned girl who is described by a schoolmate as "stuck up, and she don't want to be colored"—a film that combined and went beyond *Imitation of Life* and *These Three*, as its trailer pointed out), and *The Notorious Elinor Lee* (1940). None of his films is in distribution today, though prints survive at the Library of Congress. The films averaged one hour in length and often looked rough: Most of them had few sets and fewer retakes, and some had scratchy sound or problems with screen direction—as when characters in separate shots run away from each other into each other. But even when the stories were corny, the films were exciting because they showed blacks living lives far more genuine than anything Hollywood had even thought of offering. (The white-made breakthrough films include Stanley Kramer's *Home of the Brave*, 1949; John Cassavetes's *Shadows*, 1959; and George Romero's *Night of the Living Dead*, 1968, the first film in which the lead, Duane Jones, was cast regardless of the fact that he was black, not because he was black. The TV-movie breakthrough came in 1974: John Korty's *The Autobiography of Miss Jane Pittman*, starring Cicely Tyson.) A diversely talented man who, as Freeman said, "wouldn't let *anyone* tell him what to do," Micheaux got the films made, and he got them shown. He was the first black filmmaker anywhere in the world to become widely known, and not coincidentally the most persistent.

One of the challenges the narrative film has regularly set itself is that of adapting a literary work for the screen. From Griffith's *The Avenging Conscience* and von Stroheim's *Greed* to John Huston's *The Maltese Falcon* (1941) and Stanley Kubrick's *Barry Lyndon* (1975), the problem—and the solution—has been to discover cinematic ways of conveying the essence as well as the characters, style, plot, and point of the purely verbal original. In 1928 one of the greatest of all avant-garde teams—in effect, the American rivals of the Surrealists Luis Buñuel and Salvador Dali (who made *Un Chien andalou*, 1929, and *L'Age d'or*, 1930)—independently shot and released their masterpiece, *The Fall of the House of Usher*, based on the story by Edgar Allan Poe; they were James Sibley Watson (director and cinematographer) and Melville Webber (writer and art director). This one-reel Expressionist film—a silent whose music track was added later—uses torn and multiplied images, ominous shadows, stylized figures and sets, superimposed graphics, extreme shooting angles, every special effect in the book, and jagged, dizzying movement to conjure a mood—entirely true to Poe—of intermingled beauty and horror. (The same year, in France, Jean Epstein directed a four-reel Impressionist version, *La Chute de la maison Usher*.)

Watson and Webber's only other film was *Lot in Sodom* (1933), a Biblical adaptation whose sexual content proved too strong for audiences of the day.

As a producer reporting to, but given a free hand by, Thalberg at MGM, Lillian Gish took on the challenge of filming Nathaniel Hawthorne's *The Scarlet Letter,* a project that had been opposed by every women's club in the country because its plot concerns adultery with a capital A, not to mention with a clergyman. (When MGM told her "it wasn't allowed," she said, "What do you mean it's not allowed? It's an American classic, and I'm an American and I want to make it!") When Gish visited the women's clubs and told them she would be in charge of the project, their respect for her good taste and judgment led them to drop all opposition. To direct *The Scarlet Letter* (1926), she brought Victor Sjøstrøm (who signed his American pictures Seastrom) to Hollywood from Sweden. The picture was a great success—as were Gish's other productions, including the 1926 *La Bohème,* a silent version of Puccini's opera. But her greatest production, and the second film Sjøstrøm directed for her, was *The Wind* (1928), based closely on the 1925 novel by Dorothy Scarborough and shot in the Mojave Desert. In this film Gish gives one of her very finest performances—her best since *Way Down East* and until *The Night of the Hunter* (1955)—as a woman driven mad by the relentless, demonic, almost sexually charged wind that drives the sand across the Texas plains and through every crack in the shack she shares with her husband. Originally ending with the same powerful scene as the novel, in which the heroine—after killing and burying the man who assaulted her—walks into the oblivion of madness and blowing sand, *The Wind* was given a happy ending (in which she and her husband stand together at the open door, powerfully facing the wind) at the insistence of exhibitors.

Other women worked in Hollywood, and not just in front of the camera. A great many were script supervisors, screenwriters, film editors, and negative cutters. As a producer of narrative films, Mary Pickford was one of the most important figures in the industry. Margaret Winkler Mintz was the first woman to produce and distribute cartoons; in 1922, when she was twenty-five, she founded M. J. Winkler & Co. in New York, and within a year it became the world's largest distributor of shorts. Earlier, when she had been working as Harry Warner's secretary and found that Warner Bros. had turned down Pat Sullivan's offer of a *Felix the Cat* series, *she* bought it. In 1923 Walt Disney asked her to distribute his first series, *Alice in Cartoonland* (which used live and animated figures in the same shots, a device that continued to interest Disney throughout his career), and she not only agreed but helped him improve it. Her husband, Charles Mintz, produced the *Krazy Kat* cartoons.

In the teens and early 1920s there were at least thirty women directors active in Hollywood, many of them at Universal Pictures. Perhaps the most accomplished of them all was Lois Weber, who was born in Pennsylvania in 1882, became a church missionary and then an actress, and joined Universal as a contract director in 1912. Between then and the end of the silent era, she was the best known American woman director; she was also the most highly paid female director in the world. In 1917 she set up her own Los Angeles studio, Lois Weber Productions. Her husband, Phillips Smalley, was her "advisory director" and co-author, but she was by far the dominant creative figure. Between 1912 and 1927 she wrote, directed, and in most cases produced forty films, many of which starred either herself or the woman she made a star, Claire Windsor. Weber was deeply concerned with social and moral issues; like Griffith (*What Shall We Do With Our Old?*), she was a pioneer in what would later be called the "problem picture," and the issues addressed in her timely, insightful, compassionate, powerful, superbly crafted films remain relevant today. Her works include *Hypocrites* (1914), *Where Are My Children?* (1916, about birth control), and *The Blot* (1921, about underpaid professors). She lost her studio in 1923 when she and Smalley divorced. In the late 1920s she made a few pictures for Universal and her last silent (*The Angel of Broadway,* 1927, about a Salvation Army worker) for DeMille. She directed one talkie (*White Heat*) in 1934.

Dorothy Arzner, who was to become the best known American woman director of the

1930s (as Ida Lupino was in the 1940s), was born in San Francisco in 1900. She worked as a waitress in her father's Hollywood café before becoming an ambulance driver in World War I. At Paramount she went from secretary to script clerk to negative cutter to film editor. Her brilliant editing of the bullfight scenes in the Valentino hit *Blood and Sand* (1922) won her the chance to edit *The Covered Wagon*. For the next few years she was a highly respected editor and screenwriter. To keep her from leaving, Paramount made her a director in 1927. That first year, she directed what Paramount considered appropriate projects for a woman: *Fashions for Women, Ten Modern Commandments,* and *Get Your Man*. But soon she was making the films that would make her famous: *The Wild Party* (1929), *Honor Among Lovers* (1931), *Working Girls* (1931), *Merrily We Go to Hell* (1932), *Christopher Strong* (1933), *Nana* (1934), *Craig's Wife* (1936), and *Dance, Girl, Dance* (1940).

Many other directors made interesting films in the twenties. Some of them would be remembered primarily for one picture, as Rupert Julian is for *The Phantom of the Opera* (1925), starring the incomparable Lon Chaney. Some of them would never make the transition to sound; some of them had only begun a career that would take clearer shape in the era ahead. James Cruze, whose specialty was satire, made the most celebrated western epic of the decade, *The Covered Wagon* (1923). Rex Ingram, whose most famous film was *The Four Horsemen of the Apocalypse* (1921, the movie that made Rudolph Valentino a star), was a pictorial master of composition and atmosphere. Josef von Sternberg—a Viennese Jew born Josef Sternberg and raised in New York—began his control of physical detail and cinematic atmosphere in *The Salvation Hunters* (1925), *Underworld* (1927, the first in a decade of great gangster pictures), and *The Docks of New York* (1928). He also helped von Stroheim edit Part I of *The Wedding March,* though their version was rejected by the studio (neither of them had anything to do with the final cut of Part II, released in Europe as *The Honeymoon*). John Ford— born Sean Aloysius O'Feeney, the son of a Maine saloonkeeper—who began by taking over his brother Francis's acting troupe to shoot program westerns with Harry Carey,

made his first western as epic history, *The Iron Horse,* in 1924.

King Vidor effectively mixed wartime humor, antiwar propaganda, and a touching love story in *The Big Parade* (1925), the fifth or sixth top-grossing film of the decade (at the box office, it did as well as *The Jazz Singer*), then followed it with his masterpiece, *The Crowd* (1928), a brilliantly composed film full of powerful and daring camera movements, made deliberately without stars, that tells the story of an ordinary man—and his long-suffering wife— who can't stand the thought that he's not marked out for some special destiny, that he's not better than everyone else. In the extraordinary final shot, when the man and wife and their surviving child are shown having a good time in a theatre, reconciled to each other, to their little triumphs, and to being ordinary, the camera rapidly pulls back to reveal row after row of patrons, leaving the momentary hero behind in the crowd—a crowd of theatre patrons facing, in the real movie theatre, a crowd of moviegoers. Among Vidor's many subsequent films, the one that most complements and opposes *The Crowd* is his superb adaptation of Ayn Rand's *The Fountainhead* (1949), which takes for its hero a man who *is* presented as morally and intellectually superior to most of those around him and who is last seen atop a skyscraper, well above any crowd. The hero of *The Fountainhead* is an uncompromising architect who makes his own dreams come true, and perhaps that is the key to Vidor's idealistic puzzle: that some of his characters are practical dreamers, like the heroes who bring water to their commune in *Our Daily Bread* (1934) or the architect who builds his skyscraper; and that some, whose ambitions are frustrated or self-contradictory from the start, or who *just* dream, are destroyed by their dreams, like the heroine of *Duel in the Sun* (1947), if they do not learn to find joy in what they have, like the hero of *The Crowd*—but that all of them are compelling in their idealism, however misguided or on target it may be, and in the emotion and the sense of being that they pour into their obsessions. Only King Vidor, working with Barbara Stanwyck, could make the self-denying/self-fulfilling obsessive project of *Stella Dallas* (1937) so deeply credible and involving. (In

1925 and 1990, others tried.) It is tempting to wonder just what, as uncredited co-director of both pictures, he added to the determination of Scarlett in *Gone With the Wind* and the dreams of Dorothy in *The Wizard of Oz* (both 1939).

Among the most important of the newcomers was a German director, Ernst Lubitsch. Hollywood had begun importing many of the leading directors of Europe: Mauritz Stiller, Victor Sjøstrøm, Fritz Lang, F. W. Murnau, E. A. Dupont, Maurice Tourneur. But none found Hollywood so comfortable and so amicable a home as Lubitsch. Mary Pickford imported him specifically to direct a costume spectacle, *Rosita,* for her. Pickford, like her husband, sought to change her adolescent image: to grow up, cut her curls, and show she was a woman. Lubitsch, who had directed a string of costume pageants in Germany (*Gypsy Blood, Passion, Deception*) that had become popular in America for their comic "humanizing" (i.e., sexualizing) of history, was Pickford's choice. *Rosita* proved the beginning of the end of Mary Pickford's career and the beginning of Lubitsch's. He immediately turned to polite, witty, understated drawing-room comedies: *The Marriage Circle* (1924), *Lady Windermere's Fan* (1925), *So This Is Paris* (1926).

Lubitsch's comedy derived from one essential theme: the limits and defects of human vision. Characters see either too little or too much in Lubitsch's silent comedies. They see too little because their views are blocked—either by their own willful blindness, the prejudices of their society, or the simple physical fact that they can see only part of the whole picture, framed by some window or door that obscures as much as it reveals. When Mary Pickford quarreled with Lubitsch, she called him a director of doors, not of people. Lubitsch would use these doors (and windows) to reveal something about people: that human vision is always limited—by assumption, attitude, and prejudice.

If Lubitsch's people see too little, they also see too much when they make some inference about another character based on the mere sight of a physical object—the straw hats, canes, and fans that play such a large role in Lubitsch's comedies of manners—because they

Fig. 6-16
Nanook.

imply where and *with whom* a character has been. To make movies about the fallibility of human vision is a highly appropriate piece of cinematic irony and self-reference, since cinema itself depends on structuring human vision, framing visual limitations, and encouraging us to draw inferences from sights of material objects. Lubitsch's clever ability to manipulate the cinema frame and to imply so much with seemingly trivial details would soon allow him to make some of the very best early American sound films.

Many directors of the 1920s worked outside the fences of the Hollywood formulas. One of them was Robert Flaherty, the father of the documentary film, who had been taking his camera to Hudson Bay since 1913; the eventual result was *Nanook of the North* (1922). It was not the first documentary, to be sure (for films had been documenting actual human activities since Lumière). But *Nanook* was the first feature-length documentary to become a huge commercial hit. Flaherty had discovered that only as a documentary filmmaker could he enjoy the freedom of the solitary, individual artist, shaping his material with his own methods according to his own perceptions. Others found such freedom in the avant-garde, another world where filmmaker, camera, and idea could be one, without studio middlemen.

Flaherty's *Nanook* is significant for the beauty of its photography of the white, frozen plains of ice and for its care in revealing the life and life-style of the man—and the family—who lived there. Flaherty's greatest asset was Nanook's lack of inhibition before the camera. Although he was clearly conscious of being watched, and he knew he was performing, he did not quite know what a camera and movie were. Nanook was carefully directed to perform his specific business—hunting, building an igloo with his family, feeding the dogs—while Flaherty's camera recorded and, inevitably, commented. From *Nanook* on, the documentary has been defined as a nonfiction film that organizes factual materials in order to make a point—as distinguished from the actualité, which simply records an event. (A newsreel might be either one.)

One comment, of course, was that Nanook's life was hard, a perpetual struggle for two absolute necessities, food and shelter. But Flaherty's making of the film itself mirrored the hardness of Nanook's life, for Flaherty could only record the severity of ice and snow if he lived through the blizzards he was recording. The making of the film was a metaphor for the subject of the film, and out of that endurance came a work of art, a product of human accomplishment, like an igloo with an ice window. For Nanook, life was not hard, it merely was. In Nanook's simplicity, in his strength, his competence, his ability to survive, and his humor, Flaherty depicted a life of fulfillment. Life, in fact, could be no fuller.

Flaherty's later sound film, *Man of Aran* (1934), also develops the difficulties and fulfillments of the hard, vital life. By then Flaherty had fled to England. Hollywood, rewarding the dollar success of *Nanook* with more dollars, asked Flaherty to make pictures for commercial release. For Paramount he made *Moana* (1926)—an idyllic study of life on a South Seas island. Hollywood, which expected native girls dancing the hula, was disappointed and teamed Flaherty with other directors, W. S. Van Dyke and F. W. Murnau, for his later films, of which the greatest was his and Murnau's exquisite, troubling *Tabu* (1929–1931). To preserve his independence, Flaherty left for England where a whole group of filmmakers applying his principles had begun to produce films.

In America, the success of Flaherty's first documentary stimulated his contemporaries, Merian C. Cooper and Ernest Schoedsack. Their silent documentaries, *Grass* (1925) and *Chang* (1927), were also close and sensitive studies of people whose existence was totally dependent on the earth, the cycles of nature, and their own skills at adapting to them. With screenwriter Ruth Rose and stop-motion animator Willis O'Brien, Cooper and Schoedsack would later make the most famous and effective mixture of Hollywood fiction, documentary anthropology, and parody of Hollywood's justification for documentary anthropology—*King Kong* (1933).

The Comics

One other group of 1920s films maintained an inventiveness and individuality that remain as fresh today as they were over half a century ago. The silent film, which had already proved itself the ideal medium for physical comedy, continued to nurture its most legitimate children. Several new comic imaginations joined the established Sennett, who still supervised films, and Chaplin, who had begun to make features: most significantly, Harold Lloyd, Buster Keaton, Harry Langdon, and Laurel and Hardy. Laurel and Hardy perfected their material late in the silent period, then became the most popular comic team of the sound era. Laurel and Hardy had been put together by Hal Roach, Sennett's major rival as a producer of comedies, who reasoned that one of his fat players and one of his thin ones might go well together. The premise was entirely Sennett-like, and indeed Laurel and Hardy's method was a return to the completely comic, externalized, surface world of Sennett gags.

But Laurel and Hardy films were far more controlled and far more tightly structured than the Sennett romps. Their films demonstrate the "snowball" principle that Bergson had developed in *Le Rire*. Like the snowball rolling down the mountain, the Laurel and Hardy film gathers greater and greater momentum and bulk as it hurtles toward the valley. Their films demonstrate the classic structure of farce — from Plautus to Feydeau: to begin with a single problem and then multiply that problem to infinity. If an auto gets dented in a traffic jam at the start of the film, every car on the highway gets stripped by the end of it; if a Christmas tree branch gets caught in a door at the start of the film, the tree, the house, the salesmen's car must be totally annihilated by the end of it; if the two partners have trouble with a few nails and tacks when starting to build a house, the film must inevitably end with the house collapsing into a pile of rubble. There is an insane yet perfect logic about the whole process.

As does every great silent-film comedy, the Laurel and Hardy films depend on physical objects; the visual medium demands the use of concrete, visible things. But for Stan Laurel (the brains of the team and, like Chaplin, a Fred Karno alumnus) and Oliver Hardy, an object is something to throw, fall over, or destroy; most of their films are built around breaking things. The "adults" of this world are all overgrown, spiteful children squashing each other's mud pies. Stan is the weepy, puling, sneaky, why-blame-me, covertly nasty kid, while Ollie is the pompous, bullying, show-off, know-it-all, inherently incompetent kid. His dignity is as false and inevitable as Stan's tearfulness; they are both ploys to get away with something or get even. If the premise of the films is much thinner than Chaplin's, it is also true that the spiteful emotion they capture is a genuine one. They mirror our feelings when another car zips in to steal the parking place that we have been patiently waiting for. Their single-keyed emotion and their taut, unidirectional structure ensured their success in the short film. The best loved of their sound features are *Sons of the Desert* (1933), *Our Relations* (1936), and the great *Way Out West* (1937, in which Stan — exploiting the potential of the sound film to play with sound/picture relationships — sings a song in three voices, two of which are impossible but in perfect sync).

Harold Lloyd, another Hal Roach product, was almost a combination of Chaplin and Fairbanks. Like Charlie, he was a little guy, slightly inept, trying to succeed. Like Fairbanks, he was energetic, athletic, and engagingly charming, with a smile calculated to snare us as well as the girl. Like Charlie, he had trouble both with objects and with the world while trying to achieve his desires. But unlike Charlie — and like Doug — he invariably does achieve those desires, and they are the same material and romantic treasures that Doug always wins. Also like Doug — and unlike Charlie — Lloyd films never imply that the prize he has won was not worth the winning.

Rather than developing character or social commentary, Lloyd generates pure comedy from the situation, from topical satire, from his own limber body, and from the daring stunts he would dream up. In *High and Dizzy* (1920), the first of his high-rise comedies of thrills, he demonstrates the variety of his comedy. The film is constructed in three loosely related episodes. In the opening sequence, Lloyd plays a young doctor whose practice is so dismal that his phone is gathering cobwebs. He falls madly in love with a patient who, it turns out, walks in her sleep.

In the second sequence, he strolls down the hall and gets stinking drunk with another young doctor who has distilled some hooch in his medicinal laboratory. Lloyd's topical satire of doctors, admittedly rather gentle, is the same kind that he would use to portray the twenties' college generation in *The Freshman* (1925). The comic premise of two drunken doctors also allows Lloyd to demonstrate his ability and agility as pure physical comic, as the two friends, one fat, one thin, dizzily weave down the street and into their hotel, much like Charlie and Fatty in *The Rounders*.

Lloyd introduces his "comedy of thrills" in the film's third section. It just happens that the sleepwalking patient with whom he is in love lives in the same hotel. She starts sleepwalking out on the hotel ledge, many frightening stories above the hard pavement below. Harold goes out on the ledge to save her and, predictably, gets locked out there when she decides to stroll inside. Lloyd tightropes, trips, and stumbles on the ledge, playing on many emotions in us at the same time. We feel suspense because he might fall; yet we laugh because we know he won't. We wonder if he was really on the ledge when he shot the sequence (the camera angle and lack of editing trickiness make us suspect he really performed the stunt). We laugh at the

Fig. 6-17
High and Dizzy: *Harold Lloyd with a sleepwalking Mildred Davis on a scary ledge.*

man's fright and perplexity; we admire his underlying competence and control. It was this same synthesis of cliff-hanging serial and burlesque comedy that created the excitement and success of his feature *Safety Last* (1923).

Unlike the comedy of Chaplin and Keaton, Lloyd's remains content with emotional and psychological surfaces, never cutting very deeply, never going beyond comic sensations to confront us with ironies and paradoxes. Lloyd's films effectively distill the urges and values of American society as a whole in the 1920s—the success ethic of get up and get. Further, the Lloyd comedies reveal an extremely cunning and complex sense of comic construction, setting up a comic problem, developing it clearly and cleverly, and driving it to such dizzying heights (quite literally in the high-rise films) that an audience becomes helplessly hysterical in the presence of Lloyd's comic ingenuity (as opposed to Chaplin's comic genius).

Harry Langdon was Lloyd's opposite: His comic style was constructed almost exclusively of internal sensations and emotional reactions with almost no dependence on external business and physical gags. His career was also the shortest of any of the comic stars of the silents. He broke into films at Mack Sennett's studio in 1924, reached stardom with a series of features directed by Frank Capra in 1926 and 1927, and fell from popularity just as suddenly in 1928

when Langdon went off to direct his own films and when sound invaded Hollywood.

The union of Capra and Langdon was significant for both men, for like Capra's later heroes, Langdon was a figure of innocence trapped in a mean, brutal world where foolish angels should indeed fear to tread. Langdon was a Mr. Deeds or Mr. Smith distilled into their essential and purest naïveté. He was an overgrown baby with a puffy baby body, pudgy baby face, and tiny, slow baby brain. The Langdon–Capra films put this innocent hero into difficult and dangerous situations from which the child-man could escape only by a miracle (for only a miracle could save an infant in a lion's den).

In *Tramp, Tramp, Tramp* (1926) Harry enters a cross-country walking race to try to win enough money to save his father's business from ruin (a clear Capra motif). Harry's opponents in this athletic contest include not only men who are bigger, tougher, and stronger, but eventually the natural universe itself. Harry miraculously triumphs over an awesome cyclone that levels an entire town but turns around and goes away when Baby Harry hurls a few pebbles at it. In *The Strong Man* (1926) Harry is a weight lifter's assistant who is unexpectedly forced to substitute for his boss. He miraculously manages to subdue a whole gang of bootleggers in the course of his act, ridding a small town of the nasty mobsters who have usurped it (more Capra). Harry's small-town girlfriend in this film, Mary Brown, is blind, a figure as physically helpless and spiritually pure as little Harry himself (and a possible influence on Chaplin, who used a blind woman in *City Lights*). At the end of *The Strong Man* the couple of meeklings inherit the earth. But in *Long Pants* (1927) Harry is unhappy with the purity and innocence of small-town life. He deserts the small-town gal and runs off to the "Big City" in pursuit of an exotic "Bad Woman." Harry discovers, however, that the lady of his dreams is no lady, and he scampers back to his small-town family and sweetheart, a sadder and wiser child.

Although Harry Langdon lacked the comic range and physical gifts of the other silent clowns, his comic style revealed how restrained, how subtle, how slow, how unphysical a silent,

Fig. 6-18
The babyish Harry Langdon flirts with the vamp (Alma Bennett) in **Long Pants.**

physical comedian could be. His films were constructed so that a tiny smile, a blink of the eyes, the wave of a hand, or even, as James Agee observed, a twitch of the muscles at the back of the neck were as significant as a whole sequence of Lloyd's spectacular slips and falls.

Of the new comics, only Buster Keaton could rival Chaplin in his insight into human relationships, into the conflict between the individual man and the immense social machinery that surrounds him; only Keaton could rival Chaplin in making his insight both funny and serious at the same time. The character Keaton fashioned—with his deadpan, understated reactions to the chaos that blooms around him—lacks the compassionate yearnings and pitiable disappointments of Chaplin's tramp, but Keaton compensates for this apparent lack of

passion with the terrific range of his resourcefulness and imagination. A vaudevillean from childhood, Keaton was far more a classic American type than the more European workingclass tramp. Born in Kansas in 1895, Keaton's dour face and dry personality are reminiscent of Grant Wood's farmers in "American Gothic." Beneath this "Great Stone Face," Keaton's inventive brain conceived one outrageously imaginative gag after another, many of them based on bizarre machines and gadgets. The idol of Keaton's generation was Thomas Alva Edison, the supreme inventor as tinkerer, and Keaton loved to tinker with machines (especially trains) as much as anyone. One of those machines was the camera and, very unlike Chaplin, Keaton loved to find new ways to manipulate cinematic gadgetry. For his 1921 short

The Playhouse, Keaton (together with his designer of special effects, Fred Gabourie) came up with a special matte box, capable of splitting the cinema frame into as many as nine fragments. The device allowed him to play every member of a minstrel line, every member of the orchestra, or an entire audience within the same shot. He was by far the most cinematically innovative comedian in film history, but he never saw himself as a genius; he just thought he was good at gags.

On the road to the success he achieves (like saving his train and sweetheart in *The General*, 1927, or growing up in *The Navigator*, 1924) or the goals he is forced to redefine (the house in *One Week*, 1920, will never be perfect and is wrecked by the end of the film, but the honeymooners are happy with each other), the environment throws staggeringly huge obstacles into Buster's path. While Chaplin typically plays with objects he can hold in his hand or sit on, Keaton plays against huge things: an ocean liner he must navigate by himself, a locomotive, a steamboat, a spinning house, a waterfall, a cyclone, a herd of cattle. When he runs into trouble with men, it is rarely with a single figure (an Eric Campbell); he runs into rivers of antagonists, into gangs of opponents: a whole tribe of jungle savages, the entire Union and Confederate armies. Like Charlie, Buster has his troubles with cops, but never with one or just a few cops; in *Cops* (1922), Buster runs into the entire police force. Given the size and complexity of his problems, Buster can take no reliable action, despite his most sensible, practical efforts. The perfect metaphor for the Keaton man is in the three-reel *Day Dreams* (1922) in which Buster, to avoid the police force, takes refuge in the paddle wheel of a ferryboat. The wheel begins turning; Buster begins walking. And walking. And walking. He behaves as sensibly as a man can on a treadmill that he cannot control, but how sensible can life on a treadmill ever be?

Keaton's most magnificent contrast between sensible human behavior and an absurd and uncooperative universe is *Sherlock Jr.* (1924), one of the greatest of comic movies about movies themselves. Buster plays a projectionist in a small town (similar to the town where Kea-

Fig. 6-19

Fig. 6-20

The montage sequence of Sherlock Jr.: *Buster's dive into the sea (Fig. 6-19) splashes down in a snowy forest (Fig. 6-20).*

ton was born) who falls asleep to dream himself into the movie he is projecting. The film-within-a-film that follows permits Buster to demonstrate spectacular physical skills; Keaton was one of the greatest performer-athletes in film history, and his chase sequences are among the greatest of cinema chases. As opposed to Sennett's miscellaneous chases of frantic mechanical puppets and Chaplin's chases as choreographed ballets, Keaton's chases (in *Sherlock Jr.,* in *Seven Chances,* 1925, and in *The General*) are breathtaking exercises by a single racing body—running faster, leaping higher, falling more gracefully than any human body ever seemingly could—or maneuvering a vehicle at top speed through an impossible situation.

In the most celebrated sequence of *Sherlock Jr.,* Keaton is not in motion but at rest. It is the world itself that moves, thanks to the cinema's ability to shift spaces instantaneously by means of editing. Buster, a mortal physical being, has been trapped in the universe of cinema, which operates according to spatial and temporal laws unknown to physical reality. He simply stands, sits, or jumps, occupying the identical space within the frame, while the physical universe surrounding him switches from desert to ocean to mountain top to city street. It is perhaps the ultimate comic gag created by and commenting upon the cinematic apparatus itself.

Chaplin and Keaton are the two poles of silent comics. Chaplin is sentimental; his gentle smiling women become idols to be revered. Keaton is not sentimental; he stuffs his females into bags and hauls them around like sacks of potatoes; he satirizes their finicky incompetence and even shakes the daylights out of the young lady in *The General* who feeds their racing locomotive only the unblemished pieces of wood— then he kisses her. It was especially appropriate and touching to see the two opposites, Chaplin and Keaton, united in *Limelight* (1952), both playing great clowns who were losing their audiences and feared they were losing their touch. It may be no accident that one of the most important theatre pieces of our era, *Waiting for Godot,* was produced in the same year as *Limelight* and used the same metaphor of two old tramps whose act (in *Godot* their act is their life) has become a bomb. If the Godot of Samuel Beckett's title suggests Charlot, it should also be remembered that Beckett wrote a film script especially for Buster Keaton, *Film* (1965, directed by Alan Schneider), and that in the 1930s Beckett studied the works of Eisenstein and Pudovkin.

No two films more clearly reveal the contrasting strengths and interests of the two clowns than *The Gold Rush* (1925) and *The Gen-*

eral (1927). Like Chaplin's short comedies, *The Gold Rush* is an episodic series of highly developed, individual situations. The mortar that keeps these bricks together is a mixture of the film's locale (the white, frozen wastes), the strivings and disappointments of Charlie, and the particular thematic view the film takes of those strivings (the quest for gold and for love, those two familiar goals, in an icy, cannibalistic jungle). *The Gold Rush* uses one of Chaplin's favorite figures, the circle, to structure the sequence of episodes: Prologue (the journey to Alaska), the Cabin, the Dance Hall, the Cabin, Epilogue (the journey home)—a perfect circle.

The individual sequences of *The Gold Rush* are rich both in Chaplin's comic ingenuity and in his ability to render pathos. Several of the comic sequences have become justifiably famous. In the first cabin scene, a hungry Charlie cooks his shoe, carves the sole like a prime rib of beef, salts it to taste, and then eats it like a gourmet, twirling the shoelaces around his fork like spaghetti, sucking the nails like chicken bones, offering his disgruntled partner (who has been chewing the upper half of the shoe as if it were just a shoe) a bent nail as a wishbone. This is the Chaplin who treats one object (a shoe) as if it were another kind of object (a feast), the same minute observation he used in dissecting the clock in *The Pawnshop;* it is also the definitive example of the tramp as a gentleman—that is, of comic contrast. And unlike the Sennett world where bullets can't kill, the funny business here has permanent consequences: Characters really die in *The Gold Rush,* and once his boot has been boiled, Charlie spends the rest of the picture with his foot wrapped in rags.

But the comic business is matched by the pathos that Charlie can generate, often growing out of the comic business itself. Charlie's saddest moment is when Georgia (played by Georgia Hale), the woman he loves, whose picture and flower he preserves beneath his pillow, callously stands him up on New Year's Eve. When Charlie realizes that it is midnight and she is not coming, he opens his door and listens to the happy townspeople singing "Auld Lang Syne" (an excellent translation of sound—a song— into purely visual terms). The film cuts back and forth between Charlie, the outsider, stand-

Fig. 6-21
The Gold Rush: *Charlie's forks dance the "Oceana Roll."*

ing silently and alone in a doorway, and the throng of revelers in the dance hall, clasping hands in a circle and singing exuberantly together. But this pathetic moment would have been impossible without the previous comic one in which Charlie falls asleep and dreams he is entertaining Georgia and her girlfriends with his "Oceana Roll." Charlie's joy, his naïve sincerity, his charm, his gentleness, all show on his face as he gracefully makes the two rolls kick, step, and twirl over the table on the ends of two forks. The happiness of the comic dream sequence sets up the pathos of the subsequently painful reality.

If the reality proves painful for Charlie, it is because the lust for gold makes it so. The film's theme is its consistent indictment of what the pursuit of the material does to the human animal; as in *Greed,* it makes them inhuman animals. Charlie has come to the most materialistic of places—a place where life is hard, dangerous, brutal, uncomfortable, and unkind. Unlike the life of Nanook, whose hardness becomes a virtue in itself, the men who have rushed for gold want to endure hardship only long enough

to snatch up enough nuggets to go home and live easy. The quest for gold creates a Black Larsen who casually murders and purposely fails to help his starving fellows. It creates a Jack, Georgia's handsome boyfriend, who treats people like furniture. Just as Charlie's genuine compassion reveals the emptiness of Jack's protestations of love, Chaplin's film technique makes an unsympathetic bully out of the conventional Hollywood leading man.

The rush toward gold perverts both love and friendship. Georgia herself, though Charlie perceives her inner beauty, has become hardened and callous from her strictly cash relationships with people in the isolated dance hall. And Charlie's partner, Big Jim McKay (Mack Swain), is one of those fair-weather friends whose feelings are the functions of expediency. When Big Jim gets hungry, he literally tries to eat Charlie; although Jim's seeing his buddy as a big chicken is comic, the implied cannibalism is not. Later, Big Jim needs Charlie to direct him to his claim; once again Charlie becomes a friend because he is needed. But when Jim and Charlie get stuck in the cabin that teeters on the edge of a cliff, the two men turn into dogs again, each trying to scramble out of the cabin by himself, stepping on the other to do so.

Whereas *The Gold Rush* combines a thematic unity with the episodic structure that exhausts individual situations, the thematic coherence of *The General* is itself the product of the film's tight narrative unity. *The General* is the first, probably the greatest comic epic in film form. Like every comic epic, *The General* is the story of a journey, of the road (albeit a railroad). As in every comic epic (think of *The Odyssey*), the protagonist suffers a series of hardships and dangerous adventures before achieving the rewards and comforts of returning home. As in every comic epic (think of *Don Quixote*), there is a comic insufficiency in the protagonist and a disparity between his powers and the task he sets out to accomplish—but Buster triumphs despite his insufficiencies. Everything in the Chaplin film, every gag, every piece of business, every thematic contrast, is subordinate to the delineation of the tramp's character and the qualities that make him both lonely and superior to the men who have betrayed their humanity to keep from being lonely. Everything

Fig. 6-22
The General: *Johnny Gray (Buster Keaton) goes about his business while his train carries him behind the enemy's lines.*

in *The General* — every gag, every piece of business — is subordinate to the film's driving narrative, its story of Johnny Gray's race to save his three loves: his girl, his country, and, most important of all, his locomotive (whose name is "The General").

The great question posed by *The General* in the course of its narrative is how to perform heroic action in a crazy universe, where the easy and the impossible are reversed, as are the heroic and the mundane. Buster, with his typical deadpan expression, merely tries to go about his business while the world around him goes mad. A metaphor for the whole film is the shot in which Johnny/Buster is so busy chopping wood to feed his engine that he fails to notice that the train is racing past row after row of

blue uniforms marching in the opposite direction; he has inadvertently crossed behind the enemy's lines. Johnny Gray simply wants to run his train; unfortunately, the Union Army has stolen the train and wants to use it to destroy his fellow Confederates. In the course of trying to save the train, Johnny rescues his lady love and accidentally wins a terrific victory for the South.

That heroism occurs as a series of frantic yet graceful accidents in *The General* is at the center of its moral thrust. It is an accident that the cannon, aimed squarely at Johnny, does not go off until the train rounds a curve, discharging its huge ball at the enemy instead of at the protagonist. It is an accident that Johnny's train comes to a rail switch just in time to detour the

Fig. 6.23
The pragmatist turns obstacles into tools.

pursuing train. Just as wealth, material success, is accidental in *The Gold Rush* (and an accident not worth waiting for—whereas Georgia is), heroism and successful military strategy are accidental in *The General*. How less heroic, how less pretentious, less grand can a man be than the pragmatic and unassuming Buster?

The denigration, or redefinition, of the heroic is as constant an element in *The General* as the denigration of gold (the redefinition of wealth) is in *The Gold Rush*. The plot is triggered by Johnny Gray's rejection by the Confederate Army. He fears he has been found wanting, but the Confederacy vitally needs him at home, running his locomotive. Nevertheless, his girl and her family ostracize Johnny as an unheroic coward, a shirker, and the rest of the film demonstrates what heroism really is and what it is really worth. Johnny uses the most

practical, least heroic of available tools to defeat the northern army: boxes of freight, pieces of wood, the locomotive's kerosene lantern. Hardheadedness and improvisation, not ego and gallantry, win the day.

Such antiheroism is common to all the Keaton comedies; he debunks chivalric mountain feuds in *Our Hospitality* (1923), pugilistic prowess in *Battling Butler* (1926), athletic prowess in *College* (1927), and riverboat romance in *Steamboat Bill, Jr.* (1928). What distinguishes *The General* is that the senseless object, the immense infernal machine of this film, is war. Men themselves have been transformed into a machine (an army), and the business of this machine is murder and destruction.

The film is as shrewd, as caustic, as hard-edged as Johnny Gray himself. His sweetheart (played by Marion Mack), a typical figure of sentiment and romance (her name is Annabelle Lee!), is degraded into an incompetent and feeble representative of romantic notions—until she learns the ropes. In the course of the film, pursuing "The General," Johnny becomes an actual general and Miss Lee grows up.

The ultimate proof of the power of *The Gold Rush* and *The General* is that they need not be referred to as great silent films; they are merely great films. For both of them, silence was not a limitation but a virtue. It is inconceivable that the two films could have been any better with talk; by removing our complete concentration on the visual they could only have been worse. With such control of physical business, thematic consistency, appropriate structure, placement of the camera, and functional editing, neither *The Gold Rush* nor *The General* requires speech to speak.

Hollywood and the Jazz Age

American movies of 1915–1927 are important collectively as a social barometer, indicating the evolving spirit, values, and attitudes of American society during that period. But the cinema was only one of the American arts that grew to maturity at this time. There were startling innovations in American fiction (with the first major novels of Ernest Hemingway, John Dos Passos, William Faulkner, F. Scott Fitzgerald, and Sinclair Lewis), in American drama (whether the tragedies of Eugene O'Neill or the fast-paced social comedies of George S. Kaufman and Marc Connelly, of Ben Hecht and Charles MacArthur), in American poetry (with Ezra Pound, T. S. Eliot, Gertrude Stein, Wallace Stevens, and the flourishing little magazines, like Harriet Monroe's *Poetry*), in American theatre music (with Jerome Kern, George and Ira Gershwin, Richard Rodgers and Lorenz Hart), and in American painting, journalism, and dance as well (when Grant Wood, Ben Shahn, H. L. Mencken, Martha Graham, Katherine Dunham, and Virgil Thomson first appeared on the American scene).

It was a period of creative excitement and invention—the profuse flowering of an American artistic tradition over the full spectrum of arts and letters. A later generation of critics

would find a name—Modernism—for this energetic explosion of artistic activity that rebelled against the forms and norms of a previous generation. And somewhere in the middle of it were the movies. They may not have been as consistently committed to experimental innovation as some of the other arts, but all the artists went to the movies, and so did everyone who read their novels, saw their plays, discussed their poems, and hummed their tunes. As both John Dos Passos and Gertrude Stein readily admitted, they were doing what the cinema was doing.

The postwar years of the late teens and twenties saw many important changes in American life. It is all too easy to mystify history by selecting a single image to stand for a whole period, but there is something inevitable about the image of a flapper, a "jazz baby," in a short beaded dress and bobbed hair, wearing a jeweled headband, holding a glass of champagne, dancing the Charleston. More than anything else, the Jazz Age seems a period of contradictions. Conservative Republican presidents (Harding, Coolidge, and Hoover) explicitly pledged to return the nation to "normalcy" in the 1920s, one of the least conservative and least "normal" decades of the century. The sale and purchase of liquor may have been against the law, but more Americans, law-abiding citizens in every other way, drank more booze than they ever had before. Readers who devoured Fitzgerald's stories about the wild lives of the very rich were themselves solidly bourgeois, middle class. There were Lubitsch's and DeMille's film comedies about the lives of the rich elite, who lived either in Europe or on Long Island, alongside Lloyd's film comedies about the most normal mid-American, middle-class aspirations. There were Chaplin's film comedies that despised the pursuit of merely material goods, while American society seemed hell-bent on acquiring as many of those goods as possible—the first generation of automobiles, refrigerators, and radios. Those domestic machines and mechanical gadgets by which modern American life itself is often defined first entered middle-class American lives in the twenties.

The word *jazz* entered the American language at the same time. It didn't mean anything

Jazz Age partying of the Veddy Veddy Rich in MGM's **This Modern Age** *(1931)—with Joan Crawford, Neil Hamilton, and champagne poolside.*

Fig. 6-24

Fig. 6-25

very precisely; for those who hated it, jazz meant musical noise that was loud and vulgar, no doubt stimulating to the baser animal passions. For those who loved it, jazz was the rhythmic music you danced to and made love to, whether by black composers and musicians like Fats Waller, Bessie Smith, Ethel Waters, and Duke Ellington or white composers and musicians like George Gershwin, Paul Whiteman, Bix Beiderbeck, and Helen Kane. Jazz meant about the same thing that Rock did a half-century later—the rhythmic, exuberant, liberating music to which young Americans dance.

At the center of these changes and contradictions was the new American woman—or, rather, women. The many new types of women on movie screens indicated the conflicting varieties of experience in modern American life. At one extreme there was Mary Pickford, "America's Sweetheart," who, along with Chaplin, was one of the two greatest stars of the late 1910s. She personified the woman as child—sweet, innocent, virgin (for sure), but perky, bright, and charming too. Pickford's sexual identity was so abstractly pure that she was as likely to

play boys as girls in many of her films. Despite the attempts of historians to consign her to D. W. Griffith's earlier Age of Innocence, Pickford survived as a star throughout the roaring twenties. At the opposite pole there were several alternatives to Pickford. One was the woman of adventure and daring, personified by Pearl White, the Queen of American serials, beginning with *The Perils of Pauline* in 1914. White represented the woman less as suffering victim than as active and aggressive challenger of villainy—descending from the kind of heady courage displayed by Blanche Sweet in Griffith's *The Lonedale Operator*. Another alternative was the more adult, dignified, and controlled woman of grace and manners, represented by such stars as Gloria Swanson, Lillian Gish, Lois Wilson, and Pauline Frederick —women who personified the era's notions of a true Lady.

The rebellious alternative to Pickford's adolescent spunk was Clara Bow, the "It Girl," and *It*, like jazz, was another of the important if vague words that indicated the values of the decade. *It* was coined and popularized by British author Elinor Glyn in a series of books from

Fig. 6-26

Fig. 6-28

Fig. 6-27

American and European It. Fig. 6-26: Clara Bow, the
"It Girl." Figs. 6-27, 6-28, 6-29: Greta Garbo.

Fig. 6-29

Three Weeks (1907) to *It* (1927)—sexually scandalous bourgeois novels by a woman for women readers. *It* was a vague euphemism for sex (hence the deliberate irony of Cole Porter's 1928 song hit, "Let's Do It") and implied a wide range of sexual suggestions: sex appeal, sexual energy, sexual drive, the sex act itself, or a more general attitude toward that sexual activity. The girl, like Clara Bow, who had It both exuded bouncy sexual energy and appeared as if she might welcome a sexual invitation (even if she coyly never accepted It). One could have It, want It, show It, or think about It, but not *do* It.

American It was somewhat different from European It. While American-born stars with It (Clara Bow, Joan Crawford, Mae McAvoy) were bouncy flappers with get-up-and-go, European-born stars with It were mysterious Circes (Greta Garbo, Pola Negri) with lie-back-and-wait. Louise Brooks was the rare American It girl who flowered in German soil (*Pandora's Box*, 1928, and *Diary of a Lost Girl*, 1929, both directed by G. W. Pabst). Brooks and Garbo (who did her best work in such MGM films as *Flesh and the Devil*, 1926; *Mata Hari*, 1931; *Grand Hotel*, 1932; *Queen Christina*, 1933; *Anna Karenina*, 1935; *Camille*, 1937; and *Ninotchka*, 1939) were more than international stars: They were essential mysteries, icons of the cinema, whose intimate relationship with the camera promised but withheld absolute knowledge. The camera studied the endlessly fascinating Garbo—her face, her moods, the mask of her thoughts—as it had no one else, and always came away with a rich set of questions, energized rather than satiated by the enigmatic power of her being, which felt as simple and complex, as familiar and strange as one's own; in that sense she was the cinema's first truly Existential figure.

In the 1920s, these European It goddesses distilled and incarnated the experience of that generation of American males who marched off to France singing "Over There," met the mademoiselles about whom they sang "Hinky Dinky Parley Voo," and returned to America singing "How Ya Gonna Keep 'Em Down on the Farm, After They've Seen Paree?"

Americans of the 1920s were both attracted to exotic foreignness and distrustful of its strangeness. If one type of European exotica dominated American screens in the 1920s, the decade was also the first to impose strict limitations on immigration from Europe to America, consistent with the suspicious hostility that lurked beneath the trial and execution of Sacco and Vanzetti as dangerous anarchists. If Europe sent Hollywood its dangerous Circes, it also sent America its dangerous ideas that produced revolutions.

When Hollywood reflected on its own cultural history, with the writing of those explicit moral instructions that became the Production Code of 1930, it confessed that its films of the 1920s were more lascivious and suggestive than they ought to have been. The writers of the Code then blamed that permissiveness on the mores of the period itself, whose "roaring" hedonism and "wonderful nonsense" came tumbling down with the Wall Street Crash of October 1929. This recantation of Jazz Age values indicated not only the differences in American social attitudes just one decade later, but also the changes in an industry seeking not to lose the patronage of its most dependable middle-class customers.

The powerful images of female stars are among the most enduring, interesting, and revealing traces of this era's films. There were exceptional male figures—the virtuoso comics (Chaplin, Keaton, Laurel and Hardy), the masculine counterparts of European exotica (Valentino, Ramon Novarro, Rod La Rocque), the jazzy Jolson, the dashing American "It boys" (Fairbanks, John Gilbert), and the unclassifiable Lon Chaney. But relatively few male faces and figures from the 1920s have survived in our cultural memory. Of course, many of the films themselves have been lost, so little did anyone think of preserving them, and many others are disintegrating in the vaults of studios and museums, rarely—if ever—shown. The faces of the era's women suggest a portrait of American life as a whole. As Norma Desmond (played by Gloria Swanson) put it in *Sunset Boulevard:* "We had faces then." For most of us, those faces are the Jazz Age.

7

The German Golden Age

In the final year of World War I, the German government wondered whether preferring bullets to pictures had been a tactical error. Whatever the results of the battles at the front, the German nation and German character were losing terribly on the screens of the world. In the early years of the war, the American film, mirroring the nation's neutrality, did not take a consistent side in its view of the conflict in Europe. Some American films expressly advocated neutrality; others, like *Civilization* and *Intolerance,* preached pacifism. But as America itself prepared to enter the war, its films began to prepare it to prepare. In 1916, Vitagraph's J. Stuart Blackton made *The Battle Cry of Peace,* the first of a series of films urging "defenseless America" to defend itself. Blackton was continuing his tradition of making patriotic war films some twenty years after *Tearing Down the Spanish Flag.* The American war films predictably painted the enemy as a villainous, vicious Hun; the evil, sinister, outwardly polished and inwardly corrupt Erich von Stroheim was the perfect stereotype of this newest movie bad guy.

There was no screen antidote to this single stereotypic portrait, so the German government decided to produce one. In November 1917, the government collected the tiny, cha-otic fragments of the German film industry together into a single, large filmmaking unit, Universum Film A.G., known subsequently to the world as Ufa. Ufa's job was to make movies that would boost the German spirit at home and sell the German character and position abroad. The war ended before Ufa could accomplish either goal; but the huge movie company, with its studios at Neubabelsberg near Berlin, was still standing after the armistice had been signed. The great era of German films was born in those studios.

The German Golden Age of film was a very short one, from the making of *The Cabinet of Dr. Caligari* in 1919 to Hitler's absorption of the German film industry in 1933. The great burst of artistic activity that followed the fall of the Kaiser and the founding of the Weimar Republic, the new spirit of intellectual and creative freedom in Germany, made itself felt in all the arts (in the pictorial and plastic arts, the founding of the Bauhaus group by Kandinsky and Klee; in the theatre, the plays of Brecht and the staging of Erwin Piscator), but especially in the cinema. The great German contribution in these years of intellectual freedom and artistic innovation was, as almost all post-Griffith cinematic innovations have been, a refinement of one of the potentialities of the medium that Griffith had discovered. If Griffith's two great accomplishments were his realization of the power of atmosphere, decor, and texture within a shot and the power of editing to join shots, it was the genius of the German film to refine and develop the former (the Soviet film developed the latter). The German film, in an era of silence, made the aura, the mood, the tone of the shot's visual qualities speak—so well that the best German films of the era contain the barest minimum of intertitles, or none at all.

Further, the German filmmakers realized that the emotional tensions and sensations in a film need not be performed solely for a passive, objective camera. The camera, rather than taking the stance of an impartial observer, could itself mirror the subjective feelings of a single character experiencing an event. To use an analogy with the novel, the German filmmaker realized that the camera, like the pen, could narrate a story in the first person as well as the third. Griffith used an occasional flight into subjectivity—his cut-aways to reveal a character's thoughts, the tracking camera galloping with the horses to the rescue—but Griffith's subjective moments were always in brackets. He used specific conventions to inform the audience that it was entering the personal experience of a character. The subjectivity in the German film is rarely set off in brackets; the boundary between subjective and objective perceptions becomes indefinite: The world might look crazy because someone sees it that way or because it *is* that way, burdened with wordless meaning. To this idea—that the look and style of the visible, external universe can take its shape, color, and texture from internal human sensations—critics assigned a single term: Expressionism. The principle dominated the early twentieth century painting and drama of Germany as well as its cinema.

The dependence of the German film on the evocations of its *mise-en-scène* led to its becoming completely a studio product. The only way to make sure that the lighting, the decor, the architectural shapes, the relationships of blacks, whites, and grays were perfect was to film in a completely controlled environment. Even outdoor scenes were shot inside the four walls and ceiling of a studio. The vastness, the freedom of the outdoors that had become one of the sources of power of both the American and the Swedish film, was rejected by the Germans. The result was not only a perfect control of style and decor but also a feeling of claustrophobia that enhanced the mood of many of the best films, which were also claustrophobic in content. The totally studio-produced films emphasized the importance of the designer, whose job was to conceive and decorate enormous indoor cities. These designers—later called art directors or in some cases production designers—came to films from painting, theatre, and architecture, having absorbed the styles of many of the new artistic movements of postwar Europe: Expressionism, Cubism, Constructivism, and other forms of abstraction and analysis. The German film could never have exerted its influence without its talented painter–architect designers, the most notable of whom were Hermann Warm, Walther Röhrig, Walther Reimann, Robert Herlth, Albin Grau, and Ernö Metzner.

The emphasis on the studio production and the consolidation of talent in a single company produced a studio system very different from Hollywood's. Unlike the competing factories of Hollywood, the German studio was far more a combination of artists working with each other because they were devoted to their product rather than to receipts. Although there were competitors with Ufa in the twenties, many of them worked so closely with the major producer that merger was inevitable (Decla-Bioscop, for example). Ufa's great producer, Erich Pommer, was a man of artistic judgment and taste who stimulated mediocre directors to do their very best work (E. A. Dupont's *Variety*, 1925, for example) rather than the reverse. Instead of building a star system, the German studio developed a repertory company, emphasizing the play and not the player, the character and not the personality. The German film actor needed variety and range, not a single trait to be milked over and over again. The greatest of the German repertory actors were Emil Jannings, Werner Krauss, Conrad Veidt, Fritz Körtner, Lil Dagover, Asta Nielsen, Lya de Putti, and Pola Negri. Hollywood imported most of them and tried to turn them into stars;

the attempt was inconsistently successful. Many of these actors had been trained by the greatest German theatre director of the period, Max Reinhardt, who had conceived a style of theatre that depended as much on visual decor as on the actor and playwright. Reinhardt was influential on the German cinema of the Weimar Republic, not only for his actors and Expressionist visual conceptions but also for the style of play he pioneered, the *Kammerspiel*, a "chamber theatre" for small audiences, with small casts, intimately psychological portraits, and dim lighting (with spotlights to isolate part of the stage or action and with extensive use of *chiaroscuro*). Many of the greatest German films of the 1920s would also be intimate "chamber" dramas, a genre called the *Kammerspielfilm*.

The German studio also gave a great deal of freedom to its cameramen; they were encouraged to develop new and revealing ways of looking at things. The Hollywood cameraman had become more and more tied to the most functional, most familiar way of recording a scene. Two German cameramen in particular, Fritz Arno Wagner and Karl Freund, used their freedom to show how much a camera could really do.

The German films of this great era were of two types: either fantastic and mystical or realistic and psychological. One was steeped in the traditional German Romanticism of love and death; the other revealed the new German intellectual currents of Freud and Weber. In the films of fantasy and horror, the action revolves around the occult, the mysterious, the metaphysical. These are films of fantastic monsters in human dress, of what lives beyond the grave, of dream kingdoms of the past and of the future. The German architect–painters could use their imaginations to turn these eerie, abstract, intangible regions into concrete, visual domains. In the psychological film, the action revolves around the inner thoughts and feelings of the characters, their needs, their lusts, their frustrations. Of the Americans, only von Stroheim and von Sternberg, perhaps showing their Teutonic origins, made such internalized, sensation-centered films. Unlike the fantasy films, which usually are set in some romantic time and place, the psychological films are set in a squalid, seamy, and often middle-class

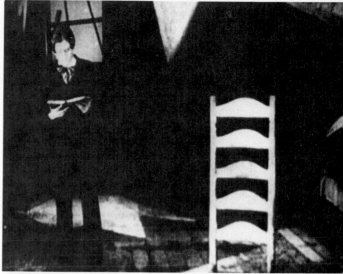

Fig. 7-1
The Cabinet of Dr. Caligari: *a madman's vision of the world—impossibly shaped windows, exaggeratedly high furniture, and geometric shadows.*

present. The architect–painters could use their imaginations to turn the tawdry, dirty, depressing rooms and streets into complex, detailed, realistic studio slums.

Fantasy

The film that signaled the start of the new German era in 1919, *The Cabinet of Dr. Caligari* (released 1920), appropriately combined both the mystical and the psychological. Its central plot was a story of horror, of murder, of superhuman powers. An enigmatic and menacing hypnotist (Werner Krauss) opens a stall at a fair in the town of Holstenwall; his act demonstrates his mastery over a sleepwalker he has apparently hypnotized, Cesare (Conrad Veidt). A rash of murders breaks out in the town. The police have no clues. The film's narrator–protagonist, Francis, suspects Caligari, shadows him, and eventually discovers that he forces his slave, Cesare, to murder the victims while the hypnotist substitutes a life-sized dummy resembling Cesare in the coffin-like box (the cabinet) to fool the police. Francis continues to follow the master who, it turns out, is also the director of the state insane asylum. The keeper of the insane is himself insane, a monster who has discovered the medieval formula of Caligari for subduing men's minds and who has set out to "become Caligari." Francis exposes the monster; the monster goes mad. The orderlies stuff Caligari into a strait jacket and lock him in a cell. This is as far as the central plot of *Caligari* goes. It is also as far as its writers, Carl Mayer (who would become the most influential of the German scenarists) and Hans Janowitz, wanted it to go.

But *Caligari* goes further. The entire central plot is bracketed by a frame, conceived by Fritz Lang. The film begins with Francis informing a listener (and us) that he has a dreadful story to tell. To set a horrific, supernatural tale within a frame is, of course, a traditional literary device (as in Mary Shelley's *Frankenstein* or Henry James's *The Turn of the Screw*), the means to anchor a fantastic story in reality (as well as isolate it, fence it in) and thereby increase our credulity. The setting of this opening, framing sequence seems like a park — there are trees, vines, a wall, benches. But there is something disturbing about it: It is too bare, too cold; the woman who walks past seems somnambulistic, ethereal. Only at the end of the film do we discover that the opening and closing framing sequences are set not in a park but on the grounds of an asylum, that Francis himself is a patient, that many of the characters in his tale (like the gentle Cesare) are also patients, and that the so-called Caligari is the director of the asylum. And it is not Caligari who winds up in a cell with a strait jacket but Francis, whose feverish accusations about the director have necessitated his confinement. The surprise at the end of the film is our discovery that the tale we assumed to be one of horror and of superhuman powers is really a paranoid's fantasy.

Our discovery of the disease in the narrator's brain suddenly illuminates the principle of the film's unnatural decor. Throughout the film the Expressionist world of the horror tale has been striking: the grotesque painted shadows on streets and stairs; the irregular, nonperpendicular chimneys, doors, and windows; the exaggerated heights of the furniture; the boldly painted makeup. This grotesque world is not simply a decorative stunt; it is, thanks to Lang's psychological "twist," the way Francis sees the world. That was how Lang, the original director assigned to the project, saw it; how Robert Wiene did direct it; and why the writers objected. Rather than expose an insane world (that could tyrannically send an innocent — or soldier — like Cesare to kill against his will), their story now implied that the world is fine, Francis is nuts, and Caligari knows best.

The striking effect of the film's design (by Warm, Röhrig, and Reimann) is not just the look but the unnatural feel of it. Walls, floors, and ceilings bear a structurally impossible relationship to one another; buildings so constructed could never stand. Skin, that soft and malleable material of nature, becomes caked and frozen with paint. Most unnatural of all, the world of *Caligari* is a world without sunlight. Shadows of light and dark, shafts where the sun would normally cast its shadow, have been painted on the sets. To use paint to make a shadow where the sun would normally make one emphasizes the fact that no sun exists. The outdoor scenes feel as if they were shot indoors. And they were. Here was the perfect use of the total studio film. It showed that an entire world (whether expressionistic *or* realistic) could be created artificially, as *Caligari*'s obviously had to be.

The interest in *The Cabinet of Dr. Caligari* is not only in the way the film looks but in the ambiguities that the film-within-a-film generates. The narrative is no simple tale told by an idiot. Is there no truth at all in Francis's story of the Holstenwall murders? And if the kindly doctor is really not the demented Caligari, why does it feel so creepy when he says, at the very end, that he now knows "how to cure" Francis? And why does the asylum look no more natural in the closing framing sequence (supposedly an objective point of view) than it did in Francis's narration? And what is the relevance of the film's clear antagonism to bureaucracy? Wiene ridicules the police and the authorities with their ridiculously high, skinny desks and their red tape. The insane asylum that the doctor heads is yet another bureaucratic enterprise with its procedures, methods, and assistants. Is one bureaucracy better than the other? Are we

Fig. 7-2   *Fig. 7-3*

Caligari's faces of paint. Fig. 7-2: Dr. Caligari (Werner Krauss); Fig. 7-3: Cesare (Conrad Veidt).

crazy, or is it the government? Is this the world of Kafka come true?

Perhaps there are no answers. Perhaps the film's ambiguities and internal contradictions stem from the conflict between the writers, who conceived one kind of story, and the director, who accepted another. Whatever the underlying reason, the ambiguities and ambivalences of *Caligari* enrich it.

Perhaps no major work in film history has attracted as many theoretical sticks and stones as *Caligari*. Theorists André Bazin, Erwin Panofsky, and Siegfried Kracauer are unanimous in believing that the film is a cinematic mistake, that it "prestylizes reality," that it violates the inherent photographic realism of the medium, that it substitutes a world of painted artifice for the rich resources of nature. Despite these later arguments, the film had an immense influence on other filmmakers, not only in Germany but in France, where "Caligarism," though detested by some, inspired many of the early avant-garde experiments in abstract cinema, in film as "painting-in-motion" rather than as realistic narrative of natural events in natural set-

tings. If it was the first "art film" and the first feature that *had* to be shot in a studio, *The Cabinet of Dr. Caligari* has also been capable of intriguing and fascinating audiences, of weaving its mysterious, hypnotic spell, for over seventy years.

Of the mystical children of *Caligari*, Fritz Lang's *Destiny* (1921) is among the most interesting. Lang, in collaboration with his author-wife, Thea von Harbou, who wrote most of his German films, is more famous for a series of psychological studies of the activities of gamblers, murderers, master criminals, and spies (*The Spiders; Dr. Mabuse, the Gambler; Spies; M*). But he also made several metaphysical-fantasy films. In *Destiny*, a young woman and her lover enter a new town; on the road they encounter a shadowy, spectral stranger. The stranger has bought a piece of land near the town's cemetery and has enclosed it with an immense stone wall that lacks a door or any other physical means of entering. The girl's lover disappears; when she discovers that he is a prisoner beyond the wall, she frenziedly starts to drink a poisonous drug. Lang cuts to the huge wall where she sees the transparent images of souls entering the region beyond the wall. The way in is metaphysical, not physical.

The wall surrounds the kingdom of death; the mysterious stranger is Death himself, and a tired, sad Death he is, superintending the candles of human life that inevitably flicker out. The girl pleads for the life of her lover; Death tiredly offers her a chance to save him, pointing out three candles whose lights have begun to flicker. The girl claims that love can conquer death, and she sets off to save at least one of the three lights.

Each of these "lights" is a story in a faroff land: a middle-eastern Moslem city, Renaissance Venice, and a magical China. In all three the girl and her lover are reincarnated as two young lovers whose monarchs have declared war on their love. In all three reincarnations, the young man dies; the girl's love does not conquer death. After her failure, Death gives the girl one more chance; she can return to life and redeem her lover's being if she can offer another life in trade. She soon runs into a burning hospital to save an infant trapped there. Death meets her inside and asks her for the child as the pawn. She considers and then refuses; she will not kill the infant to save her lover. Instead, the girl herself dies in the fire; her soul and her lover's are thereby reunited as their transparent images climb a hill and stand against the sky. Love, in dying, has ironically conquered death.

The power of the film lies in its combination of the pictorial sense of the director and the magnificent visual creations of the designers (Warm, Röhrig, Herlth). The huge, gray wall of Death dwarfs the black-clad human figures who stand in front of it; its horizontal and vertical lines run off the frame at top, right, and left—a powerful visual metaphor for the infiniteness and inaccessibility of fate. Death's cave of the candles—a dark, hazy (a special distortion-lens effect), smoky den, with its numberless collection of thin, white candles with bouncing, waving flames—just as effectively and unpretentiously symbolizes the fragility of human life, the irreversible direction of its progress, and the inexorable control of fate over that progress. Equally memorable is

Fig. 7-4
Destiny: *the Cave of the Candles (Lil Dagover and Bernhard Götzke).*

the care taken in creating each of the fantastic kingdoms for the stories of the three lights: the minarets and mosaics of the Arabian city; the canals, the flights of steps, the arched bridges streaming with revelers in the Venice sequence; the flying horse, the flying carpet, the tiny army that emerges from beneath the magician's legs in the China sequence. Lang uses the trick effects of the camera as well as the atmospheric architecture of the designers: superimposition (to depict the souls of the dead), the dissolve (to show a dead infant materializing in Death's arms), vertical masking (to emphasize the height and narrowness of arches and steps), Mélièsian stop-action (to metamorphose a man into a cactus or a pig).

All these gimmicks may make *Destiny* seem as superficial an exercise as DeMille's *Male and Female* or Fairbanks's *The Thief of Bagdad,* with which it has obvious affinities. Like the DeMille film, *Destiny* uses multiple locales and hence is enhanced by the splash of multiple sets, costumes, and customs. Like the Fairbanks film, it presents an entertaining series of surprising cinematic tricks. The Lang film, however, keeps its artistic seriousness because of the unity and consistency of its theme (the war of love and death), because of the clear purpose of its structure (a film descendant of the medieval romance in which the protagonist must face the challenge of a series of tests), and because of the fatalism and melancholy of its tone. If the film resembles DeMille or Fairbanks, it also has unmistakable affinities with the work of the later film metaphysician, Ingmar Bergman. The opening scene in the forest in which the coach stops for the stranger feels like the opening of *The Magician;* the awesome, black-cloaked figures of Death in *Destiny* and *The Seventh Seal* are cousins. In its mysticism, in its romantic struggle of love and death, which ends in a romantic truce (both triumph), *Destiny* is more than a surface picture of visual splash.

The same cannot be said of a later Lang film, *Metropolis* (1926, released 1927). Although *Metropolis* is a fantasy of the future and technology rather than a fantasy of the past and romance, like *Destiny* it uses its fantastic setting to demonstrate an abstract theme. Unfortunately, *Metropolis* is all eyes and no brain, all visual with no convincing vision. The film depicts a world of the future where the rich and intelligent live on the earth's surface with their airplanes and trams and skyscrapers, and the workers—who make the society go—live beneath the surface in a drab, utilitarian "city," below which are dark, labyrinthine caverns. Here was Lang's visual translation of the class structure. The hero (played by Gustav Fröhlich), a young rebel, rejects the sheltered lifestyle of the rich—his father, who dresses and behaves like a modern executive, runs Metropolis—and goes to live and struggle with the workers of the underworld. There he meets the spirit of the workers—Maria (played by Brigitte Helm), a proletarian version of the Virgin Mary and Christ all in one—who urges peaceful change and nonviolent progress. Maria is a Christian-Democrat-Humanist (literally Christian since she delivers her political

Fig. 7-5

Fig. 7-6

Fig. 7-7

Metropolis*: human beings reduced to dispirited masses of architecture.*

sermons in a candle-lit cave full of crosses) who formulates the film's political argument: The heart must mediate between head and hands.

The young hero's father, the Master of Metropolis, will have none of this. He hires the evil scientist, Rotwang (played by Rudolf Klein-Rogge: the direct ancestor of Dr. Strangelove, even to the black glove), to manufacture a sexy, vicious robot (Brigitte Helm) who looks exactly like Maria and who will incite the workers to riot; the father's troops can then use the riot to enslave the workers. The workers riot, flood their underground city, and almost destroy the whole society, until the real Maria appears to tranquilize them with her abstract words of political love—and the hero shows up to kill Rotwang. The Master learns his lesson, and his enlightened son, who has lived in both worlds, is designated the society's official "heart" to mediate between head (his daddy) and hands (he shakes hands with the foreman of the workers).

The film demonstrates the dangers of the purely architectural-pictorial premise of many of the German studio films. *Metropolis* is a series of stunning pictures held together by the silliest, wateriest intellectual and dramatic paste. Lang's primary compositional device was to create vast geometrical patterns: row upon row of black-clad workers in boxy elevators; the geometrical machines and the geometrical patterns of workers who serve them; the circle of workers around the warning gong as water seeps into the lower city; the fleeing workers in the flooded streets, a river of bodies that parallels the river of rushing water engulfing their homes; the final triangular configuration of head, heart, and hands.

The emptiness of the film, however, lies in the way it reduces people to patterns—to units of geometrical architecture. What is most fascistic about *Metropolis* is its portrayal of the general lot of human beings as a mass of plodding sheep or wild rioters—in either case, indistinguishable ciphers. Unable to take care of themselves, swayed just as easily by the robot as they are by Maria, the workers are utterly dependent on the beneficence of the ruler above.

The implications of *Metropolis* did not pass unnoticed in its time. It was one of Hitler's fa-

Fig. 7-8

Fig. 7-9

The triumph of Metropolis: *Human beings become architecture again in Leni Riefenstahl's 1935 Nazi celebration film,* Triumph of the Will.

vorite films, and after he had seized control of the government, he invited Lang—a leftist and half Jew—to make films for the Nazis. That Lang diminished people into puppets, crowds into patterns, and political problems into

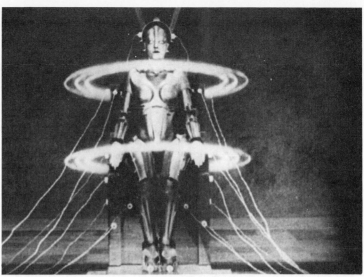

Science as magic: bringing the robot to life in Metropolis.

Fig. 7-10

romantic abstractions exactly suited Hitler's purposes. Lang, however, fled the country; Thea von Harbou stayed, joined the Nazis, and took the job, which she held until she was displaced by Leni Riefenstahl.

Much as *Caligari* had a decisive influence on the horror film, *Metropolis* foreshadowed many developments in the science fiction film (as did Lang's *Woman in the Moon*, 1928, which introduced the countdown), particularly in its vision of the futuristic upper city, in its use of telescreens for spying and communication (seen in Universal's *Flash Gordon* serials as well as in Chaplin's *Modern Times*), and in the design of Rotwang's laboratory, where scientific apparatus, Expressionistic magic, and pure light bring the robot to life (much as in the labs designed at Universal to conduct the juices of life into Frankenstein's monster and, later, the monster's bride).

Of the other films of fantasy and the supernatural, Paul Leni's *Waxworks* (1924) combined the setting of *Caligari* (a fairground "cabinet") with the structure of *Destiny* (three separate stories—of Haroun Al-Raschid, Ivan the Terrible, and Jack the Ripper—in three bizarre and decorative locales). Paul Wegener and Henrik Galeen's *The Golem* (1920, but previously made by the pair in 1914)—the story of a magician-rabbi who brings a clay statue to life

to protect the Jews in the ghetto—is significant for the twisted architecture of its settings (designed by Hans Poelzig) and the fiery, demonic special effects in the scene when Rabbi Loew brings the man of clay to life (more clear evocations of the later Frankenstein series, including the monster's attraction to an innocent playing child). Galeen's version of *The Student of Prague* (1926, previously made by Stellan Rye in 1913) is the mythical story of the double, or *Doppelgänger*, a genre dating back at least to Poe's "William Wilson" and Dostoyevsky's *The Double,* in which a man sells his shadow or reflection only to effect a divorce between his internal and external selves—and to leave on the loose a bad guy who looks just like him. Arthur Robison's *Warning Shadows* (1923) is interesting for its complex and consistent use of shadows: as an element of the film's action; as the profession of one of the main characters, who, like a filmmaker, entertains audiences with shadow plays; as a means of creating a mysterious mood and mystical atmosphere; and as one of the film's key metaphoric motifs.

Perhaps the most noteworthy of the purely horrific descendants of *Caligari* was F. W. Murnau's *Nosferatu, a Symphony of Horror* (1922), an unauthorized adaptation— with a script by Galeen—of Bram Stoker's *Dracula. Nosferatu,* Murnau's first major

Fig. 7-11
Nosferatu: *The vampire (Max Schreck) brings the demons of hell into the regions of nature.*

success, was distinguished in the aura of horror and gloom with which it surrounded the vampire's activities. Unlike later incarnations of Dracula—Bela Lugosi, Christopher Lee, and many others—Murnau's vampire (Max Schreck) was no sexy, suave, intriguing gentleman who, if he chose, stole the lady's heart before he stole her blood. Murnau's vampire was hideous—a shriveled, ashen man with pointed nose, pointed ears, and pointed head. This ugliness made the sexual implications of the vampire's relationship to humans—particularly the use of a bedroom for the primary setting of the nighttime bloodsucking—even more horrifying.

The relatively long relationship of the vampire with each victim, together with the towns-people's assumption that they are the victims of a rat-borne plague, gives *Nosferatu* a feeling of mystical parasitism, of the way that death perpetually feeds off the living. Also memorable are the shots that evoke the deadly emanations of the vampire: the rats in the streets; the phantom ship sailing by itself; the tricky use of negative film and single-frame exposure to depict the gulf between the natural world and the supernatural world of the vampire's castle; the bare, stony walls of the castle itself. Unlike many German filmmakers of the period, Murnau had cinematographer Fritz Arno Wagner shoot these sequences outdoors, in nature; rather than "prestylize" reality as *Caligari* had, Murnau and Wagner and art director Albin Grau found ways to make reality creepy—in many respects, the most crucial and impressive of *Nosferatu*'s achievements. They rejected the typical studio-sculpted forests and hillocks to reveal the conflict of nature and artifice in the narrative, to emphasize that the existence of this vampire in the world was a subversion of the natural order itself.

Significantly, the underlying theme of *Nosferatu* is similar to *Destiny*'s: the conflict of love and death. The film's heroine consciously seduces the deadly menace, who is attracted to her beauty. She keeps him out of his coffin until after the sun rises, and he dissolves into the morning air. Love is the strongest power in the mystical German film.

Psychology

F. W. Murnau's *The Last Laugh* (*Der letzte Mann*, 1924) is the most influential of the psychological sons of *Caligari,* and is probably the most even and most satisfying film of the whole German era. *The Last Laugh* teamed the greatest of Ufa's talents: director, Murnau; producer, Erich Pommer; writer, Carl Mayer; photographer, Karl Freund; designers, Röhrig and Herlth; and central figure, Emil Jannings. The plot is as simple as the plots of the mystical-fantasy films were complex; its emotions are as personal and as carefully motivated as the concepts of the metaphysical films were abstract.

A porter-doorman at a posh hotel (Emil Jannings) bases his self-respect and centers his being on his belief in the importance of his job, which is symbolized by his passionate devotion to his ornate porter's uniform. The almost military uniform (he salutes when he wears it) both defines his existence and is the only feature that impresses his status-conscious, less fortunate neighbors. Because he is old and feeble the porter is stripped of this uniform and given a new one: the white linen jacket of the lavatory attendant. The film then details the impact of this loss of dignity on his emotions and on his family and acquaintances, who reject and taunt him. Rather than leaving the old man stooped in abject despair, the film "takes pity on him" and gives him a happy ending: a sudden inheritance of money that turns him into a kindly but gluttonous gobbler of caviar. The effect of this deliberately contrived ending will be discussed in a moment. Worthy of the fullest and most immediate attention in the film is the rendering of the steady deterioration of the old man's soul once he has lost the uniform that covers his body.

One of the film's great virtues is the performance of Jannings, his clear yet subtle portrayal of the two states of the porter's mind. Wearing his uniform, Jannings walks quickly and erect; his gestures are smart and precise; his smile and buoyancy almost make him seem young. His whole body exudes pride and self-esteem, as well as smugness and vanity. Without the coat he ages fifty years—his body stoops; his gestures are vague and languid; he barely moves at all—he becomes a hunched, shuffling, broken man.

The director and cameraman give Jannings a new and useful ally—the camera itself. Freund's camera tracks and swings and tilts and twirls at key moments in the film. The key principle is not just that the camera moves for the sake of visual variety, but that it has been freed from its stationary tripod in order to illuminate narrative and psychological content. The camera actually serves as the emotional mirror of the old man's soul; sometimes its lens becomes his own eyes. When the world becomes blurry or confusing or insufferable for him, the camera photographs the way the world looks and feels to him, the way he responds to it. The camera becomes, in effect, the other major character with whom Jannings plays his scenes, and they work so well together that verbal explanations (titles) become almost unnecessary. (*The Last Laugh* has no intertitles for dialogue, but it does have one narrative intertitle—to introduce the unrealistic ending—and several shots of objects that we read: a newspaper article about the legacy, a wedding cake. For export prints, shots were taken of cakes decorated and newspapers printed in French, English, and other languages, just as the one intertitle was translated.)

The power of the liberated camera strikes the viewer in the very opening of the film. In the first shot, the camera (mounted on a bicycle) rides down the elevator of the Hotel Atlantic; after a barely perceptible cut,

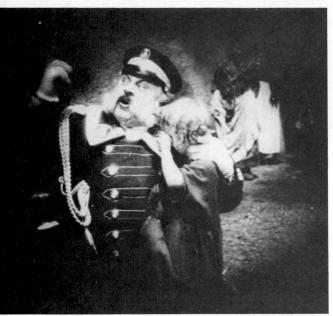

Fig. 7-12

Fig. 7-13

The Last Laugh: *the old man (Emil Jannings) in the treasured, prestigious uniform of a porter (Fig. 7-12) and in the humble uniform of a lavatory attendant (Fig. 7-13).*

it tracks through the bustling lobby, as if it were a guest who had walked out of the elevator and over to the constantly revolving door, where it stops to look through the door at the rainy night and the porter, with his big umbrella, ushering patrons to and from cabs. In the next shots, the camera joins the old man in the rain. This fast, busy sequence imparts excitement with its movement, but also establishes every crucial expository detail the film's action requires: the size and importance of the hotel, the conscientious devotion of the porter to his job, the difficulty and triumph of his managing a heavy trunk in the rain (which leads him to take a rest, which leads the manager to decide he's too old for the job, which precipitates the catastrophe and motivates the rest of the story), and the indifference of that symbol of the inhuman, continuous efficiency of business, the revolving door.

When the porter receives his notice of demotion from the manager, the camera shows us the letter and then blurs; the porter can no longer read the piece of paper. When the porter gets drunk at his daughter's wedding

party, the room starts whirling around; the spinning camera mirrors the porter's spinning head. In his drunken reverie (a classic Expressionist dream sequence in which he demonstrates his power by tossing and catching a trunk while guests and bosses marvel and clap), the world becomes blurred and distorted: The hotel's revolving door, now immensely tall, casts sharp, bizarre shadows, and the faces of the musicians (who wake him) have been squeezed, stretched, and curved like faces in the mirrors of a funhouse. Murnau even translates sound into subjective visual effects by blurring the shots of the musician's trumpet, implying that the porter can hear it only as a blur. Whereas the distortion and superimposition in a film like *Destiny* reveal the supernatural and the immaterial, those same techniques in *The Last Laugh* reveal natural sensations and responses; the effect of a technique is defined by the narrative context of the whole film.

Compared with the externalized, narrative emphasis of Hollywood films, the emphasis on the internal state of the character in *The Last Laugh* is striking. With rare exceptions like

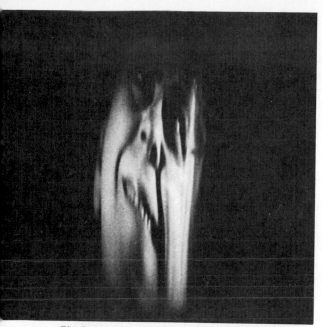

Fig. 7-14

Fig. 7-15

Subjective camera in **The Last Laugh:** *the distorted face of a neighbor (Fig. 7-14); the hung-over porter's view of a woman (Emilie Kurz) bringing his morning coffee (Fig. 7-15).*

Chaplin or von Stroheim, Hollywood filmmakers consistently subordinated character development to telling a story. Another radical departure of *The Last Laugh* from the Hollywood films of the twenties was its depiction of a world of moral grays rather than blacks and whites. On the one hand, the film condemns the callous social process that values the man's function rather than the man himself. On the other hand, our particular hotel porter is foppish, vain, egotistical, and falsely self-satisfied. For a man to define his essence by a uniform is false and foolish.

On yet another side, the other members of the porter's own working lower-middle-class world are themselves callous and petty, unsympathetic and inhumane, and prone to define a man by his uniform. They gossip at top volume. They are as vicious as the hotel manager is indifferent. They snigger behind his back when the former porter walks down the street and into his apartment. Even his own family turn their backs on him. And the porter, to some extent, deserves this, for his earlier attitude toward them, as he smugly paraded down the street in his uniform like a peacock, was as class-conscious as their present one. Although he gave candy to the children, he did it as a benevolent celebrity. He was his neighbors' connection to the military and economic ruling classes, and they honored him only until he fell, when they could take their revenge on him (now that he had become ordinary, one of them, or even lower) and on the oppressive social system he once incarnated. The complexity of the film's moral system contributes to the feeling that it mirrors life rather than forms some simplistic paradigm for it. In its rendering of character and its relativity of values, *The Last Laugh* was not only a mature contrast with the escapist Hollywood product; it also set a kind of pattern that has, with exceptions of course, continued through the years: The Hollywood film has traditionally been the film of action and clear-cut values, the European film of character and moral ambiguities.

The one odd note in the whole film is its ending: the old man's unexpected discovery of a pot of gold at the end of the rainbow. In a way like *Caligari, The Last Laugh* has an ending that doesn't "fit," dividing the film against itself in an act of deliberate self-contradiction, in this case in the service of irony. Before our eyes, a tragedy switches to a comedy. It even uses an American character to motivate the happy ending, which is a parody of a Hollywood happy ending, seen from a Brechtian distance. We see the man poor, then we see him rich, then we think about it for maybe the rest of our lives; it's like that sometimes with the movies, when you get lucky.

Wrenching us out of the story and announcing that the rest of the film is chimera, Carl Mayer's title card reads: "Here the story should really end for, in real life, the forlorn old man would have little to look forward to but death. The author took pity on him, however, and has provided a quite improbable epilogue." Whereas the film had not previously required a single title to clarify the thoughts or feelings of its characters, it suddenly uses one to show that the writer is sticking something on with narrative paste. Then, after shots of people laughing in the hotel as they read the paper, an insert shot of the article allows us to read with them that an American millionaire had left his fortune to the man who would be by his side when he died. We gather immediately that the rich man died in the washroom of the Atlantic Hotel. The German title of the film, *Der letzte Mann*, translates as *The Last Man* but also connotes "the least of men" — our martyred hero, when he is at his lowest ebb, as well as our restored hero, the "last man" of the will. But he does, in any case, have the last laugh.

Like the endings of Chaplin's *Easy Street* and Brecht's *Threepenny Opera,* the artificiality of the film's conclusion is so obvious, the solution so facile, so inconsistent with the social realities that the film itself has defined, that our minds immediately sniff parody and social comment. However, our hearts are also gladdened by the man's good fortune, particularly because he shares that fortune with the only person who showed compassion for his suffering — the night watchman (who becomes, in effect, his lover). The old man's goodness showers on all those who really need it; he discovers the humanity, the compassion for his fellows — notably, the current lavatory attendant and, at the very satisfying end of the film, a beggar —

that he once lacked. He has no compassion, however, for those who turned their backs on him. He makes the hotel manager eat crow, and his own family is noticeably absent in his moment of good fortune. The ending satisfies our sense of poetic justice at the same time that it reveals the insufficiency of social justice. We just don't know whether — or, more precisely, *how* — to believe it.

If one kind of German realist film was the close examination of a single psyche (usually a man's), the other examined the whole political or social milieu. These films, which have since acquired the label "Street films," consistently use "street" in their titles: Karl Grune's *The Street* (1923), Bruno Rahn's *Tragedy of the Street* (1927). They use the unifying locale of the street as a means of tying together diverse kinds and classes of people and diverse activities. The street becomes a microcosm of society as a whole. And it's rough out there.

Perhaps the most interesting of the street films is *The Joyless Street* (1925), the first important film of the Austrian G. W. Pabst. Pabst's street runs through postwar Vienna, a city of striking contrasts: of rich and poor, of feast and starvation, of family traditions and whoring. The street of Pabst's film is the synthesis of Vienna's two faces: the ugly, starving reality and the courtesan's painted mask. On Pabst's street the poor wait doggedly and frustratedly in line in front of a butcher's shop, hoping that the brutal man (Werner Krauss, who played Dr. Caligari) will give them a shred of meat. In the same building as the butcher's shop is Mrs. Greifer's night club, a frivolous, orgiastic late-night gathering spot for the rich, which also serves as a brothel. The film examines several lives on that street of contrasts where the women must choose between the poverty of standing in the slow line for the butcher's meat or the fast line to riches at Mrs. Greifer's (where the butcher is a steady customer). Two women take opposite paths. One (Asta Nielsen) sells her body and eventually commits murder; the other (Greta Garbo) holds out as long as she can and is rescued from selling herself at the last minute. *The Joyless Street* was so realistic, controversial, and disturbing that it was banned in England and recut for distribution in many countries, including Italy, France, and even Austria.

Pabst typically combines a social theme with melodramatic action. Despite the artificiality and contrivance of the film's tubercular whore who murders one of her rivals, the real unity of the film lies in Pabst's consistent condemnation of the society that allows such poverty and opulence to exist at the same time, that gives no choice to the poor except starvation or capitulation to the perverted values of the rich. But while we are thinking about these social and moral issues, we are also rooting for Garbo; we are still in the world of melodrama, where goodness confronts evil and emotions are extreme.

Pabst is a psychological realist, and a great one. His forays into Expressionism, as in the Freudian *Secrets of a Soul* (1926), are visually creative but have no conviction. They lack the tortured drivenness of Expressionist art, the need one sees in the paintings of Van Gogh to get the vision *out,* to express its truth and its energy with raw, bold brilliance; nor do they show Murnau's gift for transforming the world into a new kind of nightmare (*Nosferatu*) and then turning with equal success to a completely different genre, the *Kammerspielfilm* (in *The Last Laugh*). Pabst belonged to the third major movement in German film (after the Expressionist and *Kammerspiel* movements), the "New Objectivity" (*die neue Sachlichkeit*); this "new realism," which included but went beyond the Street films, took a close look at the surfaces and circumstances of reality without "prestylizing" it or pouring on the symbolism. So although he dabbled in Expressionism, Pabst was better at looking at people from the outside. From that vantage point, his psychological insight is flawless. Although some of his villains are as hissable and cruel as the butcher in *The Joyless Street* or the con artist in *The Love of Jeanne Ney* (1927), and some of his heroes are as brave and true-hearted as Jeanne Ney and her Bolshevik lover, there are also characters who are scrutinized profoundly and yet remain impossible to label or sum up, like the complex and fascinating Lulu (Louise Brooks) in *Pandora's Box.* Both in the terms of melodrama and in those of social and ethical consciousness,

everything in a Pabst film is examined for its value, to see what values it possesses or reflects. And the answers are not always simple.

In keeping with his psychological objectivity, in his greatest films Pabst strives for a realistic *mise-en-scène* — whether in the studio-made worlds of Ufa (*The Joyless Street,* like *The Last Laugh,* was shot entirely in the studio) or on the actual streets of Paris (*Jeanne Ney* seamlessly combines location and studio footage). He defines characters through their possessions and surroundings as well as their behavior, using *mise-en-scène* in a way that is both relentless and subtle, telling but not overstated. *The Love of Jeanne Ney* opens not with an establishing long shot but with a close-up of the worn-out shoes on the villain's feet (with one foot nervously flexing), which goes exactly against narrative convention, puts extreme emphasis on a realistic detail, and does establish a great deal about this cheap character (the despicable con artist Khalibiev, played by Fritz Rasp). As the shot continues, the camera moves down his legs — he's lying on a shabby couch in cheap pants — and over to survey what is on the table alongside him: a mess of papers, a crudely drawn pornographic sketch, a lamp, some half-smoked cigarettes. After the camera has held on the tabletop for a few seconds, a dirty hand with manicured nails reaches into the frame and fumbles for one of the butts; the camera pans right, following the hand, to reveal at last the face that we are not surprised to find weak and unpleasant, as the man puts the cigarette in a holder decorated with an amorous couple, lights it and finds it bitter, tosses it away, and sulks with the cigarette holder slack in his teeth. A few shots later, the holder goes up when he looks at a sexy picture and down when he looks at a bill. That is a psychological realism that is daring, insightful, material, and precise.

But what Pabst is most known for is the fluidity of his camerawork and editing. He might well be thought of as the director who perfected classical film continuity. His camera tracks so readily, pauses or turns so appropriately, that we accept it as an almost natural element of the film's world and as the natural vehicle of our attention. But if he wants us to notice the camera (as Hitchcock, who received

Fig. 7-16
The realistic mise-en-scène *of Pabst's* **The Love of Jeanne Ney;** *Fritz Rasp as the seedy villain.*

some of his training at Ufa, so often does), we *do*—as in the scene in *Jeanne Ney* when an old woman screams and the camera moves in so close and so fast that the cracks in her tongue nearly fill the screen. His lighting can appear natural but can just as easily plunge us into a world of shadows, madness, and evil (as in the murder of Jeanne Ney's greedy uncle, a sequence as darkly perverse and horrifying as anything in von Stroheim). And his editing is so rapid and smooth that we can watch sequences in *Jeanne Ney* that contain more than ten shots per minute (like the one in which Khalibiev meets Jeanne and her father) and hardly be conscious of a cut. At its most extreme, this is called "invisible editing," the exact opposite of the Soviet practice of calling attention to montage. But Pabst did not hide every cut; his skillful combination of cross-

cutting and the moving camera often produces vividly effective cuts that are meant to be noticed. Between *The Joyless Street* and *The Love of Jeanne Ney* Pabst saw Eisenstein's *Battleship Potemkin* and Pudovkin's *Mother* (which were great hits in Germany, as *The Last Laugh* was in Russia), and that is why *Jeanne Ney* is so much more intricately edited than any previous German film, why it was based on a novel in which the heroine's true love is a Bolshevik, and why it implies socialist solutions that had not been available to the characters of *The Joyless Street.*

The smoothness of Pabst's cuts depends on the absolute coordination and integration of camerawork and editing, which themselves work in concert with the movements of the actors and even the movements of the audience's eyes. Pabst discovered that one could charge a scene with invisible energy by cutting in the middle of a character's motion. The moving hand or leg, the rising body, the opening door all hide the camera's shift in distance and angle while propelling the eye into the next shot. Pabst also cut on *eye* movement—as when we watch one thing or person move from the left side of the screen ("screen left") to the center, and then something totally different move at the same pace from the center to screen right, and the trajectory of our eye movement is neither changed nor interrupted, so that it feels as if we're watching one motion even if the moving subject changes. Having mastered this, Pabst could direct a movie so that it became a dance for the eye.

His adaptation of Bertolt Brecht and Kurt Weill's *The Threepenny Opera* (1931), undaunted by the technical difficulties of sound filming (which in lesser hands drastically reduced camera movement and slowed if not killed the pace of editing), reveals Pabst's continuing interest in mixing social commentary and melodrama, the sharpness of his mercilessly realistic eye, and his love of the moving camera. His camera tracks through the studio-built streets of a sleazy beggar's London, descends stairways, marches along with the army of the poor. Brecht unsuccessfully sued Pabst for corrupting his play, for changing his anti-romantic, anticonventional, deliberately contrived theatre-piece into a romantic, conventionally plotted, realistic movie. Pabst converts the story into a conventional boy–girl tale; Mackie meets Polly in the first scene and their lustful amour blooms. Brecht's play avoids showing how or why Mackie and Polly first meet; he has no interest in this kind of exposition and motivation. Pabst's film milks the antics of the thieves and the pathos of the closing march of the poor (pathos is one of the emotions Brecht disdains). It blurs the deliberate contrivance of Brecht's ending by supplying Mackie's release with a motivation: His wife, Polly, and his gang have themselves founded a bank, so Mackie is respectable.

But Pabst's emendation is pointedly social. The founding of the bank is a clear jab at the extralegal power of capital and a rather explicit reference to Hitler, the crook who was becoming legitimate.

Fig. 7-17
Berlin: The Symphony of a Great City—*the geometry and visual music of everyday life.*

The End of an Era

The key question about the death of the German film is whether it ended with a bang or a whimper—with Hitler's tyranny over the imagination of the individual artist, with the gradual decay that had been afflicting the German film mind even before Hitler came to power, or with its export to Hollywood. There is evidence that the claustrophobia of the studio production, the dependence on architecture and paint, which had liberated the visual imagination in 1919, began to inhibit it by 1926. The weakest parts of *Metropolis* employed decoration for the sake of pure decorativeness. It was time to take to the streets—the real ones.

In 1927, the great writer of studio films, Carl Mayer, and the great photographer of studio films, Karl Freund, broke out of the studio completely to shoot a candid documentary of Berlin life. Directed, edited, and co-written (with Freund; Mayer, who disliked the director's purely pictorial approach, left the picture and was credited with having had the idea for *Berlin,* much as he had the idea for *The Street*) by the abstract artist and architect Walter Ruttmann, *Berlin: The Symphony of a Great City* was the antithesis of the traditional German film. It used no story; it was merely a chrono-

Fig. 7-18

Fig. 7-19

German filmmakers and film practice come to Hollywood. Fig. 7-18: Sunrise (1927); George O'Brien and Janet Gaynor get on the tram that will take them out of the big city that was built, German-studio style, on the Fox lot. Fig. 7-19: The Mummy (1932), directed by Karl Freund at Universal; Boris Karloff, as the reanimated Imhotep, takes the Scroll of Thoth from an unbeliever in a scene strongly influenced by German Expressionist horror.

logical progression of some twenty hours in the city's life, from the arrival of an early morning train to the late-night activities of the Berliners. The film lacked a human protagonist; its protagonist was the city itself, a place where people sit in cafés in the sun and where litter clogs a storm drain, a place where people see Charlie Chaplin on a screen and where a girl commits suicide by jumping off a bridge. The whole genre of the "city symphony"—a form of avant-garde documentary that includes Dziga Vertov's *Man with a Movie Camera* (1929)—was named after Mayer's idea and Ruttmann and Freund's film. The earliest examples of the genre, however, include Alberto Cavalcanti's *Rien que les heures* (1926) and Mikhail Kaufman's *Moscow* (1927; Kaufman was Vertov's brother).

The power of *Berlin* lies in its candid photography and its rhythmic cutting. To guarantee the authenticity of revealing the city at work and play, Karl Freund, the careful craftsman of both *The Last Laugh* and *Variety* (and, with Günther Rittau, the co-cinematographer of *Metropolis*), hid his camera in a truck and drove about the city, hastily and fleetingly shooting the movements that caught his eye. Though the shooting of the film was haphazard, Ruttmann's editing of it was not. His two controlled editing principles were form and rhythm (this was, after all, two years after *Potemkin*, and Ruttmann had also read Vertov's theoretical manifestos). As he cut from shot to shot, constructing the film, Ruttmann capitalized on either parallels in form (circles, verticals, heavy masses) or contrasts in form. To combine whole sections of shots he used the principles of music composition, endowing the sequence with a rhythm and tone appropriate to its content (an idea Vertov published in 1922). The opening movement of the film, the train approaching the sleeping city, is *allegro moderato*—rhythmic, pulsating, alive with expectation, but a bit cautious, sleepy, hesitant. The next sequence, of the sleeping city's waking, is a *largo*—slow, quiet, peaceful. As the city wakes and goes to work, the tempo changes to *allegro vivace*—vibrant, alive, active. There is an *andante* at the lunch hour when work stops, another *allegro* when it begins again, and another *andante* in the quiet, gear-changing hours of the evening between work and play. The film ends with a *presto finale*, a fast, frenzied sequence of neon lights, night life, dancing, music, movies. With its use of pure visual form, musical rhythms, and real life, *Berlin* is clearly an attempt to break the bounds of studio production.

Another iconoclastic film is *Kuhle Wampe* (1932), Brecht's attempt to redress his movie injury by writing a script of his own. The work rejects the lighting, the atmosphere, the compulsive control of the German studio film completely. Like *Berlin*, the film feels more Russian than German; its creators (Brecht and the director, Slatan Dudow) are clearly influenced by both Marx and Eisenstein: the montage of bicycle wheels rolling through the streets, unsuccessful at taking their riders to a job; the montage of rising prices, of evictions for not paying the rent, of the price tags on every human necessity. The film's rejection of plot, its use of actual locations, its subordination of people to political discussion are also signs of its rupture with tradition.

If the limitations of the studio film had begun to cramp the German imagination, it was also possible that the exodus of so much film talent to Hollywood had not left enough imaginations in Germany to get cramped. Murnau had gone to Hollywood to work for William Fox (whose Fox Film Corporation merged with Darryl Zanuck's 20th Century Productions in 1935, creating 20th Century-Fox). After making his formal masterpiece, the superbly lyrical study of a married couple's antagonism and reunion, *Sunrise: A Song of Two Humans* (1927, written by Carl Mayer, starring George O'Brien and Janet Gaynor, and photographed by Charles Rosher and Karl Struss), which won the first Oscar for Cinematography as well as a special Oscar for "Artistic Quality of Production" and was one of the pictures that won Gaynor the first Oscar for Best Actress—Murnau died in California in 1931, the victim of an automobile crash. Lubitsch had gone to Hollywood, never to return. Pommer had gone to Hollywood and returned, but he may have caught the dollar influenza after being exposed to it. Even those filmmakers who never went to Hollywood could not avoid its influence. As the German film industry had more and more financial difficulties, it was more and more un-

derwritten by Hollywood production dollars—
particularly from Paramount and MGM in an
agreement known by the homonym, Parufa-
met. With dollars came directives (especially
since Paramount and Metro were interested in
destroying the fortunes of their only powerful
European competitor).

If the export of German talent to
Hollywood bled the native film industry as
steadily as a Dracula kiss, it would inject its
powerful juices into the American film for the
next three decades. Many of the best directors
of American films between 1933 and 1960 had
either worked in the German industry or had
been trained there: Alfred Hitchcock, Max
Ophüls, Fritz Lang, Billy Wilder, Otto Preminger, Douglas Sirk, Michael Curtiz, Fred
Zinnemann, Edgar G. Ulmer, and Robert
Siodmak among them. The great American
horror films of the 1930s and 1940s at Universal (the various adventures of Frankenstein,
Dracula, the Mummy, and the Wolf Man) descended either directly or indirectly from the
German horror films. The great German cameraman Karl Freund—who was born in Bohemia, now part of Czechoslovakia—shot
Dracula (1931) for Tod Browning and *Murders
in the Rue Morgue* (1932) for Robert Florey,
both at Universal, before directing his own
horror classics, *The Mummy* (1932, Universal)
and *Mad Love* (1935, MGM). One of the cinematographers on *Mad Love,* Gregg Toland, was
decisively influenced by Freund—an influence
that is particularly clear in the film Toland shot
six years later, *Citizen Kane.* Freund's contributions to the American industry would extend to
his three-camera shooting technique at Desilu
(formerly RKO) for the *I Love Lucy* television
series in the 1950s.

Moody Expressionist lighting and claustrophobic decor dominate American crime films
of the 1940s and 1950s, the *films noirs*; despite
the name given them by postwar French film
critics, the disturbing themes and moods of
these films came directly from the German cinema. Like Fritz Lang's *Dr. Mabuse, the Gambler*
(1922) or *M* (1931), these are paranoid nightmares in which there is little difference between
the aims and methods of cops and crooks.
Madmen seem more sensitive and sympathetic
than the sane, while clichés of social justice

Fig. 7-20

Fig 7-21

Fig. 7-22
Sound and image in M. *As her mother calls for
"Elsie," Lang combines these still lifes of emptiness.*

grind inexorably toward logical conclusions
that never solve real problems. It is difficult to
imagine the history of American cinema without this infusion of both visual imagery and
thematic commentary from Weimar Germany.

Fig. 7-23
Spencer Tracy (right) in Fury.

It is also possible that Hitler's political victory in 1933 killed a thriving film culture with terrible suddenness. The early German sound films were as good as anyone's. Or better. *The Blue Angel* (1930), despite its American director (von Sternberg), was a completely German film. Its heritage is evident in its careful studio-controlled atmospheres (the smoky chaos of the nightclub hung with nets), in its close examination of a Jannings character's soul (Professor Immanuel Rath's steady degeneration into a humiliated clown), and in its cynical portrayal of the nasty, callous insensitivity of the German populace to human suffering. The film was as careful with sound as with pictures: the contrast of Lola Lola's singing and the traditional tune chimed by the town clock, the contrast between the noisy chaos in Rath's classroom before he enters and the deadly silence when he does.

Pabst's use of sound was also developing: the wheeze and crash of exploding shells in his antiwar study of the First World War, *Westfront 1918* (1930), the effective contrast of singing soldiers and dying ones, the use of musical leitmotifs in *The Threepenny Opera.* Pabst's *Kameradschaft* (1931), his final pre-Nazi sound film, was an extremely daring and innovative

work. In this story of international cooperation on the Franco-German border to rescue the victims of a mine disaster, Pabst shot a fiction film that looked as real, as unstaged as a documentary. In this dialogue film, dialogue itself becomes a metaphor (as it does in Renoir's *Grand Illusion*) since the conflict of languages (German and French) underlies the human and political conflicts of the narrative.

Lang's use of sound was equally astute. In *M*, his first talkie, there is the asynchronous handling of sound as a mother calls in vain for the daughter who has been murdered, while the camera reveals the empty spaces where no living being stirs. The murderer (played by Peter Lorre, whose first American film was *Mad Love*) is identified by the Grieg tune he repeatedly whistles, and Lang effectively depicts the moment when the man gets the urge to kill by the increasing intensity and urgency of his whistling. A blind man, who is totally dependent on sound, later recognizes the murderer from this whistled tune. And throughout the film, Lang juxtaposes visual imagery (shadows, a Wanted poster, the little girl's balloon flying heavenward with no one to hold it, the dishes on the table for a meal that will never be eaten, the searches and strategies, maps and machinations of the police going about their business) with ironic or contrapuntal commentary on the soundtrack. The principal cinematographer on *M* was Fritz Arno Wagner, who shot *Nosferatu* and co-shot both *Destiny* and *The Love of Jeanne Ney.*

M is also a significant example of Lang's interest in the trial as a dramatic opportunity for a society to investigate itself, or for a movie to investigate a society. In *M* the child-murderer is tried by criminals, and the insanity defense is explored. In Lang's first American film, *Fury* (1936), the apparent burning alive of an innocent man (Spencer Tracy) is explored in an equally complex trial in which movies (newsreel close-ups) provide crucial evidence against the members of the often architecturally arranged lynch mob, and the victim's showing up alive in court proves a triumph for conscience without dismissing the moral culpability of the violent mob. Lang continued to examine the nature of justice, and the complementary nature of revenge, in such American films as

Rancho Notorious (1951, released 1952, starring Marlene Dietrich), *The Big Heat* (1953), and *Beyond a Reasonable Doubt* (1956).

As for the man who played Cesare, the somnambulist conscripted by Dr. Caligari, Conrad Veidt left Nazi Germany for America, where—with a vengeance—he played the Nazi villain in Michael Curtiz's *Casablanca* (1942). Werner Krauss—Caligari—stayed and was honored as an Actor of the State. Emil Jannings, who also supported the Nazis and acted in propaganda films, received a similar high honor.

Rather than dying slowly, the German age may well have been translated abruptly from one of gold into one of iron. The German film theorist and historian, Siegfried Kracauer, even saw these German films as preparing the means that a Hitler would use to manipulate the minds of the public. The German sense of architecture and composition, the rhythms of cutting and movement, would be reincarnated in the masterful propaganda films of Leni Riefenstahl, who lent her great art to bending the German mind. The heroic architectural configurations of her documentary on the 1934 Nazi Party Convention at Nuremberg, *Triumph of the Will* (1935), are descendants of Lang's *Metropolis* and *Die Nibelungen* (1924); the stirring integration of musical motifs, the control of camera angle, the incorporation of mythic elements all aim at presenting the Führer as a combination of Pagan god of strength and Christian savior of mildness. In *Olympia* (1938), her documentary on the 1936 Berlin Olympic Games—the grand, exuberant masterpiece that took 18 months to edit and ranks her among the greatest of all filmmakers—the techniques used to consecrate and glorify the body, the athlete, the purely physical are the descendants of the rhythmic editing of Ruttmann (who assisted her) and Pabst, but taken to an entirely new level of power, notably in the diving sequence that climaxes the film. After *Olympia*, the German film failed to make any major contribution to the international cinema for almost thirty years, until the emergence of a new German cinema in the late 1960s.

8

Soviet Montage

The Russian film was born with the Russian Revolution. Before 1917 the Russian film industry was a colony of Europe—of Pathé or Lumière or Scandinavia's Nordisk. No film was shot in Russia by a Russian company until some ten years after the invention of the moving picture. The films of the next ten years (1907–1917) were strictly for local consumption (very few of them were exported). Costume films, horror films, and melodramas—the typical formulas of Europe and America—were the staples of the pre-1917 Russian film diet. The revolution changed all that.

Marxist political and economic philosophy, which had evolved in the age of machines, adopted the machine art as its own. Lenin considered the cinema the most influential of all the arts. Movies not only entertained but, in the process, molded and reinforced values. The film was a great teacher; with portable power supplies it could be shown to huge groups of people in every remote corner of the new Soviet Union. While the flickering images held their audiences captive, the events on the screen emphasized the virtues of the new government and encouraged the Russian people to develop those traits that would best further it. Whereas the American film began as an amusing novelty, the Soviet film was created explicitly as teacher, not as clown. In 1919, after a chaotic year in which the Soviets had let the film industry go its own commercial way, the Russian industry passed under government control.

"The foundation of film art is editing," wrote Pudovkin in the preface to the German edition of his book on film technique. Whereas the German innovators concentrated on the look, the feel, the psychological and pictorial values of the individual shot, the Soviet innovators concentrated on the effects of joining the shots together. Like so many of the earlier innovations in film technique, the Soviet discoveries were the products of experience and experiment rather than abstract theorizing. Two significant accidents determined the paths the experimentation would take. The first was the shortage of raw film stock. As in the rest of Europe, film stock was scarce in Russia during and just after the war years. The Russian film famine was even more severe, for the still-fighting Red and White armies erected blockades against each other to keep supplies from getting through. Lacking quantities of stock, the Soviet filmmakers had to make the most of what they had.

One of the first to make something was Dziga Vertov ("spinning top"; he was born Denis Kaufman), who traveled about the country as early as 1919, shooting newsreel footage with his camera, which he called his "Kino-Eye." Vertov then assembled this absolutely unstaged footage (Vertov insisted on unstaged reality throughout his career) into newsreels, of which the best known is the 1922–25 series called *Kino-Pravda* ("film truth"; in French, *cinéma vérité*), creating powerful emotional effects and educational results from the ways he and his wife, editor Elizoveta Svilova, joined this real footage together. Beginning in 1919, he also published theoretical manifestos that were as outrageous, energetic, and playful as they were radical. In his films, Vertov brings the ordinary, laborious tasks of building or rebuilding a nation to life (laying an airstrip, planting crops, finishing a tram line) by examining the progress of the task from many stirring and awesome angles, endowing the ordinary with wonder and revealing, as would many later Soviet films, the vitality of machines and the powerful potential, the almost sexual fertility of the union of people and machines. Of course, one of the reasons for Vertov's dynamic editing was that he had to shoot with mere scraps of film stock.

The scarcity of film stock also created the Kuleshov workshop. Lev Kuleshov, who taught a workshop class at the newly established Moscow Film School, led his students in a series of editing experiments. Pudovkin was to become the most famous of those students (Vertov was not in the workshop, but he began by editing newsreels under Kuleshov's supervision). But even those filmmakers who did not study with Kuleshov (for example, Eisenstein) could not escape his influence. Lacking the raw (unexposed) film stock to shoot whole films of their own, the Kuleshov workshop experimented in drafting scenarios, in editing and re-editing the pieces of film they already had on hand, and in re-editing sequences of feature films imported from the West.

The second of the influential accidents directly affected the Kuleshov group. In 1919, a print of Griffith's *Intolerance* successfully wriggled through the anti-Soviet blockade.

Intolerance, which Lenin greatly admired, became a Kuleshov primer. His students examined its boldness in cutting—cuts to drive the narrative, to integrate tremendously diverse and disjointed material, to imply concepts and draw conclusions, to intensify emotion with its rhythms, to mirror private thoughts and sensations. The Kuleshov workshop screened *Intolerance* incessantly, even re-editing its sequences to examine the resulting effects on the film's power and to discover the reasons for Griffith's particular choices. With such a thorough mastery of the principles of Griffith's cutting (and of the 1922 Abel Gance film, *La Roue*, as important for its rapid cutting as *Intolerance* was for its dialectical "drama of comparisons"), the Soviet directors would extend those principles to their limits—when they got the money and the film.

Until then they experimented. Each of the experiments furthered their control of the effects of editing and their conviction that editing was the basis of film art. Several of the Kuleshov experiments have become classics. In one, Kuleshov used some old footage of the prerevolutionary actor, Ivan Mozhukhin, who had fled to Paris (with the majority of the Czarist film industry). Kuleshov cut the shot of Mozhukhin's face into three pieces. He juxtaposed one of the strips with a shot of a plate of hot soup; he juxtaposed the second with a shot of a dead woman in a coffin; he juxtaposed the third with a shot of a little girl playing with a toy bear. When viewers, who had not been let in on the joke, saw the finished sequence, they praised Mozhukhin's acting: his hunger when confronted with a bowl of soup, his sorrow for his dead "mother" (their interpretation), his joy when watching his "daughter" playing. Mozhukhin's neutral expression was identical in all three pieces of film. The juxtaposed material (face + soup = hunger) evoked the concept or emotion in the audience, which then projected it into the actor. Editing alone had created the scenes, their emotional content and meaning, and even a brilliantly understated performance!

In another Kuleshov experiment the audience sees a series of five shots: (1) a man walks from right to left, (2) a woman walks from left to right; (3) they meet and shake hands, the man points; (4) we see a white building; (5) the two walk up a flight of steps. The audience connects the five pieces into a single sequence: A man and woman meet; they go off toward a building that he sees. In reality, the two individual shots of the man and woman walking were made in two different parts of the city; the building he points to is the White House, snipped out of an American film; the steps they ascend belong to a church in yet a third section of the city. Kuleshov's experiment revealed that the impression of geographical unity in a film was unrelated to geographical unity in space. Kuleshov called the result "the artificial landscape," or "creative geography." It was the same method Griffith used when he spliced Niagara Falls into the climax of *Way Down East*. A third Kuleshov experiment might, by analogy, be called "creative anatomy." Kuleshov created the impression of a single actress by splicing together the face of one woman, the torso of another, the hands of another, the legs of yet another.

The Kuleshov student learned that editing served three primary purposes in building a film. First, a cut could serve a *narrative* function. For example, a man walks toward the camera; suddenly, something to his right catches his attention and he turns his head. The audience's natural question is: What does he see? The director then cuts to an old tramp who pulls a pistol on the man. The audience's next question is: How will the man react to this attack? The director cuts back to the man to show his fear. And so forth. The narrative cut allows the director to analyze an action into its most interesting psychological elements and then to resynthesize these elements of the event into a powerful sequential action. Another kind of narrative cut is the flashback or flash forward —a cut to a past or future event. One can also cut to reveal what a character is thinking. A woman stares dreamily into space; the editor cuts to her husband in a faraway prison; the editor then cuts back to the woman's face. Yet a third kind of narrative cut is the cross-cut. While the tramp attacks the man with a pistol, the police, aware of the attack, charge to the

rescue. These lessons had all been learned from Griffith.

But the Soviet film students realized that a cut could do more than narrate: It could generate an *intellectual* response. One kind of intellectual cut was the metaphorical or associational cut. From a group of workers being mowed down by the rifles of soldiers, the director could cut to the slaughter of an ox in a stockyard (as Eisenstein did in *Strike*). The image of the slaughtered ox comments on the action of the slaughtered workers. The director can cross-cut between a procession of demonstrators and a river thawing in the spring, a mass of cracking and flowing ice (as Pudovkin did in *Mother*). The naturalness, the inevitability of the progress of the streaming ice comments on the force of the streaming workers and metaphorically treats revolution as a thaw, a breakup of the old order. A second intellectual effect could be produced by the contrast cut. The filmmaker cuts from the dinner table of a poor man, who eats only a few pieces of bread, to the table of a rich man laden with meats, candles, and wine. The contrast comments on the injustice of the fact that two such tables can exist at the same time. Such cuts can also be traced back to Griffith, who executed precisely this intellectual contrast between the table of the rich and the bread line of the poor in *A Corner in Wheat* of 1909. The parallel cut produces a third kind of intellectual response. From the condemned man sentenced to die at five o'clock, the filmmaker cuts to a thief who murders a victim at precisely five o'clock. The parallel acts of violence at the same time reinforce each other. Significantly, the intellectual cut—metaphoric, contrast, or parallel—also has an emotional dimension. The director uses not only the slaughter of the ox but also the sickening, horrifying bloodiness of the murder to make his point. He not only comments on the injustice of the rich man's dinner but also makes us hate the rich man for his gluttony and pity the poor man for his need.

The third kind of cut that the Kuleshov students discovered is a purely *emotional* one: The very method of joining the strips of celluloid together, rather than their content, produces an almost subliminal kinetic response in an audience that the director—working with or as the editor—can unobtrusively control. First, the director can cut a sequence rhythmically. He can use shorter and shorter pieces of film, increasing the tempo and tension of the action. Or he can cut a sequence with long pieces of film, producing a feeling of slowness or ease. By splicing together a series of strips of equal length the director can produce the feeling of a regular, measured beat. The tonal cut is the director's second method of manipulating an audience's emotions without its conscious awareness of manipulation. He can cut a sequence with steadily darker pictures, producing the impression of oncoming night and growing despair, or with steadily lighter pictures, producing the impression of dawn and rising hope. A third kind of emotional editing is the form cut, cutting on a similarity or difference in the form of the object in the frame. The director can cut from a spinning roulette wheel to a turning wagon wheel, from a plodding ox to an efficient tractor, from a jabbing pencil to a thrusting sword. A fourth kind of kinetic editing is the directional cut in which the director uses the direction of movement across the frame either to keep the action flowing or to produce a dynamic collision. The director can cut from a group of workers streaming from right to left, to a group of foot soldiers streaming from right to left, to a group of Cossacks on horseback streaming from right to left. Or he can cut from a group of workers streaming from right to left to a group of Cossacks streaming from left to right. Whereas the first series of directional cuts would produce the feeling of speed, continuousness, and flow, the second would produce the sensation of two huge masses smashing into one another. Significantly, a cut that is intended to have an intellectual effect—from pencil to sword—may also serve as a form cut, as part of a tonal sequence, as part of the film's increasing rhythm, and as a shift in the film's narrative structure. A single cut can function on all three levels— narrative, intellectual, emotional—at once. In fact, the Soviet directors discovered that most cuts *must* function on all three levels at once.

To this set of discoveries they gave the name "montage." In French, the word simply means

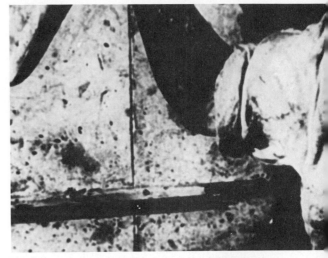

Fig. 8-1

Fig. 8-2

From the final montage sequence of Strike: *The butcher's hand thrusts downward to kill the animal, the people's hands thrust upward in an appeal for mercy.*

editing; for the Soviet directors and theorists, the word signified dynamic editing and the ways it could control a film's structure, meaning, and effect. By 1924, the Kuleshov students had acquired the film, the equipment, and the budgets to turn their lessons into films. They went out to develop their personal notions of montage. The surprise was that, despite the similarities in theory, the individual filmmakers produced strikingly individual and personal films.

Sergei M. Eisenstein

Eisenstein was the greatest filmmaker to apply the principles of Kuleshov, the greatest master of montage. Eisenstein's sense of cutting transformed his didactic lessons on the virtues of brotherhood and Marxism into dynamic, moving works of art—even for the non-Marxist. The Eisenstein silents break all the rules of "good" narrative construction. They lack a protagonist and focal characters; they move from action to commentary to analysis at Eisenstein's whim. Although they lack a conventional plot, they lack neither compelling action nor a unified structure. Although they lack individualized, rounded studies of human personality, they lack neither character nor compassion.

The Eisenstein film holds together by means of its theme rather than its story: the experience of the workers who learn what it means to strike and to take collective action against a wicked state, the ability of a single revolutionary action on a battleship to unite a whole people, the replacement of a false revolutionary government by a true one, the superiority of the new agricultural and social methods to the old ones. The theme gets its flesh from Eisenstein's depiction of the people who embody it. Although the central character of the Eisenstein film is the mass, the people as a whole, he never forgets that the mass is made up of individuals. Although the Eisenstein film is full of magnificent shots of streaming rivers of people, he invariably shows the viewer the impassioned faces of the men and women in that river. A consistent difference between right- and left-wing films is their opposite ways of depicting the worker— as a mass of indistinguishable faces (as in Lang's *Metropolis*) or as strongly individuated human types (as in the Soviet films of the period).

Like Lang, Eisenstein has the visual ability to convert huge groups of people into complex and striking geometric shapes. Unlike Lang, Eisenstein constantly reminds you that his subject is the dynamic human being, not the kaleidoscopic pattern. Eisenstein's geometric compositions, as careful and as visually attractive as they are, are never static. The individual shots are full of dynamic movement. That was one of Eisenstein's advantages in shooting outdoors; he had the freedom to move. And Eisenstein's montage increases the sense of movement and tension as the individual shots collide, crash, explode into each other.

Eisenstein defined his principle of montage as one of collision, of conflict, of contrast. He does not simply build shots with particular meanings into a whole, but sees each shot, even each frame as a unit with a dynamic visual charge of a particular kind. His goal is to bring the dynamic charge of one shot into conflict with the visual charge of the next. For example, the shots can conflict directionally—a group of men running from right to left, followed by a shot of soldiers marching from left to right. The shots can conflict in rhythm—a group of people running chaotically, followed by a group of soldiers marching steadily, slowly, inexorably. The shots can conflict in bulk—from a mass of workers to a single worker's face. The shots can conflict in emphasis—from a shot of four silent workers' faces to a shot of a single worker's fist clenched at his side. The shots can conflict in camera angle—from an extreme downward view (a high-angle shot) of a large crowd to a noble upward (low-angle) shot of a member of the crowd. The shots can conflict in the intensity of light—from a dark, dim shot to a blazing, bright one. The shots can conflict in the intensity of emotion—from a shot of fighting, struggling workers to a shot of a single worker's lifeless body, dangling quietly outside the struggle. The shots can conflict in their vitality—from a shot of a living man to a shot of a stone statue. And so forth. Eisenstein's great films are the products of his combining many and diverse gifts—his visual sense of composition, his feeling for rhythm and tempo, his ability to understand and manipulate human emotion, and his perceptive intellect, which could create meaning by joining two or more apparently unrelated images.

Eisenstein formally studied engineering and architecture. During the Civil War of 1917, he organized an impromptu theatre troupe in the Red Army. Attracted to the theatre, he started directing plays in Moscow after the war, where he was heavily influenced by the innovative, antinaturalist director, Vsevolod E. Meyerhold. In one of Eisenstein's stage productions, Ostrovsky's *Enough Simplicity in Every Wise Man* (1923), he included his first short film, *Glumov's Diary*, within the context of the play. He staged his last play, *Gas Masks* (1924), in the Moscow Gas Works. Eisenstein could go no further with stage reality; the leap into films was inevitable. His first feature film, *Strike* (1924, released 1925, made when he was twenty-seven), revealed the bold, broad strokes of a new film master. From its opening montage sequence — of whirring machines, spinning gears, factory whistles, of traveling shots along the length of the factory complex, of dynamic, dizzying movement — the film proclaimed that a brilliant cinematic imagination was at work.

Strike contains many of the traits that make an Eisenstein film pure Eisenstein. There is the director's control and alternation of moods: from the peaceful, idyllic sequences of the striking workers at rest and play to the violent, vicious slaughter of the workers in their tenements. There is the satirical treatment of the rich and the informers for the rich: The company finks are depicted as sneaky animals (a Griffith touch here); the rich factory owners sip cocktails while the workers starve and die (Griffith cross-cutting, of course). There is the director's sense of visual composition: the geometrical patterns and shapes of the factory and of the workers' tenements where the Cossacks attack. There is Eisenstein's use of metaphor to comment on the action: the sickening slaughter of the dumb and defenseless ox, which comments on the slaughter of the workers. And uniting the film is the Eisenstein vision: that the capitalistic, Czarist system is fundamentally inhuman and inhumane, an obstacle not only to physical survival but also to human fellowship, family, and brotherhood. Like many political films, *Strike* shows the effects of corrupt political systems on children and the family — as would later ones from Rossellini's *Open City* in 1945 to Tanner's *Jonah Who Will Be 25 in the Year 2000* in 1976 to Babenco's *Pixote* in 1981 — because politics determine the shape of the future that children represent.

Battleship Potemkin (1925) was Eisenstein's next film. Originally titled *1905*, the work was intended to depict the general workers' revolt in Russia of that year. Instead, Eisenstein pared down his conception to linking two separate events in that revolt — the rebellion on the battleship Potemkin and the Odessa reprisals by the Czarist army — to serve as a microcosm for the 1905 revolution, whose twentieth anniversary both *Battleship Potemkin* and Pudovkin's *Mother* (1926) were commissioned to celebrate, just as Eisenstein's *October* (1928) and Pudovkin's *The End of St. Petersburg* (1927) commemorated the tenth anniversary of the more successful 1917 revolution. The five-reel film's five parts, deliberately mirroring the five-act structure of classical drama, form a taut structural whole: from the unity the sailors build on the ship, to the unity between ship and shore, to the unity of the entire fleet. In the first part, entitled "Men and Maggots," Eisenstein builds the dramatic reasons for the sailors' discontent. Their food is infested with maggots; the Czarist doctor looks at the meat closely through his spectacles and declares the meat wholesome, although his glasses magnify the presence of the worms. The officers beat the men. Eisenstein brilliantly shows a worker's pain by merely photographing the twitching muscles of his back as he sobs.

In the film's second part, "Drama on the Quarterdeck," the men have had enough. They refuse to agree that their food is edible; when the captain orders all dissenters to be shot, the sailors rebel. By the end of this violent sequence, the ship belongs to the workers. The film's third section, "An Appeal from the Dead," is a quiet, elegiac requiem, a pause between the violent capture of the ship and the violence to follow on the Odessa Steps. One of the sailors has been killed in the battle; his body lies in state on the shore. The workers of Odessa file past it, touched and united in spirit by the sailor's sacrifice.

The fourth part of the film, "The Odessa Steps," begins gaily enough. The workers of Odessa race out to the Potemkin in their boats, carrying food and joy to their fellow workers on the ship. There is a union of ship and shore, of sailors and citizens. Other Odessans watch and wave from the shore. Suddenly, Czarist

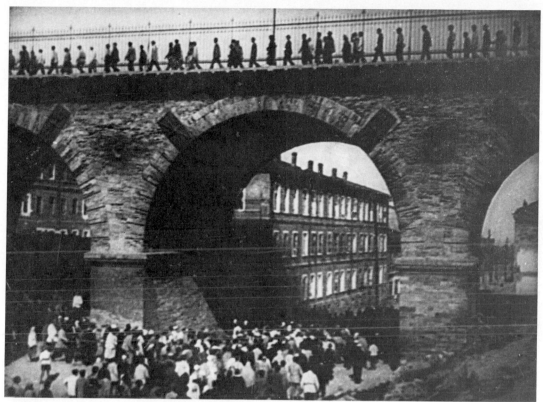

Fig. 8-3

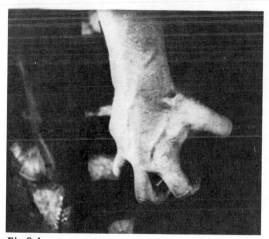

Fig.8-4

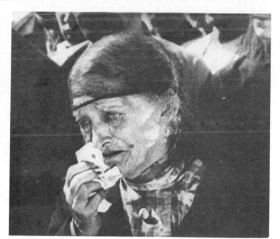

Fig. 8-5

Battleship Potemkin: *from the mass to individual detail, from geometry to people.*

troops march down the steps, shooting everyone in their path. The citizens scurry for protection. The soldiers' guns mercilessly fire, slaughtering young and old, men and women, children and mothers. The fifth section of the film, "Meeting the Squadron," is another emotional contrast. From the violence and chaos of the previous section, the mood becomes subdued, tense, expectant. The single battleship races toward the fleet; the ship prepares for battle. Eisenstein builds the suspense with shots of whirring gears, pumping pistons, rising guns. Will the fleet fire? The fleet does not. The comrades of all the fleet cheer one another. The Potemkin has united them all.

Eisenstein's uniquely powerful editing brings the film to life. At the end of section one, Eisenstein wants to emphasize that the men have had it, that the last straw has been laid on the camel's back. A sailor washing the dishes sees a plate inscribed, "Give us this day our daily bread." The biblical platitude infuriates him since they have no decent daily bread. He smashes the plate. To emphasize this act of smashing, Eisenstein divides this physical action, which takes only a few seconds, into eleven different shots, some as brief as four frames ($\frac{1}{4}$ second): (1) a close shot of the man's face reflecting his decision to smash the plate; (2) a medium shot as he pulls his arm back with the plate in his right hand; (3) a medium shot as he swings the plate over his left shoulder; (4) a medium close shot of the farthest reach of his swing, the plate behind his left shoulder; (5) a medium shot of his swinging the plate violently downward; (6) a close shot of his arm extended high above his *right* shoulder as he begins to hurtle the plate downward; (7) a close-up of his face; (8) a medium shot of his swinging the plate down from above his right shoulder; (9) a medium shot of the table as the plate smashes against it, scattering the silverware; (10) a medium close shot of his rising shoulder, the smashing completed; (11) a medium shot of the orderlies standing around the table where the plate has been smashed, a lengthy shot that ends with a fade-out. Dividing an action into such a process analyzes the event *and* makes it more violent, more purposeful, and more memorable as a pivotal point in the film. The edited version of the action (six seconds without

the fade-out) takes longer than the physical act itself.

Other sequences use a different but equally effective editing plan. No better example of tonal montage exists than in the opening passage of the film's third section, "An Appeal from the Dead." The entire sequence is saturated in the lyric calm of the sailor's death. Eisenstein cuts slowly from shot to shot, each of them growing lighter, revealing the rising of the sun through the fog. In the languid cuts, the sea is calm as glass, ships glide through the mist, gulls hover in the air. The quiet editing creates a lyrical moment of slow-moving, dark shapes sliding through a gray mist. The editing of the mourning Odessans in the final section of this "Appeal from the Dead" adds a note of strength and human determination to the moody silence. Eisenstein cuts from far shots of the immense mass of people to medium shots of three or four faces, to close-ups of single faces, clenched fists, and outstretched arms. When a bourgeois anti-Semite screams, "Down with the Jews," the half-Jewish Eisenstein shows the fierceness of the people's unity in a rhythmic editing sequence that shows heads turning in sudden, angry response to this voice of narrow inhumanity.

The most dazzling editorial sequence in all of *Battleship Potemkin* is the massacre of the citizens of Odessa on that city's great outdoor staircase: the second half of the "Odessa Steps" section. Eisenstein constructs this horrifying, brutal sequence from many different kinds of shots: far shots from the bottom of the steps showing the workers running chaotically; traveling shots along the side of the steps that flee with the workers; shots from the top of the steps showing the relentless, metric pace of the marching soldiers, only their boots, their bayonets, and their awesome shadows in the frame; close-ups of the individual citizens, their faces expressing horror, fear, pleading, confusion, anger. Eisenstein intercuts all these different shots, alternating them according to different principles of his montage of collisions, each of them sustained on the screen for the rhythmically correct number of seconds (or fractions of seconds). And as in the plate-smashing scene, the film time for the sequence on the Odessa Steps is longer than the actual time it would

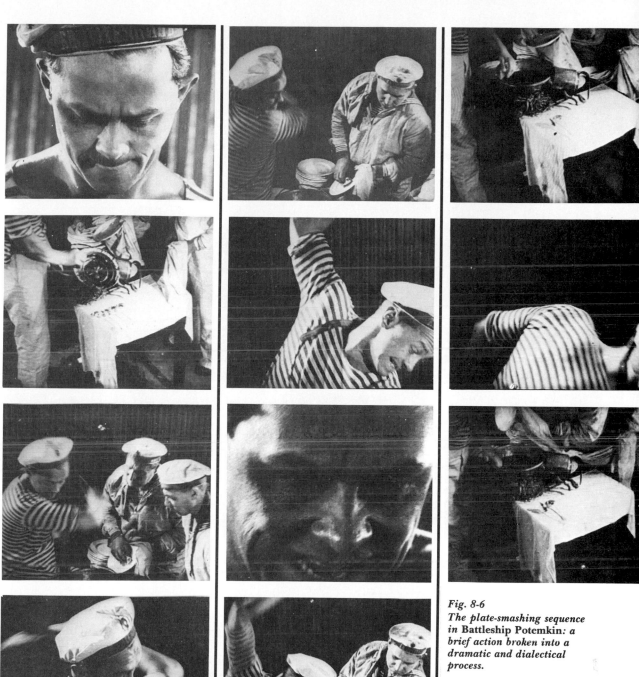

Fig. 8-6
The plate-smashing sequence in **Battleship Potemkin**: *a brief action broken into a dramatic and dialectical process.*

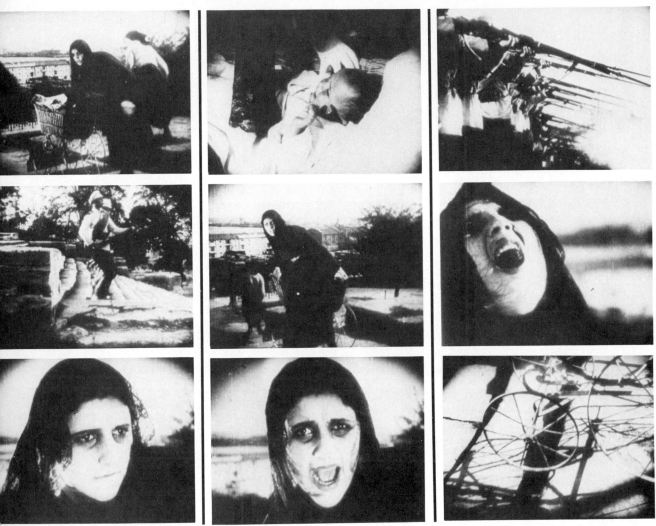

Fig. 8-7
Nine shots from the Odessa Steps sequence. Note the graphic conflicts between long and close shots, symmetrical and asymmetrical compositions, a human face and the inexorable march of an armed machine.

take a group of people to run down a flight of steps. Subjective time, the way it felt to be there, replaces natural time.

But *Battleship Potemkin* is more than montage, more than a series of dazzling editing techniques. For a film with a mass protagonist, the faces of individuals are strikingly memorable. Out of the brilliant geometric organization of sailors' hammocks emerge the faces of the young sailor who gets beaten and Vakulinchuk,

the sailor who leads his comrades in revolt. The sharp-featured, beady-eyed faces of the sneaky ship's doctor, the cunning ship's mate with the mustache of a melodrama villain, and the egomaniacal captain convey Eisenstein's condemnation of the vicious ruling class. The most maniacal face of all is that of the incongruous if not completely symbolic priest, his hair streaming in close-ups framed with light and smoke, his huge iron cross more a symbol of authority and a dangerous weapon (it sticks in the ship's deck like a hatchet) than a symbol of love and mildness. To enhance the lyrical quietness of the "Appeal from the Dead," Eisenstein evokes our sympathies with loving shots of the sorrowing faces of old and young, of men and women. But the most memorable faces of all are those in the most active and violent sequence of all—the Odessa Steps. Eisenstein creates the horror of the slaughter not just with mass murder, chaotic movement, fast cutting, and conflicting compositions, but also with the individual reactions and sensations of the people who experience the slaughter: the elderly lady with the pince-nez, the mother with her young son, the student with the glasses, the legless man scurrying at the feet of the crowd, the dark-haired, dark-clad mother with the baby carriage. As the soldiers attack, Eisenstein follows the fortunes and reactions of each of these individuals, using their emotional responses to evoke ours.

If *Battleship Potemkin* seems to be Eisenstein's most unified, satisfying, and *emotionally* effective film, it is perhaps because so many of its devices are felt rather than noticed. For example, the famous montage of the stone lions (three sequential shots of three statues—a lion sleeping, waking, and rising—edited to produce the impression of a single, natural, connected action), works because we feel the energy of, and think we see, a stone lion rising in alarm. Another element of the film that is felt rather than noticed is the sheer musicality of Eisenstein's montage. Although Eisenstein and most historians have devoted their time exclusively to discussing the intellectual and argumentative effects of montage, the editing of the strips of film in *Potemkin* also functions on a purely sensual level.

So much of the viewer's experience of *Potemkin* proceeds not from the eyes to the brain (the film's ideological statements) but from the eyes to the nerves. Like music, one *feels* the film as rhythm, mood, tone, and texture in addition to perceiving its concrete images. Eisenstein's "music" can be generally described as tensely violent, as a nervous, surging, discordant dissonance—qualities that parallel those of the modern music then being composed by his countrymen and contemporaries, Dimitri Shos-

takovich and Sergei Prokofiev. Interestingly, both composers later wrote music for the Soviet sound film, and the effective collaboration of Eisenstein and Prokofiev on *Alexander Nevsky* and *Ivan the Terrible* revealed how kindred were the spirits of these two "musicians."

Eisenstein's next film, properly titled *October* (1928, co-directed by Grigori Alexandrov), was released in a shortened and oversimplified version in the United States and England as *Ten Days that Shook the World* (for no reason other than to exploit the interest in John Reed's sensational book). In his theoretical writings, Eisenstein continually refers to the experiments with montage in *October*, which many consider the most sustained and intense attempt at defining the language of cinema since Griffith and until Godard. *October*, a loose historical survey of the months between the February Revolution of 1917 and the Bolshevik Revolution of October, is more intellectual, more satirical, and more specifically political than *Battleship Potemkin*. It is also, unfortunately, less unified dramatically, less consistent thematically, and less effective emotionally. Unlike *Battleship Potemkin*, its parts are far more striking than its whole.

October's montage makes its points and drives its rhythms. During the scenes of rebellion, Eisenstein uses extremely quick cuts (shots two frames long!) that smash the viewer with an impression of violence, shock, and frenzy. The alternation of these two-frame pieces, the one of a machine gun, the other of the gunner's face (or a different angle on the gun), creates the kinetic impression and essence of the clash and crash of gunfire, although no gun is actually firing. Eisenstein uses an opposite editing principle to emphasize that St. Petersburg has been cut in half, extending, slowing down, and intensifying the sequence of the raising of the bridges (set in July 1917), just as he expressively extends the plate-smashing scene and the Odessa Steps sequence in *Battleship Potemkin*. Two halves of a drawbridge pull apart and rise with infinite slowness. On one of the halves lies the body of a woman whose hair crosses the gap between the halves. On the other half (perhaps of another drawbridge) lies the body of a white horse, still attached to a wagon full of revolutionary banners. The horse falls into the gap; the wagon remains on the bridge; the horse remains suspended in midair as the bridge continues to rise. After an agonizing wait, the white body falls into the river. Immediately after, Eisenstein cuts to a shot of Bolshevik leaflets and banners, also falling into the river. The white pamphlets of the true revolution (*Pravda*) have been cast away, like the dead white horse. The Provisional Government, the result of the February Revolution, is portrayed as a triumph for the bourgeoisie and a failure for the real revolutionists.

Eisenstein's consistent method in this film is to use inanimate objects to comment, often sarcastically, on the activities of the living. Whereas Eisenstein used the method only once in *Battleship Potemkin*, *October* is full of "stone lions" that come to life.

A series of objects comments on the values of Kerensky, leader of the Provisional Government. As Kerensky poses, Eisenstein cuts to a statuette of Napoleon. Eisenstein further debunks Kerensky's imperial ambitions by showing all the possessions in his Czarist quarters—gleaming china plates, goblets of cut glass, chalices of silver, an army of toy soldiers—or by showing him repeatedly ascend the same staircase every time he gets promoted. Most damning of Kerensky is the series of shots that shows him fleeing in his Rolls Royce, a little American flag planted firmly on the radiator.

Eisenstein uses other objects satirically. To burlesque the glories of war, he shows a collection of gaudy medals; to burlesque the emptiness of religion (a consistent Eisenstein theme, since the church supported the Czar as well as the Provisional Government) he shows a series of icons: crosses, statues of Buddha, wooden figures of primitive gods. All of the statues emphasize the artificiality of turning the abstraction of a deity into a tangible (and expensive) object. None of this religious satire exists in the overseas release version, *Ten Days that Shook the World*. To burlesque the futility of the government officials, Eisenstein plays geometric games with the empty coffee glasses on their conference table. The glasses jump into a circle, a line, a curve, a square; though the patterns of the glasses change, the results of the conference do not. To burlesque the idealism of the Menshe-

Fig. 8-8

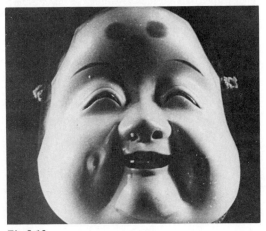
Fig 8-9

Fig 8-10
October. *Eisenstein "explodes" religion with a satiric montage of religious objects.*

viks, a group that advocated peaceful change rather than revolution, Eisenstein cuts sarcastically from one of their speakers to a group of harps plucked languidly by graceful, feminine hands. The parodic yet urgent tone of *October*, and the rigor of its montage experiments, hold together its sprawling, semihistorical structure.

Eisenstein's next film, his last silent, was *Old and New* (1929). Often called *The General Line* and also directed with the assistance of Alexandrov, *Old and New* demonstrates the difficulties and the virtues for the peasant of discarding the old ways of farming and thinking, of adopting the new collective ways and the new machines, notably a cream separator and a tractor. The film represents some departures for Eisenstein. In the manner of Pudovkin, he uses natural rather than inanimate imagery—fields, soil, animals, and crops—and he also uses a central figure—a peasant woman who supports collective farming—rather than the masses to embody the film's social progress.

But Eisenstein was beginning to run into trouble with the Soviet line and leaders. Stalin was dissatisfied with the ending of *Old and New*, finding it untrue to the spirit of the new nation and the people. Eisenstein, Jew, homosexual, and iconoclast, a devoted artist, an avid reader of everything from T. S. Eliot and Proust to Joyce and Kafka, from Dickens to Japanese poetry, began to feel the pinch of tightening state control. He did not complete another film for ten years.

Several problems contributed to this hiatus. Sound had suddenly overtaken the world's film industries, and Eisenstein needed time to study the new medium. He spent most of 1930 in America, under contract at Paramount, trying to get them to accept any of the projects he had developed (notably *An American Tragedy* and *Sutter's Gold*). Paramount decided otherwise. In 1931, Eisenstein and his cameraman, Eduard Tisse, were in Mexico with Alexandrov, filming an epic of the Mexican people, *Que Viva Mexico!*, financed by Upton Sinclair. Eisenstein fought with Sinclair, and the film was cancelled. Eisenstein never got the chance to edit the finished footage, much of which he never saw. A bowdlerized version of the film, assembled by Sol Lesser, was released in 1933 as *Thunder Over Mexico*. Marie Seton put together a better ver-

sion, *Time in the Sun*, in 1939, and Alexandrov released his own cut of the footage, as he believed Eisenstein would have edited it, in 1979. The dullness of the latter version revealed how much of an assistant director Alexandrov truly was. Returning to the Soviet Union, Eisenstein submitted several film projects that were rejected by the state film committee. Eisenstein was accused of formalism—to Stalin, a pedestrian realist, the great sin of Soviet art—of paying too much attention to the formal beauty and structure of the work and not enough to its narrative content and political utility. His methods were wasteful and time consuming. His perfectionism was demanding and inconsiderate of budgets and schedules. He seemed to be a director without a cinematic country, too political for 1930s Hollywood, too aesthetic for 1930s Moscow, and too intellectual for both of them. *Bezhin Meadow*, the project he cared the most about during the 1930s and had begun to shoot, was cancelled by official order in 1937. Finally, in 1938, he was able to complete his first sound film, *Alexander Nevsky*.

Eisenstein's theory of the sound film—expressed in a 1928 "Statement" co-signed but probably not co-written by Pudovkin and Alexandrov—was that the "talkie" was a fundamental error in the use of the medium. There was no artistic purpose in showing a man's lips move while the audience hears the words pour out. "Satisfying simple curiosity," he wrote, "increases the inertia of each shot as a montage element." For Eisenstein, sound was to be used asynchronously and contrapuntally: to become one more element of a film's montage. The visuals and sound should play *against* one another, not sing in unison. Although Eisenstein's theory of the sound film was contrary to the practice of his contemporaries—except for Vertov, who wrote in 1929 that sounds could be edited as easily as pictures, "in harmony or not" with the visuals—years of experience with the sound film have since proved the solidity of his theory.

Eisenstein, whose use of images had always been musical, was especially interested in the precise synchronization of visual images with musical passages and motifs. One of Eisenstein's best demonstrations of his musical theory is in "The Battle on the Ice" sequence in *Alexander*

Fig. 8-11
Ivan the Terrible, Part I. *A master of editing,
Eisenstein was also a master of composition.*

Nevsky, as the invading Teutonic hordes encounter the valiant Russians who have gathered to defend themselves. Aided by the power and complexity of Prokofiev's score, Eisenstein turns "The Battle on the Ice" into a cinematic symphony. The successive tones and rhythms of the Prokofiev music—slowly expectant, playfully fast, steadily victorious—play both with and against the content of Eisenstein's images of battle and the rhythms and shapes that control the editing of the images.

Eisenstein's only other completed works before his death in 1948 were two of the three intended parts of *Ivan the Terrible* (Part I released 1944, Part II [1946] released 1958, Part III [1946] unfinished). In Part II, he experimented with Expressionist color in two sequences. As with sound, Eisenstein believed that color should not be exploited for its novelty, its colorfulness, but that color should play a functional role in controlling the film's tone and effects. Again, the years would prove his sensitivity to one potential of a cinematic device. The interrelation of color, cutting, movement, and music in *Cabaret* (1972), *Saturday Night Fever* (1977), or *Flashdance* (1983) can be

related to Eisenstein's theories of using sound, color, music, and montage in film. But the most striking fact of Eisenstein's career is that he completed four pictures in his first five years and three in his next twenty. Eisenstein became a teacher and theoretician; he taught at the State Film School; he wrote lengthily and convincingly on the powers and effects of montage, although Stalin suppressed the publication of many of Eisenstein's books. But his greatest achievements in filmmaking had been accomplished before the end of the silent era. Indeed, his sound films display a self-consciousness in the handling of montage that was somewhat deadening to the vitality and exuberance of the method he applied instinctively in his youth; they also have central protagonists (Nevsky and Ivan) and relatively conventional narrative structures.

To some extent his career mirrors the artistic vitality of the Soviet film as a whole. The Russian film made the transition into the sound era with great difficulty, partly because the Soviet cinematic method was so visual, partly because the great Soviet directors became politically suspect, partly because the Soviet industry had difficulty acquiring reliable machines to shoot and project sound pictures.

Vsevolod I. Pudovkin

Pudovkin and Eisenstein were friendly opponents. Whereas Eisenstein's theory of montage was one of *collision*, Pudovkin's was one of *linkage*. For Pudovkin, the shots of the film combine to build the whole work, as bricks combine to make a wall, rather than conflict with one another in dynamic suspension. Pudovkin, a trained scientist, sometimes considered the film viewer to be a bit like the dogs in the experiments of his contemporary, Pavlov: The proper cinematic stimulus could elicit the desired intellectual or emotional response. Eisenstein, however, following the theoretical teachings of Hegel and Marx, believed that the method of argument itself must be rigorously dialectical: Shot A collides with shot B to create concept (or metaphor) C. Eisenstein's goal was to convert cinematic practice into a means of dialectical reasoning. The pictorial *thesis* in conflict with its *antithesis* would produce a new abstract *synthesis.* In the terms of later semiotic theory, Pudovkin's film theory and visual compositions tended to emphasize the signifieds of film images—*what* the images were images of, *what* they meant. Eisenstein's film theory and visual compositions tended to emphasize the complex play of signifiers themselves—*how* the images stimulated their inferences and meanings—translating Hegelian method into visual terms.

The differences between the two directors become clear by comparing their films. Whereas the tone and pace of an Eisenstein film are generally nervous and tense, exciting and jostling, the tone and pace of Pudovkin's are more languid, warm, and relaxed. He reserves the shocking, violent montage effects for sequences of fighting and rebellion—or exuberance. Whereas Eisenstein's usual human focus is the mass, Pudovkin's is the individual, a single person's revolutionary decision rather than the revolutionary action of a whole group. Whereas Eisenstein's montage is rich in intellectual commentary, Pudovkin's usually develops the emotional tone and human feelings within the scene.

Pudovkin, unlike Eisenstein, depended heavily on the performances of individual players; like Griffith, Pudovkin realized that the context of the scene, the nearly immobile face of an actor in close-up, a flickering in the eyes, could communicate more than overstated gestures. Pudovkin took Kuleshov's experiment with Mozhukhin's face seriously—far more seriously than Kuleshov himself took it (as the overacting in Kuleshov's 1926 film, *By the Law*, shows). Pudovkin believed that the "plastic material"—concrete physical objects—could communicate emotions and ideas more effectively than an actor's grimaces. He also made far greater use than Eisenstein of natural imagery: trees, rivers, mud, the wind.

After studying physics and chemistry, Pudovkin decided to work in films (originally intending to act rather than direct). His admiration for Griffith's *Intolerance* strongly influenced his decision. In 1920, Pudovkin began his studies at the State Film School, entering Kuleshov's workshop two years later. His scientific training ably suited him for his first major project, *Mechanics of the Brain* (1926), a cinematic investigation of Pavlovian research on conditioned reflexes in animals and children.

He took time off from the Pavlov picture to shoot his first fiction film, *Chess Fever* (1925), an ingenious and charming short comedy that paid homage to his teacher, Kuleshov.

Unlike the American comedies, *Chess Fever* is a comedy of editing. Pudovkin surprises us with gags that are solely the results of montage. In the opening sequence, we watch a chess game from underneath the table, seeing only the feet and arms of each of the players making his move. Only later does Pudovkin pull back to show us a single chess player playing the game by himself—he is that infected with the chess fever. Pudovkin's editing fooled us into believing that there were two players, the usual and expected number. The whole film is built out of such Kuleshovian tricks. During the filming of *Chess Fever*, an international chess tournament actually took place in Moscow. Pudovkin sent his camera crew—masquerading as newsreel photographers—to film the tournament and the champion players. Pudovkin then spliced the "newsreel" footage into the comedy, making the film's action seem to revolve around the tournament. For example, a girl is so upset by her boyfriend's fanatic devotion to chess that she throws one of his chess pieces away. Pudovkin then cuts to a shot of the chess champion, Capablanca, standing and holding a chess piece. It looks as if he caught the piece that the girl just threw. Purely an editing trick! Pudovkin took Kuleshov's notion of "creative geography" and produced "creative continuity."

Pudovkin's unique style emerged in his later fiction films. In *Mother* (1926), he reveals his ability to combine sensitive treatment of a human story, fluid narrative editing that uses the shock cutting of montage for isolated, showcase effects and natural images that comment on the action and reinforce the film's values. *Mother* is an adaptation of Gorky's novel about a woman who learns that radical action is ultimately the only protection against a wicked state. In 1905, her abusive, drunken husband is lured into helping a group of strikebreakers; he is shot and killed in a scuffle. The mother then betrays her own son, Pavel, revealing to the police, whose promises she naïvely trusts, that the youth was in collusion with the strikers. At Pavel's trial—Pudovkin's version

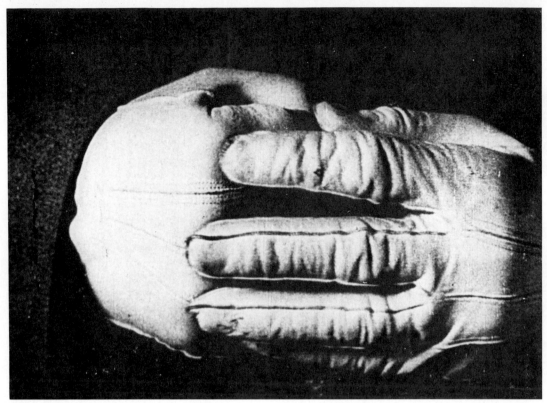

Fig. 8-12
Mother: *Pudovkin's use of the "plastic material." Defining a bureaucratic policeman by his gloved hands.*

of the Boy's trial for murder in *Intolerance* — she sees the corruption of justice. The judges are more interested in dozing or breeding race horses than in administering justice; the unsympathetic gallery has come to the trial for a good sadistic show. The unjust social process turns the old woman into a radical. She helps her son escape from prison, and together they march in the forefront of a workers' demonstration. Although both she and Pavel die, cut down by the bullets of the Cossacks and the hooves of their horses, the story of her education serves as a model for all the workers of Russia and a metaphor for the results of their education that would eventually surface in 1917.

Pudovkin's handling of actors and shaping of scenes are exceptional. His principle of acting — that the film's context, its decor, its business, its use of objects, work with the actor to create a performance — is demonstrated throughout

Mother. A most effective example is the scene of mourning in which the mother sits by the corpse of her husband. Pudovkin alternates among several shots: a far shot of the mother sitting beside the bier, the walls gray and bare behind her; a close shot of water dripping in a bucket (the scene's "plastic material"); a close shot of the mother's face, motionless. The mother's face needs no motion. The bareness of the room, the steadily dripping water, our knowledge of the husband's death create all the emotion the scene needs. Her still, quiet face mirrors all the sorrow that has been built around her.

A similar principle creates the viciousness of the strikebreakers, the Black Hundreds. As they make plans in a saloon, Pudovkin intercuts shots of the musicians playing a jolly tune, shots of a man's hands dismembering a fish (the plastic material), and shots of the strikebreakers'

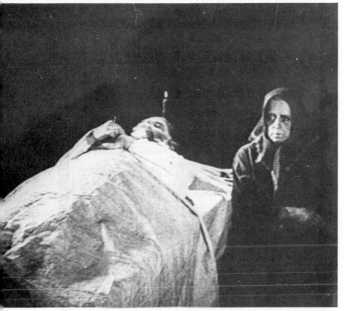

Fig. 8-13

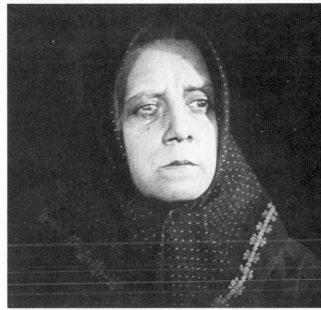

Fig. 8-14

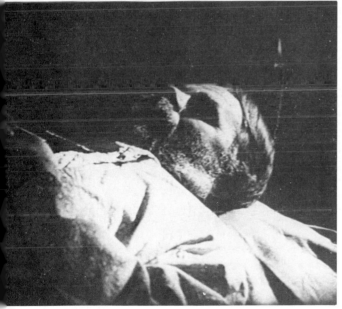

Fig. 8-15
Mother: *the scene of mourning — built with four shots.*

Fig. 8-16

faces. These men need not grimace and glower to reveal their nastiness; by juxtaposing their discussion with happy, frenetic music and the brutal gutting of a fish, Pudovkin creates all the viciousness he needs.

Significant also is the camera angle Pudovkin uses to shoot a scene. The far shot of the mourning mother beside the corpse is a downshot from a high camera position (a high-angle shot). Pudovkin discovered that the downward angle emphasizes the characters' smallness, their feeling of being alone, their insignificance. Conversely, the extreme upward angle (a low-angle shot) can magnify the self-importance of characters, their smugness and petty self-esteem —or can make them appear more formidable, like the guard outside the courthouse. Pudovkin uses extreme upward angles for his satiric shots of the factory owners, of the corrupt judges, of the egotistical, self-important policeman (played by Pudovkin himself) who comes to search the mother's house for the strikers' guns. A slight upward angle produces not satire or intimidation but ennoblement, making the character grand without delusions of grandeur. Pudovkin's final shots of the mother marching nobly at the head of the demonstration are slight upward shots. In fact, Pudovkin mirrors the state of the mother's mind and the progress of her education with his choice of camera positions. He shoots her from above before her conversion; he shoots her from below to ennoble her after it. With such control of setting and camera angle, Pudovkin helps his actress, Vera Baranovskaya, to give a brilliant performance.

Pudovkin relies primarily on the narrative cut, on the lessons he had learned from Griffith. Like Griffith, he works for fluidity in building a scene, a fluidity that hides the cut from the viewer so that we synthesize the complete emotional experience. Most reminiscent of Griffith is the subjective flashback (or mindscreen) in which the mother remembers her son hiding the guns. Such fluid, narrative cutting was infrequent in Eisenstein. But like Eisenstein, Pudovkin could also use tricky montage effects when he needed the power of a physical assault. To reveal the joy in Pavel's heart when he discovers that his comrades will soon free him from prison, Pudovkin splices together a series of images to evoke the sensation of joy. The director's sensitivity to the actor's needs told him that merely to show a smile on Pavel's face would be fakey and punchless. Instead, Pudovkin cuts from Pavel's face to a rapid series of beautiful natural images: a flowing river, tree-lined fields, a happy child playing. Pudovkin uses a similar method to reveal the other prisoners' thoughts of home: He uses shots of fields, of horses, of plowing, of hands feeling the soil. Like Eisenstein's cuts, the shots are related thematically, not narratively; unlike Eisenstein, the images are natural rather than artificial, warm and human rather than satirical. Pudovkin's famous ice shots, the parallel montage with which the film's climax begins, also echo Eisenstein's metaphorical cuts as well as Griffith's crosscutting. Pudovkin cuts repeatedly from the shots of marching workers, steadily growing in mass, rhythm, and purpose, to shots of ice flowing on the river, steadily growing in mass, rhythm, and direction. Although the image of the ice cake echoes Griffith's *Way Down East*, the intellectual function of it does not.

Like Eisenstein, Pudovkin knew how to analyze a quick action into its component movements to add emphasis, shock, and drama to the event. For example, in the climactic demonstration sequence, Pudovkin emphasizes the brutality of the slaughter by breaking the moment of the soldiers' initial attack into thirteen shots: (1) a gloved hand of the commanding officer is raised, close-up; (2) the soldiers raise their rifles, full shot; (3) the workers see the rifles and start to scurry, far shot; (4) the mother and Pavel embrace, medium close; (5) the commanding officer's gloved hand drops, close-up; (6) the rifles fire, full shot; (7) a fallen worker's body crashes in a pool of muddy water, close shot, very quick; (8) another worker plunges face first into the water, close, very quick; (9) another body falling, close on midsection, quick; (10) the red flag starts to fall, silhouetted against the sky, close; (11) the falling flag and its bearer reflected in the water as they both fall into the mud; (12) the mother and Pavel continue to embrace, medium close; (13) Pavel falls, still locked in the embrace. Out of the sudden loss and violence of this moment the mother learns her last political lesson;

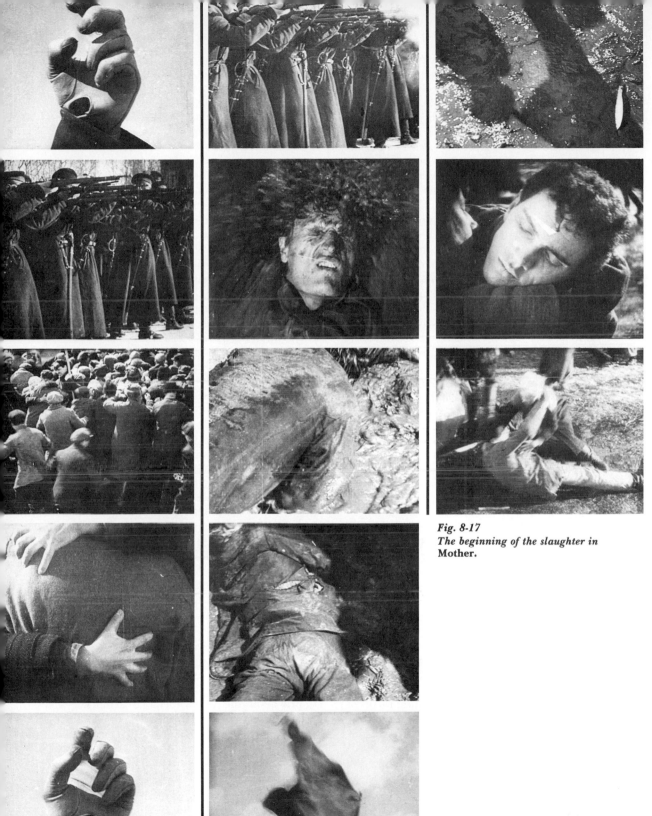

Fig. 8-17
The beginning of the slaughter in
Mother.

courageously she picks up the fallen flag and walks toward the charging troops (excellent series of cuts with contrasting directions and rhythms). Though they kill her, she dies a rebel, the metaphorical mother of the nation that is born with her death.

Like *Mother, The End of St. Petersburg* (1927) is a story of political education, of a character who betrays the revolutionists early in the film only to join them before the end of it. A young peasant boy from the country must leave for the city in order to survive; there is neither enough land nor enough food on the farm to support him. Pudovkin draws a visual contrast between city and country with the opening shots of animals, fields, rivers, and trees, and the later shots of factories and buildings and statues. The boy feels dwarfed in the city of St. Petersburg. Pudovkin shoots from high angles down at the boy, making him seem small and worthless in comparison with the huge statues, high buildings, and vast public squares.

The boy, ignorant of political realities, becomes a strikebreaker and betrays the leaders of the strike, one of whom is his own cousin. The boy feels guilty for his betrayal. He returns to the man's home to give the man's wife the piece of silver he received for his information. Pudovkin's skill in narrative cutting and manipulating detail creates a memorable scene. The boy enters the room. He and the wife look at each other, faces motionless, saying nothing. He slowly walks toward her. In a close-up of his right hand we see him slowly and fumblingly pull the piece of silver from his pocket and put it on the table, the same table where the whole family sat together earlier in the film. The wife says nothing; she just looks at his face and his coin. The boy says nothing. He slowly turns and walks out the door. The woman's grim silence, a small, seemingly trivial action, teaches him the meaning of his betrayal of another human being.

The second half of the film is a sharp structural shift. Pudovkin abandons the narrative focus on the boy to treat the political events of 1914–17 that "ended" St. Petersburg by converting it to Leningrad: World War I, the February Revolution, Kerensky's Provisional Government, and the October Revolution. Like *October, The End of St. Petersburg* was intended to commemorate the tenth anniversary of the final, Bolshevik Revolution. Although the film's second half lacks narrative unity (the thin unifying thread is the boy's development into a Bolshevik soldier), it contains some powerful thematic contrasts that Pudovkin draws with his control of montage.

The film makes a brilliant visual contrast between the idealistic glories and the horrifying realities of war. When war is declared, Pudovkin shows a procession of marching soldiers, smartly filing into formation. Pudovkin's shot reveals only their bodies from the neck down — their sabres, their uniforms, their medals, their gold braid, their boots. Not their heads. They obviously have no heads. As the parade of soldiers marches off to war, Pudovkin cuts the sequence rhythmically to look and feel like a gaudy carnival: Trumpets blare, flags flap, drums rattle, arms wave, girls throw flower petals, an orator speaks (extreme upward angle to burlesque his grandiloquence). From the rhythmic shots of celebration, Pudovkin cuts to a quiet shot of the sky; suddenly a shell explodes, splattering the earth in the foreground. The glory of war has been replaced by the reality. Pudovkin continues with horrific shots of trenches, fire throwers, smoke, bodies. Not content to let the contrast rest there, he cuts back and forth between the violent war at the front and violent men haggling at the stock exchange, in a sequence clearly inspired by *A Corner in Wheat*. While men die in the military war, other men get rich in the financial war.

Pudovkin's next film, *The Heir to Genghis Khan*, also called *Storm Over Asia* (1928), is yet another story of revolutionary education, of potential betrayal converted into political camaraderie. A young Mongol hunter learns that the value of his pelts is fixed by the greed of the capitalists, who buy them as cheaply as they can. When the Mongol is captured by his people's enemies (he has since joined the Partisan guerrilla army in their struggle against the imperialists), the young man produces papers that seem to prove him the heir of the great Genghis Khan, papers that he has acquired accidentally and that make him the hero's heir only in the sense that all Mongols rightfully share that heritage. The imperialist rulers (the British Army in the original version, the White Army in the American one), however, try to use the lad to

Fig. 8-18

Fig. 8-19

Fig. 8-20

Fig. 8-21

The End of St. Petersburg. *The deflation of war: soldiers without heads, flying flags, a fancy-speaking orator (note the upward angle to burlesque him), as men die in the smoke and carnage on the battlefield.*

keep his own people in bondage. The young Mongol perceives their viciousness, rejects the rich and soft life they offer him, breaks free from his captors, and leads his people in a successful uprising.

The film contains several masterful sequences. The most striking is a montage sequence that deflates both the sanctity of religion and the pretentions to gentility of the imperialists. Pudovkin cuts back and forth between the religious icons, which are being scrubbed and polished for a religious festival, to shots of the rich imperialists, who are also being scrubbed and powdered and dressed to attend the festival. These parallel and intercut activi-

ties turn the religious objects into pampered dolls and the pampered imperialists into dead wood.

Another, subtler device is Pudovkin's use of a puddle of muddy water, an exemplary application of his notion of plastic material. A puddle blocks the town's main road. When a soldier leads the young Mongol to be shot, the Mongol walks directly through the puddle; the soldier carefully walks around it, taking care not to soil his boots. The puddle instantly delineates the class conflict (reminiscent of Chaplin), the difference between the rulers and the people. Interestingly, when the soldier is later commanded to save the Mongol, he runs directly

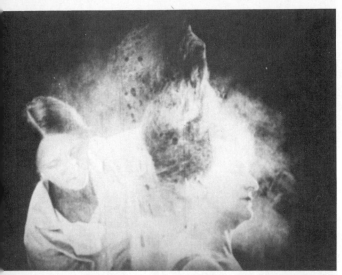

Fig. 8-22

Fig. 8-23

Satiric cross-cuts in Storm Over Asia: *from powdering and pampering a rich imperialist to polishing up a religious icon.*

through the puddle in his frenzy and haste.

The film's third remarkable device is the metaphor with which it ends, a howling, furious wind that strips the branches off the trees and the imperialist soldiers off the land. The wind, like the flowing ice in *Mother*, is a natural image; it symbolizes the spirit of the people,

rising irresistibly to blow the foreign element from their soil.

Like Eisenstein, Pudovkin believed that the value of the sound film would be its asynchronous, tonal use of sound rather than a synchronized dialogue and picture. In discussing the way he would have used sound in the silent *Mother*, Pudovkin said he would have evoked the sorrow of the mourning scene not with the synchronized sound of the mother's weeping but with the steady, hollow sound of the water dripping into the bucket. Like Eisenstein, Pudovkin had difficulty putting his theories into practice. *The Story of a Simple Case* (1932) was originally intended as a sound picture. It was finally released silent. It is uncertain whether the film's difficulties with sound stemmed from the clumsiness of the director with sound or the clumsiness of the Soviet sound machines and technicians. His next sound film, *Deserter* (1933), is his most respected: the story of a young German worker who, like the protagonists of Pudovkin's silent films, receives an education in political radicalism. Originally intended as a German-Soviet co-production, the new Hitler government forced Pudovkin to finish shooting in Russia. Pudovkin continued directing and acting in films for the next twenty years, until his death in 1953; during those twenty years he directed only about a half-dozen major films. Like Eisenstein, he was castigated for his formalism and his fictional manipulating of official Soviet history; like Eisenstein, he spent much of his later life teaching and writing. But Pudovkin's few sound films lack the stature of his silent films; his purely visual method never successfully wedded sound to his control of the plastic material.

Dovzhenko, Vertov, and Others

Alexander Dovzhenko was the third of the great Soviet directors. Though he shared both the political philosophy of Marx and the montage methods of Kuleshov with Eisenstein and Pudovkin, Dovzhenko's style was completely original. Unlike Eisenstein and Pudovkin, Dovzhenko came from the provinces, not the capital, from the Ukraine, not Moscow or St.

Petersburg. Dovzhenko's films are saturated in local Ukrainian life and customs, as well as in the folk-legend spirit and poetry of the province. Dovzhenko's films desert realism and linear construction even more completely than Eisenstein's or Pudovkin's. His is a world where horses talk, where paintings of heroes in picture frames roll their eyes at the bastardization of their principles, where animals sniff the revolutionary spirit in the air. The Dovzhenko film is structured not as story nor even as mass political action but purely as visual metaphor that develops a theme and allows the filmmaker immense elliptical jumps in time, space, and continuity.

Arsenal (1929) is the first of his mature film poems. Made after three years of apprentice directing in which Dovzhenko converted himself from painter of static scenes on canvas to director of moving ones on a screen, *Arsenal*'s subject is, roughly, the birth and growth of the revolutionary spirit in the Ukraine. Whereas Eisenstein might develop such a theme by showing the action of a human mass in relation to a single historical event, and Pudovkin might develop it by showing a single Ukrainian's radicalization, Dovzhenko seems to spread all the events of the revolutionary years before him and then to select those images and vignettes that appeal to him. The film darts from place to place, from social class to social class, from political meeting to war to church procession to factory to a train chugging through the snow.

Somewhat as in the second half of Pudovkin's *St. Petersburg*, Dovzhenko uses a central figure—a soldier who deserts the czar to serve the revolution—as a loose peg on which to hang the film's action. Scenes with the soldier flow through the film's many vignettes. In the final sequence, the White Army captures the soldier, leads him in front of a firing squad, and shoots him. The Ukrainian soldier does not die; the bullets do not strike him. He stands there defiantly. Although the forces of tyranny can capture a single arsenal, although they can shoot a single rebel, they cannot murder the spirit of rebellion and freedom in the hearts of the people. The Ukrainian becomes a metaphor for that spirit. His presence throughout the film has been as metaphor, not as traditional protagonist. Dovzhenko's films are not narratives

of events but metaphors for the feeling and the significance of the events.

Dovzhenko's striking compositions in light and space reveal the eye of a painter. Vast shots of sky and clouds, framed at the left by a tall tree and with the thinnest strip of land at the bottom with a group of tiny men trooping across it, are among Dovzhenko's favorite views. A similar principle of composition controls his snow sequences—vast expanses of white, a peasant wife huddled in black beside a grave in the lower right corner of the frame, a team of horses bearing the husband's body to the grave in the central background. Dovzhenko's painter's eye sees the power and tension of shooting with the tilted camera, on an angle to rather than parallel with the world he is filming.

But Dovzhenko's compositions are as impressive for their content as for their look. His shots of war, which dwarf men as tiny dots on the horizon or turn them into statues in silhouette against the sky, also evoke the horrors of useless human slaughter. If Pudovkin deflates war by analyzing it, Dovzhenko deflates it with haunting images of sheer horror. Dovzhenko cuts repeatedly to the frenzied laughter of a German officer who has been gassed, to a frozen smile on the face of a corpse (a smile of death), to a frozen hand sticking out of a pile of dirt (a single reminder that a whole man once breathed the air).

Dovzhenko's style is also dependent on extended metaphors. In *Arsenal*, Dovzhenko shows the journey of a train, loaded with soldiers of the czar. The train has no brakes; it hurtles faster and faster down the track until it crashes, killing the men who are still aboard. The train becomes a metaphor for the unquestioning servants of political tyranny, blindly accepting the murderous orders of their government. Dovzhenko brings the metaphor alive with his control of montage: tracking shots of the speeding train, of some soldiers frenziedly leaping from it just before the collision, of other soldiers contentedly listening to accordion music in ignorance of their doom, and swirling cuts when the train crashes into the station. Dovzhenko dramatizes the death of the soldiers by following the journey of the accordion, the former instrument of pleasure.

Fig. 8-24

Fig. 8-25

Fig 8-26

Fig. 8-27

Arsenal: *the horrors of war. Frozen statues of death in silhouette . . . a mad laugh . . . a frozen smile . . . a hand.*

Tossed from the train in the collision, the accordion lies on the ground full of air; suddenly it collapses as all the air goes out of it. The "death" of the accordion is a symbol for the death of all the soldiers on the metaphoric train.

Dovzhenko's films are composed of metaphors within metaphors, of isolated vignettes, of scenes and characters manifesting themselves without preparation or introduction, playing themselves out on the screen and then disappearing, often never returning to the film at all. The film's general theme and the unity of the director-poet's imagination keep the apparently random scenes together. Dovzhenko's second great silent film-poem, *Earth* (1930), is another series of images and vignettes, this one revolving around the earth, the harvests, the relationships of people, machines, and the cycles of life. His sound films, *Ivan* (1932), *Aerograd* (1935), and *Schors* (1939), were equally daring, episodic, and imagistic. Not surprisingly, Dovzhenko ran into stiff Soviet criticism; he was the most elliptical director of them all. How could his films be socially useful if the audiences could not follow them? Dovzhenko made only two films in his last fifteen years; he died in 1956.

The Pudovkin–Eisenstein pattern had asserted itself again—the great innovative mind stifled by the state's ever-narrowing definitions of artistic utility.

Dziga Vertov, one of the Soviet Union's pioneers in combining documentary footage with political commitment, experimental cinema with ideological statement, suffered similar artistic strangulation. His brother, cameraman Boris Kaufman, left Russia to shoot all the films of Jean Vigo in France before going to Hollywood, where he shot such pictures as *On the Waterfront* and *The Pawnbroker*. His other brother, cameraman Mikhail Kaufman, stayed to direct documentaries and shoot Vertov's *The Man with a Movie Camera* (literally, *Man with Movie Camera*; 1928, released 1929), which remains one of the most distinctive and adventurous films of any era. Like Ruttmann's *Berlin* and Mikhail Kaufman's *Moscow* (1927), the film is organized as an examination of a cross section of life in a major city—its work and play from morning to night. Unlike Ruttmann, however, Vertov depicts the ways that the cinema itself has become an intrinsic part of modern life and a marvelous aid to seeing and understanding that life. The film begins with shots of an empty movie theatre. When the patrons arrive, the seats of the theatre fold down by themselves to greet them. Thus the film begins itself. The film they see is the film we see—for *The Man with a Movie Camera* is a film-within-a-film about filmmaking. In that film-within-a-film Vertov compares the lens of the movie camera and its operations to the human eye and its operations —declaring the cinema an extension of human vision. He demonstrates the processes of editing (the movie "stops" while the editor decides which shot to use next) and the relationship of still cinema frames to moving cinema imagery. He also draws parallels between the processes of cinema and other societal occupations that depend on machines that spin circularly or cycle repeatedly—the pumping of pistons, the winding of threads, the packing of cigarette boxes, various other whirring wheels and gears for grinding, winding, spinning, and propelling. If Vertov takes the "magic" out of cinema by exposing how it does its tricks, he also endows it with another form of magic—the magic of all

Fig. 8-28

Fig. 8-29
Two consecutive frames from **The Man with a Movie Camera.**

processes of modern mechanical life that do their work in the service of human beings.

Like everyone else in the society, the man with the movie camera has a job to do—his special work being to record and reveal the work of everyone else. And like everyone else in the society, the man with the movie camera likes to play. The final section of the film allows the playful camera to dazzle us with its cinematic juggling—slow motion, accelerated motion, split screens, superimpositions, stop-motion animation—demystifying the cinema even as it gives the audience the visual treats it came to the theatre to enjoy. Grounded in daily life as much as in the theory and practice of cinema, this brilliantly reflexive documen-

Tarkovsky's Andrei
Roublyov.

Fig. 8-30

tary renders cinema and life inseparable. But
despite this impressive synthesis of radical form
and radical ideology, Vertov made few major
films after 1930, the most important being *Enthusiasm* (1931), which had a loud, complex,
contrapuntal soundtrack, exploding with the
energy of sound/picture montage, and *Three
Songs of Lenin* (1934), which combined documentary footage with lyrical passages in honor
of the founding father. He died in 1954 after
twenty years of reduced influence and enforced
idleness.

The greatest comic director of the Soviet
silent era was Boris Barnet, best known for *Girl
with the Hatbox* (1927) and the extraordinarily
inventive *House on Trubnaya Square* (1928).

Lesser film minds enjoyed healthier and
longer careers. Abram Room—whose great silent film, *Bed and Sofa* (1927), combined a sensitive study of a love triangle with the social
problems of abortion and adequate housing—
continued to make competent films in the
sound era. Room's realistic human focus and
conventional plotting were more consistent
with the new official aesthetic of "socialist realism" than were the methods of the more adventurous silent masters. Esther Shub used
montage effects to bring old newsreel footage
to life, providing a striking, imaginative, and

officially sanctioned view of what it was like to
live in *The Russia of Nikolai II and Lev Tolstoy*
(1928) and other eras.

In the early years of sound, the more
realistic and less elliptical directors triumphed.
Behind the struggle between realism and
abstraction in the cinema lay a more general
battle that was being waged between two conflicting forces in all the Soviet arts: the struggle
between socialist realism and constructivist abstraction for control of the "true path" of the
People's Revolutionary Art. The central arena
for the struggle was the theatre, where the
principles of Stanislavski's Moscow Art Theatre
(detailed, realistic characters; lucid stories of
human interaction in a clear social setting)
triumphed over those of Vsevolod Meyerhold's
"constructivism" (more abstract and symbolic
settings; epic stories of vast social forces and
movements). The official canonization of the
Stanislavski method (despite the Moscow Art
Theatre's czarist and elitist origins) led to the
vilification and ostracizing of Meyerhold.
Bertolt Brecht, who first fled Hitler's Germany
for the Soviet Union, found a very cool reception there in 1933, for Brecht and Meyerhold
held similar theories of the stage. This conflict
of values in the theatre necessarily spilled over
into the cinema, where several film directors

Tenghiz Abuladze's
Repentance.

Fig. 8-31

(Eisenstein, for example) had been extremely influenced by Meyerhold.

Nikolai Ekk, whose *Road to Life* (1931) was the first commercially successful Soviet sound film, found the new socialist-realist assumptions very congenial. His film is both a close, warm study of human feelings and exertion as well as a social lesson on how the "wild boys" of Russia —the homeless juvenile delinquents roaming the streets—found a purpose in life through collective labor. The Vasiliev Brothers' *Chapayev* (1934) became the model for the study of Revolutionary heroes, the intimate portrayal of a military leader whose great strengths are his energy, passion, humor, and love for the people, and who overcomes his great weaknesses—excessive individuality, a stubborn refusal to study the new ways — to unite his heroic band of guerrillas with the spirit of the entire Red Army.

Yakov Protazanov was another of the successful realist directors of the first decade of sound, one of the few film directors of the czarist era to return to Soviet Russia. Grigori Kozintsev and Leonid Trauberg founded the actor-oriented "FEX" group (Society for Eccentric Actors) in the silent period in answer to the montage-oriented Kuleshov group. They continued to make films into the 1960s, including the respected color version of Pasternak's translation of *Hamlet* (1964). Mark Donskoy

made the careful, literate biographical trilogy of Maxim Gorky's growth from youth to maturity (*Childhood of Gorky*, 1938; *In the World*, 1939; *My Universities*, 1940).

But for almost twenty-five years the imagination and creativity of the Soviet film were tightly reined by a government policy and aesthetic that found it exceedingly difficult to force innovative minds into the prescribed channels of film expression. The battles within the Soviet arts of the late 1920s mirrored the larger battle in Soviet politics, as Joseph Stalin seized control of the Central Soviet Communist Party in 1927 (Lenin had died in 1924) and forced Leon Trotsky, a key theorist and organizer of the Bolshevik Revolution, equal in importance to Lenin—and Stalin's most serious political and ideological rival—into exile in 1929. He also forced Eisenstein to cut Trotsky almost completely out of *October*. For the critical years from 1929 to 1937—the transitional years between silence and sound—Stalin replaced Lenin's sympathetic commissar for information, Anatoly Lunacharsky, who encouraged artistic innovation, with a flunky, Boris Shumyatsky, a business-minded bureaucrat who viewed his job as bringing the eccentric, "formalistic" artists in line. Shumyatsky's "bringing the artists in line" was as responsible for the silence of Eisenstein in those key years as the triumph of socialist realism. Stalin dismissed Shumyatsky in 1937 for failing to produce enough films and enough significant films; the Soviet filmmakers then enjoyed three years of freedom. But the war against Germany in 1940 imposed restrictions on Soviet directors again; certain kinds of films were needed to boost morale at the front and at home. After the war, Stalin clamped down on the directors again. Only since his death in 1953 have Soviet films regained prestige on international screens with such powerful and personal films as Mikhail Kalatozov's *The Cranes Are Flying* (1957), Grigori Chukhrai's *Ballad of a Soldier* (1959), Alexei Batalov's *The Overcoat* (1959), Josef Heifitz's *Lady with a Dog* (1960), Sergei Bondarchuk's *War and Peace* (1966), Andrei Konchalovsky's *The First Teacher* (1966), and Eldar Ryazanov's *A Forgotten Tune for Flute* (1987).

The three most highly respected film artists of the post-Stalinist period were Sergei Paradjanian — known overseas as Sergei Paradjanov — a musician, painter, and connoisseur of folk tales who directed the classic *Shadows of Forgotten Ancestors* (1964), *Sayat Nova* (*The Color of Pomegranates*, 1968, which circulated in Europe in an unfinished version while its maker was imprisoned for his cultural and sexual politics, and which he completed in 1978), and *Ashik Kerib* (1988); Tenghiz Abuladze, who made the great trilogy *Molba* (*Prayer*, 1969), *The Wishing Tree* (1978), and *Repentance* (1987); and Andrei Tarkovsky, whose meditative, intense works include *Ivan's Childhood* (*My Name is Ivan*, 1962), *Andrei Roublyov* (or *Andrei Rublev*, 1966, the brilliant study of an icon painter in medieval Russia, and through him of the relations between the suffering and grime of the world and the transcendent, almost impossible achievements of art and obsessive devotion — not shown in Russia until 1972, and then not widely, though it had won a prize at the Cannes Film Festival in 1966), *Solaris* (1971, released 1972, restored 1989 — a dreamlike science-fiction film about a planet of dreams, based on the novel by Stanislaw Lem), *Mirror* (1974), *Stalker* (1979, released

1981), *Nostalghia* (1983, made in Italy), and *The Sacrifice* (1986, made in Sweden shortly before his death). Upset that his films were so rarely shown in his homeland, Tarkovsky defected to the West in 1984; Paradjanov, who died in 1990, found satisfaction in making films of utter artistic purity despite his limited audience. But *Repentance* was shown to acclaim abroad and huge lines of patrons at home, its uncompromising and darkly comical anti-Stalinism proof that a new openness (*glasnost*) was indeed beginning to flourish in Mikhail Gorbachev's Soviet Union as the Cold War (1945–1990) drew to a close.

The greatest years of Soviet filmmaking, from 1922 (*Kino-Pravda*) to 1930 (*Earth*), demonstrated how powerful and significant are the effects of simply joining pieces of celluloid together. In Hollywood, Eisenstein's methods were so admired in the late 1920s that producers began installing metronomes on sets and in cutting rooms to control the rhythms of the movement and editing. In the early years of sound, Hollywood did an about-face, rejecting the discordant effects of montage in favor of what came to be called "Hollywood montage" (a series of shots bridged by rapid dissolves rather than straight cuts, often employing superimposition as well as musical underscoring, used to condense or emblematize a process taking place over a long period of time), reducing montage to an isolated effect. In the 1960s and 1970s, however, after a long period devoted to the exploration of *mise-en-scène* (augmented by the wide-screen revolution of the 1950s), the quick cutting of television commercials, the tense and violent editing of action films like *Bullitt* and *The French Connection*, the subjective flashes into the past of *Hiroshima, mon amour* and *Z* or into the labyrinth of *Last Year at Marienbad*, the satiric cross-cutting in *Medium Cool*, the symbolic montage sequences in *Scorpio Rising*, the dialectical juxtapositions that constitute Bruce Conner's *A Movie*, and the intensely charged, phenomenally rapid cutting of Stan Brakhage's *Dog Star Man* all proved that montage was once again very much "in."

9

Sound

According to legend, sound unexpectedly descended on the film industry from the skies, like an ancient god out of a machine, when *The Jazz Singer* opened on Broadway on October 6, 1927. Although the success of *The Jazz Singer* overthrew the film industry of 1927 with incredible speed, preparation for the entrance of sound had been building for over thirty years. The idea for the sound film was born with the film itself. W. K. L. Dickson even claimed to have produced a rough synchronization of word and picture with his Kineto-phonograph of 1889.

For the first twenty years of film history inventors worked to wed sight and sound. Many of the same inventors who had developed the first cinema cameras and projectors turned to sound synchronization after the film artists and industrialists had taken their toys and put them to use. In France, between 1896 and 1900, Auguste Baron, Henri Joly, and Georges Demeny patented various processes of synchronizing moving pictures with sounds recorded on a disc. Between 1900 and 1910, Léon Gaumont demonstrated various synchronized-sound pictures, both at the World Exposition of 1900 and in his own Paris theatres. In 1910, the German film pioneer Oskar Messter

produced a film with synchronized sound, *The Green Forest*. And in America, the Edison Company had produced a fifteen-minute, vaguely synchronized musical version of *Mother Goose Tales* (shot in one continuous take!) as early as 1912. Edison's six-minute *Nursery Favorites* came out in 1913, projected from what he called the Kinetophone. Like the pioneers of an earlier film era, the first sound pioneers decorated their inventions with Greco-Latin names that almost required a special apparatus to pronounce: Phonorama, Graphonocone, Chronophone. In addition to these early picture-sound apparatuses, live sounds were extremely common in the nickelodeons of 1905–1912. Not only was there the piano, organ, or trio of musicians, but live actors sometimes stood behind the screen to speak the lines accompanying the pictures; or a narrator (called the *benshi* in Japan, where this practice flourished throughout the silent era) might explain and comment upon the action as well as deliver the dialogue. It seemed inevitable that these moving pictures would acquire the ability to make their own noise.

The first practical, dependable synthesis of picture and sound came just after World War I. There were two primary problems that confronted the inventor of a sound-film process. The first, obviously, was synchronization. How were the film and the sound to be kept permanently and constantly "in sync"? The method of coupling a projected film with a recorded disc was dangerous; with two separate machines it was terribly easy for the two to slip "out of sync." The film could break; the stylus could skip. *Singin' in the Rain* (1952), a marvelous parody of the transitional era from silent to sound films, revealed the unintentionally comic results when the cavalier's voice issued from the damsel's moving lips. Although the first commercially successful American sound-film process, the Vitaphone, synchronized a disc player with the film projector, a more stable method had been developed as early as 1919. Three German inventors had discovered the means of recording the sound track directly on the film itself (optical sound). Using the principle of the oscilloscope, which converts sound into light beams, the Germans used a photocell to convert the sound into light beams, recorded the beams on the side of the strip of film next to the image, and then built a reader on the projector that could retranslate the light beams into sound. This German discovery, known as the "Tri-Ergon Process," later became the ruling sound-film patent of Europe. In America, a sound-on-film process had been developed by Lee De Forest in the early 1920s.

An earlier De Forest invention solved the second problem of the sound film — amplification. The sound not only had to be synchronized, it had to be audible. A film had to make enough noise to reach the ears of all the patrons who filled the huge movie palaces. The earliest phonographs and radios, lacking the means of amplification, could entertain only one listener, who stuck the listening tube in his ears (similar to the stereo systems on today's jets). In 1906, De Forest patented the audion tube, the little vacuum tube that magnified the sounds it received and drove them into a speaker. De Forest's tube gave birth to many children — radio, the public address system — and grandchildren — television, high-fidelity and stereo components. It also gave birth to the sound film. Whatever the system of synchronization, the audion tube magnified the sound so that an entire audience could hear it.

By 1923 De Forest was making and showing little synchronized sound films of variety acts, singers, politicians, and famous comedians. De Forest also gave a filmed lecture-demonstration of his sound-on-film process, which he called the Phonofilm. *Singin' in the Rain,* historically relevant as well as brilliantly funny, satirizes the good professor De Forest with its film clip of a horse-faced, nasal-voiced scientist, his nose and forehead grotesquely distorted by a wide-angle lens, tautologically telling the audience that it is watching a talking picture. Despite De Forest's success with his high-quality sound-on-film process, the Bell Telephone Company's research laboratory, Western Electric, developed and marketed the less dependable sound-on-disc process, christened the Vitaphone, in 1925.

Western Electric offered the Vitaphone to the biggest producer in Hollywood, Adolph Zukor. Paramount did not want it. Neither did any other major company. Their reasons for rejecting sound were obvious: It was an untried and expensive innovation that could only disrupt a business that had become increasingly stable and profitable. Sound recording was ticklish and expensive; it would slow down production schedules. Sound equipment was expensive to buy, especially for the theatre owners whose houses would have to be converted, at up to $20,000 per theatre, before any sound film could be shown. Nor did the competing sound-film processes make the decision easier. On which should the wise theatre owner place a commercial bet? The confusion was like that surrounding competing color television processes of the early 1960s, the competing home video cassette and disc formats of the late 1970s, or the competing computer formats of the 1980s. The wise theatre owner did nothing.

Rejected by the most powerful producers, Western Electric offered Vitaphone in 1926 to Warner Bros., a family of four producing brothers, whose small company had recently embarked on a costly program of major expansion. Having bought the remains of the Vitagraph Company (the last of the original Trust Companies) in 1925 and made it their distribution chain, Warners wished to expand their small network of theatres, to achieve full verti-

Will Hays welcomes moviegoers to aural wonders in the first Vitaphone program of 1926.

Fig. 9-1

cal integration, and to take on the big boys—Loew, Zukor, First National—who controlled enough theatre and distribution chains to choke the market for Warners' films. The Warner brothers bought the Vitaphone. Within three years they had swallowed First National and digested most of the theatres in that chain.

The Warner sound films started cautiously enough. On August 6, 1926, the Warners presented a program of short sound films; the first was an address by Will Hays praising the possibilities of the sound film, followed by the New York Philharmonic Orchestra and by leading artists of the opera, the concert, and the music hall. The Vitaphone shorts were no different from De Forest's earlier Phonofilm novelties. But on the same program, the Warners presented a feature film, *Don Juan* (directed, like *The Jazz Singer,* by Alan Crosland), with a synchronized musical score. A canned orchestra had replaced the live one in the pit. For over a year Warner Bros. presented a series of similar film programs: short, musical sound films and a feature with synchronized score. Because De Forest's phonofilms had failed commercially, the Warners were understandably wary of pictures that talked. Sam Warner was reported to have said, "If it can talk, it can sing."

Like the Warners, another lesser producer, William Fox, was a film businessman who gazed enviously at the Zukors and Loews on the heights; he decided to use sound the same way as the Warners did. Early in 1927 Fox began presenting mechanically scored films, the greatest of which was Murnau's *Sunrise* (planned and shot as a silent), whose music and sound effects were post-synchronized with true artistic sensitivity. Like the Warners, Fox also presented a series of short novelty films—performances by famous variety artists and conversations with famous people. In addition, Fox inaugurated the first newsreel film with synchronized narration, the Fox Movietone News. Unlike Vitaphone, the Fox system, called Movietone, was a sound-on-film process, exactly like De Forest's Phonofilm. One of De Forest's assistants, Theodore Case, had apparently pirated the inventor's system, made some slight modifications, and then sold it to Fox, who also purchased the American rights to the Tri-Ergon Process patents.

Fox exploited the novelty of coupling the sound of the human voice with the picture of moving lips. In the Movietone short referred to as *Shaw Talks for Movietone News* (1928), the audience is amused by seeing the image of the crusty playwright, by hearing his voice, by

Shaw Talks for Movietone News: *The playwright scowls his "Mussolini look."*

Fig. 9-2

enjoying his garrulous, improvised pleasantries, and by recognizing the mechanical reproduction of other natural sounds like birds chirping and gravel crackling on the garden path. Visually the film is static and uninteresting. It uses only two setups: a brief far shot as Shaw walks down the path, then a medium shot of Shaw's head and torso that lasts for the duration of the film (at least five minutes without a cut). Perhaps the only reason the film splurged with the second setup was that the honk of an automobile horn (clearly audible on the sound track) "spoiled" the first take a few minutes after the camera started rolling. The moving pictures had become a simple recording device once again. The camera stopped speaking as the movies learned to talk. The tendency of the Movietone shorts to use picture merely as an accompaniment for human speech dominated the first sound films that tried to integrate speech and fictional action.

The Jazz Singer was neither the first sound film nor the first film to synchronize picture with speech and song. It was, however, the first film to use synchronized sound as a means of telling a story. Most of the film was shot silent and the musical score later synchronized with the finished picture. In this respect Warners' *Jazz Singer* went no further than their *Don Juan*.

But at least five sequences used synchronized speech.

In one, the jazz singer returns to his Orthodox Jewish home to visit his parents. His mother (Eugenie Besserer) enjoys seeing him and listening to his "jazzy" singing of "Blue Skies." His father (Warner Oland), a cantor, does not and orders an end to all profane jazz in his house. The father's command to stop the music is the cue for the film to revert to silence. In another of the lip-synchronized sequences, Jolson sings his "Mammy" number to an audience in a theatre. The number is exactly like the vaudeville shorts recorded earlier on the Phonofilm, the Vitaphone, and the Movietone —with two differences. First, Jolson performed for two specific people who were watching him: his girl (backstage) and his mother (in the audience). Second, his song played a functional role in the thematic action of the film: The cantor's son had synthesized the sacred and profane functions of music by becoming a successful entertainer.

The schizophrenia of this first sound feature —part silent, part sound—revealed both the disadvantages and the advantages of the new medium. Whereas the silent sections of the film used rather flowing camera work and terse narrative cutting, the synchronized sections

Fig. 9-3
The Jazz Singer: *Jolson sings "Blue Skies" for his mother (Eugenie Besserer) and a frozen camera.*

were visually static and inert. For Jolson's third song, "Blue Skies," the camera was restricted to two shots: a medium shot of Jolson at the piano, and a close shot of Besserer responding (intercut sparingly). Most visually inert of all is the dialogue shot: a rambling, improvised series of Jewish jokes between choruses of the song—a full shot of Jolson and mama, one long take. The two actors obviously huddle together so that their voices can be picked up by the microphone hidden somewhere between them. When the film starts making synchronized noises, the camera stops doing everything but exposing film.

On the other hand, this moment of informal patter at the piano, though visually dull, is the most exciting and vital part of the entire movie. In the silent sequences Jolson is a poor mime, with hammy, overstated gestures and expressions. But when Jolson acquires a voice, the warmth, the excitement, the vibrations of it, the way its rambling spontaneity lays bare the

imagination of the mind that is making up the sounds, convert the overgesturing hands and the overactive eyes into a performance that seems effortlessly natural. "Wait a minute," Jolson tells an applauding audience in his first song-and-dialogue scene, "You ain't heard nothin' yet! Wait a minute, I tell ya, you ain't heard nothin'. You want to hear 'Toot Toot Tootsie'? All right, hold on . . . " The addition of a Vitaphone voice revealed the particular qualities of Al Jolson that made him a star. Not only the eyes are a window of the soul.

Problems

The Jazz Singer was a huge hit; it put new zip in a film business that had begun to sag in 1927. Warner Bros.' next Jolson vehicle, *The Singing Fool* (1928), was the top-grossing film of the 1920s and the top-grossing sound film until Disney's *Snow White and the Seven Dwarfs* (1937, released 1938). The movie czars who resisted sound because it would disrupt their stable business now had to convert to sound to stay in business. Although studio executives predicted that the sound and silent films would continue to coexist, the admission dollars of the public punctured the theory. Americans no longer wanted to see silent films. Silent films had taught them to see; the new invention of radio had taught them to hear, and its programs were free, like broadcast TV today. They would not leave their homes and spend their money if they could not both see and hear at the same time. By 1929 the silent film was virtually dead in America. Hollywood produced a few silent versions of sound films for foreign theatres and for rural American houses that were not yet equipped for sound. In 1926 a few silent films used synchronized music and sound effects as a commercial novelty; in 1929 and 1930 a few synchronized sound pictures were released silent as a commercial necessity. Only Chaplin resisted sound for aesthetic reasons, releasing *City Lights* with synchronized music but no dialogue—a silent that did tremendous business in 1931.

Although Hollywood leaped quickly into sound production, it did not leap without stumbling. The new sound film caused filmmakers and film critics three primary problems: artistic, technical, and commercial. The camera, which had spent the previous thirty years learning to take an active part in filmed fiction, suddenly became motionless and inexpressive, unless the scene was shot silent and then post-synchronized. Cuts were rare. Although the post-Griffith silent film had declared its independence from the stage, the early sound film became the vassal of the theatre once again— and rushed to hire its actors for their voices. The moving picture stopped moving and stopped using pictures. Critics and theorists sang a requiem for the film art and said amen.

Typical of the aesthetic blunders of the earliest sound films was the very first "all-talking" film, *Lights of New York* (Warner Bros., 1928, directed by Bryan Foy). The camera stood still to record scenes of seemingly endless and very bad dialogue. The film was cut sparingly if at all. The camera rarely panned more than two feet. Space was no longer charged with beauty or meaning. The decor no longer served any tonal, metaphoric, or narrative function; it was merely something to talk in. And the talking bodies huddled together so they could all be heard by the single microphone. In a scene in a barbershop, a character stops talking when he walks across the room. He could not speak unless he was parked under the mike. In a later scene, two thugs talk to their mobster boss in his office; the crooks sit on the edge of the sofa leaning toward the boss; the boss sits in his desk chair leaning toward his boys. All three actors strain to make sure that their voices can be heard by the mike, obviously buried in a canister on a ludicrous table that has no function in the scene except to hide the microphone.

Worse, the film not only strains to record the dialogue, but the dialogue, once recorded, is not worth hearing. The film's speech is crammed with mixed metaphors ("You think you can take any chicken you want and throw me back in the deck?"), with clichés ("You needed me to stick by you through all the tough times")—with the blatantly obvious and unnecessary. Especially ludicrous are the actors' attempts to render gangster slang with the most precise, theatrical diction ("Take him—for—a —ride"). Compared with the fluidity of a silent gangster film like Josef von Sternberg's *Underworld* (1927), with its completely effective moments of tough violence and subtle humor, *Lights of New York* was an abominable regression.

Many of the aesthetic shortcomings of the first sound films were less the result of theoretical problems than of the practical and technical problems of mastering the new machines. The stasis, the inertia of the early sound films resulted partially from the difficulty of silencing the whirring camera and partially from the difficulty of recording with a single, fixed microphone. To baffle the camera's clatter, the machine and its operator were imprisoned in a soundproof, windowed booth. The camera could neither tilt nor travel. The most it could manage was a slight pan. In the era before sound mixing and the boom microphone, a single mike had to be buried in a pivotal, stationary spot on the set. Of necessity, the microphone nailed the action to a tiny circle.

The comic attempts to hide the mike in *Singin' in the Rain*—in a bush, in the star's bosom—are exaggerated but accurate.

Yet another problem of the new sound equipment was its tremendous cost. Studios invested huge sums in the new machines and new soundproof buildings (sound stages) in which to use them. The theatre owner also faced enormous expenses, forced to buy new sound projectors, new speakers, and new wiring to link the two. Both studios and theatres borrowed from the banks to convert to sound. The movies, big business though they were, became subsidiaries of the banks. The two major sound processes in 1930, Western Electric's and RCA's, were themselves subdivisions of the Morgan and Rockefeller holdings. Studios borrowed from these very banks to buy the equipment that bank money had developed. The interrelationship of movies and high finance has continued ever since. By acquiring this large debt, the movie industry became dependent on Wall Street brokerage houses and banks to underwrite the costs of production. For many later historians and Marxist critics, this dependence on conservative American capital necessarily pushed the movies that the industry produced toward more conservative themes, socially and politically.

The new invention caused commercial problems with people as well as with paper. Studios suddenly discovered that popular stars and directors of the silent films were now liabilities in the era of speech. The incoming tide of foreign talent—the Negris and Jannings and Stillers—suddenly reversed and started flowing back to native shores. The actor or director with faulty English had no place in the Hollywood world of dialogue film. Lubitsch and Garbo stayed, but most returned home. (The next influx came in response to the rise of Hitler; by the time Peter Lorre arrived, colorful foreign voices were welcome.) American-born stars also had troubles with dialogue; their voices had to harmonize—as Keaton's, for example, did not—with the visual images they had projected in the silent era. The beautiful actress with a nasal rasp, the handsome Latin with a squeaky twang might as well have been unable to speak English at all. Diction coaches opened offices in the studios to polish the pronunciation of those voices that did not irreparably offend the microphone. (Stage actors with great or unique voices, like John Barrymore or the Marx Brothers, were left alone.) Along with the diction coaches came dialogue writers, many of them novelists or playwrights, whom the studios also needed. Old stars and old jobs died; new ones were born.

Eisenstein predicted that the sound film would try to solve its problems by taking the path of least resistance: by drifting into dialogue films and merely exploiting the audience's interest in seeing and hearing a person or event at the same time. Hollywood did just that, grandly advertising its films as "all-talking" and even as "100% all-talking, all-singing, and all-dancing." Gunshots, twittering birds, ringing telephones, banging doors became mandatory sound-film effects. Musical numbers became obligatory. Hollywood imported Broadway directors, players, and plays. At least the talk in a play had already been proved, and its actors had demonstrated their ability to speak it. Moving pictures were in danger of becoming hand-servants of the theatre once again, seemingly oblivious of the twenty-five years of development that had created a unique narrative art.

Solutions

While film aesthetes sang the blues, a few creative film artists worked to turn talkies into moving pictures with sound. Two of the greatest directors, René Clair and Eisenstein, refused to throw their handfuls of dirt on the film's grave, certain that the movies could absorb sound rather than the other way round. Hollywood quickly began to solve some of the technical problems. Although the noisy camera had to be encased, it could be released from its glass-windowed prison for those shots that did not require synchronized dialogue. In *Hallelujah* (1929), King Vidor let his camera roam silently over the fields, through a forest, aboard a train, and then dubbed in the singing of spirituals. Music in *Hallelujah*, its rhythms precisely synchronized with the visual action and emotional "beats," became one of the powerful sources of the film's meaning and effect—

either the exuberant joy of jazz or the soul-heavy sorrow of the spiritual. In *The Love Parade* (1929), Ernst Lubitsch shot ladies sitting in Parisian windows or soldiers marching gallantly in formation with a silent, tracking camera and then dubbed in the song that Maurice Chevalier or Jeanette MacDonald sang. In *All Quiet on the Western Front* (1930), Lewis Milestone shot battle scenes with silent, sweeping tracking shots of the lines of attacking armies and dubbed in the sounds of machine guns and grenades later. Luis Buñuel and Salvador Dali's Surrealist feature, *L'Age d'or* (1930), had its entire sound-track added after the picture was shot and edited; in a way that would have pleased Eisenstein, the "wrong" sound was often synchronized with the picture, putting the sound and image tracks in a montage relationship so that they could conflict with each other or work in counterpoint. But that was, to say the least, not a Hollywood movie.

Soon even the dialogue scenes gained mobility with the invention of the camera blimp, a device that slipped over the camera to baffle its clatter without banishing it to a soundproof booth; one blimp was invented by Lee De Forest. By 1929 Victor Fleming (in *The Virginian*) could shoot dialogue sequences outdoors, including tracking shots in which men on horseback spoke to passengers on a moving train. And by 1930 Ernst Lubitsch (in *Monte Carlo*) could shoot a long tracking shot on a gravel path in which camera movement, dialogue, and editing worked together with complete fluidity.

Hollywood solved the microphone problem, too. Rouben Mamoulian, one of the theatre directors imported from New York, revealed his filmic imagination when he suggested using two microphones to shoot a single scene, balancing and regulating the relative volumes of the two with a sound mixer. In Mamoulian's *Applause* (1929), two characters could speak to each other from opposite ends of the room without trotting together to speak into the same flowerpot. Mamoulian added zip to his film by recording indoor scenes with a moving camera, tracking toward and away from the speakers. He shot other scenes on location, taking advantage of actual and interesting New York sights

Fig. 9-4

Fig. 9-5

Fig. 9-6

Applause: *Mamoulian adds visual energy to the early talkies with silhouettes and striking camera angles (Fig. 9-4), effects shots like the split-screen that shows Helen Morgan serenading her lover's picture while he caresses the chorus girl down the hall (Fig. 9-5), and location shots to which sound could be added later (Fig. 9-6).*

like the Brooklyn Bridge, the Chrysler Building, and the subway, dubbing in the dialogue later.

An even more flexible method of capturing the voice was the invention in 1929 of the boom, a rod or mechanical arm that kept the microphone hovering above the speaker's head, just out of the camera's frame. Whenever the actor moved, the microphone could silently follow. Although the invention of the principle has been credited to either sound technician Eddie Mannix (at MGM) or actor-director Lionel Barrymore, the idea for the boom was probably born when someone improvised by tying the mike to a long stick rather than burying it in a bush or canister or telephone receiver. If the boom became a boon for fluidly mobile sound-film recording, it became the bane of lighting design. How could scenes be lit without throwing its long tell-tale shadow across the walls of the set?

Just as technicians began to conquer the mechanical problems of sound filming, directors began to discover the means of using sound artistically in a primarily visual medium. Even a deadly talkie like *Lights of New York* contained a few imaginative combinations of sound and picture: The Broadway sequence evokes the excitement of the city with a montage of city sights and city sounds; the sequence in which the gangsters shoot a cop is staged in enlarged shadows on a wall coupled with the sounds of a shout, a policeman's whistle, a shot, and the motor of the getaway car. René Clair was particularly impressed with some of the effects of MGM's first all-talking, all-singing picture, *Broadway Melody* (1929): While Bessie Love watches the departure of her lover, the director (Harry Beaumont) keeps the camera riveted on her tearful face, dramatizing the departure with sound alone—the door slams, the lover's car drives off. Then just as Bessie is about to break into tears, the picture fades out, and a single Love sob punctuates the darkness.

Ernst Lubitsch's first two sound films, *The Love Parade* (1929) and *Monte Carlo* (1930), show a creative film mind wrestling with the problems of integrating sound and picture. Although *The Love Parade* has dull, static passages (the long, posed takes for many of the musical numbers), this first Lubitsch sound film shows him beginning to weave his tapestry of witty dialogue, of clever and surprising uses of sound, and of deft images that imply much more than they show. The film contains many subtle effects that would have been impossible without synchronized sound: the coordination of the valet's physical business with the precise rhythms of his opening song, an adieu to Paris sung by a dog, Maurice Chevalier's flippant and charming asides to the camera, the parody of American tourists who do not look up from their newspapers until they hear how much the castle cost to build, the sexual implications of Chevalier's saying "Yes" in answer to the queen's question at the same time that his head is shaking "No," the parody of the wedding ceremony in which the minister emphasizes the reversal of sexual roles by pronouncing the couple wife and man, the booming sound of cannon (a typical Lubitsch use of a comic Freudian symbol, combining both picture and sound), which both implies and interrupts the couple's wedding night amours.

Several of Lubitsch's juxtapositions of sound and film are dazzling indications of the comic ingenuity that would soon develop a mature sound-film masterpiece like *Trouble in Paradise* (1932). In *The Love Parade*, as Chevalier starts to tell the queen's chamberlain a sexual anecdote (how Madame Curie cured him of a cold but gave him a French accent), Lubitsch cuts to a camera position outside the window. The rest of the scene is silent; we cannot hear the joke at all. We don't need to. The slyness of the silence, Lubitsch's joke, is funnier than the joke itself. Similarly, as Chevalier and the queen dine tête-à-tête in her boudoir, Lubitsch shows us the queen's ladies-in-waiting, ministers, and servants narrating what they can see from outside her window. Sound allowed Lubitsch to develop one of his favorite comic devices: A scene inside a room can be much more interesting and fun if the camera stays outside the room.

In *Monte Carlo*, another Jeanette MacDonald musical, Lubitsch's most famous device was to set the song "Beyond the Blue Horizon" as a duet between the soprano and a speeding train. As MacDonald sings the song, the sounds

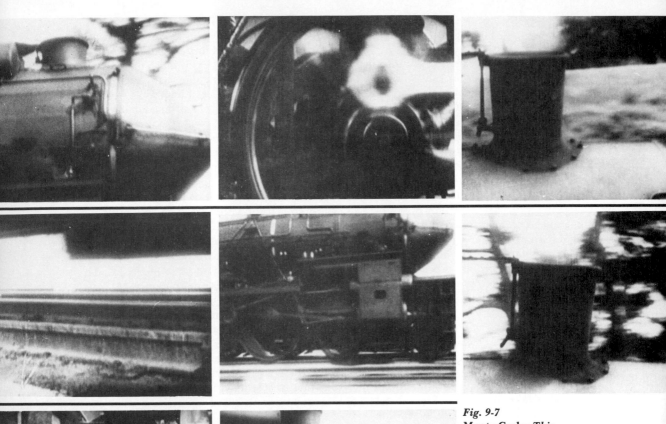

Fig. 9-7
Monte Carlo: *This rhythmic montage of eight shots of a speeding train serves as the introduction to "Beyond the Blue Horizon" — joining the Soviet adoration of machines with the exuberance of American song.*

of the train (chugging wheels, tooting whistle, puffing smoke) become her percussion accompaniment, underscored by the equally percussive rhythms of the editing. Unfortunately, the Lubitsch innovation soon became a Hollywood cliché: those outrageous combinations of speeding trains, a rhythmic song on the sound track, a superimposed calendar with the dates flying off it to mark the passage of time, or a superimposed series of newspapers whose names reveal the train's progress across the country. Lubitsch's original idea had been an innovative and ingenious combination of picture, sound, and cutting — a synthesis of Soviet montage and American musical comedy.

Fig. 9-8

Fig. 9-9

Disney's clever wedding of sound and image. Two xylophones: a cow's teeth in **Steamboat Willie** *(Fig. 9-8), a human skeleton in* **The Skeleton Dance** *(Fig. 9-9).*

The most innovative early sound films, however, were the animated cartoons of Walt Disney. Disney began as a commercial artist and cartoonist in Kansas City; he made his debut in films with animated ads and satiric, short cartoon films—*Fred Newman's Laugh-O-Grams*. He migrated to Hollywood in 1923 and produced a series of short films (called *Alice in Cartoonland*) that integrated cartoons and a living girl; Disney would again mix people and drawings in *Song of the South* (1946) and *Mary Poppins* (1964), and his studio would continue the tradition after his death with *Who Framed Roger Rabbit* (1988). By the end of the silent era, he and his animator, Ub Iwerks, had mastered the methods and art of animation. The *Alice* films were rich in the mature Disney imagination, particularly in his transposition of physical reality into almost surreal impossibility. For example, as a mouse (Mickey's progenitor) serenades his mousette (Minnie's) in *Alice Plays Cupid* (1925), a barrage of notes flies out of his guitar and streams into her face as she stands on her balcony. The mouse then uses these notes as a ladder, climbing them up to her chamber; that accomplished, he gathers them together with his tail, transposing the ladder of notes into a bouquet of flowers for his Juliet.

But it was sound that turned Disney into one of the most influential producers and respected artists in the film industry. Disney's animated cartoons, which were not compelled to photograph the real world, escaped the tyrannies of sound recording that enslaved the directors of theatrical features. Disney's drawn worlds were shot and edited with all the fluidity of the silents, as if by a real camera moving through an artificial landscape to a perfectly synchronized soundtrack; because the animation camera shot no live action and required no soundproof booth or blimp or microphone, the Disney films moved like movies. The cartoon—which is free from all natural laws, from all human and spatial realities—also granted its creator complete freedom in playing with sound. Just as the pictures could depict impossibilities—animals that act like people, physical stresses that a living organism could never endure—the soundtrack could be equally free and fanciful. Handmade pictures could combine in fantastic and imaginative ways with made-up sounds. Or the

animated film could develop a counterpoint between its fanciful, unreal sights and the concrete reality of familiar sounds. The Disney sound cartoon united three of the great traditions of silent filmmaking and carried them into the sound era: the wacky, speedy physical comedy of Mack Sennett; the fantasy world of Méliès in which what cannot happen happens; and the genius of Chaplin and Emile Cohl for transforming one kind of object into a totally different one.

Iwerks and Disney's first sound film, *Steamboat Willie* (1928, the first Mickey Mouse cartoon to be released), used the Cinephone optical sound system and shows complete mastery of the possible counterpoint of picture and sound. The most imaginative sequence is the "Turkey in the Straw" number. A billy goat has eaten a guitar and a copy of the tune "Turkey in the Straw." Mickey Mouse (voice by Disney) twists and starts to crank the goat's tail; the notes again become visible, pouring out of the animal's mouth; the music on the soundtrack accompanies the visual notes. Then Mickey runs all over the boat using whatever he can find as an accompanying percussive instrument. He rattles on a garbage pail and on a series of different-sized pots; he scratches a washboard; he swings a cat around by its tail to produce syncopated shrieks; he squeezes a duck's throat to produce rhythmic quacks; he pulls the tails of nursing piglets to produce percussive squeaks; he bangs on a cow's teeth to produce the tones of a xylophone. Whereas silent montage created meaning by juxtaposing dissimilar images, Disney perceived the similarity of apparently dissimilar sounds and images. An Eisenstein simile that the workers (visual) are like an ox (visual) contrasts with Disney's that a cow's teeth (visual) are like a xylophone (sound).

The Skeleton Dance (1929), the first of the Silly Symphonies, is an even more skillful weaving of motion, music, and rhythm. The film's opening sequence—an atmospheric painting of the mood of midnight and goblins—combines the eerie, tense whine of violins with percussive effects produced by an owl hooting, bats' wings flapping, wind whistling, and cats screeching. Then the skeletons creep out of their graves. The surprising activities of the bones are carefully coordinated with the beats of the score's rhythm. Disney is sensitive not only to the possibilities of the kinds of sound that a visual image might generate, but also to the punch of coordinating animated movement with the rhythmic effects of the score. This sensitivity to musical tones and rhythms (which, when the sound and picture beats are *too* tightly coordinated, is still pejoratively known as "Mickey Mousing") became the outstanding feature of all the Silly Symphonies, eventually culminating in the cinematic tone-poem

Fantasia (1940)—conceived by, but not credited to, the great abstract animator Oskar Fischinger—and in the wildly surreal evaporations of one object into another of the "Pink Elephants" dance in *Dumbo* (1941). Though his studio's greatest achievements were the animated features *Snow White and the Seven Dwarfs* and *Pinocchio* (1940), Disney's synthesis of image, music, and rhythm had begun with his first sound cartoons. The means of turning sound into a resource for film rather than a liability were being found.

10

France Between the Wars

The French film in the first decade of sound may have been the most imaginative, the most stimulating of its generation: a subtle blend of effective, often poetic, dialogue; evocative visual imagery; perceptive social analysis; complex fictional structures; rich philosophical implication; wit and charm. The maturity of the French film in the decade between 1930 and 1940 was partially the result of the growth of the French film in the previous decade between 1920 and 1930. The final ten years of silent films laid the foundations for the great sound structures that would follow in the next ten. Abel Gance, René Clair, Jean Renoir, Jacques Feyder, Julien Duvivier, and Jean Epstein all conquered purely visual expression before they began combining picture and word.

The sharp chasm that divided the two Hollywood film worlds before and after 1927–28 was less apparent in the Paris film world. The innovative, experimental minds of the French 1920s energetically accepted the artistic challenge of the new talking machine. Although many French plays and playwrights found a welcome on the new French sound stages, just as American plays and playwrights had in America, the French sound film never turned its back on visual expression. The French film-makers of the silent 1920s had learned some very powerful and convincing visual lessons.

Paris of the 1920s was the avant-garde capital of the world in art, literature, music, and the drama. It was the city of Picasso and Dali, of Stravinsky, Milhaud, Poulenc, and Satie, of Proust and Cocteau, and the home away from home of Joyce and Stein. The urge to experiment, to create new forms, to challenge the established artistic norms in music, painting, sculpture, poetry, fiction, and drama also dominated the new machine art of the motion picture—which had, after all, begun with Lumière and Méliès as much as with Edison and Dickson, and which depended on the French invention of photography. Paris was the city of many modern "isms"—Surrealism, Cubism, Dadaism. Painters exulted in manipulating pure shapes, textures, and colors on a canvas. The painting did not need to mirror life's external reality or depend on Renaissance codes of perspective; it could mirror life's moods, tones, and dreams, or depart from "reality" altogether. Time and consciousness were investigated to the point of reinvention, notably by Gertrude Stein, Marcel Proust, and James Joyce. The world was irrational; art could mirror that irrationality or dispense with the whole job of mirroring and description. All bets were off: Practically anything could be done in a new, modern way. In fact, given the fragmentation of the postwar world — whose ideal aesthetic, practiced in the movies as well as in James Joyce's *Ulysses*, Ezra Pound's *The Cantos*, T. S. Eliot's "The Waste Land," William Faulkner's *The Sound and the Fury,* and John Dos Passos's *U.S.A.*, was montage — the history and resources of art had to be *made* new in order to become viable and useful.

Modernist plays did not tell logical stories of rationally motivated actions; playwrights exulted in the irrational, the non sequitur. Jean Cocteau wrote a drama about an absurd wedding party at the top of the Eiffel Tower; Gertrude Stein and Tristan Tzara wrote plays whose value was in the sounds and unique uses of the words rather than in their ordinary meanings. It was the age when a premiere — like that of Igor Stravinsky's *Rite of Spring* — could spark a riot or start a movement. Colonies of artists would gather at parties or salons to show each other works they had sculpted, painted, or written — works devoted to form and sensation as well as to unconventional logic and new ways of creating meaning. At these parties some of the artists would show little movies, created on the same formal principles, to their gathered friends. They discovered that of all the arts, the moving picture was capable of the most bizarre tricks with form: a series of purely visual images, of shapes, of lights, of double exposures, of dissolves, a series of worlds out of focus, moving too fast or too slow, upside down or inside out. The lens and crank could be even more devoted to pure irrational form than chisel or brush.

Ironically, the great experimental leap forward of the French film in the 1920s was also a step into the past, analogous to Pound's lifelong effort "to gather from the air a live tradition." In 1919, at the dawn of this avant-garde decade, Louis Delluc and Ricciotto Canudo, two zealous film buffs, founded the first of many subsequent French societies for the presentation and preservation of great films of the past. Delluc and Canudo canonized the movies as the Seventh Art and urged attention to the directors of an earlier era: to Méliès, Zecca, Cohl, Max Linder, Jean Durand, Louis Feuil-

lade. The "Seventh-Art adventists" leaped back into the film past about ten years, ignoring the theatrical, stagey, Comédie-Françaiseish, Film d'Arty pictures of the decade of the war. This first generation of *cinéastes* urged a return to the wild fantasies of Méliès, to the motion-filled chases of Zecca and Sennett, to the tricks with camera speed and motion of Jean Durand's *Onésime horloger* (1912), in which a magical clock makes the world speed up so that Onésime can collect his inheritance "sooner." Like the French *cinéastes* of the sixties — Godard, Truffaut, Malle — the Paris filmmaker of the twenties used film history not only to pack movies with historical echoes and allusions but also to embellish earlier film ideas with the filmmaker's own distinct and personal extensions of them. The Parisian avant-garde filmmaker of the 1920s used one hand to rip up accepted film conventions and assumptions and the other to pull the traditions of the film past into the movies of the present.

The experimental French films of the twenties were of three approximate types: (1) films of pure visual form; (2) surrealistic film fantasies in which tricks with time, juxtaposition, transition, and form create the surrealistic-symbolic-dreamlike-irrational film universe; (3) naturalistic studies of human passion and sensation in which symbols and surreal touches help to render elusive human feelings. The three types were far from distinct. A film could begin as an essay in pure form and then change into a surreal dream-fantasy (René Clair's *Entr'acte,* 1924). Sometimes the film would begin as a surreal journey and change into a study of form (Man Ray's *Mysteries of the Chateau Dé,* 1929). Or the film could begin as an impressionistic study of human emotions and relationships only to end as a dream (Jean Renoir's *The Little Match Girl,* 1928). Dadaism, Surrealism, and poetic naturalism flowed into one another to create new and surprising compounds in the movies. There were also films and filmmakers clearly committed to the exploration of the creative possibilities of a single artistic movement, as Germaine Dulac (*The Smiling Madame Beudet,* 1923), the most important woman director of the period, was committed to Impressionism.

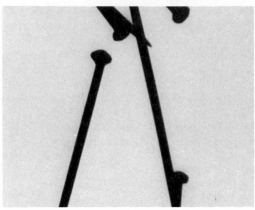

Fig. 10-1

Fig. 10-2

Man Ray's Return to Reason: *exposing the celluloid to nails and thumbtacks directly, without a camera.*

The films of Man Ray are the purest examples of movie dada—of a collage of visual shapes and patterns with no meaning other than the interesting forms themselves. Ray's films began quite literally as collages: In *Return to Reason* (1923)—a highly ironic title, since the film consciously rejects reason—he randomly scattered paint, nails, glue, salt and pepper, and scraps of paper over strips of film and then exposed the littered film to light, leaving shadows of the objects imprinted on the celluloid. Ray gradually abandoned such accidental methods for more controlled essays in form, such as *Emak-Bakia* (1927), in which visual similarities and differences of form control Ray's choice

of images. Fernand Léger's rhythmic *Ballet mécanique* (1924) and Marcel Duchamp's comic jest of spinning spirals, palindromes, and nonsense words, *Anemic Cinema* (1926), also begin with the premise of using a succession of visual images related in form, shape, and rhythm rather than in meaning.

The most famous of the Surrealist films is the Salvador Dali–Luis Buñuel fantasy, *Un Chien andalou* (1929). Like the title (*An Andalusian Dog*), the film is a series of non sequiturs, scenes that only seem to be related logically; its "logic" is that of a dream. The film teasingly suggests thematic and narrative unities amid rampant discontinuity; whatever rules it has, it makes up. Its action consistently arises from the sexual desires, tensions, and confrontations surrounding one woman. Much as in their 1930 sound film, *L'Age d'or,* Dali and Buñuel seem to contrast sexual desire and social convention: the stigmata and ants in the man's hand suggesting Christian sin and human mortality, the man fondling the woman's breasts, the two puritans laboriously being dragged along with the equally heavy burdens of pianos and burros, the doorbell in the shape of a cocktail shaker, the visual puns about pubic hair. Despite the whiffs of consistent meaning, *Un Chien andalou* is a series of daring and imaginative vignettes juxtaposed irrationally, as in the leaps of a dream, to amuse, shake up, and even attack the viewer. From the opening sequence in which Buñuel slits an eyeball with a razor in gruesome close-up (the film's continuity suggests the eye belongs to the woman, but if you look closely—rather than away, as your organ of vision is assaulted—you can see animal hair around it) to the final one in which a man and woman are apparently and inexplicably buried in the wasteland/sand of a rocky beach, the film's goal is to excite, to shock, to tickle, to surprise, to make us "see" differently rather than to preach or explain. The French writer Lautréamont defined Surrealism as the fortuitous meeting of a typewriter and an umbrella on an operating table. *Un Chien andalou* is one of cinema's most powerful demonstrations of surrealistic juxtaposition.

On the other hand, Jean Epstein's *The Fall of the House of Usher* (1928) uses gentler dream

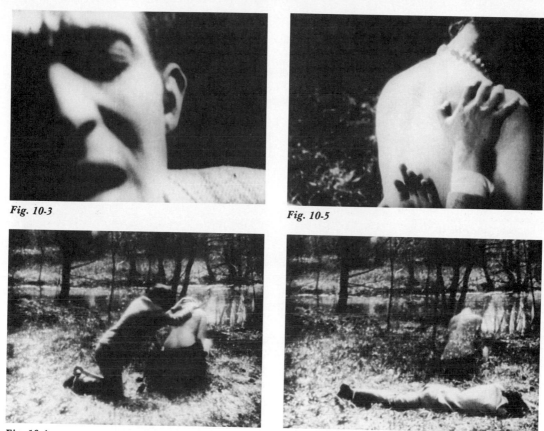

Fig. 10-3

Fig. 10-5

Fig. 10-4

Fig. 10-6

The dream-space of Un Chien andalou. *Four consecutive shots: the man falls, indoors, to slither against the torso of an outdoor nude, who promptly evaporates.*

effects to create the atmosphere for his relatively lucid Poe plot. Epstein uses the tools of cinematic Impressionism—slow-motion effects; out-of-focus lenses; multiple exposure; contrasts of light and shadow; distortion; cavernous, dreamworld sets—as a means of turning the House of Usher into a house of mirrors and visual music.

Even the naturalistic psychological studies of human interaction try to probe beneath familiar surfaces to reveal irrational, chaotic passions, often using the devices of the surrealists to illuminate this subjective world. Alberto Calvalcanti's *Rien que les heures* (1926), on the surface a documentary study of twenty-four hours of Paris life, relies on cinematic tricks to paint the city's moody picture; on freeze frames, double exposures, split-screen effects, obtrusive wipes. Louis Delluc's *Fièvre* (1921), a tense story of desire and death in a seamy waterfront saloon, weaves images of gliding ships and a symbolic rose into its tapestry of naturalistic human conflict in the café. Dimitri Kirsanov's astounding *Ménilmontant* (1925) uses quick cutting and the sordid atmosphere of Paris slums to tell its story of two sisters from the country whose parents are killed by an ax murderer in the opening montage; later, as adults in the city, they are sexually betrayed by the same man. The films of Germaine Dulac (*The Smiling Madame Beudet; The Coquille and The Clergyman,* 1928, written by Antonin

Speaking with their bodies, soldiers of the First World War spell out "J'accuse," the title of Gance's 1919 film and an accusation against the masters of war.

Fig. 10-7

Artaud, inventor of the "theatre of cruelty," whose script was more surrealistic than Dulac's impressionist movie) and Marcel L'Herbier (*The Late Mathias Pascal,* 1926) use, among other devices, slow motion, distortion, and soft focus subjectively to illuminate thought and emotion.

Even the most important commercial film director of the decade, Abel Gance, applied the surrealist's concern with visual forms, tricks, and devices to the narrative feature film. This should not be surprising, since his 1915 short, *The Folly of Dr. Tube,* used distorting mirrors to convey distorted perception and may well have been the first avant-garde film. His *J'accuse* (1919) and *La Roue* (*The Wheel,* 1922) mix an attack on varying forms of social injustice with an intimate, melodramatic study of passion and sensuality. *J'accuse (I Accuse),* which took its title from Emile Zola's 1898 article in defense of Alfred Dreyfus, let the ghosts of the soldiers of World War I ("the war to end all wars") return to discover whether their sacrifice had been effective and worthwhile. Shot in 1918 with soldiers on temporary leave from the front, who expected—correctly—to be killed within the month, so that they knew they were playing their own ghosts and trusted Gance to carry their message into a future they would not see but urgently demanded to affect, *J'accuse* was

the greatest antiwar film yet made. In 1937 Gance remade the film, hoping to stop the Second World War by re-evoking the horrors and lessons of the First; an overpowering masterpiece, the second *J'accuse* did not halt the coming conflict but remains a gesture of immense belief in the power of the cinema and a heartbreaking, almost infuriating act of faith in the good sense of humanity.

Of *La Roue,* an eight-hour movie released in the pivotal year that *Ulysses* and "The Waste Land" were published (1922), Jean Cocteau observed that "There is the cinema before and after *La Roue* as there is painting before and after Picasso." A tragic story of the wheel of fate, told with the romantic energy of a Victor Hugo and the melodramatic impact of a Euripides, this flawless and compelling picture brought its first audience to a standing ovation —no matter how long it was, they refused to leave until the final reel had been shown again —and decisively influenced the Soviets, who studied *La Roue* and *Intolerance* with equal care. Its rapid cutting—some of its shots only one frame long—came to be called "Russian cutting" once *La Roue* had, like Gance, been forgotten. Gance resembled Griffith in many ways, not the least of which is that neither could find work in the conservative studio era, though each had, through his vision of what the cinema

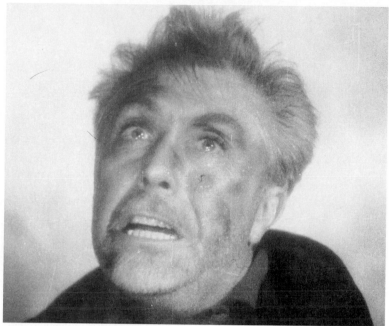

*The hero of Gance's 1937
J'accuse (played by Victor
Francen) calls up the
spirits of the soldiers of all
nations, hoping to stop
another war.*

Fig. 10-8

could be, brought the art to the peak of its powers. When they met in 1921 (between the shooting and the editing of *La Roue*), Gance and Griffith congratulated each other for having independently discovered the possibilities of the close-up, the dolly shot, and rhythmic editing. Each made films that were inseparably melodramatic and political, and each found his genius constrained by the tiny imaginations of conservative businessmen.

Although Griffith was virtually unemployed from *The Struggle* to his death, and Gance was kept from making films for periods as long as twelve years, Gance did make one great silent after *La Roue* (*Napoleon seen by Abel Gance*, 1927) and at least three important sound films in addition to the great 1937 *J'accuse*. His *The End of the World* (1931), though it was edited by a studio hack, was nevertheless the first sound film made in France. His abridged version of *Napoleon* (*Napoleon seen and heard by Abel Gance*, 1935) introduced stereophonic sound, and *A Great Love of Beethoven* (1936) used sound to convey what it meant for a composer to go deaf—and rose to the challenge as

grandly as Beethoven did, but in cinematic terms, finding visual equivalents for musical themes and structures.

Like *The Birth of a Nation*, the 1927 *Napoleon* (which ran 9½ hours) used individual human figures to explore the history of an entire nation in a period of political instability and crisis. Unlike Griffith's concentration on a group of ordinary citizens, Gance's is on Napoleon, the idealized leader, the mythic man of destiny who pulls a divided nation out of the ideological chaos of the French Revolution. Some latter-day viewers of the film have found *Napoleon* either naïvely worshipful of a heroic leader or implicitly fascist—like *The Birth of a Nation*, then, both powerful cinema and problematic politics. But one must note the stern warning delivered near the end of the film—by the leaders of the Reign of Terror—that Napoleon will fall if he betrays the original goals of the Revolution, and Gance's plans—never realized because of a lack of funding—to show Napoleon's tragic development and fall in subsequent films (*Napoleon* closes with the Italian campaign, well before the general became the

Fig. 10-9
La Roue*: Séverin-Mars as Sisif, the tragic "Man of the Wheel."*

emperor). In any case, the energy of *Napoleon* is, like that of *La Roue,* the energy of an idealized cinema: a grand, vaulting belief in what unhindered genius can accomplish. The hero of *Napoleon* is Gance.

Among the many breakthroughs of *Napoleon* was its use of multiple imagery, for which Gance's general term was polyvision. Polyvision referred to superimposition (as many as sixteen images laid on top of one another), the split screen (as many as nine distinct images in a frame), and the multiple screen (the triptych— used three times in *Napoleon,* although two of them have been lost—whereby three cameras and projectors and screens could create a single wide-screen image with an aspect ratio of 4:1, or three separate, side-by-side images that reinforced, reversed, or played against each other in counterpoint). With polyvision and rapid

cutting, Gance became the unchallenged master of montage in France. The triptych, which was later reinvented as Cinerama, was an invention whose inventor was conveniently forgotten. The final reel of *Napoleon* was also shot in 3-D and again in color, though Gance disliked the results and declined to release those experimental reels, deciding at last on the triptych.

Working on the project over a period of fifteen years, stitching together fragments of abridged and mutilated versions, British film historian Kevin Brownlow restored *Napoleon* to more than six hours; in 1975 he was joined in the effort by Robert A. Harris, who produced the final restored version, which was premiered at the 1979 Telluride Film Festival in Colorado with Gance in attendance. In 1980 Francis Ford Coppola leant his clout—and his father's music—to the project, and Harris and Coppola premiered a four-hour, sound-speed version of *Napoleon,* tinted and toned according to the original instructions, in 1981 at Radio City Music Hall in New York. (The six-hour version, with music by Carl Davis, continues to play at silent speed at festivals and archives in Europe.) To see a revival of *Napoleon,* projected from a sparkling 35mm print in a huge movie palace, supported by a live symphony orchestra and giant Wurlitzer organ, revealed not merely the grandeur of this single film but the potential magic and beauty of any properly presented "silent" epic. The power of this renovated *Napoleon* also revealed what must have been the awesome initial effect of seeing Griffith's epics in 1915–16.

The French director of the 1920s delighted in the games that could be played with the camera, in its visual surprises, in its ability to make the familiar world look bizarre. The isms of twentieth-century French painting also captured its cinema. The culmination of this decade of film painting was a feature that seemed to synthesize and incorporate the history of painting, from Renaissance religious iconography to the modern abstract concern with texture and line: Carl Theodor Dreyer's *The Passion of Joan of Arc* (1928). Despite its Danish director and German art director (Hermann Warm, the principal designer of *The Cabinet of Dr. Caligari*), the film's aesthetics and effects are also consistent with the French. Narratively, the film chronicles Joan's long trial and eventual execution at the stake; but the film's narrative structure is merely a skeleton.

The details of Joan's trial are blurry; the enormity of her suffering, her sorrow, her spiritual fire, her warmth are clear. The film examines Joan the immense emotional being rather than Joan the militant, or even Joan the religious iconoclast. The sainthood of Dreyer's Joan (played by Renée Falconetti) is not in her words or deeds; it exists within her; it is in her intense ability to feel and suffer and glow. Dreyer's Joan contrasts strikingly with Shaw's, although the film uses some of the same dialogue as Shaw's play (not because it was adapting *Saint Joan* but because both Shaw and Dreyer consulted the same historical documents, in which there was renewed public interest and to which there was greater public access after the Church canonized Joan in 1920). In Shaw's play, Joan's comments are witty and intelligent and shrewd; Dreyer's Joan, with her glowing face and shiny, tear-filled eyes, keeps her answers short and operates primarily on a level beyond verbal expression. Dreyer's film is more a musical Mass or a Passion play in film form than a suspenseful story; it presents and transcends the tale of the trial and death of Joan in the same way that Bach's *The Passion According to St. Matthew* relates, dramatizes, and goes beyond Matthew's account of the martyrdom of Christ. Like Eisenstein, Dreyer's sense of cinematic form is as musical as it is logical. Unlike Eisenstein, whose "music" was the dissonance of the twentieth-century symphony, Dreyer's music is the spiritual, passionate complexity of the organ fugue or church chorale.

To create a feature film of almost musical sensations and ritual power, Dreyer fills the frame with faces and seeks out each one's essence. His camera travels ceaselessly over the faces of the judges and Joan—or holds on one. The bare white walls of the set make the richly textured human features and makeup-free skin leap out at the viewer. Warm's decor gives the film the flavor of medieval starkness *and* the texture of modern design and abstract painting with its sharp, clean lines.

To contrast the passionate saint with her fallible and often deceptive accusers, Dreyer uses two different photographic methods. He shoots the accusers in motion. The judges, soldiers, and priests twist, pivot, and lunge with their bodies and faces; Dreyer keeps Rudolf Maté's camera moving when photographing them to sustain an even greater impression of movement. But Joan is usually still, and shot with a motionless camera. The maid's passionate calm contrasts with her accusers' nervous activity, her passivity with their action. The camera also contrasts the faults in the faces of the unenlightened accusers with the smooth, glowing perfection in the honest face of the maid. The camera prowls over the faces of judges, settling on a wart, a wrinkle, a misshapen nose or chin, a roll of fat.

For many critics, *The Passion of Joan of Arc* was the ultimate silent film, the ultimate example of the power of purely visual expression. In

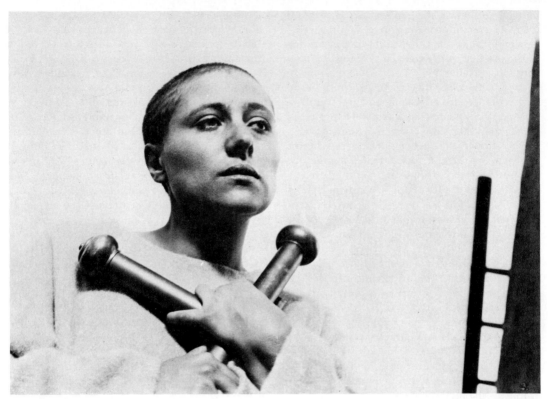

Fig. 10-10

Fig. 10-11

Fig. 10-12

The Passion of Joan of Arc—*a film of faces without makeup: Joan (Renée Falconetti, Fig. 10-10), her one compassionate accuser (Antonin Artaud, Fig. 10-11 right), and the wrinkled imperfections of the faces of her accusers (Fig. 10-12).*

comparison with its pictorial beauty and expressiveness, its artistic wholeness, its intellectual and emotional maturity, most pictures—particularly the silly, static talking pictures that were already playing at competing theatres—were ludicrous. Critics and aesthetes watched with horror as the *kitsch* of a *Jazz Singer* swallowed the high art of a *Joan.*

But even this *Joan of Arc,* as moving as its pictures were, contained its own limitations. Although sound and talking were obviously bothersome gimmicks, printed titles—the necessary evil of the silent film—became uncomfortably intrusive in Dreyer's *Joan.* Just as there is something anomalous in this Joan's uttering any words at all, there is something anomalous in interrupting the rush of compelling and brilliantly composed images and the passionate conflict of human faces to flash printed words on the screen. The intertitles disrupt the rhythm and pictorial unity of *The Passion of Joan of Arc* just as obviously as sound disrupted the pictorial imagination of early talkies. To sustain an unbroken flow of visual images, the film needed sound rather than printed words to perform vital narrative functions. *Joan of Arc* needed a nondisruptive means of showing us what those compelling faces were thinking, what those mouths were saying. Dreyer went on to make four of the greatest and most demanding of all sound films, in which people still don't talk very much, and which continued his examination of the conflict between the earthly, mortal, and material as opposed to the mystical, spiritual, and eternal: *Vampyr* (1932), *Day of Wrath* (1943), *Ordet* (1954, released 1955), and *Gertrud* (1964).

René Clair

Like so many French filmmakers of the era, René Clair mastered the purely visual cinema, the painting-in-motion of the twenties, before he began to assault both eye and ear in the thirties. Clair began as cinematic trickster, a choreographer of irrational film ballets; later he used his cinema tricks to turn the realistic and rational world into a place of fantasy and song. Clair looked back admiringly at the zany, frenetic worlds of Sennett, Zecca, and Durand, and that looking backward allowed his own

kind of zany frenzy to move forward. Despite Clair's historical influences, despite his maturing as an artist, despite the new adjustments that the talking machines forced him to make, a René Clair movie—silent or sound—is unmistakably Clair. The clearest Clair traits are his delight in physical movement and his comic fancy (falling somewhere between wit and whimsy), which converts two things that are obviously different into things that are surprisingly the same: a funeral becomes a wedding party; a prison is a factory, and a factory is a prison; a tussle for a jacket becomes a football game. Clair's constant dissolving of differences into similarities is fanciful as well as satirical, designed as much for imaginative fun as for social commentary. Clair's best silent film, *The Italian Straw Hat* (1927), and his best sound films, *Le Million* (1931) and *A nous la liberté* (1931), are those in which his flights of visual fancy drop the most explosive intellectual bombs on the director's two favorite targets—social convention and money.

Clair's first two films, both silent, contained the seeds of everything that would grow afterward. *Paris qui dort* (*The Crazy Ray,* 1923) is a fantasy, the story of a crazed scientist, appropriately named Dr. Craze, whose mechanical ray has put the populace of the world to sleep, paralyzed (in effect, by the cinema) in the midst of their activities. Only a handful of Parisians avoid the professor's sleep-ray: those who were above the beams of his machine on the top of the Eiffel Tower or in an airplane.

Clair has great fun with the human statues that dot the streets of Paris, interrupted unsuspectingly in their daily pursuits: the pickpocket paralyzed in flight with the wallet of a frozen victim, the unfaithful wife frozen in the arms of her lover, frozen diners in a café, the paralyzed waiter holding the anticipated bottle of champagne. Equally pointed is the way the characters resume their old social roles as soon as Doctor Craze reverses his ray and gets society going again. While the city sleeps, crook and cop, socialite and socialist live and play together; when the city reawakens, so do the familiar social distinctions.

Clair's second film, *Entr'acte* (1924), less satirical, less logical, and far more daring and funny than his first, was made specifically as the intermission piece, the entr'acte, for a performance of the Ballets Suedois in Paris. The film is pure movement, pure romp, the whimsical, choreographic Clair rather than the social satirist. The film begins with a series of dadaist non sequiturs: two men playing checkers on a high building, two others hunting birds on skyscrapers, a ball dancing on jets of water, a ballerina (shot from underneath) whose billowing skirt spreads and shuts like the petals of a flower. Clair quickly reveals the sly comical logic in his cinema madness. The two checker players surprisedly see the Place de la Concorde materialize on their checkerboard; the dancing ball dangles inexplicably in midair, defying gravity, after the spurting water jets have been turned off; the ballerina turns out to be a bearded man.

The delightful silliness continues in the second half of the film, in which society gathers for a funeral. But the mourners surprisingly dress in white; they throw rice at the departing hearse; a Sennett-like jet of air blows the ladies' skirts up. The hearse itself is drawn by a camel; the mourners break pieces of the funeral wreaths off the hearse and eat them like pretzels. Suddenly, the hearse starts running away by itself; the mourners rush after it. A Zecca–Sennett chase begins. Clair uses fast motion, slow motion, traveling shots, freeze-frames, interpolated cuts of racing cars and roller coasters to add energy and interest to the chase. Eventually the coffin falls off the hearse, and the corpse rises from the box and blithely makes everyone disappear. A man leaps through the screen that dares to say "The End."

Clair's silent feature, The Italian Straw Hat, set in 1895, takes its visual style from the era of the pre-Griffith French "primitives," from the decor of the Zecca and Linder films: that specific period when movies were just beginning to overturn the very nineteenth-century values that the film satirizes and to restructure our way of seeing the world. That particular visual style provides the self-referential cinematic context for the director's romping spirit and his sarcastic sniggers at the pettiness of middle-class conventions. A young bridegroom's horse eats a young lady's straw hat as the groom drives to meet his bride. Since the

young lady lost her hat while enjoying an extramarital afternoon with a beau, she must replace the rare hat to allay her husband's suspicions. The young groom, who looks suspiciously like Max Linder, must juggle his wedding party with his comically frantic attempts to replace the hat. He leads the wedding party out of the church and through the city in an energetic chase that culminates in the town jail. Throughout the chase Clair supplements the physical fun with satiric jabs at the tawdry wedding festivities, the pettiness of the silly, middle-class guests, and the inane social conventions that have created both the tacky wedding and the chase for an Italian straw hat.

The addition of sound gave Clair even more opportunities for comic inventiveness. In his first sound film, Sous les toits de Paris (Under the Roofs of Paris, 1930), Clair — always the choreographer — discovered the effectiveness of using music as a leitmotif and as a means of creating the film's fantasy-like breezy spirit. Music became the perfect unrealistic accompaniment for the balletic Clair fantasy world.

Le Million is an even more interesting mixture of movement, sound, and music. Its subject is imaginative fancy itself, the way that the line between the "real" and the "fanciful" can be erased by the power of the human imagination. The film revolves about two favorite Clair motifs — money and the chase. A poor French artist discovers that he has won a million francs in the state lottery; unfortunately, the lottery ticket is in the pocket of a coat that has been stolen by a fleeing thief. The film becomes a furious chase for the elusive jacket, carrying the artist through the streets of Paris, into a den of brainy thieves, and finally onto the stage of the Paris Opera. The balletic film appropriately ends in a joyous dance as all members of the eventually successful chase join hands in a singing, dancing circle of celebration.

On their way to this final rejoicing, Clair engages his characters in a series of wild adventures that reveal a startlingly imaginative combination of sound and image. When the artist finds his coat at the Opera, he grabs it, only to find that the vain, fat tenor insists on using the old coat as part of his atmospheric pauper's costume. The artist, the tenor, and the police engage in a mock-heroic struggle for the jacket. Clair comments on these mock-heroics by adding crowd noises, officials' whistles, and cheering to the sound track while the men play keepaway in the Opera's corridor. The coat has become a football, the struggle has become a game.

Clair's most dazzling sequence uses the sounds of the operatic performance on stage simultaneously to emphasize the difference between real love and operatic clichés of love and to erase those differences. As the film's two lovers sit behind the set on stage pledging their love, the fat tenor and fat soprano, who detest each other, pledge their troth in grandiose song. Clair juxtaposes the saccharine lyrics of the fakey aria with the sincere feelings of the genuine lovers. Clair then caps this contrast with a visual joke. The stagehands in the flies let loose a horde of artificial autumnal leaves, designed to flutter down on the two operatic lovers on stage. The wonder is that the fakey theatricality of the device underscores the artificiality of operatic love while, at the same time, it converts the equally fictional love of the movie lovers into a tender, lyrical, even magical moment of human interaction. Clair's point is not that movie love is more real than operatic love (what could be less "real" than these — or any — movie lovers?), nor that movie sets are more real than opera sets (even if Clair's camera makes sure we can see the fake backsides of all the opera's scenery). His point is that our conviction of the "realness" in any work of art has nothing to do with the realness of the fiction and everything to do with our imagination's response to the fiction. It is on this same basis that the audience in the opera house accepts operatic love as a kind of "real" story. Movies both are and are not more "real" than operas. Movies, like operas, achieve their legitimate ends only by speaking to the human fancy.

Clair's next film, *A nous la liberté (Liberty For Us)*, was to be his last masterpiece. Clair again combines his comic and musical inventiveness with the thematic wholeness and seriousness that make a great film. Two convicts escape from prison. One of them, using stolen money, builds a huge factory to manufacture phonograph records and machines; the other, his friend in prison, becomes a worker in that factory. The business tycoon eventually discovers that the life of a "respectable" factory owner, with its rules, its social obligations, its emotional infidelities, its devotion to money and machines, is no different from the life of a prisoner. Neither plutocrat nor prisoner is truly free. The film ends as the capitalist and the worker turn their backs on the factory and on money to stroll off down the road, two tramps, finally free of restraint and convention.

Uniting the film is its consistent examination of the term *liberty* in its title. For Clair, society and freedom are incompatible. Everyone attached to the factory — Clair's microcosm for society as a whole — is a prisoner of his or her role in the system: Owner, member of the board, worker, foreman, secretary, all are prisoners of their particular functions. The film's brilliance lies in the translation of this Marxist-humanist cliché into imaginative film images. The two central characters, one tall and fat, the other short and skinny, are two spirits from the world of silent comedy, reminiscent of Fatty and Charlie, of Laurel and Hardy. Their ultimate choice of vocation — tramp — also echoes the asocial yet human choice that Charlie makes over and over again. If Clair's tramps seem indebted to Charlot, Chaplin later collected the debt by borrowing one of *A nous la liberté*'s assembly-line scenes for *Modern Times* (1936). Clair's little prisoner, the Chaplinesque dreamer, sits in his place on the monotonous assembly line. As the unfinished machines roll past him on the conveyor belt, he, dreaming of his lady love, fails to put his particular screw into the destined hole. He scampers down the line following the machine, trying to remedy his error. The assembly line quickly becomes chaos, a heap of unfinished machines and brawling workers. Clair's assembly-line chaos is a perfect way of showing inhuman enslavement to the machines that humans have built.

Clair's consistent technique for illuminating the lack of liberty is visual parallel. The film opens with shots of men in prison, manufacturing little toy horses as they sit in rows on the prison's assembly line; they eat their meals as they sit in rows in the prison's dining room. Later, Clair shows the factory workers sitting

Fig. 10-13

Fig. 10-14

A nous la liberté: *Clair's visual parallels—the prison as assembly line, the assembly line as prison.*

in the same rows as the men in prison, eating in the same formations as the men in the prison mess hall. Factory and prison are visually identical. Prison uniforms have become factory uniforms; prison guards have become factory foremen; prison numbers have become workers' numbers.

The decor is used to emphasize these visual parallels. The vertical bars of the prison are echoed by other verticals throughout the film: vertical rows of flowers (like flowered bars) in front of the young girl's window, vertical wood paneling in the factory owner's office, vertical bars on the windows of the factory. The factory's bare courtyard looks exactly like the prison yard. Of course, Clair's choice of a phonograph factory is itself a part of the film's metaphorical wholeness; the factory turns music into a mechanical artifact and a commodity. Even music lacks liberty in this society.

The film hits its visual and thematic climax in the wild scene in which the social elite gather to honor the great factory owner (former crook) who has created this phonographic empire. The ceremony begins with perfect formality: the guests wearing top hats and tails (symbols of social convention), the orators sitting stiffly on the rostrum, the workers standing in formation listening to the boring, droning speeches. Suddenly a wind (both a visual and sound effect) sweeps through the factory courtyard. It drowns out the silly speech of the old rhetorician; it blows the top hats all over the courtyard; it scatters the factory's profits—paper money—all over the ground. The liberating wind turns the factory into a swarming mass of chaotic free activity. In the most Sennettesque manner, the dignitaries abandon their dignity to chase their blowing top hats and the blowing bills all over the courtyard in frenzied, choreographed patterns.

After this climax, a quiet, peaceful coda shows the effect of this whistling wind of freedom. The two prisoners become tramps; the factory's workers sit by the river dreamily fishing; the now totally automated factory continues producing phonographs by itself. In Clair's idyll, the people are free to be human, leaving the machines to tend the machines.

After two less important films in France, Clair made his first English-language film, *The Ghost Goes West* (1935), a fantasy about a social-climbing American who buys a Scottish castle and transports it, block by block, complete with ghost, back to Florida. During the war years, Clair understandably stayed in Hollywood where he made more fantasies (notably *I Married a Witch,* 1942) and the ingenious comedy-mystery *And Then There Were None* (1945). When Clair returned to France after the war, his wit was gentler, the whimsy thicker, the decor more lush. Later Clair films never matched the combination of exuberance, style, cinematic control, structural parallel, and thematic consistency of *Le Million* and *A nous la liberté.*

Jean Renoir

Like René Clair, Jean Renoir—son of the Impressionist painter Pierre Auguste Renoir—started making films in the twenties and reached the peak of his powers in the thirties. Like Clair, Renoir was a social satirist. But there

the similarities between them very clearly stop. Renoir's satire was bitter and melancholy, whereas Clair's was ebullient and whimsical. Clair's satire condemned institutions and praised the human spirit; Renoir's satire declared hollow institutions to be the inevitable products of erroneous humans. Like Clair, Renoir saw that the claims of nature and civilization were antithetical; unlike Clair, Renoir never resolves the dilemma by simplistically espousing one of the two alternatives. For Renoir realized both the attractiveness of nature that seems so innocent and the need for civilization that seems so complicated.

Renoir emphasizes the inseparable connection of civilization and nature with a favorite shot, shooting from indoors through windows and doorways that frame the outdoors with their architectural presence. His visual signature, composition in depth, allows the *mise-en-scène* to make its own statements; foreground and background figures, civilization and nature, upper and lower classes, winners and losers—all are included in Renoir's complex comedies of manners. If Clair's roots were firmly planted in ballet and in song, Renoir's were in painting, in the sensitivity to light and shadow, form and texture that he inherited from his father. Renoir's canon was fuller, richer, and longer than Clair's, with significant films stretching into the color and wide-screen eras of the 1950s. Clair was the more ingenious, Renoir the deeper, more perceptive artist.

The Renoir silent films are darker, slower, more brooding than Clair's. In his fifth movie, *The Little Match Girl* (1928), Renoir adapts Andersen's fairy tale of the little match seller who dreams of happiness in toyland and perishes in the snow of reality. The film is suffused with the heavy atmosphere of death. The opening sections, Renoir's depiction of reality in the cold, snowy city, paint the world with exaggerated harshness, with extreme blacks and whites: glaring lamps, black silhouettes, grotesque shadows. Renoir's impressionistic eye makes the real world surreal; the visual contrasts of dark and light are that intense.

In the second sequence, the little girl's dream, Renoir is free to play with all the devices of the French cinematic tricksters: double exposures, irrational sequences of images, blurred focus, superimposition. But the results are strikingly different from Clair's effusive use of the same effects. Even in the toy shop window the atmosphere is heavy and dark. The shapes of this toy world are jagged and sharp; the lighting creates harsh tones of over-darkness and extra-whiteness. Whereas Clair's lighting is appropriately even and bright, Renoir's is consistently tonal and moody. Even the toys threaten the little girl—soldiers in formation, an aggressive ball, the ominous jack-in-the-box who becomes the pursuing figure of death.

In the final section of the film, the girl and her soldier-protector futilely flee from their black pursuer. Their flight through the clouds becomes a horrifying, nightmare chase, not a joyfully Clairish one; it ends with the girl's dream-death in an impressionistic cemetery. The petals of flowers descend onto her dying body; then the petals of the dream dissolve into the snowflakes of reality. The little match girl lies frozen, buried under a mound of snow. Only a few scattered boxes of matches reveal that she once existed.

Although later Renoir films became less fantastic, the effects of tonal lighting, the overhanging mood of death, the complexity of his irony, and the sadness underlying the superficial gaiety were all constants. But Renoir's world was, even so, not utterly bitter and dark. It is characterized just as much by its vast, humanistic acceptance of life, an acceptance based on a deep understanding of the world, whose ironies, contradictions, satisfactions, and failures he observed with what can only be called wisdom. His films are among the great contributions to world culture, and their profundity deepens with every viewing.

Throughout the 1930s Renoir's films threw a cold, hard light on the crumbling social and political structures of Europe. Renoir juxtaposed the tinkle of ironic laughter with the overwhelming sense of dissolution and decay; an effete aristocracy was gradually sinking under the weight of its own artificial and lifeless conventions, and the new rising classes were barrenly following in the empty steps of their former masters. The thirties, in France as well as in America, had become the age of the scenarist, and Renoir's screenplays (which he wrote himself in collaboration with one or two other writers) novelistically emphasized parallel events, parallel structures, parallel characters, parallel reactions, parallel details. The attention to visual and intellectual parallels gave the Renoir film the richness and complexity of the novel. But the literary structures of the films were supported by Renoir's sensitivity to the visual: Shots of nature, of faces, of social groupings in deep space visually generate the film's meaning and control its tone. *La Chienne* (1931), a comedy of betrayal and survival that in Fritz Lang's hands became the depressing *Scarlet Street* (1945); *Boudu Saved from Drowning* (1932), an exuberantly comic clash between a tramp, a pure man of nature, and the stifling conventions of polite, bourgeois society; *Toni* (1935), a sensitively tragic clash between the passions of love and restrictive societal conventions—and a crucial precursor of neo-realism; *The Crime of Monsieur Lange* (1936), a comedy about a publishing house that becomes a successful co-op, almost a communist utopia, after the boss leaves; *La Marseillaise* (1938), a historical study of the French Revolution, made for the French Popular Front, which reveals its leftist sympathies by its focus on the common foot soldiers; and an adaptation of Gorky's *The Lower Depths* (1936), which attracted Renoir with its bitter microcosmic study of human beings in society—all show the director warming up for his greatest films at the end of the decade.

Grand Illusion (1937) is also a microcosmic study. Its superficial action is the story of two French soldiers who eventually escape from a German prisoner-of-war camp during World War I. Its real action is metaphor: the death of the old ruling class of the European aristocracy and the growth of the new ruling classes of the workers and bourgeoisie. The prisoner-of-war camp is Renoir's microcosm for European society. The prison contains French and Russian and English, professors and actors and mechanics and bankers, Christians and Jews, nobility and capital and labor.

At the top of the social hierarchy is the German commander, Rauffenstein (played by Erich von Stroheim, the director whose films most influenced Renoir's), and the French captain, Boeldieu (played by Pierre Fresnay). Though the two men fight on opposite sides, they are identical: They both use a monocle; they both wear white gloves; they both share the same prejudices and snobberies, the same educated tastes in wine, food, and horses. They are united by class more than they are divided by country. The supreme irony of the film is that the German commander must kill this man to whom he feels most closely allied because the rules of the war game demand that the commanding officer of the prison shoot men trying to escape, just as they demand that the prisoner (gentleman or not) attempt to escape. The two men are inflexibly, tragically responsible to their codes, their rules, and their duties.

The two tougher, hardier prisoners do escape, while Boeldieu, attired in his white gloves, smartly covers for them and gives up his life in gentlemanly sacrifice. Maréchal (played by Jean Gabin), a mechanic, and Rosenthal (played by Marcel Dalio), a Rothschildean Jew whose family owns banks, land, and several chateaux, escape together from the German prison. The animosities, the tensions, the prejudices of the two men surface as the going gets rough, but the two finally make it to Switzerland —and they make it together. They are the new Europe.

Grand Illusion opens on a gramophone horn; the machine plays "Frou-Frou," a popular French song; we are in the French camp. A few minutes later, the camera captures a second gramophone horn; the machine plays a Strauss waltz; we are in the German camp. The songs have changed; the camps are the same. Most indicative of the film's tone and statement is the drag-show sequence in which the French prisoners entertain each other dressed as cancan girls in the latest imported Paris frocks. Just before the show, the French prisoners receive word that the German army has captured the French town of Douaumont. Despite their sadness, the show must go on—to show their *esprit*. In the middle of the drag show, the French receive word that the Allies have recaptured Douaumont. Maréchal makes the announcement; the cancan boys stop dancing and rip off their wigs to cheer; they all sing the "Marseillaise." Renoir's shots of these rouged, lipsticked men singing the patriotic hymn—moments before, they had been singing a frivolous tune— reveal the irony and paradoxes about a notion

Fig. 10-15

Fig. 10-16

Grand Illusion. *Fig. 10-15: the coldness of stone and metal; Rauffenstein (von Stroheim), Boeldieu (Pierre Fresnay), and Maréchal (Jean Gabin) in the German fortress. Fig. 10-16: Maréchal finds warmth on the little farm; a farm instead of a prison, straw instead of stone, loose clothing instead of uniforms, farming tools instead of rifles.*

such as patriotism, simultaneously serious and silly, deadly and tawdry, transcendent and transvestite.

Music is used to create leitmotifs. The trifle "Frou-Frou" recurs several times. When the captured French prisoners first hear a German military band, united by the rhythmic tramping of marching feet and the soaring descant of piping fifes, Boeldieu remarks, "I hate fifes." Another unifying musical motif is "Il était un petit navire," which we hear played for the first time by Boeldieu on a little toy fife as a ruse to help Maréchal and Rosenthal escape; the tune diverts Rauffenstein's attention but leads to the death of the man who hated fifes. Later, on the icy road, when the crippled Rosenthal and the impatient Maréchal quarrel and threaten to separate, Rosenthal starts singing "Il était un petit navire" in defiance and anger. As Maréchal stalks away from his lame comrade, he starts to sing the same song. The song ultimately brings Maréchal back to his slower comrade; he will not desert him again.

Consistent visual imagery is another source of the film's unity. Renoir's camera contrasts things that are hard, cold, and dead with things that are soft, warm, and vital. The final sequences of the film take place during the winter; the consistent pictures of snow and frozen ground throw their cold, damp shadow over the entire film. The two escaped prisoners must struggle across an immense meadow of snow to reach safety in Switzerland. Yet ironically, the Swiss border, the place of refuge, is invisible. It is impossible to distinguish different nations beneath a common blanket of snow. Only the German officer's announcement that the two have made it—to freedom, in one of Renoir's characteristically open endings— informs us where the snow of Germany ends and the snow of Switzerland begins. That one can make such nationalistic distinctions between lands that are really the same is one of the film's grand illusions, an illusion that freezes the human heart and condition to death.

Equally cold is the bare, stony castle that keeps the prisoners captive. And unforgettable is the piece of iron that replaces Rauffenstein's chin; it supports his face since his real chin has been shot away. Rauffenstein himself is literally held together by metal—in the chin, the back, the knee—the living embodiment of the film's contrast of the vital and the dead. The one warm thing in the prison-castle is Rauffenstein's little geranium, which he carefully guards and nurtures. When Boeldieu dies, Rauffenstein lops off the one blossom himself; he knows that his world is dead. Emphatically warm and vital are the woman and child, Elsa and Lotte, that Maréchal and Rosenthal encounter on their flight. Elsa's warmth touches the soldier Maréchal, as does her little daughter, Lotte, with her sparkling blue eyes. Maréchal vows to return to this warmth after the war is over. But will he? He tells her he will return in French, a language she cannot understand. His promise is never received; will it ever be kept?

It is, of course, another sign of Renoir's brilliance that he has built this dialogue film around the ironies of language (the soundtrack is crowded with French, German, and English; the most educated, upper-class characters speak them all with equal facility), languages that separate people or bind them together as effectively as national boundaries. Indeed, language differences are national differences. So in this film that is full of disastrous political illusions, it is difficult to determine which is the "grand" one. That war can resolve political issues? That old social and political ideals remain viable? That national boundaries exist? That national boundaries do not exist? That national distinctions are stronger than class distinctions? That class distinctions are stronger than national distinctions? Or perhaps it is simply that the First World War was the "war to end all wars," since none of the conflicts for which it was fought— drawing acceptable national boundaries, declaring racial supremacies, bridging linguistic barriers, resolving class differences—had been resolved in the Europe of 1937.

Grand Illusion shows how, with the Great War, the aristocracy of Europe committed elegant suicide. To turn life into a cold murderous game with a series of artificial rules is ultimately to turn life into death. But how can a class that has lived according to certain codes and manners for centuries suddenly change to fit the new bourgeois and proletarian times? Rather than being villains, Rauffenstein and Boeldieu are admirable for their taste, their elegance, their consistent integrity, and their honor. Is it their fault that they have been condemned by history to live in a century that barely understands those virtues? As Renoir would put the problem in his last film of the decade, "Everyone has his reasons."

These ironies and paradoxes become the central issues of that last 1930s film, perhaps Renoir's greatest, *The Rules of the Game* (*La Règle du jeu;* shot, released, censored, and banned in 1939; restored in 1956). The film depicts the dead values of a dead society—two dead and mutually dependent societies, in fact —the society of wealthy masters and the society of genteel, parasitic servants who ape their masters. Both masters and servants value good form over sincerity and the open expression of human emotion; both are equally aware of class distinctions. The inevitable result is death. But as in *Grand Illusion,* the dancers in this dance of death are sincere, elegant, honorable human beings, trying to balance the demands of social form with the demands of human spontaneity. Like the aristocrats of *Grand Illusion,* they find that the conflicting demands are ultimately, and unfortunately, mutually exclusive and unbalanceable.

Renoir's complex structural parallels play two love stories against each other. In the main plot, a young romantic aviator, André Jurieux, openly confesses his love to a stylish upper-class married lady, Christine de la Chesnaye. Although the rules of the game do not prohibit adultery, they do condemn such frank, open, sincere expressions of it. In the subplot, the lady's maid begins her own adulterous dabbling with a new servant, Marceau: a poacher, an outsider (like André), not a genteel (if excitable) servant like her own husband, Schumacher. The servants, who ostracize Marceau, are just as snobbish and conventional as their masters who ostracize André because he is romantic and Christine because she is foreign. Other subplots concern Christine's husband's attempts to break off a boring love affair and André's best friend's discovery that he, Octave, loves Christine. The love plots cross paths, as in a dance with changing partners or a wildly complicated bedroom farce. The maid's jealous husband,

who also has problems observing the rules of the game, mistakenly shoots the aviator, thinking that André is really Octave (played by Renoir himself), and that Octave has become his wife's new lover (he has not), and that the woman wearing his wife's coat is his wife (it is Christine). The romantic aviator dies, and the game of lies goes on, but both represent codes that are dying out. The Marquis de la Chesnaye, Christine's husband (played by Marcel Dalio), formally announces to his guests that André has met with a "regrettable accident"; the group admires and accepts the baron's lie as a gentlemanly display of good form.

Renoir's sense of style and imagery again sustain the film. Its most memorable visual sequence is the rabbit hunt, a metaphor for the society's murderous conventionality and insensitivity. The wealthy masters go off to shoot rabbits; this hunt, like the lives of the rich, has its etiquette, its rules, its gentility. It is a totally destructive yet conventionalized form of killing. The servants also serve as accomplices in the murder, for their job is to beat the trees and bushes, driving the pheasants and rabbits out of cover and into the open where they can be gunned down. Servants and masters are partners in this murderous game. Renoir fills the screen for five minutes with an agonized ballet of helpless, dying animals: They run across the screen accompanied by the bushy scamper of their little feet on the sound track, we hear a shotgun, the furry animal stops, flips, spins, and stretches out (in slight slow motion) to die. The sickening, horrifying beauty of this dance of death is at the heart of the film's meaning and tone. The whole film is a dance of death. While the skeletons dance on stage at the marquis's evening party, men shoot real bullets at one another in the audience. And when André, in some ways as natural, impulsive, innocent, and naïve as an animal, is killed with a shotgun, he rolls over and dies "like a rabbit."

One of the film's key visual metaphors is the marquis's collection of mechanical toys— ornate, clockwork birds and music boxes. The marquis collects people—his wife and mistress —the way he collects toys, and he prefers stuffed but predictable machines to breathing,

Fig. 10-17
The Rules of the Game. *The perfect orderliness of conventionalized murder: the aristocrats at the hunt.*

unpredictable people. But even the machines break down—chaotically but momentarily, like the supposedly inviolable rules of correct behavior. All those, the marquis can restore—but what dies cannot be fixed.

And yet Renoir's method is not so naïve as to condemn artifice and praise the simplicities of spontaneity. For one thing, the Marquis de la Chesnaye—Renoir's representative of civilization—is a compassionate, considerate man who is trying not to hurt anyone, whereas the aviator—Renoir's representative of spontaneity—is a selfish, blundering fool. Although the music boxes are indeed mechanical, they also represent a degree of orderly and delicate perfection toward which human life might well aspire. De la Chesnaye's problem is that he would like to achieve an impossible ideal: a world in which the demands of love and order are harmonious rather than mutually exclusive—or at least are pursued with restraint and good manners, with "class." As he

tells his gamekeeper, he wants no fences around his property and he also wants no rabbits. It is not De la Chesnaye's fault that the perfect grace of the eighteenth century (the century that produced his chateau, his life-style, and the Mozart on the sound track), a world in which the demands of spontaneity and convention may seem to have been properly balanced, no longer exists in the twentieth century with its airplanes, motor cars, radios, and bourgeoisie, and its Nazis massing on the borders of France. As in *Grand Illusion*, the source of evil in *The Rules of the Game* is extremely complex: It is rooted partly in the human personality, partly in the demands of social convention, partly in nature itself, and partly in history, which has posed dilemmas greater than the powers of people to solve.

Renoir's comedies of manners were dark, bitter, and very uncomical. The death, the decay, the anti-Semitism, the organized murder that Renoir depicted in his films prophetically

216   A SHORT HISTORY OF THE MOVIES

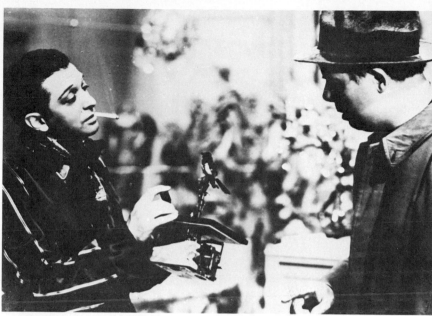

*The marquis (Marcel Dalio, left)
with one of his mechanical pets
and Octave, the sponger (played
by Renoir).*

Fig. 10-18

surfaced with the Second World War. Renoir,
like Clair, made films in the United States dur-
ing the war: *Swamp Water* (1941), *This Land Is
Mine* (1943), *The Southerner* (1945), *Diary of a
Chambermaid* (1946). After the war, he, like
Clair, returned to France. But he took a while
to get there. In India, where he inspired
Satyajit Ray, he made his first color film, *The
River* (1949–51). By way of Italy and another
movie, he was back in the Paris studios by 1954.
The greatest of his postwar French films was
French Cancan (1954), starring Jean Gabin. One
episode of his last picture, *The Little Theatre of
Jean Renoir* (made for TV in 1969, released
theatrically in 1970), was a remake of *The Little
Match Girl*. His eye, his sense of style, his perception of social structures and human relationships were still keen. Renoir would serve as
a historical bridge, uniting the tradition of
French "literary" filmmaking with the emerging cinematic breeziness of the *nouvelle vague*.

Vigo, Carné, and Prévert

Not all French films were successful at combining literariness with the visual powers of mov-

ing pictures. As in America, the early sound
years in France produced a curious and inert
hybrid, the filmed play. "Canned theatre" became one obvious but clumsy way to solve the
dialogue problem in French as well as American
films. The success of the French playwright,
Marcel Pagnol, as a producer and director of
dialogue films was symptomatic. But in translating plays for the camera, Pagnol showed
more cinematic sense than did many theatre-
inspired Hollywood directors. He often preferred shooting outdoors to shooting on the
sound stage, a very untheatrical choice. He also
had the vision to ask cinematically minded directors to work for him, like Jean Renoir (*Toni*).

The young iconoclast, Jean Vigo, however,
was totally unfettered by the theatrical and literary biases of the early thirties. Vigo made
only four films—two shorts, one of medium
length, one feature—before his death in 1934
at the age of twenty-nine. That Vigo should be
free of the deadening conventions of canned
theatre was entirely appropriate, for freedom
was his primary theme. Vigo's films show the
determined and successful efforts of his characters to create temporary pockets of freedom in
the midst of the society that confines them.

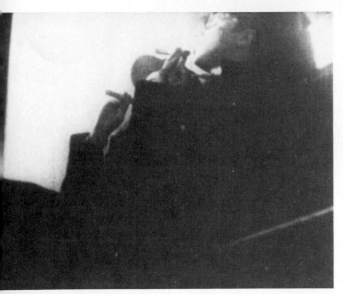

Fig. 10-19

Fig. 10-20

Zéro de conduite (*Zero in Conduct,* 1933) contrasts the energetic, joyous freedom of boyhood with the constrictive restraint of the prison-like school that the children must attend. The boys eventually rebel against their captors, staging a demonstration on alumni day in front of all the wooden guests. They lower the flag of France and raise the skull-and-crossbones. They stand against the sky as the film ends. The freedom of Vigo's surprising images reveals the spirit of this film about freedom, which strongly influenced both Truffaut's *The 400 Blows* (1959) and Lindsay Anderson's *If . . .* (1969).

Vigo's primary visual choice is to subvert realistic, three-dimensional, deep-focus space and replace it with an imaginative, metaphoric sense of space that takes its spatial coordinates not from the architecture and scenery of the physical world but from the emotions and sensations of his characters. In the opening sequence, two boys, in a moment of youthful communion, transform the cramped space of a train compartment into an imaginative realm of play and joy, almost a mental universe. There are surprising shots from varied angles and perspectives in the tiny train compartment, brilliantly photographed by Boris Kaufman, the emigré brother of Dziga Vertov. Kaufman's

Fig. 10-21

Zéro de conduite. *The subversion of three-dimensional space: two boys puffing cigars in the train car, the slow-motion procession after the feathers fly, the final ascent toward the sky.*

ability to shoot improvisationally in real locations would contribute significantly to the 1950s American film. The spatial magic of the opening sequence is matched by that of the final shot, as four young rebels, apparently climbing to the peak of a tiled roof, seem to ascend into the sky itself, since Vigo has deliberately stripped the shot of all familiar spatial coordinates.

Surprisingly beautiful in the film is the slow-motion pillow fight in the bare, sterile dormitory. This scene—another radical transformation of space, this time achieved by transforming time, and obviously influenced by the pillow fight in Gance's *Napoleon*—is a metaphor for the whole film: In the midst of the confining, regularized room the children leap and bound, swing pillows, spill feathers in balletic slow motion, the feathers falling about their bodies and laughing faces like snow. Indicative of the film's tone is Vigo's handling of the teacher–jailers as comic grotesques with sharp, ugly faces or fat, round bodies. They sneak around corners; they steal the kids' candy. Most grotesque of all is the school's principal—a three-foot dwarf with a pointed beard. The highest authority of the system is the smallest man; his mind is as small as his body. The only good teacher has an irreverent sense of humor and mimics Chaplin. Not surprisingly, this wild, iconoclastic film was banned by the French government in 1933 because it ridiculed authority. The film was not shown in France until after the war in 1946, when all forms of repression and restraint became understandably unpopular.

If *Zéro de conduite* was the young director's anarchical, sarcastic swipe at authority and the system, his next film and only full-length feature, *L'Atalante* (1934), is a mature, romantic investigation of two people discovering what is important within the system. Two young people, recently married, discover each other's love, then drift apart and separate, and then find each other again, now knowing how empty their lives are without each other. Tying the film together is the river barge, L'Atalante, where the newlyweds must live. The young man (Jean, played by Jean Dasté) owns the barge, and running the boat is his life. Juliette (the bride, played by Dita Parlo) longs for life on the shore. The barge becomes the source of the plot's complication, the rival that drives the couple apart. Although Juliette does not know it, the open space of the shore, which seems so attractive, is really more confining, less free than the apparently cramped space on the barge. As in *Zéro de conduite*, Vigo has set himself the problem of translating emotion into spatial coordinates, and the cramped, cluttered, but at times unforgettably lyrical space on the barge is spiritually and emotionally richer than the deep but dead space on shore, where excitement and "fun" turn out to be loveless, pointless, and unfulfilling. The barge, adrift on the river, gliding on the water, in the sunlight, through the fog, becomes, like the community established by the boys in *Zéro de conduite*, an ideal community—man, wife, old crew member, young apprentice—because it is not contaminated by contact with "official" society at all.

The film's opening sequence begins the contrast of ship and shore. Jean and Juliette are married on shore; the wedding party is stiff, formal, wooden; the marriage ceremony feels more like a funeral; the guests wear black. Only on the barge do the lovers loosen up and begin to feel what getting married really means: not a deadening social ceremony but a fertile union of two minds, hearts, and bodies. Vigo's gorgeous traveling shots of the barge on the water, often from extremely high or low angles, consistently evoke the beauty of river life. His understated sincerity in rendering human emotions is evident in the images that imply much more than they say: Juliette's desire to listen to the radio, her one contact with the shore; the lonely Juliette sitting huddled up alone in the fog; the man and woman sleeping alone in separate beds (before, they had always slept together). Vigo's sense of the grotesque— another carryover from *Zéro de conduite*—adds a unique and symbolic air to the old sailor (played brilliantly by Renoir's Boudu, Michel Simon), who has made the water his home, and the clownish peddler who evokes Juliette's longings for the life on shore. Because the two young people really love each other, and because Vigo has rendered that love so intimately and so sincerely, we feel complete relief and delight when they return to each other and life on L'Atalante. The barge casts off and continues its journey up river.

Like the films of Renoir, the films of Jacques Feyder and Marcel Carné took their literariness from the novel rather than the stage. In this age of the scenarist, both directors enlisted talented minds to write their scripts. Charles Spaak (who also wrote *Grand Illusion* for Renoir) wrote for Feyder the scripts of *Le Grand jeu* (1934), *Pension Mimosas* (1935), and *Carnival in Flanders* (1935). Even more fruitful was the collaboration of the novelist-poet, Jacques Prévert, and Carné. Prévert, whose poetic obsessions with fatalism and death dominated both romantic melodramas (like *Le Jour se lève*, 1939) and light comedies (*Bizarre Bizarre*, 1937), wrote Carné a series of scripts in which admirable men die (for no reason other than that men die), in which people are dragged against their wills into complicated webs of human interactions from which there is no escape, in which people lose what they want and achieve what they do not want, in which symbolic figures of death weave pointedly through the realistic action, in which images of fog and gloom and chaos dampen the film's tone and symbolize the world's emptiness.

Like Renoir, Clair, and Vigo, Carné and Prévert explore what is clearly the key theme of the 1930s, freedom. But for Carné and Prévert the limit to human freedom is human life itself: its fallibility, its mortality, its existence in a completely irrational, indifferent universe. Prévert's existential void is the precursor of Camus's or Beckett's; his characters not only wait for Godot (love is clearly their Godot), but wait for it incompetently, never attaining the desired love because of some failing within themselves, within the desired lover, or within the cosmos itself. Although the Carné–Prévert films echo the decay, the waste, the death of Renoir's, they lack the surface level of ironic comedy, of polished manners, of genteel laughter. The seriocomic irony of Renoir contrasts with the hollowness, the sadness, the profound despair of Carné.

In *Port of Shadows* (1938), a young soldier, past unknown (we know only that he is a deserter), is steadily dragged into a complicated net of murderers, thieves, and outcasts, all because of the woman he loves, who loves him in return. One of the film's leitmotifs is a small dog that follows the soldier (played by Jean Gabin) everywhere, instinctively, attached to this man who helped save his life at the beginning of the film. In the same way, the soldier is instinctively, irrationally attached to Nelly (Michèle Morgan). He abandons his own attempts to escape, protects Nelly instead, and is suddenly and unexpectedly gunned down at the end of the film, the victim of his love, his self-sacrifice, his commitment to a human being outside of himself.

Port of Shadows is dominated by the empty, seamy people who surround the soldier and Nelly: the owner of the toy shop, Zabel (Michel Simon), who is Nelly's foster father and also her lecherous captor; the nihilistic artist (a Prévert surrogate) who paints death in all his pictures; the criminal boss, Lucien. The film is dominated by images of shadows and fog—of rain, of dimly lit streets, wet pavements, shadowy figures in silhouette, the perfect visual accompaniment to the inexorable closing of the jaws of the trap around the soldier and his love. The trap is life itself.

The richest and most complex of the Carné–Prévert films is *The Children of Paradise* (1943–45). As with Dostoyevsky, Hugo, Tolstoy, or Dickens, the viewer of *Les Enfants du paradis* lives through a novelistically complicated series of interlocking events with many complex and interesting figures over a long period of time. There are six central characters: two actors, two women, an aristocrat, and a murderous thief. All have difficulty deciding what they really want; each achieves material success only to discover that it is meaningless.

Central to the film is the contrast between the two actors: one, Frédérick Lemaître (Pierre Brasseur) is the man of words who acts with his mouth; the other, Baptiste Deburau (Jean-Louis Barrault), is the mime who acts with his body. Although both Frédérick and Baptiste are historical figures—two famous French actors of the nineteenth century—the film treats them as metaphorical opposites rather than as biographical subjects. Frédérick is the man of surfaces, of words, of fine talk and phrases; he becomes a huge success in cheap, hack dramas that he saves with his own imaginative theatrics; he also runs up debts, trifles

Fig. 10-22

Fig. 10-23

Les Enfants du paradis. *Fig. 10-22: the theatre as life and life as the theatre; Frédérick (Pierre Brasseur, left) as Harlequin, Garance (Arletty) as the Moon Lady, and Baptiste (Jean-Louis Barrault) as Pierrot, acting out a version of their off-stage love triangle in a pantomime scripted by Baptiste. Fig. 10-23: the seething activity in "the gods."*

with the ladies, treats his colleagues with contempt. His life is richly barren. Baptiste is the man of real feeling and the real artist, moonstruck and vulnerable; his ability to feel and love makes him the artist that he is. Although Frédérick is the matinee idol of Paris, Baptiste's ethereal mime is the delight of artists, thinkers, and the common people.

Between the two actors stands a woman named Garance (Arletty), after the flower. She casually becomes Frédérick's mistress, although Baptiste is the shy man who really loves her. The young Garance thought that love was simple, that bodies were to be tasted and then tossed away when the flavor had departed. Her view of love's simplicity conflicted with the complexity of Baptiste's passion; when she casually offers him her body, he, seeing her as a pure spirit of beauty, declines the offer. Only years later, after she has found wealth and glamor as the mistress of a rich count (Louis Salou), does she realize the power of Baptiste's passion, the power that makes him a great mime. And only then does Baptiste realize that he should never have declined Garance's offer. But when she returns, Garance sees that Baptiste is saddled with a possessive wife he does not love (Nathalie, played by Maria Casarès, who later starred in Cocteau's *Orpheus*) and a child. The two are just as far apart as ever.

The last major character, Lacenaire (Marcel Herrand), is not a man of the theatre but a thief with a taste for murder, a man who lives his life as though it were the theatre. Lacenaire, like Frédérick, is a man of words; in private he writes plays and in public he makes embroidered, fatalistic, lengthy speeches about the futility of life. He is a man of costumes: of overstarched, overwhite shirts, fancy canes, curled hair, finely spun words—a glossy, empty servant of death who treats both life and the living as banal jokes. His one passion is indulging his contempt for others and his vain love for himself.

Carné and Prévert use the theatre as the film's central metaphor. The first and second parts of the film both open on a theatre curtain; the curtain rises to reveal the world of *Les Enfants* behind it. Both the first and second parts of the film end with the curtain coming down.

Although the theatre is the key symbol, the film never degenerates into the static talkiness of the canned-theatre films. (Ten years later, both Max Ophüls and Jean Renoir would also use the theatre or circus tent as a metaphor without inhibiting the film's cinematic freedom.) Carné and Prévert sustain the theatre metaphor by paralleling the dramatic, fictional roles of the actors on stage with their actual longings and choices as human beings off stage. In the playlets on stage there are bandits, lovers, police, and deaths; in their off-stage lives there are bandits, lovers, police, and deaths. The on-stage character played by Frédérick—Harlequin—is, like Frédérick, bouncy, playful, spirited, charming, superficially happy. Baptiste's dramatic role as Pierrot is like Baptiste himself: sad, moonstruck, tender, unfortunate. Just as Pierrot loses the beautiful moon lady (played by Garance) to Harlequin, Baptiste loses Garance to Frédérick. The theatre is life and life is the theatre.

The title of the film itself is part of its theatrical metaphor. The "Paradise" of the title is not a heavenly, metaphysical one but an earthly one: It is the slang name for the second balcony (in English theatre, "the gods"), the highest, cheapest seats in the theatre, the seats where sit the masses, those who love the theatre and mix intimately in all its passions. The chaotic, energetic masses (the "gods" who watch, who are to be pleased, and without whom the entertainers would not exist) in "Paradise" parallel the masses just outside the theatre on the teeming, vital, packed Boulevard du Temple, also known as the "Street of Crime." There is no particular order or reason or meaning for all the human activity in "Paradise" or the "Street of Crime." The life merely is; it exists in all its contradictions, its desires, its disappointments.

Weaving through the film is a dirty, vulgar old-clothes man called Jericho (Pierre Renoir), who is Prévert's symbolic reminder of the sordid, mortal realities behind all our dreams of the ideal. Jericho, with his prophetic biblical name of death and dissolution, is also a thief, an informer, and an eavesdropper. He spies on people's lives, spreading gloom and doubt wherever he goes. Baptiste hates Jericho, for the old tramp reminds him of the etherealness, the unreality of the idealized sentiments on which he bases both his life and his art. Baptiste hates Jericho so much that he creates a character just like him (for one of his mime plays) whom Pierrot kills. In an early version of the script, Baptiste was also going to kill Jericho.

At the end of the film, Baptiste loses Garance once more, perhaps never to see her again. He follows her through the "Street of Crime," vainly calling her name, trying to attract her attention. But Garance cannot hear him; the swirling masses of humanity slow Baptiste's pursuit, effectively choking him off, keeping him from reaching his love. At his side we glimpse Jericho, a metaphor for broken dreams, unfulfilled hopes, irrational fate, human mortality — the true "crimes" of human existence. Surrounded by all this human activity, so alive and yet so senseless, Baptiste is swallowed by the crowd, by his "audience," and the curtain falls.

Les Enfants du paradis could not be finished and released until after the Liberation freed both the distributors and the necessary francs. For the first fifteen years after the war, the best French films — those of Ophüls, Bresson, Tati, and Renoir — very clearly looked backward to the literary-scenario films of the prewar era, a "tradition of quality" whose major wartime expression was Les Enfants du paradis itself. Not until 1959 — when the New Wave (la Nouvelle Vague), which had been building since the mid-1950s, crested and broke on the shores of the film world it was to transform — would the French cinematic imagination strike off in a new direction.

11

The American Studio Years: 1930–1945

In the 1930s Americans went to the movies; in the 1990s they go to a movie. The difference is not merely semantic. In 1938 there were some eighty million movie admissions every week, a figure representing 65 percent of the population of the United States. In 1990 there were some twenty million movie admissions every week, less than 10 percent of the population of the United States. Over five hundred feature films were produced by the major studios in the United States in 1937, but fewer than one hundred in 1983. In the relatively active year 1987, the major studios released 135 features, and the independents another 380. The film industry of the 1930s thrived on a felicitous circle of economic dependence on attendance, exhibition, and production. The huge number of movie admissions necessitated a huge number of theatres, which necessitated a huge number of films to be shown in the theatres, which necessitated large, busy studios that could produce enough films to keep the theatres filled. Only after the Second World War did the circle of dependence reverse itself and turn vicious.

The need for enormous quantities of films guaranteed the survival of the studio system, which was geared for production in quantity. The huge studios of the 1920s converted to sound by merely adding new departments to their already complex organizations; specialization and division of labor, two pillars of the silent-film factories, became even more essential to the sound-film factory. New departments of music, of sound mixing and dubbing, of sound technicians and machinery joined the older, established departments on the studio lot. The writing department became even more specialized; some writers roughed out general treatments, others broke the treatment into its shot-by-shot elements, and still others added the necessary dialogue.

The film property traveled through the studio, from department to department, from story idea to finished script, until it finally landed in the hands of its director, often on the day before shooting began. After fifteen to thirty shooting days (for a typical "program picture"), the director relinquished the negative to the cutting department, which edited the film into its final form, as instructed by the film's producer. Only the most important directors of the most special, unprogrammatic films enjoyed the opportunity to shape the script before shooting and to cut the exposed footage afterward. From the cutting department the film went to distribution offices, and from them to the waiting chains of theatres that the company itself owned. The film product rolled down the assembly line from the original idea to final showing, all stages controlled by the studio factory. The film industry had evolved its structure for the next sixteen rich years, from 1930 to 1946.

The years of wealth were not without their moments of worry. At first, the Wall Street crash of 1929 exerted curiously little effect on the film business. Although America was officially broke, Americans kept scraping up dimes, quarters, and dollars to see movies. The economic sag first hit the movie industry in 1933; admissions declined, theatres closed, production dropped. But prudent studio economy measures, the aid of government dollars, and a new moralistic path of righteousness nursed the film business back to health.

In 1930, Martin Quigley, a Roman Catholic layman, and Daniel Lord, S.J., drafted the Hollywood Production Code, another in a series of the motion picture industry's official statements on the proper moral content of films. But the Code might never have been enforced if the Catholic Legion of Decency had not threatened an economic boycott in 1933, the same year that movie revenues first began to feel the Depression. In July of 1934, Joseph I. Breen, another Roman Catholic layman, went to work for the "Hays Office" (see Chapter 6) as the head of its new Production Code Administration (PCA), an agency that would award the industry's seal of approval only to those films that observed the Code's moral restrictions. Any producer or distributor who released a film without the industry's seal would be fined $25,000. Because every major producer and distributor was a member of the Motion Picture Producers and Distributors of America (MPPDA), they all subscribed to the PCA's rulings.

The Code declared that movies were to avoid brutality (by gangsters and especially by the police), they were to avoid depicting any kind of sexual promiscuity (unwedded, extramarital, or "unnatural"), and they were to avoid making any illegal or immoral life seem either possible or pleasant (goodbye to the gangsters who lived well until the law gunned them down). The Production Code viewed marriage as more a sacred institution than a sexual one; even the sophisticated Nick and Nora Charles of *The Thin Man* (1934) slept separately in twin beds — which became known as "Hollywood beds." Even more restrictive were the new Code's specific prohibitions against certain words. Not only were "sex," "God," "hell," and "damn" forbidden, but so were such flavorful and healthy Americanisms as "guts," "nuts," "nerts," and "louse," which were considered deficient in gentility and "tone." Ironically, the Code, which Hollywood adopted for business reasons in 1934, perished some thirty years later for the same reasons. The very words and deeds that crimped sales in the 1930s spurred them in the 1960s.

There is considerable confusion today about precisely what this Production Code was. Some historians see the Code as the era's institutional means for eliminating political dissent and narrowing discussion of the important social issues. The large banks, whose investment capital allowed the movie industry to function, could dictate the conservative content of films through the Code, constricting political change and cultural consciousness. Within the film industry at the time, the Code was a particularly useful instrument for studios to keep writers in their place. A producer could always settle a dispute with a writer simply by claiming that the Code said No.

But its administrators claimed that the purpose of the Code was not to keep films from being made, but to allow them to be made — without damaging the commercial health of the film, the studio that made it, and the industry as a whole. Americans inside and outside the film industry knew that adultery, crime, and moral aberration were not only a part of life but the elementary materials of playacting and storytelling from their beginnings. The Code was a unique historical document that attempted to formulate, concretely and precisely, the publicly admissible mores of an entire culture—the kinds of deeds suitable for public depiction and, especially, the kinds of words (now that movies could talk) suitable for public utterance.

In advising producers and writers—particularly about adaptations of prestigious plays and novels—the Production Code Administration trimmed as little of the original material as possible but as much as was necessary to conform to the moral sensibilities of an American majority—as envisaged and articulated by the Code. There is very little difference between the values of that majority in 1934 and those of what was called the Moral Majority in 1984.

In addition to soothing its audiences' moral sensitivities, Hollywood pulled itself out of the Depression by offering a bargain. Double features—two pictures for the price of one—became standard in all but the poshest of first-run theatres. Hollywood added a third attraction to the two movies (plus trailers, cartoons, shorts, and a newsreel): Audiences could play exciting games between the films—Keno, Bingo, Screeno—that sent the winner home with cash or a set of dishes. The studios survived the financial crisis of 1933, and profits shot up in 1935; they survived the crisis of 1938, and profits shot up in 1939. The boom years of the war eliminated all money crises for several more years. (The Second World War itself lasted from 1939—1941 in America—to 1945.) The film industry enjoyed its biggest business year in 1946. (Despite the blockbuster years of the late 1970s and 1980s, the film industry's profits have never been proportionately higher than those of 1946, when over 78 million Americans went to the movies. In 1989, for example, domestic grosses topped $5 billion for the first time, but the dollar wasn't what it used to be—what cost nine cents in 1946 cost a dollar in 1989—the films cost much more to make and to see, independent distributors took their cut off the top, and a much smaller percentage of the population was buying tickets.)

The studio system produced an obvious tension between film art and film business. Art cannot be mass produced; creativity does not flourish in departments and on schedules. The unexceptional program picture was the resulting rule, the fresh and original film the vital exception.

Despite this tension between commerce and creativity, there are surprising parallels between the Hollywood film of 1930 to 1945 and the richest era of English drama, 1576 to 1642. Like the Renaissance drama, the studio films were tremendously popular with vast audiences of diverse social, economic, and educational backgrounds. The Elizabethan plays and players were products of repertory theatre companies with a permanent staff of writers, actors, technicians, managers, costumers, and designers; the films were products of repertory film studios with similar permanent staffs. Like the Elizabethan theatre company, the film studio spread the acting parts among its regular stable of actors, each of whom played a specific kind of role over and over again—old man, comic, juvenile, leading man or lady, dancer, singer, child. Just as Shakespeare's Will Kemp and Richard Burbage bounced from comic or tragic part to comic or tragic part, Mickey Rooney and Clark Gable bounced for MGM. And like the films of the studio era, the Elizabethan plays were drenched in the theatrical customs, clichés, and conventions of their age: the tragic scenes of Senecan gore, the bawdy use of the comic Vice, the pastoral convention of a magical, fanciful forest. And just as a Shakespeare, a Marlowe, or a Jonson could turn a convention into a trait of personal style, so too a Lubitsch, a von Sternberg, or a Ford could make a studio convention completely his own. The most striking differences between Elizabethan plays and the studio films are that the studios produced no Shakespeare (but then neither has any other art at any other time) and that thousands of the hack, conventional, and clichéd films of the 1930s still survive, but only a few hundred (presumably the best) of the thousands of plays written between 1576 and 1642 have not been lost.

There are two ways of looking at the artistic products of a repertory system for the manufacture of popular dramatic entertainment. The critic can look at the greatest products of the system—its Shakespeares and Jonsons—or at its most typical and conventional products.

Any fair assessment of the studio system must do both.

Film Cycles and Cinematic Conventions

The studio system controlled both the subjects of film narrative and the cinematic styles in which they were shot. Formulas for fictional construction, characterization, decor, music, and photography dominated Hollywood's films. A key principle in the selection of story material was—and remains—simply that an idea that had worked before would probably work again. Films were not seen as special, individual conceptions but tended to bunch together as types, in cycles.

The new sound equipment introduced audiences to the hard-bitten, tough argot of mobsters; Hollywood produced a cycle of pictures that made the tough talk of gangsters as familiar as polite conversation around the family dinner table. The first gangster cycle condemned and glorified the brutality of the underworld: *Little Caesar, Scarface, The Public Enemy.* Later gangster cycles, purified by the antiviolence, antiillegality sections of the Breen Code, merely put the tough-talking guys on the right side of the law—that is, on the other side of the badge—*Public Hero Number 1, The Last Gangster.* A cycle of films about prisons, "the big house," spun off from the mobster films; the big house also had its slang, its underworld morality, its tough characters both behind bars and behind the warden's desk: *The Big House, San Quentin, The Criminal Code.* Yet another close relative of the mobster cycle was the journalism cycle. The newspaper reporters often seemed like gangsters who had accidentally ended up behind a typewriter rather than a tommy gun; they talked and acted as tough as the crooks their assignments forced them to cover: *The Front Page, Big News, The Power of the Press.* It is no accident that Ben Hecht, the greatest screen writer of rapid, bullet-like, flavorful tough talk as well as a major comic playwright, wrote gangster pictures (including the 1927 prototype, *Underworld,* for which he won the first Oscar for best story), prison pictures,

Fig. 11-1

Fig. 11-2

The assault of gangsters on American life. Fig. 11-1: Paul Muni as the hero/villain of the 1932 Scarface; *Fig. 11-2: George Raft as his coin-flipping friend.*

and newspaper pictures. And Hecht, of course, had scores of imitators.

A succession of musical cycles accompanied the cops-and-robbers cycles. Just as synchronized sound brought the pungent, brittle crackle of thug talk to American audiences, synchronization also brought the possibility of complex rhythmic and musical effects. Singing and dancing could be synchronized to the exact beat; picture and sound could be wed in their own kind of audio-visual montage. The first talking pictures were inevitably singing pictures. De Forest's earliest Phonofilms and the Warners' earliest Vitaphone shorts used singers and vaudeville entertainers. *The Jazz Singer* was more a singie than a talkie; even *Lights of New York*—the first of the gangster talkies—used several long musical numbers in Hawk Miller's night club. Musical sequences were almost obligatory in early talkies (even *The Blue Angel* and *Morocco*), just as most 1940s films included at least one song—whether integral and relevant, as in *Casablanca,* or unnecessary, as in *The Big Sleep.* Among the first "100 percent" talkies released by every major studio in 1929 was a musical—MGM's *Broadway Melody,* Fox's *Sunny Side Up,* and *Paramount on Parade.*

The first musical films were either filmed versions of Broadway shows with their original stars or suave, continental musical-comic pictures à la Lubitsch with Maurice Chevalier, Jeanette MacDonald, Jack Buchanan, or Miriam Hopkins. The second cycle of musicals was a series of "backstage" stories—the struggling young composer, the young hopeful in the chorus (who is catapulted to stardom when the leading lady falls ill), the down-and-out director who needs one last hit—epitomized at Warner Bros. by those films with musical numbers directed by Busby Berkeley.

The Berkeley musicals were highly contradictory mixtures of the blandest, thinnest dramatic sections (which Berkeley himself did not usually direct) and the most dazzling kaleidoscopic visual style for the musical sections. Berkeley's accomplishment was not merely that space itself became a "dancer" in these numbers but that his radical shifts of camera position stripped the frame of any clear geographical or theatrical referents. Berkeley's numbers invite us into a visual labyrinth; the viewer's eye absorbs a kind of visual "music," scored solely by abstract contrasts of black and white, circle and line, light and darkness, camera angles and editing rhythms.

But for all this dazzling dancing geometry, feminist critics remind us that Berkeley's evolv-

ing abstract forms are based on smiling female faces and shapely female limbs, presented for the display and delight of primarily male viewers, just like Florenz Ziegfeld's seminude showgirls on the Broadway stage (and Berkeley had worked for Ziegfeld). The keepers of the Production Code had similar suspicions about the Warners' backstage musicals. Although less than six months separate *42nd Street* from *Gold Diggers of 1933*, there is a clear contrast between the suggestive sleaziness and sexuality of *42nd Street* and the innocent showgirls of the later film, unjustly accused of amorous and mercenary intentions.

A parallel musical cycle was the smoother, more integrated comedies-of-romance-with-music starring Fred Astaire and Ginger Rogers at RKO. For Astaire and Rogers, dancing was not merely a generic inevitability of backstage musicals but a means of human interaction and connection. The characters embodied by Astaire and Rogers discovered one another's feelings through the dances they performed together, discovered that, no matter what social obstacles confronted them, they belonged together because they danced so perfectly together. Their dancing celebrated not just rhythm, motion, grace, and style but the way that physical activity can become a spiritual expression and spatial extension of inner feelings and harmonies.

America's greatest composers for the musical theatre wrote original songs and scores for Hollywood films: the Gershwins (*Shall We Dance?* and *A Damsel in Distress* for Astaire at RKO in 1937); Jerome Kern (*Swing Time,* 1936, and *You Were Never Lovelier,* 1943, also for Astaire); Irving Berlin (*Top Hat,* 1935, *Follow the Fleet,* 1936, and *Carefree,* 1938, for Astaire; *Alexander's Ragtime Band,* 1938, for Fox); Rodgers and Hart (*Love Me Tonight,* 1932, for Chevalier and MacDonald at Paramount); Cole Porter (*Born to Dance,* 1936, and *Broadway Melody of 1940* for MGM's Eleanor Powell).

There were the ornately costumed operettas at MGM with Nelson Eddy, Jeanette MacDonald, and Allan Jones—musicals that brought the stage hits of a previous generation to life for a new one in cinema. There were musicals for children (Shirley Temple and Bobby Breen), musicals for fresh, young ingenues

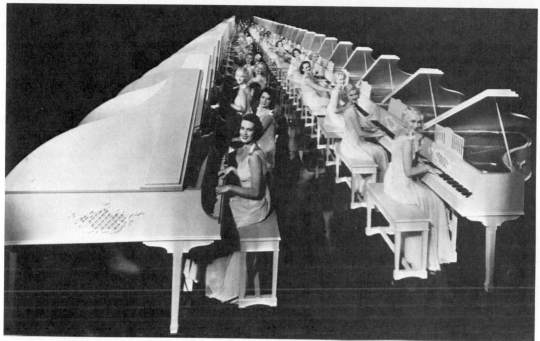

Fig. 11-3

Fig. 11-4

Fig. 11-5

The monochrome musical. Fig. 11-3: Busby Berkeley's kaleidoscopic white pianos on a black floor (Gold Diggers of 1935). Fred Astaire's variations on black and white, circle and line, light and shadow (Top Hat, Fig. 11-4; Swing Time, Fig. 11-5).

(Deanna Durbin and Gloria Jean), musicals on ice (Sonja Henie), and musicals under water (Esther Williams).

Any successful Hollywood film spawned several dozen imitations, just as one successful television show begets a dozen progeny on all three networks. Like television, the Hollywood of the thirties faced the weekly pressure of entertaining a huge percentage of the national population; as in television, fear of a dollar disaster was a constant spur to produce safe mediocrities. The parallels with television programming are even more obvious with those successful films that spawned not only imitations but sequels. The film series was the ancestor of the television series: the Andy Hardy pictures, the Maisie series, the Charlie Chan films, Mr. Moto, Philo Vance, Henry Aldrich, and — the closest parallel with television of all — the series of films springing from MGM's *Young Doctor Kildare.* Yet another studio formula was to patch together a film with all the available stars on the lot, using some flimsy narrative thread to sew the stars' fragments: Paramount's *Big Broadcasts* (of 1932, 1936, 1937, and 1938), MGM's *Broadway Melodies* (of 1936, 1938, and 1940). The studios made the same films over and over again, with similar titles or different ones.

Formulas for style were as binding as formulas for plotting. Hollywood films of the decade, with surprisingly few exceptions, looked strikingly alike. The studio system was as pervasive in erasing stylistic differences as it was in blurring differences of theme and story. The director inherited not only an unalterable, detailed scenario, but also a completed series of sets and costumes and a studio crew of cameramen, electricians, and soundmen. Many directors' impulses toward personal style were suppressed before shooting began by the studio's general policies of lighting, design, cinematography, and cutting.

The key characteristic of film style in the studio era was that sound films were talking films. The talk was better now that writers of screen dialogue knew how to write screen dialogue. The scenes of talk were smoother now that the speakers could move from place to place and both camera and microphone could follow them. The careful decor added insightful nuances and contrapuntal resonances to the scenes of talk. But talk still propelled the talkies.

The reign of talk produced further stylistic consequences. The camera's position and angle illuminated the speaker and the other characters' reactions to the speech rather than obscuring them in the hope of illuminating something else. Extreme high and low angles, extreme close shots, extreme far shots, tilts, and whirls were uncommon in even the most visually imaginative films. Cutting was as functional as the shooting. Quick cutting distracted the audience from the speaker's words. Rapid montage was reserved for occasional and obvious showcase effects: passage of time, summary of a character's activities. Scenes were lit first for the stars, then for the dramatic atmosphere. Designers and cameramen used light to make the pretty people even prettier, shaping their heads with light to make those box-office faces stand out from the backgrounds. Yet for all their apparent standardness, the movies never demonstrated a higher degree of craftsmanship and artisanship — neither in America nor elsewhere — than in these fifteen years of Hollywood studio style.

Despite their common assumptions and conventions, each of the studios displayed a unique personality in applying them. Perhaps the two giants — MGM and Paramount — were the most distinctive and the most different from one another. MGM was the studio with almost dictatorial central control — exerted by Louis B. Mayer and Irving Thalberg. Paramount, under B. P. Schulberg, was a much looser organization, granting more freedom to individual producers, directors, and writers. MGM was a studio of stars: Greta Garbo, Jean Harlow, Joan Crawford, Norma Shearer, Katharine Hepburn, Clark Gable, James Stewart, Lionel Barrymore, Spencer Tracy. Paramount was a studio of writers and directors: Ernst Lubitsch, Josef von Sternberg, Cecil B. DeMille, Leo McCarey, Preston Sturges, Billy Wilder. In the early 1930s Paramount was the iconoclast's haven: the home of Mae West, W. C. Fields, and the Marx Brothers. The studio permitted the sensual excesses of von Sternberg and the sexual sniggers of Lubitsch. MGM flattened all excesses into a shiny, respectable, beautifully lit wholesomeness. When the Marx Brothers left Paramount for MGM, they lost much of their lunacy and spark. Ironically, in the 1930s the MGM policy seemed the wiser of the two, for Louis B. Mayer's devotion to family entertainment made MGM the most respected and successful film factory in Hollywood—a studio that could bring out *The Wizard of Oz* and *Gone With the Wind* in the same year (1939)—while B. P. Schulberg's chaotic individuality ran Paramount into severe financial difficulties, resulting in the studio's loss of many of its stars (Jeanette MacDonald accompanied the Marx Brothers to MGM) and Schulberg's loss of his job.

Warner Bros., which invested less money in production values (sets, costumes, crowds), was more dependent on good talk, and the dialogue in the early Warners pictures was as sharp, as fast, and as good as anyone's. The studio specialized in gangster films, biographies, and musicals, directed by William Wellman, Mervyn LeRoy, William Dieterle, Michael Curtiz, Lloyd Bacon, and Busby Berkeley, and starring such sharp talkers as James Cagney, Edward G. Robinson, Paul Muni, Humphrey Bogart, Bette Davis, Ida Lupino, Dick Powell, Ruby Keeler, and Joan Blondell. Warner Bros. was also the studio most committed to the depiction of contemporary social problems—whether in its musicals ("The Forgotten Man" and "Shanghai Lil" numbers of Berkeley musicals), its gangster pictures (like *Little Caesar* and *The Public Enemy*), its problem pictures (like *I Am A Fugitive From A Chain Gang*), its socially conscious "biopics," as *Variety* called them (the biographies of Zola, Pasteur, and Curie), or its "woman's pictures"—the choices and conflicts of women in contemporary American society (often embodied by Bette Davis). Warners was also the most pro-Roosevelt of the studios: the most supportive of his New Deal and, like FDR, openly critical of the Nazi menace abroad.

Twentieth Century-Fox excelled in historical and adventure films directed by John Ford, Henry King, and Henry Hathaway with Tyrone Power and Henry Fonda, in show business musicals with Don Ameche and Alice Faye (and, later, with Betty Grable and Dan Dailey), and in the folksy comedies of Will Rogers and Shirley Temple. If Warners was committed to general social problems, Fox was committed to the problems of American family life. Even Fox musicals confront a woman (the Fox stars of musicals were always women—from Janet Gaynor to Marilyn Monroe) with the difficult choice between career and family.

RKO, the least financially stable of the major studios, was most memorable for the smooth musicals of Fred Astaire and Ginger Rogers, the suave comedies with Cary Grant, the literate horror B pictures produced by Val Lewton, and the occasional film by Howard Hawks (*Bringing Up Baby*), Orson Welles (*Citizen Kane, The Magnificent Ambersons*), and John Ford (*The Informer*)—not to mention *King Kong*. Universal excelled in the horror films— *Frankenstein, Dracula,* and *The Wolf Man*— directed by James Whale, Tod Browning, and others, in the later comedies of W. C. Fields, and—at the opposite extreme—in the saccharine singing pictures of Deanna Durbin and Gloria Jean.

Columbia was the creation of a single producer, Harry Cohn, who hitched his "Poverty Row" studio to director Frank Capra in 1928 and rode to respectability on the coattails of Capra's many later successes (especially *It Happened One Night* in 1934). Although Cohn was the Hollywood mogul whom more actors and writers hated more deeply than any other, he respected directors (like Capra, Howard Hawks, and George Cukor) and left them alone to do some of their finest work.

The two "minor" studios, Republic and Monogram, specialized in cheap westerns and cheap hoodlum pictures, respectively, and —like Universal—serials. A later generation of French *cinéastes* has subsequently canonized the B-picture offerings of these cheapie-quickie studios as superior to many of the glossier offerings of the major studios.

The studios forced their directors to be eclectic. A director jumped from jungle adventure to backstage musical to historical pageant to contemporary comedy to operetta. The director's sole qualification for handling so many styles and settings was the ability to get any job done well.

Typical of the competent impersonality of the studio era are the careers of Warner Bros.' Mervyn LeRoy and MGM's W. S. Van Dyke.

Fig. 11-6
RKO's I Walked with a Zombie, *produced by Val Lewton and directed by Jacques Tourneur.*

LeRoy, within a three-year period, directed *Little Caesar*, the tough story of a mobster's rise and fall; *I Am A Fugitive From A Chain Gang*, a tough tale of brutality in a southern prison; and the "dramatic" sections of the backstage musical *Gold Diggers of 1933*. In those same three years, 1930–1933, LeRoy directed twenty other films, including journalism pictures, homespun comedies, and show-business musicals. LeRoy's later work was just as eclectic, from the patriotic adventure, *The F.B.I. Story*, to the heavy, sour musical pancake, *Gypsy*. Although a director like LeRoy obviously knew his craft, it seems impossible to say whether he knew or felt anything else. Woody Van Dyke's films are equally diverse; there was adventure (*Trader Horn; Tarzan, the Ape Man*), light comedy (the *Thin Man* series), costume pageant

(*Marie Antoinette*), disaster movie/historical romance with music (*San Francisco*), operetta (*Rose Marie, Sweethearts*), as well as contributions to MGM series pictures (*Andy Hardy Gets Spring Fever, Dr. Kildare's Victory*).

The studio era produced several of these "smorgasbord" directors who could be depended upon to cook up a slick, palatable, powerful product regardless of its particular ingredients: Michael Curtiz (*Mystery of the Wax Museum, The Walking Dead, The Charge of the Light Brigade, The Adventures of Robin Hood* [co-director, William Keighley], *Dodge City, The Private Lives of Elizabeth and Essex, Yankee Doodle Dandy, Casablanca, Mildred Pierce, Life with Father*), William Dieterle (*The Firebird, The Story of Louis Pasteur, The Life of Emile Zola, Juarez, The Hunchback of Notre Dame, Love*

Fig. 11-7
RKO's **The Curse of the Cat People:** *another Lewton masterpiece, this one directed by Robert Wise and Gunther Von Fritsch.*

Letters, Portrait of Jennie), Lewis Milestone (*All Quiet on the Western Front, The Front Page, Rain, Anything Goes, Of Mice and Men*), Victor Fleming (*Red Dust, Treasure Island, The Wizard of Oz, Gone With the Wind* [begun by George Cukor and finished by Fleming with help from King Vidor], *A Guy Named Joe*), King Vidor (*The Big Parade* and *The Crowd* in the silent era, then *Our Daily Bread, Stella Dallas, Duel in the Sun,* and *The Fountainhead*).

In addition to asking their directors to select from the smorgasbord, the studios found that some directors did a better job with a single dish. Some directed comedies primarily: Gregory LaCava (*She Married Her Boss, My Man Godfrey*), Sam Wood (*A Day at the Races; A Night at the Opera; Goodbye, Mr. Chips*), Leo McCarey (*Duck Soup, Ruggles of Red Gap, Going My Way*), Edward Sutherland (*Mississippi, Poppy*). Other directors specialized in adventure, horror, or mystery: Tod Browning (*The Unholy Three, Dracula, Freaks*), William Wellman (*The Public Enemy, The Ox-Bow Incident, The Story of G. I. Joe, The High and the Mighty*), James Whale (*Frankenstein, The Old Dark House, The Invisible Man, Bride of Frankenstein*), Henry Hathaway (*Come On Marines, Lives of a Bengal Lancer*). Clarence Brown, who worked well with actors and dialogue, specialized in adapting stageplays — not to mention Faulkner's novel *Intruder in the Dust* — into films; Mark Sandrich and Roy Del Ruth directed musicals primarily. But even

Universal's Frankenstein, *directed by James Whale, was influenced more by German Expressionism than by Mary Shelley's novel; sets by Charles D. Hall.*

Fig. 11-8

the specialists took their turn at the smorgasbord table—the comic director occasionally being served a swashbuckler, the adventure director dishing up a musical.

If the most conventional studio films displayed any personality, it often reflected the general moral assumptions and values of the era as a whole. Almost all the films took the view that the sincere, the sensitive, the human would inevitably triumph over the hypocritical, the callous, the oppressive. American audiences, escaping from the realities of the Depression outside the movie theatre, withdrew inside to see grit triumph over suffering and kindness triumph over financial, political, and moral chicanery. If the optimism of Hollywood films provided the audiences with the tranquilizer they needed, it also strengthened the audience's belief that eventually good people would make bad times better.

The American film offered not only escape but also subtle propaganda. Whereas many Americans lacked the money to buy warm clothing, American movie characters wore fashionable gowns and well-tailored suits. Whereas many Americans lacked the money to pay the rent, American movie characters lived in elegant apartments filled with expensive fur-

niture. The tasteful richness of the studio films, supported by the inexorable workings of poetic justice in their plots, answered a very deep need in a people working hard to achieve the kind of comfort, ease, and plenty that it saw in the films every week. Just as the cynical materialism of the 1920s succeeded the innocence and honor of the Griffith era, the optimism and wholesomeness of the 1930s succeeded the values of the jazz age.

Did that tide of optimistic commitment flow from the genuine sentiments of the American people, from the covert ideological operation of American institutions, or from the overt manipulation of the people by the forces of Big Business? With social revolutions in Russia, Germany, Italy, and Spain—whether on the right or the left—and with the spread of trade unionism in Depression America, it certainly suited the American business establishment to administer a reassuring sedative. But the movies could never have pushed their sugared pills of populist prosperity and Christian commitment were Americans unwilling to swallow them. There was ideology in even the most escapist Hollywood movies, but whether that ideology sprang from a capitalist conspiracy (as some Marxist critics claimed a generation ago), from a Communist conspiracy (as conservative members of Congress claimed a generation ago), from the invisible operation of cultural institutions (as current Marxist historians argue), or from some spontaneous search for value by "the people" themselves seems very much a matter for conjecture.

The Comics

Some of the most distinctive American films of the 1930s, like those of the previous two decades, were comedies. Chaplin survived the transition to sound by making no apparent transition at all. His first two sound films, *City Lights* and *Modern Times,* used a synchronized score and clever sound effects but little synchronized speech (none at all in *City Lights*). Chaplin was certain that Charlie, the little tramp, was a man of mime, a character not made for a world of words.

In *City Lights* (1931), Charlie's pantomime takes him into the society of the rich, where he makes friends with a suicidal millionaire who is friendly and generous when drunk, cold and callous when sober—and forgetful of whatever had happened while he was drunk. Charlie's intermittent closeness to the world of the rich, as the millionaire remembers or forgets him, allows him to help a poor blind girl (Virginia Cherrill) who, significant in the Chaplin symbolism, sells flowers to keep herself alive. Charlie scrapes up enough money to pay for the girl's operation; she recovers her eyesight, opens a flower shop, and eventually discovers her benefactor. But Charlie perceives that he and the girl are further apart than ever; she longs for the rich, respectable suitor the tramp had pretended to be, not the bum she can now see, to whom she had just given a rose out of pity—but whom she has recognized by touch. An agonizingly poignant close-up of Charlie's face ends the film with an unanswered and perhaps unanswerable question. Does the girl accept Charlie for what he is, and can the two possibly share a life together? Or are their worlds too far apart and must the tramp take leave of his lady of the flowers? (Or is he just saying, "Yes, it's me"?) The final shot of *City Lights* is so memorable because it is so open; it stops at the climax and refuses to provide a resolution. A two-shot of Charlie and the flower-seller together would imply one answer (their union); a shot of Charlie alone, walking away from the camera, as he so often does, would imply the other. Chaplin hauntingly denies either kind of closure by not providing either shot.

In *City Lights* Chaplin raises the question of whether the tramp is capable of finding a romantic partner; in *Modern Times* (1936) Chaplin asks whether the tramp is capable of achieving marriage, for marriages require homes, and homes require payments, and payments require jobs. So in *Modern Times,* the little tramp, as always, is at the mercy of the social order, especially of the immense industrial machinery of our increasingly technological society. At the end of *Modern Times,* the tramp and his "wife" (Paulette Goddard, soon to become Chaplin's actual wife) walk away from the camera and from society, literally heading for the hills, for their kind of marriage cannot survive in such a society.

Modern Times would be Chaplin's last stand against the modern dialogue times and the last pure incarnation of the Everyman Tramp. Consistent with the metaphors of enslaving machinery in *Modern Times,* Chaplin depicts the synchronized soundtrack as another enslaving machine—a television with which the factory boss monitors his workers' most private activities or a phonograph that subordinates human movement to a recorded verbal message. Chaplin lets us hear the record and the boss's voice as it blasts from the monitor's speaker, but when people talk normally to each other, we read their words. In the climactic restaurant sequence of the film, Charlie finally makes synchronized sounds, but with a sly difference: not talking sense but singing nonsense. Otherwise, only the machines talk. The silent intertitle, and Chaplin's performance and music, convey a more human language; the talking picture is a talking machine.

In his next picture, the talkie *The Great Dictator* (1940), Chaplin played two roles: a Jewish barber, closely akin to his underdog tramp, and the villainous top-dog Führer, whom Chaplin —with his short, toothbrush moustache— resembled. The comic action of the film pleads eloquently and ironically for the rights of individual human expression against the stifling,

Fig. 11-9

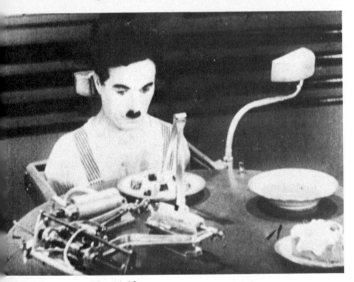

Fig. 11-10
Modern Times: *A televised Boss spies on Charlie in the washroom, then feeds him by machine.*

murderous power of the tyrant. Unfortunately, Chaplin discovered that the dialogue film could plead with speeches as well as with comic action. The overt didacticism of the film's final speech, a fervent and sincere but overlong and sentimental appeal for world peace, is a dramatic letdown.

The same overt moralizing and sentimentality cloud the brilliance of Chaplin's last two masterpieces, *Monsieur Verdoux* and *Limelight*. *Monsieur Verdoux* (1947), like *The Great Dictator,* begins with a brilliant seriocomic premise (said to have been suggested to Chaplin by Orson Welles): A delightful, witty, urbane gentleman marries a series of rich women specifically to bump them off, using the dead ladies' legacies to support his crippled wife and child on an idyllic country estate. The film necessarily questions the relationship of the means of an action to its end, whether murder is justifiable if its ultimate purpose is virtuous. The film develops its theme with a series of acidly hilarious vignettes in which Verdoux goes about his murderous business in the most fastidious, matter-of-fact way. Most hilarious of all are his frustrating attempts to dispose of the coarse, clumsy, big-mouth wife played in perfect counterpoint to Chaplin's diminutive suaveness by Martha Raye.

But as in *The Great Dictator* Chaplin deserts comic objectivity at the end of *Monsieur Verdoux* to spell out the film's implications in bald prose: Society commits the same crimes and accepts the same assumptions as Monsieur Verdoux, except on a much larger scale. The explicit accusation was unnecessary. The same blend of comic insight and uncomfortable sentimentality pulls *Limelight* (1952) in two directions. The flashback scenes that recreate the music-hall routines of the old vaudevillian, Calvero (Chaplin), are brilliantly funny and touching, the former music-hall clown's ultimate tribute to the world that fostered his mime and art. The scenes in the present—of Calvero's trying to control another human destiny (that of a dancer, played by Claire Bloom in her screen debut, whom he saves from suicide and despair) suffer from overstatement and melodrama.

Chaplin maintained his power and individuality in the studio era because he needed to make no concessions to Hollywood's commercial structure. Chaplin produced and owned his own pictures, ran his own studio, and released through United Artists; the success and popularity of his films guaranteed him theatres in which to exhibit them and profits to make more pictures just as he wanted to make them. (At

Fig. 11-11

Fig. 11-12

Fig. 11-13

Fig.11-14

Chaplin's women. With the ideally beautiful statue (Fig. 11-11) and flowerseller (Virginia Cherrill, Fig. 11-12) in City Lights; *with the unbeautiful realities of his "wives" (Margaret Hoffman, Fig. 11-13; Martha Raye, Fig. 11-14) as the bigamist in* Monsieur Verdoux.

the opposite extreme, the career of Buster Keaton, who in the sound era was "just an actor," turned into a disaster.) Chaplin's cinematic technique, even in the silent era, was never dependent on montage or intrusive camera work. For Chaplin, the frame was as much a mental arena as a spatial area, a site where physical action mirrored the movement of the mind. The antagonism of Cold War America ended the American career of that mind in 1952. Only after twenty years did Chaplin end his self-imposed exile in Switzerland, where he died in 1977.

Walt Disney, like Chapin, made the transition into the studio era by maintaining his commercial and, consequently, artistic independence. Disney, whose fantasies of sight and sound, drawing and music, movement and

rhythm had evolved in the first years of sound, found one further ally in the 1930s—color. Whereas the realistic, live-action studio films were trying to tame the effects of color, to blur its garishness, to make its hues mirror nature rather than some color-mad dream world, Disney's animated fantasies could use such color madness as one more fantastic, unreal element. The counterpoint of picture and music in the Disney cartoon acquired a third contrapuntal line. Shifts in color could accompany the shifting tones of the music and action. Expressive color, like rhythm and music, became a kinetic element. The same advantage that Disney enjoyed over realistic films in the free use of sound also gave him the freedom to manipulate color—surrealistically, as in the "pink elephants" sequence of *Dumbo* (1941), or realistically, as in most of *Bambi* (1942). Disney brought color to his Silly Symphonies, to his animal characters (Mickey, Donald, and Pluto), and eventually to his first feature film, *Snow White and the Seven Dwarfs* (1937, released 1938).

The Disney fantasies of color and motion were perfectly suited to the audience's craving for happiness, wholesomeness, and optimism in films—even if they often terrified children. His "Who's Afraid of the Big, Bad Wolf?" from *The Three Little Pigs* (1933) became not only a popular song but also a metaphor for the whole country's cheerful defiance of the big, bad "wolf at the door," the Depression. The film itself was a socially acceptable Protestant-ethic lecture: to build with bricks, not straw. (Less acceptable anti-Semitic elements have been deleted from most prints still in circulation.) But Disney's happy cleanliness began taking its toll on his visual imagination. Disney gradually deserted the short for the feature, the fantasy-abstract film of color, music, and movement for the sentimental story film that attempted to blend fantasy and realism. Even in 1938 critics noticed a tension in *Snow White* between the fantastic rendering of the animals and dwarfs and the clumsy, sticky attempts at realism in rendering Snow White and her prince. After the climactic *Fantasia* (1940), his films took fewer and fewer visual chances, and even their soundtracks soon became conventional. Everything became too controlled and perfect—an aesthetic he extended to Disneyland.

Ernst Lubitsch, whose camera had learned to comment on a character or situation by shooting an apparently insignificant detail that was loaded with implications, discovered that sound, as well as pictures, could make such touches. In his first sound films, the continental musicals, he mastered the new machines and learned to make the sound film as fluid and effortless as the silent one. But his greatest sound films were dialogue pictures, slick comedies of manners, translated by his cinematic imagination from the stage into his unique film terms: *Design for Living* (1933), *Angel* (1937), *Ninotchka* (1939, with Garbo), *To Be or Not To Be* (1942, with Jack Benny and Carole Lombard), and, especially, *Trouble in Paradise* (1932). *Trouble in Paradise* is such a subtle, deceptively artless film that its bold, imaginative mixture of picture and sound seems completely consistent with the shiny conventionalities of studio-era films.

Trouble in Paradise is the story of an urbane, elegant crook whose charm and social graces allow him to work his way into the hotels and houses and hearts of the very rich where he performs his clever, high-stake thievery. Eventually the master crook, Gaston Monescu (Herbert Marshall), finds himself caught between his love for two women, Mariette Colet (Kay Francis), the rich perfume heiress he is swindling, and Lily (Miriam Hopkins), his clever accomplice in crime. Because he is a thief, because he is merely a pretender to propriety in the gleaming world of the rich and proper, because his past has determined his future, Monescu eventually leaves Mariette for Lily.

Lubitsch brings his droll carnival of thieves to life with his dry, witty control of picture, sound effects, and speech. The film opens on a shot of a garbage pail. A man picks up the pail and tosses its contents into his "truck." Except that "truck" turns out to be a gondola, for this is a garbage man in Venice, city of romance. As the garbage gondola journeys on its route, Lubitsch shoots the gleaming water of the canals and the picturesque *palazzi* surrounding them; the garbage gondolier sings plaintively, "O sole mio." The romantic song continues as the garbage gondola continues offscreen. Not only has Lubitsch deflated picture-postcard romance, one of the film's themes, but he also has underscored, metaphorically, the film's action, which reveals the "garbage" beneath the pretty surfaces in the lives of the film's "beautiful people."

A later blending of music and picture similarly deflates the world of the rich. When the characters go to the opera, a symbol of snobbery and social status, Lubitsch summarizes the proceedings by concentrating on the conductor's score. With the camera riveted on that score, the soprano torridly sings (offscreen), "I love you, I love you." Then the pages begin to riffle, steadily turning by themselves to some point near the end of the opera. The soprano just as torridly sings (still offscreen), with the same notes, "I hate you." The device is a

Trouble in Paradise: *elegant veneers. The two thieves (Miriam Hopkins and Herbert Marshall, right) use an elegant supper as an occasion for fleecing one another.*

Fig. 11-15

brilliant means of handling the passing of time, of ridiculing opera plots and passions, and of burlesquing the values of high society that force people to pursue fashionable amusements that do not amuse them.

Lubitsch handles Monescu's sexual relationships with his two ladies with the greatest wryness and subtlety. In the first sequence, Lily and Monescu fall in love by discovering each other's crooked cleverness. The two sit in Monescu's elegant hotel suite, eating supper and drinking wine. Like the opening's garbage gondola, the scene plays the elegant, polite surfaces off against the genuine corruption beneath: The two are not Baron and Countess enjoying a slyly seductive supper but two crooks trying to fleece one another. As the two trade polished banalities, they subtly steal each other's watches, wallets, jewelry. After they discover and sort out each other's goods, Monescu bends over to kiss Lily as she sits on a sofa. Lubitsch dissolves to an empty sofa. Then he cuts to a male arm, its

white sleeve implying a discarded dinner jacket, hanging a "Do Not Disturb" sign on the door of his hotel room. Later, in a dazzlingly clever series of cuts, Lubitsch implies the direction of Madame Colet's and Monescu's intentions by throwing the intertwined shadows of their embracing bodies on the coverlet of her bed. The implications of such juxtapositions are obvious, clearly a sign of the screen's pre-Breen sexual suggestiveness.

Add to Lubitsch's subtle images and clever music his satiric handling of the minor characters, themselves rich fools or covert crooks (Edward Everett Horton, Charles Ruggles, C. Aubrey Smith), and Samson Raphaelson's sparkling, effortless dialogue, which consistently pins a new tail on an old cliché: "A bird in the hand is worth two in jail"; "If you behave like a gentleman, I'll break your neck"; "I love you as a crook, but don't become one of those useless, good-for-nothing gigolos"; "a member of the *nouveau* poor." The combined

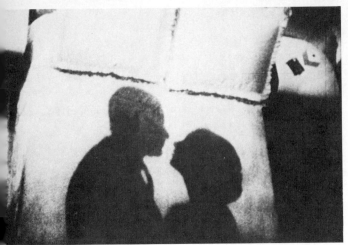

Fig. 11-17
Lubitsch's sexual wit in Trouble in Paradise—*from a reflection of the embracing lovers in the mirror to the shadows of their intertwined bodies on the bed.*

ingredients make *Trouble in Paradise* the most polished comedy of manners in the history of American film.

Frank Capra also turned to comedies of manners in 1934. But instead of the suave manners of Lubitsch's shiny Europe, Capra, born in Sicily, focused on the ingenuous, homespun manners of the most American America. Although Capra's career in films stems from silent comedy when he was a gag

man and staff director at both the Sennett and the Hal Roach studios, Capra became an important director in the era of the talkies after he signed with Columbia Pictures, where producer Harry Cohn guaranteed him creative freedom. At Columbia, he met Robert Riskin, the man who was to write most of his important scripts. The Capra–Riskin film was generally a witty contemporary morality play that pitted a good man—usually a "little guy" who is naïve, sincere, folksy, unaffected, unintellectual, apolitical—against evil social forces: money, politics, affectation, social status, human insensitivity. The "little guy" emerges from the struggle not only victorious but also wiser about the ways of the world—but so does a good, intellectual, political man like the hero of Capra's *Lost Horizon* (1937).

It Happened One Night (1934) examines the clash of a snooping newspaper reporter (Clark Gable) and a rich society girl (Claudette Colbert) fleeing her wealthy father to marry a worthless boyfriend. The two travel cross-country by bus, discovering the hazards as well as the charms of rural, uncitified America—motels, bad roads, hitchhiking, and, most significantly, people. Among the people they discover are themselves and one another—what makes them alike and makes them like others despite the gulf between their material and intellectual backgrounds.

In *Mr. Deeds Goes to Town* (1936), a young man from the country (Gary Cooper) inherits a pile of money and comes to the city to discover how to spend it. The city folk belittle the country ways of the hero "hick," and leading the laughter is the snobbish lady reporter (Jean Arthur) with whom Deeds has fallen in love. Deeds eventually converts the lady, discovers that he must use his money to help the poor and starving, and vanquishes the rich who try to prove him insane so they can control his fortune. A whole family of happy, poor, humane eccentrics struggles comically against the forces of money, sophistication, and industrialization in *You Can't Take It With You* (1938). In *Mr. Smith Goes to Washington* (1939), Mr. Deeds has changed his name to Smith, Gary Cooper has changed to James Stewart, and his problem has changed from money to politics. Although Capra's vision may seem corny and populistic

Fig 11-18

It's A Wonderful Life. *"Little guy" George Bailey (James Stewart, right) refuses to abandon his values and sell out to the heartless big capitalist, Potter (Lionel Barrymore, seated).*

today, the consistency of Capra's material, his solid scripts, the perceptive comic characterizations, the informal, understated acting in his films and their crisp comic tempi make them sincere, clever, and intelligent statements of the era's conventional optimism and folksy humanism.

But there is a dark side to the Capra films as well, despite their eventual affirmations. Mr. Deeds must endure the courtroom malice of his accusers for an agonizingly long time, until the judge finally pronounces him the sanest man who ever entered his courtroom. Mr. Smith suffers another ordeal, a Senate filibuster that pushes both his physical and moral endurance to their limits, until his enemy finally capitulates

to the strength of his will and courage. In *Meet John Doe* (1941) Capra demonstrates that the folksy slogans of an ordinary John Doe (Gary Cooper again) are uncomfortably close to the fascistic slogans of an Adolf Hitler (personified by the American millionaire, D. B. Norton, and played by Edward Arnold, Capra's inevitable representative of plutocratic oppression). Like so many Capra heroes, John Doe is a Christ figure who must endure a painful Gethsemane, and it eventually takes a miracle to save him from crucifixion.

In *It's A Wonderful Life* of 1946, one year after the World War and widespread knowledge of the Nazi death camps, Capra's Christ figure, George Bailey (James Stewart), has become so frustrated by his drab middle-American existence that only a heavenly miracle can rescue him from suicide and restore his faith in his own accomplishments. The legions of God and the Devil struggle mightily in these allegorical Capra comedies, and it takes a terrifyingly long time for justice, truth, and salvation to triumph.

Like Frank Capra and unlike Ernst Lubitsch, Preston Sturges wrote and directed witty moral comedies on American subjects. But like Lubitsch and unlike Capra, Sturges was an ironist and satirist who stood many of the era's wholesome and optimistic conventions on their ear. *The Great McGinty* (1940), the first film Sturges directed after a distinguished career in the 1930s as a Hollywood screenwriter (he wrote the script for Mitchell Leisen's brilliantly clever *Easy Living,* 1937), ridicules American democratic politics and the naïve notion that the voter really controls the government. *Christmas in July* (1940) ridicules the American dream of getting rich quick without hard work; the hero thinks up snappy advertising slogans. *The Lady Eve* (1941) is a burlesque of American sexual-romantic conventions, particularly the naïve, Puritanical insistence on virginity, purity, and innocence. It may well be his funniest work, rivals *Sullivan's Travels* as his best, and gave Henry Fonda and Barbara Stanwyck their greatest comic roles. *Sullivan's Travels* (1941) is the story of a Hollywood director (Joel McCrea) who is weary of making entertaining fluff and aspires to make films laden with Serious Moral and Social Significance; he decides that in order to make such films, he must learn firsthand what it feels like to be poor. In the course of his travels, the director discovers true love (Veronica Lake) as well as the social utility and human nobility of "merely" making people laugh.

During the war years, Sturges courageously extended his satire to American perceptions of the war, our role in the conflict, our confused sexual standards in wartime (*The Miracle of Morgan's Creek,* 1943, which D. W. Griffith found hilarious), and our superficial definitions of heroism and patriotism (*Hail the Conquering Hero,* 1944). Sturges could get away with his audacious iconoclasm because of the comic richness and subtlety of his scripts, the spirited

wit and charm of his acting ensemble, and the ingenuity of his physical slapstick comedy. Very much like Capra, Sturges suggested that the real disease was a slight case of social and moral myopia rather than an inoperable cancer in both the American people and the American way of life. If Capra's films are moral crusades in the real social, political, and economic world, Sturges's films are moral crusades in a fictional world of Hollywood's imagining — ironic, reflexive movies that comment on the way movies themselves view and create a world that never existed and never could.

George Cukor was another comic ironist and another crusader, but of a very different sort. A Broadway director who became a protegé of Lubitsch, Cukor also made comedies of sexual manners; but more like Capra than Lubitsch, these were the manners of monogamous America rather than of an elegantly hedonistic Europe. And as in Sturges's films, these were American manners filtered through the lens of Hollywood vision and convention.

Cukor's personal style was far less obtrusive than that of Lubitsch, Capra, or Sturges, so subtle that Cukor hardly seemed a distinct personality at all — merely a competent interpreter of well-written scripts, known best as a "woman's director." He specialized in adaptations of Broadway plays — by Philip Barry and others — often for Katharine Hepburn at RKO and MGM (*A Bill of Divorcement,* 1932; *Dinner at Eight,* 1933; *Holiday,* 1938; *The Women,* 1939; *The Philadelphia Story,* 1940). He also teamed with Ruth Gordon and Garson Kanin on a series of Spencer Tracy–Katharine Hepburn vehicles at MGM (notably *Adam's Rib,* 1949) and Judy Holliday vehicles at Columbia (notably *Born Yesterday,* 1950). From Hepburn to Harlow to Garbo (*Camille,* 1936, released 1937) to Holliday to Judy Garland (*A Star Is Born,* 1954) to another Hepburn (Audrey in *My Fair Lady,* 1964), Cukor elicited superb performances from female stars.

The reason was Cukor's consciousness that the sharp distinctions between male and female sexuality and identity were not as simple as they seemed in Hollywood's male-dominated mythology. Cukor was the one major director of Hollywood's studio era who was gay — or, at least, was willing to admit it in the 1970s, when

Sullivan's Travels. *Aided by his valet (Eric Blore, left), millionaire director John L. Sullivan (Joel McCrea) tries on his hobo outfit.*

Fig. 11-19

it was safe to come out. He disguised his alternative sexual taste behind heterosexual comic arguments that stood the prevailing assumptions of male domination on their heads. How was the all-female society of *The Women* different from any other society? Why shouldn't the male lawyer, Adam (Tracy), and the female lawyer, his wife Amanda (Hepburn), adopt fundamentally different strategies of law in *Adam's Rib*, since these laws have been written by men for men? How do male courts of law define the infidelity of male and female spouses in different ways, and how do they respond differently when those spouses seek revenge?

Cukor's films never provide answers to these questions; the director quietly pokes, observes, and presents his carefully balanced and amusingly paradoxical evidence. He is very much an outside observer looking in, refusing to take a side in the battle of the sexes. He presents his own oblique self-portrait in *Adam's Rib* — Kip Lurie, a successful composer for Broadway shows, a sort of Cole Porter or Noël Coward who lives across the hall from Adam and Amanda. Like Cukor, Kip is clearly gay — as

clear as Hollywood could make such matters in 1949 — an outsider to the marriage of Adam and Amanda (just as, offscreen, Cukor was a friendly outsider to the relationship of Tracy and Hepburn). In *Adam's Rib*, there is a difference between male and female, Adam and Amanda, Tracy and Hepburn, and yet there is no difference. *"Vive la différence,"* Adam concludes, yet no one can say very precisely what that difference happens to be.

Cukor's cinematic style presents these ironies and paradoxes with a balanced detachment that creates a dialectic between characters and incidents in the plot as well as within the frame itself. In Cukor's carefully balanced frames, conflicting decor and symmetrical composition often indicate the moral and social paradoxes of the film. Though less idiosyncratic than the social comedies of his contemporaries, Cukor's films have worn wonderfully well, for social and sexual consciousness have finally caught up with his subtle ironies.

As with the silent comedies, many of the sound comedies wore the personalities of their comics rather than their directors. Because

Fig. 11-20

Fig. 11-21
Adam's Rib: *Cukor's perfectly balanced frames imply the spiritual equality of Tracy and Hepburn.*

Langdon and Keaton and numerous other clowns who were schooled in the silent tradition never successfully combined talk and movement, Hollywood imported clowns from Broadway who had already effected the combination. The Marx Brothers even shot their first

films in New York. In 1929 they recreated their current stage hit, *The Cocoanuts,* for the screen. The Marx Brothers combined the great traditions of American physical comedy with a verbal humor that perfectly suited their physical types (which may be why the physically undistinguished Zeppo, the fourth brother, dropped out of the act). The Marx Brothers looked funny: Groucho's moustache and eyebrows and baggy pants, Chico's hats and sly beady eyes, Harpo's frizzy hair and silly smiles. The Marx Brothers talked funny: Groucho's nasal gravel, Chico's accent, Harpo's beeps. And the Marx Brothers walked funny. Like the Sennett silent comedies, the plots of the Marx Brothers' films were irrelevant; providing occasions for gags and for irreverent parodies of conventional behavior: self-important worlds into which the zany comics dropped and, while the court or college or high-society gathering went about its predictable, Hollywood business, did their own outrageous, unpredictable things.

Those unpredictable things were either visual or verbal insanities. The great silent comedies have no funnier sequences than many of those in the Marx films: the football sequence in *Horse Feathers* (1932), the mirror scene in *Duck Soup* (1933), the stateroom packed with human sardines or the split-second timing of the bed-shifting sequence in *A Night at the Opera* (1935), the scene in which the brothers invade the midget's teeny room with the teeny furniture in *At the Circus* (1939), the "more wood" sequence in *Go West* (1940). And for brilliant verbal double talk there is the "Why-a-duck?" sequence in *Cocoanuts* in which Groucho tries to sell Chico a piece of island property with a viaduct (why-a-duck), the "Party of the First Part" sequence in *A Night at the Opera* in which Groucho and Chico burlesque legalistic jargon by tearing apart a contract (literally) clause by sanity clause, and there is the "Tootsie Frootsie Ice Cream" sequence of *A Day at the Races* (1937) in which Chico sells Groucho a coded manual for betting the ponies, and then another manual to decode the first manual, and then yet another manual to decode that manual, and so forth to infinity. The Marx Brothers films revealed the key elements of American sound comedy—comic physical types, suited to their comic personalities, suited to the physical-comic situations, suited to the verbal wit. Comic talkies had to move as well as talk.

Another Broadway import—Mae West—fulfilled a similar comic formula. West had her comic personality, a parody of the amoral, sensual female hedonist who frankly enjoyed nice clothes, nice food, and a nice tumble in the hay. She physically suited that personality. No petite, lithe, virginal ingenue was Mae, but a buxom, hefty broad. Her rolling eyes, her gyrating hips, her falling, throaty voice consciously tried to unmask an opponent or undress a friend. And her comic lines fit the eyes, the voice, and the body: "Beulah, peel me a grape"; "Are you packin' a rod or are you just glad to see me?" Even her croaking "Oh" was more a sigh than an exclamation and said much more than oh. Like the Marx Brothers' plots, Mae West's film stories, which she wrote herself, were slender lines on which to hang her own personal business: her gyrations, her groans, her comments, her songs. The films' action inevitably ran Mae up against the wall of respectability and legality. And if she avoided prison and legal censure at the end of the film, it was primarily because her impulses were human and sympathetic even if her activities were somewhat under the table (or under the bed). Not surprisingly, a later generation of feminist critics has found Mae West both a central and a disturbing figure. While her very being defies male assumptions of female purity, submission, and domesticity, she merely manipulates those assumptions to attain her own material ends—wealth and power over men and other women—the same as those of her male oppressors.

Ironically, only one of her films, *She Done Him Wrong* (1933), is, because of its pre-Breen date, fully a Mae West film. Most suggestive (and most characteristic of Mae's style) in the film are her songs. One of them is her set of dirty lyrics to the familiar tune, "Frankie and Johnny"; after all, Frankie didn't shoot Johnny just because she saw him with another woman in a public bar. The second song was often referred to as "THAT song"; its noneuphemistic title was "I Like a Guy What Takes His Time" and its subject was exactly what the title implies it to be. A third song, "I Wonder Where My

Fig. 11-22

Mae West: The caricature of female sensuality poses beside a caricature of her own sensuality in a 1932 publicity photo.

Easy Rider's Gone," was not about horseback or motorcycle riding.

The effect of the Breen Code was obvious in her next film, which was forced to change its title from *It Ain't No Sin* (with its obvious implications) to *I'm No Angel* (1933), although the plot of the film allowed Mae to defend her personal code of morality against the sanctimonious assumptions of the bluenoses. And in *Belle of the Nineties* (1934), when Mae sings "My Old Flame," although the significance of the flame is clear in the innuendoes of her eyes and voice, it has no explicit life in the song's lyrics. Despite

W. C. Fields caught in the trap of respectable American bourgeois life in **The Bank Dick.**

Fig. 11-23

the financial success of *She Done Him Wrong,* Mae West's film career was cut up and cut short by the moralistic scissors of the Breen sanctions against sexuality and the glamorous portrayal of vice. In her later films — *Goin' to Town* (1935), *Klondike Annie* (1936), and even *My Little Chickadee* (1940) with W. C. Fields — Mae West becomes a clean-scrubbed caricature of her own sexuality, which was, in its original frankness, a caricature of sexuality in the first place.

W. C. Fields was another great comedian of the sound stage. Like Mae West and the Marx Brothers, Fields's comedy stemmed from himself rather than from the stories in which he found himself. Like Mae West and the Marxes, Fields combined a comic personality, a comic physical type, and a style of verbal wit that fitted both his mind and his body. Fields also came to films from the stage, but the former vaude-villian, famous today for his gravelly, whiskey voice, began his film career in silent comedies directed by Edward Sutherland, Gregory

LaCava, and — of all people — D. W. Griffith. Although it is impossible to imagine Fields without his voice, an occasional sequence from one of the sound films reveals his powers as pure physical clown: his clumsy attempts to play croquet in *Poppy* (1936), the battle with bent pool cues in *Six of a Kind* (1934), his deft juggling in *The Old-Fashioned Way* (1934), and the car crashes in *If I Had A Million* (1932). Physically funny, too, is the Fields body — the booze-bloated nose, the beer belly — which he tries to dignify with the spiffiest, most fastidiously selected period costumes.

Like his physical appearance, the Fields character is a mixture of external polish and inner nastiness. Fields is the great spinner of words — of melodious euphemisms, euphonious malapropisms, florid rhetoric. His affectation of polite speech is like all his other pretentions to politeness — pure sham. Beneath the fancy waistcoats and purple prose beats the heart of a dirty old man who drinks, smokes, swears, and gambles, who hates women (especially sweet old ones), children (especially cute little ones), animals, sobriety, and all respectable social institutions (especially marriage, work, honest business dealings, and the law). In *Never Give a Sucker an Even Break* (1941), he tells the audience that the soda-shop scene he is in was supposed to have been set in a bar. In films like *Tillie and Gus* (1933), *It's a Gift* (1934), and especially *The Bank Dick* (1940), Fields—like the Marx Brothers and Mae West—was the foe of everything sentimental and nice. In an era of glamorized sentimentality and niceness, their essential vulgarity and comic crudeness were especially refreshing. They provided the era's comic snore to puncture the Hays Office's American Dream.

Von Sternberg, Ford, Hawks, Hitchcock, Welles

Of the noncomic directors whose films were powerful exceptions to the studio rule, the films of Josef von Sternberg have perhaps worn the least well. Visually the von Sternberg films were gleaming gems, rich in atmospheric detail, shimmering pools of light and contrasting shadow, the excitement of a perpetually moving, prowling camera, the luminous face of Marlene Dietrich—in shadow, in blazing light, veiled, feathered, powdered, hazed. But beneath von Sternberg's gleaming surfaces—the exotic locales, the symbolic details, the smoke, the shafts of light, the audacious sexual innuendoes that could only have gotten past the censors because they didn't understand visual symbols—his films reveal certain problems of plotting and characterization.

The Blue Angel (1930), von Sternberg's second sound film, is one of his best, for it suffers least from a hollowness underneath. It was shot in Germany for Ufa. In the early sound years, Hollywood suddenly discovered a new problem —breaking the language barrier. The silent cinema—a genuinely international language —simply substituted new titles in new languages as a film leaped from country to country. But with sound, before film distributors discovered dubbing and subtitling, Hollywood's plan was to shoot the same film in Europe with different languages and sometimes even different casts. Von Sternberg went to Germany to take part in this cinematic internationalism and direct Ufa's first talkie.

The Blue Angel is a Circe story. A bewitching woman, the nightclub singer Lola Lola (Marlene Dietrich), steadily turns a compulsively orderly school teacher (Emil Jannings) into a beast; he even crows like a cock to show his transformation. It is also the tale of a siren (or, in German terms, a Lorelei) whose singing lures men to their doom. Professor Rath eventually dies from this dramatic change of air, his humiliating conversion from school teacher to nightclub clown. If the film is among von Sternberg's best it is because the director renders every step in Professor Rath's demise with the greatest intimacy and clarity, and he renders the sexual energy that destroys the man with an equal clarity. Atmosphere and visual images in the film are not independent entities but the means to depict the two conflicting characters and life-styles. Both picture and sound establish the two opposite worlds at the beginning of the film. Professor Rath's classroom is white, clean, bright, with desks arranged in geometric regularity; the Blue Angel club where Lola sings is smoky, hazy, chaotic, dim, and hung with entangling nets. Professor Rath's classroom is silent except for the drone of his voice; the Blue Angel is noisy, bustling, full of shouts and song. The antiseptic silence of Rath's classroom is emphasized by the song of a choir that drifts in through an open window; in the bustling, noisy Blue Angel, Lola sings songs of a far less spiritual kind.

Like the great films of Jannings's past, *The Last Laugh* and *Variety*, *The Blue Angel* refuses to draw simplistically sentimental or romantic conclusions. Professor Rath's ascetic life is sterile, schematic, so crammed with routine that it lacks the breath of life; like his caged bird, he is dead. Lola's sensual life is totally selfish, amoral, blind to the existence of any other being but herself; she is committed to love, not to loving someone—as her famous song, "Falling in Love Again," so clearly indicates. Neither of the two lives is superior to the other. The film's business is not moral comment but the tragic story of what happens to a man from one life who tastes a drop of another. The wine that at first makes Rath drunk eventually poisons him. Although Lola frees him from his

Fig. 11-24

Fig. 11-25

The Blue Angel. *Fig. 11-24: the hazy, chaotic clutter of the nightclub; Marlene Dietrich on stage.*
Fig. 11-25: the antiseptic order and clarity of Emil Jannings's classroom, invaded by the influence of Lola Lola.

cage and makes him sing, his song, like the man himself, becomes cracked and empty. His final metamorphosis is not into the singing bird but into the kind of pathetic clown that he saw in Lola's dressing room when he first met her.

That clown both foreshadows Rath's fate and implies that Lola's collection of human husks is endless. The shattered professor creeps back to his old classroom to die. The only consistent moral comment in the film is against the professor's callous students, who pervert his name to *Unrat* ("garbage") and who fail to see that, as both strict disciplinarian and broken clown, Rath is a human being who deserves understanding. The students are vicious, inhuman vultures, like the fallen doorman's neighbors in *The Last Laugh,* and rather obviously Nazis-to-be.

The von Sternberg–Dietrich American films are as dazzling visually as *The Blue Angel* (in fact, even more so). They have individual moments of keen psychological insight, suffused with a pervasive sexual energy. They consistently rely on brilliant surfaces—in particular, the glimmering close-ups of Dietrich's face—to imply the sexual and psychological intensity beneath the surface. But how clearly and how fully do these images reveal that underlying material? Take, for example, the final shot in *Morocco* (1930), the first of von Sternberg's Dietrich films made in this country. The hero (Gary Cooper), a member of the Foreign Legion, has marched off over the sands of the desert to fight. Marlene, in a wildly romantic moment, rejects her rich suitor and plunges off to follow Cooper over the sands, just as each peasant Arab woman follows her beloved Legionnaire, dragging her goods and her goats behind her. Now Marlene is not the kind of woman to travel with goats. The awkwardness of her crossing the desert is emphasized by her need to remove her high-heeled shoes before setting off over the sand dunes. To make such a wildly romantic gesture believable, the director's responsibility is to structure the whole film so that we believe Marlene really loves the soldier *that* much. But the Dietrich–Cooper relationship has no life in the film's scripted narrative at all. He falls in love with her in public (she is a nightclub singer again). They play few scenes together *in camera,* in which little is said and nothing is done. The ending remains an incredible romantic pose. On the other hand, if the final shot is narrative nonsense, it is visually gorgeous: a beautiful composition of waves of blowing white sand, a sliver of dark sky, black specks of human figures dotting the sand at the corners of the frame.

There are other beautiful things in *Morocco*. There is von Sternberg symbolism in the scene in which Marlene must decide between life with the rich suitor (Adolphe Menjou) and life with the man she loves. To emphasize the struggle and decision, Marlene hears the military trumpet call (fine use of sound as symbol) announcing the Legion's departure from the town; at the same time, she nervously fingers a string of pearls her suitor has given her (a symbol of the rewards of the wealthy life). As Marlene makes up her mind, she unconsciously tugs so hard at the necklace that the string breaks and the pearls scatter all over the floor. The meaning of her decision is clear. The film's finest moment is Marlene's first appearance in the Moroccan nightclub. She is dressed as a man in tails; she sings, Eve-like, about selling apples, which she offers as she sings. A lesbian is obviously attracted to the male-clad performer. Marlene, knowing the woman's intentions, toys with her while singing and then matter-of-factly walks up to her and kisses her on the mouth. It is a stunning moment of psychological intensity and energy.

Shanghai Express (1932), the fourth von Sternberg–Dietrich feature, is a story of the reawakening and reaffirmation of love between Marlene (now the shady Shanghai Lily) and Captain Harvey (Clive Brook), a proper officer in the British Army—played against a backdrop of robbers and revolutionaries in exotic China. As in *Morocco*, von Sternberg captures the texture and look of an exotic locale with a brilliant opening sequence, relying on Lee Garmes's constantly moving camera to capture the bustling activity and scurrying people of the eastern railway station. As in *Morocco*, the pictures of Dietrich are luminous, her face radiant in a streak of light against a darkened backdrop; they look striking even in the stills.

But also as in *Morocco*, much of the overt psychological narrative has been suppressed, von Sternberg relying instead on the sexual energy implied by the Dietrich close-ups and the film's calm and cool rhythm, reinforced by agonizingly long dissolves. The past relationship between Lily and Harvey fell apart when he refused to trust her, believing he had been sex-

ually betrayed. The plot of *Shanghai Express* gives him a second chance to put his faith in her, and he eventually passes this test. Clearly, Lily, like the Asian prostitute who shares her compartment (Anna May Wong), has her own powerful and personal system of morality, as opposed to the superficial and self-righteous moralism of the European passengers on the train. When Lily offers her body to the Chinese bandit in exchange for Captain Harvey's eyesight, the officer, unaware of her sacrifice, condemns her a second time for her apparent sexual licentiousness. Without any concrete information to the contrary, he must learn to abandon his smug moralism and to accept Lily's fidelity as a matter of trust alone, "purely a question of faith." It is only on the basis of this faith—whatever the sexual surfaces and moral appearances—that love between human beings becomes possible. But we audiences also accept much of the film's psychological material—primarily that there is anything worth loving about the cold, priggish Harvey in the first place—solely on our faith in von Sternberg's visual imagery rather than because of the film's character or story logic.

The final three von Sternberg–Dietrich films became progressively more bizarre, as if the director were (like von Stroheim) daring the race of Puritans to stop him and, at the same time, were (like Lubitsch) laughing at the sexual childishness of the Puritans for believing these Circean parables. *Blonde Venus* (1932)—which contains enough plot for four films—features Marlene as loving wife, tempted adulteress, devoted mother, cheap whore in a southwestern border town, and international sensation of the music hall. Despite the film's wandering and globe-circling plot, it is redeemed by its moments of intensity and audacity: the sensuous, tactile liquidity of the opening scene as Dietrich swims in a shimmering, limpid stream (and as Herbert Marshall, impersonating a Boy Scout—at the age of forty-two!—voyeuristically watches this hypnotic Lorelei); the dusty, smoky chiaroscuro of the cheap dive in the Tex-Mex border town; the astonishing visual contrasts of the "Hot Voodoo" number, in which the Blonde Venus, complete with platinum fright wig, pokes her head out of the gruesome black body of a gorilla costume; Miss

Fig. 11-26

Fig. 11-27
Von Sternberg putting his Blonde Venus through hoops. Dietrich as sleazy whore and international star.

Dietrich in white top hat and tails (the lesbian motif again), the very masculine guise that attracts the applause and adoration of her male admirers. More than anything else, von Sternberg seems to wonder how many grotesque and outlandish hoops he can make his Blonde Venus jump through without his audience's catching on to the sardonic and satirically contemptuous game.

The coming of the Code and the Hays Office in no way inhibited the director's sexual fantasies but seemed to spur them to new heights. *The Scarlet Empress* (1934), his most sumptuous exercise in *mise-en-scène*, begins with the dreams of the sweet blonde seven-year-old Sophie who later becomes Catherine the Great of Russia. The child's nighttime visions are sadomasochistic fantasies, including the agonizing screams of tortured men on the rack and, in what may be the most de Sade-like image ever presented in a "respectable" studio-era film, the hanging of a male body inside a huge bell, so that his swinging legs and heels can bang against the bell and send its reverberating peals out over the town and countryside. This image of swinging torture dissolves into a shot of Sophie herself, moving in rhythm on her childhood swing. What sexual sensations connect these two parallel acts of swinging?

Later, the grown-up author of these swinging dreams marries the madman who is the heir to the Russian throne, an idiot whose sexual activities are confined to drilling holes in people's walls so he can watch them and whose favorite playthings are inert toy soldiers (clearly von Sternberg implies something about the Prince's own inert toy soldier). The frustrated bride conceives a son by casually offering herself to one of the palace guards, and with the eventual support of the entire army, she leads the Revolution and seizes the throne (riding a milk white stallion and wearing a white hussar's costume — the white/black and male/female tensions again). The bells of all Russia (and those bells have been a consistent visual and aural motif of the film since the opening dream sequence) peal out with something resembling joy.

What is equally striking about *The Scarlet Empress* is that it is essentially a silent film. Von Sternberg reveals his roots in the visual rich-

ness of the silents by shooting whole scenes with only musical accompaniment: the spectacular wedding ceremony that alternates long shots of the immense cathedral, its columns and candles, with agonizingly immense close-ups of Dietrich's face shot through her lace veil; the Bacchanalian wedding feast with its sensational traveling shot spanning an immense table covered with steaming broths, littered plates, and the sugared carcasses of beasts. Most of all like the silent film, *The Scarlet Empress* does not attempt to tell its story with dialogue; the film probably devotes more screen time to printed titles than any made since 1930.

Von Sternberg broke away from Dietrich to direct films without her after the ultimate study of Circean hypnosis, *The Devil Is a Woman,* in 1935: the unfinished *I, Claudius* (1937), with Charles Laughton, Emlyn Williams, and Merle Oberon; *The Shanghai Gesture* (1941) and *Macao* (1952), with their exotic locales; *The Saga of Anatahan* (1953), a film he directed for the Japanese film industry and in which he returned brilliantly to the theme and image of the *femme fatale.* But von Sternberg's period of greatest influence — on both cinematic and cultural fashions — ended when he and Dietrich separated. In von Sternberg's hands, Dietrich became a modern goddess of Sexual Mystery — a celluloid icon of Circe, Aphrodite, Leda, Helen, and Galatea, all wrapped into a single key-lit face. And seven movies.

John Ford is a spiritual descendant of D. W. Griffith. Like Griffith, Ford's values are traditional and sentimental: father, mother, home, and family; law, decency, democracy. Like Griffith — and like two other major Roman Catholic directors of the studio era, Frank Capra and Leo McCarey — Ford was a populist. He praised the little people and the fallible institutions that protected them while he damned those who twisted the system to grab money and power for themselves. More like Griffith than Capra or McCarey, Ford emphasized visual images rather than talk and counterpointed violent dramatic action with rich comedy and wringing pathos. In his westerns, Ford used the settling of the frontier as his basic myth and central metaphor for the emerging American spirit — the bringing of civilization and fruitfulness to the savage wilderness. But Ford's

Fig. 11-28
The Scarlet Empress: *the spectacular wedding sequence.*

films were neither naïve nor simple in their mythic vision. The savage evil could be awesomely powerful, and the forces of civilization could be blind, cold, constricting, rigid, or cruel.

The Ford films are as striking visually as von Sternberg's. Like von Sternberg, Ford paints with extremes of dark and light. But von Sternberg used darkness to emphasize the luminescence of his shafts of light; Ford used shafts of light to emphasize the darkness. The dominant photographic method of von Sternberg is his Germanically moving camera; Ford's camera, often managed by Joseph August or Gregg Toland, composes in space, in width and depth. Dominating Ford's films are the vast vistas of the plains, mountains, and sky, the shots-in-depth of a group of human faces or figures, tensely composed, shot slightly from below. But Ford never substituted picture taking for picture making. Although the films became complex allegories of good and evil—the misty lighting, the settings, the weather, the characterizations all supporting the allegory—Ford never forgot the studio prescription that a film must tell a good story.

Ford's directorial career began in 1917 with a series of informal, inexpensive program westerns starring the good badman, Harry Carey. He did not achieve wide national recognition, however, until 1935 with *The Informer*, written by Ford's frequent collaborator, Dudley Nichols, and which brought him the first of his many Academy Awards. *The Informer* is a story of the Irish Revolution, with which Ford, the son of an Irish immigrant, was understandably in sympathy. Ford would return frequently to Irish, Catholic, or Irish-American themes—as in *Mary of Scotland* (1936), *The Plough and the Stars* (1936), *The Quiet Man* (1952), and *The Last Hurrah* (1958). In *The Informer*, Gypo (played by Victor McLaglen), a former member of the I.R.A., betrays his closest friend and former comrades to the hated British. The film traces the consequences of his succumbing to this weakness and eventually paying, both physically and mentally, for his betrayal. The film's power lies in Ford's achievement in making Gypo's tortured mind manifest, in showing the man's hurts, hopes, fears, and conflicts.

Ford accomplishes his psychological translation by the consistently subjective use of Joseph

Fig. 11-29

The Informer: *Ford's feeling for people is reflected in the strength and uniqueness of their faces.*

August's camera, which mirrors Gypo's mind with dissolves, blurred focus, and physical projections of the man's frightened mind. Ford bathes the film in fog. The fog is not only the perfect visual climate for the dim, damp story; it is also a metaphor for the era's moral fog and the psychological fog inside Gypo's head. Also memorable in *The Informer* is the metaphorical blind man—dressed in black, silhouetted in the mist, tapping steadily with his cane—who seems to follow Gypo everywhere. The blind man is both an internal and external symbol: of Gypo's internal sense of guilt, which he cannot escape, and of the literal pursuit of the revolutionaries, whose justice he also cannot escape. If Ford's blind man is reminiscent of Fritz Lang's in *M*, he serves as a reminder that German expressionist lighting and psychology were powerful influences on Ford's work.

Like many of Ford's prestigious projects of the late 1930s and early 1940s, *The Informer* was an adaptation of a respected literary work, a novel by Liam O'Flaherty. So were his adaptations of Eugene O'Neill's one-act plays about men at sea, *The Long Voyage Home* (1940), of John Steinbeck's *The Grapes of Wrath* (also 1940), and Richard Llewellyn's *How Green Was My Valley* (1941), three of his most respected prewar films. These adaptations were less impressive for their faithfulness to the original source material than for Ford's fondness for his characters and his feeling for the visual surroundings in which they lived, worked, loved, and died. With their awesome contrasts of dark and light, photographed in deep focus (twice by Gregg Toland), these three films convert light and space into both tactile and moral qualities. Indoors, there is the warmth, peace, light, and comfort of family life; outdoors, the dark uncertainty of the world—in the depths of a Welsh mine, in the dark at sea, in the night of a California desert.

Whether indoors or out, Ford invests his faith in "the people"—working people, poor people, religious people, family people—never in commercial institutions like banks, mining companies, or government camps.

Even more than his literary adaptations, Ford poured his feelings for America—its history, its destiny, and its people—into his westerns, the kinds of films in which he and brother Francis began. Francis played a small but pivotal role in almost every John Ford film, like the hard-drinking but fair-minded frontiersman in the coonskin cap who serves as a choric member of the jury in *Young Mr. Lincoln*. For John Ford, the coonskin-cap spirit of the frontier suggests the true spirit of American aspiration and civilization, the link between a Lincoln, a Harry Carey, a Francis Ford, and a John Wayne. Two of Ford's major westerns—*Stagecoach* (1939) and *My Darling Clementine* (1946)—are allegorical studies of American history in the years just before and just after the Second World War.

The coach itself of *Stagecoach* becomes Ford's metaphor for civilized society. Like the train in *The Iron Horse* (1924) and *The Man Who Shot Liberty Valance* (1962) and the truck in *The Grapes of Wrath*, the stagecoach is a machine built by civilized hands that sets out to tame the vast western wastes. Although Ford's films examine what civilization does *to* people as well as *for* people (particularly in *The Searchers*, 1956, *Liberty Valance*, and *Cheyenne Autumn*, 1964), in *Stagecoach* the key dramatic conflict is between the human microcosm inside the coach and the savagery of the land and the Apaches outside it.

Inside Ford's stagecoach is a whole society of white people, of different social classes and mental habits: banker, sheriff, outlaw, salesman, doctor, prim wife, dance-hall "singer," gambler, stage driver. Ford and Dudley Nichols carefully distinguish between the human traits of each: the gambler's chivalry and polish, the outlaw's sense of fairness, the doctor's drunken kindness, the delicate lady's shedding of her prejudices, the sheriff's concern for the outlaw's safety, the salesman's citified, dude-like cowardice. Beneath their superficial tensions and differences, all these people (with one exception) eventually reveal an underlying warmth, kindness, and camaraderie that make them equally decent human beings. Doc Boone sobers up to deliver the lady's baby; the whiskey salesman overcomes some of his antiwestern squeamishness; the sheriff lets the good-hearted outlaw get away with Dallas, the singer (a euphemism for prostitute), at the end of the film; Dallas, despite her toughness, gently helps Doc Boone bring a baby into the world; the outlaw, the Ringo Kid, loves Dallas despite the societally defined shadiness of her past.

The single unredeemed character in the film is Gatewood, the rich banker, who has stolen $50,000 from his own bank and is now running away with it. Despite his selfish violation of the law, Gatewood is the most outspoken on the immorality of the doctor, singer, and outlaw, and the most dogmatic in pontificating on the government's duty to protect his own self-important person. The banker, who views the law as written for his personal convenience, is pure Griffith. Ford's preference for the good-hearted, simple people—good-hearted despite their human fallibilities—over the evil-hearted rich is another Griffith dichotomy. And the prim, proper, moralistic, uplifting society of old hens, who viciously toss Doc and Dallas out of town at the beginning of the film, seems to have leaped directly out of *The New York Hat, Intolerance,* or *Way Down East*. Despite the brilliantly exciting staging and cutting of the stagecoach's climactic battle with the Apaches, *Stagecoach* is a film about character and the important human values.

So is *My Darling Clementine*, although the enemy has shifted from Native American "savages" to savage members of the white race, and the battleground has shifted from the desert to

Fig. 11-30

Fig. 11-31

Stagecoach. *Bringing white civilization to the wilderness. Fig. 11-30: Ford's stagecoach slices through the barren beauty of Monument Valley.*
Fig. 11-31: Inside a rustic shack, a microcosm of European-American society breaks bread.

Fig. 11-32   11-33

More civilization in the wilderness: the dance at the dedication of My Darling Clementine's *church; the architectural expanse of its saloon and hanging lamps.*

a town. On its surface *My Darling Clementine* is an installment in the legend of Wyatt Earp. He and his brothers no longer enforce the law but live the private life of ranchers, away from civilization, out on the plains. The riot and disrule of a frontier town bring him back to "civilization" and its law. Earp, played by Henry Fonda, Ford's embodiment of American backwoods, self-educated social consciousness (Lincoln and Tom Joad), restores peace to the town. It builds a church and holds a dance, two of Ford's favorite emblems of communality.

Despite its western surfaces, the film's allegorical suggestions link it closely to the war in Europe and the Pacific that had just ended. Ford soldiered with his camera in the Pacific, often at the front, where he made documentary films for the Navy (*The Battle of Midway,* 1942; *December 7th,* 1943). "What kind of a town is this?" Wyatt asks when he cannot even get a shave and haircut in peace—two marks of a civilized man. Ford might just as well be asking, "What kind of a world is this?"

The nighttime sneak attack of the vicious Clanton family on the youngest and unarmed Earp brother parallels the attack of the Japanese on Pearl Harbor or the Nazi invasion of Poland. Wyatt parallels the American fighting forces—peacekeeper in a former time (World

War I), now withdrawn and isolated from the battle, steadily drawn into it when it engulfs him. Between the Earps and the Clantons stands Doc Holliday, a man of science (he is a doctor) and culture (he can quote Shakespeare), a former citizen of Boston (the most Eastern and European of American cities, and a favorite center of decadent mischief for Ford). Doc has fallen into the Slough of Despair—into decadence and drink. He no longer practices medicine but makes his living at cards; he has deserted the faithful girl back home, Clementine, for the dance-hall slut, Chihuahua; he is also dying of tuberculosis. Holliday seems the emblem of a sick and degenerate Europe, unable to defend itself, dependent on America—as Doc is dependent on Wyatt—to restore it to moral health.

Even the town's saloon is a mythic edifice: Row upon row of hanging lanterns stretch into the deep space of the frame, illuminating the perfectly planed and proportioned architecture of the building, which is less a frontier drinking place than a monument to civilization. For Ford, this saloon—and this town—are not images of the way the West was but the way it ought to have been, what it meant to bring civilization's architecture to the wilderness. The question of the film (and of many Ford westerns) is not how can such a structure be built but how can civilization be protected, how can it survive.

Ford's usual answer is that civilization requires a vigilant gunfighter to keep the peace. Many Ford films (from *Young Mr. Lincoln* to *The Man Who Shot Liberty Valance*) define two conflicting principles of "Law" that are mutually exclusive. On the one hand, the Law is a book—a series of abstract rules, principles, and statutes that can be understood and practiced by all rational and responsible persons in a society. On the other hand, there are certain gifted persons in a society, like the biblical prophets, who carry the Law within them because they write or interpret the books. They are the Law because they embody the idea of Law; sometimes, like Fonda in *Fort Apache* or Raymond Massey in *The Hurricane* (1937), they are inflexibly bound to the rules and must choose between bending the Law (which often involves situational ethics, compromise, and forgiveness) and destructive rigidity. Given the Fall of Man (Ford's Catholic background shows clearly in his view of history), many human beings are not rational and responsible—whether they are Nazis or Clantons. Civilized human society cannot exist without its soldiers, within whom the Law is as strong as villainy in the wicked and whose ability and determination match those of the wicked.

My Darling Clementine expresses grave doubts as to whether a civilization can survive without the vigilant gunfighter and peacekeeper who carries the Law within him. Ford's westerns for the next fifteen years (from the cavalry films—*Fort Apache*, 1948; *She Wore a Yellow Ribbon*, 1949; and *Wagon Master*, 1950—through *The Searchers* to *The Man Who Shot Liberty Valance*) would continue the exploration of this mythic theme. That the movies (and our culture) haven't entirely settled this question about the relationship of abstract law and the individualist gunfighter can be seen in the Clint Eastwood and Charles Bronson films of the 1970s and 1980s.

If John Ford was the sound film's Griffith, Howard Hawks was its Ince. Compared with Ford's, Hawks's films are more brutal and less sentimental, more active and less mythic. Like Ince's, Hawks's movies are striking in their driving narratives rather than their examinations of psychology or emotional interaction. The psychological insight in a Hawks film functionally serves the narrative line. If Ince used his "soul fights" to move his narratives, the Hawks pictures contain similar conflicts between a man's outer actions and his inner urges.

Howard Hawks is the most deceptively artless of the great Hollywood "studio" directors: His visual style lacks the tricky idiosyncracies of a von Sternberg or a Lubitsch; his narrative style lacks the political and moral allegories of a Ford or a Capra. Hawks films merely seem to be well paced, well told, functionally shot genre pictures—gangster films, westerns, screwball comedies, and the like. But the ultimate testimony to Hawks's powers and abilities may well be that he created at least one film that might serve as the very best representative example of almost every American genre: the best gangster film (*Scarface*, 1930, released 1932), prison picture (*The Criminal Code*, 1931), western (*Red River*, 1948; *Rio Bravo*, 1959), backstage comedy (*Twentieth Century*, 1934), newspaper picture (*His Girl Friday*, 1940), whodunit (*The Big Sleep*, 1946), and screwball comedy (*Bringing Up Baby*, 1938). When a director succeeds so deeply and so broadly with these genre films, it is necessary to look more closely at the unique spirit and talent that created them.

That these films are at least arguably the very best examples of their genres is perhaps due to two facts. First, Howard Hawks was not really a studio director, a staff member employed by a single studio (like Ford at Fox and von Sternberg at Paramount). He was an independent producer for much of his career, and his films were released by various studios (Warner Bros., RKO, and Columbia among them). He was not *assigned* genre pictures; he made the films he wanted to make in the way he wanted to make them. Second, Hawks was one of the greatest storytellers—perhaps the greatest—of the entire studio era (he is von Sternberg's opposite in this strength). He wrote or co-authored every script he shot, and his ability to shape the scenes he wanted to shoot and eliminate those he did not was so extraordinary that he was frequently called in to help other directors solve particular narrative problems with whole films or single scenes. Hawks's special skill was an ability to convert plays and novels into cinematic narratives that were invariably richer, tighter, more complex, and more perceptive than the originals.

The aesthetic of omission, of implying what is not explicitly and overtly stated, is an essential feature of Hawks's narrative mastery. Beneath the generic surfaces of his narratives lie complex tensions between the characters' verbal façades and their unverbalized feelings. In both the comedies and the adventure films, Hawks characters tend not to talk about their feelings overtly—first, because words can be easily and hollowly manipulated; second, because Hawks characters attempt to protect themselves, either through silences or torrents of chatter, not wanting to make the costly emotional mistake of investing their trust in someone unworthy of it. Most of the great Hawks films are stories of the evolution of trust, of growing faith in another human being, and the goal of the entire narrative is to reveal to the central pair (either two men or a man and a woman) that they have good reason to invest their faith in one another. The Hawks films, then, are primarily subtextual and psychological studies of the ego and of intellect, a counterpoint between mind and feeling (in contrast to many other Hollywood directors, like Ford, Capra, or von Sternberg, for whom the central interest is exposing the naked heart). The intellect controls the character's surface; the genuine feelings lie beneath; and the resolution of the Hawks narrative almost always brings the characters to a synthesis of the perceptions of the brain and the affections of the heart.

On the surface, *Twentieth Century* is a battle of wills, a study of two egomaniacal theatre people (played by Carole Lombard and John Barrymore) who fight to the egoistic death. Beneath the battle there is love (for they would not fight if they did not love), respect for each other's abilities, each other's strength, each other's egos. In the same way, although Hildy (Rosalind Russell) in *His Girl Friday* thinks she wants a sweet, normal married life with an insurance salesman (Ralph Bellamy), the fact is that she belongs with Walter Burns (Cary Grant) because, beneath their arguments and banter and battles, they complete each other. They are both newspaper "men." Hildy's life

Fig. 11-34

Fig. 11-35

Going screwball in **Bringing Up Baby:** *Katharine Hepburn nets Cary Grant; singing "I Can't Give You Anything but Love" to a leopard on a rooftop in Connecticut.*

can be full only if she *does* what she does well, not if she tries to feel what she feels she ought to feel (this tenet is as central to the Hawks philosophy as any). And in the same way, the scientist David (Grant) in *Bringing Up Baby* can free himself from his emotional and psychological cage only by experiencing the spontaneity and unpredictability of a Susan (Katharine Hepburn) rather than by working joylessly with his more proper fiancée, Miss Swallow. Although the plot of *Bringing Up Baby* seems to be a loony chase after dinosaur bones and escaped leopards, it really is an adventure in emotional education (like Antonioni's *L'avventura*) in which David learns how to be a complete human being. The journalistic adventures of *His Girl Friday* and the theatrical adventures of *Twentieth Century* teach their characters the same lesson.

Hawks's alterations of Raymond Chandler's *The Big Sleep* clearly reveal both his psychological interests and his thematic commitments. With the aid of screenwriters William Faulkner, Leigh Brackett, and Jules Furthman, Hawks builds the surface of the film as a maze of murders and bewilderingly proliferating names (Sean Regan, Eddie Mars, Joe Brody, A. G. Geiger, Carol Lundgren, Harry Jones) designed to lead the central pair, Marlowe (Humphrey Bogart) and Vivian (Lauren Bacall), to the knowledge that they can trust each other, if only because they work well together. It would be both foolish and dangerous for Marlowe to trust her if she is not really "wonderful" (as he ironically describes her); many of the film's murdered men go to their "big sleeps" because they trust the wrong women. The twists of Hawks's narrative allow Vivian (a less romantic character in the Chandler novel) to demonstrate her loyalty and sincerity, not by telling Marlowe about them but by demonstrating them as she helps him escape his big sleep.

Despite its apparently different cowboy surface, *Red River* is a similar narrative. The prologue (which does not exist in the Borden Chase story on which Hawks's film is based) carefully and cleverly establishes every narrative detail the film will require for its conclusion. Thomas Dunson (John Wayne) builds an immense cattle spread from the mating of his bull with the calf of a young boy, Matthew Garth (Montgomery Clift). After the Civil War, it becomes necessary to drive the now huge herd a thousand miles to market, from Texas to Kansas City. During the drive, Dunson's inflexibility—his refusal to change his mind or alter a decision, his strict sense of vengeful justice—threatens the success of the entire venture. Matthew usurps Dunson's authority and proves more flexible and more popular with the men he leads. The younger, "softer" man succeeds by altering the ultimate destination, bringing the herd to the new railroad line in Abilene and establishing the Chisholm Trail.

Beneath the surfaces of this familiar American western lie several deliberate epic and biblical parallels. The founding of the herd itself, with its suggestion of mythic animal coupling, echoes any number of similar copulations in Greek mythology. As in the Old Testament's Exodus and Homer's *Odyssey*, the group must make a long and arduous journey, beset with many kinds of enemies—natural and human, geographical and psychological, external attackers (Indians, rustlers) and internal conflicts stemming from human insufficiency and unreliability. As in Homer's *Iliad* and *Odyssey*, there is a wise old choric Nestor or Mentor (the cook, Nadine Groot, played by Walter Brennan), who serves as the work's narrator and moral barometer (Groot is a minor figure who plays no such role in Chase's story). As in Exodus the group must cross a body of water named "The Red" at the beginning of their journey. And as in Exodus, Moses's hubris, his tendency to judge the weaknesses of mortals too harshly, leads to a change in leaders; Joshua, not Moses, takes the Children of Israel to the Promised Land, and Matthew, not Dunson, takes the herd to Abilene. The herd, like the Children of Israel, is both the progeny and the responsibility of its father-leaders, Dunson (always called by his last name) and Matthew (always called by his first).

In transferring the materials of older epics to these new American surroundings, Hawks sought to accomplish several ends. First, he argues that the history of America—part fact and part legend—is exactly the kind of material out of which those earlier epics were made. *Red River*, part story and part history, is, as a work of art, parallel to an *Iliad*, *Odyssey*, or Exodus in both content and spirit. Second, Hawks uses the epic context to examine his essential notion of human completeness and complementariness. Dunson is so purely hard and male ("the man with a bull" and without

Fig. 11-36
The climactic gun battle that doesn't take place in Red River: the unswerving determination of Dunson (John Wayne) overcome by the quiet, loving strength of Matthew Garth (Montgomery Clift), producing—with the help of the tough woman (Joanne Dru, offscreen in Frame 7) who shoots at them and tells them they love each other—the final reunion of "father" and "son."

a woman) that his virtue is an extremely solitary one; he can build a civilization out of the wilderness but he cannot keep the civilization together once he has built it. Matthew ("the boy with a calf") has the milder gifts of fertility and civilizing; he can bind men and societies together. The historical process examined by Hawks in the film is, in effect, the passing of America's need from the one kind of leader to the other. But only with both can one produce a whole civilization; one needs both the builder and the binder, the hard and the soft, the bull and the calf.

The climax of the film, an apparent showdown gunfight between the two leaders, reveals the usual and ultimate Hawks synthesis of love and trust demonstrated by action. Although some find the ending of *Red River* an optimistic, arbitrary avoiding of the gunfight toward which westerns invariably build, this opinion reflects a lack of understanding of both Hawks in general and the particular narrative he has carefully built. Dunson has come gunning for Matthew because he views the boy's taking the herd from him as a disloyal act, a usurpation, a denial of their love and work together that built the immense herd in the first place. (Hawks fills the frame with hundreds of cows at the start of the promised duel, the very tangible, visible proof of the fertility of the Dunson–Matthew union.) Matthew, on the other hand, has taken the herd from Dunson as an extension of his love and loyalty, knowing that only his leadership can bring their invested labors to fruition. Matthew knows (from that very prologue added by Hawks) that Dunson will not shoot a man who does not intend to shoot him; he also knows (again established in the prologue) that Dunson reads a man's eyes to determine if and when he intends to shoot. As Dunson strides toward Matthew, the younger man's eyes (carefully scrutinized by the camera) reveal that he will never shoot. One does not shoot the people one loves. Dunson must observe that love in action, and Matthew accordingly demonstrates in action (as every major Hawks character must do) exactly what he feels beneath the surface. The film ends with an affirmation of love, friendship, fraternity, paternity, and "marriage," as almost every Hawks film does.

As opposed to Ford, who saw American history as the movement of pioneers, prophets, and soldiers, followed by the spread of their civilized institutions—the Law, the cavalry, the church, the dance, the home—Hawks saw American history as the assertion of individual wills. It is as Protestant an ethic of individualism and professionalism as Ford's is a Catholic view of fallible mortal groups within earthly institutions that interpret and administer for them. While Ford's films test the responsiveness of those groups and institutions, Hawks's films test the firmness and responsiveness of human wills, both their resoluteness and their recognition of limits and limitations—the point at which they require the complementarity of another.

Unlike the decor and lighting of Ford's frontier saloon in *My Darling Clementine,* the typical Hawks setting suggests the fragility of human existence and institutions—a small circle of men (and a woman or two) huddled together under the light from a single oil or electric lantern in a ramshackle cabin barely able to withstand the assault of wind and rain. The more cynical Hawks would take one look at his good friend John Ford's monumental saloon in Monument Valley, then playfully ask, "Where the hell did they get all that wood?"

Alfred Hitchcock was not a product of the American studio system at all, but a combination of the German studio style and the British studio industry. But the British film industry has maintained a symbiotic relationship with Hollywood since the end of World War I (Hitchcock's first film job was with a British branch of Paramount), made even more dependent by the common language after the conversion to sound. Hitchcock's affinity with the American system is clear in the popularity of his British films in America and in his smooth, effortless emigration from London to Hollywood in 1939.

Hitchcock served part of his apprenticeship as an art director at Ufa. The German influence would persist throughout Hitchcock's career—in the murky shadows and studio-controlled expressionist lighting of his black-and-white films, in the equally controlled universe of his color films, in the paranoia that consumes his characters and spreads to his audience, in the claustrophobic decor that con-

fines his figures, in the inexorable and implacable sense of fate from which his characters cannot escape. Perhaps more British is Hitchcock's dry irony, which allows him to chortle at this doom and gloom that he finds as funny as it is alarming.

Although Hitchcock directed his first film in 1925 (*The Pleasure Garden*), he did not become a major figure until sound allowed him to complement his visuals with talk. Hitchcock's—and perhaps England's—first sound film, *Blackmail* (1929), already reveals the Hitchcock style in miniature. There is odd sexuality (a painter invites a woman to his flat so he can rape her while she wears a special costume), a brutal murder (the woman defends herself with a handy knife), paranoid psychology (she fears both the forces of law and the blackmailer pursuing her, seeing and hearing their menace in every ordinary conversation), a brilliant climactic chase in an ironic public place (the British Museum), and a moral twist at the end (the woman gets away with the murder, although the painter's clown picture still laughs at her). But the first three Hitchcock films to make a major impact in America were *The Man Who Knew Too Much* (1934), *The 39 Steps* (1935), and *The Lady Vanishes* (1938), all of them rich in subtle psychology, ironic humor, and gripping suspense.

The 39 Steps is a prototype Hitchcock film of his British period. The plot is a mad chase from London to Scotland and back again. The chase throws the crime-tracking runners into the most wildly diverse and incongruous settings: a Scottish farmhouse, a plush manor house, a vaudeville theatre. The action is a mad attempt to solve the film's great riddle (the single question that glues the entire film's intriguing incidents together, which Hitchcock called the "MacGuffin"), the meaning of "the 39 steps." That riddle is buried inside the head of the vaudeville performer, Mr. Memory, who, when publicly confronted with the question in front of an audience, is torn by his commitment to his art (he prides himself in knowing all) and his commitment to his fellow conspirators.

As in so many of his films, Hitchcock delights in showing the most horrible crimes taking place in the most public places: amusement parks, concert halls, trains. And like so many

Fig. 11-37

Fig. 11-38

Subjectivity in Hitchcock's first sound film,
Blackmail: *The fleeing woman sees an electrified
cocktail shaker become the knife with which she
murdered her assailant.*

Hitchcock films, *The 39 Steps* is a completely
apolitical story of political intrigue. Except for
the war-time films (*Saboteur, Foreign Correspondent, Notorious,* and *Lifeboat*), which are explicitly anti-Nazi, and *North by Northwest,* which is
fuzzily anti-Communist, the two political sides

in Hitchcock films are us and them. He deliberately refuses to cloud a good story with ideology. For the same reason, Hitchcock films
frequently take place in the world of the rich;
they are divorced from such social-realist problems as poverty and hunger. The Hitchcock
actors are smooth, slick males like Cary Grant,
Ray Milland, and James Stewart and cold, sleek
ladies (usually blonde with strong, almost sterile
features) like Grace Kelly, Kim Novak, and Eva
Marie Saint. *The 39 Steps* uses the slick Robert
Donat and the cool Madeleine Carroll.

The Hitchcock films are a unique blend of
story, style, mood, and a deceptively complex
technique. Hitchcock mixes the macabre and
the funny, mystery and whimsy, suspense and
sardonic laughter. While the gripping story
drives relentlessly forward, Hitchcock takes
time out to focus on a subtle physical detail or
ironic element. The plots revolve about the
wildest improbabilities: vast, international con-
spiracies; little old ladies who are really spies;
psychotic killers who impersonate their dead
mothers; secret codes memorized by vaudeville
entertainers; chases that culminate on carou-
sels, in concert halls, in theatres, on the Statue
of Liberty, or on Mount Rushmore. Beneath
almost every Hitchcock film is the structure of
the Sennett chase, the accelerating rush toward
a climactic solution. But Hitchcock personalizes
the improbable chase by making each of the
racers surprisingly familiar and vulnerable, fal-
libly credible. Murderers, psychotics, and spies
become as human as the little old lady next
door. The most insane, exotic tales hang on the
tiniest, most trivial details—a rare brand of
herb tea, a glass of milk, a bird cage, a glove, a
native folk song, a cigarette lighter, an inquisitive cocker spaniel. Frenzied suspense and wry
understatement are the ultimate Hitchcock ingredients, bizarre psychological states beneath
the most banal surfaces the essential Hitchcock
theme.

That Hitchcock theme, which personalizes
his vision and makes him more than the supreme technician and trickster, is the fuzzy but
inexorable line between normal and abnormal
behavior. The ordinary fears of normal human
beings—of heights, of being falsely accused,
of being alone in a sleazy motel room—are
subtly transformed into bizarrely abnormal

occurrences. Perhaps the best early example of this transformation is in *The Man Who Knew Too Much* (1934), in which everyone's fear of a trip to the dentist is transformed by the fact that this particularly menacing dentist is a member of an international conspiracy of murderers. Hitchcock would blur the line between normal and ordinary, sane and psychotic, even more in his films of the 1950s, in which the most ordinary human pursuits shade gradually into the most forbidden sexual-social taboos.

Hitchcock's two greatest technical tools are his command of editing and his control of what Pudovkin called the "plastic material." Hitchcock's films are rich in tiny yet revealing plastic details, from facial tics to physical objects, from the body in clothes to embodied dreams. *Strangers On A Train* (1951) is as much about a cigarette lighter and a pair of glasses as it is about two men, one "normal" and one "crazy."

Hitchcock's awareness of the power of concrete detail is such that when the detail is not exactly right in its natural state he fixes it up to emphasize it. In *Suspicion* (1941), to hypnotize us with a glass of milk that Joan Fontaine thinks is poisoned, Hitchcock puts a tiny light inside the glass to make the milk truly glow in the darkness. In *Spellbound* (1945), he makes a revolver dominate the foreground by photographing an immense, six-times-larger-than-life model. The power of these objects in Hitchcock films reveals the origins of his style in art direction and the dependence of his technique on "storyboarding" his shots. Hitchcock planned a film by drawing pictures of exactly the way he wanted every image to look, then set up each shot to duplicate the drawing.

In an era of functional narrative cutting, Hitchcock's editing alone tightened the screws of suspense. As Sylvia Sidney slices roast beef at the dinner table in *Sabotage* (1936), Hitchcock's cutting shows her passion building until she drives the knife into her villainous husband. The same quick cutting creates the suspense of the final fight in *Saboteur* (1942) as the Nazi spy slips off the Statue of Liberty to his death, the frenzy of the spinning carousel at the end of *Strangers On A Train*, the brutality of Janet Leigh's death in *Psycho* (1960) as

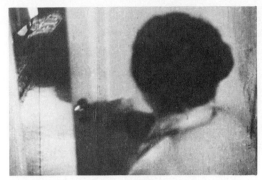

Fig. 11-39

Fig. 11-40

Fig. 11-41
The 39 Steps*: the sound-and-picture montage, from cleaning woman's discovery to train's scream.*

Hitchcock cuts from shots of the victim's face, to shots of the slashing knife, to shots of the bloodstreaked water swirling down the drain of the shower.

Hitchcock films provide perfect examples of how to cut picture and sound together. In *The 39 Steps,* the charwoman walks into a room

264 A SHORT HISTORY OF THE MOVIES

where she sees the shadow of a corpse; her eyes widen and her mouth begins to erupt into a scream. Hitchcock immediately cuts to the shriek of a train whistle and a shot of the train racing toward Scotland. The screaming train replaces the human scream and startles us with its unnatural shrillness.

In *Strangers On A Train*, Hitchcock weds sound and cutting perfectly in the tennis sequence. The hero (Farley Granger) must play a tennis match knowing that the murderer (Robert Walker) is, at that very moment, trying to plant a false clue that will establish his guilt. To avoid suspicion, Granger must finish off the tennis match before he finishes off the killer. Hitchcock makes the suspenseful delay unbearable with languid, rhythmic cutting from one player to the other to the crowd, player to player to crowd, underscoring the plodding sequence with a radio announcer's drone, the spectators' applause, the steady plop, plop, plop of racquet hitting ball.

In *The 39 Steps*, the major alteration Hitchcock made when adapting John Buchan's World War I spy story for film was to build numerous scenes around sexual confrontations that did not exist in the original. In the opening scene between Robert Donat and the female spy who is subsequently killed, Hitchcock enjoys the sexual matter-of-factness of the woman's inviting herself to a stranger's flat, where she calmly sits eating haddock and telling her outlandish story. In the scene in the Scottish crofter's house, Hitchcock deftly sketches with a few subtle strokes a whole lifetime's relationship between the moralistic crofter and his sympathetic wife. Most ironic of all the sequences is the one in which the fleeing Donat escapes his pursuers by spending the night in a hotel room with Madeleine Carroll, handcuffed in bed to a woman who detests him, since he earlier escaped the police on the train to Scotland by barging into her compartment and kissing her on the mouth.

The flair of Hitchcock's breathless construction and subtly ironic sequences is matched by his complete control of his craft. To depict the death of the spy, a necessary but potentially dangerous starting point for the story, Hitchcock underplays the sequence by making the woman rush into Donat's room obviously upset and flustered, run toward the camera, and then suddenly collapse on his bed, a knife sticking out of her back in the foreground of the frame. Then the phone rings (brilliant juxtaposition of visual and sound). To underscore Mr. Memory's confusion about telling the audience the truth about the 39 steps, Hitchcock shoots the man's face in tight close-up from below and on a tilt; the composition of the shot dramatizes the tension in his mind. Hitchcock subtly points the road back to Mr. Memory all along because Robert Donat unconsciously whistles the theme song of the man's act throughout the film. But Donat, no Mr. Memory, cannot remember where he heard the tune that keeps running through his head. Hitchcock repeatedly uses sound to build entire films around musical leitmotifs, from the original themes Bernard Herrmann composed for *Vertigo* (1958) and *Psycho* to the "*Merry Widow* Waltz" in *Shadow of a Doubt* (1943) and "The Band Played On" in *Strangers On A Train*.

The final scene of *The 39 Steps* is a brilliant synthesis of its action, irony, comedy, and psychology. Mr. Memory lies dying on the floor in the wings of the theatre. Though he is dying, he insists on telling the police the complicated formula he has memorized — his pride in his work is that great. Meanwhile, a line of chorines dances on stage (in the background of the frame). Meanwhile, Robert Donat puts his arm around Madeleine Carroll (in the foreground), and suddenly we discover the same dangling handcuff on his wrist that has been there for the last hour of the film, during much of which Donat and Carroll have been cuffed together involuntarily. This final detail ironically undercuts the romance of the ending, a perfect indication of the British Hitchcock style and tone as well as a vivid anticipation of the endings of such American Hitchcocks as *Rear Window* (1954).

When he moved from England to America at the invitation of producer David O. Selznick, Hitchcock turned the dry drollery of his English wit to observations of the American scene with even more corrosive subtlety. One of Hitchcock's favorite subjects became the superficial placidity of American life, whose clean, bright surfaces disguised the most shocking moral, political, psychological, and sexual

Fig. 11-42

Subjectivity in Strangers On A Train. Fig. 11-42: the "normal" American, Farley Granger, drawn into the shadows of Robert Walker's psychotic aberration; Fig. 11-43: the maniac as a tiny black blot on the white marble monuments of American values.

Fig. 11-43

aberrations: the wealthy members of an American cultural elite who happen to be Nazis (*Saboteur*); the small-town Americana wholesomeness that protects a psychopathic killer (*Shadow of a Doubt*). For Hitchcock, the most striking, funny, and terrifying quality of American life was its confidence in its sheer ordinariness. Beneath the surface, ordinary people and normal life were always "bent" for Hitchcock.

This conviction would make him one of the most insightful and irreverent directors of the 1950s, when American culture retreated behind a façade of cheerful normality.

Unlike Hitchcock, Lubitsch, Chaplin, Hawks, or Ford, whose reputations rest on a great number of impressive films, critical respect for Orson Welles rests primarily on one film, *Citizen Kane* (1941), widely considered the greatest sound film ever made. *Kane*'s greatness can be discussed on several different levels: its technical innovation, structural complexity, complicated handling of narrative point-of-view, controversy as a biography of a famous American, philosophical search for meaningful values, sociological study of the "American Dream," acting, literacy, individuality. Orson Welles, the young sensation of both the stage and radio, had been invited to bring his Mercury Theatre group to Hollywood in 1939 to make any film he chose. Welles was twenty-four when he signed with RKO. The film, *Citizen Kane,* was both his first and the last he would ever be so free to make. Like an earlier *enfant terrible* of Hollywood, Erich von Stroheim, Welles insisted on participating in every production detail: acting, directing, writing, editing, sound, design. And like von Stroheim, Welles soon saw the Hollywood lords giving his negatives to other hands for slicing and later found the gates of the lords' studios locked against him.

From its opening sequence, *Citizen Kane* is no ordinary film. It begins in quiet and darkness: a wire fence with a "No Trespassing" sign; a series of tracking shots and dissolves past a weird menagerie that brings us closer to the creepy mansion, Xanadu, and eventually into the room of the dying man; his expressionistic death, with the echoing, rasping sound of the word "Rosebud" on his lips; the glass ball dropping through space in slow motion before shattering; the distorted view of the nurse, seen through the curved glass of the fallen globe as she enters the room to attend to the dead man. As if this beginning were not elliptical enough, Welles shatters the dark mood of death with the blaring music and glaring images of a newsreel documentary. From moody Expressionism, the film jumps to a brilliant parody of *The March of Time*: the musical fanfare, the booming "voice-of-God" narration, the overly descriptive printed titles, the purple prose, the diagrams and maps, the lifeless newsreel photography, the tendency to reduce motion pictures to stills that merely illustrate a verbal commentary. The newsreel ends as abruptly as it began and is followed by a scene in the projection room in which the reporters discuss the newsreel's defects, a scene played entirely in

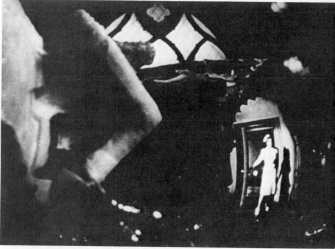

Fig. 11-44
Citizen Kane: *the expressionistically distorted and richly symbolic image of Kane's death.*

shadow, drenched in smoke, backlit by shafts of light from the projection booth. The scene is as garishly shadowed as the preceding news footage was flat and overexposed. Three sequences, three completely different film styles.

The film's technical brilliance continues throughout. Even today it seems striking in its extreme low-angle shots (how conscious were we that Hollywood sets before *Citizen Kane* had ceilings?), its consistently extreme contrasts of dark and light, its vast shots in depth revealing interaction between foreground and rearground. Welles was lucky to have the cinematic eye of Gregg Toland behind his camera and the designer's eye of Perry Ferguson in front of it.

But Welles also shows personal cinematic flair in editing several of the sequences. (*Kane* was edited by Robert Wise, but Welles gave the orders.) One striking sequence— as much a matter of good writing and choice of camera position as it is of cuts, timing, and swish-pans—reveals the widening emotional gulf between Kane and his first wife (Ruth Warrick). As the two eat breakfast together at the dining table, Welles executes a montage series of vignettes, each of which shows the two moving further apart physically. At the end of the sequence, the two, who had begun sitting next to each other, talking cheerily, sit at opposite ends of the long table, not talking at all; she is reading a competing newspaper—the supreme insult to a newspaper publisher.

Welles's control of sound is as careful as his manipulation of image. The years in radio made him aware of sound's dramatic power, an advantage he enjoyed over those directors who graduated to sound from the silents. The over-loud narration of the news digest, the echoing emptiness of Thatcher's mausoleum-library, the contrast between the amplified and unamplified human voice at Kane's political rally, the flat tones of the ungifted opera singer, the flat smallness of the voices in the immense rooms of Kane's huge chateau, all are examples of an ear trained in the power of the microphone and the loudspeaker to create aural space. The sound field in this movie has as much depth as the deep-focus visual field.

Citizen Kane, one of the most complexly structured pieces of film narrative in cinema history, resembles nothing so much as William Faulkner's *Absalom, Absalom! Citizen Kane* is, like the Faulkner novel, an immense jigsaw puzzle (like the puzzles Susan assembles in Kane's castle). Welles and screenwriter Herman J. Mankiewicz (whose favorite novel, F. Scott Fitzgerald's *The Great Gatsby,* also had its influence) lead the audience through a seemingly chaotic collection of events and personal fragments until all the pieces of the puzzle are fitted together—the last piece being the identity of "Rosebud." Although both Welles and Faulkner seem to wander confusingly over an immense expanse of time and space, both artists carefully follow a well-charted if intricate map to the ultimate revelation. Although Welles and Mankiewicz may not have been directly influenced by Faulkner (though Toland knew and had worked with him), Welles had gone to RKO with the original intention of adapting Joseph Conrad's *Heart of Darkness* (rejected by the studio because Welles planned to use subjective camera throughout), whose complex story-within-a-story, imagery, theme, and central character (Kurtz) bear obvious affinities to *Kane* and themselves had some influence on *Absalom, Absalom!*

The cinematic structure of *Citizen Kane*'s first sequence is a microcosm of the whole film. Just as Welles's camera begins outside the fence of Charles Foster Kane's house and then steadily moves closer until it comes to rest on the

Fig. 11-45

Fig. 11-46
The deliberate overexposure of the peeping news camera, trying to catch a glimpse of Kane, and the shafts and shadows of the projection sequence, lit almost totally from behind.

man himself (played by Orson Welles), so the whole film begins on the outside of Kane and steadily moves inward, seeking the man's core. The first section that sets out to convey a vision or interpretation of Kane, the news digest, is the most externalized report of all, a sweeping summary of the facts and dates of Kane's life with no attempt at understanding his motivation. The newsreel is useful for the film, not only because it gives us a completely surface report but also because it gives us a series of road signs—concrete incidents, images, and dates—to which Welles will return later in the film and which keep the film's sprawling structure moving in a clear, coherent direction.

The film's second section is narrated by Thatcher (George Coulouris), the banker who first brought young Charles to the city. Or rather it is narrated by Thatcher's memoirs, since the man is now dead. Thatcher's section primarily covers Kane's boyhood and youth, from the time he left his parents in Colorado to the time he took over the newspaper in New York, though it goes all the way to the Depression, when Kane's empire foundered. Since Thatcher never cared for Kane and since, as a banker, he concentrates on Kane's financial history, his report remains very much on the outside of Kane. It is, however, part of the narrative game of *Citizen Kane* that many of the events narrated by "Thatcher" (and the others) could not possibly have been perceived in the way we witness them (the closeness of mother and boy captured in the tight close-up of their faces; the boy's sled, Rosebud, lying alone in the snow, as the howl of a train whistle on the soundtrack implies that Thatcher and the boy have already departed and Bernard Herrmann's music sounds the haunting "Rosebud" theme). Despite the human narrative voices in the film, the primary narrator is the camera, which sees more clearly and crosses more barriers than any mortal observer.

The film's third section, narrated by Bernstein (Everett Sloane), Kane's business associate, begins to turn inward. Bernstein begins more or less where Thatcher left off—from the founding of the newspaper through the marriage with the first Mrs. Kane. But because Bernstein idolized Kane and never deserted

Fig. 11-47
The shot in depth. Jed Leland (Joseph Cotten) and Bernstein (Everett Sloane) speak in the foreground while Charlie Kane (Orson Welles) dances with chorus girls in the background.

Fig. 11-48
Welles's "dissolve-montage." As Leland tells his story in the foreground, the events dissolve into the frame in the background—a technique borrowed from the stage.

him, the section concentrates on the young, energetic, iconoclastic "Charlie" Kane, the man with spirit and vision.

The fourth section, Jed Leland's, begins the depth sounding. Jed (Joseph Cotten) is Kane's former best friend, now his cynical enemy. Kane fired Jed when Jed refused to desert his principles to suit his boss; Jed's very presence reminded Kane of the principles he had left behind. Jed's section picks up where Bernstein's leaves off: from the marriage with the first Mrs. Kane to the Chicago opera debut of Susan Alexander, who has become the second Mrs. Kane. Bernstein's section takes Kane to the peak of his happiness and success; Jed's shows the beginning of Kane's bitter descent.

The film's fifth section, Susan Alexander's, continues the descent. Now a singer in sleazy cafés, Susan (Dorothy Comingore) begins her tale with her operatic career under Kane (which was, as she says, all his idea) and continues it through their horrifying life in the huge castle, Xanadu, that Kane supposedly had built for her; she ends with the time she finally walked out on him (which was *her* idea). Kane, attractively youthful and rebellious in the film's early sections, is now seen as a broken, loveless, ugly old tyrant.

The film's examination is complete except for the epilogue, which, like the prologue, focuses on Xanadu, the house, as well as Kane, the man. Its narrator is the butler, Raymond (Paul Stewart), his final human contact, a hired companion who parallels the hired nurse in the prologue. In the epilogue, Thompson (William Alland), the journalist who made the newsreel and whose presence has tied together all the film's sections, tries once more to find the meaning of the clue that has propelled his search, the meaning of Kane's last word, "Rosebud." Raymond tells how Kane trashed her room after Susan left (but said "Rosebud" when he picked up the glass ball). The reporter, who has remained faceless throughout the film (as a sort of audience surrogate — like the camera, a vehicle of our curiosity), gives up. The reporter will never find Rosebud. After Thompson resigns the search for the "missing piece" of the puzzle, Welles shows some workmen throwing into a furnace the least valuable of the items that Kane had col-

lected during his lifetime. One of the pieces of junk is Kane's childhood sled; we see that its name is Rosebud. The wood goes up in flames; the object becomes a column of smoke, ascending into the night sky as Herrmann's "Power" and "Rosebud" leitmotifs are finally resolved. The opening "death" of a glass ball containing a snowy scene ends with the cremation of a sled. The camera pulls and dissolves steadily away from the mansion until it stands once more outside the fence with the "No Trespassing" sign. Having trespassed to discover as much as could be known about any human being, the camera now leaves Kane his privacy.

The film's key moral question is what happened to Charles Foster Kane. What, if anything, went wrong? What destroyed his youthful hopes and excitement? The answer is a dark, sickly spot at the heart of Kane's values and, by implication, at the heart of the values of American life. The three abstract themes that constantly flow through *Citizen Kane* are wealth, power, and love. The questions that the film raises are whether the first two exclude the third, and whether a life that excludes the third is worth living at all. Kane obviously has wealth; his wealth bought him newspapers and his newspapers brought him power. But Kane thinks that money and power can buy him the affection of human beings. Kane is a man of quantities. He collects things in quantity: newspapers, *objets d'art,* junk. When he runs for governor, he attempts to collect the people's hearts in the same way that he collects statues and paintings. The word "love" echoes through his whole political campaign. But hearts cannot be bought and stored like statues.

Failing to earn the people's love, Kane decides to demonstrate his power by making them love his creation, the opera singer Susan Alexander. But Kane is no Svengali; his Trilby is a dud. Kane fails to collect the people's hearts with his creation much as he failed to get their votes. And so instead of collecting the hearts of the people *en masse,* Kane decides to collect a single human heart — Susan's. He becomes her absolute tyrant; he builds her a huge house, a private universe, where he is sole master of a single human destiny. The house becomes Susan's prison, and she merely one more piece of stuff that Kane has collected. Susan rebels;

Fig. 11-49

Fig. 11-50

The erosion of time. The youthful Leland, Kane, and Bernstein (Cotten, Welles, Sloane) and the aged Thatcher, Kane, and Bernstein (George Coulouris, Welles, Sloane). In his youth, Kane signs a "Declaration of Principles"; broken by both age and the Depression, he signs away his holdings.

she leaves. Kane has not succeeded in collecting a single heart. The most appropriate epitaph at his death is the silent cellar full of crated marble and stone, the dead objects he has ravished with his checkbook from the museums, cathedrals, and chateaux of Europe.

Rosebud, the sled, is also an object. But it is an object of Kane's youth, an object that he did not buy, something he loved—and lost, given to him by parents he loved and lost. He kept Rosebud (from his mother's estate) because, like his mother's old wood stove, it had great sentimental value. He was also sentimentally attached to Susan's glass ball, whose snow scene deliberately recalls the snowy images of Thatcher's visit to young Charles in Colorado. Young Kane was ripped away from his snowy childhood, his family, and life with Rosebud, by the discovery of the Colorado silver lode on the land that Kane's mother (Agnes Moorehead) fortuitously owned. And so Rosebud, in Kane's mind anyway, represented the opposite of everything his life had become, youth rather than corrupt maturity, genuine human emotion (with his mother particularly) rather than cash substitutes. Rosebud was, in Robert Frost's words, the road not taken.

Significantly, no human observer discovers the meaning of "Rosebud." The camera alone discovers the answer to the film's opening riddle, completing the work's artistic pattern. Works of art are much more knowable, more discoverable and recoverable, than living human beings—especially great and complicated ones. The pattern completed by the discovery of Rosebud is, arguably, the only Elizabethan tragedy—in spirit and shape—that Hollywood ever produced out of American materials.

Like the hero of Marlovian tragedy, a Dr. Faustus or Tamburlaine, Kane is an immense human being with immense social power. Like Marlowe's Faustus or Shakespeare's Macbeth (a favorite Welles role), Kane is an overreacher, a man who dares the cosmos by seeking to accomplish more than a mortal can. The very virtues of such a figure—his energy, will, ambition—lead directly to his tragic flaw, as virtues inevitably do in classical tragedy. Finally, as in the classical tragedy, there is something inevitable about Kane's tragic journey;

Fig. 11-51

Fig. 11-52

The final views of Kane. Fig. 11-51: as a tiny dark figure, dwarfed by exotic arches. Fig. 11-52: as a mystery—holding the glass ball and walking between mirrors, his reflection multiplied to infinity.

elements inherent in the man's character and in the human condition itself conspire to produce the tragic result. Kane would not be Kane, the most powerful and interesting being in the film, if he were not the overreacher he is. Being

that overreacher, he is necessarily doomed to his particular tragic failure. And if Kane's desire to translate spiritual values into material objects seems lamentable, isn't it also an inevitable human response to mortality? Aren't Thatcher's library, Kane's Xanadu, and all works of art—even *Citizen Kane* itself—translations of abstract spiritual aspirations into artifacts that might "last forever"?

Citizen Kane was both shocking and confusing to its audiences in 1941. Instead of Hollywood's flat gloss, the film was sombre and grotesque. The action sprawled over more than sixty years, requiring its performers to make tremendous transitions in acting and appearance. There were no last-minute changes of heart, no romantic reconciliations. *Citizen Kane* followed its tragic premises to their logical, gloomy end. Even more disturbing for Hollywood was the enmity the film produced in the press, particularly in the Hearst chain. William Randolph Hearst saw obvious and infuriating parallels between himself and Charles Foster Kane; between Susan Alexander and his own artistic protégée, Marion Davies; between Kane's Florida castle, Xanadu, and his own California castle, San Simeon. The pressures of the Hearst press—refusing advertisements for the film, pressuring theatres that showed it with threats not to print any future ads or notices—and the film's unspectacular showing at the box office led RKO to deny Welles total artistic control over his next project, an adaptation of Booth Tarkington's *The Magnificent Ambersons.* From then on, his life and career became a struggle to make films and have them released intact—which they virtually never were.

The Magnificent Ambersons (1942) might have been as great as *Kane* if Welles had not left the country—after he and Robert Wise, who also edited *Kane,* had assembled a rough cut—to shoot the ill-fated documentary *It's All True.* With the help of the cutting instructions Welles cabled from South America, Wise presented RKO with a lengthy masterpiece that flopped with preview audiences. Some new scenes were shot and old ones rearranged, disastrously wrapping up the film's last hour in a few rushed minutes. Like *Greed,* the complete *Ambersons* has proved impossible to restore, but what remains is extraordinary.

Fig. 11-53
The Magnificent Ambersons: *Agnes Moorehead and Tim Holt on the grand staircase.*

Its story of a vain, selfish brat (Tim Holt as George Amberson Minafer) who finally gets his "come-uppance" and sees the world more clearly once he has been brought down a peg allowed Welles to tell the larger, more nostalgic story of the old ways—incarnated in the rich, graceful, high-society Amberson family—that perished with the coming of the automobile. It was a movie designed for the moving camera (manned by Stanley Cortez, whom Welles taught what Gregg Toland had taught him); the great staircase in the Amberson mansion was built to facilitate the phenomenally varied use of a crane. As in *Kane*, scene elements moved fluidly from one to the other through changes of camera angle and composition, not with the

Fig. 11-54

The Lady from Shanghai: *Orson Welles and Rita Hayworth prove that love has many angles.*

previously obligatory cuts. Figures moved in and out of shadow, as if into their own ominous or unknown depths, as the camera kept pace with the action or stopped for an intense slow look. The superb cast included Dolores Costello, Joseph Cotten, and—in the performance of a lifetime—Agnes Moorehead.

Even without a Hearst seeking its destruction, the abridged version of *The Magnificent Ambersons* opened to dismal business. RKO relieved Welles of his duties on his next film, *Journey Into Fear,* in the middle of production.

Later Welles films—*The Stranger* (1946), *The Lady from Shanghai* (1946, released 1948), *Macbeth* (1948), *Othello* (1952), *Mr. Arkadin* (1955), *Touch of Evil* (1958), *The Trial* (1962), and *Chimes at Midnight* (1966, also known as

Falstaff)—are, like *Citizen Kane,* obsessed with the themes of the corrupting influence of power and money, with treachery and desire, with guesswork in a labyrinth, with egotism and gamesmanship, with the dark side of greatness and the limits of ambition and friendship. These later films also reveal unmistakable traces of Welles's visual style, regardless of their cinematographers: baroque, back-lit contrasts of dark and light; claustrophobic interiors whose ceilings squash their occupants; a seemingly infinite depth-of-field, often surveyed from a very low angle; and magnificently planned, complexly choreographed tracking shots.

The opening shot of *Touch of Evil*—the last true *film noir*—which begins with the close-up setting of a time-bomb, travels high above the streets of Tijuana, and concludes, over three minutes later, with medium-shot reactions to the explosion, is one of the most complicated and impressive crane shots in cinema history. But the studio ran the opening credits over it. The climactic shootout in *The Lady from Shanghai,* as Everett Sloane and Rita Hayworth shoot repeatedly at each other's reflections in a house of mirrors, is one of the most memorable metaphors of cinematic death, translated into the shattering crash of glass and the annihilation of visual images.

Until his death in 1985, Welles was forced to contend with inadequate budgets and production schedules. He acted to make money to make films. Like Griffith and Gance and von Stroheim before him, he was a great artist rejected by the industry. Like Kane, he left many things unfinished. But even when the script, the budget, the other actors, or his own conception let him down, a Welles film never looked like anything other than a Welles film.

Fig. C-1

Fig. C-2

Fig. C-3

Coloring of black-and-white silent films. Fig. C-1: Edison's **Annabelle Dances;** *swirls of motion and hand-painted color. Fig. C-2: Méliès's* **Paris to Monte Carlo;** *the hand-painted automobile is always red. Fig. C-3: Porter's* **The Great Train Robbery;** *the dude dances to a volley of hand-painted golden gunfire. Fig. C-4: Griffith's* **Intolerance;** *worshipping the fiery red Ishtar in a tinted and toned frame. Fig. C-5:* **Intolerance;** *in this blue-toned frame, mashed to create a wide-screen image, the invading hordes rush toward Babylon.*

Fig. C-4

Fig. C-5

Fig. C-6

The Technicolor musical. Cyd Charisse with Gene Kelly in Singin' in the Rain *(Fig. C-6)* and with reflections of herself in the "Girl Hunt Ballet" from The Band Wagon *(Fig. C-7)*. Fig. C-8: "You Were Meant For Me" —stylized unreality in Singin' in the Rain, *with Gene Kelly and Debbie Reynolds as abstract shapes of magenta light against an artificial sky.*

Fig. C-7

Fig. C-8

Fig. C-9

Fig. C-10

The Technicolor musical — An American in Paris: the ballet. Gene Kelly tempted by seductive Furies (Fig. C-9), hoofing with GI buddies (Fig. C-10), alone with Leslie Caron in misty silhouette (Fig. C-11), and among Manet flower stalls (Fig. C-12).

Fig. C-11

Fig. C-12

Fig. C-13

*Outdoor and indoor
cinematography. Fig. C-13:*
McCabe and Mrs. Miller, *shot
by Vilmos Zsigmond. McCabe
(Warren Beatty) tracking his
enemies in the wet and icy
outdoors. Fig. C-14:* The
Godfather, *shot by Gordon
Willis. Don Vito Corleone
(Marlon Brando) transacting
his business in the indoor cave of
his office.*

Fig. C-14

Fig. C-15

Sight gags and subtle politics. Fig. C-15: Eyes as windows in Jacques Tati's Mon oncle (My Uncle); *relatives peer from their suburban home at M. Hulot's noisy disruptions in the darkness. Fig. C-16:* Do The Right Thing; *Da Mayor (Ossie Davis) offers flowers to Mother Sister (Ruby Dee). Whereas Hollywood used to maintain that black actors could not be photographed well, using that as one excuse to keep them out of leading roles, this frame with its painted building offers one of many color compositions designed to show that black is beautiful; note the use of starch-white and rose-red, here and in Fig. C-14, to organize the color schemes.*

Fig. C-16

Fig. C-17

Fig. C-18

Fig. C-19

Fig. C-20

*The color system of **Red Desert**. Giulia (Monica Vitti) in the drab, imprisoning environment of contemporary reality (Fig. C-17); Giulia and Corrado (Richard Harris) in the sexual atmosphere of the red-walled shack (Fig. C-18); rocks like flesh in the brilliant sunshine (Fig. C-19); the hotel room gone pink after sexual consummation (Fig. C-20).*

Fig. C-21

Bold colors in the darkness. Red, white, and blue star-spangled horror in Brian De Palma's Carrie *(Fig. C-21); Sissy Spacek as the prom queen covered with blood and coming into her witchlike powers. Fig. C-22: David Lynch's* Blue Velvet; *Dennis Hopper as the murderous pervert, sucking an unidentified gas and striking Isabella Rossellini for looking at him, while light and color create a seductive, intimate mood.*

Fig. C-22

Fig. C-23

Wide-screen cinematography: Lawrence of Arabia. *Fig. C-23: an extreme long shot. Fig. C-24: a close shot; Peter O'Toole as T. E. Lawrence. Directed by David Lean,* Lawrence *was shot in Technicolor on 65mm stock by Frederick A. Young; Figs. C-23, C-24, C-25, C-26, and C-27 were made directly from an original 70mm print (the extra 5mm allowed room for the soundtrack).*

Fig. C-24

Fig. C-25

Camera movement and composition for the wide screen: the attack on
Aqaba. Figs. C-25 and C-26 are from the beginning and end of a single
sequence. In Fig. C-25, the heroes begin their charge toward screen right,
filling the huge screen wth movement. Fig. C-26 is the end of a shot in
which the camera pans right to follow the invaders (seen in extreme long
shot) as they ride into and through the city, all the way to the gun. The
gun makes attack from the sea—that is, from screen right—impossible;
this brilliant view of the gun and coast is composed both laterally and in
depth—as well as in relation to the rightward camera movement.

Fig. C-26

Fig. C-27

*Depth of field and the wide screen. While the preceding frames from
Lawrence of Arabia (notably Fig. C-26) have a broad depth of field, the
depth of field in Fig. C-27 is shallow: The statue in the central
background, though only a few feet behind O'Toole and the match, is out
of focus. The meticulously composed image from 2001: A Space Odyssey
(Fig. C-28) is in focus from foreground to background, drawing our
attention to the set and props as well as to the astronaut (Keir Dullea).*

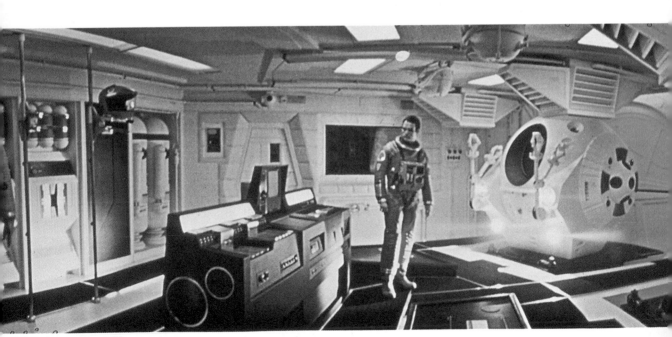

Fig. C-28

Fig. C-29

Anything goes! Fig. C-29: **Indiana Jones and the Temple of Doom** *opens with the classic American tune "Anything Goes"—sung in Chinese; the color is as flashy, controlled, and outrageous as everything else in this number. Fig. C-30:* **WarGames** *presents the War Room as the ultimate video arcade.*

Fig. C-30

Fig. C-31

Disney color animation. Fig. C-31: The Three Little Pigs. The Big Bad Wolf huffs and puffs until he turns purple in the face. Fig. C-32: Fantasia. The sorcerer's apprentice, afloat in the darkness on a flood of his own making, searches desperately in the sorcerer's book for a solution.

Fig. C-32

Fig. C-33

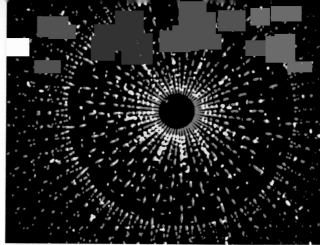

Fig. C-34

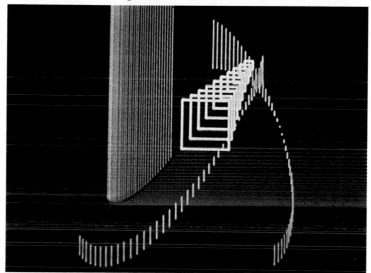

Fig. C-35

Abstract color animation.
Fig. C-33: Oskar Fischinger's
Allegretto. Fig. C-34: Jordan
Belson's Allures. Fig. C-35: John
Whitney's computerized Matrix.
Fig. C-36: Norman McLaren's
Begone Dull Care — painted,
scratched, and drawn directly on
celluloid.

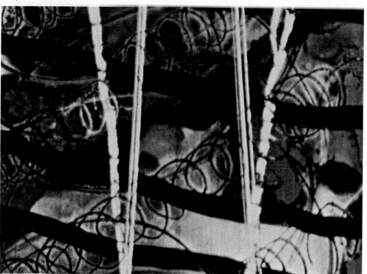

Fig. C-36

Fig. C-37

Fig. C-38

Fig. C-39

*Experimental color films.
Fig. C-37: a real fern in Stan
Brakhage's* Mothlight. *Fig. C-38:
three consecutive frames from
Robert Breer's* Blazes. *Fig. C-39:
Kenneth Anger's* Scorpio Rising
*—the biker's sensuous dream
image. Fig. C-40: using color,
light, and focal length to alter
the same space in Michael Snow's*
Wavelength.

Fig. C-40

Fig. C-41

Painting and film. Fig. C-41: Stan Brakhage's existence is song, painted directly on Imax film. Fig. C-42: the energy of painting, captured in this frame from Life Lessons, *Martin Scorsese's contribution to* New York Stories.

Fig. C-42

12

Hollywood in Transition: 1946–1965

In 1946 the American film business grossed $1.7 billion domestically, the peak box-office year in the fifty-year history of the American film industry. Twelve years later, in 1958, domestic box-office receipts fell below a billion dollars; by 1962 domestic receipts had fallen to $900 million, slightly more than half the 1946 gross. And inflated ticket prices hid an even more devastating statistic: By 1953, weekly attendance at film theatres had fallen to about 25 percent of the 1948 figure. While box-office income steadily fell, production costs — unionized labor, new equipment, costly materials — steadily rose along with the nation's soaring, inflated economy. The two vectors of rising costs and falling revenues seemed to point directly toward the cemetery for both Hollywood and the commercial American film. And there were no government bailouts for the film industry, as there would be for a shrinking automobile industry of the late 1970s.

Yet in 1968, theatre box offices collected $1.3 billion (domestic box-office receipts having risen every year since 1963). In 1974 American theatres grossed almost $2 billion. By 1979 domestic box-office grosses neared

$2.5 billion, and by 1983 were well over $3 billion. In 1989 they exceeded $5 billion for the first time. The figures indicate that the American film industry emerged from a difficult transitional period and solidified itself commercially by redefining its product and its audience. Between 1948 and 1963 lay fifteen years of groping.

Even before World War II, the two forces that would crush the old Hollywood had begun their assault. First, United States courts had begun to rule that the film industry's methods of distributing motion pictures represented an illegal restraint of open trade. Block booking was unfair to the individual competitive exhibitors, requiring them to book many pictures they did not want in order to get the few they did. Over the course of the 1920s and 1930s, the general tendency of American judicial and legislative pressure was to reduce the number of films the independent exhibitor could be forced to buy as a block. The studio-owned chains of theatres gave even greater monopolistic control of the market to the "Majors," the five biggest Hollywood production companies, who could use their commercial and artistic power to control the industry's profits and practices. The industry knew that the day would come when the line that tied theatre to studio would have to be cut. The war postponed that day.

Second, by the mid-1930s a new electronic toy that combined picture and sound—television—had been demonstrated by its scientist creators. At first Hollywood laughed at the silly toy whose programs—like those of its parent, radio—were both live and free; by the late 1940s, Hollywood had begun to fight. In 1949, there were only a million television receivers in America. By 1952, there were ten million; by the end of the decade, fifty million, and Hollywood had surrendered.

The World War helped postpone the domestic battle because fighting America needed movies to take its mind off the war. Both soldiers overseas and their families at home needed to escape to the movies. America also needed films for education: to train the soldiers to do their jobs, to teach them "why we fight," to give both information and encouragement to the folks at home who wondered how the fight was going and whether the fight was worth it. Hollywood sent many of its best directors—Frank Capra, William Wyler, George Stevens, Fred Zinnemann, John Huston, John Ford, Garson Kanin—to make documentary films for the government and the armed forces. Hollywood also sent 16mm prints of its newest releases for distribution—without charge—to the fighting men at thousands of "Beachhead Bijoux."

While Hollywood did its part, its profits conveniently rose. The government added special war taxes to theatre tickets and sold bonds in the lobby; Americans who went to the movies not only enjoyed themselves but patriotically contributed to the war effort. Many Hollywood writers, directors, and producers took new pride in the educational and documentary projects. Frank Capra's *Why We Fight* series (1942–44), Ford's *The Battle of Midway* (1942), Wyler's *The Memphis Belle* (1944), Huston's *The Battle of San Pietro* (1945) and *Let There Be Light* (1946), and Disney's *Victory Through Air Power* (1943) were among the most powerful wartime documentaries.

Even fictional feature films of wartime battles borrowed the visual styles of documentary

authenticity: Delmer Daves's *Destination Tokyo* (1943), Howard Hawks's *Air Force* (1943), Lewis Milestone's *A Walk in the Sun* (1945), William Wellman's *The Story of G. I. Joe* (1945). It was almost obligatory in these war films that an American fighting platoon was composed of one Italian from Hackensack, one WASP mainliner from Philadelphia, one Jew from Brooklyn, one farmboy from Kansas, one Irish-Catholic from Boston, one Pole from Chicago—a mythical cross section of America, pulling together to win the "big one." Not until Wellman's *Battleground* and Mark Robson's *Home of the Brave* (both 1949) did a black soldier join that cross section.

The government's Office of War Information established a Bureau of Motion Picture Affairs, while Hollywood responded with its War Activities Committee. After the war, the relationship between the industry and the government would not be so cozy.

The Supreme Court's 1948 decision in *U.S. v. Paramount Pictures, Inc.* was the ultimate in a lengthy series of court rulings that the studios must sell ("divest" themselves of) their theatres. The guaranteed outlet for the studio's product—good, bad, or mediocre—was closed. Each film would have to be good enough to sell itself. Meanwhile, more and more Americans bought television sets. Special events like the 1948 Rose Bowl game and parade and the 1948 political conventions, or regular ones, like Milton Berle, "Uncle Miltie," on the *Texaco Star Theatre* every Tuesday night at eight, kept Americans looking at the box in their living rooms or, more likely at first, in the living rooms of their neighbors. The movies declared war on the box. Until 1956, no Hollywood film could be shown on television; no working film star could appear on a television program. So Americans stayed home to watch British movies on the box and the new stars that television itself developed.

These specific legal and commercial woes were accompanied by a general shift of American mood in the years following the war that also contributed to the ills of a troubled industry. The Cold War years of suspicion—dislike of foreign entanglements in general and the increasing fear of the "Red Menace" in particular—also produced a distrust of certain institutions within the United States. Because the film industry was so active in the war effort against the Nazis, because so many Hollywood producers and screenwriters were Jewish, because so many Jewish intellectuals seemed sympathetic to liberal political positions, and because the most extreme right-wing American opinion saw the entire war as a sacrifice of American lives to save the Jews in German concentration camps and help the Soviets defend the Eastern front, it was not surprising that these rivers of reaction coalesced into an attack on the motion picture industry as a whole. Whereas for four decades American suspicion had concentrated on Hollywood's sexual and moral excesses, in the decade following the war distrust shifted to Hollywood's political and social positions: to the subversive, pro-Communist propaganda allegedly woven into Hollywood's entertainment films.

The first set of hearings of the House Committee on Un-American Activities (pejoratively referred to as the House Un-American Activities Committee, or HUAC) in 1947, investigating Communist infiltration of the motion picture industry, produced the highly publicized national scandal of the "Hollywood Ten." Ten screenwriters, directors, and producers, who had been accused of Communist leanings — among them, screenwriters Dalton Trumbo, Ring Lardner, Jr., and John Howard Lawson (former president of the Screen Writers' Guild), and director Edward Dmytryk — attacked the committee itself as an unconstitutional violation of America's first-amendment guarantees of freedom of speech. The Ten were sentenced to a year in prison for contempt of Congress, and the motion picture industry reacted fearfully by instituting a blacklist — no known or suspected Communist or Communist sympathizer would be permitted to work in any capacity on a Hollywood film.

The second set of Congressional hearings (1951–52) gave witnesses two choices. If they admitted a previous membership in the Communist Party, they were obligated to name everyone else with whom they had been associated at that time or suffer a contempt of Congress sentence as had the Hollywood Ten. The other choice was to avoid answering any questions whatever on the basis of the Consti-

tution's fifth-amendment guarantee against self-incrimination. Although "taking the Fifth" kept the witness out of prison, it also kept the witness out of work — thanks to the industry's blacklist. The result of these hearings — and the controversial blacklist, the damaging publicity in the press, the threats of boycott against Hollywood films by the American Legion, the lists of suspected Communists or Communist sympathizers in publications such as *Red Channels* — was an even greater weakening of the industry's crumbling commercial and social strength.

The biggest, richest studios were hit the hardest. Two former assets suddenly became liabilities: property and people. In 1949, MGM declared wage cutbacks and immense layoffs. The giant studio's rows of sound stages and acres of outdoor sets became increasingly empty; the huge film factories now owned vast expanses of expensive and barren land. Even more costly than land were the contracts with people — technicians, featured players, and stars — that required the studio to pay their salaries although it had no pictures for them to make. MGM allowed the contracts of its greatest stars, formerly the studio's richest commercial resource, to lapse. Every big studio extricated itself from the tangle of its obligations with financially disastrous slowness. A minor studio like Columbia, with very few stars under contract, a small lot, and no theatres, stayed healthier in those years of thinner profits. Columbia also showed foresight by being the first film studio to establish a television-producing division, Screen Gems, in 1951, when television was still an infant. The big movie houses suffered with the big studios. On a week night, only a few hundred patrons scattered themselves about a house built for three thousand. One by one the ornate palaces came down, to be replaced by supermarkets, shopping centers, and high-rise apartment buildings.

Television was not the sole cause of the film industry's commercial decay. The American demographic shift from the cities to the suburbs began just after the war. Movie theatres had always been concentrated in the city centers, and the multiplex cinemas of suburban shopping malls were two decades away. There were also many new ways to spend leisure time and the leisure dollar. Professional and collegiate sports events, stimulated by television exposure, drew increasingly larger audiences. Golf, tennis, and skiing attracted more middle-class enthusiasts than ever before—not only taking them away from movie theatres, but taking plenty of their dollars for clothing, equipment, and travel. The DC-6 and DC-7 airliners and, by 1960, DC-8 and 707 jets made long-distance travel more accessible and affordable. The 33⅓ RPM, long-playing microgroove phonograph disk made its debut in 1948; first hi-fidelity, then stereo music systems became household necessities within the next decade. A booming music industry ate into former movie dollars as voraciously as television did.

By 1952 Hollywood knew that television could not be throttled. If films and television were to coexist, the movies would have to give the public what TV did not. The most obvious difference between movies and TV was the size of the screen. Television's visual thinking was necessarily in inches whereas movies could compose in feet and yards. Films also enjoyed the advantage of over fifty years of technological research in color, properties of lenses, and special laboratory effects; the infant television art had not yet developed color or videotape. Hollywood's two primary weapons against television were to be size and technical gimmickry.

One of the industry's first sallies was 3-D, a three-dimensional, stereoscopic effect produced by shooting the action with two lenses simultaneously at a specified distance apart. Two interlocked projectors then threw the two perspectives on a single screen simultaneously, the audience using cardboard or plastic Polaroid glasses (with red and blue lenses for black-and-white films, polarized clear lenses for color films) to meld the two images into a single three-dimensional one. The idea was not new; even before the twentieth century, a viewer could see a three-dimensional version of a still photograph by looking at two related photos through a stereopticon. A popular American commercial toy, the Viewmaster, uses the same principle of fusing two pictures to present a single three-dimensional scenic view. Kodak had been marketing "stereo" still cameras since 1901, and Edwin S. Porter and William E. Waddell had presented the first 3-D movie

(non-narrative scenes of New York and New Jersey) in 1915. Abel Gance had even shot a 3-D roll for *Napoléon* in 1927, but decided not to use it.

Despite the familiarity of the stereoscopic principle, to see it in a full-length, active feature film was a great novelty. The first 3-D feature was Harry K. Fairall's *The Power of Love* (U.S., 1922); Russia released its first 3-D film, *Day Off in Moscow,* in 1940. Hollywood rushed into 3-D production in 1952 with Arch Oboler's *Bwana Devil,* which was followed by pictures like *House of Wax, It Came From Outer Space, Fort Ti, Kiss Me Kate,* and *I, the Jury* (all 1953); *Creature from the Black Lagoon, The French Line, Gog,* and *Taza, Son of Cochise* (all 1954); and finally, *Revenge of the Creature* (1955). Audiences eagerly left their television sets to experience the gimmick that attacked them with knives, arrows, avalanches, stampedes, vats of chemicals, Ann Miller's tap shoes, and Jane Russell's bust; the thrill of 3-D was that the formerly confined, flat picture convincingly threatened to leap, fly, or flow out of its frame at the audience.

Some blame the death of 3-D on the headache-inducing glasses that it required, but the more obvious cause of death was that any pure novelty, like the earliest filmstrips, becomes boring when it is no longer novel. 3-D was pure novelty; the thrill of being run over by a train is visually identical to that of being run over by a herd of cattle. Further, because 3-D required the theatre owner to make costly additions and renovations to the equipment, the exhibitors declared a war of neglect against the process and hastened its demise. Business for 3-D films fell off so quickly that Alfred Hitchcock, who had shot *Dial M for Murder* (1954) in the new process, released it in the conventional two dimensions. Among the later attempts to revive 3-D have been a few "sex-ploitation" films (for example, *Kiss My Analyst* or *The Stewardesses*) that promised especially titillating sequences for those who visited the "skin houses." Paul Morrissey's 3-D version of *Andy Warhol's Frankenstein* (1974) reduced the possibilities to three effects: the horrific, the pornographic, and the "camp." Nevertheless, in the 1980s a single-projector 3-D system, with improved resolution and simplified installation,

Fig. 12-1
Hollywood executives watch 3-D dailies in 1952 behind glasses both Polaroid and rose-colored.

gave audiences everything from *Friday the 13th Part 3* (Steve Miner, 1982) to the 3-D release of *Dial M for Murder*.

A second movie novelty also promised thrills. Cinerama, unlike 3-D, dazzled its patrons by bringing the audience into the picture, rather than the picture into the audience. Cinerama originally used three interlocked cameras and four interlocked projectors (one for stereophonic sound). The final prints were not projected on top of one another (superimposed, as in 3-D), but side by side. The result was an immense wrap-around screen that was really three screens. The wide, deeply curved screen and the relative positions of the three cameras worked on the eye's peripheral vision to make the mind believe that the body was actually in motion. The difference between a ride in an automobile and a conventionally filmed ride is that in an automobile the world also

moves past on the sides, not just straight ahead. Cinerama's huge triple screen duplicated this impression of peripheral movement.

Like 3-D, the idea was not new. As early as the Paris World's Exposition of 1900, the energetic inventor-cinematographers had begun displaying wraparound and multi-screen film processes. (Multi-screen experiments have long been popular at world fairs, for example, the New York fair of 1963–1964 and Expo '67 in Montreal.) As early as 1927, Abel Gance had also incorporated triple-screen effects, both panoramic and triptych, into his *Napoléon*. In 1938, Fred Waller, Cinerama's inventor, began research on the process. But when *This Is Cinerama* opened in 1952, audiences choked — quite literally — with a film novelty that sent them racing down a roller coaster track and soaring over the Rocky Mountains. A magnificent six-track (in later Cinerama films, seven-

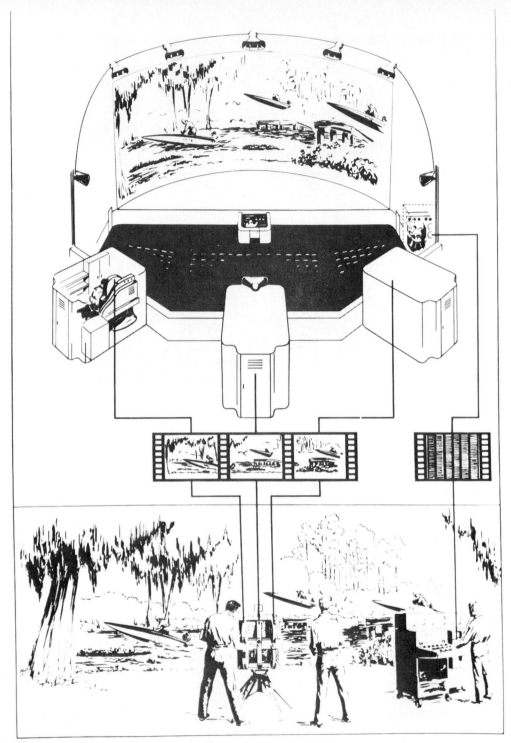

Fig. 12-2
A contemporary diagram of Cinerama: the widest of screens broken into three frames with six-track stereo sound.

track) stereophonic sound system accompanied the galloping pictures; sounds could travel from left to right across the screen or jump from behind the screen to behind the audience's heads.

For all its gimmicky newness, *This Is Cinerama* was aware of its roots in film history. The immense color image unfolded only after a small-screen, black-and-white display of *The Great Train Robbery*, America's first great box-office smash. Co-produced by Merian C. Cooper and the great showman Mike Todd, and partly directed by Ernest B. Schoedsack (Cooper and Schoedsack made both documentaries like *Grass*, 1925, and spectacular fictions like *King Kong*, 1933), *This Is Cinerama* had one foot in show business and the other in documentary filming.

Cinerama remained commercially viable longer than 3-D because it was more carefully marketed. Because of the complex projection machinery, only a few theatres in major cities were equipped for the process. Seeing Cinerama became a special, exciting event; the film was sold as a "road-show" attraction with reserved seats, noncontinuous performances, and high prices. Customers returned to Cinerama because they could see a Cinerama film so infrequently. (The second, *Cinerama Holiday*, came out three years after *This Is Cinerama*.) And although Cinerama repeatedly offered its predictable postcard scenery and its obligatory rides and chases, the films were stunning travelogues.

Cinerama faced new troubles when it too tried to combine its gimmick with narrative: *The Wonderful World of the Brothers Grimm* (1962), *It's a Mad Mad Mad Mad World* (1963), *How the West Was Won* (1963). As with 3-D, what Aristotle called "Spectacle" (he found it the least important dramatic element) overwhelmed the more essential dramatic ingredients of plot, character, and ideas. In 1968, Stanley Kubrick's *2001, A Space Odyssey* subordinated a modified Cinerama (shot with a single camera but projected on a Cinerama screen) to the film's sociological and metaphysical journey, letting the big screen and racing camera work for the story rather than letting the story work for the effects. Despite the artistic and commercial success of *2001*, Cinerama is now even deader than 3-D, partially because the mid-1970s combination of 70mm film and Panavision lenses (which Kubrick also used), enhanced by Dolby Stereo soundtracks, comes close to reproducing the immense sights and sounds of Cinerama without the clumsy multi-machine methods of the earlier process. In 1952 the gimmick successfully pulled Americans away from the small screen at home, but not enough of them at once to offer the film industry any real commercial salvation.

A third gimmick of the early 1950s also took advantage of the size of the movie screen. The new format, christened CinemaScope, was the most durable and functional of them all, requiring neither special projectors, special film, nor special optical glasses (this lack of special equipment especially pleased the theatre owners). The action was recorded by a single, conventional movie camera on conventional 35mm film. A special anamorphic lens squeezed the images horizontally to fit the width of the standard film. When projected with a corresponding anamorphic lens on the projector, the distortions disappeared and a huge, wide image stretched across the curved theatre screen. Once again the "novelty" was not new. As early as 1928, a French scientist named Henri Chrétien had experimented with an anamorphic lens for the motion picture camera; in 1952, the executives of Twentieth Century-Fox visited Professor Chrétien, then retired to a Riviera villa, and bought the rights to his anamorphic process. The first CinemaScope feature, Henry Koster's *The Robe* (1953), convinced both Fox and the industry that the process was a sound one. The screen had been made wide with a minimum of trouble and expense. A parade of screen-widening "scopes" and "visions" followed Fox's CinemaScope, some of them using an anamorphic lens, one nonanamorphic process (VistaVision) printing the image sideways on the celluloid strip, and some of them achieving screen width by widening the film to 55mm, 65mm, or 70mm, notably Todd-AO, MGM Camera 65, CinemaScope 55, Super Panavision 70, and Ultra Panavision 70. The first 70mm film of the 1950s was *Oklahoma!* (1955, directed by Fred Zinnemann and shot in Todd-AO).

Ultimately it was size and grandeur that triumphed, not depth perception or motion effects. As early as 1930, Eisenstein advocated a flexible screen size, a principle he called the "dynamic square." He reasoned that the conventional screen, with its four-to-three ratio of width to height (an aspect ratio of 4:3, or 1.33:1), was too inflexible. The screen, he reasoned, should be capable of becoming very wide for certain sequences, narrow and long for others, a perfect square for balanced compositions. But Eisenstein's principles were much closer to Griffith's use of masking or irising than to the wide screen's inflexible commitment to width. George Stevens complained that CinemaScope made photographing a python more appropriate than a person. How could a horizontal picture frame, with a five-to-two ratio of width to height, enclose a vertical subject?

Despite these complaints, which echoed those about synchronized sound in the late 1920s, some directors came to clever terms with the new frame format right away. In the wide-screen musical *It's Always Fair Weather* (1955), directors Gene Kelly and Stanley Donen could make a little in-group joke. When Dan Dailey retires to a telephone booth, a sign informs us that a call to California costs only **$2.50** for **1** minute, with the numbers in boldface. That ratio of 2.5 to 1 was merely the CinemaScope format of this very film, made in California. (The actual aspect ratio of this and other early CinemaScope films was 2.55 to 1. CinemaScope later changed to 2.35:1, which is also the aspect ratio of the current 35mm anamorphic format, Panavision.)

The film also demonstrates that the familiar American object most like a CinemaScope frame is a dollar bill. The plot of *It's Always Fair Weather* rips a dollar bill into three pieces, one for each of three American GIs, to remind them of their reunion ten years later. In the same way, Kelly and Donen repeatedly rip the CinemaScope frame into three compositional pieces, one for each of the buddies. The movie industry hoped it would rake in plenty of dollar bills from this frame that resembled a dollar bill.

Like sound in the early years, the new technological invention was a mixed blessing, adding some new film possibilities and destroying many of the old compositional virtues. What many critics of the wide screen did not perceive at the time was that just as deep focus permitted contrapuntal relationships between near and far within the frame (as in Renoir's films or *Citizen Kane*), the wide screen permitted contrapuntal relationships between left, center, and right.

George Cukor's *A Star Is Born* (1954), a great remake of Wellman's great 1937 melodrama, provides powerful proof of this potential. Cukor, who always planted subtle information by balancing the composition of his frames, now had a large, new frame to balance. Two sequences demonstrate not only Cukor's mastery of the format but also his awareness of its history and value. In one scene, Oliver Niles (Charles Bickford), the head of the studio, fires the aging matinee idol, Norman Main (James Mason). Main's popularity has been slipping and the studio itself has been slumping. The cause? Television. During this conversation, the men stand between two flickering black-and-white images on the far left and right edges of the frame. To the far left is a television set; Niles has been watching the fights on TV (even a studio head cannot stay away from a TV screen). To the far right of the frame is a motion picture, projected in the next room for Main's party guests. The discussion between Main and Niles takes place precisely between a video image and a film image—a visual translation of the historical crossroads where all the studio heads and studio stars found themselves in 1954.

Cukor uses television again in the film's Academy Award ceremony. While Cukor shoots Vicky Lester's (Judy Garland) triumph with the CinemaScope lens in medium long shot, a tiny television monitor in the upper-right-hand corner of the frame displays the moment in typical television close-ups. The shot is simultaneously a long shot and a close-up, a wide-screen color image and a small-screen black-and-white TV image, a revelation of CinemaScope's visual power and television's cultural power, capable of bringing this moment, "live," into people's homes in close-ups.

The wide CinemaScope frame enabled Cukor to shoot whole sequences, like Garland's entire rendition of "The Man That Got

Composition for the wide screen in It's Always Fair Weather. *Fig. 12-3: tearing the CinemaScope frame into three parts of a dollar bill (center to right: Gene Kelly, Michael Kidd, and Dan Dailey, with David Burns behind the bar). Figs. 12-4, 12-5: Each buddy gets a third of the screen.*

Fig. 12-3

Fig. 12-4

Fig. 12-5

Fig. 12-6

Fig. 12-7
Composition for the wide screen in A Star Is Born. Fig. 12-6: Judy Garland surrounded by jazz musicians for "The Man That Got Away"; primary interest at center. Fig. 12-7: Garland, with Jack Carson, surrounded by the photographic faces of stardom; primary interest at the sides, in a CinemaScope approach to the two-shot.

Away," in a continuous, complexly choreographed shot without a cut. (Of course, Welles and Toland had done that with the standard frame in *Citizen Kane*.) In the work of Cukor, Donen, Ophüls, Preminger, and others, the 1950s saw an explosion of interest in the uses of the wide screen, an interest that remained evident in the 1960s works of such directors as Lean, Kurosawa, Leone, Peckinpah, Kubrick, and Godard. The majority of later "scope" films use the frame more conservatively (now that broadcast, cable, and video sales contribute significantly to the financing of most movies, and since most films are not letterboxed when shown on TV), making sure the compositions are "TV-safe," aware of the cropped television fate of any wide-screen image that uses the entire canvas.

The wide screen, like sound, became an inescapable fact of film life, and the artists eventually came to terms with it. By the mid-1960s the wide-screen revolution was as complete as the sound revolution of the late 1920s, and the wide screen, like sound, would become the basis of a new generation's film aesthetics.

The battle with television was partially responsible for another technical revolution in the 1950s—the almost total conversion to color. From the earliest days of moving pictures, inventors and filmmakers sought to combine color with recorded movement. The early Méliès films were hand-painted frame by frame. Most silent films (Griffith's, Lubitsch's, and Gance's most notably) were bathed in color tints, adding a cast of pale blue for night sequences, sepia for interior or daylit scenes, a red tint for certain effects, a green tint for others. Such coloring effects were obviously tonal, like the accompanying music, rather than an intrinsic part of the film's photographic conception. As early as 1908, Charles Urban patented a color photographic process, which he called Kinemacolor. But business opposition from the then-powerful Film Trust kept Kinemacolor off American screens.

In 1917, the Technicolor Corporation was founded in the United States. Supported by all the major studios, Technicolor enjoyed monopolistic control over all color experimentation and shooting in this country. Douglas

Fairbanks's *The Black Pirate* (1926) and the musicals *Rio Rita* (1929) and *Whoopee!* (1930) used the early Technicolor process, which added a garish grandeur to the costumes and scenery. In the 1920s Technicolor was, like Urban's Kinemacolor, a two-color process: two strips of film exposed by two separate lenses, one strip recording the blue-green colors of the spectrum, the other sensitive to the red-orange colors, then bonded together in the final processing. But by 1933 Technicolor had perfected a more accurate three-color process: three strips of black-and-white film, one exposed through a filter to cyan, the second to magenta, the third to yellow, originally requiring a bulky three-prism camera for the three rolls of film. The first two-strip Technicolor feature had been *The Toll of the Sea* (1922). The first film made in the three-strip process was Disney's cartoon *Flowers and Trees* (1932). RKO's *La Cucaracha* (1934) was the first three-strip Technicolor live action short, and Rouben Mamoulian's *Becky Sharp* (1935) the first three-strip Technicolor feature. Hollywood could have converted to color at almost the same time it converted to sound. But expenses and priorities dictated that most talkies use black-and-white film, which was, itself, becoming faster, subtler, more responsive to minimal light, easier to use under any conditions. Color was reserved for special novelty effects—for cartoons or lavish spectacles that needed the decoration of color and could afford the slowness and expense of color shooting (for example, Michael Curtiz's *The Adventures of Robin Hood*, 1938; Victor Fleming's *Gone With the Wind* and *The Wizard of Oz*, both 1939).

Before World War II, color was both a monopoly and a sacred mystery. Color negatives were processed and printed behind closed doors; special Technicolor consultants and cameramen were almost as important on the set of a color film as the director and producer. Natalie Kalmus, the ex-wife of Herbert Kalmus who invented the process, became Technicolor's artistic director and constructed an official aesthetic code for the use of color (she preferred mutedly harmonious color effects to discordantly jarring ones), a code as binding on a film's color values as was the Hays Code on its moral values. Until 1949, every film that used

Technicolor was required to hire Mrs. Kalmus as "Technicolor Consultant."

The war, which demanded that the film industry keep up production while tightening its belt, generally excluded the luxury of color filming. A notable English exception was Laurence Olivier's *Henry V,* in 1944, which evoked the color system of the Duc de Berry's *Trés riches heures,* and in which the splendid color intensified the film's propagandistic appeal to the Englishman's traditional sense of courage. Most wartime American color films also had propaganda value—Minnelli's *Meet Me in St. Louis* (1944), which depicted the homespun life and traditions that the boys were fighting to save; DeMille's *The Story of Dr. Wassel* (1944), a hymn to an American war hero.

After the war, Hollywood needed color to fight television, which—at least until the 1960s —could offer audiences only black-and-white. Technicolor, formerly without competitors, had kept costs up and production down. Hollywood began encouraging a new competing color process, Eastmancolor. The new process was one of the spoils of war, a pirated copy of the German Agfacolor monopack. The monopack color film bonded three color-sensitive emulsions onto a single roll of filmstock. A color film could be shot with an ordinary movie camera. Color emulsions became progressively faster, more sensitive, more flexible. A series of new color processes—DeLuxe, Metrocolor, Warnercolor—were all variations of Eastmancolor. What these monopack color processes gained over Technicolor in cheapness and flexibility they sacrificed in intensity and brilliance. (Technicolor's clean dyes were picked up and transferred directly onto the print by each of the three strips, but the Eastman dyes were *in* the stock and had to go through chemical processing in the lab.) So unstable and impermanent were their color dyes that Eastmancolor prints of the 1950s have already faded badly. Not until the development of the CRI (color reversal internegative) printing process of the 1970s—and Martin Scorsese's successful campaign of the 1980s for an Eastman stock that would hold its color values for at least 50 years —would monopack prints approach the clarity, brilliance, and permanence of three-strip 1940s and 1950s Technicolor.

During the 1950s black-and-white gradually became the exception, and color, even for serious dramas, little comedies, and low-budget westerns, became the rule. As the technology of color cinematography became more flexible, film artists learned, as they did with sound, that a new technique was not only a gimmick but also a way to fulfill essential dramatic and thematic functions.

Sound quality improved drastically after the Second World War, thanks to the introduction of magnetic tape (another of the spoils of war, invented in Nazi Germany). Until 1949, only optical film was used to record all film soundtracks. From the 1950s to the present, a release print might have a magnetic or an optical soundtrack, but magnetic tape and magnetic film (called "mag stock") are used for virtually all sound recording, editing, and mixing.

Although the movies fought TV by offering audiences audio-visual treats that television lacked, Hollywood finally capitulated to television by deciding to work with it rather than against it. If television would not die, then it would need old movies and filmed installments of a series to sustain its diet. Columbia Pictures, Walt Disney (*Disneyland*), Warner Bros., Twentieth Century-Fox, MGM, and Universal all began making 30- and 60-minute weekly shows—as well as commercials—for TV, while several new companies bought old film studios expressly to make television films: Revue bought the old Republic studio and Desilu the RKO studio. Hollywood also lifted its ban against films and film stars appearing on television. In 1956, Hollywood first sold its films to television, the sole provision being that the film had to have been produced before 1948. Since 1956, however, Hollywood has sold more and more recent films to the networks or cable stations; many of last year's movies appear on this year's television. In a sense, TV has replaced the old fourth- and fifth-run neighborhood movie houses, all of which had disappeared by 1965—much as the rentable videocassette has nearly wiped out the revival house.

The battle between the film and television industries was less a struggle between competing formats—film vs. video—or competing fare—movies vs. TV programs—than between competing methods of distribution. It was a struggle between the broadcast networks, which had evolved historically from 1920s electronic research and radio broadcasting, and the theatre chains, which had evolved from turn-of-the-century nickelodeons and theatre circuits. Television needed both film and films; it didn't need theatres.

The theatre owners, who had always held the largest share of power in the film industry (they collected the revenues), were hit hardest by a medium that could deliver entertainment directly to the home. Theatres countered by offering sights and sounds that television could not deliver. They still do. To see *Raiders of the Lost Ark* or *A Star Is Born* on television — whether broadcast or on cassette — is not really to see it at all. The brightness, the brilliance, the immensity, the complex composition, the fullness of sound in the movie theatre remain persuasive reasons to go there. Although the most gimmicky innovations of 1952–1953 have disappeared, the principle of supplying sights and sounds that television cannot has dominated the feature film industry ever since.

By 1956, the war with television was over, and although the armistice had clearly defined the movies' future relationship with its living-room audiences, the future with its audiences in theatres was still uncertain.

Films in the Transitional Era

With the collapse of the studio structure, the dictatorial head of production, and the quantitative demands of a large yearly output, producing films became similar to producing stageplays. Like the theatre producer, the new film producer concentrated on shaping and selling a single project at a time rather than a whole year's output of more than a dozen films. Like United Artists, David Selznick, and Samuel Goldwyn of earlier years, Hollywood feature-film production, even within the studios, had "gone independent." The more independent producer selected the property, the stars, and the director, raised the money, and supervised the selling of the finished film. Perhaps the production company rented space on a studio lot; perhaps it used the studio's distribution offices to help sell the film. But the producer, not the studio, made the picture. With no lot, no long-term contracts with stars, no staffs of

writers and technicians, the producer assembled a production company for a particular film, disbanded it when the film was finished, and assembled another for the next film.

Although independent production freed filmmakers from dictatorial studio heads, the new system had its own tyrannies. Veteran directors like Howard Hawks complained that he spent more time making deals than making movies. Now the director-producer handled all the petty problems — dickering to raise the money, compromising with bankers to get it — that a studio previously managed for him. And the large pool of expert studio craftsmen and technicians began to dry up — with fewer films to make and (since many were no longer full-time studio employees but were hired for one film at a time) no way to know when or whether they would make them.

The individual producers, forced to make each film pay for itself, searched for stable, predictable production values. One of the axioms they discovered was that the most dependable films were either very expensive or very cheap. A very expensive film could make back its investment with huge publicity campaigns and high ticket prices at road-show engagements. The theory translated itself into practice with big films like *The Robe, Oklahoma!, The Ten Commandments, The Bridge on the River Kwai, Ben-Hur,* and *Spartacus.* Even unpretentious directors of fast-paced action pictures like Howard Hawks and Nicholas Ray joined the parade of Colossal Spectacles (*Land of the Pharoahs,* 1955, and *King of Kings,* 1961, respectively). The Biblical-Historical dinosaurs disappeared after *Cleopatra* (1963) cost and lost more than any film ever had before.

But the 1950s were also the years of *I Was a Teenage Werewolf, I Was a Teenage Frankenstein, Hercules, Not of This Earth, Joy Ride,* and *Riot in Juvenile Prison.* American-International Pictures, the only new producing company to be founded in a decade of studio collapse, built itself entirely on low-budget films with topical teenage themes — horror, science fiction, rock and roll, juvenile delinquency, and beach parties — that could be shot in less than two weeks and budgeted at under $250,000. Joseph E. Levine built himself a commercial empire on Steve Reeves and a cast

Fig. 12-8
Moses (Charlton Heston) leads a cast of thousands out of Egypt in **The Ten Commandments.**

of Italians, films that were produced for under $150,000 in Italy and then dubbed into English. Roger Corman built his empire by teaming Vincent Price with Edgar Allan Poe. The very inexpensive film could make back its investment in two weeks of saturation booking at neighborhood theatres and, most of all, drive-ins, yet another 1950s innovation to pull teenagers out of their parents' living rooms. In an era of unstable business values the movies had become a lure for daring speculators, just as they had been before 1917.

For major productions, the studio and independent producer became dependent on popular novels, musicals, and plays, properties that had excited the public in other forms and might excite it again. American movies had been using the commercial power of a popular novel or play for forty years, ever since Kalem adapted *Ben-Hur* in 1907 and later paid $25,000 in damages for failing to obtain legal rights to the book. In 1920, D. W. Griffith paid $175,000 for the rights to the nineteenth-century stage melodrama *Way Down East,* and although no one had ever previously paid so much for a property, Griffith's investment was still a wise one. Throughout the studio years, both silent and talking, Hollywood adapted successful novels, from *The Four Horsemen of the Apocalypse* to *Gone With the Wind.* But the percentage of adaptations that attempted to reproduce a book faithfully in return for trading on the book's popularity was rather low. Studios employed dozens of writers either to invent totally original screenplays or to fashion almost original scripts loosely based on little known stories and plays.

If the period preceding World War II could be called the Age of the Original Scenario for screenwriters, the years following the war must be called the Age of the Adaptation. Lacking large, permanent staffs of screenwriters, both studio and independent producers bought established, already written properties that merely needed translating into film form: *The Caine Mutiny, Exodus, From Here to Eternity, Not as a Stranger, Tea and Sympathy, My Fair Lady, Sweet Bird of Youth,* and so forth. It was easier for a producer to raise money for a film that was considered "presold"; it was easier to sell one of these familiar properties back to the public after the film had been finished.

Because both fiction and the stage have traditionally remained freer of sexual and moral restrictions than films—the official codes for books and plays in America have been much looser and more informal, responsive to "Freedom of the Press"—it was inevitable that fresh breezes would blow from the original works into the screen adaptations of them. Because television applied even stricter moral regulations to its programs than the Production Code did to films, producers could lure audiences to the movie theatre with promises of franker, racier, "more adult" entertainment. Films adapted from novels like *Peyton Place, From Here to Eternity, Compulsion, Advise and Consent, Lolita,* and *Butterfield 8* could not possibly avoid references to adultery, fornication, or homosexuality, topics perfectly suited to Hollywood's audience war with television.

The war against the Code began officially in 1953 with Otto Preminger's decision to release *The Moon Is Blue* without the Code's seal of approval. Not only was Preminger's the first major American movie since 1934 (when the first was awarded) not to bear a seal; it also demonstrated the commercial and publicity value of not receiving a seal of moral approval. The war declared by Preminger would end in 1968 with the elimination of the 1930 Production Code (already modified in 1966) and the adoption of the more flexible system of rating the "maturity" of a film's content. During the fifteen years between 1953 and 1968, the strict moral principles of the Code repeatedly slid and bent, for in the search to find a lure that television lacked, the film industry seized upon sexual relationships and social criticism.

A landmark Supreme Court ruling, the so-called *Miracle* case of 1951 (formally, *Burstyn* v. *Wilson*) made these attacks on the Code easier. Not until 1951 did the Supreme Court declare that movies were part of the nation's "press," entitled to Constitutional guarantees of freedom of speech. A 1915 Supreme Court ruling *(Mutual Film Corp* v. *Ohio Industrial Commission)* had decided exactly the opposite—that movies were a novelty and amusement, conducted solely for profit, not "speech" at all. That ruling stood until a foreign "art film," *Ways of Love,* opened in New York in 1950. It was composed of three unrelated segments (one of which was Jean Renoir's *A Day in the Country,* made in 1936), the most important of which was Roberto Rossellini's *The Miracle,* starring Anna Magnani.

The story of a delirious peasant woman, seduced by a beggar, who believes she has been impregnated by St. Joseph, the film was condemned as sacrilegious by the archdiocese of New York and seized by New York's commissioner of police. After repeated losses in lower courts, Joseph Burstyn, the film's American distributor, took the case to the Supreme Court, which ruled that the term "sacrilegious" had no clear meaning and that films could no more be suppressed than any other forum for public debate. That it took a foreign "art film" to effect this important change in American law foreshadowed many other changes that "art films" would effect within the decade. Produced outside America and shown in little theatres whose owners were not members of the Motion Picture Association, these "art films" were never subject to the industry's Code.

The resulting sexual-social films of the transitional years were very different from the 1970s' "liberated" films. The sharp producer of the 1950s had merely found a clever way of injecting sexual tidbits and social questions into the old 1934 formulas for morality, motivation, and plotting. Otto Preminger and Stanley Kramer were particularly good at turning "explosive," "controversial" material into films that could offend almost no one.

Preminger, a Lubitsch protégé, had begun with ironic, unpretentious genre films at Twentieth Century-Fox (from *Laura* in 1944 to *River of No Return* in 1954) only to move toward more monumental, controversial, and socially conscious literary adaptations in the era of independent production. His *cause célèbre, The Moon Is Blue,* merely added a few "naughty" words (for example, *virgin* and *mistress!*), leering eyebrows, and bedroom situations to a completely conventional, and stale, comedy of manners. Equally puerile is Preminger's *Advise and Consent* (1962), which, in the best Joe McCarthy style, turns the crusading leftist into an unscrupulous villain and the bigoted, filibustering southern crook into a sweet old soul. Two of Preminger's most enjoyable adaptations, *The Man With the Golden Arm* (1955) and *Anatomy of a Murder* (1959), use quiet, understated acting and evocatively moody jazz scores (by Elmer Bernstein and Duke Ellington, respectively) to make the stories of drug addiction and rape more absorbing and the social commentary less obvious. Later, Preminger was instrumental in vanquishing the blacklist, as he had challenged the Code; he hired Dalton Trumbo, one of the Hollywood Ten, to write the script for *Exodus* (1960) under his own name. At approximately the same time, Kirk Douglas hired Trumbo to write *Spartacus* (1960), and the release of those two films broke the power of the blacklist.

Stanley Kramer became the era's sentimental liberal. In *The Defiant Ones* (1958), he examined race relations by showing a black man (Sidney Poitier) and a white man (Tony Curtis) escaping from a southern prison. Chained together, they are forced to come to terms with one another. Although the terms, the problems, and their solutions are completely predictable from the moment the men flee, Kramer's loud and clear plea for racial tolerance would dominate his career from *Home of the Brave,* which he produced in 1949, to *Guess Who's Coming to Dinner?,* which he directed in 1967. In *On the Beach* (1959), the last of the human race is about to perish from atomic fallout. Kramer's film depicts the sentimental consequences of universal death, but none of its political or social causes. Just so we don't miss the point (as if we could), the film's final image issues an explicit warning — "There is still time, brother."

Perhaps the conscience of Stanley Kramer is best presented by the judge in *Judgment at Nuremberg* (1961). Played by Spencer Tracy (who, along with Henry Fonda, was everyone's favorite movie liberal), the head judge at the Nuremberg trials defines himself as a Maine Republican who thought FDR was a great man. Such a definition is specially designed to offend no one's principles. Amazingly, the film's *scène à faire,* its obligatory scene that *must* be played, in which the judge explains the legal principles on which he is going to find the German defendants guilty, never takes place. Kramer cuts from the judge asking for dissenting opinions, a clear forum for possible debate, to the judge pronouncing sentence on the guilty. The precise standard of guilt remains unclear. The film remains a vehicle for a predictable, melodramatic display of war horrors.

The impetus for these socially committed films is clear enough — Kramer and his brethren wanted to do something meaningful, important, relevant. But their films lend unintentional support to one of Samuel Goldwyn's classic pronouncements: "If you want to send a message, go to Western Union." The tension between social consciousness and Hollywood cliché is uncomfortably strong in these message films. That tension accounts for some of their pretentiousness and staleness today.

William Wyler's *The Best Years of Our Lives* (1946) maintains its freshness because its topical theme — the problem of the returning serviceman's adjusting to civilian life — has been completely absorbed by a compelling story, a credible study of more general problems of human relationships, and because of Gregg Toland's deep-focus camera work. But Elia Kazan's *Gentleman's Agreement* (1947), a study of suburban anti-Semitism, and *Pinky* (1949), a study of a black girl who passes for white, seem both worn and thin because a rather obvious statement of a social problem has been substituted for both plot and people.

Kazan, a Cold War liberal in the era of Hollywood blacklisting, had the problem of making social-problem films that would neither offend an audience nor cost him his job. He solved the problem in his public life by cooperating with HUAC; he solved the problem in his films

Fig. 12-9

Fig. 12-10

Fig. 12-11

Fig. 12-12

Two films shot by Boris Kaufman. On the Waterfront: *the realism of "Method" acting; Marlon Brando with Eva Marie Saint (Fig. 12-9) and Rod Steiger (Fig. 12-10).* The Pawnbroker: *Steiger trapped in the cage of his pawnshop (Fig. 12-11) and in the cage of New York's modern architecture (Fig. 12-12, with Geraldine Fitzgerald).*

by turning social statements into "human" statements—*A Streetcar Named Desire* (1951), *Viva Zapata!* (1952), *On the Waterfront* (1954), *East of Eden* (1955), *A Face in the Crowd* (1957) —all of which sustain their social issues with dynamic performances by Marlon Brando (the prototypic Kazan actor), Vivien Leigh, James

Dean, Jo Van Fleet, Rod Steiger, Andy Griffith, and others. In these films Kazan brought the earthy, introspective "Method" acting style of the Group Theatre (founded in New York in 1931 by Lee Strasberg, Harold Clurman, and Cheryl Crawford) and of the Actors Studio (founded in New York in 1947 by Crawford,

Fig. 12-13
Humphrey Bogart (left) and Elisha Cook, Jr. in **The Maltese Falcon.**

Robert Lewis, and Kazan; Strasberg was the key teacher and artistic director) to Hollywood. Because of their intelligent scripts and powerful acting, Kazan's literary adaptations of the 1950s look better than his social-problem films of the 1940s.

Several other American filmmakers of the era also used New York styles to escape the studio clichés of Hollywood — in particular, the use of real New York locations and established New York actors (*Marty,* 1955; *12 Angry Men,* 1957; *A View from the Bridge,* 1962; *The Pawnbroker,* 1965). Many of these "New York films" owed their texture and impact not only to their director (usually Sidney Lumet, the most perceptive and unsentimental of the "message picture" directors, whose *The Hill,* 1965, and *Prince of the City,* 1981, are among the most powerful and complex examples of the

genre) but to their informal origins in television styles and to the apparent spontaneity of location shooting and lighting. The improvisational "look" of these New York films can usually be attributed to Boris Kaufman, the cinematographer who shot most of them and who had demonstrated the same spontaneity in his collaboration with Jean Vigo two decades earlier.

John Huston also faced the tension between cinematic style and significant statement. Some of his films, like *The Maltese Falcon* (1941, the first film he both wrote and directed) and *The Asphalt Jungle* (1950), match style and statement so unobtrusively that the results have classical status; others, like *Moulin Rouge* (1953), foreground their experiments at the expense of stylistic balance but remain of interest; and still others, like *Freud* (1962) and

Fig. 12-14

The Treasure of the Sierra Madre: *from left, Tim Holt, Humphrey Bogart, and the director's father, Walter Huston.*

Reflections in a Golden Eye (1967), experiment in a manner that comes to seem pretentious. Most of his works are literary adaptations, and again it can be said that some, like *The Maltese Falcon* and *The Treasure of the Sierra Madre* (1948), brilliantly convey the essence of their originals through a careful adaptation of literature and film to each other's demands, and a perfect balance of tone and substance; some, like *Fat City* (1972), *Wise Blood* (1979), and *Under the Volcano* (1984), strong films in their own terms, share enough of the tone, power, and intent of the original works to be considered valid, intriguing adaptations; and some, like *Moby Dick* (1956) and *The Bible* (1966), utterly fail to rise to—or even to understand—the challenges posed by the original material.

If Kazan's films, with their credibly earthy acting, revealed his background in the theatre, Huston's revealed his background as a screenwriter with their taut and subtle scripts

in which individual human weaknesses usually destroy the best-laid plans of mice and men. In Huston's films, the characters who survive are usually those who accept the limits of their humanity and navigate a moral crisis (the detective in *The Maltese Falcon*) or are flexible and resourceful enough to modify their projects (*The African Queen*, 1951). Those who fall—or fail, but remain of consuming interest—are obsessed, inflexible overreachers possessed by their projects (*The Man Who Would Be King*, 1975; *Wise Blood*) or people who are too good at their jobs, or trapped in them, to give them up (*The Asphalt Jungle; Prizzi's Honor*, 1985). Of the three men who set out to mine gold in *The Treasure of the Sierra Madre*, it is the one driven mad by gold—who abandons his humanity and forgets that of others, who is utterly consumed by the project, and who talks the most about ideals—who is destroyed, while the other two are able to accept the loss of the gold and do

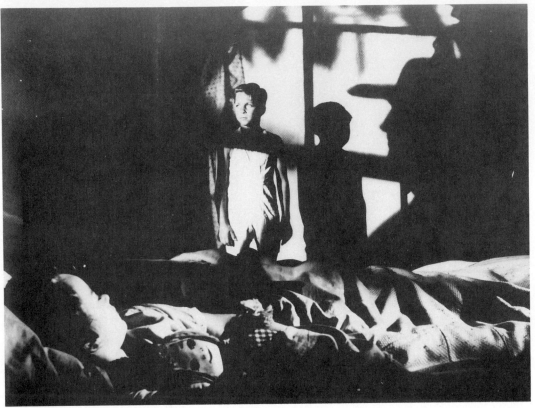

Fig. 12-15
The children and the shadow of their pursuer: an expressionistic moment from **The Night of the Hunter.**

not lose sight of larger values. The "black bird" or its equivalent is the quest object in most Huston films: the dangerous, problematic, and possibly worthless icon of desire, riches, and power. The best of Huston's moral tales are both idealistic and ironic; behind them one senses the shrewd, wry cackle of a student of the aspirations and failures of human nature.

One of the greatest films of the 1950s was a study of values, a literary adaptation, and a compelling story realized in purely cinematic terms: *The Night of the Hunter* (1955). Scripted by James Agee from the novel by Davis Grubb, it was the only movie ever directed by actor Charles Laughton. This hauntingly photographed, lyrically evocative film tells of two children, on the run from a killer (Robert Mitchum), who find sanctuary in the home of a

tough, practical, loving woman (Lillian Gish in her best sound-film performance). In place of money and horror, the film finds value in the enduring power of love, and it does so without the least trace of sentimentality.

The rise of New York in the early 1950s as both a production center and a production style suggested the growing uncertainty within the film industry itself. Not since before World War I had New York been a major center of American film production, although there had been a brief return to both New York studios and styles in the first years of synchronized sound. When Hollywood ran into trouble—as it did with the addition of dialogue or the loss of its audiences—it turned to New York for help.

In 1950 New York was not only the center

of American theatre—as it had been for a century—but the center of American television production as well, with a large pool of talented actors, writers, and directors. Many of them would move from television to New York "little" movies and then on to Hollywood itself. In the era before videotape, color, and its own move to Hollywood, television was very much a medium for writers and actors, not designers or producers, and for intimate direction. Television directors were more like theatre directors, interpreters of the dialogue rather than manipulators of *mise-en-scène*.

Many important screenwriters of this generation came from television: Paddy Chayefsky (*Marty*; *The Bachelor Party*, 1957; *The Goddess*, 1958; *Middle of the Night*, 1959), Reginald Rose (*12 Angry Men*), Abby Mann (*Judgment at Nuremberg*), Rod Serling (*Patterns*, 1956; *Requiem for a Heavyweight*, 1962; *Seven Days in May*, 1964). A generation of new directors also came from television: Sidney Lumet, Daniel Mann (*Come Back, Little Sheba*, 1952; *The Rose Tattoo*, 1955), Delbert Mann (*Marty*; *Separate Tables*, 1958; *Middle of the Night*), Arthur Penn (*The Left-Handed Gun*, 1958; *The Miracle Worker*, 1962; *Bonnie and Clyde*, 1967), Sam Peckinpah (*Ride the High Country*, 1962; *The Wild Bunch*, 1969), Irvin Kershner (*A Fine Madness*, 1966; *The Empire Strikes Back*, 1980), John Frankenheimer (*The Manchurian Candidate*, 1962; *Seven Days in May*; *Seconds*, 1966). Although many of these directors would later adopt Hollywood's familiar genres, most of them were initially committed to detailed social and psychological portraits of either very typical (like Ernest Borgnine in *Marty*) or atypical (like Kim Stanley in *The Goddess*) human beings.

Although it was not apparent at the time, the most enduring Hollywood movies of the period wore the disguises of familiar genres. The two basic metaphors for American life—the open frontier and the dense modern city—had been the movie means for examining the promise and exposing the failures of American society since even before D. W. Griffith. The western provided the generic terms for mythifying American history, its aspirations in building a nation from a wasteland, the actions that hindered or furthered it. The gangster film established the generic terms for diagnosing the corruption and diseases of the present. It depicted America after the Fall, after the virgin wilderness had been cleared and densely packed with stone buildings and people.

The western remained one of the most exciting and entertaining genres of the transitional era: George Stevens's *Shane* (1953), Fred Zinnemann's *High Noon* (1952), Nicholas Ray's *Johnny Guitar* (1954), as well as several by Budd Boetticher, Anthony Mann, and Samuel Fuller. But in the transitional era the conventions of this long-lived Hollywood genre began to stretch in several different directions. Some western films—most notably Anthony Mann's (*Winchester 73*, 1950; *Bend of the River*, 1952; *The Man from Laramie*, 1955) and Budd Boetticher's (*Decision at Sundown*, 1957; *The Tall T*, 1957; *Ride Lonesome*, 1959)—maintained the conventional attitudes of the genre toward violence and killing. Violence was a legitimate means of establishing law and civilization or a legitimate assertion of one's self and self-respect against elemental enemies. Like Ford's *Stagecoach* and Hawks's *Red River*, they were attempts to examine the essential human and social qualities that produced the American nation (and its ideals) in the first place.

But other westerns of the fifties began bending the conventions of the genre to other ends. On the one hand, a filmmaker could use the mythic background of the Old West to attack contemporary American values (disguise was an especially useful ploy in an era of blacklisting). *High Noon*, in its attack on the timidity of the respectable majority and in its contempt for the think-alike, act-alike mentality, is clearly about the American social climate of 1952 and mixes contemporary moralizing with the western's setting and action. On the other hand, a filmmaker could take the violence of westerns as symptomatic of deranged behavior and imply that the forging of this "ideal" American nation was corrupt from its very beginning. Hence the nearly psychotic gunman in *Shane* and the rich man he works for. *Johnny Guitar* may be one of the most bizarrely deranged westerns ever made, its tense hysteria magnified by the screeching gaudiness of its Trucolor, a two-color process as false as its name, favored by the quickie Republic studio because of its cheapness.

Fig. 12-16
Reflection of death: Tom Neal and Ann Savage in Edgar G. Ulmer's film noir, Detour *(1945).*

The gangster film began turning very dark, concentrating on the inevitability of crime in urban America, on crime as a symptom of the society's disease, on criminals who are not simply selfish and tough (like Rico or Scarface) but deranged (like the giggling maniac played by Richard Widmark in Henry Hathaway's *Kiss of Death*, 1947), on policemen who are as diseased as the men they track down, on peripheral characters who are frequently physical or mental cripples, and on visual images that are consistently shadowy, dark, and dim. French critics coined the name for this genre—the *film noir* —a term derived from the black covers of crime novels in the French *Série noire*, many of which were translations of American novels by Dashiell Hammett, James M. Cain, Raymond Chandler, and (later) Mickey Spillane and Jim Thompson. But both the style and the spirit of these *films noirs* were unmistakably German,

from their fatalism to their claustrophobic decor and shadows. Some were even directed by Germans (Wilder, Preminger, Ulmer, and Siodmak among them).

Edward Dmytryk's *Crossfire* (1947) is a dark mixture of murder, anti-Semitism, and homosexuality. Robert Rossen's *Body and Soul* (1947) and Abraham Polonsky's *Force of Evil* (1948) both use John Garfield as a child of the slums facing the inevitable decision between an unprofitable honesty and lucrative crookedness. Garfield, who would be literally hounded to death by right-wing suspicion, was the prototypic *film noir* hero and the "bad girl"—Gloria Grahame, Jean Hagen, Shelley Winters, the early Marilyn Monroe—its prototypically used and abused woman. Another prototypical *noir* figure is the *femme fatale*: the seductive woman who is deadly dangerous (for example, the women played by Barbara Stanwyck in Billy

Fig. 12-17

Out of the Past: *shadows in a world of traps and betrayals*—the **femme fatale** (*Jane Greer*) *left, the hero (Robert Mitchum) in a trenchcoat, and the blackmailer (Steve Brodie) speaking from the darkness; before the film ends, all three will die.*

Wilder's *Double Indemnity*, 1944, and Jane Greer in Jacques Tourneur's *Out of the Past*, 1947). The titles of Dassin's *Night and the City* (1950), Joe Lewis's *Gun Crazy* (1950), and Huston's *The Asphalt Jungle* themselves evoke the *noir* world. Though anticipated by films ranging from *The Blue Angel* to *The Maltese Falcon*, the first true *noir* appears to have been Frank Tuttle's *This Gun For Hire* (1942); the last—the film that marked the end of the *noir* cycle—was Welles's *Touch of Evil* (1958).

The *noir* world was a dark place, psychologically and morally as well as cinematographically. In Robert Siodmak's *Cry of the City* (1948), the cop becomes possessed with the task of tracking down the criminal, who happens to be his boyhood pal as well as a man that the cop secretly envies. James Cagney stars in Raoul

Walsh's *White Heat* (1949), in which the old-style breezy Cagney gangster has become psychotic. Jules Dassin depicts the brutality of prison life (*Brute Force*, 1947), the brutality of urban life (*The Naked City*, 1948), and the commercial brutality of the San Francisco vegetable market (*Thieves' Highway*, 1949). In Fritz Lang's *The Big Heat* (1953) women become mere pawns (and the victims of gruesome crimes) in the war between cops and criminals.

An outgrowth of the *film noir* was a new genre that also showed marked affinities with the western. The "rebellious youth" films of the 1950s—particularly Laslo Benedek's *The Wild One* (1953) and Nicholas Ray's *Rebel Without a Cause* (1955)—were also a violent reaction against a decaying and diseased society. But whereas the gangster chose violence as a

Fig. 12-18

Fig. 12-19

Icons of 1950s rebellion: Marlon Brando in **The Wild One** *(Fig. 12-18) and James Dean in* **Rebel Without a Cause** *(Fig. 12-19).*

defense against the brutal hardness of city life, the youths rebel against the sterility, monotony, and conformity of normal adult life.

Despite Ray's ironic title (from the book, by psychiatrist Robert Lindner, on which the film was loosely based), these rebels most certainly do have a cause. Just as the western hero has his horse, his means to freedom, and the gangster his automobile, his means of destruction, the youths have their motorcycles and automobiles, which are instruments of both freedom and destruction. The machines take the youths away from the confined mediocrity of adult life and give them the exhilaration of movement in open spaces (like the cowboy's horse); but the machines also destroy property, people, and even their masters themselves. "What are you rebelling against?" someone asks the smirking Johnny (Marlon Brando) on his motorbike in *The Wild One*. "What'cha got?" he answers. The highway death of the young James Dean not only robbed Hollywood of a rich acting talent and translated an actor into a legend; it also seemed a metaphor for the ultimate rebellion against what'cha got.

While a western looked at the past and a gangster film at the present, the science fiction fantasy set its sights on the future. Inspired by both the new fear of atomic annihilation and hope of interplanetary travel, science fiction films brought atomic mutants and extraterrestrial visitors to Earth or sent Earthmen to the Moon, Mars, and other galaxies. In *The Thing* (1951), directed by Christian Nyby and produced by Howard Hawks, atomic science and outer space combine to produce a death-defying, vegetable monster. But in *Forbidden Planet* (Fred M. Wilcox, 1956), Earthlings take their monster with them into space—a very Freudian menace, emanating from the unbridled id of the scientist himself. Martians attack Earth in *The War of the Worlds* (1953), directed by Byron Haskin and produced by the great special-effects designer, George Pal—until vanquished by some mundane mortal malady like the common cold. But in Robert Wise's *The Day the Earth Stood Still* (1951), a sage interplanetary visitor brings reason, sense, and peace to an Earth intent on destroying itself and everything else in the galaxy.

Fig. 12-20

Fig. 12-21

Fear of the intergalactic unknown: **The Thing** *(Fig. 12-20) and* **The War of the Worlds** *(Fig. 12-21).*

Interplanetary travel took humans into space in Kurt Neumann's *Rocketship X–M,* George Pal's *Destination Moon* (both 1950), and Joseph Newman's *This Island Earth* (1955) while Earth was overrun by atom-strengthened ants in *Them!* (1954), overspread with intergalactic slime in *The Blob* (1958), and munched by atom-wakened dinosaurs in many films from Japan (*Godzilla, King of the Monsters,* 1954, U.S. version 1956; *Rodan,* 1956, U.S. version 1958; both originally directed by Inoshiro Honda)—which had suffered the reality of atomic devastation. *It Came From Outer Space* (1953, 3-D, directed by Jack Arnold) could serve as a metaphoric title for the entire genre, and no matter what that antecedent turned out to be, you knew that this It would not be nearly so pleasant as "It" used to be in the Roaring Twenties.

One of the most political of science fiction films was Don Siegel's *Invasion of the Body Snatchers* (1956, from the novel by Jack Finney), in which vegetable pods from outer space replace the Earth's inhabitants, resembling the Earthlings in every way but one: They have no feelings. These pods seem (but were not meant as) a possible allusion to Communism: the way

some Americans, who appear "normal," are really selfless agents of an evil foreign power—the Red Menace of the Cold War 1950s. But the pods also strongly suggest an indictment of American conformity, a uniform society that appears human but lacks the essential human qualities of emotion, moral judgment, and independent action. Either way, the point is that all the pods think alike. Don Siegel later said Hollywood was full of pods. While American horror films of a previous generation (like *Frankenstein* and *The Mummy*) doubted the ability of science to transcend the limits of mortality and the mysteries of experience ("There are some things man is not meant to know . . . "), American science fiction films of the 1950s surveyed a universe with no limits whatever on our knowledge or potential for either creation or destruction.

The newest comic performers were Danny Kaye at Goldwyn and Bud Abbott and Lou Costello at Universal. Abbott and Costello seemed to be built on the old physical premises of teams like Laurel and Hardy—one fat, one thin; one smart, one dumb; one clumsy, one suave. But despite their physical humor, Abbott and Costello were primarily verbal comics (their most famous routines, like "Who's on First?," originated on radio); the only way to use them in a film was to plunge the bungling, cowardly, klutzy Lou into dangerous or horrifying situations. And so Abbott and Costello went into jungles or the Army or met all the monsters under contract to Universal—the Mummy, Frankenstein, Dracula, and the Wolf Man—in an attempt to squeeze laughs from spine-tingling contrasts of humor and horror. The Danny Kaye films also juxtaposed comedy and danger, surrounding Kaye with rings of murderers, kidnappers, spies, and thieves who gave him his trademark comic jitters and stutters, which complemented his tongue-twisters (*The Kid from Brooklyn*, 1946; *A Song Is Born*, 1947; *On the Riviera*, 1951; *Knock on Wood*, 1953; *The Court Jester*, 1956).

Succeeding Abbott and Costello in 1950 were Dean Martin and Jerry Lewis at Paramount, another team combining a zany clown and a slick "straight" man. Martin and Lewis contrasted both physically and mentally: the one brash, noisy, nasal, infantile; the other oily, loose, controlled. But their wacky personalities were frequently drowned in predictable, overplotted situation comedies (many of the American classic comedians were notoriously independent of plotting).

The same overplotting plagued the films that Jerry Lewis made alone after 1956. Although some French intellectual critics rate Lewis alongside Chaplin and Keaton, few Americans over fourteen can sit through a Jerry Lewis film. Lewis's problem seems to be a conflict between character and plot, a zany conception forced to march through a completely formulaic story. The first reel or two of a Lewis film is brilliantly funny as Lewis reveals the particular comic nuttiness of the main character. But then, the exposition at an end, the nutty professor, shopkeeper, or errand boy must trudge through more than an hour of, Will he get the girl? or, Will he keep his job? Unlike most of the great film clowns, Lewis's funniness stems more from technique than from a unique personality and vision of experience.

The director-crafted comedy of manners also declined after the war. After Frank Capra made his dark comedy of postwar doubt, *It's A Wonderful Life* (1946), his lightweight comedies that followed (*State of the Union*, 1948; *Riding High*, 1950; *A Hole in the Head*, 1959) were feeble shadows of his greatest work. Even Preston Sturges, cramped by a production contract with Howard Hughes, made less successful comedies after the war, though each had great moments (*The Sin of Harold Diddlebock*, 1947, starring Harold Lloyd—badly recut by Hughes and released as *Mad Wednesday* in 1950; *Unfaithfully Yours*, 1948; *The Beautiful Blonde from Bashful Bend*, 1949).

Among the best postwar comedies of manners were Billy Wilder's, who with his co-author, I. A. L. Diamond or Charles Brackett, preserved the tradition of comic collaboration between director and scenarist. Wilder's comedy juxtaposed verbal wit with a sinister, morally disturbing environment: the corruption of a postwar Berlin in rubble (*A Foreign Affair*, 1948), the dark estate of a psychotic has-been of the silent screen (*Sunset Boulevard*, 1950), a concentration camp (*Stalag 17*, 1953), the gangster underworld (*Some Like It Hot*, 1959), the corruption of Madison Avenue (*The Apartment*, 1960), and the Cold War in the now rebuilt and industrialized Berlin (*One, Two, Three*, 1961).

The films vary in their balance of comedy and moral seriousness. *Sunset Boulevard* is most interested in the perversion of human values that turns Norma Desmond (Gloria Swanson) into a fanatic worshipper of her dead past and screenwriter Joe (William Holden) into a male prostitute willing to sell head, heart, and body for the hope of an equally dead future (the film is narrated by Joe after his death). Wilder's film examines the human dreams and emotions a person must sell to purchase success. *Some Like It Hot*, the opposite extreme, tries to get as many gags as it can out of Jack Lemmon and Tony Curtis in drag with an all-girl orchestra. If *Some Like It Hot* looks backward to the classic screwball comedies (its references to Cary Grant and its reversals of male and female roles and clothes), it also looks forward to the transvestite comedies of the 1980s like *Victor/Victoria* and *Tootsie*. Marilyn Monroe, the stereotypical "dumb blonde" of the 1950s, with the body of velvet and the head of air, both plays that stereotype (named Sugar Cane) and suffers the pain of its sexist application in this powerful Wilder comedy.

Musicals in the postwar years were also undergoing a transition, one that produced Hollywood's greatest musical films. Before the war, Hollywood musicals were slight concoctions (focusing mostly on the doings of show folk). Musical numbers wove through a scanty plot about love among entertainers as Ruby Keeler, Dick Powell, Fred Astaire, Ginger Rogers, Eleanor Powell, or Rita Hayworth sang and danced in the show-business world of theatres and nightclubs. The 1930 musicals had few pretensions to psychological realism or complex (as opposed to complicated) human relationships; the plots were almost invisible trifles to hold the brilliant musical numbers together. By the mid-1950s, however, filmed musicals, following the pattern of Broadway shows (which, of course, they were often adapting), became more realistic and psychological. World War II and street gangs and death had become subjects for Broadway musicals like *West Side Story* and *South Pacific.* The unserious fluff of Rodgers and Hart had been replaced by the romantic seriousness of Rodgers and Hammerstein.

In the "integrated" musical, as the Rodgers–Hammerstein type and its successors came to be known, one did not assume that singing and psychological interaction were mutually exclusive (as they were in earlier Broadway shows and Hollywood musical films). The "integrated" show tried to imagine under what conditions a human being might sing in reality —or, in some cases, "think" a song. Although it was difficult enough to convince a Broadway audience that a group of juvenile delinquents would sing to each other before cutting each other's throats, the task was even more difficult for films. The stage, at least, enjoys the unreality of cardboard and plaster and paint and spotlight. The stage musical could draw on the conventions of two other theatrical forms— opera and the dance—as its stylized means of translating song and dance into a representation of reality. But how to make a film audience believe that a group of juvenile delinquents

would pirouette down a real New York street with real graffiti on the walls and real garbage in the gutter? How to make an audience believe that a woman would sing a song standing on a real tugboat in the middle of New York harbor?

The director of early musical films did not have such problems. Musical films were obviously unreal, unserious spoofs that never tried to be believable. A director like Busby Berkeley could twirl his camera, his dancers, their pianos, fiddles, and fountains, in grandiose and grotesquely imaginative patterns precisely because his musical numbers owed no allegiance to either spatial logic or social reality. Although it is almost taken for granted that color is the musical's natural medium, it is worth mentioning that without black-and-white there would have been no Busby Berkeley or Fred Astaire—or not the same ones. Berkeley's kaleidoscopic visual conceptions depended on the contrast of white and black (say, white dresses gleaming off a polished black floor), and Fred Astaire, in top hat and tails, literally *was* black and white. Significantly, every Astaire color movie of the 1940s and 1950s conceived at least one musical number in which contemporary color was translated into the monochrome values of his 1930s musicals (for example, the title song in *Funny Face,* performed exclusively in the red-oranges of a photographic darkroom).

Musical films just after the war, while they did become lavish, ornate, Technicolor spectaculars (as so many films did), maintained their stylized unreality. The MGM musicals produced by Arthur Freed in particular combined surrealistically imaginative musical numbers, pleasant scores, an exciting use of color, and funny, spoofing plots that often still revolved around showfolk.

Of the directors of musicals for Freed's unit, Vincente Minnelli was most conscious of the traditions of painting and modern art. His musicals (*The Pirate,* 1948; *An American in Paris,* 1951; *The Band Wagon,* 1953) are dazzling in their attention to color and light, to details of costume and decor, and to their layering of perspectival space for the cinema lens. Charles Walters was most sympathetic to individual performers, especially to the manic moods of

Judy Garland (*Easter Parade*, 1948; *Summer Stock*, 1950). Stanley Donen (with or without Kelly) was most committed to defining visual space itself as an emanation and external projection of musical energy, movement, and feeling (*On the Town*, 1949; *Singin' in the Rain*, 1952; *Seven Brides for Seven Brothers*, 1954; *It's Always Fair Weather*).

The best of the Freed musicals were those with musical numbers conceived and choreographed by Gene Kelly, particularly *An American in Paris* and *Singin' in the Rain*. In the former, Kelly's ballet, combining George Gershwin's tone poem with French impressionistic painting, received the most critical attention. Although the lengthy ballet borders on the pretentious and fits very loosely into the film's plot, the dream-ballet by itself is a brilliant demonstration of the powers of a purely abstract cinema. Its integration of music, color, dance, decor, costumes, editing, and camera movement is as sensually and formally "pure" cinema as any abstract filmmaker has ever attempted. Equally exuberant and imaginative was the staging of "By Strauss" in a Paris bistro, the staging of "I'll Build a Stairway to Paradise" on a Paris music-hall stage, and Kelly's casual singing, hoofing, and whistling of "I've Got Rhythm" for a group of Paris kids.

Singin' in the Rain boasts perhaps the funniest screenplay of any musical film, the best of Betty Comden and Adolph Green's many Hollywood spoofs, both in films and on the stage. Every musical number in *Singin' in the Rain* combines music and fun, pleasant movement and wry spoof: the opening musical montage in which Kelly rises from sleazy hoofer to movie star, the staging of the title song in which Kelly tap dances in rain puddles (!), the surrealistic ballet, "Broadway Melody," in which Kelly romanticizes a young entertainer's rise to the top.

In addition to its parodic historical representation of Hollywood's conversion to synchronized sound, the technology that made musicals possible, *Singin' in the Rain* contains its own reflexive history of MGM musicals, from their 1929 beginning to the 1952 present. The film's score, with music by Nacio Herb Brown and lyrics by Arthur Freed (the film's producer), is a virtual compilation of hit tunes from MGM musicals, from the 1929 *Hollywood*

Fig. 12-22
The exuberance of song and dance: Gene Kelly Singin' in the Rain.

Revue and *Broadway Melody* through the succeeding *Broadway Melodies* and the Rooney–Garland "barnyard musicals," like *Babes in Arms*, of the 1930s and 1940s. All but two of the songs in *Singin' in the Rain* come directly from earlier MGM musicals, for which they were written by the same man who now produced MGM musicals.

The Band Wagon is equally reflexive and retrospective. Its main character, Tony Hunter, is a veteran song-and-dance man whom modern fashion considers old and out of date. Hunter is played by Fred Astaire, about whom modern fashion held similar suspicions in 1953. The film's title is, not coincidentally, the same as that of Astaire's last Broadway show with his sister, Adele. Many of the film's songs, by Arthur Schwartz and Howard Dietz (who, like Freed, now worked for MGM) come directly from that 1931 show. Hunter's trademark is

Astaire's trademark—the top hat—now considered so old that it can't even attract a minimal bid at auction. In the end, however, Hunter (like Astaire and Freed) proves that he knows what entertains most—not the "High Arts" of ballet and drama, but good old song-and-dance.

"That's Entertainment" is not only the most familiar new song written for this film but could well be the anthem for all of Freed's MGM musicals. Its lyrics clearly proclaim these film musicals as the contemporary American descendants of Shakespeare, melodrama, and farce, the true twentieth-century art of the people. But there is also a sadness beneath the exuberant proclamation, a nostalgic realization that the tradition of entertainment sustained by these MGM musicals was coming to an end. Though Tony Hunter (or Fred Astaire) knew more about this kind of entertainment than anyone else, because he carried its traditions within him, there were no new Hunters (or Astaires, or Kellys) on the entertainment horizon. Like Chaplin's *Limelight,* made at almost the same time, *Singin' in the Rain* and *The Band Wagon* both celebrate a tradition and sing a requiem for its demise.

That the tradition was dead can be seen in the differences between the love song, "You Were Meant for Me," of *Singin' in the Rain,* and the love song, "One Hand, One Heart," of *West Side Story* (1961). In the earlier film, Gene Kelly leads his lady (Debbie Reynolds) onto a sound stage, turns on atmospheric colored lights, turns on an artificial wind machine, and then sings, surrounded by stylized unreality. In *West Side Story,* girl and boy pledge their troth in the bridal shop where she works, surrounded by the realistic artifacts of her trade. The pair enacts a metaphoric marriage ceremony, supported by all these concrete props (and duplicating the action and dialogue of the stage production, word for word), just before they consummate their "marriage" in a suggestive fadeout. Whichever style you prefer, the psychological and visual differences between them are obvious.

By the mid-1950s, MGM had already begun deserting original musical ideas, assigning Vincente Minnelli to adapt stage shows like *Brigadoon* and *Kismet.* The original screen musical died with the original screenplay. It also died with the studio system that produced a certain number of musicals each year and kept a stable of musical talent stocked expressly for that purpose. With the death of the studios that developed such musical talent, the world was condemned to a future with no new Kellys, Garlands, and Astaires, who no longer had a school for study nor a showcase for displaying their wares. The repertory musical performer needs a repertory system. The road for independent production was being cleared.

The next great musicals would come out in twenty years—notably those directed and choreographed by Bob Fosse (*Cabaret,* 1972; *All That Jazz,* 1979), who had danced in 3-D in *Kiss Me Kate;* those that truly re-imagined stage musicals for the cinema (Luis Valdez's *Zoot Suit,* 1981); and those that experimented with the form and idea of the musical (Herbert Ross's *Pennies from Heaven,* 1981, based on Dennis Potter's British teleplay, which was the primary experimental work).

By the turn of the 1960s, there were signs that a new sense of cinema was on the way—not just from the New Wave films arriving from Europe, but from such brave American black-and-whites as John Cassavetes's *Shadows* (1959), Alfred Hitchcock's *Psycho* (1960), Robert Rossen's *The Hustler* (1961), David Miller's *Lonely Are the Brave* (1962), and Frank and Eleanor Perry's *David and Lisa* (1963).

Surfaces and Subversion

To understand those American films of the fifties that seem most interesting four decades later requires a careful look at the differences between the clear values on their narrative surfaces and the more complicated social questions beneath. Unlike the American message films and European "art films" of the period, these Hollywood films, as in past decades, wear thick disguises, masquerading as ordinary westerns or thrillers or weepies—the derogatory term for "women's pictures," itself a derogatory enough term. To wear a thick disguise was an understandable strategy in an era of blacklisting, when it was safer to make films with no apparent "message" at all. But these genre films, like those of the previous era, felt comfortable raising the important questions within the

Fig. 12-23
Three consecutive shots from the opening sequence of Pickup on South Street: *The victim (Jean Peters) waits alluringly, a hand fingers her purse, and the thief (Richard Widmark) gazes intently.*

Southeast Asian "conflict," the one in Vietnam. For the subject of his last war film, *The Big Red One* (1980), he returned to World War II. In 1982 he made a film about racism, *White Dog,* that was judged too controversial to release.

On its surface, *Pickup on South Street* is a simple enough story about a petty thief, Skip

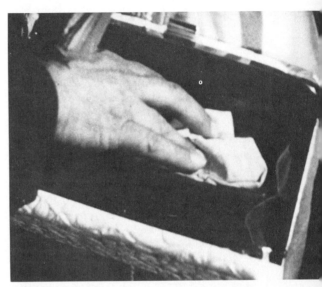

Fig. 12-24

boundaries of familiar genres. Although few critics took even the best of these genre films seriously in the 1950s, most of the movies made money—accomplishment enough in that decade—and many of them have proved more durable than the critics who casually dismissed them.

Beginning in 1949, Samuel Fuller directed, wrote, and often produced a series of inexpensive genre films, which fell somewhere between "A" and "B" pictures in their budgets, styles, stars, and shooting schedules: westerns (*I Shot Jesse James,* 1949; *Run of the Arrow* and *Forty Guns,* both 1957), gangster films (*Pickup on South Street,* 1953; *Underworld U.S.A.,* 1961), and disturbing melodramas (*Shock Corridor,* 1963; *The Naked Kiss,* 1964). Fuller's war films were among the few about the Korean "conflict" (*The Steel Helmet* and *Fixed Bayonets,* both 1951), that very euphemism indicating uncertain public reaction to a war neither enthusiastically supported nor condemned. Fuller's Korea films—especially *The Steel Helmet*—are shockingly violent and honest, and his *China Gate* (1957) is uncannily prophetic of the next

Fig. 12-25

McCoy (Richard Widmark), who picks the purse of a woman (Jean Peters) passing atomic secrets to the Russians. The thief finds himself surrounded by powerful enemies. The police want to send him back to prison, the FBI wants the secret documents and the spy ring, the woman wants the documents to appease her boyfriend, the boyfriend and his Communist allies want the documents at any human cost. The thief has only himself to depend on; a real model of individualism and free enterprise, he plays the parties off against one another until he lands on his feet.

Fuller brought this curious mixture of political espionage and petty crime to life by scrambling its moral system, shifting audience allegiances to characters that most Americans (and the Production Code itself) found loathsome. The studio was as surprised as Fuller when *Pickup on South Street* won at the Venice Film Festival.

The thief's urge to steal is uncontrollably sexual, as the film's opening sequence in a crowded subway car makes powerfully clear. He sidles up to his attractive victim and eyes her closely, hiding his hand behind a newspaper as he slides it toward her body. Then, without her realizing it, he bumps against her, enters her purse, removes its contents, and withdraws. But if the thief is a kind of rapist, and certainly no ordinary hero, his victim is a prostitute. She does the bidding of her boyfriend (Richard Kiley) because he offers her nice clothes and a nice apartment, and she uses her body as bait to retrieve the stolen documents from the thief. The FBI agents are no more appealing. In the film's opening sequence they stare intently at the thief's entry of the woman's purse but do nothing about the violation. Are they callously disinterested citizens, cops forced to keep a low profile, or voyeurs (surrogates for the movie audience, vicariously participating in the sexual scene)? The film's title suggests its deliberate mixing of the criminal and the sexual: A cop "picks up" a crook, a stranger "picks up" a lover, a prostitute "picks up" a trick.

The Communists are the most repellent figures in the film, willing to use any means — prostitution, bribery, murder — to achieve their ends. They embody several of the period's notions about "Commies" (as Fuller's films always call them), from the highly publicized alleged activities of the Rosenbergs and Alger Hiss to the equally publicized cliché that for Communists the end justifies the means. But these Commies are the most comfortable materialists in the film. They wear the nicest clothes, live in the fanciest apartments, smoke the largest cigars. Without dialogue, these Commies could be mistaken for stockbrokers, corporate executives, and bankers — the filthy capitalists in the films of Eisenstein and Pudovkin.

While Fuller's Commies look like plutocrats, his thieves are the embodiment and protectors of capitalism: They are all in the business of selling. One of the film's quirkiest creatures is "Lightning Louie," a fat informant who picks up and pockets his bribery fees with the same chopsticks he uses to shovel Chinese food into his face. Even the thief's close friend, "Moe" (Thelma Ritter), sells him out several times — for her business is selling information to anyone who pays her price. Nothing personal, she tells him, just business. And the one time "Moe" refuses to sell him out, she dies for her loyalty.

The one moral precept for these thieves — one Fuller shared — is that it's better to be a patriotic crook than a rotten Commie. Unfortunately, the capitalist thieves live worse than anyone else in the film: They reside in sleazy, claustrophobic rooms and ramshackle waterfront cabins without electricity. Unlike the wealthy Commies, they live like rats — hardly models of the benefits of capitalist enterprise. But they are resourceful. By the end of the film the Commies have been caught, the documents have been recovered, and the thief's past record of convictions has been wiped clean. He and the prostitute have forged a permanent romantic alliance. Although poetic justice has been done, it is unclear what system of morality might justify this justice. Fuller's supposedly simple story spins a complicated web of sexuality, thievery, politics, law, government, business, loyalty, and love.

If the opening scene of *Pickup on South Street* implicates the movie viewer's voyeurism, most of Alfred Hitchcock's work from *Rope* (1948) to *Psycho* (1960) makes voyeurism its major theme. Hitchcock's films of this period seem convinced of two things: that normal American life is shockingly abnormal, and that one of the clearest signs of this abnormality is the devotion to watching movies. Like *Pickup on South Street, Rope* begins with an odd sexual climax—but the camera must wait outside a penthouse apartment, its curtains drawn, not permitted an *in flagrante* view of the brutal homosexual murder, modeled on the sensational Leopold–Loeb murder case, in the dark. Only after the murderous climax can the camera and the light be invited inside, to permit the audience's identification with the two handsomely murderous boys, in the throes of the murder's post-coital exhilaration. The Code prohibited the depiction of explicit sexual and "unnatural" acts, and films cannot be shot in the dark. In a similar way, *Strangers On A Train* (1951) balances the audience's antipathies between a maniacal homosexual murderer, Bruno (Robert Walker), and a bland model of straight American normality, the tennis pro, Guy (Farley Granger).

In this decade committed to the "straight" and normal, Hitchcock's sly examinations of sexual aberration beneath the placid surfaces of 1950s American life were deliciously subversive. He took particular delight in exposing the dark sexual undersides of familiar movie stars —James Stewart and Cary Grant in particular —so familiar and safe as sexual beings: the calm rationality of Stewart, astonished that he has a libido; the superficial suavity of Grant, always verging on the hysterical and scatterbrained. Near the conclusion of *Vertigo* (1958), James Stewart grasps the female fantasy of his own construction, embodied by Kim Novak, in his arms. Hitchcock's sleazy hotel room begins spinning slowly, its walls, bathed in aqueous blue-green light, dissolving into Stewart's memory of that location where he last encountered this fantasy woman before her apparent death. While the embracing couple stands at the center of this vertiginous, dizzying twirl, Stewart pulls away slightly from Novak to glance over his right shoulder, as if to ask, "Where the hell am I?" These great American stars didn't quite know where they were in Hitchcock films; like the audience, they were often kept off-balance.

Rear Window (1954), written by John Michael Hayes from a story by Cornell Woolrich, puts all these disturbing themes together in a masterful comic thriller that, on its surface, seems merely an exciting whodunit. A professional photographer, L. B. Jeffries (Stewart), confined to his apartment with a broken leg, has just one amusement during the hot summer days: gazing at the activity in the courtyard surrounding his apartment window. As he watches the activities of his neighbors, he notices something wrong in one of the apartments: A man's nagging wife mysteriously disappears. After a lengthy period of puzzling, spying, poking, and piecing the evidence together, Jeffries exposes the missing woman's husband, Thorwald (Raymond Burr), as her murderer. Jeffries avoids his own demise by means of a last-minute rescue with striking affinities to D. W. Griffith's *The Lonedale Operator,* over forty years earlier.

The difference between the Griffith melodrama and a Hitchcock psychological thriller is the latter director's dissection of movies themselves as the source of the thrills. Jeffries's experience with the life outside his window is identical to the spectator's experience at the cinema. He sits immobilized and powerless; his only activity is mental: to watch, to comment, to make inferences, to sympathize, and to get excited. Jeffries extends his vision with parallels to the movie camera—a pair of binoculars and his still camera's telephoto lens. This immensely long lens frequently sits in Stewart's inert lap— one of the slyest comic phalluses in the history of cinema.

Jeffries is more turned on by the activity outside his window than by the visits of his flesh-and-blood girlfriend, Lisa (Grace Kelly). There is something odd about their relationship. The couple shares far more sexual excitement when they work on the murder case together—when she enters the frame of his movielike fantasies—than when they sit together in his apartment (when and where sexual intimacy is expected to occur).

Hitchcock fills the frame with other frames, drawing a parallel between Jeffries's vicarious experiencing of other people's lives and the moviegoer's. Through the courtyard's many

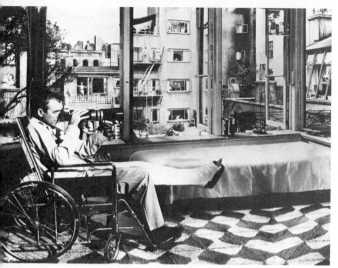

Fig. 12-26

Fig. 12-27

Fig. 12-28

Rear Window: *window frames as movie frames. The spectator-voyeur (James Stewart, Fig. 12-26) observes the framed stories of the newlyweds (Fig. 12-27), "Miss Lonelyhearts" (Fig. 12-28), "Miss Torso" (Fig. 12-29), and the murderer, Thorwald (Raymond Burr, Fig. 12-30).*

Fig. 12-30

Fig. 12-29

window frames, Jeffries catches glimpses of other human beings, whom he converts into characters. There is a shapely dancer he names "Miss Torso," a typical movie pinup in some typical movie musical. There is a spinster he names "Miss Lonelyhearts," itself a reference to the novelist and screenwriter Nathanael West; her heart is so lonely that her typical movie melodrama seems likely to end with suicide. There is a young male composer, probably gay, a Ned Rorem type whose sophisticated friends include a much older man (played by Hitchcock himself). There is a newlywed couple —the shades of whose apartment are perpetually drawn, since the Production Code prohibited any direct view of their sexual intimacy. Finally, there is Thorwald, the murderer, whose marital movie genre (murder) conforms more to the Code than does the passion of the newlyweds. The courtyard full of window frames—suggesting long shots and close-ups, paralleling the varied formats of frames through film history—is really full of movie shots within a movie shot and of movie sets within a movie set. Or the courtyard is his television set, with a choice of channels.

The spectator gets into trouble when experience violates his voyeuristic privacy. Because movies need the darkness that outlines the light-filled frame, Jeffries retreats into the darkness of his apartment for a better view of Thorwald's light-filled apartment. But when Thorwald discovers Jeffries's prying gaze (and, in person, Lisa snooping), he steps out of the movie frame of his own apartment and into the auditorium of Jeffries's apartment. Unable to fight or move, Jeffries depends on yet another trick of photography and vision. His exploding flashbulbs temporarily blind his assailant. Jeffries clings desperately to the ledge of his windowsill—Hitchcock's literal visualization of that classic movie metaphor, the "cliffhanger" —just as Hitchcock heroes hang from such "cliffs" as the Statue of Liberty (in *Saboteur*, 1942), the edge of a roof (*Vertigo*), and Mount Rushmore (*North by Northwest*, 1959). L. B. hangs there just long enough for rescue by those typical enforcers of movie closure, the police.

Because Hitchcock knows that all properly constructed Hollywood fictions require this closure, he confers happy endings on the courtyard's many window frames. The couple with the inquisitive dog, which was murdered by Thorwald, trains a new puppy. Miss Torso finds her mate—not one of her many handsome dancing partners but a short and dumpy soldier, the loving husband to whom she has remained movie-faithfully true. The composer finishes the melody on which he has been working for the entire film, and he plays it for none other than Miss Lonelyhearts, who has come to his apartment to hear it. Hollywood can always tie up two loose ends with an impossible marriage between a spinster and a homosexual. The one sour note comes from the newlyweds, now arguing rather than making love. The shade that perpetually covered their window, blocking our view, can now be lifted since the Code permits movies to spy on arguments. Jeffries seems more contented with (or resigned to) the idea of marrying Lisa, but now that he has two broken legs he is even less mobile and less able to perform the acts of intimacy with her than when the film began.

The curtains on Jeffries's window, which opened to begin the film, finally close, to cover his view (and ours) of the courtyard world— just as the curtains covering a movie screen open and close for each screening. No director made films that were simultaneously such exciting movies and such ironic critiques of movie excitement as Alfred Hitchcock in the 1950s.

A loner and a rebel, Nicholas Ray began making films in 1948. Like Fuller, Ray became a director on the fringes of the Hollywood establishment with films that he often wrote himself. Although he began in the theatre and came to Hollywood as Elia Kazan's assistant, Ray would feel more comfortable with Hollywood genres rather than theatrical ones: westerns (*Johnny Guitar*, 1954; *The True Story of Jesse James*, 1957), war films (*Flying Leathernecks*, 1951), the combination of *film noir* and wild youth (*They Live By Night*, 1948, released 1949; *Knock on Any Door*, 1949; *Born to Be Bad*, 1950). Ray's movie about the industry itself, *In a Lonely Place* (1950), features Humphrey Bogart as a Hollywood screenwriter who is unjustly suspected of murder but who *is* emotionally destructive. Like Vincente Minnelli's *The Bad and the Beautiful* (1953) and Robert Aldrich's

A new and more perfect union in Rebel Without a Cause: *from left, Sal Mineo, James Dean, and Natalie Wood at Falcon's Lair.*

Fig. 12-31

The Big Knife (1955), Ray's film was one of the period's best to bite the Hollywood hand that fed it.

Rebel Without a Cause (1955), which gave birth to the James Dean legend (Dean appeared in only two other films: Kazan's *East of Eden*, earlier in 1955, and George Stevens's *Giant*, 1956), is one of Ray's most personal works. The rebellion in the film's title is the only detail Ray borrowed from a best-selling 1944 case study of a psychotically destructive youth. The title is a smokescreen for the film's real issue — the attempt of three outsiders, strangers alike to the coldly impersonal materialistic values of their weak but rigid parents and the desperately insecure values of their teenage contemporaries, to form an alternative community of genuine human sympathy.

Jim Stark (Dean) begins the film as a hopeless drunk because he sees no value in a future represented by the enslavement of his father (Jim Backus — the voice of Mr. Magoo) to material possessions and a nagging wife. "Jimbo's" father is a man of no commitments or aspirations, except to keep the peace amongst the sterile bric-a-brac of his bourgeois home. Judy (Natalie Wood) also has problems with a father who spurns her confusedly provocative need for affection, sending her off in search of thrills

and easy sensual power over boys her own age. Plato (Sal Mineo), the rich kid who never sees his divorced parents, is the most vulnerable and intellectual of the three, and implicitly homosexual. Plato recognizes the fragility of human experience in a cold and awesome universe — suggested by the hypnotic planetarium show, a spectacle of sound and light analogous to movies themselves. Plato, like Judy, searches for love and finds it in the same source — Jim.

Ray chronicles Jim's discovery of what it means to be a man and what it means to be a responsible human being. The seeming alternative to his father's emasculation is the world of his contemporaries, no less corrupt than that of the adults and a distorted mirror of the same materialistic values. These youths believe that manhood can be defined by possessing automobiles and girlfriends, proving their right to them with knife fights and chicken runs, car races that may be to the death. Jim, Judy, and Plato try to be good — and they are — but always seem to end up being called bad. Only love can unscramble their hearts, can give an uncontradictory message, can let them find themselves beyond the empty and unfulfilling hypocrisy of imposed social roles.

The trio withdraws — from both worlds of adult bourgeoisie and adolescent *machismo* — to found a perfect community in a private oasis. The deserted mansion in the Hollywood Hills, Falcon's Lair, serves as home to this alternative community. Without electricity, furniture, automobiles, or any of the artifacts or ornaments of materialistic comfort, the single quality that fills this home is the intimate affection of its three inhabitants. The conventional distinctions of bourgeois existence melt away—rich and poor, body and soul, love and friendship, male and female, homosexual and heterosexual—to be replaced by the amorphous tenderness of their feelings. This amorphous sensitivity is what the James Dean myth came to mean for his generation in the first place. The outside world, however, invades this fragile oasis— both adolescents seeking revenge and the police trying to clean up the mess by making more mess. With the death of Plato, the sacrificial victim, Jim understands that the world cannot be abandoned, but the only values worth keeping are the personal ones he defines for himself.

Rebel Without a Cause had great power for young audiences in the 1950s, urging them to abandon any simple conformity to seek values that made personal sense. At the same time, it urged parents to face up to their own problems. The film's visual power—Ray's first in CinemaScope and color—contributed to its moral argument. The awesome horizontal sweep of the CinemaScope frame, as Ray used it, suggested a passion for openness that contrasted with the cramped and confined interiors of bourgeois homes. Ray described Dean's red jacket, in contrast with his black Mercury, as a danger sign, a personality about to explode. Natalie Wood's verdant green sweater was a sign that said "go," while Sal Mineo's socks, one black and one red, were a sign not only of imbalance but also of his adopting the same danger colors that defined Dean. Ray consistently identified with oddballs and loners who saw themselves as different from everyone else.

Ethan Edwards of John Ford's *The Searchers* (1956) was another oddball and loner, different from everyone else. In *The Searchers* Ford continued his mythic investigation of American history, which began in 1924 with *The Iron Horse* and stretched through 1939 with *Young Mr. Lincoln* and *Stagecoach*. Like Ford's postwar

My Darling Clementine, the cavalry trilogy of 1948–1950 (*Fort Apache, She Wore a Yellow Ribbon, Rio Grande*), and the 1962 *The Man Who Shot Liberty Valance, The Searchers* exposes the conflict of irresolvable historical forces: the clash between inflexible civilized institutions designed to patrol the peace and individual qualities of human will required to fight for peace; between the struggle to establish and protect a civilization and the values of civilization that make it worth establishing and protecting. If the shadow of the recent World War fell darkly across *My Darling Clementine,* an even longer shadow—of the World War, Korea, and the Cold War—falls across *The Searchers.*

On its surface, *The Searchers* seems the story of *a* searcher, Ethan Edwards (John Wayne), accompanied by a sidekick, Martin Pawley (Jeffrey Hunter), who is one-eighth Cherokee. Ethan's brother, Aaron, and Aaron's wife, Martha, whom Ethan had himself once loved, are brutally slaughtered in a Comanche attack soon after the film begins. The Comanches carry off two daughters, Debbie and Lucy. Though Lucy is raped and murdered, Debbie remains among the Comanches as both servant and squaw. Ethan's search for Debbie, which consumes him for five years, is an act of determination and revenge: to murder the man responsible for the death of his kin (the Indian brave, Scar) and to rescue Debbie from the Comanches before she has suffered sexual contamination—or to murder her if he is too late (since, for Ethan, to be a white squaw is worse than death for a Christian woman).

Ethan refuses to surrender the search, just as he has never surrendered any cause—he still reveres the sword of the Confederacy. Ethan and Martin pursue the search in winter and in summer, on the plains and through the mountains, living nomadically, like the Comanches they pursue. Ethan far more resembles the people for whom he searches than the "Texicans" he defends: He knows Comanche customs, habits, rituals, and strategies. He knows the way they think and thinks the way they do. Martin, however, strongly feels the pull back toward Texas: His sweetheart, Linda Jorgensen (Vera Miles), will not wait forever for him to conclude his search for Debbie.

Fig. 12-32

The Searchers: *Ethan Edwards (John Wayne) in a comfortable, settled moment indoors, then alone and outdoors—searching.*

Fig. 12-33

The film's dominant contrast is between those who settle and those who search. Perhaps Ford's title is plural because Ethan is one of an old race of people condemned to searching. Ethan feels uncomfortable indoors, within the comforts of a home, covered by a ceiling. Ford's beautiful and parallel shots, which begin and conclude the film, looking outdoors into the glaring sunlight through the dark arch of a doorway, are visual metaphors for the contrasting regions—of indoors and outdoors, civilization and wilderness, garden and desert, settling and searching. In Ford's metaphor, these two regions are contiguous; the warm familial peace indoors cannot be secure without taming the threat from the outdoors. There can be no settlers without searchers—and perhaps, in Ford's view, no peace without war. The settlement needs its searchers and fighters to allow it to be settled.

Ethan remains connected to but apart from the world of settlers; he is not just more comfortable outside, but an outsider. Even he must, however, occasionally suffer the constraints, sometimes comic, of those institutions that civilizations have designated to protect them, whether the posse sworn in by Clayton (Ward Bond) or the United States Cavalry. In a neat historical irony, the comically clumsy embodiment of military rules, regulations, and propriety is played by Wayne's own son, Pat. But then Ford has cast Harry Carey, Jr. in the film as well, the son of the star with whom Ford's career in films and westerns began. The film not only portrays a history of the American West but contains its own history of the American western. The evolution of the individualist, John Wayne, into the mere military cog, Pat Wayne, may be Ford's own encapsulation of American history, parallel to the evolution of the personal gun law of Tom Doniphon (John Wayne again) into the codified book law of Ransom Stoddard (James Stewart) in *The Man Who Shot Liberty Valance.*

In the film's climax, Ethan chases the fleeing Debbie (Natalie Wood). Martin runs after them, terrified that Ethan intends to kill her, but Ethan sweeps her into his arms, up on his horse, and simply says, "Let's go home, Debbie." Like the film's opening and closing shots, this action completes a circle, for Ethan had lifted Debbie in much the same way when she was a little girl. This act of loving acceptance makes the civilized family possible and brings Ethan's obsessive quest for revenge to an unexpected but appropriate solution. Like the by-the-rules, code-driven official (Raymond Massey) in Ford's *The Hurricane* (1937), but unlike the rigid officer (Henry Fonda) in *Fort Apache,* Ethan rises above his own inflexibility. From *The Informer* to *The Quiet Man* (1952), Ford tells stories of moral education whose heroes learn the meaning of honor, courage, love, and law (and, often, how and when to fight). *The Searchers* is typical in the way its les-

son comes clear only at the end, with no sense of the formulaic or pat: Up to the last moment, the audience cannot predict whether or not Ethan will tragically set his rigid code above the demands of love.

In contrast to Ford's complex, energetic, and mutually enriching opposition of the settler's hearth and garden and the loner's wide open spaces, Douglas Sirk shrinks the world into a modern, bourgeois interior that has been arranged and ordered to death. Born in Denmark, Sirk moved to Germany, where he began making films in the 1930s. A leftist, he left Germany in 1937 and arrived in America in 1939 to direct anti-Nazi war films (*Hitler's Madman,* 1943), *films noirs* (*Sleep My Love,* 1948), and domestic comedies (*No Room for the Groom,* 1952). Sirk's major work began in 1954 after his move to Universal, where he became a director of glossy melodramas (adult soap operas, at the time called weepies or women's pictures) under producer Ross Hunter.

Universal was one of Hollywood's few success stories of the 1950s, when it climbed from the industry's doormat to become one of its great powers, for which Hunter was largely responsible. Universal, merged with the huge talent agency, MCA, stocked a large stable of youthful contract talent—Rock Hudson, Sandra Dee, Troy Donahue, Suzanne Pleshette, John Gavin, John Saxon—which Hunter combined with aging stars, cast off from the declining studios, to add both box-office recognition and star stature—Jane Wyman, Lana Turner, Cary Grant, Lauren Bacall, Dorothy Malone. Hunter's two dependable products were the Sirk melodramas and the Doris Day comedies of virginity—threatened but preserved till marriage.

The Sirk melodramas are odd mixtures of contradictory qualities. On the one hand, they seem slick depictions of the most tawdry values of materialistic, middle-class life. On the other hand, they seem brutally funny comments on this very tawdriness, on the values of bourgeois life that the characters automatically accept and on the values of movies and movie audiences that accept them just as automatically. To see a Sirk film, like *Imitation of Life,* in a 1959 movie theatre was like walking into a clinic for schizophrenics: half the audience sobbing hysterically into very wet handkerchiefs, the other half laughing hysterically in sheer disbelief. These same contradictory reactions have divided audiences of Sirk films ever since.

The reason is that Sirk films are powerful bourgeois melodramas and, at the same time, powerful comments on the assumptions of bourgeois melodrama. In *All That Heaven Allows* (1955, U.S. release 1956) an attractive, middle-aged widow (Jane Wyman) falls for a younger man (Rock Hudson), her own gardener, depicted as Thoreau's "man of nature." Her own friends find the man unsuitable — not rich enough, not old enough, not a member of her own social class. The single attraction they see in him is physical — what they can see. She sees him as spiritually different. But if he is such a "natural spirit," why does nature play such a tame visual role in the film — embodied by one symbolic deer behind a plate-glass window in a sound-stage forest? "Nature" is a pitiful visual metaphor in many Sirk films, like the hurricane of paper leaves that opens *Written on the Wind* (1956); to say the least, we are not in Ford's Monument Valley. Why is every scene of nature in *All That Heaven Allows* so obviously an indoor imitation of the outdoors? Is it a mere studio convention, or is Sirk debunking both the conventions and the contrast between nature and artifice on which the film depends? This question is always at the center of a Sirk film. We are never quite sure who is kidding whom.

Sirk shoots his bourgeois world filtered through reminders of Hollywood's presence. Doorways, partitioning screens, window panes, glass mirrors, plate-glass windows, reflective surfaces (even the glass screens of television sets) dominate Sirk frames, calling attention to the fact that we look not at life but at a frame. Grotesquely unnatural prismatic lighting effects in Sirk's color films raise questions about the source and purpose of this oddly colored light. Is the *mise-en-scène* merely decorative, or is Sirk "deconstructing" the very images he constructs (pointing out their internal contradictions) or using Brechtian distancing devices to separate the audience from the illusion of the work? Or is he, without irony, simply giving the audience what it wants: the slickly artificial and maudlin? Does the Sirk film proclaim that everything about it is manufactured — from the way it looks, to the characters who inhabit it, to their value and moral systems?

Imitation of Life (1959) is the ultimate Sirk film — both his last and his most powerful at posing these questions. It is a story about race relations, one of the few serious social subjects that films could explore between 1949 and 1959 without fear of right-wing protests and boycotts. An unemployed white actress (Lana Turner) meets a black woman (Juanita Moore) early in the film while their daughters play together on a crowded beach. The actress rises to success, aided by the financial support and household service of the black woman, who has moved in with her. The white woman's daughter (Sandra Dee) enjoys a typical upper-middle-class adolescence (boarding school and college), while the black daughter (Susan Kohner), who looks white, suffers the pain of social exclusion. She tries to escape her black heritage, seeking sexual affairs with white boys, working as a showgirl in a white nightclub — but returns in the end for her mother's funeral to suffer orgiastic agonies of grief, accompanied by the sorrowful singing of Mahalia Jackson and the sobbing ecstasies of the film's audience.

In remaking this Fanny Hurst novel (originally directed by John M. Stahl for Universal in 1934, starring Claudette Colbert and Louise Beavers), Sirk and Hunter made a crucial change. While in the original (novel and film), the white woman makes a public success of the black woman's private recipe for pancake flour (a clear allusion to Aunt Jemima), the black woman in the 1959 film has no direct relation to the white woman's vocational success. The unglamorous world of pancake mix has been abandoned for the glittering world of Broadway stardom. What happens to Annie, the black woman, in this new world? Quite simply, she becomes Lora's maid — the star's servant and domestic.

There is no indication in the film of why this black woman — the social and financial equal of the white woman at its beginning — should automatically accept her "place" as the white woman's servant. Annie (even her diminutive name is demeaning) does all the household chores, supervises the kitchen, serves as Lora's dresser, arranges Lora's dinner parties without

Fig. 12-34

Fig. 12-35

Imitation of Life. *Whether in a dressing room (Fig. 12-34) or a kitchen (Fig. 12-35), Annie (Juanita Moore) finds it "natural" to become the maid of her friend and equal, Lora (Lana Turner).*

any agreement that she will be paid for these services. What she gets in return is room and board (an arrangement once called slavery). Lora wears a seemingly infinite number (actually thirty-four) of shapely, high-fashion,

bright-colored outfits (designed by Jean-Louis), decked with rings, necklaces, bracelets, and dangling earrings. But Annie wears baggy nondescript sackcloths of indescribable noncolor — some drab variation of brown or gray — with plain round collars, baggy sleeves, and little jewelry. However many of these outfits she wears, they all look the same and always suggest the domestic. Neither Annie nor Lora sees anything odd in this visual inequality (as if it were "natural" for a black woman to become or resemble the servant of a white woman, supposedly her social equal). The question is, does Sirk? Is this a plea for interracial respect and personal authenticity, or a sentimental exaltation of the problems of racism and role-playing?

And how could anyone take Susan Kohner, so obviously white and glamorous, for Sarah-Jane, the daughter of that very dark-skinned, very drably dressed woman in the same frame? And how could Lora ever rise to stardom on the Broadway stage (particularly since her performances are never shown)? Once Lora becomes a star, her problem shifts to whether she can also find love. Annie doesn't hope for love; she has no aspirations for herself at all, only a mother's hope that Sarah-Jane might be happy. Are black women only mammies, never women? Although these white and black women inhabit the same house, the same film, and the same frame, they don't inhabit the same universe. Class and race have nothing and everything to do with their friendship. Who's kidding whom here?

Does *Imitation of Life* want us to recognize it as purely an imitation, a Hollywood fake that purports to depict American race relations in 1959? Or does it really imitate life — the way white movie audiences *view* the two races? Does it show what makes Lora's and Sarah-Jane's lives empty and unreal? Even if its melodramatic plot of Lora's stardom and Sarah-Jane's rebellion is the disguise, and friendship and understanding (and suffering) between women the film's official underlying subject, the ways it is actually about — or an example of — the contradictions of its culture and period can be found in plain sight: for example, in the differences between Lana Turner's and Juanita Moore's wardrobes. If Sirk's melodramas are about surfaces, that does not make them superficial.

Whatever adjective one might seek to describe these films by Fuller, Hitchcock, Ray, Ford, and Sirk, escapist wouldn't be one of them. The moral, economic, social, psychological, and sexual ambiguities of such films suggest an America that was itself as genuinely confused as it was superficially assured about its purpose and direction.

Finding the Audience

Despite the gimmicks, despite the wide screen, despite the sexual innuendos, despite the industry's claim that movies were better than ever, movie income and movie admissions continued to fall throughout the 1950s. In an effort to give the public what television could not, Hollywood had to discover who its public was. It could not assume, as studio moguls Mayer and Zukor and Cohn did in the thirties, that its public was all of the people all of the time.

The signs that would eventually point the way had begun to appear just after the war. A series of foreign films — with De Sica's *The Bicycle Thief* (1948) being the first highly publicized import — proved that a particular kind of film, inexpensively produced, more obviously sociological and less idealized than the Hollywood film, could attract interested audiences to small theatres while slick Hollywood films played to empty houses in large ones. More and more little neighborhood theatres that could no longer do business as fourth-run houses for Hollywood films found a second life as "art houses" by replacing the popcorn machine with an espresso maker and showing foreign pictures like *Rashomon* (1950), *Seven Samurai* (1954), *La strada* (1954), *Les Diaboliques* (1955), and *The Seventh Seal* (1956). In 1959, for example, the art houses' competition wasn't all *Ben-Hur, Some Like It Hot,* and *North by Northwest.* Two of the dumbest American films ever made (Martin Ritt's *The Sound and the Fury* and Edward D. Wood, Jr.'s *Plan 9 From Outer Space*) were released in 1959 — but so were such foreign films as Marcel Camus's *Black Orpheus,* François Truffaut's *The 400 Blows,* Jack Clayton's *Room at the Top,* and Ingmar Bergman's *Wild Strawberries.* The better

films were better received, and many patrons even went back to see them again and talked about them seriously with their friends.

A foreign film was certainly unlike anything that the networks could or would present on television: introspective, with dialogue requiring the audience to read subtitles, sensitive to intellectual and political questions, treating sexual interaction not as salaciously marketable but as a basic and important fact of human experience, with refreshing insights into other cultures, other values, and other ways of seeing. And these foreign imports had never been required to submit themselves to the moral approval of the Hays Office Code. There had been a call for "art houses" and an "art movement" in the 1930s, which had been answered in a few major cities by a few theatres. But the small art house of under 500 seats, with its elite fare, ran contrary to the old financial tides of the 1940s when the movie palaces of several thousand seats filled up every night with customers eager to see Cary Grant or Greer Garson. With television, however, the commercial tides had turned.

Hollywood discovered that movies had indeed become an elite as well as a popular art. Just as the legitimate theatre had been the art for *some* in the thirties when movies were the art for *everyone,* so movies had become the art for some when television became the art for all. Whereas movies had been the casual everyday form of entertainment before the war, television supplied that kind of entertainment after it. Movies, then, had to be aimed at the minority audience that wanted the kind of show that television could not or would not provide; *Psycho* found that audience in 1960, as did *Dr. Strangelove* in 1964, *Bonnie and Clyde* in 1967, *Faces* in 1968, and *Medium Cool* in 1969. The elitism of the movie audience by 1970 becomes clear when comparing the average cost of a ticket in 1946 and 1970. Although films grossed almost the same amount of money in both years, in 1946 the average movie seat cost a bit over forty cents; in 1970 the average seat cost a bit under two dollars. By 1980 the average cost had risen to $3.50, and in 1990 it was normal to pay $5.50 (top big-city prices rose to $4.00 in 1978 and to $7.00 in 1989). Even adjusting for inflation, movies were no longer the "nickel" entertainment, the easiest to get for the least cost, that they had been since the turn of the century. But the programs on television, like those on radio, were free.

To keep any share of the entertainment market at all, the motion picture industry needed to reflect about who still went to movies and why. Families were one answer; movies still provided an outing for the whole family. But the combined cost of four, five, or six tickets, not to mention the cost of getting to the theatre, meant that the outing would be rare and special—perfect for those family-oriented "specials," like the Biblical Blockbusters of the 1950s or the Musical Blockbusters of the 1960s.

The professional, college-educated elite, who still lived in the cities or frequently visited them, was another answer. A strongly committed moviegoing generation of upwardly mobile Americans had discovered the cultural importance of movies—both American and foreign, both classic and new—during their college days.

Finally, there were the young, aged about fourteen and upwards, for whom movies were (and had been since the nickelodeon era) an essential part of the socialization process. These young people used movies to get out of the house, away from the society of their parents (increasingly symbolized by that television set), into a society of their own contemporaries.

It was easy for the movie industry to attract members of these two groups—the cultural elite and the adolescent—away from the television set. Hollywood aimed its films at their values, their interests, their styles, using their themes, their music, their moral codes. If movies were directed at the young, educated, and urban, television, like films in the thirties, was aimed at rural and suburban families—at the kind of audience who went to the movies in the thirties and forties; in fact, much of its audience in the 1950s was composed of those very people. Television formulas—family comedies, mysteries, westerns, hospital dramas, courtroom dramas—were the old movie formulas (with a strong dash of radio, evident not only in the soaps and news, but also in variety shows, situation comedies, dramatic series, and the many programs that began on radio, rang-

ing from *Dragnet* to *The Jack Benny Show*). They did not change because the audience did not change. Films and film audiences had changed. The audience for movies in theatres has remained surprisingly constant—in both its size and composition—for over two decades.

Even before the days of MTV, the VCR, and electronic cinema, the movies learned to coexist with television. They made TV movies and licensed their films to be shown on television. They recruited directors, writers, and actors with television experience. (Ultimately, in the mid-1980s, Fox launched its own network.) They scrapped their huge movie palaces and replaced them with 500-seat theatres that were easier to fill despite their high ticket prices. They chopped big theatres into two or three or more multiplex theatres on the same property, a much more economical use of land and space, whether in the big cities or suburban shopping centers. Even the few great movie palaces that still survive—the Criterion in New York, the Empire in London, the Egyptian in Los Angeles—are multiplex cinemas now. In 1973 the MGM and Twentieth Century-Fox back lots were both sold to make room for apartment houses, office buildings, stores, and restaurants.

Television, which threatened to swallow the film studios, also subsidized them. Over 75 percent of the film footage shot in Hollywood is for television production. The old studios survived the years of drift and struggle—if they survived at all—thanks to the steady income from TV filming. The old economic hierarchy—Specials, "A" pictures, programmers, and "B" pictures—of the studio era still determines types of theatrical and television production: Theatrical movies are Hollywood's special product; the mini-series and made-for-TV movies parallel the A pictures and programmers; the weekly television shows are Hollywood's B staples.

Because of pressures and problems ranging from the blacklist to "the box," in the 1950s there was terrific uncertainty about what might be said, how it might be said, and to whom it might be said—an uncertainty that increased with every passing year until the film business bottomed out in the early 1960s. The best films of the postwar era preserved the old studio styles, structures, and genres, even as the studios were crumbling — or took wild creative chances in spite of those conventions. Hollywood stumbled through the maze of conflicting production values and social controversies, eventually emerging from what a science fiction film of the fifties might call a time warp.

Note that in the last sentence "Hollywood" has been personified. It has been personified since at least the Jazz Age, always implying a cultural assumption rather than a geographical location. While the personification once meant "the Movies" or "the Movie Business," by 1965 it had come to symbolize the entire American entertainment business. There are hundreds of pink ceramic stars, encased in the black terrazzo sidewalks of Hollywood Boulevard, honoring those who have contributed to Hollywood. Each name is accompanied by one of four brass symbols — a television set, a radio microphone, a phonograph disc, or a movie camera. This sidewalk, designed in the mid-1960s, already implied that the movies occupied only a fraction of the entertainment capital's business.

Although the American film business — yearly gross, weekly admissions, audience vitality and interest — has been thriving for over two decades, the theoretical capital of that business, Hollywood, is no longer *the* production center of American theatrical films. With so many companies filming in or near New York, San Francisco, Toronto, Montreal, London, all over the continent of Europe, and even in developing regional production centers of America (where states have established film boards specifically to lure production companies), Hollywood is still the name of the movie game. It is no longer the only stadium where that game is played.

13

Neorealisms and New Waves

After the Second World War, European directors did exactly what they did after the First World War. They climbed out from under years of wartime rubble and disrupted production, somehow scraped together enough money and film stock to assemble a motion picture, and began making films that showed extraordinary sincerity, insight, and artistic control. While American films groped for a new identity, many of the films that struck audiences and critics as the best came from Europe. The films seemed best not because they often revealed portions of naked bodies, not because they were bathed in obscure, symbolic meanings, and not because American audiences had become cultural snobs—as so many chauvinistic American film critics and executives claimed. The films seemed best because they raised the same questions in cinematic form that had been raised in the best novels, plays, poems, and philosophical essays of the twentieth century. And the adult Americans who had become the new movie audience, those who found it easy to leave their television sets, were precisely those who were reading the books.

It was not that the best American films were mindless (the great European directors

never believed them to be) but that the best films from Europe were so explicitly serious, more aggressively existential, modernist, and adult than the familiar genres and attitudes of Hollywood. In the tradition of Mann, Proust, Pirandello, and Sartre (and, by the way, of Renoir, Carné, Murnau, and Pabst), the new European film searched for meaningful, life-giving values in a world in which absolute values had crumbled. Nor could the social and psychological problems of these European films be solved by Hollywood's two most frequent forms of closure—the killing of a bad guy or the marriage of John and Jane. Many European films began with a marriage rather than ended with one.

The great films of postwar Europe, despite the individuality of the particular directors, shared several traits that contrasted with the typical American film. First, very few of them were faithful adaptations of familiar books and plays. The films were often original conceptions, carefully shaped by the director and scenarist working in unison (in fact, the director was usually credited as co-author). This collaboration of director and scenarist revealed a continuity in the European film tradition (before the war, many of its great films had been produced with collaborations like Murnau–Mayer and Carné–Prévert).

Second, those postwar European films that reached American viewers continued the prewar tradition of structuring themselves around a theme or psychological problem more than around a story. Like *Grand Illusion, The Children of Paradise, Battleship Potemkin,* or *The Last Laugh,* the films of Roberto Rossellini, Vittorio De Sica, Federico Fellini, Ingmar Bergman, Alain Resnais, Jean-Luc Godard, and Michelangelo Antonioni were not so much linear narratives as they were experiments in cinematic narration, often concerned with political and philosophical issues, as well as investigative comparisons of human conduct, emotional states, and conflicts between the social whole and the personal unit.

Third, the focus on psychology and theme brought these films back into the mainstream of twentieth-century thought and literature. The thematic and psychological questions in these films, and to some degree the ways they were handled, were closely related to those in Kafka, Pound, Joyce, Proust, Mann, Woolf, Faulkner, Beckett, Camus, Ionesco, and others.

Fourth, European directors discovered different ways to define film style, realizing that certain kinds of thematic inquiries or psychological states required a totally different handling of the *mise-en-scène,* camera, and soundtrack. The makers of *The Cabinet of Dr. Caligari, The Last Laugh, The Smiling Madame Beudet, The Fall of the House of Usher, Vampyr,* and *A nous la liberté* had earlier realized the same principle.

In effect, the postwar European cinema brought the movies into the mainstream of Modernism, the key twentieth-century movement that produced nonrepresentational painting, atonal music, absurd drama, and the stream-of-consciousness novel, and whose tenets included the self-conscious questioning of all social and moral values, the duty to "make it new," the study of perception, the determination to work creatively with fragmentation (from Cubism to montage), and the self-conscious manipulation of the conventions of the art itself. Like the great European directors before 1940, the great postwar European filmmakers were both thinkers and poets. And the postwar film audience, especially in America, was receptive to their films, bringing in some of the money that allowed them to make more films. Although several American critics shuddered at the thought of "Antoniennui" (boring films about boredom) or "come-dressed-as-the-sick-soul-of-Europe" pictures, the years after 1945 were a great period in film history, one in which wave after wave of European directors and writers had something to say and knew how to say it.

Italian Neorealism

Not since 1914 had Italy been an important international film power. The huge silent spectacles of 1912–1914 were swiftly replaced by the Griffith films, which were not only big but active. Early Italian sound films traveled between the two poles of pro-Mussolini propaganda and escapist comedies, historical spectacles, and musical romances, so-called "White Telephone" pictures (because of the inevitable white telephone in the fancily decorated apartments that served as sets for these films). Mussolini extended considerable aid to the film industry, founding both a huge film studio (Cinecittà) and a film school (Centro Sperimentale). Although opposite the Soviets in ideology, Mussolini believed just as firmly in the persuasive power of cinema to shape a people. Like the Germans and Japanese, Mussolini banned the importation of American films—an isolation that protected the Italian populace from American contamination and the Italian film industry from American competition, allowing its consolidation into a native cinema that was commercially vigorous if artistically dead. The occasional work of great artistic merit that dared to concentrate on important social, political, and philosophical matters—such as Goffredo Alessandrini's *We the Living* (1942; U.S. release 1988), based on the novel by Ayn Rand—was confiscated by the Fascist authorities or—like Visconti's *Ossessione*—recut after a brief release. If society, art, sex, politics, and independent thought were problematic, economics was untouchable: Any portrayal of unemployment was absolutely forbidden.

After the overthrow of Mussolini and the expulsion of the Nazis, the Italian filmmakers, highly experienced in film production, used the new freedom to combine their skill in making pictures with the subjects about which they wanted to make pictures. Just as the freedom following World War I unlocked the minds of the German and Soviet directors, the freedom following World War II released the Italian imagination. The influx of American movies brought a fresh view of America to Italian moviehouses—just as it did to those in France, Germany, and Japan. And the influx of American capital brought a fresh view of Italy to American moviehouses.

Even as the Nazis were evacuating Rome, Roberto Rossellini began to work on *Open City (Roma, città aperta, 1945)*. An "open city" is one that is immune from attack because it has been declared demilitarized, as Rome was. Rossellini made the film under the most difficult conditions, closely resembling the early production problems of the Soviet filmmakers: Raw film stock was scarce, money for constructing sets was even scarcer, actors were difficult to find, slickness and polish were impossible without the controlled lighting of studio filming. Rossellini turned defects into virtues. He willingly sacrificed polish for reality, settings for real locations, fiction for life. Rossellini often preferred laborers and peasants to actors (another parallel with Eisenstein and Pudovkin). He and cinematographer Ubaldo Arata carried their camera all over the city and fleetingly shot the real city on the run.

Open City (written by Sergio Amidei, Rossellini, and Fellini, who also collaborated on *Paisan*) contrasted the humane, committed, unified struggle of the Italian people for freedom—the unity of priests, workers, intellectuals, adults, children—with the brutality of the Nazi invaders who used the most loathsome methods (torture, bribery, manipulation of dependence on drugs or sexual gratification) to enslave the weakest Italians or to force them to betray their fellows. The two styles of the film—the natural, open, realistic, crisply lit texture of the scenes with the Resistance figures; the cramped, stilted, artificial, shadowy texture of the scenes with the Nazis—supported the film's thematic contrast.

Fig. 13-1

Fig. 13-2

Open City. *From the death of a single valiant priest (Fig. 13-1; Aldo Fabrizi), the boys walk back to the city, arm in arm (Fig. 13-2).*

At the end of the film a single member of the Resistance, a committed priest (Don Pietro, played by Aldo Fabrizi), is executed by the Nazi oppressors for his service to the people. This priest is a notable political exception (the Italian clergy generally supported Mussolini's Fascist government), and his alliance with the Resistance is also an alliance with the Communists who led it. As the partisan priest dies, Rossellini's camera captures the activities of the children of Rome and a far shot of the city itself, for from the death of this one man will come a solidarity that was to be the hope of the new Rome. *Open City* became the unofficial cornerstone of a new movement in Italian cinema—neorealism.

Rossellini's next film, *Paisan* (1946), further defined the filmmaker's commitments. A collection of separate vignettes, each of the film's six sequences moves progressively north with the Allied invasion and Nazi retreat. Despite its documentary structure, mirroring the movement of the campaign, Rossellini concentrates on the human texture within each of the vignettes—some lighter and some more brutal, some dominated by the imagery of battle-scarred cities and some by the apparent placidity of the countryside. As is usual for Rossellini, he neither makes simple judgments nor takes simple positions, neither for nor against the insensitivities of the invading liberators, neither for nor against the Italians, themselves terribly divided by the struggle. Rossellini's camera, managed by Otello Martelli, records the luminous Italian countryside in which the struggle takes place, seemingly unaffected by the brutal battle within it. The counterpoint between human action and the visual landscape that contains it would remain Rossellini's dominant visual technique and personal theme.

Cesare Zavattini, scenarist for most of De Sica's neorealist films, defined the principles of the movement: to show things as they are, not as they seem, nor as the bourgeois would prefer them to appear; to write fictions about the human side of representative social, political, and economic conditions; to shoot on location wherever possible; to use untrained actors in the majority of roles; to capture and reflect reality with little or no compromise; to depict common people rather than overdressed heroes and fantasy role models; to reveal the everyday rather than the exceptional; and to show a person's relationship to the real social environment rather than to his or her romantic dreams. As can be seen from the last of those tenets, the movement was as opposed to Expressionism as it was to Hollywood. The neo-realist film developed the influence of the social environment on basic human needs: the need for food, shelter, vocation, love, familial comforts, sexual gratification. In the tradition of Marxist thought (yet another parallel with the classic Soviet films), the neorealist films repeatedly show that unjust and perverted social structures threaten to warp and pervert the essential and internal human values.

Vittorio De Sica became the most popular Italian neorealist with American audiences, probably because his melodramas effectively combined the political, the sentimental, and the traditional story—as opposed to the detached ironies, paradoxical observations, conceptual framing, and elliptical narratives of Rossellini. De Sica, a popular stage and film actor in the 1930s and director of escapist fluff films in the early 1940s, directed the neorealist *Shoeshine* in 1946 (script by Zavattini), a brutally poignant study of the perversion and destruction of a pair of Roman boys by both the gangsters and the police who are using them. *The Bicycle Thief* (1948, Zavattini's most important script) is another study of degradation and pain. Its original title, *Bicycle Thieves,* is far more appropriate than the accepted American translation, simply because there are two bicycle thieves in the film: the man who steals the protagonist's bike and the protagonist himself (Antonio, played by Lamberto Maggiorani), who eventually becomes a bicycle thief out of necessity.

From the film's opening shots De Sica and Zavattini begin their relentless development of the kind of social environment that turns men into bicycle thieves: There are many men without work; there are very few jobs; the men have wives and children to support; the man with a bicycle is one of the lucky working few. To get his bicycle out of the pawn shop (for a job pasting up posters all over the city—for a glamorous American movie), Antonio's wife takes her wedding sheets to pawn in exchange for the bike. The poignancy of her sacrifice is underscored by De Sica's long shot of row upon row of pawned bridal sheets—others have been forced to make the same sacrifice of sentimental mementos for practical necessity. De Sica's camera constantly emphasizes the quantities of people and of things that are

Fig. 13-3
The Bicycle Thief. *Father (Lamberto Maggiorani) and son (Enzo Staiola) search desperately in a downpour for the irreplaceable bicycle.*

embraced by this story rather than implying that this is a tale of the exceptional few. The film is filled with panning or tracking shots of rows and rows of men, of houses, of bicycles, of bicycle parts.

The film's narrative premise is Antonio's desperate need to find his stolen bicycle. Without the bicycle he has no job; without a job his family starves. The man and his young son, Bruno (Enzo Staiola), roam the streets, catching an occasional glimpse of the bike or the figure who stole it. Throughout the film the boy's relationship with his father serves as barometer of the effects of the agonizing search on the man's soul. Father and son drift further apart; the man even strikes the boy. When Antonio

finally corners the thief, he discovers that the young man is as poor as he is. Even more pathetic, the thief is epileptic. The thief's mother and neighbors protect the young man against Antonio, and neither the police nor the local Mafia are any help, since Antonio has no evidence.

Realizing the impossibility of ever getting his own bicycle back, Antonio is tempted by the sight of the many unattended bicycles around him. In his extremity, the man cannot resist the temptation. He steals a bicycle himself, is swiftly caught, and then is beaten and abused by the angry citizens who denounce him as a villainous thief. The man's degradation is complete. Bruno both sees and hears his father's ultimate degradation. Just before this ignominious defeat, the father sits alone — empty, hurt, beaten — his son silently beside him. The boy slowly slips his hand inside the father's. Once again after the attempted theft, when the father tries to hurry away from the boy in shame, Bruno catches up with him and slips his hand inside his father's. Despite the terrible social humiliation, the humanity and affection of father and son have been restored. Then they disappear into a crowd of people who, the film implies, are struggling with analogous problems; this tragedy, made from such unglamorous materials, is one among thousands.

De Sica claims that an American producer offered him millions to make *Bicycle Thieves* with Cary Grant as Antonio. De Sica rejected both the money and the star. Instead, he cast a metal worker, a nonactor, as the desperate father. De Sica's preference reveals many of the principles of neorealism: reality rather than pretense, earthiness rather than sparkle, the common man rather than the idol. Instead of Hollywood's bright sets and stylish clothes, these films showed primitive kitchens, squalid living rooms, peeling walls, baggy, torn clothing, streets that almost stank of urine and garbage (no telephones here, much less white ones!). Instead of the Hollywood love goddess, the neorealist heroine incarnate was Anna Magnani: coarse, fiery, indefatigable, plump, strong, sweaty. Zavattini claimed that the neorealist film was as attached to the present as sweat was to skin.

The essential theme of the neorealist film was the conflict between the contemporary common man and the immense sociological forces that were completely external to himself and yet completely determined his existence: first the war, after it the means of making a living and the struggle to keep a home and family together. In the three or four years following the war, many Italian directors developed their own variations on this essential theme: Rossellini's *Germany Year Zero* (1947) examined the rubble, hunger, and unemployment of postwar Berlin, completing the "War Trilogy" that began with *Open City* and *Paisan*; Alessandro Blasetti's *Un giorno nella vita* (1946); Luigi Zampa's *Vivere in pace* (1946), *L'onorevole*

Angelina (1947), *Anni difficili* (1948, script by Amidei); Alberto Lattuada's *The Crime of Giovanni Episcopo* (1947) and *Senza pietà* (1948); Giuseppi de Santis's *Caccia tragica* (1947) and *Bitter Rice* (1949). In many of these films, despite the social squalor and economic misery surrounding them, the central figures succeed in asserting the human and the humanity within themselves. The films are about misery without surrendering to misery.

But by 1950 neorealism had either run or begun to change its course. Either the new stability of postwar Europe, the new prosperity of the Italian film industry, or the new Andreotti Law (which simultaneously supported film production but denied export permits to any film that depicted Italian society unfavorably) shifted the Italian film's focus away from the sociological struggle with squalor. The films became increasingly psychological and less sociological. Although critics tried to elucidate the continuity of the movement by coining terms like poetic neorealism, romantic neorealism, or historical neorealism, such terms were not quite compatible with the original neorealist premise. The Italian film for the international market, while still valuing the realist actor and the realist milieu, had begun to use more polished scripts, more carefully constructed sets, more conventional fictional structures and themes, and highly professional actors. Even the original neorealist directors wandered away from earlier styles and themes.

Roberto Rossellini tracked inward from cross-sectional surveys of an entire society to close studies of personal moralities and internal sensations — featuring Ingrid Bergman, the great star who defied Hollywood propriety and world opinion by abandoning her husband to remain with Rossellini in Italy. (Their daughter, Isabella Rossellini, became a famous actress in her own right, particularly with the 1986 release of David Lynch's *Blue Velvet*.) In *Stromboli* (1949), scripted by Sergio Amidei, Bergman plays a war refugee from Northern Europe, desperately seeking a new life with an Italian husband on a tiny island off the Italian coast. The isolation of the primitive island and its brutal people, the craggy rock of the treeless volcanic soil, the gleaming white houses baking in the brilliant and brutal sun all meta-phorically imply the woman's loneliness, frustration, and isolation. Rossellini's landscape serves as an objective correlative of the woman's internal state, a stranger in a strange land, tied to a small-minded, old-fashioned man, as unresponsive to her needs as the parched soil on which she walks. At the end, she both transcends her situation and comes to terms with it.

Viaggio in Italia (Voyage to Italy, 1953) is one of Rossellini's greatest works, if also one of his greatest critical disappointments. A British couple (Ingrid Bergman and George Sanders) travels to Naples to settle the property and business affairs of a deceased relative. Rossellini depicts their emotional distance from one another by their emotional distance from the surrounding countryside and its customs. Driving in their car (even its steering wheel on the wrong side for the road), encased by its glass windows and windshield, wearing dark glasses that block them from seeing or being seen, the couple travels through the world as if in an armored tank. Their clothing is wrong for the weather; their habits are insensitive to native custom. But simply by walking around and observing—Rossellini's awesome visual recording of the statues in a museum, of the ruins of Pompeii, of the bubbling volcanic lava of Vesuvius—the woman especially begins to feel the fertile energy of that vital setting called "Italy."

Sightseeing becomes a powerful moral and emotional force. By seeing these sights, the couple begins to internalize their visual resonances, giving them at least some hope of continuing together in the future. For Rossellini to convert sightseeing into a poetic force is especially appropriate for cinema, for what else is a film but sights seen and felt? Rossellini's ability to render the moral, emotional, architectural, philosophical, and poetic power of sights and systems would make him a major influence on a new generation of directors in both Italy and France.

De Sica and Zavattini made a utopian folk fantasy, *Miracle in Milan* (1950), a joyous combination of political and Christian myth, and *Umberto D* (1952), a wrenching film of typical

Fig. 13-4
The power of sightseeing in Viaggio in Italia.

De Sica pathos, far more interested in Umberto's personal feelings than in the social problem of old-age benefits. The old man's relationship with his dog, Flick, was almost identical to Antonio's relationship with his son in *Bicycle Thieves,* including the dog's rejection of Umberto when he attempts an act of debasement (suicide), followed by an identical reconciliation. De Sica, however, probably strayed least from the original neorealist principles, as his later *The Roof* (1956) and *Two Women* (1960) show. Sophia Loren won an Academy Award for her ability to play an unglamorous, Anna-Magnaniesque woman in *Two Women* (written by Zavattini), valiantly fighting the classic problems of neorealism: the war, hunger, and the assault on her family. In *The Garden of the Finzi-Continis* (1971), De Sica again depicts the struggle of individual people and whole families against the viciousness of social systems and the brutalities of war. But this late film—with its nostalgic look backward at the world of the rich; its softer, more sentimentalized human beings; its dependence on lengthy discussions; and its lush color pictorialism—seemed antithetical to the style and spirit of the earlier, earthier De Sica. But in their final collaboration, *A Brief Vacation* (1973, De Sica's last film), they told the story

Fig. 13-5
The Sicilian fishing boats of **La terra trema.**

of a working-class woman who, to cure herself of TB, takes the only vacation of her life in *The Magic Mountain*-like retreats of the rich. Here the glossy look of the sanitarium—and the concerns of the rich—contrast most effectively with the dim, brutal, unchanged world to which she must return.

The potential direction of Italian realism was predicted by a much earlier film: Luchino Visconti's *Ossessione* (1942). Visconti's film, an unauthorized adaptation of James M. Cain's novel of sexual sordidness and murder, *The Postman Always Rings Twice,* uses squalid settings and realistic rather than romantic human types as background for its personal, psychological action. Social realism becomes the film's milieu, its soil, rather than its subject. Visconti's films consistently depart from the

Zavattini definitions, using the social reality to define the personal problems of the characters rather than to be the focus of the films themselves. For this reason, Visconti felt equally comfortable in the social reality of contemporary squalor: *Ossessione, La terra trema (The Earth Trembles,* 1948), *Rocco and His Brothers* (1960)—or historical sumptuousness: *Senso* (1954), *The Leopard* (1963), *The Damned* (1969), *Death in Venice* (1971).

That Visconti's interest was more in the interrelationship of human passion and stylistic decor than in societal forces can be clearly seen in the difference between his films in color and those in black-and-white. For Visconti (as, perhaps, for De Sica) black-and-white was the medium for depicting poverty, deprivation, and raw passion; color was the medium for depicting the rich, the elegant, and the more complex and contradictory thoughts and feelings. In *The Damned* the corrupt, decadent characters; their business, manufacturing weapons; and their social games were literally equated with the opulently decadent decor, which was itself the mirror of the vicious political system these Nazis had created and nurtured.

Visconti's late films put many of the commonly accepted views about film to their most severe test: particularly that human beings are the focal interest of narrative films, and that film might be defined as a moving image. In his late color films, people seem to be reduced to mere puppets, mere elements of decor, and the image not only does not move but, in *Death in Venice* especially, seems subservient to the musical track. In his discussion of *La terra trema,* André Bazin referred to the extreme length — three to four minutes — of Visconti's shots as they tracked and panned endlessly, observing the characters' actions. In *Death in Venice* the shots are equally lengthy, and the camera tracks and pans as much, assisted by a new ally — the zoom lens — that seems to slide through three or four maneuvers in every shot.

But unlike *La terra trema,* the dominant photographic subject of *Death in Venice* seems to be the characters' nonactions, as if they are posing for stills. They sit motionless — almost a Panavision postcard — allowing the eye to soak up the magnificent details of the decor: its elegance, its accurate recreation of a historical era, its visual taste and beauty. And as the eye absorbs this static scene, the only thing other than the camera that moves is the music of Mahler on the soundtrack, rising to heights of ecstasy. Whether the music successfully recreates and transmits the passion in the main character's soul (clearly its intention) is a matter for debate, but the result (despite the film's pictorial and musical beauties) seems less complex and less compelling than the original novella by Thomas Mann.

Fellini, Antonioni, and Others

Although Federico Fellini's apprenticeship was to Rossellini and Amidei on the scenarios for *Open City, Paisan,* and *The Miracle,* Fellini's own films reveal the flamboyant romantic. He prefers the places of mystery, magic, and make-believe — the circus, the variety theatre, the nightclub, the opera house — to the squalid slums of reality. His characters search for happiness, for love, for meaning, not for social security. If Anna Magnani or Ingrid Bergman is the soul of Rossellini's neorealism, Giulietta Masina is the soul of Fellini, his wife offscreen and the central figure of many of his films, including *La strada (The Street,* 1954) and *Nights of Cabiria* (1956), two of his greatest. Giulietta Masina, with the glowing eyes, the smirking mouth, the deep dimples, wildly joyful, wildly sad, is to Anna Magnani or Ingrid Bergman as a sunbeam is to a lion or an icicle. In both *La strada* and *Nights of Cabiria* Masina plays a pure spirit of love, a being of the heart and not the mind.

In the earlier film, she is Gelsomina, the clownish fool, apprenticed to the strong man, Zampanò (Anthony Quinn), who uses her as servant, performer, cook, and concubine — human chattel. Despite her rough treatment from the boorish animal-man, Gelsomina comes to love this human with whom she shares her life. But he — afraid of human commitment, of emotional strings — betrays her, leaves her alone to die in the snow. He kills her in the same careless and callous way that he killed that other clownish soul, the acrobat (Richard Basehart), who had felt the rays of Gelsomina's hypnotic passion. Only after Gelsomina is dead, when the strong man hears the haunting, sweet-sad song that she once played on her trumpet, does the supposedly strong man learn how weak and alone he is as he sobs helplessly in a vast cold empty universe of sand, sea, and sky.

As Cabiria, Giulietta Masina plays once again the spirit of pure love trampled by the realities of human selfishness. Cabiria is the purehearted whore, forced to sell her love since no one wants it for nothing. The film opens with a boyfriend's stealing her purse and throwing her in the river. Every sequence duplicates the disillusionment of this opening one. When Cabiria goes to a music hall, a hypnotist entrances her into enacting all her romantic, childlike fantasies, symbolized by the appear-

Giulietta Masina in **La strada.**

Fig. 13-6

ance of her ideal lover, named "Oscar." Cabiria's tender dreams become merely sport for the hooting, crass members of the audience. But a gentleman who has watched the performance, claiming that his name really is Oscar, introduces himself to Cabiria and begins her most serious romantic hope in the film. After she sells her house and her furniture, gladly leaving her old life behind for the love of a man she knows almost nothing about, she discovers that he too wants only her purse.

Though he takes her money, he cannot throw her into the sea as he had planned. Cabiria's final disillusionment is the ultimate magnification of the opening scene, the ultimate disappointment, the comedy of the opening scene turned tragic and horrifying by the compelling events between the two scenes. But Cabiria does not die. In one of the most truly ironic and metaphorical endings in film history, closely paralleling the ending of *The Children of Paradise,* the weeping, sobbing Cabiria encounters a group of festive, singing youngsters as she walks on the road back to town (and, metaphorically, to life). They sing as she

sobs; they do not notice her tears; their singing does not stop her tears, but she continues walking with them, participating vicariously in their song. The laughter and tears of Cabiria's life, of Everyman's life, have been brilliantly juxtaposed.

Fellini's greatest works are inevitably works of laughter and tears. His sheer romanticism is underscored by his composer, Nino Rota, whose scores mix melodiousness and mysteriousness, exoticism and sweetness. Fellini gets into trouble when he deserts feeling for thought. *La dolce vita* (*The Sweet Life,* 1960), however great, is an overstated contrast of Sensuality versus Spirituality. In the film's first sequence, a helicopter pilot, towing a wooden statue of Christ, looks down and waves at three women in bikinis, sunning themselves on a Roman roof. The film, intellectually, is over. Christ has been petrified; he is the tool of modern machinery (the helicopter); people are more interested in bosoms and bikinis than in Christ. Although the film has nothing more to say, Fellini continues for almost three hours, contrasting sensual things — nightclubs,

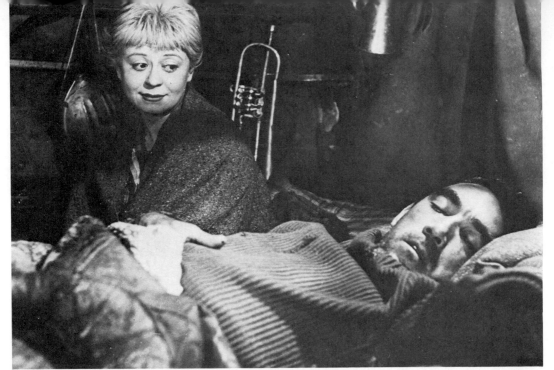

Fig. 13-7

Fig. 13-8
La strada: *Gelsomina (Giulietta Masina) and Zampanò (Anthony Quinn). Love despite the obstacles.*

orgiastic parties, chic gatherings—with the corruption of spiritual things—a verbose intellectual commits suicide, a group of crazy children pretend to see a miraculous vision.

Juliet of the Spirits (1965), another examination of the same duality—Sensuality versus Spirituality, which must be considered Fellini's primary theme—suffers from a similar overschematization. Its most striking virtue is a dazzling use of color that Fellini manipulates to underscore the thematic opposition (pale cool green and lavender versus brilliant white, red, orange, and yellow). If black-and-white had been Fellini's medium for analysis and conflict, color in the 1970s was to become his medium for synthesis and accord. *Fellini Satyricon* (1969) synthesized the Sensual and the Spiritual by pushing the purity of sensual expression to its limit, so that this elevation of the sensual became an apotheosis of spirit as well (*Casanova*, 1976, attempted the same synthesis). Fellini never interrupts the flow of his visual-sensual circus in *Satyricon* for symbolic dichotomies and abstract generalizations. The result is a hypnotic journey through a surrealistic dream world that, like Fellini's other circuses (his primary image for the world of art), has no function other than to be savored and experienced for the way it looks and feels.

What substitutes for thought in Fellini is a romantic rebelliousness and an ambivalent reaction to the grotesque. A consistent Fellini target is the Roman Catholic Church. For Fellini, the Church is a hypocritical and empty show that bilks its public by playing on its insecurities and fears. The Church is the arch-sensualist masquerading as a spiritualist. In *La strada*, Fellini photographs a solemn Church procession with a neon sign reading "Bar" prominently in the foreground; he further debases the religious spectacle by showing the tacky cardboard backing on the glowing pictures of the saints. One of Fellini's most devastating blows at the Church is in *Night of Cabiria*. A society of human unfortunates takes a desperate outing to a religious festival, where they are greeted by canned prayers on loudspeakers (prominently in the foreground of Fellini's frame) and greedy vendors hawking sacred candles and secular candies. Fellini transforms a spiritual event into a commercial carnival. Even more grotesque, this delegation of prostitutes is led by a crippled pimp and dope pusher who has come to the festival specifically to be made to walk again. Perhaps he needs healthy legs to collect even more profits from the sales of body and needle. A much later Fellini swipe at the Church that rivals *Nights of Cabiria* in its venom and cynicism is in *Fellini Roma* (1972) with its monstrously funny fashion show of clerical clothing and priestly paraphernalia.

Whereas Fellini treats organized religion with grotesque bitterness and comical contempt, he treats the glamorous world of the rich with a stylish grotesqueness that reveals both its emptiness and its fascination. Fellini films are jammed with the faces and costumes of the *haut monde*, ladies in long silken gowns and geometrically shaped lorgnettes, their teased hair climbing to the ceiling and their aquiline noses dragging toward the floor, effete gentlemen with fleeting eyes and fluttering hands. The lesbian in the posh nightclub of *Nights of Cabiria*, the society party in *La dolce vita*, the patrons of the health spa in *8½* (1963), the Roman revellers at feasts and orgies in *Fellini Satyricon*, the first-class passengers in *And the Ship Sails On* (1983), are all examples of the grotesque—in costume, make-up, gestures, features, shapes, sizes—that Fellini finds hauntingly attractive. In *Juliet of the Spirits,* his first color film, Fellini uses flashing, blinding color to make the wealthy sensualists even more beautiful-ugly. (The previous year, Antonioni put color to subtler uses in *Red Desert.*) Fellini's social criticism of the fashionably idle pulls him one way; his hypnotized attraction to their visually stunning exteriors and their uncompromising sensuality pulls him another.

Fellini's greatest film, his most impressive synthesis of dramatic power, personal vision, and cinematic control, may well be *8½*. (Before this, Fellini had directed six features and three "half films"—two episodes in compilation films and one co-directed feature; *8½* is named only as Fellini's 8½th movie.) Perhaps the quintessential modernist feature film, the subject of *8½* is simply itself. It is not merely about filmmaking (like Truffaut's *Day for Night*); it is about the making of this very film, a film which the director finds impossible to make

Fig. 13-9
8½: Fellini faces.

but which has been made nonetheless. The protagonist of the film (Guido, played by Marcello Mastroianni) is a film director himself. Because of his nervousness and tension, he is relaxing, preparing for his next film, at a fashionable health spa. Preparing for the project, the director is flooded with images out of his film and memories out of his life, which get thoroughly and inextricably confused. He puts his living relationships into fictional structures; he draws his fictional ideas from his personal experiences of the past and present (just as Fellini does with more tenderness and less agony a decade later in *Amarcord,* 1973, another color film of synthesis and reconciliation). The director's emotional problem in the film—and undoubtedly Guido represents Fellini here—is wondering whether he is successful at either life or art, wondering whether he

hasn't prostituted his life for his art and his art for his life, whether he has the right or the ability to make films.

Although *8½* tempts critics to treat it as an abstract Pirandellian disquisition on life and art, reality and illusion, its major strength, like Fellini's, is as human drama. Fellini successfully roots the drama in Guido's thoughts and sensations. The film begins with Guido's nightmare: He feels trapped inside a hot, smoky automobile during a mammoth traffic jam. He longs to escape from the car, to fly high above the earth. The remainder of the film works on the man's anxiety and longing, his desire to break free of the bonds of his life, his desire to soar in life and art. He searches throughout the film for an actress to portray a pure lady in white. Is she the illusory panacea that will make sense of both his personal relationships and his artis-

Fig. 13-10

Fig. 13-11

8½. Fig. 13-10: the artist (Marcello Mastroianni) among his memories and fantasies; Fig. 13-11: the circle and circus of the film director's life.

tic purpose? Is she a reference to the symbolic girl in white in *La dolce vita,* whom Fellini sees as a facile and naïve solution to a complex artistic and human problem? By the end of the film, Guido seems to renounce the search. He attends a gala party for his film. The party be-

comes a gigantic circus composed of all the characters of his memories and of his film. Fellini's camera swirls in an excited circle as the parade of Guido's creatures dances about a circus ring, that familiar Fellini setting. Guido stares at the dancing creatures; he then steps into their circle and joins the dance. His life is what it is; his art is what it is. There is nothing for him to do but live it and create it. The artist's tension has been resolved; he cannot be separated from the dancing ring of his thoughts, his loves, his creations, his memories. The film that could not be made has been made because whatever Guido's (and Fellini's) deficiencies as a human being, he is a maker of films. That is his dance.

That dance has never been particularly political for Fellini. Despite his apprenticeship in engaged cinema, Fellini came to depend more on his childhood memories (whether in *8½* or *Amarcord*), on the magic of the theatre and the circus, and on his dreams. Late Fellini films suggest sharp twinges of political conscience, for Italy has been one of the most politically divided countries of postwar Western Europe. Fellini's *Orchestra Rehearsal* (1979) uses the dissolution of a symphony orchestra — its rebellion against the traditional authority of its conductor — as a metaphor for postwar Italian history: breaking free from fascist autocracy only to fall into the bickering chaos of trade unions and splinter political parties, until the wrecking ball mercifully knocks the entire edifice to the ground. The cost of liberation has been the loss of social harmony and its music.

And the Ship Sails On also uses the making of music (and, by implication, films) as its central metaphor. This political allegory sails even further into the past — the death of the old and gracious Europe before the First World War, the Europe once represented by archdukes and opera singers. The glittering first-class passengers cannot avoid the hunger and misery of the politically displaced peasant refugees in steerage. Like the fat and bloated prince, Europe is a woozy hippopotamus with a terminal disease. For all Fellini's sympathy for the film's drab figures of poverty, virtual incarnations of neorealism's past, he cannot disguise his visual attraction to the rich and splendid artists and aristocrats in the first-class dining salon nor his affection for the shimmering cloth and sparkling color of his stylized decor. Although Fellini knows that films cannot avoid the pleas of misery and social justice, he prefers the magic, beauty, and dreams of art.

Like Fellini's, Michelangelo Antonioni's roots are in neorealism. While Rossellini and De Sica were making their documentary-style features, Antonioni was making documentary shorts about the lives of street cleaners and farmers. But Antonioni soon deserted the documentary for the highly polished and stylized drama of personal sensations—eventually to return to documentary filmmaking for the 1972 *Chung Kuo Cina,* shot in the People's Republic of China. Antonioni is as much an abstract expressionist painter as a documentary photographer. His series of 184 paintings, which he titled "Montagne Encantate" (Enchanted Mountain), reveals his visual values. These are colorful representations of living rocks, vaguely sensuous landscapes of soft blobs and hard shapes, dominated by clashes of color and contrasts of forms. These enchanted mountains of sensuous shapes would dominate Antonioni's films as well (from the rocks of *L'avventura* to the rocks of *Red Desert*), their evocative landscapes far closer to Rossellini's disciplined psychological imagery (and, in France, Robert Bresson's pure, severe, unsentimental, understated intensity) than to Fellini's flamboyance or Zavattini's neorealism.

Whereas that neorealism used the external social environment to define a human being, Antonioni uses the emotions of a human being to define the external physical environment— a subtle Expressionism in the service of psychological, sociological, and philosophical insight. For Antonioni, the world takes its color from the character, rather than the character taking color from the world. Or, rather, as in Rossellini films, they take their color from one another. When Antonioni finally adopted color photography in *Il deserto rosso* (*Red Desert*) in 1964, the above metaphor for his method became a cinematic reality. After making seven short documentaries (1943–1950) and directing his first features, including *Cronaca di un amore* (*Chronicle of a Love,* 1950) and *I vinti* (*The Vanquished,* 1952), and doing even better

work on *Le amiche* (*The Girlfriends,* 1955) and *Il grido* (*The Cry,* 1957), Antonioni achieved complete mastery over his method with *L'avventura* (*The Adventure,* 1960).

Rather than using the camera and microphone merely to record dialogue, movement, and facial reaction, Antonioni's method concentrates as much on the scenic environment as on the people in the environment. The environment reflects the people in it. And not just socially. The emotional resonances of the environment convey the internal states of the people within it. Among Antonioni's favorite photographic subjects are the slick, hard-surfaced materials of modern architecture: glass, aluminum, terrazzo. The angular furniture, the stony objects, and the glossy floor of the apartment at the beginning of *L'eclisse* (*Eclipse,* 1962) brilliantly evoke the coldness, the emptiness, the deadness in an alienated relationship as Vittoria (Monica Vitti) breaks off with her lover. Significantly, Antonioni underscores the scene's shiny, hard look with silence—no music, almost no words, a few scraping sounds of hard objects on stone-like floors and furniture. *La notte* (*The Night,* 1960) begins with a similar feeling of hollowness and death, created by the slick, shiny glass windows and bare white corridors of the hospital where an author and his wife (Marcello Mastroianni and Jeanne Moreau) visit a dying friend. The beginning of *Blowup* (1966, based on a story by Julio Cortázar) surrounds a group of carnivalesque merrymakers with wet, shiny terrazzo courtyards and hard, cold aluminum-and-glass apartment buildings. The beginnings of Antonioni films consistently use the scenic environment to define both the film's social milieu and its emotional climate.

Other Antonioni environments come to mind, many of them reminiscent of his paintings: the rocky barren island where the empty, barren holidaymakers search for Anna in *L'avventura;* the steel flagpoles with the ropes hollowly clanging against them in *L'eclisse;* the gray-brown ugliness of the factory belching smoke in *Red Desert;* the endless desert of *Zabriskie Point* (1970). Perhaps Antonioni's favorite object for emotional definition is the white wall: Sandro's flat in *L'avventura,* the

Fig. 13-12

Fig. 13-13

The white wall in L'avventura. *Fig. 13-12: Sandro (Gabriele Ferzetti) and Anna (Lea Massari); Fig. 13-13: Sandro and Claudia (Monica Vitti).*

hospital corridors in *La notte,* the hotel corridor in *Red Desert,* the photographer's studio in *Blowup.* The Antonioni character's feeling of affinity with the hard white wall is emphasized by a piece of business that recurs through nearly all of the films—the character stands against the wall and then circles around the room, back and palms pressing against the plaster.

A tendency of criticism of Antonioni is to push his films into one of two clichéd and comfortable categories. The first tendency is to turn the artistic principle of the films upside down by taking the subordinate social and material environment as the real stuff of the film. According to such critics, *L'avventura* is about the evils of wealth, *L'eclisse* condemns the stock exchange, *Red Desert* denounces industrialization, *Blowup* contrasts illusion and reality. However, Antonioni accepts the fact that people today live with the stock exchange, with factories, with ambiguities. What else can he do with a fact? What he is interested in is how they live with them, how it feels to do so, what the problems are in doing so.

The second cliché of Antonioni criticism is that all his characters live lives that are boring and empty, meaningless and sterile, and that his subject is sterility and meaninglessness in the abstract. Ironically, most of the Antonioni characters manage to survive (Jack Nicholson in *The Passenger,* 1975, is an obvious exception); they do not commit suicide, even if they consider the possibility (as Giulia perpetually does in *Red Desert*). Most of the central Antonioni figures find some value that helps them live, and most of the Antonioni films end with some cautiously positive implication. Sandro and Claudia in *L'avventura* come together in a moment of mutual sympathy—beautifully and sensitively depicted by her placing her white hand on his black hair—without saying a word. The photographer at the end of *Blowup* realizes that his life has a meaning to him, if to no one else—that, like the carnival clowns with their invisible tennis ball, he can play his own life's game with the same energy and conviction, even if that game has no grounding in absolute being or any absolute meaningfulness to anyone else.

The ending of *Red Desert* is explicitly positive. Giulia walks by the factory exactly as she did in the film's opening sequence; the smoke stack still belches its poisonous smoke. Giulia's young son asks her whether the smoke will kill the little birds that might fly through it. Giulia answers that the birds have long since learned not to fly through the smoke. The parallel of the birds to Giulia, and the smoke to the industrial world surrounding her, implies that Giulia too has learned something.

The real subject of the Antonioni films is education. So many of the films are circular; *L'eclisse, Red Desert, Blowup* seem to end where they began. Although the characters walk around in a physical circle, they do not walk around in an emotional one. In the course of their journeys, they learn the pervasiveness of emptiness and the possible if temporary ways of combating it. For such a theme, Antonioni's visual images are the only means of rendering each emotional stage of the journey clearly, convincingly, and sensitively. The images become Antonioni's "objective correlatives"; he is as dependent on visual images for these correlatives as were the designers and directors of *Broken Blossoms, The Cabinet of Dr. Caligari, The Last Laugh,* and *Greed.* No other director of sound films is more dependent on pictures and more free of words than Antonioni.

He rejects words for two reasons. First, words are not a very effective tool for communicating internal states of feeling. Vague, imprecise feelings of loneliness, uneasiness, and *angst* do not lend themselves to the terse summary required of movie dialogue. The more lucidly and lengthily a person talks about his or her own internal feelings (either in life or in art), the more we distrust the sincerity of the feelings and the depth of the self-awareness. Second, Antonioni does not trust words as a genuine means of human communication. "Our drama," he once said, "is noncommunication." If his characters succeed in discovering anything meaningful at all, they do so by physical contact, by moments of laughter or calm, by a union of temporarily harmonizing vibrations rather than by discussion and conversation. The emotional climax of *Red Desert* contains Antonioni's ultimate metaphor for the irrelevance of words when Giulia addresses her lengthiest and most explicit revelation of her innermost feelings to a Scandinavian sailor who cannot understand a word of the Italian she is speaking.

L'avventura is probably Antonioni's most whole, most careful, most completely realized film. Despite the impression that the plot wanders, it travels steadily toward its final moment of reconciliation and compassion in which Claudia can feel sympathy for the weakness of Sandro and in which Sandro can feel the terrible pathos of his need to betray Claudia. The plot is a series of betrayals. Anna betrays her friend, Claudia, by making her wait downstairs while she viciously devours Sandro in an afternoon of casual lovemaking. The middle-aged couple (Giulia and Corrado) survives daily on little betrayals—stinging, hateful words that hurt. Giulia betrays Corrado with the adolescent boy who paints nothing but nudes. Sandro has betrayed his talent as an architect by selling out to the pressures of finance. Antonioni brilliantly captures Sandro's bitterness as the former architect deliberately spills ink on a young architectural student's careful line drawing of the town's cathedral. Sandro's betrayals are also sexual. He betrays Anna by lusting after Claudia before Anna disappears. And even after the touching, fulfilling moments with Claudia, he callously flirts with the tasteless American publicity seeker in the very hotel where Claudia waits in bed for his return.

But if Sandro's education is to discover the human weakness that makes betrayal so inevitable, Claudia's education is to discover that betrayal is a fact of human life and to ignore that fact is to cut herself off completely from the human. "Human" and "betrayal" are unfortunately synonymous; any meaningful human relationship must start from that definition. *L'avventura* is a journey and adventure that bring Sandro and Claudia to that starting point.

If *L'avventura* is the fullest and most sensitive statement of Antonioni's vision, *Red Desert* is the most revealing of his technique. *Red Desert,* Antonioni's first color film, is a film about colors, as its title indicates. Its revolutionary, self-conscious use of color inspired Bergman, Godard, and others to work in color, though few were so bold as to repaint real landscapes to get the hues they desired, as Antonioni did in *Red Desert* and *Blowup.* After *Ivan the Terrible, Part II* (1946), *Black Narcissus* (1947), and *Vertigo* (1958), *Red Desert* is the next crucial step in the history of genuinely expressionist color filmmaking; the next major step would be Kurosawa's *Dodes'ka-den* (1970).

Fig. 13-11
Clutching at love. Monica Vitti and Gabriele Ferzetti in L'avventura.

Giulia's troubles with reality are mirrored by her troubles with colors. Color in the film is not Fellini's flamboyant, saturated show but Antonioni's subtle use of the environment to mirror the character's internal states and, ultimately, to communicate the film's subject. *Red Desert* often uses a long lens that blurs the background into a mass of indistinguishable colors; that effect mirrors the way Giulia herself sees color: frightening, aggressive, uncontrollable, indistinguishable, out of focus. She is so uncomfortable with colors — in fact oppressed, threatened, overwhelmed, and even erased by them — that she cannot pick one to cover the walls of her shop. Giulia's discomfort with colors is a metaphor for her discomfort with the reality that surrounds her — all of its sights, sounds, smells, uncertainties. In a later sequence in the engineer's hotel room, the walls change color from their original hard gray to warm pink. The walls are now pink be-

cause Giulia feels them pink, with her body next to a warm, strong man. He, ironically, cares neither how she feels nor how she feels the walls.

Though Antonioni's method disparages words, he does not forget sounds. Sound is a crucial element in *Red Desert* and in all Antonioni films (even his deliberate silences reveal a knowledge of the power of sound). In *Red Desert* sound and color operate similarly. Giulia sees her everyday life as a grayish, poisonous, choking existence, punctuated by the frightening grotesque colors of the factory pipes (hence the gray-brownishness of the shots of the factory, the mud, the fog, and the striking blues and oranges of the pipelines). Accompanying the shots of the oppressive factory are the incessant thumping, beating, chugging noises of the factory machines on the soundtrack.

Later in the film, Giulia tells her child a beautiful fairy tale of an ideally serene life on a far-off paradisiacal isle. Suddenly the screen changes from its sordid browns and grays to shots of brilliant blue waters and sparkling pink sand—a pink similar to that in the hotel room, and carefully dyed by the director to look that way. With the appearance of beautiful, clear, inviting images, the irritating noises on the soundtrack melt away to be replaced by the sound of waves lapping on the beach and the siren song of a mystical soprano. The rocks of the island seem as inviting as human flesh. Indeed, the entire island sequence—with its brilliant colors, sensuous terrain, and hypnotic music—is a temptation to escape, to the very suicide Giulia has already attempted, not to a place of beauty and harmony but into the comfort of nothingness, the ease of nonexistence. For this reason, Corrado's hotel room turns the same pink as the island's rocks; Giulia has discovered a temporary island of sensuous nonbeing—which she discovers to be as false and lifeless as the fairy tale she tells her son. By his careful control of image, color, and sound, Antonioni tells the story of this woman's mental journey, her attempts to learn, like the little birds, to avoid the poisonous smoke of reality by acknowledging its existence.

Pietro Germi was Italy's greatest film satirist of the postwar period. Germi made several neorealist films just after the war, the most interesting being *In the Name of the Law* (1948), a contrast between social hypocrisies and the underlying moral realities in a Mafia-dominated Sicily. This contrast of the appearance and the reality, the external show and the internal emotion, later became Germi's dominant theme in his great satirical comedies, *Divorce—Italian Style* (1961; Academy Award, 1962), *Seduced and Abandoned* (1963), and *The Birds, the Bees, and the Italians* (1966; literal title, *Ladies and Gentlemen*). In the first of these films, murder seems a practical social tool, there being no easier legal way to break a stifling marriage contract. In *Seduced and Abandoned*, a Sicilian family insists on maintaining its honor to the death. And death is precisely the result of the worship of the dead word, honor, despite the hilariously comic machinations to get the deflowered daughter engaged, disengaged, and eventually married. The code of honor becomes a rigid absurdity that the char-

acters uphold with the most frenzied, ludicrous, hypocritical, and silly seriousness.

Although it received less critical attention than the two earlier films, *The Birds, the Bees, and the Italians* is equal to Germi's greatest work; it is another powerful mixture of stinging social commentary and farcical social comedy. In a town of grotesque lechers, drunkards, and gossips, a society whose every thought (if not deed) is lewd, two unmarried people dare to live together openly. The town lechers, hypocritically supporting the official moral code, refuse to let the two people live together warmly and sincerely while their own emotional lives remain blunted and covert. Using the moral clichés, the townspeople drive the couple apart, forcing her to leave town and him to jump off a roof.

Despite the obvious seriousness of the film's stand against hypocrisy, Germi carries the story off with almost the flavor of farce. Every lecher is comically and grotesquely individuated. Richly comic are their social gatherings when they all get together, gossiping viciously out of one side of the mouth and excitedly arranging a liaison out of the other. Equally comic and telling is the scene in a sleazy nightclub, supposedly a lurid strip joint, where the tawdry bourgeois townspeople go for a night of "fun." The nightclub seems a deliberate parody of the posh nightclubs of Fellini and Antonioni. Neither chic nor exotic, the tacky café wakes up and puts on its *dolce vita* only when the soused customers enter. The most lurid entertainment comes not from one of the hired strippers but from a nymphomaniac wife who suffers from the constant desire to take off her clothes. The Germi world in this film is the Fellini world gone bourgeois —with warts. By mixing farcical grotesques with the enormous suffering that the comic hypocrites inflict on less callous, more innocent beings, Germi achieves his particular serio-comic blend.

The paths of neorealism took several other directions. Mario Monicelli's *The Organizer* (1963, U.S. release 1964) applied neorealist principles to a historical study, the fight for fair wages and working conditions by a group of early-twentieth-century strikers. Vittorio De Seta, a documentary filmmaker, combined doc-

Fig. 13-15
The Battle of Algiers: *political fiction as newsreel reportage.*

umentary and fiction for his first feature, *Bandits of Orgosolo* (1961), one of the precursors of *cinéma vérité*. After his debut film, the ferociously iconoclastic *Fists in the Pocket* (1965), Marco Bellocchio satirically examined the clumsy attempts of the bored rich to carve a meaning out of their lives by dabbling in romance and Marxist politics in *China Is Near* (1967). And Lina Wertmüller, who served her apprenticeship with Fellini, sought to combine broad satire with sharp political analysis. Her major films (*The Seduction of Mimi,* 1972; *Love and Anarchy,* 1973; *Swept Away . . . ,* 1974; *Seven Beauties,* 1976) reveal both a Marxist analysis of contemporary social problems and an exuberant comic sensitivity to the dilemmas of sexuality, power, morality, and survival. In *The Battle of Algiers* (1965), Gillo Pontecorvo combined *Open City*'s tale of political resistance with a visual style that suggested newsreel actuality — to document the Algerian struggle for freedom from the French.

Most neorealistic of the second-generation postwar directors is Ermanno Olmi. In *Il posto* (*The Job,* also called *The Sound of Trumpets,* 1961), Olmi studies an adolescent boy's absorption into the machinery of bureaucratic industrialized society. The boy leaves home, takes a civil service examination, gets a job as messenger, and finally earns a clerk's desk in the bureaucratic office. The film ends with a brilliant sound effect, not the glorious sound of trumpets but the cranking of a mimeograph machine. The boy has been "duplicated," cranked through the industrial process to emerge as one more identical sheet of paper on which his future for the next fifty years has been printed.

Although Olmi clearly condemns the dehumanizing mechanistic pattern that turns a boy into a faceless man, he handles his subject from two perspectives: from his own view, which judges and condemns, and from the boy's, who sees the whole process as something exciting and adult. The job frees him from his home; it gives him some sense of financial security; it brings him into contact with girls. Whereas Olmi's view condemns the prison-like regimented process of taking a civil service examination, the boy excitedly, earnestly tries to pass it. Whereas Olmi's view exposes the hollow sterility of the company's New Year's Eve party, a sad evening of manufactured fun that is no fun at all, the young boy fights his initial fright, drinks a bit of wine, dances, and actually enjoys himself. Perhaps Olmi's point is that "the piece of paper" is ignorant about being ground through a machine and hence can enjoy it. The two contrasting views of the same social process add a touching humanness and artistic richness to the film.

Olmi's masterpiece, *The Tree of Wooden Clogs* (1978), set in Northern Italy around 1900, relates economic conditions and "minor" subjects to the crucial concerns of real life as rigorously as any of its neorealist predecessors. A brilliantly shot color study of a year in the lives of three peasant families, it focuses on the story of a man who cuts down a small tree to make a new pair of clogs for his son (who has a six-kilometer walk to school and has broken one clog); for this act, the family is evicted.

The two most interesting and influential Italian *auteurs* to emerge in the 1960s were Pier Paolo Pasolini and Bernardo Bertolucci. Like most of the earlier neorealists, both were Marxists who sought to combine a passion for politics with a passion for cinema. Pasolini's career began neorealistically enough with *Accattone* (*Beggar,* 1961), a study of a brash, poor young man in a Roman slum, trying to earn enough money to survive and, at the same time, preserve enough of his spiritual identity so that his survival is worth it. Pasolini later drifted from neorealism to elliptical poetic allegories of moral and political degradation. Bertolucci's first major success, *Before the Revolution* (1964), set the pattern for his more famous films to follow—a study of the interrelationship between political structures and sexual or emotional fulfillment. While Pasolini's films are more abstract, more elliptical, more complexly structured, and more ferociously aggressive moral-political investigations, enlivened and propelled by dazzling bursts of unforgettable imagery, Bertolucci's conform to a more familiar narrative pattern, which combines political events in a particular society with richly rendered characters, lush color settings (often of the recent past), and carefully structured strings of narrative action, sinuous but linear (like the rich movements of his camera). Bertolucci might be thought of as combining the leftist social conscience of a Zavattini with the more intimately psychological and sexual perceptions of a Visconti or Antonioni. Pasolini was more the Eisenstein or Vertov of Italian political cinema (like the two Soviet masters, Pasolini wrote rich and complex theoretical essays on film "language" as a form of visual-intellectual poetry) while Bertolucci is more its Pudovkin.

In Pasolini's *Teorema* (*Theorem*, 1968), its very title informing us that it is a logical demonstration, a beautiful young man—a kind of angel—succeeds in blasting apart the apparently solid foundations of an apparently solid bourgeois family by making every member of it fall in love with him—the maid, daughter, artist son (whose notions of truth and beauty are so devastated by the confrontation that his "action painting" becomes a process of urinating on canvas), mother, and high-finance, businessman father. At the end of the film, the businessman has been so overwhelmed by his passion, his commitment to a forbidden, anti-bourgeois love, that he wanders about the town's railroad station, seeking to pick up hustlers or make quick sexual contacts of the most degraded sort. The final image of the film shows him wandering in a wasteland, naked, the rocks and sand of the hilly desert

seething with volcanic steam. The grand bourgeois has been absolutely stripped of all the moral, social, and political apparatus by which he lived his life—no clothes, no sense of direction, no civilization, no concrete location, no purpose, a total moral and social leper. The theorem that underlies this stripping process is, quite simply, that sexual passion knows no moral or social boundaries and that those who least know this truth—the grandest, *hautest* bourgeoisie—are most easily and completely overwhelmed by the discovery of the flimsy assumptions on which their entire lives are based. His next film, *Pigpen* (1969), was about cannibalism, bestiality, and capitalism.

Salò (1975) was Pasolini's last film before he was murdered in a sexual incident that might well have occurred in one of his films. Based on the Marquis de Sade's *120 Days of Sodom* (which also inspired the ending of Buñuel and Dali's 1930 *L'Age d'or*) and named for the northern lake town that was Mussolini's last capital (as the Fascist government withdrew steadily toward the Austrian border), *Salò* is an even more extreme, aggressive, and repellent allegorical theorem than *Teorema*. In this piece of cinema cruelty (in Antonin Artaud's sense of the term), the audience is subjected to a horrifying vision of political totalitarianism disguised as sadomasochistic sexuality. In 1943, four pillars of Italian Fascistic society—a duke, a priest, a judge, and a general (indeed, the same four pillars of society that recur in the plays of Jean Genet)—gather a specially selected group of extremely beautiful young boys and girls in a large palatial house and then proceed to make them perform every imaginable sexual atrocity for their own pleasure. The beautiful young people are permitted to indulge in any sexual wish, so long as it is not a normal, natural, or tender one. Pasolini fills the screen for two hours with orgies of sexual torture and oppression—buggery, voyeurism, casual murder, pornographic songs and stories (a vital part of the dirty old men's pleasure), mutilation, branding, scalping, the consumption of human feces. One of the points Pasolini makes in this *reductio ad absurdum* of sexual decorum is that these sexual perversions, the very opposite of bourgeois society's standards

Fig. 13-16
Salò: sexual slavery as a metaphor for moral and political bondage.

and beliefs, are, like Fascism itself, a product of bourgeois society—of its ruling nobility, clergy, laws, and armies. Pasolini's other films alternate between this shattering allegorical mode (*Pigpen*) and more distanced visual style pieces with political underpinnings (*The Gospel According to St. Matthew*, 1964; *Medea*, 1969).

The political films of Bernardo Bertolucci are more sensuous, more meticulous in their stylish attention to visual detail, and less schematic in their abstract arguments. As a result, they are also much more popular. In *Before the Revolution, The Conformist* (1971), and *Last Tango in Paris* (1972), Bertolucci examines the interrelationship between political issues and sexual drives not, as Pasolini does, by revealing the radical anarchic power of sexual passion but, instead, by showing that political and sex-

ual commitments weave together in complex and mysterious ways. The rich, bored dilettantes are no more committed to Marxist ideology than they are to their own lusts and seductions in *Before the Revolution*. They play around with both and succeed in fulfilling neither. In *The Conformist* the central figure's ideological emptiness is intimately connected with his lack of sexual identity, his need to assert his masculine *machismo* while covering up his intrinsic homosexuality. He can betray ideals, his friends, his professor, his lover, his wife, his principles because he is a zero—both ideologically and sexually. *Last Tango in Paris* was not one of Pasolini's abstract sexual theorems but an intimate and detailed portrait of human carnality, dominated by the pervasive lust and persuasive confusion of the lost Amer-

Fig. 13-17
Landowner (Robert De Niro) and worker (Gérard Depardieu) in Bertolucci's 1900.

ican portrayed by Marlon Brando, in one of his greatest screen roles.

1900 (1976), a mammoth, epic history of Italy in the twentieth century (cut from 320 to 243 minutes for U.S. release), might be considered a sort of Marxist Italian *The Birth of a Nation* or *Gone With the Wind*, as if shot by Pudovkin in color. Bertolucci shifts his personal focus from sexual lust to friendship—a study of the limits on and the possibilities for friendship of two men, born on the same day on the same estate in 1900 (on the day that Verdi died, signifying the death of nineteenth century Romanticism) but in the two opposite classes of landowner and peasant. Bertolucci examines the closeness of the two boys (their comradely discoveries of nature, sex, and death together; the genuine emotional ties that bind them) and the barriers to that friendship (their different financial, educational, and moral backgrounds; their different sexual and sensual tastes; their different attitudes toward the phenomena of the century—two wars; the

rise and fall of Fascism; the labor, union, and workers' movements—and toward private property itself). Ultimately, Bertolucci's synthesis (and, in contrast to Pasolini, there is a synthesis, not an insistently irreversible analysis) is that the two men are and are not close, can and cannot be friends, can and cannot overcome the facts of social history that both bind and separate them. Even as cantankerous old men, the two "friends" can only agree to differ.

A third generation of Italian realists emerged in the 1970s—Ettore Scola, Paolo and Vittorio Taviani, and Francesco Rosi—all of them fully conscious of their neorealist roots (indeed, Rosi had been making films for decades before attracting wider international attention). Scola is the subtle ironist and comic stylist of the group (*We All Loved Each Other So Much*, 1974; *A Special Day*, 1977; *La Nuit de Varennes*, 1982). Like many of his contemporaries, Scola is dedicated to exploring the processes of history: political history, like the

French Revolution (in *La Nuit de Varennes*, scripted by Sergio Amidei, whose scripts were so important to Rossellini), or cinema history, like Scola's explicit homage to De Sica (*We All Loved Each Other*) and the succeeding quarter century of Italian film styles.

The Taviani brothers closely examine Italian social structures within periods of historical crisis. *Padre Padrone* (1977) is a careful dissection of Italy's paternalistic familial structures, collapsing beneath the attack of modern literacy. *The Night of the Shooting Stars* (1982) pays explicit homage to Rossellini and *Paisan* in the same way that Scola's *We All Loved Each Other* pays homage to De Sica. The Tavianis capture a child's magical and mythic recollection: a memorable night and day, over three decades earlier, of civil-war brutality between Fascists and Partisans in the last hours of Mussolini's Italy—much as the Taviani brothers themselves recall the magic of seeing such battles in *Paisan* as children, over three decades earlier. The Taviani films might also be described as explorations of language: the language of cinema in *Good Morning, Babylon* (1987, about *Intolerance*), literacy itself in *Padre Padrone,* and storytelling in *KAOS* (*Chaos*, 1984—a group of stories by Pirandello, followed by one about him).

The films of Francesco Rosi (*Salvatore Giuliano*, 1961; *Christ Stopped at Eboli*, 1979; *Three Brothers*, 1981) are also attracted to periods of historical crisis and to a stylistic alternating of realistic depictions of events with the interpretation and imaginative experiencing of those events. As a political tragedy, *Salvatore Giuliano* has been compared to both *Julius Caesar* and *Citizen Kane*. Like *Night of the Shooting Stars,* Rosi's *Three Brothers* contrasts present and past, the experiences of childhood with the responsibilities of adults and old age. In its depiction of the crumbling social structures of contemporary Italy—the bloody battles between the Marxists of the North and the Mafia of the South, which Italian law must adjudicate; the demands of the Italian working class; the effects of juvenile delinquency, drug addiction, and crime—*Three Brothers* reveals the devastating effect of contemporary social problems on the old familial structures of Italian society.

For forty years the Italian film has started with the surface of reality as its initial premise. But the Italian filmmaker has been free to manipulate the realistic surfaces of rich or poor, of past or present, and to probe beneath those surfaces with sociological commentary, psychological insight, sexual allegory, farcical comedy, philosophical ennui, bizarre romance. The postwar Italian film has been so rich and diverse because the filmmakers have been encouraged to use their imaginations and because, ironically, the Italian film industry was supported first by American dollars, and later by the Italian government to stimulate even more production.

The Hollywood dollar stimulated not only postwar Italian "art films," but several cycles of trash films as well. In the 1950s, a series of quasi-Roman, quasi-Biblical "spectacle" films starring the American muscleman, Steve Reeves, could be shot for under $150,000 in Italy and then dubbed into English for mass release in American neighborhood theatres and drive-ins. In the 1960s, a series of Italian "spaghetti westerns," the best of which (*For a Fistful of Dollars*, 1964, released in the United States as *Fistful of Dollars* and very closely based on Kurosawa's 1961 *Yojimbo; For a Few Dollars More*, 1965) starred Clint Eastwood and were directed by Sergio Leone, not only made money but attracted a cult, a coterie of intellectual admirers: many of them French, many of them the same fans who admired the raw garish violence of the Roger Corman horror films of the same era. Leone's success with the cheap violent western was so great that he was given the chance to shoot a major high-budget western, *Once Upon a Time in the West* (1968), which perhaps serves as an example of the slowest paced, most naturalistically detailed, and most visually dazzling collection of western clichés ever assembled—but with a difference (Henry Fonda smiles as he shoots a child . . .). The West is demystified, shown in all its grossness, while Leone weaves a new myth. A film of sudden, intense close-ups and boldly composed long shots, enthusiastically filling the wide screen and magnificently scored by Ennio Morricone (who had composed the music for all of Leone's films—becoming well known for the theme from *The*

Fig. 13-18
New York's Lower East Side, recreated for Leone's
Once Upon a Time in America.

Good, the Bad and the Ugly, 1966 — and who would go on to score *1900* and *Days of Heaven,* 1978), *Once Upon a Time in the West* shared much with the Eastwood "man with no name" westerns but explored a wider range of tones.

Over a decade later, Leone's companion piece continued his Italian exploration of American genres — moving from the Westerner to the Easterner, the cowboy to the gangster. *Once Upon a Time in America* (1984) was a tactile, gauzy, nostalgic return to Hollywood's gangster past and the central motif of that genre — the conflict between power and friendship (this time the gangster buddies were Jewish, not Italian).

In its early years the postwar Italian cinema showed the American industry how to combine ideas, social comment, realistic human observation, and poetic visual techniques with the mo-

tion picture form; in its later years it seemed to pander more and more to the very movie conventions and practices it previously had tried to subvert. In the late 1970s, with its greatest directors either dead (De Sica, Visconti, Pasolini, Germi) or working all over Europe on international co-productions or on multimillion-dollar visual extravaganzas (Bertolucci, Fellini, Antonioni), the Italian cinema no longer enjoyed the artistic influence and international importance of a decade earlier. In the 1980s, however, the Italian cinema regained considerable international respect with the films of Scola, Rosi, and the brothers Taviani.

France — Postwar Classicism

The postwar Italian film sprang from the reality that the filmmaker sought to capture with camera and film; the postwar French film sprang from the filmmaker's stylistic concern with the way a camera can capture reality. That the postwar French cinema should be committed to style and form is not surprising; the prewar French cinema was just as committed to formal experiment, from the powerfully innovative silents of Gance, Dulac, Ray, Kirsanov, Duchamp, Epstein, and others to the musical romps of Clair and the literariness of Renoir and Carné. To approach reality through the conscious manipulation of style and artistic form has been an aesthetic premise of the French creative mind from Racine to Proust to Ionesco. The postwar French cinema is very much in the same tradition.

The sameness is emphasized by the fact that the great prewar directors — Clair, Renoir, Carné, Cocteau — also made films after the war. René Clair returned to France to combine fantasy, song, and social satire once again in films that were frothy mixtures of physical movement, stylized decor, and music — among them *Le Silence est d'or* (*Silence is Golden,* 1947, starring Maurice Chevalier; U.S. title, *Man About Town*), a nostalgic tribute to the Zecca-Méliès years of the French film; *Beauty and the Devil* (1949), an ironic treatment of the Faust legend; and *Beauties of the Night* (1952), the romantic reveries of a daydreaming musician.

Whereas Clair returned to France to make films that were softer, sweeter, and weaker than his earlier work, Renoir returned to make at least three films that are arguably as great as his masterpieces of the 1930s. The three films —*The River* (his first in color; shot 1949–1950, released 1951), *The Golden Coach* (1952), and *French Cancan* (1954)—might be considered a kind of trilogy. All three use color not only beautifully but also as a metaphoric and thematic element in their investigations. All three are set in periods or places far from postwar France: India's Bengal region (*The River*), South America of the 1700s (*The Golden Coach*), and Montmartre of the 1890s (*French Cancan*). And all three examine the conflicting human choices of contempt and consent, commitment and alienation, vocation and love. The primary duality of all three films is the usual Renoir conflict between art and nature (or life), but in these late films the conflict becomes a communion as the very artfulness of the films themselves—their visual beauty as well as their structural complexity—reveals how one can indeed make life into art and thereby synthesize the opposites of art and nature.

The River, shot in India by a French director with a French and Bengali crew, featuring a cast of both Indians and Westerners, is about this clash of cultures and values. Using the vibrant colors of the Indian landscape, the pulsing music of the sitar, the myths of the Hindu religion, and the contemplative philosophy of the Indian people, *The River* (based on the book by Rumer Godden, who co-wrote the script with Renoir) shows a group of "crippled" Westerners—crippled physically or spiritually by the war, by political chaos, and by personal disappointment—healing their minds and feelings by seeking to achieve a harmony with the eternal cycles of nature: birth, life, and death. *The Golden Coach* continues the examination of clashing cultures. A group of Spanish aristocrats has imported their decadent political structures and social rituals from Old World Europe, attempting to duplicate them in the New World. Ironically, another group of Europeans, the members of an acting troupe (led by Anna Magnani), are far more successful at communicating with their New World audience. Art is a more powerful force than politics, and the director, through his leading

actress, argues for the validity of art as a human vocation. And *French Cancan* addresses the same issue. Renoir depicts a theatrical producer (played by the aging Jean Gabin who, like Renoir, was almost twenty years older than he was when he made *Grand Illusion*) who, also like Renoir, defines art as his life.

Marcel Carné, deprived of Jacques Prévert's scripts, never regained the power of *Les Enfants du paradis* although he made almost a dozen films examining failure, lost love, and inexorable death. Jean Cocteau, whose only prewar film was the 1930 *The Blood of a Poet* (an experimental, personal attempt to "picture the poet's inner self"), made several films in strikingly different though equally formalistic film styles: the claustrophobic realism of *Les Parents terribles* (1948), a complicated tangle of sexuality, incest, parental rivalry, and jealousy; the poetic symbolism of *Orphée* (*Orpheus,* 1950), an expressionistic study of the artist's ambivalent relationship with love and death as well as a rich realization of some of the ways that poetry and film can work together; and *Beauty and the Beast* (1946), a perfectly realized fairy tale that mixed Cocteau's surreal romanticism and evocative symbolism quite effectively in the story of Belle's growing love for the physically ugly yet humanly loving beast. The impression of these stylistically eclectic Cocteau films is that they are the works of a cinematic amateur (in the original sense of the word). The artist, having given birth to his personal and symbolic world on the stage, on the page, and on canvas, also decided to people the screen with his personal fantasies, images, motifs, and symbols. Like Renoir, Cocteau's primary theme was that only the work of art was capable of effecting a synthesis of the conflicting demands of art and nature, of form and freedom. Cocteau's commitment to art is even more fervent than Renoir's, for Cocteau sees the artist alone as capable of achieving immortality through the created work, which cannot wither into ugliness and die like the body of the mortal artist itself. As befits his deification of art, Cocteau's films are generally more fanciful, more symbolic, more claustrophobically stylized, more otherworldly than Renoir's who, even in his late period, holds the demands of art and social reality in balance.

Cocteau's union of opposites in Beauty and the Beast — *loveliness (Josette Day as Beauty) and ugliness (Jean Marais as the Beast), human and animal, nature and artifice, animate and inanimate (note the candelabra's arm).*

Fig. 13-19

Of the new directors of French cinema in the fifteen years following the war, the three greatest were Max Ophüls, Robert Bresson, and Jacques Tati. All three of them made films very much in the Clair–Carné–Renoir tradition; all three of them had, in fact, made films before 1945. Whereas the end of the war signaled a shift in an entirely new direction for the Italian film, the end of the war in France extended an earlier one. The break with French tradition came in 1959, and, as we shall see, it was not a complete break at all.

Max Ophüls made films in Italy, Holland, and the United States after fleeing his German homeland and Hitler in 1933 (he was Jewish). Ophüls's reputation today rests primarily on the last films he made in America (*Letter from an Unknown Woman,* 1948; *Caught* and *The Reckless Moment,* both 1949) and the four he

directed and co-wrote in France before his death: *La Ronde* (1950), *Le Plaisir* (1952), *Madame de . . .* (*The Earrings of Madame de . . .* , 1953), and *Lola Montès* (1955); all the French films were shot by Christian Matras and are noted for their fluid, highly charged camera work. Ophüls is clearly an international rather than a French director. And yet he found a place in French studios at a particularly apt time for his particular talents — a time when French film values favored the literate, almost theatrical script and the ornate, carefully styled studio production. Ophüls's greatest artistic resemblance is to two other internationalized Europeans, the German Ernst Lubitsch and the Austrian Erich von Stroheim, whose contrasting qualities he seems to synthesize. Ophüls's films combine Lubitsch's light, mocking, sexually wise touch with von

Stroheim's perception of human desire and social corruption.

The last Ophüls films all revolve around sexual intrigue in conflict with social regulations. The Ophüls characters continue to carry on their intrigues while either hypocritically ignoring the social tensions (as the liars do in *La Ronde* and *Madame de . . .*) or openly defying social convention (as Lola does). In developing a consistent theme, Ophüls also prefers consistent stylistic conventions. Each film's plot is less a single driving narrative than a string of vignettes, held together by the setting (the Vienna of *La Ronde,* the circus tent of *Lola Montès*), by an object (the earrings of *Madame de . . .* , which are passed from person to person in a fatal circle), or by a concept (in *Le Plaisir,* which retells three stories by Guy de Maupassant, how pleasure is found easily but happiness is elusive). By deemphasizing story, Ophüls illuminates key structural balances, comparisons and contrasts of similar actions in different circumstances or different actions in similar ones. Such balancing—itself both intellectually distant and passionately involved— takes the viewer directly to the center of Ophüls's moral statement on love, feelings, and social custom. And Ophüls's deliberate choice of an artificial, theatrical setting (the soundstage in *La Ronde,* the circus tent in *Lola Montès*) provides a nonrealistically appropriate setting for Ophüls's comedies of sociosexual manners and also raises intentional questions about the shams of real human activity and the realness of acting and impersonation.

La Ronde is one of the finest translations of a stage work (Arthur Schnitzler's *Reigen*) into film. The film is completely theatrical and completely cinematic. Ophüls effected the translation much as Olivier did with his *Henry V* six years earlier—by coming to terms with the aesthetic fact that the stage is primarily verbal and stylized and that the cinema is primarily visual and intensely real-seeming. Ophüls erases neither the stage's artificiality (as so many American adaptations of stage plays try to do) nor the cinema's visual realism: The setting in *La Ronde* is both an undisguised soundstage and the city of Vienna around 1900. The camera wanders about the soundstage at will between the two poles of obvious stage set and realistic bedroom, between a metaphorical carousel, symbolic of the film's everturning dance of sexual relationships (a conjugal merry-go-round in which A loves B who loves C who loves A), and a real boudoir. "To wander" is an especially appropriate verb, for Ophüls keeps the camera perpetually on the move, spinning, flowing, traveling around the soundstage. Ophüls's German heritage is especially clear in his use of the moving camera and emphasis on *mise-en-scène.* The gliding photography adds not only visual energy but also continuity between the potentially disparate vignettes. And Ophüls's wandering camera has an ally: The director has invented a narrator, a character who does not exist in the original play, who speaks directly for the filmmaker to the audience. The urbane, perceptive, witty narrator (Anton Walbrook) wanders, as the camera wanders, as he speaks for Ophüls. Director, camera, and narrator are one.

The single view they present is of sexual desire and the lies people tell to others and to themselves to obtain the objects of their desires. Ophüls's view of human relationships is much the same as Arthur Schnitzler's (both Lubitsch and von Stroheim also liked Schnitzler). Schnitzler's play is a series of ten wryly comic seductions, all of which, except the last, denote the sexual climax with a line of asterisks in the text. The play's unique structure gives its author several interesting perspectives, which Ophüls pointedly borrows. Because the scenes do not depict sexual activity but show only the events leading up to and away from the activity, the obvious focus of each scene is on the emotional reactions before (usually sexual excitement, clichéd lies, mental fencing) and after (usually disillusionment, callousness, and guilt) the asterisks. The play's aim (and Ophüls's aim, too) is decidedly psychological, not sexual. Furthermore, Schnitzler's play uses each character in two successive seduction scenes, leading to obvious comparisons of each character's actions, words, poses, and emotions in each sexual situation. And third, the Schnitzler play is constructed with an increasing complexity; the lies that each of the characters tells get fancier and fancier with each

Fig. 13-20
Max Ophüls's urbane narrator-chorus (Anton Walbrook) with the whore (Simone Signoret) and the metaphoric carousel of **La Ronde.**

subsequent scene; the sexual confrontations steadily climb the social and intellectual ladder, beginning with whore and ending with count. All classes, all people, play the same games, each in his or her own way.

Ophüls filmically preserves the intentions of Schnitzler's witty play: the stylized settings, the graceful camera, the subtly stylized acting, the charming waltz that plays as the characters change beds, the elegant and careful details of each setting, the urbane and confidential patter of the narrator. Especially clever is Ophüls's discovery of cinematic equivalents for Schnitzler's asterisks, usually handled on the stage by dimming and then brightening the lights. To denote the sexual climax, Ophüls's camera often gracefully tracks away from the

lovers, riveting itself on an object, and then later (perhaps after a dissolve) tracks back to them. His cleverest device is the sequence in which the film abruptly stops and jump-cuts to the narrator holding up a strip of film and a pair of editing scissors, shaking his head in concern over the lewdness of the scene he is about to censor. The narrator snips the sensual strip from the reel, and the film jumps back to the two sated lovers.

The moral view of Ophüls's *La Ronde* is not simply that sex is frothy and fun. The film poses a moral tension between natural human responses and unnatural social restrictions. The result is that the only time the characters cannot lie to each other is when they are lying with each other, during the "asterisks" of each scene. There is an underlying sad antithesis of human feeling and human callousness; the human brain's subjection to social rules and theories of proper human responses devastatingly turns both men and women into masses of contradictions of which they are totally ignorant.

The same antithesis between experience and convention propels *Lola Montès,* but Lola (Martine Carol) resolves the contradiction by remaining unflinchingly true to her feelings, regardless of the risk, regardless of the consequences. The story of Lola is the fictional biography of a real person, a famous (or infamous) courtesan of the nineteenth century, who took a series of brilliant lovers—a famous composer (Liszt), a ruling Bavarian prince (Ludwig). But Lola falls on evil fortune; she becomes a circus performer, forced to parade her life's story before a crass and ogling audience, selling gossip and kisses for a quarter. Lola has, on the surface, fallen from great lover to circus freak and two-bit whore. Her new lover is the fat and slimy ringmaster (Peter Ustinov) who, though he loves her, salaciously revels in Lola's past, his present mastery over her, and the money he makes from her life. Lola's conquerors are those common mortal ones, circumstance and time, as her sick and aging body requires more and more whisky to keep it going.

Despite the change in her fortunes, despite the public tawdriness of her new life and lover, Lola is still Lola. She refuses to bow to convention, to play safe. Even her deliberate public display of her past is an unconventional act of defiance. If people want to look at her, let them. If the past is all that remains of her life, then she will live in that past, even in front of a paying audience that gets a vicarious thrill from it. Though her doctor advises her that she is too weak, too ill to make her high platform leap that climactically ends her act, she insists on making the leap. And contrary to all circus film clichés (for example, DeMille's *The Greatest Show on Earth* of 1952), Lola doesn't leap to her demise at the end of *Lola Montès* (although she will, of course, leap to it one day). Lola cannot live her life in any way other than a series of dangerous leaps. What is important is not whether the leap is successful but that she always makes the leap.

But *Lola Montès* is more than an examination of a romantic life-style. It is one of the most dazzling of visual shows—in both color and CinemaScope. The circus within the film is matched by Ophüls's visual circus of mammoth action, swirling colors, and brilliant decor. Each of the sequences has its own unique color and tone: the warm browns, oranges, and ambers of the rustic affair with the composer; the cold whites, silvers, and pale blues of the affair with the prince; the dazzling reds and golds of the circus, glowing in the blackness of the circus tent. The film's composition is as dynamic as its color. Ophüls was one of those early directors to compose not *in* the wide screen but *for* the wide screen. The big shots—in the circus tent, in the palace—truly fill the frame. Ophüls's constantly moving camera, his panoramic staging, and his careful decor decrease the impression of the screen's great width by adding fullness and balance to the frame. Ophüls constantly splits the wide screen with contrapuntal verticals, breaking the horizontal expanse with lamps, chandeliers, ropes, drapes, pillars.

For his intimate close ups, Ophüls rejects the conventional single face in the center of the frame, a composition that clashes with the wide screen; he either frames two faces that tensely balance one another on opposite sides of the screen or frames a single face that is balanced asymmetrically by an object or rearground action elsewhere in the frame. Ophuls's favorite camera maneuver in the film is the circular track that moves round and round the action, keeping the figures contrapuntally balanced around an invisible pole in the center of the wide frame. The circular motion is not only active and interesting pictorially; it is the perfect cinematic parallel for the film's metaphorical circus tent, which becomes a microcosm for all earthly places and all human experience. Ophüls's turning camera, his metaphorical setting, and the very structure of *Lola Montès* turn all human experience into a vivid circus and all spectators in the movie theatre into spectators in the circus tent.

Although *Lola Montès* was Max Ophüls's final film before his death in 1957, his name gained a posthumous asterisk while losing its umlaut. His son, Marcel Ophuls, became a

Fig. 13-21

Fig. 13-22

Lola Montès—*composition for the wide screen. Fig. 13-21: Filling the frame; Fig. 13-22: contrapuntal verticals (Martine Carol and Anton Walbrook).*

Fig. 13-23
Diary of a Country Priest.

major documentary filmmaker of the next generation (*The Sorrow and the Pity,* 1969; *The Memory of Justice,* 1976; and *Hotel Terminus: The Life and Times of Klaus Barbie,* 1988). These personal, political films were quite the cinematic opposite of his father's elegantly formal romances.

Robert Bresson, though equally careful with narrative structure, details of decor, and pictorial composition, is a completely different kind of filmmaker. Subdued rather than flamboyant, quiet rather than gaudy, introspective rather than extrovertedly spectacular, Bresson's and Ophüls's films are as far apart as Brittany and Vienna. Bresson has made fewer than a dozen films in a career of forty-five years, the most important of them being *The Ladies of the Bois de Boulogne* (1945), *Diary of a Country Priest* (1950), *A Man Escaped* (1956), *Pickpocket* (1959), and *Mouchette* (1967), followed by *Une Femme douce* (1969, his first in color), *Lancelot du lac* (1974), and *L'Argent* (1983). Bresson takes two, three, even five

years to make a single film. His slowness and care as a craftsman seem to mirror the quietness, the slow pace, the internalized probing of his films. Like Antonioni, Ozu, and Dreyer, Bresson is a purist and a perfectionist. Whereas the Ophüls films are dizzying visual shows, the Bresson films feel more like ascetic, introspective novels. Bresson's favorite transitional device is the slow fade out and fade in, rather like the novelistic end of one chapter and beginning of the next. Like the novelist, Bresson can tell his story through an omniscient third person (*The Ladies of the Bois de Boulogne*) or a confessional first person (*Diary of a Country Priest*). The *Diary* even uses the narrator's voice as the priest makes entries in his journal.

Bresson's primary theme is the battle of spiritual innocence with the corruption of the world. Bresson, a devout Roman Catholic, searches for spiritual meaning and salvation in a world that has obviously lost them. In *Diary of a Country Priest,* a young, innocent curé faces the worldly evils about him: A cynical, nihilistic doctor commits suicide; a wealthy count substitutes money and influence for morality and faith; the faith of the count's wife wavers at the loss of her son; the count's neurotic daughter viciously implicates the priest in the countess's death; the peasants of the countryside remain indifferent and hostile. As a priest, the man fails. He succeeds only in bringing a moment of faith and peace to the countess. The other members of his parish remain tied to their selfish cares and material concerns. But as a man, the priest succeeds completely. He dies of cancer, unshaken in his faith to the end, certain that "all is grace." His spirit wins the battle with his body. Bresson's cinematic technique—unselfconscious, unspectacular, rigorously dispassionate, effortlessly transparent—never diverts our attention from the man's internal struggle and the thematic basis of that struggle, spiritual and physical health.

Fig. 13-24
The first entrance of M. Hulot (Jacques Tati, right) in Mr. Hulot's Holiday.

Jacques Tati is the great comic of the French film, probably the greatest film mime and visual comic since Chaplin and Keaton. Like Bresson, Tati works slowly, controlling every detail of the film himself from script to cutting; like Bresson, Tati refuses to compromise with either technicians or producers. As a result, though Tati's first film appearance was as early as 1932, he made only six feature films: *Jour de fête* (1949), *Mr. Hulot's Holiday* (1953), *My Uncle* (1958, his first in color), *Playtime* (1967, in 70mm), *Traffic* (1970), and *Parade* (1973). Like Chaplin and Keaton, Tati came to films from the music hall. Before taking to the stage, Tati took to sport—tennis, boxing, soccer. Tati's comedy—for example, his famous tennis pantomime—often combines the athletic field and the music hall. But Tati is sensitive not only to the comic possibilities of his body but also to the visually comic possibilities of film.

Like Chaplin and Keaton, Tati plays essentially the same character in each picture. The character Tati plays is inevitably a loner, an outsider, a charming fool whose human incompetence is preferable to the inhuman competence of the life around him. Tati's Mr. Hulot (even the name Hulot recalls Charlot) merely goes about his business, totally unaware that the world around him has gone mad and that

his naïve attention to his own business turns its orderly madness into comic chaos. Like Chaplin and Keaton, Tati's Hulot neither looks nor moves like anyone else in the universe. He leans forward at an oblique angle—battered hat atop his head, pipe thrusting from his mouth, umbrella dangling at his side, trouser cuffs hanging two inches above his shoes—an odd human construction of impossible angles, off-center and off-kilter. His bouncy walk implies an elastic spring, ready to launch him into space and off the earth, where he simply doesn't belong.

In his first feature film, *Jour de fête* (a feast-day or holiday), Tati plays a clumsy rural postman who discovers the apparent efficiency and speed of the American postal system. Tati's zany attempts to convert himself into a speedy efficient machine produce great visual gags as well as chaos in the little town. As always with Tati, that which seems efficient and modern is ultimately inefficient and wasteful.

For *Mr. Hulot's Holiday,* his second feature film, Tati created Monsieur Hulot, an apparently conventional, pipe-smoking, easygoing, middle-class gentleman who comes to spend a conventional week at a completely conventional middle-class resort. Monsieur Hulot, again like Chaplin and Keaton, runs afoul of objects. His troubles with bathers on the beach, with his sputtering little car, with a violently bucking horse, even with the twang of the hotel's dining-room door, and, finally, with a warehouse full of fireworks, reduce the conventional, routinized tourist resort to unconventional hysteria. Tati's comic attack exposes the resort—supposedly a place devoted to leisure and fun—as the domain of the dull, the monotonous, the dead. M. Hulot is the force who converts the dead place of play into a genuine funhouse by bombarding it (quite literally at its climax) with uncanny objects, sounds, and movements. We in the theatre, like those few vacationers who take the time to notice Hulot's spontaneous, disruptive activities, also discover what genuine, active fun really is.

My Uncle features Monsieur Hulot again—this time as an old-fashioned, simple, mild uncle of a family of upper-middle-class suburbanites. Hulot's simple, unaffected ways contrast with the complicated machinery of his suburban relatives' lives: their fancy gadgets that open the garage doors and kitchen shelves (inconsistently); their bizarrely shaped furniture that is designed for everything but comfort and function; their gravel-lined flagstone-paved "garden" that is suitable for everything but growing things and enjoying the sun. In this struggle of humanity versus the artifact, the gadgets win the battle (they always do in physical comedy), but M. Hulot wins the satirical war.

Playtime brings a group of American tourists to Paris. Hulot, more a passive observer than the central figure of the film, accompanies a group on their tour of a modern industrial exposition and a fancy nightclub that has just been glued together for fashionable Parisians and American tourists. The film's joke, as well as its serious point, is that Paris—the Paris of the travel folders and romance—does not exist. The old Paris has been replaced by aluminum-and-glass skyscrapers and neon-lit prefabricated restaurants. Paris is no different from New York—hence the irony of the American tourists. The film is a clear extension of *My Uncle*, the ultimate blow at "modernity."

But the blow wears a comic glove. Tati ridicules the slick surfaces of modern life with hilarious visual gags: The tiles of the dance floor have been pasted down so recently that they stick to the dancers' high-stepping shoes; a plate-glass door has been cleaned so well—to the point of invisibility—that the customers cannot tell whether the doorman actually opens the door or merely mimes it. Tati also uses sound brilliantly. Although *Playtime* has so little dialogue that it requires no subtitles, Tati develops sound gags like a plastic-and-foam-rubber sofa that makes grotesque breathing and sucking noises when Hulot sits on it and a miraculous modern door that makes absolutely no noise even when slammed with the most violent force.

Like *Mr. Hulot's Holiday,* the underlying theme of *Playtime* is the creative use of leisure and the genuine fun that can result from active perception rather than the passive acceptance of planned and canned routines. The American tourists of *Playtime* parallel the vacationers in *Holiday,* and in *Playtime* they eventually do have fun, despite their overly packaged tour, simply by observing the oddities of Hulot and, even more important, the surprising oddities of the world itself. Like *Mr. Hulot's Holiday, Playtime* is very much about itself, about our having fun by watching a film closely and by finding its comic inventions for ourselves rather than being fed them by a prepackaging film director. Shot in 70mm, its geometric modern city planned and constructed by Tati himself (humorously called "Tativille," its cost drove him into bankruptcy, from which he never recovered), *Playtime* invites us to explore its vast spaces without a dictatorial guide. There is not a single close-up in the film; our eye must pick out visual and comic significance for itself. In their blend of social satire, wry charm, imaginative physical gags, and the creative use of the visual and aural devices of the cinema itself, the films of Jacques Tati have not been surpassed by those of any other postwar film comic, French or otherwise.

Two other major French directors of the years just following the war were Henri-Georges Clouzot and René Clément. Clouzot is, like Hitchcock, an assured director of extremely suspenseful melodramas. Both *The Wages of Fear* (1953) and *Les Diaboliques (Diabolique,* 1955) mix chills, horror, sexual intrigue, and taut suspense. *Les Diaboliques* is the

more celebrated of the two, a story of a supposedly dead man who keeps reappearing to
terrify his living wife — and a shrieking audience. But *The Wages of Fear* is a purer representative of the Clouzot method: an
agonizingly tense, long journey of two trucks
transporting nitroglycerin through the jungles
of South America (pretentiously remade by
William Friedkin as *Sorcerer* in 1977).

Clément's most important film is *Forbidden
Games* (1952), a wartime story of two children
who are both affected and infected by the murderous world of their elders. A young girl's
parents and puppy are machine gunned by a
strafing German airplane. The girl, too horri-
fied by the death of her parents, fixes her fascination on the dead puppy, refusing to believe
it is dead; she tries to keep it and play with it.
She is adopted by a family of Pyrenees farmers
who, through their young son, teach her that
dead things must be buried. The girl buries the
puppy. She becomes so fascinated with burying
things that she and the young boy go about the
countryside killing living beings — flies,
spiders, toads — specifically so they can bury
them.

Attached to all the burials is that symbol of
the cemetery, the cross. Clément equates
Christianity, the forces of death, and the problem of dealing with death. In their quest to
bury bigger and bigger things the two children
attack bigger animals and steal crosses out of
the town cemetery for them. Eventually their
private cemetery is discovered; they are punished for their activity, which ironically merely
mimics that of their elders. The little girl is
sent back to Paris as an orphan, separated from
the boy and the family she has come to love.

But Clément's later films fail to duplicate
the thematic seriousness and artistic integrity
of *Forbidden Games*: *Gervaise* (1956), a heavy
and stilted translation of Zola; *Purple Noon*
(1959), a psychological, picture-postcard mystery that uses Alain Delon's body in the same
way that Roger Vadim used Brigitte Bardot's
and Jane Fonda's; *Rider on the Rain* (1970), a
horrific suspense story with sexual overtones
(like *Purple Noon*) in which Clément attempted
to show the New Wave directors that he too
could out-Hitchcock Hitchcock — but not even

Clouzot or Chabrol, let alone Clément, could
really do that.

1959 and After

In the years following the war a new generation of the French became addicted to the
movies. These *cinéastes* first became film critics
rather than filmmakers, simply because in
France, as in America, the studio establishment
had solidified enough to keep new minds and
small budgets out. These cinephiles did not
like the film establishment's ornately staged,
heavily plotted, overscripted, unspontaneous,
leaden films. In *Cahiers du cinéma*, the journal
founded by film theorist André Bazin, the
young critics François Truffaut, Jean-Luc
Godard, and Claude Chabrol ripped apart the
films of Clément, Clouzot, the screenwriters
Aurenche and Bost (*Symphonie Pastorale*, 1946;
The Red and the Black, 1954), and others of
what they considered the same literary, talky,
tasteful, studio-crafted, theatrical type. It was
Roberto Rossellini, one of the idols of these
critics, who urged them to stop writing about
films and start making them.

These *Cahiers* critics retreated a generation,
to the 1930s of Clair, Renoir, and Vigo, where
they found the zest and spontaneity of what
they considered the authentic French tradition.
Just as the French directors of the 1920s
leaped backward to the primitive exuberance
of Cohl, Zecca, and Sennett, the French directors of the 1960s leaped backward to the films
of the 1920s and 1930s. Just as the French
films of the 1920s combined echoes of the past
with bizarre innovations for the future, the
films of Truffaut and Godard were to be full
of echoes of Vigo, Bogart, Hitchcock, Ray,
Hawks, Renoir, Walsh, combined with ingeniously elliptical, irrational techniques. The
year 1959 was the year that the critics, heeding
Rossellini's advice, became filmmakers — the
year of Truffaut's *The 400 Blows* (*Les Quatre
cents coups*) and Godard's *Breathless* (*A bout de
souffle*, shot 1959 but released 1960).

The young François Truffaut, like the
young Vigo and the young Renoir, built his
early films on the central artistic idea of freedom, both in human relationships and in film

Fig. 13-25
The 400 Blows: *Antoine Doinel (Jean-Pierre Léaud) in the classroom. Both the feeling and the candid style of Vigo's Zéro de conduite.*

technique. Truffaut's early protagonists are rebels, loners, or misfits who feel stifled by the conventional social definitions. Antoine Doinel (Jean-Pierre Léaud), the thirteen-year-old protagonist of *The 400 Blows* (its title a reference to the proverbial 400 blows—from disappointments to beatings—a boy must endure to become a man), must endure a prison-like school and a school-like prison, sentenced to both by hypocritical, unsympathetic, unperceptive adults. Charlie Kohler (Charles Aznavour) of Truffaut's *Shoot the Piano Player* (1960) has deliberately cut himself free of the ropes of fame and fortune as a concert pianist, preferring his job in a small smoky bar, where he thinks he can remain—uncommitted, unburdened, unknown. Catherine of *Jules and Jim* (1961, released 1962) feels so uncomfortable with all definitions—wife, mistress, mother, friend, woman—that she commits suicide. Truffaut's

early cinematic style was as anxious to rip the cords as his characters were. The early films are dazzlingly elliptical, omitting huge transitional sections of time and emotional development. His construction emphasizes the key moments of interaction and conflict rather than the motivational gaps between the moments. This elliptical leaping—and a camera that moved unpredictably but always effectively, as if possessed by a vision of cinema and its renewed possibilities—gave the Truffaut films an intensity, a spontaneity, a lightness that other films lacked.

Truffaut also delighted in mixing cinematic styles. Breezy, startling, and deeply moving, *The 400 Blows* ranges from sentimental traveling shots of Antoine's tear-stained face, underscored by Jean Constantin's lush music, to scenes shot on the streets with the unpretentious intensity and insight of the neorealists

Fig. 13-26
Antoine at the sea: the final scene of **The 400 Blows.**

out further comment. In *Jules and Jim,* Truffaut undercranks the camera for Sennettesque effects; he uses a subjective traveling shot as the three characters race across a bridge; he uses newsreel footage of World War I that is horribly distorted by his contemporary anamorphic lens; he uses a brief freeze-frame to capture a moment of Catherine's beauty; he uses slow motion as Catherine drives her car off a pier to her death, prolonging the suicide, making the moment sad and slow. The trick and the surprise were intrinsic to Truffaut's method. They perfectly accompanied the stories and characters he had chosen to film. They gave the film's action the Truffaut spirit.

Charlie Kohler finds it impossible to divorce himself from commitment and emotion in *Shoot the Piano Player.* Charlie, as a flashback reveals, was once the famous concert pianist, Edouard Saroyan. After his wife's suicide, for which Saroyan's absorption in himself and his career is largely responsible, the pianist indulges his guilt by changing his identity, becoming Charlie Kohler, honky-tonk pianist, determined to avoid any further human involvement, human conflict, love. He sits at his piano expressionless, grimly banging out his honky-tonk tunes.

But life catches up with Charlie, forcing him to respond—just as it catches up with Bogart in *Casablanca* and Jean Gabin in *Port of Shadows,* both of whom are specifically evoked by the film. Charlie cannot stop himself from helping Lena (Marie Dubois), from defending her against the bullying owner of the bar (whom he accidentally kills), from falling in love with her despite his decision not to love. And as with his wife, he is again responsible for the death of a beloved when Lena is accidentally caught in the middle of a gunfight between Charlie's brothers and two gangsters. Accidents in the film are ironic and horrifying, senseless yet pervasive. Truffaut captures the pathos of Lena's death in her long, poignant slide down a hill of white snow. Charlie has lost his love again. In the film's final shot, he has returned to his piano to bang out the same haunting tune—grim, expressionless, determined. The film paradoxically maintains that it is the nature of love to be lost but that to pro-

—but in scope—to candid comic scenes in the schoolroom, echoing Vigo's candid work with school children; from a *cinéma vérité* interview between Antoine and a prying social worker (actually, Léaud's screen test, with Truffaut offscreen asking the questions; the social worker's voice was dubbed in later), to long, subjective traveling shots as Antoine escapes the reform school and races toward the sea. The film then ends with a deliberately startling surprise, a freeze frame of the boy staring ahead, presumably implying the ambiguity of the future that lies ahead of him. *Shoot the Piano Player* contains a most audacious, irrelevant interruption. A character swears that he is telling the truth. "May my mother drop dead if I'm lying," he says. Truffaut then cuts to a shot of an old lady by a stove who suddenly clutches her heart and collapses to the floor. Truffaut then returns to the story with-

tect oneself from the pain of loss by not loving is not to live at all.

Jules and Jim is another study of the relationship of love and life. Catherine refuses to live any longer than she can love, feel, respond freely, act impulsively. She travels with a bottle of vitriol as a potential means of escape from a life that might one day hang too heavily about her neck. She is a creature of whim, of impulse, of change. She can dress up like a Jackie-Cooganesque kid; she can race across a bridge; she can dive into the Seine to shake up her complacent companions. Catherine's impulsiveness later drives both her and Jim off a pier to their deaths. Truffaut establishes Catherine as a pure spirit, determined to be free. Her face and smile match the statue of the love goddess that Jules and Jim first encounter in a friend's slide show, then track down. But the pure spirit of love has difficulties surviving in the real world of geographical boundaries, marriage laws, child bearing, and political wars. Though Catherine (Jeanne Moreau) enjoys supremely sunny moments with Jim (Henri Serre), with Jules (Oskar Werner), with the two of them together, the moments lose their sunlight when they become months and years. She cannot remain happy with anyone for very long. And so she cuts the rope that binds her both to life and to Jules and Jim by driving her car off a pier, taking Jim with her, while Jules, like us in the audience, can only watch.

The Truffaut filmography splits into two unequal halves—a group of early films in black-and-white (which earned him his initial respect and reputation) and two decades of films in color (which, despite their craft and subtlety, have never achieved the critical recognition of his first three films). The two recurrent themes of Truffaut's later films are education and art, both of which grow out of his earliest work. *The 400 Blows* most explicitly—and apprehensively—concerns itself with education, while both Charlie Kohler of *Piano Player* and Catherine of *Jules and Jim* have converted themselves into characters, into works of art. After several transitional pieces in a variety of styles—the melodramatic love triangle of *The Soft Skin* (1964), a repressive, anti-

Fig. 13-27

Fig. 13-28

Jules and Jim: *Fig. 13-27: supremely sunny moments; Fig. 13-28: Jeanne Moreau.*

literate world of the future in *Fahrenheit 451* (1966, based on the novel by Ray Bradbury), and a Hitchcock dissertation in *The Bride Wore Black* (1968, two years after he published his book-length interview with Hitchcock)—the second half of Truffaut's career begins with the return to Antoine Doinel in *Stolen Kisses* (1968).

Antoine Doinel is Truffaut's alter ego; his adventures on film parallel Truffaut's own personal experiences as a child and young man; the maturing of the actor who plays Doinel, Jean-Pierre Léaud, parallels the maturing of the film director behind the camera who discovered the young boy and nurtured his early career. Léaud is Truffaut's spiritual son, much as Truffaut claimed André Bazin as his own spiritual father. But the maturing experienced together by Truffaut and Léaud (like the relationship between Truffaut and Bazin) comes about solely because of the cinema, because of sharing the experience of that art. And so the Doinel films allow Truffaut to unite both of his primary themes—education and art—simply because the mutual experiencing of art produces their shared education.

In *Stolen Kisses,* young Doinel blunders at both love and work, clumsily groping toward self-fulfillment in both. In *Bed and Board* (1970), Antoine is married, with a child of his own (the educational cycle has begun again) as well as a mistress who fulfills his fantasies. (Antoine is still a half-committed blunderer, the consistent trait of his adult life.) And in *Love on the Run* (1979) Antoine gets divorced (still the blunderer), but his novel has finally been published (his own creation of a work of art)—a novel that is really an autobiographical exploration of his own experiences with women, transmuted into art (like the novel in *The Man Who Loved Women,* 1977, and the Doinel cycle as a whole).

Despite his creation of this work, Antoine continues to run after the same women in his life/novel (running is the essential Doinel metaphor, established in the magnificent running sequence that closes *The 400 Blows*). So the transforming of life into art in no way erases or resolves the aches and tensions of life (it does not resolve them for Charlie Kohler or the man who loved women either); the work of

art merely exists alongside the life it depicts, a separate but closely related chronicle. *Love on the Run* reinforces this conclusion with a cinematic metaphor—its compilation of film clips from all the previous Doinel movies (including the brief "Antoine et Collette" from *Love at Twenty,* 1962)—for the film is not only the story of an adult Doinel looking back on his life but of the adult Truffaut looking back on the entire cycle of Doinel films, which are, in a sense, his own life.

The Wild Child (1969, released 1970), on its surface an almost documentary-style study (Truffaut's only black-and-white film after *The Soft Skin*), is also devoted to education. A late eighteenth-century scientist succeeds in taming a wild boy—a child who had spent his entire early life as a beast in the forest—and introduces him to the luxuries of civilization: speech, clothes, shelter, discipline, and love—which make him unfit for life in the wild. That the film is much closer to the Doinel cycle than it might seem from its case-history surface can be seen in Truffaut's dedication of the film to Jean-Pierre Léaud, that Truffaut himself played Dr. Jean Itard, the scientist who taught the boy (just as Jean Renoir played roles in many of his own films), and that the Truffaut–Léaud relationship is unmistakably significant to *The Wild Child.* Just as both the boy and the scientist are changed as the result of the educational process in *The Wild Child,* both Truffaut and Léaud, themselves outlaws and outcasts, grew into mature and full human beings under the tutorship of the director and in the process of creating works of art, the ultimate product of civilization.

The central Truffaut theme had evolved into one that was quite close to Renoir's: the relationship of art to nature and the ability of art to contain nature and to become its own nature. *The Wild Child* looks more ambivalently at the claims of nature than *The 400 Blows* or *Jules and Jim;* though civilization necessarily constricts, it also humanizes. As in the films of Renoir, socialization is a tragic necessity (most tragic in the film when Itard unjustly and arbitrarily locks the boy in a closet to teach him the meaning of injustice). In contrast to the exuberant spontaneity of Truffaut's earlier rebels is the savagery of the wild child (Victor, played by Jean-Pierre Cargol) who is unfettered but, in civilization's terms, less than human. Truffaut's camera, managed by the great Cuban-born cinematographer Nestor Almendros, consciously evokes the visual values of that earlier, more primitive cinematic era of Feuillade, Gance, and Griffith: the use of irising, pure silence, and black-and-white, whose silvery monochrome looks more like the older orthocromatic film than the newer panchromatic stock, as well as the decision to shoot in the old aspect ratio of 1.33:1 (most of his films were shot in European widescreen [1.66:1, flat] or in scope [2.35:1, anamorphic])—all reveal the director's retreating into the cinematic past for his study of the historical past. For Truffaut, as for Renoir and Rossellini (in *The Rise to Power of Louis XIV*, 1966), the cinema is a time machine —although its views of past centuries can only be manufactured by the mechanics, optics, and attitudes of the twentieth century.

Precisely the same tension between art and nature propels *Day for Night* (1973), a film that Truffaut was seemingly destined to make, since its subject is the process of filmmaking itself. As with *The Wild Child*, Truffaut plays a role in his own film—a similar role—the patient, paternal teacher-master who is responsible for the success of a complex project. As with *The Wild Child*, the film develops the conflict and resultant synthesis of art and nature, for the filmmaking process is none other than that of converting the totally artificial into the seemingly natural. A film produces candle effects with electric lights, rain and fire with valves and hoses, snow with suds of foam, an artfully "artless" ironic touch (a kitten eating the remains of an amorous breakfast) with a specially selected (and unnaturally uncooperative) cat, and deadly accidents with the leaps of a nimble stuntman. The term that gives the film its title, *day-for-night* (in French, *la nuit américaine*—"American Night"), is itself a synthesis of art and nature, the term that Hollywood coined in the era when the movies invariably produced the effect of nighttime by shooting during the day with a blue filter.

But the synthesis of art and nature in *Day for Night* goes even deeper. Those in the film business ultimately turn their lives into the service of art. Whatever happens in their lives,

Fig. 13-29
Day for Night: *Life as art as life as art. An adult Jean-Pierre Léaud (with Valentina Cortese) as a love-sick actor, playing a love-sick character, in a Truffaut movie, featuring Truffaut in the role of a film director.*

they make the picture —for ultimately, as in the late Renoir films, the dedication to art becomes natural for people who define themselves as being artists. That Truffaut's film is close to Fellini's *8½* is obvious not only in its subject but in the recurring dream sequence that deliberately echoes the anguished fantasies of Fellini's film as well as Ingmar Bergman's ominous dream sequences in *Wild Strawberries*. But Truffaut turns this potential dream of *angst* into a joke; each successive repetition reveals more and more glee as Truffaut's little boy unashamedly seizes possession of his great prize —the stills for *Citizen Kane* (just as Antoine Doinel steals film stills in *The 400 Blows*). Truffaut's director dreams of how the commitment to art turns the fears of death into a celebration of life.

Two major Truffaut films of the late 1970s —*The Story of Adèle H.* (1975) and *Small Change* (1976)—respectively develop the compulsive surrender to a fixation that leads to madness and death and the commitment to education that leads to a celebration of life. Adèle H. (short for Hugo—the novelist's daughter), like Ophüls's Madame de . . . , another woman with an incomplete name but a completely consuming passion, follows her passion wherever it leads her—Nova Scotia, Barbados—converting her quest for the romantic absolute into such a deeply perfect work of art that it seals her life off completely from the influence or even awareness of social reality. In *Small Change* Truffaut returns to the classroom of *The 400 Blows* of two decades earlier (and to that of Vigo's *Zéro de conduite,* two decades before that). As opposed to the black-and-white psychological repression and emotional torture of the earlier films, *Small Change* is a thoroughly sunny color film in which the old, dark wooden desks of both the Vigo and the earlier Truffaut schoolrooms have been replaced by bright, light, modern ones; the old repressive, vicious teachers have been replaced by a genuinely concerned and kind one (he parallels the patient father-teacher played by Truffaut himself in *The Wild Child* and *Day for Night*); and, in this happier world, when kids fall out of buildings, they land unharmed. A much more complex and coldly affecting treatment of the problems of life, *The Green Room* (1978), stars Truffaut as a figure taken from two Henry James stories (notably "The Beast in the Jungle") who is obsessed with art and death virtually to the point of missing out on life.

Truffaut was never a committed political filmmaker. Like Renoir, he was too much the sympathetic but detached observer and ironist who saw the validity of competing ideological positions. And like Ophüls, he was too much the romantic and formalist in his quest for emotional satisfaction and artistic perfection. Truffaut faced his evasions directly in *The Last Metro* (1980), his most political film and his most successful—commercially and critically—in France. The beautiful director of a Parisian acting ensemble during the Nazi Occupation (Catherine Deneuve) insists on continuing business as usual, performing the escapist plays the public and the authorities expect of her, refusing to take a stand against the anti-Semitic regulations that devastate her own acting company. Although her detachment angers the new leading man of the troupe (Gérard Depardieu), he discovers her apolitical stance is a ruse to protect her own husband, the company's former director and leading man, who is hunted by the Occupation authorities and hiding in the basement of the theatre.

Truffaut makes two points about his own apolitical films—in response to the activism of his colleague and contemporary, Jean-Luc Godard, who took quite the opposite path. First, the genuine political effects of art are frequently unknowable on the surface; second, the business of artists is to make art. The artist who rejects his *métier* for explicit political and rhetorical programs might well produce bad politics and bad art. In this final major film before his death in 1984, Truffaut reaffirms his belief in the human value of making art and making movies.

Jean-Luc Godard took the idea for his first feature film, *Breathless* (*A bout de souffle,* 1959, released 1960), from Truffaut. Michel Poiccard, the gangster-lover-hero of the film, is very much a Truffaut figure, a synthesis of Charlie, Catherine, and Antoine Doinel. But *Breathless* and Michel Poiccard were as close as Godard's films ever came to Truffaut's. Whereas Truffaut's films are consistent in both theme and technique, the Godard films are consistent in their inconsistency, their eclecticism, their mixing of many different kinds of ideas and cinematic principles.

Godard, paradoxically, supports several contradictory ideas and filmic methods at the same time. On the one hand, he finds human experience irrational and inexplicable: the sudden, accidental, almost arbitrary deaths at the end of *Vivre sa vie* (1962), *Contempt* (1963), and *Masculine Feminine* (1966), the chance murder of the policeman in *Breathless.* On the other hand, Godard embraces Brechtian devices and politics, and Brecht's premise was that both art and human problems must be viewed as strictly rational and hence solvable. The parable of turning a man into a soldier in *Les Carabiniers* (*The Riflemen,* 1963) echoes that parable in Brecht's *A Man's a Man* (written in 1924); the explicitly numbered scenes of *Vivre sa vie, A Married Woman* (1964), and *Masculine Feminine* and the concrete references to B. B. in *La Chinoise* (1967) are unmistakable. On the one hand, Godard is fond of allegorical, metaphorical parables: *Les Carabiniers, Alphaville* (1965), *Weekend* (1967). On the other, he is fond of recitations of concrete facts and figures: the prostitution figures in *Vivre sa vie,* the Maoist students' speeches in *La Chinoise,* the truck drivers' debate in *Weekend,* the discussions of imagemaking in *Le Gai savoir* (1968, released 1969) and of both radical politics and democracy (a tape-recorded interview with a character named Eve Democracy) in *One Plus One* (1968)—also known as *Sympathy for the Devil,* from the hit song by the Rolling Stones, whom the film features.

Godard unsentimentally depicts both irrational moments of fleeting sensation and long-winded speeches of abstract rational argument, both moments of violent action and hours of inactive discussion, outrageous intrusions of the director's favorite film sequences and book titles and long unedited scenes in which the director attempts to efface himself completely. Like Truffaut's, Godard's film career breaks into two parts—the works preceding and following 1968. But Godard's films never evolve toward Truffaut's synthesis of life and art; instead, Godard's films progressively reflect a fear that the familiar solutions of art are precisely antithetical to the necessary solutions for life, particularly political life. Bourgeois films cannot solve bourgeois problems, let alone Marxist and Maoist ones. And so Godard's films become not progressively whole and controlled but progressively fragmented and questioning, in search of "new forms for new contents," as the director (Yves Montand) says in Godard and Jean-Pierre Gorin's *Tout va bien* (1972). Rather than resolving his contradictions, Godard's evolving work seeks to explore and emphasize those very contradictions. To the extent that he characteristically presents a dialectic rather than its resolution and that he thinks so deeply about the cinema as a language, Godard may well be considered the filmmaker who picked up where Eisenstein left off.

Breathless, his very first feature, remains the most realistic, most whole, and strongest narrative of the Godard films. Godard examines the life of Michel Poiccard (Jean-Paul Belmondo), alias Laszlo Kovacs (the same name as the American cinematographer who began by filming B pictures for American-International and

Fig. 13-30
The first shot of **Breathless:** *Jean-Paul Belmondo playing Michel Poiccard playing Humphrey Bogart.*

who later shot *Easy Rider* and *Five Easy Pieces*). Poiccard is indeed a petty crook in the Monogram, B-picture tradition, a casual car thief who kills a policeman virtually by chance, gets emotionally entangled with his girl (Jean Seberg), whom he wants to run away with him, and is eventually gunned down by the police after the girl tips them off. The remarkable thing about the film is not just its simple story and the choppy, exciting, refreshing way it is told, but its Bogartesque character: brazen, charming, free, refusing to warp emotions into words or conduct into laws. Remarkable also are the emotional moments of the film: the startlingly real interaction between Michel and Patricia in her room and bed, Michel's buoyant good humor as he drives the car just before he sees the cop, the sentimental but touching ending (a possible echo of Lucy's dying gesture in *Broken Blossoms*) as the dying Michel bids a funny-sad farewell to the woman who betrayed him because she was afraid to love him.

To like Godard for *Breathless* is perhaps to wish he were another Truffaut. But even in *Breathless* the unique Godard devices—the logical assault against logic, the sudden and abrupt event, the detachment of the viewer

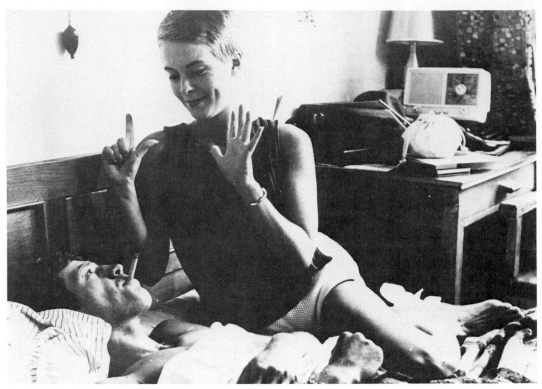

Fig. 13-31
Breathless: *Michel (Belmondo) and Patricia (Jean Seberg) in the bedroom.*

from the illusion of the film—control the work. As Michel drives the stolen car, his lengthy monologue on life and the countryside is addressed directly to us, an artifice that Godard emphasizes with his jump cutting, which destroys—or excitingly charges—the visual continuity of time and space. Michel's shooting of the policeman becomes a distant puppet show because of Godard's nonfluid, jumbled cutting of the sequence and his games with camera speed. As Michel walks on the Champs Elysées, an automobile suddenly strikes and kills an unsuspecting pedestrian. Again Godard's jump cutting and Raoul Coutard's hand-held camera give the event the convincing feeling of accident, chance, the unexpected. Michel takes a casual look at the dead pedestrian, shrugs, and keeps walking. The fragments of human passion, the juggled editing and jiggled camera, are pure Godard, not Truffaut.

The primary strength of Godard films of the next half decade is the director's continuing ability to catch flashing, elusive moments of passion, joy, or pain with the most surprising and unconventional narrative techniques. *Vivre sa vie (My Life to Live)*, a supposedly cold, detached, rational study of a woman (Nana, played by Godard's first wife, Anna Karina), who drifts into prostitution (a consistent Godard metaphor for the relationships of people under capitalism) and is shot to death when one pimp tries to sell her to another (in an understated, realistic scene of almost arbitrary violence—as far from a big "Hollywood ending" as possible) contains perceptive and revealing moments of human interaction. In the film's first scene, Nana and her husband separate; Godard catches the emptiness, the hollowness of the relationship by shooting the scene in a café, full of the sounds of tinkling cups and passing traffic, behind the two speak-

Fig. 13-32

Fig. 13-33

Vivre sa vie. Fig. 13-32: going about the business of prostitution (Anna Karina as Nana). Fig. 13-33: sudden, meaningless death during a business transaction.

ers' backs. The faces of the man and woman never appear in the scene, except in a brief reflection in the mirror opposite the counter at which they are sitting. Also effective in the film is Nana's going about the business of being a prostitute—with the very old, the very young, the ugly, and the handsome—in the most matter-of-fact way while Godard's soundtrack gives us, in counterpoint, a dry recitation of facts and figures on prostitution. The girl's teasing of a young man in a pool room, her weeping at a screening of Dreyer's *Joan of Arc* (the film itself moves her, and she also recognizes her own suffering on the screen), and her lengthy but touching discussion of the meaning of life with an old philosopher in a café also contribute to the roundness of her portrait.

Masculine Feminine, too, succeeds because of its charming or touching moments as well as its hard-edged analyses. Godard seeks to capture the world, the politics, the vitality of the young, the generation of "Marx and Coca-Cola." Godard relies on improvisational interviews with his young central figures, whose charm, spontaneity, and honesty in front of the camera are infectious. The suddenness of the boy's chance death (Jean-Pierre Léaud again) at the end of the film parallels the irrational abruptness of the deaths in *Breathless* and *Vivre sa vie*. Godard again handles death anticlimactically. We discover that the boy has fallen off a building to his death only when his girlfriend reports the accident to the police. The clicking clatter of the bureaucratic typewriter recording the account in the coldest, most mechanical manner contrasts poignantly with the breathing, vital energy of the living boy. Life and death, radical energy and officious indifference are that close and that far apart in the world of Godard.

Les Carabiniers and *Weekend* get their energy from the power of Godard's fable rather than the charm of his characters. *Les Carabiniers,* based on an idea by Rossellini, is a wryly comic Brechtian parable of two country bumpkins—ironically named Michelangelo and Ulysses, a synthesis of classical, Renaissance, and modern civilization—who leave the farm to go to war. The recruiting officer promises them the world; instead, the yokels merely bring back picture postcards of the world. Except, ironically, those postcards *are* the world, for the world itself has been transformed by the twentieth-century media into images—in souvenir or newspaper photographs, on television or movie screens. Throughout the film the two soldiers have described their travels and exploits to the women at home (Cleopatra and Venus) on wry picture postcards that make no separation between the pleasant places they visit and the people they butcher. This naïvely bitter, comic, Brechtian device points directly to the film's statement: Those who butcher get butchered in return.

Weekend, another film about butchery, begins realistically enough; Godard takes realistic man's animal-like possessiveness toward his automobile as the film's starting point. As the central couple travel on a highway to a weekend with their in-laws, Godard transports them from the land of the living to parable land. Using an agonizingly long, stifling traffic jam on the highway—shot in one long take— Godard leads us gradually from reality into metaphor: from traffic jam to a land of wrecked automobiles and mutilated crash victims, to a land of open human hostility and warfare, to a land of cannibalistic savages slaughtering pigs and people with equal appetite. In *Weekend,* cannibalism becomes the ultimate metaphor for modern society.

But on his way to this ultimate reduction, Godard cannot restrain himself from adding capricious, playful touches. The secret code employed by the cannibalistic bands is based entirely on film titles and characters— Potemkin, Gösta Berling, Arizona Jules. The latter is one of the innest of in-group jokes, apparently a combination of Arizona Jim (the parody of Rio Jim in Renoir's *The Crime of Monsieur Lange*) and *Jules and Jim.* Godard is wry when serious and serious when wry.

If Godard's overall career reveals a consistent pattern, it is that he began by using bizarre devices of cinematic perception as a means to tell rather conventional narratives—the means to bring his characters to life—and he became progressively more concerned with a critique of cinematic perception as an end in itself. The one subject Godard's films consistently explore is the cultural process of making and receiving images—on film, television, radio news, printed advertisements, billboards, book jackets, popular songs. The first shot in Godard's first feature captures Jean-Paul Belmondo gazing upon a sexy pin-up in a tabloid newspaper. While this shot in *Breathless* served to define the interests, the cultural level, and the sexual commitments of the character, successive Godard films became increasingly interested in precisely what people were seeing and reading in those magazines and other media of cultural dissemination rather than in who these people were—or, rather, Godard became convinced that people unwillingly and unconsciously become the products of those very drawings and advertisements.

Three of Godard's pre-1968 films are most clearly committed to a study of imagemaking. *Contempt* is a film explicitly about the making of film images (with Fritz Lang in the role of a director and Brigitte Bardot as a sex-object star); *A Married Woman* is an analysis of the commoditization of women, marriage, "beauty," and "romance" in modern society; and *2 or 3 Things I Know About Her* (1967) is a return to the milieu of prostitution of *Vivre sa vie* but with the emphasis on the milieu (cafés, cars, city streets, architecture) and on the making of movies about it rather than on the business of prostitution. As his films moved toward 1968, Godard became increasingly convinced that one cannot make movies—or any other kind of art work—about anything without first understanding how one is making them and why.

The Paris riots of May–June 1968 intensified Godard's political commitments, leading him to organize a political cell (he and co-founder Jean-Pierre Gorin called it the Dziga Vertov film collective, after the Soviet innovator of *Kino-Pravda*) for making films, in opposition to the Appollonian, bourgeois model of the individual artist-creator. The character played by Yves Montand in *Tout va bien* is, like Godard, a film director who explains that he could no longer continue making auteurist feature films after the events of 1968 (Montand obviously speaks for Godard here). But Montand's choice becomes a cynical one; he decides to shoot the most vapid and exploitative television commercials exclusively. Unlike this character, Godard has decided to become the analyst rather than the manipulator of modern cultural packaging.

Another important influence on Godard's work must have been the revolutionary political films from embattled Third World countries (like the mammoth *Hour of the Furnaces* from Argentina), which were first shown frequently in Europe the same year as the Paris riots. The political discussions in Godard's films, beginning with *La Chinoise* (especially the colonialism debate in *Weekend* and black radical rhetoric in *One Plus One*), seem to have been inspired by similar discussions in Third World films. But while these Third World films advocate stirring political actions and passionately address a unified working-class audience, Godard's discussions are highly abstract, distant, and dry analyses of semiotic theory addressed to the highly educated elite (a good deal of post-1968 film theory has the same problem). After making many films of and about both political and communication theory (*Pravda* and *Vent d'est* [*Wind from the East*], both 1969; *Letter to Jane*, 1972; *Numéro deux* [*Breathless Number Two*], 1975), Godard began to retrieve his lost public with *Sauve qui peut/ La vie* (*Everyone for Himself/Life,* 1980). Distributed commercially in America by Francis Ford Coppola, the film combined its semiotic study of making messages (the film's main character is a television director named Godard) with another close study of prostitution. The films made in collaboration with Gorin and the Dziga Vertov collective (late 1968–1972) were the most radical of Godard's career, and *Wind from the East* is rightly considered a breakthrough investigation of the language and politics of the cinema.

The investigation of language is an aspect of every Godard film, but it reaches its philosophical peak in *2 or 3 Things* and its political apex in *Wind from the East.* Beginning in 1968, Godard also made films for TV about language (*Le Gai savoir,* released 1969); working with his post-1976 collaborator, Anne-Marie Miéville, he made two important series for TV, the 1976 *Communication* (*Six fois deux/Sur et sous/ la communication*) and the 1978 *France/Tour/*

Détour/Deux/Enfants. Godard's controversial *Hail Mary* (1985) opened with a short film by Miéville—which many preferred to the Godard feature; that same year they made *Soft and Hard (A Soft Conversation on Hard Subjects).* Godard's more commercial, theatrical films after *Sauve qui peut* include *Passion* (1982), *First Name: Carmen* (1983), *Detective* (1985), *Hail Mary,* and what turned out to be a disastrous adaptation of *King Lear* (1989).

First Name: Carmen contains no surrogate for Godard (like film director Jean-Pierre Melville in *Breathless,* or the fictitious directors in *Tout va bien* and *Sauve qui peut*); instead, Godard himself plays "Uncle Jean" Godard —a cranky film director committed to a sanitarium, who has had trouble raising money and finding subjects for films. He stares at blank walls and blank paper in his typewriter. Part romance (the classic temptress who lures a man to his doom), part movie parody (cops and robbers), and part tactile exploration of eroticism (like *Breathless*), *First Name: Carmen* was the first Godard film in fifteen years to attempt his earlier balance between human spontaneity, emotional intensity, and reflexive commentary on the way images are shot, edited, ordered, and synchronized with a soundtrack.

The tension between formal experiment and political commitment is also central to the work of Alain Resnais. Although Resnais has been consistently linked with both Truffaut and Godard, he is a completely different kind of filmmaker. Ten years older than Truffaut and Godard, Resnais's career in films began not as *cinéaste* and critic but as film editor and documentary filmmaker. His most important early films were documentaries that studied the works of artists (Van Gogh, Gauguin, Picasso's "Guernica") or examined the horrors of the Nazi concentration camps (*Night and Fog,* 1955). But as with Truffaut, 1959 was the year of Resnais's first feature, *Hiroshima, mon amour,* and critics considered his work part of the same "wave," despite the differences in his films.

The New Wave ("la Nouvelle Vague") was a term coined in France to describe the sudden appearance, on many fronts, of brilliant films by new directors. Although there were several directors (such as Louis Malle) affiliated with neither camp, the New Wave consisted primarily of two parts: the *Cahiers* group of critics-turned-directors (Claude Chabrol, Jean-Luc Godard, Jacques Rivette, Eric Rohmer, and François Truffaut) and the "Left Bank" group of Chris Marker, Alain Resnais, and Agnès Varda. The Left Bank group has often been characterized as taking literature, philosophy, politics, and the possibilities of documentary (from realism to investigation) more seriously than the *Cahiers* group. They were also the more professionally experienced filmmakers, and Varda's *La Pointe Courte* (shot and privately premiered in 1954, released in 1956, and edited by Resnais) has been called by some the first New Wave film; it is certainly the crucial precursor, as *Ossessione* prepared the way for neorealism.

In France as well as abroad, the perceived crest of the New Wave was *The 400 Blows*, which was completed and released in France in 1959 and—something almost unprecedented—released in America that same year. America saw *The 400 Blows, The Lovers, Look Back in Anger,* and *Room at the Top* in 1959; *Hiroshima, mon amour* in 1960; *Breathless, La dolce vita,* and *L'avventura* in 1961; and *Jules and Jim* and *Last Year at Marienbad* in 1962—and perceived itself in the midst of something new and exciting: A wave of films was breaking on its shores, a wave of films from England, Italy, and especially France.

Resnais begins with a far more literary premise than Truffaut or Godard. His films are neither improvised nor spontaneous. Like Bresson and Renoir, Resnais begins with detailed, literate, highly polished scripts. Although Resnais does not adapt novels into films—he believes a work must be written specifically for film—he asks novelists to write his original scripts: Marguerite Duras, Alain Robbe-Grillet, Jean Cayrol. Resnais respects literateness, complex construction, and poetic speech. His films are thoughtful, astonishing, tightly controlled, and operatic in comparison with the breezy, erratic, makeshift feeling of the early Truffaut and Godard films. Because one of the key Resnais themes is the effect of time, the interrelation of past, present, and future, of memory and event, his narratives are frequently elliptical, jump cutting in time and space even more freely than Truffaut's or Godard's.

In *Hiroshima, mon amour* (1959), a French woman and a Japanese man try to build something more between them than a single night in bed. She is an actress who has come to Hiroshima to make a peace film; he is an architect trying to build the ruined city up from its ashes. But they are separated by more than cultural distance. Between them is the past. For him, there is Hiroshima, the burned-out home of his youth. For her, Nevers, the little French town where she loved a German soldier in the occupation army whom the villagers murdered when the Nazis evacuated. Both have burned-out pasts.

To show the intrusion of these pasts into the present, Resnais, the sensitive editor, continually cuts shots of Nevers and the Hiroshima carnage into the shots of the present. At the film's opening, the two embracing lovers' arms seem to be covered with radioactive dust. As they make love, Resnais's camera tracks through the Hiroshima war museum, showing the burnt buildings and mutilated bodies. When the woman (Emmanuele Riva) glances at the twitching hand of her sleeping lover (Eiji Okada), Resnais cuts to a short, sudden flash of her experience in Nevers: the moment she held her German lover and saw his hand twitch as he died. The result of this assault of the past on the present is an emotional gulf between them that can never be bridged.

Last Year at Marienbad (1961) is a dazzling film of the living dead. Resnais captures the ornate details of an elegant and elaborate chateau: its mirrors and chandeliers, its carved walls and ceilings, its formal gardens. His editing adds to the visual excitement, jumping about the castle so freely that he erases—or renews—time and space completely. Alain Robbe-Grillet, who wrote *Marienbad*, said that "elsewhere" and "formerly" are impossible in the continuously renewed present tense of cinema, so that whether a given shot or sequence presents objective or subjective material (fantasies, dreams, memories), the events of *Marienbad* happen not in two years at two chateau-resorts, nor in a week at one resort, but in the hour and a half it takes to project the film. Resnais (whose early features were edited by Henri Colpi and Jasmine Chasney) treats virtually any cut as a leap in time, not only as a shift from one physical or mental space to another; this is most clear in his science fiction film about love and memory, *Je t'aime, je t'aime* (1968), but it begins in *Night and Fog* and catalyzes all the features. In *Marienbad,* time and space have been so thoroughly redefined that every character and event in the film is totally ambiguous. A man (X, played by Giorgio Albertazzi) may or may not meet a woman (A, played by Delphine Seyrig) at what may or may not be a health resort; he may or may not have met her there one year before. He may or may not ask her to leave the resort with him, to flee the man (M, played by Sacha Pitoeff) who may or may not be her husband. At the end of the film, they may or may not leave the chateau together.

Fig. 13-34

In this maze of time and faces, several dominant themes are quite clear. One of them is the contrast between sincere emotional interaction and stifling artificial conventions, as evoked by the cold, baroque ornateness of the castle itself and the woman's sinister "husband," who is both murderous (he enjoys the pistol range) and infallible (he cannot be defeated at the matchstick game). A second clear theme is time itself. The man claims to have met the woman last year, but what exactly is a year? She has photographs in her room, clear mementos of the past, but the pictures seem to be of her in the present. At one point in the film a man bumps into a woman and spills her drink. Some forty-five minutes of film time continue from this point. Then Resnais returns to the spilled-drink sequence, with the characters in exactly the same positions as when the drink was spilled. Has Resnais equated forty-five minutes of screen time with an instantaneous flash of thought and feeling in a particular character's mind? And if it is a subjective flash, whose is it? Although the film's structure strikingly resembles the stream-of-consciousness narration of modern fiction, it is difficult to determine whose consciousness is streaming in the film—the man's, the woman's, the director's, the writer's, or some combination of all of them?

Fig. 13-35

Fig. 13-36

Framing and space in Last Year at Marienbad. *Fig. 13-34: the man (Giorgio Albertazzi) watching a couple in a framed mirror; Fig. 13-35: almost-checkers against a painted checkerboard; Fig. 13-36: the woman (Delphine Seyrig) posed in front of a formal garden that might be either real or trompe l'oeil.*

La Guerre est finie (1966), a much less her-
alded Resnais film, is much warmer than either
of his first two features; it is also more lucid
and comprehensible. Like the earlier films, *La
Guerre est finie* asks how a man lives in the
present given the fact of his past and, further,
how he makes personal sense of his life if it
makes no absolute sense.

Thirty years after the Spanish Civil War,
Diego (Yves Montand) continues to work for
the Spanish underground, making regular trips
into Spain from France to bring the Spanish
workers revolutionary literature and strategy.
Though the war is indeed over, it is not over
for the man who has defined his life by fighting it and whose relationships with other people
—friends, lover, mistress—are defined by his
vocation. The climactic moment of the film
comes when his vocation is challenged by a
group of young leftists who find his methods
and his crusade archaic, worthless, ineffective;
they advocate not intellectual conversion and
organization of the workers but violent revolution and dynamiting the society. Diego rejects
their callous challenge and continues to make
his trips to Spain, fighting the finished war in
his own way. But his lover, Marianne (Ingrid
Thulin), intervenes (in the final sequence, to
save him from being captured), and one is left
with the sense that he will at last let the war be
over.

Resnais's later films have been formal color
style pieces: some of them as elegantly and effi-
ciently structured as operas, some as rigorous
as investigations. *Je t'aime, je t'aime* used a
science fiction format to experiment with the
tenses of film narrative—suggesting that *Last
Year at Marienbad*'s dizzying spatiotemporal
leaps would make perfectly ordinary sense if
we knew that the consciousness of the central
character was being manipulated by a time machine. For Resnais, the true time machine is
cinema itself. While some Resnais color films—
notably the great *Muriel, or The Time of a
Return* (1963), which continues the theme of
the intrusion of the past (both romantic and
political) on the present, and the controversial
Stavisky (1974)—maintain a political focus,
Providence (1977, his first film in English) uses
his athletic, subjective editing to examine the

narrative process itself. Resnais studies a novelist's consciousness, wandering back and forth
between the novel he is writing and the life he
is living. In *Mon oncle d'Amérique* (1980), an almost clinical study of stress, Resnais likens the
edited pieces of film to the tiny tiles of a mo-
saic, gathered into a unity by the codes of cinematic narration and the audience's perception
of formal connection. Resnais's embracing of
these purely formal (and formalistic) questions
—whatever the psychological beauties of the
films—has led to an obvious lessening of critical and box-office attention to his work. His
films of the 1980s—*La Vie est un roman*
(1983), *L'Amour à mort* (1984), *Melo* (1986),
and *I Want to Go Home* (1989, written by Jules
Feiffer)—were barely released in France and
had little or no exposure abroad.

Several other French filmmakers—though
not of the stature of Godard, Truffaut, and
Resnais—also contributed to the reputation of
the French film in the 1960s. Claude Chabrol
was the first of the *Cahiers* critics to make a
film (*Le Beau Serge*, 1958). In films such as *Les
Cousins* (1959), *A double tour* (*Leda*, 1959;
also called *Web of Passion*), *Les Bonnes femmes*
(1960), *Landru* (1962), *Les Biches* (1968), *Que
la bête meure* (*This Man Must Die*, 1969), *Le
Boucher* (1970), *La Rupture* (1971), *Wedding in
Blood* (1973), and *Violette* (1978), Chabrol
reveals—rather like Hitchcock, whom he
often emulates—an interesting contrapuntal
tension between the sexual passions of his characters and the carefully detailed, stiflingly
bourgeois social environment. Chabrol specializes in case studies of bizarre psychological
types and personal relationships that inevitably
culminate in a grotesque murder. Beyond that,
however, he is a filmmaker who takes women
seriously and portrays them insightfully, notably in *La Rupture*, *Violette*, and *Story of Women*
(1988, the story of a female abortionist in
Nazi-occupied France).

Roger Vadim's first film, *. . . and God
created woman* (1956), also preceded the 1959
Wave. Vadim began with a rough, honest sexuality that made Brigitte Bardot a star, but his
subsequent films became ponderously ornate,
tasteless style pieces that leer as coyly at sex as
Cecil B. DeMille ever did: *Les Liaisons danger-*

euses (1959), *Circle of Love* (1964), *Barbarella* (1968), and the sexually frank but rather dull 1987 remake, *And God Created Woman.*

If Vadim was France's DeMille, Jacques Demy was its Busby Berkeley. In *The Umbrellas of Cherbourg* (1964), which introduced Catherine Deneuve to the screen, Demy took the tritest of melodramatic plots (boy loves girl; he goes into the army; she marries a rich suitor; he returns; their love can never be again) and decorated it with the richest frosting he could find. The film is 100 percent all-singing; even the most banal ideas—needing a penicillin shot, asking for a liter of gas—get the benefit of Michel Legrand's lush score in what may be the first opera written for the cinema. And the film's art director, Bernard Evein, adopted the aesthetics of the department-store window: If the wallpaper is orange with lavender flowers, then the women must wear lavender dresses with orange flowers. When people match the wallpaper, more subtle and psychological principles of fictional construction may get overlooked; nevertheless, the color scheme of *The Umbrellas of Cherbourg* was fabulously creative, and it had the good luck to come out the same year as *Red Desert,* when self-conscious color was newly being scrutinized and valued. His later films include *Les Demoiselles de Rochefort* (1966) and *Donkey Skin* (1970); he died in 1990.

Demy's wife, Agnès Varda, is a totally different kind of filmmaker: probing, thoughtful, intellectually sensitive to the problems of the artist and the difficulty of making life both happy and full.

Her first film, *La Pointe Courte,* was inspired by William Faulkner's *The Wild Palms,* a novel written in what Eisenstein would have called parallel montage (two short, systematically opposite novels about the nature of love and freedom, presented in alternating chapters), two of whose characters leave the city to nurture their love in the woods. That image of hard-won romantic freedom and sense of place dominates *La Pointe Courte* and shows up, somewhat more simplistically, in other New Wave films— notably Godard's *Pierrot le fou* (1965)—as an image of romantic escape. Eventually Godard adapted the *structure* of *The Wild Palms:* two films—*Made in U.S.A.* (1967) and *2 or 3 Things*

I Know About Her—both shot in the summer of 1966 and meant to be shown in alternating reels (but never shown that way, since *Made in U.S.A.* was banned before *2 or 3 Things* was released). Godard acknowledged both Varda and Faulkner by having Patricia read *The Wild Palms* in *Breathless.* A cinematic generation later, Wim Wenders acknowledged Godard with the same novel in *Kings of the Road* (1976).

The film that made Varda famous was *Cleo from 5 to 7* (1961, released 1962), which follows a woman (Corinne Marchand) in virtually real time while she confronts the possibility that she has cancer. *Le Bonheur* (*Happiness,* 1965), shot in deliberately beautiful color, tells the moral tale of a happily married man who has a happy extramarital affair and decides to share his happiness with his wife, who takes the news rather badly. *Daguerréotypes* (1975), one of her many documentaries, presents the people who live on her street, which is named after Daguerre. (All her documentaries are personal as well as objective; perhaps the most moving is *Jacquot de Nantes,* 1991, a film about Demy.) *One Sings, the Other Doesn't* (1977) returns to fiction to examine, in feminist terms, a long friendship between two women. *Sans toit ni loi* (*Without Roof nor Law,* 1985; U.S. title, *Vagabond*) investigates the rewards and costs of a free life, recreating the final weeks in the life of a young drifter (Sandrine Bonnaire); the film is appropriately dedicated to the French writer Nathalie Sarraute, author of *Tropisms* and master of the neutral observation of the behavior of organisms. *Kung-Fu Master!* (1989) —the name of a video game favored by a fourteen-year-old boy who forms a romantic attachment with the forty-year-old mother of one of his classmates—reveals the same knowing sensitivity, the same sharp insight into the growing pains of children and adults, that informs all of her films. A true *auteur,* Varda writes, directs, and edits or co-edits her films, which are characterized by her great eye for strong compositions and colors and by the complex, painful problems with which she forces her characters to deal.

Chris Marker, who was born Christian François Bouche-Villeneuve, established himself as an author and world-travelled journalist

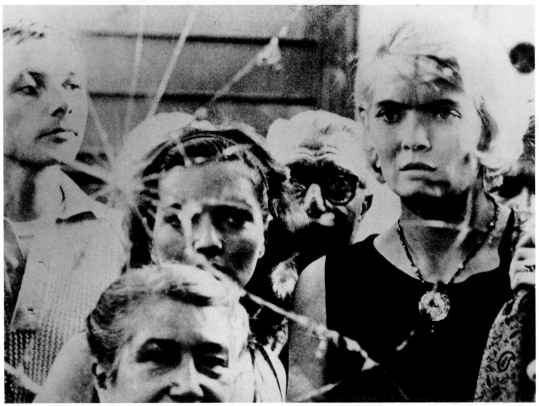

Fig. 13-37
Cleo from 5 to 7: *a look at life and death (Corinne Marchand, right).*

before co-directing his first documentaries with Resnais in the early 1950s. His own documentaries have enlarged the possibilities of the art; he has worked in the neglected genres of the letter (*Letter from Siberia,* 1957), the essay (*Cuba sí!,* 1961), and the meditation (*Sans soleil,* 1983). Some of his narrative films are as much fiction as nonfiction (one would be hard pressed to call *The Koumiko Mystery,* 1965, a pure fiction); what drives them is narration itself. Even his science fiction short, *La Jetée* (1962, released 1964)—perhaps the best film ever made on the subject of time—is told in words, voice-over, as much as it is shown, and it is shown almost entirely in a paradoxically cinematic succession of stills (frozen moments in the museum of the main character's memory, like the fragments of time caught and held as individual, still frames of movie film). In the

early 1960s Marker experimented with *cinéma vérité;* in the mid-1960s he organized the SLON film cooperative (the Society for the Launching of New Works), through which he produced several highly political compilation films—the most important of which was *Far from Vietnam* (1967), for which Resnais, Godard, and others made short films about what it meant to be far from the combat (making movies in safety) but inevitably, philosophically, politically involved in it—and released such controversial films as the long, powerful documentary *The Battle of Chile* (directed by Patricio Guzmán; Parts I and II, 1973–77).

Eric Rohmer began making his "Six Moral Tales" in 1962 and found a worldwide audience with the fourth one, *My Night at Maud's* (1969), a tale of love and religion and serious conversation. The mental battle over desire

Fig. 13-38
A frozen moment from **La Jetée.**

was joined again, almost as memorably, in the last two films in the series, *Claire's Knee* (1970) and *Chloe in the Afternoon* (1972; literally, *Love in the Afternoon*). In 1976 he turned his austere eye to literature, adapting Heinrich von Kleist's *The Marquise of O,* and in 1978 he retold Chrétien de Troyes's twelfth-century version of the legend of the grail-seeking Parsifal according to the conventions and in the imagery of medieval art (*Perceval*). He then began another cycle, "Comedies and Proverbs," which notably includes *The Aviator's Wife* (1981), *Le Beau mariage* (*The Perfect Marriage,* 1982), *Pauline at the Beach* (1983), and *My Girl Friend's Boy Friend* (1987). Rohmer, like Chabrol, Truffaut, and Godard, graduated to the making of cinema from the *Cahiers du cinéma,* which he edited after Bazin's death.

A fifth of the *Cahiers* critics to make films, Jacques Rivette, explores the magic, the mystery of making and responding to movies, plays, and stories in the first place—in *Paris nous appartient* (*Paris Belongs to Us,* 1961; produced by Truffaut, the movie the family goes to see in *The 400 Blows*), *L'Amour fou* (1968, which mixed 16mm and 35mm footage), *Out one* (1971, nearly thirteen hours), *Out one spectre* (1974, a different film, lasting one-third

as long, made from the footage of *Out one*), and especially the exuberant, intricate, and playful *Céline and Julie Go Boating* (1974).

Louis Malle is one of the most eclectic of the New Wave directors. After studying political science and then filmmaking, he virtually co-directed Jacques-Yves Cousteau's underwater documentary *The Silent World* (1956), which won an Academy Award; then he assisted Bresson on *A Man Escaped,* a totally different kind of project. His first feature, *Frantic* (1957, released 1958), was a thriller scored by Miles Davis, starring Jeanne Moreau, and shot by Henri Decaë (who was soon to shoot *The 400 Blows* and *Le Beau Serge;* Decaë was the vital cinematographer for the *Cahiers* group before the advent of Raoul Coutard, who worked primarily with Godard, and Nestor Almendros, who worked primarily with Rohmer and Truffaut). In later years he would make a multipart documentary on India as well as two of the best movies ever to attempt to sort out the moral complexities of living in France under the Nazi occupation: *Lacombe Lucien* (1974) and *Au revoir les enfants* (1987). His first contribution to the New Wave was *The Lovers* (1958), a graceful literary study of the manners and world of the very rich, culminating in the woman's throwing over both industrialist husband and polo-playing lover to leave with the young student with whom she spends the night. *Zazie dans le Métro* (1960) is a delightfully breezy, illogical, spirited film that uses cinematic tricks to recreate the literary and linguistic gags of Raymond Queneau's novel. The film is one of surprise and freedom, the director's hymn to the spontaneous and unfettered. The zany illogic of the film's story, editing, and staging mirrors the illogic that little Zazie embodies by being a petite eight-year-old who knows how to talk dirty. *Murmur of the Heart* (1971) seems a synthesis of these earlier styles with its child's-eye view of the restraints of adult life and a wealthy, attractive mother's attempts to manage both her family and her love life. Malle would later desert his French environment for the American scene—*Pretty Baby* (1978), *Atlantic City* (1980, a Canadian-French co-production), *My Dinner with Andre* (1981)—a prime example of the internationalization of film production since the late 1970s.

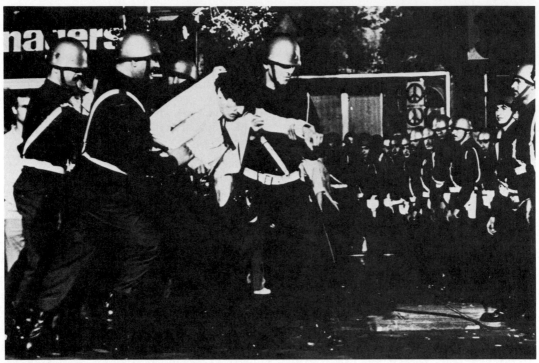

Fig. 13-39
Z: the synthesis of spy thriller and revolutionary political document.

French filmmakers of the second Wave, those to emerge in the late 1960s and 1970s, fit the paradigm suggested by the opposite evolutions of Truffaut and Godard. One group of younger filmmakers concentrates entirely on personal, experiential studies of human sensation and interaction while the other makes explicitly activist political films. The most popular films of the latter group have been the French productions of another international director: the Greek-born Constantin Costa-Gavras. His violent and probing political films (*Z*, 1969; *The Confession*, 1970; and *State of Siege*, 1972), like the films of Godard and Resnais, mix their political radicalism with deliberately erratic and radical film styles: mixtures of driving suspense and social comment, human spontaneity and political commitment, elliptical jumps into the past and future, freeze frames and slow motion, satirical comedy and passionate sincerity. Costa-Gavras's New Wave ancestry is especially apparent in the refreshing

camera work of Raoul Coutard—prowling over faces, running through a crowd—whose work added similar insight and energy to *Breathless, Les Carabiniers,* and *Jules and Jim.* His American films, particularly *Missing* (1982), maintain an active political focus and continue Costa-Gavras's investigation into the differences between true and false accounts of events. Costa-Gavras, like Rossellini before him, uses the surfaces of documentary and *cinéma-vérité* realism to give both life and immediacy to his studies of commitment and liberation. Of course the discovery and development of the *cinéma vérité* documentary style was also a French contribution (as its name implies) of the New Wave era, the most influential films in that style probably being Jean Rouch's *Chronique d'un été* (1961) and Chris Marker's *Le Joli mai* (1962, released 1963).

Foremost of the personal, domestic group is Alain Tanner, who applies a Marxist political analysis to the personal lives of middle-class citizens. Though Tanner is Swiss, his films are very French in look, language, and psychological theme. *The Salamander* (1971), *The Middle of the World* (1974), *Jonah Who Will Be 25 in the Year 2000* (1976), and *In the White City* (1983) examine the tangled interconnections of erotic sensitivity, familial responsibility, vocational fulfillment, and political sensibility. The Tanner characters, who tend to be just slightly offbeat, mildly extraordinary people living extremely ordinary, middle-class lives, attempt to break away to form an alternative, more responsive human community.

Much of the experimental energy of the New Wave has been diluted by more comfortable and amiable stories of bourgeois French life in the 1970s: The middle-class comedies of Claude Sautet are the most popular French films in France. Although the sense of a unified cinema movement has evaporated, the French cinema still provides visions of erotic and familial experience that look very different from the domestic, American variety. Among the later French directors of promise are Tanner's Swiss countryman, Claude Goretta (*The Wonderful Crook*, 1975; *The Lacemaker*, 1977) and Truffaut's assistant, Bertrand Blier, with his odd studies of male sexuality (*Going Places*, 1974; *Get Out Your Handkerchiefs*, 1977). Jean Eustache made one of the more interesting experiments in cinematic form and sexist commentary before his suicide (*The Mother and the Whore*, 1973; considered by many the last film of the New Wave). Claude Miller made one of the few French feature films to explore repressed homosexual feelings (*The Better Way*, 1975). A much less sensitive, if far more popular, examination of homosexual relationships was the Italo-French *La Cage aux folles* (1978, directed by Edouard Molinaro), a gay sit-com that unaccountably became the highest grossing foreign-language film yet released in America.

Four women directors have also joined the newer generation of French filmmakers — two of whom work within the French film industry, and two of whom work very much outside it. Diane Kurys (*Peppermint Soda*, 1977; *Entre nous*, 1983; *C'est la vie*, 1990) and Nelly Kaplan (*A Very Curious Girl*, 1969; *Néa*, 1976; *Charles et Lucie*, 1979) moved from apprenticeships with Gance, Resnais, and Truffaut to direct their own films, frequently concentrating on young women or maturing adolescents at turning points in their lives. The novelist Marguerite Duras moved from writing scripts for Alain Resnais (*Hiroshima mon amour* — she spelled it without the comma that appears in many prints of the film) to writing and directing films, often based on her own novels and plays (*La Musica*, 1966; *Destroy, She Said*, 1969; *Nathalie Granger*, 1973; *The Woman of the Ganges*, 1974; *India Song*, 1975; *Days in the Trees*, 1976; *Le Camion*, 1977). Like her novels, Duras's films experiment with both narrative form and psychological representation — often in the interplay between minimal visual imagery and densely rich soundtracks. Chantal Akerman is influenced by experimental filmmakers on both sides of the Atlantic — Godard, Michael Snow, Stan Brakhage. In her first ten years as a filmmaker, she directed seventeen movies. Her films (especially *Jeanne Dielman, 23 quai du commerce, 1080 Bruxelles*, 1975, and *Meetings with Anna*, 1978) reduce plot and dialogue, emphasizing the power of sounds, the duration of uninterrupted temporality, and the resonances of spaces in depicting fleeting moments of action, sensation, and recollected experience. Like Varda, these directors have given France the claim to the longest of female-centered cinematic narrative traditions, one that goes back to Germaine Dulac and Marie Epstein. Duras's films, which carry out avant-garde experiments with narrating voices and minimal plotting, are like those of her predecessors in that they are outside the mainstream of commercial narrative filmmaking, as those of Kurys are not. The works of Kaplan and Akerman are, in their own distinct ways, radical in form and feminist in politics.

Of the newest generation of French directors, Bertrand Tavernier is the most conscious of uniting the traditions of old and new storytelling, past and present cinema. Although a committed leftist, Tavernier, like Renoir of the 1930s, gives ordinary bourgeois citizens their dignity in their attempts to understand the political structures that contain them, for "everyone has his reasons." Although the middle-class clockmaker (*The Clockmaker*, 1974) cannot understand his son's acts of political

Fig. 13-40
Destroy, She Said: *written and directed by Marguerite Duras a decade after she wrote* **Hiroshima mon amour.**

radicalism, he comes to understand that his son must have a reason for them. *Coup de torchon* (1981) satirizes the political commitments of both right and left, while *Deathwatch* (1979) imbeds its critique of cinema's exploiting the images of women within the framework of science fiction fantasy. His greatest commercial success of the 1980s was *Round Midnight* (1986), an evocative realization of the jazz scene in 1950s Paris; it experimented with jazz rhythms in its own structure and starred Dexter Gordon as an expatriate master of the tenor sax. *Life and Nothing But* (1989) took a complex look at grief in the aftermath of the First World War, concentrating on a soldier whose job is to identify corpses.

Most reminiscent of Renoir is *A Sunday in the Country* (1984)—from its title, which evokes Renoir's 1936 film, *A Day in the Coun-*

try, to its central character, an aging impressionist painter and a contemporary of Auguste Renoir, the film director's father. Set early in the twentieth century, at the time that photography and the cinema had come to supplant or supplement painting as the culture's dominant mode of pictorial representation, Tavernier's elderly painter comes to realize that the process of making images is not simply an act of craft or beauty but a reflection and a shaper of moral commitment. Like *Daddy Nostalgia* (1990), *Sunday in the Country* is also an affecting, carefully observed movie about fathers and daughters.

Among the New Wave characteristics these later films share are their careful rendering of the textures of internal human sensations and experiences, their anti-studio look, their interest in political analysis (including the politics of gender), and their elliptical narrative structures that emphasize psychological and thematic development rather than a linear, chronological presentation of events.

The French (and Italian) Revolution

Perhaps the most important contribution of the French and Italian postwar cinemas was not the addition of at least a dozen masters of the film art and dozens of masterpieces to the body of world cinema. Even more significant—from the vantage point of three decades of hindsight—is the way that these two national movements revolutionized the values and aesthetics of the motion picture, affecting and influencing the entire world's cinema in the sound era as much as Griffith, Murnau, or Eisenstein did in the silents. The stylistic revolution that began in Italy and culminated in France spread worldwide, eventually capturing the cinema of America, Eastern Europe, and even the Third World. The Italian movement was generally more concerned with content than style—the close, careful observation of ordinary human beings in their social contexts; hence its great impact on national cinemas, like those of Czechoslovakia or Third World nations, which produced films that juxtaposed sympathetic, close studies of working- and lower-class people with a discussion of political issues. If the Italian cinema created a new style through content, the French cinema created a new content through style; hence the impact of both in America, at a time when the American cinema groped for a new content and style.

As often happens, a technological discovery produced a new style that determined a new content. Whereas the old narrow-screen black-and-white film was a more distant, objective, tonally graduated, balanced, even rational experience (perfectly suited to lengthy scenes of dialogue, narrative continuity, and images that essentially supported a film's story and issues), the new wide-screen color film was a more immediate, subjective, and kinetic experience (in which the physical sensations produced by the images and sounds were often the primary

bases for understanding a film's story and issues). Composition in the Academy Frame (or Academy ratio, as the narrow, 1.33 to 1 screen was called) was indeed composition *in* the frame, deriving from classical conceptions of space, balance, proportion, and perspective. Although the best Hollywood directors noted how poorly suited was the stretched-out wide screen's shape to such compositional values, many merely tried to apply them as best they could. But effective wide-screen composition was to become composition *out* of the frame, in the sense that the screen no longer produced compositions of images to be viewed but instead used its images to strike, assault, and prod the viewer into experiencing sensations that mirrored those of the characters. The sheer size and grandeur of the wide screen aided and necessitated its physical assault. And so all the cinematic tricks—the freeze frames, the jiggling hand-held camera, the zoom lens, the unconventional uses of music and voice-over, the elliptical jumps in the plot, the jump cuts and shock cuts—all became ways of conveying subjective sensations to an audience.

This new stylistic assumption determined the content of the two kinds of film that primarily used it. The subject of the films either became experiential itself—the feelings, sensations, and experiences of people living through an ultimate or exquisite moment of their lives, often ending with a Joycean "epiphany" of discovery (Truffaut, early Godard, Antonioni, Fellini, Rohmer). Or the subject of the films became political, using radical stylistic devices to produce a fuller perception of political and social realities, obviously and even admittedly influenced by Brecht (such as the later Godard, Costa-Gavras, and Pontecorvo films). Or the subject of the films became some mysterious and personal combination of politics and experiential sensations (Rossellini, De Sica, Marker, Varda, Resnais, Bertolucci, Pasolini, Duras, Kaplan, Akerman, Tanner, Tavernier). Ultimately, the films were about perception—either of emotional or social, inner or outer, realities. And they used all the cinema's devices of perception to make the audience perceive.

It is interesting (and perhaps ironic) that so many of these discoveries were made by the disciples of André Bazin, for Bazin's view was that cinema was the ultimate transcriber of reality, the ultimate discovery of the means of getting nature into our power by reproducing it. For Bazin, the filmmaker's role was to disappear completely, making the film reveal the reality in front of the lens rather than to mirror the personal perceptions of the filmmaker. Bazin's favorite filmmakers—von Stroheim, Welles, Renoir, Flaherty, Chaplin, Rossellini—were those who "put their faith in reality" rather than in the image, as did Eisenstein (who constructed his own reality by means of montage). Bazin's New Wave disciples are much more in the modernist tradition of defining reality as only that which each person can subjectively perceive. (There is no reality; there are only our own realities.) As a result, the cinematic tricks of these French directors were far more intrusive and self-conscious in their manipulations of "reality"—of spatial, temporal, and causal continuity—than Bazin's theory encouraged.

But then Bazin, who died in 1958, did not live to see the total conversion to the wide screen and color. In all fairness to Bazin, he did envision the possibility of a future period when the stylistic demands of the cinema would change. He noted that the cinema had attained a stability of style and technique that had remained constant for over two decades (as indeed they had since the introduction of synchronized sound), and he predicted that the introduction of a radically different technology might well produce a radically different cinema style and content. Then came the technological revolution, and the postwar cinemas of Italy and France (Bazin's disciples among them) brought the rest of the world into its next cinematic era.

14

Emerging National Traditions 1: The 1950s and 60s

The postwar decades have seen the emergence of other distinctive and important national movements, the products of many of the same causes that produced the postwar French and Italian successes. First, the postwar period encouraged personality and individuality in the cinema—new things to "say" and new ways to "say" them—because the old formulae and stylistic assumptions were breaking down. Second, the audience, the technology, and the world were all changing. Times of instability and change tend to encourage originality rather than formula. Third, the American film industry was in severe trouble artistically and commercially. Prizes at international film festivals (a new sign of the times) brought not only honor to previously unknown film artists and industries but, perhaps more important, bookings. American films were no longer powerful or attractive enough to keep foreign films off the screen, either abroad or in America itself.

Finally, feature film production has been either directly or indirectly supported by government policies in every country of the world except the United States. Foreign governments have established quotas to limit the importation or exhibition of American films, have levied exorbitant taxes on profits from showing American films or limited the currency that American companies could export, and have invested directly in film production or invested indirectly through state-supported television systems. While the American film industry has always had to sink or swim on its own, in the lean postwar years of shrinking feature-film production, the American government let the Hollywood industry sink, while other governments kept their industries afloat. In the mid-1970s the wheel came full circle. By adopting the styles and assumptions of the foreign film movements, the American cinema not only became strong enough again to keep most foreign competition off American screens but began winning the prizes at the international film festivals as well.

Sweden

The name of Ingmar Bergman is as synonymous with the new cinematic directions of the past four decades as those of Fellini, Antonioni, Resnais, or Godard. Bergman, like Truffaut and Godard, is the product of a rich national film tradition. The Swedish film industry, though never producing a great number of films, enjoys a long and distinguished history. Bergman, an actor, playwright, and stage director, learned his film craft from Alf Sjöberg, Sweden's most important director in the first two decades of sound production. And Sjöberg learned his craft in the silent era of Victor Sjöström and Mauritz Stiller. If the French and Italian filmmakers descended from the spiritual paternity of Rossellini and Bazin, Bergman's spiritual father was the cinema's Danish metaphysician, Carl Theodor Dreyer.

Stiller, Sjöström, and Dreyer combined the visual and poetic power of the northern landscapes with stories of realistic passions and mystical influences — exactly as Bergman would do forty years later. The three consistent traits of the Swedish silents were, first, their use of natural imagery to evoke and convey human passions as in Sjöström's use of the sea in *A Man There Was* (1916, released 1917), and of the mountains and fjords in *The Outlaw and His Wife* (1918), and Stiller's use of the lake of ice in *Sir Arne's Treasure* (1919), and of the snow and mountains in *The Story of Gösta Berling* (1924, starring Garbo); second, their satirical and critical condemnation of social hypocrisies and injustices, as in Sjöström's *The Outlaw and His Wife* and Stiller's *Erotikon* (1920); and third, Dreyer's great theme, the influence of cosmic, metaphysical forces in human affairs. The eerie, ghostly carriage that comes for the tramp who dies at precisely midnight on New Year's Eve in Sjöström's *The Phantom Chariot* (1920, released 1921) is clearly the ancestor of the hearse that comes for Isak Borg in Bergman's *Wild Strawberries,* and Sjöström's figure of death with his scythe is an equally clear ancestor of Death in Bergman's *The Seventh Seal.* The metaphorical unity in the Swedish film tradition is striking, for Victor Sjöström — Sweden's first film master — played the role of the old doctor in Bergman's *Wild Strawberries.*

Bergman directed his first film, *Crisis,* in 1945. For ten years Bergman and his first cinematographer, Gunnar Fischer, felt their way together within the film form, discovering how to synthesize the drama (Bergman's first love) with the visual image, building a stock company of actors sensitive to each other and to the director: Max von Sydow, Gunnar Björnstrand, Eva Dahlbeck, Ingrid Thulin, Harriet Andersson, Bibi Andersson. Later regulars would include Gunnel Lindblom, Liv Ullmann, and Erland Josephson. *Smiles of a Summer Night* (1955) was probably Bergman's first fully mature work, although critics in retrospect now point to signs of the Bergman mastery in *Thirst* (1949), *Monika* (1952), and especially *The Naked Night* (*The Clown's Evening,* 1953; also known as *Sawdust and Tinsel*). But it was *The Seventh Seal* (1956, released 1957) that first conquered audiences throughout the world, and within a year Bergman had produced two more films, *Wild Strawberries* (1957) and *The Magician* (*The Face,* 1958), to cement his reputation. These three films — *The Seventh Seal, Wild Strawberries,* and *The Magician* — make up a central unit in the Bergman canon, a complementary trilogy of films despite their differences in tone, style, and historical milieu. The films represent the best of Bergman's early period; they are also a pool of ideas and images from which all his later work seems to be drawn.

The key question about *The Seventh Seal* is whether it is a metaphysical allegory told in earthly terms, or whether it is an earthly allegory told in metaphysical terms. Its story is of a medieval knight who returns home from the crusades only to encounter Death waiting for him on a desolate, rocky beach. The knight (Antonius Blok, played by Max von Sydow) challenges Death (Bengt Ekerot) to a game of chess, knowing the inevitable result but playing for time. He wants the time for one reason: to discover the value of living. Everywhere around him he sees death: from the crusades, from the plague, from flagellation and superstition. Is there life?

At the end of the film, the knight loses the chess game and Death overtakes him and his party. But as the knight himself says, the delay has been most significant, for he has accomplished one vital action. He has helped a young family of simple innocent folk escape the clutches of Death. This happy family of father (significantly named Joseph), mother (named Mary), and infant becomes the film's trinity of

Fig. 14-1
The Seventh Seal: *Death as confessor. The equation of black, death, darkness, restraints, and the Church; from left, Bengt Ekerot and Max von Sydow.*

life. At the end of the film, they stand in the sunlight, watching Death lead the knight and his party across a hilltop in shadow.

The film's central contrast is the opposition of the ways of life and the forces of death. The Church—organized, dogmatic religion—becomes emblematic of everything in the film connected with superstition and death. The Church instigated the deadly crusades. The Church decorates its walls with pictures and statues of death. The Church inspires men to frenzies of prayer and mourning and mortification. The Church burns human scapegoats. The men of the Church wear black, the color of death. In fact, the knight mistakes the figure

of Death for a priest when he makes confession. Bergman underscores the minions of death with darkness, shadows, and the religious smoke of the censer or the stake. This "holy" smoke dominates the religious sequences, befouling the clarity of the film's deep-focus cinematography with a substance that seems like both fog and poison.

Opposed to the film's dark moments are its moments of life, clarity, and light. The scenes between Joseph (Nils Poppe) and Mary (Bibi Andersson)—the two strolling players—are slightly overexposed, brilliantly bathed in light. Actors and the theatre would remain a perpetual source of joy for Bergman, as he demon-

Fig. 14-2
The Seventh Seal. *Mary (Bibi Andersson) and Joseph (Nils Poppe): two actors in the sunlight.*

strates in *Fanny and Alexander* (1982). The scene in which the knight partakes of their happiness, when the group sits in the sunshine to eat wild strawberries, is natural, peaceful, and bright. The real religion, the real humanity in the film stems from the sincere, unselfish feelings of the characters for one another—husband for wife; parent for child; the cynical squire (Gunnar Björnstrand) for his master, the knight, and for the tormented farm girl. In the course of the film, the knight discovers the value of those feelings and feels them himself.

In Bergman's allegory we all play chess with Death. Life and death are inseparable. One of the film's most haunting and, at the same time, most comic sequences is the one in which Death

chops down the tree in which Skat, an actor, is hiding. Skat plummets to his death while Bergman's camera remains riveted to the sawed-off trunk of the tree. Immediately after the sound of the crashing tree, a cute little squirrel jumps on the tree stump and twitches its nose. Life and death are that close. And so are comedy and tragedy, for Bergman uses comedy as sardonic earthy comment on a serious film's weighty and philosophical themes. Like the gravedigger in *Hamlet*, the squire in *The Seventh Seal* (and Granny in the later *Magician*) treats death as a bitter, hopeless joke. Since we all play chess with death and since we all must suffer through that hopeless joke, the only question about the game is how long it will last and how well we will play it. To play it well, to live, is to love and not to hate the body and the mortal as the Church urges in Bergman's metaphor. In this sense the knight wins the game with Death; it is the only way that game can be won.

Wild Strawberries puts the same theme in modern dress. The film begins with a vision of death, the old man's dream in which he sees a hearse roll down a desolate street, in which he sees himself inside the hearse's coffin (Bergman's homage to Dreyer's *Vampyr*), in which the vision of himself in the coffin grabs hold of the dreamer and tries to pull him into it, in which he sees that time has stopped, that the clocks have no hands. Bergman increases the dream's impression of whiteness, of desolation, of unreality by overexposing the whole vision, giving the dream world the pale texture of a ghostly shroud. Then the old doctor wakes up. Since he perceives the closeness of death, he is haunted by questions about the value of the life he has lived. Ironically, this doctor, Isak Borg (played by Sjöström), aged 78, is about to be honored by society for the value of his life's work; a university is to award him an honorary degree. Despite the university's assessment of his life's worth, the doctor is not so certain about it. The rest of the film shows him groping for an answer, through his memories and through the events of the day (as well as a final dream). Like *The Seventh Seal*, the film is structured as a journey. As Borg travels along the road toward the university, three kinds of encounters influence his thought: encounters with his present relationships (son, housekeeper, daughter-in-law, mother), encounters with people on the road (three young, robust hikers and a bickering, middle-aged married couple), encounters with visions of his past that keep crowding into his brain.

When Borg examines his present relationships, he sees nothing but emptiness and sterility. He has tyrannized his old housekeeper of some forty years, taking her completely for granted, never realizing that she has served him as faithfully and as lovingly as any wife ever could. His mother is a shell of a human being, living totally in the past, measuring her life by the little scrapbook mementos and childhood trinkets that she has dutifully preserved. But

Fig. 14-3
Wild Strawberries. *Official societal definitions of a meaningful life — the doctor (Victor Sjöström, right) honored by the university.*

even worse is Borg's relationship with his son and daughter-in-law. He has tyrannized them, too, refusing to allow his son the financial means to be independent. Borg's great legacy to his son has been to transfer his bitterness, his nihilism, his contempt for life. So successfully has Borg passed on this dowry that the son and daughter-in-law are in danger of separating. The son hates life so bitterly that he refuses to bring children into it.

The two groups that Borg encounters on the road are diametric opposites. The young hikers are shining, vital, energetic; they devour life with a callous yet honest robustness (Ibsen called it the Viking Spirit), unfettered by social convention, disillusionment, and failure. The middle-aged couple are slaves of a now empty passion, tied to one another by habit, by argument, and by the need to share futility. Both encounters trigger Borg's visions. The pair with blasted lives evokes Borg's bitterest dream-moment in which he attends a hell-like school (the scene echoes the school scene in Strindberg's *A Dream Play*) and fails an examination administered by the husband. The doctor's life has been as uncompassionate as that schoolroom.

Fig. 14-4
Wild Strawberries. *Summer, sunlight, whiteness, and the memories of youth.*

But the young trio, particularly the girl (Bibi Andersson), stimulates Borg to dream of his childhood, his dazzling summers at the family summer house, where he felt both bitter disappointment (in romance) and the blinding happiness of youth. Bergman shoots these summer scenes with a clarity, a brilliance, and a whiteness that echo the scenes between Mary and Joseph in *The Seventh Seal.* Summer and sunshine, in fact, are consistent Bergman metaphors for moments of happiness in *Smiles of a Summer Night, Monika, Summer Interlude* (1950, released 1951), and *The Virgin Spring* (1959, released 1960). As in *The Seventh Seal,* there are wild strawberries, tart and sweet, alive, fresh. As he goes to sleep at the end of the day, Borg's final vision of his summer youth is of a brilliant sunshiny day, the whole family outdoors in the clear bright air, the girls and boys in white, his mother and father, despite their emotional difficulties, alone together in a boat on the lake.

Like the knight of *The Seventh Seal,* Isak Borg translates his vision into human action. At the end of his journey, he realizes the irrelevance of the university's social pageant. Instead,

he shows his human responsiveness by proposing marriage to his housekeeper (a proposal she does not accept), by offering to ease his pressure on his son, and by, in effect, reconciling son and daughter-in-law to one another. Borg has taken a journey toward life, and the film's implication is that he has helped his son do the same, preparing him to procreate new life. Borg contentedly falls asleep, no longer haunted by clocks without hands.

In *The Magician,* Bergman turns from the relationship of death to life to examine the relationship of art to life. *The Magician* is also a story of the road. A nineteenth-century magic lanternist (who is also a "mesmerist," or hypnotist) and his assistants travel by coach to a town where they are stopped by the local authorities. These bureaucratic devotees of reason are anxious to see the lanternist display his wares, to see whether his illusion is powerful enough to unsettle their conventional understanding of reality. The magician's art is indeed powerful enough to drive one spectator to hang himself and another to the point of madness. And yet the bureaucrats judge the man's performance a failure. In the midst of his dejection, word comes to the illusionist that his presence is desired at court. He will be honored by both the coin and the prestige of the throne. In an unexpected mood of joy and triumph and (of course) sunshine, the magician's coach sets out for the court.

The great power of *The Magician* is that it operates on two levels simultaneously. There are, in fact, two magicians: Vogler, the lanternist (played by Max von Sydow), and Bergman, the filmmaker. Both Vogler and Bergman work on the principle that the trick, the fake, the illusion can seize the mind more powerfully than the expected reality. Vogler's life is a tissue of lies and tricks. He is not mute as he pretends to be; his hair is dyed; his assistant is not a boy but his wife. Everything about the man is false —a game of mirrors and deceptive appearances like his lantern show. But Bergman plays tricks on *his* audience as ruthlessly as Vogler plays them on his.

The film opens in a forest during a thunderstorm; it is a dark and ominous one: murky, shadowy, back-lit in a gothic manner that consciously evokes John Ford. In this first sequence, Bergman introduces us to a dark, shadowy figure who seems to be an apparition of death and who appears to die in the coach before the magician arrives at the town. But later in the film we discover that the figure is not dead at all. The director has simply tricked us into believing him dead. He also tricks us with the magician's apparent muteness and his assistant's gender. But his ultimate trick on us is also the magician's ultimate trick on the bureaucrat: Vogler mysteriously lures the official to an attic, locks him in, and then reduces him to absolute terror with thumping sounds, invisible attacks, and the vision of a detached eyeball swimming in an inkwell. Bergman reduces us to terror, too; the sequence is inexplicable, evocative of the powers of the unknown, tensely controlled in its rhythm of sounds and cutting.

As though Bergman hasn't demonstrated the magician–director's powers convincingly enough, he ends the film with a grand artistic caprice. The film director has the instant power to change failure to victory, gloom to triumph: He can introduce a messenger with a letter from the king; he can add the music of trumpets and triumph to the soundtrack; he can shoot the scene in bright sunshine rather than murky shadow. The artistic principle behind all this conscious trickery is simply to show that reason, that the forces of society, have an undeniable power; society can put people in jail or decree their failure. But the irrational, the weapon of the artist, also has an undeniable power; its appearances can capture not reason but feelings and the imagination. Feeling and imagining, as both *The Seventh Seal* and *Wild Strawberries* assert, are the essential human functions, and the cinema is, like the title of Bergman's favorite Strindberg work, a dream play.

The later Bergman films return again and again to the same ground as these central three. The films that Bergman himself designated as his trilogy—*Through a Glass Darkly* (1961), *Winter Light* (1962), and *The Silence* (1963)—all seek meaningful personal values—love—in a world in which human life has no absolute purpose other than to be. *Cries and Whispers*

(1972) returns to the issue of *Wild Strawberries*: the way that the awareness of an impending death defines the values of living. And *Persona* (1965; released 1966) combines the self-conscious cinematic tricks of *The Magician* with a psychoanalytic study of a mind that, like Isak Borg and the knight, views the experience of living as a bleak and lifeless lie. That *Persona* parallels *The Magician*'s concern with art and illusion is especially clear in the surname of the actress, Vogler, which is the same as the magician's.

But despite the similarities of these to the earlier films, the Bergman cinematic style had altered radically. Whereas the earlier films generated their philosophical meanings through lucid dialogue, supported by appropriate images and well-plotted literary structures (revealing Bergman's origins in the theatre), the later films incorporated the elliptical and irrational cinematic devices of the French masters, their disruption of spatial, temporal, and causal continuity. Bergman's stylistic shift may be partly the result of his observing these French manipulations of cinematic perception, partly the result of his realizing that the probing of human perception and psychology required a more elusive technique, and partly the result of his switching to a more experimental cinematographer, Sven Nykvist, who replaced Gunnar Fischer in the 1960s. The late Bergman films are increasingly concerned with psychology—the fears, anguish, and even diseases of individual human brains—as though devoting themselves entirely to the anguished dream world of Isak Borg or the irrational illusionistic world of magician Vogler's attic.

Persona is Bergman's last black-and-white masterpiece, his most complex and difficult film, and his most dazzling display of technical virtuosity. On its surface, the film is a psychological case study of Elisabeth Vogler (Liv Ullmann), a famous and successful actress who went blank onstage during a performance of *Electra* and has refused to speak since. Her refusal to communicate is symptomatic of her feeling that human existence is merely a collection of meaningless lies, that there is nothing to achieve, that success is an illusion and happiness is the biggest lie of them all. For Elisabeth, to speak is to lie. (The problem is, to be silent is not necessarily to be honest and good.) She is treated in a mental hospital by the young, energetic, and dedicated nurse, Alma (Bibi Andersson), and the cure then takes both of them out of the hospital to the seaside home of the hospital's head psychiatrist. At that seaside retreat, where the nurse does all the talking, the two women share moments of tender intimacy and of intense hatred. The end of this process is the actress's apparent return to communication, to her life on the stage and with her family, and Nurse Alma's return to her job, somewhat shaken by the experience but continuing on her way.

What complicates the case study is Bergman's elliptical and nonlinear way of telling this story, which gives rise to several motifs that extend far beyond a simple examination of an aberrant human mind. First, Bergman presents his film not as a mirror of human events but quite frankly as a film about human events. The process of making and watching the film plays a role in the film. *Persona* begins with the illumination of an arc-light projector, with the spooling of a reel of film on the projector, with the familiar projection leader that counts down the numbers—11, 10, 9 . . .—on a screen before a film begins, and with several miscellaneous clips of other films interspersed (a slapstick comedy, an animated cartoon). It ends with a loop of film slipping out of the projection gate, with sprocket holes, with the white glare of a blank screen and the extinguishing of the projection arc with which the film began. Between these two self-referential devices the film repeatedly refers to itself—at one point, showing the camera filming a scene (it is the scene of the actress onstage in *Electra* and gives rise to the question of whether she is acting on the stage or on a soundstage), and, at another, by the film's appearing to stop, rip, and burn in the projection gate.

Bergman calls attention to the film as a film because he wants to emphasize that what follows is a fiction, an illusion—a sequence of light and shadow on a flat screen. The audience has entered the world of art and chimera—of magic—not of nature and reality. But Bergman's film then gives this clear dichotomy another twist, for is the world of nature any

more solid, any more real than the one of artistic illusion? That is the question that propels the rest of the film after its projectionist prologue. For example, at one point in the film Alma believes she hears Elisabeth Vogler speak to her—and we believe we hear her too. But Elisabeth denies speaking, and indeed the words were so soft and so misty that we begin to doubt what we thought we heard and wonder if she really did speak or if Alma merely imagined it. At another point in the film, Alma believes she hears a noise in the house and discovers Elisabeth's husband, who mistakes the nurse for his own wife and begins making love to Alma as Elisabeth watches. And yet he cannot possibly be there in that house; he must be the product of Alma's imagination. And yet there he stands, concretely before us and before the nurse. These are only two of the film's sequences that intentionally cast doubt on the reliability of the senses. Is the concrete world any more tangible, any more "real" than the "intangible" world of the imagination?

This phenomenological collapse of the familiar distinction between illusion and reality leads Bergman to collapse another familiar kind of distinction. Nothing is usually so unique and consistent, in art or in the psychoanalyst's definitions, as individual human personality. Bergman has titled his film *Persona*, a term that can refer either to a role in the drama (as in *dramatis personae*) or to a psychological type in reality (as in Jungian terminology or split persona-lity). One of the assumptions of such terminology is that individual and distinct *personae* exist. The film apparently presents us with two opposite, antithetical *personae*—nurse and patient (can an opposition be clearer?). Each has her own part to play and even her own "costume" (patient's gown, nurse's uniform).

The patient is "ill" because she has discovered the futility, the instability, the lies of all life's definitions: success, marriage, family, wealth. The head psychiatrist explains this illness as Elisabeth's escape from the lies of life by silence, as merely a role (like her roles on the stage) created out of apathy and of which she will become bored. That the psychiatrist is right is irrelevant, for the doctor fails to perceive that the very truths, terms, and definitions of her science are indeed the very lies that Elisabeth (and Bergman) has discovered and cannot accept.

Nurse Alma would appear to be Elisabeth's opposite: contented with her job, with her fiancé (whom she admittedly does not love), with her optimistic and unquestioning acceptance of reality's ambiguities as solid verities. And then Bergman collapses these two opposites—nurse and patient—into one. For the nurse does all the talking; she ironically is the one actually undergoing the psychoanalytic treatment while Elisabeth plays the psychiatrist and merely listens. (A further irony is that Alma describes herself as a good listener. And perhaps she is, for she starts listening to herself.) The film is Alma's psychodrama as much as Elisabeth's. It is Alma who confesses her doubts and insecurities; it is Alma who is driven to acts of violence, inconsistency, jealousy, frenzy, and paranoia. One suspects that Elisabeth is playing her psychiatrist's role rather deliberately, if only to prove that she is capable of reaching another human being, no matter how vicious that reaching becomes.

Bergman's film constantly emphasizes that the two women are one and the one is two. First, the two women look strikingly alike. Second, there is the magnificent ghostly scene before the mirror (which may or may not be a dream since it looks as if it were shot through a fog or gray gauze), in which the two women embrace, their two heads seemingly emerging from a single body. Finally, there is the lengthy scene at the kitchen table that Bergman shoots in its entirety twice. First, he shoots Alma's entire tale (ironically, Alma speaks aloud Elisabeth's silent thoughts about her child) from Alma's point of view, camera riveted on Elisabeth—who is wearing a black sweater and black headband—moving the camera steadily toward Elisabeth's face with a series of lap dissolves (four shots that overlap and seem to melt into one another). Then Bergman shoots the scene over again from Elisabeth's point of view, camera riveted on Alma (a conventional film would shoot the scene twice but cut back and forth between the two points of view in the final editing)—who is wearing an identical "costume" of black sweater and black headband—the camera again moving steadily closer to the subject's face with another series of four identi-

cal lap dissolves (at exactly the same points of the speech as in Elisabeth's previous sequence). The faces begin to mirror each other. Finally, Bergman literally blends the two faces into one (thesis-antithesis-synthesis), using half of each woman's face to make the entire composite portrait. The two opposite *personae* become literally, tangibly one—a concrete illusion that Bergman has produced by means of the filmmaker's art.

Persona was followed by the grim, powerful, nightmarish trilogy of *Hour of the Wolf* (1966, released 1968), *Shame* (1967, released 1968), and *The Passion of Anna* (1969), all of which starred Liv Ullmann and Max von Sydow. After several more emotionally painful works— notably *Cries and Whispers* and *Scenes from a Marriage* (1974, condensed from the 1972 TV version)—Bergman returned to the sustaining vision of theatricality. His later films reaffirm his faith in illusion, in the imagination, in art, and in magic. The three-part structure of *Fanny and Alexander,* fashioned from a longer version made for Swedish television, seems Bergman's own spiritual autobiography. It begins happily, surrounded by family, in the theatre—the place where Bergman began, the place of joyous illusion, the place of smiles and light (as in Bergman's early films like *Smiles of a Summer Night* and the sunny passages of *The Seventh Seal* and *Wild Strawberries*). It then plunges into a middle section of dark despair, dominated by Calvinist severity and mortification—which parallels Bergman's darkly despairing black-and-white films of the 1960s. But it escapes once again into the light, with the aid of a Jewish merchant, back to the celebration of magic and theatre (and the performance of Strindberg's *A Dream Play*).

If Bergman's film of *The Magic Flute* (made for TV in 1974, then released theatrically) is one of the most successful opera films, it is because it is so sympathetic to Mozart's theatrical spell of magic and joy. *Fanny and Alexander* ends with a parallel affirmation: Bergman knows despair, but puts his faith in magic. What art can work such concrete magic (like Alexander's seeing the ghost of his father) as cinema?

After *Fanny and Alexander,* Bergman officially retired from filmmaking, then promptly

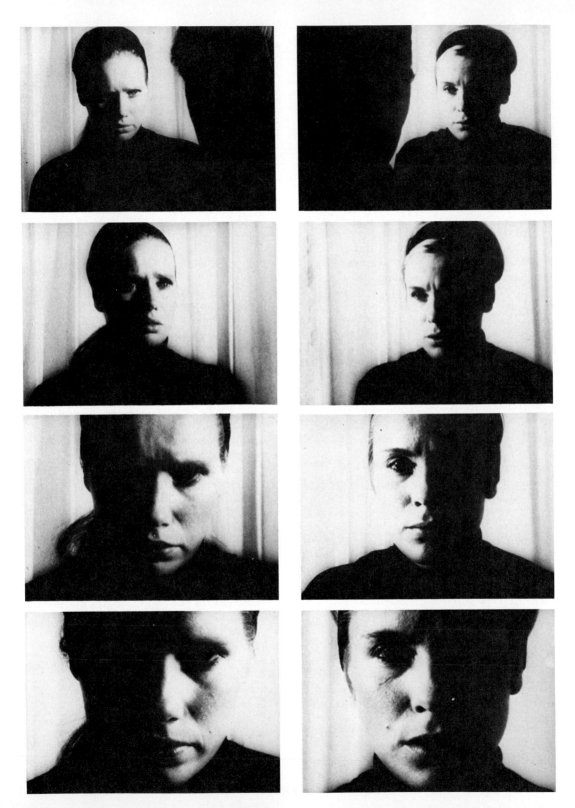

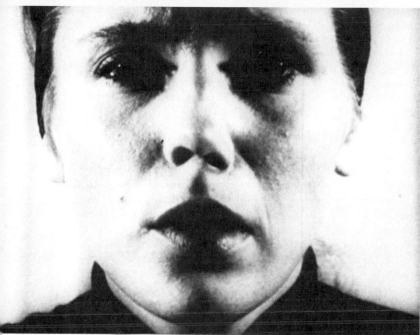

Fig. 14-5

Persona. *Blending two* **personae** *into one: the joining of Elisabeth Vogler (Liv Ullmann, left column) and Sister Alma (Bibi Andersson, right column). As the two women face each other across a table, the scene is side-lit, from Alma's right and Elisabeth's left, leaving complementary halves of each character's face in darkness; at the end of the last shot, with the illuminated side of Alma's face on the left side of the screen, the dark half is filled in with the lit side of Elisabeth's face.*

made *After the Rehearsal* (1984, for TV but soon shown in theatres) and a short, personal film about his mother (in the form of a look through the family scrapbook).

Although Ingmar Bergman is the unquestioned directorial star of the postwar Swedish industry, several later and lesser lights have appeared in the past two or three decades: the lush, pictorial, fatalistic romanticizing of Bo Widerberg's *Elvira Madigan* (1967); the close, affectionate observation of Swedish immigrants in Jan Troell's two-part epic, *The Emigrants* (1971) and *The New Land* (1972); the frank sexuality and the probing of the relationship between mind and body in Vilgot Sjöman's *I Am Curious (Yellow,* 1967, and *Blue,* 1968) or the elegant depiction of incest in Sjöman's *My Sister, My Love* (1969). These last works were very close to a Swedish "subgenre" that became familiar to many American audiences who may never even have heard of Ingmar Bergman. Using its reputation as one of the world's most sexually liberated nations, Sweden unleashed a series of sexploitation films on the world market—*Inga, Helga, 491, I a Woman* (Parts 1,

2, and 3!)—that played extended runs on New York's 42nd Street and in the seamier neighborhoods of many other cities. Like the Italian cinema, the Swedish industry discovered it could make money from its trash as well as its art.

England: From Masterpiece Theatre to Social Realism to *Masterpiece Theatre*

With certain notable exceptions, the British film has never quite recovered the experimental and artistic uniqueness of the era of Hepworth, Urban, Smith, Williamson, and Collings, which disappeared just before the First World War. The common language made England such a Hollywood colony that in 1927 the British government first passed special quota laws to protect the native cinema in the era of the talkies. A British theatre owner, to stay in business, was obliged to show a certain quota of British-made films. These quotas protected no one and produced a flood of artless, craftless cheapies—called "quota quickies"—that served as second features (sometimes screened at 10 A.M.) for the American films that everyone came to see.

If a British film did score an international success in the 1930s—such as Alexander Korda's *The Private Life of Henry VIII* (1933) or Hitchcock's *The 39 Steps*—its director or star almost immediately departed for Hollywood. Charles Laughton, Cary Grant (born Archibald Leach in Bristol), Laurence Olivier, Stan Laurel, Charles Chaplin, and Leslie Howard were as much a part of the Hollywood of the past as Richard Burton, James Mason, David Niven, Sean Connery, Albert Finney, Dirk Bogarde, Maggie Smith, Julie Andrews, Anthony Hopkins, Julie Christie, Peter Sellers, Glenda Jackson, Alec Guinness, Michael Caine, Peter O'Toole, and Ben Kingsley have been of the "Hollywood" of the past several decades (Peter Cushing and Alec Guinness were even in *Star Wars*). Alfred Hitchcock's conversion to Hollywood budgets and procedures anticipated similar changes in the careers of David Lean and Carol Reed, who began by making disciplined, effective, black-and-white dramas and went on to direct spectacles in which more was sometimes less. Though Lean proved himself the absolute master of the intelligent big movie, *Ryan's Daughter* (1970) was so big that its little story collapsed. And it is ironic that *Oliver!* (1968) is the last well-known film in the career of Carol Reed, who made his mark with far less extravagant films as diverse as *The Stars Look Down* (1939) and *Outcast of the Islands* (1951), doing his very best work in the tightly constructed, haunting thrillers *Odd Man Out* (1947) and *The Third Man* (1949).

David Lean's first great film was the restrained, deeply moving romantic melodrama *Brief Encounter* (1945); he followed it with two of the most highly regarded of all Dickens adaptations, *Great Expectations* (1946) and *Oliver Twist* (1948). He first revealed his eye for the sumptuous in *Summertime* (1955), then began directing a series of spectacles, literate and long and flexibly paced, that were overwhelmingly pictorial, organized around complex characters, and designed to open and explore moral questions rather than baldly settle them. The

first and best of these were *The Bridge on the River Kwai* (1957) and *Lawrence of Arabia* (1962, written by Robert Bolt and shot by Frederick A. Young); they were followed by *Doctor Zhivago* (1965), *Ryan's Daughter,* and *A Passage to India* (1984). At the time of his death in 1991, Lean was working on an adaptation of Joseph Conrad's *Nostromo*.

For fifteen years after the Second World War, the British film seemed synonymous with four cinematically conventional, although carefully crafted, genres. London was—and still is—the world capital of a style of English theatre and literature that has evolved over many centuries. These literate, well-spoken films displayed the taste, style, grace, and intelligence that also account for the popularity of programs like *Masterpiece Theatre* on American television. Perhaps these films were a bit bookish and musty, lacking the energetic vitality of American genre films, a bit too conscious of their "masterpieceness," but they represented a unique stylistic response of the British industry to the genres that Hollywood produced with such worldwide success.

First, there were the highly polished, fluently acted adaptations of the literary classics: Lean's films of Dickens, Anthony Asquith's adaptations of Rattigan (*The Winslow Boy,* 1948; *The Browning Version,* 1951) and Wilde (*The Importance of Being Earnest,* 1952), and Olivier's later adaptations of Shakespeare (*Hamlet,* 1948; *Richard III,* 1955). Olivier's *Henry V* (1944) created much of the momentum for this genre: More than an effective wartime propaganda film, it showed how brilliant and cinematically original a literary adaptation could be; beyond that, its bold use of color and artificial sets put it in the company of the fantasy films of Powell and Pressburger.

Second, there were the tightly edited, subtly acted, intelligently written contemporary dramas. Some of these concerned themselves with wartime military assignments or postwar political cabals, but the majority were romances (*Brief Encounter*), thrillers (*Odd Man Out*), mysteries (Sidney Gilliat's *Green For Danger,* 1946), and horror films (*Dead of Night,* 1945, directed by Alberto Cavalcanti as well as Charles Crichton, Robert Hamer, and Basil Dearden).

Fig. 14-6
Olivier's Henry V: *France as an English Renaissance audience might have imagined it while watching Shakespeare's play, thanks to an art direction based on the art of the period.*

Third, there were the understated, brilliant, satirical "little" comedies made at the Ealing Studios by Robert Hamer (*Kind Hearts and Coronets*, 1949; *Father Brown*, 1954), Alexander Mackendrick (*Tight Little Island*, 1949; *The Man in the White Suit*, 1951; *The Ladykillers*, 1955), Charles Crichton (*The Lavender Hill Mob*, 1951), and Anthony Kimmins (*The Captain's Paradise*, 1953). Many of these masterpieces of comic construction, irony, and understatement—including some not made at Ealing, such as Ronald Neame's *The Horse's Mouth* (1958)—featured the protean performances of Alec Guinness, who could transform himself into any kind of comic character—

fuddy-duddy scientist, bohemian painter, suave bigamist, little old lady.

And fourth, there were the elegant Technicolor spectacles produced by the Archers, an independent company formed by Michael Powell, who directed the films, and Emeric Pressburger, who wrote them; their collaboration was attested to by the credit they always used, "Written Produced and Directed by Michael Powell and Emeric Pressburger." Powell learned his trade on low-budget quickies, but he learned even more as one of the directors of the grand 1940 fantasy, *The Thief of Bagdad*. The Archers were best known for their intense use of color, their spectacular fantasies,

Fig. 14-7
Dead of Night *is constructed so that it might be, in its entirety, a prophetic dream. Here, at the start of the climax, the dreamer strangles a skeptical psychoanalyst.*

and their social and psychological boldness. Their key works include *The Life and Death of Colonel Blimp* (1943, an epic satire), *A Matter of Life and Death* (1946, a fantasy released in the United States as *Stairway to Heaven*), *Black Narcissus* (1947), and *The Red Shoes* (1948). *Black Narcissus*, which is convincingly set in India, high in the Himalayas, was shot (by Jack Cardiff) entirely at Pinewood Studios, London; the intent, in Powell's words, was to create "a perfect color work of art." As realistic as the world of *Black Narcissus* looks and sounds, its artificiality is complete, and its contrast of cultures, expectations, moods, and personalities develops as a contrast and metamorphosis of colors as well as of music and sound effects. The story concerns a group of nuns, led by Sister Clodagh (Deborah Kerr), who attempt to set up a school and dispensary in an old palace on a mountain shelf above a remote Indian village. The longer they stay, the more their former,

organized ways of doing and thinking about things come to seem irrelevant. Each of the nuns is disturbed by the place, some more than others. One sister, assigned to work in the garden, finds herself listening to the endless wind, looking through the clear air at the great mountains, thinking too much, spacing out, and —caught up in an almost metaphysical simplicity—planting flowers instead of potatoes; another sister, assailed by the forces of desire and madness, turns murderous. This sensuous, rigorous film was banned in many countries. And *The Red Shoes* was no fairy-tale backstage musical, but another beautiful, disciplined, adult film made with absolute artistic control. Like the ballet danced within it— "The Red Shoes," based on Hans Christian Andersen's story—*The Red Shoes* tells of a woman (Moira Shearer) who puts on the red shoes, cannot take them off, and dances to her death. She is torn between two men, the im-

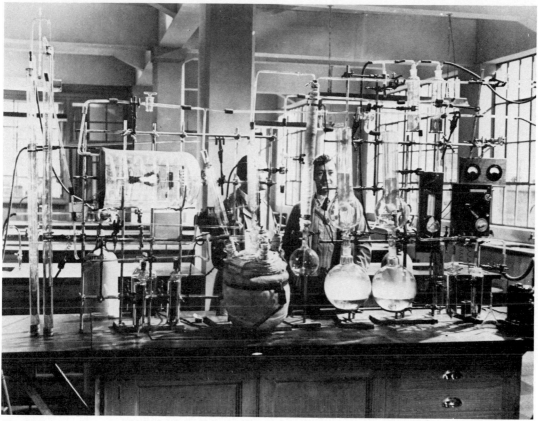

Fig. 14-8
The Man in the White Suit: *the realistic texture of the British documentary tradition flavoring the comedy of Alec Guinness, surrounded by the tubes and wires of his scientific apparatus.*

presario who offers her the great career she wants and deserves, and the young composer who wants her to quit dancing and love him. Neither of these men will give her a break, and the conflict they represent is, in any case, between the lover and artist in herself; the choice proves impossible, and she is destroyed—in a moment that intricately represents the triumph of artifice. Powell and Pressburger collaborated from 1942 to 1956; Powell went on to direct the savage, brilliant *Peeping Tom* (1960), to advise Coppola on the creation of artificial worlds (during the development of electronic cinema and of *One from the heart,* 1982), and to script an adaptation of Ursula K. Le Guin's *The Wizard of Earthsea* before his death in 1990. *Peeping Tom,* released the same year as Hitchcock's *Psycho,* is, like *Psycho,* a forerunner

of the slasher film, a disciplined masterpiece, and an ironic mixture of voyeurism and murder —reflexively linked by the making of photographic images.

The general traits of all four of these British genres were a subtle understatement, expert acting, detailed decor, and a firm control of taut narrative construction.

Among the most distinctive and significant work in the British film between the era of Charles Urban and 1959 was the documentary film movement of the 1930s and 1940s. Sponsored by the government and directed by filmmakers like John Grierson, Paul Rotha, Basil Wright, Harry Watt, Edgar Anstey, and Humphrey Jennings, the British documentaries developed the craft of capturing the surfaces of reality to illuminate the essences beneath

Fig. 14-9

Black Narcissus: *two worlds. Fig. 14-9: Sister Clodagh (Deborah Kerr) tries to find comfort in the well-organized, Christian world of her office, where everything fits within the frame assigned to it.*
Fig. 14-10: Having renounced her vows, Sister Ruth (Kathleen Byron) runs through the rich darkness of the old palace, losing her scarf on a Hindu wall sculpture. Production designed by Alfred Junge.

Fig. 14-10

Fig. 14-11
Peeping Tom: *Carl Boehm as the photographer who, spied on and abused as a child, has become obsessed with recording the ultimate private moment — the confrontation with one's own fear and death. In the background, Anna Massey as his observant friend.*

them. The realist texture that seemed to distinguish British fictional films from Hollywood's was especially obvious in the purely realist documentary films. To some extent, the new British film of 1959 began with a similar premise. This new British film was the product of several influences: of the British documentary tradition; of the new class-conscious British novels and plays by authors like John Osborne, John Braine, Arnold Wesker, Alan Sillitoe, and Alun Owen; of the Italian neorealist films; and of the new spirit of free cinema that was emerging in France at the same time. The result of these many influences was a series of films that was radically different from the polished, elegant films of Lean, Asquith, and Reed.

The new British films, like the Italian neorealist ones, emphasized the poverty of the worker, the squalor of working-class life, the difficulty of keeping a home and keeping one's self-respect at the same time, the social assumptions that sentence a person with no education and a working-class dialect to a lifetime of bare survival. To emphasize the dreary mediocrity of the working-class life, the British directors turned their cameras on the oppressive smoke of factories, the dull and drizzly weather at their stifling seaside resorts, the dingy and smoky feel of the pubs where they try to escape, the bare and faded austerity of the rooms they can afford to rent. In the midst of this intentionally barren and gray world, the directors focus on a common man reacting to his surroundings — bitter, brutal, angry, tough. These heroes of the films, traditionally labeled "angry young men" (a term first applied to the writers and antiheroes of the plays on which many of these films were based), react in one of two ways to the working-class prisons of their lives: They try to grab some of the swag of the upper-class life for themselves, or, failing that, they get nasty and break things. Their tragedy is usually that their only talent is loving and society does not reward that kind of talent. Angry young men aside, Tony Richardson's *A Taste of Honey*, 1961, and Bryan Forbes's *The L-Shaped Room*, 1962, were among the best of the new films whose central characters were female.

Jack Clayton's *Room at the Top* (1958) was the first of the working-class British films to earn an international reputation and to make money. Clayton came to films not as a young rebel but as a tireless perfectionist-craftsman who had worked his way up in the British film industry. Clayton's care and craftsmanship were as responsible for the film's success as was its sociological content. Joe Lampton (Laurence Harvey), an ambitious young man with a provincial accent and a provincial education, takes a job at Brown's factory in a northern industrial city. Joe quickly learns the economic facts of life. He becomes enamored of a posh residential area of the city known as "the top," a hill that dominates the town. Most attractive of all the houses on "the top" is that of Mr. Brown (Donald Wolfit), the owner of the factory and commercial lord of the town. Brown himself had worked his way out of the working class, only to don class snobbery and to join the Conservative Club once he had gotten to "the top."

Joe sets his sights on Susan (Heather Sears), Brown's daughter, a rich, pretty, but emotionally shallow girl who responds to affection with the same intensity as to a brisk set of tennis. On his way to capturing Susan, Joe meets Alice, an older, warmer woman (Simone Signoret) who reveals to him what two people are capable of feeling for one another. She, escaping her callous, brutal husband, falls in love with Joe, and he falls in love with both the strength of her mind and the warmth of her body. But fate grabs hold. Just when Joe has decided that the relationship with Susan Brown is valueless, Susan becomes pregnant and her father compels Joe to marry her. When Joe tells Alice that he is going to marry Susan, she becomes so upset that she kills herself in an automobile accident. And so Joe marries Susan. He gets his room at the top. Only now he does not want it.

Clayton's handling of this distinctly adult film shows his experience and craft. He gets the best English-language performance of her career from Simone Signoret and the most virile, least mannered performance of his career from Laurence Harvey. Compositionally, Clayton has not only exerted great care in bathing the film in wet, dreary, smoky grays but also in surrounding the characters with signs of the importance of Brown's name and power in the industrial town. On billboards, outside railway windows, reflected in the puddles on the street, hanging on one of his smokestacks, is the name of Brown, an ever-present reminder of the temptation of money and power, the temptation to which Joe yields, damning himself.

That Clayton's commitment is more to his craft than to his class-conscious subject matter becomes clearer in his subsequent films — *The Innocents* (1961), *The Pumpkin Eater* (1964, script by Harold Pinter), and *The Great Gatsby* (1974). *The Innocents* leaves the gray dirty world of the present for the costumed grace of a country manor house of the nineties. Clayton adapts Henry James's *The Turn of the Screw*, a novella with one of the most debated critical questions in literary history. Has James written a story of real ghosts or a story of phantoms created by the neurotic brain of a sexually repressed governess (played by Deborah Kerr)? Clayton decides, as have many literary critics,

that the ambiguity in the story is intentional, that James deliberately refuses to show whether the ghosts are real or imaginary. His problem is to translate this ambiguity into cinema, for the camera can be quite convincing in its demonstration that a being either is or is not there. By letting the governess's point of view control every shot of the ghosts — we never see them except from her vantage point — the director ingeniously sustains the doubt about their existence apart from her. The result of this careful manipulation of point of view is a chilling story of terror and evil with a psychological mystery at its heart. Does the evil in the universe torture and frighten the child to death, or does the evil in the human mind kill him?

Tony Richardson was the first and most fortunate of the British directors to take advantage of the success of *Room at the Top*. In 1959, Richardson directed the film version of John Osborne's *Look Back in Anger*, three years after he had directed the sharp, tongue-lashing stageplay at London's Royal Court Theatre. Within three years Richardson had directed three similar films: two adaptations of realist, class-conscious plays (*The Entertainer*, 1960, starring Laurence Olivier, from the play by John Osborne; *A Taste of Honey*, starring Rita Tushingham, from the play by Shelagh Delaney) and an adaptation of Alan Sillitoe's antiestablishment, class-conscious novel *The Loneliness of the Long Distance Runner* (1962, starring Tom Courtenay). These four early Richardson films are similar in their strengths and weaknesses. All depend heavily on the literateness of the original works. All are brilliantly acted, both in the major roles and in the tiny character parts. Richardson's experience as a stage director no doubt aided his actors, but actors like Richard Burton, Claire Bloom, Mary Ure, Laurence Olivier, Brenda DeBanzie, Rita Tushingham, Murray Melvin, and Tom Courtenay made his task somewhat easier. Cinematically, the Richardson films feel like stageplays, punctuated by shots of grimy slums, run-down rooms, unamusing amusement parks, and dirty children. *The Loneliness of the Long Distance Runner* is the most adventurous of the films cinematically, allowing the freeness of the novel and the new cinematic winds blowing

Fig. 14-12

Fig. 14 13
Two angry young men surrounded by the shabby respectability of their working-class lives: from right, Laurence Harvey, Hermione Baddely, and Simone Signoret in Room at the Top *(Fig. 14-12); Richard Burton and Mary Ure in* Look Back in Anger *(Fig. 14-13).*

from across the channel to help Richardson escape the tyrannies of stage dialogue and stage setting, of stage time and stage place.

Later Richardson films—*Tom Jones* (1963), *The Loved One* (1965), *The Charge of the Light Brigade* (1968), *Joseph Andrews* (1977)—leave the grime of working-class England and the bitterness of social-outcast laborers far behind. (Success seems to take its toll on anger and agony.) The angry naturalistic sincerity of the four early films is replaced by higher budgets, bigger casts, and colorful settings, thousands of miles or hundreds of years distant from industrial Britain.

Richardson's collaboration with playwright John Osborne indicates that English fashions in its cinema are inseparable from fashions in its theatre. As British playwrights moved away from working-class characters and themes, so did British cinema. A parallel movement can be seen in the collaboration of playwright Harold Pinter and the blacklisted American director Joseph Losey, who emigrated to England. While Pinter began writing plays that arose from his own working-class background, his later plays were close psychological studies of upper-middle-class, well-educated characters, suffering primarily sexual doubts and indecisions. Losey turned a number of similar Pinter filmscripts into elegantly acted, coolly mysterious, and psychologically insightful films—*The Servant* (1963), *Accident* (1967), *The Go-Between* (1971)—that had nothing to do with grimy social realism and angry young men.

For more than five years English directors made film variations on the original Clayton Richardson themes: the young, uneducated, often unintelligent working man or woman sentenced by industrial society to an inescapable yet unendurable life of drabness and mediocrity. Quite significantly, not one of these social-realist films was shot in color. Color was as antithetical to the smoke and fog of working-class Britain as it was to the poverty of neorealist Italy. Karel Reisz's *Saturday Night and Sunday Morning* (1960) and *Morgan, a Suitable Case for Treatment* (1966) and Sidney J. Furie's *The Leather Boys* (1963) mix stories of rebellious young have-nots with a carefully realistic depiction of the social milieu that

Fig. 14-14
The Servant: *Dirk Bogarde and James Fox (right) as the manservant and master who exchange roles in Losey and Pinter's brilliant study of decadence and power.*

energy in brief bits, in edited snippets, rather than whole films. The technique produces tensions in some Lester films between the stylistic demands of the whole and his commitment to the bits. Lester does best when his bits propel a whole that is conceived as a string of bits—

Fig. 14-15

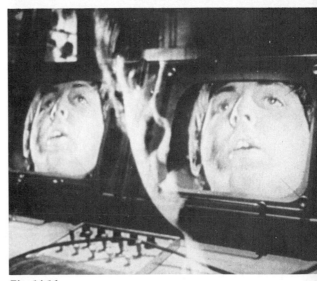

Fig. 14-16
A Hard Day's Night—*cinematic fun and games with the Beatles.*

condemns them to the prison of their economic class. Other British films of the same era, with widely different themes and characters, share the same texture and smell of cinematic Naturalism—from the factory tensions of Guy Green's *The Angry Silence* (1960), to the realistically brutal world of success in Lindsay Anderson's *This Sporting Life* (1963), to the neurotic occultism of Bryan Forbes's *Seance on a Wet Afternoon* (1964), to the realism of a Midlands mining town in Jack Cardiff's *Sons and Lovers* (1960), to the fashionable social world of John Schlesinger's *Darling* (1965).

One obvious exception to this school of social realism was the work of Richard Lester, an American expatriate who united the Beatles with the cinematic ellipticality of Truffaut and Godard. The results—*A Hard Day's Night* (1964) and *Help!* (1965)—were buoyant, seemingly effortless romps through the streets and fields of illogic. Lester, who began by making television commercials, invests his imaginative

Fig. 14-17
King Arthur (Graham Chapman, central foreground) and his knights receive their mission from God in **Monty Python and the Holy Grail.**

from the Beatles films and *How I Won the War* (1967) to *The Three Musketeers* (1974), *The Four Musketeers* (1975), and *Superman II* (1981). Lester's most impressive combinations of bits and wholes are the psychological drama *Petulia* (1968) and the historical romance *Robin and Marian* (1976).

From the Renaissance stage to the music hall, the British have enjoyed a witty and often outrageous comedic tradition. In the 1950s, some of the best working talent was on the radio, as it was on television in the 1970s, and the stars of these shows often went on to significant film careers. The BBC's *Goon Show,* one of the most bizarre and hilarious programs in the history of radio, starred Spike Milligan, Harry Secombe, and Peter Sellers. Lester's first comedy, *The Running, Jumping and Standing Still Film* (1960), was a short that starred the Goons, and for sheer craziness and comic energy the only Lester that can match it is *A Hard Day's*

Night. Peter Sellers, whose voice was as protean as Lon Chancy's face, became one of England's great screen comedians, starring in films as diverse as *The Mouse That Roared,* 1959; *I'm All Right Jack,* 1959; *The Wrong Arm of the Law,* 1962; *Lolita,* 1962; *The Pink Panther,* 1964, and its sequels; *Dr. Strangelove,* 1964; *The World of Henry Orient,* 1964; and *Being There,* 1979. Just over a decade after the Goons, the BBC's silliest and most creative comedians were the Pythons: Graham Chapman, John Cleese, Terry Gilliam, Eric Idle, Terry Jones, and Michael Palin. They broke into film in 1972 with *And Now For Something Completely Different* (directed by Ian McNaughton), an anthology of routines from their TV show, *Monty Python's Flying Circus.* Their first original feature, *Monty Python and the Holy Grail* (1974)—which made cinematic, literary, and historical jokes with equal skill in an outrageous sendup of the Arthurian legend—was directed by Terry

Jones and Terry Gilliam (an American; the troupe's animator); the ones after that were directed by Jones alone and include *Monty Python's Life of Brian* (1979), the tale of a fellow whose life runs parallel to that of Jesus, and *Monty Python's The Meaning of Life* (1983), a guide to the universe. Cleese, Idle, and Palin went on to establish themselves independently as actors and writers in such films as Richard Loncraine's *The Missionary* (1982) and Charles Crichton's *A Fish Called Wanda* (1988), and Gilliam became a controversial director with *Brazil* (1985).

Economically and internationally, England's biggest hit was the James Bond series, based on the spy novels of Ian Fleming and starring Sean Connery (succeeded by Roger Moore and others). Released through United Artists and becoming one of that company's chief assets, the Bond films of the 1960s, 1970s, and 1980s offered sophisticated adventure, witty dialogue, state-of-the-art gadgetry, spectacular sets, elaborate action sequences, and generous helpings of sex and death. The series began with *Dr. No* (1962, directed by Terence Young), won over the critics with *From Russia With Love* (1963, Terence Young), and consolidated its position at the center of the new spectacle — displacing all those Hollywood ancient-world extravaganzas — with *Goldfinger* (1964, Guy Hamilton). Hammer Films also attracted loyal audiences with its boldly colored, bloody horror films, beginning with Terence Fisher's *The Curse of Frankenstein* (1957), which starred Peter Cushing and Christopher Lee — two actors who soon became as important to the studio as its head writer, Jimmy Sangster. But Britain still turned out a number of restrained but relentless black-and-white chillers — such as Jacques Tourneur's *Curse of the Demon,* 1957 — that were at least as effective as the elegantly gruesome Hammers.

Since the mid-1960s, the line dividing London and Hollywood has blurred again. Stanley Kubrick, an American, has been making British films since *Lolita.* Many who rushed to see that very English import, *The Servant,* did not realize Joseph Losey was American, let alone the director of *The Prowler* (a 1951 *noir*) and the controversial antiwar film *The Boy With Green Hair* (1948). Tony Richardson's desertion of native themes for Hollywood production values was a paradigm for the British industry as a whole. Karel Reisz deserted the slums for the Technicolor internationalism of *Isadora* (1968) and the literary pretentions of *The French Lieutenant's Woman* (1981, script by Pinter); Lindsay Anderson's surface realism continued in *If . . .* (1969), augmented by the new Hollywood conventions of youthful romanticism, lush Technicolor pictorialism, and Pirandellian games with the inseparability of reality and illusion (games that turned Brechtian in his next major feature, *O Lucky Man!,* 1973, and that had been abandoned by the time he directed his first American film, *The Whales of August,* 1987); Bryan Forbes directed the Technicolor all-star disaster *The Madwoman of Chaillot* (1969); John Schlesinger was almost as comfortable with the American social fringes in *Midnight Cowboy* (1969) as he was with the British ones in *Darling.* British and American styles were so indistinguishable that there were few essential stylistic differences between two parallel film adaptations of historical stageplays, Fred Zinnemann's *A Man for All Seasons* (1966) and Anthony Harvey's *The Lion in Winter* (1968), except for Zinnemann's superior ability to translate a talky drama into a moving picture.

By the mid-1970s a new group of British directors had solidified their positions as the most interesting of their generation. Ken Russell was the most audacious and gaudy British stylist, a director with a brilliant sense of decor and a strong yearning to say things of Significance — the significance of which was frequently buried beneath the scenery and wallpaper. Russell, whose training came in filming biographies (mostly of composers) for television, directed his first highly acclaimed film in 1969, *Women in Love.* The solidity of the D. H. Lawrence characters and the effectiveness of the novel's symbolism helped anchor Russell's visual flights of fancy in solid fictional ground. His film of *The Boy Friend* (1971) avoided the tension between style and ideas by having none of the latter; it (like his later *Tommy,* 1974) was as pure a style piece as has ever been made, a self-contained history of the musical film. But Russell's "psychological" studies of Tchaikovsky (*The Music Lovers,* 1970) and medieval religious fanaticism (*The Devils,* 1971) seemed to have more to do with stereotypic romantic and sexual poses than psychological subtlety and revelation, and both seemed to lose their intended intellectual and psychological complexity beneath the striking but simple surfaces of the decor. As *Altered States* (1980) and *The Lair of the White Worm* (1988) affirmed, Russell remains the "trippiest" and "spaciest" of British directors.

John Schlesinger is a completely different kind of stylist, the most literate, verbal, and psychological of the new British directors. Schlesinger's primary concern is to reveal the normal, ordinary sense behind the lives of people whom society would define as most abnormal, freaky, and bizarre. For Schlesinger, "abnormal," "aberrant" people live lives that seem completely normal and make perfect sense from their point of view, and the Schlesinger films develop precisely this subjective point of view. The young man's erratic and erotic fantasies in *Billy Liar* (1963), the bizarre sexual and career values of the world of high fashion in *Darling,* the complex desires and problems of those who live *Far from the Madding Crowd* (1967, based on Thomas Hardy's novel and, like *Darling,* scripted by Frederic Raphael and starring Julie Christie), the down-and-out lives of hustlers and bums in *Midnight Cowboy* (one of the first American films to be rated X), the bisexual triangles in *Sunday, Bloody Sunday* (1971) are not examples of human freaks but examples of the way even the most bizarre-seeming human types are not so bizarre, but merely people trying to satisfy the most common human needs: security and love. With *The Day of the Locust* (1975, from the novel by Nathanael West), however, Schlesinger seemed to have lost some of the insight and solidity beneath the freaky façade. And *Yanks* (1979) looked as if it might have been made by any British director thirty years before. Schlesinger's promise of the 1960s and early 1970s has not been fulfilled since.

Nor has Lindsay Anderson's, who remained the British director most devoted to rebellion against a stagnant and repressive bourgeois society and bourgeois mentality. Anderson's rebellion was embodied by his violent central characters who usually want to break (or machine gun) the elements in society that repress them: Richard Harris in *This Sporting Life* and Malcolm McDowell in *If . . .* and *O Lucky Man!* Anderson's rebellion also determines his cinematic style; he avoids the literate coherence of a Schlesinger or the lush pictorialness of a Russell by making violent attacks on the continuity of space, time, and action. Whereas structure, character, and dialogue are Schlesinger's strengths (the dramatic values) and spatial composition is Russell's (the pictorial values), Anderson's primary strength is his battle with continuity at the editing table. Anderson is the British director most obviously influenced by the French, particularly by Godard (and Godard's interpretation of Brechtian theory). Like the French New Wave directors, Anderson was a film critic (and editor of a film journal, *Sequence*) who turned filmmaker.

Nicolas Roeg was a cinematographer (he did second-unit work on *Lawrence of Arabia,* then shot *The Masque of the Red Death,* 1964, for Roger Corman, *Fahrenheit 451* for Truffaut, *Far from the Madding Crowd* for Schlesinger, and *Petulia* for Lester) who moved to directing his own films. His dominant interests are sexual ambiguity, the power of the supernatural, and the mystical influence of cultural myth — sometimes drug-induced or -related and sometimes featuring rock stars (Mick Jagger in *Performance,* 1970, which Roeg co-directed with Donald Cammell, and David Bowie in *The Man Who Fell to Earth,* 1976). His superb horror film, *Don't Look Now* (1973), intercuts subjective and objective visions as rapidly and complexly as it intercuts the past, present, and future; the daring, originality, and narrative significance of montage in his films put Roeg in the tradition of Eisenstein and Resnais. But he is also, as *Don't Look Now* plainly reveals, a master of *mise-en-scène.* His Australian production, *Walkabout* (1971), proved enormously influential, suggesting themes and images that the new Australian feature-film industry would explore later in the 1970s, particularly in films such as Peter Weir's *The Last Wave* (1977). From *Performance, Walkabout,* and *Don't Look Now* to *Insignificance* (1985) and *Track 29*

(1988), his films have proved mysterious and fascinating, laying out labyrinths that circle back on themselves in a trap of revelation. Yet he is also capable of turning out a polished, linear narrative whose very simplicity is elegant, such as the Jim Henson film he directed in 1990, *The Witches*.

Peter Watkins, who began as an editor for the BBC, is the most distinguished British documentarist of the past thirty years. His *The War Game* (1965) was so powerful an indictment of atomic competition and British vulnerability to its terrifying consequences that it was banned from British television and has never been shown on the BBC. Watkins's biographical recreation of the life of painter *Edvard Munch* (1974) is its formal opposite—one of the most tactile cinematic examinations of a painter's creative activity, scratching and scraping his obsessive images onto the canvas. His politically radical fiction films—which often deal, much as *The War Game* does, with the urgency of finding, circulating, and preserving an image of the truth, despite government censorship—include *Privilege* (1967) and *Punishment Park* (1971).

After Roeg, the most labyrinthine and intellectual of the new British directors is Peter Greenaway; his *The Draughtsman's Contract* (1982) attracted nearly as many attempts at explanation as *Blowup* had. At once cold and sensual, Greenaway has pursued the trails of desire and signification through films that are constructed like elegant traps: *The Draughtsman's Contract*, *Drowning By Numbers* (1988), and *The Cook, The Thief, His Wife & Her Lover* (1989).

Stephen Frears began by directing Albert Finney in *Gumshoe* (1972) but hit his stride in the 1980s. Provoked by the sexually and politically conservative regime of Prime Minister Margaret Thatcher, Frears made films that took homosexuals for their central characters (*Prick Up Your Ears*, 1987), unsentimentally portrayed the nihilistic, anarchistic spirit that swept England's new generation of rebels (*Bloody Kids*, 1983—perhaps his best film), and examined racial and economic conflicts in an England grappling with everything from new sexual attitudes to old colonial attitudes, illuminated now by fluorescents and now by the fires of a street riot (*My Beautiful Laundrette*, 1985;

Sammy and Rosie Get Laid, 1987). He also displayed a talent for the slow-paced, beautifully shot, moody crime drama (*The Hit*, 1984) and for the cruel tale of the manipulative, sexually charged war for power (*Dangerous Liaisons*, 1988; *The Grifters*, 1990).

The mainstream British film keeps its roots in the theatre for the simple reason that British stage actors, directors, and playwrights remain expert delineators of a lengthy English-language tradition. From Laughton, Olivier, and Guinness to the Redgraves, Maggie Smith, Ben Kingsley, and Jeremy Irons, British actors, trained by the two great acting academies, RADA (the Royal Academy of Dramatic Arts) and LAMDA (the London Academy of Musical and Dramatic Art), are among the most proficient in the world. The latest generation of British films has maintained this theatrical "Tradition of Quality": *The Dresser* (Peter Yates, 1983) and *Betrayal* (David Jones, 1983, script by Pinter) were both adapted, rather literally, from stageplays; *Chariots of Fire* (Hugh Hudson, 1981) and *Gandhi* (Richard Attenborough, 1982) brought England two successive Academy Awards for "best picture," and *A Room with a View* (James Ivory, 1985) did nearly as well—perfect examples of the Masterpiecery that impresses many Americans as "best." Like television's *Masterpiece Theatre*, this literate, careful, "correct" kind of production is the sort of film the British really know how to make.

Czech Renaissance and Polish Solidarity

No cinema better demonstrates the interrelationship of film art and political freedom than the cinema of Czechoslovakia (now the Czech and Slovak Federative Republic), a country that has probably been invaded, occupied, and liberated more times in this century than any other. The Czech Golden Age of cinema (or "Czech film miracle" or "Czech New Wave" as it has also been called) was an extremely short one (roughly, 1963 to 1969), during which time over a dozen Czech films won major awards at the important international film festivals, including the Academy Awards for Best

Foreign Language Film of 1965 (*The Shop on Main Street*) and 1967 (*Closely Watched Trains*, Czech release 1966). The years of Czechoslovakian film mastery coincided with the only years since the Munich Agreement of 1938 that the Czech people and Czech artists enjoyed a measure of intellectual and creative freedom. Before this brief eruption, the Czech cinema was one of startings and stoppings, of promising beginnings cut short by political repression and artistic censorship. Although the American filmmaker suffered the commercial repression of a Louis B. Mayer and the moral suppression of the Production Code, the history of the Czech cinema reveals that the censorship of bureaucratic political committees can be even more devastating to the individual artist.

In the late silent and early sound periods, the Czech cinema had begun to develop an integrity and individuality (as in the films of Gustav Machatý, Otakar Vávra, Karel Lamač, and Martin Frič) that was destroyed by the Nazi occupation of 1939. After the war the Czech cinema made another new beginning. Led by a group of young filmmakers who had organized their intentions in the final year of the Nazi occupation, the cinema was the first of the industries that was nationalized after the liberation. But this promise was cut short by the Soviet occupation and Stalinization of 1948, and there followed over a decade of repressive rule: the purges, the hardening of the Iron Curtain, the cultural isolation of the Cold War. The fears and repressive climate of the McCarthy years in the United States were marked and mirrored by parallel (and much more severe) activities on the other side of the Iron Curtain (as can be seen in Costa-Gavras's *The Confession,* as well as in Jaromil Jireš's 1969 Czech film, *Joke*). Signs of a political thaw began to appear in 1961, and the Czech Golden Age of cinema sprang up through the cracks until the Soviet tanks rolled into Prague in August, 1968.

During the decades of occupation and repression, two significant institutions were founded that would later contribute to the greatness of the Czech film in its years of freedom. Just as the Fascists founded a film school and built an efficient studio in Mussolini's Italy that would later be put to use by significant artists in a period of artistic freedom, the noted Czech film school, the F.A.M.U., was founded in 1947, and the Barrandov Studios were built into one of the best-equipped production facilities in Europe during the Nazi occupation. The great Czech films and filmmakers would come from this film school (five intensive years of training at state expense) and film studio as soon as the filmmakers were free to combine their artistic imaginations with their technical capabilities.

The Czech masterpieces were of four general types, including two that had undergone a transformation in the previous years of Soviet repression. One of these was the story of Resistance to the Nazi Occupation, a safe subject in the Stalinist era since opinion of the Nazis was quite unanimous. But under the Soviets, the Resistance film mirrored the values of socialist realism, primarily by presenting a positive, heroic, almost superhuman figure as the embodiment of political resistance — like Schors and Chapayev in those Soviet sound films. In the mature Czech films of the 1960s, however, the central figures of Resistance are frequently weak, lazy, slovenly, and comic — nonheroic, ordinary, all-too-human figures who eventually choose or are forced to take a political stand. This study of the comic antihero confronted by the demands of war is a long-standing Czech literary tradition, perhaps most memorable in Karel Hašek's famous novel *The Good Soldier Schweik.*

Such are the "heroes" of Jiří Weiss's *The Coward* (1961), the study of a cowardly rural schoolteacher who eventually decides to sacrifice himself rather than to select ten of his fellow townspeople to be slaughtered by the Nazis; of Ján Kadár's and Elmar Klos's *Death Is Called Engelchen* (1963), the study of a wounded Czech partisan who wonders whether his sacrifice has been worth the struggle; of Otakar Vávra's *Golden Rennet* (1965), a study of intellectual cowardice; of Zbyněk Brynych's *The Fifth Horseman Is Fear* (1964), the story of the tenants of an apartment house in Nazi-occupied Prague, particularly an old Jewish doctor who must choose between protecting himself and helping a fugitive who has dedicated himself to helping the doctor's people; as well as of both *The Shop on Main Street* and *Closely Watched Trains.*

A second genre, the historical costume drama, also popular during the years of suppression, was less popular in the 1960s. As in Hitler's Germany and Mussolini's Italy, a film could avoid delicate political issues by avoiding contemporary life altogether. In the sixties this escapist tendency continued, but of special note are František Vláčil's *Markéta Lazarová* (1967), a mammoth and carefully detailed historical spectacle set in thirteenth-century Bohemia, and Jiří Weiss's *The Golden Fern* (1963), a beautiful adaptation of a Czech fairy tale. In the forest on midsummer eve, a shepherd discovers and steals the mystical golden fern, a magical token that allows him to fulfill all his wishes as long as he keeps possession of it. Of special interest and beauty in the film are its attention to the styles of decor and costume (there are three —peasant village life, Hapsburg nobility, and High Turk) and its ability to translate such fanciful and mystical material into the concrete reality of cinema (in particular, Weiss's use of natural imagery, lighting, and camera movement to develop the conflict of man and nature for possession of the fern). Both *Markéta Lazarová* and *The Golden Fern* were shot by the same talented cinematographer, Bedřich Baǐka, who now shoots films and teaches cinematography in the United States.

The third of the Czech genres of the 1960s —the film of contemporary life, of contemporary human and social problems—had a very different analogue in the era of Soviet suppression. Under the Soviets, Czech cinema eulogized the noble worker, sang the praises of the collective society, depicted the beauty of the factory, and dedicated itself to the idealistic proposition that with hard work and collective cooperation Life Would Be Beautiful. The mature Czech films of the 1960s doubted the values of collectivization, suggested that work did not equal happiness, refused to glamorize the everyday, and implied that the essential human problems were internal, psychological, and personal rather than external and societal.

These films of contemporary life tend in two opposite directions. Many of them set their studies of human personality against a clear social and political background. Věra Chytilová, among the most important and accomplished women directors of postwar Europe, made careful studies of feminist problems (*Ceiling*, 1961; *Daisies*, 1966; *The Fruit of Paradise*, 1970). Jan Němec's *Report on the Party and the Guests* (1966), a satire on conformity, was banned for over a year, even in the liberalized Czechoslovakia. Jaromil Jireš's *Joke* is an explicitly anti-Stalinist and anti-Soviet film, the story of a man who seeks revenge for his earlier imprisonment and injustice in the 1950s era of the purges. Evald Schorm's *Courage for Everyday* (1964) and Jiří Weiss's *Ninety in the Shade* (1964, a British co-production) both use suicide as a means of exposing the potential alienation and sterility of living in such a constrained, highly regulated, and at times brutally absurd society. Indeed, the number of these Czech films that use the motif of suicide (either attempted or successful) is striking.

The other tendency of the contemporary films is to concentrate more on character than on politics, to study the human comedy. These "experiential" films—studies of experience— represent one of the truly unique (and most influential) accomplishments of the Czech cinema: personal, subtle, touching, probing. Many have very simple plots; much as in Chekhov's plays, almost nothing happens. But in the course of this nothing the audience discovers how it feels to be these people, how they feel life and how they feel about life. The purest expressions of these "experiential" films are the sympathetic satires by Miloš Forman (*Black Peter*, 1963; *Loves of a Blonde*, 1965; *The Firemen's Ball*, 1967) and the delicately sensitive, perfectly constructed comedy, *Intimate Lighting* (1965), by Ivan Passer, who began as Forman's scenarist and later made movies in America (*Cutter's Way*, 1981; *Creator*, 1985; *Haunted Summer*, 1988), as Forman did. Regardless of their settings, the primary focus of the great Czech films of the 1960s is the internal quality and texture of human experience.

Precisely the same is true of the fourth genre of Czech films of the period, the surreal or futuristic allegory. Jan Schmidt is the master of this genre, and his short film *Josef Kilian* (1963), co-directed by Pavel Juráček, has been frequently compared with the work of another Czech master, Franz Kafka. Josef K's world becomes a frightening, hysterical nightmare, and the experiential quality that Schmidt and

Juráček develop is that of wandering in a labyrinth of terrifying dreams. Schmidt's riveting, post-apocalyptic film, *The End of August at the Hotel Ozone* (1966, released 1968), script by Juráček, is a brutal and frightening odyssey of survivors from atomic holocaust, all of them women, roaming about the countryside on horseback, killing—a snake, a dog, a cow—for the sport of it. They are desperately searching for a male to renew the species, and when they find him—a gentle, civilized old man—they murder him too. Schmidt's point seems to be that such a race is better off perishing.

Perhaps the most anarchic and surreal director of the era was Juraj Jakubisko, a Slovak. The Slovak and Czech production centers are separate (the Czech studio, Barrandov, is in Prague, the Slovak in Bratislava), the cultures and traditions are separate, the religions were originally separate (the Czechs Protestant, the Slovaks Catholic). Jakubisko seems to have the same relationship to the Czech cinema as Dovzhenko, a Ukrainian, had to the Moscow-based Soviet cinema. Like some of the works of Dovzhenko, Jakubisko's films (*Deserters and Nomads*, 1968; *Birds, Orphans, and Fools*, 1969) seem anarchically poetic: a series of striking images that mix a blunt sexuality, politics, religion, audacious visual stunts, and experiential frenzy, cohering neither in plot nor in temporal continuity. As in many of the Czechoslovakian films there is also an undercurrent of fatalism and nihilism in Jakubisko. It is no wonder that Juráček and Jakubisko, two of the most daring and pessimistic of the period's directors, were not permitted to make films by the new authorities.

Although they might have picked some of this up from the example of John Cassavetes (*Shadows*, 1959), the Czech cinematic style reveals the pervasiveness and influence of both the French and Italian movements and might be described as a perfect synthesis of Italian neorealism—particularly its emphasis on the problems of ordinary people and its rejection of the "studio look"—and the compositional and editing spontaneity of the French New Wave—its elliptical cutting, its jumbling of film time, its hand-held camera and *cinéma vérité* authenticity. No surer sign of French influence exists than the half-dozen major Czech films—

Forman's *Black Peter* and Passer's *Intimate Lighting* among them—that end with a Truffaut freeze frame.

Although the Czech filmmakers usually preferred to shoot in real locations, the dominant imagery of this cinema is not nature (though nature often plays a memorable role as a film's supporting and secondary imagery) but the human face. By keeping the camera much closer to the faces of the actors, who were often nonprofessionals, the Czech films avoided the glossy facial lighting of Hollywood. These Czech films reduced the apparent artfulness of the cinema's handling of human beings, substituting a feeling of naturalness, imperfection, spontaneity, and absolute authenticity. This feeling of spontaneity was essential to the films' stories as well as their styles, for the films were frequently about the ability of people to act spontaneously.

Another trait of these films is their intermingling of comedy and seriousness, producing films that were quite remarkable in their range of emotions, from hilarity to pathos to sudden horror. And this range of effects was also one of the ideas and subjects of the films, for the Czech films implied that life was indeed a mixture of lightness and seriousness, of living through a time fraught with dangers and demanding the most difficult choices (this often-subjugated people knows about difficult choices). A most difficult existence still remains rich in smiles and jokes, though death waits (and not even unexpectedly) around the next corner. In their seriocomic blend the Czechs distilled the tragic modern history of their tyrannized little nation into a positive vision of life that saw humor in even the darkest moments and that (with a few exceptions) refused to surrender its faith in human exertion, commitment, and integrity.

Jiří Menzel's *Closely Watched Trains* (1966) is as good an example of this Czech spirit as any. The film's story (scripted by Bohumil Hrabal, from his short story) is of a comical young man, Miloš Hrma, who has taken a job as an apprentice at a train station during the Nazi Occupation—primarily to avoid any serious or difficult labor. Despite its wartime setting, the film seems to be a sex comedy, concentrating on the sexual inadequacies, failures, and fears

Fig. 14-18
Closely Watched Trains. *The human texture of Czech realism. Miloš (Václav Neckár) whispers his sexual secret to the pro-Nazi train inspector (Vlastimil Brodsky).*

of the inexperienced boy, who is a clumsy apprentice at love as well as at work. Menzel spends most of his time developing the boy's comic qualities: his ridiculously gawky body; his bird-skinny legs; his naïve adoration of his train controller's uniform (he wears the cap even in bed); his comical ancestors (the grandfather, a magician who attempted to conjure the Nazi tanks out of Czechoslovakia; the father, a former train employee who retired at the age of forty-eight to spend the rest of his life in bed); his naïve, bird-like, eyes-closed attempts to peck a kiss at his girlfriend, Maša, usually without success (in contrast to his co-worker,

Hubicka, for whom sexual intimacy is as natural as breathing). Comic sexual symbols dominate the film, from the long neck of a goose that the station master's wife rubs continually up and down, up and down, to force the food down its neck, to the perpetual rip in the station master's leather sofa, a hole opened by the athletic sexual activity on the sofa.

But beneath the sexual comedy are darker elements, even while Menzel refuses to desert his comic spirit and pratfalls. The boy attempts to ease his sexual failure and frustration with another act of impotence: to commit suicide by slashing his wrists as he sits in a steamy bathtub.

But even the suicide has a comic balance, for the boy's final act of bidding the world goodbye is to remove his precious cap (he doesn't want to dishonor it), and Miloš is saved from death only when a comically clumsy workman punches a hole in the bathroom wall and sees the scrawny, limp form in the tub.

The ultimate surfacing of seriousness is the film's climax, when the boy performs the mission of blowing up a Nazi ammunition train (just as successfully as he made love, the night before, with Viktoria Freie, the woman who brought him the explosives) and is suddenly and unexpectedly machine-gunned by a Nazi guard. The term *climax* is especially relevant to this final act, for the explosion is presented as a kind of orgasm.

Menzel's point is clearly that a clumsy boy has become a man, both sexually and politically. But our intellectual understanding of that positive point is balanced and complicated by our emotional awareness that he will never exercise his manhood again and that in gaining his manhood he has lost his life. Maša's sad realization parallels the audience's, for she knows that Miloš is dead when the wind of the explosion blows his cap (which he would never willingly remove) to her feet. Details count for Menzel, and he transforms the comic symbol of the cap into a touching monument to the boy's memory. In this strange variation on the familiar *Bildungsroman*, the long comic apprenticeship produces a period of maturity that is strikingly and tragically brief.

The Shop on Main Street (1965), produced and directed by Ján Kadár and Elmar Klos, also mixes the comic and the serious, although not so exuberantly or contrapuntally as *Closely Watched Trains*. According to Kadár, in his collaboration with Klos he took responsibility for the shooting and the handling of the actors while Klos served as producer and supervised the cutting. If so, *The Shop on Main Street* owes its greatest debt to Kadár's work with actors, and the earlier *Death Is Called Engelchen*, with its brilliant leaps backward and forward in time and space, was more dependent on the editing of Klos.

Of the pure comedies, Miloš Forman is the master. An affectionate satirist who pokes fun at human folly, he also realizes that folly is what makes people human. Forman's satire is gentle and compassionate rather than corrosive and vicious. Two of Forman's Czech films (*Black Peter, Loves of a Blonde*) and three of his American films (*Taking Off*, 1971; *Hair*, 1979; *Amadeus*, 1984) are youth films that examine the generation gap, whether for young Mozart or for ordinary young people. His other major films, *The Firemen's Ball, One Flew Over the Cuckoo's Nest* (1975), *Ragtime* (1981), and *Valmont* (1989), examine the follies and insanities of adulthood, a secondary theme of the youth films.

Forman's primary satirical subjects are youthful clumsiness and adult boredom. The folly of youth for Forman is that it is so earnest and so clumsy. Sexual pursuit is the primary activity, but the pursuit is awkward, callous, and mechanical. Sexual success is the only emblem of human importance, and Forman's youths devote their lives to feeding their egos and vanities with this kind of food. Forman's adults, meanwhile, spend their lives in their apartments, conversing about the evils of their children, bored with the books they read, with the television they watch, and especially with one another. If it were not for the follies of youth, the adults would seemingly have nothing to occupy their lives at all. In *Taking Off*, however (and here Forman senses the difference between American and Czech parents), the adults also occupy themselves by imitating the follies of youth, which is a double folly.

Forman's three favorite domains are the dance hall, the kitchen, and the bedroom — three distinct and essential social centers. Dances are society's and youth's institutionalized means of sexual pursuit, and Forman delights in examining the clumsy and self-conscious games that people play in the dance hall. Using a *cinéma vérité* method of photographing actual dance halls and mixing his players with the real "revellers" (as Mack Sennett did in *Tango Tangles*), Forman continually reveals how difficult it is for young people to act naturally and effectively in such a situation, how the major business of a dance is not dancing but finding a dance partner, and how most of the people at a dance spend most of their time defending themselves against the very thing they have come to the dance to get.

Fig. 14-19
Loves of a Blonde: *comic stabs at adolescent love and tenderness (Vladimir Brecholt and Nana Brechkova).*

The kitchen is the social center of the family, the place where the boring, painful, yet inevitable discussions of the worthlessness of youth take place. The clumsiness that Forman captures in this social center is that no one listens to what the others are saying (or cares), no one (father, mother, child) agrees on the issues of the discussion, and no one cares about the results of the discussion, since there will obviously be none (everyone in the kitchen already knows this but feels compelled to continue anyway). The bedroom is the personal and private social center where the results of the sexual pursuit culminate. The clumsiness that Forman brilliantly captures in these scenes (in particular the seduction scenes between Mila and Andula in *Loves of a Blonde*) reveals how such monumentally important matters of human experience find expression in such awkward, pedestrian, and limited physical acts.

One further contribution of the Czech cinema that cannot be overlooked is its accomplishments in cel animation and in puppet cinema, most notably the work of Jiří Trnka (*The Devil on Springs,* 1946; *The Czech Year,* 1947; *The Emperor's Nightingale,* 1948; *Song of the Prairie,* 1949; *Cybernetic Grandma,* 1962; *The Hand,* 1966) and Karel Zeman (*Christmas Dream,* 1945; *The Invention of Destruction,* 1957; *Baron Münchhausen,* 1961; *On a Comet,* 1970).

The other cinemas of Eastern and Central Europe endured the same Stalinist and anti-Stalinist twists and turns as the Czech cinema, producing similar periods of fertility and barrenness. After the Czech cinema, the Polish cinema is the most interesting. The most fertile period of the Polish cinema preceded the Czech era by almost a decade (1955–1964), produced primarily by the founding of another major film school (the Lódź Film School in 1948) and the splitting of the Polish industry into individual artistic production units in 1955. These smaller production units granted the Polish directors a new freedom and allowed the exercise of

Ashes and Diamonds: the death of a political assassin (Zbigniew Cybulski).

Fig. 14-20

more individuality; the two most talented directors, Andrzej Wajda (of the KADR unit) and Roman Polanski (of the KAMERA unit), took advantage of this new opportunity.

As in Czechoslovakia, the Nazi Occupation and the Resistance to it were favored subjects of the Polish cinema, and no one made more powerful films on the Occupation era than Andrzej Wajda, whose first feature, *Generation* (1955), became the first work of the new "Polish school." As opposed to the seriocomic, neorealist, intimately personal style of the Czech war films, Wajda's style is more active, more violent, more baroque, and less internalized. The greatest early Wajda films (*Kanal*, 1957; *Ashes and Diamonds*, 1958) consistently use arresting, grotesque visual imagery (for example, the claustrophobic Warsaw sewers in *Kanal*), often dwelling on shots of rubble, ashes, and garbage, but these images can turn suddenly beautiful and unforgettably disturbing, as do the sheets hung out to dry in *Ashes and Diamonds,* which become a deadly labyrinth even as they wave neutrally in the breeze. *Ashes and Diamonds* is a spectacularly visual film, with

expressionistically vivid lighting effects (its extreme backlighting and low-angle camera work influenced by *Citizen Kane*), with two brilliantly climactic murder scenes that juxtapose the deaths with striking images (the startling eruption of fireworks at the moment of death, the dark stains of blood oozing into a white sheet drying in the sun), and with the compelling performance of one of the most interesting (and least known) stars in the history of cinema, Zbigniew Cybulski—in many ways the Polish James Dean.

Wajda's filmmaking career is itself a miniature of the political history of Poland over the past three decades. With the constriction of Polish freedoms in the mid-1960s (and the early death of Cybulski, Wajda's close friend and leading actor), Wajda's work became more introspective (particularly the devastatingly ironic film he made in response to Cybulski's death, *Everything for Sale,* 1969) and more ambiguous in its treatment of political issues. But with the return of Polish dissent in the 1970s, symbolized by Lech Walesa's Solidarity organization of workers and intellectuals, Wajda's films again became openly political. He identified strongly with Solidarity in *Man of Marble* (1977, another film influenced by *Kane*) and *Man of Iron* (1980), the latter of which condemned the spineless vacillation of a journalistic flunky who refused to take a political stand and in which Walesa himself appeared. As in *Open City* or *The Battle of Algiers*, *Man of Iron* mixed fictional filming with suggestions of documentary footage, giving a fiction the immediacy and conviction of newsreel reportage.

Wajda's *Danton* (1982) feels the weight of Solidarity's defeat beneath the Polish capitulation to Soviet policy. A French-Polish co-production shot in France (many of Wajda's films were shot outside Poland), ostensibly detailing the ideological battle between Danton and Robespierre during the French Revolution, the film uses the familiar strategy of paralleling historical conflicts to contemporary events. When Danton dies beneath the blade of Robespierre's guillotine, the red drops of his blood suggest the color and design of the familiar Solidarity insignia. Wajda implies that although Walesa's Solidarity movement may be as dead as Danton, the ideas for which both stand are very much alive. In the late 1980s, when Walesa proved victorious, Wajda was free to mix politics and melodrama without reaching for big symbolic effects. The best of his mid-1980s films, *A Love in Germany* (1984, starring Hanna Schygulla) and *The Possessed* (1988, from Dostoevsky's novel), cannot match *Ashes and Diamonds* or *Man of Marble,* but they are still the work of a master.

Roman Polanski's career represents another kind of historical metaphor. Even beginning with his early Polish films, Polanski's primary theme is not the rubble of war but the ominousness of the universe itself. Polanski's black-and-white films use an extremely simple situation built around a single object and very few characters (two men carry a wardrobe out of the sea in *Two Men and a Wardrobe*, 1958; three people sail a boat out to sea in *Knife in the Water,* 1962; a woman descends into madness in *Repulsion,* 1965). But Polanski endows these simple events with allegorical significance, primarily by charging the entire universe with a menacing, hostile spirit that turns the most simple and commonplace human events into

terrifying combats of great magnitude. In *Knife in the Water* he endows the simple meeting of the three with menace by his use of lenses (primarily wide-angle lenses that magnify and distort distances), by his camera placement (using grotesque angles so that characters or objects dominate others or even blot them out entirely), and by the muted tension and jousting beneath the spare dialogue, props (that hypnotic knife), and movement. In *Repulsion* (shot in England) the most commonplace settings — the walls, ceilings, and doors of an ordinary apartment — become horrifyingly tactile and mysterious enemies, magnified by the increasing hysteria of the film's paranoid protagonist (Catherine Deneuve).

Polanski's visions of cosmic paranoia and malevolence were incompatible with any socialist theory of human justice. Imprisoned as a child of eight in a concentration camp, where his mother died, Polanski could only resolve his nihilistic conflict with a repressive state by escaping to a more indulgent West to make films in England, France, and the United States (*Repulsion*; *Cul-de-Sac*, 1966, a black comedy; *The Fearless Vampire Killers or: Pardon Me, But Your Teeth Are In My Neck,* 1967, a parody; *Rosemary's Baby,* 1968, a straightforward horror film and his first American picture; *Macbeth,* 1971, a version of Shakespeare's play that is short on verbal poetry and long on visual violence; *Chinatown,* 1974, his best American film; *The Tenant,* 1976, his best horror film since *Repulsion*; *Tess,* 1979, from the novel by Thomas Hardy).

There were other Polish directors who made effective films in its greatest decade: Aleksander Ford, who had been making films since 1929 (*Border Street,* 1949; *Five Boys from Barska Street,* 1954; *Knights of the Teutonic Order,* 1960); Andrzej Munk (*Eroica,* 1957; *Bad Luck,* 1959), who died in an automobile accident before he could complete his major work, *The Passenger* (1961, released 1963); and Jerzy Kawalerowicz, who hides his political statements within the walls of convents (*Mother Joan of the Angels,* 1961) and Egyptian pyramids (*Pharaoh,* 1966) when he is not declaring them overtly, as he does in *Night Train* (1959).

Jerzy Skolimowski was, like Polanski, a younger-generation Polish filmmaker who fled

Poland. After serving as scriptwriter for both Wajda (*Innocent Sorcerers*, 1960) and Polanski (*Knife in the Water*), he wrote and directed *Identification Marks: None* (1964), *Walkover* (1965), and *Barrier* (1966) in Poland; after his anti-Stalinist *Hands Up!* (1967) was banned, he made *Le Départ* (1967) in Belgium, *Deep End* (1970) in Germany, and *The Shout* (1978) and *Moonlighting* (1982) in England. Unlike Polanski, Skolimowski has made powerful, incisive political films (*Hands Up!*, *Moonlighting*) as well as complex, disturbing, apolitical films (*The Shout*).

The early Hungarian cinema is probably most notable for the talents it exported to the rest of the world after their Hungarian apprenticeships: Béla Lugosi; Hollywood directors Michael Curtiz, André de Toth, and Paul Fejos; the noted British producer and director, Alexander Korda; and the international film theorists, László Moholy-Nagy and Béla Balázs. The best-known international representative of the new Hungarian cinema of the 1960s and 1970s is Miklós Jancsó (*Cantata*, 1962; *The Red and the White*, 1967; *The Confrontation*, 1968). Jancsó's films combine Hungarian folk tales and history with extremely lengthy and carefully planned tracking shots that choreograph cinema space as complexly as an Orson Welles in the West; his use of the wide screen, especially in *The Red and the White*, is among the most impressive in the history of the art. István Szabó, originally a member of Balázs's experimental workshop, makes psychologically detailed portraits of contemporary citizens who must make difficult choices between personal interest and political responsibility. The actor of *Mephisto* (1981, starring Klaus Maria Brandauer) refuses to take a stand against the Nazi oppressors because he's "only an actor." He indeed becomes the slave of his satanic role, both onstage and off.

The primary contribution of the Yugoslavian cinema is its famed Zagreb animation studio, the most innovative, imaginative, and influential source of animated films in the world since 1957. In live-action films, the Yugoslavian cinema is one of the youngest in Europe, with no native production until after the Second World War. Its most influential New Wave director is the brilliantly clever political

and social satirist, Dušan Makavejev (*Man Is Not a Bird*, 1965; *Love Affair, or The Tragedy of a Switchboard Operator*, 1967; *Innocence Unprotected*, 1968; *W. R.—Mysteries of the Organism*, 1971; *Sweet Movie*, 1974). Makavejev's *Montenegro—or Pigs and Pearls* (1981), his first crowd-pleaser, starred Susan Anspach as an American married woman who collides with a colony of Yugoslavian immigrants in Stockholm. While the Yugoslavians seem bizarrely out of place in the coldly rational northern capital, the American woman responds to their oddness and sensuousness. Despite her apparent normality, she is the least predictable person in the film. *Montenegro,* like the other Makavejev films, is a very odd mixture of social allegory and absurd comedy, of solid plotting and outrageous intrusion and disruption — outlandish cinematic mixtures of laughter and thoughtfulness quite unlike anyone else's.

These Eastern European films suggest that no matter how the map of Europe might be drawn, moral, psychological, and stylistic concerns transcend political borders even as they respond to political conditions. Descendants of a rich cultural heritage in literature, painting, and music, the best films from Eastern Europe are as complex, thoughtful, and stylistically idiosyncratic as the best films from anywhere in the world.

Cinemas East

The Japanese cinema first conquered the West when Akira Kurosawa's *Rashomon* won the Grand Prize at the Venice Film Festival of 1951. In the wake of *Rashomon* followed a series of imaginative and impressive films from Japan, directed by Kurosawa and by other masters of a cinema that had previously been unknown to most Western audiences: Kenji Mizoguchi, Yasujiro Ozu, Teinosuke Kinugasa, Kon Ichikawa, Hiroshi Inagaki, Masaki Kobayashi, Tadashi Imai, Mikio Naruse. The decade of the 1950s proved to be Japan's richest cinematic era—both commercially and artistically—as a result of many of the same forces that stimulated the new Western film industries in the same period: the receptivity to new forms of film expression, the new market for non-American films, and the new period of political and intellectual freedom. Like many of the European nations, the Japanese cinema emerged from over a decade of political constraints caused by the Second World War and its aftermath of normalization. What was equally surprising for both Western audiences and critics was not simply the maturity of Japanese films in this decade but the richness and depth of the Japanese film tradition; Mizoguchi, Ozu, and Kinugasa had been directing great films since the 1920s.

The Japanese cinema developed under conditions that kept it approximately ten years behind the cinemas of the West, a lag that worked in its favor in the 1950s, for the Japanese film industry felt the crippling effects of television almost a decade later than the industries of America and Europe. So too, the early period of primitivism lasted a decade longer in Japan, at least into the mid-1920s. Although there were commercial and technological reasons for this—a lag in organizing the industry, problems with machines and film—the primary reasons were aesthetic. First, women did not appear in Japanese films until the mid-1920s, women's roles being played by female impersonators called *oyama* (Kinugasa began his career as an *oyama*). This sacrifice of naturalness and authenticity tended to keep the Japanese cinema tied to its theatrical roots (where men also played the female roles, as they did on the Elizabethan stage) and kept it from asserting the kind of naturalness and spontaneity that gradually evolved in the films of the West between 1905 and 1915.

Second, the Japanese cinema used a narrator to explain the film to the audience. Called the *benshi*, this narrator's presence eliminated the need for printed titles and partly accounts for the way the Japanese cinema developed its own cinematic grammar and rhetoric, which had nothing to do with the Griffith tradition. Although narrators occasionally accompanied film screenings in American nickelodeons, their influence was minimal and they disappeared with the nickelodeons. In Japan, where the commentary of a narrator was a convention of Kabuki theatre, the film became so dependent on a human speaker that the cinema itself did not need to "speak" in its own unique and powerful terms. All the early Western masters of the cinema—Griffith, Eisenstein, Murnau, et al.—were specifically those who discovered ways to make a purely visual "language" communicative. A rare exception of the Japanese silent cinema is Kinugasa's tale of devotion and insanity, *A Page of Madness* (*Crazy Page*, 1927), as elliptical in its construction as anything by the French surrealists, as daring in its editing as Kirsanov's or Eisenstein's montage, and with fewer printed titles than *The Last Laugh*, more stream-of-consciousness sequences than *Napoleon*, and a more cinematic grasp of Expressionism than *Caligari* (which had not yet been shown in Japan). Kinugasa's *Crossroads* (1928) was the only Japanese film before *Rashomon* to be shown widely in the West, and his *Gate of Hell* (1953) was one of the biggest hits to follow *Rashomon*, along with Mizoguchi's *Ugetsu* (1953), Ozu's *Tokyo Story* (1953), Kurosawa's own *Seven Samurai* (1954), and of course, Inoshiro Honda's *Godzilla, King of the Monsters* (1954; U.S. version, co-directed by Terry Morse, 1956).

Third, lacking an active tradition of popular, bourgeois prose fiction (even though the first known novel was written in Japan in the early eleventh century: *The Tale of Genji*, by Lady Murasaki Shikibu), Japan's cinema descended exclusively from the rich theatrical traditions of Noh, Kabuki, and Bunraku, as well as the highly developed arts of painting, poetry, and design. While Western cinematic conventions evolved as combinations and compromises between enacted and written story-telling, the indigenous Japanese cinema evolved from the stylizations of its theatrical and visual arts. Not only did the *oyama* and *benshi* come to Japanese cinema from the theatre but, according to Japan's foremost film critic, Tadao Sato, so did a key distinction between two types of leading men. One was the *tateyaku*—strong, powerful, virile (to be embodied by Sessue Hayakawa and Toshiro Mifune—parallel to America's Clark Gable and John Wayne); the other was the slighter, sweeter, milder figure, the *nimaime*—literally, the "second lead" of Kabuki (parallel to such American stars as Richard Barthelmess, Henry Fonda, and

Montgomery Clift). Many Japanese film stories derive from expectations about these two opposite types of actors.

The confining Japanese cinematic traditions died slowly and unwillingly. The *oyama* disrupted film production in 1922 by calling a strike when they saw they were to be replaced by women. The *benshi,* who had made themselves into one of the primary attractions of the Japanese cinema (often an audience attended a film merely to enjoy the commentary of a clever and popular *benshi*), fought extinction even more vigorously. In 1932 the *benshi* and the theatre musicians called a strike against the entire film industry; some *benshi* turned off the soundtracks of the early talkies so they could do their act; on at least one occasion the *benshi* union hired thugs to assault an official of one of the studios that was converting to sound.

When sound finally came to the Japanese cinema it too came almost a decade later than to the film industries of the West. (For that matter, the first unhidden kiss scene was shot in 1946.) Although the first successful sound film was shot in Japan as early as 1931 — *The Neighbor's Wife and Mine,* directed by Heinosuke Gosho — in 1932 only 45 of some 400 Japanese films used synchronized sound. Ozu did not shoot his first sound film until 1936, and silent production did not die completely until 1937.

The coming of sound to Japan was quickly followed by the coming of war, and the Japanese government demanded that the film industry support the war effort with films reflecting national militaristic policies. An equally repressive policy restricted the Japanese film industry after the war when the American Occupation Forces created a cultural "reorientation" committee, which banned certain subjects (for example, all Japanese period dramas because they were feudalistic and militaristic) and demanded others (for example, the values of peaceful living and democratic institutions).

On the other hand, the Japanese film industry had developed a number of practices and traditions that would work for rather than against it when a period of commercial, technical, and political equality would enable it to compete on the world's screens. First, the Japa-

nese film industry, like the American one, was composed of several competing commercial companies, with their own writers, directors, actors, and technicians working under contract, which were in the business of conceiving, making, and selling films. The four Japanese studios that became most familiar to Western audiences were Nikkatsu (the oldest, founded in 1912 — Ichikawa's studio); Shochiku (founded in 1920 and for three decades the commercial leader — Ozu's studio); Toho (founded in the 1930s by the amalgamation of several smaller companies — Kurosawa's primary studio; exploiter of Japanese monster pictures, like *Godzilla*; developer of Japan's own wide-screen, anamorphic process, Tohoscope); and Daiei (founded during the war — producer of *Rashomon, Gate of Hell,* and Mizoguchi's later films).

One of the obvious implications of such a studio system is production in quantity, and the Japanese industry regularly produced over four hundred feature films each year, second only to Hollywood in its most golden Studio Era and leader in quantitative output when American production fell in the 1950s. As in the United States, this production in quantity guaranteed a very large number of very bad to passably mediocre films every year. But as in the United States, it also guaranteed a significant number of films every year that would rank among the art's finest achievements.

The Japanese studio system avoided many of the evils of the American system, but it produced others. A primary advantage was that the system was built around the director rather than the producer or star. The Japanese "producer" is comparable to the production manager in Hollywood who manages production details but makes no creative decisions. The Japanese director is a more powerful audience attraction than a film's star, and it is the director's name — not the star's — that frequently appears above the title in Japanese films. As a result, Japanese stars earn far less money than their counterparts in the West and enjoy far less power. The Japanese director is the paternalistic head of his own production "family" — the Japanese film industry being modeled to some extent as a mirror of Japanese society. The disadvantages of such a system —

more comfortable and less competitive than Hollywood's—are, first, that talented directors must serve long apprenticeships in order to work themselves up the familial ladder (in the case of a mentorship under a great senior director, this may be an advantage). Japan does not import instant talents from outside its studio system—no Rouben Mamoulians or Bob Fosses who come from the theatre; no Jean-Luc Godards or Lindsay Andersons who come from film journals. A second disadvantage is that the paternalistic system may perpetuate mediocrity and incompetence (for no member of any family is thrown out of it for mediocrity) as well as keep women from rising to positions of authority.

In its film subjects the Japanese cinema also bears a striking resemblance to American movies; Japanese films tend to bunch themselves in clear-cut genres and cycles. In fact, Japanese genres are even more specifically defined and definable than their American counterparts. The basic division is between the *jidai-geki,* a period or costume film set in Japan's past (in most cases, in the feudal period before the 1868 Meiji Restoration), and *gendai-geki,* a film of modern life. But within these two basic genres there are many subgenres. The *jidai-geki* can be further subdivided into the particular period of Japanese history it depicts (for example, the Tokugawa era, 1615–1868). As the terms are used in the Japanese industry, however, the *jidai-geki* treats only the Tokugawa period, the *Meiji-mono* treats the period from the Meiji Restoration to 1912, and there is no specific term for films set before the Tokugawa era (such as *Rashomon,* which is set in the Heian period, no later than the twelfth century). The *gendai-geki* has such subgenres as the *shomin-geki* (the drama or comedy of middle-class and lower-middle-class life), the "mother picture" (a mother's relationship to her children), the "wife picture" (the difficulties of marriage for women), the "nonsense picture" (farcical comedies), the *yakuza* or gangster picture, and the "youth picture" (the wild doings of youth).

Two consistent structural traits do seem to dominate the best Japanese films, and both are descendants of the Japanese theatrical traditions of the Kabuki and the Noh.

First, the best films are ruthlessly economical in their concentration on the central theme. Rather than fill up the script with flavorful and atmospheric events to "flesh out" a film—in a sense diverting an audience from the central issue and giving the film a feeling of life's randomness—the great Japanese films seem to rivet every incident of the plot, every character, every visual image, and every line of dialogue to the film's central thematic question or dominant mood. A second, and related, structural trait is the Japanese concern for symmetry. Many of the best Japanese films are not close studies of individual people or pairs but of a fairly large group of people, a whole "family" of characters, who make different choices, take different paths in life, and thereby come to different ends. This structural feeling for symmetry keeps these multipath "journeys" moving along side by side in the audience's mind, united, of course, by the single thematic issue that has produced the "journey" in the first place.

Unlike the Czech cinema, there is no single consistent trait of visual style that dominates the Japanese cinema. Those three directors who, at least from a Western perspective, appear to be Japan's greatest film artists—Akira Kurosawa, Kenji Mizoguchi, and Yasujiro Ozu—have three completely different visual senses and use three completely different cinematographic principles. These very visual differences make them such unique and individual stylists.

Akira Kurosawa is the Japanese director most popular in the West—perhaps because he has been so obviously influenced by films of the West (he once listed Gance's *La Roue* and the works of Hawks, Stevens, Capra, Ford, and Wyler as major influences—and Antonioni and Mizoguchi as favorites rather than influences). He is one of the only filmmakers to have made effective movies in both the *jidai-* and *gendai-geki.* Kurosawa's *samurai* films are closely related to American westerns (and have been remade as westerns); some of his films move with the swift pace of American films rather than the more leisurely pace of Japanese films; many of his films, including *Rashomon,* use music that sounds more Western than Japanese; and he is clearly influenced by Western cinematic styles, especially the use of the subjective traveling camera, the wide-screen revolution, the expressionist color experiments of Eisenstein's *Ivan the Terrible, Part II,* the use of extreme deep-focus photography, and, consequently, the use of very fast film stock. Kurosawa also seems to share an artistic trait with such Western directors as Hitchcock and Godard—the urge to tackle very difficult stylistic problems that require him to push himself beyond the artistic frontiers he has already charted and conquered.

Rashomon (1950) clearly demonstrates Kurosawa's thematic concerns and stylistic maturity (he had been directing films since 1943, and he has edited and either written or co-written all of his pictures). The film is famous as the essential cinematic demonstration of the relativity and subjectivity of truth—and that it is. But of greater interest in the film is, first, Kurosawa's stylistic control that conveys and convinces us of that subjectivity and, second, what he says people should do with their lives given the relativity and subjectivity of truth as well as the imperfection of human beings.

Rashomon uses what might be described as six different cinematic styles, six separate camera strategies, each corresponding to one of the levels of the film's realities. Two of the six sections are "frames," not the central incident itself but ways of telling or finding out about the incident. One of these two frames is primary: two men telling a third about the incident as they sit beneath the ruins of the Rashomon Gate during a rainstorm; the other is, in effect, a frame-within-a-frame: the testimony of the three participants in the incident to a "judge" who is attempting to discover exactly what happened and why. The remaining four sections are four different versions of what happened and why, each of them mirroring the attitudes, perceptions, and personality of the witness. The single concrete fact is that a man lies dead in the forest; but what emerges as worse, the real moral problem, is that the inquest into that man's death has been filled with lies. Since people need to assign a cause, to see a reason for a catastrophic fact, the film becomes a search for answers and reasons: how he died, why they lied, and whether people are any good.

The film's primary frame introduces this search as two men, a Woodcutter and a Priest (representatives of the secular and sacred orders), feel compelled to tell their story to a stranger, perhaps to aid their search, perhaps to ease their suspicion that the search has no end. Kurosawa sets this frame during a furious rainstorm, from which the only refuge is a pitiful shelter of architectural ruins. Although rainstorms are almost a cliché of the Japanese cinema, Kurosawa clearly uses this storm as a concrete external image of both the internal mental agony of the unfulfilled search and the chaotic social instability of the era: a period of lawlessness, bandits, plagues, famine, civil war, and, like the Rashomon Gate itself (and the old values it represents), ruins. Kurosawa is a master at using natural imagery to evoke abstract and internal human sensations, a technique he brings to perfection in his later *Throne of Blood* (1957). What is intriguing about the Woodcutter's introduction is that he tells the Listener that this incident is especially terrible, worse even than the social chaos of the present. The Listener, whose curiosity is understandably aroused—he serves as the viewer's surrogate in this respect—agrees to listen to the tale in the course of waiting out the storm.

For these scenes at the Gate, Kurosawa uses a conventionally objective cutting and shooting method. He cuts freely—from various distances and angles—to make the viewer a privileged observer, leading us from place to place, always giving us the most interesting and revealing point of view. The dominant motif is the driving sound and image of the incessant rain. But for his frame-within-a-frame—the testimony before the "judge"—Kurosawa uses a totally different visual principle. Kurosawa keeps his camera in a single spot, at about the eye level of a seated observer, while the speakers stare directly at the camera to tell their story. The implication is obvious; the camera is the "judge" and has become the new viewer-surrogate; the camera-judge takes the evidence, attempting to provide the viewer-judge with the means to draw a conclusion. Kurosawa returns to this courtyard (it is not a court*room,* since the camera-judge, as well as the witnesses, are obviously sitting on the ground outdoors) after each of the versions of the tale, just as he returns to the Rashomon Gate after each of the testimonies in the court.

The first three versions of the incident are those of each of the three principal participants. Each is completely different in human motivation, sequence of events, emotional tone, and visual style. The first version is that of the boastful, impulsive bandit, Tajomaro, played as a sensual, virile, exuberant male animal by Toshiro Mifune, the film's *tateyaku*. Tajomaro's version emphasizes the physical sensations of the confrontation—the heat of the day, the glare of the sun, the sting of the gnats that he repeatedly swats—that Kurosawa depicts subjectively, from Tajomaro's point of view. When Tajomaro first sees the woman, he describes her in sensual terms—as a cool breeze—and the camera watches a gust of wind ripple through the leaves and lift the woman's veil, accompanied by the rippling tinkle of a celeste. Kurosawa's primary subjective device in the sequence, however, is the violent, furious pace of his tracking and panning shots, the camera's incessant energetic movement, translating Tajomaro's predatory stalking into visual terms. It is also Kurosawa's way of translating the way Tajomaro sees himself: aggressive, restless, dominant, assertive.

According to Tajomaro, his conquest of the woman was exactly that: an assertive masculine act in which he subdues the woman first by his strength and then by his passion. The bandit then bests the husband in fair, violent, valiant combat ("He fought marvellously"), again the virile male displaying the theoretical characteristics of masculinity. Kurosawa's camera catches the flashy *samurai* swordsmanship and the final kill as Tajomaro perceives it—or, more to the point, describes it: with violent movement of the participants, violent camera movement, and violent cutting.

The woman (Machiko Kyo) tells a version that is completely different in style, tone, emphasis, and action. According to the way she sees both herself and the event, she is a "poor helpless woman" (she depicts herself as stereotypically "feminine," just as Tajomaro is self-stereotypedly "masculine"). Although her version begins after the sexual consummation, her obvious implication is that she had no choice but to submit meekly to the rape of a

Fig. 14-21
Rashomon: *the bride fighting the bandit like a tiger cat (Toshiro Mifune and Machiko Kyo).*

strong and determined animal (as opposed to the bandit's description of her struggling like a tiger cat). It serves both her self-image and her credibility for her to avoid any references to the sexual act itself. So too, the bandit plays a very small role in her version of the incident, and the few glimpses she provides are of a whooping savage, a grotesque caricature of the bandit's masculinity in his own version. She presents herself as a selfless, proper wife; the bandit scarcely exists for her because the real object of her concern is her husband, the only one whose reactions to the rape matter. And his reaction is a cold, pitiless, piercing stare. She retrieves her dagger, still stuck in the trunk of a tree (a point of agreement with Tajomaro's version), and he continues to stare. She starts moving toward him, the dagger erect, and his hypnotic stare continues. The music on the

Fig. 14-22

Fig. 14-23

Rashomon. *Fig. 14-22: husband (Masayuki Mori) and bandit (Toshiro Mifune); Fig. 14-23: husband, wife (Machiko Kyo), and the lethally connecting dagger.*

soundtrack (which sounds unfortunately close to Ravel's "Bolero") pulses and swells, mirroring the tension of the moment for the wife who has been caught in a kind of trance. The result, however, is that she faints, and upon awaking she finds the dagger in her husband's chest (different murder weapon than in Tajomaro's story). Interestingly, Kurosawa does not depict her discovery of the knife visually but merely lets her tell that part of the story to the camera-audience-judge.

The ghost of the husband tells the third version of the story, a feat that Kurosawa accomplishes mystically by using a female medium to summon the man's spirit from the other world and to serve as the vessel of the husband's perceptions. As "he" tells "his" story, Kurosawa uses uniquely cinematic devices to convert this intangible and metaphysical presence into a tangible, credible reality.
A dead man's voice issues from the woman-medium's lips, and that voice is not only foreign to the apparent gender of the speaker but also strange in its pitch, tone, and timbre — echoing, breathy, hollow, sounding like a phonograph record played at too slow a speed in an underground cavern. Kurosawa supports the bizarre sound with a striking visual image: The medium's white veils float and flap violently in the wind that has suddenly entered the courtyard, clashing with its previous stillness. The wind is, or is like, a blast from the supernatural.

In contrast to the writhing agony of the medium is the stillness and quiet of the husband's version of the incident itself, toward which his attitude is one of sad resignation. For the husband (the film's *nimaime*, played with majestic silence by Masayuki Mori), the woman hardly exists. For him, the essential relationship is between himself and the bandit, two honorable men both caught in the trap of a worthless woman. According to the husband, he does not die by being bested in combat (Tajomaro's version) nor as a result of a hypnotic trance that impels his wife toward him with the dagger (as in hers) but as a result of his own decision — to commit *seppuku* (*harakiri*, or ritual suicide) according to the *samurai*'s precepts of honor.

But the Woodcutter, who we know (from an earlier traveling shot) discovered the body and

who we now find out actually witnessed the entire incident, sees all three versions as concoctions of lies — even the dead man's: "There was no knife." One cannot even depend on supernatural beings for the truth. The Woodcutter then tells his version of the incident, the "objective account" of an outside observer. Interestingly, the Woodcutter is played by Takashi Shimura, a regular member of the Kurosawa acting family and a figure whom Kurosawa uses consistently as the objective, rational, balanced center of an intense human action (Shimura plays the leader of the *Seven Samurai* who survives to bury his fallen comrades; he plays the equivalent of the Macduff role in *Throne of Blood*).

In the Woodcutter's "objective" account, all three characters are weaker, smaller, and sillier than in their own. The bandit sentimentally begs for forgiveness and blubberingly offers to marry the woman he defiled; the husband is a jittery coward; the wife is a selfish and cackling shrew who wants the two men to fight over her. Because both men are so cowardly and so comical in this version, they have a good deal of trouble working up a fight. They both shake with fright, their hands and swords trembling. Their whoops are not masculine assertions of strength (as in the bandit's version) but nervous squeals of terror. Each offers a very tentative poke of a sword thrust only to scurry away for cover. Eventually the fight blunders to its climax as the husband loses his weapon and backs away (a long, slow tracking shot rather than a rapid, violent one), trips, and is killed. Even as he whines for mercy, the bandit sobbingly and quiveringly pushes his sword home.

Several questions arise, however, from this "objective" report. Can an outside observer actually feel the personal and internal resonances of such an intense event? Does his comical, low, and essentially deflating view of human passion and action accurately present the participants' feelings? The Woodcutter's consistent tendency in the film has been to see all forms of human exertion as essentially low and vile. Is he any more to be trusted than the others? If he is to be trusted (however warily), what does his version imply about human behavior? Are the participants "lying" — as the

Woodcutter believes—or are they telling the "truth" as they perceive it? Are they distorting their stories to make themselves look good, or are they simply telling what they "know" to be true—even if each of them, including the Woodcutter, "knows" something different to be true?

Rashomon's final sequence, which returns us to the ruins of the Rashomon Gate, provides Kurosawa's synthesis of the conflicting versions and resolution of the ambiguity through human action. As the Woodcutter's story finishes, the three men hear the cries of an infant, obviously abandoned to the storm and the ruins by its parents. The Listener's reaction is to steal the baby's clothes and blanket: "We can't live unless we act selfishly these days." The Woodcutter protests, but the Listener accuses him of not being so perfect himself and correctly guesses that the Woodcutter stole the valuable dagger. Because the Woodcutter left that out of his supposedly objective report, he too is a liar as well as a thief, and he is in no position to play holier than thou. The Listener leaves with the baby's clothes. The Woodcutter reaches for the baby, but the Priest interferes—assuming now that this second thief wants to steal what little protection against life's harshness the infant still has. When the Woodcutter explains that he wants to adopt the child, that he already has six children and another won't make much difference, the Priest becomes ashamed of himself for having judged the man too harshly (thus every major character has proved fallible and done something wrong). The Priest hands over the baby and finds that the Woodcutter's selfless, generous act has restored his faith. People can be kind, and the world can make sense. The rain stops, and the Woodcutter leaves with his new child. The sun finally shines.

Many of Kurosawa's films, particularly the later ones, are battles with despair, and like the majority of Japanese films (even those with "happy endings"), they end on a sad or emotionally mixed note. *Seven Samurai*, for example, ends with a shot of the graves of the samurai who fell in battle, rather than a shot of the survivors. If *Rashomon* gives us a happy ending, it is only after showing us that the search for truth must lead to ambiguity; that people can be cowardly, vain, and immoral; that ideals, codes of honor, and roles may not be lived up to; and that nostalgia for goodness and honor is a sad emotion, since for every moral success one finds many more moral failures and brutal acts. These points are made with equal conviction in Kurosawa films from *Ikiru* (*To Live*, 1952) to *Ran* (*Chaos*, 1985). In response to the essential ambiguity of life and our knowledge of it—clearly a central theme of *Rashomon*—Kurosawa shows in film after film that a person is what he or she *does*, simply because it is impossible to discover what anything is in any other way; for this reason Kurosawa might be considered the most existential of the Japanese directors.

Kurosawa's two most interesting *samurai* films—*Seven Samurai* and *Yojimbo* (*Bodyguard*, 1961)—work the theme of existential action into two opposite situations, both borrowed from the American western. *Seven Samurai* is a variation on the farmers-against-the-ranchers western (like George Stevens's *Shane*, 1953), except in Kurosawa's film they are the farmers against the bandits. *Yojimbo* is the story of the paid gun (sword) for hire who rides (stalks) into a small town that is split between two warring but equally crooked rival factions and succeeds in cleaning up both sides. *Seven Samurai* develops the theme of human assertion and action through cooperation—regardless of differences in temperament, background, social class, and personal style. *Yojimbo* develops the theme of self-assertion and individual integrity, the man who can sell his sword but not his values. Kurosawa paid his debt to the American western when both *Seven Samurai* and *Yojimbo* were made into westerns (John Sturges's *The Magnificent Seven*, 1960, and Sergio Leone's *For a Fistful of Dollars*, 1964, respectively). His *samurai* films also had a significant effect on another genre: The plot of George Lucas's *Star Wars* owes as much to Kurosawa's *The Hidden Fortress* (1958) as it does to *The Wizard of Oz*, and the editing and pace of both *Star Wars* and *The Empire Strikes Back* (1980) were strongly influenced by the editing of *Seven Samurai*.

Kurosawa's most important *gendai-geki* is *Ikiru*, another extension of his belief in the assertion of human dignity through action. *Ikiru* is the story of a petty bureaucrat (played by Takashi Shimura) who has wasted most of his life and who discovers that he is dying of cancer. He decides to dedicate his final days to accomplishing one important thing before his death. The film is as sensitive, as personal, as close in its human observation as the *samurai* stories are active and violent.

But perhaps no two films reveal Kurosawa's stylistic range so well as his two films of 1957, both of them film adaptations of Western classics of the drama: Shakespeare's *Macbeth* (*Throne of Blood*) and Maxim Gorky's *The Lower Depths*. The two literary texts pose opposite cinematic problems: Shakespeare's magnificent language and sprawling terrain; Gorky's claustrophobic, discursive, and philosophic study of a social mass rather than a single protagonist. Kurosawa solved these opposite stylistic problems in opposite ways. He dispensed altogether with Shakespeare's text and translated the spirit of the play's theme and poetry into visual symbols; he kept the text of the Gorky play almost verbatim (it is a far more literal translation of the play than Renoir's 1936 version) and shot the entire film in confined and cramped settings.

In *Throne of Blood* Kurosawa translated Shakespeare's poetry (the references to blood, to the chaos in nature), theme (the valiant man tempted and destroyed by the evil in himself and in the cosmos), and characters (the strong warrior, the ambitious wife) into visual terms. Kurosawa's dominant method here is to depict the interrelationship and interpenetration of natural, supernatural, and psychological forces. At the beginning of the film, nature is "out of joint" — there is a violent wind and furious rainstorm. Lord Washizu (the Macbeth figure, played by Mifune) and his friend, Miki (Banquo), attempt to ride through a forest, which attacks them on every side with lightning, tortuous branches, and diverting bypaths. (Kurosawa's tracking shots again increase the impression of violence and fury.) The tangled, "breathing" forest is metaphoric of the internal maze in Washizu's mind as well as of the ensnaring temptations of the supernatural order, which is about to angle for his soul. This im-

prisoning forest in the film's early sequence is mirrored by the liberating forest in the late sequence when a moving, man-made forest (the forest's new "soul" is human, not superhuman) restores the balance of nature and purges the results of the initial human experience with a forest.

Another of Kurosawa's images linking man, nature, and the supernatural is fog: the misty white smoke of steamy clouds rising as if from beneath the earth. The fog is metaphoric of the universe's poisonous temptations as well as the moral fog in Washizu's mind. When Washizu first sees the Witch, she is sitting on the earth, seemingly rising out of the fog that blankets her legs and feet. And her skin is the same chalk white as that pestilential mist. And then Kurosawa makes a dazzling leap from the metaphysical to the psychological plane, for Lady Washizu (Lady Macbeth) has the same chalk-white skin, and she continually sits motionless — while she "argues" with her husband, while he performs the murder — in a position identical to that of the Witch. (In effect, Kurosawa has turned *Macbeth* into a cinematic Noh play. There is far less of the theatrical in *Ran*, his later adaptation of *King Lear*.) The Witch and Lady Washizu and the fog are deathly, white, and earthbound. While Washizu argues with his wife about their course of action, he continually stands up and paces about (the camera pacing with him) as he defends the selfless, humane position; but when he relents and accepts her arguments, he too sits down — earthbound, motionless. At the end of the film, when the wood comes to the castle to reclaim the initial debt of the forest, Washizu's own men shoot him full of wooden arrows, and he collapses to the earth, dying in a cloud of mist. He is now permanently bound to the earth and the fog.

The Lower Depths avoids such stunning natural images and uses, instead, the imagery of the human face and the social grouping. Rather than make a dazzling pictorial film, Kurosawa emphasizes the cramped dwelling that serves as the physical boundary and the shelter of a social microcosm. He also uses a broad depth of field, turning the film's primary visual principle into a contrasting series of planes of depth,

Fig. 14-24

Fig. 14-25

Consistent imagery in **Throne of Blood.** *Fig. 14-24: The witch sits blanketed by the mist of the forest;*
Fig. 14-25: the usurper collapses into the mist at the feet of the moving, human forest.

usually by basing his compositions on some variation of the receding triangle. (There are very few shots in which there is only a single being in the frame. Even in a character's most isolated moments there is a face or a body or two in the rearground.) *The Lower Depths* is a study of a social whole, and these triangulations in depth continually emphasize that the whole is inescapable and omnipresent.

In addition to this deliberate stylistic confinement, the film mirrors Kurosawa's vision of life as clearly as any. At its conclusion a group of characters erupts into an exuberant, rhythmic, vital dance — an absolutely compelling mixture of rhythmic sounds, physical movement, and film editing. At the same time, another character commits suicide. That juxtaposition is the Kurosawa statement, a point he greatly emphasizes, in comparison to the Gorky play, by inventing this dance. There is life and death, dance and suicide, elation and annihilation, but life and the dance go on.

Despite his own drinking and suicidal depressions, Kurosawa's work has also gone on. His late films — in splendid color — rework the concerns of his earlier ones. *Dodes'ka-den* (1970) is an expressionist color version of *The Lower Depths* — a cross section of social refuse with no objective reason to live, persisting nonetheless in the hope that life will be brighter. *Dersu Uzala* (1975), a Japanese-Soviet co-production, contrasts the committed and meaningful values of a hunter who dwells in the forests, living close to the land and its creatures, with the aimlessness of modern, indoor city-dwellers who have lost their contact not only with nature but with life itself. And *Kagemusha* (1980) is a return in color to the feudal world of *Seven Samurai* and *Yojimbo,* more critically dissecting the political inequities, class distinctions, and illusions of identity that supported this superficially chivalric society. The stylized dream sequences of *Kagemusha* and *Dodes'ka-den,* painted by Kurosawa himself, are among the most spectacular displays of brilliant color in the Japanese cinema. Five years after *Kagemusha, Ran,* Kurosawa's adaptation of *King Lear,* appeared to worldwide praise. In this version, Lear has three sons rather than daughters, and several of Shakespeare's characters are condensed and combined. Visually gorgeous and philosophically bleak, *Ran* was as pessimistic as *Lear* and as action-packed as *Seven Samurai.* And it made full use of the Dolby Stereo soundtrack, as have all of his films since *Dersu Uzala,* which was made in 70mm. *Akira Kurosawa's Dreams* (1990) is a series of sequences, each about ten minutes, that recreate dreams the director felt were the most significant ones in his life — often with the feeling of a real dream, sometimes with little more than artfulness. *Dreams* ends with a plea for ecological awareness; his next film, *Rhapsody in August* (1991), depicted the horrors of nuclear war.

Kenji Mizoguchi was a director of an earlier generation whose career came to its artistic culmination as Kurosawa's began to expand. Compared with Kurosawa, Mizoguchi employs a more consistent and single visual style, a more consistent theme and setting, and a much narrower range of emotion and tone. Mizoguchi specializes in period dramas, and his milieu is not simply the past but the past as seen in folk legends, fairy tales, plays, and paintings. Whereas Kurosawa saturates the past with modern realism and intellectual issues, Mizoguchi develops the distant mildness and stateliness of that past as well as some of its harsher realities. His primary attraction to the past is its apparent synthesis of art and nature — the way the natural life of the past has been frozen (and enshrined) by the art of the legend and the drawing. Many of Mizoguchi's central figures are themselves artists: the actress Taki no Shiraito in the 1933 silent film of the same name; the troupe of Kabuki players in *The Story of the Last Chrysanthemum* (1939); the artist Utamaro in *Utamaro and His Five Women* (1946); the potter in *Ugetsu* (1953). For Mizoguchi, the business of the artist is the conversion of life into the perfection and precision of art, and the business of the cinema is both the conversion of life into art and the reverse conversion of art (a folk tale, for example) into the "living" vitality of cinema. No clearer blending of the domains of art and nature exists than in the opening of *Ugetsu,* which begins with paintings of nature (under the titles) and dissolves into shots of nature.

In his photographic style Mizoguchi mirrors this art-as-nature-as-art synthesis, which is typical of Japanese aesthetics. Where Kurosawa often uses a traveling camera and deep focus, Mizoguchi uses a generally fixed camera (when it travels, it does so slowly and gracefully) and softer focus. Mizoguchi's shots of Japanese settings — fields, mountains, lakes (often shot by cinematographer Kazuo Miyagawa, who also shot *Rashomon*) — are much softer and flatter than Kurosawa's shots of nature, deliberately turning these natural settings into evocations of Japanese prints and paintings. Mizoguchi tends to use back- and side-lighting for these outdoor shots, not only softening them and reducing the depth of field but also giving them a hazy, limpid glow. Even in the moments of human agitation (for example, the sister's suicide in *Sansho the Bailiff*, 1954), nature remains soft, still, and quiet. The woman drowns herself in a placid pool of glassy water, framed by statuesque, motionless, and gauzy trees that watch but do not react (as opposed to Kurosawa's nature whose tumult mirrors human agitation). Like Akerman, Antonioni, Bergman, and Cukor, Mizoguchi is a great director of women, and many of his movies are centered around the lives, perceptions, and ordeals of women (*Sisters of the Gion*, 1936; *Women of the Night*, 1948, which so realistically revealed the lives of prostitutes that it affected legislation; *The Life of Oharu*, 1952; *Sansho the Bailiff*).

In his structure, Mizoguchi is also more classical than Kurosawa; Mizoguchi's major films are perfect examples of the Japanese sense of symmetry. Whereas Kurosawa's symmetry (in *Rashomon*, *Seven Samurai*, and *Throne of Blood* — but not in *High and Low*, 1963) is often blurred by the violence and energy of his action, Mizoguchi's stately pace emphasizes his structural purity (and symmetry is another of the ways that art resembles nature). Mizoguchi's primary structural device is the separation of the leading characters, each of them traveling different paths — quite literally, since the journey is essential to many Mizoguchi films. *Taki no Shiraito* traces the separate paths of the actress and the young law student until fate draws the paths together; *Utamaro* follows the artist's "journey" as well as that of each of his women; *Sansho* is a series of separations — father from wife and children, mother from children, son from daughter — and eventual reunions with both the living and dead. The symmetry of *Sansho* is so perfect that there are two fathers in the film (Sansho and Zushio's father), two sons (Taro and Zushio), two separations (the mother from Zushio and Anju; Zushio from Anju), two children (Zushio and Anju), two reunions with the living (Zushio with Taro and Zushio with his mother), and two reunions with the dead at their shrines (Zushio at his father's tomb and at the lake where Anju drowned).

Ugetsu is a perfect Mizoguchi film in structure, theme, visual style, and tone (and it ought to be, since he edited and co-wrote the movie as well as directed it, and thought about it for years before making it). There are four central characters — a potter and his wife, the potter's brother and his wife — each of whom travels a separate path and comes to a different end. The men, pursuing the false goals of money, fame, and lust, both discover the worthlessness of these goals, primarily because the wives — in many respects, the main characters — trod a road that led to their rape (one is murdered by soldiers, the other becomes a prostitute). Mizoguchi brings the film to life by the elegance of this symmetry and the magnificence of his visual technique, which dissolves nature into the mystical and concretizes the mystical into nature.

As the characters travel by boat on a misty lake to bring their goods to market (the potter is driven by his desire for riches), Mizoguchi converts the lake into a misty, ethereal Acheron; the thick fog converts the natural lake into an apparently supernatural netherworld. As opposed to Kurosawa's fog, which seethes, breathes, and floats, Mizoguchi's fog seems to sit and stifle. Out of this fog, the characters see a boat floating toward them, a mystical and eerie boat, seemingly floating on the fog itself. Inside the boat lies a chalk white, corpselike figure who looks like a ghost and is even taken for a ghost by the characters. No, he says, he is not a ghost but a man who has been beaten and robbed by pirates. He warns the characters against going further — especially because of the danger to the women. But the potter presses onward.

Not heeding this warning from a man who looks like a ghost, the potter comes face-to-face with ghosts who look like people. First, the potter falls under the spell of Lady Wakasa (Machiko Kyo), who tempts him by flattering his artistry and gains possession of his body by satisfying his sensuality. Their moments of sensual union are echoed by the diaphanous, shiny glow of nature in Mizoguchi's typically luminous cinematography. But Mizoguchi keeps his comment on the action clear by continually cross-cutting between the other characters on their "paths." While the potter falls under the dreamily sensual spell of Lady Wakasa, his wife is murdered by a group of soldiers on the road, his brother cheats his way into fulfilling his dreams of becoming a *samurai,* and his brother's wife is raped on the road by bandits.

The potter's diaphanous dream world collapses when he awakes one morning to discover that Lady Wakasa has been dead for years and that her house is a mere pile of ruins (Mizoguchi has this "morning after" discovery shot in a much harsher and brighter light than is usual for him). The potter, penniless and broken, returns home to join his wife (the usual Mizoguchi reunion after separation). Although his wife greets him, he discovers the next morning from his neighbors that she has been killed and that he has spent the night with yet another ghost (a second "morning after" discovery—and a clear example of the Mizoguchi symmetry). He decides to devote his life to honoring his wife's grave (just as the son honors the graves of his sister and father in *Sansho*), and the spirit of his wife returns to him again—this time as an incorporeal voice. She tells him that her spirit will remain perpetually beside him (a beneficent supernatural presence, in contrast to the deleterious Lady Wakasa) and that he should return to his pottery. Both the potter and the brother renounce their false ambitions and return to the normal cycles of their lives. (The warrior brother's renunciation was insisted upon by the studio; Mizoguchi considered it out of character.)

Mizoguchi's moral system is more conventional than Kurosawa's. He advocates the usual humanistic virtues of love, fidelity, and selfless-

Fig. 14-26

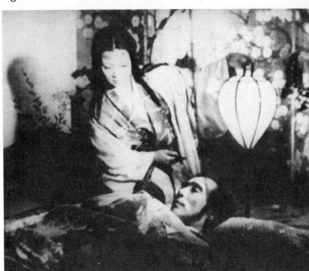

Fig. 14-27

Ugetsu. *Fig. 14-26: Mizoguchi's elegantly balanced composition as the potter enjoys a picnic with a ghost; Fig. 14-27: the physical concreteness of ghostly confrontation—Lady Wakasa (Machiko Kyo) and the potter (Masayuki Mori).*

ness as opposed to the selfish drives of lust, power, and money, but he mixes these values with the traditional Japanese virtues of patience, honor, self-control, humility, and resignation.

Yasujiro Ozu, Mizoguchi's contemporary, is the master of the *shomin-geki*—the modern-day, middle-class comedy. Ozu's primary subjects are the surfaces, forms, rituals, and processes of middle-class life itself. His films are dominated by scenes of conversing and eating, both at home and in restaurants; scenes at the office; scenes of men drinking together in bars. They are films about the central social processes: work, marriage, family life, friendship. And they are films that mirror the modernization of Japanese life: television sets, neon lights, modern architecture, furniture, and offices. The women gossip, the men play golf, and the children both go to school and watch television.

As a stylist Ozu is a real oddity, in many ways challenging most of the West's cinema theory. It is probably not unfair to say that of all the world's highly respected directors in the entire history of film, there is none more visually spare than Ozu. He abjures the visual conventions of Western cinema—traveling shots, rapid montage, movement within the shot, dissolves, fades, even the boundary of the 180° line, whose crossing within a Hollywood scene is thought to confuse the viewer. And all his pictures are alike, so that it is almost impossible to tell one from the other. In truth, the titles of many of Ozu's films are so similar that they are hard to keep straight (*Late Spring*, 1949; *Early Spring*, 1956; *Late Autumn*, 1960—a color remake of *Late Spring*; *End of Summer*, 1961; *An Autumn Afternoon*, 1962). In truth, their subjects are similar—parents and children; whether, when, and whom to marry—and the actors recur from one film to another (as in the work of Griffith or Bergman). In truth, all of them have a similar tone: a subtly understated pathos and comedy that play against one another in delicate counterpoint. And their endings are more likely to be wistful and complexly balanced than simply "happy"; virtually all of them share an attitude or tone the Japanese call *mono no aware:* a wistful acceptance of the way things are, a kind of satis-

Fig. 14-28

Fig. 14-29
Late Autumn: *the modern domestic world of Ozu—women in the home, men at the bar.*

faction at the changes—and the deaths and losses—that life brings to all of us in its course.

There is perhaps a higher percentage of talk in an Ozu film than in anybody else's ever—but there are also moments of contemplation and silence. Sometimes the camera will hold for as long as ten seconds on a room the characters have left. If these talky family melo-dramas and comedies are "soaps"—as some Ozu-bashers have suggested—they are the kind of soaps made by Dreyer (*Day of Wrath*, *Gertrud*) and Antonioni (*La notte*, *Eclipse*); Ozu's style is as spare, rigorous, and subtly flexible as Bresson's. The color is unspectacular; the editing is functional; the camera rarely moves (when it does move, the shot is momentous). The camera is often confined to a low eye level —as if it were the view of someone sitting on the floor in a Japanese house—but even if it has been invited, so to speak, to sit at the family table, it remains neutral, an impersonal but not unkind observer.

Ozu's strengths are structural and psycho-logical as well as visual. Like Kurosawa and Mizoguchi, Ozu inevitably uses the multiple human focus, examining parallel actions, reac-tions, and choices in the lives of different peo-ple. Unlike Kurosawa and Mizoguchi, Ozu tends toward parallelism, the similarity of re-sponses that play against one another contra-puntally, rather than contrast; unlike Kurosawa's multiple points of view in *Rashomon* and Mizoguchi's multiple paths in *Ugetsu*, Ozu builds his films as very subtle variations on a single issue—say, getting married—revealing the attitudes of old and young, married and single, parents and children, widowers and ad-olescents toward the central issue. Ozu is the master of counterpoint; in his purity, delicacy and deceptive complexity, he is a kind of J. S. Bach of cinema. An inevitable Ozu effect is that just at that point when one wonders if anything is going to happen and if the film is going any-where (some forty-five minutes into it), the film's structure, idea, warmth, subtlety, and charm grab hold of the viewer and refuse to let go until the end.

Ozu's *Ohayo* (*Good Morning*, 1959), which is not one of his "seasonal" studies of marriage, is a good example of his method and concerns. The film's subject is etiquette, the formal pleasantries of life (like saying "Good Morn-ing") that enable human beings to live together. The film reveals the social tensions of life— women's gossip, the suspicion of a neighbor's dishonesty, the fear of being snubbed—and demonstrates that the social niceties are truly necessities for easing these tensions. At the center of the film are two children (Ozu has always liked the world of children, beginning with his first silent triumph, *I Was Born But . . .* , 1932). The two boys want their fa-ther to buy them a television set; when he refuses they get angry and he tells them that they talk too much. The oldest boy says that adults talk too much, too, that they say useless things like "Good Morning." And so the two boys refuse to talk altogether, throwing the neighbors, their teachers, their friends, and their own family into confusion. Ozu comically and deftly shows that the "useless" amenities of life are extremely useful for keeping society at peace. Ironically, the boys have their own social ritual—a marvelous little amenity in which they have developed the ability to fart automatically when they are pushed on the forehead. To the boys that is a useful ritual, while to say "Good Morning" is useless. Ozu, without any specific comment and over-emphasis, reveals how necessary all our social rituals are—including a father's giving in to his kids and buying them a TV. From such a film one can see that Ozu's true subject is the extra-ordinary ordinary and the interesting boring.

Ozu's masterpiece, *Tokyo Story* (1953), is a film about ordinary life that must be called extraordinary. It tells of an elderly couple— Shukichi, the father, played by Chishu Ryu, and Tomi, the mother, played by Chieko Higashiyama—who take their first trip to the big city to visit their children. Shortly after their arrival in Tokyo, it becomes clear that the son and daughter are far more interested in their own problems than in devoting respectful, loving attention to their parents. (In this film, unlike *Good Morning* but like the later novels of Henry James, the amenities reveal and conceal matters of the greatest emotional seriousness; watching it, one flinches at a disrespectful line or tone.) Only Noriko (Setsuko Hara), the widow of their second son, is genuinely glad to see them, spends time talking with them, and sincerely extends them the proper hospitality. In the loud, fast world of the town, Noriko is a rarity; much of the film concerns the differ-ences between old and modern ways as well as between small town and big city living *and* be-tween generations, and all these themes become especially clear, both intellectually and emotionally, in the scenes with Noriko and her parents-in-law.

The son and daughter send their parents to a resort—obviously to get rid of them, but supposedly because the old couple will enjoy themselves more there. The mother's strength, which has been failing, takes a turn for the worse, and shortly after they reach home, she dies. Now it is the children and in-laws' turn to travel from Tokyo to the small town (a good example of symmetry in Ozu's work); they pay their respects, but leave soon enough. Noriko stays longer, to comfort the father and keep him company, but he tells her that he is content to be alone. His acceptance of life and the solitude to which it has brought him—*mono no aware*—is beautiful, profound, and unforgettably moving.

After Kurosawa, Mizoguchi, and Ozu, Kon Ichikawa is among the most interesting directors of that generation. Ichikawa's primary distinction is in the intensity and savagery of his ideological argument, which openly criticizes political, social, and personal corruption as it examines the depravity and degeneration of the human animal. Ichikawa's first noted film, *The Burmese Harp* (1956), is one of his milder studies: the examination of a soldier in Burma in the final days of the Second World War who first disguises himself as a priest in order to survive and then becomes a true convert to the priestly values, primarily as a result of the war horrors he has seen (and Ichikawa's camera occasionally has shown). But his *Fires on the Plain* (1959), which has been called the most powerful antiwar film ever made in Japan, concentrates exclusively on the horrors of the final days of the war, on a man's determination to survive (although he is ill with consumption), even if it means murdering and eating other human beings to stay alive. Ichikawa's *Odd Obsession* (*The Key*, 1959) is set in the Ozu environment of the middle-class and lower-middle-class family, but this family occupies itself with bizarre sexual games that eventually destroy all the players.

Mikio Naruse, a contemporary of Ozu, also begins within the same *shomin-geki* world. As opposed to Ichikawa's brutal dissection of its perversities, Naruse's pessimistic bourgeois melodramas (*Floating Clouds*, 1955; *As a Wife*,

Fig. 14-30
Tokyo Story: *Noriko (center) extends her hospitality to her parents-in-law; from left, Chishu Ryu, Setsuko Hara, and Chieko Higashiyama. Note the position of the camera.*

As a Woman, 1961; *Yearning*, 1963) observe postwar white-collar workers trapped by modern life—stifling marriages, boring jobs, and inadequate salaries—for whom adultery and theft promise escape but lead to ruin. Like Mizoguchi, Naruse takes women seriously and portrays their situation under patriarchy with brilliance and conviction (*When a Woman Ascends the Stairs, Flowing Night, Autumn is Beginning,* and *Mother, Wife, Daughter*—all 1960).

Kinugasa's *Gate of Hell* and Inagaki's *Samurai* (both 1953) were two of Japan's first color films and are visually magnificent in their application of splendid color photography to the *jidai-geki*. Inagaki went on to make a color, wide-screen version of the Legend of the Loyal 47 Ronin (a favorite subject of the Japanese drama and of many films), the 1962 *Chushingura*. Hiroshi Teshigahara's *Woman in the Dunes* (1964) is remarkable for its minute, tactile examination of a change of heart. A man from a modern city on vacation in the dunes is imprisoned by the people who live there, forced to serve as the husband of a woman who lost her previous one. He begins by resisting this imprisonment, trying to escape, loathing the pervasive and omnipotent sand that seeps into his hair, clothes, food, bed, and soul. Only when he ceases to fight the sand and decides instead to study its laws and work with it (he calculates a way to distill precious, life-giving water from the sand) does his prison suddenly become a home. He discovers that sand is certainly no worse a physical environment than the sterile technological society from which he came.

Masaki Kobayashi's first great work was the nine-hour trilogy *The Human Condition* (1958–61), a wide-screen epic, in black-and-white, about the treatment Manchuria received at the hands of the Japanese during World War II and the efforts of a man to escape a prison camp (he drowns a particularly oppressive guard in a vat of excrement) and walk home. The greatest of his later films are *Harakiri* (1962)—which simultaneously resembles the work of Orson Welles, Alain Resnais, and Peter Watkins with its story, told through flashbacks, of an atrocity and a revenge that are both covered up—and *Kwaidan* (1964), a wide-screen, expressionist color anthology of extremely effective ghost stories adapted from the writings of Lafcadio Hearn.

The Japanese film industry, like the industries of the West, underwent severe commercial changes in the decade following 1950. The Japanese discovered that many of their cheaper and exploitative productions—monster pictures (*Godzilla, Rodan*), invasions from outer space (*The Mysterians*)—could make money abroad. And so Japan was continually invaded by prehistoric monsters or visitors from another planet who stomped or incinerated models of Japan's major cities before they were repulsed by some new weapon or by each other. As the Japanese bought (and manufactured) more and more television sets, Japanese film attendance dropped. The Japanese film industry had learned from the West, however, that this was one monster that could not be repulsed. The Japanese studios began production for television from the start—and even began operating television stations themselves. Then they invented the VCR. . .

Of the younger generation of directors, Nagisa Oshima, who mixes radical film techniques, radical politics, and a radical sexuality, is among the most promising. Like the films of Godard, *The Man Who Left His Will on Film* (1970) is both a deconstruction of film imagery and a disquisition on the making of film images. *Death by Hanging* (1968) is a Brechtian attack on easy definitions of both social crime and personal identity in bourgeois society. *Cruel Stories of Youth* (1960) links big business and big crime. *Boy* (1968) is the dispassionate story of a boy whose parents have trained him to get hit by cars so that they can extort money from the drivers. *In the Realm of the Senses* (1976), a Japanese–French co-production, falls among several genres—the pornographic film in its explicit sensuality, the feminist critique of sexist values and male dominance, and the romantic pursuit of an imperishably perfect love. *Merry Christmas, Mr. Lawrence* (1983) contrasts the values of British prisoners and their Japanese captors in a war camp, with strong undercurrents of homosexuality and an attack on the parallel class distinctions within Eastern and Western societies that transcend the wars between nations. This Japanese–British co-production, drastically cut before its American release, featured British stars Tom Conti and David Bowie. The film suggests that Oshima, more like Kurosawa than Mizoguchi or Ozu, deliberately seeks audiences and influences beyond his native Japan.

Shohei Imamura seems a descendant of both Ozu, for whom he worked, and Godard, whom he admires. Called the "cultural anthropologist" of modern Japanese cinema, Imamura's films (*The Pornographers*, 1966; *A Man Vanishes*, 1967; *Vengeance Is Mine*, 1979; *The Ballad of Narayama*, 1983) deliberately mix fictional and documentary styles, dissecting primitive Japanese societies that either resist or suffer modernization.

Although there are still other notable young Japanese directors—Kinji Fukasaku, Yoji Yamada, Kohei Oguri, Hiroto Yakoyama, Mitsuo Yanagimachi—the overall quality of Japanese film production has declined since the late 1960s. The studios are less willing than they were in the past to finance art films—which might not break even, let alone make profits—but have turned out hundreds of features each year in the popular genres of light comedy, soft-core pornography, *yakuza*, and animal adventure (two abandoned dogs work their way across Antarctica), along with the usual monster and youth films. Late in the 1980s, having cornered the world market on televisions and video equipment, the Japanese reached out to acquire several American studios in order to have more films, of demonstrated quality, to own, license, and duplicate for playback on all those machines. The hottest Japanese film of the 1980s was the superbly animated *Akira* (1988), directed by Katsuhiro Otomo from his multi-volume comic book (or graphic novel) of the same name. A metaphysical epic about bikers and orphans with superhuman powers, set in "Neo-Tokyo" three decades after World War III, *Akira* makes electrifying use of the wide screen, the resources of computer animation, and more than two hundred colors.

The West discovered the Indian cinema much as it did the Japanese. Satyajit Ray's *Pather Panchali* (*Song of the Road,* 1955) won a special prize at the 1956 Cannes Film Festival, and his next film, *Aparajito* (*The Unvanquished,* 1956) won the Golden Lion Award at Venice the following year. *The World of Apu* (*Apur Sansar,* 1959) completed the trilogy. Unlike the Japanese cinema, Indian cinema offered no rich unknown cache of artistry. Not that the Indian film industry was not prolific: India produced some three hundred feature films in 1958, second only to Japan (but ahead of America) in the quantity of feature production. In the 1970s, India became the world leader in the number of feature films produced each year. In the 1980s, India remained the world's largest film producer, releasing an average of two films a day (one-fifth of all the features made worldwide). But several causes—unique both to Indian society and to its film industry—keep quantity up and quality down, generally confining distribution for many Indian films to local markets. (It should be noted, however, that some of the most formulaic, mass-market Indian films are exported to more than one hundred nations—primarily in the Third World—where they have long proved extremely popular.)

First, India is a vast nation of over eight hundred million people, and movies remain the only form of popular entertainment accessible to the masses. Although the videocassette industry is very much on the rise, there are still relatively few television sets in India per capita. The pressure on the studios to provide film after entertaining film for a huge, uneducated audience has led to a consistent mediocrity, a devotion to formula and convention, and a fear of experimentation. The dominant narrative formula calls for a lengthy love story, many problems standing in the way of the lovers' happiness (he might be from the wrong caste, she might be kidnapped by gangsters . . .), endless musical numbers, a great deal of violence, a happy ending in which all problems are resolved, and three hours of footage.

Second, and even more difficult for the film industry, India is a nation without a common language. There are over a dozen Indian languages, not counting dialects—every one of them a mystery to the speakers of the others—the most common of which are Hindi, Urdu, Bengali, Telegu, Marathi, and Tamil. This language barrier caused little difficulty in the silent era. The Indian silent film industry, effectively established in 1913 by the magical, mythological films of Dadasaheb Phalke and developed by pioneers such as Dhiren Ganguly, Debaki Bose, and Chandulal Shah, may well have been more artistically advanced than the silent Japanese cinema. But the coming of sound, which liberated the Japanese cinema from the *benshi,* imprisoned the Indian cinema in the Tower of Babel.

Most films for the all-India market are now made in Hindi in the commercial film capital, Bombay. In Madras and elsewhere, many films —some more mainstream than others— are made in regional languages for regional and, in rare cases, international distribution. The art film, or "alternative cinema," has flourished in Bombay and elsewhere and runs "parallel" to the commercial film establishment, never touching it. This New Indian Cinema produces work of considerably greater interest than the Hindi popular melodramas, finds little distribution in India, and acknowledges the inspiring example of Ray (most of whose films are shot in Bengali, adopt a lyrical-realist aesthetic, and have found a worldwide audience).

Third, the Indian cinema has been subject to ruthless government intervention and censorship. Under the British, themes of independence were forbidden; under the government of free India, "decadent" Western influences were forbidden. Kissing scenes appeared only in the 1970s. In addition to limiting its artistic freedom, the Indian government taxes the film industry heavily; its huge audiences provide handsome revenues, even with the low ticket prices. Further, the government levied severe import quotas that restricted the supply of raw film stock. Even more ironic, an Indian print that had been shown abroad was subject to duty as an "imported" film upon returning home. If the government restricted the movement of commercial films, it encouraged alternative production by financing personal films. Satyajit Ray's first films—as well as those of Mrinal Sen, Shyam Benegal, and Aparna Sen—were supported by the Indian government.

Fourth, the Indian film industry itself is a victim of corrupt profiteering practices. Independent producers who want to make a quick killing, rather than established film companies, are the rule. In the 1930s, however, India's studios were more solid organizations; the most famous of them, Bombay Talkies, was a co-operative familial studio—modeled on Germany's Ufa, where Bombay Talkies' married owners, Himansu Rai and Devika Rani, had worked. But the independent speculator, who usually did not have enough money to complete a film once it was started and therefore needed to beg, borrow, deal, and swindle more as the shooting went along, came to dominate the industry in the 1940s.

The speculator could get that money only because, fifth, the Indian film industry has been totally dominated by the star system since the familial studios collapsed in the 1940s. And it has been a star system with a vengeance, making the power and salaries of the Hollywood luminaries look puny. Because only a producer with a major star could get the money to finish a film, stars became so popular and enjoyed such power—even political clout—that they commanded immense salaries (at least half of it paid under the table in untaxable "black money") and might work on as many as two dozen films at once, dropping in periodically on each of the production units as the star's schedule and inclinations permitted. Music was

the supporting "star" of an Indian film (the music director is the second highest paid position in the Indian film industry); for decades, of the hundreds of films shot each year in India, there was *not one* without singing and dancing. The Indian film became so conventional that its foremost historians (Barnouw and Krishnaswamy) described the formula succinctly as "A star, six songs, and three dances." These formulaic Hindi films are called *masala* films; "masala" means a mixture of spices, and the sense of the term is that these films consist of a number of standard ingredients in combinations that vary only slightly from film to film—as if one were adding a little more garlic to a successful recipe or substituting turmeric (pirates) for fenugreek (gangsters).

To such assumptions and conventions Satyajit Ray was, and remains, a stranger. His father was a friend of Rabindranath Tagore, the greatest Indian poet of the twentieth century. Well read in Indian literature and philosophy, Ray studied painting after receiving a degree in economics. But Ray was also a *cinéaste*; with Chidananda Das Gupta, Ray was co-founder of the first film society in India, the Calcutta Film Society, in 1947. So one might see Ray as uniting the traditions of Indian culture, painting, and music with those of Western cinema. The meeting of Western and Indian values is one of his recurring subjects. The influence of Western films is unmistakable in Ray's films, particularly Italian neorealism and the graceful structure of the classical French cinema of the 1930s—though when he was a young man, he preferred Hollywood movies. Ray was particularly influenced by observing Jean Renoir make *The River* in Calcutta in 1949–50, when he spoke frequently with the classical French director. Although Ray is a Bengali, his outlook is international.

In the Indian cinematic tradition, the two dominant genres are "socials" and "mythologicals." The mythologicals, as the name suggests, use the cinema to bring to life the traditional tales and settings of Indian folklore, ancient literature, and myth. The socials, or contemporary melodramas, address social problems but use them primarily as plot complications. In the most general sense, Ray's films could be classified as socials. Though he is not hostile to the mythologicals and once hoped to make one, he does poke gentle fun at the genre in the film-within-a-film sequence of *The World of Apu,* which parodies a mythological whose hokum is undiluted by reality but also shows the audience's intense devotion to the movie. Ray avoided the majority of Indian film traditions, from the sentimentality of the conventional socials to the conventions of the studio system — in other words, not just how films were conceived but how they were produced. *Pather Panchali,* which he was inspired to begin after seeing *Bicycle Thieves* in London, had no star (in the manner of the Soviets, Italians, and Czechs, Ray even used some nonprofessional actors), no songs and dances (although there was a terrific instrumental score by Ravi Shankar), a cinematographer who had never shot a motion picture before (the still photographer Subrata Mitra), and was shot on location (Indian films were exclusively studio films, even for outdoor scenes, a choice that aided their flight from reality and linked them with the stylized conventions of Indian theatre). Ray's film wanted to have as much to do with reality as possible.

Ray's Apu trilogy (*Pather Panchali, Aparajito,* and *The World of Apu*), adapted from two mammoth novels by Bibhutibhusan Banerjee (*Pather Panchali,* which covers the first film, and *Aparajito,* which covers the last two), employs a complex, carefully conceived structure that is apparent in the unity of the individual films as well as in the overall conception of the trilogy. The subject of the trilogy is the growth of a young Indian boy (Apu) from his peasant, rural youth to a mature and educated adulthood in the city — an Indian *Bildungsroman.* The three films devote themselves to childhood, adolescence, and adulthood, respectively. In all three films, deaths play a pivotal role in the boy's growth and development: the death of the old aunt and his sister in *Pather Panchali;* the death of his father and mother in *Aparajito;* the death of his wife (the hardest one for him to accept) in *The World of Apu.* In counterpoint to these deaths, all three films end identically: Apu is on the road ("Pather Panchali" means "Song of the Road"), moving from the country to the city, implying the continuity of life and growth.

At the end of *Pather Panchali,* the remains of the family leave their village to try to live better in the city (Benares). At the end of *Aparajito,* Apu pulls himself together after the death of his mother and takes the path back to the city (Calcutta) and the university. At the end of *The World of Apu,* Apu is back on the road, returning to Calcutta again, his son on his back. For Apu, it is also his most explicit return to life, on which he had turned his back after the death of his wife. A sign of the complexity and precision of Ray's structural conception is that at the end of this final installment Apu's young son is almost exactly the same age as the child Apu in the first one, living a similar life (unfettered but fatherless), now on his way to the city with a newly returned father. The song of the road has come full circle.

Ray's themes and concerns are clear in the trilogy. First, there is his sympathetic and microscopic examination of the points of view of all the major characters. Although much of *Pather Panchali* gives the child's-eye view of life (and death), the mother's view of that struggle also gets Ray's careful attention. She often seems cross and vicious, but she has the heavy responsibility of keeping the family together and alive with her husband not only penniless but absent. In *Aparajito* the same (but older) mother is caught between her selfish need to keep her son with her and her selfless desire to see him do well in life; the boy is caught between his attachment to his mother and his ambition to succeed and to study. Ray's films excel in the many-sidedness of these human portraits.

Perhaps Ray's essential theme, however, is his ultimate commitment to life, to human exertion, and to the cycles of nature of which man is a small and uncomprehending part. Ray's films are acutely aware that life is often painful, that people can be petty, that sorrow is inescapable and death inevitable, and that nature is an ever-present mystery.

Ray's dominant technique for rendering the human feelings that are so central to his films may be described as the prolonged reaction shot: a device that he uses constantly. Ray's concern is not human action but the essential moment of human reaction to an event of great personal significance; the prolonged moment

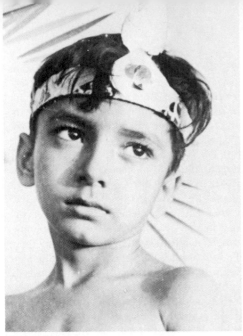

Fig. 14-31

Pather Panchali: *the worlds of youth and age. The young Apu (Subir Banerji) and the old aunt (Chunibala Devi).*

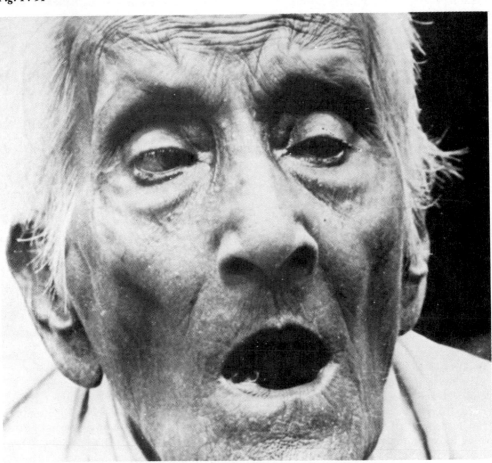

Fig. 14-32

of reaction serves as the culmination and ultimate definition of that significance. Ray leaves his camera riveted on the person's face, a face that usually remains as motionless as his or her body, and the camera simply continues watching.

These reaction shots, so still and yet so long, convert a totally external objectivity into a truly internal experience for both the character and the audience. One of the best (of many possible) examples is the painful moment of parting between mother and son in *Aparajito* as he goes off to the city, to the university, and, in effect, to his own life. Ray's camera holds on her face and body; she stands still in the dusty arch of a doorway that seems to frame and to fix her forever, watching his back recede down the village path. She stands there, and stands — her feelings of loss flickering beneath the surface of her placid face, locked into the doorway of her own now empty life. It is *the* moment of separation.

Another of Ray's tools is his masterful visual imagery, often charged with symbolic connotations. In *Pather Panchali* there is the magnificent sequence of the mother's nighttime vigil beside the bed of her feverish daughter. Outside the house a storm rages, sending gusts of wind through the cracks, trying to blow out the little candle of light at the bedside. The storm personifies the attack of nature and death on the household, and the mother, in trying to save her daughter, is in effect trying to bar those forces from her shaky home. Nature and death win, however, as a gust slips through to extinguish the candle. Another haunting and symbolic image from the same film is the magnificent shot of a speeding train, powerfully slicing through fields of flowering grasses, leaving behind its trail of floating smoke. With the train, awesomely depicted as the child Apu perceives the magical monster, Ray juxtaposes the old and new worlds (one of his constant themes): the adult, modern world outside the little village and the little world of the child. (Apu's globe of the world in *Aparajito* serves a similar symbolic function, but Apu is then old enough to understand the relationship between region and world.) Trains play an increasingly important role in Apu's life, carrying him from city to village and back to the city again, and

Fig. 14-33
The child's-eye view of the train, slicing through fields of kaash flowers in Pather Panchali.

so the wondrous image of his boyhood becomes a commonplace method of transportation in his adulthood.

Ray's other films are equally interesting in their careful views of Indian life and are often quite as effective. In *The Music Room* (1958) Ray examines the collapse of the old India — its traditions and its art — and the rise of the new bourgeoisie. *Devi* (*The Goddess*, 1960) is also a clash of old and new, a study of the old religious prejudices and fanaticism that can destroy happiness. *Mahanagar* (*The Big City*, 1963) examines family life in the new Calcutta, particularly the new status of women. *Three Daughters* (1961, released abroad in a shortened version, *Two Daughters*) and *Charulata* (1964) are both based on stories by Tagore; the latter is as much about the late nineteenth-century impact of British ideas on Bengali intellectuals as it is an insightful exploration of a love triangle. *Kanchanjungha* (1962), his first color film, is socially and psychologically observant, precise and powerful in its evocations, and tightly constructed; it tells of the problems and frustrations of the members of a wealthy family on vacation in Darjeeling and how they and other characters rebel against the aristocratic, authoritarian father—and, implicitly, the patriarchy he represents. *Days and Nights in the Forest* (1970) seems to combine the complex, subtle insightfulness of Chekhov with Mozart's elegant sense of variation and play. *The Chess Players* (1977), Ray's first film in Urdu rather than Bengali, is the chilling-amusing story of two men who concentrate so much on the chess games they play with each other that they do not notice—or pretend to be above—how the political world is playing games with *them*. All of these films are memorable for their careful and sensitive development of human relationships, their social analysis, their music (often by Ray), their resonant visual imagery, and their subtle philosophical psychology. Their setups are long, but their payoffs are intellectually and emotionally moving.

In 1983, Ray suffered a heart attack while shooting *The Home and the World* (1984); it was finished by his son. Ray spent several years recuperating, then directed *Ganashatru* (1989, an adaptation of Ibsen's *An Enemy of the People*) and *Shakha Proshakha* (*Family Meeting*, 1990).

But Ray's are not the only non-mainstream films made in India. One of his most significant contemporaries, in many ways his opposite (loud sound effects, jarring editing, a ruthless vision of the interconnected evils of the world), was Ritwik Ghatak, whose masterpiece is *Meghe Dhaka Tara* (*The Cloud-Capped Star* or *The Hidden Star*, 1960); he followed that with *Komal Gandhar* (*E Flat*, 1961), *Subarnarekha* (1962), and *Jukti Takko ar Gappo* (*Reason, Debate, and a Tale*, 1974), then drank himself to death. Ray's other great contemporary, Mrinal Sen, is a Marxist whose denunciations of the exploitation of the poor (*Akaler Sandhaney/In Search of Famine*, 1980) and of women (*Ek Din Pratidin / And Quiet Rolls the Day*, 1979), and whose attacks on middle-class hypocrisy (*Khandhar/The Ruins*, 1983) have found an international audience. Sen is a major Third World filmmaker, influenced by Godard (*Calcutta '71*, 1972) and an influence on the many new *auteurs* who have found the political content of his works inspiring. A younger filmmaker of special interest is Adoor Gopalakrishnan, the director of *Elippathayam* (*The Rat Trap*, 1981) and *Mukhamukham* (*Face to Face*, 1984).

A significant movement, the New Cinema, began in the late 1960s. As mentioned before, this parallel or alternative cinema is completely distinct from the artificial worlds of the Hindi romances and violent adventures—whose color and camerawork are flashy, whose sets range from the studio-realistic to the theatrical and fantastic, and whose heroes spring up from vicious beatings as free from permanent damage as the heroes of cartoons. The New Cinema examines social problems (often from a Marxist perspective), prefers to shoot on location, seeks to create a neorealism for the expression of Indian reality, rejects formulaic narrative structures, uses the camera subtly and effectively, occasionally uses Brechtian and reflexive devices, and promotes the concept and creative authority of the *auteur*. None of these notions has any place in Bombay's mainstream industry.

The New Cinema began with Mrinal Sen's *Bhuvan Shome* (*Mr. Shome*, 1969), an irreverent comedy that had been financed by a loan from the government's Film Finance Corporation (FFC). When *Bhuvan Shome* proved to be a critical and popular success, the FFC made more money available for quality, low-budget films, much as the French government helped to finance the New Wave. The key *auteurs* fall into two groups, those in Bombay and those in the south of India. In Bombay: Shyam Benegal (*Ankur/The Seedling*, 1974; *Manthan/The Churning*, 1976), Mani Kaul (*Duvidha/In Two Minds*, 1973), Ketan Mehta (*Mirch Masala/ Spices*, 1986), Govind Nihalani (*Aakrosh/Cry of the Wounded*, 1980; *Ardhsatya/Half Truth*, 1983), and Kumar Shahani (*Tarang/The Wave*, 1984). In the south: Malayali G.Aravindan (*Chidambaram*, 1985), Adoor Gopalakrishnan (see above), Girish Karnad (*Kaadu/The Forest*, 1973), Girish Kasaravalli (*Ghatashraddha/The Ritual*, 1977), and Pattabhi Rama Reddy (*Samskara/Funeral Rites*, 1970).

Although few Indian films other than those of Ray have been widely seen outside India, many Western films have been shot there. India was both the visual setting and primary metaphor of Renoir's *The River* and Lean's *A Passage to India*. Roberto Rossellini (*India*, 1958) and Louis Malle (*Phantom India*, 1969) made careful documentary studies of Indian

Fig. 14-34
Salaam Bombay! After working hard at a wedding, Krishna (Shafiq Syed, second from left), Manju (Hansa Vithal, right), and their friends are paid practically nothing but allowed to eat their fill.

life and culture, both commissioned by European television. An American director, James Ivory, and his Indian partner, producer Ismail Merchant, began their career with Calcutta films (*Shakespeare Wallah*, 1965; *Bombay Talkie*, 1970), heavily influenced by the films of Satyajit Ray, only to switch loyalties to the novels of Henry James (*The Europeans*, 1979; *The Bostonians*, 1984) and E. M. Forster (*A Room with a View*, 1985; *Maurice*, 1987); most of their later films have been British or American productions.

The New Cinema has brought new opportunities for women directors. Aparna Sen was already a famous actress when she began directing. Her best known film may be *36 Chowringhee Lane* (1981), the perceptive, understated, carefully detailed story of an

Anglo-Indian schoolteacher (played by Jennifer Kendal) who must come to terms with loneliness and old age. Sen's *Parama* (1985) examines women's changing roles in India and takes a feminist look at the problem of adultery. Mira Nair's first feature, *Salaam Bombay!* (1988), which is "Dedicated to the children on the streets of Bombay" and whose profits have funded shelters for homeless children, is the story of a nice, honest, trusting, soft-spoken boy (Krishna, played by Shafiq Syed) who tries, while making a living on the street at menial jobs, to save enough money to go home to his family and village. Like the homeless kids in *The 400 Blows* and *Shoeshine*, Krishna and his friends endure rough times until they are taken under the care of the social services, which make things worse. After his money has been stolen, his girlfriend (Manju, played by Hansa Vithal) has been made a ward of the state, and he has knifed a pimp (Manju's father), Krishna ends up alone on the street. First he cries; then his cold, hurt look turns to hatred. He has come to a different kind of fixity—more realistic and in many ways more chilling—than the freeze-framed hero of *The 400 Blows*: His attitudes and destiny are set.

Japan and India are by no means the only film-producing nations across the Pacific. The People's Republic of China, founded in 1949, has for the most part encouraged film production. Between 1949 and the beginning of the Cultural Revolution (1966–1976), the state abolished commercial filmmaking and then nationalized and completely subsidized the industry, ten major studios were built, and the number of theatres increased from 646 to 20,363. As in the Soviet Union, the films' essential task was to communicate the ideals of the revolution to a huge and far-flung population; not surprisingly, the best Chinese films have been works of art as well as of propaganda. Zheng Junli's *Lin Zexu* (1959), for example, told a patriotic war story *and* attempted to find visual equivalents for the subtle tropes of Chinese poetry. During the Cultural Revolution censorship was at its most formidable, many filmmakers were sent away from the cities and studios to learn from the peasants, and very few pictures were made. By 1978, however, the "rehabilitated" filmmakers were back at work, determined to make artistic movies, and they encountered no government opposition. In the early 1980s the studios were given the responsibility of planning their own budgets, working with only partial government financing, and raising the rest of their production money at the box office. In 1983 an astounding 27 billion movie tickets were sold. In 1984 Wu Tianming's *Life* portrayed both peasants and intellectuals as good characters. Things were opening up.

The first major work of "the fifth generation"—a group of younger directors—appeared in 1985: Chen Kaige's *Yellow Earth,* a magnificently photographed, complexly constructed drama about a Maoist who goes to a remote, feudal village to learn folk songs that he can adapt for use by the army; the effect he

and the villagers have on each other; and a girl who must choose between going through with an arranged marriage (the old ways of the peasants, which—as most Chinese films emphasize—tend to oppress women) and leaving the village and her world to join the army, for which she would very much like to write inspiring songs. As so many Chinese films do, *Yellow Earth* dramatizes the confrontation of new and old ways, presenting the Red Army representative as the bringer of new information and attitudes ("Men can sew," says the amazed heroine of *Yellow Earth* when the Maoist takes up needle and thread), but its deep sense of character goes well beyond the simple, allegorical role assignment (you be Capital, you be Labor) typical of propaganda.

Wu Tianming, who headed the Xi'an studio for most of the 1980s and helped to make it the center of fifth-generation filmmaking during the short-lived Chinese New Wave, directed *Old Well* in 1987, a film that not only told the story of a Party member with a better idea for a well and a village woman who cuts her ties to the dowry system, but also made extraordinary use of the only true Technicolor lab in the world, which happens to be in China. (In the West, Technicolor laboratories have processed only Eastmancolor stock or its equivalent since the mid-1970s; the last American film shot in Technicolor and imbibition printed was Coppola's *The Godfather Part II,* 1974.) The colors in *Old Well* and in Zhang Yimou's *Red Sorghum* (1988) are intense beyond words.

Red Sorghum has an additional level of intensity, however: outright exuberance. Although like virtually all Chinese films it keeps sexual activity offscreen, *Red Sorghum* is full of raw sexual energy, which it celebrates along with life, love, the earth, action, resistance. Although the movie is, like most Chinese art, subtly and carefully structured, it pulls no punches: Its violent scenes are absolutely violent, its scenes of collective action are irresistibly inspiring, its humorous scenes are outrageous, its tender moments and fine characters ring true, and its wild beauty is stunning and uncompromised. In the summer of 1988, when Chinese politics were at their most liberal, young people expressed their idealism, energy, determination, and revolutionary optimism by

Fig. 14-35
Red Sorghum: *Gong Li (right, as Nine) carries food for the resistance fighters through a field of sorghum.*

humming and singing the songs from *Red Sorghum*. But in the summer of 1989, when a pro-democracy demonstration, held primarily by students in Beijing's Tiananmen Square, was brutally put down by the government, China entered another oppressive phase. "Stupid Old People Should Resign Quickly," read one banner hung in Tiananmen Square; they didn't. The Xi'an studio was virtually shut down. Wu Tianming left the country. And Zhang Yimou's next film, *Ju Dou* (1990), which is both more politically critical and more sexually frank than *Red Sorghum,* became an international hit at film festivals but was not allowed by the censors to be shown in China.

Although Hong Kong production has seemed synonymous with Bruce Lee and Kung Fu, the films of King Hu (*A Touch of Zen*, 1969; *The Valiant Ones*, 1975) convert the acrobatics of martial art into extended choreographic sequences that resemble the lengthy dream ballets of American musicals.

The Philippines produces some fifty feature films each year, almost entirely for local consumption, with Lino Brocka and Mike de Leon its most forceful figures. These Philippine films must balance several conflicting commitments —to entertain a large local audience, to seek financing for more ambitious productions, to stimulate political reform, and to avoid offending the ruling authorities. Many Brocka films rejected the Marcos policy of showing only "the beautiful side" of Filipino life and had to be smuggled out of Manila for exhibition abroad. This balance between provoking dissent within a nation and presenting a case against a ruling government outside it mirrored the goal of many Third World films, whose influence has been widely felt since about 1970.

15

Hollywood Renaissance: 1964–1976

It is not entirely certain when the old American movie reawakened as the new American cinema: *Bonnie and Clyde* (1967)? *Seconds* (1966)? *The Pawnbroker* (1965)? *Dr. Strangelove* (1964)? *David and Lisa* (1963)? *Lonely Are the Brave* (1962)? *The Hustler* (1961)? *Psycho* (1960)? The exact film that marked the metaphoric reawakening is neither important nor discoverable. Since the American cinema never completely dozed off, it could never really wake up either. Hollywood arose for its fifth era, its renaissance, gradually, just as it slipped into its transitional fourth phase—quite unlike its sudden leaps into the second era of the feature film and its third era of synchronized sound.

All eight of the above films (of which only *Bonnie and Clyde* is in color) contain some seeds of the period's values: the offbeat antihero protagonists; the sterile society that surrounds them; the explicit treatment of sexual conflicts and psychological problems; the glorification of the past and the open spaces; the slick but tawdry surfaces of contemporary reality; the mixing of the comic and the serious; the self-conscious use of special cinematic effects (slow

motion, quick cutting, ironic juxtaposition of picture and sound, and so forth).

Most of the films give evidence of the two clichés that critics used to describe films of the era: sex and violence. But films have always used sex: whether it was the sexiness of Griffith's Friendless One, of Valentino's Sheik, of Dietrich's veiled face in a key light, or of bare breasts and buttocks in a Paris apartment. And films have always been violent—whether it was violent death on a Civil War battlefield in *The Birth of a Nation*, the violent death of a hoodlum on the cathedral steps in *Little Caesar,* or the violent deaths on the highway in *Easy Rider* (Dennis Hopper, 1969). The key question about any film style is not whether it uses sex and violence but how it uses them. More than anything else, the sex and violence of this "new" Hollywood cast a cynical look back on the genre films of the old Hollywood, suggesting that their assured and optimistic conclusions simplified the unresolved and perhaps unresolvable divisions in American life.

This new cinema in America evolved for several reasons. The first and most obvious was a negative cause: The old, steady movie patrons now stayed home to watch television. The industry had to find new steady customers, not those who would go to the occasional movie that seemed special enough but those who would go every week—who still liked movies and considered them important to their social and leisure experience.

For another, the new cinema of Europe eventually converted American producers. The innovations of Godard, Truffaut, and Antonioni had already conquered the rising generation of young filmmakers and audiences at the art houses. Even more convincing, Truffaut and Antonioni could make money. The years 1959 and 1960 were as important as any to the future American film: the years of *Breathless, The 400 Blows, Shoot the Piano Player, Hiroshima, mon amour, L'avventura,* and *La dolce vita.*

Third, though Hollywood repeatedly scoffed at the Underground Cinema, the underground crawled up into Hollywood to enjoy the last laugh. Not only did underground filmmakers succeed by Hollywood's financial standards—for example, Andy Warhol, Robert Downey, and Brian De Palma—but the underground films conditioned a whole generation of young filmgoers (precisely those who became the steady customers for Hollywood films) to understand and accept innovations in cinematic form, visual stimulation, and elliptical construction.

Fourth, the film industry pushed its discovery of the elitism of the new film audience to its limits. Rather than attempt to make all of the films for all of the people, producers and exhibitors realized they must appeal to very special tastes. They made a few family pictures to serve that special need. They capitalized on the racial makeup of urban audiences by making "blaxploitation" cops-and-robbers films (Gordon Parks's *Shaft,* 1971, and its descendants). They made "sexploitation" films for that special audience, catering even further to particular tastes by aiming the films at the specific sexual orientation of the viewers (heterosexual, homosexual, or bisexual) and at their preferred voyeuristic fantasies within those orientations (oral, anal, sadomasochistic, whatever). *The Devil in Miss Jones* (1973), *Deep Throat* (1972),

and *Boys in the Sand* (1971) were three of the most commercially successful pornographic features. There could even be special cult films at midnight for young, late-night "film freaks" in the cities. Among the most popular of these cult films have been Philippe De Broca's *King of Hearts* (1966), Alexandro Jodorowsky's *El Topo* (1969), John Waters's *Pink Flamingos* (1971), Hal Ashby's *Harold and Maude* (1971), Jim Sharman's *The Rocky Horror Picture Show* (1975), David Lynch's *Eraserhead* (1977), and Slava Tsukerman's *Liquid Sky* (1983). There were also old films that attracted cults (*Casablanca*) and cult films that never became "midnight movies" (David Lynch's *Blue Velvet,* 1986).

In the same way, the American industry aimed its "art films" (those directed by Arthur Penn, Mike Nichols, Robert Altman, and others) at the minority audience that liked such films, a group that represented a fraction not only of the American population but also of the filmgoing public. These films, however, were precisely those that served as America's best examples of film art and the most important representatives of its fifth era.

Finally, the values of these new American "art films" reflected the sexual and social values of American film audiences in the period. The American college student, the core of this audience, had discovered the sensual pleasures of the body and the joint as two concrete values in a world of conflicting ideals and hypocritical rhetoric. The vision of reality on the screen did not entirely shape its audience; as in the 1930s, the screen still reflected the values of those who sat in front of it. Those values had changed.

Arthur Penn's *Bonnie and Clyde* was perhaps the first full statement of the new cinema's values; it was as influential on the American films that followed it as *Breathless* was in France or *Open City* in Italy. In the years after *Bonnie and Clyde,* the innovations it introduced hardened into almost obligatory conventions; these conventions of the new cinema can be assembled easily into a list.

In most cases, the protagonists of the films were social misfits, deviates, or outlaws; the villains were the legal, respectable defenders of society. The old bad guys became the good guys; the old good guys, the bad guys. The

Fig. 15-1
Love, thrills, and bullets. Michael J. Pollard, Faye Dunaway, and Warren Beatty (right) in Bonnie and Clyde.

surprising element in *Bonnie and Clyde* (and *Easy Rider, Cool Hand Luke, The Wild Bunch, Butch Cassidy and the Sundance Kid, Thieves Like Us,* et cetera) was not simply that the protagonists were criminals, for films had depicted their Little Caesars and Bonnie Parkers for decades. The surprise was that these new murderers were also charming, warm, loving, compassionate, good-humored. The pursuers with badges were inevitably the humorless, inhuman ones. Given the outlaw protagonists, the new obligatory ending was the unhappy rather than happy one. The protagonists die; law—or the Establishment—triumphs over lawlessness. However, good did not triumph over evil, for law and good were often antithetical. There were also counter-culture movies with happy endings, like Alan Myerson's *Steelyard Blues* (1973), or open ones, like Tom Laughlin's *Billy Jack* (1971).

The crucial thing about the new antihero heroes was not that they died, since death is inevitable, but that they lived as they did—free, unchained, unswervingly true to themselves. Ironically, despite this reversal of moral values, the American film was still essentially romantic and Manichean, just as it was in the 1920s and 1930s. There were still film characters who lived profoundly beautiful lives and others who lived profoundly vile ones—even if the definitions of beauty and vileness had changed.

Allowing for such exceptions as *Medium Cool* and *Faces*—and the new use of painfully realistic gore makeup—the new American cinema did not ask to be taken as reality but constantly announced that it was artificial. Rather than effacing the film's artfulness, as a Ford or Hawks intentionally did, the new directors threw in as many cinematic tricks as possible, which both intensified the film's moods and reminded the audience that it was watching a film. Slow motion, freeze frames, jump cutting, mixtures of black-and-white and color were all standard tricks of the new trade. This deliberate artificiality had several consequences.

The first was that there was an emotional power in the visual assaults of the medium itself. One of the advantages that film enjoys over television is that its big screen is more hypnotic, its stereophonic sound more overwhelming. And it is not interrupted by commercials. In McLuhanesque terms, television is a much cooler medium than cinema, more distant from its viewers, who are able to remain more detached. A second consequence of the film trickery was that the quick cutting, the flashes both forward and backward in time as well as into and out of a character's private mental experience (sometimes confusingly interwoven) totally broke down the definitions of time and space, of now and then, of reality and fantasy, of "proper" linear continuity.

The new films played as trickily with sound as they did with images. Gone was the old principle of studio scoring—to underscore a scene with music that increases the action's emotional impact without making the viewer aware of the music's existence. This early principle of film scoring was a clear extension of the piano's function in the nickelodeon. In the new films, there was little of this kind of background music. If there was to be music it had to be either clearly motivated (playing on a radio or record player nearby) or deliberately artificial (a song on the soundtrack that existed specifically to be noticed and played either in harmony or in counterpoint with the sequence's visuals). In George Roy Hill's *Butch Cassidy and the Sundance Kid* (1969), the story stops for an idyllic bicycle ride accompanied by a Burt Bacharach tune. In Haskell Wexler's *Medium Cool* (1969), the patriotic speeches and songs inside the Democratic Convention hall accompany the riots between students and police in Grant Park. The soundtrack of Altman's *Thieves Like Us* (1974) is a compendium of 1930s radio broadcasts, serving to show how central the radio was to American life in that era, saturating the film with period color, and often commenting ironically on the action (for

example, an installment of *Gang Busters* during a bank robbery or a radio version of *Romeo and Juliet* during a love scene).

Some sequences in the new films distorted sound purposely (for example, Coppola's *The Conversation*, 1974, whose subject is sound recording); others were completely silent, contrasting with the other sequences of song or noise. Rock and jazz composers wrote many of the new film scores, and the most popular groups performed them. The new films used rock music heavily (the scores of *Easy Rider*, Martin Scorsese's *Mean Streets*, 1973, and George Lucas's *American Graffiti*, 1973, were anthologies of highly relevant rock hits), for rock was the other artistic and social passion of the young audiences who supported the movies.

The new cinema in America became self-consciously concerned with style—with visual texture, a careful attention to the dress, decor, and dialects of the historical era (usually from America's recent past), with a specific use of the camera and soundtrack to capture and mirror that style authentically. Fewer films were shot on soundstages; directors preferred the authenticity of shooting on location. Whereas the old Hollywood style was devoted to eliminating the imperfections of reality—graceless rooms, uneven lighting, uncontrollable noise—the new American films required accident and imperfection for their visual style and human credibility. The lighting styles of Bergman's Sven Nykvist and of the New Wave cinematographers (Raoul Coutard, Nestor Almendros, Henri Decaë), who bounced light off the ceilings of rooms and caught it as it poured through windows, influenced a new generation of American cinematographers—Haskell Wexler, Gordon Willis, Vilmos Zsigmond, Robert Surtees, Lucien Ballard, Laszlo Kovacs, John Alonzo. Inside the old studios, the only light that poured through a window flowed from an electric pitcher.

The new American films were gladly influenced by French films, Italian films, Czech films, British films, underground and avant-garde films, and even rediscovered films (old Hawks movies in Bogdanovich's *Targets*, 1968; *Battleship Potemkin* in *Targets* and *Bonnie and Clyde*). Many of the new American films, like the new European films, depicted how actions *felt*, not just actions, so that character became more important than plot; they also tackled big issues, much as the Europeans did (whereas the 1980s would be considered a decade in which big issues were generally evaded).

However Europeanized the fifth American era had become, it still maintained its old inclination toward rigid genres and repetitive cycles. Producers still felt safer with a formula that had succeeded before, and so a series of films about compassionate thieves followed *Bonnie and Clyde*, a series of films about the last assertive gasp of the old frontier followed *The Wild Bunch*, a series of violent police-chase films followed *The French Connection*, a series of Mafia films followed *The Godfather*, a series of sci-fi adventures followed *Star Wars*, et cetera. Despite their new experiential and stylistic commitments, the new films were descendants of the old genres: the western, the gangster, the *policier*, the screwball comedy, and so on. The basic generic division in the new films was between city films and country films. Beyond these lay the road films (*Easy Rider*), the wilderness of horror (George Romero's *Night of the Living Dead*, 1968), and the worlds of fantasy (*Willy Wonka and the Chocolate Factory*, 1971, directed by Mel Stuart).

The city films, which invariably examined the harried and hurried quality of American city life, were dependent on the imagery of the city: hard, close, flat, artificial, cold—stone and neon. Many of the city films developed a thematic opposition between the unnaturalness and brutality of the city and the freedom and openness outside the city. (*Midnight Cowboy* is the story of a country mouse, played by Jon Voight, and a city mouse, played by Dustin Hoffman.) Such new films were clearly descendants of the *film noir* of the transitional era (the toughness of life and death in the big city), which itself owed much to the reporter pictures (tough reporters were indigenous to the big city) of the Studio Era. While the city of that previous era shoved law and crime, promise and corruption up against one another in tempting proximity, the city films of the "new" Hollywood suggest a seething human hell. Automobiles become vehicles of destruction during brutally extended breakneck chases, whether through San Francisco (*Bullitt*, directed by

Peter Yates, 1968) or New York (*The French Connection*, directed by William Friedkin, 1971). The cities breed paranoid fantasies, whether the sounds of San Francisco (*The Conversation*) or the sights of New York viewed through a windshield—smoke, steam, and brimstone rising from the entrails of the city itself (Martin Scorsese's *Taxi Driver*, 1976). There were also paranoid glimpses of cities of the future (George Lucas's *THX-1138*, 1971; Richard Fleischer's *Soylent Green*, 1973).

Close cousins to the city films, thematically as well as geographically, were the suburb films —such as Mike Nichols's *The Graduate* (1967), Paul Mazursky's *Bob & Carol & Ted & Alice* (1969), Robert Altman's *The Long Goodbye* (1973), George Romero's *Dawn of the Dead* (1978, released 1979), and Paul Schrader's *American Gigolo* (1980). Appropriately, many of these films used Los Angeles, that city of suburbs and the capital of the movie business, as both setting and metaphor. If, compared to the densely packed older cities, these suburb-cities were clean, bright, and new, they were also rootless and soulless. They lacked a center —either geographical or spiritual.

Even those films that did not assail the inhumanity of the city or suburb took advantage of shooting in Manhattan, using its real settings and gifted actors for the same natural offbeat feeling that the British realist films evoked from London, Manchester, and Birmingham: *A Thousand Clowns* (1965), *A Fine Madness* (1966), *You're a Big Boy Now* (1966), *The Producers* (1968), *The Night They Raided Minsky's* (1968), *Little Murders* (1971), *Next Stop, Greenwich Village* (1976), and *Manhattan* (1979), to name just a few.

The new, "experiential" western—for example, Sam Peckinpah's *The Wild Bunch* (1969), George Roy Hill's *Butch Cassidy and the Sundance Kid*, and Robert Altman's *McCabe and Mrs. Miller* (1971)—revealed the internalization and sensualization of a previously more externalized, active genre. For the new films, the West, the vast plains and deserts, were the last outposts of the free spirit of man and the original pioneer spirit of America. Just as the city films needed the country for contrast, the country films needed the city—the place where sheriffs and police and bankers and mer-

Fig. 15-2
Pike (William Holden) gets shot in the back at the climax of Sam Peckinpah's masterpiece, **The Wild Bunch.**

chants reside. Both *The Wild Bunch* and *Butch Cassidy* were set in an era when the Old West was crumbling, when the city's values were swallowing the country's. The heroes of both films prefer to remain anachronisms rather than surrender to "decency" and the machine. The slow-motion sequences in these new westerns existed to heighten, lyricize, and magnify the moment of death, in effect turning that moment into a prolonged sensual experience. If the new western differed from the old one it was not because it was more violent; plenty of men were shot dead in the old westerns. But in the old western the audience merely saw a man shot dead; the emotional effect came from the suspense before the shooting (who will win the gunfight, when, and how?) and the relief after it. The new western turned the moment of death and the causing of death into the emotional epiphany.

The new gangster film mirrored the same basic generic division between past and present, city and country. The crime films concerned themselves with rural gangsters of the past or urban gangsters of the present or near-present. The country-crime genre was essentially a sub-genre of the new western. Whereas the protagonists of the western depended on their horses, the central figures of *Bonnie and Clyde, Thieves Like Us*, and Terrence Malick's *Badlands* (1973) used the automobile as their means of slicing through the open prairies. Contrasted with the happy freedom of Bonnie and Clyde is a nation of economic slaves, the hungry and the poor who are victims of a political system that dwarfs people and undermines their lives with its Depressions. Contrasted with the happy freedom of Bowie, Masefield, and Chickesaw in *Thieves Like Us* is the boring banality of middle-class drawing rooms and dinner tables, lives that are so dull that those corny radio shows serve as their only glimpse of a more exciting existence.

As opposed to Nicholas Ray's *They Live by Night*, of which *Thieves Like Us* is an explicit remake, Altman's work views the earlier film's dream of a secure, materialistic home as a living death.

A synthesis of past and present, city and country, gangster and cowboy existed in the idealization of sky, plain, and mountain in *Easy Rider*; the horse had become the motorbike; civilization was personified by the small-town bigots, the county sheriff, institutionalized love (a New Orleans whorehouse), institutionalized fun (Mardi Gras), and institutionalized death (an immense cemetery). But even the free and romantic West is being sullied; a commune of transposed, hip city kids feels as much hostility toward the two easy riders as the "straight" bigots in the towns and city. The only freedom, the only joy is being on the road itself, and even that, as the film's ending shows, can never be enjoyed for long.

Whereas the country-crime films tended toward a softness and slowness, softening human brutality and luxuriating in the luminous beauty of nature, the city-crime films were hard, fast, and cold. If the special-effects death sequence was obligatory in the western and country-crime film, the breathlessly rapid and assaultive chase was obligatory in the city-crime and police films. The essential technical tool of the city film was editing rather than composition as in the country films, and the basic subjective device was the violent rushing of the traveling or hand-held camera rather than the subjective prolongation of an event in slow motion. Cops in the city-crime films (*Bullitt*; *The French Connection*; Richard Fleischer's *The New Centurions*, 1972; Sidney Lumet's *Serpico*, 1973; William Friedkin's *Cruising*, 1980) usually faced two sources of tensions: within themselves (are they just doing their job or are they neurotically driven to violence and sadism?) and within their own departments (the pressures of politicians, bureaucrats, and incompetents). The *film noir* of the transitional era (for example, Lang's *The Big Heat*, 1953) was a truly transitional link between the detective films of the Studio Era in which the cop fought crime and of the new era in which a cop fights himself and cops fight each other. The new focus of the gangster city films was less on the push to the top and the inevitable fall (*Little Caesar* or *Scarface*) and more on the mundane problems of living legitimately once the top had been reached (the conflict between the old life of crime and the new respectability in *The Godfather Part II*).

The most obvious link between the New Hollywood and the old was the one "new" genre of the 1970s—what might be called the genre genre. These films parodied the plot structures, stylistic conventions, and movie stars of Hollywood Past, usually by compiling a catalogue of Studio Era clichés—the Neil Simon–Robert Moore comedies (*Murder by Death*, 1976; *The Cheap Detective*, 1978), Dick Richards's *Farewell, My Lovely* (1975), Stanley Donen's *Movie Movie* (1978), some of the early Woody Allen films (*What's Up, Tiger Lily?*, 1966; *Take the Money and Run*, 1969; *Play It Again, Sam*, 1972, written by Allen but directed by Herbert Ross, as *What's New, Pussycat?*, 1965, had been directed by Clive Donner), and, of course, almost everything by Mel Brooks (*The Producers*, 1968; *Blazing Saddles*, 1974; *Young Frankenstein*, 1974; *Silent Movie*, 1976; *High Anxiety*, 1977).

If a single American film of the 1970s put all these themes together, it was *Chinatown* (1974). Like many of the most perceptive film dissections of American society—from Chaplin to von Stroheim to Lang to Hitchcock—*Chinatown* was not directed by an American. Roman Polanski—whose view of life, American or otherwise, stretched from a Nazi concentration camp to Bel Air and the brutal Manson murder of Sharon Tate, Polanski's wife—directed the film from a masterful script by Robert Towne. The film explored American political corruption in a supposedly saner, cleaner social era of "wholesome values"—the 1930s of Frank Capra and the New Deal. While the 1930s films reaffirmed the myths of American purpose and destiny (after serious setbacks and struggle), *Chinatown* exposed the myths themselves as naïve falsehoods.

On its surface, *Chinatown* is a detective movie set in Los Angeles—like the studios themselves and like the Dashiell Hammett and Raymond Chandler novels that the studios made into movies like John Huston's *The Mal-*

Fig. 15-3
Chinatown: *disguising a vision of contemporary social and political corruption as a 1930s detective thriller or 1940s film noir (from left, Jack Nicholson, Perry Lopez, Faye Dunaway).*

tese Falcon and Howard Hawks's *The Big Sleep.* Huston himself appears in *Chinatown* as its master villain. Instead of traveling with Jake Gittes (Jack Nicholson) toward a successfully solved case, the film conducts him on a tortuous journey through a bewildering maze of murders and sordid sexual encounters to arrive at the core of moral corruption within American life itself. Polanski weds the country's "Watergate mood"—the suspicion of invisible strands of corruption binding everyone in high places— to a Technicolor, Panavision world of beautiful images (shot by John Alonzo), which intensify the terrifying ugliness beneath an apparently beautiful surface. The American Dream is a nightmare of power, lust, and money. In its paranoia, its many specific references to American film history and genres, its depiction of a modern city perverting the essential natural resource (water) of the Edenic garden, and its explicit sexual corruption (from mere adultery to layers of incest), *Chinatown* captures the mood of an entire era.

The new American cinema was not a shift in direction so much as a new use of the traditional themes and images of American literature and American film. Instead of the indoor, studio-built, dialogue-centered films of the first thirty years of sound, the new films preferred to go outdoors, to real locations rather than sets; they emphasized the kinetic effects of film as movement, picture, music, rather than as well-made, logical story. The best new American films were like those that had always been best —a unified blend of story (pared down in the quantity of incident), human insight (carefully textured in the quality of an experience), thematic vision (more ambivalent in its moral positions), and cinematic style (more intrusive and idiosyncratically stylized than ever).

It may seem odd for a multibillion-dollar capitalistic industry to sell subversive products.

Many of the era's best films rip the social, moral, sexual, and political fabric of American life — tearing holes in the cultural myths that passed for American truths, even lacerating the movies that advertised those myths. But this was an era with three devastating assassinations of figures identified with progressive social change, dominated by an unpopular war that became more burdensome every year, and climaxed by a government scandal that justified any paranoid's worst fears about those who held the reins of American power.

The era that began with the assassination of one president ended with the disgrace of another after his replacement casually pardoned him. The national mood of anger, doubt, and distrust understandably differed from the optimism, commitment, or vigilance of prewar, wartime, and postwar America. Not every American shared that mood, but the most vocal Americans against the war and in favor of civil rights — who marched on Washington in immense numbers and disrupted college campuses — were the very ones who went to the movies. The American film business — much leaner than it had been a decade earlier —could afford to play a central role in this national debate.

Not coincidentally, the old Hollywood Production Code, which had always been a hypocritical compromise between the facts of life and the pressures of public opinion, came to an end as this era began. After several years of hedging, of making exceptions for prestige films like *Lolita* (1962), Lewis Gilbert's *Alfie* (1966), or *Who's Afraid of Virginia Woolf?* (1966), in 1968 the Motion Picture Association of America (MPAA, formerly the MPPDA) finally replaced the PCA (Production Code Administration) with the CARA (Classification and Rating Administration). The new board — which, as a service to parents, rated the "level of maturity" a film assumed of its audience rather than prohibited certain kinds of material altogether — instituted four categories: originally, G (for all audiences), M (suggested for mature audiences — which became GP, then PG), R (restricted to audiences of eighteen years and older, except when accompanied by an adult), and X (restricted to audiences of eighteen and over). PG-13, a warning stronger than PG (parental guidance suggested) but

weaker than R, was added in 1984. In 1990 the new NC-17 (no children under seventeen) rating replaced the X. In CARA's first twenty years, half of the nearly nine thousand features rated received an R, one-third a PG.

While the new MPAA ratings system unleashed more explicit sexual talk and activity and a more open critical attack on the society's norms than had ever been seen in movies before (or since), there was still plenty of uncertainty, bargaining, and hypocrisy. Who was to say what a seventeen-year-old did or should know? CARA repeatedly revised the guidelines and the age limits. Since young people comprised such a large share of the movie audience, just to drop the cutoff age one year, from eighteen to seventeen, translated into a major increase in a film's potential audience. So there was considerable bargaining between film producers and CARA over what a film might cut to receive a more commercially "desirable" rating — just as there had always been bargaining between producers and the PCA over what a film could show or say.

In 1968 and 1969 many respected commercial films with sex and violence and anti-Establishment messages received an X rating (*Medium Cool, Midnight Cowboy*). Originally conceived to describe films with serious adult content, the X quickly became a euphemism for "porn" — films that were never rated at all. Shot by producers and exhibited in theatres that never belonged to the MPAA, these films rated themselves as X to attract customers. By 1971, the debasement of the X had so shaken CARA's standards that a film like Robert Altman's *McCabe and Mrs. Miller*, rated R, contains words, shots, and actions that could never have received an R rating in 1968; the same could be said of William Friedkin's *The Exorcist*, which received its R in 1973. To distinguish rated films with adult content from unrated films brimming with prurient sex (or uncompromised violence, as in the case of *Dawn of the Dead*, which Romero refused to re-edit for an R), the MPAA instituted the NC-17, hoping that certain films could be rated "adults only" without falling prey to the many ordinances that prohibited X-rated films from advertising in local papers or playing in local theatres. But many organizations simply urged the boycotting of NC-17 films. Another 1990 change in the ratings system was that CARA was required to give the reasons (sex, violence, language) a picture had been rated R. The industry's new rating system changed the shape of public debate about the relationship of personal morality and public exhibition but certainly did not end the discussion.

Although the $10 million blockbusters with G ratings could make a lot of money (Robert Wise's *The Sound of Music*, 1965, starring Julie Andrews), they could also lose a lot of money (Robert Wise's *Star!*, 1968, starring Julie Andrews). The iconoclastic, risk-taking films, which cost near or less than the 1970 industry average of $3 million, made consistent, if modest, profits. If smashing the idols of American myth and exposing the ideals of American genres made money, then movie executives could only assent to the evidence of their balance sheets.

The New American Auteurs

Like the film industries of Europe and Japan, the American cinema became more a directors' cinema, granting proven directors a higher measure of control over the scripting, production, and editing decisions, allowing them more freedom in selecting their projects and giving them more credit for their contribution than the studios once did in their golden era. A film is frequently labeled *by* or *of* its director (an attribution that the Writers Guild of America vigorously opposed for decades), whose name often appears above the film's title. The American director became one of the film's stars, and it is significant that many 1970s directors were allowed to make films without any major star at all (*The Last Picture Show, Thieves Like Us, Days of Heaven*), an unheard of practice for major studio films until 1968 (and Kubrick's *2001*).

When François Truffaut in France and Andrew Sarris in America developed the "*auteur* theory" (or *auteur* policy), they did so as a means of distinguishing directorial individuality in the Studio Era, since individuality was often buried beneath the decisions of producers and the scripts of the scenario department. The new American *auteurs* are film authors in the full sense of a Griffith, Gance, Dreyer, Ford, Hitchcock, Godard, Fellini, Bergman, or Kurosawa—the ones who control the responsibility for the entire project so that their own personal visions and visual styles get recorded on film. Though the following list of these new *auteurs* must necessarily be tentative (most of them are still in mid-career), each has created a large body of work that demonstrates considerable power and imagination as well as a clear consistency of style and vision.

Woody Allen is the new American comic *auteur* who is most conscious of the older American comic-film tradition that he inherits. His glasses create a "glass character" who resembles Harold Lloyd, his physical clumsiness and unattractiveness parallel Harry Langdon's, and his dryly quiet, offbeat comic ironies suggest the flavor of Buster Keaton and the wit of Groucho Marx. But more than anyone else, Allen resembles Chaplin as an observer and chronicler of the contemporary American social scene. Although his characters wear different names (Fielding Mellish in *Bananas*, 1971; Miles Monroe in *Sleeper*, 1973; Boris Grushenko in *Love and Death*, 1975; Alvy Singer in *Annie Hall*, 1977), a device that parallels Keaton's different names and costumes, Woody Allen's comic persona is a single, familiar, established being, like Charlie, who wanders across the landscape of contemporary urban life, contrasting that persona with the less observant, less sensitive society dwellers who surround him. One might call Woody Allen's entire *oeuvre* "Modern Times," and if the problem for Allen's city dwellers has shifted from the external ones of finding a job and founding a home to the internal one of feeling secure enough to survive between appointments with the analyst, that shift is symptomatic of five decades of change in American life itself. Like Charlie (the British tramp), Woody (the Jewish *schlemiel*) is terribly out of tune and out of step with the society around him. On the one hand, he is physically, mentally, and emotionally unequipped to accept its norms, values, and definitions. But on the other (also like Charlie), he longs to accept those values and be accepted by them in return, thereby turning his attempts at winning acceptance into parodies of society's attitudes and rituals themselves. (For example,

Fig. 15-4
New American archetypes: the neurotic Jewish schlepp and the arty Gentile kook (Diane Keaton and Woody Allen in Annie Hall*).*

flip—in two senses of the term. First, it was casual and flippant, taking nothing as serious or sacred (racial and religious stereotypes, political philosophies, politicians, intellectuals, revolutions, conformity, cultural crazes, sexuality, psychology, et cetera), especially the making of the movie itself. He was also flip in that he leapt from gag to gag with astonishing rapidity, often wearing the audience (and his ideas) out before the end of the film and often establishing funny situations that he failed to develop (two dangers of flipping). But Allen's three late 1970s films (*Annie Hall*; *Interiors*, 1978; *Manhattan*) show far more care and consciousness of cinematic style and "art"—possibly because all three were shot by Gordon Willis (cinematographer for all three of the *Godfather* films, *All the President's Men*, and others), the most distinguished cinematographer with whom Allen had yet collaborated. At the end of *Annie Hall* two young actors attempt to reproduce the farewell scene between Annie and Alvy at the outdoor health-food restaurant. That falteringly funny attempt may be taken as a metaphor for Allen's evolution in the use of comedy —the desire to objectify, to concretize personal experiences and private obsessions into comic works that can be publicly performed for others.

Interiors parallels Chaplin's *A Woman of Paris* —a serious study of the artist's concerns (for Allen, family life, the artistic vocation, and sexual fulfillment) that dispenses with the familiar comic persona as a focus and anchor for the study. And *Manhattan* is clearly Allen's *City Lights*—its use of the urban setting, the nostalgic Gershwin music to evoke the 1930s, the equally nostalgic but visually glorious use of black-and-white (indeed, the film's combination of old-movie monochrome with the new movie's ultrawide Panavision frame makes the film's visual style a synthesis of past and present). And, of course, *Manhattan* ends with the same kind of agonized, unanswered question as did *City Lights*. The difference between Chaplin and Allen, however, may lie in the difference between the two unanswered questions posed by the two endings. The question Chaplin raises—can the once blind woman possibly love him for what he is rather than for

when trying to look cool with some friends in *Annie Hall*, he sneezes into the cocaine.)

Allen's comic persona is deliberately close to Allen's off-screen personality—introspective, cynical, neurotic, self-conscious, self-indulgent, hip, flip—though the real Woody Allen is powerful and well organized. Both Woody and Allen look for love and make nervous jokes about death. Allen's films come closer to psychoanalysis, to psycho-comedy, than the work of any other American comedian —except, of course, Lenny Bruce, another important (but nonfilmic) Allen ancestor.

Allen's cinematic technique in his earliest films was, like that of Mack Sennett, truly

what she thought he was, see beneath what he *appears* to be—seems so much larger than the Allen question—can he possibly trust her, and himself, for six months, until (if ?) she returns from London. Won't she have found someone else to love? Worse, won't *he* have found someone else to love? Allen's films are painfully aware that his own affections are as transient and undependable as everyone else's. That gap —between the terrible importance and permanence of the final question in *City Lights* and the terrible triviality and transience of the final question in *Manhattan*—may be Allen's comment on the differences between life in 1930 and 1980.

Since *Love and Death*, Allen's movies have become increasingly reflexive, committed to exploring the condition of comic movies rather than his own fixed comic persona. *Love and Death* alluded to Soviet cinema—from Einsenstein's images to Prokofiev's film scores—as often as to nineteenth century Russian fiction; it reimagined Russian history in the terms of Russian art, as well as in the personal terms of Allen's comedic mythology. *Stardust Memories* (1980), like Fellini's *8½*, which it deliberately echoes, shows the way a popular artist can be trapped by his own success and the expectations of fans and critics—their unwillingness to let the comedian follow his dreams and their insistence on his retracing the paths of his past. *A Midsummer Night's Sex Comedy* (1982) combined Shakespeare's *A Midsummer Night's Dream* and Bergman's *Smiles of a Summer Night*, linked by midsummer sexuality, the confusions of lust-blinded lovers, and the magic of cinema itself— as symbolized by the inventor Allen's "spiritball," capable of projecting images from air and light. Thanks to Gordon Willis's hard work, inserting Woody's image into old film clips and making new footage look old, *Zelig* (1983) is virtually an entire movie in the style of *Citizen Kane*'s newsreel—an ironic examination of the way American hype converts anonymous nonentities into media superstars. *Broadway Danny Rose* (1984) accomplishes the unlikely task of dumping a Jewish *schlemiel* into a gangster film like *The Godfather*. *The Purple Rose of Cairo* (1985) contrasts the grim realities of Depression America with the glorious, esca-

pist joy of Depression Hollywood's films, symbolized by Allen's contrast of realist color cinematography with dreamlike black-and-white. To bring an impossibly naïve representative of Hollywood's imagining into the reality of American life required that Allen remove his own perceptive persona from the film altogether.

Hannah and Her Sisters (1986)—its title lifted from Thomas Mann's *Joseph and His Brothers*—starred Allen, Mia Farrow, Barbara Hershey, Max von Sydow, and others in an intricately plotted examination of love and marriage, guilt and personal growth. But Allen's most complex and troubling film since *Manhattan* (allowing for the fact that most of his films since *Annie Hall* have put their audiences through emotional wringers) was *Crimes and Misdemeanors* (1989). Although *Manhattan* ends by urging Woody—and the audience— to learn to have a little faith in people, *Hannah* and *Crimes* make it clear that few people, including one's most intimate friends and lovers, deserve the honor.

The question raised in *Crimes* is whether God sees the evil that goes on in the world and does anything about it. The villains are a superficial media star (Alan Alda) who leads a charmed life and gets everything and everybody he wants, and an eye doctor (Martin Landau) who gets away with adultery and murder. Contrasted with them both is Woody, who would like to be as famous as Alda and who has an adulterous affair—but the woman (Farrow) ends up with Alda, and Woody's desires and failings become the misdemeanors that we compare with Landau's crimes. Landau suffers from the guilt he entirely deserves (unlike the neurotic guilt and anxiety typical of Allen's personae); he unburdens himself to a rabbi (Sam Waterston—who is going blind but sees ethical problems clearly, in contrast to the confused eye doctor) and worries for months— until he simply stops worrying. So far it appears that the good and evil in the world are neither rewarded nor punished appropriately. But at the very end, with Landau and Alda enjoying their lives and Woody trying to make sense of his own, Allen the writer-director gives us an overwhelmingly powerful image: the now blind rabbi dancing at a family wedding. With that image of ethical continuity, of acceptance, and of personal strength, Allen arrived at last at a profound closure that would have pleased Chaplin.

Robert Altman made fifteen feature films in the 1970s alone. Like Allen he would rather make movies than masterpieces, a large number of attempts rather than a few highly polished gems. As a result, Altman's work is extremely inconsistent, varying from film to film and even from part to part within individual films. Altman's work comes in two narrative sizes. The first is a smaller, closer study of a bizarre central figure or figures who lead bizarre lives or are possessed by bizarre dreams—the boy who wants to become a bird and fly in *Brewster McCloud* (1970), the incompetent gunslinger and the drug-addict dancehall doll in *McCabe and Mrs. Miller*, the picaresque lifestyle of a hiply updated Philip Marlowe in *The Long Goodbye*, the thieves who want to rob enough banks to settle down to respectable middle-class lives in *Thieves Like Us*, the possessed gambler-friends of *California Split* (1974), the two young water therapists living in the arid desert of *Three Women* (1977), Nixon in a room (*Secret Honor*, 1984).

The second Altman narrative structure requires a much larger canvas. It is a broad sociological and psychological study of a particular American institution, built from a great number of interwoven characters, adding up to a cross-sectional view of American life itself. *MASH* (1970), Altman's first major success, used the sexy, funny, gory activities of a group of American medics in Korea to examine (at the height of the Vietnam crisis) American attitudes toward war, particularly wars against other races in distant parts of the world. *MASH* led to a hit TV series, *M*A*S*H*, and to more advanced experiments in complex film soundtracks. *Nashville* (1975), probably Altman's most solid and respected film, used the American country-and-western recording industry—and all the people it touched or who wanted to be touched by it—to investigate American political, sexual, and economic structures, as well as the American dreams of fame and success. *Buffalo Bill and the Indians, or Sitting Bull's History Lesson* (1976), one of Altman's more disap-

pointing films (the worst is *Quintet*, 1979), used the wild west show to examine the rape of the American continent and the debasement of the pioneer spirit. And *A Wedding* (1978) used a suburban upper-middle-class wedding ceremony to examine the relationship of love and lucre in contemporary American life.

One of the consistent Altman strengths is the compelling spontaneous authenticity of the moments of human interaction. Altman works improvisationally with his actors, and the scenes they build together (between Donald Sutherland and Elliott Gould in *MASH*, Julie Christie and Warren Beatty in *McCabe and Mrs. Miller*, Gould and Sterling Hayden in *The Long Goodbye*, Keith Carradine and Shelley Duvall in *Thieves Like Us*, Gould and George Segal in *California Split*, Barbara Harris or Lily Tomlin and everybody else in *Nashville*, Duvall and Sissy Spacek in *Three Women*) are hypnotic encounters with acting that feels like life.

The second Altman strength is his perceptive scrutiny of American social institutions, which he explores with haunting and startlingly memorable visual images. *Brewster McCloud* is dominated by images of the bare, sterile Astrodome. In *The Long Goodbye* there are fleeting yet repetitive glimpses of the exercising dancers who provide the scenic view from Marlowe's apartment, and in *Three Women* the similarly fleeting yet repetitive glimpses of the perfectly matched twins; in both films these images, which weave through the narrative like musical motifs, are summaries of a purely physical, empty-headed American life-style. In *A Wedding* the unforgettable visual splendor of a totally mirrored bathroom converts this place of physical necessity into a gleaming American temple for worship of the shiny, the surface, and the body. The brilliance of Altman's improvised, spontaneous human performances and perceptive, evocative visual imagery frequently overcomes the dreamlike meanderings of his weaker narratives.

Consistent with the spirit of the era, Altman's work attacked the myths of American life as articulated in the genres of American movies. *McCabe and Mrs. Miller* does to the western what *The Long Goodbye* does to the detective film: explode its assumptions and pick up only a few of the pieces. In this ragged

Fig. 15-5
McCabe and Mrs. Miller: *no idealized civilization in this wilderness. The dirty frontier town of Presbyterian Church, blanketed by perpetual snow, rain, and mud — its church spire barely visible in the background.*

frontier town, ironically named Presbyterian Church, there is no mythic showdown between good and evil in the glaring light of high noon. The "good guy," McCabe, is a drunken profiteer from gambling and prostitution, who shoots his assailants in the back. The sun never shines in this muddy town; the rain or snow never stops. The "bad guys" are not desperadoes but methodical hired killers, employees of the mining company that first tries to buy McCabe out but finds it easier to blow him away. The "dance-hall girls" are not euphemisms but whores, plain and simple, and their madam, Mrs. Miller, reveals no heart of gold when trouble comes but retreats into her opium haze.

This is a western concerned not with decency but with sanitation — obsessed with the way people smell, belch, fart, and rid themselves of bodily wastes. Despite the town's name, its church, that great icon of civilization

in John Ford westerns, is only half-built (the film's pre-release title was *The Presbyterian Church Wager*). Its major purpose in the film is to catch fire and distract the town's citizens from the real battle between McCabe and the hired killers — just as western movies, Altman implies, distracted American citizens from political realities with mythic façades.

Since the mid-1970s, and the passing of that era's attack on movie myth, Altman has found it increasingly difficult to finance projects and please audiences. In the 1980s he turned to theatre (where he had never previously worked) — staging productions and then filming them cheaply, sometimes using television equipment and techniques (*Come Back to the Five and Dime, Jimmy Dean, Jimmy Dean*, 1982; *Streamers*, 1983; *Secret Honor*). His most ambitious and disturbing recent films, *Fool for Love* (1985, written for the screen by playwright Sam Shepard) and *Vincent & Theo* (1990, the story of the brothers

Van Gogh), attracted critics and audiences but still failed to convince producers that Altman could be trusted to turn out a commercially viable project; during this period Altman lost several assignments when he told studio heads that he intended to make an Altman film rather than, for example, an MGM film. The future course of this industry outsider and antagonist is unclear.

If Robert Altman was a foe of movie myth and industry during the 1970s, Francis Ford Coppola virtually *was* the American film industry in this period. Coppola is less a film director or *auteur* than an all-around man of the movies. He began as an assistant to Roger Corman—where he learned to cut, dub, write, and shoot films. He has written scripts for other directors (from the Oscar-winning *Patton*, 1970, for Franklin Schaffner, co-written by Edmund H. North, to the terrible *The Great Gatsby*, 1974, for Jack Clayton), and he has become a major producer or co-producer of others' films—whether for a younger generation of American directors (George Lucas, Carroll Ballard), an established generation of non-American directors (Kurosawa, Godard, Wenders), or the forgotten masterpiece of a silent director (Abel Gance's *Napoléon*). More than anything else, Coppola is committed to the cinema—to its past and its future, its genres and possibilities, and to the people who make it. He is the single most important film figure of his generation, a combination of D. W. Griffith and Thomas Ince.

For his personal projects, Coppola's films tend to be either big commercial epics (*Finian's Rainbow*, 1968; *The Godfather*, 1972; *The Godfather Part II*, 1974; *Apocalypse Now*, begun in 1976 and finally released in 1979; *The Cotton Club*, 1984; *The Godfather Part III*, 1990) or smaller, more offbeat style pieces (*You're a Big Boy Now*, 1966; *The Rain People*, 1969; *The Conversation*, 1974; *One from the heart*, 1982—spelled like an Italian film title, one way Coppola announced that this film did come from his heart; *Rumble Fish*, 1983; *Gardens of Stone*, 1987; *Tucker: The Man and His Dream*, 1988). *The Conversation*, with its clever use of sound as both the central subject and the dominant stylistic device of the film, with its furtive and recurring *cinéma vérité* sequences shot in

Union Square that are an exact visual equivalent of the sound-recording process, with its effective settings (the modern, barren, absolutely impersonal and Kafkaesque office building; the matter-of-fact detail of the commercial exposition displaying the newest products for snooping and bugging), was among the first of his films to proclaim a social conscience and intellectual consciousness. Like Polanski's *Chinatown*, the film very effectively exploited the nation's Watergate paranoia. One might see the film's theme as the clash between a person's craft and conscience, the pure devotion to artisanship as opposed to the moral responsibilities of engaging in any business that affects the lives of other human beings.

The three parts of *The Godfather*, adapted from Mario Puzo's best-selling novel, constitute a monumental American epic about the conflict between doing business and living according to meaningful values—a conflict built into the very familial and economic structure of American society. *The Godfather* opens with a wedding—a family celebration of fertility, union, and the future. Vito Corleone (Marlon Brando) spends his time not outdoors, in the bright and open sunlight, but in his dark cavelike office, where he does business with his wedding guests. Although his may seem a special, unethical business (using his power and influence to do "favors" for his extended family), he is no different from other American businessmen, who often discuss business at weddings.

The negotiations indoors represent the dark underside of the brightly visible activity outdoors; for Coppola, every American business has this dark underside. One can never separate business and family—the way the Mafia chieftains pretend to do. The result of this wedding will be barren: The son-in-law will betray his own father-in-law and will be murdered by the family in return; the daughter will be unhappy and alone. As an Italian-American, Coppola is terribly conscious of the suspicion that all Italian immigrant families are branches of the illegitimate Mafia tree. Instead, Coppola argues that no American and no American business, of whatever ethnic extraction, can escape the conflict between business dealings and personal values. The Mafia is not a disease within American life; it is a symptom of American life itself.

Fig. 15-6
The Godfather: the public dance, outdoors, in the sunlight. Family ceremony in contrast to the dark interior of family business (Marlon Brando, Talia Shire, and guests).

The Godfather Part II extends the examination historically into both past and future—an epic chronicle of debasement and degradation, the dissolution of the American Dream that brought immigrants to this country in the first place. The temporal leaps in Coppola's narrative—late-nineteenth-century Sicily, the arrival of immigrants at Ellis Island, life in New York's Little Italy in the 1910s and 20s, Batista's corrupt Cuba of the 1950s, Las Vegas of the 1960s—produce a political conversation between the simple hopes of the past and the complex corruption of the present, as the stories of Vito's and Michael's careers are cross-cut. Like the Ricos and Tony Camontes of Hollywood Past, Michael Corleone (Al Pacino) accumulates wealth and power at the expense of losing everyone close to him—associates, friends, wife, children, brother. Unlike those earlier gangsters, Michael himself does not lose his life but remains—a lonely, stripped, but powerful head of a corporation of crime. He becomes the model for the ultimate American businessman—all business and no man. The film is not so thematically distant from *The Conversation* after all.

The Godfather Part II, one of the few sequels as good as or better than the original, is so different in style and structure that the two parts also form a "conversation," a genuine historical dialectic. Although no Marxist, Coppola's dialectical method within and between the two films suggests a historical analysis of the assumptions of American capitalism. When the two films were re-edited for television in strict chronological order, they lost both dramatic and thematic power, missing the careful dialectic of Coppola's conception. *The Godfather Part II* is the most ambitiously constructed parallel montage since *Intolerance*. It may also reveal the depths of character and the tragic paradoxes of power more effectively—and formally—than any American film since *Citizen Kane*.

Paramount was determined from the start that *The Godfather Part III* would have a linear narrative, as *The Godfather* did, rather than pursue the narrative experiments of *The Godfather Part II*. Even if both films had won the Oscar for best picture (an unprecedented achievement), the studio felt that *Part II* was confusing. What Coppola and Puzo (who co-wrote all three scripts) wanted *Part III* to do was give Michael an opportunity to redeem himself spiritually, to suffer as he had made others suffer. In *Part III*, then, Michael completes his project of shifting all the family's business interests to legitimate activities—but everywhere he turns, even the Vatican, he encounters corruption and more enemies. After confessing his sins to an insightful cardinal (soon to become Pope John Paul, and soon to die), Michael asks God for an opportunity to atone for killing his brother (Fredo, at the end of *Part II*—the most important of his sins, since it was against the family), and he gets it: By the end of the film, Michael loses the person he loves the most —his daughter, who is shot to death right in front of him. His silent scream as he holds her body is the beginning of his penance and is one of the strongest moments the American cinema had produced in years. From then till the end of his life, Michael remains in Sicily and, we assume, does no evil. If the intrigues and subplots of *Part III* are not as riveting as those in the first two films, *Part III* is still to be praised for adhering to the tragic, emotional, and ethical logic of its predecessors, and its intricate climax (cross-cut killings and rituals climax all three films) is as fine as anything Coppola has ever done.

Coppola's Vietnam epic, *Apocalypse Now*, is more ragged and less whole (not at all surprising, given the grief, money, and time— three years—to complete it). Coppola's foe is again the system itself, the military mentality that produces a Kurtz (Brando), insane with power; a Willard (Martin Sheen), who, like Ethan Edwards in *The Searchers*, must search for Kurtz by becoming Kurtz; and a Kilgore (Robert Duvall), who can make little distinction between the fun of surfboarding and the fun of napalming. Coppola's metaphoric journey upriver—adapted from Joseph Conrad's *Heart of Darkness*—is dominated by powerful images: Playboy bunnies entertaining the troops (deliberately reminiscent of those Bob Hope GI shows); the psychedelic nighttime carnival in which Willard wanders through an eerie wasteland of stoned, "tripping" soldiers; the horrifying collection of severed human heads that decorates Kurtz's camp.

Coppola's musicals (*Finian's Rainbow, One from the heart, The Cotton Club*) are stylistic exercises that explore the central paradoxes of the musical as a genre—the relation of convention to credibility, stylization to reality, number to story, and entertainment to social commentary. In these films, Coppola sacrifices his characters and their actions for intrusive style: references to a trunkful of other movies in *Finian's Rainbow* (*Hallelujah, Our Daily Bread, Strike, Monte Carlo, Mary Poppins*); deliberately intrusive color and lighting shifts and painted, stylized decor in *One from the heart*; another trunkful of filmic references in *The Cotton Club* (*The Gold*

Rush, Lights of New York, Little Caesar, Twentieth Century, Goin' Hollywood, Sunset Boulevard). Unfortunately, these musicals have at times (despite that title) very little heart—the ultimate element that gives a musical its artistic sense.

Martin Scorsese combines the improvisational acting spontaneity of Altman with the urban, Italian-American sensibility of Coppola. Scorsese seems to succeed most with carefully textured psychological portraits of Americans deeply entangled in their neorealistically detailed social environments—New York's Little Italy (*Mean Streets*, 1973), a diner in the arid American Southwest (*Alice Doesn't Live Here Anymore*, 1974), a paranoid hell of New York street life (*Taxi Driver*, 1976). *Raging Bull* (1980) was ostensibly a biographical case history of boxer Jake La Motta, but it went much deeper. Combining Italian neorealism and the visual style of 1950s New York films (set in that period, shot primarily in black-and-white), *Raging Bull* paralleled the violence of American boxing to American sexual violence in general; the male's *machismo* and misogyny suggest a self-destructiveness turned against others and a repressed homosexual paranoia.

As fast and violent as Scorsese's films often are, they are also intensely meditative; many even have thoughtful voice-over narrators. He moves the camera with more zest and authority than anyone now making movies. He is scrupulously attentive to technical quality and wildly excited about the work of classic craftsmen like Michael Powell—or Hitchcock, Lean, Rossellini, Bresson, Hawks, and others, because this is one director who knows his film history and loves watching movies as well as making them. The visceral editing (often by Thelma Schoonmaker), the evocative music (often old, carefully selected rock'n'roll; Bernard Herrmann composed the music for *Taxi Driver* shortly before his death), the state-of-the-art soundtracks, and beyond all that the ironies and depths of Scorsese's films have vaulted him to the first rank of American directors. As a professional and as an artist, he may well be the most highly respected filmmaker of his generation.

"I'm God's lonely man," says Travis Bickle (Robert De Niro), the psychopathic taxi driver

Fig. 15-7
Apocalypse Now: *the grotesque juxtaposition of surfboards and napalm.*

who wants to cleanse the world of sin—and many of Scorsese's central characters are isolated (often within the limits of an obsession, whether it be an idea, a desire, or a view of the world) and do think about God. At the beginning of *Mean Streets*, Charlie (Harvey Keitel) observes, voice-over, "You don't make up for your sins in church. You do it in the streets; you do it at home." Charlie would like to do penance for his sins on his own, in his own terms, with actions rather than words. For a character like Jake La Motta (De Niro) in *Raging Bull*, punishing himself and impulsively, blindly seeking redemption might mean screaming at and fighting with everyone he loves or getting punched to a pulp in the ring and destroyed through all his mistakes. In *The Color of Money* (1986, the sequel to *The Hustler*), Fast Eddie Felson (Paul Newman) has to face himself, find himself, and in fact redeem himself not before a conventional altar, but at the spiritual and profane battleground of a pool table.

But not all of Scorsese's pictures are as upbeat and as morally and psychologically conventional as *The Color of Money*; most of them are as disturbing as *Raging Bull*, where we watch a man stupidly wreck his life, or *Taxi Driver*, where we share the meditations and worldview of an oddly innocent but genuinely crazy and violent man as he prepares a private apocalypse—and both La Motta and Bickle are characters we cannot shake, scary mysteries whose solution is completely emotional.

The King of Comedy (1983) transfers the obsessiveness of *Taxi Driver* to the world of entertainment (*Raging Bull* was already there; at one point Scorsese cuts from the line "That's entertainment!" to a loud, bloody smash to the face): Rupert Pupkin (De Niro), whose single-

Fig. 15-8
Mean Streets: *Charlie (Harvey Keitel) in church, crossing himself before the lighted candles and thinking of "the pain of Hell," the burning heat "from a lighted match increased a million times. Infinite."*

minded desire to appear on a talk show leads him to kidnap its host (Jerry Lewis), becomes a celebrity with his own show when he gets out of prison. *After Hours* (1985) is a relentless view of a night in Manhattan, a night full of promise during which everything goes wrong; the movie doesn't let up any more than Rupert Pupkin or Jake La Motta does.

GoodFellas (1990), the true story of a boy (Ray Liotta) who grew up to join the "wiseguys"—the friendly brotherhood of criminals who ran his neighborhood—and thought it was great until some of the crazy murderousness of his buddies (Joe Pesci, Robert De Niro) got out of hand, is Scorsese's return to the world of *Mean Streets*, this time with the matured skills of a world-class film-maker. Highly charged, fast-paced, full of sudden violence, and very funny, its tones and rhythms masterfully varied and controlled, *GoodFellas* presents the work- and home-life of its gangsters in a realistic, understated manner (unlike the romanticized *Godfather*)—at a

hundred miles an hour and changing direction without warning.

The great question in the majority of Scorsese's films is whether this is a world in which one can attain salvation; it is assumed that one cannot be saved by the church. When Scorsese turned at last to his long-delayed adaptation of Nikos Kazantzakis's *The Last Temptation of Christ* (1988; it took ten years to find a studio that would not be intimidated by Fundamentalist protests), he showed that even Jesus might have had trouble finding salvation, that even he might have felt that his destiny was bound up with the entanglements of this world—and that when Jesus accepted his true destiny, which was to be martyred rather than live out the life of an ordinary man (the last temptation), he entered a state of radical isolation, chose suffering, and expressed his spiritual conviction in an active, physical language of pain and blood, along with a few intense words. In all these respects Jesus is a prototypical Scorsese character, one whose suffering and

Fig. 15-9
Raging Bull: *Jake La Motta (Robert De Niro), at home, fighting with his first wife (Lori Anne Flax).*

confusion Scorsese has learned to understand. Although *The Last Temptation* was deeply devoted to celebrating the Christian sacrifice, albeit in Kazantzakis's and Scorsese's terms, it became the most controversial film of the late 1980s; around the world, screens were slashed and theatres were picketed, mostly by people who had not seen the movie and had no intention of dirtying their imaginations with it.

Scorsese has also produced films directed by others (starting with *The Grifters*, with which he was involved from 1986 to 1990) and has directed documentaries (*The Last Waltz*, 1978). Both he and Thelma Schoonmaker edited and were the assistant directors of Michael Wadleigh's *Woodstock: 3 Days of Peace & Music* (1970). In the 1980s, as a direct result of Scorsese's efforts, Eastman Kodak began to manufacture camera and printing stocks that would

hold their colors far longer than any previous Eastman film; these extremely high-quality filmstocks are now used throughout the American film industry.

Paul Mazursky specializes in psychological-sociological case histories, usually of city dwellers, but he adds offbeat comic ironies to his very solidly and charmingly acted portraits (*Bob & Carol & Ted & Alice*, 1969; *Harry and Tonto*, 1974; *Next Stop, Greenwich Village*, 1976; *An Unmarried Woman*, 1978; *Down and Out in Beverly Hills*, 1986, a remake of Renoir's *Boudu Saved from Drowning*; *Enemies, A Love Story*, 1989; *Scenes From A Mall*, 1991). Hal Ashby also made a string of solidly scripted, subtly acted, wryly comic films (*The Landlord*, 1970; *Harold and Maude*, 1971; *The Last Detail*, 1973; *Shampoo*, 1975; *Bound for Glory*, 1976; *Coming Home*, 1978; *Being There*, 1979), often about

Fig. 15-10
The Last Temptation of Christ: *Willem Dafoe as Jesus.*

oddballs in conflict with the assumed values of American life and sometimes about the process of defining those values.

Terrence Malick, who has been influenced by Murnau as much as by George Stevens, and who once taught philosophy, is the film poet of this generation, though he has directed only two features: *Badlands* and, five years later, *Days of Heaven* (1978). Both these films manipulate several complexly contrapuntal lines; both juxtapose violent narrative events with a spectacularly lush and rhythmically languid series of stunning visual images; both use ironic, immature voice-over narrators (Sissy Spacek in *Badlands*, Linda Manz in *Days of Heaven*) who understand, to varying degrees, the events they are involved in and whose unpolished voices contrast tonally with the rigorous, magnificent shots. The radiant, almost transcendent look of *Days of Heaven* (shot by Nestor Almendros), supported by the superb music of Ennio Morricone and a Dolby Stereo mix that could unforgettably put one in the middle of a fire fight or a windswept field of wheat, had a luminous beauty, a richness of texture, and a subtle palette that aspired to see into the heart of the physical world and to present the full range of its essential being on film. Both films are parables of good and evil, but *Badlands* is more flat —and for that, more funny and frightening; its love anthem is the strange rock song "Love Is Strange," and its narrator thinks in clichés (which, as we compare what she says with what we see, generate narrative complexity). The narrator of *Days of Heaven*, however, is a reliable commentator whose remarks are on target

and have their own poetry and wit, without being the least bit arty.

Paul Schrader, like Coppola and Scorsese, came to filmmaking from film school. His scripts for Scorsese (*Taxi Driver*), Brian De Palma (*Obsession*), Sidney Pollack (*The Yakuza*), and others, led to directing his own scripts. Raised in a strict Calvinist home and not permitted to see a movie until he was eighteen (a background reflected in his *Hardcore*, 1979), Schrader's films explore the repressions and guilt of characters with enormous sexual appetites and inflexible moral codes, characters who are fanatically attracted to ritual and seek redemption through discipline and violence or find it through grace. His first feature, *Blue Collar* (1978), took a hard and intensely political look at labor unions and at the "divide and conquer" strategy that frustrates class awareness in America. The later films have been more psychological and philosophical than political: *Hardcore, American Gigolo* (1980), *Mishima* (1985).

Brian De Palma began with offbeat projects (*Greetings*, 1968; the film version of the environmental theatre work, *Dionysus in 69*, and *Hi, Mom!*, both 1970). He graduated to reflexive parodies (*Phantom of the Paradise*, 1974), powerful horror films (*Carrie*, 1976; *The Fury*, 1978), and thrillers combining Hitchcock psychoses with Roger Corman atrocities (*Sisters*, 1973; *Obsession*, 1976; *Dressed to Kill*, 1980). De Palma makes the sexual repressions of his characters and the psychological aggressions of movie voyeurism increasingly explicit. *Dressed to Kill* is an attack on movie voyeurism as sexist pornography, a theme De Palma takes further in *Blow Out* (1981) and *Body Double* (1984).

Blow Out, modeled both on Antonioni's *Blowup* (as its title makes clear) and Coppola's *The Conversation*, combines Antonioni's quasi-pornographic fashion photographer with Coppola's sound recorder into a soundman for cheap horror movies. While Antonioni's photographer puts together the pieces of a puzzle by examining photographic stills and Coppola's by listening to tapes, De Palma's soundman puts together the pieces of a puzzle by combining still photographs with a soundtrack, just as movies do. And the focus of *Blow Out*'s investigation is not Antonioni's vaguely romantic

Fig. 15-11
Linda Manz, the narrator of **Days of Heaven.**

murder mystery but a political conspiracy and assassination.

Body Double, De Palma's "*Vertigo Meets Rear Window*," demonstrates the inherent similarities of three widely different types of movies—the hard-core pornographic film (such as those featuring porn-star Holly Body), the soft-core, trashy horror movie (such as those performed by the film's aspiring actor), and "legitimate" commercial films (such as those by Hitchcock, Antonioni, or De Palma). In De Palma's violent examination of film violence, a porn star is like any Hollywood star (her name, Holly Body, implies the conjunction of Hollywood and gazing at bodies)—an irony De Palma increases by casting Melanie Griffith, daughter of Tippi Hedren, star of Hitchcock's *The Birds* and *Marnie*, as Holly. The idea of a body double, of joining (by means of editing) an alluring, alternative torso to a star's beautiful face is as inherently voyeuristic and pornographic as it is cinematic. Indeed, it demonstrates the classic Soviet montage method of "creative geography," the montage technique Hitchcock used in *Psycho*'s slashing knife-murder of Janet Leigh

in the shower and De Palma himself used with a body double for Angie Dickinson in the shower sequences of *Dressed to Kill*.

The relationship of Hitchcock, Antonioni, and De Palma suggests a general historical evolution over three generations of film narrative (and storytelling in general). Critics summarize this evolution with the descriptive terms traditional, modernist, and postmodern. Hitchcock's stories seem "traditional" because he subordinates his subtle dissection of movie voyeurism to the film's primary narrative line—say, the solving of a murder in *Rear Window* or *Vertigo*. One could respond to a *Rear Window* without recognizing its ironic self-analysis of audience responses to cinema (indeed, audiences and critics responded in precisely this unselfconscious way in the 1950s).

Antonioni seems "modernist" because his primary narrative line cannot be understood literally; *Blowup*'s self-conscious theme (making inferences by connecting photographic images —as the photographer does to discover a murder) overwhelms its literal plot. The film's conclusion (the symbolic clowns with their invisible tennis ball, and the final disappearance of the hero-photographer as the frames on which we see *him* are drastically enlarged) cannot be interpreted literally; the film only achieves closure—a comprehensible, coherent conclusion—by relating the invisible ball to the film's abstract themes of vision and interpretation.

De Palma seems "postmodern" not only because his work comes after and refers to Antonioni's, but because this critical term suggests a *return* to conventional narrative structures (like Hitchcock's) that also *require* metaphoric, self-conscious interpretation (like Antonioni's). *Blow Out* and *Body Double* both tell a story and dissect the procedures of storytelling, a reflexive double duty. This evolution over three generations of film narrative suggests not extreme differences in kind but subtle differences in emphasis and degree: whether a film story (or any story) should be primarily an engaging tale, a challenging attack on storytelling, or both. Many American filmmakers of the current generation share De Palma's assumption—Altman (*Brewster McCloud*), Coppola (*One from the heart*), Scorsese (*The King of Comedy*), and Schrader (*Mishima*) among them—but De Palma has been particularly successful at pushing his films to violent extremes in both opposite directions of this narrative double duty.

Several other directors, not so many years ago, seemed much more interesting than they do today—a further warning about the ephemerality of directorial reputations and the difficulty of assessing artists in mid-career. Peter Bogdanovich was the new American *auteur* who was most influenced by the *auteur* theory and its application to the old Hollywood movie. Like many of the French New Wave directors, Bogdanovich began as a film critic, his favorite subjects being Hawks, Ford, and those lesser known studio directors (Raoul Walsh, Allan Dwan) whose individuality and consistency had not been previously appreciated. Bogdanovich's first film, *Targets* (1968), in many ways his cleverest, is a film buff's film, taking its style from the Roger Corman Technicolor-terror genre (Corman produced the film), complete with Boris Karloff as its star. For *The Last Picture Show* (1971) and *Paper*

Moon (1973) Bogdanovich recreated the dry, dusty aridity of America's rural past—of the 1950s and 1930s, respectively. He also used the textures of American films of those decades, in particular his radical decision to use black-and-white. The danger of Bogdanovich's pure universe of art and homage is clear in *What's Up, Doc?* (1972) and *At Long Last Love* (1975), heavy-handed and empty attempts to combine 1930s musical and screwball comedy with contemporary acting techniques and production values. Unlike the *Cahiers* critics who became filmmakers in France, Bogdanovich seems to have little to make movies about except movies themselves. Some of his later films have succumbed to Hollywood formulas (*Mask*, 1985), while the best have avoided or undermined them (*Saint Jack*, 1979).

William Friedkin is the tightest and most impersonal technician of the new directors, a man who sees each project as a specific tactical problem to be solved and who then proceeds to solve it in a dazzling way. Among the problems he has posed himself are translating talky stage plays into cinema (*The Birthday Party*, 1968; *The Boys in the Band*, 1970); capturing the texture and flavor of the old burlesque houses, customers, and performers (*The Night They Raided Minsky's*, 1968); translating the violence of urban police life into imagery (*The French Connection*); bringing the devil to the screen with convincing and terrifying effectiveness (*The Exorcist*); and capturing the social and sexual atmosphere of New York's sadomasochistic homosexual underworld (*Cruising*). Friedkin's solutions are as eclectic as the problems themselves: developing the human texture of *Boys in the Band*; exercising great care with atmosphere and color textures in *The Brink's Job* (1978) and *The Night They Raided Minsky's*; editing *The French Connection* with overwhelming dexterity and virtuosity; and employing one of the most disturbingly agonizing soundtracks—and Dick Smith's special effects make-up—for *The Exorcist*. Friedkin described his own intention in all his films as that of producing powerful but crude emotional effects—terror, tension, suspense. With the exception of *To Live and Die in L.A.* (1985), most of Friedkin's later films—*Sorcerer* (1977, a remake of *The Wages of Fear*), *Deal of the Century* (1983), *The*

Guardian (1990)—have struck audiences as more crudely leaden than crudely exciting.

Of the older generation of Hollywood directors, Mike Nichols (*Who's Afraid of Virginia Woolf?*; *The Graduate*; *Catch-22*, 1970; *Carnal Knowledge*, 1971; *The Day of the Dolphin*, 1973), a very successful director of Neil Simon comedies on the stage, made his most important film in 1967 when *The Graduate*—released a few months after *Bonnie and Clyde*—seemed to summarize the attitude of the entire younger generation toward the stifling world of bourgeois adulthood. Since *The Graduate* and *Carnal Knowledge* (script by Jules Feiffer), Nichols proved with every film that he was very good at observing human beings during comic scenes of offbeat dialogue and very weak at everything else to do with cinema. In the 1980s, Nichols spent most of his time back in the theatre but made two commercially successful films, *Silkwood* (1983) and *Working Girl* (1988). Elaine May, his partner in the 1950s nightclub-and-LP comedy team Nichols and May, has directed several films, the most important of which are *The Heartbreak Kid* (1972, a studio comedy with lots of bite) and *Mikey and Nicky* (shot 1973, released 1976, re-edited and re-released in the 1980s; strongly influenced by the work of John Cassavetes, and starring Cassavetes and Peter Falk).

Arthur Penn is a director of the old school (*The Miracle Worker*, 1962) who came to the movies from television dramas and converted to the new school. His dominant interest is the creation of folk legends out of outlaws or offbeat social rebels (*The Left-Handed Gun*, 1958; *Mickey One*, 1965; *Bonnie and Clyde*; *Alice's Restaurant*, 1969; *Little Big Man*, 1970), a concern that, like *The Graduate*, made its greatest impact on younger audiences in the anti-myth late 1960s and early 1970s. Of his later films, the most interesting and underrated is *Night Moves* (1975). The least appreciated of his great films is *Alice's Restaurant*.

Martin Ritt, who acted with the Group Theater in the 1930s, directed hundreds of TV shows and dramas before he was blacklisted. He spent the early 1950s at the Actors Studio, teaching Paul Newman, Joanne Woodward, Rod Steiger, and others how to act. His first feature film, *Edge of the City* (1957)—a realistic look at race relations and corrupt union practices in and around the docks of New York, starring Sidney Poitier and John Cassavetes—indicated Ritt's great skill with actors and the controversial, nonconformist direction the best of his films would take: *Paris Blues* (1961), *Hud* (1963), *The Spy Who Came In From The Cold* (1965), *Sounder* (1972), *The Front* (1976, about the blacklist).

Other blacklisted directors who went on to do major work, but outside the country, include Jules Dassin (*The Canterville Ghost*, 1944; *Brute Force*, 1947; *The Naked City*, 1948; *Night and the City*, 1950, a *noir* filmed in England; *Rififi*, 1955, French, a great caper movie famous for its long, silent burglary sequence; *Never on Sunday*, 1960, Greek; *10:30 PM Summer*, 1966, French, from a novel by Duras; *A Dream of Passion*, 1978, Greek, his response to *Persona*) and Joseph Losey (*The Boy With Green Hair*; *The Prowler*; *The Big Night*, 1951; *Stranger on the Prowl*, 1953, Italian; *The Damned*, 1962, British, released in the United States as *These Are the Damned*; *The Servant*, British, script by Pinter; *King and Country*, 1964, British; *Accident*, 1967, British, script by Pinter; *The Go-Between*, 1971, British, script by Pinter; *The Romantic Englishwoman*, 1975, British; *Mr. Klein*, 1976, French; *Steaming*, 1985, British).

Like Lumet, Penn, and Ritt, John Frankenheimer directed for TV before making movies; his first feature, *The Young Stranger* (1957), was a remake of a TV drama he had directed. One of his best pictures, *The Manchurian Candidate* (1962, from the novel by Richard Condon), was withdrawn from distribution after the assassination of President Kennedy because it included a number of political assassinations, one virtually at the presidential level. For similar reasons, Bogdanovich's *Targets* was withdrawn after the murder of Robert Kennedy, never again to be shown theatrically—but *The Manchurian Candidate* had better luck and was re-released in 1987; theatre owners and film distributors were surprised that the late-80s audience would be so interested in an old black-and-white movie that took politics seriously and played games with perception (near the beginning, it cuts between what is seen by characters who have been hypnotized and by those who have not), especially when the revival houses

Fig. 15-12
The Manchurian Candidate: *The brainwashed Raymond (Laurence Harvey) enjoys a little game of solitaire and goes into a trance as his mother (Angela Lansbury) watches.*

evitability of violence in human experience and the necessity of defining one's relation to it (*Straw Dogs*, 1971), or both (*The Wild Bunch*, 1969).

Most of Peckinpah's films were recut by the studios before release—even *The Wild Bunch* lost half an hour. Charlton Heston once stood outside the cutting room with a rifle so that Peckinpah could edit *Major Dundee* (1965) without interference—but the film was simply recut after Peckinpah delivered it. MGM executive James Aubrey told Peckinpah to cut an hour from *Pat Garrett and Billy the Kid* (1973)— in three weeks!—when he had no intention of using that cut; while Peckinpah slaved away, managing to remove forty minutes without changing the picture's structure, Aubrey had the editing department prepare the shortened, straightened-out, ruined release version. Among Peckinpah's lesser works, the films that best managed to survive such mutilation include *The Ballad of Cable Hogue* (1970, in which the Old West figure is run over by the first car he has ever seen), *The Getaway* (1972, from the novel by Jim Thompson, which has a much nastier ending; however, Thompson's hellish conclusion was not cut from the film, as one might by now imagine—it isn't in the script and was never shot), and his only war film, *Cross of Iron* (1977). *Pat Garrett* and *Bring Me the Head of Alfredo Garcia* (1974) at this point just look incoherent. The final film of this artist who was, in his own way, an embattled last survivor of the Old West—and whose work amounted to much more than the bloody, slow-motion death sequences that became his trademark—was *The Osterman Weekend* (1983); to see it was not only to feel that it could have been better but to know that it *had* been better.

John Cassavetes got his start in television, but as an actor. Like Orson Welles, he acted in features (*Rosemary's Baby, The Fury*, Robert Aldrich's 1967 *The Dirty Dozen*) primarily in order to pay for the films he directed, the most significant of which are *Shadows* (1958, recut 1959), *Faces* (1968), *Husbands* (1970), *Minnie and Moskowitz* (1971), *A Woman Under the Influence* (1975), *The Killing of a Chinese Bookie* (1976, recut 1978), *Opening Night* (1978), *Gloria* (1980), and *Love Streams* (1984). His films reveal a unique fusion—of narrative cin-

were closing and old movies had been relegated to the world of video. The best of his later works is the medical thriller *Seconds* (1966), a cautionary tale about the desire to recapture one's youth, starring Rock Hudson in his most intriguing performance. Others that merit a good look include *Seven Days in May* (1964), *The Fixer* (1968), *The Iceman Cometh* (1973), and *Black Sunday* (1977).

Sam Peckinpah, who also came to films from television (where he was primarily a writer), is another director who achieved his greatest success in the anti-myth era. Without question, he made the greatest westerns of the 1960s. Peckinpah's three best films study the crumbling old men (Randolph Scott and Joel McCrea) who personify the last gasp of the free spirit of the Old West (*Ride the High Country*, 1962), the in-

Fig. 15-13
Gena Rowlands and John Marley in **Faces.**

ema, candidly documentary shooting styles, confessional explorations of character, and an unswerving commitment to filmmaking as personal statement—that remained fresh, experimental, honest, and intense throughout his career (he died in 1989). As a director, he was an actor working with actors, trying to get them to reveal the essential being and unstylized behavior of their characters; as a writer, he strove to present the ways people really talk and behave, charting a fine line between the too tightly organized and the pointlessly rambling; as a complete filmmaker, he sought an invisible style that would not be arty, pretty, or in the way. His wife, Gena Rowlands, and his friends Seymour Cassel, Peter Falk, and Ben Gazzara gave their finest performances in his films, probing their own, their characters', and Cassavetes's vital energies and personal mysteries in an atmosphere that was kept utterly free of artificiality, phoniness, and formulaic solutions.

As an independent who freelanced on the fringes of the studio system, Cassavetes wrote, produced, directed, distributed, and sometimes acted in his films, all of which conceptualize experience in terms of the interactions of a tightly knit cluster of individuals. One acts out one's destiny in front of an audience in Cassavetes's work, whether that be a paying audience and a metaphoric family (*The Killing of a Chinese Bookie*), a literal family (*A Woman Under the Influence*), or a group linked by a dynamic system of intimate relationships (*Faces*). However deeply personal its sources, experience is public and social. Cassavetes's characters function within a force field of social "influences" that can never be escaped or avoided. The only course of survival is to master these evershifting, often fiercely predatory forces; the alternatives are misery and destruction. As his characters maneuver for position, power, and self-knowledge within volatile networks of mutal responsibility, Cassavetes reveals just how complex living can be. The intricacy of Cassavetes's depiction of his characters' negotiations with each other — along with the deliberately unpolished quality of his shooting and editing — give his scenes the appearance of having been improvised, but the fact is that all these hesitations, ellipses, and obliquities of expression were scripted and rehearsed in advance.

Although the relentless pressures and the fierce conflicts in his work gave Cassavetes the reputation of being a pessimist, he repeatedly denied the accusation that his films were negative or despairing. He argued that he was as idealistic as Capra (who, with Dreyer, was among his favorite filmmakers), that he was actually only updating Capra's work for the postwar era. In his own view of his work, he was celebrating his characters' virtually heroic capacities of creative response to the dangers and problems they confront.

That heroic creative response is one Cassavetes shared with his characters. A Hollywood outsider fighting the studios, distribution systems, and publicity machinery for his vision of the feature film not as a commercial product but as a personal expression, this fiercely independent, embattled filmmaker was not discouraged but challenged and energized by the forces that sought to destroy or dismiss his uniquely demanding, historically significant work.

Sidney Lumet began as an off-Broadway director, then became a highly efficient television director. His first movie was typical of his best work: a well-acted, tightly organized, deeply considered "problem picture," *12 Angry Men* (1957). Since then, Lumet has divided his energies among idealistic problem pictures (*Fail-Safe*, 1964; *The Hill*, 1965; *Serpico*, 1973; *Prince of the City*, 1981; *The Verdict*, 1982), literate adaptations of plays (*Long Day's Journey Into Night*, 1962) and novels (*The Pawnbroker*, 1965; *The Group*, 1966; *The Deadly Affair*, 1967), big stylish pictures that tend to go nowhere (*The Wiz*, 1978), and New York-based black comedies (*Bye Bye Braverman*, 1968; *Dog Day Afternoon*,

1975; *Network*, 1976). For over three decades, from *12 Angry Men* to *Q & A* (1990), Lumet's sensitivity to actors and to the rhythms of the city have made him America's longest-lived descendant of the 1950s neorealist tradition and its urgent commitment to ethical responsibility. Beneath the social conflicts of Lumet's best films lies the conviction that reason will eventually prevail in human affairs, that law and justice will eventually be served.

The films of Clint Eastwood represent the continuation of a very different tradition — the American genre film's classic definition of moral stature through the assertion of individual will and the exercise of personal style. From the 1960s "spaghetti westerns" directed by Sergio Leone (*A Fistful of Dollars*; *For a Few Dollars More*; *The Good, the Bad and the Ugly*) through the "Dirty Harry" city-crime films of the 1970s and 1980s directed by Don Siegel (*Dirty Harry*, 1971), Ted Post (*Magnum Force*, 1973), and Eastwood himself (*Sudden Impact*, 1983), the Eastwood films depict a society ungovernable by laws, lawmakers, principles, procedures, and bureaucrats. Only a vigilante Enforcer like Harry Callahan can bring criminals to a primitive justice, for he is as mean and "dirty" (if neat in appearance and methodical in strategy — the name means that he gets stuck with all the dirty jobs) as the dirty menaces he blows away.

Harry brings no order to his world — the way Ford's Wyatt Earp can — for the world cannot be ordered. The destruction Callahan wreaks is at least as messy and bloody as that of the criminals he tracks. So of course he is the enemy of conscientious bureaucrats who keep their noses clean behind desks. Ultimately, Harry demonstrates his personal honesty, will, skill, and style — nothing more. If Harry's fondness for big guns that make large holes seems both Freudian and sexist, the Eastwood films are certainly conscious of it.

Aside from his screen personae of Harry Callahan and Leone's "Man with no name," Eastwood is an accomplished director of action films (*The Enforcer*, 1976), westerns (*High Plains Drifter*, 1973), and thrillers (*Play Misty for Me*, 1971) who also has a serious interest in jazz — evident not only in his ambitious biography of Charlie Parker, *Bird* (1988), but also in his having persuaded Warner Bros. to co-finance Tavernier's *Round Midnight*.

Eastwood learned the trade by watching Don Siegel, an action director with a tough sense of humor, whose major works include *Riot in Cell Block 11* (1954), *Invasion of the Body Snatchers* (1956), *Baby Face Nelson* (1957), *The Killers* (1964, not broadcast because it was too violent, but the first movie made for TV), *Madigan* (1968), *The Beguiled* (1971), *Dirty Harry, Charley Varrick* (1973), *The Shootist* (1976), and *Escape from Alcatraz* (1979).

A new generation of horror directors appeared during this period, though some (in America, John Carpenter and Wes Craven; in Canada, David Cronenberg; in Italy, Dario Argento) were not widely known until after 1976. While studio pictures from *Rosemary's Baby* and *The Exorcist* to *Jaws* (Steven Spielberg, 1975) and *Carrie* kept the genre alive in the mainstream, independently produced films catered to the drive-in crowd with explicit gore (Herschell Gordon Lewis's *Blood Feast*, 1963, was the first gore film), sadistic sex and violence (Wes Craven's *The Last House on the Left*, 1972), troubling fantasy (Herk Harvey's *Carnival of Souls*, 1962), and gruesome humor (Joel Reed's *Blood Sucking Freaks*, 1978).

The most important American horror film since *Psycho* was George A. Romero's *Night of the Living Dead* (1968), a gory, low-budget, black-and-white, tightly organized shocker that remains as frightening and revolting as it is thought-provoking. *Night of the Living Dead* takes a hard look at the world that is in danger of being taken over by flesh-eating zombies, and few of the living measure up; most are selfish, violent, stupid. The strongest, smartest, most resourceful character is played by a black man (Duane Jones—in the history of film, the first black actor to be cast in a leading role *regardless* of the fact that he was black, rather than because of it), and though he survives the night, he is shot and burned the next morning by a redneck posse—shown in grainy stills and brief shots that resemble 1960s news coverage of racist incidents in the South. The Vietnam War and the civil rights movement made their presence felt in this film, though it did not set

Fig. 15-14
Kept back by fire, but not for long: the flesh-eating zombies of George Romero's **Night of the Living Dead.**

out to be a political or racial allegory and simply happened to express—as expressionist horror often does—the tension of the time with unprecedented force.

The sequels, however, took on social issues deliberately—for as an officially despised genre, the low-budget horror film was (and still is) free to take outrageous creative chances and adopt controversial attitudes toward the issues of the day—or of eternity. Daring and iconoclastic, *Dawn of the Dead* (1978, released 1979) did not just satirize consumerism (the heroes are isolated in a besieged shopping mall this time, not in a besieged farmhouse) but presented the imminent death of the whole racist, sexist, materialistic world—and the media, too; at the end of this film, which in its uncut version may well be the 1970s' greatest satire, the survivors are a black man and a pregnant white woman. The besieged humans in *Day of the Dead* (1985), who are in an underground government storage facility (another museum of human culture, like the mall in *Dawn*), are viciously divided: on one side the bad guys—racist, sexist, militaristic—and on the other a group of intelligent, resourceful workers and scientists (one of whom is, of course, mad); at the end, the few survivors include a white woman and a black man. Romero's *Dead* trilogy puts a completely new face on the end of the world—murderous, ravenous, mindlessly compulsive, inarticulate, dead—and makes it clear what is, or was, worth saving about humanity. Romero's other horror films include *Martin* (1976), a complex, disturbing, formally experimental tale about a young man who is not your average vampire; *Creepshow* (1982, script by Stephen King), an attempt to capture the look and spirit of 1950s EC horror comics on film; and *Monkey Shines* (1988), whose vindictive-mad-scientist ending was deleted—and dumb ending inserted—over Romero's objections.

The Texas Chain Saw Massacre (1974) was another independent first feature made far from Hollywood (in Texas; *Night of the Living Dead* came from Pittsburgh) that put its director, Tobe Hooper, in the permanent annals of the genre. A deranged family melodrama that lives up to its title, *The Texas Chain Saw Massacre* is painfully violent, grossly repulsive, and full of ghoulish art (like *Psycho*, it was inspired by the case of Ed Gein, the Wisconsin ghoul), for one of its principal subjects is the art of horror. Hooper's most brilliantly reflexive horror film, *The Funhouse* (1981), and his most commercially successful film, *Poltergeist* (1982, produced by Spielberg), have higher production values but continue to investigate, as *Texas Chain Saw* did, the nature of the "normal" and "abnormal," particularly in terms of the family. Larry Cohen's *It's Alive* (1974) takes another approach to the institution of the family: a monstrous killer baby, destroyed by killer police and representatives of a killer society. Cohen's tongue-in-cheek monster films (*Q*, 1982) prepared the way for his sharpest satire, *The Stuff* (1985), in which the monster is a truly organic health food as addictive as cocaine.

Discussions of science fiction in this period inevitably come around to one film: Stanley Kubrick's *2001: A Space Odyssey* (1968), released one year before the first moon landing but still offering a completely realized vision of outer space—which is not surprising, since Kubrick is such a meticulous and demanding artist. In the early 1960s, Kubrick detached himself from the constraints of American studios to produce films in England, but his work remains rooted in American values and culture. A perfectionist who, like Welles and Bresson, controls every detail of the film himself, from

Fig. 15-15

Fig. 15-16

Full Metal Jacket: *Kubrick's relentless parody of the Vietnam War takes the recruits from the point where they are taught by the machine to be part of the machine (Fig. 15-15) to their survival or death in combat (Fig. 15-16, one of the few images to acknowledge the high number of black casualties in the war).*

scripting to editing—but with the advantage of being his own producer—Kubrick works very slowly. His reputation rests on only nine films: *The Killing* (1956), *Paths of Glory* (1957), *Lolita* (1962), *Dr. Strangelove Or: How I Learned To Stop Worrying And Love The Bomb* (1964), *2001, A Clockwork Orange* (1971), *Barry Lyndon* (1975), *The Shining* (1980), and *Full Metal Jacket* (1987). Kubrick's early films, *Fear and Desire* (1953) and *Killer's Kiss* (1955), are melodramatic apprentice work; and on *Spartacus* (1960), Kubrick was more doctor than director, having been brought in by Kirk Douglas to help save an immobile and overstuffed patient.

Kubrick films are often unpopular with American critics. In none of the films is there a successful fulfilling love relationship; there is something very cold about the Kubrick world. Kubrick has also been attacked for being a pure craftsman and a careful imitator of other directors' cinematic styles. *Paths of Glory* undeniably recalls the elegant, polite, hypocritical world of Renoir's *Grand Illusion* combined with the Germanic camera movement of Murnau and Pabst. The back-lit, shadowy, low-angle cinematography of *Dr. Strangelove* irresistibly recalls *Citizen Kane*. But Kubrick's work does not borrow from the work of Renoir and Welles so much as echo it. Like Renoir and Rossellini, Kubrick begins with a deep thematic conviction and a refusal to compromise in developing that conviction.

The essential Kubrick theme is man's love affair with death. Kubrick seems to be a social critic in that his films consistently rip apart the hypocrisies of polite society: the military society of World War I France, the pseudointellectual society of suburbia, the political society of the White House and Pentagon, the scientific society that can develop rockets that fly to the moon as well as bombs to annihilate nations, the sterilized banality of a society of the future, the elegant hypocrisies of Europe's eighteenth-century aristocracy. As with Renoir, Kubrick's social evils are human evils; people created society, not the other way around. Without a society men slaughter each other individually, as they do in "The Dawn of Man" sequence in *2001* after the first ape/man discovers the use of a weapon. With society men slaughter each other *en masse* under the pretext of patriotism, military justice, or national defense.

Kubrick's great cinematic gift is not just his ability to develop this bitterly ironic theme but his gift for finding the perfect ironic tone—part horror, part humor, a mixture of burlesque and Grand Guignol—for developing it. This ironic tone resembles that of Jonathan Swift as well as that of Renoir in his bitterly satiric human comedy of manners, *The Rules of the Game*. Few American directors have been able to handle social satire without turning it into a pie-throwing farce. The cold, hard intellectual edge of Kubrick's satirical knife never lets the sad farce become silly farce.

Dr. Strangelove is the fullest expression of the Kubrick theme and the Kubrick tone. The film begins with an audacious visual joke. Two jet planes, one refueling the other in mid-air, appear to be copulating. Kubrick emphasizes the gag by underscoring the planes' passion with a lush romantic version of the popular tune, "Try a Little Tenderness." As it turns out, the whole film synthesizes copulation and murder. The American general, Buck Turgidson (George C. Scott) acts the same in the bedroom with his sweetie as he does in the war room discussing the bomb crisis. The crazed army commander, Jack Ripper (Sterling Hayden), develops his whole theory about the Commies attacking his "precious bodily fluids" with fluoridated water based on how he felt after making love. The American pilots in the atomic bomber work feverishly to drop their bomb on the Rooskies although the plane has been critically damaged. When they finally succeed in dropping it, the plane's commander (Slim Pickens) rides the bomb down to his destruction, whooping like a cowboy on a bronco, the bomb looking exactly like an enormous surrogate phallus.

The ultimate symbol of man's romance with death is Dr. Strangelove himself, the "converted" Nazi scientist (like Wernher von Braun, the former Nazi who headed America's atomic weaponry research), who still delights in the means of mass murder and who, despite his platitudinous respect for American democracy, cannot keep his black Rotwang glove from rising into an instinctive "Sieg heil." (Strangelove was one of three roles played by Peter Sellers in this film; the others were Lionel Mandrake and President Merkin Muffley. All three names include sexual puns.) The film ends as it began, with a romantic orgy performed by death-dealing machines. The bombs explode in hypnotizingly beautiful rhythms, while Vera Lynn sings her optimistically romantic tune of the 1940s, "We'll Meet Again"—the audience and the Bomb, that is; "some sunny day," we have a hot date.

For more than four decades Americans have made films about the threat of nuclear disaster. If *Dr. Strangelove* still seems as fresh and pointed as any of them, it is because it never deserts its caustic analysis of causes for the

Fig. 15-17

Fig. 15-18
Dr. Strangelove: *Farcical madmen decide the fate of the world. Dr. Strangelove (Peter Sellers, Fig. 15-17) and General Buck Turgidson (George C. Scott, right, Fig. 15-18) in the War Room.*

effects of pathos (*On the Beach*), suspense (*Seven Days in May* and *Fail-Safe*), horror (*The War Game*), or reassuring solutions.

Kubrick's virtuosity as a stylist tempted him into adapting two essentially unadaptable literary style pieces—Vladimir Nabokov's *Lolita* and Anthony Burgess's *A Clockwork Orange*. Both of the novels are totally dependent on a virtuoso's manipulation of language; Kubrick turned both into films with many remarkable moments and sections, but both films ultimately fail to reproduce the complexity of the original works. And for the same reason. Both novels use a first-person narrator; both narrators use language in an idiosyncratic way (Humbert Humbert's effusive intellectualizations; Alex's private argot, Nadsat); and both novels use such unique language because this language *is* the mind of the narrator, the way he sees the world, and that narrator's mind *is* the subject of the book. That mind is not Kubrick's subject (or interest), and in losing the central intelligence of both novels Kubrick loses the essence of both original works, though he of course creates—with his own additions, substitutions, deletions, and selective emphases—works that are themselves original. Fans of Stephen King's *The Shining* have had to make the same kind of peace with Kubrick's film, which has its own merits but pays little or no attention to King's version of the story. Kubrick's dominant concerns—social violence, social satire, and social sterility—pull the original psychological novels in interesting but more superficial directions.

To some extent, the same is true of *2001: A Space Odyssey*, which is really two films, one mystical, one cynical, which Kubrick attempts to hold in balance. On the one hand, Kubrick's astronauts travel toward the meaning of life itself, the life force that has specifically planted metal slabs on Earth, beneath the surface of the moon, and near Jupiter at the "dawn of time," in order to influence human progress—and reward it at the correct stage, for in order to find the moon's monolith, human technology would have to have developed to the point of landing people on the moon. Thus the mysterious silent slabs are both beacons and goads. The first slab provokes the discovery of the first tool, a discovery that culminates in the invention of rocket ships and computers, which are further extensions of human beings. Kubrick's brilliant cut from the soaring bone to the floating space shuttle visually establishes the connection between these tools. The second slab provokes the Jupiter Mission, which takes human beings to their next stage of evolution, "beyond the infinite." After some form of education and maturation in a strange room, the life mystery sends the reborn astronaut back to Earth in a different kind of space capsule—a womblike bubble. Presumably a new species of human beings—or stage of evolution—begins with this starchild. This metaphysical theme necessarily remains fuzzy and elusive in the film; the monoliths and the force behind them are never explained—which leaves the feeling of metaphysical mystery intact.

On the other hand, the film's social commentary is quite clear, a satirical study of a race that can improve its machines and weapons but not its mind and instincts. The first tool that the ape-man discovers becomes a weapon. When humans travel to the moon, they take their capitalistic establishments with them—Pan Am, Howard Johnson's, Bell Telephone. The scientist also takes his nationalistic prejudices and loyalties, not being free to discuss scientific problems with his colleagues from other countries. When human beings build super machines —the computer, HAL—they build them with human weaknesses. HAL is a superbrain; he also kills because he has been programmed with the human emotion to distrust his associates. The Jupiter Mission becomes a battle between man (Keir Dullea) and tool (HAL): which one is more "human," more evolved, more deserving of reaching the outermost monolith and learning its secrets. Despite the tensions in the film's two quests, 2001 remains one of the most intelligent "big" films ever made. Always intriguing, often breathtaking, it still looks absolutely fresh and contemporary—even after decades of progress in space operas, special effects, and computerized motion graphics.

The Independent American Cinema

The Independent American Cinema has been called by many names: the American Under-

ground, the American Avant-Garde, The New American Cinema, and the Experimental American Cinema among them. By whatever name, an alternative cinema tradition has existed in the United States since the 1920s with a series of assumptions that differ markedly from those of the commercial American cinema. This cinema is highly personal and individual (often one person literally makes the entire film); like poetry, it has virtually no commercial aspirations; and it is necessarily revolutionary in structure, or visual technique, or intellectual attitude, or all three. These personal, experimental films first attracted wider American attention in the mid-1960s, contemporaneous with *Bonnie and Clyde, Blowup*, and *2001*. Nevertheless, the American avant-garde, independent, poetic cinema was not particularly a 1960s movement. Rather, a tradition of avant-garde filmmaking that had grown along with, and been influenced by, the avant-garde cinema of Europe since the 1920s, and that had its own major films and figures and movements all along, went through a particularly creative phase just when public interest in film as an art was at its height.

There are three conflicting critical attitudes about the Independent Cinema. For some, this cinema represents the narcissistic visual scribblings of the lunatic fringe whose work is ultimately irrelevant to the development of serious film art (that is, commercial, feature-length "art films"). In support of this position, it is probably true that a vast majority of American filmgoers has never even heard of the most respected Independent filmmakers. A second position finds the Independent American Cinema a fertile testing ground for techniques and devices that are later absorbed and practiced by the mainstream of filmmaking (that is, commercial, feature-length narrative films). In support of this position one can point to the influence of the French avant-garde on the later features of Clair, Epstein, Renoir, and Buñuel (all of whom came out of the avant-garde), as well as the fact that many of the stylistic devices and moral attitudes of the commercial films of the 1960s and 1970s (their sensuality, the use of slow motion, accelerated motion, rock music, *musique concrète*, computer graphics, shock cutting, split screen) were first seen in Independent films. Many of the experiments undertaken by New Wave directors were inspired by those they had seen in 1958 (at the Brussels World's Fair and, a week later, in Paris) at screenings of films by Kenneth Anger, Jordan Belson, Stan Brakhage, Robert Breer, Jim Davis, Maya Deren, Ian Hugo, and others. Yet a third position finds the Independent American Cinema the only significant and serious works of film art in America. In support of this position, they observe that these are the only films free of commercial pressures, totally dependent on the vision of a single artist, and totally aligned with the parallel modernist movements in painting, music, and poetry. The business of these Independent films is perception: the way the devices of an art can aid, extend, and complicate a human being's ability to perceive inner and outer realities. That goal might be taken as the ultimate intention of all the modernist arts.

Rather than engage in this controversy of values, it would be useful simply to trace the history of this movement, to define its principles and principal types, and to mention the accomplishments of its most distinctive filmmakers. The tendency of the earliest avantgarde American films (in the 1920s and 1930s) was to avoid the Hollywood assumptions by making films of pure visual form, films that were, in effect, moving paintings that had little content beyond the visual content of forms in motion. Although Robert Florey and Slavko Vorkapich's *The Life and Death of 9413 — A Hollywood Extra* (1928, shot by Gregg Toland) protests against the facelessness and inhumanity of the modern industrial system (using the movie business as its industry), it is really a series of expressionist paintings made to move, combining the visual settings of the German expressionists (especially *Caligari*) with the camera trickery of the French surrealists. Another avant-garde film that tells a story but is primarily a triumph of pure Expressionism is James Sibley Watson and Melville Webber's *The Fall of the House of Usher* (1928). Ralph Steiner's *H₂O* (1929), which is composed exclusively of images of light reflecting on water, begins with beautiful and recognizable images (say, raindrops splashing in a rippling stream) and steadily becomes more abstract, so that the shots of

Fig. 15-19
H₂O: the abstract play of moving light and water.

light and shimmering water cease to look like anything except waving abstractions (a sort of moving Klee or Pollock painting). Among the few early exceptions to this purely formal rule were Joseph Berne's sensitive *Dawn to Dawn* (1934) and Watson and Webber's sexually symbolic *Lot in Sodom* (1933).

The best early films of pure form, movement, rhythm, and (later) music were made not in America, however, but in Europe. In the silent era, Hans Richter and Viking Eggeling excelled in rhythmically moving forms that also manipulated the restrictions of black-and-white. For example, Richter's *Rhythmus 21* (1921) features a variety of kinds of rhythmic movement: Rectangular shapes move about the screen, they change their sizes and shapes (expanding and contracting into lines, squares, trapezoids, and so forth); and they change their shades (shifting from white on black to black on white to gray on black, et cetera). Fernand Léger's *Ballet mécanique* (1924) was another film that strongly influenced the Americans. In the 1930s, Len Lye (whose *A Colour Box*, 1935, was animated without the use of a camera) in

England and Oskar Fischinger in Germany developed the film of pure form and movement to its height by using color and by accompanying the dizzily spinning and changing forms with appropriate musical backgrounds. In effect, these films became dances—the dance of color and shape.

The most important American independent filmmaker of the 1940s was Maya Deren, a woman who combined her interest in dance, in voodoo, and in subjective, phenomenological psychology in a series of surreal perceptual films. *Meshes of the Afternoon* (1943, soundtrack added 1959), *At Land* (1944), and *Ritual in Transfigured Time* (1946) defy the continuity of space and time, erase the line between dream and reality, and turn the entire vision of the film into the streaming consciousness of the filmmaker. In *Meshes* and *At Land*, she is the central performer—both the mind behind the film and the body within it. *Meshes of the Afternoon* uses a series of repeating motifs—a shadow walking dreamily down a garden path, a flower, a key, a knife, a telephone receiver, attempts to mount a flight of stairs—that prefigure the use of similarly repeating motifs in *Last Year at Marienbad* almost two decades later. Deren attacks objective reality by metamorphosizing the knife into the key, the flower into the knife, by making the act of climbing a flight of stairs seem impossibly difficult and tortuous (by her use of lenses, camera angles, and slow motion), and by combining suggestions of chastity, sexuality, and death without the audience's ever being able to pull the complexly woven themes apart to make solid and coherent sense out of them. The motifs weave together musically rather than rationally, tangling the viewer in a systematic labyrinth of unresolvable resonances. As such, the film serves as a clear bridge between the Surrealism of *Un Chien andalou* and the dream-realities of *Marienbad*, *Persona*, and *8½*. Her very brief *A Study in Choreography for Camera: Pas de Deux* (1945), which, like most of her films, is silent, combines Deren's two dominant interests—the movement within space of dance and the movement of space through editing—to reveal how editing may create the impression of continuous motion through discontinuous space.

Greatly influenced by Maya Deren, the

Fig. 15-20
Maya Deren with her 16mm camera.

American avant-garde began building itself into a movement in the mid-1950s—aided by the expanding availability of 8mm and 16mm equipment—with the recognition of the work of a great many major filmmakers. Joseph Cornell, who preceded Deren, made his first film in 1939. Those who began to make films in the 1940s, and of course continued to work for decades, include Kenneth Anger, James Broughton, Maya Deren, Curtis Harrington, Hy Hirsch, Ian Hugo, Willard Maas, Gregory Markopoulos, Marie Menken, Sidney Peterson, James Whitney, and John Whitney. The 1950s saw the first films of Jordan Belson, Stan Brakhage, Robert Breer, Shirley Clarke, Bruce Conner, James Davis, Ken Jacobs, Larry Jordan, Kurt Kren, Peter Kubelka, Christopher MacLaine, Ron Rice, Harry Smith, Jack Smith, and Stan VanDerBeek. In the 1960s, they were joined by Bruce Baillie, Jack Chambers, Bruce Elder, Hollis Frampton, Ernie Gehr, James Herbert, George Kuchar, Mike Kuchar, George Landow, Jonas Mekas, Gunvor Nelson, Andrew Noren, David Rimmer, Carolee Schneemann, Paul Sharits, Michael Snow,

Chick Strand, Andy Warhol, Joyce Wieland, and others.

Since the 1950s, the Independent Cinema has tended to gravitate toward four vague but recognizable "genres": the formal, the social-satirical, the sexual, and the reflexive. As with the avant-garde French films of the 1920s, these categories are neither rigid nor mutually exclusive. A film devoted primarily to the visual effects of imaginatively dancing forms can imply a social and a reflexive dimension (most notably Robert Breer's *Jamestown Baloos*, 1957, *Horse Over Teakettle*, 1962, and *Fist Fight*, 1964). A sexual film almost invariably satirizes the assumed social values of normality (say, Kenneth Anger's *Scorpio Rising*, 1963). And many of the films devoted to a reflexive meditation on the processes of film and filming necessarily devote themselves to dazzling manipulations of visual forms.

The film of pure form, one of the oldest experimental styles of cinema, persisted in the American Underground, much of it influenced by the earlier work of Fischinger, Léger, and Lye. Among the outstanding formal dances are the computer films of John Whitney, who, like Fischinger, combines his ceaselessly moving color-forms with appropriate accompanying music (*Catalog*, 1961; *Permutations*, 1968; *Matrix*, 1971). Whitney's films differ from Fischinger's in being more precise and mathematical in their symmetrical visual forms (not surprising, since those forms are being spun to symmetrical perfection by a computer) yet looser and freer in their jazz or raga music. The best known work of his brother, James Whitney, is *Lapis* (1963–66).

Other films in the formal tradition include those of Jordan Belson (*Mandala*, 1953; *Allures*, 1961; *Re-Entry*, 1964; *Phenomena*, 1965; *Samadhi*, 1967), who uses his colorfully amorphous evolutions of circular blobs as mandalas, indescribable objects of spiritual reflection and contemplation. Belson's meditational colors and forms flowed into the commercial mainstream with the astronaut's shimmering visions in Philip Kaufman's *The Right Stuff* (1983). Many of the animated films of Robert Breer are sorts of spatial dancing: *Blazes* (1961), which assaults and smashes the viewer with twenty-four different images per second (more

an attack than a "dance"); *66* (1966), another sequence of cleverly evolving forms and colors. Scott Bartlett's stroboscopic *Offon* (1967) succeeds in turning more concrete referents (the eye, eyeball, human forms, a bird, a face) into purely kaleidoscopic forms in ceaseless motion, accompanied by *musique concrète*. Indeed, this form of modernist "music"—usually a rhythmic assemblage of various abstract sounds such as buzzing, scratching, grinding, whining, and the like—is one of the primary accompaniments of many avant-garde films, though it is also true that many are silent.

Bruce Conner is the funniest of the social satirists; he is essentially an editor, and his best films (*A Movie*, 1958; *Cosmic Ray*, 1961; *Report*, 1963–67; *Marilyn × Five*, 1965) cleverly splice together existing stock footage to make their satirical point. Conner's point is that men are murderous, violent, destructive, and ultimately suicidal, conducting an assault against their fellows and against nature itself that will eventually kill everyone. Conner supports his view in *A Movie* with found footage of violence and destruction exclusively: planes dropping bombs and then diving to earth in a retributive burst of flames; Indians and cowboys on the warpath; tanks in battle; collisions of racing automobiles; the burning of a zeppelin; the collapse of a bridge; the detonation of the atomic bomb. Conner's movie implies that the business of the movies is to chronicle catastrophe; he splices these catastrophes together with such rhythmic, repetitive, and rapid insistence that the impression of cataclysm is complete. Man is his machines (and the movie is also the product of a machine), and the machines produce death and disaster. Stanley Kubrick's juxtaposition of stock footage with ironic music in the closing sequence of *Dr. Strangelove* clearly derived from Conner's *A Movie*.

Equally satirical is Stan VanDerBeek's *Breathdeath* (1963), which combines his interest in collage and cartooning with his own apocalyptic vision of a society warring, breathing, and boring itself to death. Tom DeWitt's *Atmosfear* (1967) is a satirical view of "pollution": of the air, of the landscapes (with ugly factories and smokestacks and architecture), of the cities (with repressive and restrictive signs), and, ultimately, of the mind. In this same satirical tradition are the films of James Broughton (*Mother's Day*, 1948; *Loony Tom the Happy Lover*, 1951; *The Pleasure Garden*, 1953, in 35mm; *The Bed*, 1968) and Robert Nelson (*Confessions of a Black Mother Succuba*, 1965; *Oh Dem Watermelons*, 1965; *The Great Blondino*, 1967; *Bleu Shut*, 1970).

Yet another kind of satirical Underground film burlesques the business of aboveground movie making (also an implication of the Bruce Conner films), for society's art mirrors society's values. The comical, usually camp films in this tradition are those of the Kuchar brothers (*Sins of the Fleshapoids*, 1965, by Mike, and *Hold Me While I'm Naked*, 1966, by George) and some of the early films of Andy Warhol (*Harlot*, 1965; *The Chelsea Girls*, 1966), though Warhol was also an important minimalist (*Sleep*, 1963). Paul Morrissey directed the majority of the later features (*Flesh*, 1969; *Trash*, 1970; *Andy Warhol's Frankenstein*, 1974, in 3-D), which Warhol produced.

As can be seen from the Warhol films, the satirical Independent films are close cousins to the sexual ones, for in their studies of "abnormal" sexuality, Underground filmmakers often comment satirically on society's concepts of normality. The master in the field was Kenneth Anger, the son of a famous Hollywood agent of its Golden Age. The young Anger translated his Hollywood experiences into a scandalous book about Hollywood sexual practices, *Hollywood Babylon*, which includes such gossipy morsels as the "real" murder weapon in the Virginia Rappe murder case, the "real" reasons for the deaths of Thomas Ince, William Desmond Taylor, and Paul Bern (Jean Harlow's husband), and the various genital sizes of the Hollywood matinee idols. Anger's outrageousness also dominates his films, beginning with his first major work, *Fireworks* (1947), which he made when he was only fifteen. The film is clearly his own adolescent and masochistic fantasy, the symbolic dream journey of a lonely, horny boy (played by Anger himself) who is picked up, beaten, and raped to satiety by sailors, climaxing (literally and figuratively) with the image of a penis metamorphosizing into a Roman candle.

Fetishism and sadomasochism dominate Anger's most important film, *Scorpio Rising*, an

Fig. 15-21

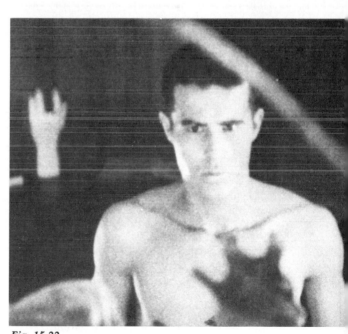

Fig. 15-22

Maya Deren meets herself in **Meshes of the Afternoon** *(Fig. 15-21); Kenneth Anger seeks to complete himself in* **Fireworks** *(Fig. 15-22).*

examination of the practices, perversions, and paraphernalia of the motorcycle "man": his attachment to costume and symbol (chains, boots, belts, leather, Levis, jacket), his idolization of Marlon Brando (in *The Wild One*) and James Dean (another motorcycle freak), his hatred of society's lifeless symbols of goodness (personified by recurring shots of a kitschy Christ in film clips from DeMille's *King of Kings*) and his adoration of cruelty (personified by film clips and stills of Hitler). The motorcycle freak's worship of the macho external is, Anger implies, a literal cover-up of his homosexual essence, and Anger uses the soundtrack to comment contrapuntally (and comically) on this gap between self and projected self-image. Popular rock-and-roll tunes of the era (a clear precursor of *Easy Rider* and *American Graffiti*) dominate the soundtrack, and at one point, as the cyclist adoringly dons his macho Levis, the song goes, "She Wore Blue Velvet." Anger's film was also important in serving as the basis for several of the country's crucial obscenity test cases, first seized and then judged not obscene by the State of New York in 1965. This film alone was responsible for the demise of that censorship board, a reminder that "underground" films, because of their artistic seriousness, have played a major role in American social history — as test cases for definitions of pornography.

One of the famous sexual films that has not yet been thus exonerated is Jack Smith's *Flaming Creatures* (1963), an outrageous, funny, and violent attack on sexual definitions, propriety, and normality. Smith's friend, Ken Jacobs, has made films in the sexual-social-satirical tradition (*The Death of P'town*, 1961; *Blonde Cobra*, 1963), though he is better known for his structuralist, reflexive films (*Little Stabs at Happiness*, 1963; *Soft Rain*, 1968; *Tom, Tom, the Piper's Son*, 1971). Some of Warhol's early work — in particular, *Blow Job* (1964), a thirty-minute reaction shot of the face of a man apparently receiving one — are not only attacks on normal and accepted sexual practices but also Warhol's attack on the normal definition of a movie.

The fourth kind of Independent film, the cinematically self-conscious, self-reflexive one, also attacks the commonly accepted assumptions of what a movie is or ought to be. As the term *reflexive* (or *self-reflexive*) implies, these films are meditations on themselves — as works of film art. As meditations on themselves, these films consciously test the possible definitions of cinema and its processes, revealing the different visual and psychological purposes to which cinema can be put. The underlying commitment of these films is to the act and art of perception itself, to "seeing" (in both senses of sight and insight) — the ways that cinema records the world and the things we can discover about both the world and the cinema as a result.

Stan Brakhage is the most lyrical, poetic, and romantic of the reflexive filmmakers. Brakhage combines a Wordsworthian adoration of nature and child-like innocence with the modernist's meditation on the processes and materials of his art. For Brakhage, the love of film intensifies the love of life and nature, and his films simultaneously celebrate both the world and the remaking of the world with cinema. Brakhage treats celluloid itself as a living, organic substance — growing mold on it (which he calls "a little garden"), baking film in the oven, cutting individual frames of film into pieces and reassembling them as celluloid collages, scratching and etching patterns directly onto the celluloid, assembling an entire film (*Mothlight*, 1963) by scattering bits of leaves, flowers, seeds, and moths' wings on pieces of mylar splicing tape and then processing the results (a completely unphotographed film — and a link with Man Ray's scatterings of the 1920s, except that Man Ray never used organic materials). Brakhage combines these nonphotographic film methods with photographic and montage manipulations like the extreme use of superimposition (up to four images printed in the same frame), radical varying of the focus and exposure settings within individual shots, and elliptical yoking of images that demand mythic and allegorical interpretation as well as a quick eye.

Brakhage's early films tended to be sexual mood pieces in black-and-white, partly influenced by Kenneth Anger's tortured dream-fantasies (*Reflections on Black*, 1955; *Flesh of Morning*, 1956). But he converted to color and to the autobiographical recording of his own family and life in 1959 with *Window Water Baby Moving*, in which the filmmaker lovingly observed and captured the birth of his own first child. One of Brakhage's most important works is *Dog Star Man* (1961–1964), a seventy-nine-minute silent work (no sound, exclusive concentration on the dense visual imagery) in four parts plus a Prelude (a clear Wordsworthian echo). The mythic film combines adoration of nature (mountains, forests, snow, moon, mists, clouds, sun) with the tortuous journey of a man (Brakhage himself) and his dog up a mountainside to create Brakhage's cosmological view of man's relation to the universe, shaped by his ability to translate his visions into works of art. Perhaps the most stunning of his later achievements is *The Dante Quartet* (1982–1987), a series of four hand-painted films that takes the viewer from Hell to Paradise: *Hell Itself, Hell Spit Flexion* (on 35mm stock), *Purgation* (on 70mm stock), and *existence is song* (on Imax stock, each frame a nearly 3″ × 4″ layered painting, up to an eighth of an inch thick). These short, hypnagogic films are fast, gripping, visionary. The title of one of Brakhage's major works, *The Text of Light* (1974), a lengthy abstract study of the prismatic play of light beams in a glass ashtray, might serve as the key to all his texts of light.

Bruce Baillie combines Brakhage's romantic consciousness of nature with the social analyst's perception of the corruption of modern life. *Mass for the Dakota Sioux* (1964) and *Quixote* (1964–1965) examine the ways that the pioneer spirit of America—as symbolized by its original inhabitants—has been corrupted by the building of cities, the buying and selling of food, the digging and erecting of edifices by machines. *To Parsifal* (1963) contrasts the natural imagery of woods and water with the modern machines of fishing boat and railroad train. *Castro Street* (1966) explores the relationships among consciousness, film, and the environment—in this case a train yard and an oil depot. Just as Brakhage recorded his own life in a cinema diary, *Scenes from Under Childhood* (1967–1970), Baillie constructed his own autobiographical cinema diary, *Quick Billy* (1967–1971). Perhaps the most dedicated of

the film diarists is Jonas Mekas, who seeks subjective and objective authenticity with the concentration of a jazz musician on the moment, recording his life and the course of his art: *Diaries, Notes and Sketches (Walden)* (1968); *Lost Lost Lost* (1976).

The films of Hollis Frampton were more logical exercises than romantic quests. *Zorns Lemma* (1970), a complex, three-part, hour-long film, was probably Frampton's most important—and most difficult—work. In its first section, about four minutes long, the viewer sees a completely black, blank screen during the reading of an alphabetical lesson out of the *Bay State Primer*, one of those early moralistic texts for teaching Puritan children their ABCs. The second section, about forty-five minutes long, is also alphabetical—a silent series of images of New York signs, each one beginning with a different letter of the alphabet. Frampton holds each sign on the screen for exactly one second (twenty-four frames), and he reduces the English alphabet to the Roman one of twenty-four letters (combining i and j, u and w)—so that the number of letters and the number of frames is identical. Frampton then goes through the entire alphabet with this metronomic, one-second rhythm 108 times—but as he does so, he systematically substitutes a visual image for each letter of the alphabet (a fire replaces x, a shot of waves replaces y, a shot of woods replaces another letter, beans filling up a jar replaces another). The second section concludes when, on its 108th cycle, all twenty-four letters have been converted to twenty-four visual images, producing, in effect, an entirely new alphabet of purely visual cinema imagery.

The first section of the film used sounds without images—dominated by blackness; the second, images without sounds—dominated by colors; its third part combines word and image—dominated by whiteness—in a single, apparently unbroken twelve-minute shot (whereas the second part used editing extensively—2,692 images of one second each). A man, woman, and dog cross a snowy white field (perhaps an allusion to *Dog Star Man*) as a group of female voices recites a visionary text according to a strict, one second, metronomic beat (the aural equivalent of twenty-four frames per second). The point of Frampton's mathematical and alphabetical games is to reveal how insidiously our vision and knowledge are constricted by our methods of seeing and knowing. To create a new alphabet of images is to see the world and the means of recording it differently. The film's thesis, antithesis, and synthesis also chart an optimistic history of American consciousness itself—from the narrow, moralistic beginning of merely hearing, reading, and repeating prepared texts, to the broader but still limited ability to see and use letters for ourselves, to the ultimately liberated ability to see, hear, and feel the world itself.

Perhaps the most celebrated and controversial of the reflexive films came from Canada rather than America: Michael Snow's *Wavelength* (1967)—the film credited with establishing the structuralist film movement—which is, on its surface, nothing more than an agonizingly slow forty-five minute zoom shot through a single loft, beginning with a full shot of the entire room and the street outside, ending as an extreme close-up of a portion of a photograph on the far wall of the room. In the course of this inexorable forward zoom, human figures wander into the space of the frame—two men who move a bookcase, two women who listen to the radio, a man who breaks into the loft and collapses on the floor, a young woman who uses the telephone—but all of these humans leave the frame (or the frame leaves them—as it does the man on the floor, when it zooms past his body), never to return. These people, and whatever pattern of narrative causality has brought them to this particular space at this particular time, are never developed, investigated, or explicated. The usual center of human interest for the usual movie is not at all central to this film.

The central concern of *Wavelength* is the space itself—indeed, space itself. As in *Zorns Lemma*, the structural logic of the film is rigidly formal and precisely deductive. It begins with a three-dimensional space that might be defined as 12 feet high, 22 feet wide (the usual width of a New York brownstone), and, say, 100 feet deep (the length of the room plus the signs visible outside its windows across the street). The

film ends with a two-dimensional space less than 8 inches high and less than 10 inches wide (part of an 8 × 10 photograph). It also begins as a moving picture in color and ends, in effect, as a still photograph in black-and-white (and out of focus at that, so that no shape, texture, or depth is discernible at all). The film's structural logic is this implacable narrowing of spatial depth, which is the film's subject as well.

As the lens slides through this space, it attempts to divert us (in both senses of the term) with the differing qualities and characteristics of the space itself. Snow uses different lighting exposures (some of which emphasize the signs outdoors, others of which emphasize the indoors by washing out the outdoors with bright, overexposed whiteness), different color filters, different intensities of printing grain, different times of the night and day, producing different qualities and conditions of light; and, of course, the shifting focal lengths of the zoom lens produce different perceptions of the room and the shapes and textures of its objects (not coincidentally, the zoom lens flattens the visual field the most when it is at its telephoto setting—and it is at that setting when it shows the still, two-dimensional photograph). The usual movie chooses to shoot in a particular space, to frame a particular area, because some important human action, necessary for understanding the narrative, takes place in that space. In the usual movie, space is the background, the necessary container, for significant human action. But Snow's *Wavelength* takes its chosen space as its most important characteristic (and the most important characteristic of any framed image); what else does a frame frame other than space itself? So for Snow, human actions are only significant when and if they happen to intersect with that framed space—and they are no more important than anything else in that space.

A film like *Wavelength* once again raises the question about the value and significance of the Independent American Cinema. On the one hand, the critic can respond to *Wavelength* with a "So what?" Space that is empty of human significance is truly empty (and very boring). Cinema space is meaningful only if it has been invested with meaning. On the other hand, the critic can respond to *Wavelength* as one of the most perfect expressions of the cinema condition (that movies necessarily frame spaces) as well as one of the most perfect means of educating us about the human condition—that cinema can provoke viewers to perceive the mystery, the expressiveness, the variety, and the "spaceness" of the shapes around them, not only in the frame but in the world.

16

Emerging National Traditions 2: The 1970s and 80s

As in the first two decades after the Second World War, new national cinemas have attracted international attention since 1965, promoted by the international film festivals, supported by their governments or national television systems, and welcomed by audiences and critics in America and Europe. The most important new movements were those in Germany, Australia, and that collection of developing nations vaguely called the Third World, although the increasing internationalism of film production in the 1970s and 1980s was as striking as any single national movement.

Das Neue Kino

Although it would be an exaggeration to say that for thirty-five years, from 1932 to 1967, the film industry of Germany did not produce a single film of international significance (with the exception of Leni Riefenstahl's controversial documentaries of the 1930s), the exaggeration would be a slight one. Among the scattered postwar German films to be seen in America

were Rolf Thiele's *Rosemary* (1959), a neorealist study of the life and death of a Berlin prostitute; Kurt Hoffmann's *Aren't We Wonderful?* (1958), a political comedy; and Swiss-born Bernhard Wicki's *The Bridge* (1959), the poignant, ironic chronicle of a group of German schoolchildren, slaughtered while defending a worthless bridge against the invading American army in the final days of the war. Volker Schlöndorff's *Young Törless* (1966), which parallels sadomasochistic torture in a boy's school with the moral and psychological conditions for Nazism in Hitler's Germany, was either the last of these occasional German films to achieve international recognition or the first representative of the new and genuine German film movement.

In 1960 the German film industry produced some seventy feature films, almost exclusively for local consumption in their simple themes and conventional styles. The Oberhausen manifesto, formulated by twenty-six German screenwriters and directors at the Oberhausen Film Festival of 1962, called for a "new

German cinema," free from the stifling habits and conventions of the German film industry. Through its leaders, especially Alexander Kluge (*Yesterday Girl*, 1966; *Strongman Ferdinand*, 1975), the group successfully pressured the West German legislature to set up a film board and allocate subsidies for film production in 1967. The new German cinema flowed from these subsidies.

In the late 1960s and early 1970s appeared the first feature films of three young German filmmakers — Werner Herzog (*Signs of Life*, 1968), Rainer Werner Fassbinder (*Love Is Colder Than Death*, 1969), and Wim Wenders (*The Goalie's Anxiety at the Penalty Kick*, 1971). All three were born within four years of each other (Herzog in 1942, Wenders in 1945, Fassbinder in 1946); each was about twenty-five when his first feature appeared; each has been supported by government subsidy, either directly, through the Film Subsidies Board, or indirectly, through subsidized television production. These three young directors, who have steadily achieved greater international recognition, formed the nucleus of the most interesting, promising, and productive new national film movement since the French New Wave of 1959.

Although American and European critics and festivals had realized as early as 1972 that something important was happening in West Germany — particularly after watching *The Goalie's Anxiety*, Herzog's *Aguirre, the Wrath of God* (1972), and Fassbinder's *The Bitter Tears of Petra von Kant* (1972) — American audiences did not take to the New Cinema (*das neue Kino*) as rapidly as they had to the films of the New Wave. There were both cultural and commercial reasons for the slow American reception of the New German Cinema. First, in the 1970s there were fewer small "art cinemas" in America devoted to showing foreign-language films than there had been in the 1950s and 1960s (in the 1980s there were even fewer). The reduced number of theatres meant a much smaller audience for such films than in the period when significant numbers of American filmgoers first turned hungrily to the European imports to escape the predictable Hollywood pap. As in the 1980s, many student audiences in the 1990s seem contented with Hollywood's offerings (and unwilling to read subtitles), while the older audiences who continue to patronize foreign-language films prefer the same older kinds of French, Swedish, Japanese, and Italian styles and subjects that attracted them decades earlier (many of them made, of course, by the same directors).

Second, the new German films were not more difficult than the previous generations of European films, but they were difficult in a different way — colder, harder-edged, more stylized, more austere, more ironic, less romantic, less warm, and less charming than Fellini, Truffaut, Tanner, Bertolucci, or Forman. There was consequently not much money to be made from these films, which diminished not only their American theatrical distribution but also the attention they received in the American press. Most of these German films were and still are shown primarily on college campuses in America by film societies in 16mm or in an occasional retrospective by a big city art house or museum of modern art.

The surprising commercial success of Fassbinder's *The Marriage of Maria Braun* (1979) accompanied international financing for English-language productions by Fassbinder (*Despair*, 1977), Wenders (*The American Friend*, 1977; *Paris, Texas*, 1984) and Herzog (*Fitzcarraldo*, 1982). The major American publicity campaigns for these films, Wenders's collaboration with Coppola and playwright Sam Shepard, and the posthumous interest in Fassbinder's last films — from the epic *Berlin Alexanderplatz* (1980, 15 hours, made for TV) to *Querelle* (1982) — indicate that these filmmakers have begun to attract not only the critical attention but also the audiences they deserve in the United States.

That the New German Cinema initially made little impact in America was ironic, for one of its traits was a conscious debt to the American cinema. Wenders's *Kings of the Road* (1976) is both a western (two buddies riding in open spaces) and a road movie like *Easy Rider* (they ride in a truck rather than on horseback, accompanied by American rock music). His *American Friend* is a *film noir* that evokes many American movies: Hitchcock's *Strangers On A Train* (one stranger proposes the murder of another stranger; the film is based on *Ripley's*

Game, a novel by Patricia Highsmith, who also wrote *Strangers On A Train*), Bette Davis's *Dark Victory* (a man is going blind as a result of a mysterious terminal disease), *The French Connection* (an international Mafia-style conspiracy, shot in various cities all over the globe), American westerns (the American wears a cowboy hat and describes himself as "a cowboy in Hamburg"—and that cowboy is played by American actor Dennis Hopper, the director of *Easy Rider*). There are also appearances by American directors Nicholas Ray (who directed Hopper in *Rebel Without a Cause*) and Samuel Fuller (who, like Ray, specialized in 1950s stories of masculine self-assertion)—homages to living heroes of the cinema.

Fassbinder's films are packed with conscious homages to Douglas Sirk and Max Ophüls. One Fassbinder film, *Ali: Fear Eats the Soul* (1973), is a remake of Sirk's *All That Heaven Allows,* and another, *The Bitter Tears of Petra von Kant,* dissects the same female conflicts among love, success, and power as Sirk's *Imitation of Life.* Fassbinder's repetitive use of glass reflections on windows, mirrors, and table tops deliberately recalls Sirk's complex use of windows and mirrors; the graceful, lengthy tracking shots in many of Fassbinder's films recall the camera style of Max Ophüls. And one of the more interesting lines of movie genealogy can be traced with the appearance of Eddie Constantine in *Beware of a Holy Whore* (1970), who comes to Fassbinder via Godard's *Alphaville,* and came to Godard via a series of low-budget French crime films based on American Monogram mysteries. Fassbinder also acknowledges Godard as a way-station between American movies and the New German Cinema by using Anna Karina, Godard's first wife and lead actress, as the French mistress in *Chinese Roulette* (1976). Although Werner Herzog's conscious debt to American culture and American movies may be smaller than Wenders's or Fassbinder's, *Stroszek* (1977) contains a brilliant satire of the plastic surfaces of American life (mobile homes, fast-food restaurants, formica furniture) as well as of American bank-robbing westerns. Herzog's homages are more likely to be paid to Murnau.

If one characteristic of the New German films is their debt to foreign movies, another is their debt to a native German film tradition— the expressionist masterpieces of the 1920s. The Fassbinder films unmistakably evoke the stylized, symmetrical, highly patterned visual world of Fritz Lang—as well as the cushy, carefully arranged interiors of Sirk, but the films can be streetwise and dirty too. At times he shares with Lang the visual emphasis on slow choreographic actor movements and statuesquely frozen poses, sharply defined by the bare, hard white walls behind the actors, linked by the traveling of a typically German moving camera. The opening shots of *Fox and His Friends* (1974) at a circus sideshow clearly link Fox, who performs as "the talking head," with Cesare of *The Cabinet of Dr. Caligari.*

If some of Fassbinder's films recall the visual stylization of Lang's, Herzog's recall the spiritual, mystical trances of such films as *The Cabinet of Dr. Caligari, Destiny, Warning Shadows,* and *Nosferatu*—the last one quite literally, since Herzog modeled his *Nosferatu* (1978) on Murnau's. The slow rhythms of the Herzog films, their lengthy shots of frozen figures and hypnotically entrancing landscapes, evoke the dreamlike mysteries and rhythms of the expressionist world, as opposed to Fassbinder's evocation of its look. Like the characters of many expressionist films, Herzog's central figures are possessed by manias and demons that drag them inexorably into the realms of their desires and their imaginations. One of Herzog's most expressionist experiments was *Heart of Glass* (1976), in which he hypnotized virtually the entire cast during shooting, to achieve the impression that the world of the film had been plunged into a deep trance.

Although Wenders is the most apparently realist of the three directors (in the sense that Fassbinder is theatrical and Herzog is visionary), his work can be compared with such German classics as the more realistic works of Murnau and Pabst—in particular Wenders's unsentimental look at characters in undistorted environments (as in Pabst's *Pandora's Box* and much of Murnau's *The Last Laugh*) and his contrast of cramped, indoor architectural spaces with open, freer outdoor spaces (as in Murnau's *Nosferatu* or Pabst's *Jeanne Ney* and *Kameradschaft*). Nevertheless, of the three directors only

Fassbinder could present a world as *grossly realistic* as the opening of *Jeanne Ney*.

Most of the films of *das neue Kino* are "new narratives." Rather than forging stories that are credible chains of chronological events, the German films push narrative construction in its two opposite directions—either the distanced political parable in the manner of Bertolt Brecht or the internalized rendering of human emotion and experience. Fassbinder's work is the most consciously Brechtian—the title of one of his films, *Mother Küster's Trip to Heaven* (1975), is a deliberate echo of Brecht's *Mother Courage and Her Children*. The Fassbinder narratives, like those of Brecht, develop a detached irony that prods the audience to perceive the broad political, psychological, or moral outlines of the tale rather than to become intimately attached to the feelings and fortunes of its central character or characters. Fassbinder's parables, however melodramatic (and in that sense unBrechtian) they may become, tend toward the allegorical and take the form of complex and explicit elaborations of a simple moral-political lesson: that personal catastrophe gives one great economic power in contemporary society (*Mother Küster*), that certain forms of sexual-romantic love require the antagonism of bourgeois society in order to exist (*Ali*), that even social outcasts like homosexuals are more loyal to their economic class than to their sexual comrades (*Fox*), that the myth of the bourgeois artist—tyrannically reducing everyone in life to slaves for the sake of Art—is also the myth of Fascism (*Satan's Brew*, 1976), that the political and economic recovery of postwar Germany was achieved by acts of moral prostitution (*Maria Braun*). On the other hand, Herzog and Wenders make internalized experiential narratives that are less political, less detached, more tactile, and more engrossing than Fassbinder's. Herzog depends almost exclusively on the shadings, textures, and rhythms of his visual imagery to transfer the sensations of his characters directly to the conscious and unconscious perceptions of the viewer. Wenders's narratives, deceptively closer to the movie norm, still depend on a highly elliptical and subtle interplay of external narrative event and sensuously evocative and internalized visual imagery.

Rainer Werner Fassbinder was the most prolific of the new German directors until his death from a drug overdose in 1982. Directing some forty feature films in a dozen years, in addition to producing television programs and radio plays, as well as writing and staging theatrical productions in the same period, he drove himself to death on a relentless alternation of work and drugs. Fassbinder's roots, like Ingmar Bergman's, were in the theatre, and his films never deserted the theatre's elegant, economical stylization. (In 1969 he played the title role in Brecht's play *Baal*, directed for TV by Schlöndorff.) Like Bergman and D. W. Griffith, Fassbinder preferred the theatrical method of working with an acting ensemble rather than with individual types and stars, and over the 1970s the faces of the Fassbinder players became almost as familiar as the Griffith or Bergman stock companies—Irm Hermann, Margit Carstensen, Hanna Schygulla, Brigitte Mira, Kurt Raab, Volker Spengler, Marquard Böhm, Harry Baer. Despite the speed of his production and shooting, Fassbinder's style and control evolved slowly and steadily. His frenetic productivity of eleven films in 1969–1970 slowed greatly to permit greater investment of his time, care, and control. The stylistic experiments of these early films, which tended in any number of contradictory directions—the mannered *film noir* of *The American Soldier* (1970), the maniacal mixture of movie making and lovemaking in *Beware of a Holy Whore*, a chaotic movie about movie chaos, and the undramatic, almost *cinéma vérité* study of dull, drab middle-class life of *Why Does Herr R. Run Amok?* (1969) —fused into a consistent Fassbinder look, style, and tone.

There are three primary Fassbinder visual and social settings: the drab, stifling, tawdry world of the working- and middle-class—their apartments, bars, offices, and shops (*The Merchant of the Four Seasons*, 1971; *Mother Küster*; *Ali*); the cold, hard, shiny elegance of the world of the rich and famous (*Petra von Kant*; *Fox*; *Chinese Roulette*; *Satan's Brew*); and the detached, frigid elegance of the world of the near or distant past (*Effi Briest*, 1974; *Despair*). The visual characteristic that links these three social realms is their unrelenting hardness and coldness, their lack of comfort, softness, or human charm. Both private homes and places of public habitation become uninhabitable in the Fassbinder world; they are mausoleums or, like Fox's apartment, museums. Whether cutely cluttered or chicly bare, Fassbinder films are set in the Land of the Dead. For this reason, Fassbinder films are almost exclusively indoor films, claustrophobically enclosed by the rooms his characters are forced to inhabit (another clear parallel to the tradition of German Expressionism and to the American Sirk and Ophüls films, which depicted similarly claustrophobic, indoor worlds).

Fassbinder's favorite images in these settings are gleamingly bright, reflectively repellent surfaces—the gleaming white tiles of the public toilet in *Satan's Brew*, the white marble where Fox lies dead in *Fox and His Friends*, or the white walls and transparent glass shelves of *Chinese Roulette*. Given his visual preoccupation with the hard and shiny, it is not surprising that Fassbinder's favorite visual material was glass— windows (broken into many panes or whole in huge sheets), mirrors (small or large, ornately carved or simply framed, uniquely shaped or purely rectangular), and glass-panelled doors. In *Chinese Roulette*, even the tables and shelving are made of glass. Although the fascination with glass also comes to Fassbinder via Ophüls and, especially, Sirk, the material serves several explicit symbolic and metaphoric purposes in the Fassbinder world.

Glass is both a means and a barrier to communication. It both permits one to see through it and confines one's vision to its surface. It is both transparent and solid, invisible and visible, revealing and blinding. In *Petra von Kant*, Marlene (Irm Hermann), Petra's loving secretary, observes Petra's tender scenes of affection with other women from the other side of a window —she is both screened off from the scene she is witnessing and a visual participant in that scene, both distant from it and close to it. Effi Briest is perpetually surrounded by the windows, mirrors, and doorways of her upper-class life. She is capable of seeing herself and seeing the life around her, but she is also screened from the outdoors and limited to observing only her surface characteristics in a mirror. The glass of *Effi Briest* becomes a metaphor for Effi's being ineffably stuck in her world of glass and,

Fig. 16-1
Effi Briest: *Effi (Hanna Schygulla) engulfed by the curtains, carvings, mirrors, and paintings of her world.*

at the same time, incapable of seeing it or penetrating it at all.

Although both Ophüls and Sirk used glass for social and psychological commentary, Fassbinder's glass imagery is more insistent and more consistently Brechtian—a deliberate distancing device, Brecht's *Verfremdungseffekt* or "Estrangement Effect," also called the "Alienation Effect," which is designed to remove or estrange the spectator from the illusion of reality in the spectacle and from the temptation to empathize with its characters, so that the critical, dispassionate spectator can study and judge the characters as well as the political and ethical implications of their problems and of the measures taken to solve them. Not only does the glass in *Effi Briest* separate Effi from her world without her knowing it, it separates us from Effi, reducing her to a social marionette rather than building her into an attractive and rounded psychological being. The glass reflections in Fassbinder films deliberately push us, too, behind windows (quite literally, since we see films through frames constructed by lenses of glass). This distancing coldness allows the Fassbinder films to achieve their goal as parable-like allegories of the bourgeois social condition — accompanied by a savage comic irony that, in Brecht as well as Fassbinder, almost inevitably accompanies this kind of narrative.

The central theme of Fassbinder's work, as consistent as his panes of glass, is power — social power, economic power, psychological power, erotic power, often translated into specific scenes of sadomasochistic dominance and subservience. The characters in Fassbinder films exercise terrible power over others, just as the filmmaker exercises a terrible power over his audience. *Satan's Brew* begins and ends with a quotation from Antonin Artaud, and the union of Artaud and Brecht, the theatre of cruelty with the theatre of ideas, mental punishment with political discussion, is as important to Fassbinder as it was to Pasolini and Polanski. Appropriately enough, one of Fassbinder's final works was an adaptation of Jean Genet's *Querelle de Brest*, for Genet, like Fassbinder, evolved a radical politics based on sadomasochistic, homosexual alternations of dominance and subservience. Many central Fassbinder figures are completely mistaken in the power they think they possess — the sexual power of Effi Briest and Fox is much lighter than the social and economic power that engulfs them, and the mercantile power of the merchant of the four seasons is equally illusory and inadequate. As in the plays of Jean Genet, the characters in Fassbinder films love to dominate and to be dominated, and many of the films chronicle the revolutions of this sadomasochistic circle.

Ali: Fear Eats the Soul (in German, simply *Fear Eats the Soul*) is one of Fassbinder's most popular and accessible works, the strange love story of a middle-aged widow and a young, almost-black Moroccan who meet, marry, and confront the societal rejection and isolation that could be expected to greet such a marriage. The film is clearly based on Sirk's *All That Heaven Allows*, but the differences between the Sirk film and the Fassbinder show a degree of psychological perceptivity and artistic courage in the German work that the American one either did not or could not achieve. Sirk's middle-aged widow, Carrie, is an upper-class, graceful, and attractive woman (played by Jane Wyman); Fassbinder's widow, Emmi, is an old, wrinkled, frumpy, working-class cleaning lady (played by Brigitte Mira, who plays most of Fassbinder's matrons). Sirk's young sexual male, Ron, was impersonated by Rock Hudson, who played a gardener (which put him in a different social class from those whose trees he pruned, but also gave him a "natural" dignity — a quality that the film emphasized by frequent references to Thoreau's *Walden*). Although Sirk's film made it fairly clear (or as clear as a 1955 Hollywood film could) that the gardener was an attractive sexual object, his embodiment by the picture-perfect Hudson converted the sexual male into a pretty mannequin. Fassbinder's Ali (El Hedi Ben Salem), on the other hand, is a total social outcast (a black, unlettered stranger in a strange land) but a very powerful, graceful male presence, seething with energy and sexuality — and anxiety — as well as an underlying spiritual wholeness and tenderness.

Whereas the central narrative question in Sirk was "Can she marry this man?" — a marriage opposed by all her friends, family, and social set — Fassbinder goes beyond to a more ironic and challenging problem. Of course the same groups oppose the widow's marriage at first (her family, her neighbors, her grocer, the people with whom she works), but the two actually marry at the conclusion of the film's first third (the marriage was merely implied by the final scene in Sirk's film), leaving the final narrative sections for several ironic twists. The animosity of the social milieu that surrounds the married couple softens — particularly when people find there is something (usually financial) to be gained by befriending the strange

Ali: Fear Eats the Soul. *Emmi (Brigitte Mira) and Ali (El Hedi Ben Salem) as Fassbinder's radically odd couple.*

Fig. 16-2

couple. And only when the animosity of the society softens does the central couple suffer an emotional crisis. Their love has been nurtured and intensified by the antagonism that separates them from everyone else. How can they maintain their affection without those outside enemies? Without living in a world of their own? That question for Fassbinder is the most interesting one about such a relationship—not Can they marry? but Can they stay married?

Fox and His Friends, despite its homosexual milieu, is a similarly ironic parable of the conflict between personal erotic relationships and the surrounding bourgeois economic and moral landscape. Fox, a working-class boy–man (played by Fassbinder) who survives by working in carnivals and as a hustler, wins 500,000 Marks in the lottery. The money gives him an entry into the world of "finer things," and he manages to acquire a very pretty new lover, a "smart set" of new friends, a fancy apartment stocked with paintings and antique furniture, an expensive sports car, fashionable clothes, and other cultural benefits such as pretentious meals in French restaurants and exotic vacations in far-off Marrakech. He lends immense amounts of money to Eugen, his lover, which

help prop up the boy's tottering family business, and he carelessly signs legal contracts that will defraud him of both his money and his property.

Fassbinder carefully details the conspiracy of the entire surrounding society to fleece Fox, particularly showing that everyone with whom he does business is, like Fox himself, a homosexual—the antique dealer, the clothes salesman, the lawyer, and Eugen. Although they all share this apparently anti-bourgeois sexual preference, all of these homosexuals are perfectly acceptable in the proper bourgeois world (represented by Eugen's father and mother or the travel agent) because they accept all the bourgeois assumptions about money and property. Their economic loyalties are much stronger (and more socially significant) than their sexual ones. Fox, who has blindly, romantically, sincerely, willingly done everything for the love of Eugen, ends completely stripped of everything—no lover, no friends, no car, no apartment, no money, and no life. In a truly ironic final image, Fox lies dead of an overdose on the cold white shiny tiles and stones of a public building—appropriately enough, one of those new underground shopping emporia— while two teenage boys rob the corpse of its

Fig. 16-3
Fox and His Friends: *Fox (Fassbinder, left) with his lover, Eugen (Peter Chatel), in the overstuffed, overdecorated, bourgeois "museum" that is their home.*

remaining Deutschmarks and the denim jacket that has been Fox's trademark, accompanied by the bitterly cold gaiety of carnival music. Fassbinder's death as Fox grimly foreshadows his own, seven years later.

Werner Herzog makes both documentaries and fictional feature films, but the differences between them are not nearly so great as such terms imply. Even Herzog's documentaries are far less concerned with the objective recording of events, processes, or conditions than with the subjective and symbolic aspects of undergoing a particular event, process, or condition. *Fata Morgana* (1970) is a transcendental documentary shot in the Sahara and as concerned with creation myths as it is with looking at the desert through new eyes. *Land of Silence and Darkness* (1971) attempts to recreate the sensation of experiencing the world as a blind and deaf person (quite a task for film, whose two tools are images and sounds). *The Great Ecstasy of the*

Sculptor Steiner (1974) attempts to transfer the ski jumper's sensation of flying from the film's subject to its audience. And *La Soufrière* (1976), a documentary about an anticipated volcanic catastrophe on the island of Guadaloupe that does not take place, is more interested in transferring the mysterious emptiness of the evacuated city of Basse Terre than in chronicling a seismic event. Whether in his documentaries or in his fictional films, Herzog depends entirely on the poetic sensations and evocations of his visual imagery, invariably distinguished by its intense silence, its haunting colors, its mysterious impenetrability, its hypnotic slowness, its stare through the surface of light. One of the most memorable and essential of these images is the shot of ten thousand windmills in Herzog's first feature — *Signs of Life.* Herzog's camera slowly and silently pans across the valley of a Greek island filled with all those windmills, each of them turning silently, hypnotically, continuously from the silent force of an unseen wind.

Among Herzog's favorite images are natural settings that are barren, rough, mysterious, fascinating, and untamed. He once said that he searches this planet for extraterrestrial landscapes. The arid rocky island of Cos in *Signs of Life*, the lushly dense, green Amazonian jungle of *Aguirre, the Wrath of God* (1972) and *Fitzcarraldo*, or the flat dusty brown Wisconsin plains of *Stroszek* are typical of the visual environments to which Herzog's German characters have been transported. Herzog's soundtracks are as careful as his visual imagery; he gives particular attention to musical themes and to the musical scoring of both speech and noises — the repetitive use of intense and mysterious silences; the calls, cries, and hoots of birds in *Aguirre, the Wrath of God*; the use, in film after film, of music by South American Indians; the intensely moving music that opens *The Mystery of Kaspar Hauser* (the German title translates, *Everyone for Himself and God Against All,* 1974); the clash of languages (German and English) and of musical styles (German glockenspiel music as opposed to American pop-rock) in *Stroszek,* or the breathlessly rapid, almost incomprehensible chant of the auctioneer in the same film, a chant that is both a jumble of language and a complex musical passage.

Fig. 16-4
Aguirre, the Wrath of God: *Aguirre (Klaus Kinski) demonically enclosed in his universe of one.*

At the center of most Herzog narratives is a single character who follows his single-minded determination to an inevitable and irreversible end. The Herzog characters are driven by destinies—or inner compulsions—that can be neither softened nor averted. Aguirre (played by Klaus Kinski, whom Herzog once called the only true demon of the cinema), the Spanish conquistador, is driven to seek the mythical city of El Dorado in the depths of the South American jungle. He tyrannically and unswervingly pushes his band of steadily dwindling Europeans into the heart of the immense, unknown continent, refusing to alter his determination despite the murderous natives, the devastating heat, the crippling diseases, the dense forest, and the angry uncharted waters. Aguirre becomes a relentless, wrathful god who ignores the evidence and arguments of men and nature. The result is complete catastrophe: the death of everyone on the pathetically small raft that Aguirre—the stranded imperialist, the demon of European power, the self-proclaimed wrath of God,

a Hitler before his time—has forged to tame the continent. The final shot of the film is both a dazzling cinematic device and Herzog's brilliant visual metaphor for Aguirre's mind and world. As the leader stands firmly atop his raft, littered with the bodies of his followers and the frenetic scrambling of what seem like ten thousand monkeys, Herzog's camera (now in a helicopter) hovers above Aguirre and circles the raft, ringing the man and his kingdom of monkeys off from the rest of the world, revealing that Aguirre's physical and mental universes are essentially a circumscribed world of one—and that one a figure of pure will, helpless but unwilling to capitulate, locked in the world of his obsession—where not even he can live for long.

Other Herzog figures similarly attempt to mold the physical world according to the shapes of their imagination, and they predictably run into trouble when the world resists. Like Aguirre, the residents of a small German town in *Heart of Glass* become obsessed with a mythical quest that leads to death and destruction—not the search for El Dorado but the attempt to rediscover a secret formula for making the perfect ruby-red glass for which the town is famous. Like Aguirre, the innocent child–man Kaspar Hauser (played by Bruno S., who had been institutionalized as a schizophrenic before Herzog starred him in *Kaspar Hauser* and *Stroszek*) sees the universe with a singleness of personal vision that clashes with the assumptions of all those citizens who teach him to see it differently by teaching him to speak. Like Truffaut's *The Wild Child*, *Kaspar Hauser* shows what it means to live with and without language, but it goes further, adding the problem of language's inability to describe what lies outside the realm of words and of well-ordered perceptions. Fitzgerald (Kinski again), of *Fitzcarraldo*, is determined to haul his ship up and over the top of a mountain, contrary to gravity and the natural medium—water—in which it was built to travel, so that he can bring the voice of Enrico Caruso to the jungle and raise money for an opera house. The journey of that ship—all to create an edifice for art, the opera house Fitzgerald envisions—seems an emblem for Herzog's characters and for Herzog himself: fixing one's sights on an impossible task

Fig. 16-5
Alice in the Cities: *Rüdiger Vogler, Wenders's alter ego in the early black-and-white features, surveys the bleak American landscape with his Polaroid.*

and refusing to look away from it until the film is finished.

Wim Wenders's films are more like American movies in both style and content. They are also about American movies—and the pervasive force of American culture in West Germany. Characters in Wenders films drink Jack Daniel's whiskey, listen to American rock music on American juke boxes, discuss American novels, drive American cars, delight in American names, and, in effect, attempt to recreate the life-styles and values of characters— particularly male characters—in American films. The goalie in *The Goalie's Anxiety at the Penalty Kick* attends a showing of Howard Hawks's *Red Line 7000* (1965), and a newspaper in *Alice in the Cities* (1973) announces the death of John Ford. If Wenders's films glorify—and investigate and critique—American culture and American movies, they also pay homage to cinema itself. French directors Jean Eustache

and Gerard Blain play roles in *The American Friend*, as do American directors Ray and Fuller. The two buddies of *Kings of the Road*, in explicating a passage from Faulkner's *The Wild Palms*, also pay their respects to Godard's *Breathless*, in which Patricia and Michel discuss a passage from the same novel. Such internationalism (an American author and a French filmmaker in one scene of a German movie) is typical of Wenders's films, many of which show Germans and Americans trying to figure each other out.

The vocation of one of the two major characters in *Kings of the Road* is to service motion picture projectors, maintaining the machines that allow the cinema to exist. The shadow-show that the two friends mime behind a movie screen, their three-dimensional bodies converted into two-dimensional silhouettes by the worklight behind them, is a tribute both to the magic of silent comedy (their routine echoes

Laurel and Hardy) and to the hypnotic image of cinema in general (their antics captivate a group of noisy children, impatient for the equipment to be repaired and the film to begin, into adoring silence). This "live" shadow-show becomes itself a piece of cinema—two-dimensional, moving, silent silhouettes on a white screen, created by the powers of light. The crimes against life in *Kings of the Road* are crimes against cinema—projectionists who do not care whether the image is properly framed or focused, whether their equipment is clean and well-oiled; filmmakers who debase the art by turning love into pornography and violence.

The central narrative issue and interest of *Kings of the Road* is this intersection of life and cinema. As its overseas release title indicates (the German title translates, *In the Course of Time*), the film is a story of people on the road—like Chaplin's Tramp, like Huck Finn and Jim, like Jack Kerouac's wanderers, like the "searchers" of American westerns. The road is a place of total freedom from social entanglements; the two men in the truck, like the cowboys on their mounts, belong everywhere and nowhere—perhaps like Wenders, whose films have been said to manifest "a worldwide homesickness" and whose independent production company is called Road Movies. Robert, the projector repairman, is a figure of entertainment, joy, amusement, life. His decision to disentangle himself from the world, to live on the road, to keep his life moving by keeping himself moving, is a long-standing one. His new traveling companion and passenger, Bruno, a child psychologist who has just broken with his wife and incompetently tried to kill himself, is still emotionally entangled and confined by his life—his unfulfilling relationship with his father, his wife, and with children themselves (an irony, given his vocation). In riding along and spending time together (one sense of the German title), the two "kings of the road," who begin as opposites, achieve a synthesis; the tangled Bruno discovers the openness, the cleanness, the simplicity, the wholeness of the road, of being at one, and at home, with himself.

The American Friend is also about achieving a synthesis of opposites and a wholeness with oneself. At the center of the film is another contrast of two men—Tom Ripley (Dennis

Fig. 16-6

Fig. 16-7

The American Friend: *the framemaker (Bruno Ganz, Fig. 16-6) and the cowboy (Dennis Hopper, Fig. 16-7), each framed within the frame.*

Hopper), an American wheeler-dealer engaged in various shady business transactions (the "cowboy in Hamburg"), and Jonathan Zimmerman (Bruno Ganz), a Swiss framemaker and art restorer who lives in Hamburg with his wife and child. The men come together when Zimmerman makes the frame for one of the paintings Ripley sells, a picture by a noted American painter presumed dead. On the surface, the two men appear to be as opposite as Switzerland and the American West—the one a quiet, careful, devoted craftsman and family man, the other a rootless, slippery, shuffling wanderer, attached to nothing and no one. But the two are not so different as they seem. There is an emptiness at the center of each man's life. The framemaker's life is all frame and no picture; it has shape but no image to shape. Wenders emphasizes this condition with images of empty frames that Zimmerman carefully scrutinizes, despite their emptiness. Ripley's life is also all surface, all style, and no accomplishment. He may look like a cowboy, talk like a cowboy, walk like a cowboy, but all he does is serve as middleman for a mildly unethical scheme to drive up the prices of a painter's works. Both do work that is peripheral to the world of painting—concerned with how the painting is presented to an audience, how its value is asserted. Both are foreigners in Hamburg. Both are spiritually homeless.

Closely related to the contrast of these two men is a contrast of vision and action. The film is built around metaphors for vision: The framemaker suffers from a terminal disease that attacks the eyes; Wenders packs the film with a little history of objects and devices that have extended the powers of human vision—painted canvases, a Stereopticon, a Zoetrope, peephole viewers, an illuminated electrified painting (significantly, it is of a train named "The General"), a Polaroid Land camera, and television. The references to movies are the most central of these visual metaphors (just as they are in *Kings of the Road*) yet among the most subtle. The framemaker, Zimmerman, is a surrogate for a filmmaker, whose business is also making frames. And the cowboy, Ripley, is the typical subject of movies—quirky, active, aggressive, violent, intriguingly unpredictable. In order to achieve a whole movie, one needs

both frame and subject, shape and content. In the same way, for Ripley to become whole he needs a frame, a shape for his actions; and for Zimmerman to become whole, he needs an action, a content, for his frames.

The film unites the two men by plunging them into just such a unifying action: a proliferating series of murders, violent confrontations, and breathless escapes. There is, of course, a sense in which the accelerating and expanding violence into which the two men are drawn is a terrible trap, a sense that Wenders emphasizes throughout this latter-day *film noir* with images of confinement, entanglement, and enclosure (tunnels, narrow escalators, confined passageways of trains, labyrinthine corridors). But there is also a sense in which the violence becomes an assertive, existential act of human defiance against emptiness, inactivity, and meaninglessness—a sense that Wenders emphasizes with the extremely open, vast images (parallel to the open images of *Kings of the Road*) that dominate the final scene of the film.

Given Wenders's affection for the styles, themes, and images of American film, it was no surprise that he began to make films in America: *Hammett* (1983), produced by Francis Ford Coppola (and employing the advanced technology developed for *One from the heart*), a fictionalized biography of Dashiell Hammett, the American detective novelist who was so influential on movies (*The Maltese Falcon, The Thin Man*), and *Paris, Texas* (1984), written by Sam Shepard, which won the Cannes Golden Palm award for that year. In this return to *Alice in the Cities* and *Kings of the Road*, the two wandering "buddies" are father and son, searching (in a conscious homage to Ford's *Searchers*) the Hollywood Hills and Texas plains for a missing woman (the wife and mother, played by Nastassia Kinski, Klaus's daughter); when they find her—since this is a western (a form that both Shepard and Wenders continually explore) rather than a weepie—the husband heads for the hills.

Wings of Desire (1987), a French-German co-production, was written by Wenders and novelist Peter Handke (author of *The Goalie's Anxiety* and other works adapted by Wenders). It tells of two angels (Bruno Ganz and Otto Sander), assigned to Berlin since prehistoric times, who move through the city in 1987, eavesdropping on people's thoughts and wondering what it would be like to be human, to live in time rather than eternity. Since the angels can remember everything that ever happened on a particular street, Wenders can show that street in the present, then during the Third Reich, then in the present again or after an Allied bombing, summarizing all that Berlin has been, has done, and has endured. The movie takes the long view of history and of the fates of individuals, but it also moves in close to show all the concerns and uncertainties of the present and of individuals—and so does the camera, which may look at Berlin from above or at people straight on (or may reflexively imitate the camera movements from a shot in Murnau's *Sunrise*; this is, after all, a Wenders film). What the angels see is in black and white, while mortal experience is in color; angels hear the thoughts of others (sometimes the soundtrack is a chaos of minds), while people hear only themselves. The ultimate questions this movie raises about life are posed by Rainer Maria Rilke, one of whose poems is quoted repeatedly, and by the everyday/cosmic attitude the movie adopts with such calm, authority, and love. It turns out that some angels may become mortal; Peter Falk plays one of these "former angels," and the film is dedicated to three more: Ozu, Truffaut, and Tarkovsky. *Wings of Desire* is certainly the *It's A Wonderful Life* of the 1980s, but it is also a movie that feels on the verge of some great historical change. A film about the present and for the future, it ends on a note of setting out on the adventure of life, its story to be continued. When Germany was reunified in October, 1990, after forty-five years of division, that seemed to fit perfectly into the film's worldview—and rather than become dated, *Wings of Desire* became even more relevant and inspiring.

The new German cinema has not been confined to its three major voices. Alexander Kluge has already been mentioned. Volker Schlöndorff excels in stylish literary adaptations—of Heinrich von Kleist (*Michael Kohlhaas*, 1969), Heinrich Böll (*The Lost Honor of Katharina Blum*, 1975), Günter Grass (*The Tin Drum*, 1979, the most popular German film of all time in Germany), and Marcel Proust (*Swann in Love*,

1983). His wife, Margarethe von Trotta, frequently writes Schlöndorff's scripts, co-directed *Katharina Blum*, and writes and directs films of her own (*Sisters, or The Balance of Happiness*, 1979; *Marianne and Juliane*, 1981; *Sheer Madness*, 1982; *Rosa Luxemburg*, 1986; *Three Sisters*, 1988). Though all of the twenty-six filmmakers who signed the Oberhausen Manifesto were men, there are now many women directors active in Germany, notably Helma Sanders-Brahms (*Germany, Pale Mother,* 1980), Ulrike Ottinger (*Freak Orlando*, 1981), and Doris Dörrie (*Inside the Whale*, 1984). Jean-Marie Straub, the most radical of filmmakers who work in Germany, has been influenced by Bresson as well as Brecht and Godard. With his wife and collaborator, Danièle Huillet, Straub is committed to deconstructing both the ordinary processes of film narrative and the usual strategies of film imagery. Straub/Huillet, as they are usually referred to, together write, produce, and direct their films, which include *Not Reconciled*, 1965; *Chronicle of Anna Magdalena Bach*, 1967; *History Lessons*, 1972; *Moses and Aaron*, 1974; *Class Relations*, 1983; and *The Death of Empedocles*, 1987. Films from the "Berlin Underground" include Frank Ripploh's *Taxi zum Klo* (1981), an amusingly frank account of Germany's gay subculture. At the opposite extreme, Hans-Jürgen Syberberg makes operatic films on an epic scale. While his *Parsifal* (1982), a staging of Wagner's opera, recalls the German traditions of Romanticism and Expressionism (and puts a Nazi parade inside Wagner's head, which is used as a set), *Our Hitler* (1977) confronts those traditions and German history in search of the roots of Nazism.

It remains to be seen just how the reunification of Germany will affect the film industries on either side of what used to be the Berlin Wall. East-West co-productions can be expected, and perhaps even a unified industry, but the biggest difference may be made by the fact of a unified audience.

Third World Cinemas

The term "Third World film" does not so much describe a national tradition as provide a heading for many politically and economically related but geographically scattered national cinemas: those films from the underdeveloped emerging nations of Africa, Asia, and Latin America that explicitly examine the political, social, and cultural issues of those nations. Although Brazil is one of those countries that has produced Third World films, the popular romantic-erotic fantasy *Dona Flor and Her Two Husbands* (Bruno Barretto, 1978), with its escape from social realities, would probably not be considered one of them. Nor would either the personal, psychological studies of Satyajit Ray or the spectacles and action films produced for India's vast popular audience (but the films of Mrinal Sen would). Nor would the Kung Fus from Hong Kong. On the other hand, some European films (*The Battle of Algiers, State of Siege*) and some American black or Latino films (like Melvin Van Peebles's *Sweet Sweetback's Baadasssss Song*, 1971; John Singleton's *Boyz N the Hood*, 1991; and Anna Thomas and Gregory Nava's *El Norte*, 1983) have been considered spiritual products of the Third World even though the films were produced or directed by Americans or Europeans. *Yol* (1982), a realistic, socially critical Turkish film directed by Şerif Gören and written by Yilmaz Guney—who wrote the script while in jail and had to smuggle it out—is certainly a Third World film. To keep an already muddy metaphor from becoming any more murky, it would make sense to define a Third World film by both its national origin and its cultural content.

These developing, often post-colonial countries produce films either to educate their own citizens about the cultural history and contemporary conditions of the nation or to present that nation's problems and positions to the citizens of the rest of the world—or both. To make feature films up to the stylistic and technical standards of the international market costs a lot of money—particularly for countries with limited economic resources. Those Third World films that have been widely screened outside local markets must pass a strict test of social utility—serving a country's national and international interests. Their clearest historical analogy is to the Soviet silent classics of the 1920s. Like the new Soviet Union, these nations are emerging from decades or even centuries of cultural exploitation—economic domination by foreign interests, political domi-

nation by autocratic governments that concentrated power in the hands of the few for the benefit of the few and kept the bulk of the population largely illiterate and very poor. As in the new Soviet Union, films could be used to educate an audience unable to read and ignorant of the goals and methods of a new government. As in the Soviet Union, films could be projected in the most remote regions of these often topographically tortuous countries with the aid of portable power supplies. One Cuban documentary, Octavio Cortázar's *For the First Time* (1967), describes the wondrous introduction of motion pictures—Charlie Chaplin's among them—to a village of Cuban peasants. As in the Soviet Union, films could combine their political lessons with moving stories of human action, often mingling native symbols and folk elements with their didactic tales of social values.

No clearer parallels with the early Soviet movement can be found than in several specific devices of these Third World films. The ending of the Cuban film *The Last Supper* (1976), directed by Tomás Gutiérrez Alea, reflects the influence of Pudovkin: A montage of metaphoric cross-cuts links the uprising of an oppressed people with the inevitable and irreversible processes of nature. The ending of Miguel Littin's Chilean film *The Promised Land* (1973; never released in Chile), like Pudovkin's *Mother*, shows a failed revolution of the past passing on its spirit to the future and, like Dovzhenko's *Arsenal*, develops the mystically unkillable power of the people. The Argentinian *The Hour of the Furnaces: Notes and Testimonies on Neo-Colonialism, Violence and Liberation* (1968), directed by Fernando Solanas and Octavio Getino—which rejects what it calls the "first cinema" of Hollywood and the "second cinema" of *auteurs* in search of a revolutionary "third cinema" energized by neorealism and the documentary, politically engaged and collaboratively produced—includes such specific Eisenstein echoes as the use of stone statues in a Buenos Aires cemetery as a metaphor for cultural deadness (paralleling Eisenstein's similar use of statues in *Potemkin* and *October*) and the metaphoric killing of beasts in a slaughterhouse (parallel to the famous montage symbolism of *Strike*—except that the Argentine film's soundtrack ironically juxtaposes its slaughter with the jaunty counterpoint of the merry Swingle Singers). Finally, like the Soviet cinema, the cinema of the Third World includes many works that are mere propaganda (telling the audience what to think) and many that present ideas for the audience to think about (comparable to a Brechtian theatre of ideas). Third World cinema is both an international phenomenon and a set of national cinemas, bursting with important movements (*cinema novo* in Brazil) and exciting director/theorists (Solanas and Getino in Argentina, Glauber Rocha in Brazil, Tomás Gutiérrez Alea in Cuba) and essential films (Rocha's 1969 *Antonio das Mortes*) whose international influence has been enormous.

The methods and goals of film production in these Third World countries can be divided into three very broad categories. First, one country, Cuba, with an extremely well-developed, sophisticated, and nationalized film industry, can rival the industries of all but a few countries of the world in the quality and quantity of its output. Like Lenin, Fidel Castro declared the cinema the most important and socially useful of the arts; as a result, the Cuban government, like the Soviet Union, founded and funded a national film school and film production company (ICAIC — Instituto Cubano del Arte e Industria Cinematograficos). Although ICAIC produces mainly documentaries, it also makes several narrative feature films each year, for the Cubans discovered, as did the Soviets, that the populace preferred Hollywood-style stories to didactic documentaries. These feature films, too, help Cuba forcefully argue its case abroad — particularly in Paris, where there is less political resistance to them than in New York. ICAIC also produces a weekly television program, *24 Frames Per Second*, which contributes to the Cuban audience's sophisticated appreciation of cinema processes as well as the political implications of image making — the semiotic problems that so haunt and consume Godard.

During the brief periods of the progressive Torres regime in Bolivia and the Allende regime in Chile, the cinemas of these two South American nations began to move toward a Cuban-style nationalized industry. But the right-wing *coups d'état* that ended both leftist regimes also ended their developing cinemas and forced many leading artists into exile. Conversely, expanding political freedoms in 1980s Brazil stimulated Brazilian film production.

Second, several Third World countries make a small number of feature films for both national consumption and international distribution (for example, Senegal, Egypt, Ethiopia). Because the population of many of these countries is small, these films seek international distribution to expand their impact and justify their cost. And because the governments of some of these countries are still politically repressive, the political content of these films is often guarded and metaphoric — more ironic, less radical, less explicitly Marxist, less dominated by revolutionary rhetoric than the films of Cuba or those of the third group.

That third group of films comprises those from countries with such repressive totalitarian governments that the films become underground acts of rebellion and sedition in themselves — films from Argentina, Chile, Bolivia, Peru. Because these films are so dangerous to make, they could never be shown in the countries that produced them without a revolutionary change in their governments; two outstanding examples are *The Hour of the Furnaces* and *The Battle of Chile* (1973–79, directed by Patricio Guzmán and edited in Cuba, a Chilean-Cuban co-production released by Chris Marker's radical film collective, SLON — the Society for the Launching of New Works — which had produced *Far from Vietnam* in 1967). These films have been produced almost exclusively for international distribution, to rally international opinion against the ruling regimes of those countries.

Despite these differences in the methods of their production and distribution, Third World films share several general themes. The first is an attack on the dominating cultural presence of the more affluent nations of Europe and America — the British presence in *The Night of Counting the Years* (Egypt, 1969), a film by Shadi Abdes-Salam, the French presence in the films of Ousmane Sembene (Senegal), the American presence in South American and Vietnamese films. These movies often reveal the power of

Fig. 16-8

Clashes of cultures. Black African song and a sleeping white aristocrat in The Last Supper *(Fig. 16-8); native African costumes and customs with Westernized gifts at the wedding in* Xala *(Fig. 16-9).*

Fig. 16-9

foreign influences in their conflict between imported products, processes, or customs and strictly native ones—the bottles of Evian water, Coca-Cola, and J & B Scotch whiskey in Sembene's *Xala* (Senegal, 1974) or the conflict of both Christianity and Islam with native African religious rituals in his *Ceddo* (Senegal, 1977); the magazine advertisements for American consumer products in *The Hour of the Furnaces*; the juxtaposition of the ritual magic of black African slaves with the rituals of Christian Easter in Tomás Gutiérrez Alea's *The Last Supper*; the presence of the American "Progress Corps" in Jorge Sanjiné's *Blood of the Condor* (Bolivia, 1969).

A second major theme is the crushing, unimaginable poverty of vast segments of the peasant population—whether of the Andes Indians of *Blood of the Condor*, the feudal farmers of Haile Gerima's *Harvest: 3000 Years* (Ethiopia, 1975), the migrant workers of Miguel Littin's *The Jackal of Nahueltoro* (Chile, 1969) and *The Promised Land* (1973), the impoverished family in the barren drought-burned plains of Brazil's Northeast in Nelson Pereira dos Santos's *Vidas secas* (*Barren Lives*; Brazil, 1963), or the impoverished street children in the Rio de Janeiro slums of Hector Babenco's *Pixote* (Brazil, 1981).

A third theme, like the original title of Eisenstein's 1929 film, might be called "Old and New," the contrast of the old backward ways of farming, living, thinking with newer, more progressive ones—the conflicts of national and tribal laws in *The Night of Counting the Years*, of ancient and modern customs in *Xala*; the examinations of the new systems of education and the new social role of women in the Cuban documentaries *The New School* (1973) and *With the Cuban Women* (1975), and of the general patterns of historical evolution in the Cuban fictional classic, *Lucía* (1968). Some of these films, of course, celebrate the old ways, the founding rituals and unique look of their land and culture—as Souleymane Cissé treats black Africa in *Brightness* (1987). A final theme that unites many of these films is the implication that these scattered countries, continents, and peoples are indeed united by common cultural problems and common cultural goals—that the exploited peoples of India, Vietnam, Africa, Cuba, Argentina, Bolivia, Chile share a common need and common enemy.

Like Humberto Solas's *Lucía*, many of these Third World films have been recognized as contemporary classics from world class directors. *Lucía* is a film in the tradition that stretches from Griffith's *The Birth of a Nation* to Bertolucci's *1900*: the mammoth political epic that juxtaposes personal human dramas with immense historical events and political processes. Solás divides his epic into three periods—1895, 1932, and 196 . . . —each of them reflecting a particular political struggle of the Cuban people (first, the War of Independence from Spain; next, the first Cuban political revolution against the dictator Machado; finally, the continuing worker's revolution under Castro). Uniting the film is a woman named Lucía—or rather, three different women with the same name (the female focus and the recurrent name parallel similar unifying devices in Griffith's *Intolerance*). In each of the film's eras, there is a conflict between Lucía's romantic love and the political events that surround and threaten that love.

The 1895 Lucía surrenders to her sexual passion for Rafael, although such a passion is forbidden in the proper, highly Europeanized upper-class world of 1895 Cuba. Her Rafael, an undercover Spanish agent, seduces Lucía as a means of capturing an arsenal held by the Cuban guerrilla army. The result is that Lucía becomes the unknowing cause of her country's defeat, of her brother's death, and of her own horrifying rape. The 1932 Lucía is a member of the *haute bourgeoisie* who falls in love with and marries Aldo, a young radical student. She supports his political struggle by, in effect, joining the working class (she goes to work in a factory) and participating in the street demonstrations of the Cuban women. After the success of the insurrection against Machado, Aldo discovers that their revolution has become corrupt (this was, after all, an insurrection of the bourgeoisie—and Batista would be its end product). Aldo continues his fight against the new status quo, machine-gunning the mayor of Havana on the steps of the city hall (this assassination is a piece of Cuban history), himself dying in the struggle. Lucía remains alone with both her personal and political futures shattered.

Fig. 16-10

Fig. 16-11

Lucía: *political history as pictorial history.*
Fig. 16-10: the 1895 Lucía (Raquel Revuelta)
surrounded by the formal elegance and symmetry of
her aristocratic world. Fig. 16-11: the 1960s Lucía
(Adela Lagra) and her Tomás (Adolfo Llaurado)
surrounded by the bustling vitality of her worker's
world.

The 196 . . . Lucía is a member of the working class who has recently married her very energetic and attractive Tomás. Unfortunately, Tomás, in addition to his masculine charm, is also enslaved by the old masculine ways of thinking; he converts his new wife into his domestic prisoner, refusing to allow her to work in the fields, to be seen in public, or to learn to read and write, all because of his sexual jealousy and macho possessiveness. Lucía rebels and deserts him, but the two live very unhappily apart. (The section sets itself the propagandistic problem of supporting marriage while opposing the enslavement of the wife.) In the film's final shot, after their reunion, Lucía continues to insist on her right to be free and Tomás on his right to possess her. The film (like *1900*) ends on this unresolved argument—implying that the battle has not been won and that the struggle of Cuban women still continues.

In its individual narratives and its general political philosophy—that it is impossible to be happy in love without also being happy in a just society—the film is certainly no richer or clearer than Griffith's *Intolerance.* But also like the Griffith film, *Lucía* gets its power from the broader intellectual plan that integrates the individual tales and, especially, from the careful visual style, texture, and detail that convey each of the historical periods. The 1895 sequence is dominated by ultrasharp contrasts of white and black. Solas defines the upper-class Europeanized world of the first Lucía by its extremely sunny whiteness, its brilliant clarity, and the perfectly symmetrical order of everything in Lucía's world—the photographs on the walls, the arrangements of furniture, even the shapes and patterns of trees in her garden. But when Lucía is ripped from her garden world and plunged into her nightmare one, the film stock emphasizes a world that has gone grainy, contrasty, and overblack—the personal experiencing of horror in the visual terms of a cinematic nightmare. The 1932 sequence is dominated by much softer contrasts, giving the sequence the gauzy, overdecorated, Art Deco look of 1930s Hollywood films.

If *Lucía* is a history of Cuba from 1895 to 196 . . . —particularly its steady descent of the class ladder, from upper-class plantation dwellers to the urban *haute bourgeoisie* to working-class rural laborers—it is also a history of film lighting, film stocks, and cinematic visual values—from high contrast to soft contrast to deep focus. The 1895 section is set in the year the Lumière brothers first projected their

Fig. 16-12
Vidas secas: *the homeless family of "Nordestinos."*

films. And the 196 . . . section is shot with fast panchromatic film in deep focus, mirroring the visual values of both contemporary cinema and, not coincidentally, Italian neorealism. The film mirrors the problems of contemporary life by capturing the look of contemporary cinema.

Nelson Pereira dos Santos's *Vidas secas* is in a very different style and single key—a hard, close, unflinching look at the desperate poverty of a single family of "Nordestinos," the rural peasants of Brazil's Northeast, in 1940. This family—husband, wife, two boys, and faithful dog—roams the barren, burned plains in search of a farm or ranch where they can earn their keep. The couple's great goal in life is to save enough money for a leather bed—a bed with a sheet of leather to cover the bony wooden branches that serve as its "mattress." Fabiano, the very hard-working husband, runs into trouble with a petty government police-man, but rather than take the path of rebellion (he gets the opportunity both to join a band of guerillas and to murder this toad in uniform), he remains the hard-working docile slave. The film's setting in the past implies that the man's political docility is a sign of an incompletely evolved political consciousness.

One of the film's remarkably effective devices is its brilliantly cinematic use of available light for both indoor and outdoor sequences. The scorching, blazing power of the sun, the cause of the land's dryness, is also the film's central metaphor and the source of its abso-

lutely authentic depiction of people living in the midst of their genuine surroundings, either outdoors when exposed to its pitiless glare or indoors when trying to escape into the temporary shade of rooms and houses. Although the film pretends to be set in the past (many radical Brazilian films, like *Antonio das Mortes*, must masquerade as apolitical and unconnected to the present), it nevertheless successfully implies that the journey of such people continues, un-solved and unresolved, even into the present.

A later Santos film, *How Tasty Was My Little Frenchman* (1971), is a political allegory of a very different type. A period film photo-graphed in lush color, it depicts the experiences of a seventeenth-century Portuguese mercenary captured by a native Brazilian tribe. They sen-tence him to death because they believe him to be French, the tribe's enemy. They fail to un-derstand that he is Portuguese—also an enemy of the French—and that he came to South America to fight the French. Portuguese look just like Frenchmen to the natives, and the dif-ferent European languages sound indistin-guishable to their ears—an ironic comment on the way Europeans of that period believed all "savages" to look and talk alike.

Their law ("savage" by European standards) demands that he live for a year with the tribe, in material comfort and wedded bliss, after which they will ceremonially kill him and eat him. The "Frenchman" spends his time both trying to escape from the tribe and luxuriating in the simple beauty of its natural life. He can-not believe that they will actually murder him after a year of such community and compan-ionship. But they do—with his sensuously lov-ing wife leading the ceremony. (As the title says, he was *her* tasty little Frenchman.) The film im-plies that, whether French or Portuguese, the white European is an exploitative colonizer who deserves to experience both the integrity of na-tive custom and the severity of its justice. The film depicts Europeans as the real "savages" in their exploitation of this New World and its native people.

The Third World political documentaries, like Solanas and Getino's *The Hour of the Fur-naces*, have a very different kind of artistic power and political purpose. *The Hour of the Furnaces* is a three-part, 260-minute analysis of

Fig. 16-13
The Hour of the Furnaces: *testament to political oppression and social violence.*

the political, economic, and cultural landscape of Argentina, past and present. Part 1 examines Argentinean political-cultural life in the present and the roots of that life in the past — the dependence on foreign investments and capital, the domination by foreign culture and customs, the concentration of wealth in the hands of the few, the political alienation of the working class, and the extreme impoverishment of the native Indian population. Part 2 examines Perónism, which the film calls the only genuine working-class political movement in Argentinean history — first, the decade of Perón rule, 1945–1955, then the decade of underground Perónist sentiment and activity following the coup that overthrew the Perón regime. Part 3 is a call to arms, urging armed revolution and resistance as the only way to establish a just and equitable government in Argentina. The film's three parts, which might be titled Present, Past, and Future, exhibit the three-part argument of Marxist dialectic: thesis, antithesis, and synthesis.

The Hour of the Furnaces is interesting on a number of levels and for a number of reasons. First, like the great political documentaries of Marcel Ophuls (*The Sorrow and the Pity*, 1969;

The Memory of Justice, 1976), the film shakes its audiences — regardless of their political convictions — with the sense of witnessing and participating in a series of historically important and humanly shattering events. The film presents the country's social chaos and cultural antagonisms so sharply, so clearly, and so comprehensively that audiences from more stable, less divided cultures in happier times can only marvel at a spectacle with the intensity of historical fiction but the authenticity of historical fact. Second, the film adopts the stance of Marxist (rather than fascist) rhetoric asking the audience to think about the issues it has presented, to discuss them (indeed there are sections where the film deliberately breaks off and asks the audience to discuss), to formulate questions and to argue about them. This request for conscious and active participation seems antithetical to the fascist propaganda strategy (also common to bourgeois cinema) of hypnotizing viewers by manipulating ideologically loaded plots (where only the right people get the happy endings or the audience's sympathy) and symbols that strike beneath the viewer's threshold of conscious awareness.

But these differences may be only superficial. Plenty of propaganda remains in the film; much is also left unsaid. For example, *Hour of the Furnaces* treats the Roman Catholic Church very gingerly (a clear departure from Marxist theory and from Eisenstein's satiric practice), occasionally linking a bishop visually with the forces of governmental repression but never accusing the Church as a whole of any role in subjugating the people. Given the close attachment of the South American working classes to the Church, the film would rather not raise this sensitive issue at all. On the other hand, the soundtrack is a stream of verbal rhetoric that repeats its accusations like a litany. We hear the accusations that the government of Argentina is an oligarchy, that the oligarchy is supported and controlled by the American CIA, that Argentinean intellectuals and universities are mere servants of decadent European tastes and culture (the film purposely develops an antagonism between workers and intellectuals), but we see little or no precisely documented evidence. The film assumes that merely to flash images on the screen of classic European paintings or of modern magazine ads is in itself an indictment of America, Europe, and Western civilization as a whole.

A great documentary that makes its case with precision and force is Guzmán's two-part, 191-minute *The Battle of Chile* (released in 1977; a third part was added in 1979), which chronicles the six months of social agitation that led to the military *coup d'état*—the bloodiest in South American history—against the constitutionally elected left-wing government of Salvador Allende in 1973. Less than a decade later, Costa-Gavras's *Missing* (1982) could make commercial Hollywood fiction—but not a Third World film—from almost as radical an interpretation of the same political events (as long as it was primarily the story of an American victim; otherwise there would have been no studio interest in the project).

Unlike the Marcel Ophuls documentaries, these Third World chronicles tend to be ideologically one-sided. Ophuls is painfully aware of the complexities and ironies in the commitment to any single political position. These enriching ironies and complexities are luxuries that only pluralistic democratic nations can

Fig. 16-14
Memories of Underdevelopment: *the bourgeois intellectual surrounded by books, physical embodiments of his attitudes and values; the book in his hands is* **Lolita.**

usually afford. Two Third World directors, Tomás Gutiérrez Alea of Cuba, who received his cinema education at Italy's Centro Sperimentale, and Ousmane Sembene of Senegal, a novelist who was educated in France and studied filmmaking in Moscow, reveal many of the same broader ironies and complexities of a more international outlook.

Alea's first major work to be seen in the United States, *Memories of Underdevelopment* (1968), is an extremely ironic portrait of a member of the bourgeoisie (Sergio Corrieri) who, unlike many other members of his class, remains in Cuba after the fall of Batista. This highly influential film carefully and comically reveals the man's difficulty in finding a place for himself in the new Cuban society. His sexual tastes (rather graphically recorded), his cultural tastes (in books, paintings, music) simply do not belong in the new Cuba, and the film simultaneously condemns the man's spiritual emptiness and ironically sympathizes with his isolation. But an even more careful, controlled, and elegant Alea film is *The Last Supper* (1977), a costume drama in splendid color. *The Last Supper* is, like the first section of *Lucía*, set in the Cuba of the late eighteenth century—on a sugar cane plantation owned by the aristocracy and worked by black African slaves. As the film's title indicates, the story takes place during Easter week, and the entire work is built on a religious, allegorical foundation. The land-owner of the plantation suffers a seizure of aristocratic *Weltschmerz*—he knows not why he is living or what the value of life may be. In order to regain his faith, he decides to perform an ideal act of Christian penance and charity; he selects twelve of his own slaves, washes their feet, and invites them to sit at his table as his disciples. The meal they eat together is in-tended to mirror the ideals of Christian charity and equality—master with slave, all equals in the eye of God.

The lengthy supper sequence becomes a rare moment of emotional togetherness and ideological separation. As the diners consume more and more wine, they feel closer to one another. (Like Brecht's *Herr Puntila* and Chap-lin's *City Lights*, the film uses alcohol as the great eradicator of class barriers.) The one slave who refuses to be seduced by the master's kindness is Sebastian (whose Christian name ironically evokes passive martyrdom). Although the master refers to Sebastian as Judas, it re-mains to be seen who is the true Judas at this table. Only when the host falls asleep does Se-bastian tell his own mythic story, a pagan ver-sion of the "Fall of Man," which sees humankind as a mixture of man and beast— the head of a pig surmounts the heart of a man. The master will indeed reveal that, despite his kindly sentiments, a pig's head rules this man's heart. The pig's head is economic interest—a Cuban metaphor for vicious capitalism—that draws a sharp distinction between business and religious sentiment; in other words, the master has no trouble believing in both slavery and Christianity.

The next day is Easter Sunday, and the slaves —according to the master and the sympathetic plantation priest (another deliberate attempt to attack not the spirit of Christianity but its bastardization)—are to spend the holy day at rest and worship. But the brutal foreman of the plantation can think of nothing but pro-ductivity. This foreman represents the hard economic reality beneath the spiritual and phil-osophical façade of the master, the man who does the ruling class's dirty work. He demands

that the slaves get to work. A violent rebellion of slaves results—led by those very twelve dis-ciples who sat at the master's table and believed in his commitment to the sanctity of the next day. In the struggle, the slaves deliberately kill the vicious foreman (a man who had earlier cut off Sebastian's ear as punishment), accidentally kill his wife, and set fire to the plantation. The master's pigheaded answer is the equally violent subduing of the rebellion by armed force and the deliberate murder of every one of the twelve slaves who, the night before, sat with him at table—as an example of the price of revolution.

But Sebastian manages to escape, using the magic dust he brought with him from Africa, the spirit of his homeland, to convert himself into a tree, a rock, a river, a bird. With Sebas-tian's escape—Alea cross-cuts between the running Sebastian and images of a tree, a rock, a river, a bird—we understand that his re-bellious spirit is, like the spirit of Christ, an un-killable human force that will be reborn in later generations of followers. The black African spirit of Sebastian becomes the film's metaphor for the spirit of the Cuban working-class people —most of them descendants of these African slaves—that would arise and rebel against the shams of Christian social justice in 1959.

Ousmane Sembene has been adapting his own stories and novels into film since 1966 when he made *Black Girl*, a sensitive study of an African woman who feels stifled, deceived, and corrupted when brought to the South of France to work as a cleaning lady. One of Sembene's most complex films is his adaptation of his novel *Xala*, an ironic study of the diffi-culty of exercising power well after having seized it. The film's prologue is a comic allegory of political change—the native-dressed black Africans enter a marble-halled, mausoleum-like European-style building, the Chamber of Com-merce, and jauntily evict its white occupants and their symbols—busts of European figures, army boots, institutional paintings—spouting rhetoric about "Africa for the Africans." But in the very next shot, the African deputies sit in the Chamber's conference room, dressed in European tuxedos and tailcoats; in succeeding shots, a white commander, one of those previously expelled from the Chamber, directs

Fig. 16-15
Xala: *Native Africans in the Chamber of Commerce with Westernized clothing and identical, geometrically arranged attaché cases.*

a perfect line of metronomically marching black policemen; two other formerly expelled white deputies present attaché cases stuffed with greenbacks to each of the current deputies, who sit in perfect symmetrical lines around the conference table. (Sembene deliberately uses the unnaturally straight line and the overperfection of sharp, rectangular compositions as satiric devices.) The prologue's point is clear: A group of Africans throw the rascals out of the Chamber of Commerce and become the rascals themselves; they are not true revolutionaries, charting a new and indigenously African course, but examples of mere neocolonialism. The prologue poses the question whether it is possible to inhabit the Chamber of Commerce without becoming a practitioner of the same sort of commerce purveyed by the white Western world.

The rest of *Xala* tells the story of one of those bureaucratic deputies, a highly respected businessman, whose business, significantly, is importing food. This minister has decided to indulge his sexual appetite by taking a third wife. (Sembene ironically reveals that the sexist Africans have preserved those vestiges of African culture that suit their pleasure under the guise of perpetuating "Africanness.") The wedding party is a curious mixture of African customs (the groom need not even attend the church service) and Western ones (the guests

drink cocktails and Coca-Cola; gifts include African ones, like gold and native jewelry, and a Western one, a red-ribboned automobile; a band plays a very terrible and funny pastiche of pop-rock music). This marriage begins the minister's downfall—he sinks steadily into debt, beggary, and social disgrace.

Unfortunately, the minister is mysteriously incapable of sexual arousal with this new young bride he took for sexual purposes. The minister believes that someone has put a curse—a *xala* —on his virility. So he seeks a variety of native magical cures (again Sembene shows that these Westernized Africans become very Africa-conscious when it suits their needs), but his inadequacy is incurable. At the end of the film, the minister has fallen lower than the outcast poverty of a group of beggars and cripples that has wandered symbolically through the film's narrative—beggars who have been swindled out of the food they need to survive by the minister's own economic machinations. The man's true *xala* is that he is a stranger to his own people—not white and not black, not traditional and not modern, not African and not Western. Like all of the hypocritical swindlers and thieves in the outwardly respectable Chamber of Commerce, he is a not.

One of the film's consistent motifs is to draw a contrast between men and women in this society—a sure sign, for Sembene, that the new culture is as stagnant, as immature, as unresponsive to the genuine needs of the African people as the one it replaced. The men in the film all speak French, while the women all speak the native language, Wolof. The men all dress in black-and-white Western clothing, while the women dress in colorful native garb. This contrast of neutrality and color plays a consistent symbolic function in this color film. The single colorful object in the conference room of the Chamber of Commerce is the table around which they sit (which is, in effect, their altar); it is green, like dollars. The minister's male sexual problem becomes a metaphor for the general sexist and material corruption of the "new" African male, the continent's true *xala*. In *Xala*'s ironic contrasts of Black and White, Old and New, Male and Female, Africa and Europe, Third World and Western World, political justice and political repression, economic freedom and economic dependence, the film brilliantly, maturely, comically, perceptively summarizes the essential issues of Third World cinema as a whole.

Up from Down Under, Down from Up Above

If the British film industry has been a Hollywood colony, ruled by the common language, the English-language film industries of former British colonies—from Australia to Canada—have faced even greater difficulty. While England possessed the economic and cultural resources to develop projects that Hollywood could not do at all or as well, the film industries of British colonies struggled to find both the economic means and the cultural distinctiveness as an alternative to both London and Hollywood.

Australia's film-production problem paralleled that of any Third World nation—with important differences. Founded by the British as a penal colony in 1788 (which it remained until 1840), not federated as a commonwealth until 1901, Australia has a population 95 percent of which descends directly from Britain. While an emerging country of Africa or Latin America could draw upon its own native culture, customs, and language that had been usurped by colonizers, the dominant customs and language of Australia came from England, and it was this culture that would produce its films.

Given its direct British descent, Australian culture is not without its parallels to America's. As opposed to the verdant unity of the English countryside, Australia remains a largely untamed frontier continent with awesome topographical contrasts—plains, seas, mountains, deserts, forests. Like modern America, it has both vast modern cities and vast open spaces. Also like America, it has an indigenous native culture that the European white settlers pushed back and pushed aside but could neither ignore nor assimilate. The cultural clash of European immigrants and Australian aborigines paralleled that between white American pioneers and North American Indians. While some Australian films (notably Peter Weir's *The Last Wave*, 1977) set Australian whites in the context of aboriginal culture, as colonizers who need to learn from or at least stop oppressing the natives, the majority (like Weir's *Gallipoli*, 1981) celebrate white Australian culture in itself and bitterly resent the ways Australians are treated by *their* imperialist oppressors, the stuck-up and sometimes cruel British. The Australian films of the 1970s defined their identity by combining local themes with models from both London and Hollywood: British traditions of literary elegance and polished acting (many Australian actors and directors have trained at the London dramatic academies and have apprenticed in British repertory companies) with the vitality of American images and Hollywood genres.

Before there could be films, there had to be budgets. Shot in Australia, Nicolas Roeg's British film, *Walkabout* (1971) was among the first to demonstrate the power of Australian themes and visual imagery (the contrast of white and aboriginal children's worldviews in the frontier Australian Outback). If the British could make such films (or a Canadian—Ted Kotcheff's *Outback*, also 1971), why couldn't Australian directors make them as well? As in so many film production centers outside America, the stimulus came from governmental subsidies for feature films with "local content," consistent with international standards of technical expertise and stylistic polish, through the Australian Film Development Commission, established in 1970 (which became the Australian Film Finance Corporation, or FFC).

Although many Australian films try to sort out modern Australian life (for example, Gillian Armstrong's comic rock-musical, *Star Struck*, 1983), some of the most impressive Australian films look back at the nation's history—particularly the two decades between the Boer War in South Africa and the First World War in Europe, the very period of Australian confederation. Australian troops had fought for the British in both wars, with great loss of life and little Australian gain—except for clichés like defending the Empire, serving the Queen, or protecting "the race" against "the wogs" (that most offensively racist and chauvinistic term of British imperialism). Australian troops had been forced to fight British economic wars against colonial insurgents very much like themselves. Bruce Beresford's *Breaker Morant* (1980) and Peter Weir's *Gallipoli* are two powerful depictions of the Australian soldier as pawn and cannon fodder, under the yoke of sneering British superiors.

If the British and New Zealanders have often characterized the Australians as rough and uncouth, Beresford's *The Adventures of Barry Mackenzie* (1972, sequel 1974), a film in extreme bad taste, only confirmed their suspicions. Beresford's breakthrough film was *Don's Party* (1976), and he captured the international market with *Breaker Morant*. If *Breaker Morant* suggests the American war in Vietnam (a foreign power fighting an imperialistic war against native guerillas, thousands of miles from home), it also suggests the debate in John Ford's cavalry films between the laws of peace and the necessities of war. Morant's platoon had been specially trained to fight the Boer guerillas by using the enemy's informal and improvisational tactics rather than the rules of British military protocol. But when Morant's Australian platoon performs one of the actions for which it was expressly created, the British disown it for political and diplomatic reasons, court martial Morant and his fellow officers as criminals, and execute two of them on a beautiful morning.

The films Beresford later directed in America include several distinguished "small" films (that is, independent productions in which studios had no interest until they won Academy Awards, characterized by low budgets, excellent scripts, focus on just a few people, and superb acting) and a few big studio mistakes (he directed *King David* for Paramount in 1985). The best of the "small" films is *Tender Mercies* (1983), which won its author, Horton Foote, his second Oscar (the first had been for Robert Mulligan's *To Kill a Mockingbird*, 1962). That Beresford works best when he has a good script (and is otherwise in trouble) is clear from *Breaker Morant, Tender Mercies*, and *Driving Miss Daisy* (1989). With Beresford's move to Hollywood, the filming of "rough" Australian types was left to Paul Hogan and Peter Faiman, whose *Crocodile Dundee* (1986) was a major international hit.

Gillian Armstrong's *My Brilliant Career* (1979), set in the same period as *Breaker Morant*

Fig. 16-16
Edward Woodward in **Breaker Morant:** *Even the pose suggests John Wayne's in* **The Searchers** *(see Fig. 12-33).*

and within the same visual environment, is a *Bildungsroman*—the coming of age of Australia's first major woman novelist (Miles Franklin, played by Judy Davis). The film is a close look at both the social disadvantages of women in colonial Australia and the unspoken cultural prejudices against Australian thought and art within the entire British Empire. The woman's lowly status in her patriarchal and colonial society mirrors the country's lowly status in the Empire. Her growing maturity and confidence suggest the growth and confidence of Australia itself in the same period—and of creative, powerful women in any period.

Both Peter Weir and Fred Schepisi have contrasted Australia's Europeanized culture with that of its aboriginal natives. Schepisi's *The Chant of Jimmy Blacksmith* (1978) is another study of a brutally disturbing incident in Australian history, like the execution of Morant or the slaughter of Australian troops at Gallipoli. Jimmy Blacksmith is a native Australian who gives up his values, his customs, even his name to serve the whites. When he discovers that he has been betrayed, that he has gained neither the promised material wealth nor social equality, he goes berserk and murders as many white settlers as he can find. He is of course sentenced and executed by white courts of law. Schepisi's film is both a political plea for the rights of Australia's exploited blacks as well as a warning about inevitable retribution—a persistent fear of British colonialism. Rebellion and punishment also play major roles in his semi-autobiographical study of sexual repression in a 1950s parochial school (*The Devil's Playground*, 1976). Schepisi later made a number of fine films in America, including *Plenty* (1985, starring Meryl Streep), *Roxanne* (1987, with Steve Martin as Cyrano), *A Cry in the Dark* (1988, again with Streep; a U.S.-Australian co-production based on an Australian infanticide case), and *The Russia House* (1990, a spy thriller much of which was shot in Moscow and Leningrad with the full participation of the Soviets—the first post-Cold War film).

Peter Weir's *The Last Wave* also envisions black retribution—not as vengeful violence but as a quietly subversive power, more psychic and metaphysical than physical. In contrast to the rational modern man of law (Richard Chamberlain), Weir's aborigines are in touch with mystical and supernatural influences, capable of summoning a destructive wave that will drown the puny white civilization. More than any other Australian director, Weir suggests the doubt and paranoia beneath the surfaces of Australian culture—that "modern," "rational," "civilized" white European society is itself a mere shadow and delusion in the mystical eyes of Australia's native inhabitants. One of the most elegant films of the late-1970s horror renaissance, *The Last Wave* is in the same league as Roeg's *Don't Look Now*. Weir's previous film, *Picnic at Hanging Rock* (1975), is a very elegant mystery—the inexplicable disappearance of three girls and a teacher from a

proper boarding school during an outing, leaving no physical traces behind. Set in the same Commonwealth period as *Breaker Morant* and *My Brilliant Career*, Weir's film contrasts the rational, orderly appearances of repressive white European society (the school itself) with the mystical operations of an inexplicable universe—just as *The Last Wave*, his best film, does in modern dress.

Gallipoli was the last film Weir made in Australia. His American films have been very well received (*Witness*, 1985; *Dead Poets Society*, 1989; *Green Card*, 1990), except when they depart markedly from Hollywood formulas (*The Mosquito Coast*, 1986). Only *The Year of Living Dangerously* (1982) has some of the hypnotic quality, the unsettling and rich imagery, the compelling rhythms, and the mysterious overtones of his great Australian films.

George Miller's Mad Max films—*Mad Max* (1979), *The Road Warrior* (*Mad Max 2*, 1981), and *Mad Max Beyond Thunderdome* (1985)— are futuristic fantasies that combine several genres and traditions while creating an original myth; together they constitute an epic. The central character, Max (American born Mel Gibson, who emigrated to Australia with his parents), is an "enforcer" like Dirty Harry, a searcher and a loner like Ethan Edwards, a wanderer of the wasteland like an Arthurian knight, a founder like Aeneas, a fighter like Achilles, and a wily if not amoral survivor like Odysseus. He makes his own rules and establishes his own loyalties (the reason he helps the good guys in *The Road Warrior* is that the bad guys killed his "horse"—his V8—and his dog). The setting is the Australian Outback after a war that has destroyed the old world, which depended on fossil fuels and collapsed without them; now gasoline is the most precious commodity, and most of the characters spend their time killing each other—for fun, and to steal gas from the losers' disabled vehicles. A burned-out ex-cop whose wife and son were run down by murderous bikers, Max is incapable of settling down but makes vital contributions to the pockets of civilization that are humanity's only alternative to an age of barbarism. *The Road Warrior* tells how Max helps a besieged group—occupying a refinery that resembles a fort in a John Ford western but also echoes

The Feral Kid (Emil Minty, left) and Mad Max (Mel Gibson) after the climactic chase in **The Road Warrior.**

Fig. 16-17

the tiny, walled city of Troy—escape to found "the great northern tribe" (much as the Trojans were said to have founded Rome), and *Thunderdome* ends with a foundation story that is also a creation myth. The Mad Max films draw, then, on the genres of the biker film, the action-adventure spectacle, and the road movie as well as the older, related traditions of the medieval romance and the ancient epic—but more than anything else, they are westerns: from *Thunderdome*'s wide-open town to *The Road Warrior*'s climactic chase, which converts Ford's stagecoach into a speeding truck and his Indians on ponies into brutal crazies driving wild cars. The Mad Max films are clear examples of the vital Australian blending of classic American genres and images with uniquely modern and Australian issues: What would happen to an immense, isolated continent like Australia after an atomic holocaust, in a world already plagued by oil embargoes?

If Australian thought and culture suffered the domination of British rule, it enjoyed the cultural oddity of isolation as a Western society in the Pacific world of Southeast Asia. Even more severe have been the cultural handicaps on a Canadian cinema, not only a former British colony, but also a former French colony, a divided nation of two cultures and two languages, just across the northern border from the country with the West's most powerful film industry. For decades, Canadian cinema was synonymous with the National Film Board of Canada, founded by the British documentarist John Grierson in 1939. Government-supported and famous for the experimental films of Norman McLaren (*Fiddle-de-dee*, 1947; *Begone Dull Care*, 1949; *Neighbours*, 1952; *Blinkity Blank*, 1955; *Pas de deux*, 1967), the Film Board was committed almost exclusively to short films —documentary or animated, in English or in French. Canadian feature-film production, though it dates from 1914, and though the National Film Board did produce a few features— few, but superb, like Don Owen's *Nobody Waved Goodbye* (1964)—was a relatively minor activity. Instead, Canada's international prestige rested on its animated films and documentaries. Many feature-oriented Canadian directors (Norman Jewison, Arthur Hiller) and actors (Donald Sutherland, Christopher Plummer) left to work south of the border.

The changes in Canadian feature-film production began in 1978, stimulated (as usual) by government policy—seed money for film investment through the Canadian Film Development Corporation (established in 1967) and new, attractive tax laws for film companies to shelter profits. While postwar European governments used tax laws to combat American films, the Canadian government used tax laws to lure film projects, many of which seemed thoroughly American. Louis Malle's *Atlantic City* (1980) was officially a Canadian film, despite its French director, American setting, and clear relationship to American genres like the gangster film and *film noir*. Other Canadian productions included apparently Italian films, like Ettore Scola's *A Special Day* (1978), and French films, like Claude Lelouch's *Us Two* (1979).

Finding Canadian subjects for Canadian films has been more difficult. Although *Nobody Waved Goodbye* and Paul Almond's *Act of the Heart* (1970) justifiably attracted international attention, Ted Kotcheff's *The Apprenticeship of Duddy Kravitz* (1974), based on a best-selling Jewish-Canadian novel and supported by the Canadian Film Development Corporation, was the first thoroughly Canadian feature film to make a great deal of money outside Canada. Canadian themes have since been seen in Richard Benner's affectionate tribute to Canadian transvestite performer Craig Russell (*Outrageous!*, 1977), Ralph L. Thomas's tracing the paths of Canadian youth to the brainwashing camps of the "Moonies" (*Ticket to Heaven*, 1981), and Phillip Borsos's exploring the legends of Canada's own Wild West and exotic outlaws (*The Grey Fox*, 1983).

One of the first French-Canadian directors to reach an international audience, with his small-scale *Mon oncle Antoine* (1971) and grand-scale *Kamouraska* (1974), Claude Jutra first made animated films and "direct cinema" documentaries (helping to found Canada's vastly influential *cinéma vérité* movement) at the National Film Board. In the late 1980s the most intriguing and popular French-Canadian films were those of Denys Arcand: *The Decline of the American Empire* (1986), a witty, sexy comedy of manners, and *Jesus of Montreal* (1989), a reflexive satire about the production of a Passion Play and the role of ethics and religion in modern life.

Of the newer English-language directors who established their reputations with Cana-

dian features and continued to pursue the themes of their early works in the films they made in the United States and elsewhere, perhaps the best known are Ted Kotcheff and David Cronenberg. Kotcheff left Canadian TV to make films in England (*Life at the Top*, 1965, the sequel to *Room at the Top*) and Australia (*Outback*, 1971 — a richly atmospheric and disturbingly violent film that may be his best and that was released in the same violent year as *Straw Dogs* and *A Clockwork Orange*) before returning to Canada to make *Duddy Kravitz*. His most successful American film, *First Blood* (1982), inaugurated the Rambo series but was more thoughtful and intense than its sequels. The heroes of all these films are at war with the world around them, either because they have been forced to fight groups they detest (*Outback*, *First Blood*) or because they have chosen to "conquer" groups they want to join (*Life at the Top*, *Duddy Kravitz*); in all these battles, whether physical or verbal, the hero's moral values and self-definition are at stake — and not every hero survives, or wants what he wins. Kotcheff has continued to make films in America (such as *Winter People*, 1989, which features much the same kind of battle), returning to Canada to direct *Joshua Then and Now* (1985 — made for TV, then cut for theatrical release), based on the novel by Mordecai Richler, the author of *Duddy Kravitz*.

The horror films of David Cronenberg are even more tightly interrelated, taking for their essential subject the nature of evolution, both of "the flesh" and of consciousness. The changing body is a cancerous horror in some of his films, a paradox in others, and it is usually accompanied by a scary but fascinating change in mental ability and perspective. There is no thematic break between his major Canadian films (*They Came From Within*, 1975; *Rabid*, 1977; *The Brood*, 1979; *Scanners*, 1980, released 1981, his first international hit; *Videodrome*, 1982, released 1983) and American ones (*The Dead Zone*, 1983; *The Fly*, 1986; *Dead Ringers*, 1988). Instead of a break, one notices the career continuity, and the repetition and variation of developing themes, that characterize an *auteur*. In *The Brood*, the story of a woman whose angry thoughts cause her to give birth to little monsters who kill her enemies —

Fig. 16-18
Videodrome: Max (James Woods), a cable TV programmer, gets his first look at a sadistic Videodrome program.

so that they are the children of her anger, "the shape of rage"—the horror is characteristically mental and physical. The hero of *Videodrome* (Max) attains a new level of consciousness partly as the result of a brain tumor induced by a video signal, and the hero of *The Dead Zone* (one of the best Stephen King adaptations and the first Cronenberg film not based on his own story) gains telepathic abilities, from brain injuries, that allow him to save the world. In *They Came From Within*, sluglike venereal parasites infect the bodies and drastically affect the minds and behavior (compulsive erotic violence) of everyone living in a fancy bourgeois housing complex; rather than evolve, they devolve. But *Videodrome*'s Max evolves morally and metaphysically—and suffers vivid hallucinations—as his body evolves into "the new flesh," the incarnated Word of video philosopher Brian O'Blivion (inspired by Canadian media theorist Marshall McLuhan). Experimental flesh grafts turn skin-flick star Marilyn Chambers into the carrier of a plague in *Rabid*. The "mad scientist" villain in *The Brood* is a psychiatrist, as the one in *Rabid* is a plastic surgeon. *Scanners* concerns a generation of telepaths whose projected thoughts have physical effects, created through *in utero* chemistry by a scientist who wants to accelerate human evolution—unlike the mad scientist who invents *They Came From Within*'s squirmy parasites

in order to pull humanity back to a primitive level of development. In the original version of *The Fly* (Kurt Neumann, 1958), the scientist ends up with the fly's head and arm immediately, as soon as the teleportation experiment goes wrong; in Cronenberg's version, the emphasis is on the scientist's slow evolution into a man–fly, and on the way he learns to enjoy, as his body changes, the way a fly thinks. And the end of *Scanners* shows two brothers in one body (one's mind and voice in the other's body), as *Dead Ringers* examines the problem of twin brothers with disturbingly separate minds in disturbingly similar bodies, who come together to die.

The New Wave films of Germany and Australia demonstrate that national cinemas not only need financial support, they also need subjects of national concern and issues of cultural debate to make films about. The international future of Canadian feature-filmmakers depends on their ability to find powerful subjects of local and national concern that also suggest the social and personal problems of people everywhere—just as every national cinema, from Hollywood to Sydney, has done before.

This survey of alternative English-language cinemas requires a footnote calling attention to the small but developing industries of New Zealand (Roger Donaldson's *Smash Palace*, 1981), Scotland (Bill Forsyth's *Gregory's Girl*, 1981), and Ireland (Jim Sheridan's *My Left Foot*, 1989), as well as independent productions such as Jamie Uys's *The Gods Must Be Crazy* (1981), from Botswana.

The problem faced by governments that support English-language alternatives to Hollywood and London is, oddly, success—for that is when so many of the newly proved talents, from directors like Weir, Forsyth, and Cronenberg to actors like Mel Gibson, depart for Hollywood (or London!) just as British stars and directors did in the 1930s.

The New Internationalism

The most striking change in film commerce since the mid-1960s has not been the introduction of individual national traditions but the leveling of national boundaries that has created a truly international market. The extent of international distribution, the extent of American investments in foreign production and foreign investments in American production, the number of international co-productions, the number of international film festivals, and the number of directors working outside their native industries have become more significant than any particularly national statistics.

Directors had, of course, changed residence before; for example, both Billy Wilder and Fred Zinnemann left Vienna for Hollywood, as Hitchcock left England, and stayed, while Lang and Renoir worked in Hollywood for awhile and then left. But in the 1970s and 1980s it became more common to find directors working in several countries—like Louis Malle, who continued to make films in France after he began directing in America; or Andrei Tarkovsky, who left Russia to make *Nostalghia* in Italy and *The Sacrifice* in Sweden; or Wim Wenders, who made *Paris, Texas* in America, then hit the road for Tokyo (the documentary *Tokyo-Ga*, 1985) and Berlin. International crews and casts flourished as filmmakers satisfied the desire to work with the right people in the right place (Tarkovsky wanted his Swedish film to be shot by Sven Nykvist) and learned from each other: Pavel Lounguine's Soviet-French *Taxi Blues* (1990) was one of the first Soviet films to be shot with live sound—because it had a French sound crew.

It also became far more common to find films financed by groups or industries in several countries: international co-productions such as the French-German *Wings of Desire* or the Italian-British-Chinese *The Last Emperor* (1987), which was directed by Bertolucci and shot by Vittorio Storaro (both Italian) on location in China—notably in the Forbidden City, where no Westerners had previously been allowed to film—and which starred John Lone (from Hong Kong), Joan Chen (from Shanghai), and Peter O'Toole (from Connemara). Just as *The Last Emperor*'s location shooting was itself an event in the history of international cooperation, three years later *The Russia House* spread Moscow and Leningrad across the wide screen as no non-Soviet film had been allowed to show them before—and did just as well with Vancouver and Lisbon; it also had an Australian director and co-producer (Fred Schepisi), a British literary source and screenwriter (playwright Tom Stoppard's adaptation of John le Carré's *glasnost*-era spy novel), European co-financing and an American releasing company (MGM-Pathe), a distinguished supporting cast from America (Roy Scheider) and England (James Fox, director Ken Russell), and in the leading roles a Scot (Sean Connery), an American (Michelle Pfeiffer), and a German (Klaus Maria Brandauer).

International filmmaking has cross-fertilized the cinema. To take only one example: When John Ford decided to film *The Fugitive* (released in 1947) in Mexico, he hired a Mexican cinematographer, Gabriel Figueroa. Figueroa had been trained in Hollywood and had been particularly impressed by the style and example of Gregg Toland—not just in *Citizen Kane* but also in the films Toland shot for Ford and Wyler. One result was that *The Fugitive* looks almost as if Toland had shot it for Ford, but it also reveals Figueroa's own rich, developing style. Figueroa brought his international eye to many of the films he shot in Mexico, from Buñuel's *Los olvidados* (1950) and *The Exterminating Angel* (1962) to John Huston's *Under the Volcano* (1984). He also worked regularly with the greatest Mexican director of the 1940s, Emilio Fernandez, shooting—among others—his *María Candelaria* (1943) and the dramatically powerful, visually stunning *The Pearl* (1946). *The Pearl* was itself the product of an international collaboration, for John Steinbeck wrote its script for Fernandez before rewriting it as a short novel. And Fernandez passed some of his tricks along to Peckinpah, for whom he played the role of General Mapache in *The Wild Bunch*.

There have always been three reasons for film production to cross national boundaries—political, economic, and thematic. The first exodus of filmmakers from their homeland for political reasons was of Germans and other Europeans (Renoir and Clair, for example) from Hitler's Europe. Blacklisted American directors left the United States in the 1950s for England (Joseph Losey) or Greece (Jules Dassin), while the young Costa-Gavras left right-wing Greece to study and make films in a more politically receptive France (*Z*) and the United States

Fig. 16-19
The Pearl: *a Mexican classic written by John Steinbeck, directed by Emilio Fernandez, and shot by Gabriel Figueroa.*

(*Missing*; *Music Box*, 1989). Since the mid-1960s the political exodus has been from Eastern Europe. Miloš Forman, Roman Polanski, Jerzy Skolimowski, Andrzej Wajda, Dušan Makavejev, Ján Kadár, and Ivan Passer are among the many Eastern Europeans who have deserted native production—temporarily or permanently—for the West.

International co-productions also solve economic problems. Through this internationalism flows American investment capital for a Kurosawa to make a film deemed too extravagant and unpopular for the Japanese studios to support (like *Kagemusha*); capital also flows the other way, allowing American filmmakers to raise money wherever they can find it (as Paul Schrader did for his Italian-American *The Comfort of Strangers*, 1990). International co-productions often imply international casts— William Hurt, Raul Julia, and Sonia Braga in Hector Babenco's *Kiss of the Spider Woman* (1985), Klaus Kinski and Claudia Cardinale in *Fitzcarraldo* (originally Jason Robards and Mick Jagger), Robert De Niro, Burt Lancaster, Donald Sutherland, Dominique Sanda, Stefania Sandrelli, Sterling Hayden, and Gérard De-

pardieu in *1900*. An international assortment of stars guarantees box-office appeal in more than a single country.

Finally, some filmmakers shoot outside native boundaries because thematic commitments require the alternative visual or social environment. Both Louis Malle and Wim Wenders inspect American culture, while Werner Herzog requires savage and alien landscapes. *The Last Emperor* was a much better film for having been shot in China; the same is true of *The Sheltering Sky* (1990), which Bertolucci made in North Africa, and *Last Tango in Paris*, which just as obviously had to be shot in Paris. Conversely, the only place Terrence Malick could find the look of 1916–17 Texas for *Days of Heaven* was on the plains of Canada. The effortless migration of Bruce Beresford, Fred Schepisi, and Peter Weir from Australian to American themes and settings reveals the close connection between these two cultures.

Perhaps the model for this internationalism is the career of the vagabond director Luis Buñuel, for fifty years a man without a cinematic country—making films in France, working as an editor and translator in America, then

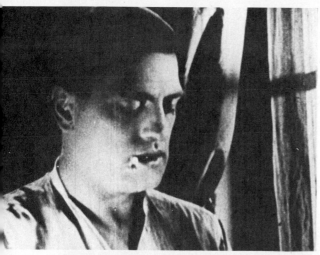

Fig. 16-20

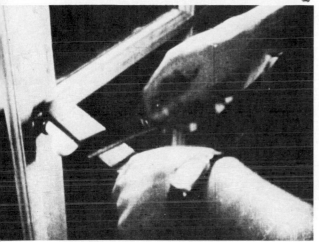

Fig. 16-21

The beginning of Buñuel's film career and of Un Chien andalou — *the filmmaker (Buñuel himself, Fig. 16-20) sharpens his razor to assault and alter human vision.*

making films in Mexico, returning again to France, and only occasionally making a film in his native Spain. Although the Spanish have a rich tradition of painting, poetry, theatre, and fiction, the decades of political repression have constrained the country's filmmakers until only recently—with the death of Franco and the emergence of Spanish directors Victor Erice (*Spirit of the Beehive*, 1973), Carlos Saura (*The*

Hunt, 1966; *Cría cuervos*, 1977; *Blood Wedding*, 1981; *Carmen*, 1983; *El amor brujo*, 1985—the last three choreographed by Antonio Gades), and Pedro Almodóvar (*Labyrinth of Passion*, 1982; *Matador*, 1986; *Women On The Verge Of A Nervous Breakdown*, 1988).

Buñuel, a descendant of the Surrealism of Paris in the 1920s where he learned his craft from Jean Epstein, made films in a variety of styles: symbolic-surrealist (*Un Chien andalou*, 1929; *L'Age d'or*, 1930), documentary (*Las Hurdes*, or *Land Without Bread*, 1932), social-realist *(Los olvidados)*, psychological case study (*El*, 1952), religious allegory (*Nazarin*, 1958; *Viridiana*, 1961), psychological-surrealist allegory (*Belle de jour*, 1967), religious-surrealist allegory (*The Milky Way*, 1969), political-surrealist erotic drama (*That Obscure Object of Desire*, 1977), and social-surrealist allegorical comedy (*The Discreet Charm of the Bourgeoisie*, 1972; *The Phantom of Liberty*, 1974). Through these differing styles over an amazingly long career shine the consistent Buñuel traits: the surrealist's perception of the insubstantiality of reality coupled with the surrealist's savage humor (for to smash the solidity of reality is an act of joy as well as destruction); the psychologist's interest in the inner workings of the human brain (particularly its sexual fantasies and personal visions of experience that violate all the norms of the realists, the professional psychologists, and the Church); and, finally, his preoccupation with the Church itself (for Buñuel, its fundamentally and comically naïve and false definitions of man). Just as Ingmar Bergman, the son of a Lutheran minister, rebelled against his religious heritage in films that ironically used the images, the terms, the metaphors of that religion, Buñuel, educated by the Jesuits, broke the icons of his childhood faith and used those icons as the central artistic metaphors of his work. But whereas Bergman could supplement the northern preacher's view of life as a vale of tears with the notion that it was also a vale of sunlight, Buñuel could only supplant the Roman Catholic cathedral of gold and silk and ruby with a pile of mortal manure.

The inadequate budgets of Buñuel's pre-1960 black-and-white films led to his reliance on two great strengths: the imaginativeness of his film's abstract idea and the ferocious

Stirrings of a new Spanish cinema: two internationally popular examples. Fig. 16-22: Antonio Gades and Laura Del Sol in Carlos Saura's Carmen. *Fig. 16-23: Carmen Maura (right) in Pedro Almodóvar's* Women On The Verge Of A Nervous Breakdown.

Fig. 16-22

Fig. 16-23

Fig. 16-24
Alfonso Mejía as Pedro in Buñuel's **Los olvidados,** *one of the greatest of his Mexican features;*
cinematographer, Gabriel Figueroa.

energy of its translation into a concrete fictional
metaphor.

The first event in Buñuel's first film was a
close-up of a razor slicing an apparently human
(though actually animal) eyeball. The brutality,
the nausea, the visceral attack of this first action
dominate the Buñuel canon. One of the most
unflinchingly sadistic and brutal scenes ever
filmed is in the assault of the juvenile delinquents in *Los olvidados* (*The Forgotten Ones*; U.S.
title, *The Young and the Damned*) on a legless,
armless beggar (cripples, dwarfs, blind men,
hunchbacks, and other assorted physical freaks
are as common in the Buñuel world as priests).
The delinquents pull the helpless cripple out of
his cart, roll the man over on the ground, kicking the stump of his body, then gleefully send
his cart careening down the street so he can
never retrieve it. The hero, a relatively innocent boy, ends up dead on a pile of garbage. As
realistic as this depressing, nasty, ironic movie

is, it still contains surreal dream sequences —
and a certain perverse tone — that make it
utterly unlike any of the other children of
neorealism.

Viridiana, one of Buñuel's richest and most
evenly balanced works, as well as one of his
most blasphemous, was filmed in Spain; apparently Franco and the Church misunderstood
what it was going to be about and approved the
production. (When it was finished, they tried
to suppress it.) It begins in a monastery with the
music of Handel's *Messiah*; it ends in the bedroom of a young lecher with rock-and-roll
music. The music and the settings mirror the
film's journey. The young woman, Viridiana
(Silvia Pinal), is a novitiate in a convent on the
threshold of taking her final vows. Before taking those vows she makes the customary trip
back to the secular world to be sure that she
wants to leave it. She visits her rich uncle's
estate. He falls under the sexual spell of her

beauty. Carried away by his passion, he drugs his niece with the intention of raping her insensate body. But instead of actually committing the rape, he merely tells her that she has been violated, daubing the sheets of her bed with blood to convince her of the physical fact of her sin. The blood of lust on her sheets convinces her that she no longer carries the blood of the lamb in her soul. She decides not to return to the convent; her uncle kills himself in his shame.

Rejecting the formal teachings of the Church as a means of saving her soul, Viridiana takes the next step on the film's allegorical path. She turns to natural religion — good works, charity — as a means of helping humankind. Viridiana uses the money and the grounds of her deceased uncle's estate to establish a utopian community for the poor. Viridiana feels her soul strengthened by this Christian-communist colony in which all work together and none go hungry. But one day when Viridiana and the other masters leave on an excursion, the peasants break into the house, set out the fancy linen and china, and begin to devour a banquet of their own. They raucously break furniture and dishes; they drunkenly bloody the white linen with wine. One of the beggars takes a picture of the loathsome group; they pose in the positions of the disciples in da Vinci's "Last Supper"; the beggar woman "snaps the picture" of the gathering by raising her skirt and exposing her naked groin. This lewd burlesque of the sacred scene deflates any hope that this human scum can be improved or helped by any means whatever. Viridiana has failed at both faith and charity. Seeing no hope at all, Viridiana wanders into the bedroom of her sensual cousin where he "plays cards," as he euphemistically puts it. As Viridiana sits down at the card table, her cousin tells her that he has always known she would one day play cards with him. Buñuel's allegory of the vile reality of the human flesh is complete.

Nazarin is also an allegory that develops the gap between the abstract, ideal teachings of Christ and Buñuel's concrete definition of the bestial human animal. *The Discreet Charm of the Bourgeoisie* develops the gap between the simple concrete reality that the bourgeois expectations assume (the banality of property, success,

money, social intercourse, and, especially, eating dinner) and the complex levels of super-realities (wishes, dreams, imaginings, fancies) that actually exist. One of the funniest, cleverest, and most challenging of the late Buñuel films that combines these two themes is *The Milky Way*, a film named after the route of pilgrimage from Paris to San Sebastian in Spain, where Christian pilgrims of the Middle Ages traveled to view the tomb of St. James. Buñuel's film is more a pilgrimage in time than in space, for as his two modern "pilgrims" (one old, one young; both of them bums, reminiscent of Chaplin or Laurel and Hardy) make the same journey, their "stopping places" are a series of religious heresies that might have existed on or near that route over the past five centuries. Buñuel's film skips among the centuries, making it completely natural for the two twentieth-century pilgrims to meet two young men who continually walk back and forth between events in the seventeenth and twentieth centuries.

The heresies that the two pilgrims visit are magnificently bizarre, all of them based on actual historical testimony, as one would expect from Buñuel. The bizarre authenticity of these "actual" heresies is essential to Buñuel's attempt to show how bizarre are all religious beliefs and to raise the question of what makes heresy heretical. Among the bizarre heretics are a group of worshippers who combine their Latin prayers with sex orgies, continuing to speak in Latin and wear their priestly robes even as the Bacchanalia begins; a convent of nuns who literally re-enact the Crucifixion, driving nails into the palms of the chosen sister (she is so inspired that the nails do not hurt her at all); a bishop who exhumes the body of one of his predecessors, presumed a saintly cleric, excommunicating his bones for his now heretical opinions. Even in the posh restaurants and country inns of the present, the waiters and customers seem to have nothing better to discuss than matters of religious controversy, such as transubstantiation and the credibility of miracles.

Buñuel's comic (and serious) point is that today's orthodoxy is tomorrow's heresy: Heresy is simply a matter of contemporary opinion. For example, when the pilgrims finally arrive

Fig. 16-25
Viridiana: *Buñuel's beggars and cripples at his parody of "The Last Supper."*

in San Sebastian they discover that no other pilgrims have journeyed there because the Church long ago decided that the presumed bones of St. James that lay entombed there were not the bones of St. James. (The Church can decide whose bones are whose as it pleases, just as it decides whose views are heretical and why.) Buñuel finds it amusing that a body of men, calling themselves the Church, can presume to define such insubstantial matters with such certainty—especially when history (as Buñuel's film shows) reveals the force of that insubstantiality with great clarity.

The cinema is a useful tool for Buñuel to use in making such a point, since it is so able to make the solid appear insubstantial and the insubstantial appear solid. The film is capable of showing us historical phantoms in corporeal dress, of showing us supernatural figures (a clairvoyant man with a flowing black cape) in a completely natural guise; even of showing us miracles (the appearance of both the Virgin and of Christ) more concretely than any vision ever appeared to any saint. One of Buñuel's most vigorous demonstrations of the insubstantiality of the concrete and the concreteness of the insubstantial is a sequence in an inn where two

men each go to their separate rooms alone. In one of the rooms, however, a beautiful and naked woman miraculously appears in the bed beside one of the men, although he has not opened the door and it is impossible to enter the room in any other way. As he lies in the room next to the tempting woman who cannot possibly be there, a priest begins giving him a lecture on abstinence and chastity (what else?), sitting outside the bedroom door. Except that the priest suddenly appears inside the room, facing the man and woman (who also is not there) while he lectures, although he too cannot possibly have entered the room. But there he is inside the room!

In the same way, the single female object of desire in *Obscure Object* cannot possibly be embodied by two different women, but there the two women concretely are, both of them the single beloved a man would like to possess. The fact that she is two underscores the impossibility of ever fulfilling the desire to *possess*, let alone define, another human being. For Buñuel the cinema has always been the realm of the impossible actual: Phenomena, which in the reality of time and space cannot possibly occur, can occur before the viewer's eyes because the cinema is free of reality's time and space. But for Buñuel this feature makes the cinema *more* like life and experience (not less), for reality is composed of thoughts, dreams, ideas, and desires as much as of tangible objects. The heresy that happened in a farmhouse *is there* on that Milky Way just as clearly as that farmhouse is there. The alternating objects of abstract desire —one sweet and virginal, the other fiery and sensual—*are there*, just as clearly as each of those actresses is there. In Buñuel's view, only when people realize the insubstantiality of our supposedly "objective reality" and of our opinions based on it will we be able to avoid doing violence both to reality and to one another. It was a view Buñuel maintained ferociously throughout a film career of over fifty years, until his death in 1983.

The Return of the Myths: 1977–

17

At some point in the late 1970s, the American cinema abandoned its attack on the genres of American movies and the myths of American life to embrace them both again. Though some critics sneeringly compared the new films to computerized video games, American movies were born as close cousins to the electrical and mechanical novelties in amusement arcades. The new films self-consciously defined movies as both the repository for cultural myths and the contemporary medium for their dissemination. They saw the movies as myth machines. The new films viewed these myths and mysteries not with the jaded eye of adulthood but with the hope and wonder of childhood; they set out to recapture or invent a kind of innocence.

In this period, muscular heroes in T-shirts, robots with hearts of gold, tough cops, resourceful teens, and benevolent masters rose up to vanquish purely evil villains, and what came from outer space was peaceful, wise, and endearing. Instead of the intellectual and emotional complexity of such previous big films as *Lawrence of Arabia* and *The Godfather*, the typical blockbuster of the late 1970s and 1980s offered a wide-screen, color, stereophonic *ride*,

constructed for speed and thrills rather than contemplation, with a simple, forceful, unthreatening message (for example, cheaters never prosper). Both audiences and producers preferred what were called "feelgood" movies to "downers" and "bummers"; by far the majority of films had heroes one wanted to root for, villains one could only hate, and happy endings. Movies fit once more into recognizable genres and embraced their conventions, even while harmlessly making fun of them. Films that tackled difficult political or psychological material often had their endings changed by executives—although a few subversive, questioning films did manage to sneak by. It was the period of the blockbuster (a movie that sells more than $100 million worth of tickets), the sequel, the Dolby soundtrack, the videocassette and laserdisc, the direct-to-video release, and the all-powerful talent agent—a time that began with the science-fiction spectacles of George Lucas and Steven Spielberg and grew to include the creepy ironies of David Lynch and the political fables of Spike Lee. And though this period of American film history has continued into the early 1990s, so that its end remains unknown, its aesthetic, technical, and economic elements are already clear enough. It is not an extension of the Hollywood Renaissance but an entirely new period.

Three criteria have traditionally marked the transition from one American film era to another, although the three may not operate with equal force or absolute congruence in every period of film history.

The first is the structure of the film business —the system of marketing films to the public. The Nickelodeon Era evolved out of the period when films were viewed as peep shows in penny arcades or were projected as single items on vaudeville bills when marketing procedures radically changed: The film strips were no longer sold, but rented. The shifts to feature films, to talking films, to the nonvertically integrated studio films of the Transitional Era, and to the breakthrough films of the Hollywood Renaissance were similarly produced and accompanied by changes in the financing, distributing, or exhibiting of the film product.

The second criterion is a major advance or shift in film technology. The change from the Nickelodeon Era to the Silent Feature Era accompanied significant technological progress; films became not only physically longer but also more fluent, coherent, and complex in order to sustain their greater narrative length. The transition from the Silent Era to the Sound Era began with the introduction of synchronized sound—and its acceptance by the public and the industry. The wide screen accomplished a similarly technological and aesthetic revolution.

The third criterion for defining a period is a shift in film content that mirrors a shift in cultural values as a whole. The German cinema left its Golden Age behind when its Nazi Period began. In America, each of the previous eras reflected a dominant cultural value and attitude: the working-class unpretentiousness of the Nickelodeon Era; the middle-class materialism of the Silent Feature Era; during and after the Depression, the optimism and populism of the Studio Era; the apparent retreat from political problems of the postwar Transitional Era; and the rebellious, anti-Establishment pessimism of the Hollywood Renaissance.

The late 1970s saw major changes in all three of these areas. The film business adopted a "blockbuster mentality," preferring to finance and distribute a few big films with the potential for enormous profits rather than a larger slate of modest films with modest profits. One "monster hit" a year could keep a studio in business and support the less expensive movies it also produced. *The Godfather, Jaws, Star Wars, Close Encounters of the Third Kind, Grease,* and *Superman,* all of them films of the 1970s, were among the top-grossing films of all time—as were their 1980s cousins *The Empire Strikes Back, E.T., Raiders of the Lost Ark, Return of the Jedi, Ghostbusters, Back to the Future,* and *Batman.* Although *The Birth of a Nation* and *Gone With the Wind* may still be considered more commercially successful than most of these blockbusters—they made more profit in relation to their cost—even when the figures are adjusted for inflation, *E.T.* remains ahead of them all. In the hope of repeating that success, the studio attitude became to spend a lot of money to make a lot of money. "Small" films with relatively low budgets—many of which were "picked up" from independent producers and simply released by the studio—were given smaller openings and often had to make their profits overseas or on video. (Video itself made a difference, to be discussed later.) Given the cost of these spectacles—as high as $60 million, when the average feature cost $11 million in 1981 and $23.5 million in 1989—the films required tremendous advertising campaigns, which cost even more, and the theatre owner had to send a higher percentage of ticket earnings back to the distributor. Theatres learned to make their profits at the concession stand, not at the box office. Theatres also were remodeled, or built, to house two or four—or twenty—screens; the multiplex cinema marked the era's biggest, if not best change in the practice of theatrical exhibition.

The major technical advances of the late 1970s were the introduction of the Dolby noise-reduction process, which drastically improves sound quality whether the final soundtrack is optical or magnetic; the Dolby Stereo Variable Area soundtrack, which allows 35mm prints to have four-track stereophonic *optical* soundtracks with a subtlety, clarity, depth, and

Fig. 17-1

Fig. 17-2

Lessons from Vietnam in The
Deer Hunter, *an epic of post-
combat stress: The naïve view
from here (Fig. 17-1) matures
with the experience of over there
(Fig. 17-2). Fig. 17-1, from left:
John Cazale, Chuck Aspegren,
Robert De Niro, John Savage,
Rutanya Alda, Christopher
Walken, Meryl Streep.*

range previously possible only with magnetic
sound; and the Steadicam, which combines the
mobility of the hand-held camera with the
smoothness of the old Mitchell studio camera
mounted on a dolly. Just as it became normal,
in the course of the 1960s, for features to be
shot in color, stereo became the norm by 1980.
In *Raging Bull* and *Days of Heaven*, the quality
and aesthetics of the sound are as significant as

those of the picture. It can now take more time
to record, edit, and mix a movie's soundtrack
than it does to shoot and edit its footage.

Finally, a new cultural attitude—a conser-
vatism associated with but not limited to the
presidency of Ronald Reagan—seems to have
produced and been reflected by a shift in film
content. The rebels, misfits, loners, and oddballs that dominated American films from

Bonnie and Clyde and *Midnight Cowboy* to *MASH* and *Taxi Driver* were replaced by more ordinary citizens who sought to find a meaningful place for themselves within conventional American society. With the final singing of "God Bless America," the working-class, small-town protagonists of Michael Cimino's *The Deer Hunter* (1978) reintegrate themselves, both as individuals and as a group, into the fabric of American moral and social life, despite the agony their country has forced them to endure. The working-class hero of John Badham's *Saturday Night Fever* (1977) also seeks some meaningful place in American social life, beyond the escapist dream-dance world of the disco and the narrow moral and political provinciality of Bay Ridge. In the mythic sequel, *Staying Alive* (Sylvester Stallone, 1983), all of the hero's fantasies—not of social, moral, and political growth but of dancing his own way in a big show—are fulfilled in an unbelievable manner, and the substance of his victory is simply that the Disco Kid keeps his personal style. The Dustin Hoffman of *Kramer vs. Kramer* (Robert Benton, 1979), who just wants to live lovingly with his son, would not give a dime on a cold day to the Dustin Hoffman of *Midnight*

Cowboy. The young welder of *Flashdance* (Adrian Lyne, 1983) wants to exchange her blue-collar job for the opportunity to express herself in ballet. The majority of 1980s studio pictures reflected a movement away from social rebellion and toward something else: something not to be angry about but to believe in. What might have been hissed or laughed off the screen in the politicized late 1960s and early 1970s became the stuff of dreams in the 1980s. As the song in *Flashdance*—and President Reagan—repeatedly asserted, anyone with determination and talent could "have it all," and that sweet hope fit well into a culture in which people tried to fulfill all the roles they thought they should (wife–mother–executive); in which they were encouraged to want more and buy more, even on credit; and in which poverty, disappointment, and suffering (the homeless could not "have it all") went unacknowledged.

These developments took place throughout the industry and across the country, but if any single film can be credited with opening the era —as *The Jazz Singer* cleared the way for the talkies—that film is George Lucas's *Star Wars* (1977), whose unprecedented use of Dolby

Star Wars: *left to right, Peter Mayhew, Mark Hamill, Alec Guinness, Harrison Ford.*

Fig. 17-3

Noise Reduction from the beginning to the end of production and whose Dolby Stereo soundtrack led to what has been called "the second coming of sound," a complete revolution in the technology and aesthetics of film sound; whose special effects changed the look not only of science fiction but of the fiction film in general —not to mention what they and the film's sound effects did to video games; whose phenomenal earnings led the industry to concentrate on big films designed for relatively young audiences; whose creative interest in sequels was clear from the start, when *Star Wars* declared itself "Episode IV" of an otherwise unproduced series; and whose successful integration of Zen philosophy, of Joseph Campbell's researches into mythology and heroism, of serials and their heroes, of fantasy, of science fiction, and of fast-paced action and adventure announced the return of the myths.

In addition to the *Star Wars* series and Spielberg's *Close Encounters* and *E.T.*, whose mythic figures come from outer space—and Lucas and Spielberg's *Indiana Jones* series, whose myths come from ancient and biblical mythology or from the movies—two other films helped to form the mythic consciousness of this period: Richard Donner's *Superman* (1978) and John G. Avildsen's *Rocky* (1976). The comics have their own mythology, and the perfect, moral, likable, mighty Superman—an

Achilles whose "heel" is his vulnerability to Kryptonite—was a refreshing figure in whom the audience wanted to believe. *Rocky*, a small film that became an unexpected hit, created its own life-sized but mythic hero in Rocky (Sylvester Stallone), the underdog who won't quit, the boxer who wins in spirit whether or not he wins a fight, the working-class Italian-American who believes utterly in America. A hero created by the movies and its formulas, a figure whose physical strength adds to his mythic stature, and a character whose success is so unlikely in the real world that it might well be called "mythical," Rocky became the prototype for working-class overachievers like the heroine of *Flashdance* and, from Stallone's own Rambo to Sigourney Weaver's Ripley, at least another fifteen years of winners. There were very few films about losers.

The mythic, often escapist films generally had high production values, impressive stunts and special effects, and attractive heroes— many of whom, in this conservative period, were police. Both *48 HRS.* (Walter Hill, 1982), starring Eddie Murphy and Nick Nolte, and *Lethal Weapon* (Richard Donner, 1987), starring Mel Gibson and Danny Glover, pit a team of police officers—one black and one white, whose temperaments are comically mismatched but who come to like and depend on each other, and most of whose lines are jokes (they

Fig. 17-4
From Kinetoscope parlors to video arcades: WarGames *(with Matthew Broderick, right) makes explicit the long kinship between movies and novelty arcades.*

Fig. 17-4

spar like the mates in screwball comedies) —
against extremely violent and not at all funny
villains. The hero of *RoboCop* (Paul Verhoeven,
1987) is both a man and a machine, and both
are good cops. The hero of *Blue Thunder* (John
Badham, 1983) is a good cop and the skillful
pilot of an armed surveillance helicopter. The
hero of *Top Gun* (Tony Scott, 1986) is a hotshot
jet pilot who wins tests of skill and gets the girl.
The kids in *Fame* (Alan Parker, 1980) want to
develop their skills, survive their personal trials,
and become famous, and at the end it looks as
if many of them have learned something about
life, art, and themselves and may even have a
chance; compared to the slew of 1980s films
about dancers and singers and groups who desperately want to succeed and, of course, do,
Fame was almost realistic. So was Robert
Townsend's *Hollywood Shuffle* (1987), which
quite reasonably pointed out that if the hero
couldn't make it as a Hollywood director, he
could always find honest work at the post office.

Not every myth was of a hero; mythic villains are part of the same system. The young
stockbroker in *Wall Street* (Oliver Stone, 1987),
who wins morally even if he suffers, must defeat a tremendously powerful antagonist, a
takeover artist who incarnates every evil known
to capitalism. Although many of these films
simply had nasty but mortal bad guys, others
presented villains who might look human but
were virtually impossible to defeat or kill
(James Cameron's *The Terminator*, 1984). The
most common unstoppable villain of the era
was the slasher, the compulsive madman (occasionally a woman) who kills one person after
another — with a knife, with his bare hands, or
with whatever happens to be around. If the
original slasher was Cesare in *Caligari*, and if
there have been others in such films as *M*,
Peeping Tom, and the crucial *Psycho*, the subgenre of the slasher film was defined and codified by John Carpenter's *Halloween* (1978),
which brought together the essential elements
of vengeance, madness, immortality (previous
slashers could be killed), one-by-one teenage
victims, hints of the supernatural (the killer,
who is compared to the Boogey Man, is fueled,
at least in part, by the energy and folklore
of Halloween, when the dead are said to
come home), the butcher knife, the mask, the

unspeaking killer, the resourceful female survivor, and sex (that is, sex scenes that are associated with death). *Halloween* was cloned by its
own sequels as well as by countless low-budget
independent productions, but its most famous
imitator was the *Friday the 13th* series. In
Friday the 13th itself (Sean S. Cunningham,
1980), as in the opening of *Halloween*, the camera shows not the killer but what the killer sees
(not so the audience will identify with the
slasher but so it won't discover her identity),
and the villain turns out to be a woman who
blames all sexually active teenagers for the
death of her son, Jason; in the sequels, the
larger-than-life slasher is Jason. The next major
slasher series, in many ways the most creative,
began with Wes Craven's *A Nightmare on Elm
Street* (1984), whose slasher attacked his victims
in their dreams.

Most of the pro-myth films had little interest
in politics — in *Footloose* (Herbert Ross, 1984),
a bad government is one that forbids people to
dance — but some of them were aggressively
opposed to the politics, and particularly the
feminism, of the 1960s and 1970s. One example of the backlash against feminism was *Die
Hard* (John McTiernan, 1988), a film that was
equally popular with male and female audiences. The hero, a New York City policeman
(John McClane, played by Bruce Willis), is an
ordinary man who copes with an incredibly
dangerous situation in order to save his wife
(Holly Gennaro McClane, played by Bonnie
Bedelia). John is strong, intelligent, witty,
nonracist, professional, and a regular guy.
Holly is also strong and intelligent and good at
her job. As the story begins, the policeman visits
his estranged wife in Los Angeles on Christmas
Eve; he goes to meet her at work, where he is
irritated to find that she is listed only under her
maiden name. He also finds that she has just
been awarded a Rolex watch for being especially good at her job. Then the high-rise office
building is taken over by criminals pretending
to be terrorists. After a lot of sound and fury,
during which most of the criminals and some
of the hostages are killed, we find the last and
worst villain dangling from a thirtieth-floor
window — holding on for dear life to Holly,
who is being held and braced by her husband.
John notices that the villain's grip is actually on

Fig. 17-5

Halloween: *The ritual of formally arranged bodies, later imitated by* **Friday the 13th,** *created an atmosphere of eerie significance (Nancy Loomis as Annie).*

the Rolex, not on Holly's forearm (the villain has his gun-hand free), and so he unlatches the watch—the explicit symbol of her independent professionalism—and the criminal falls to his death. When Holly and John finally leave the building, she identifies herself by her married name.

Two baseball pictures, Phil Alden Robinson's *Field of Dreams* (1989) and John Sayles's *Eight Men Out* (1988), clearly demonstrate that in this period, the escape from politics was a step into fantasy and mythmaking, and to confront political and economic corruption was to dismantle a myth. In *Field of Dreams*, an Iowa farmer (Ray, played by Kevin Costner) obeys a voice that tells him, more or less, that if he builds a baseball field on his property, the great "Shoeless" Joe Jackson will come there to play. Jackson had been one of the "Black Sox," members of the Chicago White Sox who conspired to throw the 1919 World Series and

were barred forever from professional baseball; he represents a scandal this film would like to heal. In fact, the movie sets out to forgive and heal all of the failings of the century, both personal and political. The key is to believe in one's dreams, to follow them with the childlike, innocent part of one's heart in spite of what might be rational or practical. And in this definitively mythic film, every dream comes true. When Ray builds the baseball diamond, the ghosts of Shoeless Joe and his teammates do appear; their suspension from the game has, in this magical time and place, been lifted, their sins forgiven. Given this second chance, the Sox think the Iowa field must be heaven, because heaven is where dreams come true. Another deceased ballplayer, whose dream of playing in the majors had almost but not quite been fulfilled, finally gets to go to bat against a major-league pitcher here. Even Ray gets a second chance and a wish fulfilled: to reconcile with his dead father. Most significantly, the dreams of a black, leftist writer (played by James Earl Jones) come true. He had been a major novelist and a concerned activist in the 1960s, but finally lost faith in causes and in the improvability of American society; bitter and disillusioned, he had stopped writing. The writer's dream, which the hero helps to fulfill, is not to see social justice but to watch a great baseball game with the innocent eyes of his youth. In this film, to believe in the dream is to undo the failures of the past (the fixed World Series, Watergate) and set aside everything that has divided us (the hero's unfortunate fight with his father, the aroused political consciousness of the 1960s). And in a decade that saw thousands of farmers lose everything, the urgent financial problems of Ray and his family are solved when vast audiences drive to their farm to watch the games. The myth of America—the genuine America, as unspoiled as the ideal of baseball, which can be a "heaven" where dreams come true—is renewed, and whatever was bad about the bad old times, including all those disruptive political struggles, is forgiven and forgotten; the past has been given back its innocence, and the present looks better too.

Eight Men Out, on the other hand, tells the true story of the Black Sox scandal in a firm, realistic style. If the myth of baseball is taken down a peg—the players are workers, the boss is cheap and hateful, and even the gamblers treat the players unfairly—the spirit of the game still does come forcefully across in this film. (Because of the depth with which it treats betrayed idealism, *Eight Men Out* manages to deal authentically with idealism.) America, like baseball, is presented in a less-than-mythical light—a place that can be so hypocritical, unfair, and economically corrupt that it is almost a fixed World Series in itself, full of betrayed, believing fans. The moral conflicts and disasters this film explores are serious, even tragic matters. They need to be understood, not set aside —as history needs to be remembered and learned from. Erasing history is no way to defend or recapture the essence of an ideal. Better to examine that ideal as it was tested in history, Sayles would argue, in the context of real human pain and struggle, and to confront head-on the corrupt figures and forces that can sometimes make America a difficult place in which to be an idealist. *Field of Dreams*, which did much better at the box office, is a feelgood movie; *Eight Men Out* is a bummer that inspires a complex mix of emotions and judgments and does not offer simplistic solutions. Distrustful of official institutions and taking legendary figures with a grain of salt, *Eight Men Out* is an example of the period's "anti-myth" movies.

Some of the anti-myth films were low-budget independent productions; a few were studio extravaganzas. Tim Hunter's *River's Edge* (1986), which presented the American family as a dying institution and contemporary teenagers as unable to love or to feel anything deeply, and Gus Van Sant, Jr.'s *Drugstore Cowboy* (1989), which rejected the images of the 1980s' anti-drug campaigns (suggesting instead that junkies might take drugs because they enjoy them) and dramatized the junkie mind-set and life-style without becoming judgmental, were among the most forceful and thought-provoking of the small films. Kubrick's *Full Metal Jacket*, a war film; Ridley Scott's *Alien* (1979), a horror film set in outer space; and Michael Cimino's *Heaven's Gate* (1980), a western, spent their big budgets on unflattering portraits of militarism and big capitalism. If Barry Levinson's *Good Morning, Vietnam* (1987) implied that all the Americans and Vietnamese needed was to play a good baseball game together, *Full Metal Jacket*—released the same year—exploded the myths of the Vietnam War and closed with an image of marching soldiers singing the "*Mickey Mouse Club* Song," whose "C: See you real soon" is ironically reminiscent of *Dr. Strangelove*'s "We'll meet again." *Alien* has a strong, intelligent, fast-acting hero (Ripley, played by Sigourney Weaver), a metamorphosing monster as indestructible and rapacious as Ripley is heroic, and a bad-guy robot, all of which would seem to make this a mythic film. But the real villain—undefeated at the film's conclusion—is the company that owns the spaceship and wants it to bring back the Alien, even at the cost of the crew, as a specimen from which to develop new weapons and troops. Since the company wants it and approves of what it does, the Alien comes to sym-

Fig. 17-6
Heaven's Gate: *In the community center where they go to enjoy themselves and to debate political matters, the immigrants are entertained by the violinist of the Heaven's Gate Band (David Mansfield).*

bolize the company: the inhumanity of the military – industrial complex.

Heaven's Gate told the story of the Johnson County Wars in 1890s Wyoming, substantially increasing the body count and drawing explicit political connections between the federal government and the rich cattlemen who, in the course of the film, exterminate virtually all of the peasant immigrants whose desire to work their land stands in the way of the cattlemen's plans. Read as "cattlemen vs. farmers," this is a standard western conflict, waiting for its Shane. But the marshal (Kris Kristofferson as Jim Averill) is not particularly effective, finally committing himself to the defense of the immigrant community only in the climactic battles, where he puts his Harvard education to use by organizing a Roman military strategy; the rest of the time he is either drinking to quiet the pain of disappointed idealism or courting a

prostitute (Isabelle Huppert as Ella Watson) who loves someone else (Christopher Walken as Nate Champion). The head of the Cattlemen's Association (Sam Waterston as Frank Canton) is far better organized than the marshal, as well as cruel and cold, prejudiced and patrician. Canton's government connections are part of the upper-class world in which he moves — for Heaven's Gate makes the Old West the site of a class war. The members of the lower class gather in their community center, "Heaven's Gate," to dance in good times and debate in bad; they are not fancy folks, not all of them speak English, and some of them have stolen cattle (a capital offense) to feed their families, but they have the right to live and work in America despite what the Cantons think. When the peasants, at the cost of most of their number, are on the verge of winning the final battle, the cavalry, guided by Canton, rides to the rescue—of the bad guys. This cynical development, which causes a woman fighter to blow her brains out, climaxes the anti-mythic, disillusioned vision of *Heaven's Gate* and marks how far the narrative and thematic device of the last-minute rescue had developed since Griffith.

Heaven's Gate was the biggest box-office disaster in Hollywood history. United Artists, which produced the film and was virtually destroyed by it, had to write off its $44 million cost and was acquired by MGM within a year (forming MGM/UA in 1981). *Heaven's Gate* opened for a week at its original length, 219 minutes, but was savaged by a New York critic. UA pulled the film, cut it to 147 much less interesting minutes, and forced Cimino to apologize publically for his extravagance and poor artistic judgment. The original version, which has not played in a U.S. theatre since that first engagement, did very good business in Europe throughout the 1980s, in 70mm and Dolby Stereo. The common domestic judgment was that *Heaven's Gate* had no story, was depressing, and indicated the folly of letting an obsessive *auteur* get too far out of (studio) control. The complete version had no chance to win an audience and pay back its cost, and the shortened version was too lame to do well at the box office. The complete version did in fact have a story (well beyond its *Shane* aspects and the love triangle, a narrative comparable to an epic novel) and was, for some, an astoundingly powerful cinematic experience. Even if its story sometimes becomes diffuse or hard to follow, *Heaven's Gate* is a major film. Its clearly articulated leftist message, which just as clearly referred to the social, economic, and political problems of the present, may have offended studio executives (as Cimino's arrogant behavior on the set certainly did) or may have been too out of step with current attitudes. Painfully re-evaluating the myths of the western, of fair government, and of the hero, *Heaven's Gate* pushed the anti-myth position farther than Hollywood was willing to go in this period. That same year, Lucas's *The Empire Strikes Back* (1980, directed by Irvin Kershner) took creative mythology even beyond the achievements of *Star Wars* and took the box office along for good measure.

Emerging Directors

The master mythmakers of the era are George Lucas and Steven Spielberg. They are also the most powerful creative figures in the contemporary American film industry. Like P. T. Barnum, they are producers, showmen, masters of the revels; like Hitchcock, they are known by those who might not recognize the names of any other directors. As much captains and architects as personal stylists, they have worked with large teams of creative collaborators: the composer John Williams; special effects artists like Douglas Trumbull (whose work includes *2001* and *Blade Runner* as well as *Close Encounters*), Dennis Muren, John Dykstra, and Richard Edlund; sound designers like Walter Murch and Ben Burtt; writers like Melinda Mathison and Lawrence Kasdan; directors like Robert Zemeckis and Joe Dante; and armies of cinematographers, editors, production designers, and highly skilled technicians. Dolby Noise Reduction and Dolby Stereo owe much of their success to the impact of the *Star Wars* soundtrack. The special effects house Industrial Light & Magic is part of Lucas's company, Lucasfilm Ltd. Lucas also pioneered—and, as THX Sound, implemented—a system of standards for the quality and balance of theatrical sound. He has been a major force in the development of new editing technologies (SoundDroid, a digital sound-editing system, and EditDroid, a computerized editing station that allows movies to be edited on video) as well as in the marketing of movie-related merchandise and the creation of live amusements. As a producer who controls a vast, multifaceted creative enterprise and whose cinematic fantasies have had an immense influence on more than a generation of children, Lucas has become the next Disney. As the director of the world's most popular spectacles, Spielberg has been called the next DeMille, but he also combines elements of Thomas Ince and Victor Fleming.

Lucas's first feature was *THX-1138* (1971), a stylized science-fiction drama about a passionless, mechanized, regimented dystopia. *American Graffiti* (1973), a comedy about teenagers cruising the streets of a small town, was a major hit. (As previously mentioned, soundtracks of *Easy Rider*, *Mean Streets*, and *American Graffiti* all achieved influential breakthroughs in the use of rock'n'roll.) His next film combined the adolescent coming-of-age drama with science fiction: *Star Wars*. Giving up directing to concentrate on producing, Lucas followed *Star Wars* with *The Empire Strikes Back* and *Return of the Jedi* (1983, directed by Richard Marquand); they are the fourth, fifth, and sixth episodes, or central trilogy, of a nine-part epic conceived as three trilogies. The only characters set to appear in all nine films are the two robots, C-3PO and R2-D2.

Raiders of the Lost Ark (1981) began the equally lucrative Indiana Jones trilogy, which Lucas produced and Spielberg directed. With their cliffhangers and nonstop action, the Indiana Jones films owe even more to the 1930s and 1940s serials than *Star Wars* does. One of the most entertaining and imaginative action pictures of the 1980s, *Raiders* deserves to be ranked with the greatest films ever made in the genre of action-adventure. *Indiana Jones and*

the Temple of Doom (1984), a more violent film with a less interesting heroine (Kate Capshaw instead of *Raiders'* Karen Allen), in its best moments was as fast as a roller coaster and nearly as spellbinding as *Gunga Din* (George Stevens, 1939). *Indiana Jones and the Last Crusade* (1989) set archaeologist Jones (Harrison Ford) on the trail of the Holy Grail, in the company of his father—played by Sean Connery, who as James Bond was the definitive hero of the action-adventure spectacle that leapt from one big action scene and exotic location and reflexive joke to another, and thus *was* the cinematic father of the Indiana Jones films and their hero.

From *Duel* (1971) to *Temple of Doom*, it is Spielberg who established the movie as ride. His control of tension and pace is both tight and expansive; he may be better at grand, sweeping effects than any director since David Lean, and he has a firm, efficient sense of narrative structure. Spielberg's one flaw—which in some of his films works as a strength—is his belief that

Fig. 17-7
Raiders of the Lost Ark: *Things get rolling for Indiana Jones (Harrison Ford).*

audiences respond only to scenes and emotions that are depicted with bold, powerful strokes, that scenes have to be "big" to work. For example, at the climax of *The Color Purple* (1985, from the novel by Alice Walker) he almost chokes the screen with purple, failing to convey the point, which is the importance of an isolated, out-of-the-way patch of purple—or person. *Always* (1989, a remake of a movie he loved, Victor Fleming's 1943 *A Guy Named Joe*) paints the subtleties of emotion with such a broad brush that the result is emotionally unaffecting; *1941* (1979) has so much action that it's boring. But the majority of his films are rich, intense experiences, both emotionally involving and kinetically charged, whose full, direct manner is appropriate and successful. *Close Encounters of the Third Kind* (1977, revised 1980) and *E.T.—The Extra-Terrestrial* (1982) are engrossing spectacles whose science-fiction visions are awesome and whose domestic, terrestrial scenes are well-observed. *Duel* (about a motorist pursued by a crazy truck driver; his last TV movie) and *The Sugarland Express* (1974, about a couple fleeing the police to keep their baby; his first theatrical movie) have relentless, effective, linear trajectories—they know where they're going and keep moving. In the very best of his films, *Jaws* (1975; a horrific variant of Henrik Ibsen's problem drama *An Enemy of the People*) and *Raiders*, his style has the authority, economy, and grace of a master.

Like Lucas, Spielberg is also a producer (his company is Amblin Entertainment). Though he never interfered with their directors, his creative stamp is evident in the films he produced, from the less memorable (*The Goonies*, 1985, directed by Richard Donner) to the unforgettable: *Poltergeist* (1982), directed by Tobe Hooper; *Gremlins* (1984), directed by Joe Dante; and *Back to the Future* (1985), directed by Robert Zemeckis.

Close Encounters depicts a battle between earthly authority, which attempts to limit our knowledge of extraterrestrial life, and the higher power of the imagination—of people who *know*, without knowing how they know, that the beings exist. Those who know—a man, woman, and child from separate families —become a new and truly "nuclear" family,

rejecting the earthly constraints of suburban homes and bourgeois marriages. They are bound not by contractual law and material interest but by imagination and myth. The interplanetary visitors communicate the same way movies do—with visual images and music—translating ideas into pictures, sounds, and colors, transmitting them through space. The scientist who passionately seeks contact with the unknown is played by the film director François Truffaut. As filmmaker-scientist he *produces* the climactic encounter between earthly and extraterrestrial beings and shares it with his audience in a dazzling display of sound and light, music and color—the resources of movies themselves. In Spielberg's mythology, the essential close encounter is between filmmakers and their audiences, for whom the dreams and myths of the imagination become concrete celebrations of sound, light, color, and space.

E.T.—The Extra-Terrestrial begins where *Close Encounters of the Third Kind* ends. Instead of an Earthling who departs with the extraterrestrials, the extraterrestrial creature is abandoned on Earth by his own people. E.T. is merely Christ, sent to Earth from above, announced by a shining spaceship-star, a mythic idea in mortal dress. His miracles of healing make converts among the innocent and pure of heart—the children who come unto him. All he asks in return is Faith. He both dies and rises again, to return "home" to the heavens. And his disciples fly with him, their bicycles magically transformed into space vehicles. E.T.'s spaceship leaves a rainbow in its wake—a reference to *The Wizard of Oz*. E.T. refers to yet another magic kingdom where you "wish upon a star," both Disneyland and Disney's *Pinocchio*, which earlier transformed a wooden puppet into a human child—just as Spielberg transforms a short actor in a mechanical costume into E.T. Spielberg can't resist having a little fun with his puppet child, demonstrating the answers to such comical questions as: How do you get a space creature drunk? Or how do you dress him in drag? Like *Close Encounters of the Third Kind*, *E.T.* is as much a hymn to the wonder of movies as to the mysteries of outer space. How else can you perform the miracle of raising the dead—of animating a nonexistent being like E.T. (or Mickey Mouse, or King

Fig. 17-9

Fig. 17-8

Close Encounters of the Third Kind: *the wonder of childhood vision (Fig. 17-8, Cary Guffey) and the wondrous sight of the Mother Ship's landing (Fig. 17-9).*

Kong, or Charlie the Tramp)—except with cinema? Even the ark in *Raiders of the Lost Ark* is a movie machine, a dazzling display of sound and light, capable of destroying anyone who looks at it. Indiana informs us of the only de-

fense against its power—"Don't look!" Once you look (and listen), the movies will get you. To see or make movies requires light, and the lighting instrument that movies have traditionally used is itself called an arc.

Many film critics and theorists deplore the manipulations of these movie arks or arcs. The death of film storytelling had been announced a decade ago—as had been the death of myth, of closure (clear-cut endings), and of Hollywood itself. For such critics, these films are deplorable regressions, their open appeal to childhood (even the slaves in the Temple of Doom are children) less like Wordsworthian Romanticism than a crass pandering to the juveniles who comprise the bulk of the American movie audience. But then, critics of movies and television have tended to impersonate schoolmarms, deploring the terrible tastes of the young and noting that movies pose dangers to their mental and moral health, since the movies began.

Nobody ever got lost trying to follow a Spielberg or Lucas film, but the films of David Lynch are something else. A unique stylist with a unique vision, Lynch has a fearlessly bizarre approach to the aesthetic challenges of narrative tone and structure. Whether set in the past or outer space or small-town America, the world he presents is—as his characters often remark—a strange place. Of all the directors whose first features appeared during or after 1977, Lynch is by far the most experimental.

An abstract painter and something of a cartoonist (in his long-running strip about the angriest dog in the world, the picture never changes), Lynch learned a great deal from the avant-garde. If the mechanical robin at the end of *Blue Velvet* (1986) can be traced directly to George Kuchar's *Hold Me While I'm Naked*, Lynch's emphasis on intriguing, unexplained images whose presence not only *is* a mystery but also points obliquely to related mysteries can be traced back to the poetic devices of avant-garde cinema in general. The sound for Lynch's first four films—*Eraserhead* (1977), *The Elephant Man* (1980), *Dune* (1984), and *Blue Velvet*—was designed by Alan Splet, whose complex, ominous sound composites perfectly complement Lynch's haunting images.

Lynch's films—along with *Twin Peaks* (broadcast 1990–91), the enigmatic TV series he created with Mark Frost—present and rework a number of recurring themes and images. Life has a mystery. What lurks below the surfaces of ordinary reality may be horrible, unbearable (*Eraserhead, Blue Velvet*). Or there may be a secret knowledge, to uncover which is to solve a problem, grow in spiritual power, and fulfill one's destiny (*Dune, Twin Peaks*). The human body, though it may be kept squeaky clean (*Twin Peaks*), can be seen as fundamentally repulsive (*Eraserhead, The Elephant Man, Dune*). Sex is dangerous, unpredictable, and uncontrollable (*Eraserhead; Blue Velvet; Wild At Heart*, 1990). Children want love and suffer horribly (*Eraserhead, The Elephant Man*). The squirmy white things in *Eraserhead*—particularly a small one that opens its mouth, into which the camera plunges—resemble the sand worms of *Dune*, and both raise the question of creation from the body. As the camera moves into the severed ear in *Blue Velvet*, part

of the ear is briefly seen as a sphere shaped by shadow, and a windlike but unnatural sound is heard; it is the sound heard in *Eraserhead* when the mysterious sphere, "the planet," is seen or entered. Jeffrey Beaumont (Kyle MacLachlan) explains the lure of the mystery in *Blue Velvet* this way: "I'm seeing something that was always hidden. . . . I'm in the middle of a mystery, and it's all secret." Judging from *Eraserhead* and *Blue Velvet*, what was always hidden may well be the primal scene, the child's first look at parental sexual activity. In any case, what one discovers in a Lynch film about people's private lives is usually awful. The innocent look of too-ordinary reality is clearly hiding something, and the secret—the vision of the way life really is—may be the stuff of soap operas (*Twin Peaks*), of cosmic poetry (*The Elephant Man*), of witchcraft (*Dune, Wild At Heart*), of the darkest *noirs* (*Blue Velvet*), or of nightmares (*Eraserhead*).

Eraserhead makes love and marriage, intercourse and reproduction, life and living all utterly horrible. Henry Spencer (John Nance), who is "on vacation," marries Mary X (Charlotte Stewart) after they produce a baby—although the hospital staff isn't sure that it is a baby: a skinless, screaming, goatlike head, linked by its skinny neck to a torso held together with swaddling. Mary is pitifully unhappy, makes weird sounds in her sleep when she can sleep, can't stand the baby's constant painful crying, and finally goes home to her nutcase parents. Henry, who has a dream in which his brain is made into erasers, eventually kills the baby (after it frightens away a beautiful woman Henry has had sex with, then *cackles*—the only time it's done anything but cry or eat) and perhaps ends up with the girl of his dreams, a tiny imaginary lady with huge cheeks whom he has watched perform on a stage inside the radiator. This is not the stuff of Hollywood romance. Its outdoors is geometric and muddy and bleak, its indoors claustrophobic and depressing, its characters maddening and unattractive and hurting bad. Dreams of creativity are squished in this wildly creative black-and-white black comedy, which became a major cult hit.

The Elephant Man, also in black and white (shot by Freddie Francis), is the essentially true story of John Merrick (John Hurt), a hideously deformed young Englishman, and Dr. Frederick Treaves (Anthony Hopkins), the anatomist who discovers him in a Victorian freak show and arranges for him to live in London Hospital and to meet members of London society—but, as an object of study, still to be on view. In the company of Mrs. Kendal (Anne Bancroft), an actress who believes that the theatre is "romance," Merrick even attends a play, where for the first time he can be in the audience rather than on stage (although at the end of the scene, Mrs. Kendal calls attention to him, and the audience gazes and applauds, this time without cruelty). Mrs. Kendal and Merrick's long-dead mother are the two beautiful women who almost magically accept him; he keeps their portraits together on his night table. When he dies, it is as if he projects his soul into starry space and toward the face of the mother. As she softly declares, "The heart beats—nothing dies," the camera pulls into a white space between her eyes, and the screen fills with light.

Dune, a science-fiction spectacle based on the novel by Frank Herbert, was made for producer Dino De Laurentiis on the condition that Lynch would next be allowed to write and direct a smaller film entirely the way he wanted. Ironically, the smaller film, *Blue Velvet*, made far more at the box office than the epic—and although that word is often misapplied to films that are simply long and expensive, *Dune* really is an epic. Even if much of the explanatory voice-over is irritating, the complex story of interplanetary rivalry for a spice that allows one to "fold space" and teleport is clearly told, the coming of a new order to the planet Dune is definitively epic material, and the unifying tale of the development of the young hero (Kyle MacLachlan) is as mythic as the period could demand. Nevertheless, many judged *Dune* too difficult to follow and at times—in scenes like those of the probing of a ruler's pimples—upsettingly gross.

Blue Velvet was Lynch's most popular film and the ancestor of another complicated mystery set in a small town, *Twin Peaks* (it is in *Blue Velvet*'s Lumberton, but could just as well be in Twin Peaks, that radio station WOOD announces, "At the sound of the falling tree, it's 1:30!"). At the beginning of the film, everything is bright and clean and in peaceful slow

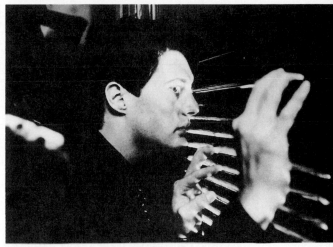

Fig. 17-10
Blue Velvet: *Jeffrey (Kyle MacLachlan) hides in Dorothy's closet and peeks at the mystery.*

motion—until a man who has been watering his lawn suddenly falls, stricken with an ailment that is never identified. His son, Jeffrey (MacLachlan), comes home from school to work in the family store; he falls for a sweet girl, Sandy (Laura Dern), and everything is apple-pie normal—or, more precisely, heightened apple-pie normal—until Jeffrey finds a man's ear on the ground and sets out, with Sandy's help, to solve the mystery it poses. The key figures in that mystery are a violent psychopath named Frank (played by Dennis Hopper, whose performances here and in *River's Edge* are astounding) and a sexual masochist named Dorothy (Isabella Rossellini). Dorothy does whatever Frank wants—sing "Blue Velvet," for example—because Frank and his cohorts have kidnapped her husband (whose ear Jeffrey found) and child. Sandy and Jeffrey have a love theme, played on a church organ; it is heard under their first kiss and under the scene in which Sandy expresses her hope that everything will be all right again, which will happen magically when the robins come back. The counter-theme, "Blue Velvet," is the song of irresistible sexuality and dark, obsessive perversity: Frank's terrifying abuse (and the evidence that he was sexually traumatized when young, making him kin to the suffering children in *Eraserhead* and *The Elephant Man*), Dorothy's desperate performing onstage and off, the whole criminal and deviant world hidden beneath the clean, bright, artificial surface of Lumberton. When sung by Rossellini, it is a siren song that leads, so to speak, through a severed ear into the darkness that everyone hides. Like their leitmotifs, the innocent and corrupt worlds of *Blue Velvet* are as distinct as day and night. They are also equally stylized, extreme, and distant from reality. In the Happy Ending, when Jeffrey's Dad has recovered and the flowers are again too bright against fences that are too white, Sandy and Jeffrey see a robin, an artificial one, with an artificial beetle in its beak.

If Anne Bancroft plays the Good Witch of the Theatre in *The Elephant Man*, Diane Ladd plays the Wicked Witch of Motherhood in *Wild At Heart*, a road movie filled with off-the-wall references to *The Wizard of Oz*; for example, two butchered men try to gather their blood and body parts together, losing a hand to a hungry dog, in an allusion to the scarecrow whose straw has been scattered by the flying monkeys but is stuffed back in by his friends. In this film, sex is hot and dangerous, like a struck wooden match; weirdness and corruption are everywhere in a world that is dangerous, crazy, rough, and passionate ("wild at heart and weird on top"). Dreams come true here ("If you're truly wild at heart, you'll fight for your dreams"), but through painful and fantastic means. The innocence of the young lovers (Laura Dern and Nicolas Cage) is relentlessly tested, destroyed, and celebrated. *Wild At Heart* is both a parody of 1980s mythic romance and the real thing, as *Twin Peaks* is and is not a soap. (When asked the relationship between *Wild At Heart* and *Twin Peaks*, Lynch replied that they both had a lot of wood in them.) *Wild At Heart* is an ironic artifice in the postmodern mode of *Blue Velvet*, but it also has scenes of violence and of sexual self-knowledge that are acutely realistic. Like Lynch's previous films, it deals with innocence, pain, and transformation in a stylized, mysterious world; unlike them, it was censored for U.S. release.

Jim Jarmusch is a minimalist who constructs his films according to strict formal principles. *Stranger Than Paradise* (1984) was conceived as

Fig. 17-11

Fig. 17-12

Realistic mise-en-scène *and carefully balanced composition: Jim Jarmusch's* Stranger Than Paradise *(Fig. 17-11: foreground, Richard Edson; background, Eszter Balint and John Lurie) and* Down By Law *(Fig. 17-12: from left, John Lurie, Tom Waits, and Roberto Benigni).*

a black-and-white film consisting of nothing but sequence shots (each scene is presented in a single long take) linked by blackouts. While the scenes in *Stranger Than Paradise* follow one another in chronological order, those in *Mystery Train* (1989) are presented in an artificial order —simultaneous events are presented one after the other—that reflects a formalized approach to time. As simple as it sounds, he also plays with the number three: two men and a woman on the road in *Stranger Than Paradise*, three prisoners in *Down By Law* (1986), three interrelated but separated sequences in *Mystery Train*. Each of his films is a self-conscious response to a formal problem, almost in the manner of Godard; each patiently observes the so-called minor, aimless, and boring stretches of everyday life, almost like a Czech comedy; and each has a deadpan wit, an uncrowded *mise-en-scène,* and a love of rock'n'roll that are reminiscent of Malick's cool, weird, ironic *Badlands,* whose runaway lovers dance to "Love Is Strange." He is as likely to allude to Elvis (*Mystery Train*) as to Ozu (the horse "Tokyo Story" in *Stranger Than Paradise*). His first film, *Permanent Vacation* (1980), was shot for $12,000 in ten days and took its title from the lyrics of "My Boyfriend's Back." Eva (Eszter Balint), the immigrant heroine of *Stranger Than Paradise* (and the "Stranger In Paradise"), calls Screamin' Jay Hawkins her "main man" and repeatedly plays her favorite song, "I Put A Spell On You." In *Mystery Train,* Screamin' Jay Hawkins himself plays the role of a desk clerk at the Memphis hotel where the main action takes place.

Jarmusch is a minimalist in another sense as well; to quote him: "My aesthetic is minimal. I make films about little things that happen between human beings." He avoids putting in too much, refusing to burden the film with extra props and dialogue and events that would get in the way of the subtleties that interest him — the peculiar, fortuitous way things happen. Very little takes place in his mundane scenes, but as they grow on you, they become very funny. Steering away from what Hollywood calls "action," he spends narrative time with matters Hollywood would skip over. As he told an interviewer, "In most films, if a guy gets a phone call from his girlfriend, who says 'Come over,' the editor will cut to him at her door. I'm more interested in the guy on the way to his girlfriend's house than I am in the other two scenes. What did he see on the train? What did he eat? I'm more interested in those things in between." Jarmusch rejects Griffith's aesthetic of cutting out the inessential (and of calling attention to what is important in a scene through editing and camerawork) in order to dramatize what is, in another way, essential. He avoids cutting within scenes in order to present them in real time while reminding the audience — which gets restless when denied continuity editing — that it is watching a movie. If his films have, via their rock idols, a touch

of the mythic, no one could mistake them for "return of the myths" material; the lavish, conservative fantasies turned out by Hollywood in the late 1970s and 1980s are Jarmusch's polar opposite. In this period, the narrative filmmakers most unlike each other are Jarmusch and Spielberg, who might be considered a maximalist.

John Waters is an ironist, like Lynch and Jarmusch, a writer-director of satirical comedies that at first were cult films in bad taste, then crossed into the mainstream when Waters restrained himself to what he calls "good bad taste." Shot and set in Baltimore, his home town, many of his films starred his childhood friend, the transvestite actor Divine (Harris Glenn Milstead), who died shortly after starring in *Hairspray.* Among their first films together were *Multiple Maniacs* (1970), *Pink Flamingos* (1972), and *Female Trouble* (1974), milestones in the history of trash art. Waters established the outer limits of cinematic taste in *Pink Flamingos,* which ends with an unfaked shot of Divine's eating dog excrement, then moved on to the sense of smell in *Polyester* (1981), which was released in "Odorama." There had been olfactory films before (Jack Cardiff's *Scent of Mystery,* 1960, in "Smell-O-Vision," identified a central character not with visual or sound cues but with her perfume), but they either circulated and dispelled odors through the theatre's air conditioners (AromaRama; *The Great Wall of China,* 1959) or shot perfumy mists into the audience's faces from tubing attached to the backs of the seats (Smell-O-Vision). Waters's system — reflecting his lifelong love of schlock movies, the gimmicks of William Castle, and the outrageous in general — was scratch and sniff. Each viewer of *Polyester* was given a card. In one of the cleverest gags in the history of film/viewer interaction, Divine reaches for some flowers; a number flashes on the screen instructing the audience which area on the Odorama card to scratch off; the audience scratches, expecting flowers and dropping its guard (some of the earlier odors were vile), then smells instead the disgusting thing that is suddenly thrust in Divine's face. The viewer literally shares the character's sense of surprise as well as her unpleasant experience — a real step toward Bazin's "myth of total cinema."

Waters's eleventh film, *Hairspray* (1988), was his first hit with those who go to the movies before midnight; it was followed by *Cry-Baby* (1990), a high-energy teen romance with some gutsy musical numbers and, as usual, arresting casting (from Patty Hearst, Polly Bergen, Troy Donahue, Traci Lords, and Dave Nelson to Kim McGuire as Hatchet Face).

Hairspray, set in Baltimore in the spring and early summer of 1963, takes a nostalgic *and* parodistic look at the clichés of the period — but if that were all it did, it might have been nothing more than another *Grease*. However, into this apolitical world of dancing, romancing, feuding teenagers come the social and political struggles of the early 1960s. It is as if we were seeing a 1963 teen picture that dealt with the turbulent real world of 1963, something no such film ever did. The result is a humanistic political fable that is also a put-on and an engaging, hilarious comedy. In this movie the vain, popular, attractive girl (Amber, played by Colleen Fitzpatrick) continually loses to the sincere, feisty, energetic fat girl (Tracy, played by Ricki Lake). Divine plays Edna Turblad, Tracy's hefty mother, as well as Arvin Hodgepile, the racist manager of the TV station that broadcasts the Corny Collins show, Baltimore's answer to American Bandstand. Corny (Shawn Thompson) is not a racist, but he has been going along with the station policy that "Negro Day" is the last Thursday of every month and that on all other days, the dancers are only white. (The majority of the songs played on the show were recorded by blacks.) When Tracy becomes one of the dancers on the show — the hottest and baddest — she and her best friend, Penny (Leslie Ann Powers), determine to integrate the show. And they succeed. The racism of the older generation, from Hodgepile to Amber's parents (played by Debbie Harry and Sonny Bono), is portrayed vividly even if it's funny. Waters himself plays a psychologist hired by Penny's mother to brainwash Penny into breaking up with her black boyfriend; "Negro," he says, and zaps her with a large blue neon prod. Tracy's parents, on the other hand, become aware of their own racism and reject it. A black woman who works on the show and owns a record store (Motormouth Maybelle, played by the great singer Ruth Brown) joins

the push for integration — blacks and whites dancing together to music that itself integrated black and white musical traditions. And what ties all this together is hairspray, which is used by the vain characters to enhance their image but also is used by the high school rebels whose hair-dos are "hair-don'ts" and who are punished by being put in a homeroom reserved for social misfits — and blacks. When Edna gets her first high hair-do, Tracy welcomes her to the 1960s. The expression and enjoyment of who one is, a staple of adolescent drama, and the good feeling that comes when the right people win, a staple of 1980s mythology, become inseparable in *Hairspray* from the momentum of positive social transformation.

Each of the Coen brothers' first features tackled a separate genre — *Blood Simple* (1983), the *film noir*; *Raising Arizona* (1987), the romantic comedy; and *Miller's Crossing* (1990), the gangster melodrama. Joel Coen directs, Ethan Coen produces, and they write the scripts together. Although their tight, witty films are primarily concerned with style, calling attention to their clever camerawork, rich detail, and self-conscious distance from their subjects, each movie is also a genuine, effective genre work: *Blood Simple* is a superb *noir*, as wickedly dark as *Raising Arizona* is wickedly funny. The result is that one admires the Coens' recreation of particular cinematic modes as well as their breezy modernity. In their movies the old is made new — something many 1980s films attempted but few managed. They also write better voice-over narration than anyone now working, Malick and Duras excepted; "Down here you're on your own" launches *Blood Simple* as brilliantly as "Maybe it was Utah" wraps up *Raising Arizona*. Like Waters, Jarmusch, Sayles, and many of today's most original writer-directors, the Coens are independent filmmakers, working without studio interference and free to follow their creative impulses and intuitions where the business mentality of Hollywood fears to tread.

The plot of *Blood Simple* is so complex, so full of betrayals and misunderstandings, that none of the characters ever completely figures it out. To the audience, however, it makes perfect sense. As when watching a Hitchcock film, one is rewarded for paying attention to details

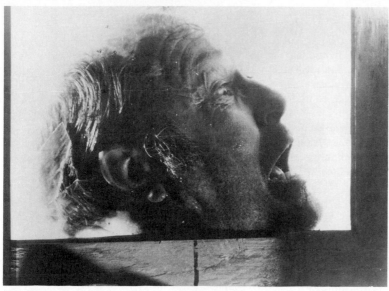

Fig. 17-13

Blood Simple: *The detective (M. Emmet Walsh) finds that no matter who you are, something can "all go wrong."*

—in this case, for keeping track of a cigarette lighter and a pearl-handled .38 (and the three bullets inside it), which are narrative elements as central as the main characters: an unnamed detective (M. Emmet Walsh); bar owner Julian Marty (Dan Hedaya); Marty's wife, Abby (Frances McDormand); and Abby's lover, Ray (John Getz). The violence, passion, pessimism, and look of *noir* are all here, and the tone is set at the start, as the detective observes voice-over that "nothing comes with a guarantee"—anybody can have something just go all wrong. When things do go wrong for the detective and he lies dying in the bathroom of Abby's apartment, shot by her with the last bullet in the revolver, the film ends with a marvelous death image. Lying on the floor, the detective looks up at the underside of the sink, which has been dripping throughout the climax; taking as long as the rest of his life, another droplet begins to form, grows—and falls, with a cut to black.

Jonathan Demme has also worked in a number of genres, sometimes with an ironic edge and sometimes with scrupulous neutrality. In his concert films, *Stop Making Sense* (1984) and *Swimming to Cambodia* (1987), the camera observes the performers—the Talking Heads and Spalding Gray, respectively—and lets their own styles come through directly. This is not something that can be achieved simply by turning the camera on and recording the show, *Queen Elizabeth* style; it requires intense discipline and clarity as well as a perfect understanding of the performer's aesthetics. Demme's restraint in *Stop Making Sense* is refreshingly different from the authorial intrusiveness of most concert films. Demme's stylistic integrity and directorial authority are clear from his films but not foregrounded by them. His gangster comedy, *Married to the Mob* (1988), has none of *The Godfather*'s rich romanticism or *GoodFellas*'s muscular precision, but a light, clean, sharply ironic touch and a zippy pace of its own. His lean, mean thriller, *The Silence of the Lambs* (1991, from the novel by Thomas Harris), is full of ferocious, gruesome characters and events, portrays them without compromising their horrific nature, and becomes troubling without being troubled. The film neither wallows in psychotic violence nor judgmentally keeps its distance but is engaged and perfectly balanced, and over repeated viewings it stands up better than the films made from Harris's previous novels, *Black Sunday* (John Frankenheimer, 1977) and *Manhunter* (Michael Mann, 1986, a mannered adaptation of *Red Dragon*). The best of Demme's earlier narrative films—*Citizens Band* (1977), *Melvin and Howard* (1980), and *Something Wild* (1986)—are more offbeat, friendly, even affectionate in tone than *The Silence of the Lambs*, but in all his works Demme appears to like and care about his central characters as well as to understand them.

Terry Gilliam, the American member of England's Monty Python group, first became well known as the creator of the animated sequences in their TV series, *Monty Python's Flying Circus*, and as the co-director (with Terry Jones) of *Monty Python and the Holy Grail*. After directing another two British pictures (*Jabberwocky*, 1977; *Time Bandits*, 1981), Gilliam shot two American-backed pictures in Europe: *Brazil* (1985) and *The Adventures of Baron Munchausen* (1989). *Brazil*, shot in 1984, is a dark social satire based loosely on George Orwell's novel *Nineteen Eighty-Four*. *Brazil*'s dystopia is an oppressive "free society" that spies on its citizens—a huge, inefficient, ruthless bureaucracy devoted to red tape. The government has been under terrorist attack for thirteen years but dismisses that as "beginner's luck." Crude instruments and cheap furniture dominate the cramped, ugly work environment; ducts are everywhere, particularly at home, and it is a crime to fix or have anything fixed without going through Central Services (Robert De Niro plays an outlaw repairman, Harry Tuttle). The hero (Sam Lowry, played by Jonathan Pryce) begins by tracking down a bureaucratic error and ends by falling in love with a terrorist (Jill Layton, played by Kim Greist). Sam meets his fate in Gilliam's version of Orwell's "Room 101," where a friend tortures him; Sam's escape is to retreat mentally—forever—to an idyllic fantasy inspired by the song "Brazil." In the American version of the film, what happens to Jill is not made explicit; in the English version, she definitely is murdered. *Brazil*'s biting, depressing wit proved too much for the picture's American producer, MCA-Universal; the studio wanted the picture to end when the lovers are united and have not yet been captured—leaving out the entire dream sequence, 27 minutes in the original cut—and in the meantime refused to release this expensive, risky movie. Gilliam began a public

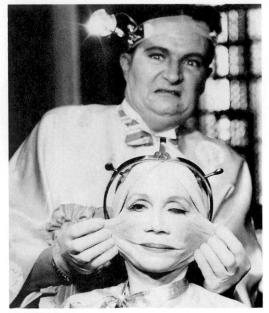

Fig. 17-14
Brazil*: Dr. Jaffe (Jim Broadbent) tries a new kind of plastic surgery on the hero's mother, Mrs. Lowry (Katherine Helmond).*

campaign, placing ads in the trade papers that "asked" when Universal planned to release his film. The studio reluctantly opened *Brazil* for a week and found that it did great business, so the film went into wide release—but this "American version" was, and still is, missing over twelve minutes (mostly from the ending) that can be seen only in the English release version. The American version also has extra fantasy-in-the-clouds sequences, particularly at the very start, that Universal felt would make the film more enjoyable. Taking an ironic, prodigiously creative look at stupidity, incompetence, vanity, and short-sightedness, the drab and dull and confused—with an undercurrent of passion and rebellion—*Brazil* is the best representative yet of Gilliam's satiric side. His next film, *The Adventures of Baron Munchausen*, shows the other side of his work, exuberant fantasy, at its height. The roots of both *Brazil* and *Munchausen* are in his satiric, fantastic work with the Pythons. *Jabberwocky* is a satire, though not a distinguished one—a film on the way to *Brazil*—as *Time Bandits* is a fantastic adventure, a rehearsal for *Munchausen* that is more technically than dramatically impressive. As *Brazil* opens at "8:49 PM / Somewhere in the 20th Century," *Munchausen* opens in the "Late 18th Century / The Age of Reason / Wednesday." Munchausen tells the tales of his fabulous adventures in a theatre whose sets and props are elegant versions of some of Gilliam's Python cartoons. But in this era of logic and certainty, Munchausen feels out of place. (However, no Gilliam world is entirely rational, regardless of what it thinks of itself; here the Age of Reason is an age of wars.) Soon he goes on new adventures, and at the end it becomes clear that his impossible stories were true, that he really is a magical figure, and that the rational world cannot do without the wild beauty and nonsense of fantasy.

The years since 1977 have also produced some filmmakers interested more in political and social problems than in the irrational, ironic, reflexive, and fantastic. Michael Cimino's works are not devoid of irony, but he appears to have no sense of humor. What he does have is a rich, grand, grave style—style to spare. In his big films, the politically conservative *The Deer Hunter* and the politically radical *Heaven's Gate*, this style works brilliantly, from the intelligently moving camera to the overwhelming sense of place. Whatever one thinks of his at times incoherent plotting and inconsistent politics, watching those two movies one feels in the presence of a visual powerhouse. *The Deer Hunter* is a bit sophomoric in its symbolic use of Russian roulette, not to mention the deer, but it is a very fine study of postcombat stress. *Heaven's Gate*—speaking always of the uncut version—is a bit careless about conveying essential narrative information, but it is visually magnificent, bears a coherent political and socioeconomic message, and is the only great western of the 1980s. In the later films, however—none of which has been even as good as his debut picture, *Thunderbolt and Lightfoot* (1974)—his style not only gets in the way but is unmotivated and irritating, vain and pushy; this is particularly true of both the release version and the uncut director's version of *The Sicilian* (1987, from the novel by Mario Puzo—a book that could easily have been made into a terrific movie but appears hardly to have been consulted). *Year*

of the Dragon (1985) has problems with psychological and narrative credibility, revealing a shallow understanding not just of character but of people—but it is more disciplined and watchable than the films that followed (such as *The Desperate Hours*, 1990). *Year of the Dragon* is the interesting work of a showoff trying to keep a low profile after the disaster of *Heaven's Gate*, his masterpiece, the film for which he had to apologize.

Oliver Stone began as a screenwriter, receiving an Oscar for Alan Parker's *Midnight Express* (1978), then writing De Palma's hamfisted remake of *Scarface* (1983) and Cimino's *Year of the Dragon*. All this time he was trying to sell *Platoon*, a script based on his experiences in Vietnam. After directing *Salvador* (1986), a buddy film whose view of the politics of El Salvador was left of center, he was given the chance to direct *Platoon* himself; released in the last days of 1986, it quickly attracted large audiences who proclaimed it the first film to portray accurately the experience of the American foot soldier in Vietnam. (The next film about which that was said was Patrick Duncan's *84 Charlie Mopic*, 1989.) Each of Stone's films is centered on a man who faces the darkness in himself and in the world around him, then has to decide what to do about it. Although there are many characters in *Platoon*, the most important is first-timer Chris (Charlie Sheen). Like many of Stone's heroes, Chris is torn between two fathers, a good one (Sgt. Elias, played by Willem Dafoe) and a bad one (Sgt. Barnes, played by Tom Berenger). The good one opposes the massacre of civilians, takes care of his men, and even smokes dope with them. The bad one takes care of his men too, but he is contemptuous and ruthless; "There's the way it ought to be, and there's the way it is," he says to Chris, articulating the all-time argument against the value of idealism and incarnating "the way it is." After Barnes kills Elias, Chris kills Barnes (either because Chris is an idealist or because he is one no longer—the film gives no clue); his conclusion about the war is that Americans were really just fighting each other on foreign soil. Politics aside, *Platoon* does convey the experience of protracted jungle warfare, putting the audience through a rough and unbroken tour of duty.

The opposed fathers in Stone's next film, *Wall Street* (1987), are an honest, hardworking businessman (Martin Sheen as Fox) and an unscrupulous corporate raider (Michael Douglas as Gekko). The hero is Fox's son, Bud (Charlie Sheen, Martin's real son), a stockbroker who learns from Gekko how to use confidential information and get rich in the inflated market of the mid-80s, making money without creating anything, sometimes even by destroying. When Bud realizes that his father's company — which Bud helped Gekko take over — is going to be broken up and sold off piece by piece, Bud does something like Chris's shooting Barnes: saves his father's company (using against Gekko the tricks Gekko taught him), then turns himself in, telling the truth about Gekko's illegal practices. Gekko's fatherly parting shot to Bud is "I gave you your manhood, I gave you everything!" Bud chooses the honesty represented by his literal father — the terms Barnes mocks, "the way it ought to be." *Wall Street* drew on some earlier scandals and remarkably anticipated several that broke years later. Stone's style may not be subtle — he always makes sure we get the point — and not all his camera movements may be aesthetically necessary (like Cimino and unlike Demme, Stone foregrounds his style), but he does make forceful, well-researched films on political subjects and other important aspects of contemporary life (for example, the assassination of a provocative talk-show host in *Talk Radio*, 1988, starring and co-written by Eric Bogosian). To appreciate how *Wall Street*'s material could have been treated from a more right-wing perspective — and, in fact, very profitably was — consider that the male lead (Richard Gere) in Disney's *Pretty Woman* (1990, directed by Garry Marshall) does for a living exactly what Gekko did (without breaking the law) but is portrayed as a basically good person. Also, both films are about the discovery that there are things more important than money, but *Pretty Woman* lets money itself remain OK and ends with the rousing instruction, like something out of *Flashdance*, "Always time to dream, so keep on dreamin'!"

Near the end of *Wall Street*, an old broker (Hal Holbrook as Lou) gives Bud this Hemingwayesque advice, and it resonates through all of Stone's films: "Man looks in the abyss. There's

nothin' staring back at him. At that moment, man finds his character. And that is what keeps him out of the abyss." That confrontation and salvation occur in *Midnight Express, Salvador, Platoon, Wall Street*, and *Born on the Fourth of July* (1989, starring Tom Cruise as a paralyzed Vietnam veteran who becomes an activist; Stone has not yet done better work than the sequences in the veterans' hospitals). The hero of *The Doors* (1991) embraces the abyss, and the hero of *Talk Radio* dances around it until someone pushes him in. For Oliver Stone, hell is where you find it.

John Sayles is an insightful writer with a good ear for dialogue and a skilled director whose style is understated, meticulous, economical, and evocatively realistic. Most of his films offer slices of life, which made him the logical choice to script the slice-of-life tragicomedies of Grace Paley for the screen (*Enormous Changes at the Last Minute*, 1978–82, released 1983, directed by Mirra Bank and Ellen Hovde). Like *Enormous Changes*, the films he writes and directs reject sexism, racism, and big capitalism and stick up for ordinary people. The best example of his openness to feminism is *Lianna* (1983), in which a woman comes to terms with her discovery that she is a lesbian; *Baby It's You* (1982, released 1983) — a high-school-and-after romantic comedy best known for inventing "lip-syncing" (pretending to sing while a recording plays) — adopts a slicker but just as revealing approach to the emotional development of a young heterosexual woman. Sayles's deep understanding of character and his leftist politics are central to all his works, from his novel *Union Dues* and his first feature, *Return of the Secaucus 7* (1980), a comedy about a reunion of 1960s radicals, to *City of Hope* (1991), an epic study of life in a blue-collar town. Both *City of Hope* and the tragic *Eight Men Out* (like *Platoon*, Sayles's first script idea, long put off because studios and producers considered the idea box-office poison) demonstrate that one way to gauge the health or corruption of a society is to examine the conditions under which people work and the decisions they feel they have to make. *Matewan* (1987) — another film about workers, this time coal miners in the 1920s — may be the most compelling pro-labor film of the 1980s. As funny and knowing as his realistic comedies are, Sayles also has a talent for comic horror, naturally with a sociopolitical twist — evident in his clever scripts for Joe Dante's *Piranha* (1978) and Lewis Teague's *Alligator* (1980) and in his brilliant script for Dante's *The Howling* (1980, released 1981, co-written by Terence Winkless). His science-fiction fable, *The Brother from Another Planet* (1984), performs a twist on *E.T.* for good reason: Sayles was one of *E.T.*'s uncredited writers, dropped from the project because he disagreed about the direction it should take. What he did instead was to make his own *E.T.*, in which the visitor from outer space is black.

Spike Lee, son of jazz musician Bill Lee, was born in Atlanta; as a graduate student in NYU's film program, he made a thesis film — *Joe's Bed-Stuy Barbershop: We Cut Heads* (1983) — that won a Student Academy Award. Now an independent filmmaker based in New York — writing, producing, directing, and (like Sayles) usually acting in his "Forty Acres and a Mule" productions, the most recent of which have been backed and distributed by major studios — Lee is the most important black filmmaker of his generation. His frank, saucy, brash, reflexive style can best be described as "in your face."

Like *Bed-Stuy Barbershop*, a realistic drama about a barber who is more interested in cutting hair than in letting his shop be a front for the numbers racket, many of Lee's films are set and shot in the Bedford-Stuyvesant section of Brooklyn. His films tackle the clichés about black character and experience that pervade American culture, investigating and radicalizing them until the clichés are dismantled and — in the best of his works, but not all — the personal and social realities step forward. His first two features, *She's Gotta Have It* (1986) and *School Daze* (1988), addressed the images blacks have of each other, while the next, *Do The Right Thing* (1989), looked at interracial constructs. *School Daze*, a big-studio but low-budget musical, attacked assimilation and black fraternity life while exploring the prejudices that sometimes divide light- and dark-skinned blacks. *She's Gotta Have It* — a film as important as *Stranger Than Paradise* and Wayne Wang's *Chan Is Missing* (1982) in stimulating the 1980s' independent production movement, since all

three won festival prizes and attracted enthusiastic audiences without any help from Hollywood — is the story of a free spirit (Nola Darling, played by Tracy Camilla Johns) whose lovers want to change and control her; above all, each wants her for himself alone. Nola is passionate about Brooklyn, sex, honesty, and black consciousness. It is she who has to tell Spike Lee (who plays Mars Blackmon, one of the lovers) when Malcolm X's birthday is. Nola decides that no one but herself is going to control her body, her mind, her desires, and her self-image, which leaves the possessive ex-boyfriends (and one lesbian) on their own, explaining to the camera their interpretations of Nola's character and their memories of loving her and being frustrated by her. The "it" in *She's Gotta Have It* at first appears to be promiscuous sex — particularly since that is what one of the lovers says she's "gotta have" — but it turns out to be personal autonomy, the freedom to explore and define and be herself. Opening with a quote from a black woman writer, Zora Neale Hurston, *She's Gotta Have It* is about a woman who repudiates the clichés that surround her and refuses to be controlled by blacks or whites, sexists or racists, attitudes or platitudes. (It is unfortunate that at the end of *Jungle Fever*, 1991, Lee's occasionally brilliant treatment of interracial sex, the clichés win.)

Do The Right Thing is set on a single block in Bedford-Stuyvesant on the hottest day of the year. Although it is a black neighborhood, there are no black-owned businesses, only a market owned by Koreans and a pizzeria owned by Italians (Sal, played by Danny Aiello, and his two sons). The Koreans are newcomers, but Sal has been in business for twenty-five years; although it is not his neighborhood, Sal is proud that its residents have grown up on his pizza. When Sal confides his pride and his dreams to his sons, sappy family-melodrama music can be heard beneath the dialogue; when Da Mayor (Ossie Davis) and Mother Sister (Ruby Dee), two of the neighborhood's older residents, remark how hot it is, the music plays variations on "Summertime"; this is one way that the movie identifies artistic and social stereotypes reflexively, urging the audience to recognize and think about them. A stammering

Fig. 17-15
Do The Right Thing: *Radio Raheem (Bill Nunn, left) and Buggin Out (Giancarlo Esposito).*

white man, Smiley (Roger Guenveur Smith)—mentally retarded in a way that makes him the film's "innocent"—begins the film by holding up a photo of Martin Luther King, Jr. and Malcolm X standing together and smiling; although the sociopolitical goals and tactics Malcolm proposed were more radical and revolutionary than those of King, who argued for nonviolent civil disobedience, the two assassinated leaders and their programs are linked in this photo. As the film's many characters go about their business, three men sit at a streetcorner in front of a bright red wall and comment on the action; these "Cornermen" are much like the chorus in a Greek tragedy, and their judgments are those of the attentive community.

The heat provokes confrontations and brings out latent racial antagonisms. Buggin Out (Giancarlo Esposito) demands that Sal add pictures of African-Americans to the pizzeria's Wall of Fame, which has pictures only of

famous Italian-Americans; Sal refuses, and Buggin Out tries to organize a boycott. Mookie (Spike Lee), who delivers Sal's pizzas and has no developed political consciousness, unsuccessfully tries to defuse the suddenly growing antagonism between Buggin Out and Sal. At one point Da Mayor gives Mookie the simple, venerable advice, "Always do the right thing." "That's it?" says Mookie, who will find, along with the audience, that it is not always simple to know what the right thing is. Mookie's best friend, Radio Raheem (Bill Nunn), carries his prized radio (a portable stereo called a boom box) wherever he goes, playing Public Enemy's "Fight the Power," a call to "fight the powers that be."

As tensions increase, Sal and the police are clearly revealed as the powers that be. As the pizzeria is closing for the night, Buggin Out and Radio Raheem repeat the demand that Sal acknowledge his black customers by putting up new photos; Raheem refuses to turn down the

Do The Right Thing: *Da Mayor (Ossie Davis, left) offers Mookie (Spike Lee) some advice that will prove problematic: "Always do the right thing."*

Fig. 17-16

volume on his box, and Sal loses his self-control, allowing his latent racism to surface. Swinging a baseball bat, Sal smashes the radio to "kill" the music and all it stands for. Raheem attacks Sal in a rage, and they end up fighting in the street. The police break up the fight, arrest Buggin Out, and kill Radio Raheem with a chokehold. The Cornermen denounce the killing. When the police leave, Sal and his sons face the outraged community; Da Mayor urges everyone to think before doing something irrevocable. Politicized by the death of his friend — caused indirectly by Sal, directly by the police, and generally by institutionalized white power — it is Mookie who starts the riot, picking up a garbage can and tossing it through one of the pizzeria's large windows. He does this dispassionately, not in a rage; his decision to do what he now considers right is a rational judgment. The pizzeria burns down; Smiley pins his photo of King and Malcolm on the burning wall. The next morning Sal and Mookie come to some kind of mutual understanding, but the political barriers between them remain clear.

Both Mookie and the neighborhood have taken a stand against racist oppression; the question is whether they were right to meet violence (Sal's destroying the boom box; the killing of Radio Raheem) with violence (destroying the pizzeria). This question is im-

plicit in the two equally long, dialectically opposed quotations that end the film, one from King and one from Malcolm X. King argues against violence as a way of achieving racial justice: "The old law of an eye for an eye leaves everybody blind. [Violence] is immoral because it seeks to humiliate the opponent rather than win his understanding; it seeks to annihilate rather than convert. . . . It destroys community and makes brotherhood impossible. . . . Violence ends by defeating itself. It creates bitterness in the survivors and brutality in the destroyers." Malcolm argues that however many good people there are in America, "there are also plenty of bad people . . . who seem to have all the power and be in these positions to block things that you and I need. Because this is the situation, you and I have to preserve the right to do what is necessary to bring an end to that situation." Malcolm advocates violence in the cause of self-defense, calling it "intelligence." These positions are absolutely opposed, since the community cannot decide to be violent and nonviolent. Yet there is something on which King and Malcolm agree: the need to recognize oppression and take an unalterable stand against it. The synthesis possible between them — as heroic, murdered champions of black power — is seen in the photo of the two together, which fades in just before the quotations have finished scrolling up the screen and is the movie's final image. The synthesis that may emerge from their irreconcilable positions may have to be achieved over time and in history, as Hegel argued dialectical oppositions do collide and mutate. In the present historical moment, these different visions of the correct means to social, economic, and political change force a choice, and Mookie chooses the position articulated by Malcolm X. But Mookie and Lee are not the same here, any more than they were in *She's Gotta Have It*. Lee chooses to dramatize the dialectic; like Brecht, he wants the audience to judge what it sees—decide for itself what "the right thing" is—rather than be spoon-fed a resolution. He does not vacillate between action and inaction; he knows that active resistance is necessary and that the choice is between ways of resisting. His great project in *Do The Right Thing* is to expose the structure of racism. And as in all his films, his rude, upfront, catalytic technique is to come right out with what many people leave unsaid, or live with in silence—in this case, the injustice and racism that underlie the politics of contemporary America and determine its social conflicts. Once those conflicts have surfaced and been irrefutably articulated, there is no turning back for the community or the movie. Given what Malcolm X called "the situation," the one unquestionably right thing is to fight the powers that be—"by any means necessary" (to quote the tail credits), including Mookie's violent decision and Lee's nonviolent one, to make a movie that explodes racial stereotypes and poses essential questions. The day may be hot, in fact inflammatory, but it is not any "Summertime" imagined by Gershwin.

Luis Valdez, the founder of El Teatro Campesino, began as a playwright and stage director. Working with his brother, Daniel Valdez, who composed the music and played one of the two leads (Henry Reyna), Luis Valdez wrote and directed *Zoot Suit*, a Brechtian musical about Chicano consciousness, which was produced in Los Angeles by the Center Theatre Group. Like the film adapted from it, *Zoot Suit* starred Edward James Olmos in the role of El Pachuco, the spirit of *machismo* and political awareness, who is part of Reyna's being, a figure of destiny, and the narrator of the work.

Zoot Suit (1981), rewritten for the screen and directed by Luis Valdez, was shot entirely in a theatre; sometimes it shows the audience watching the play, sometimes it is a movie with stage sets, and sometimes it is a movie shot as if the event were happening on location. It employs theatrical transitions, devices, and conventions as well as cinematic ones, all of which work together in a reflexive and blazingly cinematic style. El Pachuco calls for a cut to a new scene with a snap of his fingers, or snaps to stop the action for commentary; he gestures for a swish pan or walks from one set to another as the stage revolves; he inhabits the stage as a solid presence only Henry can see—or through cutting momentarily becomes one of the characters; he interrupts the happy ending for the sober ending and then cues the dance ending. If the crucial film of the 1940s with which to study the relations between theatre and cinema is *Henry V*, the film of the 1980s is *Zoot Suit*. It is also one of the most colorfully designed, strikingly choreographed, and rhythmically edited films of the decade, with an extremely sophisticated narrative structure and a direct, engaging tone. Politically intense in its portrayal and analysis of the 1942 Sleepy Lagoon murder case, which was exploited in a racist anti-"Mexican" campaign that unjustly sent many *pachucos* (who today would call themselves Chicanos) to prison, the film is also irresistibly energetic and sardonically, boldly funny. What it projects and is about is Style, inseparable from political awareness and incarnated in the zoot suit (a perfect example of the "objective correlative"). "Our *pachuco* realities will only make sense if you grasp their stylization," El Pachuco tells the audience. "To put on the zoot suit," he says, was "to play the myth" and to find "a style of urban survival." Tough, proud, and cool in the advice he gives Henry Reyna, one of the Sleepy Lagoon zoot-suiters sentenced to life (but freed on appeal two years later), El Pachuco becomes Henry's worst enemy and best friend, for the *macho* attitudes he represents and the advice he gives are both imprisoning and inspiring, keeping him back and thrusting him forward. One of the few significant musicals of the period (only Bob Fosse's *All That Jazz*, 1979, and Herbert Ross's *Pennies*

Fig. 17-17
Zoot Suit: *Alice (Tyne Daly, left) offers her help to Henry Reyna (Daniel Valdez, center) and his co-defendants (in the background: Mike Gomez, left, and Kelly Ward). At the far right, in a skeptical mood, El Pachuco (Edward James Olmos).*

From Heaven, 1981, approach it), the most important Chicano film of the 1980s, and one of the most brilliantly conceived conjunctions of theatre and cinema in film history, *Zoot Suit* was given a very limited theatrical release. Few people were lucky enough to see it on the big screen in 1981; ten years later it still had not been re-released (though it did finally appear on video late in 1991). Valdez's next movie, *La Bamba* (1987), was a more conventional approach to the mythic theme of Chicano heroism, a biography of rock star Ritchie Valens that was made in simultaneously released Spanish and English versions.

Both racial and sexual politics are explored in the understated, elliptical films of Wayne Wang (*Chan Is Missing*, 1982; *Dim Sum: a little bit of heart*, 1984; *Eat a Bowl of Tea*, 1989; *Life is Cheap—But Toilet Paper is Expensive*, 1990) and the sensitive, powerful dramas of Robert

M. Young (*Alambrista!*, 1977, released 1978; *Short Eyes*, 1977; *The Ballad of Gregorio Cortez*, 1982; *Extremities*, 1986; *Dominick and Eugene*, 1988—and, as cinematographer and co-director, Michael Roemer's *Nothing But a Man*, 1964). These honest and unassuming film-makers are vitally interested in people (as Kubrick, to take an obvious example, is not) and explore characters, and their relationships and options, with great and delicate skill. In their different ways, they are the most humanistic of the new independent directors.

Feminist politics significantly affected American film theory as well as the makers of avant-garde and short narrative films in this period, but the feature-length narrative films, including those made by women, rarely were programmatically feminist. Mainstream cinema responded to the feminist movement of the 1960s and 1970s by creating more roles for strong women (or superficially revising the old roles) and putting sexism in the same "sensitive" category as racism—not to be treated in an offensive manner. But that was a far cry from exploring a gynocentric cinema, as women directors in Germany and France—and in the American avant-garde—were doing. Feminism was a subtext and a secondary concern in the American features directed by women, the majority of whom were fighting their way into the studio system with films that would entertain mainstream audiences—which is certainly one route to power in Hollywood, and often the only way to get a chance to direct *again*. Among the most interesting and accomplished of the women directors to have come to prominence since the mid-1970s are Radha Bharadwaj (*Closet Land*, 1990), Kathryn Bigelow (*Near Dark*, 1987; *Blue Steel*, 1990), Lizzie Borden (*Born In Flames*, 1983; *Working Girls*, 1986, wide release 1987; *Love Crimes*, 1991), Martha Coolidge (*Not a Pretty Picture*, 1975; *Valley Girl*, 1983; *City Girl*, 1984; *Real Genius*, 1985; *Rambling Rose*, 1991), Lisa Gottlieb (*Just One of the Guys*, 1985), Amy Heckerling (*Fast Times at Ridgemont High*, 1982; *Look Who's Talking*, 1989), Barbara Kopple (*Harlan County, U.S.A.*, 1976; *Keeping On*, 1981), Mary Lambert (*Siesta*, 1987), Penny Marshall (*Big*, 1988; *Awakenings*, 1990), Yvonne Rainer (*Film about a woman who . . .*, 1974; *Kristina Talking Pictures*, 1976; *The Man Who Envied Women*, 1985), Susan Seidelman (*Smithereens*, 1982; *Desperately Seeking Susan*, 1985; *Cookie*, 1989), Joan Micklin Silver (*Hester Street*, 1974; *Between the Lines*, 1977; *On the Yard*, 1978; *Head Over Heels*, 1979; *Crossing Delancey*, 1988), and Claudia Weill (*Girlfriends*, 1978; *It's My Turn*, 1980).

Comparable male directors who came to prominence at the same time, whose dramatic features were well crafted, carefully thought out, and well received, include John Badham (*Saturday Night Fever*, 1977; *Dracula*, 1979; *WarGames*, 1983), Carroll Ballard (*The Black Stallion*, 1979; *Never Cry Wolf*, 1983), Warren Beatty (*Heaven Can Wait*, 1978, co-directed by Buck Henry; *Reds*, 1981; *Dick Tracy*, 1990), animator Don Bluth (*The Secret of NIMH*, 1982; *An American Tail*, 1986), Charles Burnett (*Killer of Sheep*, 1977; *My Brother's Wedding*,

1984; *To Sleep With Anger*, 1990) James Cameron (*The Terminator*, 1984; *Aliens*, 1986; *The Abyss*, 1989; *Terminator 2: Judgment Day*, 1991), James Foley (*After Dark, My Sweet*, 1990), Walter Hill (*The Warriors*, 1979; *The Long Riders*, 1980; *48 HRS.*, 1982), Ron Howard (*Splash*, 1984; *Cocoon*, 1985; *Parenthood*, 1989), Jonathan Kaplan (*White Line Fever*, 1975; *Over the Edge*, 1979; *The Accused*, 1988), Lawrence Kasdan (*Body Heat*, 1981; *The Big Chill*, 1983), Philip Kaufman (*The White Dawn*, 1974; the remake of *Invasion of the Body Snatchers*, 1978; *The Wanderers*, 1979; *The Right Stuff*, 1983; *The Unbearable Lightness of Being*, 1988; *Henry and June*, 1990, the first film to be rated NC-17), John Landis (*Schlock*, 1971; *National Lampoon's Animal House*, 1978; *The Blues Brothers*, 1980; *An American Werewolf in London*, 1981; *Trading Places*, 1983), Barry Levinson (*Diner*, 1982), David Mamet (*House of Games*, 1987; *Things Change*, 1988), John McNaughton (*Henry: Portrait of a Serial Killer*, 1986, wide release 1990), Robert Redford (*Ordinary People*, 1980; *The Milagro Beanfield War*, 1988), Alan Rudolph (*Remember My Name*, 1978; *Choose Me*, 1984), Richard Rush (*The Stunt Man*, 1978, released 1980), Jerry Schatzberg (*The Panic in Needle Park*, 1971; *Street Smart*, 1987), and Joel Schumacher (*The Incredible Shrinking Woman*, 1981; *The Lost Boys*, 1987; *Flatliners*, 1990).

Four British directors joined the American film industry in the 1980s, making pictures that were either rich and hotly debated (Ridley Scott, Alan Parker) or apparently simple and uncritically enjoyed (Tony Scott, Adrian Lyne). The courses of their careers were determined not only by their considerable visual talents but also by what their respective audiences demanded, and so they become particularly interesting as a guide to the Reagan era itself. When Tony Scott and Adrian Lyne uncharacteristically made intricate, resonant, risk-taking films that departed from conservative mythic formulas, required some thought, and included unpleasant material, audiences stayed away; such was the fate of Tony Scott's *The Hunger* (1983, starring David Bowie and Catherine Deneuve as vampires) and Lyne's *Jacob's Ladder* (1990, a montage of memories, visions, and alternate realities in the mind of a soldier killed in battle). And when Ridley Scott made empty thrillers (*Black Rain*, 1989) or Alan Parker carelessly and offensively rewrote history (*Mississippi Burning*, 1988), *they* lost fans in droves. Even though Ridley and Tony Scott are brothers, the audiences for Tony's *Top Gun* (1986) and Ridley's *Blade Runner* (1982) were distinct camps: the former, much larger and more self-centered, looking to be blatantly entertained and subtly reassured; the latter preferring artistically ambitious films that tackled significant matters in complex, revealing, *and* entertaining ways.

All four directors had made commercials in Britain before turning to features; Tony Scott's fast-moving, seamlessly edited commercials were extremely influential in America, as were those of Adrian Lyne. Lyne's first major hit, *Flashdance* (1983), was the standard-bearer for the Reagan era, a movie that seductively preached that anyone who worked and dreamed hard enough could have everything she wanted. With its music-video colors and rhythms, likable heroine (Jennifer Beals), and denial of political and socioeconomic realities, *Flashdance* encouraged its audience to be uncritical. Like all Lyne's films, *Flashdance* worked hard on its sex scenes, trying to make them unconventional and exciting, while it took potshots at feminism. A Lyne woman doesn't need any sociopolitical movement, she just needs to be Cinderella (*Flashdance*), explore her sexuality (*9½ Weeks*, 1986), and be a good shot in case she needs to defend her family against another woman (*Fatal Attraction*, 1987); beyond that, considering how much water Lyne dumps on his heroines, leans them against, or seats them in, she needs a towel. *Fatal Attraction* was as popular with adults as *Flashdance* was with teenage girls; it argued that committing adultery was the same as allowing a killer into the family (perhaps a reaction to the spread of AIDS) and that a single woman who looked autonomous and professional could secretly be crazy and demanding. Tony Scott's big films (*Top Gun*; *Days of Thunder*, 1990) also had the look and pace of feature-length music videos and a feelgood reliance on formula, but they were not quite as programmatically anti-feminist as Lyne's; nevertheless, they reinforced conventional sex

roles and demonstrated by their good box office that the mainstream audiences of the period were happy with clichés.

Alan Parker's often violent and menacing films showed the dark side of dreams: a vacation that lands its drug-smuggling hero in a Turkish prison (*Midnight Express*, 1978), the real-world problems with which aspiring artists may have to deal—for example, an "audition" that ends in sexual humiliation (*Fame*, 1980), the nightmare of crazy divorce at the end of a marriage (*Shoot the Moon*, 1982), the madness that engulfs a successful rock star and reflects the oppressive horrors of the world (*Pink Floyd —The Wall*, 1982, a British production; script and music by Roger Waters), a murder case whose successful solution destroys the detective (*Angel Heart*, 1987). Occasionally Parker let a happy dream appear to prevail (*Birdy*, 1984) or freed a character from a trap (*Midnight Express*), but the movies were more memorable when the overpowering dream was a kind of doom with its own implacable reality (*The Wall*, *Angel Heart*).

Ridley Scott's first picture, *The Duellists* (1977, British), was based on a story by Joseph Conrad; like all of his films, it was superbly designed and shot in Panavision and color. The ore-laden ship in his next film, *Alien*, was named the "Nostromo" in reference to Conrad's *Nostromo* (part of whose plot concerns the corrupting effect of a hoard of silver), an allusion that identified the militaristic and greedy owners of the ship as the primary villains. A nonsexist, nonracist, worker's perspective made itself felt in that film, and the ruthless gulf between masters and slaves—and between cops and "little people"—dominated the society portrayed in his next picture, *Blade Runner*, which was based loosely on a dystopic novel by Philip K. Dick. His next films (*Legend*, 1985; *Someone to Watch Over Me*, 1987; *Black Rain*) set leftist politics and ethically complex literature aside, but they were as brilliantly composed and moodily lit as their predecessors; *Thelma & Louise* (1991) struck that perfect balance of genre (the road movie), politics (sexual), and look (engrossing) that characterizes all his best films, whatever the politics or the genre. A master of *mise-en-scène*, Scott has worked with some of the best cinematographers,

Fig. 17-18
Alien*: A search party from the "Nostromo" finds the remains of a nonhuman pilot, the "space jockey" who radioed a warning. Production design, Michael Seymour; Director of Photography, Derek Vanlint; Costume Design, John Mollo; "Alien" Design, H. R. Giger; Art Directors, Les Dilley, Roger Christian; Set Decorator, Ian Whittaker; Concept Artists, Ron Cobb, Jean Giraud, Chris Foss; Visual Design Consultant, Dan O'Bannon.*

production designers, art directors, concept artists, and special effects wizards in the business. The look of *Blade Runner*—a *noir* set in the Los Angeles of 2019, some of whose scenes were shot in The Bradbury, a downtown building featured in many of the original *noirs*—with its towering buildings, endless rain, inescapable ads, richly dark color scheme, low-key lighting, and stunning special effects, survives in the release version. Unfortunately, the producers found the director's cut of *Blade Runner* too negative and confusing for their taste (it also angered preview audiences, who apparently expected another *Raiders*), so they added a voice-over narration that simplistically explained the story, then gave the film an astoundingly bad ending: a sequence that shows the lovers driving in a clean, sunny landscape (up to this point, a blue sky has been seen in

only one shot—when the soul-like bird of a dead Replicant flies heavenward), accompanied by a voice-over that, like the sunny pictures, takes off all the pressure by announcing that the heroine (a robot, or Replicant, with a built-in four-year life span) just happens to have been constructed without a termination date. This self-destruct feature is what motivates most of the *Frankenstein*-like plot, in which the virtually human beings, artificially created and born full-grown, seek out their creator (Tyrell, played by Joe Turkel) to demand that he use his skills to extend their lives; the lead Replicant (Roy, played by Rutger Hauer) even quotes Blake, as Frankenstein's creation quotes Milton, and it is through Roy and his slave revolt that the film—again like Mary Shelley's *Frankenstein*—raises the issues of the moral responsibilities of creators, the tunnel vision of

The Breakfast Club: *from left, the Princess (Molly Ringwald), the Brain (Anthony Michael Hall), the Athlete (Emilio Estevez), the Basket Case (Ally Sheedy), and the Criminal (Judd Nelson).*

Fig. 17-19

those who concentrate obsessively on doing a job, the nature of humanity, however created, and the suffering and anger of rejected children, along with themes Shelley did not address, such as the injustice of the class system and the ruthless politics of big capitalism. The rest of the plot concerns the efforts of Deckard (Harrison Ford), a "blade runner"—an assassin who works for the police—to locate and kill the rebellious Replicants. To watch *Blade Runner* in something like its original glory, ignore the entire voice-over track, pretend that you have been given a few extra hints that Deckard might be a Replicant himself, and leave the theatre right after the shot in which the lovers, Deckard and Rachael (Sean Young), leave Tyrell's office and the elevator door closes.

Some of the period's comedies broke away from standard sex-role constructs, satirized contemporary society, or knowingly portrayed the traumas of growing up. Many of the latter were "teenpix," made for a target audience of adolescents. Among the more insightful teenpix were those written and directed by John Hughes, whose *The Breakfast Club* (1985) spent a day in detention with five adolescents as they raised and lowered their social and personal shields until they came to understand each other and themselves—a high-school version of *The Iceman Cometh*, but with a psychologi-

cally convincing and emotionally satisfying happy ending. Although some of his comedies were silly without being funny, and some were entertaining without touching the nerve of self-recognition, one of them—*Home Alone* (1990), directed by Chris Columbus, written and produced by Hughes—became the highest grossing comedy ever made; as of April, 1991, with $270 million in domestic receipts (U.S. ticket sales), it was third on the list of all-time domestic box-office champs, only $52 million behind *Star Wars* and $130 million behind *E.T.*

Paul Brickman's *Risky Business* (1983) was a commercially successful and surprisingly ironic satire of capitalism, in which the perfect model for capitalistic individualism and enterprise turns out to be converting an upper-middle-class suburban home into a house of prostitution. Although Altman's *McCabe and Mrs. Miller* and many of Godard's films had suggested a similar metaphor long before, the capitalist entrepreneur of *Risky Business* was no outsider like the sleazy McCabe, but a fresh, attractive, all-American lad (played by Tom Cruise) who comes of age, both financially and erotically, by selling sexual merchandise—thanks to the help of a fresh, attractive, all-American prostitute (played by Rebecca De Mornay). As a result of this risky enterprise, the hero's entire American Dream comes true —fame, fortune (though temporary), sexual ecstasy (also temporary), and admission to Princeton. It is significant, and typical of the period, that preview audiences preferred this ending to the one originally planned and shot, in which the hero does not get into Princeton. As said before, it was a time for winners. Unlike the Barrows, McCabes, and Gitteses of a decade earlier, the enterprising young people in *Flashdance, An Officer and a Gentleman, Footloose, Beverly Hills Cop*, and so on, all slay the social dragons that confront them, usually by doing things their own way.

While most of the comedies were strictly boy-meets-girl, a few explored the complexities of sexual identity. Reversals of sexual roles and clothes are common motifs of films such as *Victor/Victoria* (Blake Edwards, 1982), *Tootsie* (Sydney Pollack, 1982), and *All of Me* (Carl Reiner, 1984), which consciously descend from screwball comedy. For example, *Victor/Victoria*, set in the Paris of Lubitsch (a Hollywood soundstage calling itself Paris), refers explicitly to the Lubitsch "touch" of suppressing visual information from the frame. The year of the film's action, 1934, is—not coincidentally—the very one in which Hollywood officially enforced its Production Code. *Victor/Victoria* seems a conscious return to the explicit sexual matters that the pre-Code Lubitsch had treated so deftly but that the Code expressly restricted.

Screwball comedy has always been interested in role reversals and gender definitions: Cary Grant wears a dress in several screwball comedies, while the genre's smart and strong women (Katharine Hepburn, Rosalind Russell, Carole Lombard, Barbara Stanwyck) are the equals and even the competitive rivals of their male partners. The philosopher Stanley Cavell has argued that in these screwball "comedies of equality," the modern American professional woman—strong, smart, independent, and assured—made her first film appearance. The underlying question of so many screwball comedies—from *His Girl Friday* to *Adam's Rib* to *Some Like It Hot*—was what mental or spiritual consequences derive from the biological differences between men and women. Although they never suggested a clear answer, they always suggested that the smart woman

was an oddity and exception, different from the culture's anticipated norm.

This traditional comic issue (which can be traced at least as far back as Shakespeare's transvestite comedies, like *Twelfth Night* and *As You Like It*) receives new energy and irony in an era when the norms of gender difference and definition are themselves matters for open cultural debate. Both women's and gay liberation movements have forced reflection about what typical maleness and femaleness mean. Feminist concerns—freedom of choice, the ERA, equal pay for equal work—raise questions about the ways our society has traditionally divided male and female activity as well as the sexist assumptions underlying that division. Gay and lesbian activists similarly question why the gender of sexual preference should in any way influence judgment about the ability or productivity of human beings. Out of this cultural concern with the natures of femininity and masculinity came the transvestive comedies of the early 1980s.

Blake Edwards has long been a clever comic chronicler of American sexual mores—from *Breakfast at Tiffany's* (1961) to *10* (1979). The cabaret singer of *Victor/Victoria* (played by Edwards's wife, Julie Andrews) appears to be a gay man—high singing voice, slight build, effeminate gestures, and companion to a notorious Parisian homosexual. Ironically, the gay characters in the film are those who do not *appear* gay at all—the beefy behemoth bodyguard, Bernstein (played by ex-footballer Alex Karras—who doesn't look like anyone named Bernstein either), and the hefty man who becomes his lover, Victoria's vocal coach, Toddy (played by Robert Preston). The film also makes a sly allusion to *My Fair Lady*, another musical about vocal coaching and social masquerade—and a film role denied Julie Andrews, considered not pretty enough by the sexist Hollywood standards of 1964. Edwards brings the film's audience, like its gangster protagonist, King (the aptly titled gangster played by James Garner—and what American archetype is more typically "masculine" than the gangster?), from sexist confidence to a more questioning confusion: How valid are definitions of sexual attraction and gender identity based solely on appearances?

Fig. 17-20
Deceptive surfaces in Victor/Victoria: *four "guys" out on the town (from left, Robert Preston, Julie Andrews, James Garner, and Alex Karras).*

The female soap-opera star of *Tootsie* (played by Dustin Hoffman) also learns about the power of appearances and their ability to deceive. Disguised as a woman, Dorothy Michaels, the temperamental male actor, Michael, suffers the same indignities that women might endure daily from their male bosses, co-workers, and dates. The soap-opera nurse he embodies becomes a strong and independent spokesperson for the rights and respect of women, while, at the same time, the male actor inside Dorothy discovers his own sexist presumptions.

All of Me forces Lily Tomlin (Edwina) and Steve Martin (Roger) to share Martin's body. Martin acts the roles of both Edwina and Roger — not androgynously, but as separate male and female personalities in a male body; the audience sees Edwina when Roger does: when he looks in a mirror. They fight, and learn from each other, and learn to love each other. Eventually the soul of a conventionally attractive *femme fatale* (Terry, played by Victoria Ten-

nant) ends up in the body of a horse, allowing Edwina's spirit to inhabit Terry's body and to explore another kind of intimacy with Roger — the kind that uses two bodies rather than one. But we and Roger have come to prefer Edwina to the "more attractive" woman, so when Roger and Edwina-in-Terry's-body begin to dance in the final scene, director Reiner rewards us by panning from Roger and Terry to a mirror that shows Roger and Edwina, so that we can celebrate the genuine romantic couple. Carl Reiner, who was Sid Caesar's straight man on 1950s television and a cohort of Mel Brooks, also directed — among many other works — *The Comic* (1969, a tragicomedy based partly on the life of Buster Keaton) and *Oh, God!* (1977, in which George Burns is convincing as God, a role never previously filmed with any success). His son, Rob Reiner, began as an actor on the TV show *All in the Family*, then went into directing with *This Is Spinal Tap* (1984), a parody of a rock documentary; that and *When Harry Met Sally . . .* (1989) may be his funniest comedies, and they share with his two best dramas (*Stand By Me*, 1986, and *Misery*, 1990 — both adapted from works by Stephen King) and his tale of romantic adventure, *The Princess Bride* (1987), an unfailingly precise ability to strike the right note at the right time, be it sad or uproarious, frightening or wistful. In both the Reiners' films, from *All of Me* to *Stand By Me*, interpersonal relationships are deeply explored, and what results is a moving understanding of the ways people bond together, the comedy and the drama of acceptance.

If Roger Corman can be credited with discovering and apprenticing Bogdanovich, Coppola, Dante, Demme, Sayles, and Scorsese — to name just a few — Spielberg's greatest discoveries to date are Frank Marshall (*Arachnophobia*, 1990, an extremely clever horror comedy) and Robert Zemeckis (*I Wanna Hold Your Hand*, 1978; *Used Cars*, 1980; *Romancing the Stone*, 1984; *Back to the Future*, 1985; *Who Framed Roger Rabbit*, 1988; *Back to the Future Part II*, 1989; *Back to the Future Part III*, 1990). Zemeckis's nonstop comedies are intricately plotted and intelligently conceived, full of zingy jokes and impressive, dramatically and aesthetically relevant special effects. Both as a single film and as a trilogy, *Back to the Future* is one of the most complicated treatments of time travel ever attempted on film, and certainly the funniest. *Romancing the Stone* pits fantasy against reality as deftly as *Back to the Future Part II* juxtaposes versions of the same character from different temporal continuums and *Who Framed Roger Rabbit* puts live actors and cartoon figures ("toons") in the same shots. Co-produced by Spielberg's Amblin Entertainment and Disney's Touchstone Pictures, shot in London at Cannon Elstree Studios, with special visual effects by Lucas's Industrial Light & Magic, and putting together on screen for the first time the stars of both Disney and Warner Bros. cartoons — not to mention MGM and Fleischer cartoons — *Roger Rabbit* called on an extraordinary spectrum of major talents to create the most technically advanced and visually seamless cartoon-with-people ever made. *Roger Rabbit*'s reflexive conceits range from the wild notion that cartoons are *acted* in real time (so that when a refrigerator falls on Roger's

head and he sees tweeting birds instead of stars, he is accused of blowing his lines) to an ending that is inseparably Warner Bros. and Disney (after Porky says "That's all, folks," Tinker Bell closes the film as if it were an episode of *Disneyland*). This is a world in which Daffy Duck and Donald Duck perform together on stage, with Daffy accusing Donald of having a speech impediment; in which Betty Boop *is* in black-and-white, as her films were, and has had trouble getting work in color cartoons — and Roger's wife can say "I'm not bad, I'm just drawn that way"; and whose detective story looks like and uses major plot elements from both *The Maltese Falcon* and *Chinatown*. The 1940s Los Angeles of this film still has its streetcars and a convenient, reliable system of public transportation ("Who needs a car in L.A.?"). The villain — like the villain of *Chinatown*, who wants to control the city's expansion and the region's water — has a vision of shopping centers and gas stations, freeways and air pollution, and wants to begin creating that Los Angeles on the site of Toontown. The villain is destroyed, the mystery is solved, Toontown and the streetcars are saved, and Roger and his wife are reunited — but anyone familiar with today's Los Angeles must find this happy ending a bit wistful, since the streetcars are gone, freeways and pollution are everywhere, and no Toontown can be found on the maps. Alternate realities are indeed central to the comedies of Robert Zemeckis.

The boldly designed films of Tim Burton, who once worked as an animator at Disney, turn to bright and dark subjects with equal zest. His lightest and brightest was *Pee-wee's Big Adventure* (1985), in which the childlike Pee-wee Herman (Paul Reubens) sets off in search of his stolen bicycle; his darkest was the blockbuster *Batman* (1989), whose look and mood were inspired not by the early Batman comics but by the later Batman graphic novels, from Frank Miller's *The Dark Knight Returns* to Alan Moore's *The Killing Joke*. If both those films have elements that make them seem cartoons brought to life, Burton's other films — *Beetlejuice*, 1988, and *Edward Scissorhands*, 1990 — are horror fantasies revived as divine comedy. *Beetlejuice* takes an original look at the exasperations of the afterlife. *Edward*

Fig. 17-21
Who Framed Roger Rabbit: *Detective Eddie Valiant (Bob Hoskins) finds himself in the same frame — and desk — as Roger.*

Scissorhands, a fable about why it snows, stars Johnny Depp in a brilliant re-imagining of both the novel and the 1931 movie *Frankenstein*. A film with heart and wit, *Edward Scissorhands* is set in a bland modern suburb that happens to adjoin a gothic castle inhabited by an old inventor (Vincent Price) and his creation, Edward (Depp). The inventor, as much a lonely, loving Gepetto as a Dr. Frankenstein, dies before he can give Edward normal hands; instead Edward's fingers are shears and blades — the tools of his art (sculpting) and the fate that separates him from others, whom he cannot readily embrace without cutting. In the end, when this sensitive artist has been exiled to the castle by a Tupperware torch party, Edward uses the scissors — his mark of Cain and the sign of his origin — to express his love in art, shaving ice sculptures to make the snow that falls on his beloved.

The definitive late-1980s comedy of manners was independent Steven Soderbergh's first feature, *sex, lies, and videotape* (1989). This film did for the video generation what *Carnal Knowledge* and *Trouble in Paradise* had done for their generations — addressed the present terms of intimacy. It has four major characters: John (Peter Gallagher), a lawyer; Ann (Andie MacDowell), his wife; Cynthia (Laura San Giacomo), her sister; and Graham (James Spader), John's old friend. John and Cynthia are having an affair (sex and lies). Graham (videotape) moves to town, offering Cynthia and especially Ann the unusual opportunity to talk with a completely honest man. For years, Graham has been conducting an experiment in self-control that is also an investigation of honesty and sexuality; he has been doing this in order to prove to an old flame and to himself that he is no longer a compulsive liar, that he can control

Momentarily turning the tables, Ann (Andie MacDowell) takes charge of the camera in sex, lies, and videotape.

Fig. 17-22

his sexual urges, and that he can express all his feelings verbally—because he used to act out his feelings nonverbally, including sexually, in a way that used to scare people. He makes videotapes of women, for his eyes only, asking them questions about sex and allowing them to relax and reveal themselves entirely, "for the camera"—which is the mediator of intimacy here. A paradoxical privacy, perhaps comparable to that of the confessional, is created for each woman by the presence of the camera and Graham, two silent listeners and observers. Graham, who says he is impotent except when he is alone (and watching the tapes), is the celibate in the confessional and the eunuch in the harem, and he asks better questions than the psychiatrist Ann is seeing. After Cynthia makes a tape, she breaks up with John. Ann makes a tape after discovering evidence of the affair; she breaks up with John too. John beats Graham up, tosses him out of his own place, and watches Ann's tape. It is through watching an electronic recording—not through any previous intercourse of any kind—that John learns Ann's true feelings about sex as well as the fact that she has never had an orgasm. In revenge, John reveals to Graham that the old flame he's been trying to make himself perfect for was not so perfect herself; she had even cheated on Graham with John—and lied

about it. In a disillusioned rage, Graham destroys all his tapes and video equipment—and finds he is free to begin his life again, however vulnerable he will be without a screen. At the end, he and Ann set out together on the uncharted road to unmediated intimacy.

A tremendous number of horror movies were released in the late 1970s and 1980s, the majority low-budget slasher films in which victims were picked off by mortal or immortal psychopaths. The immediate paradigms for this subgenre were Carpenter's *Halloween*, Cunningham's *Friday the 13th*, and Steve Miner's *Friday the 13th Part 2* (1981); models within the past two decades included *Peeping Tom*, *Psycho*, *Blood Feast*, *The Texas Chain Saw Massacre*, and *Black Christmas* (Bob Clark, 1975, Canada). More significant than the slasher clones, major horror pictures continued to appear from George Romero, David Cronenberg, Tobe Hooper, Larry Cohen, and Brian De Palma, who were joined in the late 1970s by Wes Craven, John Carpenter, Joe Dante, and many others. Among the most interesting English-language horror films to have appeared since 1977, aside from works by those just named, are *Alien*, *The Driller Killer* (Abel Ferrara, 1979), *Terror Train* (Roger Spottiswoode, 1980), *Motel Hell* (Kevin Connor, 1980), *Dead & Buried* (Gary Sherman,

1981), *Wolfen* (Michael Wadleigh, 1981), *Basket Case* (Frank Henenlotter, 1982), *The Sender* (Roger Christian, 1982), *The Evil Dead* (Sam Raimi, 1983), *The Return of the Living Dead* (Dan O'Bannon, 1985), *Re-Animator* (Stuart Gordon, 1985), *Aliens, Henry: Portrait of a Serial Killer, A Nightmare on Elm Street 3—Dream Warriors* (Chuck Russell, 1987), *Hellraiser* (Clive Barker, 1987), and *Pumpkinhead* (Stan Winston, 1988). The "gore boom" that lasted from the 1970s to the mid-1980s was dampened by CARA, which began to make it much more difficult for violent horror films to get an R rating; in the late 1980s, producers afraid of the X—like those of the *Friday the 13th* series —left in the sex scenes but drastically trimmed the kill scenes. Romero and Hooper released some of their films unrated (Hooper's 1986 *The Texas Chainsaw Massacre 2* and Romero's *Day of the Dead*, following in the steps of *Dawn*), which translated into a self-imposed X, smaller audiences, and artistic integrity.

Hollywood Boulevard (1976), directed by Joe Dante and Allan Arkush, is a fine example of the comedies Roger Corman produced, full of outrageous gags and film jokes (beginning with the title, an allusion to Wilder's *Sunset Boulevard*) and clearly made fast and on the cheap. Arkush went on to direct another Corman comedy, *Rock'n'Roll High School* (1979). Dante's next picture for Corman was *Piranha*, a parody of *Jaws* (and at least ten other movies) and a violent nibble at the military, the Vietnam War, Bob Hope, and capitalist priorities; *Piranha* and the first film Dante made without Corman, *The Howling*—a tragicomic and satiric tale of werewolves, the media, and psychological fads—were co-written by John Sayles. All of Dante's films are crammed with references to other films; for instance, after the tail credits of *The Howling*, Dante sends the audience on its way by cutting in part of a scene from the classic *The Wolf Man*, in which the old gypsy (Maria Ouspenskaya) tells Lon Chaney, Jr., "Go now, and heaven help you!" Horror, reflexivity, and comedy are the mainstays of his movies, and they reinforce each other perfectly in *Gremlins* (1984), the first of Dante's films produced by Spielberg.

Wes Craven's first film was the utterly shocking, ruthlessly violent *The Last House On The Left* (1972, produced by Sean Cunningham), a remake of Ingmar Bergman's *The Virgin Spring*. The rape and murders—and water symbolism—of Bergman's film are all in *Last House*, but stripped of Bergman's civility; updating the story to the bourgeois American present, Craven realistically shows the cruelty and horror that are possible in the world. Most people consider this film terminally sick, but it is a crucial example of the reality-oriented horror film and a key to the most important of Craven's later films (it has at least one knockout dream sequence, anticipating *A Nightmare on Elm Street*, and it pits two families against each other—one civilized, the other wild— anticipating *The Hills Have Eyes*, 1977). Like it or not, *Last House* is as significant in the historical development of the genre as *Night of the Living Dead* and *The Texas Chain Saw Massacre*. The film that made Craven famous was *The Hills Have Eyes* (the Museum of Modern Art created a scandal by showing it, implying that cruel, violent horror films could be art); it is both aggressively stylish and relentlessly painful, a movie with no time for clichés and formulas. When Craven turned to the slasher film in *A Nightmare on Elm Street* (he had little or nothing to do with the sequels), he sliced the formula to fit his own purposes. The slasher is not silent but talkative and witty, teenagers are not killed for having sex (though they are killed), and the means of attack—from within the victim's dreaming consciousness—is approached as a *cinematic* problem: how to interweave reality and dream in such a way that the audience, like the dreamer, believes a dream to be real until the moment of waking. Some of the dreams looked realistic, which added to the surprise when Craven cut to reality or veered into nightmare, and the others were expressionistic from the start, offering a *mise-en-scène* (designed by Greg Fonseca) the likes of which had not been seen since the cannibal family's house in *The Texas Chain Saw Massacre* (designed by Robert A. Burns). *Elm Street* also judged the police, and the current generation of parents, harshly—not just because they are self-important, out of it, and unwilling to listen to their kids, like the older generation in *The Blob* and *Rebel Without a Cause*, but also because it is the parents' sins that slasher Freddy

(Robert Englund) is out to avenge by killing their children. (This theme was carried forward in the first episode of the TV series *Freddy's Nightmares*; the episode was directed by Tobe Hooper.) Within the history of the horror film, *A Nightmare on Elm Street* deserves comparison with Dreyer's *Vampyr*, whose cinematic world is upsetting and equivocally real in an analogous way. *Shocker* (1990) tackled the dangerous dreamworld of television—offering a slasher capable of riding an electronic current or a broadcast into the home—while continuing Craven's investigation of the contemporary family. One chase from channel to channel deliberately alluded to the montage of landscapes in *Sherlock Jr.*

Halloween was not John Carpenter's first film; that was *Dark Star* (1974), many of whose design and plot elements collaborator Dan O'Bannon reworked in his script for *Alien*. Carpenter proved himself as an action director with the tightly paced *Assault on Precinct 13* (1976), then became famous with *Halloween*. (He was a distant observer on the first two sequels, then completely lost interest.) Carpenter usually writes or co-writes the music for his films—and often writes their screenplays, using his own name or various pseudonyms. *The Fog* (1980) attempted to capture the mood of a gory ghost story told around a campfire. *Escape From New York* (1981) combined science fiction with the action film and was remarkable not only for its futuristic but contemporary vision of Manhattan (as a prison island), but also for the vivid use it made of punk costumes and hairstyles. *The Thing* (1982), his best film since *Halloween* and until *Prince of Darkness* (1987), was a remake of the 1951 film produced by Hawks, directed by Christian Nyby, and homaged in *Halloween* as it plays on the late show: *The Thing From Another World*. It is one of the very few remakes in this period that compares favorably with its original. Using the full resources of Panavision, color, and stereo, *The Thing* returns to the original story, John W. Campbell, Jr.'s "Who Goes There?," presenting not a single, easily identified adversary but a shape-shifter that can take on the form of any living being; thus anyone might be the enemy—an idea utterly foreign to Hawks, who preferred to show

a group of isolated humans fighting a known enemy and growing closer as each person's character and the bonds between people are tested. Carpenter lets the group disintegrate until only a black man and a white man are left, establishing a tentative truce on the verge of death. Interracial cooperation and multiculturalism are important themes in most of Carpenter's films, from *Assault on Precinct 13* to *Prince of Darkness* and *They Live* (1988). In *Prince of Darkness*, an interracial team of professors and graduate students work together to prevent the triumph of Satan; it is characteristic of Carpenter's dialogue that the scientific discussions are literate, carefully researched, and intriguingly credible. The ending, and the ending implied beyond that one, are frightening and moving with all the complexity of great horror, as we realize that love may be responsible for bringing about a spiritual and metaphysical catastrophe in the future.

They Live, Carpenter's most brilliantly conceived film—and in many respects the most political American film of the 1980s—is radical down to its very choice and use of aspect ratio: Panavision, with full-screen compositions and important visual information on the right and left sides of the screen, making it impossible (short of letterboxing) for the film to be shown intact on television, because in this film television is an important part of what's wrong with America. *They Live* was the first film to portray the hardships of blue-collar workers and others who lost their homes and jobs during the Reagan era, while big capitalism flourished—analogous in theme to *Heaven's Gate*, but set in 1988 Los Angeles. The nameless hero (Nada—Spanish for "nothing"—played by wrestler Roddy Piper) is a union worker, forced to seek work in Los Angeles after the banks folded in Denver (as the Savings and Loans did fold less than two years after the film's release); he makes friends with a black worker (Frank, played by Keith David) who was laid off when the steel mills closed in Detroit—though the factory owners escaped without financial harm—and had to leave his family there. (It is significant that the working-class heroes of *They Live* are not big stars.) They camp in a downtown, outdoor shelter for the homeless, an

Fig. 17-23
Aliens disguised as riot cops attack the rebels: a black-and-white shot from **They Live.**

environment utterly free of racism and sexism. A nearby mission is the center of a guerrilla rebellion; a blind street preacher (Raymond St. Jacques) urges passers-by to "wake up" and see that their "owners" and "masters" are all around them, enjoying wealth and social power while the lower classes struggle on in poverty. In the same tone, graffiti proclaim that "they live; we sleep." "They" are aliens from Andromeda—and the human collaborators they have recruited—who control all the big corporations, the government, the banks, and most of the media and the police. The Earth, which they are developing, exploiting, and polluting (so that our atmosphere will become like theirs), is "their Third World."

They Live argues that a revolution can be brought about by, and consists of, a new way of seeing—having the veil lifted and seeing things as they are. "Nada" finds that the rebels are passing out special dark glasses; wearing a pair, he sees the world as it is—but in black and white. He sees the ghastly aliens, who appear normal only because a conditioning signal (one that forces people to see things as if they were normal) is being sent all over the world—through TV sets, whether or not they are switched on. He also sees otherwise invisible surveillance equipment and the evidence of a massive conditioning effort: loudspeakers that repeatedly say "sleep, sleep"; paper money bearing the legend "This Is Your God"; magazines and billboards that read "Obey," "Watch TV," "Consume," "Submit," "Buy," "Stay Asleep," "Do Not Question Authority," and "Conform"; and, typically, a billboard with a sexy photo advertising a beach vacation, which turns out to read "Marry And Reproduce." A political speech "Nada" watches on TV, delivered by an alien, wryly echoes the rhetoric of genuine 1980s politicians: "It's a new morning in America—fresh, vital. The old cynicism is gone. We have faith in our leaders. We're optimistic as to what becomes of it all. It really boils down to our ability to *accept*. We don't need pessimism. There are no limits. We must look to the strength of our nation, our ideals, a *vision*. We don't want to just survive; we want to succeed." And vision is indeed what is at stake. After a violent, five-minute fight (many of Carpenter's films, such as the 1986 *Big Trouble in Little China*, include elaborate fight sequences, but this one goes on so long that we realize just how hard it is to get someone to try looking at things differently), "Nada" makes Frank put on the glasses, and from then on they work together against the aliens and the "human power elite." Most of the rebels are wiped out by police attacks, but "Nada" and Frank manage to infiltrate a banquet being held for the city's elite; then, at the cost of their lives, they locate and "Nada" destroys the instrument that is sending the conditioning signal, along with a cable TV station's programs, to a satellite where it is bounced around the world. The result is that people suddenly can see, in *color*, things as they are. On a television, an alien—standing in front of a sign that reads "No Independent Thought"—is saying, just as the veil is lifted, "All the sex and violence on the screen has gone too far for me. I'm fed up with it. Filmmakers like George Romero and John Carpenter have to show some restraint." The unrestrained ending that follows shows the uncompromised truth of the situation—as horror films, however metaphorically, very often do—and implies that now that people have been awakened, the aliens, together with their economic and ecological crimes, will quickly be vanquished. Both politically and reflexively, Carpenter argues, movies are a site of vision, while TV is a lulling realm of sleep, empty diversion, socioeconomic conditioning, and false reassurance. When *They Live* begins, the audience and the characters see a false vision that is in color and appears normal. With the glasses (later, contact lenses), we and the heroes see a black-and-white vision that is more truthful; for the next hour, we look at the color world and imagine the hidden black-and-white reality. At the end, we see a truthful vision in color. Our ability to see correctly, and film's to record

correctly, have been restored; the film has *redeemed vision*.

It's A Wonderful Deal

Throughout the late 1970s and 1980s, the American film industry appeared to be more interested in making deals than in making movies.

The reins of production passed into the hands of several kinds of executives: young business majors fresh out of college, former talent agents, corporate bigwigs, and producers of recent hits. Most of these new decision-makers were skilled at identifying projects that could turn into hit movies, but almost none of them had any visual training, on-the-set filmmaking experience, or grasp of film history (Chaplin, *Citizen Kane*, and *Casablanca* about covered it). They rarely thought about what would make a good *film*, not just a good story or a good business opportunity. And they were desperate for appealing, entertaining, sure-fire projects.

Most film ideas were approved for production on the basis of market research and guesswork rather than experience and confident instinct. New ideas were rare, and when they succeeded, they were repeated in sequels. No period in film history ever saw so many sequels. Nor so many remakes—attempts to discover the old magic in old ideas, updating what had worked before. *The Big Clock* (as *No Way Out*), *The Blob*, *Cape Fear*, *D.O.A.*, *The Fly*, *A Guy Named Joe* (as *Always*), *Here Comes Mr. Jordan* (as *Heaven Can Wait*), *Invasion of the Body Snatchers*, *A Kiss Before Dying*, *Out of the Past* (as *Against All Odds*), *The Postman Always Rings Twice*, and *Stella Dallas* (as *Stella*) were just a few of the films that were remade, sometimes with a lame change of title and rarely with success. Screenwriter and novelist William Goldman summed up the 1970s and 80s studio mentality with the motto "NOBODY KNOWS ANYTHING."

Today's studio executives listen as writers pitch stories, producers outline projects, and agents present packages; put a hundred projects into development when they know they will make only ten; and order changes in completed films in response to the reactions of preview audiences and other executives. Making a good picture has come to seem a matter of luck (which is to confuse a picture's box-office performance, which may involve luck, with its inherent merit), with the only defense an educated guess based on past performance — or, in unusually happy cases, inspired delight and conviction in the presence of a first-class new idea. The great goal is to reach the desired ("target" or targeted) audience and earn its repeat business, then to reach other age and population groups, and to see a picture with "legs" (the ability to grow in popularity on its own, without needing extra advertising, and to move from a few theatres to many) do so well that it becomes a blockbuster (a film that earns more than $100 million at the box office), which can be kept in release a long time, be profitably distributed overseas and profitably licensed to networks and video companies, become the basis of a sequel, and perhaps even be re-released. The "blockbuster mentality" characteristic of studios in this period consisted of (1) spending a lot of money in the hope of earning a lot of money, (2) with rare exceptions, making only those pictures likely to appeal to large audiences, and (3) planning to subsidize the studio's less expensive or less successful pictures with the income from one or two immense hits each year, which allowed them to take a chance on a few pictures that might have an inherently limited appeal.

For Hollywood executives, the new world began in 1975, when *Jaws* made oceans of money faster than any picture since *The Birth of a Nation*, catalyzing the blockbuster mentality and identifying teenagers and young adults as the movie audience to please. Fifteen years of teenpix came from this conception of the primary audience, but so did an unprecedented interest in and development of new sound technologies and special effects. *Star Wars* confirmed these priorities: special effects, young audiences, open endings leading to sequels, and impressive soundtracks. And *Rocky,* released between them, showed that a medium-budget movie could make zillions and that the public was looking for heroes. *Rocky II* (Sylvester Stallone, 1979) and *Rambo: First Blood Part II*

(George P. Cosmatos, 1985) provided what for many executives was the final revelation: that a sequel could earn more than the film on which it was based.

But not every studio executive was in Hollywood, or even in a studio. Beginning in the 1960s, many of the studios were taken over by bigger corporations, conglomerates whose executives saw filmmaking as part of their company's business rather than all of it, and strictly as a profit-making venture. (Imagine the difference it would have made if Mayer and Thalberg had had to answer to General Motors.) Universal-International was taken over by MCA (1962), Paramount by Gulf + Western (1966), United Artists by Transamerica (1967), Warner Bros. by Kinney (1969), and Columbia by Coca-Cola (1982) — and many of those went on to change hands. For example, investor Kirk Kerkorian gained control of MGM in 1969 and United Artists in 1981, forming the MGM/UA Entertainment Company; in 1985 Ted Turner, the owner of several major cable-TV stations, bought MGM and UA, but in 1986 he sold them back to Kerkorian, keeping the films. (In 1986, Turner also sold the MGM lot and laboratory to Lorimar.) Kerkorian sold MGM again in 1990 to Giancarlo Parretti of Pathe Communications (no relation to the legendary Pathé Frères). Parretti rang down the curtain on UA and formed MGM-Pathe, but he ran the studio for less than six months; in 1991 he was replaced as chairman and chief executive, and MGM-Pathe went on under new management. Like Turner's, Parretti's was a highly leveraged buyout. Little of the $1.3 billion Parretti paid Kerkorian for his 80 percent interest in MGM/UA was cash — the rest a transfer of paper assets, borrowed money, and anticipated revenues pledged by other companies for rights to the not-yet-owned films — and when it came to running the studio, the Italian financier had trouble paying the bills. In comparison, MCA's purchase of Universal for $11.25 million in 1959 (and in 1959 dollars) was a simple transaction, as was Matsushita's acquisition of MCA in 1990 for $6.59 billion.

Although the studios survived, they no longer had permanent staffs of skilled artists and artisans — no Script Department with its group of experienced writers, no pool of directors, no costumers who worked for the studio on film after film and both understood and helped to create the studio's style, and not even the costumes themselves. Studios emptied their warehouses of props and costumes, from "Rosebud" to the dresses worn in *Gone With the Wind*, which saved them storage costs but made them no longer the rich producing entities they once had been, cornucopias of props, costumes, sets, and equipment. Just one result of this housecleaning was that far fewer period pictures were made; most films were set in the present, using costumes and props that could be bought in ordinary stores or rented from a supply house. A more significant result was that filmmakers became freelancers; everyone was hired to work on a specific project—and without a project was out of work, hoping for a call.

There was no studio staffed like the old MGM, which had actors like Judy Garland, Mickey Rooney, Clark Gable, and Spencer Tracy on the payroll, available to work on anything, as it had writers like Jules Furthman and Frances Marion, designers and choreographers and costumers who knew how to make an MGM musical, acres of outdoor sets, and even its own film laboratory. The MGM lab, Metrocolor, was closed in the late 1980s. As of 1991, MGM itself had only a skeleton staff, housed in a few office buildings. The old MGM back lot was sold long ago (by Kerkorian) to real estate developers, and the rest of the lot, with its soundstages and office buildings, passed from the control of MGM/UA to Lorimar-Telepictures to Warner Bros. to Columbia, which itself was finally bought by Sony. Even a highly successful studio like Disney, which has never changed ownership, now hires "talent" on a film-by-film basis, only in rare cases going so far as to contract with an actor or director on an exclusive basis for a set number of pictures.

In the studio era, a Paramount picture was approved, made, and released by Paramount, whether or not it was shot on the Paramount lot. Today a Paramount picture is just as likely to have been made by an independent production company and "picked up" (as *Friday the 13th* was) by Paramount for release as "A Paramount Picture." In a "negative pick-up" deal, an independent producer sells the completed negative—the finished film—to a studio, thus recouping the costs of production and in most cases securing the rights to a portion of the film's earnings. But the deal may be made earlier, even before the film is shot, with the studio paying some or most of the cost of production; in this case the filmmakers get more of their money at the "front end" of the deal—that is, right away—and are entitled to less of the film's profits. Generally, those who spend their own money or defer their compensation, whether they be producers, studios, or actors, receive more money at the "back end" of the deal, after the film has been released. (The contracts involved in making a film are no longer comparable to those one might sign when buying a house—or a neighborhood; the average feature now calls for hundreds of contracts, even thousands.) All of the studios make pick-up deals—and there's no secret about it; it's made plain in credits like "MGM presents a GMT Production . . ." or when a studio logo (such as MGM's shot of the roaring lion) is followed by "Acme Films Presents." The important thing to realize here is that the studios themselves are not producing as many films as it appears, but are working in partnership with independents more than ever before.

Throughout this period, a number of studio heads and major producers were former talent agents who brought their clients along with them. But the talent agencies themselves are now at least as powerful as the studios. The sales of Columbia and Universal—whole studios—were arranged by talent agents. Michael Ovitz, the head of Creative Artists Agency—the most powerful in the business—not only acted as middleman between Matsushita and MCA in 1990, but in 1991 was instrumental in selecting the new chairman of Paramount Pictures. With virtually everyone now working on a contract basis—contracted to work on *a* film, with a profession but not a regular job—agents assemble prominent "elements" into a "package," which in business terms is the seed from which the movie grows: the basic idea (a script, an adaptable book, or sometimes just a title and a notion) and the key people who will make the film and attract the audience. This constitutes putting a picture together, constructing the picture-as-deal and deciding, as studio producers once did, which movies would be made by whom. Indeed, the major agent's list of clients, from whom the package of writer, director, and stars typically is selected, is today's version of the studio's "stable" of talent. If Mickey Rooney and Judy Garland regularly appeared together in pictures today, it would be because they had the same agent, not because they worked for the same studio.

The agent offers this package to the highest bidder or to a favored business associate. One agency whose clients included John le Carré, Tom Stoppard, Fred Schepisi, Sean Connery, and Michelle Pfeiffer constructed the following package: *The Russia House* (the literary property —a novel by John le Carré), to be scripted by Stoppard and directed by Schepisi and to star Connery and Pfeiffer. Pathe bought that package, produced that film with those people, and released it as one of the first MGM-Pathe pictures; Pathe had a great deal to do with how the movie was made, but at the initial creative level only approved rather than conceived it.

The cost of making films went up throughout the 1970s and 1980s, but it was not simply a matter of inflation when the average "negative cost" of a studio feature (the expenses involved in producing the negative, in other words the cost of making the movie) jumped from $11 million to over $20 million in the 1980s. The blockbuster mentality fed on itself. If a star's last picture had cost $10 million and earned $50 million, his or her fee on the next picture would be at least $1 million, probably $5 million, and possibly $15 million. If a picture was expected to do well—perhaps because it was the sequel to a hit—it appeared a safe investment, and more money was spent on it; thus *Die Hard 2* (1990) cost much more than *Die Hard*. Studios spent more in the hope of making more—not from a string of medium-budget pictures but from a single big gamble. But if one spends $70 million on a *Die Hard 2*, and if conventional practices dictate that a film must take in at least three times its negative cost at the box office in order to break even (to cover the costs of advertising, prints, distribution, and interest as well as the cost of production), that overburdened sequel would have to sell at least $210 million in tickets—megahit

status—before earning a penny. *Total Recall* (Paul Verhoeven, 1990) cost $65 million, made almost twice that at the box office, and was a financial disappointment—but *Batman* cost $53.5 million and grossed over $253 million, and that was just the domestic ticket sales.

Studios hedged these enormous bets by selling subsidiary rights to the picture even before it was shot: licenses to distribute the film theatrically in other countries, to show it on cable, to broadcast it on network TV, to reproduce and sell it on videocassettes and laserdiscs, to distribute it nontheatrically in 16mm, to sell a novel based on its plot, to consider it for a TV series, and even to make toys and clothes inspired by its characters and other trademarked items. These secondary revenues, especially the ones from video, could equal those taken in at the box office, and they had an effect on the way the film was shot: to play well in a theatre and acceptably on a TV set (in color, with more close-ups than long shots, and with crucial action confined to the "TV safe area," a rectangle the shape of a TV screen). Another commercial practice that had a marked effect on film content was "product placement," which amounted to selling advertising space within the movie. Sometimes the product would show up subtly— everyone in the movie just happened to drink Budweiser or drive a Ford or fly TWA—but it could also make its presence felt blatantly. When a father and son go shopping in *Manhunter*, the boy asks his dad what kind of coffee he likes, then says "You like that Folgers stuff, don't you? Mom likes it too." In older films, most products were anonymous (studio-made boxes marked "Corn Flakes") or bore invented names ("Wham" ham in *Mr. Blandings Builds His Dream House*, 1948), but in 1990 the Teenage Mutant Ninja Turtles ordered Domino's Pizza.

An independent can still make a picture for under $5 million, even under $1 million (but not, of course, with a $5 million star). And the less it costs, the less it has to earn in order to get out of the red. To pick only two mysteries —the Coens' *Blood Simple* and the big-studio *Presumed Innocent* (Alan J. Pakula, 1990)—the low-budget, independent film was not only more experimental and entertaining, but also more profitable.

The studios are no longer the only game in town, though they remain extremely powerful. Many independent producers, directors "shopping projects" (trying to interest studios in them), and writers with finished scripts "written on spec" (on speculation—that is, on one's own, gambling one's time and effort with no guarantee that anyone will buy the work) visit the studios in the hope of selling an idea or a script, obtaining co-financing to produce a film, or convincing the studio to make the film the director wants to direct or the actor wants to star in. But just as many independents make films with no guidance or interference from any studio. Independent filmmakers who feel strongly about what they have made can make pick-up deals with studios when the film is completed, on a take-it-or-leave-it basis, refusing to make cuts, but it is more common for them simply to deal with smaller releasing companies or independent distributors. Many other independent filmmakers strike co-financing deals with studios, instantly raising much of the production money they need, gaining prestige, validating the payroll, and getting rid of the worry of finding a distributor in one fell swoop. Or they let the studio finance the project completely and more or less take over. The biggest problem independent artists have found in working with studios on a creative level is that once they have sold their scripts or seen their productions become studio productions or turned in their footage—subtly or grossly, the studio makes its own version of the film, not theirs. The most frustrating preproduction experience any writer, producer, or director undergoes at the hands of today's studios is called "development hell," which well describes the years one may spend waiting for a studio to make up its mind to produce a project, ordering rewrites and other substantial but tentative revisions in the meantime—until one finds that the project has been put in "turnaround," offered to any other studio that might want it in exchange for reimbursement of the project's cost so far . . . where the cycle of indecision can begin again.

Yet the studios need these outsiders—the writers, who give them some of their best ideas, and the independents, who give them films. If Hollywood demonstrated anything in the 1980s, it was a hunger for ideas; it didn't seem to know what to make. It wanted the lucid and the unexpected, material with a twist, a hook, a spin—in short, the simple-complex and the bold-subtle. Most consistently, Hollywood wanted the new-old. It wanted sequels to documented hits (*The Godfather Part III*); it wanted updated remakes of classics (*Heaven Can Wait*) and Americanized remakes of overseas hits (*3 Men and a Baby*, 1987); it wanted revitalized genres (Indiana Jones and the serials; *Body Heat* and *noir*). The art of the sequel is one of repetition with variation (the *Godfather* films are quite different from each other, but each of them opens with a ceremony that is both familial and religious, and each climaxes with a montage of murders), and the same can be said of the remake, the genre revival, and—according to 1980s Hollywood—the aesthetics of the sure-fire investment.

The art most anxiously but consistently pursued by producers and agents in this period, whether or not they were also executives, was that of putting creative people together to work on viable projects. In many respects, the package was the deal, and the deal was the movie. Cinematography, sound, editing, and other cinematic matters were rarely considered; to hire a director was to indicate a preference for a certain style and pace. Since the agents and executives saw movies simply as stories acted out by stars in a repeatable medium, it was enough for them to determine the story, the stars, and the director, which were not only the key elements of the film as they saw it, but also the basis of its marketing campaign. And if overseas and video markets were willing to commit to this film, and if Chrysler wanted to donate all the cars for the chase scenes, so much the better. Even if the executives couldn't quite envision the movie they were approving, they could see the deal and knew precisely how to evaluate it.

The conditions of film exhibition changed drastically in the late 1970s and 1980s. Thanks to Dolby Stereo, theatres with optical sound projectors could present movies in four-channel stereo (before, stereo usually required a magnetic sound projector—a scarce item in 35mm). The theatrical sound experience became more important, and sound editing and mixing became far more sophisticated than ever before, both technically and aesthetically. The battle of the aspect ratios, which began with the wide-screen revolution of the 1950s, was settled in favor of two formats: American widescreen, a flat (nonanamorphic) format with an aspect ratio of 1.85 to 1, and Panavision, a scope (anamorphic) format with an aspect ratio of 2.35 to 1. Few theatres were able to show films made in the old Academy ratio of 1.33 to 1; unless they were dedicated revival houses, most theatres showed old films through 1.85 : 1 aperture plates that masked off the top and bottom of the frame.

The first 18-screen theatre was built in Toronto in 1979; it was conceived by veteran exhibitor Nathan A. Taylor, who together with Garth Drabinsky founded Canada's Cineplex Odeon Group. The cineplex (or multiplex cinema), now found in most cities, standing alone or in shopping malls, houses at least four — usually six or more — small theatres, each an auditorium with Dolby Stereo and a relatively small screen. In the 1980s virtually no new theatres were built except multiplex cinemas. Many drive-ins and revival houses closed. Some older theatres were upgraded to show the new spectacles, but many were partitioned, making way for two or three additional screens, to pull in more patrons. The new exhibition spaces were smaller, but they were easier to fill than the cavernous single-screen theatres that had been built in times when far more people went to the movies. A 1990 study found that only 25 percent of Americans went to more than five films a year. The price of admission crept ever higher; by 1990 most theatres were not allowed to sell tickets for less than $5 except at bargain matinees, and the big-city theatres were charging as much as $7. To take a family to the movies became an expensive proposition. The big films with big soundtracks were, audiences judged, worth seeing and hearing in big theatres (or in a cineplex, even with the sound turned down so it wouldn't be heard in the other theatres — because even if the screen was small, what one saw on it was a *movie*, not a video). In the 1980s, audiences saw motion pictures in big theatres with state-of-the-art projection and sound equipment, in multiple-screen theatres with their many selec-

tions, in the older single-screen theatres that kept alive the "ordinary" moviegoing experience, or at home. Trading quality for convenience and economy, a family of four could rent a video copy of a recent movie, watch it on TV, and save at least $20. At that rate, a good videocassette recorder or laserdisc player could pay for itself with a few dozen skipped movies.

The growing expense of movie tickets made audiences more choosy. Since the 1960s they had been going to "a movie" rather than "the movies," but now they were going to a movie only when they felt confident they would enjoy it. The impulse just to go out and see a movie was expensive to indulge; the audience was less experimental in its taste and less widespread in its patronage. In particular, audiences proved willing to pay to see sequels, new versions of movies they already knew they liked. The sequel phenomenon was not simply dreamed up by executives who needed safe investments; to the audience, too, a sequel seemed a safe investment.

The drama of buying, selling, merging, and taking over studios reached a historic climax in the late 1980s when Columbia and Universal were bought by Japanese companies and Warner Bros. merged with Time Inc. Movie companies had long been corporately linked with the publishing and recording companies that had, like them, been absorbed by conglomerates. Now the conglomerates renamed themselves "communications" enterprises and flung their nets of information and entertainment across the globe. Paramount remained a Gulf + Western company, but Gulf + Western (the parent company) changed its name to Paramount Communications Company and made oil a sideline; the filmmaking division is Paramount Pictures, and there is also a Paramount Television. Time, which owns several publishing and recording companies as well as Home Box Office (HBO, which shows new movies on cable), merged with Warner Bros. Communications in 1989 to form Time Warner, the world's largest communications conglomerate. The Walt Disney Company stayed Disney; it also opened two new divisions (Touchstone and Hollywood, in that order) for its more mature titles. But the other four majors were acquired by foreign companies. In 1985, Twentieth Century-Fox was bought by Rupert Murdoch's News Corporation, which is based in Australia; in the process Fox dropped its hyphen. Within a few years, the television arm of Fox had launched its own broadcasting network. In 1990 Fox sold its DeLuxe Laboratories to Britain's Rank Organisation, leaving no Hollywood studio with its own film processing and printing facilities, as hard as that is to believe (it's as if a professional photographer had no darkroom). MGM/UA was bought by the European company Pathe in 1990, as previously discussed; when United Artists went out of business in 1990, its chief assets were the Rocky and James Bond series. Columbia, which had merged with Tri-Star early in 1989, signed a merger agreement with Sony late in the year, and Columbia Pictures Entertainment became a Sony company — as did CBS Records soon after. Finally, in the last days of 1990, Matsushita Electric Industrial Co. Ltd. bought MCA Inc., the parent company of Universal as well as of many recording companies, a television division, and a publisher (and the company that manages Yosemite National Park, which the United States got to keep); Matsushita also owns Panasonic, Quasar, and Technics, which manufacture stereo and video equipment. When Columbia and Universal passed into Japanese hands, the new owners made it clear that they did not want to influence or supervise the studios' filmmaking activities; their primary interest was the *software* for their hardware: the music for their CDs and CD players, the movies for their videocassettes and videocassette recorders (VCRs), laserdiscs and laser players, monitors and television sets — much as Time and HBO needed movies for their videocassette and cable operations. (As if to confirm this, Columbia Pictures Entertainment, Sony Music Entertainment, and Sony Electronic Publishing became the Sony Software Corporation in 1991.) Magazines, books, records, tapes, data, movies — all had become information to be partially or entirely generated, stored, manipulated, formatted, and retrieved electronically, on machines the majority of which were made in Japan or depended on Japanese components. Sony, the inventor of Betamax (the first popular VCR and half-inch video format), and Matsushita, its archrival and one of the chief developers of VHS (the competing format that finally took over the U.S. half-inch video market), now each had a studio to supply them with new films and old, grist for the mills of video.

Movies in the Age of Video

Throughout the 1980s and into the 1990s, video has played important roles in the production, consumption, and destruction of feature films.

In the 1950s and 1960s, television was at first the chief competitor and then the partner of the film industry. As a broadcasting medium, it began as an inexpensive alternative to the cinema and a revolutionary upgrading of radio. By the 1950s, when TV's visual quality had improved enough to represent a threat, the movies were deliberately doing things TV couldn't do — be in color, in 3-D, in CinemaScope, in stereo — and TV was doing what movies couldn't do: present events as they unfolded, live rather than canned, with no admission charge. However, the television industry soon found that it needed old movies and newly filmed programs to keep its schedules full and to attract more viewers. Movie companies found that they could make money from licensing the broadcasting rights to old films and could keep their facilities busy filming TV shows and, eventually, TV movies. Some studios even established television divisions. From then on, the relationship between the film and TV companies became close and mutually beneficial, even if they remained official rivals for the public's leisure hours.

In the 1970s, when a great many homes were first wired to receive cable TV, the studios found themselves with two actively competitive and lucrative markets for their classics and new features — network TV (which is broadcast: sent through the air to all antennas) and cable TV (which is a restricted access system whose signal is sent directly, via electronic cables, only to paying subscribers). At the same time, public television stations became (as they remain) the chief subsidizers of independent documentary filmmaking. Typically, studios and independents licensed their new features to be shown first on cable and then on network TV, obtaining some of the production money they needed by pledging these exhibition rights. Soderbergh financed *sex, lies, and videotape* almost entirely by selling the video rights to the as-yet-unshot film to RCA/Columbia Home Video.

Video (closed-circuit television; another meaning of "video" is art made to be seen on a television) entered the consumer market in the mid-1970s and became a fact of life in the 1980s; by 1991, more than 76% of the American homes that had TVs also had VCRs. By then it was typical for a new film to be released first to domestic theatres, then to foreign theatres, then to video manufacturers and outlets, then to cable, then to 16mm distributors (a step often skipped), and then to network TV. In some cases, video distribution became as important to the studio as theatrical exhibition. If a film was not expected to do well, it might open theatrically for as little as a week (to get reviews, to earn theatrical status, and to test the market for cable and video release), or it might even be released "direct to video" without appearing in theatres at all. Roger Corman was incensed when the first film he had directed in twenty years, *Frankenstein Unbound* (1990), went to video in a matter of weeks. In addition to using video as a dumping ground for big- and low-budget films that died in theatres or were considered too expensive (in relation to expected revenue) to advertise for theatrical exhibition, the film companies found that the sale of video copies of hit films could realize tremendous amounts of money. Disney's *Lady and the Tramp* (1955) made $50 million in theatres — counting its first release and all revivals — but it made $90 million on video. (Film companies made their money not when video copies were rented but when they were sold to rental outlets and to individuals — and, of course, when the duplication rights were first sold to the video companies.) Even films with smaller followings were profitable to re-release on video; 50,000 devotees would not be enough to pay for a nationwide theatrical run, since 50,000 is not many tickets to sell, but it is quite a respectable number of cassettes.

There used to be very few ways to see an old movie — not just a 1930s or 1940s movie, but any movie that was no longer playing in theatres. Films were released, played for a few weeks or months, then faded into memory. With luck, an old film might show up in 35mm at a revival house or in 16mm on a college campus. If for some reason one needed to see a particular film and couldn't wait for it to happen to show up in a theatre, on late-night TV, or in a film series, one would have to rent it in 16mm (if the film was in nontheatrical distribution and could be found in catalogs), buy it (illegal, if the film was still protected by copyright), find it in a collection, watch it at the Library of Congress, or pay a studio to get a copy out of its archive for a very expensive private screening. Then, in August, 1976, the first prerecorded videocassettes were offered for sale.

Videotape recording was conceived by a Russian scientist, Boris Rtcheouloff, in 1922; he was awarded a Soviet patent in 1927 but never built any instrument, let alone the tape to run through it. Videotape was invented in America in the early 1950s (a primitive black-and-white recorder was built by Bing Crosby Enterprises in 1951), and RCA developed a color videotape recorder, too big to use outside a studio, in 1953. Ten years later, Ampex marketed a home videotape recorder as big as a freezer and as expensive as a house. Portable video recorders that used reel-to-reel tape were widely used by TV reporters, underground political groups ("the video underground"), and video artists in the late 1960s and 1970s. Sony invented the videocassette recorder (VCR) in 1974, keeping the one-half-inch-wide videotape prethreaded in a plastic case (as audiocassettes do) rather than on open reels. Sony called its machine the Betamax, and the Beta format proved convenient and of high quality. Sony's first self-contained, portable VCR went on the American market in 1976 (earlier models came inside special console TVs). Then JVC introduced the VHS format, which also housed one-half-inch tape in a plastic cassette, and RCA and Matsushita joined JVC in developing VHS VCRs and tapes, which became widely available in 1977 — the same year that Twentieth Century-Fox, sensing a trend, licensed Magnetic Video to sell its films on videocassette. From 1979 to 1984, Sony was in court, accused — primarily by Disney — of encouraging copyright infringement on a massive scale by facilitating the home recording of TV programs and particularly of movies; the Supreme Court finally ruled that home taping was legal as long as the tapes were only for personal use. That 1984 decision made it legal for people to build their own collections of video copies of films, taping them off the air for purposes of entertainment and reference (buying legally prerecorded cassettes never posed copyright problems). It was also in 1984 that Woody Allen's *Manhattan* was released on video, at his insistence, in what became known as the "letterbox" format: displaying the complete, original wide-screen image, with black bars above and below. As VCRs developed the ability to scan and locate images rapidly, to record and play back in stereo, and to display single frames for several minutes, they became very useful tools for the study of motion pictures. Even more versatile and useful was the laserdisc player, developed throughout the 1970s by Philips (in the Netherlands) and finally put on the market in 1978; its single-frame display was perfectly steady, and the visual quality of the laserdisc image far surpassed anything possible with tape, as did the quality of its digital sound (the laserdisc is the ancestor of the compact disc). A competing product, the videodisc—which read the disc with a stylus, not a laser beam—came and went in the early 1980s. The first laserdisc of a movie, marketed in December, 1978, was MCA DiscoVision's *Jaws*, a three-disc boxed set. Portable VHS and Beta color video cameras became available in the early 1980s (and Sony's 8mm camcorder in 1985), and when the prices of those cameras went down, the home-movie business dropped Super8 film in favor of videotape, which didn't need to be processed and offered effortlessly synchronized sound. As the small-gauge market shrank, a number of film labs closed down, and film manufacturers made fewer kinds of film; 8mm black-and-white was the first to go.

The situation now is that tens of thousands of movies are available on videocassette and laserdisc, inexpensive to buy and downright cheap to rent. Anyone with a VCR or a laser player can rent or purchase a video copy of a movie to watch at home; anyone with a VCR can tape a home library, and, given a camcorder, can shoot home videos in color and lip-sync sound; any scholar can pull a video copy of a movie off the shelf as easily as a reference book. Since both cassettes and discs are encoded with the film's complete, original soundtrack (including any surround tracks), anyone with a top-quality VCR or a laser player and the right decoding and stereo equipment can play the movie at home with no loss of sound quality and in full theatrical stereo—an opportunity the majority of 16mm prints cannot provide, since most of them are monaural. If the video image has been letterboxed, the composition of the film image can be studied and appreciated—frame-by-frame, in slow motion, or at normal speed. Furthermore, thanks to the practice of releasing both rated and unrated versions of some films on video—which extends to releasing the directors' cuts of some films as well as the release versions—the video viewer may be in a position to see more of "the real movie" than the theatregoer can. As of 1990, the only way to see the uncut *Heaven's Gate* was on VHS, the only way to see the unrated *Angel Heart* was on VHS or laserdisc, and only the Japanese laserdisc of Douglas Trumbull's *Brainstorm* (1983) allowed one to follow all the changes of aspect ratio in that film and to experience how they were coordinated with the surround track.

But not even a laserdisc can truly reproduce a film image; even on the best monitor, what one sees is a televised image. The film frame contains far more information than the video "frame," in most cases hundreds of times more; if the image on a TV were blown up to the size of a conventional (pre-cineplex) movie screen, it would be a mass of swirling dots sliced by very thick horizontal lines. Film grain is simply much finer than television's array of dots. Nor has any TV screen been invented that can reproduce film's colors, let alone the full range of its black-and-white scale. Film colors are created chemically, TV colors electronically. Film colors are thrown on a screen as the projector's perfectly white light shines through the dyes on the film; TV colors emanate from the screen as clusters of glowing dots (each dot keyed to a primary color). The TV image is projected *at* the viewer, while the film image is projected from behind the viewer; the glowing TV tube is both projector and screen, while the movie screen reflects the light thrown onto it. Film can shift instantly from a dazzling to a dark field, but a very bright light "burns" itself onto the video camera's tube, leaving an afterimage that can take a second or more to disappear; this makes a video camera incapable of responding rapidly and accurately to all the light-level changes in a film that is being copied or telecast and may even make some picture tubes incapable of showing films correctly. Black-and-white TV can only approximate the subtle values and brilliant definition of black-and-white film. The televised film image is like a film image that has gone to sleep, like a landscape behind a screen door, like an oil painting copied in colored lights; its palette is utterly different, as are its elements. Even if television were not inferior to film in sharpness and resolution, it would still be uncinematic in its phosphorescence.

The TV image is also much smaller than the projected film image, so that a close-up does not have the impact—the sudden bigness—it would have in a theatre, and an extreme long shot loses so much detail that it becomes unreadable. As essential as letterboxing is to the proper presentation of a wide-screen image, it leaves that image even smaller and less detailed than normal. And without letterboxing, even a film shot with an aspect ratio of 1.33 : 1 (the same aspect ratio as TV) is not televised in its entirety, since the TV tube "eats" the perimeter of any image in order to stabilize it electronically (the inner part of such an image, the 90 percent or so that is displayed, is the "TV safe area," and that rectangle is drawn or etched on the viewfinders of most Hollywood cameras so that when the movies are shot in the first place, crucial actions and titles are kept within the purview of the tube). Because most TV watchers want the image to be as large as possible, letterboxing is a rarity. When wide-screen films are copied for broadcasting or for video release—or, scandalously, for release in 16mm—most of them are "panned and scanned"; in other words, only a 1.33 : 1 area of the image is recorded, and this image area is moved around in order to keep the "essential" action within the frame, sometimes by panning and sometimes by introducing cuts so that the action area can leap from one part of the frame to another. Thus someone who watched a pan-and-scan version of *West Side Story* could think that the elegant long-take opening was a rapidly edited montage and would have no access to the original compositions nor any vestige of the wide screen itself. In the absence of letterboxing, *any* film that is shown on TV is cropped—missing some of its top, bottom, and sides. A CinemaScope film that is not letterboxed and also suffers the usual loss of perimeter is cropped so drastically that half the image is lost.

All this applies to "uncut," full-length versions, but matters become even worse when to all these problems are added those introduced by the practices of commercial television—notably the interruption of a film to show commercials, which ruins the editing, narrative, and cinematographic rhythms of the movie; the deletion of shots and scenes that might offend a family audience, even if that renders the plot and characterization hard to follow; and the silencing or bleeping of naughty words, which throws off the rhythm of the dialogue, breaks the spell of the picture as abruptly as a commercial does, and may deprive the viewer of important information (for example, "We're going to _____ the _____").

From the point of view of the film production and distribution companies, the worst thing about video is the ease with which movies can be pirated. It is not unusual for a movie to be circulated in unauthorized video copies even before it first appears in theatres, and it is terribly easy for even an authorized video to be illegally copied; both of these practices constitute theft—grand theft, in fact. And from the point of view of 16mm film distributors, the worst thing about video is that many people are renting video copies rather than movies; this is particularly unfortunate in the case of film professors, whose tight budgets sometimes appear to justify the showing of videos instead of films in film classes. The fewer prints are rented, the more distributors have to charge for them; the less a particular print is rented, the less incentive the distributor has to strike a new copy of that movie when the old print has deteriorated. Thus many films are going out of 16mm distribution, as distributors are going out of business. (And with the closing of most revival houses, the distribution of old films in 35mm has suffered equal casualties.) As much as professors enjoy the ability to stop a video on a frame and talk about it, it is literally essential that students also be exposed to the actual movie — what might these days be called the film version of the film — uncut, uncropped, uninterrupted, and projected at the correct speed. Beyond that it is valuable, convenient, and cost-effective to use a video copy for further study in the classroom, library, or home, particularly since that protects the celluloid print from excessive handling. In a nutshell, then, a good video copy of a movie can reproduce its theatrical soundtrack with no loss of information or quality, but it cannot reproduce the film image without inevitably and sometimes grossly altering it. Video has wonderfully improved public access to copies of films, but the films themselves are becoming ever harder to locate.

Colorization is the practice of electronically adding color to video copies of black-and-white movies. The first films to be colorized, in 1984, were a few Laurel and Hardy shorts and the features *Topper* (1937) and *Of Mice and Men* (1939). The colors are not film dyes but the glowing hues of color TV, assigned by computer to specific areas of each frame (blue to Cary Grant's jacket, brown to his hat). Nor do the colors have any necessary relationship to the original colors of whatever was photographed; in the computer-colored version of *Suddenly* (1954), Frank Sinatra's famous blue eyes are brown. The colorizer establishes a palette of video colors and assigns them in a pattern that is almost always aesthetically bland.

Movies are colorized in order to make them better TV programs, in line with the assumptions that a color TV is wasted if it's not showing a program in color and that black-and-white films *lack color* rather than *have* their own unique scale of tones. Many colorizers argue that black-and-white films would have been made in color if the money or technology had been available. But such presumptuous arguments ignore the fact that even if the film in question had been shot in color, it would have been *film* color — Technicolor or Eastmancolor — not video color. Colorizers also maintain that one can turn down the color on a TV set and watch a colorized picture in black-and-white, but the actual result is a gray mush. To colorize a movie is comparable to taking crayons to an Ansel Adams photograph; not only does it have nothing to do with the aesthetics of the original and the intentions of the artist, it also does nothing to improve the photo and, in fact, takes a great deal away from it.

As Eisenstein recognized, color and black-and-white raise extremely different aesthetic problems and opportunities. John Huston could have made *The Maltese Falcon* in color, but he chose not to; when Ted Turner (whose purchase of the MGM/UA film library also netted him the pre-1950 Warner Bros. films controlled by UA, among them *The Maltese Falcon* and *Casablanca*) had the film colorized over his objections, Huston said the result was like a roast that had been covered with teaspoon after teaspoon of syrup.

Fortunately, colorization does not mutilate the actual, physical film; it only creates a new, false, electronic version (which *can* be transferred onto fresh celluloid but rarely is). But it does mutilate the movie on an abstract level, it does prevent audiences from seeing the work even approximately as it was meant to be seen (*The Maltese Falcon* was not made to be seen on a TV, but that is minor compared to how much it was not meant to be in phony color), and it does keep younger audiences — who see new color films in theatres and most old films on television — from discovering the world of black and white. It is also a deeply felt insult to the makers of the films. When *It's A Wonderful Life* went into the public domain (that is, when its copyright expired), Frank Capra and Jimmy Stewart begged and reasoned and screamed bloody murder, defending the integrity of the film's cinematography and shivering at the prospect of Donna Reed with a blotchy pink-orange face. Nevertheless, five different colorized versions of *It's A Wonderful Life* were put on sale or broadcast within days of the copyright's expiration, and each of those versions was copyrighted as a new work. Even if that constituted moral and intellectual thievery, there was an ironic honesty in the admission that any computer-colored version of *It's A Wonderful Life* was not *It's A Wonderful Life* but a completely different, newly composed text that could legally be copyrighted.

These stills from It's A Wonderful Life *give a sense of the eloquent range of visual tones in this black-and-white film, which was not shot in color and needs no color added to it. Fig. 17-24: James Stewart and Donna Reed. Fig. 17-25: the dark world of Potterville.*

Fig. 17-24

Fig. 17-25

Video is not film, but as a technology and art of the moving image, it is film's nearest relative. One example of the influence the two arts had on each other in the 1980s is the music video, imitated in film as often as it imitated film. But there is more to their relationship than aesthetic exchange. From the late 1970s to the present, video technology has played an ever-increasing role in film production. On the set, most of what is shot on film is simultaneously recorded on video; some directors watch the monitor rather than the actors in order to evaluate how the action works within the frame. The video camera allows actors and directors to walk through a scene and evaluate it before shooting. Video rehearsals, played back immediately, allow actors to polish their performances without waiting for dailies. It is also becoming common practice to edit films on video: Shots are copied onto videotape or laserdisc and computer-catalogued; the editor calls up the shots in the desired order to see how they play, and by punching in a few frame numbers (instructing the computer which part of the shot to display) can trim a shot to the desired length; the film negative is then cut and assembled by conventional methods, with the negative cutter working from the shot and frame numbers on the video workprint.

One of the most creative applications of video is the "electronic cinema" championed by Coppola and used extensively in *One from the heart*. Coppola uses the video camera, a computer, and a video-effects generator as a painter might use a sketchbook and as a writer might assemble a first draft. On a single screen he combines a background (a sketch or photo rather than a fully constructed set), the actors, and any materials to be superimposed or matted in; the soundtrack can be roughly assembled just as the picture is, adding music and effects to the dialogue to see how the whole thing plays. Or he might string together photos and sketches of the backgrounds he intends to use, from first scene to last. A cross between a rough draft of the film and an extensively illustrated script, the computer-generated composite lets Coppola see just how much of the set will actually show up on camera and have to be constructed, how the actors and dialogue work

in this visual context, how the scene looks with and without camera movements or lab effects, and which visual elements yield the most effective composites; it also lets him present to co-workers and possible backers an electronic sketch of his vision of the film. Generally defined, electronic cinema is the practice — still largely experimental — of shooting a movie with a high-definition television camera; the video images are transferred onto film in the lab. Coppola has further ambitions for electronic cinema, including the possible satellite transmission of high-definition images for playback in theatres. Whether this leads to a cinema without film (a contradiction in terms, but in the movies anything is possible) remains to be seen.

The Look of the Future

A number of educated guesses may be made about the directions the American cinema will take in the last decade of the millennium. Some of these are projections of established trends — for example, since there were practically no women directing in Hollywood in 1980, and since the Directors Guild of America reported that 10 percent of all film and TV directing assignments in 1990 went to women, it is to be hoped and expected that more films will be directed by women. Considering the primary reason that studios were bought and sold in the late 1980s — to provide movies for the cable stations and cassette makers of the video marketplace — it appears certain that video will become an even more significant market for movies. Film and TV companies will continue to work together, in most cases as divisions of the same communications giants, and the technologies of film and TV will surely continue to influence each other, if not converge. The video market should expand the audience for low-budget and beginning filmmakers, many of whom may start with direct-to-video features, as well as provide theatrical filmmakers with the money they need to make their films (as the sale of its video rights made possible the production of *sex, lies, and videotape*). In time, the consumer might have access to complete, uncropped, uncolorized copies of most of the world's surviving films, perhaps with the sale of videos funding the restoration of prints. Those consumers who are film students and scholars will rely increasingly on video as a tool for the study of motion pictures, and if nothing else, critical descriptions of shots, scenes, and sequences can be expected to become more precise. Movies will continue to be made with an eye to their ultimate appearance on TV, but if the primary consideration is not how they appear in theatres, there will be no reason to see them in theatres. The consumer practice of "waiting for the video" may well become as entrenched as "waiting for the paperback," putting the movies under even more pressure to earn their theatrical keep by making the fullest possible use of the resources of sound and screen. Within the film business, the "new internationalism" of film production can be expected to increase, as will the power of agents and the number of independent filmmakers — but the days of the blockbuster mentality and the sequel, and perhaps even the new mythology, appear to be numbered. The year 1990 saw the box-office failure of "sure thing" *Rocky V* (John G. Avildsen), the unexpected success of such mid-range bourgeois films as *Ghost* (Jerry Zucker) and *Home Alone*, and the announcement that *A Nightmare on Elm Street* would call it a night with Number Six. With smaller pictures paying off better than big films, Hollywood can be expected to balk at paying $5 million to a star whose last picture didn't perform to its wild expectations, and a cycle may begin toward more reasonable film budgets — back in the direction of $10 or $15 million — making it possible for more films to be made (and for ticket prices to drop, though that is surely too wishful a prediction). But the most interesting trend of all is the boom in the restoration of classic films. In many respects the look of the future is the look of the past.

Restoration is the art of taking an old, perhaps damaged film, many of whose shots may be missing or out of order, and undoing the damage, finding and assembling the best surviving prints and fragments — and doing a staggering amount of research — in order to strike a new print that is as close as possible to the film as originally released. Ever since the enthusiastic reception of Kevin Brownlow's painstaking restoration of Abel Gance's *Napoleon* (produced and presented in 1981 by Robert A. Harris and Francis Ford Coppola), the commercial value of the pictures gathering dust and turning to nitrate soup in their vaults has impressed itself on film companies both in America and abroad. (Re-releasing a picture is cheaper than remaking it and is not that far in spirit from 1980s Hollywood's constant search for old successes to renew and repeat.) Harris's own restoration of *Lawrence of Arabia*, which took three years and resulted in the best possible 70mm print of the film as David Lean had intended it to appear — a good twenty minutes longer than the abridged version that had been in circulation, including every shot that had been cut (at the producer's orders) shortly after the picture first opened — was one of the most significant film events of 1989. Indeed, Columbia's re-release of *Lawrence* received as much public attention as its purchase that same year by Sony, the former as important in the history of the art as the latter is in the history of the business. Spectacularly visual, elegantly paced, sweepingly historic, intellectually and emotionally profound, and with a perfectly clean soundtrack, the restored *Lawrence* hit a generation of film students right between the eyes — students who had seen films projected in 70mm (like *Alien*, blown up from 35mm) but nothing *shot* in 70mm (that is, nothing with the perfect detail and invisible grain of the 65mm camera negative), who had seen movies that were exciting but not *compelling*. In a time of action-adventure teenpix and little adult pictures with two characters who come to appreciate each other, *Lawrence* appeared like the conscience of narrative film. The first time *Lawrence* came out, it permanently impressed teenagers like Spielberg and Scorsese; the new generation may turn out to acknowledge the oasis of *Lawrence* as earlier filmmakers acknowledged *Citizen Kane*: as *the* fountain of inspiration and dispeller of complacency, the movie that showed them what a film could be.

In 1987, Paramount began to inventory and preserve its film and television archives — 200,000 cans of material; in 1990 it opened a state-of-the-art building for the archive and an-

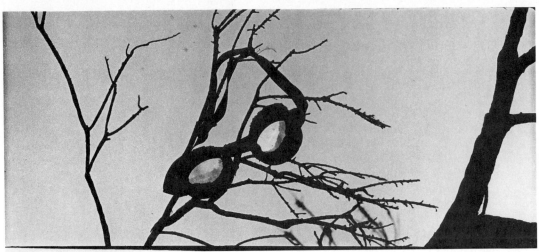

Fig. 17-26
Lawrence's goggles, snagged on a branch: the last shot in the sequence of Lawrence's fatal motorcycle accident and the first shot restored to **Lawrence of Arabia.**

nounced a program of re-releases. By June, 1990, both Warner Bros. and Columbia had announced their own film preservation campaigns, and eight filmmakers—Woody Allen, Francis Coppola, Stanley Kubrick, George Lucas, Sydney Pollack, Robert Redford, Steven Spielberg, and the president of the board, Martin Scorsese—had formed The Film Foundation to raise at least $30 million for restorations to be carried out jointly by studios and archives. That same year, Disney completed a scrupulous restoration of *Fantasia* for the film's fiftieth anniversary, the first time in decades that it had been seen full-frame. Also in 1990, at France's Gaumont, Pierre Philippe and Jean-Louis Bompoint restored Jean Vigo's masterpiece, *L'Atalante*, which had been released in 1934 in a version recut by the producers, who found the director's cut gloomy and uncommercial—the only version available from 1934 to 1990 (when Vigo's cut was found in the archives of the British Film Institute), the one that earned classic status and has been analyzed shot-by-shot for years. The restored version of *L'Atalante* is a real historical surprise, ten minutes longer and with a more flowing, less jumpy rhythm, revealing a complexly mature break with the style of *Zero for Conduct*; it

is also as stunningly beautiful, as clean and fresh and strange, as it was in 1934.

Colorization, which disregards the filmmakers' creative intentions and decisions, is the opposite of restoration. In Joe Dante's *Gremlins 2—The New Batch* (1990), a cable station, modeled on one of Ted Turner's, announces a showing of *Casablanca*, "Now in color, with a happier ending." As of 1990, Turner owned 2,200 MGM films, 750 RKO films, and 750 pre-1950 Warner Bros. films—not just their TV rights but the movies themselves as well as their domestic theatrical distribution rights. He showed them on two of his stations, exposing millions of people to films that had not been out of the archives for decades. But Turner had the most popular of the black-and-white films colorized, convinced that he was improving them, and he upset many people with his widely announced plans to colorize *Citizen Kane*. As it turned out, a clause in Welles's original RKO contract, which remained binding on any owner of the film, specified that no changes could be made in *Citizen Kane* without Welles's approval (or that of his heirs, who were not about to give it). Welles had the right of final cut on *Kane*, and even from the grave the final word: No. Denied the right to colorize *Kane*,

Turner did two utterly contradictory things: colorized *The Magnificent Ambersons* and had *Citizen Kane* restored. A new 35mm negative was prepared under the supervision of the film's original editor, Robert Wise, and Turner arranged for the new prints to be distributed theatrically by Paramount. *Citizen Kane* opened in ten cities on May 1, 1991, exactly fifty years after its opening at the RKO Palace in New York. The more great pictures are restored to their original look and length, the more the history of film will come alive.

Appendix: For Further Reading and Viewing

The following books and films, correlated with each chapter of the text, give the reader an idea of available material for further research. The filmography contains a representative sampling of the major films of each director; the date after each film is the year it was released in its country of origin. Most of these films are available for rental in 16mm prints. Just which distributor rents which title, however, changes quite often—too often for any comprehensive listing to remain useful for long. The most reliable way to find out who currently carries a given title is to look through the current catalogs published by each distributor. A list of 16mm distributors, with addresses and telephone numbers, follows at the end of the Appendix.

1. General Histories of Film and Reference Works

Allen, Robert C., and Douglas Gomery. *Film History: Theory and Practice.* New York: Knopf, 1985.

Armes, Roy. *French Cinema.* New York: Oxford University Press, 1985.

Armour, Robert A. *Film: A Reference Guide.* Westport, Conn.: Greenwood, 1980.

Barsacq, Léon. *Caligari's Cabinet and Other Grand Illusions: A History of Film Design.* New York: New American Library, 1978.

Barsam, Richard. *Nonfiction Film: A Critical History.* New York: Dutton, 1973.

Bogle, Donald. *Toms, Coons, Mulattoes, Mammies, and Bucks: An Interpretive History of Blacks in American Films.* rev. ed. New York: Crossroad, 1989.

Bohn, Thomas W., and Richard L. Stromgren. *Light and Shadows: A History of Motion Pictures.* 2nd ed. Sherman Oaks, Calif.: Alfred, 1978.

Bowser, Eileen, ed. *Film Notes.* New York: Museum of Modern Art, 1969.

Brakhage, Stan. *Film Biographies.* Berkeley: Turtle Island, 1977.

Brownlow, Kevin. *The Parade's Gone By . . . .* New York: Knopf, 1968.

Carr, Robert E., and R. M. Hayes. *Wide Screen Movies: A History and Filmography of Wide*

Gauge Filmmaking. Jefferson, N.C.: McFarland, 1988.

Casty, Alan. *Development of the Film: An Interpretive History*. New York: Harcourt, Brace, 1973.

Clarens, Carlos. *An Illustrated History of the Horror Film*. New York: Capricorn, 1968.

Conant, Michael. *Anti-trust in the Motion Picture Industry*. Berkeley and Los Angeles: University of California Press, 1960.

Cook, David A. *A History of Narrative Film*. 2nd ed. New York: Norton, 1990.

Cook, Pam, ed. *The Cinema Book*. New York: Pantheon, 1986.

Cowie, Peter. *A Concise History of the Cinema*. 2 vols. London: Zwemmer, 1971.

Cripps, Thomas. *Slow Fade to Black: The Negro in American Film*. New York: Oxford University Press, 1977.

Crowther, Bosley. *The Lion's Share*. New York: Dutton, 1967.

——— . *The Great Films: Fifty Golden Years of Motion Pictures*. New York: G. P. Putnam's Sons, 1967.

Dickinson, Thorold. *A Discovery of Cinema*. New York: Oxford University Press, 1971.

Dunn, Linwood, and George E. Turner, eds. *The ASC Treasury of Visual Effects*. Hollywood: American Society of Cinematographers, 1983.

Ellis, Jack C. *A History of Film*. Englewood Cliffs, N.J.: Prentice-Hall, 1979.

Everson, William K. *The American Movie*. New York: Atheneum, 1963.

——— . *American Silent Film*. New York: Oxford University Press, 1978.

Fell, John L. *A History of Films*. New York: Holt, Rinehart, 1978.

Fielding, Raymond. *A Technological History of Motion Pictures and Television*. Berkeley and Los Angeles: University of California Press, 1967.

Finler, Joel W. *The Hollywood Story*. New York: Crown, 1988.

Fischer, Lucy. *Shot/Countershot: Film Tradition and Women's Cinema*. Princeton: Princeton University Press, 1989.

Fulton, A. R. *Motion Pictures: The Development of an Art from Silent Films to Television*. rev. ed. Norman: University of Oklahoma Press, 1980.

Griffith, Richard, and Arthur Mayer. *The Movies*. New York: Simon & Schuster, 1970.

Halliwell, Leslie. *Halliwell's Filmgoer's Companion*. 9th ed. New York: Scribner's, 1988.

——— . *Halliwell's Film Guide*. 7th ed. New York: Harper and Row, 1989.

Harpole, Charles, general editor. *History of the American Cinema*. 10 vols. New York: Scribner's, 1990–

Haskell, Molly. *From Reverence to Rape: The Treatment of Women in the Movies*. New York: Holt, Rinehart, 1974.

Jacobs, Lewis. *The Rise of the American Film: A Critical History*. 2nd ed. New York: Teachers College Press, 1968.

Jowett, Garth. *Film, The Democratic Art: A Social History of American Film*. Boston: Little, Brown, 1976.

Katz, Ephraim. *The Film Encyclopedia*. New York: Lippincott, 1979.

Kawin, Bruce F. *How Movies Work*. Berkeley and Los Angeles: University of California Press, 1992.

Kay, Karyn, and Gerald Peary, eds. *Women and the Cinema: A Critical Anthology*. New York: Dutton, 1977.

Knight, Arthur. *The Liveliest Art: A Panoramic History of the Movies*. rev. ed. New York: Mentor, 1978.

Leab, Daniel J. *From "Sambo" to "Superspade": The Black Experience in Motion Pictures*. New York: Houghton, Mifflin, 1975.

Luhr, William, ed. *World Cinema Since 1945*. New York: Ungar, 1987.

Lyon, Christopher, ed., and Susan Doll, asst. ed. *The International Dictionary of Films and Filmmakers*. 4 vols. Chicago and London: St. James, 1984–86.

Macgowan, Kenneth. *Behind the Screen*. New York: Delacorte, 1965.

Manvell, Roger. *The International Encyclopedia of Film*. New York: Crown, 1972.

Mast, Gerald, ed. *The Movies in Our Midst: Documents in the Cultural History of Film in America*. Chicago: University of Chicago Press, 1982.

Monaco, James. *How to Read a Film: The Art, Technology, Language, History, and Theory of Film and Media*. rev. ed. New York: Oxford University Press, 1981.

The New York Times Film Reviews, 1913–1970.
7 vols. New York: Arno, 1971.

Pratt, George C. *Spellbound in Darkness: A History of the Silent Film.* rev. ed. Greenwich, Conn.: New York Graphic Society, 1973.

Ramsaye, Terry. *A Million and One Nights.* New York: Simon & Schuster, 1964.

Randall, Richard S. *Censorship of the Movies.* Madison: University of Wisconsin Press, 1968.

Rhode, Eric. *A History of the Cinema from its Origins to 1970.* New York: Hill & Wang, 1976.

Robinson, David. *The History of World Cinema.* New York: Stein & Day, 1973.

Rotha, Paul, and Richard Griffith. *The Film Till Now.* rev. ed. Boston: Twayne, 1960.

Russo, Vito. *The Celluloid Closet: Homosexuality in the Movies.* New York: Harper & Row, 1981.

Ryan, R. T. *A History of Motion Picture Color Technology.* New York: Focal Press, 1978.

Sadoul, Georges. *Histoire Générale du Cinéma.* 5 vols. Paris: Editions Denoël, 1946–54.

———. *Dictionary of Film Makers.* Translated and updated by Peter Morris. Berkeley and Los Angeles: University of California Press, 1972.

———. *Dictionary of Films.* Translated and updated by Peter Morris. Berkeley and Los Angeles: University of California Press, 1972.

Salt, Barry. *Film Style and Technology: History and Analysis.* London: Starword, 1983.

Sarris, Andrew. *The American Cinema: Directors and Directions, 1929–1968.* New York: Dutton, 1968.

Sitney, P. Adams, ed. *Film Culture Reader.* New York: Praeger, 1970.

Sklar, Robert. *Movie-Made America: A Cultural History of American Movies.* New York: Random House, 1975.

Slide, Anthony, with Paul O'Dell. *Early American Cinema.* New York: Barnes, 1970.

Spottiswoode, Raymond, et al. *The Focal Encyclopedia of Film and Television Techniques.* Stoneham and London: Focal Press, 1969.

Thomson, David. *A Biographical Dictionary of Film.* New York: William Morrow, 1976.

Wagenknecht, Edward. *Movies in the Age of Innocence.* Norman: University of Oklahoma Press, 1962.

Willis, John. *Screen World.* annual vols. New York: Crown, 1946–

2. Birth (1825–1900)

BOOKS

Ceram, C. W., *pseud.* See Marek.

Conont, Robert, *A Streak of Luck.* New York: Seaview, 1979.

Dickson, W. K. L., and Antonia Dickson. *A History of the Kinetograph, Kinetoscope, and Kinetophonograph.* New York: Arno, 1970.

Hendricks, Gordon. *The Edison Motion Picture Myth.* Berkeley and Los Angeles: University of California Press, 1961.

———. *Eadweard Muybridge: The Father of the Motion Picture.* New York: Grossman, 1965.

———. *Origins of the Motion Picture.* New York: Arno, 1972. (Contains *The Edison Motion Picture Myth, The Kinetoscope,* and *Beginnings of the Biograph.*)

Hepworth, Cecil M. *Animated Photography.* 2nd ed. London: Hazell, Watson, & Viney, 1900.

Hopwood, Henry V. *Living Pictures.* London: Optician & Photographic Trades, 1899.

Jenkins, C. Francis. *Animated Pictures.* Washington, D.C.: McQueen, 1898.

MacDonnell, Kevin. *Eadweard Muybridge.* Boston: Little, Brown, 1972.

Marek, K. W. (Ceram, C. W.) *Archaeology of the Cinema.* New York: Harcourt, Brace, 1965.

McBride, Joseph, ed. *Persistence of Vision.* Madison: University of Wisconsin Press, 1968.

Münsterberg, Hugo. *The Photoplay: A Psychological Study.* New York: Appleton, 1916. (Reprinted as *The Film: A Psychological Study: The Silent Photoplay in 1916.* New York: Dover, 1970.)

Muybridge, Eadweard. *Human and Animal Locomotion.* 3 vols. New York: Dover, 1979.

Newhall, Beaumont. *The History of Photography: From 1839 to the Present Day.* rev. ed. New York: Museum of Modern Art, 1964.

———. *Latent Image: The Discovery of Photography.* Garden City, N.Y.: Doubleday, 1967.

Quigley, Martin, Jr. *Magic Shadows: The Story of the Origin of Motion Pictures.* Washington, D.C.: Georgetown University Press, 1948.

Sadoul, Georges. *Louis Lumière.* Paris: Seghers, 1964.

Sanderson, Richard A. *A Historical Study of the Development of American Motion Picture Content* and *Techniques Prior to 1904.* New York: Arno, 1977.

Wackhorst, Wyn. *Thomas Alva Edison: An American Myth.* Cambridge, Mass.: MIT Press, 1981.

FILMS

LOUIS (1864–1948) AND AUGUSTE (1862–1954) LUMIÈRE

Workers Leaving the Lumière Factory (1895)

Excursion of the French Photographic Society to Neuville (1895)

L'Arrivée d'un train en gare (*Arrival of a Train at the Station,* 1895)

L'Arroseur arrosé (*The Sprinkler Sprinkled* or *Watering the Gardener,* 1895)

Le Repas de bébé (*Baby's Breakfast* or *Feeding Baby,* 1895)

Friendly Party in the Garden of Lumière (1895)

Sack Race (1895)

Demolition of a Wall (1896)

Flood at Lyons (1896)

Boat Leaving the Port (ca. 1897)

THOMAS ALVA EDISON (1847–1931)

Fred Ott's Sneeze (1894)

Chinese Laundry (1894)

Dickson Experimental Sound Film (ca. 1895)

The Execution of Mary, Queen of Scots (1895)

The Irwin-Rice Kiss (1896)

Feeding the Doves (1896)

The Black Diamond Express (1896)

Morning Bath (1896)

A Wringing Good Joke (1899)

Uncle Josh at the Moving-Picture Show (1902)

3. Film Narrative (1900–1913)

BOOKS

Addams, Jane. *The Spirit of Youth and the City Streets.* New York: Macmillan, 1909.

Arvidson, Linda. *When the Movies Were Young.* New York: Benjamin Blom, 1968.

Balshofer, Fred J., and Arthur C. Miller. *One Reel a Week.* Berkeley and Los Angeles: University of California Press, 1968.

Barnes, John. *The Beginnings of the Cinema in England.* New York: Harper and Row, 1976.

Bowen, Louise de Koven. *Five and Ten-Cent Theatres.* Chicago: Juvenile Protective Assn., 1911.

Crafton, Donald. *Before Mickey: The Animated Film 1898–1928.* Cambridge, Mass.: MIT Press, 1982.

———. *Emile Cohl, Caricature, and Film.* Princeton: Princeton University Press, 1990.

Elsaesser, Thomas, ed. *Early Cinema: Space—Frame—Narrative.* London: BFI, 1990.

Fell, John L. *Film and the Narrative Tradition.* Norman: University of Oklahoma Press, 1974.

———, ed. *Film Before Griffith.* Berkeley and Los Angeles: University of California Press, 1983.

Frazer, John. *Artificially Arranged Scenes: The Films of Georges Méliès.* Boston: Twayne, 1980.

Grau, Robert. *The Theater of Science.* New York: Broadway Publishing, 1914.

Low, Rachel, and Roger Manvell. *History of the British Film (1896–1918).* 3 vols. London: Allen & Unwin, 1948–50.

Musser, Charles. *Before the Nickelodeon: Edwin S. Porter and the Edison Manufacturing Company.* Berkeley and Los Angeles: University of California Press, 1991.

———. *The Emergence of Cinema: The American Screen to 1907.* vol. 1 of Harpole, ed., *History of the American Cinema.* New York: Scribner's, 1990.

Musser, Charles, and Carol Nelson. *High-Class Moving Pictures: Lyman H. Howe and the Forgotten Era of Traveling Exhibition, 1880–1920.* Princeton: Princeton University Press, 1991.

Niver, Kemp R., and Bebe Bergsten, eds. *Biograph Bulletins 1896–1908.* Los Angeles: Artisan Press, 1971.

———. *Motion Pictures from the Library of Congress Paper Print Collection 1894–1912.* Berkeley and Los Angeles: University of California Press, 1967.

North, Joseph H. *The Early Development of the Motion Picture: 1887–1909.* New York: Arno, 1973.

Slide, Anthony. *The Big V: A History of the Vitagraph Company.* Metuchen, N.J.: Scarecrow, 1976.

Smith, Albert E., and P. A. Koury. *Two Reels and a Crank.* New York: Garland, 1984.

Vardac, A. Nicholas. *Stage to Screen.* Cambridge, Mass.: Harvard University Press, 1949.

FILMS

GEORGES MÉLIÈS (1861–1938)
A Game of Cards (1896)
The Conjuror (1899)
The Dreyfus Affair (1899)
A Trip to the Moon (1902)
Jupiter's Thunderbolts (1903)
The Magic Lantern (1903)
The Palace of the Arabian Nights (1905)
The Doctor's Secret (*Hydrothérapie fantastique,* 1910)
The Conquest of the Pole (1912)

EDWIN S. PORTER (1869–1941)
The Life of an American Fireman (1903). Completed 1902
The Gay Shoe Clerk (1903)
Uncle Tom's Cabin (1903)
The Great Train Robbery (1903)
The Ex-Convict (1904)
The Kleptomaniac (1905)
The Whole Dam Family and the Dam Dog (1905)
Dream of a Rarebit Fiend (1906)

OTHER FILMS OF THE ERA
The Funeral of Queen Victoria (1901, R. W. Paul)
Tom, Tom, the Piper's Son and *A Kentucky Feud* (1905; Biograph)
Rescued by Rover (1905, Cecil Hepworth)
Scenes of Convict Life and *Slippery Jim* (1905, Ferdinand Zecca)
The Black Hand and *The Paymaster* (1906; Biograph)
The Story of the Kelly Gang (1906, Charles Tait)
A Skater's Debut (1906, Max Linder)
The Pumpkin Race (1907, Louis Feuillade and Romeo Bosetti)
Rescued from an Eagle's Nest or *The Eagle's Nest* (1908, J. Searle Dawley; Edison). Completed 1907
The Music Master (1908; Biograph)
The Assassination of the Duc de Guise (1908, Charles Le Bargy and André Calmettes; Film d'Art)
Drame chez les Fantoches or *A Love Affair in Toyland.* (1908, Emile Cohl)

Une Dame vraiment bien! (*A Truly Fine Lady,* 1908, Louis Feuillade)
Meeting of the Motion Picture Patents Company (1909; Biograph)
The Airship Destroyer (1909, Charles Urban)
The Joyous Microbes (1909, Emile Cohl)
The Vampire (1910; Selig)
Little Nemo (1911, Winsor McCay)
Onésime horloger (1912, Jean Durand)
Queen Elizabeth (1912, Louis Mercanton; Film d'Art)
Fantômas (1913–1914 serial, Louis Feuillade)

4. D. W. Griffith (1908–1931)

BOOKS

Barry, Iris, and Eileen Bowser. *D. W. Griffith: American Film Master.* New York: Museum of Modern Art, 1965.

Bitzer, G. W. *Billy Bitzer: His Story.* New York: Farrar, Straus, 1974.

Bowser, Eileen. *The Transformation of Cinema: 1907–1915.* vol. 2 of Harpole, ed., *History of the American Cinema.* New York: Scribner's, 1990.

Geduld, Harry M., ed. *Focus on D. W. Griffith.* Englewood Cliffs, N.J.: Prentice-Hall, 1971.

Gish, Lillian, with Ann Pinchot. *The Movies, Mr. Griffith, and Me.* Englewood Cliffs, N.J.: Prentice-Hall, 1969.

Griffith, D. W. *The Man Who Invented Hollywood: The Autobiography of D. W. Griffith.* Edited by James Hart. Louisville, Ky.: Touchstone, 1972.

Gunning, Tom. *D. W. Griffith and the Origins of American Narrative Film: The Early Years at Biograph.* Urbana and Chicago: University of Illinois Press, 1991.

Henderson, Robert M. *D. W. Griffith: The Years at Biograph.* New York: Farrar, Straus, 1970.
———. *D. W. Griffith: His Life and Work.* New York: Oxford University Press, 1972.

Huff, Theodore. *Intolerance: Shot-by-Shot Analysis.* New York: Museum of Modern Art, 1966.

Jesionowski, Joyce E. *Thinking in Pictures: Dramatic Structure in D. W. Griffith's Biograph*

Films. Berkeley and Los Angeles: University of California Press, 1987.

Niver, Kemp R. *D. W. Griffith: His Biograph Films in Perspective.* Los Angeles: John D. Roche, 1974.

O'Dell, Paul, with Anthony Slide. *D. W. Griffith and the Rise of Hollywood.* New York: Barnes, 1971.

Silva, Fred, ed. *Focus on* The Birth of a Nation. Englewood Cliffs, N.J.: Prentice-Hall, 1971.

Slide, Anthony. *The Griffith Actresses.* Cranbury, N.J.: A. S. Barnes, 1973.

Stern, Seymour. *Griffith: I—"The Birth of a Nation." Film Culture* #36, Spring–Summer 1965. New York: Film Culture, 1965.

Williams, Martin. *Griffith: First Artist of the Movies.* New York: Oxford University Press, 1980.

FILMS OF D. W. GRIFFITH (1875–1948)

Griffith's Biograph films, including: *The Adventures of Dollie* and *After Many Years* (1908); *Those Awful Hats, The Drunkard's Reformation, What Drink Did, The Lonely Villa, Country Doctor, The Mended Lute, 1776, or The Hessian Renegades, In Old Kentucky, Pippa Passes, A Corner in Wheat,* and *The Redman's View* (1909); *The Way of the World, The Unchanging Sea, Ramona, Over Silent Paths,* and *The Sorrows of the Unfaithful* (1910); *His Trust* and *His Trust Fulfilled, The Two Paths, What Shall We Do With Our Old?, The Lonedale Operator, The Broken Cross, Enoch Arden,* and *A Country Cupid* (1911); *An Unseen Enemy, The Painted Lady, The Musketeers of Pig Alley,* and *The New York Hat* (1912); *The Mothering Heart* (1913); *The Battle at Elderbush Gulch,* and *Judith of Bethulia* (1914)
Home, Sweet Home (1914)
The Avenging Conscience (1914)
The Birth of a Nation (1915)
Intolerance (1916)
Hearts of the World (1918)
A Romance of Happy Valley (1919)
True Heart Susie (1919)
Broken Blossoms (1919)
The Greatest Question (1919)
Way Down East (1920)
Orphans of the Storm (1921)

The White Rose (1923)
America (1924)
Isn't Life Wonderful? (1924)
Lady of the Pavements (1929)
Abraham Lincoln (1930)
The Struggle (1931)

5. Mack Sennett and Charles Chaplin (1911–1931)

BOOKS

Agee, James. "Comedy's Greatest Era." In *Agee on Film: Reviews and Comments.* Boston: Beacon Press, 1964, pp. 2–19.

Asplund, Una. *Chaplin's Films.* Translated by Paul Britten Austin. London: David & Charles, 1971.

Chaplin, Charles. *My Autobiography.* New York: Simon & Schuster, 1964.

Huff, Theodore. *Charlie Chaplin.* New York: Henry Schuman, 1951.

Lahue, Kalton C., and Terry Brewer. *Kops and Custard.* Norman: University of Oklahoma Press, 1968.

Manvell, Roger. *Chaplin.* Boston: Little, Brown, 1974.

Mast, Gerald. *The Comic Mind: Comedy and the Movies.* 2nd ed. Chicago: University of Chicago Press, 1979.

McCabe, John. *Charlie Chaplin.* Garden City, N.Y.: Doubleday, 1978.

McCaffrey, Donald W., ed. *Focus on Chaplin.* Englewood Cliffs, N.J.: Prentice-Hall, 1971.

Payne, Robert. *The Great God Pan.* Garden City, N.Y.: Hermitage House, 1952.

Robinson, David. *Chaplin: His Life and Art.* New York: McGraw-Hill, 1985.

Sennett, Mack. *King of Comedy.* New York: Doubleday, 1954.

Smith, Julian. *Chaplin.* Boston: Twayne, 1984.

Tyler, Parker. *Chaplin: Last of the Clowns.* New York: Horizon, 1972.

FILMS

MACK SENNETT (1880–1960)
Comrades (1911)
Barney Oldfield's Race for a Life (1913)

Mabel's Dramatic Career (1913)
Tango Tangles (1914)
Tillie's Punctured Romance (1914)
The Surf Girl (1916)
His Bread and Butter (1916)
His Bitter Pill (1916)
A Clever Dummy (1917)
Teddy at the Throttle (1917)
Mickey (1918). Completed 1916
Astray from the Steerage (1920)

CHARLES CHAPLIN (1889–1977)
Chaplin's Keystone films, including: *Making A Living, Kid Auto Races at Venice, Mabel's Strange Predicament, Tango Tangles, His Favorite Pastime, Twenty Minutes of Love, Caught in a Cabaret, Caught in the Rain, The Knockout, Mabel's Married Life, Laughing Gas, The Property Man, The Face on the Bar Room Floor, The Masquerader, The Rounders, The New Janitor, Dough and Dynamite, His Musical Career, His Trysting Place, Getting Acquainted,* and *His Prehistoric Past* (all 1914)
Chaplin's Essanay films, including: *His New Job, A Night Out, The Tramp, Work, A Woman, The Bank,* and *A Night in the Show* (1915); *Charlie Chaplin's Burlesque on Carmen,* and *Police* (1916)
Chaplin's Mutual films: *The Floorwalker, The Fireman, The Vagabond, One A.M., The Count, The Pawnshop, Behind the Screen,* and *The Rink* (1916); *Easy Street, The Cure, The Immigrant,* and *The Adventurer* (1917)
A Dog's Life (1918)
Shoulder Arms (1918)
Sunnyside (1919)
The Kid (1921)
The Idle Class (1921)
The Pilgrim (1923)
A Woman of Paris (1923)
The Gold Rush (1925)
The Circus (1928)
City Lights (1931)
Modern Times (1936)
The Great Dictator (1940)
Monsieur Verdoux (1947)
Limelight (1952)
A King in New York (1957)
A Countess from Hong Kong (1967)

Unknown Chaplin (1983, Kevin Brownlow and David Gill)

6. The American Film (1914–1927)

BOOKS

Barr, Charles. *Laurel and Hardy.* Berkeley and Los Angeles: University of California Press, 1968.

Barsam, Richard. *The Vision of Robert Flaherty: The Artist as Myth and Filmmaker.* Bloomington: Indiana University Press, 1988.

Blesh, Rudi. *Keaton.* New York: Macmillan, 1966.

Brooks, Louise. *Lulu in Hollywood.* New York: Knopf, 1982.

Brownlow, Kevin. *Behind the Mask of Innocence: Sex, Violence, Prejudice, Crime: Films of Social Conscience in the Silent Era.* New York: Knopf, 1990.

Brownlow, Kevin, and John Kobal. *Hollywood: The Pioneers.* New York: Knopf, 1979.

Cooke, Alistair. *Douglas Fairbanks: The Making of a Screen Character.* New York: Macmillan, 1940.

Croy, Homer W. *How Motion Pictures Are Made.* New York: Harper, 1918.

Curtis, Thomas Quinn. *Von Stroheim.* New York: Farrar, Straus, 1971.

Dardis, Tom. *Keaton: The Man Who Wouldn't Lie Down.* New York: Scribner's, 1979.

DeMille, Cecil B. *Autobiography.* Englewood Cliffs, N.J.: Prentice-Hall, 1959.

Everson, William K. *The Films of Laurel and Hardy.* New York: Citadel, 1967.

Finler, Joel. *Stroheim.* Berkeley and Los Angeles: University of California Press, 1968.
——— , ed. Greed: *a film by Erich von Stroheim.* (Includes the script.) New York: Simon & Schuster, 1972.

Gabler, Neal. *An Empire of Their Own: How the Jews Invented Hollywood.* New York: Crown, 1988.

Hall, Ben S. *The Best Remaining Seats.* New York: Bramwell House, 1961.

Herndon, Booton. *Mary Pickford and Douglas Fairbanks.* New York: Norton, 1977.

Irwin, Will. *The House that Shadows Built.* New York: Doubleday, 1928.

Keaton, Buster, with Charles Samuels. *My Wonderful World of Slapstick.* Garden City, N.Y.: Doubleday, 1960.

Kerr, Walter. *The Silent Clowns.* New York: Knopf, 1975.

Koszarski, Richard. *An Evening's Entertainment: The Age of the Silent Feature Picture, 1915–1928.* vol. 3 of Harpole, ed., *History of the American Cinema.* New York: Scribner's, 1990.

Lebel, J. P. *Buster Keaton.* Cranbury, N.J.: Barnes, 1967.

Lindsay, Vachel. *The Art of the Moving Picture.* New York: Macmillan, 1915.

Lloyd, Harold. *An American Comedy.* New York: Dover, 1971.

MacCann, Richard Dyer. *The First Tycoons.* Metuchen, N.J.: Scarecrow, 1987.

Marsh, Mae. *Screen Acting.* Los Angeles: Photostar Publishing, 1922.

May, Lary. *Screening Out the Past: The Birth of Mass Culture and the Motion Picture Industry.* rev. ed. Chicago: University of Chicago Press, 1984.

McCabe, John. *Mr. Laurel and Mr. Hardy.* New York: Dutton, 1975.

Moews, Daniel. *Keaton: The Silent Films Close Up.* Berkeley and Los Angeles: University of California Press, 1977.

Moore, Colleen. *Silent Star.* Garden City, N.Y.: Doubleday, 1968.

Münsterberg, Hugo. *The Photoplay: A Psychological Study.* New York: Appleton, 1916.

Norris, Frank. *McTeague, A Story of San Francisco.* New York: Doubleday & McClure, 1899.

Oberholtzer, Ellis Paxson. *The Morals of the Movie.* Philadelphia: Penn Publishing, 1922.

Petrie, Graham. *Hollywood Destinies: European Directors in America, 1922–1931.* London: Routledge & Kegan Paul, 1985.

Reilly, Adam. *Harold Lloyd: The King of Daredevil Comedy.* New York: Macmillan, 1977.

Robinson, David. *Buster Keaton.* Bloomington: Indiana University Press, 1969.

———. *Hollywood in the Twenties.* Cranbury, N.J.: Barnes, 1968.

Rubinstein, E. *Filmguide to* The General. Bloomington: Indiana University Press, 1972.

Sampson, Henry T. *Blacks in Black and White.* Metuchen, N.J.: Scarecrow, 1977.

Wead, George, and George Ellis. *The Film Career of Buster Keaton.* Boston: Twayne, 1977.

Weinberg, Herman G. *The Complete* Greed *of Erich von Stroheim.* New York: Dutton, 1973.

———. *The Complete* Wedding March *of Erich von Stroheim.* Boston: Little, Brown, 1974.

———. *Stroheim: A Pictorial Record of His Nine Films.* New York: Dover, 1975.

FILMS

ITALIAN SPECTACLE PICTURES
Quo vadis? (1912)
Cabiria (1914)
Antony and Cleopatra (1914)
Spartacus (1914)

MERIAN C. COOPER (1893–1973) AND ERNEST B. SCHOEDSACK (1893–1979)
Grass (1925)
Chang (1927)
The Four Feathers (1929)
The Most Dangerous Game (1932)
King Kong (1933)
This Is Cinerama (1952). Co-producer, Mike Todd

CECIL B. DeMILLE (1881–1959)
The Squaw Man (1914)
Joan the Woman (1917)
Don't Change Your Husband (1919)
Male and Female (1919)
Why Change Your Wife? (1920)
The Affairs of Anatole (1921)
Forbidden Fruit (1922)
The Ten Commandments (1923)
The King of Kings (1927)
Madame Satan (1930)
The Sign of the Cross (1932)
Cleopatra (1934)
The Plainsman (1936)
Union Pacific (1939)
Northwest Mounted Police (1940)
Samson and Delilah (1949)
The Greatest Show on Earth (1952)
The Ten Commandments (1956)

DOUGLAS FAIRBANKS (1883–1939)
His Picture in the Papers (1916)
Flirting With Fate (1916)

The Mystery of the Leaping Fish (1916)
The Americano (1916)
Wild and Woolly (1917)
Reaching for the Moon (1917)
The Mark of Zorro (1920)
The Mollycoddle (1920)
The Three Musketeers (1921)
Robin Hood (1922)
The Thief of Bagdad (1924)
The Black Pirate (1926)
The Iron Mask (1929)

ROBERT FLAHERTY (1884–1951)
Nanook of the North (1922)
Moana (1926)
Tabu (1931). Co-director F. W. Murnau.
Man of Aran (1934)
The Land (1942)
Louisiana Story (1948)

THOMAS INCE (1882–1924)
The Taking of Luke McVane (1915). With W. S. Hart
Keno Bates, Liar (1915). With W. S. Hart
The Coward (1915). With Charles Ray
The Deserter (1916). With Charles Ray
Civilization (1916)

BUSTER KEATON (1895–1966)
Shorts, including: *One Week, Convict 13, The Scarecrow,* and *Neighbors* (1920); *The Haunted House, The Goat, The Playhouse, The Boat,* and *The Paleface* (1921); *Cops, My Wife's Relations, The Blacksmith, The Frozen North, Day Dreams,* and *The Electric House* (1922); and *The Balloonatic* (1923)
The Three Ages (1923)
Our Hospitality (1923)
Sherlock Jr. (1924)
The Navigator (1924)
Seven Chances (1925)
Go West (1925)
Battling Butler (1926)
The General (1927). Completed 1926
College (1927)
Steamboat Bill, Jr. (1928)
The Cameraman (1928)
Spite Marriage (1929)

HARRY LANGDON (1884–1944)
Shorts, including: *Picking Peaches, Smile Please, The Luck of the Foolish, All Night Long,* and *Feet of Mud* (1924); *Remember When?, Boobs in*

the Woods, and *Lucky Stars* (1925); and *Saturday Afternoon* (1926)
Tramp, Tramp, Tramp (1926)
The Strong Man (1926)
Long Pants (1927)

STAN LAUREL (1890–1965) AND OLIVER HARDY (1892–1957)
Shorts, including: *Finishing Touch* and *The Call of the Cuckoo* (1927); *Leave 'Em Laughing* and *Two Tars* (1928); *Liberty, Big Business, Double Whoopee, Perfect Day, Wrong Again,* and *Bacon Grabbers* (1929); *Brats, Below Zero,* and *Another Fine Mess* (1930); *Beau Hunks* (1931); *County Hospital* and *The Music Box* (1932); and *Thicker Than Water* (1935)
Pardon Us (1931)
Sons of the Desert (1933)
Our Relations (1936)
Way Out West (1937)
Blockheads (1938)
A Chump at Oxford (1940)

HAROLD LLOYD (1893–1971)
Early shorts, including: *Lonesome Luke* (1915); *The Cinema Director* (1916); *Birds of a Feather* (1917); *The Non-Stop Kid* and *Nothing But Trouble* (1918); *The Chef, Don't Shove, Just Neighbors, Chop Suey & Co.,* and *Going, Going, Gone* (1919)
Haunted Spooks (1920)
High and Dizzy (1920)
Never Weaken (1921)
Grandma's Boy (1922)
Dr. Jack (1922)
Safety Last (1923)
Why Worry? (1923)
Girl Shy (1924)
Hot Water (1924)
The Freshman (1925)
For Heaven's Sake (1926)
The Kid Brother (1927)
The Sin of Harold Diddlebock (1947)

OSCAR MICHEAUX (1884–1951)
The Homesteader (1918). First New York showing, 1920
Within Our Gates (1920). Completed 1919
The Brute (1920)
Birthright (1924)
Body and Soul (1925). First version completed 1924
Spider's Web (1926)

Wages of Sin (1928)
The Exile (1931)
Ten Minutes to Live (1932)
Harlem After Midnight (1934)
Lem Hawkins' Confession (1934)
God's Step Children (1938)
The Notorious Elinor Lee (1940)
The Betrayal (1948)

ERICH VON STROHEIM (1885–1957)
Blind Husbands (1919)
Foolish Wives (1922). Completed 1921
Greed (1924)
The Merry Widow (1925)
The Wedding March (1928)
Queen Kelly (1932). Shot 1928–1929

LOIS WEBER (1882–1939)
Suspense (1913)
Hypocrites (1914)
Where Are My Children? (1916)
The Hand That Rocks the Cradle (1917) Original title: *Is a Woman a Person?*
The Blot (1921)
The Angel of Broadway (1927)
White Heat (1934)

REPRESENTATIVE FILMS (1912–1928)
Vitagraph Comedies: *Stenographer Wanted* (1912), *Goodness Gracious, or, Movies As They Shouldn't Be* (1914), *Professional Patient* (1917)
Broncho Billy's Capture (1913, Gilbert M. Anderson)
Traffic in Souls (1913, George Loane Tucker)
Gertie the Dinosaur (1914, Winsor McCay)
The Perils of Pauline (1914 serial). With Pearl White (Louis J. Gasnier)
A Fool There Was (1915). With Theda Bara (Frank Powell)
The Miracle Man (1919). With Lon Chaney (George Loane Tucker)
The Toll Gate (1920). With W. S. Hart (Lambert Hillyer)
Miss Lulu Bett (1921). With Lois Wilson (William C. de Mille)
Tol'able Dàvid (1921). With Richard Barthelmess (Henry King)
The Four Horsemen of the Apocalypse (1921). With Rudolf Valentino (Rex Ingram)

Blood and Sand (1922). With Rudolf Valentino (Fred Niblo)
Salomé (1922). With Alla Nazimova (Charles Bryant)
The Hunchback of Notre Dame (1923). With Lon Chaney (Wallace Worsley)
The Covered Wagon and *Hollywood* (1923, James Cruze)
The White Sister (1923). With Lillian Gish (Henry King)
The Phantom of the Opera (1925). With Lon Chaney (Rupert Julian)
The Big Parade (1925, King Vidor)
The Unholy Three (1925). With Lon Chaney (Tod Browning)
Tumbleweeds (1925). With W. S. Hart (King Baggot)
Dancing Mothers (1926). With Clara Bow (Herbert Brenon)
Sparrows (1926). With Mary Pickford (William Beaudine)
Ben-Hur (1926, Fred Niblo)
The Scarlet Letter (1926). With Lillian Gish (Victor Sjöström)
Son of the Sheik (1926). With Rudolf Valentino (George Fitzmauricc)
What Price Glory? (1926, Raoul Walsh)
Wings (1927, William Wellman)
It (1927). With Clara Bow (Clarence Badger)
Hotel Imperial (1927, Mauritz Stiller)
The Wind (1928). With Lillian Gish (Victor Sjöström)
The Crowd (1928, King Vidor)

7. The German Film (1913–1940)

BOOKS

Armour, Robert. *Fritz Lang.* Boston: Twayne, 1978.
Atwell, Lee. *G. W. Pabst.* Boston: Twayne, 1977.
Barsam, Richard Meran. *Filmguide to* Triumph of the Will. Bloomington: Indiana University Press, 1975.
Berg-Pan, Renata. *Leni Riefenstahl.* Boston: Twayne, 1980.
Bogdanovich, Peter. *Fritz Lang in America.* New York: Praeger, 1967.
Eisner, Lotte H. *The Haunted Screen: Expressionism in the German Cinema and the*

Influence of Max Reinhardt. Berkeley and Los Angeles: University of California Press, 1969.

———. *Murnau.* Berkeley and Los Angeles: University of California Press, 1973.

———. *Fritz Lang.* New York: Oxford University Press, 1977.

Hinton, David. *The Films of Leni Riefenstahl.* Metuchen, N.J.: Scarecrow, 1978.

Hull, David Stewart. *Film in the Third Reich.* Berkeley and Los Angeles: University of California Press, 1969.

Infield, Glenn. *Leni Riefenstahl: The Fallen Film Goddess.* New York: Crowell, 1976.

Jenkins, Stephen, ed. *Fritz Lang: The Image and the Look.* London: BFI, 1981.

Jensen, Paul M. *The Cinema of Fritz Lang.* Cranbury, N.J.: Barnes, 1969.

Kaplan, E. Ann. *Fritz Lang: A Guide to References and Resources.* Boston: G. K. Hall, 1981.

Kobal, John, ed. *Great Film Stills of the German Silent Era.* New York: Dover, 1981.

Kracauer, Siegfried. *From Caligari to Hitler: A Psychological History of the German Film.* Princeton: Princeton University Press, 1947.

Leiser, Erwin. *Nazi Cinema.* New York: Macmillan, 1974.

Manvell, Roger, with Heinrich Fraenkel. *The German Cinema.* New York: Praeger, 1971.

Ott, Frederick. *The Films of Fritz Lang.* Secaucus, N.J.: Citadel, 1979.

Petley, Julian. *Capital and Culture: German Cinema, 1933–45.* London: BFI, 1979.

Petro, Patrice. *Joyless Streets: Women and Melodramatic Representation in Weimar Germany.* Princeton: Princeton University Press, 1989.

Prawer, S. S. *Caligari's Children: The Film as Tale of Terror.* New York: Oxford University Press, 1980.

Taylor, Richard. *Film Propaganda: Soviet Russia and Nazi Germany.* New York: Barnes & Noble, 1979.

Usai, Paolo Cherchi, and Lorenzo Codelli, eds. *Before Caligari: German Cinema, 1895–1920.* Madison: University of Wisconsin Press, 1990.

Vogel, Amos. *Film as a Subversive Art.* New York: Random House, 1974.

Wollenberg, Hans H. *Fifty Years of German Film.* New York: Arno, 1972.

FILMS

Fritz Lang (1890–1976)
The Spiders (1919)
Destiny (Der Müde Tod, 1921)
Dr. Mabuse, the Gambler (2 parts, 1922)
Die Nibelungen (2 parts, 1924)
Metropolis (1927). Completed 1926
Spies (1928)
M (1931)
The Testament of Dr. Mabuse (1933)
Fury (1936)

F. W. Murnau (1888–1931)
Der Januskopf (1920)
Schloss Vogelöd (1921)
Nosferatu, a Symphony of Horror (1922)
The Last Laugh or *The Last Man* (1924)
Tartuffe (1926). Completed 1925
Faust (1926)
Sunrise: A Song of Two Humans (1927)
Tabu (1931). Co-director, Robert Flaherty

G. W. Pabst (1885–1967)
The Joyless Street (1925)
Secrets of a Soul (1926)
The Love of Jeanne Ney (1927)
Pandora's Box (1928)
Diary of a Lost Girl (1929)
Westfront 1918 (1930)
The Threepenny Opera (1931)
Kameradschaft (1931)
The Trial (1947)
The Last Ten Days or *The Last Act* (1955)

Leni Riefenstahl (1902–   )
The Blue Light (1932)
Triumph of the Will (1935)
Olympia (1938)
Tiefland (1944)

Representative German Films (1913–1933)
The Student of Prague (1913, Stellan Rye)
The Golem (1914, Paul Wegener and Henrik Galeen)
Homunculus (1916, Otto Rippert)
Madame Du Barry (U.S. title: *Passion,* 1919, Ernst Lubitsch)
The Cabinet of Dr. Caligari (1920, Robert Wiene). Completed 1919
The Golem: How He Came into the World (1920). Script by Paul Wegener and Henrik Galeen (Paul Wegener and Carl Boese)

Warning Shadows (1922, Arthur Robison)
The Street (1923, Karl Grune)
Waxworks (1924, Paul Leni)
The Hands of Orlac (1924, Robert Wiene)
Variety (1925, E. A. Dupont)
The Student of Prague (1926, Henrik Galeen)
Tragedy of the Street (1927, Bruno Rahn)
Berlin: The Symphony of a Great City (1927, Walter Ruttmann)
The Cat and the Canary (1927, Paul Leni)
Überfall (*Accident*, 1929, Ernö Metzner)
Mädchen in Uniform (1931, Leontine Sagan)
Kuhle Wampe (1932, Slatan Dudow and Bertolt Brecht)
Hitlerjunge Quex (1933, Hans Steinhoff)

8. The Soviet Film (1917–1991)

BOOKS

Babitsky, Paul. *The Soviet Film Industry.* New York: Praeger, 1955.

Barna, Yon. *Eisenstein.* Bloomington: Indiana University Press, 1974.

Birkos, Alexander S. *Soviet Cinema: Directors and Films.* Hamden, Conn.: Archon, 1976.

Constantine, Mildred, and Alan Fern. *Revolutionary Soviet Film Posters.* Baltimore: Johns Hopkins University Press, 1974.

Dickinson, Thorold and Catherine de la Roche, eds. *Soviet Cinema.* London: Falcon Press, 1948.

Dovzhenko, Alexander. *Alexander Dovzhenko: The Poet as Filmmaker.* Translated by Marco Carynnyk. Cambridge, Mass.: MIT Press, 1973.

Eisenstein, Sergei M. *The Film Sense.* Edited and translated by Jay Leyda. New York: Harcourt, Brace & World, 1947.

——— . *Film Form: Essays in Film Theory.* Edited and translated by Jay Leyda. New York: Harcourt, Brace & World, 1949.

——— . *Notes of a Film Director.* rev. ed. Translated by X. Danko. New York: Dover, 1970.

——— . *Immoral Memories: An Autobiography.* Translated by Herbert Marshall. Boston: Houghton Mifflin, 1983.

——— . *Non-Indifferent Nature: Film and the Structure of Things.* Translated by Herbert Marshall. Cambridge and New York: Cambridge University Press, 1987.

Feldman, Seth R. *The Evolution of Style in the Early Work of Dziga Vertov.* New York: Arno, 1977.

Geduld, Harry, and Ronald Gottesman. *Sergei Eisenstein and Upton Sinclair: The Making and Unmaking of* Que Viva Mexico! Bloomington: University of Indiana Press, 1970.

Kuleshov, Lev. *Kuleshov on Film.* Translated by Ronald Levaco. Berkeley and Los Angeles: University of California Press, 1974.

Leaming, Barbara. *Grigori Kozintsev.* Boston: Twayne, 1980.

Le Fanu, Mark. *The Cinema of Andrei Tarkovsky.* London: BFI, 1987.

Leyda, Jay. *Kino: A History of the Russian and Soviet Film.* 3rd ed. Princeton: Princeton University Press, 1983.

——— , ed. *Eisenstein: Three Films* — Battleship Potemkin, October, Alexander Nevsky. Scripts translated by Diana Matias. New York: Harper and Row, 1974.

Leyda, Jay, and Zina Voynow. *Eisenstein at Work.* New York: Pantheon, 1982.

Marshall, Herbert. *Masters of Soviet Cinema: Crippled Creative Biographies.* London: Routledge & Kegan Paul, 1983.

——— . *Soviet Cinema.* London: Russia Today, 1945.

——— , ed. *Sergei Eisenstein's* The Battleship Potemkin. New York: Avon, 1978.

Mayer, David. *Eisenstein's* Potemkin: *A Shot-by-Shot Presentation.* New York: Grossman, 1972.

Montagu, Ivor. *With Eisenstein in Hollywood.* New York: International, 1967.

Nilsen, Vladimir. *The Cinema as a Graphic Art.* Translated by Stephen Garry. New York: Hill and Wang, 1959.

Nizhny, Vladimir. *Lessons with Eisenstein.* Translated by Ivor Montagu. New York: Hill & Wang, 1962.

Pudovkin, V. I. *Film Technique and Film Acting.* London: Vision Press, 1959.

Sadoul, Georges. *Dziga Vertov.* Paris: Champ Libre, 1971.

Seton, Marie. *Sergei M. Eisenstein.* New York: Grove Press, 1960.

Swallow, Norman. *Eisenstein: A Documentary Portrait*. New York: Dutton, 1977.

Tarkovsky, Andrey. *Sculpting in Time: Reflections on the Cinema*. Translated by Kitty Hunter-Blair. Austin: University of Texas Press, 1989.

Taylor, Richard. *The Politics of the Soviet Cinema: 1917–1929*. Cambridge: Cambridge University Press, 1979.

Taylor, Richard, and Ian Christie, eds. *The Film Factory: Russian and Soviet Cinema in Documents 1896–1939*. Cambridge, Mass.: Harvard University Press, 1988.

Thompson, Kristin. *Eisenstein's* Ivan the Terrible: *A Neoformalist Analysis*. Princeton, N.J.: Princeton University Press, 1981.

Tsivian, Yuri, with Paolo Cherchi Usai, Lorenzo Codelli, Carlo Montanaro, and David Robinson, eds. *Silent Witness: Russian Films 1908–1919*. London: BFI, 1990.

Vertov, Dziga. *Kino-Eye: The Writings of Dziga Vertov*. Edited by Annette Michelson and translated by Kevin O'Brien. Berkeley and Los Angeles: University of California Press, 1984.

FILMS

ALEXANDER DOVZHENKO (1894–1956)

Zvenigora (1928)
Arsenal (1929)
Earth (1930)
Schors (1939)

SERGEI M. EISENSTEIN (1898–1948)

Strike (1925). Completed 1924
Battleship Potemkin (1925)
October (1928). Co-director, Grigori Alexandrov
Old and New or *The General Line* (1929). Co-director, Grigori Alexandrov
Que Viva Mexico! (1930–32). Unfinished. Co-director, Grigori Alexandrov. Portions of the footage assembled and released as *Thunder Over Mexico* (1933, Sol Lesser), *Time in the Sun* (1939, Marie Seton), and *Que Viva Mexico!* (1979, Grigori Alexandrov)
Alexander Nevsky (1938). Co-director, Dmitri Vasiliev
Ivan the Terrible I, II (1944–1946)

VSEVOLOD I. PUDOVKIN (1893–1953)

Chess Fever (1925)
Mechanics of the Brain (1926)
Mother (1926)
The End of St. Petersburg (1927)
The Heir to Genghis Khan or *Storm Over Asia* (1928)
Deserter (1933)

ANDREI TARKOVSKY (1932–1986)

Ivan's Childhood or *My Name is Ivan* (1962)
Andrei Rublev or *Andrei Roublyov* (1966). Shown abroad since 1966; Soviet release, 1972
Solaris (1972)
Mirror (1974)
Stalker (1981). Completed 1979
Nostalgia or *Nostalghia* (1983)
The Sacrifice (1986)

DZIGA VERTOV (1896–1954)

Kino-Pravda (1922–1925)
Kino-Eye (1924)
The Man with a Movie Camera or *Man with Movie Camera* (1929). Completed 1928
Enthusiasm (1931)
Three Songs of Lenin (1934)

SOVIET MISCELLANY

Father Sergius (1918, Yakov Protazanov)
Shackled by Film (1918). Script by Vladimir Mayakovsky (Nikandr Turkin)
Extraordinary Adventures of Mr. West in the Land of the Bolsheviks (1924, Lev Kuleshov)
The Cloak (1926, Grigori Kozintsev and Leonid Trauberg)
By the Law (1926, Lev Kuleshov)
Moscow (1927, Mikhail Kaufman)
Bed and Sofa (1927, Abram Room)
Girl with the Hatbox (1927, Boris Barnet)
House on Trubnaya Square (1928, Boris Barnet)
The Russia of Nikolai II and Lev Tolstoy (1928, Esther Shub)
Road to Life (1931, Nikolai Ekk)
Chapayev (1934, Sergei and Georgy Vasiliev)
Lieutenant Kije (1934). Score by Sergei Prokofiev (Alexander Feinzimmer)
The Youth of Maxim (1935, Grigori Kozintsev and Leonid Trauberg)
The Gorky Trilogy (1938–1940, Mark Donskoy)
Boris Godunov (1955, Vera Stroyeva)

The Quiet Don I, II, III (1957, Sergei Gerasimov)
The Cranes Are Flying (1957, Mikhail Kalatozov)
The Overcoat (1959, Alexei Batalov)
Ballad of a Soldier (1959, Grigori Chukhrai)
Lady with a Dog (1960, Josef Heifitz)
Hamlet (1964, Grigori Kozintsev)
Shadows of Forgotten Ancestors (1964, Sergei Paradjanov)
War and Peace (1966, Sergei Bondarchuk)
The First Teacher (1966, Andrei Konchalovsky)
The Color of Pomegranates or *Sayat Nova* (1968– 1978, Sergei Paradjanov). Early version released 1971
Molba (*Prayer,* 1969, Tenghiz Abuladze). Completed 1967
King Lear (1971, Grigori Kozintsev)
Slave of Love (1976, Nikita Mikhalkov)
The Wishing Tree (1978, Tenghiz Abuladze). Completed 1977
Repentance (1987, Tenghiz Abuladze). Completed 1985
A Forgotten Tune for Flute (1987, Eldar Ryazanov)
Little Vera (1988, Vassili Pitchul)
Ashik Kerib (1988, Sergei Paradjanov)
Defense Council Sedov (1989, Yevgeny Tsimbal)
Get Thee Out! (Dmitri Astrakhan)

9. The Transition to Sound (1927–1930)

BOOKS

Baxter, John. *King Vidor.* New York: Monarch Press, 1976.
Brown, Bernard. *Talking Pictures.* London: Pitman, 1931.
Cameron, Evan W., ed. *Sound and the Cinema: The Coming of Sound to American Film.* Pleasantville, N.Y.: Redgrave, 1980.
Carringer, Robert, and Barry Sabath. *Ernst Lubitsch: A Guide to References and Resources.* Boston: G. K. Hall, 1980.
Durgnat, Raymond, and Scott Simmon. *King Vidor, American.* Berkeley and Los Angeles: University of California Press, 1988.
Feild, Robert. *The Art of Walt Disney.* New York: Macmillan, 1943.
Franklin, Harold B. *Sound Motion Pictures.* Garden City, N.Y.: Doubleday, 1930.

Geduld, Harry M. *The Birth of the Talkies: From Edison to Jolson.* Bloomington: Indiana University Press, 1975.
Green, Fitzhugh. *The Film Finds Its Tongue.* New York: Putnam, 1929.
Leebron, Elizabeth. *Walt Disney: A Guide to References and Resources.* Boston: G. K. Hall, 1979.
Milne, Tom. *Rouben Mamoulian.* London: Thames & Hudson, 1969.
Paul, William. *Ernst Lubitsch's American Comedy.* Cambridge, Mass.: MIT Press, 1983.
Poague, Leland. *The Cinema of Ernst Lubitsch: The Hollywood Films.* South Brunswick, N.J.: Barnes, 1978.
Schickel, Richard. *The Disney Version: The Life, Times, Art, and Commerce of Walt Disney.* New York: Simon & Schuster, 1968.
Thomas, Bob. *Walt Disney: An American Original.* New York: Simon & Schuster, 1976.
Thomas, Frank, and Ollie Johnston. *Disney Animation: The Illusion of Life.* New York: Abbeville, 1982.
Thrasher, Fredric. *Okay for Sound.* New York: Duell, Sloan, & Pierce, 1964.
Vidor, King. *King Vidor on Film Making.* New York: McKay, 1972.
——— . *A Tree Is a Tree.* New York: Monarch, 1976.
Walker, Alexander. *The Shattered Silents: How the Talkies Came to Stay.* London: Elm Tree, 1978.
Weinberg, Herman G. *The Lubitsch Touch.* 3rd ed. New York: Dutton, 1977.
Weis, Elisabeth, and John Belton, eds. *Film Sound: Theory and Practice.* New York: Columbia University Press, 1985.

FILMS

WALT DISNEY (1901–1966)
Alice in Cartoonland Series (1923–27)
Steamboat Willie (1928)
Plane Crazy (1928)
The Skeleton Dance (1929)
Flowers and Trees (1932)
Mickey's Pal Pluto (1933)
The Three Little Pigs (1933)
Thru the Mirror (1936)
Moving Day (1936)

The Old Mill (1937)
Snow White and the Seven Dwarfs (1938).
  Completed 1937
Pinocchio (1940)
Fantasia (1940)
Dumbo (1941)
Bambi (1942)
The Three Caballeros (1945)
Make Mine Music (1946)
So Dear to My Heart (1948)
Seal Island (1948)
The Adventures of Ichabod and Mr. Toad (1949)
Cinderella (1950)
Treasure Island (1950)
Alice in Wonderland (1951)
Peter Pan (1953)
The Living Desert (1953)
20,000 Leagues Under the Sea (1954)
Sleeping Beauty (1959)
Mary Poppins (1964)

ERNST LUBITSCH (1892–1947)
Gypsy Blood or *Carmen* (1918)
Passion or *Madame Du Barry* (1919)
Rosita (1923)
The Marriage Circle (1924)
Lady Windermere's Fan (1925)
So This Is Paris (1925)
The Love Parade (1929)
Monte Carlo (1930)
Trouble in Paradise (1932)
Design for Living (1933)
The Merry Widow (1934)
Angel (1937)
Ninotchka (1939)
The Shop Around the Corner (1940)
To Be or Not To Be (1942)
Cluny Brown (1946)

ROUBEN MAMOULIAN (1897–1987)
Applause (1929)
City Streets (1931)
Dr. Jekyll and Mr. Hyde (1932)
Love Me Tonight (1932)
Queen Christina (1933)
Becky Sharp (1935)
Golden Boy (1939)
The Mark of Zorro (1940)
Blood and Sand (1941)
Silk Stockings (1957)

KING VIDOR (1894–1982)
The Big Parade (1925)
The Crowd (1928)
Hallelujah (1929)
Street Scene (1931)
Our Daily Bread (1934)
Stella Dallas (1937)
Duel in the Sun (1947)
The Fountainhead (1949)

ILLUSTRATIVE TRANSITIONAL FILMS
Sunrise: A Song of Two Humans (1927, F. W.
  Murnau)
The Jazz Singer (1927, Alan Crosland)
Shaw Talks for Movietone News (1928; Fox)
The Sex Life of the Polyp (1928; Fox)
St. Louis Blues (1928, Dudley Murphy)
Lights of New York (1928, Bryan Foy)
The Singing Fool (1928, Lloyd Bacon)
Broadway Melody (1929, Harry Beaumont)
The Virginian (1929, Victor Fleming)
The Cocoanuts (1929, Joseph Santley and
  Robert Florey)
Whoopee! (1930, Thornton Freeland)
L'Age d'or (1930, Luis Buñuel and Salvador Dali)
All Quiet on the Western Front (1930, Lewis
  Milestone)
Scarface (1932, Howard Hawks). Uncensored
  version completed 1930
Vampyr (1932, Carl Theodor Dreyer)
Minnie the Moocher (1932). With Betty Boop
  and Cab Calloway (Max and Dave Fleischer)
Modern Times (1936, Charles Chaplin)

10. France Between the Wars
(1918–1945)

BOOKS

Abel, Richard. *French Cinema: The First Wave,
  1915–1929.* Princeton: Princeton University
  Press, 1984.
——— . *French Film Theory and Criticism: A
  History / Anthology, 1907–1939.* 2 vols.
  Princeton: Princeton University Press, 1988.
Bazin, André. *Jean Renoir.* Edited by François
  Truffaut. New York: Simon & Schuster, 1973.

Bordwell, David. *Filmguide to* La Passion de Jeanne d'Arc. Bloomington: Indiana University Press, 1973.

Braudy, Leo. *Jean Renoir: The World of His Films.* Garden City, N.Y.: Doubleday, 1972.

Brownlow, Kevin. Napoléon: *Abel Gance's Classic Film.* New York: Knopf, 1983.

Clair, René. *Reflections on the Cinema.* London: Kimber, 1953.

————. *Cinema Yesterday and Today.* New York: Dover, 1972.

Durgnat, Raymond. *Renoir.* Berkeley and Los Angeles: University of California Press, 1973.

Ehrlich, Evelyn. *Cinema of Paradox: French Filmmaking Under the German Occupation.* New York: Columbia University Press, 1985.

Faulkner, Christopher. *Jean Renoir: A Guide to References and Resources.* Boston: G. K. Hall, 1979.

Flitterman-Lewis, Sandy. *To Desire Differently: Feminism and the French Cinema.* Urbana and Chicago: University of Illinois Press, 1990.

Fraigneau, André. *Cocteau on the Film.* New York: Dover, 1972.

Gilliatt, Penelope. *Jean Renoir: Essays, Conversations, Reviews.* New York: McGraw-Hill, 1975.

Gilson. René. *Jean Cocteau.* New York: Crown, 1974.

Leprohon, Pierre. *Jean Renoir.* New York: Crown, 1971.

Lourie, Eugene. *My Work in Films.* New York: Harcourt Brace Jovanovich, 1985.

Mast, Gerald. *Filmguide to* Rules of the Game. Bloomington: Indiana University Press, 1973.

McGerr, Cecilia. *René Clair.* Boston: Twayne, 1980.

Mitry, Jean. *René Clair.* Paris. Éditions Universitaires, 1960.

Ray, Man. *Self Portrait.* Boston: Little, Brown, 1963.

Renoir, Jean. *My Life and My Films.* New York: Atheneum, 1974.

Sadoul, Georges. *French Film.* London: Falcon Press, 1953.

Salles Gomes, P. E. *Jean Vigo.* Berkeley and Los Angeles: University of California Press, 1971.

Sesonske, Alexander. *Jean Renoir: The French Films, 1924–1939.* Cambridge, Mass.: Harvard University Press, 1980.

Smith, John M. *Jean Vigo.* New York: Praeger, 1972.

Vigo, Jean. *The Complete Jean Vigo.* Surrey: Lorrimer, 1983.

Welsh, James M., and Steven P. Kramer. *Abel Gance.* Boston: Twayne, 1978.

Williams, Linda. *Figures of Desire: A Theory and Analysis of Surrealist Film.* Urbana and Chicago: University of Illinois Press, 1981.

FILMS

MARCEL CARNÉ (1909–)
Bizarre Bizarre (1937)
Port of Shadows (1938)
Le Jour se lève (1939)
Les Visiteurs du soir (1942)
The Children of Paradise (1943–1945)

RENÉ CLAIR (1898–1981)
Paris qui dort (The Crazy Ray, 1923)
Entr'acte (1924)
The Italian Straw Hat (1927)
Sous les toits de Paris (1930)
Le Million (1931)
A nous la liberté (1931)
The Ghost Goes West (1935)
I Married a Witch (1942)
It Happened Tomorrow (1944)
And Then There Were None (1945)
Silence is Golden (1947)

JULIEN DUVIVIER (1896–1967)
Poil de carotte (1932)
Pépé-le-Moko (1937)
Panique (1946)

ABEL GANCE (1889–1981)
La Folie du Docteur Tube (The Madness of Dr. Tube, 1915)
The Tenth Symphony (1918)
J'accuse (1919)
La Roue (1922)
Napoléon vu par Abel Gance (Napoleon, 1927)
Napoléon Bonaparte vu et entendu par Abel Gance (1935)
Un Grand amour de Beethoven (1936)
J'accuse (1937)

MARCEL PAGNOL (1895–1974)
Marius (1931)
Fanny (1932)
César (1936)

MAN RAY (1890–1976)
Return to Reason (1923)
Emak-Bakia (1927)
L'Etoile de mer (1928)
Les Mystères du Château du Dé (1929)

JEAN RENOIR (1894–1979)
The Little Match Girl (1928)
La Chienne (1931)
Boudu Saved from Drowning (1932)
Toni (1935)
The Crime of Monsieur Lange (1936)
The Lower Depths (1936)
A Day in the Country (1936). Unfinished; first
  showing, 1946
Grand Illusion (1937)
La Bête humaine (1938)
La Marseillaise (1938)
The Rules of the Game (1939)
This Land Is Mine (1943)
The Southerner (1945)
The River (1951)
The Golden Coach (1952)
French Cancan (1954)

JEAN VIGO (1905–1934)
A propos de Nice (1930)
Taris (1931)
Zéro de conduite (1933)
L'Atalante (1934)

REPRESENTATIVE FILMS
Fièvre (1921, Louis Delluc)
Crainquebille (1922, Jacques Feyder)
The Smiling Madame Beudet (1923, Germaine
  Dulac)
Ballet mécanique (1924, Fernand Léger)
Ménilmontant (1925, Dimitri Kirsanov)
Anemic Cinema (1926, Marcel Duchamp)
Rien que les heures (1926, Alberto Cavalcanti)
The Late Mathias Pascal (1926, Marcel
  L'Herbier)
The Seashell and the Clergyman (1928,
  Germaine Dulac)
The Fall of the House of Usher (1928, Jean Epstein)
The Passion of Joan of Arc (1928, Carl Theodor
  Dreyer)

Un Chien andalou (1929, Luis Buñuel and
  Salvador Dali)
Carnival in Flanders (1935, Jacques Feyder)

11. The American Studio Years (1930–1945)

BOOKS

Adamson, Joe. *Groucho, Harpo, Chico, and Sometimes Zeppo.* New York: Simon & Schuster, 1973.

Adler, Mortimer J. *Art and Prudence.* New York: Longman's, 1937.

Affron, Charles. *Cinema and Sentiment.* Chicago: University of Chicago Press, 1982.

Arce, Hector. *Groucho.* New York: Putnam, 1979.

Balio, Tino. *United Artists: The Company Built by the Stars.* Madison: University of Wisconsin Press, 1976.

——— . *United Artists: The Company That Changed the Film Industry.* Madison: University of Wisconsin Press, 1987.

Basten, Fred E. *Glorious Technicolor: The Movies' Magic Rainbow.* Metuchen, N.J.: Barnes, 1980.

Baxter, John. *The Cinema of John Ford.* London: Tantivy, 1971.

——— . *The Cinema of Josef von Sternberg.* London: Tantivy, 1971.

——— . *Hollywood in the Thirties.* Cranbury, N.J.: Barnes, 1968.

Bazin, André. *Orson Welles: A Critical View.* Translated by Jonathan Rosenbaum. New York: Harper, 1978.

Behlmer, Rudi, ed. *Memo from: David O. Selznick.* New York: Avon, 1972.

Benchley, Nathaniel. *Bogart.* Boston: Little, Brown, 1975.

Bergman, Andrew. *We're in the Money: Depression America and its Films.* New York: New York University Press, 1971.

Blumer, Herbert. *Movies and Conduct.* New York: Macmillan, 1933.

Bogdanovich, Peter. *John Ford.* Berkeley and Los Angeles: University of California Press, 1968.

——— . *Allan Dwan: The Last Pioneer.* New York: Praeger, 1971.

Bordwell, David, Kristin Thompson, and Janet Staiger. *The Classical Hollywood Cinema: Film Style and Mode of Production to 1960.* New York: Columbia University Press, 1985.

Brunas, Michael, John Brunas, and Tom Weaver. *Universal Horrors: The Studio's Classic Films, 1931–1946.* Jefferson, N.C.: McFarland, 1990.

Capra, Frank. *The Name Above the Title.* New York: Macmillan, 1971.

Carringer, Robert L. *The Making of* Citizen Kane. Berkeley and Los Angeles: University of California Press, 1985.

Cavell, Stanley. *Pursuits of Happiness: The Hollywood Comedy of Remarriage.* Cambridge, Mass.: Harvard University Press, 1980.

Charters, W. W. *Motion Pictures and Youth.* New York: Macmillan, 1933.

Corliss, Richard. *Talking Pictures.* Woodstock, N.Y.: Overlook, 1974.

Cowie, Peter. *The Cinema of Orson Welles.* New York: Barnes, 1965.

Croce, Arlene. *The Fred Astaire & Ginger Rogers Book.* New York: Dutton, 1977.

Curtis, James. *Between Flops: A Biography of Preston Sturges.* New York: Limelight, 1984.

Cywinski, Ray. *Preston Sturges: A Guide to References and Resources.* Boston: G. K. Hall, 1984.

Dale, Edgar. *The Content of Motion Pictures.* New York: Macmillan, 1933.

Doane, Mary Ann. *The Desire to Desire: The Woman's Film of the 1940s.* Bloomington: Indiana University Press, 1987.

Durgnat, Raymond. *The Strange Case of Alfred Hitchcock.* Cambridge, Mass.: MIT Press, 1975.

Eames, John D. *The MGM Story: The Complete Story of Fifty Roaring Years.* New York: Crown, 1964.

Eyles, Allen. *The Marx Brothers: Their World of Comedy.* New York: Barnes, 1966.

Facey, Paul W. *The Legion of Decency: A Sociological Analysis of the Emergence and Development of a Pressure Group.* New York: Arno, 1974.

Fielding, Raymond. *The March of Time.* New York: Oxford University Press, 1978.

Finler, Joel W. *The Hollywood Story.* New York: Crown, 1989.

Forman, Henry James. *Our Movie-Made Children.* New York: Macmillan, 1933.

Freeman, David. *The Last Days of Alfred Hitchcock.* Woodstock, N.Y.: Overlook, 1984.

French, Warren. *Filmguide to* The Grapes of Wrath. Bloomington: Indiana University Press, 1973.

Gallagher, Tag. *John Ford.* Berkeley and Los Angeles: University of California Press, 1985.

Gehring, Wes. *Leo McCarey and the Comic Anti-hero in American Film.* New York: Arno, 1980.

Glatzer, Richard, and John Raeburn, eds. *Frank Capra: The Man and His Films.* Ann Arbor: University of Michigan Press, 1975.

Goldner, Orville, and George E. Turner. *The Making of* King Kong: *The Story Behind a Film Classic.* New York: Ballantine, 1976.

Gottesman, Ronald, ed. *Focus on* Citizen Kane. Englewood Cliffs, N.J.: Prentice-Hall, 1971.

——— . *Focus on Orson Welles.* Englewood Cliffs, N.J.: Prentice-Hall, 1975.

Grierson, John. "Directors of the Thirties." In *Film: An Anthology,* Daniel Talbot, ed. Berkeley and Los Angeles: University of California Press, 1966, pp. 110–29.

Gussow, Mel. *Don't Say Yes Until I Finish Talking.* Garden City, N.Y.: Doubleday, 1971.

Halliwell, Leslie. *Mountain of Dreams: The Golden Years of Paramount Pictures.* London: Hart-Davis, MacGibbon, 1978.

Harley, John Eugene. *World-Wide Influence of the Cinema.* Los Angeles: University of Southern California Press, 1940.

Harris, Robert A. *The Films of Alfred Hitchcock.* Secaucus, N.J.: Citadel, 1976.

Hays, Will H. *The Memoirs of Will H. Hays.* Garden City, N.Y.: Doubleday, 1955.

Henderson, Brian, ed. *Five Screenplays by Preston Sturges.* Berkeley and Los Angeles: University of California Press, 1985.

Higham, Charles. *The Films of Orson Welles.* Berkeley and Los Angeles: University of California Press, 1970.

——— . *Hollywood Cameramen.* Bloomington: University of Indiana Press, 1970.

——— . *Warner Bros.: A History of the Studio.* New York: Scribner's, 1975.

Hirschhorn, Clive. *The Warner Bros. Story.* New York: Crown, 1979.

Hochman, Stanley, ed. *From Quasimodo to Scarlett O'Hara: A National Board of Review Anthology, 1920–1940.* New York: Ungar, 1982.

Huettig, Mae D. *Economic Control of the Motion Picture Industry.* Philadelphia: University of Pennsylvania Press, 1944.

Hurst, Richard M. *Republic Studios: Between Poverty Row and the Majors.* Metuchen, N.J.: Scarecrow, 1979.

Inglis, Ruth A. *Freedom of the Movies.* Chicago: University of Chicago Press, 1947.

Jewell, Richard B. *The RKO Story.* New Rochelle, N.Y.: Arlington, 1982.

Kael, Pauline. (Includes the script) *The* Citizen Kane *Book.* Boston: Little, Brown, 1971.

Karpf, Stephen. *The Gangster Film: Emergence, Variation, and Decay of a Genre, 1930–40.* New York: Arno, 1973.

Kawin, Bruce F., ed. *Faulkner's MGM Screenplays.* Knoxville: University of Tennessee Press, 1982.

Kindem, Gorham, ed. *The American Movie Industry: The Business of Motion Pictures.* Carbondale: Southern Illinois University Press, 1982.

Klingender, F. D., and Stuart Legg. *Money Behind the Screen.* London: Lawrence & Wishart, 1937.

Kobal, John, ed. *Hollywood Glamor Portraits: 145 Photos of Stars 1926–1949.* New York, Dover, 1976.

Koszarski, Richard. *Hollywood Directors: 1914–1940.* New York: Oxford University Press, 1976.

Lambert, Gavin. *On Cukor.* New York: Putnam, 1972.

LaValley, Albert, ed. *Focus on Hitchcock.* Englewood Cliffs, N.J.: Prentice-Hall, 1972.

Leff, Leonard J., and Jerold L. Simmons. *The Dame in the Kimono: Hollywood, Censorship, and the Production Code from the 1920s to the 1960s.* New York: Grove Weidenfeld, 1990.

Lewis, Howard T. *The Motion Picture Industry.* New York: Van Nostrand, 1933.

Loos, Anita. *Kiss Hollywood Goodbye.* New York: Viking, 1974.

Maland, Charles. *American Visions: The Films of Chaplin, Ford, Capra, and Welles, 1936–41.* New York: Arno, 1977.

——— . *Frank Capra.* Boston: Twayne, 1980.

Manvell, Roger. *Films and the Second World War.* New York: Dell, 1976.

Martin, Olga. *Hollywood's Movie Commandments.* New York: Wilson, 1937.

Marx, Arthur. *Goldwyn.* New York: Norton, 1976.

Marx, Groucho, with Richard J. Anobile. *The Marx Brothers Scrapbook.* New York: Norton, 1973.

Marx, Samuel. *Mayer and Thalberg: The Make-Believe Saints.* New York: Random House, 1975.

Mast, Gerald. *The Comic Mind: Comedy and the Movies.* 2nd ed. Chicago: University of Chicago Press, 1979.

——— . *Howard Hawks, Storyteller.* New York: Oxford University Press, 1982.

——— . *Can't Help Singin': The American Musical on Stage and Screen.* Woodstock, N.Y.: Overlook, 1987.

Mayer, Arthur. *Merely Colossal.* New York: Simon & Schuster, 1953.

McBride, Joseph. *Orson Welles: Actor and Director.* New York: Viking, 1977.

McBride, Joseph, ed. *Focus on Howard Hawks.* Englewood Cliffs, N.J.: Prentice-Hall, 1972.

——— . *Hawks on Hawks.* Berkeley and Los Angeles: University of California Press, 1981.

McBride, Joseph, and Michael Wilmington. *John Ford.* New York: Da Capo, 1975.

McCarthy, Todd, and Charles Flynn. *Kings of the B's.* New York: Dutton, 1975.

McGilligan, Pat, ed. *Backstory: Interviews with Screenwriters of Hollywood's Golden Age.* Berkeley and Los Angeles: University of California Press, 1986.

Miller, Don. *"B" Movies.* New York: Curtis, 1973.

Moley, Raymond. *Are We Movie Made?* New York: Macy-Masius, 1938.

——— . *The Hays Office.* Indianapolis: Bobbs-Merrill, 1945.

Mueller, John. *Astaire Dancing.* New York: Knopf, 1985.

Naremore, James. *The Magic World of Orson Welles.* New York: Oxford University Press, 1978.

——— . *Orson Welles: A Guide to References and Resources.* Boston: G. K. Hall, 1980.

Nizer, Louis. *New Courts of Industry.* New York: Longacre, 1935.

Parish, James R. *The Golden Era: The MGM Stock Company*. New Rochelle, N.Y.: Arlington, 1974.

———. *The Great Gangster Pictures*. Metuchen, N.J.: Scarecrow, 1976.

Perlman, William, ed. *The Movies on Trial*. New York: Macmillan, 1936.

Perry, George. *The Films of Alfred Hitchcock*. New York: Dutton, 1965.

Peters, Charles C. *Motion Pictures and Standards of Morality*. New York: Macmillan, 1933.

Phillips, Gene. *George Cukor*. Boston: Twayne, 1982.

Place, J. A. *The Non-Western Films of John Ford*. Secaucus, N.J.: Citadel, 1979.

Poague, Leland. *Frank Capra: An Approach to Film Comedy*. South Brunswick, N.J.: Barnes, 1975.

———. *Howard Hawks*. Boston: Twayne, 1982.

Quigley, Martin. *Decency in Motion Pictures*. New York: Macmillan, 1937.

Rohmer, Eric, and Claude Chabrol. *Hitchcock: The First 44 Films*. Translated by Stanley Hochman. New York: Ungar, 1979.

Rosow, Eugene. *Born to Lose: The Gangster Film in America*. New York: Oxford University Press, 1978.

Rosten, Leo C. *Hollywood: The Movie Colony and the Movie Makers*. New York: Harcourt, Brace, 1941.

Rothman, William. *Hitchcock: The Murderous Gaze*. Cambridge, Mass.: Harvard University Press, 1982.

Salt, Barry. *Film Style and Technology: History and Analysis*. London: Starword, 1983.

Sarris, Andrew. *The Films of Josef von Sternberg*. New York: Museum of Modern Art, 1966.

———. *The John Ford Movie Mystery*. Bloomington: University of Indiana Press, 1975.

Seldes, Gilbert. *The Movies Come from America*. New York: Scribner's, 1937.

Sennett, Ted. *Warner Bros. Presents*. New Rochelle, N.Y.: Arlington, 1971.

Siegel, Joel E. *Val Lewton: The Reality of Terror*. New York: Viking, 1973.

Sinclair, Andrew. *John Ford*. New York: Dial, 1979.

Sinclair, Upton. *Upton Sinclair Presents William Fox*. Los Angeles: the author, 1933.

Smith, Steven C. *A Heart at Fire's Center: The Life and Music of Bernard Herrmann*. Berkeley and Los Angeles: University of California Press, 1991.

Spoto, Donald. *The Art of Alfred Hitchcock*. New York: Hopkinson and Blake, 1976.

———. *The Dark Side of Genius: The Life of Alfred Hitchcock*. Boston: Little, Brown, 1983.

Stott, William. *Documentary Expression and Thirties America*. New York: Oxford University Press, 1973.

Taylor, John Russell. *Hitch: The Life and Times of Alfred Hitchcock*. New York: Pantheon, 1978.

Taylor, Robert Lewis. *W. C. Fields: His Follies and Fortunes*. Garden City, N.Y.: Doubleday, 1949.

Telotte, J. P. *Dreams of Darkness: Fantasy and the Films of Val Lewton*. Urbana and Chicago: University of Illinois Press, 1985.

Thomas, Bob. *King Cohn: The Life and Times of Harry Cohn*. New York: Putnam, 1967.

———. *Thalberg: Life and Legend*. Garden City, N.Y.: Doubleday, 1969.

———. *Selznick*. Garden City, N.Y.: Doubleday, 1970.

Thomas, Tony. *The Busby Berkeley Book*. Greenwich, Conn.: New York Graphic Society, 1969.

Thomas, Tony, and Aubrey Solomon. *The Films of Twentieth Century-Fox: A Pictorial History*. Secaucus, N.J.: Citadel, 1979.

Thorp, Margaret. *America at the Movies*. New Haven: Yale University Press, 1939.

Truffaut, François. *Hitchcock*. rev. ed. New York: Simon & Schuster, 1984.

Tuska, Jon, ed. *Close Up: The Contract Director*. Metuchen, N.J.: Scarecrow, 1976.

Tyler, Parker. *Magic and Myth of the Movies*. New York: Simon & Schuster, 1970.

———. *The Hollywood Hallucination*. New York: Simon & Schuster, 1970.

Von Sternberg, Josef. *Fun in a Chinese Laundry*. New York: Macmillan, 1965.

Walsh, Raoul. *Each Man in His Time: The Life Story of a Director*. New York: Farrar, Straus, 1974.

Weinberg, Herman G. *Josef von Sternberg*. New York: Dutton, 1967.

Wellman, William. *A Short Time for Insanity: An Autobiography*. New York: Hawthorn, 1974.

West Mae. *Goodness Had Nothing to Do with It.* Englewood Cliffs, N.J.: Prentice-Hall, 1959.

Willis, Donald C. *The Films of Frank Capra.* Metuchen, N. J.: Scarecrow, 1974.

——— . *The Films of Howard Hawks.* Metuchen, N.J.: Scarecrow, 1975.

Wood, Robin. *Hitchcock's Films.* New York: Barnes, 1965.

——— . *Howard Hawks.* rev. ed. London: Secker and Warburg, 1979.

——— . *Hitchcock's Films Revisited.* New York: Columbia University Press, 1989.

Yacowar, Maurice. *Hitchcock's British Films.* Hamden, Conn.: Archon, 1977.

Zukor, Adolf. *The Public Is Never Wrong.* New York: Putnam, 1953.

FILMS

DOROTHY ARZNER (1900–1979)
The Wild Party (1929)
Honor Among Lovers (1931)
Working Girls (1931)
Merrily We Go to Hell (1932)
Christopher Strong (1933)
Nana (1934)
Craig's Wife (1936)
Dance, Girl, Dance (1940)

FRANK CAPRA (1897–1991)
Platinum Blonde (1931)
American Madness (1932)
The Bitter Tea of General Yen (1932)
It Happened One Night (1934)
Mr. Deeds Goes to Town (1936)
Lost Horizon (1937)
You Can't Take It With You (1938)
Mr. Smith Goes to Washington (1939)
Meet John Doe (1941)
Why We Fight Series (1942–1944)
Arsenic and Old Lace (1944). Completed 1941
It's A Wonderful Life (1946)
State of the Union (1948)

GEORGE CUKOR (1899–1983)
A Bill of Divorcement (1932)
Dinner at Eight (1933)
David Copperfield (1935)
Sylvia Scarlett (1935)
Camille (1937)
Holiday (1938)
The Women (1939)
The Philadelphia Story (1940)

A Woman's Face (1941)
Gaslight (1944)
Adam's Rib (1949)
Born Yesterday (1950)
Pat and Mike (1952)
A Star Is Born (1954)
Les Girls (1957)
My Fair Lady (1964)
Travels With My Aunt (1972)
Rich and Famous (1981)

MICHAEL CURTIZ (1888–1962)
Doctor X (1932)
Mystery of the Wax Museum (1933)
Captain Blood (1935)
Black Fury (1935)
The Walking Dead (1936)
The Charge of the Light Brigade (1936)
Kid Galahad (1937)
Angels With Dirty Faces (1938)
The Adventures of Robin Hood (1938). Co-director, William Keighley
Dodge City (1939)
The Sea Hawk (1940)
Santa Fe Trail (1940)
Yankee Doodle Dandy (1942)
Casablanca (1942)
Mildred Pierce (1945)
Life with Father (1947)

WILLIAM DIETERLE (1893–1972)
A Midsummer Night's Dream (1935)
The Story of Louis Pasteur (1936)
The Life of Emile Zola (1937)
Juarez (1939)
The Hunchback of Notre Dame (1939)
Dr. Ehrlich's Magic Bullet (1940)
Love Letters (1945)
Portrait of Jennie (1948)

W. C. FIELDS (1879–1946)
Shorts: *The Barber Shop, The Fatal Glass of Beer,* and *The Pharmacist* (all 1933)
Million Dollar Legs (1932)
Tillie and Gus (1933)
Six of a Kind (1934)
It's a Gift (1934)
The Old-Fashioned Way (1934)
The Bank Dick (1940)
My Little Chickadee (1940)
Never Give a Sucker an Even Break (1941)

VICTOR FLEMING (1883–1949)
When the Clouds Roll By (1920)
Lord Jim (1925)
Mantrap (1926)
The Virginian (1929)
Red Dust (1932)
Treasure Island (1934)
Captains Courageous (1937)
The Wizard of Oz (1939)
Gone With the Wind (1939)
Dr. Jekyll and Mr. Hyde (1941)
A Guy Named Joe (1943)

JOHN FORD (1895–1973)
The Iron Horse (1924)
The Lost Patrol (1934)
The Whole Town's Talking (1935)
The Informer (1935)
The Plough and the Stars (1936)
The Prisoner of Shark Island (1936)
Mary of Scotland (1936)
The Hurricane (1937)
Stagecoach (1939)
Young Mr. Lincoln (1939)
The Grapes of Wrath (1940)
The Long Voyage Home (1940)
How Green Was My Valley (1941)
My Darling Clementine (1946)
The Fugitive (1947)
Fort Apache (1948)
She Wore a Yellow Ribbon (1949)
Wagon Master (1950)
Rio Grande (1950)
The Quiet Man (1952)
The Searchers (1956)
The Horse Soldiers (1959)
The Man Who Shot Liberty Valance (1962)
Donovan's Reef (1963)
Cheyenne Autumn (1964)

GRETA GARBO (1905–1990)
The Story of Gösta Berling (1924)
The Joyless Street (1925)
Flesh and the Devil (1926)
Mata Hari (1931)
Grand Hotel (1932)
Queen Christina (1933)
Anna Karenina (1935)
Camille (1937)
Ninotchka (1939)

HOWARD HAWKS (1896–1977)
The Dawn Patrol (1930)
The Criminal Code (1931)
Scarface (1932). Completed 1930
Today We Live (1933)
Twentieth Century (1934)
The Road to Glory (1936)
Bringing Up Baby (1938)
Only Angels Have Wings (1939)
His Girl Friday (1940)
Ball of Fire (1941)
Air Force (1943)
To Have and Have Not (1944)
The Big Sleep (1946)
Red River (1948)
I Was a Male War Bride (1949)
Monkey Business (1952)
Gentlemen Prefer Blondes (1953)
Rio Bravo (1959)
Hatari! (1962)
El Dorado (1967)

ALFRED HITCHCOCK (1899–1980)
The Lodger (1926)
Blackmail (1929)
Murder! (1930)
The Man Who Knew Too Much (1934)
The 39 Steps (1935)
Sabotage (1936)
Young and Innocent (1937)
The Lady Vanishes (1938)
Rebecca (1940)
Foreign Correspondent (1940)
Suspicion (1941)
Saboteur (1942)
Shadow of a Doubt (1943)
Lifeboat (1944)
Spellbound (1945)
Notorious (1946)
Rope (1948)
Under Capricorn (1949)
Strangers On A Train (1951)
Dial M for Murder (1954). 3-D, but released flat
Rear Window (1954)
To Catch a Thief (1955)
The Trouble With Harry (1955)
The Man Who Knew Too Much (1956)
The Wrong Man (1956)
Vertigo (1958)
North by Northwest (1959)
Psycho (1960)

The Birds (1963)
Marnie (1964)
Frenzy (1972)
Family Plot (1976)

FRITZ LANG (1890–1976)
Fury (1936)
You Only Live Once (1937)
Hangmen Also Die (1943)
Scarlet Street (1945)
Clash by Night (1952)
Rancho Notorious (1952)
The Big Heat (1953)
Beyond a Reasonable Doubt (1956)

VAL LEWTON (1904–1951)
Cat People (1942)
I Walked with a Zombie (1943)
The Leopard Man (1943)
The Seventh Victim (1943)
The Ghost Ship (1943)
The Curse of the Cat People (1944)
Isle Of The Dead (1945)
The Body Snatcher (1945)
Bedlam (1946)

THE MARX BROTHERS (CHICO, 1891–1961;
  HARPO, 1893–1964; GROUCHO, 1895–1977;
  ZEPPO, 1900–1979)
The Cocoanuts (1929)
Monkey Business (1931)
Horse Feathers (1932)
Duck Soup (1933)
A Night at the Opera (1935)
A Day at the Races (1937)
At the Circus (1939)
Go West (1940)

LEO McCAREY (1898–1969)
Duck Soup (1933)
Ruggles of Red Gap (1934)
The Awful Truth (1937)
Make Way for Tomorrow (1937)
Love Affair (1939)
Going My Way (1944)
My Son John (1952)
Rally Round the Flag, Boys! (1958)

LEWIS MILESTONE (1895–1980)
All Quiet on the Western Front (1930)
The Front Page (1931)
Rain (1932)
Anything Goes (1936)
Of Mice and Men (1939)

A Walk in the Sun (1945)
The Strange Love of Martha Ivers (1946)
Pork Chop Hill (1959)

JOSEF VON STERNBERG (1894–1969)
The Salvation Hunters (1925)
Underworld (1927)
The Docks of New York (1928)
The Last Command (1928)
The Blue Angel (1930)
Morocco (1930)
An American Tragedy (1931)
Shanghai Express (1932)
Blonde Venus (1932)
The Scarlet Empress (1934)
The Devil Is a Woman (1935)
The Shanghai Gesture (1941)
Anatahan (1953)

PRESTON STURGES (1898–1959)
The Great McGinty (1940)
The Lady Eve (1941)
Sullivan's Travels (1941)
The Palm Beach Story (1942)
The Miracle of Morgan's Creek (1943)
Hail the Conquering Hero (1944)
The Sin of Harold Diddlebock (1947). Recut
  version, *Mad Wednesday*, released 1950
Unfaithfully Yours (1948)

RAOUL WALSH (1887–1981)
The Roaring Twenties (1939)
They Drive by Night (1940)
High Sierra (1941)
They Died With Their Boots On (1941)
White Heat (1949)
Battle Cry (1955)
The Revolt of Mamie Stover (1956)

ORSON WELLES (1915–1985)
Citizen Kane (1941)
The Magnificent Ambersons (1942)
Journey Into Fear (1943)
The Stranger (1946)
The Lady from Shanghai (1948)
Macbeth (1948)
Mr. Arkadin or *Confidential Report* (1955)
Touch of Evil (1958)
The Trial (1962)
Chimes at Midnight or *Falstaff* (1966)

WILLIAM A. WELLMAN (1896–1975)
Wings (1927)
The Public Enemy (1931)
Wild Boys of the Road (1933)
The President Vanishes (1934)
Nothing Sacred (1937)
A Star Is Born (1937)
The Ox-Bow Incident (1943)
The Story of G. I. Joe (1945)
Battleground (1949)
The High and the Mighty (1954)

MAE WEST (1892–1980)
She Done Him Wrong (1933)
I'm No Angel (1933)
Belle of the Nineties (1934)
Klondike Annie (1936)
My Little Chickadee (1940)

JAMES WHALE (1889–1957)
Frankenstein (1931)
The Old Dark House (1932)
The Invisible Man (1933)
Bride of Frankenstein (1935)
Show Boat (1936)
The Man in the Iron Mask (1939)

THE WARNER BROS. BUSBY BERKELEY (1895–1976) CYCLE
42nd Street (1933, Lloyd Bacon/Busby Berkeley)
Gold Diggers of 1933 (1933, Mervyn LeRoy/Busby Berkeley)
Dames (1934, Ray Enright/Busby Berkeley)
Footlight Parade (1934, Lloyd Bacon/Busby Berkeley)
Gold Diggers of 1935 (1935, Busby Berkeley)
In Caliente (1935, Busby Berkeley)

THE RKO FRED ASTAIRE (1899–1987)/GINGER ROGERS (1911–) CYCLE
Flying Down to Rio (1933, Thornton Freeland)
The Gay Divorcée (1934, Mark Sandrich)
Roberta (1935, William A. Seiter)
Top Hat (1935, Mark Sandrich)
Swing Time (1936, George Stevens)
Shall We Dance? (1937, Mark Sandrich)
The Story of Vernon and Irene Castle (1939, H. C. Potter)

STUDIO ERA MISCELLANY (1930–1945)
Little Caesar (1930, Mervyn LeRoy)
Dracula (1931, Tod Browning)
Tarzan, the Ape Man (1932, W. S. Van Dyke)
Freaks (1932, Tod Browning)
Grand Hotel (1932, Edmund Goulding)
I Am A Fugitive From A Chain Gang (1932, Mervyn LeRoy)
The Mummy (1932, Karl Freund)
If I Had A Million (1932, James Cruze, H. Bruce Humberstone, Stephen Roberts, William A. Seiter, Ernst Lubitsch, Norman Taurog, and Norman Z. McLeod)
King Kong (1933, Merian C. Cooper and Ernest B. Schoedsack)
State Fair (1933, Henry King)
The Black Cat (1934, Edgar G. Ulmer)
Manhattan Melodrama and *The Thin Man* (1934, W. S. Van Dyke)
Imitation of Life (1934, John M. Stahl)
Magnificent Obsession (1935, John M. Stahl)
Mad Love (1935, Karl Freund)
Mutiny on the Bounty (1935, Frank Lloyd)
Flash Gordon (1936 serial, Frederick Stephani)
My Man Godfrey (1936, Gregory LaCava)
The Petrified Forest (1936, Archie Mayo)
Easy Living (1937, Mitchell Leisen)
The Good Earth (1937, Sidney Franklin)
Destry Rides Again (1939, George Marshall)
Gunga Din (1939, George Stevens)
Midnight (1939, Mitchell Leisen)
Dark Victory (1940, Edmund Goulding)
Now, Voyager (1940, Irving Rapper)
The Biscuit Eater (1940, Stuart Heisler)
The Wolf Man (1941, George Waggner)
This Gun For Hire (1942, Frank Tuttle)
The Song of Bernadette (1943, Henry King)
Since You Went Away (1944, John Cromwell)
Murder, My Sweet (1945, Edward Dmytryk)
State Fair (1945, Walter Lang)
The House on 92nd Street (1945, Henry Hathaway)
Detour (1945, Edgar G. Ulmer)

12. Years of Transition (1946–1965)

BOOKS

Agee, James. *Agee on Film.* 2 vols. (Vol. 1 contains his reviews and essays; vol. 2, his scripts, includes *The African Queen* and *The Night of the Hunter*.) New York: McDowell, Obolensky, 1960.

Allan, Blaine. *Nicholas Ray: A Guide to References and Resources.* Boston: G. K. Hall, 1984.

Alloway, Lawrence. *Violent America: The Movies, 1946–64.* New York: Museum of Modern Art, 1971.

Battcock, Gregory, ed. *The New American Cinema.* New York: Dutton, 1967.

Baxter, John. *Hollywood in the Sixties.* New York: Macmillan, 1972.

Beck, Jerry, and Will Friedwald. *Looney Tunes and Merrie Melodies: A Complete Illustrated Guide to the Warner Bros. Cartoons.* New York: Henry Holt, 1989.

Bentley, Eric, ed. *Thirty Years of Treason.* New York: Viking, 1971.

Bessie, Alvah. *Inquisition in Eden.* Berlin: Seven Seas, 1967.

Biskind, Peter. *Seeing is Believing: How Hollywood Taught Us to Stop Worrying and Love the Fifties.* New York: Pantheon, 1983.

Bowles, Stephen. *Sidney Lumet: A Guide to References and Resources.* Boston: G. K. Hall, 1979.

Brodsky, Jack, and Nathan Weiss. *The Cleopatra Papers: A Private Correspondence.* New York: Simon & Schuster, 1963.

Carmen, Ira H. *Movies, Censorship, and the Law.* Ann Arbor: University of Michigan Press, 1966.

Casper, Joseph A. *Vincente Minnelli and the Film Musical.* London: Yoseloff, 1977.

Casty, Alan. *The Films of Robert Rossen.* New York: Museum of Modern Art, 1969.

Ceplair, Larry, and Steven Englund. *The Inquisition in Hollywood: Politics in the Film Community, 1930–1960.* Garden City, N.Y.: Doubleday, 1980.

Ciment, Michel. *Kazan on Kazan.* New York: Viking, 1972.

Cogley, John. *Report on Blacklisting. I. The Movies.* New York: Fund for the Republic, 1956.

Conant, Michael. *Anti-trust in the Motion Picture Industry.* Berkeley and Los Angeles: University of California Press, 1960.

Deming, Barbara. *Running Away from Myself.* New York: Grossman, 1969.

Dick, Bernard F. *Billy Wilder.* Boston: Twayne, 1980.

Dowdy, Andrew. *The Films of the Fifties: The American State of Mind.* New York: William Morrow, 1975.

Englund, Steven. *Grace of Monaco: An Interpretive Biography.* Garden City, N.Y.: Doubleday, 1984.

Fordin, Hugh. *The Movies' Greatest Musicals: Produced in Hollywood USA by the Freed Unit.* New York: Ungar, 1975.

Garnham, Nicholas. *Samuel Fuller.* New York: Viking, 1971.

Geist, Kenneth L. *Pictures with Talk: The Life and Films of Joseph L. Mankiewicz.* New York: Scribner's, 1978.

Goodman, Ezra. *The Fifty Year Decline and Fall of Hollywood.* New York: Simon & Schuster, 1961.

Goodman, Walter. *The Committee.* New York: Farrar, Straus, 1968.

Halliday, Jon, ed. *Sirk on Sirk.* New York: Viking, 1969.

Handel, Leo A. *Hollywood Looks at Its Audience.* Urbana: University of Illinois Press, 1950.

Hardy, Phil. *Samuel Fuller.* New York: Praeger, 1970.

Hellman, Lillian. *Scoundrel Time.* Boston: Little, Brown, 1976.

Higham, Charles, and Joel Greenberg. *Hollywood in the Forties.* Cranbury, N.J.: Barnes, 1968.

Jones, Ken D., and Arthur F. McClure. *Hollywood at War.* Cranbury, N.J.: Barnes, 1973.

Kael, Pauline. "Movies, the Desperate Art." In *Film: An Anthology,* edited by Daniel Talbot. Berkeley and Los Angeles: University of California Press, 1966, pp. 51–71.

——— . "Zeitgeist and Poltergeist; Or, Are Movies Going to Pieces?" In *I Lost It at the Movies.* New York: Bantam, 1966, pp. 3–24.

——— . "*Hud,* Deep in the Divided Heart of Hollywood." In *I Lost It at the Movies,* pp. 69–83.

Kagan, Norman. *The War Film.* New York: Pyramid, 1974.

Kahn, Gordon. *Hollywood on Trial.* New York: Boni & Gaer, 1948.

Kanfer, Stephan. *A Journal of the Plague Years.* New York: Atheneum, 1973.

Karimi, A. M. *Toward a Definition of the American Film Noir.* New York: Arno, 1976.

Kitses, James. *Horizons West: Mann, Boetticher, Peckinpah.* Bloomington: Indiana University Press, 1969.

Knox, Donald. *The Magic Factory: How MGM Made* An American in Paris. New York: Praeger, 1973.

Koszarski, Richard. *Hollywood Directors: 1941–76.* New York: Oxford University Press, 1977.

Kozloff, Sarah. *Invisible Storytellers: Voice-Over Narration in American Fiction Film.* Berkeley and Los Angeles: University of California Press, 1988.

Kreidl, John Francis. *Nicholas Ray.* Boston: Twayne, 1977.

Lenihan, John H. *Showdown: Confronting Modern America in the Western Film.* Urbana and Chicago: University of Illinois Press, 1979.

Lewis, Jerry. *The Total Film Maker.* New York: Random House, 1971.

MacCann, Richard Dyer. *Hollywood in Transition.* New York: Houghton, Mifflin, 1962.

Madsen, Axel. *Billy Wilder.* Bloomington: Indiana University Press, 1969.

———. *William Wyler.* New York: Crowell, 1973.

McArthur, Colin. *Underworld USA.* New York: Viking, 1972.

McGilligan, Pat, ed. *Backstory 2: Interviews with Screenwriters of the 1940s and 1950s.* Berkeley and Los Angeles: University of California Press, 1991.

Miller, Merle. *The Judges and the Judged.* Garden City, N.Y.: Doubleday, 1952.

Minnelli, Vincente, with Victor Arce. *I Remember It Well.* Garden City, N.Y.: Doubleday, 1974.

Morgan, Hal, and Dan Symmes. *Amazing 3-D.* Boston: Little, Brown, 1982.

Ottoson, Robert. *American International Pictures: A Filmography.* New York: Garland, 1985.

Powdermaker, Hortense. *Hollywood: The Dream Factory.* Boston: Little, Brown, 1950.

Pratley, Gerald. *The Cinema of John Frankenheimer.* Cranbury, N.J.: Barnes, 1969.

———. *The Cinema of Otto Preminger.* Cranbury, N.J.: Barnes, 1971.

———. *The Cinema of John Huston.* Cranbury, N.J.: Barnes, 1977.

Preminger, Otto. *Preminger: An Autobiography.* Garden City, N.Y.: Doubleday, 1977.

Quart, Leonard, and Albert Auster. *American Film and Society Since 1945.* New York: Praeger, 1985.

Rebello, Stephen. *Alfred Hitchcock and the Making of* Psycho. New York: Dembner, 1990.

Reemes, Dana M. *Directed by Jack Arnold.* Jefferson, N.C.: McFarland, 1988.

Richie, Donald. *George Stevens: An American Romantic.* New York: Museum of Modern Art, 1970.

Ross, Lillian. *Picture.* New York: Limelight, 1984.

Schechter, Harold. *Deviant: The Shocking True Story of Ed Gein, the Original "Psycho."* New York: Pocket Books, 1989.

Schumach, Murray. *The Face on the Cutting-Room Floor.* New York: Morrow, 1964.

Seidman, Steve. *The Film Career of Billy Wilder.* Boston: G. K. Hall, 1977.

Shindler, Colin. *Hollywood Goes to War: Films and American Society, 1939–52.* London: Routledge & Kegan Paul, 1979.

Spoto, Donald. *Stanley Kramer: Film Maker.* New York: Putnam, 1978.

Steiner, Gary A. *The People Look at Television.* New York: Knopf, 1963.

Stern, Michael. *Douglas Sirk.* Boston: Twayne, 1979.

Telotte, J. P. *Voices in the Dark: The Narrative Patterns of* Film Noir. Urbana and Chicago: University of Illinois Press, 1989.

Trumbo, Dalton. *Additional Dialogue: The Letters of Dalton Trumbo, 1942–1962.* Edited by Helen Manfull. New York: M. Evans, 1970.

Tuska, Jon. *Dark Cinema: American Film Noir in Cultural Perspective.* Westport, Conn.: Greenwood, 1984.

Vaughn, Robert. *Only Victims.* New York: Putnam, 1972.

Vizzard, Jack. *See No Evil: Life Inside a Hollywood Censor.* New York: Simon & Schuster, 1970.

Warren, Bill. *Keep Watching the Skies! American Science Fiction Movies of the Fifties.* 2 vols. Jefferson, N.C.: McFarland, 1982, 1986.

Warshow, Robert. *The Immediate Experience.*
  Garden City, N.Y.: Doubleday, 1952.
Wolfenstein, Martha, and Nathan Leites.
  Movies: A Psychological Study. Glencoe, Ill.:
  Free Press, 1950.
Wysotsky, Michael Z. *Wide-Screen Cinema and
  Stereophonic Sound.* New York: Hastings, 1971.
Zolotow, Maurice. *Billy Wilder in Hollywood.*
  New York: Putnam, 1977.

FILMS

JACK ARNOLD (1912–   )
It Came From Outer Space (1953). 3-D
Creature from the Black Lagoon (1954). 3-D
Tarantula (1955)
The Incredible Shrinking Man (1957)
The Mouse That Roared (1959)

ROGER CORMAN (1926–   )
Not of This Earth (1957)
Machine Gun Kelly (1958)
A Bucket of Blood (1959)
House of Usher (1960)
The Little Shop of Horrors (1960)
The Pit and the Pendulum (1961)
X — The Man with the X-Ray Eyes (1963)
The Raven (1963)
The Masque of the Red Death (1964)
The Tomb of Ligeia (1965)
The Wild Angels (1966)
Gas-s-s-s (1970)

JULES DASSIN (1911–   )
Brute Force (1947)
The Naked City (1948)
Thieves' Highway (1949)
Night and the City (1950)
Rififi (1955)
Never on Sunday (1960)
Topkapi (1964)
10:30 PM Summer (1966)
A Dream of Passion (1978)

STANLEY DONEN (1924–   )
On the Town (1949). Co-director, Gene Kelly
Royal Wedding (1951)
Singin' in the Rain (1952). Co-director, Gene
  Kelly
It's Always Fair Weather (1955). Co-director,
  Gene Kelly
Funny Face (1957)
The Pajama Game (1957)

Two for the Road (1967)
Bedazzled (1967)
Movie Movie (1978)

SAMUEL FULLER (1911–   )
I Shot Jesse James (1949)
The Steel Helmet (1951)
Park Row (1952)
Pickup on South Street (1953)
House of Bamboo (1955)
Run of the Arrow (1957)
China Gate (1957)
Underworld U.S.A. (1961)
Shock Corridor (1963)
The Naked Kiss (1964)
The Big Red One (1980)
White Dog (1982)

HENRY HATHAWAY (1898–1985)
The Lives of a Bengal Lancer (1935)
Peter Ibbetson (1935)
Trail of the Lonesome Pine (1936)
The Real Glory (1939)
The House on 92nd Street (1945)
The Dark Corner (1946)
Kiss of Death (1947)
Call Northside 777 (1948)
Niagara (1953)
True Grit (1969)

JOHN HUSTON (1906–1987)
The Maltese Falcon (1941)
The Battle of San Pietro (1945)
Let There Be Light (1946)
The Treasure of the Sierra Madre (1948)
Key Largo (1948)
The Asphalt Jungle (1950)
The Red Badge of Courage (1951)
The African Queen (1951)
Beat the Devil (1954)
The Misfits (1961)
The Night of the Iguana (1964)
Fat City (1972)
The Man Who Would Be King (1975)
Wise Blood (1979)
Under the Volcano (1984)
Prizzi's Honor (1985)
The Dead (1987)

ELIA KAZAN (1909–   )
A Tree Grows in Brooklyn (1945)
Boomerang (1947)
Gentleman's Agreement (1947)

Pinky (1949)
A Streetcar Named Desire (1951)
Viva Zapata! (1952)
On the Waterfront (1954)
East of Eden (1955)
A Face in the Crowd (1957)
Wild River (1960)
Splendor in the Grass (1961)

HENRY KING (1888–1982)
Tol'able David (1921)
The White Sister (1923)
Alexander's Ragtime Band (1938)
The Black Swan (1942)
The Song of Bernadette (1943)
Twelve O'Clock High (1949)
The Gunfighter (1950)
King of the Khyber Rifles (1953)
Carousel (1956)
Tender is the Night (1962)

STANLEY KRAMER (1913–   )
The Defiant Ones (1958)
On the Beach (1959)
Inherit the Wind (1960)
Judgment at Nuremberg (1961)
It's a Mad Mad Mad Mad World (1963)
Guess Who's Coming to Dinner? (1967)

JERRY LEWIS (1926–   )
The Bellboy (1960)
The Errand Boy (1961)
The Nutty Professor (1963)
The Patsy (1964)
The Big Mouth (1967)

SIDNEY LUMET (1924–   )
12 Angry Men (1957)
Long Day's Journey into Night (1962)
Fail-Safe (1964)
The Pawnbroker (1965)
The Hill (1965)
The Deadly Affair (1967)
Bye Bye Braverman (1968)
Serpico (1973)
Dog Day Afternoon (1975)
Network (1976)
Prince of the City (1981)
The Verdict (1982)

JOSEPH L. MANKIEWICZ (1909–   )
The Ghost and Mrs. Muir (1947)
A Letter to Three Wives (1949)
All About Eve (1950)

Julius Caesar (1953)
The Barefoot Contessa (1954)
Guys and Dolls (1955)
Suddenly Last Summer (1959)
Cleopatra (1963)

VINCENTE MINNELLI (1903–1986)
Cabin in the Sky (1943)
Meet Me in St. Louis (1944)
The Pirate (1948)
Father of the Bride (1950)
An American in Paris (1951)
The Band Wagon (1953)
The Bad and the Beautiful (1953)
Lust for Life (1956)
Gigi (1958)
The Reluctant Debutante (1958)
Some Came Running (1959)
Bells Are Ringing (1960)
Two Weeks in Another Town (1962)

OTTO PREMINGER (1906–1986)
Laura (1944)
Where the Sidewalk Ends (1950)
Angel Face (1952)
The Moon Is Blue (1953)
River of No Return (1954)
The Man With the Golden Arm (1955)
Porgy and Bess (1959)
Anatomy of a Murder (1959)
Exodus (1960)
Advise and Consent (1962)

NICHOLAS RAY (1911–1979)
They Live By Night (1949). Completed 1948
Knock on Any Door (1949)
In a Lonely Place (1950)
Johnny Guitar (1954)
Rebel Without a Cause (1955)
The True Story of Jesse James (1957)
King of Kings (1961)

ROBERT ROSSEN (1908–1966)
Johnny O'Clock (1947)
Body and Soul (1947)
All the King's Men (1949)
The Hustler (1961)
Lilith (1964)

DOUGLAS SIRK (1900–1987)
Sleep My Love (1948)
Magnificent Obsession (1954)
All That Heaven Allows (1955)
Written on the Wind (1956)
The Tarnished Angels (1957)
Imitation of Life (1959)

GEORGE STEVENS (1904–1975)
Alice Adams (1935)
Vivacious Lady (1938)
Gunga Din (1939)
Woman of the Year (1942)
The Talk of the Town (1942)
The More the Merrier (1943)
A Place in the Sun (1951)
Shane (1953)
Giant (1956)

BILLY WILDER (1906–   )
The Major and the Minor (1942)
Double Indemnity (1944)
The Lost Weekend (1945)
A Foreign Affair (1948)
Sunset Boulevard (1950)
Stalag 17 (1953)
Sabrina (1954)
The Seven Year Itch (1955)
Love in the Afternoon (1957)
Some Like It Hot (1959)
The Apartment (1960)
One, Two, Three (1961)
The Fortune Cookie (1966)
The Private Life of Sherlock Holmes (1970)

ROBERT WISE (1914–   )
The Curse of the Cat People (1944). Co-director,
  Gunther Von Fritsch
The Body Snatcher (1945)
The Set-Up (1949)
The Day the Earth Stood Still (1951)
I Want to Live! (1958)
West Side Story (1961). Co-director, Jerome
  Robbins
The Haunting (1963)
The Sound of Music (1965)
The Sand Pebbles (1966)
Star Trek—The Motion Picture (1979)

WILLIAM WYLER (1902–1981)
These Three (1936)
Dodsworth (1936)
Dead End (1937)
Jezebel (1938)
Wuthering Heights (1939)
The Letter (1940)
The Little Foxes (1941)
Mrs. Miniver (1942)
The Memphis Belle (1944)
The Best Years of Our Lives (1946)
Roman Holiday (1953)
Friendly Persuasion (1956)
The Big Country (1958)
Ben-Hur (1959)
The Collector (1965)
Funny Girl (1968)

FRED ZINNEMANN (1907–   )
The Men (1950)
High Noon (1952)
Member of the Wedding (1952)
From Here to Eternity (1953)
Oklahoma! (1955)
A Hatful of Rain (1957)
The Nun's Story (1959)
A Man for All Seasons (1966)
Julia (1977)
Five Days One Summer (1983)

TRANSITIONAL ERA MISCELLANY (1946–1965)
The Killers (1946, Robert Siodmak)
Crossfire (1947, Edward Dmytryk)
Out of the Past (1947, Jacques Tourneur)
Easter Parade (1948, Charles Walters)
Force of Evil (1948, Abraham Polonsky)
The Senator Was Indiscreet (1948, George S.
  Kaufman)
Home of the Brave (1949, Mark Robson)
Intruder in the Dust (1949, Clarence Brown)
Winchester 73 (1950, Anthony Mann)
Gun Crazy (1950, Joseph H. Lewis). Completed
  1949
Destination Moon (1950, Irving Pichel)
Ways of Love (1950). Includes Pagnol's *Jofroi*
  (1934), Renoir's *A Day in the Country* (1936),
  and Rossellini's *The Miracle* (1948)
The Thing or *The Thing From Another World*
  (1951, Christian Nyby)
Bend of the River (1952, Anthony Mann)

Lili (1953, Charles Walters)
Salt of the Earth (1953, Herbert Biberman)
The Wild One (1953, Laslo Benedek)
The War of the Worlds (1953, Byron Haskin)
Invaders from Mars (1953, William Cameron Menzies)
The 5,000 Fingers of Dr. T. (1953, Roy Rowland)
Kiss Me Kate (1953, George Sidney). 3-D
House of Wax (1953, André de Toth). 3-D
Gog (1954, Herbert L. Strock). 3-D
Them! (1954, Gordon Douglas)
The Bridges at Toko-Ri (1954, Mark Robson)
Bad Day at Black Rock (1954, John Sturges)
The Big Knife (1955, Robert Aldrich)
Blackboard Jungle (1955, Richard Brooks)
Marty (1955, Delbert Mann)
The Night of the Hunter (1955, Charles Laughton)
Kiss Me Deadly (1955, Robert Aldrich)
This Island Earth (1955, Joseph Newman)
The Court Jester (1956, Norman Panama)
Invasion of the Body Snatchers (1956, Don Siegel)
Forbidden Planet (1956, Fred M. Wilcox)
Picnic (1956, Joshua Logan)
Sweet Smell of Success (1957, Alexander Mackendrick)
I Was a Teenage Werewolf (1957, Gene Fowler)
The Tall T (1957, Budd Boetticher)
The Blob (1958, Irvin S. Yeaworth, Jr.)
The Fly (1958, Kurt Neumann)
The Goddess (1958, John Cromwell)
Auntie Mame (1958, Morton DaCosta)
The Savage Eye (1960, Ben Maddow, Sidney Meyers, and Joseph Strick)
Elmer Gantry (1960, Richard Brooks)
The Magnificent Seven (1960, John Sturges)
The Connection (1961, Shirley Clarke)
Lonely Are the Brave (1962, David Miller)
The Manchurian Candidate (1962, John Frankenheimer)
What Ever Happened to Baby Jane? (1962, Robert Aldrich)
David and Lisa (1963, Frank Perry)
Hud (1963, Martin Ritt)
Zorba the Greek (1964, Michael Cacoyannis)
Seven Days in May (1964, John Frankenheimer)
Dr. Strangelove Or: How I Learned To Stop Worrying And Love The Bomb (1964, Stanley Kubrick)
The World of Henry Orient (1964, George Roy Hill)

Nothing But a Man (1964, Michael Roemer). Co-director, Robert M. Young
A Thousand Clowns (1965, Fred Coe)
The Spy Who Came In From The Cold (1965, Martin Ritt)

13. Postwar Cinema in Italy and France (1945–1990)

BOOKS

Allen, Don. *Truffaut.* New York: Viking, 1974.
Almendros, Nestor. *A Man with a Camera.* Translated by Rachel Phillips Belash. New York: Farrar, Straus, 1984.
Andrew, J. Dudley. *André Bazin.* New York: Oxford University Press, 1978.
Armes, Roy. *French Cinema Since 1946.* 2 vols. New York: Barnes, 1966.
——— . *The Cinema of Alain Resnais.* New York: Barnes, 1968.
——— . *French Cinema.* New York: Oxford University Press, 1985.
Bazin, André. *What is Cinema?* 2 vols. Berkeley and Los Angeles: University of California Press, 1967, 1971.
Betti, Liliana. *Fellini: An Intimate Portrait.* Boston: Little, Brown, 1979.
Bondanella, Peter, ed. *Federico Fellini: Essays in Criticism.* New York: Oxford University Press, 1978.
Braudy, Leo, ed. *Focus on* Shoot the Piano Player. Englewood Cliffs, N.J.: Prentice-Hall, 1972.
Bresson, Robert. *Notes on Cinematography.* Translated by Jonathan Griffin. New York: Urizen, 1977.
Brown, Royal S., ed. *Focus on Godard.* Englewood Cliffs, N.J.: Prentice-Hall, 1972.
Brunette, Peter. *Roberto Rossellini.* New York: Oxford University Press, 1987.
Bruno, Giuliana, and Maria Nadotti, eds. *Off Screen: Women and Film in Italy.* New York: Routledge, 1988.
Cameron, Ian, ed. *Claude Chabrol.* New York: Praeger, 1970.
——— . *The Films of Jean-Luc Godard.* New York: Praeger, 1969.

———. *The Films of Robert Bresson.* New York: Praeger, 1970.

Cameron, Ian, and Robin Wood. *Antonioni.* New York: Praeger, 1968.

Chatman, Seymour. *Antonioni, or, The Surface of the World.* Berkeley and Los Angeles: University of California Press, 1985.

Cocteau, Jean. *Cocteau on the Film.* New York: Roy Publishers, 1954.

Collet, Jean. *Jean-Luc Godard.* New York: Crown, 1968.

Cowie, Peter. *Antonioni, Bergman, Resnais.* New York: Yoseloff, 1964.

Crisp, C. G. *François Truffaut.* New York: Praeger, 1972.

———. *Eric Rohmer: Realist and Moralist.* Bloomington: Indiana University Press, 1988.

Duras, Marguerite. *Green Eyes.* Translated by Carol Barko. New York: Columbia University Press, 1990.

Durgnat, Raymond. *Franju.* London: Studio/Vista, 1967.

———. *Nouvelle Vague: The First Decade.* Essex: Loughton, 1963.

Fava, Claudio G., and Aldo Vigano. *The Films of Federico Fellini.* Secaucus, N.J.: Citadel, 1984.

Fellini, Federico. *Fellini on Fellini.* New York: Delacorte, 1976.

Flitterman-Lewis, Sandy. *To Desire Differently: Feminism and the French Cinema.* Urbana and Chicago: University of Illinois Press, 1990.

Giannetti, Louis D. *Godard and Others.* London: Tantivy, 1975.

Godard, Jean-Luc. *Godard on Godard.* Translated by Tom Milne. New York: Viking, 1972.

Graham, Peter. *The New Wave.* Garden City, N.Y.: Doubleday, 1968.

Greene, Naomi. *Pier Paolo Pasolini: Cinema as Heresy.* Princeton: Princeton University Press, 1990.

Guarner, José Luis. *Roberto Rossellini.* Translated by Elizabeth Cameron. New York: Praeger, 1970.

Guzzetti, Alfred. Two or Three Things I Know about Her: *Analysis of a Film by Godard.* Cambridge, Mass.: Harvard University Press, 1981.

Harvey, Sylvia. *May '68 and Film Culture.* London: BFI, 1978.

Houston, Penelope. *Contemporary Cinema.* Baltimore, Md.: Penguin, 1964.

Hughes, Eileen. *On the Set of* Fellini—Satyricon: *A Behind-the-Scenes Diary.* New York: Morrow, 1971.

Huss, Roy, ed. *Focus on* Blow Up. Englewood Cliffs, N.J.: Prentice-Hall, 1971.

Insdorf, Annette. *François Truffaut.* rev. ed. New York: Simon & Schuster, 1989.

Jarratt, Vernon. *The Italian Cinema.* New York: Macmillan, 1951.

Kael, Pauline. "The Come-Dressed-as-the-Sick-Soul-of-Europe Parties: *La Notte, Last Year at Marienbad, La Dolce Vita.*" In *I Lost It at the Movies.* New York: Bantam, 1966, pp. 162–76.

Kawin, Bruce F. *Mindscreen: Bergman, Godard, and First-Person Film.* Princeton: Princeton University Press, 1978.

Ketcham, Charles. *Federico Fellini: The Search for a New Mythology.* New York: Paulist Press, 1976.

Kreidl, John Francis. *Alain Resnais.* Boston: Twayne, 1979.

Leprohon, Pierre. *The Italian Cinema.* New York: Praeger, 1972.

———. *Michelangelo Antonioni.* New York: Simon & Schuster, 1963.

Liehm, Mira. *Passion and Defiance: Film in Italy from 1942 to the Present.* Berkeley and Los Angeles: University of California Press, 1984.

Lyons, Robert J. *Michelangelo Antonioni's Neorealism.* New York: Arno, 1976.

Maddock, Brent. *The Films of Jacques Tati.* Metuchen, N.J.: Scarecrow, 1977.

Manvell, Roger. *New Cinema in Europe.* New York: Dutton, 1966.

Monaco, James. *The New Wave.* New York: Oxford University Press, 1976.

———. *Alain Resnais.* New York: Oxford University Press, 1978.

Murray, Edward. *Fellini the Artist.* New York: Ungar, 1976.

Mussman, Toby, ed. *Jean-Luc Godard: A Critical Anthology.* New York: Dutton, 1968.

Nowell-Smith, Geoffrey. *Luchino Visconti.* Garden City, N.Y.: Doubleday, 1968.

Pasolini, Pier Paolo. *Heretical Empiricism.* Edited by Louise K. Barnett and translated by

Ben Lawton and Louise K. Barnett. Bloomington: Indiana University Press, 1988.

Perry, Ted. *Filmguide to 8½.* Bloomington: Indiana University Press, 1975.

Petrie, Graham. *The Cinema of François Truffaut.* New York: Barnes, 1970.

Robinson, W. R. *Man and the Movies.* Baton Rouge: University of Louisiana Press, 1967.

Rondi, Gian. *Italian Cinema Today.* New York: Hill & Wang, 1965.

Rosenbaum, Jonathan. *Rivette: Texts and Interviews.* London: BFI, 1977.

Rosenthal, Stuart. *The Cinema of Federico Fellini.* Cranbury, N.J.: Barnes, 1976.

Roud, Richard. *Jean-Luc Godard.* rev. ed. Bloomington: Indiana University Press, 1970.

Salachas, Gilbert. *Federico Fellini: An Investigation into His Films and Philosophy.* New York: Crown, 1969.

Samuels, Charles Thomas. *Encountering Directors.* New York: Putnam, 1972.

Servadio, Gaia. *Luchino Visconti.* New York: Watts, 1983.

Snyder, Stephen. *Pier Paolo Pasolini.* Boston: Twayne, 1980.

Stack, Oswald, ed. *Pasolini on Pasolini.* Bloomington: Indiana University Press, 1969.

Stirling, Monica. *A Screen of Time: A Study of Luchino Visconti.* New York: Harcourt, Brace, 1979.

Truffaut, François. *The Films in My Life.* New York: Simon & Schuster, 1979.

Van Wert, William F. *The Film Career of Alain Robbe-Grillet.* Pleasantville, N.Y.: Redgrave, 1977.

Ward, John. *Alain Resnais, or The Theme of Time.* New York: Doubleday, 1968.

Willemen, Paul, ed. *Ophüls.* London: BFI, 1978.
———. *Pier Paolo Pasolini.* London: BFI, 1977.

Williams, Alan. *Max Ophüls and the Cinema of Desire: Style and Spectacle in Four Films.* New York: Arno, 1980.

Wollen, Peter. *Signs and Meaning in the Cinema.* 3rd ed. Bloomington: Indiana University Press, 1972.

Wood, Robin, and Michael Walker. *Claude Chabrol.* New York: Praeger, 1970.

Zavattini, Cesare. *Sequences from a Cinematic Life.* Translated by William Weaver. Englewood Cliffs, N.J.: Prentice-Hall, 1970.

FILMS

ITALY

MICHELANGELO ANTONIONI (1912–)
N.U. or *Netezza urbana* (*Trash Collectors,* 1948)
Cronaca di un amore (1950)
I vinti (1952)
Le amiche (1955)
Il grido (1957)
L'avventura (1960)
La notte (1960)
L'eclisse (*Eclipse,* 1962)
Red Desert (1964)
Blowup (1966)
Zabriskie Point (1970)
Chung Kuo Cina or *China* (1972)
The Passenger (1975)
The Mystery of Oberwald (1980)
Identification of a Woman (1982)

BERNARDO BERTOLUCCI (1940–)
Before the Revolution (1964)
The Spider's Strategem (1970)
The Conformist (1971)
Last Tango in Paris (1972)
1900 (1976)
Luna (1979)
The Last Emperor (1987)
The Sheltering Sky (1990)

VITTORIO DE SICA (1902–1974)
Shoeshine (1946)
The Bicycle Thief or *Bicycle Thieves* (1948)
Miracle in Milan (1950)
Umberto D (1952)
The Gold of Naples (1954)
The Roof (1956)
Two Women (1960)
The Garden of the Finzi-Continis (1971)
A Brief Vacation (1973)

FEDERICO FELLINI (1920–)
Variety Lights (1950)
The White Sheik (1952)
I vitelloni (1953)
La strada (1954)
Il bidone (1955)
Nights of Cabiria (1956)
La dolce vita (1960)
8½ (1963)
Juliet of the Spirits (1965)

Fellini Satyricon or *Satyricon* (1969)
The Clowns (1971)
Amarcord (1973)
Casanova (1976)
Orchestra Rehearsal (1979)
And the Ship Sails On (1983)

SERGIO LEONE (1929–1989)
A Fistful of Dollars or *For a Fistful of Dollars* (1964)
For a Few Dollars More (1965)
The Good, the Bad and the Ugly (1966)
Once Upon a Time in the West (1968)
Once Upon a Time in America (1984)

PIER PAOLO PASOLINI (1922–1975)
Accattone (1961)
The Gospel According to St. Matthew (1964)
Hawks and Sparrows (1966)
Teorema (1968)
Pigpen or *Pigsty* (1969)
Medea (1969)
The Decameron (1971)
The Canterbury Tales (1972)
The Arabian Nights (1974)
Salò or *The 120 Days of Sodom* (1975)

ROBERTO ROSSELLINI (1906–1977)
Open City or *Rome, Open City* (1945)
Paisan (1946)
Germany Year Zero (1947)
The Miracle (1948)
Stromboli (1949)
Europa '51 (1951)
Viaggio in Italia (*Voyage to Italy,* 1953)
India (1958)
General Della Rovere (1959)
The Rise to Power of Louis XIV (1966)
Socrates (1970)
The Age of the Medici (1972)
The Messiah (1975)

ETTORE SCOLA (1931–   )
We All Loved Each Other So Much (1974)
A Special Day (1977)
La Nuit de Varennes (1982)
Le Bal (1984)
The Family (1987)

LUCHINO VISCONTI (1906–1976)
Ossessione (1942)
La terra trema (1948)
Senso (1954)
Rocco and His Brothers (1960)

The Leopard (1963)
The Damned (1969)
Death in Venice (1971)
The Innocent (1976)

ITALIAN MISCELLANY (1960–1989)
Bell' Antonio (1960, Mauro Bolognini)
Bandits of Orgosolo (1961, Vittorio De Seta)
Salvatore Giuliano (1961, Francesco Rosi)
Il posto (1961, Ermanno Olmi)
The Gold of Rome (1961, Carlo Lizzani)
The Fiancés (1963, Ermanno Olmi)
The Girl with the Suitcase (1963, Valerio Zurlini)
Seduced and Abandoned (1963, Pietro Germi)
The Lizards (1963, Lina Wertmüller)
Il sorpasso or *The Easy Life* (1963, Dino Risi)
The Organizer (1963, Mario Monicelli)
The 10th Victim (1965, Elio Petri)
The Battle of Algiers (1965, Gillo Pontecorvo)
Fists in the Pocket (1965, Marco Bellocchio)
China Is Near (1967, Marco Bellocchio)
Investigation of a Citizen above Suspicion (1970, Elio Petri)
In the Name of the Father (1971, Marco Bellocchio)
The Seduction of Mimi (1972, Lina Wertmüller)
Swept Away . . . or *Swept away by an unusual destiny in the blue sea of August* (1974, Lina Wertmüller)
Seven Beauties (1976, Lina Wertmüller)
Padre Padrone (1977, Paolo and Vittorio Taviani)
Bread and Chocolate (1978, Franco Brusati)
The Tree of Wooden Clogs (1978, Ermanno Olmi)
Christ Stopped at Eboli (1979, Francesco Rosi)
Three Brothers (1981, Francesco Rosi)
The Night of the Shooting Stars (1982, Paolo and Vittorio Taviani)
KAOS (*Chaos,* 1984, Paolo and Vittorio Taviani)
Cinema Paradiso (1989, Giuseppe Tornatore)

FRANCE

ROBERT BRESSON (1907–   )
Les Anges du peche (1943)
Les Dames du Bois de Boulogne (1945)
Diary of a Country Priest (1950)
A Man Escaped (1956)
Pickpocket (1959)
The Trial of Joan of Arc (1962)
Au hasard, Balthazar (1966)
Mouchette (1967)

Une Femme douce (1969)
Lancelot of the Lake (1974)
The Devil Probably (1977)
L'Argent (1983)

CLAUDE CHABROL (1930–)
Le Beau Serge (1958)
The Cousins (1959)
A double tour (1959)
Les Biches (1968)
This Man Must Die or *The Beast Must Die* (1969)
Le Boucher (1970)
La Rupture (1971)
Wedding in Blood (1973)
Violette or *Violette Nozière* (1978)
The Cry of the Owl (1987)
Une Affaire de femmes or *Story of Women* (1988)

JEAN COCTEAU (1889–1963)
The Blood of a Poet (1930)
Beauty and the Beast (1946). Asst. director, René Clément
Les Parents terribles (1948)
Orpheus (1950)
The Testament of Orpheus (1959)

JEAN-LUC GODARD (1930–)
Une Histoire d'eau (1958). Co-director, François Truffaut
Breathless (1960). Shot 1959
Le Petit soldat (1963). Completed 1960; banned until 1963
Vivre sa vie or *My Life to Live* (1962)
Les Carabiniers (1963)
Contempt (1963)
Band of Outsiders (1964)
A Married Woman (1964)
Alphaville, A Strange Adventure of Lemmy Caution (1965)
Pierrot le fou (1965)
Masculine-Feminine (1966)
Made in USA (1967)
2 or 3 Things I Know About Her (1967)
La Chinoise (1967)
Weekend (1967)
One Plus One (1968)
Le Gai savoir (1969). Completed 1968
Wind from the East (1969). Co-director, Jean-Pierre Gorin
Tout va bien (1972). Co-director, Jean Pierre Gorin
Communication (1976). Co-director, Anne-Marie Miéville

France / Tour / Détour / Deux / Enfants (1978). Co-director, Anne-Marie Miéville
Numéro deux (1979)
Sauve qui peut / La vie or *Every Man for Himself* (1980)
Passion (1982)
First Name: Carmen (1983)
Hail Mary (1985)

LOUIS MALLE (1932–)
Frantic (1958). Completed 1957
The Lovers (1958)
Zazie dans le Métro (1960)
Le Feu follet (1963)
Phantom India (1970)
Murmur of the Heart (1971)
Lacombe Lucien (1974)
Pretty Baby (1978)
Atlantic City (1980)
My Dinner with Andre (1981)
Au revoir les enfants (1987)

CHRIS MARKER (1921–)
Letter from Siberia (1957)
Cuba sí! (1961)
Le Joli mai (1963). Completed 1962
La Jetée (1964). Completed 1962
The Koumiko Mystery (1965)
Far from Vietnam (1967)
The Essence of the Air is Red (1977)
Sans soleil (1983)

MAX OPHÜLS (1902–1957)
Letter from an Unknown Woman (1948)
Caught (1949)
The Reckless Moment (1949)
La Ronde (1950)
Le Plaisir (1952)
Madame de . . . or *The Earrings of Madame de . . .* (1953)
Lola Montès (1955)

ALAIN RESNAIS (1922–)
Night and Fog (1955)
Hiroshima, mon amour (1959)
Last Year at Marienbad (1961)
Muriel, or The Time of a Return (1963)
La Guerre est finie (1966)
Je t'aime, je t'aime (1968)
Stavisky (1974)
Providence (1977)
Mon oncle d'Amérique (1980)
Life is a Novel (1983)

L'Amour à mort (1984)
Melo (1986)
I Want To Go Home (1989)

JACQUES RIVETTE (1928–)
Paris nous appartient (Paris Belongs to Us,
  1961). Shot 1957–1959
L'Amour fou (1968)
Out one (1971)
Out one spectre (1974)
Céline and Julie Go Boating (1974)
La Belle noiseuse (1991)

ERIC ROHMER (1920–)
My Night at Maud's (1969)
Claire's Knee (1970)
Chloe in the Afternoon (1972)
The Marquise of O . . . (1976)
Perceval or *Perceval le Gallois* (1978)
The Aviator's Wife (1981)
Le Beau mariage (1982)
Pauline at the Beach (1983)
My Girl Friend's Boy Friend (1987)

ALAIN TANNER (1929–)
La Salamandre (1971)
The Middle of the World (1974)
Jonah Who Will Be 25 in the Year 2000
  (1976)
In the White City (1983)

JACQUES TATI (1908–1982)
Jour de fête (1949)
Mr. Hulot's Holiday (1953)
Mon oncle (1958)
Playtime (1967)
Traffic (1970)
Parade (1974)

BERTRAND TAVERNIER (1941–)
The Clockmaker (1974)
Deathwatch (1979)
Coup de torchon (1981)
A Sunday in the Country (1984)
Round Midnight (1986)
Life and Nothing But (1989)
Daddy Nostalgia (1990)

FRANÇOIS TRUFFAUT (1932–1984)
Les Mistons (1957)
Une Histoire d'eau (1958). Co-director, Jean-
  Luc Godard
The 400 Blows (1959)
Shoot the Piano Player (1960)
Jules and Jim (1962). Completed 1961
The Soft Skin (1964)
Fahrenheit 451 (1966)
The Bride Wore Black (1968)
Stolen Kisses (1968)
The Wild Child (1970)
Bed and Board (1970)
Two English Girls (1971). Revised 1984
Day for Night (1973)
The Story of Adèle H. (1975)
Small Change (1976)
The Man Who Loved Women (1977)
The Green Room (1978)
Love on the Run (1979)
The Last Metro (1980)
The Woman Next Door (1981)
Vivement dimanche! or *Confidentially Yours* (1983)

AGNÈS VARDA (1928–)
La Pointe Courte (1956). Completed 1954
Cleo from 5 to 7 (1962) Completed 1961
Le Bonheur (1965)
Les Créatures (1966)
Lions Love (1969)
Daguerréotypes (1975)
One Sings, the Other Doesn't (1977)
Murs murs (1981)
Documenteur: An Emotion Picture (1981)
Vagabond or *Sans toit ni loi* (1985)
Jacquot de Nantes (1991)

FRENCH MISCELLANY (1950–1990)
Les Enfants terribles (1950, Jean-Pierre Melville)
Forbidden Games (1952, René Clément)
The Wages of Fear (1953, Henri-Georges
  Clouzot)
Les Diaboliques (1955, Henri-Georges Clouzot)
. . . and God created woman (1956, Roger
  Vadim)
The Red Balloon (1956, Albert Lamorisse)
Black Orpheus (1959, Marcel Camus)
Eyes without a Face (1960, Georges Franju)
Chronique d'un été (1961, Jean Rouch)
Lola (1961, Jacques Demy)

Sundays and Cybele (1962, Serge Bourgignon)
Judex (1963, Georges Franju)
Life Upside Down (1963, Alain Jessua)
The Umbrellas of Cherbourg (1964, Jacques Demy)
The Shameless Old Lady (1964, René Allio)
A Man and a Woman (1966, Claude Lelouch)
The Two of Us (1966, Claude Berri)
King of Hearts (1966, Philippe De Broca)
Jeu de massacre (1967, Alain Jessua)
Le Samourai (1967, Jean-Pierre Melville)
The Man Who Lies (1968, Alain Robbe-Grillet)
L'Enfance nue (1969, Maurice Pialat)
Destroy, She Said (1969, Marguerite Duras)
A Very Curious Girl (1969, Nelly Kaplan)
Z (1969, Constantin Costa-Gavras)
The Sorrow and the Pity (1969, Marcel Ophuls)
Rider on the Rain (1970, René Clément)
César and Rosalie (1972, Claude Sautet)
State of Siege (1972, Constantin Costa-Gavras)
The Valley Obscured by Clouds (1972, Barbet
  Schroeder)
Nathalie Granger (1973, Marguerite Duras)
Les Violons du bal (1973, Michel Drach)
The Mother and the Whore (1973, Jean Eustache)
Vincent, François, Paul . . . and the Others
  (1974, Claude Sautet)
The Mad Adventures of "Rabbi" Jacob (1974,
  Gerard Oury)
The Wonderful Crook (1975, Claude Goretta)
Cousin Cousine (1975, Jean-Charles Tachella)
India Song (1975, Marguerite Duras)
*Jeanne Dielman, 23 quai du commerce, 1080
  Bruxelles* (1975, Chantal Akerman)
Néa (1976, Nelly Kaplan)
The Memory of Justice (1976, Marcel Ophuls)
Idi Amin Dada (1976, Barbet Schroeder)
Get Out Your Handkerchiefs (1976, Bertrand
  Blier)
The Lacemaker (1977, Claude Goretta)
Peppermint Soda (1977, Diane Kurys)
La Cage aux folles (1978, Edouard Molinaro)
Meetings with Anna (1978, Chantal Akerman)
Série noire (1979, Alain Corneau)
Cocktail Molotov (1980, Diane Kurys)
Diva (1982, Jean-Jacques Beineix)
Entre nous (1983, Diane Kurys)
Shoah (1985, Claude Lanzmann)
*Hotel Terminus: The Life and Times of Klaus
  Barbie* (1988, Marcel Ophuls)
C'est la vie (1990, Diane Kurys)

14. Emerging National Traditions 1 (1945–1991): Sweden, Great Britain, Poland, Czechoslovakia, Japan, India, China

BOOKS

Andrew, Dudley, and Paul Andrew. *Kenji Mizoguchi: A Guide to References and Resources.* Boston: G. K. Hall, 1981.

Armes, Roy. *The Ambiguous Image: Narrative Style in Modern European Cinema.* Bloomington: Indiana University Press, 1976.

——— . *A Critical History of British Cinema.* New York: Oxford University Press, 1978.

Balcon, Michael. *Twenty Years of British Film.* London: Falcon, 1947.

Banerjee, S., ed. *New Indian Cinema.* New Delhi: N.F.D.C., 1982.

Banerjee, Shampa, and Anil Srivastava. *One Hundred Indian Feature Films: An Annotated Filmography.* New York and London: Garland, 1988.

Barnouw, Erik, and Subramanyam Krishnaswamy. *The Indian Film.* 2nd ed. New York: Oxford University Press, 1980.

Barr, Charles. *Ealing Studios.* London: Cameron & Taylor, 1977.

——— , ed. *All Our Yesterdays: 90 Years of British Cinema.* London: BFI, 1986.

Baxter, John. *An Appalling Talent: Ken Russell.* London: Joseph, 1973.

Bergman, Ingmar. *Four Screenplays of Ingmar Bergman:* Smiles of a Summer Night, The Seventh Seal, Wild Strawberries, The Magician. Translated by Lars Malmstrom and David Kushner. New York: Simon & Schuster, 1960.

——— . *Three Films by Ingmar Bergman:* Through a Glass Darkly, Winter Light, The Silence. Translated by Paul Britten Austin. New York: Grove Press, 1970.

——— . Persona *and* Shame. Translated by Keith Bradfield. New York: Grossman, 1972.

Bergom-Larsson, Maria. *Swedish Film: Ingmar Bergman and Society.* Cranbury, N.J.: Barnes, 1979.

Berry, Chris, ed. *Perspectives on Chinese Cinema.* 2nd ed. London: BFI, 1991.

Betts, Ernest. *The Film Business: A History of British Cinema, 1896–1972.* London: Allen & Unwin, 1973.

Bisplinghoff, Gretchen, and Virginia Wexman. *Roman Polanski: A Guide to References and Resources.* Boston: G. K. Hall, 1979.

Björkman, Stig, Torsten Manns, and Jonas Sima. *Bergman on Bergman.* Translated by Paul Britten Austin. New York: Simon & Schuster, 1973.

Blackwell, Marilyn Johns. Persona: *The Transcendent Image.* Urbana and Chicago: University of Illinois Press, 1986.

Bock, Audie. *Japanese Film Directors.* New York: Kodansha, 1978.

Bordwell, David. *The Films of Carl-Theodor Dreyer.* Berkeley and Los Angeles: University of California Press, 1981.

———. *Ozu and the Poetics of Cinema.* Princeton: Princeton University Press, 1988.

Burch, Noël. *To the Distant Observer: Form and Meaning in Japanese Cinema.* Revised and edited by Annette Michelson. Berkeley and Los Angeles: University of California Press, 1979.

Butler, Ivan. *Cinema in Britain.* London: Tantivy, 1969.

———. *The Cinema of Roman Polanski.* Cranbury, N.J.: Barnes, 1970.

Carney, Raymond. *Speaking the language of desire: The films of Carl Dreyer.* Cambridge and New York: Cambridge University Press, 1989.

Castelli, Lewis, and Caryn Lynn Cleeland. *David Lean: A Guide to References and Resources.* Boston: G. K. Hall, 1980.

Cheng, Jihua, Li Xiaobai, and Xing Zuwen. *History of the Development of Chinese Cinema.* 2 vols. Beijing: China Film Press, 1963.

Christie, Ian, ed. *Powell, Pressburger, and Others.* London: BFI, 1978.

Cowie, Peter. *Finnish Cinema.* Cranbury, N.J.: Barnes, 1977.

———. *Ingmar Bergman: A Critical Biography.* New York: Scribner's, 1982.

———. *Swedish Cinema.* Cranbury, N.J.: Barnes, 1969.

Das Gupta, Chidananda. *The Cinema of Satyajit Ray.* New Delhi: Vikas, 1980.

Desser, David. *Eros plus Massacre: An Introduction to the Japanese New Wave Cinema.* Bloomington: Indiana University Press, 1988.

Dick, Eddie, ed. *From Limelight to Satellite: A Scottish Film Book.* Bloomington: Indiana University Press, 1991.

Donner, Jorn. *The Personal Vision of Ingmar Bergman.* Bloomington: Indiana University Press, 1964.

Dreyer, Carl Theodor. *Four Screenplays.* Translated by Oliver Stallybrass. Bloomington and London: Indiana University Press, 1970.

Durgnat, Raymond. *A Mirror for England: British Movies from Austerity to Affluence.* New York: Praeger, 1971.

Erens, Patricia. *Akira Kurosawa: A Guide to References and Resources.* Boston: G. K. Hall, 1979.

Feineman, Neil. *Nicolas Roeg.* Boston: Twayne, 1978.

Gifford, Denis. *British Cinema.* Cranbury, N.J.: Barnes, 1968.

Gomez, Joseph A. *Peter Watkins.* Boston: Twayne, 1979.

Goulding, Daniel J. *Liberated Cinema: The Yugoslav Experience.* Bloomington: Indiana University Press, 1985.

———, ed. *Post New Wave Cinema in the Soviet Union and Eastern Europe.* Bloomington: Indiana University Press, 1989.

Graham, Allison. *Lindsay Anderson.* Boston: Twayne, 1981.

Hibbin, Nina. *Eastern Europe: An Illustrated Guide.* Cranbury, N.J.: Barnes, 1969.

Hirsch, Foster. *Joseph Losey.* Boston: Twayne, 1980.

Holloway, Ronald. *Z Is for Zagreb.* Cranbury, N.J.: Barnes, 1972.

Kaminsky, Stuart, and Joseph F. Hill, eds. *Ingmar Bergman: Essays in Criticism.* New York: Oxford University Press, 1975.

Kawin, Bruce F. *Mindscreen: Bergman, Godard, and First-Person Film.* Princeton: Princeton University Press, 1978.

Kulik, Karol. *Alexander Korda.* London: Allen, 1975.

Kurosawa, Akira. *Something Like an Autobiography.* Translated by Audie E. Bock. New York: Knopf, 1982.

Kurzewski, Stanislaw. *Contemporary Polish Cinema.* London: Wischhusen, 1980.

Lauritzen, Einar. *Swedish Film.* Garden City, N.Y.: Doubleday, 1962.

Leahy, James. *The Cinema of Joseph Losey.* Cranbury, N.J.: Barnes, 1967.

Leaming, Barbara. *Polanski: A Biography*. New York: Simon & Schuster, 1981.

Le Fanu, Mark. *The Cinema of Andrei Tarkovsky*. London: BFI, 1987.

Leyda, Jay. *Dianying: Electric Shadows: An Account of Films and the Film Audience in China*. rev. ed. Cambridge, Mass.: MIT Press, 1979.

Liehm, Antonín J. *Closely Watched Films: The Czechoslovak Experience*. White Plains, N.Y.: International Arts, 1974.

————. *The Miloš Forman Stories*. White Plains, N.Y.: International Arts, 1975.

Liehm, Mira, and Antonín J. Liehm. *The Most Important Art: East European Film After 1945*. Berkeley and Los Angeles: University of California Press, 1977.

Low, Rachel. *The History of the British Film: 1929–39*. London: Allen & Unwin, 1979.

Luhr, William, ed. *World Cinema Since 1945*. New York: Ungar, 1987.

Manvell, Roger. *New Cinema in Britain*. New York: Dutton, 1968.

Mellen, Joan. *Voices from the Japanese Cinema*. New York: Liveright, 1975.

————. *The Waves at Genji's Door: Japan Through Its Cinema*. New York: Pantheon, 1976.

Michalek, Boleslaw. *The Cinema of Andrzej Wajda*. Translated by Edward Rothert. Cranbury, N.J.: Barnes, 1973.

Michalek, Boleslaw, and Frank Turaj. *The Modern Cinema of Poland*. Bloomington: Indiana University Press, 1988.

Milne, Tom. *The Cinema of Carl Dreyer*. Cranbury, N.J.: Barnes, 1971.

Mosley, Philip. *Ingmar Bergman: The Cinema as Mistress*. New York: Boyars, 1981.

Pensel, Hans. *Seastrom and Stiller in Hollywood*. New York: Vintage, 1969.

Perry, George. *The Great British Picture Show*. New York: Hill & Wang, 1974.

Petric, Vlada, ed. *Film and Dreams: An Approach to Bergman*. Pleasantville, N.Y.: Redgrave, 1981.

Petrie, Graham. *History Must Answer to Man: The Contemporary Hungarian Cinema*. London: Tantivy, 1979.

Ray, Satyajit. *Our Films, Their Films*. Bombay: Orient Longman's, 1977.

Rayns, Tony, and Scott Meek, eds. *Electric Shadows: 45 Years of Chinese Cinema*. London: BFI, 1980.

Richie, Donald. *The Japanese Cinema: Film Style and National Character*. Garden City, N.Y.: Doubleday, 1971.

————. *Ozu: His Life and Films*. Berkeley and Los Angeles: University of California Press, 1974.

————. *The Japanese Movie*. rev. ed. Tokyo: Kodansha, 1982.

————. Additional material by Joan Mellen. *The Films of Akira Kurosawa*. rev. ed. Berkeley and Los Angeles: University of California Press, 1984.

————, ed. *Focus on* Rashomon. Englewood Cliffs, N.J.: Prentice-Hall, 1972.

Richie, Donald, and Joseph Anderson. *Japanese Film: Art and Industry*. New York: Grove Press, 1960.

Robinson, Andrew. *Satyajit Ray: The Inner Eye*. Berkeley and Los Angeles: University of California Press, 1989.

Rosenfeldt, Diane. *Richard Lester: A Guide to References and Resources*. Boston: G. K. Hall, 1978.

Quinlan, David. *British Sound Films: The Studio Years, 1929–1959*. Totowa, N.J.: Barnes & Noble, 1984.

Sato, Tadao. *Currents in Japanese Cinema*. Translated by Gregory Barrett. Tokyo: Kodansha, 1982.

Schrader, Paul. *Transcendental Style in Film: Ozu, Bresson, Dreyer*. Berkeley and Los Angeles: University of California Press, 1972.

Sen, Mrinal. *Views on Cinema*. Calcutta: Ishan, 1977.

Seton, Marie. *Portrait of a Director: Satyajit Ray*. Bloomington: Indiana University Press, 1971.

Simon, John. *Ingmar Bergman Directs*. New York: Harcourt, Brace, 1972.

Sjöman, Vilgot. *L. 136: Diary with Ingmar Bergman*. Translated by Alan Blair. Ann Arbor: University of Michigan Press, 1978.

Skoller, Donald, ed. *Dreyer in Double Reflection: Translation of Carl Th. Dreyer's Writings* About the Film (Om Filmen). New York: Dutton, 1973.

Skvorecký, Josef. *All the Bright Young Men and Women: A Personal History of the Czech Cinema*. Toronto: Martin, 1971.

Steene, Birgitte, ed. *Focus on* The Seventh Seal. Englewood Cliffs, N.J.: Prentice-Hall, 1972.

———. *Ingmar Bergman.* Boston: Twayne, 1978.

———. *Ingmar Bergman: A Guide to References and Resources.* Boston: G. K. Hall, 1982.

Stoil, Michael Jon. *Cinema Beyond the Danube: The Camera and Politics.* Metuchen, N.J.: Scarecrow Press, 1974.

Tarkovsky, Andrey. *Sculpting in Time: Reflections on the Cinema.* Translated by Kitty Hunter-Blair. Austin: University of Texas Press, 1989.

Taylor, John Russell. *Directors and Directions: Cinema for the Seventies.* New York: Hill & Wang, 1975.

Vasuder, Aruna. *Liberty and License in the Indian Cinema.* New Delhi: Vikas, 1978.

Walker, Alexander. *Hollywood U.K.* New York: Stein & Day, 1974.

Whyte, Alistair. *New Cinema in Eastern Europe.* New York: Dutton, 1971.

Wood, Robin. *The Apu Trilogy.* New York: Praeger, 1971.

———. *Ingmar Bergman.* New York: Praeger, 1969.

Young, Vernon. *Cinema Borealis: Ingmar Bergman and the Swedish Ethos.* New York: Avon, 1971.

Zsuffa, Joseph. *Béla Balázs, The Man and the Artist.* Berkeley and Los Angeles: University of California Press, 1987.

FILMS

SWEDEN AND DENMARK

INGMAR BERGMAN (1918–   )
Thirst (1949)
Monika (1953)
The Naked Night or *Sawdust and Tinsel* or *The Clown's Evening* (1953)
Smiles of a Summer Night (1955)
The Seventh Seal (1957). Completed 1956
Wild Strawberries (1957)
The Magician or *The Face* (1958)
The Virgin Spring (1960). Completed 1959
Through a Glass Darkly (1961)
Winter Light (1962)
The Silence (1963)

Persona (1966). Completed 1965
Hour of the Wolf (1968). Completed 1966
Shame (1968). Completed 1967
The Passion of Anna (1969)
Cries and Whispers (1972)
Scenes from a Marriage (1974)
The Magic Flute (1974)
Fanny and Alexander (1982)
After the Rehearsal (1984)

CARL THEODOR DREYER (1889–1968)
The Passion of Joan of Arc (1928)
Vampyr (1932)
Day of Wrath (1943)
Ordet (1955). Completed 1954
Gertrud (1964)

SWEDISH MISCELLANY
Torment (1944, Alf Sjøberg)
Miss Julie (1951, Alf Sjøberg)
One Summer of Happiness (1951, Arne Mattsson)
491 (1964, Vilgot Sjøman)
Dear John (1966, Lars Magnus Lindgren)
Elvira Madigan (1967, Bo Widerberg)
I Am Curious Yellow (1967, Vilgot Sjøman)
Adalen '31 (1969, Bo Widerberg)
The Emigrants (1971, Jan Troell)
The New Land (1972, Jan Troell)
The Ox (1991, Sven Nykvist)

GREAT BRITAIN

LINDSAY ANDERSON (1923–   )
This Sporting Life (1963)
If . . . (1969)
O Lucky Man! (1973)
The Whales of August (1987)

JACK CLAYTON (1921–   )
Room at the Top (1958)
The Innocents (1961)
The Pumpkin Eater (1964)
The Great Gatsby (1974)

DAVID LEAN (1908–1991)
Blithe Spirit (1945)
Brief Encounter (1945)
Great Expectations (1946)
Oliver Twist (1948)
Summertime (1955)
The Bridge on the River Kwai (1957)
Lawrence of Arabia (1962)

Doctor Zhivago (1965)
Ryan's Daughter (1970)
A Passage to India (1984)

RICHARD LESTER (1932–)
The Running, Jumping and Standing Still Film (1960)
A Hard Day's Night (1964)
The Knack, and How to Get It (1965)
Help! (1965)
A Funny Thing Happened on the Way to the Forum (1966)
How I Won the War (1967)
Petulia (1968)
The Three Musketeers (1974)
The Four Musketeers (1975)
Robin and Marian (1976)
Cuba (1979)
Superman II (1981). Completed 1980

JOSEPH LOSEY (1909–1984)
The Boy With Green Hair (1948)
The Big Night (1951)
The Prowler (1951)
The Damned or *These Are the Damned* (1962)
The Servant (1963)
King and Country (1964)
Accident (1967)
The Go-Between (1971)
The Romantic Englishwoman (1975)
Mr. Klein (1976)
Don Giovanni (1979)
Steaming (1985). Completed 1984

LAURENCE OLIVER (1907–1989)
Henry V (1944)
Hamlet (1948)
Richard III (1955)

MICHAEL POWELL (1905–1990)
The Thief of Bagdad (1940). Co-directors, Ludwig Berger and Tim Whelan
The Life and Death of Colonel Blimp (1943). Co-director, Emeric Pressburger
A Canterbury Tale (1944). Co-director, Emeric Pressburger
I Know Where I'm Going (1945). Co-director, Emeric Pressburger
A Matter of Life and Death or *Stairway to Heaven* (1946). Co-director, Emeric Pressburger
Black Narcissus (1947). Co-director, Emeric Pressburger

The Red Shoes (1948). Co-director, Emeric Pressburger
Tales of Hoffman (1951). Co-director, Emeric Pressburger
Peeping Tom (1960)

CAROL REED (1906–1976)
The Stars Look Down (1939)
Kipps (1941)
Odd Man Out (1947)
The Fallen Idol (1948)
The Third Man (1949)
Outcast of the Islands (1951)
The Man Between (1953)
Trapeze (1956)
The Key (1958)
Our Man in Havana (1960)
Oliver! (1968)

KAREL REISZ (1926–)
Momma Don't Allow (1955). Co-director, Tony Richardson
Saturday Night and Sunday Morning (1960)
Morgan! or *Morgan, a Suitable Case for Treatment* (1966)
The Loves of Isadora (1968). Condensed version entitled *Isadora*
Who'll Stop the Rain (1978)
The French Lieutenant's Woman (1981)

TONY RICHARDSON (1928–1991)
Momma Don't Allow (1955). Co-director, Karel Reisz
Look Back in Anger (1959)
The Entertainer (1960)
A Taste of Honey (1961)
The Loneliness of the Long Distance Runner (1962)
Tom Jones (1963)
The Loved One (1965)
The Charge of the Light Brigade (1968)
Ned Kelly (1970)
Joseph Andrews (1977)

NICOLAS ROEG (1928–)
Performance (1970). Co-director, Donald Cammell
Walkabout (1971)
Don't Look Now (1973)
The Man Who Fell to Earth (1976)
Insignificance (1985)
Track 29 (1988)
The Witches (1990)

KEN RUSSELL (1927–   )
Women in Love (1969)
The Music Lovers (1970)
The Devils (1971)
The Boy Friend (1971)
Tommy (1974)
Lisztomania (1975)
Altered States (1980)
Gothic (1986)
The Lair of the White Worm (1988)

JOHN SCHLESINGER (1926–   )
Billy Liar (1963)
Darling (1965)
Far from the Madding Crowd (1967)
Midnight Cowboy (1969)
Sunday, Bloody Sunday (1971)
The Day of the Locust (1975)
Marathon Man (1976)
The Believers (1987)

THE EALING COMEDIES
Kind Hearts and Coronets (1949, Robert Hamer)
Tight Little Island or *Whisky Galore!* (1949,
   Alexander Mackendrick)
The Lavender Hill Mob (1951, Charles Crichton)
The Man in the White Suit (1951, Alexander
   Mackendrick)
The Captain's Paradise (1953, Anthony
   Kimmins)
The Ladykillers (1955, Alexander Mackendrick)

BRITISH MISCELLANY (1945–1991)
Dead of Night (1945, Alberto Cavalcanti,
   Charles Crichton, Basil Dearden, and Robert
   Hamer)
Green For Danger (1946, Sidney Gilliat)
The Importance of Being Earnest (1952, Anthony
   Asquith)
The Holly and the Ivy (1953, George More
   O'Ferrall)
An Inspector Calls (1954, Guy Hamilton)
Romeo and Juliet (1954, Renato Castellani)
Curse of the Demon (1957, Jacques Tourneur)
The Horse's Mouth (1958, Ronald Neame)
Horror of Dracula (1958, Terence Fisher)
I'm All Right Jack (1959, John Boulting).
   Producer, Roy Boulting
The Angry Silence (1960, Guy Green)
The League of Gentlemen (1960, Basil Dearden)
Sons and Lovers (1960, Jack Cardiff)
Tunes of Glory (1960, Ronald Neame)

Billy Budd (1962, Peter Ustinov)
The L-Shaped Room (1962, Bryan Forbes)
Dr. No (1962, Terence Young)
From Russia With Love (1963, Terence Young)
Heavens Above! (1963, John and Roy Boulting)
Lord of the Flies (1963, Peter Brook)
The Leather Boys (1963, Sidney J. Furie)
Seance on a Wet Afternoon (1964, Bryan Forbes)
Zulu (1964, Cy Endfield)
The War Game (1965, Peter Watkins)
Marat/Sade or *The Persecution and
   Assassination of Jean-Paul Marat as Performed
   by the Inmates of the Asylum of Charenton Under
   the Direction of the Marquis de Sade* (1966,
   Peter Brook)
Georgy Girl (1966, Silvio Narizzano)
Alfie (1966, Lewis Gilbert)
The Whisperers (1967, Bryan Forbes)
Privilege (1967, Peter Watkins)
Quatermass and the Pit or *Five Million Years to
   Earth* (1968, Roy Ward Baker)
The Lion in Winter (1968, Anthony Harvey)
Romeo and Juliet (1968, Franco Zeffirelli)
The Prime of Miss Jean Brodie (1969, Ronald
   Neame)
King Lear (1971, Peter Brook)
Punishment Park (1971, Peter Watkins)
The Ruling Class (1972, Peter Medak)
The Creeping Flesh (1973, Freddie Francis)
Monty Python and the Holy Grail (1974, Terry
   Jones and Terry Gilliam)
Edvard Munch (1974, Peter Watkins)
The Rocky Horror Picture Show (1975, Jim
   Sharman)
Stevie (1978, Robert Enders)
The Long Good Friday (1980, John Mackenzie)
Chariots of Fire (1981, Hugh Hudson)
The Draughtsman's Contract (1982, Peter
   Greenaway)
Gandhi (1982, Richard Attenborough)
Betrayal (1983, David Jones)
Bloody Kids (1983, Stephen Frears)
The Killing Fields (1984, Roland Joffe)
The Company of Wolves (1984, Neil Jordan)
The Emerald Forest (1985, John Boorman)
My Beautiful Laundrette (1985, Stephen Frears)
28 Up (1985, Michael Apted)
Sammy and Rosie Get Laid (1987, Stephen Frears)
Drowning By Numbers (1988, Peter Greenaway)
Distant Voices, Still Lives (1988, Terence Davies)
The Mahabharata (1989, Peter Brook)

The Cook, The Thief, His Wife & Her Lover
  (1989, Peter Greenaway)
"Let Him Have It" (1991, Peter Medak)
Prospero's Books (1991, Peter Greenaway)

CENTRAL AND EASTERN EUROPE

MILOŠ FORMAN (1932–)
Black Peter (1963)
Loves of a Blonde (1965)
The Fireman's Ball (1967)
Taking Off (1971)
One Flew Over the Cuckoo's Nest (1975)
Hair (1979)
Ragtime (1981)
Amadeus (1984)
Valmont (1989)

JÁN KADÁR (1918–1979) AND ELMAR KLOS (1910–1970)
Death Is Called Engelchen (1963)
The Shop on Main Street (1965)
Adrift (1969–1971)

MIKLÓS JANCSÓ (1921–)
Cantata (1962)
My Way Home (1964)
The Round-Up (1965)
The Red and the White (1967)
Silence and Cry (1968)
Red Psalm (1972)
Jesus Christ's Horoscope (1989)

DUŠAN MAKAVEJEV (1932–)
Man Is Not a Bird (1965)
Love Affair, or The Tragedy of the Switchboard Operator (1967)
Innocence Unprotected (1968)
WR — Mysteries of the Organism (1971)
Sweet Movie (1974)
Montenegro — or Pigs and Pearls (1981)
Manifesto (1988)

ROMAN POLANSKI (1933–)
Two Men and a Wardrobe (1958)
Knife in the Water (1962)
Repulsion (1965)
Cul-de-Sac (1966)
Rosemary's Baby (1968)
Macbeth (1971)
Chinatown (1974)
The Tenant (1976)
Tess (1979)

JERZY SKOLIMOWSKI (1938–)
Identification Marks: None (1964)
Walkover (1965)
Barrier (1966)
Le Départ (1967)
Hands Up! (1967)
Deep End (1970)
The Shout (1978)
Moonlighting (1982)

ANDRZEJ WAJDA (1927–)
Generation or *A Generation* (1955)
Kanal (1957)
Ashes and Diamonds (1958)
Everything for Sale (1969)
Landscape After the Battle (1970)
Man of Marble (1977)
Man of Iron (1980)
Danton (1982)

MISCELLANY: CZECHOSLOVAKIA, HUNGARY, POLAND, YUGOSLAVIA
Man on the Track (1955, Andrzej Munk)
The Invention of Destruction (1957, Karel Zeman)
Dom (*House*, 1958, Walerian Borowczyk)
Ceiling (1961, Věra Chytilová)
The Passenger (1963, Andrzej Munk).
  Unfinished at his death in 1961
Josef Kilian (1963, Jan Schmidt and Pavel Juráček)
90° in the Shade (1964, Jiří Weiss)
The Fifth Horseman Is Fear (1964, Zbynčk Brynych)
Les Jeux des anges (1964, Walerian Borowczyk)
Golden Rennet (1965, Otakar Vávra)
Intimate Lighting (1965, Ivan Passer)
Closely Watched Trains (1966, Jiří Menzel)
The Hand (1966, Jiří Trnka)
Daisies (1966, Věra Chytilová)
Report on the Party and the Guests (1966, Jan Němec)
I Even Met Happy Gypsies (1967, Aleksandr Petrović)
The End of August at the Hotel Ozone (1968, Jan Schmidt). Completed 1966
Capricious Summer (1968, Jiří Menzel)
Joke (1969, Jaromil Jireš)
The Structure of Crystals (1969, Krzysztof Zanussi)
The Fruit of Paradise (1970, Věra Chytilová)
The Story of Sin (1975, Walerian Borowczyk)
Camouflage (1977, Krzysztof Zanussi)

Women (1977, Márta Mészáros)
Contract (1980, Krzysztof Zanussi)
Lulu (1980, Walerian Borowczyk)
Mephisto (1981, István Szabó)
Time Stands Still (1982, Peter Lothar)
Contest or *Orientation Course* (1983, Dan Piţa)
When Father Was Away on Business (1985, Emir
   Kusturica)

JAPAN, INDIA, AND CHINA

KON ICHIKAWA (1915–)
The Burmese Harp (1956)
Fires on the Plain (1959)
Odd Obsession or *The Key* (1959)
An Actor's Revenge (1963)
Tokyo Olympiad (1965)

AKIRA KUROSAWA (1910–)
Drunken Angel (1948)
Stray Dog (1949)
Rashomon (1950)
The Idiot (1951)
Ikiru (*To Live*, 1952)
Seven Samurai (1954)
The Lower Depths (1957)
Throne of Blood (1957)
The Hidden Fortress (1958)
Yojimbo (1961)
High and Low (1963)
Red Beard (1965)
Dodes'ka-den (1970)
Dersu Uzala (1975)
Kagemusha or *Kagemusha, The Shadow Warrior*
 (1980)
Ran (*Chaos*, 1985)
Akira Kurosawa's Dreams (1990)
Rhapsody in August (1991)

KENJI MIZOGUCHI (1898–1956)
Sisters of the Gion (1936)
The Story of the Last Chrysanthemum (1939)
The 47 Ronin I, II (1941)
Utamaro and His Five Women (1946)
Women of the Night (1948)
The Life of Oharu (1952)
Ugetsu or *Ugetsu Monogatari* (1953)
A Geisha (1953)
Sansho the Bailiff (1954)
Princess Yang Kwei Fei (1955)
Chikamatsu Monogatari (*A Story from
   Chikamatsu,* 1954)
Street of Shame (1956)

NAGISA OSHIMA (1932–)
Cruel Story of Youth (1960)
Violence at Noon (1966)
Boy (1968)
Death by Hanging (1968)
Diary of a Shinjuku Thief (1969)
The Man Who Left His Will on Film (1970)
The Ceremony (1971)
In the Realm of the Senses (1976)
Empire of Passion (1978)
Merry Christmas, Mr. Lawrence (1983)

YASUJIRO OZU (1903–1963)
I Was Born, But . . . (1932)
Passing Fancy (1933)
A Story of Floating Weeds (1934)
The Brothers and Sisters of the Toda Family (1941)
There Was a Father (1942)
Late Spring (1949)
Early Summer (1951)
The Flavor of Green Tea over Rice (1952)
Tokyo Story (1953)
Early Spring (1956)
Tokyo Twilight (1957)
Ohayo (1959)
Floating Weeds (1959)
Late Autumn (1960)
End of Summer (1961)
An Autumn Afternoon (1962)

SATYAJIT RAY (1921–)
Pather Panchali (*Song of the Road,* 1955)
Aparajito (*The Unvanquished,* 1956)
The Music Room (*Jalsaghar,* 1958)
Apur Sansar (*The World of Apu,* 1959)
Devi (1960)
Three Daughters (1961)
Kanchanjungha (1962)
Mahanagar (1963)
Charulata (1964)
Days and Nights in the Forest (1970)
Distant Thunder (1973)
The Chess Players (1977)
The Home and the World (1984)
Ganashatru (1989)
Shakha Proshakha (1990)

FAR EASTERN MISCELLANY
A Page of Madness or *Crazy Page* (1927,
   Teinosuke Kinugasa)
Mother (1952, Mikio Naruse)
Gate of Hell (1953, Teinosuke Kinugasa)

Samurai I, II, III (1953, Hiroshi Inagaki)
Muddy Waters (1953, Tadashi Imai)
Godzilla, King of the Monsters (1954, Inoshiro Honda). U.S. version, 1956
Floating Clouds (1955, Mikio Naruse)
Snow Country (1957, Shiro Toyoda)
Lin Zexu (1959, Zheng Junli)
The Mysterians (1959, Inoshiro Honda)
When a Woman Ascends the Stairs (1960, Mikio Naruse)
The Cloud-Capped Star (1960, Ritwik Ghatak)
Bad Boys (1960, Susumu Hani)
The Island (1961, Kaneto Shindo)
The Human Condition I, II, III (1958–1961, Masaki Kobayashi)
Chushingura (1962, Hiroshi Inagaki)
Harakiri (1962, Masaki Kobayashi)
Mothra (1962, Inoshiro Honda)
She and He (1963, Susumu Hani)
Kwaidan (1964, Masaki Kobayashi)
Woman in the Dunes (1964, Hiroshi Teshigahara)
Onibaba (1964, Kaneto Shindo)
Bwana Toshi (1965, Susumu Hani)
Shakespeare Wallah (1965, James Ivory)
The Face of Another (1966, Hiroshi Teshigahara)
Kuroneko (1968, Kaneto Shindo)
Bhuvan Shome (1969, Mrinal Sen)
Double Suicide (1969, Masahiro Shinoda)
Bombay Talkie (1970, James Ivory)
Eros + Massacre (1970, Yoshishige Yoshida)
Reason, Debate, and a Tale (1974, Ritwik Ghatak)
Kaseki (1974, Masaki Kobayashi)
Manthan (1976, Shyam Benegal)
Insiang (1976, Lino Brocka)
Vengeance Is Mine (1979, Shohei Imamura)
And Quiet Rolls the Day (1979, Mrinal Sen)
36 Chowringhee Lane (1981, Aparna Sen)
The Rat Trap (1981, Adoor Gopalakrishnan)
Eijanaika (1981, Shohei Imamura)
The Ruins (1983, Mrinal Sen)
Family Game (1983, Yoshimitsu Morita)
The Go Masters (1983, Junya Sato)
The Ballad of Narayama (1983, Shohei Imamura)
Face to Face (1984, Adoor Gopalakrishnan)
Life (1984, Wu Tianming)
Yellow Earth (1985, Chen Kaige)
Old Well (1987, Wu Tianming)
Red Sorghum (1988, Zhang Yimou)
Salaam Bombay! (1988, Mira Nair)
Akira (1988, Katsuhiro Otomo)
King of the Children (1988, Chen Kaige)

Ju Dou (1990, Zhang Yimou). Assistant director, Yang Fengliang
Raise the Red Lantern (1991, Zhang Yimou)

15. The American Cinema (1964–1977)

BOOKS

Agel, Jerome. *The Making of* 2001. New York: Signet, 1970.

Atkins, Thomas R., ed. *Sexuality in the Movies.* Bloomington: Indiana University Press, 1975.

Bliss, Michael. *Martin Scorsese and Michael Cimino.* Metuchen, N.J.: Scarecrow, 1985.

Brakhage, Stan. *Brakhage Scrapbook: Collected Writings 1964–1980.* Edited by Robert A. Haller. New Paltz, N.Y.: Documentext, 1982.

———. *Film at Wit's End: Eight Avant-Garde Filmmakers.* New Paltz, N.Y.: McPherson & Co. 1989.

Carney, Raymond. *American Dreaming: The Films of John Cassavetes and the American Experience.* Berkeley and Los Angeles: University of California Press, 1985.

Cawelti, John G., ed. *Focus on* Bonnie and Clyde. Englewood Cliffs, N.J.: Prentice-Hall, 1972.

Ciment, Michel. *Kubrick.* Translated by Gilbert Adair. New York: Holt, Rinehart and Winston, 1983.

Curtis, David. *Experimental Cinema.* New York: Universe Books, 1971.

Deren, Maya. See Melton.

Dunne, John Gregory. *The Studio.* New York: Farrar, Straus, 1969.

Fadiman, William. *Hollywood Now.* New York: Liveright, 1972.

Farber, Stephen. *The Movie Rating Game.* Washington, D.C.: Public Affairs Press, 1972.

Feineman, Neil. *Persistence of Vision: The Films of Robert Altman.* New York: Arno, 1978.

Geduld, Carolyn. *Filmguide to* 2001. Bloomington: Indiana University Press, 1973.

Houston, Penelope. *The Contemporary Cinema.* rev. ed. Baltimore: Penguin, 1971.

Jacobs, Diane. *. . . But We Need the Eggs: The Magic of Woody Allen.* London: Robson, 1982.

———. *Hollywood Renaissance.* Cranbury, N.J.: Barnes, 1977.

James, David E. *Allegories of Cinema: American*

Film in the Sixties. Princeton: Princeton University Press, 1989.

Johnson, Robert K. *Francis Ford Coppola.* Boston: Twayne, 1979.

Kael, Pauline. "Commitment and Straitjacket." In *I Lost It at the Movies.* New York: Bantam, 1969, pp. 55–69.

Kagan, Norman. *The Cinema of Stanley Kubrick.* New York: Grove, 1975.

Karp, Alan. *The Films of Robert Altman.* Metuchen, N.J.: Scarecrow, 1981.

Kass, Judith. *Robert Altman: American Innovator.* New York: Popular Library, 1978.

Kelly, Mary, ed. *Martin Scorsese: The First Decade.* Pleasantville, N.Y.: Redgrave, 1980.

Kolker, Robert Philip. *A Cinema of Loneliness: Penn, Kubrick, Coppola, Scorsese, Altman.* New York: Oxford University Press, 1980.

Le Grice, Malcolm. *Abstract Film and Beyond.* Cambridge, Mass.: MIT Press, 1977.

Lovelace, Linda, with Mike McGrady. *Ordeal: An Autobiography.* New York: Bell, 1983.

Madsen, Axel. *The New Hollywood.* New York: Crowell, 1975.

McKinney, Doug. *Sam Peckinpah.* Boston: Twayne, 1978.

Mellen, Joan. *Women and Their Sexuality in the New Film.* New York: Horizon Press, 1973.

Melton, Hollis, general editor. *The Legend of Maya Deren: A Documentary Biography and Collected Works.* 3 vols. New York: Anthology Film Archives, 1984– .

Phillips, Gene D. *Stanley Kubrick: A Film Odyssey.* New York: Popular Library, 1977.

Quart, Leonard, and Albert Auster. *American Film and Society Since 1945.* New York: Praeger, 1985.

Rainer, Yvonne. *The Films of Yvonne Rainer.* Bloomington: Indiana University Press, 1989.

Renan, Sheldon. *An Introduction to the American Underground Film.* New York: Dutton, 1967.

Rosenthal, Alan. *The New Documentary in Action: A Casebook in Film Making.* Berkeley and Los Angeles: University of California Press, 1971.

Rotsler, William. *Contemporary Erotic Cinema.* New York: Random House, 1973.

Schuth, H. Wayne. *Mike Nichols.* Boston: Twayne, 1978.

Seydor, Paul. *Peckinpah: The Western Films.* Chicago and Urbana: University of Illinois Press, 1980.

Sitney, P. Adams. *Visionary Film: The American Avant-Garde 1943–1978.* 2nd ed. New York: Oxford University Press, 1979.

——— . *Modernist Montage: The Obscurity of Vision in Cinema and Literature.* New York: Columbia University Press, 1990.

——— , ed. *The Avant-Garde Film: A Reader of Theory and Criticism.* New York: Anthology Film Archives, 1987.

Smith, Julian. *Looking Away: Hollywood and Viet Nam.* New York: Scribner's, 1975.

Stuart, Frederic. *The Effects of Television on the Motion Picture and Radio Industries.* New York: Arno, 1975.

Turan, Kenneth, and Stephen F. Zito. *Sinema.* New York: Praeger, 1974.

Tyler, Parker. *Screening the Sexes: Homosexuality in the Movies.* New York: Holt, Rinehart, 1972.

——— . *Underground Film: A Critical History.* New York: Grove, 1969.

Wake, Sandra. *The* Bonnie and Clyde *Book.* London: Lorrimer, 1972.

Walker, Alexander. *Stanley Kubrick Directs.* New York: Harcourt, Brace, 1971.

Waller, Gregory A. *The Living and the Undead: From Stoker's* Dracula *to Romero's* Dawn of the Dead. Urbana and Chicago: University of Illinois Press, 1986.

Whitney, John. *Digital Harmony: On the Complementarity of Music and Visual Art.* New York: McGraw-Hill, 1980.

Williams, Linda. *Hard Core: Power, Pleasure, and the "Frenzy of the Visible."* Berkeley and Los Angeles: University of California Press, 1989.

Wood, Robin. *Arthur Penn.* New York: Praeger, 1969.

Youngblood, Gene. *Expanded Cinema.* New York: Dutton, 1970.

Zuker, Joel S. *Arthur Penn: A Guide to References and Resources.* Boston: G. K. Hall, 1984.

FILMS

WOODY ALLEN (1935–)
What's Up, Tiger Lily? (1966)
Take the Money and Run (1969)

Bananas (1971)
Sleeper (1973)
Love and Death (1975)
Annie Hall (1977)
Interiors (1978)
Manhattan (1979)
Stardust Memories (1980)
Zelig (1983)
Broadway Danny Rose (1984)
The Purple Rose of Cairo (1985)
Hannah and Her Sisters (1986)
Radio Days (1987)
Crimes and Misdemeanors (1989)
Alice (1990)

ROBERT ALTMAN (1925–)
The James Dean Story (1957). Co-director,
  George W. George.
MASH (1970)
Brewster McCloud (1970)
McCabe and Mrs. Miller (1971)
The Long Goodbye (1973)
Thieves Like Us (1974)
California Split (1974)
*Buffalo Bill and the Indians, or Sitting Bull's
  History Lesson* (1976)
Three Women (1977)
A Wedding (1978)
Popeye (1980)
*Come Back to the Five and Dime, Jimmy Dean,
  Jimmy Dean* (1982)
Secret Honor (1984)
Fool for Love (1985)
Vincent & Theo (1990)

HAL ASHBY (1932–1988)
Harold and Maude (1971)
The Last Detail (1973)
Shampoo (1975)
Bound for Glory (1976)
Coming Home (1978)
Being There (1979)

PETER BOGDANOVICH (1939–)
Targets (1968)
The Last Picture Show (1971)
What's Up, Doc? (1972)
Paper Moon (1973)
Saint Jack (1979)
Texasville (1990)

MEL BROOKS (1926–)
The Producers (1968)
Blazing Saddles (1974)
Young Frankenstein (1974)
Silent Movie (1976)
High Anxiety (1977)

JOHN CASSAVETES (1929–1989)
Shadows (1959). Earlier version shown 1958
Faces (1968)
Husbands (1970)
Minnie and Moskowitz (1971)
A Woman Under the Influence (1975)
The Killing of a Chinese Bookie (1976). Recut 1978
Opening Night (1978)
Gloria (1980)
Love Streams (1984)

FRANCIS FORD COPPOLA (1939–)
Dementia 13 (1963)
You're a Big Boy Now (1966)
Finian's Rainbow (1968)
The Rain People (1969)
The Godfather (1972)
The Conversation (1974)
The Godfather Part II (1974)
Apocalypse Now (1979)
One from the heart (1982)
Rumble Fish (1983)
The Cotton Club (1984)
Gardens of Stone (1987)
Tucker: The Man and His Dream (1988)
The Godfather Part III (1990)

BLAKE EDWARDS (1922–)
Breakfast at Tiffany's (1961)
Experiment in Terror (1962)
Days of Wine and Roses (1962)
The Pink Panther (1964)
The Return of the Pink Panther (1974)
10 (1979)
S.O.B. (1981)
Victor / Victoria (1982)
Micki and Maude (1984)

STANLEY KUBRICK (1928–)
Fear and Desire (1953)
Killer's Kiss (1955)
The Killing (1956)
Paths of Glory (1957)
Spartacus (1960)
Lolita (1962)

*Dr. Strangelove Or: How I Learned To Stop
   Worrying And Love The Bomb* (1964)
2001: A Space Odyssey (1968)
A Clockwork Orange (1971)
Barry Lyndon (1975)
The Shining (1980)
Full Metal Jacket (1987)

PAUL MAZURSKY (1930–)
Bob & Carol & Ted & Alice (1969)
Blume in Love (1973)
Harry and Tonto (1974)
Next Stop, Greenwich Village (1976)
An Unmarried Woman (1978)
Down and Out in Beverly Hills (1986)
Enemies, A Love Story (1989)
Scenes From A Mall (1991)

ROBERT MULLIGAN (1925–)
Fear Strikes Out (1957)
To Kill a Mockingbird (1962)
Baby The Rain Must Fall (1965)
Up the Down Staircase (1967)
Summer of '42 (1971)
The Other (1972)
Same Time, Next Year (1978)

MIKE NICHOLS (1931–)
Who's Afraid of Virginia Woolf? (1966)
The Graduate (1967)
Catch-22 (1970)
Carnal Knowledge (1971)
Silkwood (1983)

ALAN J. PAKULA (1928–)
Klute (1971)
The Parallax View (1974)
All the President's Men (1975)
Sophie's Choice (1982)

SAM PECKINPAH (1925–1984)
Ride the High Country (1962)
Major Dundee (1965)
The Wild Bunch (1969)
The Ballad of Cable Hogue (1970)
Straw Dogs (1971)
The Getaway (1972)
Pat Garrett and Billy the Kid (1973)
Cross of Iron (1977)
The Osterman Weekend (1983)

ARTHUR PENN (1922–)
The Left-Handed Gun (1958)
The Miracle Worker (1962)

Mickey One (1965)
Bonnie and Clyde (1967)
Alice's Restaurant (1969)
Little Big Man (1970)
Night Moves (1975)
Four Friends (1981)

MARTIN SCORSESE (1942–)
Who's That Knocking At My Door (1969)
Boxcar Bertha (1972)
Mean Streets (1973)
Alice Doesn't Live Here Anymore (1974)
Taxi Driver (1976)
New York, New York (1977)
The Last Waltz (1978)
Raging Bull (1980)
The King of Comedy (1983)
After Hours (1985)
The Color of Money (1986)
The Last Temptation of Christ (1988)
GoodFellas (1990)

AMERICAN MISCELLANY (1966–1976)
A Fine Madness (1966, Irvin Kershner)
Lord Love a Duck (1966, George Axelrod)
Seconds (1966, John Frankenheimer)
The Crazy-Quilt (1966, John Korty)
Cool Hand Luke (1967, Stuart Rosenberg)
The Dirty Dozen (1967, Robert Aldrich)
In Cold Blood (1967, Richard Brooks)
In the Heat of the Night (1967, Norman Jewison)
Bullitt (1968, Peter Yates)
Night of the Living Dead (1968, George A.
   Romero)
Madigan (1968, Don Siegel)
Pretty Poison (1968, Noel Black)
Planet of the Apes (1968, Franklin J. Schaffner)
Easy Rider (1969, Dennis Hopper)
Medium Cool (1969, Haskell Wexler)
Butch Cassidy and the Sundance Kid (1969,
   George Roy Hill)
They Shoot Horses, Don't They? (1969, Sydney
   Pollack)
True Grit (1969, Henry Hathaway)
Putney Swope (1969, Robert Downey)
The Learning Tree (1969, Gordon Parks)
Tell Them Willie Boy Is Here (1969, Abraham
   Polonsky)
Woodstock: 3 Days of Peace & Music (1970,
   Michael Wadleigh)
Beneath the Planet of the Apes (1970, Ted Post)
Where's Poppa? (1970, Carl Reiner)

Patton (1970, Franklin J. Schaffner)
Five Easy Pieces (1970, Bob Rafelson)
Joe (1970, John G. Avildsen)
Dirty Harry (1971, Don Siegel)
The French Connection (1971, William Friedkin)
Shaft (1971, Gordon Parks)
Sweet Sweetback's Baadasssss Song (1971, Melvin Van Peebles)
Billy Jack (1971, Tom Laughlin)
Little Murders (1971, Alan Arkin)
The Last Movie (1971, Dennis Hopper)
The Panic in Needle Park (1971, Jerry Schatzberg)
Willy Wonka and the Chocolate Factory (1971, Mel Stuart)
Tomorrow (1972, Joseph Anthony)
The Heartbreak Kid (1972, Elaine May)
The Last House on the Left (1972, Wes Craven)
Sounder (1972, Martin Ritt)
Deliverance (1972, John Boorman)
The Sting (1973, George Roy Hill)
Badlands (1973, Terrence Malick)
The Exorcist (1973, William Friedkin)
The Way We Were (1973, Sydney Pollack)
Steelyard Blues (1973, Alan Myerson)
Hester Street (1974, Joan Micklin Silver)
The Texas Chain Saw Massacre (1974, Tobe Hooper)
It's Alive (1974, Larry Cohen)
The White Dawn (1974, Philip Kaufman)
Death Wish (1974, Michael Winner)
Smile (1975, Michael Ritchie)
The Front (1976, Martin Ritt)
Mikey and Nicky (1976, Elaine May). Shot 1973
The Shootist (1976, Don Siegel)
Rocky (1976, John G. Avildsen)
Leadbelly (1976, Gordon Parks)

AMERICAN INDEPENDENT CINEMA (1928–1990)
The Fall of the House of Usher (1928, James Sibley Watson and Melville Webber)
The Life and Death of 9413—A Hollywood Extra (1928, Robert Florey) Co-creators, Slavko Vorkapich and Gregg Toland
H₂O (1929, Ralph Steiner)
Lot in Sodom (1933, James Sibley Watson and Melville Webber)
Composition in Blue (1935, Oskar Fischinger, Germany)
A Colour Box (1935, Len Lye, England)
Allegretto (1936, Oskar Fischinger)

Meshes of the Afternoon (1943, Maya Deren) Soundtrack added 1959
At Land (1944, Maya Deren)
A Study in Choreography for Camera: Pas de Deux (1945, Maya Deren)
Ritual in Transfigured Time (1946, Maya Deren)
The Potted Psalm (1946, Sidney Peterson and James Broughton)
Dreams that Money Can Buy (1944–1946, Hans Richter)
Motion-Painting I (1947, Oskar Fischinger)
Fireworks (1947, Kenneth Anger)
The Petrified Dog (1948, Sidney Peterson)
Mother's Day (1948, James Broughton)
The Lead Shoes (1949, Sidney Peterson)
Begone Dull Care (1949, Norman McLaren, Canada)
Loony Tom the Happy Lover (1951, James Broughton)
Bells of Atlantis (1952, Ian Hugo)
Color Cry (1952, Len Lye)
Mandala (1953, Jordan Belson)
Analogies #1 (1953, James Davis)
The Wonder Ring (1955, Stan Brakhage)
Flesh of Morning (1956, Stan Brakhage)
NY, NY (1957, Francis Thompson)
Anticipation of the Night (1958, Stan Brakhage)
A Movie (1958, Bruce Conner)
Wedlock House: An Intercourse (1959, Stan Brakhage)
Window Water Baby Moving (1959, Stan Brakhage)
Pull My Daisy (1959, Robert Frank and Alfred Leslie)
The Flower Thief (1960, Ron Rice)
Catalog (1961, John Whitney)
Cosmic Ray (1961, Bruce Conner)
Guns of the Trees (1961, Jonas Mekas)
Allures (1961, Jordan Belson)
Blazes (1961, Robert Breer)
Horse Over Teakettle (1962, Robert Breer)
Normal Love (1963, Jack Smith)
Blonde Cobra (1963, Ken Jacobs)
Scorpio Rising (1963, Kenneth Anger)
Mothlight (1963, Stan Brakhage)
Sleep (1963, Andy Warhol)
Flaming Creatures (1963, Jack Smith)
Little Stabs at Happiness (1963, Ken Jacobs)
To Parsifal (1963, Bruce Baillie)
Breathdeath. A Trageede in Masks (1963, Stan VanDerBeek)

Mass for the Dakota Sioux (1963–1964, Bruce Baillie)
Fist Fight (1964, Robert Breer)
Re-Entry (1964, Jordan Belson)
Blow Job (1964, Andy Warhol)
Dog Star Man (1961–1964, Stan Brakhage)
The Art of Vision (1961–1965, Stan Brakhage)
Phenomena (1965, Jordan Belson)
Quixote (1964–1965, Bruce Baillie)
Oh Dem Watermelons (1965, Robert Nelson)
Sins of the Fleshapoids (1965, Mike Kuchar)
Hold Me While I'm Naked (1966, George Kuchar)
Relativity (1963–1966, Ed Emshwiller)
Lapis (1963–1966, James Whitney)
Film in which there appear sprocket holes, edge lettering, dirt particles, etc. (1966, George Landow)
66 (1966, Robert Breer)
Inauguration of the Pleasure Dome (1966, Kenneth Anger)
The Chelsea Girls (1966, Andy Warhol)
Castro Street (1966, Bruce Baillie)
Report (1963–1967, Bruce Conner)
Fuses (1964–1967, Carolee Schneemann)
Offon (1967, Scott Bartlett)
Samadhi (1967, Jordan Belson)
Wavelength (1967, Michael Snow, Canada)
Pas de deux (1967, Norman McLaren, Canada)
David Holzman's Diary (1967, Jim McBride)
Portrait of Jason (1967, Shirley Clarke)
Maidstone (1968, Norman Mailer)
Chinese Firedrill (1968, Will Hindle)
Permutations (1968, John Whitney)
Trash (1968, Andy Warhol and Paul Morrissey)
Diaries, Notes and Sketches (Walden) (1968, Jonas Mekas)
←——→ (1969, Michael Snow)
Invocation of My Demon Brother (1969, Kenneth Anger)
Scenes from Under Childhood (1967–1970, Stan Brakhage)
The Machine of Eden (1970, Stan Brakhage)
Multiple Maniacs (1970, John Waters)
Zorns Lemma (1970, Hollis Frampton)
La Région Centrale (1971, Michael Snow)
Reminiscenses of a Journey to Lithuania (1971, Jonas Mekas)
Tom, Tom, the Piper's Son (1971, Ken Jacobs)
Matrix (1971, John Whitney)
Pink Flamingos (1971, John Waters)
The Text of Light (1974, Stan Brakhage)

Film about a woman who . . . (1974, Yvonne Rainer)
Kristina Talking Pictures (1976, Yvonne Rainer)
Four Journeys Into Mystic Time (1978, Shirley Clarke)
Re-born (1979, Ian Hugo)
Two Figures (1980, James Herbert)
What's Out Tonight Is Lost (1983, Phil Solomon)
The Man Who Envied Women (1985, Yvonne Rainer)
The Dante Quartet (1982–1987, Stan Brakhage)
Marilyn's Window (1988, Stan Brakhage)
Remains To Be Seen (1989, Phil Solomon)
The Lost Domain (1990, Peter Herwitz)
See You Later (1990, Michael Snow)
The Book Of All The Dead (1975–present; Bruce Elder, Canada)

16. Emerging National Traditions 2 (1968–1991): Germany, Spain, Latin America, Africa, Australia, Canada

BOOKS

Alea, Tomás Gutiérrez. *Memories of Underdevelopment.* (Includes the script and source novel.) New Brunswick, N.J.: Rutgers University Press, 1990.
Aranda, Francisco. *Luis Buñuel: A Critical Biography.* New York: Da Capo, 1976.
Armes, Roy. *Third World Film Making and the West.* Berkeley and Los Angeles: University of California Press, 1987.
Baxter, John. *The Australian Cinema.* Sidney: Angus & Robertson, 1970.
Buache, Freddy. *The Cinema of Luis Buñuel.* Cranbury, N.J.: Barnes 1973.
Buñuel, Luis. *My Last Sigh.* Translated by Abigail Israel. New York: Knopf, 1983.
Burton, Julianne. *The New Latin Cinema: An Annotated Bibliography.* New York: Cinéaste, 1976.
——— , ed. *Cinema and Social Change in Latin America: Conversations with Filmmakers.* Austin: University of Texas Press, 1986.
——— , ed. *The Social Documentary in Latin America.* Pittsburgh: University of Pittsburgh Press, 1990.
Chanan, Michael. *The Cuban Image: Cinema and Cultural Politics in Cuba.* London: BFI, 1985.

————, ed. *Chilean Cinema.* London: BFI, 1976.

————, ed. *Twenty-Five Years of the New Latin American Cinema.* London: BFI, 1983.

Corrigan, Tim. *New German Film: The Displaced Image.* Austin: University of Texas Press, 1983.

————, ed. *Films of Werner Herzog: Between Mirage and History.* New York: Methuen, 1987.

Cyr, Helen W. *A Filmography of the Third World.* Metuchen, N.J.: Scarecrow, 1976.

D'Lugo, Marvin. *The Films of Carlos Saura: The Practice of Seeing.* Princeton: Princeton University Press, 1991.

Durgnat, Raymond. *Luis Buñuel.* Berkeley and Los Angeles: University of California Press, 1968.

Elsaesser, Thomas. *New German Cinema: A History.* New Brunswick, N.J.: Rutgers University Press, 1989.

Feldman, Seth, and Joyce Nelson, eds. *Canadian Film Reader.* Toronto: Martin, 1977.

Greenberg, Alan. *Heart of Glass.* Munich: Skellig, 1976.

Handling, Piers, ed. *The Shape of Rage: The Films of David Cronenberg.* Toronto: General Publishing, 1983.

Hayman, Ronald. *Fassbinder: Filmmaker.* New York: Simon & Schuster, 1985.

Higginbotham, Virginia. *Luis Buñuel.* Boston: Twayne, 1979.

Hutton, Anne, ed. *The First Australian History and Film Conference Papers, 1982.* North Ryde. NSW: Australian Film and Television School, National Library, 1982.

James, C. Rodney. *Film as a National Art: NFB of Canada and the Film Board Idea.* New York: Arno, 1977.

Johnson, Randal. *Cinema Novo x 5: Masters of Contemporary Brazilian Film.* Austin: University of Texas Press, 1984.

Khan, Mohamed. *An Introduction to Egyptian Cinema.* London: Infomatics, 1969.

Krelman, Martin. *This Is Where We Came In: The Career and Character of Canadian Film.* Toronto: McClelland & Stewart, 1978.

Kyrou, Ado. *Luis Buñuel: An Introduction.* New York: Simon & Schuster, 1963.

Luhr, William, ed. *World Cinema Since 1945.* New York: Ungar, 1987.

McFarlane, Brian. *Australian Cinema.* New York: Columbia University Press, 1988.

Mellen, Joan, ed. *Luis Buñuel: Essays in Criticism.* New York: Oxford University Press, 1978.

Molina-Foix, Vicente. *New Cinema in Spain.* London: BFI, 1977.

Mora, Carl J. *Mexican Cinema: Reflections of a Society 1896–1988.* rev. ed. Berkeley and Los Angeles: University of California Press, 1990.

Morris, Peter. *Embattled Shadows: A History of the Canadian Film, 1895–1939.* Montreal: McGill-Queens University Press, 1979.

Nevares, B. R. *The Mexican Cinema.* Albuquerque: University of New Mexico Press, 1976.

Oshana, Maryann. *Women of Color: A Filmography of Minority and Third World Women.* New York: Garland, 1985.

Pfaff, Françoise. *The Cinema of Ousmane Sembene: A Pioneer of African Film.* Westport, Conn.: Greenwood, 1984.

Phillips, Klaus, ed. *New German Filmmakers: From Oberhausen through the 1970s.* New York: Ungar, 1984.

Pines, Jim, and Paul Willemen. *Questions of Third Cinema.* Bloomington: Indiana University Press, 1989.

Reade, Eric. *History and Heartburn: The Saga of Australian Film, 1896–1978.* East Brunswick, N.J.: Fairleigh Dickinson University Press, 1981.

Rentschler, Eric. *West German Film in the Course of Time: Reflections on the Twenty Years since Oberhausen.* Bedford Hills, N.Y.: Redgrave, 1984.

————, ed. *German Film and Literature: Adaptations and Transformations.* New York: Ungar, 1984.

Roud, Richard. *Straub.* New York: Viking, 1972.

Sadoul, Georges, ed. *The Cinema in the Arab Countries.* Beirut: Interarab Centre of Film & Television, 1966.

Salmane, Hala. *Algerian Cinema.* London: BFI, 1977.

Sandford, John. *The New German Cinema.* Totowa, N.J.: Barnes & Noble, 1980.

Schmidt, Nancy. *Sub-Saharan African Films and Filmmakers: An Annotated Bibliography.* London: Hans Zell, 1988.

Shohat, Ella. *Israeli Cinema: East/West and the Politics of Representation.* Austin: University of Texas Press, 1989.

Somgyi, Lia, ed. *Hungarian Film Directors, 1948–1983.* Budapest: Interpress, 1984.

Steven, Peter. *Jump Cut: Hollywood, Politics, and Counter-Cinema.* New York: Praeger, 1985.

Veroneau, Pierre, ed. *The Canadian Cinemas.* Ottawa: Canadian Film Institute, 1979.

Williams, Linda. *Figures of Desire: A Theory and Analysis of Surrealist Film.* Urbana and Chicago: University of Illinois Press, 1981.

FILMS

THE NEW GERMAN CINEMA

RAINER WERNER FASSBINDER (1946–1982)
Why Does Herr R. Run Amok? (1969)
Beware of a Holy Whore (1970)
The Merchant of the Four Seasons (1971)
The Bitter Tears of Petra von Kant (1972)
Ali: Fear Eats the Soul or *Fear Eats the Soul* (1973)
Effi Briest (1974)
Fox and His Friends (1974)
Mother Küster's Trip to Heaven (1975)
Satan's Brew (1976)
Chinese Roulette (1976)
Despair (1977)
The Marriage of Maria Braun (1979)
Berlin Alexanderplatz (1980)
Lola (1981)
Veronika Voss (1981)
Querelle (1982)

WERNER HERZOG (1942–   )
Signs of Life (1968)
Fata Morgana (1970)
Even Dwarfs Started Small (1970)
Land of Silence and Darkness (1971)
Aguirre, the Wrath of God (1972)
The Great Ecstasy of the Sculptor Steiner (1974)
Everyone for Himself and God Against All or *The Mystery of Kaspar Hauser* (1974)
La Soufrière (1976)
Heart of Glass (1976)
Stroszek (1977)
Nosferatu (1978)
Woyzeck (1978)
Fitzcarraldo (1982)
Scream of Stone (1991)

VOLKER SCHLÖNDORFF (1939–   )
Young Törless (1966)
The Lost Honor of Katharina Blum (1975). Co-director, Margarethe von Trotta
Coup de grace (1976)
The Tin Drum (1979)
Circle of Deceit (1981)

WIM WENDERS (1945–   )
The Goalie's Anxiety at the Penalty Kick (1971)
The Scarlet Letter (1972)
Alice in the Cities (1973)
Kings of the Road or *In the Course of Time* (1976)
The American Friend (1977)
Hammett (1983)
Paris, Texas (1984)
Wings of Desire (1987)

GERMAN MISCELLANY (1956–1988)
The Captain from Koepenick (1956, Helmut Kautner)
The Confessions of Felix Krull (1957, Kurt Hoffmann)
Aren't We Wonderful? (1958, Kurt Hoffmann)
The Bridge (1959, Bernhard Wicki)
Not Reconciled (1965, Jean-Marie Straub and Danièle Huillet)
Yesterday Girl (1966, Alexander Kluge)
Chronicle of Anna Magdalena Bach (1967, Straub/Huillet)
Moses and Aaron (1974, Straub/Huillet)
Strongman Ferdinand (1975, Alexander Kluge)
The Wild Duck (1976, Hans Giessendorfer)
Our Hitler (1977, Hans Jürgen Syberberg)
The Second Awakening of Christa Klages (1977, Margarethe von Trotta)
Knife in the Head (1978, Reinhard Hauff)
Sisters, or The Balance of Happiness (1979, Margarethe von Trotta)
Germany, Pale Mother (1980, Helma Sanders-Brahms)
Marianne and Juliane or *The German Sisters* or *The Leaden Time* (1981, Margarethe von Trotta)
Freak Orlando (1981, Ulrike Ottinger)
Too Early, Too Late (1981, Straub/Huillet)
Das Boot (1981, Wolfgang Petersen)
Parsifal (1982, Hans Jürgen Syberberg)
Sheer Madness or *Friends and Husbands* (1982, Margarethe von Trotta)
Class Relations (1983, Straub/Huillet)

Inside the Whale (1984, Doris Dörrie)
Three Sisters (1988, Margarethe von Trotta)

SPAIN

LUIS BUÑUEL (1900–1983)
Un Chien andalou (1929). Co-director, Salvador Dali
L'Age d'or (1930). Co-director, Salvador Dali
Land Without Bread or *Las Hurdes* (1932)
Los olvidados or *The Young and the Damned* (1950)
El (1952)
The Adventures of Robinson Crusoe (1952)
Illusion Travels by Streetcar (1953)
Nazarin (1958)
Viridiana (1961)
The Exterminating Angel (1962)
Simon of the Desert (1965)
Belle de jour (1967)
The Milky Way (1969)
The Discreet Charm of the Bourgeoisie (1972)
The Phantom of Liberty (1974)
That Obscure Object of Desire (1977)

CARLOS SAURA (1932–   )
The Hunt (1966)
Cousin Angelica (1974)
Cría or *Cría cuervos* (1977)
Sweet Hours (1981)
Blood Wedding (1981)
Carmen (1983)
El amor brujo (1985)

THIRD WORLD CINEMA

CUBA
Lucía (1968, Humberto Solas)
Memories of Underdevelopment (1968, Tomás Gutiérrez Alea)
The Other Francisco (1975, Sergio Giral)
Alicia (1976, Victor Casaus)
The Last Supper (1977, Tomás Gutiérrez Alea)

LATIN AMERICA
The Pearl (1946, Emilio Fernandez, Mexico)
Yanco (1961, Servando Gonzalez, Mexico)
Vidas secas (1963, Nelson Pereira dos Santos, Brazil)
The Hour of the Furnaces: Notes and Testimonies on Neo-Colonialism, Violence and Liberation (1968, Fernando Solanas and Octavio Getino, Argentina)

El Topo (1969, Alexandro Jodorowsky, Mexico)
The Jackal of Nahueltoro (1969, Miguel Littin, Chile)
Blood of the Condor (1969, Jorge Sanjinés, Bolivia)
Antonio das Mortes (1969, Glauber Rocha, Brazil)
How Tasty Was My Little Frenchman (1971, Nelson Pereira dos Santos, Brazil)
The Harder They Come (1973, Perry Henzell, Jamaica)
The Promised Land (1973, Miguel Littin, Chile)
Xica (1976, Carlos Diegues, Brazil)
The Battle of Chile (1973–1979). Part I released 1975, Parts I and II released together in 1977, Part III released 1979 (Patricio Guzmán, Chile)
Pixote (1981, Hector Babenco, Brazil)
Kiss of the Spider Woman (1985, Hector Babenco, Brazil)
Danzon (1991, Maria Novaro, Mexico)

AFRICA AND ASIA MINOR
Black Girl (1966, Ousmane Sembene, Senegal)
The Money Order (1968, Ousmane Sembene, Senegal)
The Night of Counting the Years (1969, Shadi Abdes-Salam, Egypt)
Ramparts of Clay (1971, Jean-Louis Bertucelli, Tunisia)
Xala (1974, Ousmane Sembene, Senegal)
The Girl (1975, Souleymane Cissé, Mali)
Ceddo (1977, Ousmane Sembene, Senegal)
Work (1978, Souleymane Cissé, Mali)
The Exile (1980, Oumarou Ganda, Niger)
The Gods Must Be Crazy (1981, Jamie Uys, South Africa)
The Wind (1982, Souleymane Cissé, Mali)
Yol (1982, Şerif Gören, Turkey)
Brightness (1987, Souleymane Cissé, Mali)

AUSTRALIA AND BRITISH COMMONWEALTH

BRUCE BERESFORD (1940–   )
Don's Party (1976)
Breaker Morant (1980)
Tender Mercies (1983)
Driving Miss Daisy (1989)

DAVID CRONENBERG (1943–   )
Crimes of the Future (1970)
They Came From Within or *Shivers* (1975)
Rabid (1977)

The Brood (1979)
Scanners (1981). Completed 1980
Videodrome (1983). Completed 1982
The Dead Zone (1983)
The Fly (1986)
Dead Ringers (1988)

PETER WEIR (1944–   )
Picnic at Hanging Rock (1975)
The Last Wave (1977)
Gallipoli (1981)
The Year of Living Dangerously (1982)
Witness (1985)
The Mosquito Coast (1986)
Green Card (1990)

COMMONWEALTH MISCELLANY
Nobody Waved Goodbye (1964, Don Owen)
Goin' Down the Road (1970, Don Shebib)
Act of the Heart (1970, Paul Almond)
Outback (1971, Ted Kotcheff)
Mon oncle Antoine (1971, Claude Jutra)
Kamouraska (1974, Claude Jutra)
The Apprenticeship of Duddy Kravitz (1974, Ted Kotcheff)
The Devil's Playground (1976, Fred Schepisi)
The Picture Show Man (1977, John Power)
Outrageous! (1977, Richard Benner)
The Chant of Jimmy Blacksmith (1978, Fred Schepisi)
Newsfront (1978, Phil Noyce)
Murder By Decree (1978, Bob Clark)
Mad Max (1979, George Miller)
My Brilliant Career (1979, Gillian Armstrong)
The Road Warrior or *Mad Max 2* (1981, George Miller)
Lonely Hearts (1981, Paul Cox)
Gregory's Girl (1981, Bill Forsyth)
Ticket to Heaven (1981, Ralph L. Thomas)
The Grey Fox (1983, Philip Borsos)
Local Hero (1983, Bill Forsyth)
Man of Flowers (1983, Paul Cox)
Star Struck (1983, Gillian Armstrong)
My First Wife (1984, Paul Cox)
Mad Max Beyond Thunderdome (1985, George Miller)
Crocodile Dundee (1986, Peter Faiman)
The Decline of the American Empire (1986, Denys Arcand)
A Cry in the Dark (1988, Fred Schepisi)
Sweetie (1989, Jane Campion)
My Left Foot (1989, Jim Sheridan)

Jesus of Montreal (1989, Denys Arcand)
The Russia House (1990, Fred Schepisi)
An Angel at My Table (1991, Jane Campion)
A Woman's Tale (1991, Paul Cox)

17. The Return of the Myths (1977–1991)

BOOKS

Bach, Steven. *Final Cut: Dreams and Disaster in the Making of* Heaven's Gate. New York: William Morrow, 1985.

Bart, Peter. *Fade Out: The Calamitous Final Days of MGM.* New York: William Morrow, 1990.

Blake, Larry. *Film Sound Today.* Hollywood: Reveille Press, 1984.

Bliss, Michael. *Martin Scorsese and Michael Cimino.* Metuchen, N.J.: Scarecrow, 1985.

Dworkin, Susan. *Double De Palma.* New York: Newmarket, 1984.

Ellis, John. *Visible Fictions: Cinema, Television, Video.* London: Routledge & Kegan Paul, 1982.

Frank, Ronald Edward, and Marshall G. Greenberg. *The Public's Use of Television: Who Watches and Why.* Beverly Hills, Calif.: Sage, 1980.

Goldman, William. *Adventures in the Screen Trade: A Personal View of Hollywood and Screenwriting.* New York: Warner, 1983.

Kinder, Marsha. *Playing with Power in Movies, Television, and Video Games: From Muppet Babies to Teenage Mutant Ninja Turtles.* Berkeley and Los Angeles: University of California Press, 1991.

Klotman, Phyllis Rauch, ed. *Screenplays of the African American Experience.* Bloomington: Indiana University Press, 1991.

Lees, David, and Stan Berkowitz. *The Movie Business.* New York: Vintage, 1981.

Litwak, Mark. *Reel Power: The Struggle for Influence and Success in the New Hollywood.* New York: William Morrow, 1986.

Marc, David. *Demographic Vistas: Television in American Culture.* Philadelphia: University of Pennsylvania Press, 1984.

McClintick, David. *Indecent Exposure: A True Story of Hollywood and Wall Street.* rev. ed. New York: Dell, 1983.

McConnell, Frank. *The Spoken Seen: Film and*

the Romantic Imagination. Baltimore: Johns Hopkins University Press, 1975.

———. Storytelling and Mythmaking: Images from Film and Literature. New York: Oxford University Press, 1979.

Monaco, James. American Film Now: The People, The Power, The Money, The Movies. rev. ed. New York: New American Library, 1984.

Munro, Colin R. Television, Censorship, and the Law. Farnsborough, Eng.: Saxon House, 1979.

Newcomb, Horace, ed. Television: The Critical View. 3rd ed. New York: Oxford University Press, 1982.

Penley, Constance. The Future of an Illusion: Film, Feminism, and Psychoanalysis. Minneapolis: University of Minnesota Press, 1989.

Pye, Michael, and Linda Myles. The Movie Brats: How the Film Generation Took Over Hollywood. New York: Holt, Rinehart, 1979.

Quart, Leonard, and Albert Auster. American Film and Society Since 1945. New York: Praeger, 1985.

Rosenbaum, Jonathan. Film: The Front Line. Denver: Arden Press, 1983.

Schaefer, Dennis, and Larry Salvato. Masters of Light: Conversations With Contemporary Cinematographers. Berkeley and Los Angeles: University of California Press, 1984.

Schechter, Harold. The Bosom Serpent: Folklore and Popular Art. Iowa City: University of Iowa Press, 1988.

Smith, Thomas G. Industrial Light & Magic: The Art of Special Effects. New York: Ballantine, 1986.

Soderbergh, Steven. sex, lies, and videotape. (Includes the script.) New York: Harper and Row, 1990.

Vale, V., Andrea Juno, and Jim Morton, eds. Re/Search #10: Incredibly Strange Films. San Francisco: Re/Search Publications, 1986.

Wood, Robin. Hollywood from Vietnam to Reagan. New York: Columbia University Press, 1986.

FILMS

JOHN CARPENTER (1948–   )
Assault on Precinct 13 (1976)
Halloween (1978)
The Thing (1982)
Prince of Darkness (1987)
They Live (1988)

JOEL (1955–   ) AND ETHAN (1958–   ) COEN
Blood Simple (1983)
Raising Arizona (1987)
Miller's Crossing (1990)
Barton Fink (1991)

JONATHAN DEMME (1944–   )
Citizens Band or Handle With Care (1977)
Melvin and Howard (1980)
Stop Making Sense (1984)
Something Wild (1986)
Swimming to Cambodia (1987)
Married to the Mob (1988)
The Silence of the Lambs (1991)

BRIAN DE PALMA (1940–   )
Greetings (1968)
Hi, Mom! (1970)
Sisters (1973). Completed 1972
Obsession (1976)
Carrie (1976)
The Fury (1978)
Dressed to Kill (1980)
Blow Out (1981)
Scarface (1983)
Body Double (1984)
The Untouchables (1987)

BOB FOSSE (1927–1987)
Sweet Charity (1968)
Cabaret (1972)
Lenny (1974)
All That Jazz (1979)
Star 80 (1983)

SPIKE LEE (1957–   )
She's Gotta Have It (1986)
School Daze (1988)
Do The Right Thing (1989)
Mo' Better Blues (1990)
Jungle Fever (1991)

GEORGE LUCAS (1944–   )
THX-1138 (1971)
American Graffiti (1973)
Star Wars (1977)

DAVID LYNCH (1946–   )
Eraserhead (1977)
The Elephant Man (1980)
Dune (1984)
Blue Velvet (1986)
Wild At Heart (1990)

George A. Romero (1940–)
Night of the Living Dead (1968)
Martin (1976)
Dawn of the Dead (1979) Completed 1978
Day of the Dead (1985)

John Sayles (1948–)
Return of the Secaucus 7 (1980)
Baby It's You (1983). Completed 1982
Lianna (1983)
The Brother from Another Planet (1984)
Matewan (1987)
Eight Men Out (1988)

Paul Schrader (1946–)
Blue Collar (1978)
Hardcore (1979)
American Gigolo (1980)
Mishima (1985)

Ridley Scott (1939–)
The Duellists (1977)
Alien (1979)
Blade Runner (1982)
Someone to Watch Over Me (1987)
Thelma & Louise (1991)

Steven Spielberg (1947–)
Duel (1971)
The Sugarland Express (1974)
Jaws (1975)
Close Encounters of the Third Kind (1977). Revised 1980
Raiders of the Lost Ark (1981)
E.T. — The Extra-Terrestrial (1982)
Indiana Jones and the Temple of Doom (1984)
The Color Purple (1985)
Indiana Jones and the Last Crusade (1989)

American Miscellany (1977–1991)
Killer of Sheep (1977, Charles Burnett)
The Hills Have Eyes (1977, Wes Craven)
Between the Lines (1977, Joan Micklin Silver)
Short Eyes (1977, Robert M. Young)
Saturday Night Fever (1977, John Badham)
Go Tell the Spartans (1978, Ted Post)
Grease (1978, Randal Kleiser)
Days of Heaven (1978, Terrence Malick)
The Deer Hunter (1978, Michael Cimino)
Heaven Can Wait (1978, Warren Beatty and Buck Henry)
Invasion of the Body Snatchers (1978, Philip Kaufman)

Piranha (1978, Joe Dante)
The Warriors (1979, Walter Hill)
The Black Stallion (1979, Carroll Ballard)
Kramer vs. Kramer (1979, Robert Benton)
The Empire Strikes Back (1980, Irvin Kershner)
The Stunt Man (1980, Richard Rush). Completed 1978
Fame (1980, Alan Parker)
Resurrection (1980, Daniel Petrie)
Ordinary People (1980, Robert Redford)
Heaven's Gate (1980, Michael Cimino)
Friday the 13th (1980, Sean S. Cunningham)
Friday the 13th Part 2 (1981, Steve Miner)
Arthur (1981, Steve Gordon)
Body Heat (1981, Lawrence Kasdan)
The Funhouse (1981, Tobe Hooper)
The Howling (1981, Joe Dante). Completed 1980
Polyester (1981, John Waters)
Zoot Suit (1981, Luis Valdez)
Pennies From Heaven (1981, Herbert Ross)
Missing (1982, Constantin Costa-Gavras)
First Blood (1982, Ted Kotcheff)
The Ballad of Gregorio Cortez (1982, Robert M. Young)
48 HRS. (1982, Walter Hill)
Poltergeist (1982, Tobe Hooper)
Pink Floyd — The Wall (1982, Alan Parker)
Chan Is Missing (1982, Wayne Wang)
Diner (1982, Barry Levinson)
Star Trek II: The Wrath Of Khan (1982, Nicholas Meyer)
Tootsie (1982, Sydney Pollack)
Fast Times at Ridgemont High (1982, Amy Heckerling)
Born In Flames (1983, Lizzie Borden)
Brainstorm (1983, Douglas Trumbull)
WarGames (1983, John Badham)
The Big Chill (1983, Lawrence Kasdan)
Flashdance (1983, Adrian Lyne)
The Right Stuff (1983, Philip Kaufman)
Terms of Endearment (1983, James Brooks)
Risky Business (1983, Paul Brickman)
Return of the Jedi (1983, Richard Marquand)
1918 (1984, Ken Harrison)
Places in the Heart (1984, Robert Benton)
All of Me (1984, Carl Reiner)
Romancing the Stone (1984, Robert Zemeckis)
Beverly Hills Cop (1984, Martin Brest)
Stranger Than Paradise (1984, Jim Jarmusch)
Ghostbusters (1984, Ivan Reitman)
Gremlins (1984, Joe Dante)

The Terminator (1984, James Cameron)

A Nightmare on Elm Street (1984, Wes Craven)

Desperately Seeking Susan (1985, Susan Seidelman)

The Breakfast Club (1985, John Hughes)

The Stuff (1985, Larry Cohen)

Rambo: First Blood Part II (1985, George P. Cosmatos)

Back to the Future (1985, Robert Zemeckis). Part II, 1989; Part III, 1990

The Return of the Living Dead (1985, Dan O'Bannon)

Brazil (1985, Terry Gilliam)

Down By Law (1986, Jim Jarmusch)

Aliens (1986, James Cameron)

Stand By Me (1986, Rob Reiner)

River's Edge (1986, Tim Hunter)

Henry: Portrait of a Serial Killer (1986, John McNaughton). Re-released 1990

Top Gun (1986, Tony Scott)

Platoon (1986, Oliver Stone)

Lethal Weapon (1987, Richard Donner)

RoboCop (1987, Paul Verhoeven)

Hollywood Shuffle (1987, Robert Townsend)

Near Dark (1987, Kathryn Bigelow)

Who Framed Roger Rabbit (1988, Robert Zemeckis)

Die Hard (1988, John McTiernan)

Hairspray (1988, John Waters)

Bird (1988, Clint Eastwood)

Dominick and Eugene (1988, Robert M. Young)

84 Charlie Mopic (1989, Patrick Duncan)

Batman (1989, Tim Burton)

Field of Dreams (1989, Phil Alden Robinson)

Born on the Fourth of July (1989, Oliver Stone)

Drugstore Cowboy (1989, Gus Van Sant, Jr.)

Eat a Bowl of Tea (1989, Wayne Wang)

Mystery Train (1989, Jim Jarmusch)

sex, lies, and videotape (1989, Steven Soderbergh)

New York Stories (1989, Woody Allen, Francis Ford Coppola, and Martin Scorsese)

Total Recall (1990, Paul Verhoeven)

The Grifters (1990, Stephen Frears)

Jacob's Ladder (1990, Adrian Lyne)

To Sleep With Anger (1990, Charles Burnett)

Edward Scissorhands (1990, Tim Burton)

Terminator 2: Judgment Day (1991, James Cameron)

Boyz N the Hood (1991, John Singleton)

Rambling Rose (1991, Martha Coolidge)

Distributors

The following list of 16mm distributors reflects the many changes of ownership and location that took place in the late 1980s and early 90s (to July 1991). Some distributors charge for their catalogs; others provide them for free. Asterisks identify distributors whose large and diverse holdings make them particularly useful when setting up a survey course in film history, but every company listed here is an important resource.

* Biograph Entertainment
2 Depot Plaza, Suite 202B
Bedford Hills, NY 10507
(914) 242-9838
(800) 346-3144

* Budget Films
4590 Santa Monica Blvd.
Los Angeles, CA 90029
(213) 660-0187

**University of California
  Extension Media Center**
2176 Shattuck Ave.
Berkeley, CA 94704
(415) 642-0460

California Newsreel
149 9th St., Suite 420
San Francisco, CA 94103
(415) 621-6196

**Canadian Filmmakers'
  Distribution West**
1131 Howe St., Suite 100
Vancouver, B.C., V6Z 2L7
  Canada

Canyon Cinema Cooperative
2325 3rd St., Suite 338
San Francisco, CA 94107
(415) 626-2255

**China Film Import & Export
  (L.A.), Inc.**
2500 Wilshire Blvd., Suite 1028
Los Angeles, CA 90057
(213) 380-7520
(213) 380-7521
Fax: (213) 487-2089

Cinecom Entertainment Group
1250 Broadway, 33rd floor
New York, NY 10001
(212) 239-8360

* Corinth Films
34 Gansevoort St.
New York, NY 10014
(212) 463-0305
(800) 221-4720

Creative Film Society
8435 Geyser Ave.
Northridge, CA 91324
(818) 885-7288

Direct Cinema
P.O. Box 10003

Santa Monica, CA 90410
(213) 396-4774
(800) 525-0000

* Em Gee Film Library
6924 Canby Ave., Suite 103
Reseda, CA 91335
(818) 881-8110
Fax: (818) 981-5506

FACSEA
972 Fifth Ave.
New York, NY 10021
(212) 439-1400

* Film-makers' Cooperative
175 Lexington Ave.
New York, NY 10016
(212) 889-3820

* Films Inc.
5547 No. Ravenswood Ave.
Chicago, IL 60640
(800) 323-4222

First Run Features
153 Waverly Place
New York, NY 10014
(212) 243-0600

First Run/Icarus Films
153 Waverly Place

New York, NY 10014
(212) 727-1711

Frameline
P.O. Box 14792
San Francisco, CA 94114
(415) 861-5245

Samuel Goldwyn Co.
10203 Santa Monica Blvd.,
   Suite 500
Los Angeles, CA 90067
(213) 552-2255
(800) 421-5743

Grove Weidenfeld Press
Film Division
841 Broadway
New York, NY 10003
(212) 614-7850

Hurlock Cine World
2858 Mendenhall Loop
P.O. Box 34619
Juneau, Alaska 99803
(800) 327-9344

Interama
301 W. 53rd St., Suite 19E
New York, NY 10019
(212) 977-4830

International Film Exchange,
   Ltd.
201 W. 52nd St.
New York, NY 10019
(212) 582-4318

Ivy Films
165 W. 46th St.
New York, NY 10036
(212) 382-0111

The Killiam Collection
6 E. 39th St.
New York, NY 10016
(212) 684-3920

Kino International
333 W. 39th St., Suite 503
New York, NY 10018
(212) 629-6880

* Kit Parker Films
1245 10th St.
Monterey, CA 93940
(408) 649-5573
(800) 538-5838

Krypton International, Inc.
The Almi Collection
c/o Mediators
655 Madison Ave., 14th floor
New York, NY 10021
(212) 751-1396

Milestone Film and Video
275 W. 96th St., Suite 28C
New York, NY 10025
(212) 865-7449

Minneapolis Film Center
425 Ontario St. SE
Minneapolis, MN 55414
(612) 627-4430

* The Museum of Modern Art
Circulating Film Library
11 W. 53rd St.
New York, NY 10019
(212) 708-9530

New Cinema, Ltd.
75 Horner Ave., Unit 1
Toronto, ONT, M8Z 4X5
   Canada
(416) 252-4151
Fax: (416) 251-3720

* New Yorker Films
16 W. 61st St., 11th floor
New York, NY 10023
(212) 247-6110

Original Cinema
419 Park Ave. South, 20th floor
New York, NY 10016
(212) 545-0177

Pyramid Films
Box 1048
Santa Monica, CA 90406
(213) 828-7577
(800) 421-2304

* Swank Motion Pictures
201 S. Jefferson Ave.
St. Louis, MO 63166
(314) 534-6300
(800) 876-5577

   or

60 Bethpage Road
Hicksville, NY 11801
(516) 931-7500
(800) 645-7501

   or

2777 Finley Road
Downers Grove, IL 60515
(312) 629-9004
(800) 323-2292

   or

6767 Forest Lawn Drive
Hollywood, CA 90068
(213) 851-6300
(800) 421-4590

Third World Newsreel
335 W. 38th St.
New York, NY 10018
(212) 947-9277

Alan Twyman Presents
592 So. Grant Ave.
Columbus, OH 43206
(614) 469-0720

Women Make Movies
225 Lafayette St., Suite 207
New York, NY 10012
(212) 925-0606

Zeitgeist Films
247 Centre St., 2nd floor
New York, NY 10013
(617) 274-1989

Zipporah Films
1 Richdale Ave., Unit #4
Cambridge, MA 02140
(617) 576-3603

Acknowledgments

The author and publisher wish to thank the following for making available photographic stills:

from *Scorpio Rising;* courtesy of Kenneth Anger.

from *Wavelength;* courtesy of Anthology Film Archives.

A Kinetoscope Parlor and *Fred Ott's Sneeze;* reprinted by Arno Press, Inc., 1970.

from the films *Diary of a Country Priest, 8½, Closely Watched Trains, Viridiana, Pather Panchali, Throne of Blood,* and *The Bicycle Thief;* courtesy of Audio-Brandon Films.

from the films *Mothlight* and *existence is song;* courtesy of Stan Brakhage.

from *Faces;* courtesy of Ray Carney and the Estate of John Cassavetes. Frame enlargement from *Faces* reproduced by permission. Photography by Al Ruban.

from *Women on the Verge of a Nervous Breakdown;* courtesy of Cinevista, Inc.

from *Blood Simple;* courtesy of Circle Releasing Corporation.

from the films *Lawrence of Arabia*, copyright © 1962, and *On the Waterfront;* both courtesy of Columbia Pictures Industries, Inc. All rights reserved.

from *Halloween;* courtesy of Compass International Pictures.

from the films *Breathless, Vivre sa vie, The Children of Paradise,* and *A nous la liberté;* courtesy of Contemporary Films/McGraw-Hill.

from *Blue Velvet;* courtesy of DEG Communications.

from *A Trip to the Moon, The General, The Pawnshop, One A.M., The Last Laugh,* and *Easy Street;* courtesy of Em Gee Film Library.

from *La strada;* courtesy of Avco-Embassy Films.

from *Lola Montès;* courtesy of Les Films de la Pléiade.

Glossary

Academy ratio. Also known as "Academy Frame." The standard proportions of the 35mm image: four units wide by three units high, expressed as 4:3 or 1.33:1. *See also* Aspect ratio.

Actualité. A nonfiction film that records a real event in an unbiased manner.

Anamorphic. Any wide-screen process, lens, or format in which a wide field of view is squeezed (horizontally compressed) during shooting and unsqueezed (restoring normal width-to-height relationships) during projection.

Anamorphic lens. A lens that compresses or widens the horizontal dimension of an image without affecting the vertical dimension — squeezing a wide image to fit onto standard-sized film, then spreading out the skinny image to fill a wide screen.

Animation. The process of making inanimate drawings or objects appear to come to life and move — usually by shooting sequential drawings, or an object in sequential positions, one frame at a time.

Art director. The person who designs a movie's sets and decor.

ASA. A measure of the photosensitivity of an emulsion, following specifications established by the American Standards Association; the higher the ASA, the faster the "speed" and the greater the sensitivity of the film.

Aspect ratio. The ratio of the width of the image (written first) to its height (a constant). The standard 35mm Academy Frame is $1\frac{1}{3}$ times as wide as it is high; its aspect ratio ($1\frac{1}{3}$ to 1) is written 1.33:1. Other common aspect ratios are 1.66:1 (35mm European widescreen, a flat format), 1.85:1 (35mm American widescreen, also flat), 2.2:1 (70mm flat), 2.35:1 (Panavision, a 35mm wide-screen anamorphic format), and 2.75:1 (70mm anamorphic). CinemaScope (35mm anamorphic) began at 2.55:1 but soon changed to 2.35:1.

Auteur. A filmmaker — usually a director, but sometimes a producer or writer — with a distinctive style and coherent thematic vision that are developed throughout a body of work. French for "author"; thus, the primary creator of a movie, who guides the collaborative filmmaking project so that it expresses his or her creative intentions.

Barney. A padded bag placed over the camera to soundproof it. *See also* Blimp.

Base. The flexible component or vehicle of film stock, made of a cellulose compound and coated with a photographic emulsion.

Benshi. In Japan, the live narrator of a film.

Bildungsroman. A novel about the formative experiences of a central character; e.g., Goethe's *Wilhelm Meister's Apprenticeship*.

Blacklist. A list that prohibits the hiring of specific individuals and/or a particular class of people, such as left-wing screenwriters.

Blimp. A rigid cover placed over the camera to soundproof it; a "blimped camera" is one with internal soundproofing. *See also* Barney.

Block booking. The practice of forcing an exhibitor to rent a group of films rather than to bid on individual titles.

Blockbuster. A major box-office hit, usually one that grosses $100 million or more during its first domestic release.

Blocking. Planning and rehearsing the positions and movements of the actors and of the camera within a shot or scene.

Boom. (1) The arm of a crane, which supports the camera platform and moves it through the air. (2) The lightweight pole from which a microphone is suspended above the actors (whose movements it accompanies) and outside the frame.

Boom shot. A shot taken from a crane.

Bourgeois. Middle-class.

Bourgeois cinema. Films, and the industry behind them, that encourage audiences to identify with fictional characters and situations, to forget their troubles, and to feel satisfied with fictional resolutions, rather than to remain critically distant from the fiction, keep real-world problems in mind, and confront and discuss those problems with the aid of the film. Escapist fictions that make political analysis appear irrelevant and unnecessary.

Box-office grosses. *See* Gross.

B picture. (1) A film meant to appear at the bottom of a double bill. (2) A relatively inexpensive film, usually a genre picture

(e.g., a no-nonsense mystery or horror film) with character actors rather than big stars.

Breen Code. *See* Production Code.

Cameraman. Also known as "cameraperson." (1) The person in charge of shooting a movie. Also known as "cinematographer," "director of photography," "DP." (2) Loosely, the camera operator.

CARA. The Motion Picture Association of America's Classification and Rating Administration; the board that awards a film its MPAA rating (G, PG, R, etc.), determining how old one must be — implicitly, how mature one ought to be — in order to see it.

Celluloid. Transparent material chemically derived from cellulose; cut into strips to be used as film base or into sheets on which to paint individual elements of composite drawings.

Chiaroscuro. The artistic arrangement of light and dark elements in a shot or in any pictorial composition.

Cinéaste. (1) A knowledgeable film enthusiast. (2) Literally, a film producer, writer, or cinematographer.

Cinema. (1) The art of motion pictures; "the movies" in general. (2) A movie theatre.

CinemaScope. The 35mm anamorphic process introduced by 20th Century-Fox in 1953; eventually replaced by Panavision. *See also* Aspect ratio.

Cinématographe. The Lumière brothers' 35mm camera, which could also be used as a projector and a printer.

Cinematographer. Also "Director of Photography" and "DP"; sometimes "cameraman." A motion picture photographer; the head of the camera crew.

Cinéma vérité. French for "film truth"; "*kinó-pravda*" in Russian. An unscripted documentary in which the catalyzing presence of the camera, with which the subjects interact, is acknowledged. In most cases the crew is small, sometimes only one person to run the camera and one to record the sound, and the equipment is lightweight.

Cineplex. Trade name of the first multiplex cinema.

Cinerama. Triptych format (three cameras, three projectors) employing a high, wide, deeply curved, three-panel screen, yielding a panorama that extended nearly to the limits of peripheral vision; a fourth projector played the six- or seven-track stereophonic sound. Original aspect ratio variable from $2.71:1$ to $2.77:1$. Introduced 1952; changed from a multi-film system to a large-negative anamorphic system in the early 1960s.

Close shot. Also known as "CS." (1) Unlike the far shot, a shot in which the camera is (or, thanks to a long lens, appears to be) near the subject. (2) A shot whose field of view is slightly broader than that of the close-up; in terms of the human figure, the head and upper chest might fill the frame.

Close-up. Also known as "closeup," "CU." A shot whose field of view is very narrow; in terms of the human figure, a face or hand might fill the frame.

Colorization. The computerized process of adding color to black-and-white movies electronically.

Completion date. (1) The year a film is finished and ready to be released; usually the year in which it is copyrighted. (2) The day the final trial print is approved.

Composition. The arrangement of the elements of an image in relation to the boundaries of the frame and to each other.

Composition in depth. The composition of a visual field in relation to the axis that runs from the camera to infinity; in most cases, significant elements are distributed from the foreground to the background of the image.

Constructive editing. Also known as "linkage editing." A variety of montage in which many brief, distinctly individual shots (which are considered complementary and related rather than in conflict) accumulate into a whole, like a wall made out of bricks; formulated by Vsevolod Pudovkin.

Contact printer. *See* Printer.

Continuity. (1) The narrative structure of a film, laid out in sequence; the plot as a string of scenes. (2) A list and description (including dialogue) of all the shots in the final version of a film, prepared by the editor; the film as a series of shots. Also known as "cutting continuity." (3) The matching of details that allows shots taken at different times to appear to be recording a single, continuous event; the impression that conditions established in one shot continue to exist in later or related shots. (4) A list of the details—such as the length of a cigarette, the condition of a tablecloth, or the number of buttons left unbuttoned on a shirt—that have to be matched from shot to shot, either within a scene or from one scene to another. (Once the boot has been eaten in *The Gold Rush,* continuity demands that from then on, scene after scene, the tramp must have only one boot and the correct foot must be wrapped in just so many rags).

Continuity editing. Also known as "découpage." Editing to create the impression that events flow seamlessly from shot to shot; the opposite of montage, in which cuts are called to the audience's attention and discontinuity is heightened.

Contrapuntal sound. Sound that is synchronized to clash with what is shown; a soundtrack that works against the image track or in counterpoint with it. Audio-visual montage.

Co-production. A film produced by two or more business entities (studios, partnerships, independent producers, etc.).

Core. A hub on which film is wound.

Crane. A vehicle equipped with an arm (or boom); at the end of the arm is a camera platform that can be lifted and moved through the air.

Credits. Also known as "titles." A list including the name of the film, its distributor, copyright and other notices, and the names and contributions of those who worked on it, found at or near the film's start ("head credits" or "opening titles") and/or at its end ("tail credits" or "end titles").

Cross-cutting. Also known as "parallel montage." Cutting back and forth between ongoing actions—usually between scenes that are presented as occurring in different locations at the same time and that are dramatically or thematically related.

Cult film. A film with a devoted following.

Cut. (1) An instantaneous transition from one shot to another. (2) To splice one shot to another; also the splice itself. (3) The way a particular version of a film has been edited, as in "the director's cut." (4) The instruction to stop shooting or to end a shot. (5) Abridged.

Cutaway. A cut away from a shot—or setup, figure, or action—to which the editor will soon return; the return is a "cutback." A cut to a shot whose function is to provide a break from, offer information about, or evade a flawed portion of the primary shot, or to intervene between two similar shots so that their joining will not create a jump cut.

Day-for-night. Shooting in the daytime while using filters or underexposing to create the impression of night.

Deep focus. A visual field that is in sharp focus from foreground to background (extreme depth of field) and whose foreground and background planes appear to be widely separated (impression of a deep visual field, created by a wide-angle lens); often used to accentuate composition in depth.

Depth of field. A measure of the range of focus in an image. The range before and behind the plane of focus within which objects remain acceptably sharp. (A lens might be focused at an object eight feet away but still keep objects that are from five to twenty feet away in focus; at a setting yielding a greater depth of field, that same lens might be focused at eight feet and keep objects in focus from four feet to infinity.) Thus, the distance between the nearest and farthest objects that are in focus, measured along the axis from the camera to infinity.

Dialectical montage. Also known as "intellectual montage." A variety of editing in which shots "collide" or significantly conflict with each other, ideally generating a synthesis (which may be a metaphor or a concept) in the mind of the viewer; formulated by Sergei Eisenstein.

Dialectics. The theory and practice of systems that develop through conflict between opposites. The *thesis,* or first term, gives rise to its opposite or opponent, the *antithesis,* and out of their conflict emerges a *synthesis* that becomes the first term in a new dialectical cycle.

Diffusion. The dispersion, unfocusing, or scattering of light, creating "soft" rather than "hard" effects.

Director. The person who guides the actors in performance, determines the staging of the action, supervises all aspects of shooting, and works with the producer, writer, and designer before production and the film and sound editors after production in order to ensure the consistency and excellence of the movie as well as the best possible use of the personnel, materials, and resources provided by the producer.

Director's cut. The film as the director would like to see it released; the final version presented to the producer or studio, usually with the contractural understanding that it may be altered without the director's approval.

Dissolve. Also known as "lap dissolve." A superimposed fade-out and fade-in; a transitional device in which one image vanishes evenly and gradually while another gradually appears.

Documentary. A nonfiction film that organizes and presents factual materials in order to make a point.

Dolby noise reduction. Also known as "Dolby NR." A process for reducing system noise, particularly tape hiss, by compressing the signal during recording and expanding or decoding it during playback.

Dolby Stereo. (1) Also known as "Dolby SVA" (Stereo Variable Area). A Dolby NR-encoded, optical, variable area soundtrack that carries four channels (left, center, right, and surround) on two tracks; most often found on 35mm prints. (2) A magnetic soundtrack, each of whose six or more channels has been Dolby NR-encoded and is carried on its own track; most often found on 70mm prints.

Dolly. A camera platform with rubber wheels that allow it to move (be pushed) freely over a floor, unlike the earlier steel wheels that had to run on steel rails ("tracks"). *See* Track shot.

Dubbing. (1) Replacing one performer's voice with that of another (as in *Singin' in the Rain*). (2) Replacing all the performers' dialogue with dialogue spoken in another language, usually by other performers. (3) Re-recording with the same performer, especially when an actor replaces his or her dialogue as recorded during shooting with a new performance, under ideal sound conditions, of the same dialogue. Also known as "looping." (4) Copying or transferring a recording.

Dupe. A print copied from another print, usually illegally.

Editing. The art of selecting, trimming, and assembling in order the shots (film editing) and/or the tracks (sound editing) that make up the finished motion picture.

Electronic cinema. The technology and practice of shooting a movie with a high-definition television camera; the video images are transferred onto film in a laboratory.

Emulsion. The light-sensitive component of film stock.

Establishing shot. (1) A long shot, early in a movie or scene, that shows where the action takes place. (2) Any shot that introduces a location.

Exposure. (1) The amount of light that is allowed to reach the film. Overexposure indicates too much light, underexposure too little. (2) The act of allowing light to reach film; the instant in which this happens.

Expressionism. (1) The artistic movement that held that the look and style of the visible, external universe could take its shape, color, and texture from internal human sensations. The art of rendering inner states as aspects of the outer world. (2) Emotionally intense creative distortion.

Exterior. (1) An outdoor shooting location. (2) A scene that is set outdoors.

Extreme close-up. Also known as "ECU," "tight close-up." A shot with a very narrow field of view; the camera appears to be extremely close to the subject. In terms of the human figure, an eye or mouth might fill the frame.

Extreme long shot. Also known as "ELS." A shot with a very broad field of view; the camera appears to be extremely far from the subject. A human figure might be less than one tenth the height of the frame.

Fade. (1) A transitional effect in which the image gradually and evenly disappears into darkness (a "fade-out" or "fade to black") or appears from darkness (a "fade in"). (2) A dissolve to any monochromatic field ("fade to red," "fade to white," etc.). (3) To effect a fade; to fade out (rarely used alone to mean "to fade in").

Far shot. Unlike the close shot, a shot in which the camera is or appears to be distant from the subject.

Fast film. Film whose emulsion has a high "speed," making it extremely reactive to light and useful in low-light conditions.

Fast motion. Also known as "undercranking." The effect of speeded-up movement, achieved by exposing fewer than the normal number of frames per second (i.e., shooting at a rate lower than the projection rate).

Faux raccord. A jump cut with a false impression of continuity; often a match of action over a change of scene.

Feature. A movie whose running time is an hour or more.

Femme fatale. The deadly woman, found regularly in *film noir*.

Film. (1) The flexible medium, consisting of a perforated base coated with an emulsion, on which images are photographically imprinted. (2) Perforated film base coated with magnetic oxide; sound is transferred from magnetic tape to magnetic film, which is the same gauge as the film run through the camera and can easily be kept in frame-by-frame sync with the picture and with other tracks. Also known as "fullcoat," "mag film," "magnetic film," "mag stock." (3) A movie. (4) Like "cinema," a general term for the art of motion pictures. (5) To shoot a motion picture.

Film d' Art. Early silent French "art" films consisting of filmed stage productions.

Film noir. An American genre of the 1940s and 50s (named by French critics who noticed the resemblance between these "dark films" and the series of violent mystery novels—many of which were by American writers—published as the *Série noire*) characterized by sudden violence, tough romantic intensity, deceptive surfaces and emblematic reflections, unsentimental melodrama, narrative complexity, low-key lighting, and themes of entrapment and corruption, obsession and madness, betrayal and disenchantment, irony and doom.

Film stock. Also known as "filmstock," "raw stock," "stock." Unexposed film.

Final cut. (1) The right given to some directors to have the director's cut released without any changes. (2) The final version of a film, after which it will not be re-edited.

Flashback. A cut to an earlier event, usually followed by a return to the present.

Flash forward. A cut to a future event, usually followed by a return to the present.

Flat. (1) Not anamorphic; a spherical-lens format. (2) Not 3-D; a two-dimensional format.

Focal length. The distance in millimeters from the film plane (the location of the frame of film that is to be exposed) to the optical center of the lens when the lens is focused at infinity. In 35mm Academy-ratio cinematography, a "normal" lens has a focal length of 50mm, a short or wide-angle lens

has a focal length shorter than that (e.g., 28mm), and a long or telephoto lens has a long focal length (e.g., 200mm).

Formalism. Whether practiced by an artist or a critic, the emphasis on the form, structure, and strategies of a work of art, rather than on its subject or the circumstances under which it came to be created.

Format. The physical and optical characteristics of a negative or print, such as whether it is flat or anamorphic, the gauge of the film, the aspect ratio of the image, and the number of perforations per frame.

Fps. Frames per second; the rate of exposing and/or projecting frames.

Frame. (1) An individual photograph or picture area on a strip of film. (2) The perimeter or boundary line of the picture area. (3) In the narrative film, a story or narrative situation within which another story is bracketed or presented.

Frame enlargement. A printed enlargement of an individual frame from a movie.

Freeze-frame. A sudden cessation of movement created by the continual reprinting of the same frame.

Full shot. Also known as "FS." A medium long shot that offers a relatively complete view of the set and shows the human figure from head to foot.

Gate. In a camera, printer, or projector, the apparatus through which film passes as it is exposed to light.

Gauge. The width of a strip of film in millimeters.

Gendai-geki. In Japan, a film set in the present or recent past; the film of modern life.

Genre. (1) A subcategory of the narrative film, defined by the choice and treatment of subject—mystery, musical, western, and so forth. A group of films, or a narrative approach, that deals with a specific avenue of human experience in a characteristic manner (or a variation of it), structuring the story and its presentation in relation to a recurring set of terms, themes, values, figures, and images. (2) A particular genus or type of motion picture. Within the nonfiction film, for example, *cinéma vérité* and the newsreel are distinct genres.

Gross. The amount of money earned by a film before any expenses are deducted. The "domestic box-office gross" is the amount spent on tickets to a particular movie in the country where it was produced.

Hays Office. Colloquial name for Hollywood's bureau of self-censorship, the Motion Picture Producers and Distributors of America, as administered by its first president (1922–1945), Will Hays.

Head. The beginning of a reel of film or tape.

High-angle shot. A shot in which the camera looks downward toward the subject.

High-key lighting. A lighting plan in which the set is brightly lit and there is a low contrast ratio (in other words, the dark areas of the image are not much darker than the bright areas).

Hommage. A shot, a scene, or an element within either, that is reminiscent of and pays tribute to the work of an earlier filmmaker.

House. A theatre.

Ideology. A set of interlocking assumptions, values, and expectations held by a person, group, or culture.

Independent. (1) Originally, a film production company not affiliated with the Motion Picture Patents Company. (2) A filmmaker who works without studio support or interference and who may distribute the film personally or license it to a company that specializes in alternative, nonstudio products. (3) A producer or small production company that makes a film autonomously but may have a financing and distribution deal with a studio.

Insert. A shot, usually of an unmoving object, that is cut into a scene or a sequence; the principal actors, if they or any part of them should appear, are represented by doubles.

Intercutting. (1) Inserting one or more shots into another series of shots or into a master shot. (2) Interweaving shots from separate scenes, not necessarily in a cross-cutting pattern but usually to imply relatedness.

Interior. (1) An indoor set. (2) A scene that takes place indoors.

Intertitle. Any title, whether or not it is superimposed on another image, that appears anywhere between the head credits (or "opening titles") and the tail credits ("end titles") of a movie.

Iris. (1) A circular mask (*See* Mask). (2) A transitional device in which the image appears as an expanding circle (an "iris in") or disappears as a contracting circle (an "iris out").

Iris shot. A shot whose picture area appears within a circle, whether or not the circle changes size during the shot.

Jidai-geki. In Japan, a costume drama or period piece set in the feudal past.

Jump cut. (1) A cut between two shots that are so similar that the subject appears to jump from one position to another. (2) A disjunctive, disorienting cut; a sudden transition that may be illogical, mismatched, or impatient with normal continuity and that —unlike the match cut—calls attention to itself.

Kammerspielfilm. In German silent cinema, an intimate "chamber drama," relatively free of intertitles and usually concerned with the close psychological observation of a small number of characters who must deal with the problems of everyday life in realistic but evocatively lit settings; inspired by the *Kammerspiele* of Max Reinhardt (a theatre so small that the audience could see the actors' subtle gestures; also, the plays performed there); formulated by Lupu Pick in reaction against Expressionism.

Kinetograph. Edison's first motion picture camera; invented by W. K. L. Dickson.

Kinetoscope. Edison's battery-operated peephole viewer, invented by Dickson.

Laserdisc. A digitally encoded disc, resembling a silver LP record or large compact disc, that is read by a laser beam and yields a very high quality video image accompanied by digital sound. *See also* Videodisc.

Leitmotif. (1) A recurring musical theme that is associated with a recurring narrative element or theme; formulated by Richard Wagner. (2) A thematically significant narrative element that recurs and develops in the course of a movie.

Lip sync. Perfect synchronization between picture and sound, so tight that an actor's lip movements and recorded dialogue absolutely match.

Live sound. Tracks recorded during shooting.

Location. A shooting site that is not on a studio lot often a place where the film's fictional or actual events took place.

Long lens. A lens with a long focal length and a narrow field of view, which flattens depth relationships and appears to bring the subject closer; a very long lens is called a "telephoto lens."

Long shot. Also known as "LS," "far shot." A shot that gives a wide, expansive view of the visual field; the camera appears to be far from the subject. In terms of the human figure, a person might be less than half the height of the frame.

Long take. A shot that lasts longer than a minute.

Loop. (1) In the threading path of a camera, printer, or projector, a short length of film that is left slack. (2) A strip of film, tape, or magnetic film whose beginning is joined to its end. (3) To post-synchronize dialogue, specifically by "looping" (listening repeatedly to the live sound, and recording the new reading, on a loop of magnetic film loaded in a dubber that is synchronized with a projector). *See* Dubbing.

Low-angle shot. A shot in which the camera looks upward toward the subject.

Low-key lighting. A lighting plan in which the set is dimly lit, with rich shadows and occasional highlights, and there is a high contrast ratio (in other words, the dark areas of the image are much darker than the bright areas).

Mag. Short for "magnetic." Magnetic tape or film.

Magnetic film. *See* Film.

Magnetic soundtrack. One or more stripes of magnetized iron-oxide particles bearing the final soundtrack, either on magnetic film that is played by a machine synchronized with the projector, or bonded onto the release print (running alongside the frames) and played by the projector.

Mag stock. *See* Film.

Majors. Hollywood's biggest studios: Originally Fox, MGM, Paramount, RKO, and Warner Bros; later joined by Columbia, United Artists, and Universal.

Mask. A sheet of metal (a "matte plate") or cardboard (a "matte card"), painted flat ("matte") black — or a strip of exposed film (a "fixed matte") that is transparent in some areas and opaque everywhere else — that admits light only to specific areas of the frame. Used to reshape the frame or in connection with the making of optical composites. *See also* Matte.

Master shot. A long take, usually a full or long shot, that covers all the major action of a scene and into which closer or more specific views usually are intercut.

Match cut. A cut over which an action appears to continue seamlessly.

Matte. (1) Any surface or coating that is "flat" (nonreflective) rather than shiny; most photographic and lighting equipment and accessories are matte black. (2) A mask that admits light freely to certain areas of the frame and completely blocks it from reaching other areas. In most cases, a *mask* is a rigid physical object or camera accessory, and a *matte* is a selectively opaque shot or shot element; *see also* Mask *and* Traveling matte.

Matte box. A black, accordion-like device mounted in front of a camera lens (and often fitted with a sunshade or "lens hood"), capable of holding matte cards and filters.

Medium long shot. Also known as "MLS." A shot whose field of view is narrower than that of a long shot but broader than that of a medium shot. *See* "full shot."

Medium shot. Also known as "midshot," "MS." (1) A shot whose field of view is midway between those of the close shot and the far shot. (2) More precisely, a shot whose field of view is midway between those of the close-up and the full shot. In terms of the human figure, a view from head to thighs might fill the frame.

Melodrama. A popular narrative form that is characterized by intense emotion and draws strong, vivid distinctions between good and evil.

Mindscreen. The field of the mind's eye.

Mise-en-scène. The atmosphere, setting, decor, and texture of a shot. The way a scene has been designed and staged for the camera.

Mix. (1) To balance, combine, and re-record separate tracks, creating an intermediate or final composite soundtrack. (2) A "dissolve" *See* Dissolve.

Monopack. Also known as "integral tripack." A compound emulsion used in color photography; the three layers of the negative are sensitive to cyan, magenta, and yellow, respectively, yielding their complementary primaries—red, green, and blue—in the positive print.

Montage. (1) The dynamic editing of picture and/or sound. (2) The intensive, significant, and often abrupt juxtaposition of shots; *See* Continuity editing. (3) Rapid cutting. (4) A series of overlapping images; in the sound film, usually accompanied by music and used as a transitional device. Also known as "Hollywood montage."

MOS. Minus optical sound; i.e., shot silent.

Motion Picture Patents Company. Edison's patent-sharing trust, comprising the nine leading film companies of 1908 (Edison, Biograph, Vitagraph, Essanay, Lubin, Selig, Kalem, Méliès, and Pathé) as well as inventor Thomas Armat and distributor George Kleine. The combine was incorporated and activated in 1908; Méliès was included in 1909, the same year that Eastman agreed to sell perforated raw stock only to members of the MPPC. Disbanded 1917.

Movie. (1) A motion picture. (2) A feature-length narrative film.

Movietone. The sound-on-film ("optical sound") process introduced by Fox; virtually identical to Phonofilm. *See also* Vitaphone.

MPAA rating. *See* CARA.

Multiplex cinema. A theatre with many separate auditoriums.

Mutoscope. Biograph's peephole viewer; each frame was printed on paper and mounted on a card, and the cards flipped by as the viewer turned a crank.

Narration. (1) The act of telling or relating, whether or not the account is fictive, the presenter ("narrator") is personalized, the act is deliberate, or words are employed. (2) Also "narrative." A text or discourse; the words and/or images delivered by a narrator—who may be a character (*Citizen Kane*), a writer (*Nosferatu*), the writer (*The Last Laugh*), a persona (*Annie Hall*), the filmmaker (*2 or 3 Things I Know About Her*), or an impersonal voice (*Jules and Jim*). (3) In sound film, a voice-over commentary; in silent film, the intertitles attributed to a narrator (usually impersonal, but sometimes a character).

Narrative. (1) The adjective for "narration." (2) That which is narrated, whether true or false; the story (or series of events and perceptions) and the discourse in which it is presented.

Narrative film. A movie whose story is primarily or entirely fictitious.

Naturalism. A deterministic realism that accounted for behavior through the close observation of hereditary, instinctive, psychological, social, economic, and political forces, rejecting theistic explanations along with sentimentality.

Negative. (1) Film stock that turns black where it has been exposed to light. (2) The camera original; the negative film run through the camera. (3) The completed movie; the edited and perfected final negative, from which release prints may be struck.

Negative pick-up. Also known as "pickup." A deal whereby a studio buys and distributes an independently produced film.

Neorealism. Particularly in Italy after World War II, a "new realism" characterized by location shooting, scripted dialogue that sounds improvised, the use of nonprofessional actors in the majority of roles, an emphasis on the everyday struggles of common people and the unvarnished look of nonstudio reality, the rejection of bourgeois fantasy as well as of Expressionism, and the determination to present the characters in relation to their real social environments and political and economic conditions.

Net. The amount of money earned by a film after all expenses are deducted.

New Wave. (1) Particularly in France in 1959, the sudden appearance, on many fronts, of a host of brilliant films by directors who had not previously made features or whose earlier work had gone unnoticed. Also known as *"la Nouvelle Vague."* (2) Any sudden appearance of many exciting new filmmakers in a country whose films have been undistinguished—and may have done little or no international business—for a long time.

Nickelodeon. The first permanent movie theatre in America, which was converted from a store, opened in 1905; it was called a nickelodeon because admission to the theatre (*odeon* in Greek) cost a nickel.

Nitrate film. Film whose base is made of cellulose nitrate; explosive, and obsolete since 1951, but often visually superior to safety-base film.

Normal lens. A lens whose focal length is neither long nor short and that reproduces perspective much as it is seen by the human eye.

Offscreen. Also known as "OS." Outside of camera range.

Optical composite. Any image created by combining elements from two or more separately photographed images, or combining two or more complete images, usually on an optical printer.

Optical printer. A film copier in which the original and the printing stock are not in physical contact during the instant of exposure (in a contact printer, they are); instead, one or more optical systems intervene, allowing part or all of the original image to be rephotographed with or without modifications. An image might be cropped, flipped, repeated, superimposed on another, distorted, filtered, used in a special effects composite, and so forth. The optical printer itself might be thought of as a camera facing a projector. *See also* Printer *and* Special effects.

Optical soundtrack. A continuous black-and-white, sound-on-film image area running down one edge of the film (adjacent to the frames), containing the movie's final soundtrack and designed to allow varying amounts of light to pass through it to a photocell.

Orthochromatic film. Early black-and-white film stock, sensitive to blue and green (and, much less so, to yellow) but not to red or orange; replaced monochromatic film which was sensitive only to blue. *See also* Panchromatic film.

Pan. (1) To pivot the camera horizontally, turning it from side to side. (2) Also "panning shot" and "panoramic shot." A shot within which the camera pivots on a vertical axis, turning in a horizontal plane.

Panavision. The 35mm anamorphic format that replaced CinemaScope; its aspect ratio is 2.35:1.

Panchromatic film. Black-and-white film stock, in use since 1926, that is sensitive to the entire spectrum. Because its speed, or photosensitivity, was less than that of the orthochromatic film it replaced, it required wider lens-aperture settings and yielded inferior depth of field.

Paper print. A positive copy of a film, made on sheets of paper and sent to the Library of Congress (until 1907, when copyright law was revised to allow the registration and protection of materials not printed on paper) to establish copyright on each of the individual photographs that constituted the movie.

Parallel montage. Cross-cutting between two or more separate actions (often different enough to "collide" when juxtaposed) in order to imply that they are dramatically and thematically related.

Patent Company. *See* Motion Picture Patents Company.

Perforated stock. Film or mag stock that has sprocket holes along one or both edges.

Persistence of vision. Retinal retention of a bright image that is followed by darkness or flashed in the dark.

Phi phenomenon. The preconscious process of deducing and hallucinating movement from a series of stills; believing that one sees a continuous action rather than a series of consecutive but frozen fragments of motion.

Phonofilm. The sound-on-film process invented by Lee De Forest. *See also* Movietone.

Photocell. Also known as "photoelectric cell." A device that converts light into electrical impulses—for example, when responding to light that has passed through an optical soundtrack.

Photosensitivity. The degree to which an emulsion reacts to light.

Pickup. *See* Negative pickup.

Picture. (1) A movie. (2) The image track of a movie, as distinct from the soundtrack.

Pixillation. The art of animating a person or an object that is capable of moving under its own power—and may well move between exposures. *See* Stop-motion animation.

Plan-séquence. *See* Sequence shot.

Plastic material. Visually expressive material; formulated by V. I. Pudovkin.

Positive. An image or print whose color or black-and-white values correspond to those in the subject; created either by shooting reversal film (which yields a direct positive image) or by making a negative of a negative.

Post-production. The phase of filmmaking during which picture and sound are augmented and edited into final form, after the conclusion of principal photography.

Post-synchronization. (1) The process of recording, after the picture has been shot, a track that is to accompany a particular MOS (minus optical sound) shot—or to be substituted for a track recorded during production—and of synchronizing this and other wild tracks with picture; *see* Wild track. (2) The process of creating and synchronizing a soundtrack for a film shot silent or in a foreign language.

POV shot. Point-of-view shot, also known as "subjective camera." A shot in which the camera adopts the vantage point of a character's physical eye or literal gaze, showing what the character sees.

Pre-production. The practical planning phase of filmmaking, including all the work (location scouting, set construction, costume design, etc.) that must be done before shooting can get underway.

Principal photography. The process of shooting (with or without sound) the principal performers and every dialogued scene in the script; the core activity of the production phase of filmmaking.

Print. (1) A positive, projectable copy of a film. (2) Any printed copy of a film, whether positive or negative, intermediate or final. (3) To duplicate a frame, a shot, a reel, or a complete movie, with or without making alterations.

Printer. A film-copying machine that directs light through processed film (the original) onto raw stock (which, when processed, becomes the print). A "contact printer" is used for relatively simple duplication, such as making a release print from a final negative, a workprint from a camera negative, or a brighter copy of a shot that is too dark. An "optical printer" is used to create the majority of optical special effects.

Problem picture. An issue-oriented feature film, particularly one that calls attention to a contemporary, real-world topic of concern.

Producer. (1) The person who selects and hires the creative team to write and shoot a film, pays all the costs of filmmaking, owns the finished product, and arranges for the film's distribution. (2) The business entity that collectively performs the functions of an individual producer. (3) The studio or production-company executive who authorizes and directly or indirectly supervises the making of a film.

Production. (1) A filmmaking project. (2) The activity of making a film. (3) The shooting phase of filmmaking, particularly that involving the principal actors (which is called "principal photography"). It is prepared for in "pre-production" (scheduling, production design, etc.) and followed by "post-production" (editing, mixing, etc.).

Production Code. Also known as "The Motion Picture Production Code." A moralistic list of what could and could not be shown or endorsed in a Hollywood film. A producer's self-censorship guide, considered preferable to censorship by groups outside the film industry, the Code was drawn up in 1930, approved by the Hays Office, and officially adopted by producers and distributors that same year. It was first enforced in 1934, when Joseph Breen was appointed to run the Production Code Administration.

Production designer. An art director responsible for designing the complete look of a film, coordinating and integrating its sets, dressing, props, costumes, and color schemes.

Production still. (1) A photograph, shot with a still camera, that is taken on the set, often approximating a scene in the film, or illustrates some aspect of the making of the film. (2) The photographs included in a film's press kit, including production and publicity stills.

Program picture. A run-of-the-mill feature, presumably tossed off without much creative effort.

Prop. Also known as "property." A physical object handled by an actor or displayed as part of a set; the term excludes set dressings and costumes.

Property. (1) An owned work. (2) A concept, script, or pre-existing work (a "literary property") that is being considered for production. (3) A film currently in production. (4) A prop.

Rating. *See* CARA.

Raw. Unexposed and unprocessed.

Reaction shot. A cutaway or reverse shot, usually a close-up or close shot, that shows how one or more characters react to an offscreen action, usually one that has been shown in the preceding shot.

Realism. A representational style that attempts to present a state of affairs without distortion.

Rear projection. Also known as "back projection." The projection of stills or footage onto a translucent screen, from behind that screen, in order to provide a background for the live action that is performed between the screen and the camera.

Reel. (1) 1,000 feet of 35mm film — in practice, between 900 and 1,000 feet — wound on a reel; in 16mm, a full reel is 400 feet of film. At silent speed, approximately 13–16 minutes long; at sound speed, approximately 10 minutes long. (2) The sound, on tape or magnetic film, that accompanies a particular reel of film. Also known as "reel of sound." (3) Up to 2,000 feet of 35mm film, wound on the metal projection reels in use today. Also known as "double reel." (4) A metal or plastic spool on which film or tape is wound; as distinct from a core, a reel has outside rims or flanges.

Reflexivity. (1) Self-referentiality, whether displayed by a work or by its creator. (2) Also "self-consciousness." The implication that a work of art is aware of itself as a work of art, either as an artifice in a particular creative tradition or as an autonomous and self-directing structure.

Release date. The date—loosely, the year—a film is first shown to a public audience, not on a sneak-preview basis but as an official opening.

Release negative. The final negative of the release version, from which release prints are struck.

Release print. An original positive print (not a dupe of such a print) that is officially put into distribution and designed to be projected.

Release version. The approved, final cut; the text or version of a movie that is approved for release and distribution.

Restoration. Returning a film as much as possible to the condition it was in when it was new and complete.

Reverse motion. Printing or projecting a film from last frame to first.

Reverse-angle shot. Also known as "reverse shot." (1) A shot that reverses the field of view over a cut, as if the camera had turned 180° to the rear. (2) One in a series of alternating, complementary views (a "shot/reverse-shot" pattern) whose angles are usually separated by 120–160°; often used for conversations.

Safety-base film. Camera or printing stock that has a slow-burning base made primarily of cellulose tri-acetate (originally, cellulose acetate), in contrast to the explosive base of nitrate film, which it replaced.

Scenario. A film script or screenplay.

Scene. (1) A dramatic action or interaction that takes place in a single location. (2) A complete unit of action that is capable of being covered in a single shot, regardless of how many shots are actually used to cover it. (3) The shot(s) in which a scene is presented.

Scope. Anamorphic; derived from "CinemaScope."

Score. (1) The original music composed for a film. (2) The music arranged for a film, whether new or old.

Screen direction. (1) In the interests of spatial continuity and logic, the practice of keeping track of the directions in which people or objects are facing or moving. (2) The trajectory of movement (or direction of a gaze, orientation of an object, etc.) within, across, and in relation to the borders of the frame (e.g., toward screen right); its orientation to real or hypothetical three-dimensional space (e.g., toward the east window); and the continuity of that space as it is created by the continuity of trajectory from shot to shot (e.g., to indicate in a cross-cut sequence that X and Y, who are never seen in the same shot, are running in the same direction up opposite sides of the street, X runs up the west side of the street and toward screen right, and Y runs up the east side of the street and toward screen left).

Screen left. The left side of the screen, as seen by the audience.

Screen right. The right side of the screen, as seen by the audience.

Screenwriter. Also known as "scenarist." The author or co-author of a screenplay; the artist who first determines the structure, characters, themes, events, and dialogue of a film as well as many of its crucial images.

Segue. A sound dissolve; pronounced "seg-way."

Sequel. A film whose action follows or predates (as a "prequel") that of a previously released film, whose essential narrative and thematic elements it sets out to vary, extend, and repeat. Unlike the films in a series, the original and its sequels are meant to be shown in numerical order (or release order, if the films aren't numbered).

Sequence. (1) Any group of consecutive shots and/or scenes. (2) A series of interrelated shots that is not restricted to covering an action in a single location and that has its own beginning, middle, and end (subtly limited structure) and distinct project (function, style, or concern) within the whole of the film; e.g, the dream sequence that opens *Wild Strawberries* or the Odessa Steps sequence in *Battleship Potemkin*. (3) A series of interrelated scenes with a consistent dramatic project, constituting a significant unit of the structured narrative; e.g., the Bernstein sequence in *Citizen Kane* or the chain-gang sequence in *Sullivan's Travels.*

Sequence shot. Also *"plan-séquence."* A scene that is covered in a single long take whose camera movements are, in most cases, intricately blocked.

Serial. A film made of chapters that are shown at regular intervals—in most cases, weekly.

Series. (1) A set of films that feature the same main characters and generally may be shown in any order; e.g., the James Bond series. (2) Loosely, a set of sequels; e.g., the *Friday the 13th* series.

Set. (1) A decorated sound stage. (2) An artificially constructed setting, whether interior or exterior. (3) Any site where a movie is shot.

Set dressing. (1) Furniture, fixtures, and objects attached to the walls or floor of an interior set. (2) Integral parts of an exterior set. *See* Prop.

Setup. The position (location and angle) of the camera, fitted with a particular lens, at the start of a take; any number of shots may be taken from the same setup.

70mm. Film that is 70 millimeters wide; most often used for release prints, either of films that have been shot on 65mm negative stock or of 35mm anamorphic films that have been blown up.

Shomin-geki. In Japan, the drama or comedy of middle-class and lower-middle-class life; a subgenre of the *gendai-geki.*

Short lens. A lens with a short focal length and a broad field of view, which exaggerates depth relationships in the visual field; a very short lens is called a "wide-angle lens."

Shot. (1) A continuously exposed series of frames, beginning and ending with a cut or other transitional device. (2) A take. (3) In animation and special effects, a series of individual or composite frames that gives the impression of having been continuously exposed.

Shot/reverse-shot. *See* Reverse-angle shot.

Shutter. A device that, when open, allows light to reach and expose the film in a camera or printer—or shine through the film and the lens in a projector—and that, when shut, keeps out light and allows the next frame to be advanced into position.

Silent speed. (1) The most common speed was 16 fps (frames per second), though there was no fixed standard; in the 1920s, many films ran at 18 or 20 fps, and some at 24 fps. (2) On today's projectors, 18 fps.

16mm. Film that is 16 millimeters wide; the smallest professional gauge and the standard low-budget format.

Slow film. Film whose emulsion has a low "speed," requiring bright lighting.

Slow motion. Also "overcranking." The effect of slowed-down movement, achieved by exposing more than the normal number of frames per second (i.e., shooting at a rate greater than the projection rate.)

Socialist realism. The Stalinist insistence that art serve the interests of the state and be clear to anyone; to be arty was to be elitist and confusing, and to deviate from the Party line was to fail to communicate plain reality.

Sound composite. Any recording created by mixing other recordings.

Sound speed. 24 fps, although some formats have been designed for higher rates (multi-film Cinerama ran at 26 fps, early Todd-AO at 30 fps).

Sound stage. Also "soundstage." A large, windowless, soundproof building in which sound films are shot on artificially lit sets.

Soundtrack. Also "sound track." (1) The final sound composite; all the sounds heard in a film. (2) The optical or magnetic track(s) in which that composite is stored; usually an integral part of the release print.

Special effects. Also known as "SPFX." (1) Physical effects that can be staged for the camera and shot in real time (e.g., a tree crashing through a window). Also known as "production effects." (2) Production effects entailing the use of machines (e.g., an electronically detonated explosion). Also known as "mechanicals," "mechanical special effects," "special mechanical effects." (3) Photographic illusions created through nonroutine shooting or printing techniques, usually during post-production (e.g., a traveling matte in which a bicyclist crosses the face of the moon). Also known as "opticals," "optical special effects," "special optical effects," "special effects cinematography."

Speed. (1) The rate at which frames are exposed or projected. (2) The degree to which an emulsion reacts to light and the rapidity with which it does so; the "faster" —more photosensitive—an emulsion is, the less light is required for adequate exposure and the more grainy an image is likely to be. (3) A measure of the light-gathering ability of a lens.

Spherical lens. A lens that preserves the normal horizontal and vertical relationships found in the subject.

Splice. The physical bond that joins one piece of film (or magnetic stock or tape) to another; also, making such a bond.

Split reel. (1) A film that is half a reel or less in length (where a full reel is 1,000 feet of 35mm film or the equivalent). (2) A reel, one of whose sides may be unscrewed to allow the insertion or removal of film that has been tightly wound on a plastic hub (a "core").

Split screen. Also "split-screen." Any frame containing two or more separate and distinct frames or images.

Sprocket holes. Also "perforations," "perfs." The regularly spaced holes—into which the teeth of sprocket wheels precisely fit—that run along one or both edges of motion picture film and magnetic film.

Sprocket. Also "sprocket wheel." The toothed wheel that engages and advances film in a camera, printer, or projector.

Steadicam. A camera mount, worn by the operator, that allows the camera to remain steady even when the operator moves, ensuring extremely smooth hand-held traveling shots.

Still. A single photograph, taken by a conventional camera rather than a movie camera.

Stock. *See* Film stock.

Stop-action photography. Also "stop-motion photography." Stopping the camera, making a change or letting a change take place in the action area, and then restarting the camera, creating what appears to be a continuous shot within which everything suddenly shifts position or something is instantly changed into something else.

Stop-motion animation. Frame-by-frame shooting of a model (e.g., King Kong), a cutout, or any object incapable of moving under its own power. *See* "pixillation."

Studio. A large production company, on its own lot, fully equipped with everything necessary to plan, shoot, record, edit, mix, and release motion pictures.

Subjective camera. (1) A shot or setup that shows what a character sees; a POV (point-of-view) shot. (2) Loosely, a shot, scene, or sequence that shows what a character remembers, relates, dreams, hallucinates, or imagines; a mindscreen.

Subjective sound. A track that presents what a character hears, does not hear (e.g., if deaf), or imagines hearing.

Subtitle. A line of words printed near the bottom of the screen; in most cases a condensed translation of foreign-language dialogue. Considered intertitles only when part of the original movie.

Superimposition. Multiple exposure; printing or shooting one image over another.

Surrealism. An avant-garde movement that sought to pursue within artistic structures the juxtapositions, transitions, and bizarre logic characteristic of dreams and the unconscious.

Sync. Synchronization, especially between picture and sound.

Tail. The end of a reel of film or tape.

Take. (1) An unedited shot, beginning when the camera starts exposing film and ending when the camera stops. (2) An attempt to photograph a shot; the attempts that prove satisfactory are approved for printing.

Technicolor. Imbibition printing, also called the "dye transfer process," and the company that perfected it. The process of applying dyes directly onto the print (rather than putting the dyes through the film developing process) by means of a "matrix," which is a celluloid strip bearing various thicknesses of hardened gelatin that is capable of absorbing and shedding dyes. In three-strip Technicolor, each of the three matrices is a black-and-white record of the red, green, or blue in the image (in negative, the cyan, magenta, or yellow, respectively).

Telephoto lens. (1) A lens with a very long focal length and a very narrow field of view; it has a high factor of magnification (as if telescopic) and flattens depth relationships. (2) Loosely, any "long lens."

35mm. Film that is 35 millimeters wide; the standard professional film gauge.

Tilt. (1) To pivot the camera upward or downward. (2) A shot within which the camera pivots on a horizontal axis, moving in a vertical plane; a tilting movement. Also known as "tilt shot," "tilting shot." (3) A shot in which the camera is tilted to the side, so that the top and bottom of the frame are not parallel to the lateral horizontal axis of the set. Also known as "Dutch angle," "Dutch tilt shot," "off-angle shot."

Tinting. The process of evenly and monochromatically coloring an originally black-and-white shot, either by dying the film or by printing on colored stock. In a tinted shot of a face, the whites of the eyes are colored. Rarely, a shot is both tinted and toned.

Title. (1) A shot consisting primarily or entirely of words; it may appear on its own, as did most of the narrative and dialogue intertitles in silent film, or be superimposed over another shot. The term includes head and tail credits, intertitles, title cards, scrolling titles (titles that "crawl" up the screen), and subtitles. (2) The name of a work.

Title card. A stable, full-frame title; also the card (which may or may not be decorated) on which the words are drawn or printed, and the shot of the card. Includes virtually all head and tail credits and narrative and dialogue titles in silent film and the majority of superimposed titles today, but excludes crawls (unless the title or integral group of words appears on the screen by itself, however briefly, as it moves) and subtitles.

Titles. (1) The sequence of title cards that includes the name of the film. (2) The opening or closing credits. (3) The intertitles, considered as a group.

Toning. The process of chemically converting a black-and-white image to a monochromatic color image; the darker the image (i.e., the greater the concentration of exposed silver crystals), the deeper the color. In a toned shot of a face, the whites of the eyes are white. Rarely, a shot is both toned and tinted.

Track. (1) An individual recording. (2) One of the steel rails on which the steel wheels of a camera platform could smoothly ride; also one of the boards, laid over uneven terrain, on which the rubber wheels of a dolly may ride. (3) To move the camera forward, backward, to the side, diagonally, or along a curve—but not off the ground and through the air—usually with perfect smoothness.

Track shot. Also known as "tracking shot," "trucking shot." (1) A shot taken from a camera platform whose steel wheels ride on steel rails ("tracks"); characterized by smooth movement along straight lines and relatively gentle curves. (2) Any shot in which the camera moves ("tracks") forward, backward, to the side, diagonally, along a curve, or across the ground; the term excludes shots taken from a crane or plane —as well as pans, tilts, and zooms, which are not moving-camera shots. (3) A track shot taken from a dolly; often characterized by complex movements it would be almost impossible to lay out in steel and by the absence of rails on the floor. Also known as "dolly shot."

Traveling matte. (1) A matte that can vary the contours of its opaque area(s) from frame to frame; a film of a moving silhouette. (2) An optical composite that seamlessly, and without see-through ("phantom") effects, integrates elements from different shots into one image; in most cases the foreground action is matted into the quiet or active background shot.

Traveling shot. Any track shot, dolly shot, crane shot, following shot, hand-held shot, or aerial shot in which the camera moves from one place to another. The term excludes pans and tilts (in which the camera only pivots) and zoom shots (in which the lens is adjusted and the camera does nothing).

Two-shot. A shot of two people.

Uncut. Unabridged.

Underscoring. Music that accompanies a shot, scene, or sequence but is not being played by any character or object (radio, record, etc.) in the movie; nondiegetic music.

Variable area track. An optical soundtrack whose amplitude or contour varies but whose density (a measure of opacity) remains constant.

Variable density track. An optical soundtrack whose dimensions remain constant but whose uniform degree of opacity varies.

Voice-over. Also known as "voice-over narration," "VO." A commentary dialogue track (sometimes presented as an interior monologue) that is not motivated by, or being delivered aloud by, any onscreen or offscreen indigenous source; instead it is laid "over" the indigenous sounds of the scene.

Video. (1) Closed-circuit television. (2) The art and technology of television. (3) A work made to be televised. (4) A videotape or laserdisc copy of a movie or of a video work.

Videocassette recorder. Also known as "VCR." A videotape deck that electronically records and plays back audio-visual information that may be displayed on a television; the videotape is wound on cores in a permanent plastic case, so that the tape itself need not be handled.

Videodisc. An obsolete video format, resembling a phonograph record, in which picture and sound were stored in grooves read by a stylus. *See* "laserdisc."

Vitaphone. The sound-on-disc process first used by Warner Bros.; eventually made obsolete by the sound-on-film process; *see* Movietone.

Vitascope. Edison's first projector, invented by Thomas Armat and incorporating the Latham loop. *See* Loop.

Wide-angle lens. (1) A lens with a very short focal length and a very broad field of view; it deepens or exaggerates depth relationships in the visual field and produces distorted, bowed images of objects that are very near the camera. (2) Loosely, any short lens.

Wide screen. Any film, whether flat or anamorphic, that has an aspect ratio greater than 1.33 : 1.

Widescreen. A 35mm flat format whose aspect ratio is 1.85 : 1 in America and 1.66 : 1 in Europe.

Wild track. Also known as "wild recording." A recording made without camera synchronization.

Wipe. A transitional effect in which one image appears to push another off the screen (the moving boundary between the images is the "wipe line") or in which parts of one shot are removed while parts of the next shot appear in their place.

Writer. *See* Screenwriter.

Zoom. To adjust the focal length of a zoom lens while the camera is running; also a shot taken while the zoom is being adjusted. As the focal length is shortened (a "zoom out" or "backward zoom"), the lens behaves more like a wide-angle lens, exaggerating depth relationships, decreasing magnification, and widening the field of view so that the camera appears to move away from the subject; as the focal length is increased (a "zoom in" or "forward zoom"), the lens behaves more like a telephoto lens, flattening depth relationships, increasing magnification, and narrowing the field of view so that the camera appears to move closer to the subject.

Zoom lens. A lens with a variable (rather than a fixed) focal length, which allows the camera operator or assistant to widen or narrow the field of view without moving the camera or stopping to change lenses.

Index